TOTAL

Indians™

EDITED BY

JOHN THORN, PETE PALMER,
MICHAEL GERSHMAN, DAVID PIETRUSZA
AND PAUL HOYNES

PENGUIN BOOKS

PENGUIN BOOKS
Published by the Penguin Group
Penguin Books USA Inc., 375 Hudson Street,
New York, New York 10014, U.S.A.
Penguin Books Ltd, 27 Wrights Lane,
London W8 5TZ, England
Penguin Books Australia Ltd, Ringwood,
Victoria, Australia
Penguin Books Canada Ltd, 10 Alcorn Avenue,
Toronto, Ontario, Canada M4V 3B2
Penguin Books (N.Z.) Ltd, 182–190 Wairau Road,
Auckland 10, New Zealand

Penguin Books Ltd, Registered Offices:
Harmondsworth, Middlesex, England

First published in Penguin Books 1996

10 9 8 7 6 5 4 3 2 1

Official Publication – Major League Baseball

ISBN 0 14 02.5728 4

Printed in the United States of America
Set in Times Roman
Designed by Marc Cheshire with Ray Shaw

Contents

Acknowledgments

The appearance of *Total Indians* marks the first time the editors have created a team-oriented book using concepts originally developed for *Total Baseball*, the official encyclopedia of Major League Baseball. It could not have been published without the assistance of a dedicated group of writers, researchers, and editorial/production staff. The principal contributors are credited on the preceding title page and in the table of contents.

Al Silverman, our editor, made a major contribution in shaping the book and providing wise editorial counsel. His colleagues in Penguin's art, editorial, and production departments — Dolores Reilly, Susan VanOmmeren, and Jessie Reyes — were consistently helpful under exceedingly tight deadlines and helped shepherd this book through the production process in an amazingly short period of time.

The publishing department of Major League Baseball played a key role in bringing this project to fruition, and our thanks go to Michael Bernstein for editorial oversight and to his staff — Dana Williams, Samantha Fahrer, and Rich Pilling — for adding to the book's editorial and visual impact. On the image front, our thanks also go to Bryan Reilly of Photo File and Todd Radom for their All-Star efforts on the cover.

In its fabled history, the Indians franchise has had a long line of distinguished pitchers and players. We were fortunate to have stories about them from Bob Carroll, Eliot Cohen, Henry Hecht, and Havelock Hewes on historic Indians, as well as stories from Bob Klapisch and Matt Silverman on current Indians heroes.

Courier Corporation, which printed Total Baseball, did its usual yeoman job in turning our words into finished form in record time. Our thanks go to Dave Barton for overseeing the project and Bill Topaz, Tom Osenton, and Peter Clifford for their continued support.

We were fortunate to extend our relationship with Starkey & Henricks, which has been the typographer for every edition of *Total Baseball*. To Peter and Doug Bird and their extraordinary, beleaguered staff go our admiration and gratitude.

For research help, particularly into the years before 1920, we extend heartfelt thanks (alphabetically) to SABR colleagues Bill Carle, Bob McConnell, and Frank Williams. Bill helped us with biographical data, especially debut dates. Bob McConnell lent his personal expertise and his knowledge of the John Tattersall research collection to clear up a variety of perplexing areas. And Frank continued his remarkable efforts in correcting pitcher won-lost records before 1920.

CHAPTER 1

The 1995 Championship Season

Paul Hoynes

The season that always happened to the other team in the other city finally came to Cleveland. It had been so long that people didn't know how to act. Important baseball questions had gone unasked and unanswered for too many seasons in this city on the shores of Lake Erie. These questions had nothing to do with ownership changes, salaries, free agency, or arbitration. These were real baseball questions.

Who was the fastest Indian next to Kenny Lofton? Which outfielder had the best wiggle when he stepped into the batter's box? Could Albert Belle hit the scoreboard above the left field bleachers in Jacobs Field? What kind of car did Carlos Baerga drive?

That is the kind of question that gets asked when people give their hearts to a team. When that happens, wives and girlfriends watch more games on TV than their husbands and boyfriends. In music it's called a crossover hit. A country western song that rises to the top of the pop charts. A soul song that hard rockers and metal heads go out and buy.

The Indians were a crossover hit with a bullet in 1995. Not only did they reach the postseason and the World Series for the first time since 1954, but they were the kind of team that emboldened a gray-haired lady to corner Omar Vizquel, the Indians' impish shortstop, in a restaurant to request an autograph for her grandson.

"When I went to give her the autograph," said Vizquel with a smile, "her sister came up to me and said, 'She doesn't even have a grandson, she wants the autograph for herself.'"

They were a team that made a city smile, that made it jump out of its chair and scream out the window after another last at-bat, game-winning homer that the Indians seemed to hit once or twice a week.

When the championship season ended, two victories short of a World Series crown, over 6,000 fans greeted the team at the airport in the cold predawn hours on October 29. A day later, over 30,000 fans packed Public Square for a rally in the Indians' honor.

"It was a dream season,'" said manager Mike Hargrove. "Sometimes I had to pinch myself to make sure I was awake."

It is hard to say it was unexpected. The drum roll started in 1994 with the opening of Jacobs Field and the addition of legitimate free agent veterans Dennis Martinez, Eddie Murray, Tony Pena, and Jack Morris. They were players who could still actually play; for years, Cleveland had been one of the final stops for the spent husk of any player had once flourished in the big leagues. Do you associate the names Gorman Thomas, Phil Niekro, Keith Hernandez, Bake McBride, Steve Carlton,

Boog Powell, Willie Upshaw, and Oddibe McDowell with the Tribe?

How did the Indians transform themselves from elephant's graveyard to contender? Certainly not by luck.

The Tease

The sweet scent of success, unfamiliar through its long absence, was wafting its way over the city in 1994. The Indians were in a brand new ballpark, playing in front of sellout crowds every night. They trailed first-place Chicago by one game in the newly formed American League Central division. If that wasn't enough, they led the wild-card race over Baltimore and Kansas City in the new three-division alignment.

On the field they were being acknowledged as one of the best teams in baseball, a quality mix of young players nearing their peak and veterans who could still contribute. That's why the strike hurt so much.

In baseball's modern-day economics, successful teams can be kept together for only so long before they outprice themselves. GM John Hart could hear the clock ticking. Every second represented an opportunity missed.

"The strike robbed us of the possibility of doing what we did in 1995, in 1994," he said. "It's just a shame it had to happen. This could have been a great two-year run for us. In a lot of ways it still has been."

Many of the Indians' players felt the strike would end in two weeks, and they'd be back to resume the pennant race. They couldn't have been more wrong. On what would have been the last day of the regular season, Hart walked alone through an empty Jacobs Field wondering if the Indians would ever have another chance to be that good. He wondered if all the hard work had been worth it. And deep inside, he must have contemplated if this woeful franchise, steeped in bad karma, just might be impossible to turn around.

But the plan was bigger than all those dark thoughts. In the winter of 1990, Hart and Director of Baseball Operations Dan O'Dowd were returning from a nasty arbitration hearing with Greg Swindell, one of the Indians' best pitchers. Swindell had won his hearing, which meant he'd make over $2 million for the upcoming season, but he was unhappy because the Indians had pointed to some negative statistics during the hearing in an attempt to convince the arbitrator that their salary figure was more reasonable than Swindell's. "Arbitration is a loaded gun pointed at the head of the club," said Hart. "It drives a wedge between the player and the team. We were trying to think of ways to get around it."

The Plan

It started with the painful decision to turn a decent team in 1990 into the laughingstock of baseball in 1991. The Indians set a franchise record with 105 losses that year, while using a record 53 players — the majority of whom would never be called big leaguers again. The few established players they did have were released or traded for young prospects to cut the payroll to bare metal.

"We knew we were going to have to get bad before we got good," said O'Dowd. "From a revenue standpoint, it made no sense to spend a lot of money on the 1991 club to finish in the middle of the pack. We reserved our finances and put them into the farm system, and player development.

"But it was not part of the plan to lose 105 games. That was terrible."

The Indians payroll had been chopped to $8.3 million by the start of the 1992 season. It was the lowest in the big leagues, but good things were happening beneath the surface. Young players such as Baerga and Sandy Alomar Jr., acquired from San Diego for Joe Carter before the 1990 season, were getting valuable big-league experience. High-round draft picks Charles Nagy and Belle received their first extensive playing time in Cleveland in 1991. Before the start of the 1992 season, Lofton and first baseman Paul Sorrento were acquired in trades with Houston and Minnesota, respectively.

In the amateur draft, the Indians selected Manny Ramirez, Herbert Perry, and Chad Ogea with their first three picks in 1991. They would all make significant contributions in 1995. Jim Thome, a third round pick in 1989, made his big league debut in 1991.

To keep the team together, and to avoid the harsh feelings often created by the arbitration process, the Indians started signing their young players to long-term contracts. In most instances, the players weren't even eligible for arbitration — meaning the club could pay them at their own discretion provided it was at or above the major league minimum. Twelve players signed multiyear deals in the spring of 1992. Baerga, Alomar, and Nagy were among the first to do so. Baerga and Alomar were represented by the same agent, Scott Boras, at the time. He urged them not to sign.

"There was a risk on both sides," said Baerga. "The Indians were taking a risk on me being the kind of player they thought I'd be, and I was giving up my right to arbitration. But it relaxed me. I didn't have to worry about putting up big numbers every year so I'd get paid. I could just go out and play."

Lofton, Belle and Sorrento signed similar deals in the spring of 1993. "I had a lot of baseball people calling me up and saying, "You're going to do what?" said Hart. "But it worked for us. It gave our owner a chance to look down the road two or three years and see what his payroll would be, and it gave our players security."

Two more factors came into play in the forming of the 1995 Indians. One attracted the other.

Jacobs Field opened on April 4, 1994. Compared to their old home, Cleveland Stadium, it looked like the Starship Enterprise. Where Jacobs Field offered the look of an old-time ballpark with modern conveniences for players and fans, Cleveland Stadium was a rusting hulk on the shores of Lake Erie filled with flying insects, the threat of frostbite, and empty seats.

When utility infielder Alvaro Espinoza took his first look at Jacobs Field's huge locker room, he said, "I'm going to bring my bed down here and live. Why do I need an apartment? I've got everything I need right here."

The fans felt the same way. The Indians set a franchise record of 2.8 million in attendance in 1995. They sold out 57 of the 71 home dates, including the last 52 in a row.

"I don't think you can even measure the effect Jacobs Field has had on our team," said O'Dowd. "It might be bigger than anything we've done."

Still, the swiftness of the Indians' rise in 1995 was startling. Baseball started the year walking a dangerous and slippery path. With the strike still dragging on, the owners pushed the replacement movement to within hours of becoming a reality. When they finally scuttled their own creation — the Indians fired their replacement players on the night of April 1 after they played the New York Mets in a snow-filled exhibition game in Jacobs Field — the whole season was put on fast forward.

The traditional six-week spring training was reduced to 19 days after the owners invited the regular players back to work. The regular season felt the knife as well. The 162-game schedule was sliced to 144 games.

While the players rushed to spring training camps in Florida and Arizona, front office personnel, managers, coaching staffs, trainers, and other support people took a deep breath and readied themselves for Spring Training II. Every club except Baltimore had already been through one full training camp with the replacements. By the time the Indians opened the regular season on April 27 against Texas at The Ballpark in Arlington, the team, in various stages, had been quartered in Winter Haven, Florida, for over 70 days. When trainers Jimmy Warfield and Paul Spicuzza modeled T-shirts that said, "I survived the spring of 1995," it was more fact than joke.

As soon as the strike ended, the Indians added their second layer of free agents. The first layer — Murray, Martinez, Morris, and Pena — had shown them how to win in 1994. The next class — Orel Hershiser, Paul Assenmacher, Dave Winfield, and Bud Black — would help them become champions.

The Closer

The Indians were built on power. That power could be seen in the bullpen and at the plate. The offensive production was expected: the Indians had led the league in homers, runs, hits, and slugging percentage in 1994. It was the power in the bullpen that came as a surprise.

Jose Mesa started the season as the Tribe's closer for one reason — they had no one else. "Jose is going to get the first chance," said Hargrove. "If he can't do it, we'll go to the next guy in line."

Mesa had already pitched his way through two organizations when the Indians acquired him for a minor league outfielder named Kyle Washington on July 14, 1992. He gave the Indians what he'd given Toronto and Baltimore, a starter with a high-voltage arm, who had no idea where the ball was going. His theory on pitching was to throw the next pitch harder than the one before.

In 1994, the Indians moved Mesa to the bullpen for the first time in his career. He did a good job as a setup man, but choked when given a chance to close games.

In the hurried spring of 1995, Mesa closed almost every exhibition game whether or not it was a save situation. Hart, meanwhile, frantically searched for a real closer. The Indians scouted Bryan Harvey, Jeff Montgomery, Randy Myers, Rod Beck, John Hudek, and others. They would have scouted Rollie Fingers if he hadn't retired in 1985. But whenever the Indians talked trade, the other team asked for two or three of their best young players. Hart, with an eye on the future, refused to let the prospects go. That meant the job belonged to Mesa.

Mesa hit 95–98 mph consistently, but he'd done that his whole career. What he hadn't done was throw strikes as consistently as he threatened the sound barrier. That all changed in 1995. Some of it had to do with the work Phil Regan did the year before. Regan, the Indians pitching coach who been hired away to manage Baltimore in 1995, taught Mesa a two-seam sinking fastball to go with his regular fastball. It gave Mesa a pitch where he could get a ground ball out in a difficult situation. It also meant he didn't have to try to strike out every batter he faced.

Two games were vital in Mesa's development. In one of them, Hargrove learned to trust Mesa. In the other, Mesa learned to trust himself. On May 21 in Fenway Park, Mesa started the ninth inning by getting two quick outs. After a single by John Valentin, Mo Vaughn, the league's MVP, came to the plate. The Indians led, 7–5, and lefty Paul Assenmacher was warming in the bullpen. But instead of calling for the lefty, Hargrove stayed with Mesa. He struck Vaughn out for his fourth save.

"Mike showed a lot of confidence in Jose in that situation," said Hart. "After that, I think Jose knew he was Mike's guy. He just took off."

On May 28 in the SkyDome, Mesa entered the ninth with the Indians leading Toronto, 5–3. He loaded the bases on three straight singles, gave up a run on a sacrifice fly, and then walked Candy Maldonado to reload the bases. But Mesa ended the game by getting Ed Sprague to hit into a first-pitch double play.

"That game showed me I could struggle and still save games," said Mesa. "It gave me a lot of confidence. No doubt about it."

Mesa became the stud steer of the best bullpen in the league. Flanked by setup men Eric Plunk and rookie Julian Tavarez from the right side and Assenmacher, Jim Poole, and Alan Embree from the left, the Indians were 80–0 when leading after the eighth inning. Overall, the bullpen crew went 32–13 with a 3.05 ERA and 50 saves. Mesa alone saved 46 games in 48 chances. That included 38 saves in 38 opportunities, surpassing the major league record of 37 by Willie Hernandez.

Late Inning Lightning

While Mesa slammed the door, it seemed everyone else was winning games with homers in the last at-bat. Dave Nelson felt the impact of those homers in his right hand. As the first base coach, it was Nelson's duty to high five the player who hit the game-winning homer as he rounded first and headed home.

"Manny Ramirez gives you the dead fish shake when he hits one, but Albert Belle almost dislocates your shoulder when he hits a homer," said Nelson. "It's the same with Jimmy Thome. Those guys are so pumped up that they hurt your hand."

The Indians won 27 games in their last at-bat. Eleven of those victories came on homers. They were never out of a game, as their 48 come-from-behind victories showed. The melodramatic heroics started on June 4, when the Indians trailed 1994 Cy Young winner David Cone and Toronto 8-0 going into the bottom of the third. They rallied to a 9-8 win when Sorrento hit a two-out, two-run homer in the ninth. To this day Indians' fans can tell you where they were when Sorrento homered.

"The people never left the park," said Sorrento. "It was as if they could sense what was coming. The later it got in the game, the louder they cheered."

The last at-bat mania went on all season, but it reached its zenith in a three-day stretch from July 16–18. It left two of the best closers in history dazed and confused. On July 16, Ramirez faced Dennis Eckersley with two outs in the bottom of the twelfth, a runner on second base and Oakland leading, 4–3. Eckersley, a former Cy Young and MVP winner, threw two quick strikes past the 23-year-old right fielder. Ramirez, stepping out of the box to tighten his batting gloves between every pitch, worked the count back to 2-2.

Eckersley, failing to get Ramirez to chase two bad pitches off the plate, came back inside with a waist-high fastball. Ramirez drove it deep into the first section of the left field bleachers for a 5–4 victory. Eckersley watched the flight of the ball and said one word "Wow!" He said it again as he walked off the mound as Jacobs Field rocked with the sound of over 40,000 people screaming.

"Wow!" What better way to describe the Tribe's season. While Eckersley reveled in the drama, it was hard to tell if Ramirez even knew who Eckersley was. "I'd never faced him before," said Ramirez, his face void of expression, after the game. "In the dugout, they told me he had a good slider."

Saying Dennis Eckersley has a good slider is like saying the Mona Lisa has an interesting smile, but that seemed to capture Ramirez's season perfectly. He hit 31 homers and drove in 107 runs in his second season in the big leagues, but frequently forgot how many outs there were while running the bases. Several times umpires had to tell him if he'd just taken a called third strike or ball four because he'd lost track of the count.

On July 18, Lee Smith, the all-time save leader, entered the ninth protecting a 5–3 lead for California. At the time, the Angels were running away with the AL West. Although they were eventually overtaken by Seattle, at that time of the season it appeared California could have a playoff date with the Indians.

So this was more than just another game in July. At least that's what it felt like when Baerga walked to load the bases with one out. As he jogged to first, Baerga turned toward the plate and pumped both fists at Belle. The message could not be missed — do something, and do it now.

Belle hit Smith's 1–2 pitch over 400 feet into the picnic area behind the center field wall for a grand slam and a 7–5 victory.

The 50–50 Man

Belle and Mesa were the most dominant players on a team filled with heroes. Belle became the first man in history to hit 50 homers and 50 doubles in one season. In true Indian fashion, he took his time doing it. The left fielder hit 36 homers after the All-Star break. He hit 31 of them in August and September, and tied Babe Ruth's record by hitting 17 homers in September.

Belle, who refused to talk to reporters through most of the season, became just the eighth man in history to get 100 extra base hits in a season. He ended with 103; the last man to do it was Stan Musial in 1948.

His hard-line approach with reporters may have played a role in him finishing second to Vaughn in the MVP balloting, but it could not alter the fact that he led the league in homers, total bases, runs, doubles, slugging percentage, and extra base hits. He tied Vaughn for the RBI lead with 126.

The Indians were never really pushed during the season. They moved into sole possession of first place in the AL Central on May 11 and never left. They won the division by 30 games, a modern record.

How dominant were they? Kansas City finished second in the AL Central. The Indians were 11–1 against the Royals. They were so good that Cleveland fans never really saw what they'd been missing since 1954 — a pennant race. The whole season seemed to be one long victory lap, but there were a few items that kept the Indians' attention.

In late June they lost a three-game series to Chicago in Comiskey Park. The sweep, combined with a loss to Boston on June 23, ran their losing streak to a season-high four games and reduced their lead over the Royals to 5½ games. It just so happened that Kauffman Stadium was the Tribe's next stop for a three-game series in the middle of a ten-game trip.

"I was sweating bullets going into that series," said Hargrove. "I figured if we were going to win or lose the division, this is when we were going to do it."

There was no need for such dramatics. The Indians swept the Royals as starters Chad Ogea, Mark Clark, and Charles Nagy earned the wins. They won 10 of their next 14 games and went into the All-Star break with a 46–21 record and a 12-game lead.

Something else happened on that trip. Murray, the personification of the do-it-every-day-ballplayer, became the nineteenth man in history to reach 3,000 hits. After sweeping the Royals, the Indians went to Minneapolis with Murray three hits shy of 3,000. In the first game of the series on June 29, he homered and singled in his first two at-bats, and then went hitless in his next four to send the Metrodome crowd home one hit shy of witnessing history.

The wait ended on June 30. Murray walked and flied out to center in his first two plate appearances. Then he sent a clean single through the right side of the infield against Mike Trombley to all but guarantee himself an invitation to Cooperstown. Winfield, who had reached 3,000 hits in the same ballpark in 1993, was the first Indian to reach him as teammates rushed out of the dugout to greet him at first base.

"It was exciting," said Murray, a man of few words.

"This is something I'll be able to sit back and think back on when I'm done playing." Murray was just the third player to reach 3,000 hits while wearing an Indians uniform. Nap Lajoie and Tris Speaker were the others.

The Indians clinched the division on September 9 with a 3–2 victory over Baltimore at home. Hershiser and Murray, two of the players Hart had signed to win games like this, did just that. Hershiser, who finished the season with a 16–6 record, pitched 6⅔ innings for the win, while Murray drove in two of the three runs.

When the game ended, the Indians carried the AL Central division banner out to center field, and raised it onto a flagpole on top of the scoreboard. Each player took a turn pulling the banner to the top.

"I had tears in my eyes watching it go up," said Alomar. "I've been here since 1990. I went through the 1991 season when we lost 105 games. This is the first banner I've ever seen raised here. I won't forget it."

While the banner represented the present for the Indians, Hargrove did not forget the past. As the banner was pulled to its destination, a song by Garth Brooks called "The Dance" was played over the sound system. It was the favorite song of Steve Olin, the Indians' closer who was killed along with teammate Tim Crews in a spring-training boating accident in 1993.

Hargrove, who had lived through a chunk of the Tribe's bad days as a player, coach, and manager, was so overcome with emotion in the crazed locker room celebration that he could hardly speak. And what words he did say to reporters couldn't be understood.

The Indians won their last five games of the season to reach 100. They finished the year leading the league in batting average (.291) and earned run average (3.83). They were the first team to do that since the 1971 Orioles.

It's October, and We're Still Playing?

A team doesn't make its first appearance in the post-season in 41 years without something weird happening. At least the Indians didn't. The Tribe's first postseason game since 1954 lasted five hours and one minute and featured Belle's bat getting cut in half. Twice delayed by rain, the Indians finally beat Boston in Game 1 of the best-of-five division series, 5–4, on Pena's two-out homer in the thirteenth.

The game ended at 2:08 A.M. on October 4. It had started at 8:44 P.M. on October 3. Boston manager Kevin Kennedy had Belle's bat confiscated after he hit a leadoff homer in the eleventh inning to negate Tim Naehring's go-ahead homer in the top of the inning. Kennedy said the Boston front office told him to have Belle's bat checked if anything suspicious happened.

After the postseason ended, Roger Clemens, who started Game 1 for Boston, said two of Belle's teammates and a clubhouse attendant told the Red Sox before the game that he was using a corked bat. But when former AL President Dr. Bobby Brown, the league's on-site observer, had the bat cut in half, no cork was found.

Hours before the game, Pena had told teammates that if he played, he was going to hit a home run to win the game. Pena entered the game as a defensive replacement in the tenth inning.

The Indians completed a three-game sweep of Boston behind the strong pitching of Hershiser and Nagy. Buried beneath the mountains of offensive statistics compiled by the Tribe during the season, the rotation had gone unnoticed even though it went 68–31 for the best record in the league. In the postseason, however, the starters carried the team.

In Game 2 in Jacobs Field, Hershiser threw 7⅓ scoreless innings and combined with Tavarez, Assenmacher, and Mesa on a three-hitter in a 4–0 victory over Erik Hanson. The win gave Hershiser a 5–0 record in his postseason career as the series moved to Fenway Park for the next three games.

In Game 3, Nagy struggled early in the wind and rain of Fenway, but steadied himself to hold Boston to one run through seven innings in the Tribe's 8–2 victory. The offense, showing patience against knuckleballer Tim Wakefield, led 3–0 after three innings. Thome's two-run homer in the second inning was the big hit. The Indians added five more runs in the sixth to reach the American League Championship Series. The Red Sox hit .184 in the sweep with Vaughn and Jose Canseco, the number 3 and 4 hitters, taking a combined 0–for–27 with nine strikeouts.

In the Indians locker room, the celebration was low key. There was no champagne or beer in sight. "I was glad to see that," said Martinez. "You don't want to show too much emotion because you haven't won anything yet. If we win the next step, then you've got to celebrate because we're going to the big show."

The ALCS

The Indians, who finished the regular season with the best record in baseball at 100–44, opened the best-of-seven ALCS against Seattle in the Kingdome on October 10. In their three postseason series, the Indians didn't have home field advantage once.

The Mariners, appearing in the postseason for the first time in history, won Game 1 when manager Lou Piniella was forced to start rookie Bob Wolcott against Martinez and the best hitting team in baseball. Piniella had no other choice because he'd fried his rotation to a crisp in beating New York in five games in the other division series.

Twelve of Wolcott's first 13 pitches were balls as he loaded the bases. When he escaped without allowing a run, the Indians knew they were in trouble. The Mariners won, 3–2, as the Tribe stranded 12 runners.

The Indians had never seen Wolcott or the Kingdome quite like it was in the postseason. The Mariners entered the league in 1977 with Toronto, but the city had gone out of its way to ignore them until late in the 1995 season when they ran down the Angels to win the AL West in a one-game playoff. From that point on the Kingdome had become a cauldron of sound with close to 60,000 fans standing and cheering from the first pitch to the last.

It was so loud in Seattle's concrete mushroom that Baerga wore earplugs in the first game. By Game 2, he removed the earplugs, and the Indians adjusted. Behind eight good innings by Hershiser, Baerga's two-run single in the fifth, and Ramirez's two homers, the Indians coasted to a 5–2 victory to bring the series back to Jacobs Field all tied up. "That was a must win," said Hargrove.

"We did not want to go back to Cleveland down 0–2 and have to face Randy Johnson in Game 3."

Johnson, who won 18 games during the regular season, was not available for Games 1 and 2 because he'd won Games 3 and 5 against the Yankees. The Big Unit, the AL's Cy Young award winner, was the Mariners' heart and soul.

Johnson held the Indians to two runs in eight innings in Game 3, but Nagy pitched just as well as the game went into extra innings with the score 2–2. Jay Buhner, who had hit five homers against the Indians during the regular season, won it with a three-run homer in the eleventh against Plunk. It was his second homer of the game and gave the Mariners a 2–1 lead in the series.

Ken Hill, acquired from St. Louis just before the July 31 trading deadline, pitched seven scoreless innings to win Game 4, 7–0. It was Hill's second win of the postseason even though it was his first start since September 27. Murray and Thome hit two-run homers against loser Andy Benes in the first three innings to end things early. The Tribe scored seven runs even though Belle (right ankle) and Alomar (neck) missed the game with injuries.

In Game 5, Hershiser, pitching on three days rest, allowed one earned run in six innings for his third victory of the postseason. Relievers Tavarez, Assenmacher, Plunk, and Mesa finished the five-hitter for the 3–2 win. The Mariners had led, 2–1 through five innings, but Thome changed the direction of the game and the series with a long two-run homer off loser Chris Bosio in the sixth. Hershiser became the first pitcher in history to have a postseason record of 7–0. He struck out eight and allowed five runs. He also guaranteed himself the MVP award of the ALCS.

The extra rest served Martinez and his battered body well in Game 6 as the Indians clinched the pennant with a 4–0 victory. Before the game, however, Martinez looked like someone walking his last mile as he sat on the bench during batting practice. "I felt the weight of the world on me," said Martinez. "It was win or die."

Martinez pitched seven scoreless innings in his matchup with the 6'10" Johnson. Lofton, who hit .458 in the ALCS, gave him a 1–0 lead with a single in the fifth. In the eighth, the Indians closed the book on Johnson and the Mariners.

Pena opened with a double to right center. Ruben Amaro pinch ran and stole third. Lofton followed with a bunt single and stole second. Johnson, perhaps disrupted by Lofton's speed on the bases, threw a wild pitch that bounced away from catcher Dan Wilson and rolled toward the Indians' dugout.

Amaro scored for a 2–0 lead as Wilson fumbled for the ball. Then, much to the dismay of the thundering Kingdome crowd, Lofton sprinted home from second on the same play for a 3–0 lead. When Baerga followed with a homer to right center, it was clear the Indians were headed to a World Series meeting with Atlanta. The win was Martinez's first ever in the postseason. He would start two more games in the World Series, but he'd spent himself that night in Seattle. It seemed to be worth it to him.

"Finally, we gave Cleveland something it can be proud of," said Martinez. "I don't think the people will ever forget that."

Once again, the Tribe's pitching was marvelous. They held Seattle to a .184 batting average, while throwing two shutouts. Edgar and Tino Martinez, like Vaughn and Canseco before them, were helpless. They were a combined 5–for–45 with no RBI.

Wait Till Next Year

The Indians' hitters would soon share that helpless feeling. In winning the World Series in six games, Atlanta's pitchers held the Indians to a .179 batting average. Five of the six games were decided by one run, but the Tribe, which averaged almost six runs a game during the regular season, scored just 19 runs against the Braves.

The slide started in the Braves' 3–2 victory in Game 1. Hershiser, locked in a 1–1 duel with Greg Maddux, unexpectedly took himself out the game after walking the first two batters in the seventh. Pitching coach Mark Wiley went to the mound to calm him down and in the next moment Hershiser was walking toward the dugout.

On the bench, Hargrove was befuddled. Hershiser's sudden departure had put him on the defensive in his managerial chess game with Atlanta's Bobby Cox. When he called for Assenmacher to face lefty Ryan Klesko, Cox used righthanded batter Mike Devereaux as a pinch-hitter. Assenmacher walked him to load the bases.

When Hargrove called for Tavarez to face righty batsman Charlie O'Brien, Cox pinch-hit the lefthanded Luis Polonia, who sent a ground ball to short to score McGriff for a 2–1 lead after Hargrove elected not to bring the infield in. Then, with his pitchers struggling to throw strikes, and the bases still loaded, Hargrove went against his better judgment and didn't call for a pitchout with Rafael Belliard at the plate. Belliard laid down a perfect squeeze bunt to score Justice with the deciding run in a 3–2 victory.

Hershiser, the ultimate big-game pitcher, never really explained why he gave himself the hook. First he lost his release point, then he grew frustrated and talked himself out of what proved to be the pivotal game of the series.

Maddux, the four-time Cy Young winner, was nearly perfect. He gave up unearned runs to Lofton in the first and the ninth innings, allowed two hits, struck out four, and broke at least five Indians' bats.

Tom Glavine wasn't as sharp as Maddux, but he was still good as the Braves beat the Tribe, 4–3, in Game 2. The Indians ended a streak of six straight World Series defeats in Game 3, but it was not easy. Murray doubled home Espinoza in the eleventh for a 7–6 victory. Baerga, playing with a hairline fracture in his left ankle the entire postseason, started the rally with a double, and was replaced by Espinoza.

The game should have ended in regulation as the Indians led 4-1 against John Smoltz after three innings. But Nagy gave up solo homers to Fred McGriff and Ryan Klesko in the sixth and seventh, respectively, to cut the Tribe's lead to 5-3.

Hargrove let Nagy start the eighth. All year long, he'd gone to the bullpen in that situation, but Nagy's pitch count was low. The Braves scored three times in the inning to take a 6–5 lead. It could have been the deciding event of the Series since no team has ever recovered from a 3–0 deficit, but Alomar doubled home a run in the eighth to force extra innings.

Mesa pitched three scoreless innings for the win. It was the Tribe's first Series win since Game 6 in 1948 against the Boston Braves, but even in victory things did not go right. Belle, in an unprovoked profanity-riddled tirade several hours before the game, chastised several reporters for being in the Indians' dugout. He then confronted CBS reporter Hannah Storm and told her to get out of the dugout as well, but Storm wouldn't move.

The outburst heaped more negative publicity on Belle, who snapped and snarled at reporters throughout the Series. He was forced to apologize to Storm before Game 6 in Atlanta.

In Game 4 Hill and Steve Avery didn't allow a run through five innings. That ended when Klesko and Belle traded homers in the sixth. The Braves won it with three runs in the seventh on Polonia's RBI double and David Justice's two-run single against Assenmacher.

The Indians were not in an enviable position, but at least they ate well. They dined on a $600 dinner of prime rib, Cajun catfish, and lobster from clubhouse manager Stan Hunter after Game 4. It was if they were condemned men eating one last feast before heading home for the winter following their meeting with Maddux, he of the 1.63 regular season ERA, in Game 5.

Thus replenished, however, the Indians beat Maddux, 5–4, to force a Game 6 back in Atlanta. Hershiser atoned for his exit in Game 1 by holding the Braves to one run through eight innings with six strikeouts. Offensively, the Indians, after much film study, peppered Maddux with one line drive after another. It started with Belle's two-run homer in the first and continued with run-scoring singles by Thome and Ramirez in the sixth. Thome added a 436-foot homer to center in the eighth, and it turned out to be the decisive run when Klesko hit a two-run homer against Mesa in the ninth.

But it would be foolish to think Hershiser and the Tribe's hitters beat Maddux by themselves. Hours before the game, Mike Seghi, director of team travel, PR-man Bart Swain, and clubhouse attendant Tom Foster paid the ultimate price. They took Joeboo, the team's voodoo-doll mascot, to the Indians' bullpen and turned him into a sacrificial ball of flame. It helped that a younger Joeboo had taken the original's place. Swain, out of respect, preserved the moment with pictures.

"We had to do it," said Foster. "We had to get rid of the evil spirits."

Yet nothing could save the Indians from Glavine in Game 6. He beat them, 1–0, combining with Mark Wohlers to give Atlanta its first World Series championship. Glavine, the series MVP, allowed one hit in eight innings. He struck out eight and walked three.

Martinez, pitching with a stiff right shoulder, lasted 4⅓ scoreless innings, but Hargrove had the bullpen warming in the first inning. The only run of the game came on Justice's leadoff homer in the sixth off Poole.

After Baerga made the final out in Game 6, he and several teammates stayed on the bench and watched the Braves celebrate in the middle of the infield. His eyes were glazed with disappointment, but minutes later in the Indians' locker room his eyes bore a different look.

"This team will be back," he said.

CHAPTER 2

The Indians History

Paul Hoynes

When the 1995 season ended, the Cleveland Indians were one of the two best teams in baseball. Yet for most of their existence, the Indians have been a long-running version of *Heartbreak Hotel,* offering promises every spring and, as certainly as summer follows spring, leaving their fans with little cheer in the fall.

This look at 95 Indian summers is no more orderly than the franchise it chronicles. Defined by disappointment and tragedy, the Indians history nonetheless has had its moments of glory, capped by the 1995 American League Championship. That story was told in the preceding chapter; here the focus shifts to the Indians' three other World Series appearances, and the seemingly endless summers of woe that make the Cleveland Indians so enfuriating, so oddly endearing, so undeniably and intensely, *our* team.

How Bad Has It Been?

The Indians are one of eight charter members of the American League. They are one of four to play in the same city since the league began in 1901. Other than that, they've spent most of their time leaning against a lamppost watching the rest of the league rush by.

The American League Central Division title they won in 1995 was their first since the start of divisional play in 1969. In those 37 campaigns, they've had six winning seasons, including the strike-shortened years of 1981 and 1994. That stretch includes eight last-place finishes in the old AL East. It would have been worse, but the Tribe caught a break when the expansion Toronto Blue Jays entered their division in 1977. The Indians finished one step ahead of the last-place Jays for four straight seasons from 1978–81. In 1982, the Indians and Toronto tied for last.

It has often been said that the Indians' greatest accomplishment, especially during the time between 1960 and the purchase of the club by shopping mall developers Richard and David Jacobs on December 9, 1986, is that they somehow managed to stay in Cleveland. Various owners, at various times, had contemplated moving the team to New Orleans, Seattle, Minneapolis, Houston, and several other cities to escape a bad ballpark where, unsurprisingly, hardly anyone came to watch a bad team.

There has always been something achingly human about the Indians, something that keeps them attached to the pulse of Cleveland. For years attendance at Cleveland Stadium was brutal. After drawing more than 2 million fans in 1948 and 1949, in the ensuing decades they were often lucky to draw a million customers (indeed, in the years 1960-73, they went 14 straight seasons without drawing a million). Not until 1990 did they again top the 2 million mark.

"Cleveland is a good baseball town," former Baltimore manager Earl Weaver once said. "You take a cab to the ballpark, and the cabbie will tell you what's wrong with the team. You get your hair cut in Cleveland, and the barber wants to talk baseball. The people just don't go to the ballpark."

The Indians have never been lovable losers like the Chicago Cubs. Until recently, the team seemed to exist for one reason—to give long-suffering Clevelanders something to complain about.

. . . And to Pull at Their Heart Strings

Has ever a team been touched by more tragedy? Maybe that's why the Indians have endured in Cleveland. In spite of their privileged position — grown men making good money for playing a boy's game — the Indians have always seemed very much like the people who follow their fortunes.

In 1993, the Indians moved their spring training camp from Tucson, Arizona, to Florida. They had trained in Tucson from 1947–92, but Jacobs wanted the club to train in Florida so fans — himself included — could have easier access to the team. They were scheduled to move to Homestead, just south of Miami. Those plans were scratched when Homestead was badly mauled by Hurricane Andrew. The Indians eventually found a home in Winter Haven.

March 22 was the only off-day the team had that spring training. Newly acquired pitcher Tim Crews owned a ranch on Little Lake Nellie about 40 miles north of Winter Haven. He invited several of his new teammates to an all-day picnic. Most of the players had their own plans and didn't attend, but pitchers Steve Olin and Bob Ojeda and their families did.

"Steve had promised our kids that they'd go horseback riding on the ranch," said Patti Olin. "We got lost once, and almost turned back, but we finally found it."

That night Crews took Olin and Ojeda fishing on the tiny lake in his high-powered bass boat. They had been on the lake only a few minutes when someone flashed car headlights from the shore. It was a prearranged signal for Crews to come ashore and get more passengers.

He gunned the engine and began to make a long turn toward the pickup area when the boat collided with an unlighted dock that extended almost 250 feet into the lake. The three pitchers, sitting side by side in the middle of the boat, took the brunt of the collision in their upper bodies. The boat was traveling an estimated 39 mph on impact.

Olin, who had saved 29 games in 1992 and was emerging as the Indians' closer, died instantly. Crews died a few hours later, while Ojeda, who had the top of his scalp sheared off and almost died from loss of blood, survived.

Olin, drafted and developed by the Indians, left his wife and three children. Crews, a veteran who had spent the previous six years with Los Angeles, left a wife and three children. Ojeda, signed as a free agent before camp after pitching for Boston, the New York Mets, and Los Angeles, returned to pitch that season after undergoing months of rehabilitation, including plastic surgery and psychological counseling.

Tragedy continued to stalk the Indians that year. Cliff Young, another pitcher, was killed in an automobile accident near his hometown of Willis, Texas during the off-season. Young was trying to light a cigarette when he lost control of his car. It left the road and hit a tree.

In October of 1977, Andre Thornton was just starting to show why he'd become one of the best power hitters in Indians history. He led the team with 28 homers and 77 runs scored in his first season in Cleveland. At the end of the year, Thornton and his family were on the way home to West Chester, Pennsylvania, for a wedding.

During the trip, the van they were traveling in was pushed off the turnpike by a violent gust of wind during a winter storm. In the accident, Thornton's wife, Gertrude, and their young daughter, Theresa, were killed. Thornton, who was driving the van, and his son, Andy, escaped unharmed.

Thornton, a man of vast physical and religious strength, was able to overcome the deaths of his wife and daughter. He wrote a book called *Triumph Born of Tragedy* about the accident. In it, he explained how God gave him the strength and faith to continue his life. He went on to play nine years with the Indians, hitting 214 homers and driving in 749 runs. After the 1984 season, he had a chance to become a free agent, and escape the Indians' cycle of defeat. Thornton chose to stay in Cleveland, where he still makes his home today.

When Crews and Olin were killed, the Indians asked one man to speak at their memorial service in Florida. It was Thornton, the born-again Christian, who had learned firsthand how to deal with such pain and loss.

The 1970s were filled with bad news for the Tribe. Promising power-hitter Tony Horton, who hit 27 homers in 1969, suffered a nervous breakdown in 1970 and left the game at the age of 25. All-Star catcher Ray Fosse, one of the Tribe's brightest hopes, injured his shoulder in a home plate collision with Pete Rose in the 1970 All-Star game and never turned into the hitter he seemed destined to be. Ken "The Hawk" Harrelson broke his leg in the spring of 1970, missed most of the season, and retired the next year. Sudden Sam McDowell ruined a potential Hall of Fame career with fast living and alcohol.

But none of those misfortunes had the impact on the franchise that the events of May 7, 1957 did. Herb Score was going to be the lefthanded Bob Feller. The timing was perfect. Feller, the winningest pitcher in Indians' history, had retired in 1956. The torch had been passed to Score.

In his rookie year in 1955, Score won 16 games and led the league with 245 strikeouts in 227⅓ innings — still an AL rookie record. The next year he went 20–9 and again led the league in strikeouts with 263 in 249⅓ innings. Ted Williams said he was the best lefthander he'd ever seen. Williams's team, the Red Sox, offered $1 million for Score, but General Manager Hank Greenberg refused.

Score's whole future changed with one pitch in a game against the New York Yankees. Gil McDougald, the second batter of the game, lined a 2–2 pitch toward the pitcher. Score, who had fallen off the mound because of the force of his follow through, didn't see the ball until the last moment, and could do nothing to protect himself. He was struck in the right eye and fell. When he hit the ground he was bleeding from his eye, ear, and nose.

Score, who did not pitch again that year, recovered his sight, but the rest of his game was lost. He came back in 1958, but tore a ligament in his left elbow and made just 12 appearances. Four years later he was out of the majors. He's been announcing Indians' games on radio and television ever since. "Getting hit in the eye didn't end my career," said Score. "I recovered from that. It was the elbow injury that did it." To thousands of Indians' fans, however, Score's career and a large chunk of the Indians' future ended in that game in May of 1957.

There was no comparison between Don Black and Score as far as pitching ability or potential. But Black had thrown a no-hitter for the Indians in 1947, and was on the team the next year when they made their run to the pennant and World Series. By then, however, he was being used mostly as a spot starter by manager Lou Boudreau. On September 13, 1948 Black made his tenth and final start of the season and his career. He pitched two scoreless innings before suffering a cerebral hemorrhage while batting. Black recovered, but never pitched again in the big leagues. He died on April 21, 1959 at 42.

Shortstop Ray Chapman was one of the most popular players on the 1920 Indians. His teammates liked him for his sunny disposition and his fine singing voice. Chapman would often lead the team in song during the team's trips. It made the long train rides go faster.

On August 16, 1920, with the Indians in the thick of a pennant race with the Chicago White Sox and Yankees, Chapman's voice was silenced. He was hit on the left side of his head by a pitch from submariner Carl Mays of the Yankees at the Polo Grounds. Chapman, leading off the fifth inning, froze on an inside pitch by Mays and never got out of the way.

He died the next morning of a fractured skull after undergoing surgery. Chapman's death, the only on-field fatality in big league history, devastated the Indians and Cleveland. His body was shipped home and funeral services were held in St. John's Cathedral in Cleveland. Over 2,000 mourners jammed the church. Three thousand more who couldn't gain entry waited outside.

Tris Speaker, player-manager for the Indians, was so overcome by grief that he didn't attend the service. Some of the Indians were upset at Mays, who had a reputation for throwing at batters. In his book *The Pitch That Killed,* author Mike Sowell quotes first baseman Doc Johnston, one of Chapman's teammates, as saying, "Mays should be strung up."

Other teams around the league said they would boycott games that Mays pitched, but the threat never materialized. For his part Mays said it was never his intention to hit Chapman. He pitched 15 years in the big leagues, spending his final season with the New York Giants in 1929. He went on to be a scout, and the Indians were one of the teams he worked for.

The Indians' close association with the game's dark side may have had its origins with Addie Joss, one of the best pitchers in team history. Joss, who joined the team in 1902, pitched no-hitters in 1908 and 1910. The 1908 no-hitter was a perfect game in which Joss beat Chicago, 1-0, in League Park on October 2 during a tight pennant race.

Joss's health began to fade in 1910, but his overall record in eight seasons was remarkable — 160–97 with a 1.89 ERA. In 1911 he collapsed on the bench during an exhibition game in spring training and was finally sent home to Toledo, Ohio. He died of tubercular meningitis on April 14, 1911 at the age of 31.

With that kind of past, it's a wonder any player would want to wear an Indians uniform. But there has never been a lack of candidates, just a lack of talent.

They Weren't Always Called Indians

In their inaugural season of 1901, the Cleveland players of the American League were called the Blues after the color of their uniforms, and in echo of the city's former National League and American Association franchises. The players voted to change to the more macho sounding Bronchos in 1902. The next year the name was changed to the Naps in honor of second baseman Napoleon Lajoie, the franchise's first great player.

The Cleveland Americans became Native Americans, or Indians, in 1915 after a newspaper ran a contest to rename the team. A fan suggested that the team be named in honor of Louis Sockalexis, one of the first Native Americans to star in the big leagues. Sockalexis, who played for the Cleveland Spiders of the National League from 1897–99, didn't last longer in the big leagues because he fell prey to alcohol.

Under any name, however, the Indians have really had just two extended periods where they could be called a great team. Preceding the 1920 world championship, the Indians finished third in 1917 and second in 1918 and 1919. After beating the Brooklyn Dodgers in the best-of-nine World Series, they finished second by 4½ games in 1921. In those five years, the Indians were a combined 437–293 and a threat in every pennant race.

That team began to take shape in 1916. Young pitchers Jim Bagby and Stan Coveleski were brought to Cleveland to complement veterans such as catcher Steve O'Neill and middle infielders Chapman and Bill Wambsganss. Jack Graney and Elmer Smith were in the outfield.

The player who brought the team together was Speaker, the Gray Eagle. Speaker had helped Boston win the World Series in 1912 and 1915, and was already established as one of the best center fielders in the game. The Indians were able to acquire him because he was in a contract dispute with Joe Lannin, Boston's president.

Speaker was upset about the trade. The Indians were a bad ballclub coming off a seventh-place finish. At first he refused to go to Cleveland, and threatened to quit. Then he requested that he receive $10,000 of the $50,000 the Indians paid the Red Sox for his services. The request came with a stipulation — the $10,000 had to come from Lannin himself.

When the Indians home opener came around, Speaker had reached terms with the Indians. The only thing missing was the $10,000 from the Boston president. The morning of the game he informed Tribe owner Jim Dunn that he would not play until he received the money. Dunn offered to pay the $10,000 himself, but Speaker wanted Lannin's money and his alone. Finally, Ban Johnson, American League president, called Speaker and assured him that Lannin's check was on the way. It was then, and only then, that the stubborn Speaker agreed to play.

The Indians finished 77–77 in 1916, a 20-game improvement over 1915. Speaker, who won the batting title by hitting .386 to end Ty Cobb's nine-year reign, established himself as a force on the club. Lee Fohl was the manager, but he and Speaker conferred on most game strategy through a set of signs that they'd flash during the game — Fohl from the bench, and Speaker from center field.

The upward spiral was on its way. The Indians won 88 games in 1917, but still finished 12 games behind first-place Chicago. Bagby won 23 games and Coveleski 19, and Speaker hit .352. During the season, the Indians lost nine players to the military draft, but added Smokey Joe Wood from Boston, where he had been Speaker's roommate. Wood had won 34 games for the champion Red Sox in 1912, and three more in the Series, but his arm went bad and the Indians used him as an outfielder.

The Indians might have won their first pennant in 1918 if not for World War I. The season ended on September 1 by governmental decree so all players could enlist or go to work in defense jobs. The Indians had pulled to within 4 games of the pennant-winning Red Sox in late August, but ran out of time to run them down. They finished 2½ games back.

The 1919 season was played to completion following the end of the War. The Indians finished second to the White Sox by 3½ games. During the year, Speaker became the player-manager after Fohl quit following some haywire pitching strategy that allowed Babe Ruth, still with Boston at the time, to hit a game-winning homer over the right field wall in League Park. Two other important events took place that year. The Indians, leaning heavily on Speaker's advice regarding player moves, acquired outfielder Charlie Jamieson from the Philadelphia Athletics and righthander Ray Caldwell from the Red Sox.

Jamieson, who had played just 401 games in the big leagues before the trade, spent the next 14 years with the Indians and retired as a .303 lifetime hitter. He shared right field in 1920 and hit .319.

Caldwell had already drunk himself out of two organizations, the Yankees and Red Sox, when Speaker signed him to a unique contract. After giving Caldwell a raise, Speaker had a clause put in the contract that said, "After each game he pitches, Ray Caldwell must get drunk. He is not to report to the clubhouse the next day. The second day he is to report to manager Speaker and run around the ballpark as many times as manager Speaker stipulates. The third day he is to throw batting practice, and the fourth day he is to pitch a championship game."

Caldwell went 5–1 for the Tribe in 1919. In the championship season of 1920, he was 20–10. In his book, *The Cleveland Indians,* Franklin Lewis says Caldwell followed his contract language to the letter until late in the 1920 season when he stopped drinking.

The First Championship: 1920

The 1920 Indians probably weren't the most talented team in the American League. What they did have was Speaker pushing the right buttons and the three-man rotation of Bagby, Coveleski, and Caldwell combining for 75 victories. Bagby set a team record with 31 wins. Coveleski, a spitballer, won 24. On offense, the Tribe led the league with 857 runs, while hitting .303 as a team.

Perhaps more importantly, they had a rubber soul. They needed it to bounce back from Chapman's death. The Indians tried to replace Chapman with Harry Lunte, but he pulled a hamstring muscle. Desperate for another shortstop, the Indians paid $6,000 to New Orleans for Joe Sewell. The investment turned out to be a good one. Sewell hit .329 in 22 games and spent 11 years with the Indians in a career that would take him to the Hall of Fame.

On September 14, the Indians fell 1½ games behind New York. Three days later, they led the Yankees by a game and the White Sox by 1½ games. After Bagby won his 29th game on September 19, the Indians had won 17 of their last 21 games and led second-place Chicago by 1½ games with the White Sox headed to Cleveland for a three-game series.

Chicago won two of the three games and left town trailing by a half game. On September 28, the pennant was decided off the field. White Sox owner Charles Comiskey suspended eight of his players for their part in fixing the 1919 World Series between Chicago and Cincinnati after a Cook County grand jury handed down indictments against them. The demoralized White Sox lost two of their last three games, while Bagby clinched the pennant with his 31st victory on October 2.

The Indians beat Brooklyn in the World Series five games to two. Coveleski, who came out of the Pennsylvania coal mines and liked to nip on moonshine, started and won three games. Each of his victories was a five-hitter.

After Coveleski won the opener, Brooklyn took the next two games to bring the series back to Cleveland with a 2–1 lead. Dunn, who had bought the club on February 21, 1916, was a nervous wreck on the train to Cleveland. Speaker told him to relax because the Indians were going to win four straight and win the series in Cleveland.

That's exactly what they did. Coveleski won Game 4 to even the series, before Game 5 turned into a date with history. Not only did the Indians win, but Wambsganss, playing second base, became the only man in World Series history to turn an unassisted triple play, Bagby became the first pitcher to hit a Series homer, and Smith became the first man to hit a grand slam in the Series. The triple play came in the fifth with runners on first and second. Clarence Mitchell, Brooklyn's pitcher, sent a liner toward right. Wamby, as his teammates called him, made a leaping catch. He took three strides and stepped

on second to force Pete Kilduff. He was going to throw to first to get Mitchell, but by that time Otto Miller was only a few feet away, so he tagged him for the third out.

Lefty Duster Mails, a late-season pickup, won Game 6 on a three-hitter, 1–0. Then Coveleski dropped the hammer in Game 7. The Indians postseason prize money was $4,204 per player. A week after the final victory, the team was honored at Wade Park in front of 50,000 people.

The Indians, just to make sure no one forgot what they'd accomplished, had "World Champions" printed across the front of their uniforms in 1921. They played like it for most of the year, too, winning 94 games, but a four-game series against the Yankees on September 23 virtually ended the season. The Tribe trailed the Yankees by two percentage points when they came to the Polo Grounds, but with Speaker out for the season with torn knee ligaments, New York prevailed.

Veeck as in Wreck

The Indians were not heard from again in the postseason until 1948. The man who made their arrival possible walked with a limp, liked beer, hated ties, and always sat in the front seat of taxi cabs so he could talk baseball with the driver. He rarely slept, choosing to spend every conscious moment rebuilding the Indians, reading books, and partying.

The man was Bill Veeck, and he ushered in the best, and perhaps most unappreciated, period in Indians history. From 1947, Veeck's first full season as owner, through 1956 the Indians were a combined 928–614 for a .602 winning percentage. They won one world championship, two pennants, finished second five times, third once, and fourth twice. Veeck sold the team after the 1949 season, but the organization he established helped carry the Indians into their one golden era.

Veeck came from a baseball family. His father, William Sr., was president of the Chicago Cubs. His baseball education started at the ground floor. He worked the ticket windows and concession stands and helped the grounds crew in Wrigley Field. He eventually became treasurer of the ballclub, but in 1941 at 27 he quit to buy the Milwaukee Brewers of the American Association.

When he returned from World War II — while serving in the Marines in the South Pacific his right foot was crushed when an anti-aircraft gun malfunctioned — Veeck was ready to put his knowledge to work. On June 21, 1946 his group purchased the Indians from the Alva Bradley family. The Bradleys, and other prominent Cleveland families, had owned the team since 1927 and failed to produce a championship. Veeck put a World Series ring on his finger in less than two full seasons as majority owner.

Veeck never met a promotion he didn't like. The Cleveland fans felt the same way. The Indians set a club record for attendance with 1,057,289 in 1946 — and that was to watch a sixth-place club. They broke that record in 1947 when 1,521,978 fans came to the Stadium to see the Indians finish fourth. The war was over, and people were in a mood to celebrate and spend. But the best was yet to come.

One of the first things Veeck did in 1947 was move the

Indians into Cleveland Stadium fulltime. Cozy League Park, which opened on May 1, 1891 as the home of the defunct Spiders and had been the Tribe's home since 1901 (rebuilt as a concrete-and-steel park in 1910), closed on September 21, 1946. The quaint old ballpark's capacity was listed at 22,500 fans. That was much too small for Veeck's big plans.

Cleveland Stadium was the place for him. The huge park on the shores of Lake Erie was hailed as a wonder of the age when it opened on July 31,1932. That day 80,014 people saw Philadelphia's Lefty Grove outpitch Mel Harder and the Indians, 1–0. Veeck saw that sea of seats and dreamed of the money he'd make when people were sitting in them.

Until he arrived, the park was so big that the Indians had trouble filling it. From 1932–46, they'd play their weekday games in League Park and move to the Stadium for holidays, night games, and weekends when bigger crowds were expected. It was a pitcher's paradise, but the hitters hated it. The outfield was vast. With the bleachers in center field 470 feet away when the park opened, hitters from both home and visiting teams grumbled.

Veeck corrected that situation by erecting a temporary fence in the outfield in April of 1947. That season the Indians finished second in the league in homers. In his autobiography *Veeck — as in Wreck,* he said the grounds crew would move the fence in or out between series in the dead of night according to the number of power hitters the opposing team would bring to town.

The club Veeck purchased had two great players — Bob Feller and Lou Boudreau. Feller had rejoined the Indians in 1945 after serving almost four years in the U.S. Navy. Boudreau had been with the Indians since 1938. They were both one-time boy wonders. Feller was 17 when in 1936 he struck out 15 St. Louis Browns in his first major league start. Boudreau became the Indians' player-manager on November 25, 1941 at the tender age of 24.

Other veterans included Ken Keltner at third, Ray Mack at second, catcher Jim Hegan, and outfielders Pat Seerey and Hank Edwards. The pitching staff featured Feller, Allie Reynolds, Steve Gromek, and converted infielder-outfielder Bob Lemon. Veeck added second baseman Joe Gordon and little known knuckleballer Gene Bearden at the end of the 1946 season. While he was acquiring ballplayers, Veeck had part of his right leg amputated as the result of his war wound and was fitted with a wooden leg.

On July 3, 1947 he signed Larry Doby, the first black to play in the American League. Jackie Robinson officially broke the color barrier with Brooklyn earlier that season. Doby, who been playing second base for the Negro Leagues' Newark Eagles when the Indians signed him, did not adjust as quickly to the big leagues as Robinson. He hit .156 in 29 games, but he would soon make his presence felt.

The Indians went 80–74 in 1947, a 12-game improvement over 1946, but they were out of the race by June. Feller led the league with 20 wins and 196 strikeouts, while Lemon won 11 games. Gordon and Boudreau had good years in the middle of the infield, Gordon hitting 29 homers and Boudreau batting .307. Veeck, ever restless, was not satisfied.

The Second Championship: 1948

In 1948 the Indians won their first six games. Lemon had a breakthrough year, going 20–14, and throwing a no-hitter on June 30 against Detroit. Bearden, the lefthanded knuckleballer, was 20–7. Russ Christopher, a reliever Veeck signed in spite of the fact that he had a hole in his heart, saved 17 games.

On offense, Doby proved he belonged. He moved to right field and hit .301 with 14 homers and 66 RBI. In the next eight years, Doby would become one of the best power-hitting outfielders in Indians history. Gordon hit .280 with 32 homers and 124 RBI. Keltner, thought to be through, hit .297 with 31 homers and 119 RBI, while Boudreau won the MVP by hitting .355 with 18 homers and 106 RBI.

All those fine statistics didn't guarantee the Indians anything. Despite their fast start, they found themselves in a tight race with Philadelphia and the Yankees. Then the Indians slumped in July and the Red Sox moved into first. It was during that slump that Veeck pulled another rabbit out of his hat. He signed ageless Satchel Paige from the Negro Leagues.

While the rest of the baseball world howled in protest — J.G. Taylor Spink, editor of *The Sporting News,* bashed the signing in an editorial — Veeck felt Paige, who by his account was 42, could still pitch. To prove his point, Paige went through a secret tryout against Boudreau at Cleveland Stadium. He threw 20 pitches, and Boudreau didn't hit one of them hard.

Paige, rated by Feller as one of the top 20 pitchers of all time, passed his test. One of baseball's great characters, he said the secret to pitching and staying young were the following six rules:

1. *Avoid fried meats which angry up the blood.*
2. *If your stomach disputes you, lie down and pacify it with cool thoughts.*
3. *Keep the juices flowing by jangling around gently as you move.*
4. *Go very light on the vices, such as carrying on in society. The social ramble ain't restful.*
5. *Avoid running at all times.*
6. *Don't look back. Something might be gaining on you.*

Paige went 6–1 with a 2.48 ERA and one save in 21 games for the Tribe. At the end of the season, Spink wrote what amounted to a retraction.

The Indians went on an 18–4 winning streak in August to get back in the race. On August 20, Paige added to the streak by shutting out Chicago, 1–0, on a three-hitter in front of 78,382 fans in Cleveland Stadium. On Labor Day, though, the Red Sox had a 4½ game lead over the Tribe.

The Indians had one thing in their favor — Feller. After blowing hot-and-cold through the first five months of the season, he went 6–0 in September. Still, Boudreau was taking no chances. During an East Coast trip late in the season, he met with the traveling beat writers and asked them not to go into the Indians' locker room after games to interview players for fear that something would be said or written to spur the opposition. The writers, in a move which would shock their brethren today, agreed.

On September 22, Feller pitched the Indians into a first place tie with New York and Boston by beating the Red Sox, 5–2. The Indians took a two-game lead over the Red Sox with four to play when Feller beat Detroit, 4–1, on September 26, and Bearden beat the White Sox, 11–0, two days later. But the race was not over.

Needing to beat Detroit twice in the final series of the season to clinch, Lemon lost, but Bearden won to clinch a tie. On the last day of the season, Boudreau sent Feller back to the mound for the clincher. He lost, 7–1, to Hal Newhouser, while Boston beat the Yankees. The Indians and Red Sox had ended in a tie for first place. A one game playoff — the first in league history — in Fenway Park on October 4 would decide the pennant winner.

Bearden, working on two days rest, started the playoff game. The rookie, an unknown when Veeck acquired him from the Yankees at the end of the 1946 season, pitched well and the Indians won easily, 8–3. Boudreau had four hits, including two homers, Keltner hit a three-run homer in the fourth, and Doby doubled twice.

The Indians would play the Boston Braves in the World Series. Bob Feller was Boudreau's obvious choice to start the Series opener. He would win 266 games during his career with the Indians, and would have easily surpassed 300 if not for the four years he spent in the Navy.

That never bothered Feller. He enlisted on December 9, 1941, two days after the Japanese bombed Pearl Harbor. The Iowa farmboy was at his peak. He'd gone 25-13 with a 3.15 ERA and 260 strikeouts in 343 innings in 1941. He had already won 107 games by the age of 22. Years later when Feller was asked why he didn't wait until he was drafted so he could pitch another season or two, he said, "because we were getting the hell beat out of us and I wanted to help."

The one thing that bothered Feller in later years was his inability to win a game in the World Series. His best chance came in Game 1 on October 6, 1948 at Braves Field. He and Johnny Sain were in a scoreless duel until the bottom of the eighth. With runners on first and second and one out, the Indians worked a pickoff play between Feller and Boudreau at second.

Everyone in the ballpark thought Boudreau had slapped the tag on Phil Masi with the exception of umpire Bill Stewart. On the next pitch, Tommy Holmes singled past third to drive in the only run of the game in Boston's 1–0 victory. Feller had thrown a two-hitter and lost.

The Indians tied the series with a 4–1 win in Game 2. Lemon beat Warren Spahn on an eight-hitter as Boudreau and Doby each doubled in a run. The Series shifted to Cleveland and Bearden's knuckler continued to baffle hitters. He won Game 3 with his arm and bat. Not only did he throw a five-hitter, but he doubled in the third and scored on a Boston error for the only run the Indians would need in the 2–0 victory over Vern Bickford.

Boudreau kept surprising his teammates that year, not only with his play on the field, but with his decisions as manager. His choice of Bearden to start the playoff game against the Red Sox shocked many. So did his choice to start Steve Gromek in Game 4 of the series. Each time, Boudreau made the right choice.

Gromek, a spot starter most of the season, outpitched Sain, the Braves' ace, for a 2–1 win. Boudreau drove in a run in the first, but it was Doby's 410-foot homer that proved to be the winning run in front of 81,897 in Cleveland Stadium. Gromek struck out two and allowed seven hits. The Indians were one game away from a Series victory as they sent Feller to face Spahn in front of 86,288 fans in Game 5.

The Braves jumped Feller for three quick runs in the first, but the score was tied, 4–4, after five innings. The Braves, however, scored six times in the seventh to put the game away and hand Feller his second loss of the Series. The one bright spot was Paige's relief appearance. He became the first black pitcher to appear in a World Series game.

Lemon started Game 6 in Braves Field and won for the second time. He needed help from Bearden, who came on in the eighth. Bearden allowed two runs to score, but earned the save in the 4–3 win. Gordon homered, and Boudreau and Hegan drove in runs. The Indians had been in just two World Series since the club joined the American League in 1901, but now they'd won both of them.

The season was sweet from an artistic and financial standpoint. Cleveland clutched carnival barker Veeck and his Indians to its heart. A major league record 2,620,627 fans watched the club play that year — a team record that would stand for 47 years.

The machinery that drove the Indians kept chugging even though they finished third in 1949 with a record of 89–65. Veeck sold the club at the end of the season, as part of his divorce settlement, for $2.5 million to insurance executive Ellis Ryan. The Indians he left behind, headed by General Manager Hank Greenberg, would become great. There was just one problem.

The Yankees Were Better

From 1949–56 — what should have been prime time for the Tribe — New York won seven of the eight available AL pennants and six world championships. They won five straight World Series from 1949–53. The Indians finally stopped them in 1954. All it took was 111 victories. No matter what the Indians did, the Yankees did a little more.

During the Yankees' stranglehold on the league, the Indians finished second in 1951, 1952, 1953, 1955, and 1956. In those years, they averaged 92 wins a season, but could get no closer than the two games they finished behind the Yankees in 1952.

The core of the Indians began to change in 1950. Al Rosen replaced Keltner at third. He hit .287 and led the league in homers with 37. Ray Boone became the regular shortstop in place of Boudreau. Lemon moved ahead of Feller as the dominant pitcher on the staff. Mike Garcia, a rookie in 1949, won 11 games in 1950. Early Wynn, obtained by Veeck after the 1948 season, rounded off what would eventually be the Big Four — Lemon, Feller, Wynn, and Garcia — with an 18–8 record.

The Indians continued to be one of the few clubs to pursue minority ballplayers. They found Bobby Avila in Mexico and he eventually pushed Gordon off second base. After a tentative rookie year, Luke Easter, signed out of the Negro Leagues by Veeck, took over first base and hit .280 with 28 homers and 107 RBI in 1950.

The Indians won 92 games that season, but it was only

good enough for fourth place. The Yankees won the pennant with 98 wins while Detroit finished 95–59 and Boston 94–80. It proved to be the last season for Boudreau in Cleveland. Hank Greenberg, like Veeck, felt that Boudreau was a much better shortstop than manager; he hired Al Lopez to manage the ballclub and Boudreau went to Boston.

Lopez proved to be an excellent choice. The fact that Greenberg led the Cleveland media into thinking he'd rehire Boudreau kindled an already adversarial relationship into a raging fire between the Tribe's GM and the city's sportswriters. For much of the 1950s the Indians were one of the best teams in baseball. Yet no one seemed to enjoy it — not Greenberg, not the media, not the fans.

For 19 years Lopez had been one of the best catchers in the big leagues. His strongest skill as a manager was handling pitchers. In the 1950s, he was the perfect fit for a team that sometimes had more pitching than it knew what to do with.

Lopez had some help. Mel Harder served as the team's pitching coach from 1948–63. Harder, the second winningest pitcher in Indians history with 223 victories, probably knew more about the Tribe's pitchers than they knew about themselves. He played a big role in helping Lemon make the transition from position player to pitcher.

Finally, there was Jim Hegan. To this day, he's considered the best catcher in franchise history. He played in Cleveland from 1941–57 and caught two world championship teams. It's true he didn't hit much, but as Yankee catcher Bill Dickey said, "When you can catch like Hegan, you don't have to hit."

The Indians finished second in 1951 and 1952 with consecutive 93-victory seasons. The pitching was almost too good to describe. Feller, Wynn, and Garcia won 20 or more games (Feller led the league with 22), while Lemon won 17 in 1951. The next year Wynn won 23, while Garcia and Lemon won 22 each. Still, the Yankees danced just out of reach.

It was more of the same in 1953. The Big Four combined for 66 wins, with Lemon leading the way with 21. Rosen hit .336 and led the league with 43 homers and 145 RBI to win the MVP award. Doby hit 29 homers with 102 RBI, while Avila hit .286 and outfielder Dale Mitchell .300. Yet this time, the Indians finished 8½ games off the pace. Lopez was so frustrated that he went to Greenberg and offered his resignation. He had an offer to manage Cincinnati and felt a change might do the Indians good.

Greenberg wouldn't let Lopez go. It's a good thing, too, because he would have missed a great ride in 1954.

The Third Championship: 1954

It was a team without a weakness. The pitching staff may have been one of the best of all time. They had 77 complete games as Wynn went 23–11, Lemon 23–7, Garcia 19–8 and Feller 13–3. Joining Feller as a spot starter was former Tiger Art Houtteman, who went 15–7.

In the bullpen, Lopez watched rookies Don Mossi and Ray Narleski in spring training, and took them north. They formed an effective righty-lefty closer tandem as they combined for a 9–4 record with 20 saves. Old rival Hal Newhouser, picked up in 1953, went 7–2 out of the bullpen.

On offense, Avila led the league with a .341 average, while Doby led in homers with 32 and RBI with 126. On June 1, Greenberg acquired Vic Wertz from Baltimore. Greenberg liked Wertz's bat, but he didn't have a position. Lopez gave him a chance at first and he hit 14 homers in 295 at-bats. The Indians responded by going 41–17 in June and July.

Wertz brought toughness to the team as well. In 1955, he contracted polio and played in 74 games. He came back in 1956 and hit 32 homers with 106 RBI, much to the amazement of his teammates.

The Indians had a 4½ game lead over New York on the Fourth of July. By the All-Star break, Chicago had cut that lead to a half game after sweeping a four-game series from the Indians in Comiskey Park. They dusted the White Sox by going 15–3 after the break, but the Yankees were still in their rear view mirror. They stayed there until the Indians beat them in a doubleheader on September 12 in Cleveland Stadium to take an 8½ game lead. The Yankees would win 103 games that season, but the race was over.

How did Cleveland feel about its Indians? The fervor the fans poured out to the 1948 champions was missing. Three straight second place finishes to the Yankees had taken a toll on the fans as well as Lopez. Only 1,335,472 fans watched the Indians in 1954.

The Indians were considered huge favorites in the World Series against the New York Giants. A quirky ballpark and a great catch by Willie Mays changed that in a hurry. Not just for one or two seasons either. The Giants' sweep of the Indians put them on a bobsled ride to baseball hell. It wasn't until 1992 that anyone was able to apply the brakes.

The first two games of the Series were played in the Polo Grounds. Its dimensions were freakish to say the least. While the wall in straight away center was 483 feet from home plate, the distance down the foul lines were ridiculously short at 280 to left and 258 to right. The power alleys were approximately 450 feet from the plate.

In Game 1, Wertz hit a long drive to dead center field in the eighth inning with runners on first and second, no one out, and the score tied, 2–2. Wertz said it was the best ball he'd ever hit, and it would have easily been a homer in Cleveland. But Mays, his back to the plate, made an over the shoulder catch some 425 feet from the plate, spun back toward the infield, and made a strong throw toward home. It was such an accurate throw that Doby barely had time to advance from second to third, and Rosen had to hustle back to first.

The Indians proceeded to load the bases, but couldn't score. The Giants would win the game on a three-run pinch-hit homer by Dusty Rhodes in the tenth inning against Lemon, who started the game. In most parks Rhodes's 260-foot fly ball to right would have been a routine out. In the Polo Ground it was a homer.

Mays' catch has been called the best in Series history. Feller disagrees.

"I saw him make tougher catches," said Feller. "And I've seen other guys make tougher catches. On the bench, we figured he'd catch it."

No matter where it ranks, it sunk the Indians. Al Smith

gave the Indians a 1–0 lead with a leadoff homer in the first inning of Game 2, but Rhodes drove in two runs with a single and a homer as the Giants won, 3–1, to take a 2–0 lead with the Series moving to Cleveland.

The Giants bounced Garcia in Game 3 on the way to a 6–2 win. Ruben Gomez and Hoyt Wilhelm combined on a four-hitter, and the pesky Rhodes added a two-run single. Lopez came back with Lemon in Game 4. He didn't have it, and the Giants led 7–0 entering the bottom of the fifth on the way to a 7–4 win.

The suddenness of the Indians' exit gripped the city and wouldn't let go. The Giants had held the Indians to a .190 team batting average, while they laid a 4.84 ERA on the forehead of the best pitching staff in the league.

In 1956, the Indians were back in their usual position. They finished second to the Yankees by nine games. They contended for the flag one last time, in 1959, before the golden era of Indians baseball turned to lead.

The outlook wasn't brilliant for the Cleveland nine in the 1960s, '70s, or '80s; indeed it was relentlessly bleak. Hardly a man alive could recall the heady days of rebellion and the high hopes that marked the birth of the franchise and the bold venture called the American League.

Indian Summers, Many Moons Ago

In the winter of 1900, Ban Johnson needed a man with a fat bank account and a love for baseball. Johnson, a law school dropout and former sports editor of the *Cincinnati Commercial Gazette,* had a vision. He wanted to form another major league to challenge the established National League.

As president of the Western Baseball League, he had the connections. What he didn't have was the money. Charles Somers, the man of Johnson's dreams, did. He and his father were millionaires in the Cleveland coal business.

When Johnson was introduced to Somers in Cleveland, he told him about his plan to form the American League. Part of that plan had him moving what remained of his Grand Rapids, Michigan, club to Cleveland. Somers, along with partner Jack Kilfoyl, quickly agreed to finance a club in Cleveland. What Somers didn't know was that his money would eventually steer many of the American League teams through their first awkward steps.

With Johnson's nudging, Somers loaned Charles Comiskey enough cash to finish the construction of South Side Park on the south side of Chicago. He helped finance the Philadelphia A's and St. Louis Browns. When Johnson put a team in Boston to compete with the National League, Somers paid the bills for the first three years of its existence.

Baseball's voice had been silenced in Cleveland when Johnson arrived. That wasn't all that bad considering the most prominent team in town specialized in giving fans a headache the size of Texas. Maybe that has been the Indians' problem all these years: they have merely been following the example set by their predecessor.

The Cleveland Spiders played in the National League in 1889–99. Their owner, Frank Robison, built League Park in 1891. The following year the Spiders played the Boston Beaneaters for the National League equivalent of the World Series. After the first game ended in a scoreless tie, Boston won five straight in the best-of-nine series to win the championship.

The Spiders were crawling in a different direction by 1899. Robison, who had purchased the league's St. Louis franchise, sent all of Cleveland's best players to his new club. The Spiders, perhaps the worst team ever to play professional baseball, finished with a 20–134 record. When they disbanded at the end of the year not one voice of protest was heard.

National League owners didn't appreciate Johnson for starting a new league. In Cleveland, they prevented Somers from using League Park. Johnson retaliated by threatening to start a bidding war for players and moving into other National League cities. A settlement was finally reached in which Johnson agreed to keep the American League a minor league through 1900 and make his players subject to the National League draft. After that, Johnson planned to go head-to-head with the National Leaguers.

One of the National League's concessions was to allow Somers to use League Park. After their dry run in 1900, the Cleveland Blues of manager James McAleer faced Chicago on April 24, 1901 in the first game ever played in the American League. The White Sox beat the Blues, 8–2, as the other three games scheduled for that day were rained out.

Blues, Bronchos, Naps

Jack McCarthy and Erve Beck had two hits for the Blues. Bill Hoffer threw a seven-hitter, but lost. The Blues went 54–82 and finished seventh in the eight-team league.

In 1902 Cleveland started raiding the National League in earnest. They persuaded outfielder Elmer Flick to leave the Philadelphia Phillies. Two more former Phillies were acquired in June. Second baseman Napoleon Lajoie and righthander Bill Bernhard started the 1901 season by jumping leagues from the Phillies to Connie Mack's Philadelphia A's for more money. The Phillies obtained a court order in 1902 preventing Lajoie, Bernhard and any other of their league-jumping players from playing for another team.

Somers, who had lent Mack considerable money, approached him during these legal problems to see if he could acquire Lajoie and Bernhard. Mack consented and Cleveland's new team had its first headline player in Lajoie. The Phillies sued, without success, to prevent Lajoie, Bernhard, and Flick from coming to Philadelphia. As a safeguard against any past or future legal snares, the three former Phillies did not accompany Cleveland to the City of Brotherly Love for the next two years.

Another important addition that year was Addie Joss, who had pitched the year before for Toledo of the Western League. Cleveland, which had changed its name from the Blues to Bronchos, needed the help. They lost 13 of their first 17 games, but finished above .500 at 69–67 largely because of the influx of new talent. Lajoie hit .379 and Flick .297; Bernhard went 17–5 and Joss 17–13.

The public was so enthralled with Lajoie and his play

that in a newspaper contest asking fans to rename the team for the 1903 season, the name "Naps" received the most votes. That year the Naps were the preseason pick to win the pennant. Under manager Bill Armour, they finished third at 77–63, 15 games behind Boston.

In 1904, Lajoie became player-manager when Armour resigned on September 9. Armour told Somers that the team didn't want to be managed — certainly not the first or last manager to mutter such a phrase. Lajoie hit .376 that year, but the Naps slipped from third to fourth even though they won 11 more games.

The Naps made their first true run at the pennant in 1908. Lajoie entered the year as a marked man. He'd missed much of the 1905 season with blood poisoning from a spike wound. In 1907, his average dropped below .300 (.299) after he had hit .324 or better in each of the first 11 years of his career.

The Naps were nine games off the pace in late July. They went 15–3 during one stretch in August to get back in the race with Detroit, Chicago, and St. Louis. Lajoie had the best pitching in the league — Joss at 24–11, Bob Rhoades 18–12, Heinie Berger 13–8, and Charlie Chech 11–7 — and it showed in the stretch run. Rhoades, automatically nicknamed Dusty, threw a no-hitter at Boston on September 18 for a 2–1 win in League Park. The win was the Naps 12th in the last 14 games and kept them one game behind Detroit.

On October 2, Joss threw the first perfect game by a Naps pitcher. He beat Chicago's Ed Walsh, a 40-game winner that year, 1–0, in Cleveland. After the celebration, the Indians needed to win one of the next two games to clinch. They lost both — 3–1 to the White Sox and 3–1 to St. Louis in the first game of a doubleheader — and were eliminated.

The pennant belonged to the Tigers by a half-game or four percentage points: 90–63 (.588) to 90–64 (.584). The difference was a rainout that the Tigers didn't make up. The Indians protested that if Detroit had played the game and lost, a one-game playoff would have been needed to break the first-place tie. The rules was changed after the season, making it mandatory to replay tie games or rainouts if they have an influence on the pennant race. The change came too late to help the 1908 Naps.

The race took a toll on Kilfoyl, team president since 1901. He stepped down because of failing health and was replaced by Ernest Barnard, who joined the club in 1904 as traveling secretary. Barnard would succeed Johnson as American League president in 1928.

It would be a while before anyone's health was threatened again by another Cleveland stretch run. The Naps fell to sixth place in 1909. Lajoie was so discouraged that he resigned as manager on August 17, but remained as a player. Deacon McGuire took his place and would have the pleasure of telling friends in his golden years that he once managed Cy Young. Baseball's winningest pitcher returned to Cleveland that season and led the team with 19 victories at the age of 42.

Young, an Ohio native, spent his first nine years in the big leagues pitching for the Spiders. In those nine years, with the exception of his rookie season in 1890, he never won fewer than 21 games a season. If Lajoie had acquired *that* Cy Young instead of the older version, he might not have stepped down as manager.

The 1910 Naps were almost a carbon copy of the 1909 edition. Young would be out of baseball in one more year. Joss threw his second no-hitter on April 20 against Chicago, but would die a year later. They finished fifth, 32 games out of first place.

While the team suffered, it was an exceptional year for Lajoie. "Big Frenchy" and Ty Cobb were locked in a race for the batting title. The contest between the handsome Lajoie and the hated Cobb captured the nation's attention. Luxury cars were offered to the American and National batting champions by Hugh Chalmers, owner of a car company, which heightened the tension even more.

On October 6, Cobb, supposedly bothered by eye problems, sat out the last two games of the season. The *Cleveland Plain Dealer* accused Cobb of sitting on his average. He was leading Lajoie at the time, .3848 to .3841. On October 9, the Naps ended their season with a doubleheader against St. Louis. The Browns, like almost every other club in the league, hated Cobb for his ill temper and hard style of play. The smell of fix was in the air.

Lajoie tripled in his first at bat. He then proceeded to beat out six straight bunt hits for the remainder of the doubleheader. The third baseman and shortstop for the Browns played Lajoie on the edge of the outfield grass the whole day.

It appeared they had been instructed to do so by their manager, Jack "Peach Pie" O'Connor, and scout Harry Howell. Johnson took a week to investigate the matter before announcing that Cobb had won the title, .384944 to Lajoie's .384084. St. Louis fired O'Connor and Howell after the season.

The one civil thing that came out of the race was that Chalmers, saying he considered the race a tie, gave cars to both Lajoie and Cobb.

In 1902 the Indians had received a gift in the form of Lajoie and Bernhard from the A's. In the last month of the 1910 season, Mack was still in a giving mood. Shoeless Joe Jackson had not fit in well with A's. He'd been sent to New Orleans, which is where Somers heard about him. Somers worked a trade with Mack, and Jackson came to the Indians in the middle of September. He hit .387 in the last 20 games of the season.

Over the next five seasons, Jackson would hit .408, .395, .373, .338, and .327. When Somers went broke and was forced to trade him in 1915 for three players and cash, Jackson left with a .375 batting average, still the best of any Indian hitter. It would not be the first time a Cleveland owner would be forced to make an ill-advised trade to keep the team solvent.

Jackson couldn't read or write. Ridiculed by his Philadelphia teammates because of it, he was accepted warmly in Cleveland and flourished. Ruth was said to have patterned his swing after Jackson, and in left field it was written that his glove was a place where "triples went to die." Things changed when he went to Chicago. In the Black Sox Scandal, he was one of eight White Sox players indicted for fixing the 1919 World Series. He was banned for life at the age of 31. His lifetime average of .356 is the third highest in history.

In the next two years, the Indians went through three managers before settling on Joe Birmingham in late August of 1912. One of the first things the 28-year-old manager did was bench the aging Lajoie, which caused considerable disruption on the club. Yet Birmingham was asked back in 1913, and the Indians responded with a strong third-place showing at 86–66. Lajoie, back in good graces, hit .335, and Jackson drove in 71 runs. Vean Gregg and Cy Falkenberg won 20 and 23 games, respectively, as the Indians finished 9½ behind the A's.

All the promise of 1913 disappeared in 1914. The Indians lost 102 games — a franchise record until the Tribe lost 105 in 1991 — and finished last for the first time since the league began. Falkenberg jumped to the Federal League, Gregg's wins dropped from 20 to 9, and Lajoie was released at season's end.

The club was renamed the Indians in 1915 because Lajoie was no longer a member. There were few other noteworthy accomplishments as the Tribe finished 44½ games out of first and local bankers informed Somers, who had once kept much of the league afloat, that he was $1.75 million in debt and needed to sell the club. Somers sold it to a group headed by James C. Dunn, called "Sunny" by his friends, in February of 1916. The club would then enjoy six of its most successful years, while Somers set about rebuilding his fortune.

The Whooping Twenties

The Indians, led by player-manager Tris Speaker, newly imported from the Boston Red Sox, peaked during that six-year ride highlighted by the 1920 world championship. From 1922–25, they finished fourth, third, sixth and sixth. They gathered themselves for one more brush with greatness in 1926. It would be the last by the Indians until 1940.

George Burns, a knockabout first baseman, provided the impetus by having the best season of his 16-year career. He hit .358 with 64 doubles and 114 RBI to win the MVP award. Joe Sewell hit .324, Speaker .304, and Charlie Jamieson .299. Right-hander George Uhle, born in Cleveland, had a career season as well. He went 27–11 with 32 complete games. Along the way, he struck out the great Ruth 16 times.

The season turned on a six-game series against the Yankees that began on September 15 in Dunn Field — League Park's new name following Dunn's purchase of the club. The Indians lost the opener, but rallied for four straight victories to pull within two games of first-place New York. The Yankees came back to win the sixth game, and the Indians had to settle for second place by three games.

The Gray Eagle spent 1927 with Washington before ending his career with the A's in 1928. Without him, the Indians were a disaster. They played 306 games in those two years, and lost 179 of them. After the 1927 season, the Indians were purchased from Mrs. James Dunn by a group of wealthy Clevelanders headed by Alva Bradley, who owned real estate in downtown Cleveland. Billy Evans, a former umpire and sportswriter, was hired as general manager and Roger Peckinpaugh as manager.

Led by newcomer Earl Averill (acquired for $50,000) and league batting champion Lou Fonseca's .369 batting average, the Indians hit .294 as a team to finish third in 1929. Averill, the Indians all-time home run leader, hit .331 with 18 homers and 96 RBI. Wes Ferrell, who'd win 91 games from 1929–32 with the Tribe, led the staff with 21 victories. The Indians finished 24 games out of first place, but the future looked promising headed into the 1930s.

Depressing Times

The rosy outlook for the upcoming decade was only a mirage. It wasn't that the Indians were bad. Nine of the 10 teams they fielded in the 1930s had winning records, but they never finished higher than third or closer to first than 12 games back. They were, in a word, mediocre.

It didn't matter who ran the club on the field or made the trades in the front office. The Indians' pace seldom varied. During 1930–33, they finished fourth four straight times. Walter Johnson replaced Peckinpaugh 51 games into the 1933 season. The players, especially the pitchers, disliked The Big Train. Steve O'Neill, the Tribe's old catcher, replaced Johnson in 1935. The front office thought O'Neill was too easy on the players, and replaced him with whip-cracker Oscar Vitt in 1938. He ignited a player revolt that drew huge headlines and probably cost the club a pennant.

In the front office, Evans resigned at the end of 1935 when told he'd have to take a salary cut because of the Great Depression and an attendance of 397,615. Cy Slapnicka, the Tribe's best scout, replaced him.

The one thing the Indians kept doing was finding good players. They just couldn't get enough of them on one team at the same time. Harder won 158 games during the 1930s. That included 20 wins in 1934 and 22 in 1935. First baseman Hal Trosky had a great rookie season in 1934, hitting .330 with 35 homers and 142 RBI. Joe Vosmik came off the Cleveland sandlots to hit .320 with 117 RBI in his first full season in 1931. Together with Averill and Dick Porter, he gave the Tribe a fine starting outfield of graceful fielders and .300 hitters.

Then there was Feller. Slapnicka, born in Cedar Rapids, Iowa, had heard of the strong-armed Feller. He introduced himself to Feller and his father, Bill, while they were working in the wheat fields on the family farm in Van Meter, Iowa in 1935. Feller, 16, signed a contract soon after that meeting. When Slapnicka returned to Cleveland, he told team owners, "Gentleman, I've found the greatest young pitcher I've ever seen."

On July 6, 1936, Bradley and his partners watched those words come to life. In an exhibition game against the St. Louis Cardinals, the down-and-dirty Gashouse Gang, Feller pitched three innings and struck out eight. Feller, on summer vacation between his junior and senior year in high school, was 17. Leo Durocher was his first strikeout victim, and sought refuge in the dugout after taking two strikes from the hard-throwing Feller.

Feller, used carefully by O'Neill, went 5–3 in 14 games that year. After striking out 15 on August 23 against the Browns in his first big-league start, he was even better on September 13 against the A's. Feller struck out 17 for what was then a league record. When the season ended, he returned to Van Meter and spent that winter playing basketball for his high school team.

Before he returned home, Feller and his father were

summoned to Chicago for a meeting with Commissioner Landis. Lee Keyser, owner of the Des Moines minor league team, complained to the Commissioner that Slapnicka violated the rules of the day which said a major league team should not sign a sandlot player to a contract. Keyser felt Feller should be his property because minor league clubs had the rights to players in their jurisdiction.

Slapnicka had also skirted the rules with paperwork that said Feller had played for Fargo-Moorhead and New Orleans. He hadn't played with either team, going straight from the farm to Cleveland. Landis, who could have freed Feller and started a major bidding war for the youngster, ruled that Feller could stay with the Tribe. He awarded Keyser $7,000, and extracted some revenge against Slapnicka six months later. In a complaint by minor league outfielder Tommy Henrich, Landis ruled against the Indians and granted Henrich his freedom. It cost the Tribe a fine outfielder, who went on to play 11 years with the Yankees.

Feller came down with a sore right elbow in 1937. Hot-tempered Johnny Allen helped compensate by winning 15 straight games. O'Neill, however, was in danger of losing his job when the club fell out of first place in midseason. He was saved, at least for the remainder of the year, when the Tribe won 40 of its last 60 games to finish fourth at 83–71.

Vitt, a former third baseman for Detroit, was hired to shake the Indians out of almost a decade of slumber in 1938. He'd managed the Newark Bears, the Yankees' top farm club, to the International League championship by 25½ games in 1937. That seemed to be enough of a recommendation for Bradley.

What the Indians didn't know about Vitt was that he ran his mouth, criticizing players in the press and in the dugout during games. He'd tell players one thing to their face and another when their backs were turned.

Cry Babies and Boy Wonders

The Indians opened the 1940 season as favorites to win the pennant. Feller did nothing to quiet such talk by pitching the first and only Opening Day no-hitter. Still, nothing could ease the tension between Vitt and the players. A dozen players, headed by veterans such as Harder, went to Bradley and told him they couldn't win a pennant unless he fired Vitt. Trosky, believed to be the ringleader, didn't attend because he had to return home following the death of his mother.

Bradley said he couldn't make such a move. Gordon Cobbledick, the *Plain Dealer*'s beat writer, broke the story the next day. It received bigger headlines than Hitler capturing Paris. From that point on the Indians were called the Cry Babies throughout baseball. Vitt and the players, however, managed to co-exist well enough to take a 5½ game lead over Detroit on August. 22.

The Indians arrived in Detroit on September 19 tied for first with Tigers. Fans greeted them at the railroad station for the three-game series with a barrage of fruit and eggs, while screaming "Cry Babies!" At Tiger Stadium the next day, baby bottles were hung from the upper deck and dangled in front of the Tribe's dugout. Still, Harder held a 4–1 lead through seven innings in the opener. Then Vitt

brought in the overworked Feller in the eighth, and the Tigers rallied for a 6–5 win. They won the next game, too, before Feller won his 27th of the season.

The Tigers returned to Cleveland for the last weekend series of the season. The Indians had to sweep the three-game set to win the pennant. With little to lose, the Tigers used unknown Floyd Giebell in the opener against Feller. Rapid Robert pitched well, but the Tribe lost the game and the pennant, 2–0.

The Indians finished second by one game to Detroit. Vitt never managed another game in the big leagues.

Roger Peckinpaugh, who managed the Tribe with little distinction in 1928–33, was brought back to manage in 1941. The Indians finished tied for fourth with Detroit that season, and Slapnicka resigned as general manager. Peckinpaugh took his place.

Lou Boudreau, following two years as the regular shortstop, became the Tribe's boy manager on November 25, 1941.

There was much Boudreau had to learn about managing. The one thing he had in his favor was that when things were at their worst, he had one helluva shortstop to back him up. Boudreau's play at short — he was declared 4-F because of bad ankles — was one of the few things the Indians had going for them during the War years. He won a batting title in 1944 by hitting .327, yet between 1942 and 1945 the Tribe finished fourth, third, fifth and fifth.

Boudreau would become a much better manager when the War ended and players such as Feller returned from overseas. Not to mention an owner named Veeck. But the talented Tribe of the late 1940s to the mid-'50s,which brought two pennants to the city by the lake, fell into a black hole from which they did not emerge until 1994–95.

A Near Death Experience

Symbolically, that black hole may have been the pocket of Willie Mays's glove. For a more realistic starting point, however, one must go to 1957. After finishing second in 1955 and 1956, the Indians were aging in 1957. Herb Score's eye injury, Bob Lemon's sore right arm and Al Rosen's retirement at the relatively young age of 32 because of a salary dispute contributed to the problems.

The Indians fell from second to sixth place. Yet there was still promise, especially in the outfield where Rocky Colavito and Roger Maris combined to hit 39 homers. They were products of the farm system Hank Greenberg built after Veeck's sale of the club in 1949.

But at the end of the 1957 season, Greenberg was fired. Tradin' Frank Lane was about to lay waste to the farm system Greenberg had worked so hard to develop.

The Indians finished fourth in 1958 at 77–76 as Lane set about rebuilding the club in his image. He wanted speed and flash in his team. By 1959, he had what he wanted in such players as Woodie Held, Vic Power, Minnie Minoso, Billy Martin, Jimmy Piersall, Tito Francona, and George Strickland. Among those swept away in the trading frenzy were Early Wynn, Ray Narleski, Don Mossi, Jim Hegan, Bobby Avila, Vic Wertz, and Roger Maris.

People liked the 1959 Indians. They drew almost 1.5

million fans, an increase of 834,171 over 1958, and the most since 1951. But for all his frantic dealings, Lane couldn't do enough to catch the White Sox.

Lane did good things in 1959. The pitching staff was steady with Cal McLish (19–8), Gary Bell (16–11), Mudcat Grant (10–7), and Jim Perry (12–10) The offense was even better as it led the league in homers with 167, a .263 batting average, and a .408 slugging average. Francona hit .363, Minoso drove in 92 runs, and Held hit 29 homers.

Don't Knock the Rock

And in right field, there was Colavito. Groomed to be a bookend power-hitting outfielder with Maris, he hit .257 with 111 RBI and tied Harmon Killebrew for the league lead in homers with 42. He instantly became the hero of every 8-year-old boy in Cleveland — not to mention their fathers.

The Rock hit 129 homers, including four in one game on June 10, 1959, in not quite four full seasons in Cleveland. He was 26 and fans came to the Stadium just to see how high he could hit foul balls.

But Lane could not leave well enough alone. He started ripping apart the second-place Tribe with another batch of trades in preparation for 1960. Then he committed a mortal sin. On April 17, just before the start of the 1960 season, he traded Colavito to Detroit for Harvey Kuenn, the 1959 batting champion. Clevelanders treated the move as if Lane had traded one of their sons.

Attendance dropped from 1.5 million to just over 950,000 and the Indians fell from second to fourth. Kuenn would have had to be Superman to replace Colavito, and he wasn't. He hit .308 with nine homers and 54 RBI and was dealt to San Francisco at the end of the season. Colavito hit .249 with 35 homers and 87 RBI for the Tigers.

The day after Colavito was traded, Lane sent Score, Colavito's roommate and best friend, to the White Sox. A trade that preceded both those deals also backfired. On April 12, Lane sent Norm Cash, whom he acquired from the White Sox in December 1959, to the Tigers for third baseman Steve Demeter. Cash went on to have an outstanding career as a first baseman, while Demeter was given a four-game trial before disappearing into the minors.

Nothing seemed to discourage Lane. On August 10, 1960, in a move that captured the state of the team, Lane traded managers with Detroit. Jimmy Dykes came to the Tribe, while Gordon went to the Tigers. Lane, who did such serious damage to the franchise in a such short period of time, was fired after the 1960 season.

The Turbulent Sixties

Gabe Paul replaced Lane as general manager for the 1961 season. Paul, a baseball lifer, rose from PR man to general manager of the Cincinnati Reds from 1937–60. He was a smiling, gracious man. Reporters could call him in the middle of the night to check out a rumor, and Paul would gladly confirm or deny it.

When Paul ran the Reds from 1949–60, he record was not great. He left them to become general manager in Houston, found out that he didn't like the situation, and landed in Cleveland with the blessing of Nate Dolin and Bill Daley, two longtime Tribe stockholders. Dolin and Daley were swayed because the Reds, a team that still bore Paul's imprint, reached the World Series in 1961.

In Cleveland, Paul's thoughts dealt with survival, not pennants. The Indians finished 30½ games out of first place in 1961. With attendance dropping, the owners started cutting back. First to go was the farm system. The Indians, who had nine farm teams in 1956, were down to five in 1961 and four in 1963.

After finishing sixth in 1962 in spite of Dick Donovan's 20 wins, ownership reorganized before the 1963 season. When Paul couldn't form a syndicate to buy the club, Daley picked up the pieces. Paul threw in $600,000 of his own money to be the group's front man.

After watching attendance drop for four straight seasons, Daley put the squeeze on Cleveland in 1964. He started negotiating with Seattle as a possible new home for the team. Oakland and Dallas made offers. He wanted a new lease and improvements in the stadium. Finally, in October, the city met Daley's demands. Cleveland corporations pushed a ticket-buying campaign to keep the Indians in town. Still, Paul traded Pedro Ramos to the Yankees in September for $75,000 and two players to keep body and soul together.

Through all the politicking, the Indians remained a second-division club, finishing in a sixth-place tie with the Twins. The one thing they had was pitching. Sam McDowell, Luis Tiant, Sonny Siebert, and Tommy John were all young and talented. One of them would have to go so Paul could put more fannies in the seats.

In 1965, Paul brought Colavito back to Cleveland. In a three-way deal with Kansas City and Chicago, Colavito returned, while Paul sent John, outfielder Tommy Agee and catcher John Romano to the White Sox. The city rejoiced, but the price for Rocky was high. John, 21 at the time, would win 288 games — 286 of them with teams other than the Indians. Agee turned into a quality outfielder, helping the Mets win the 1969 World Series.

The Tribe enjoyed a short-term gain as Colavito hit .287 with 26 homers and a league-leading 108 RBI. McDowell went 17-11 and led the league with a 2.18 ERA and 325 strikeouts. Attendance jumped almost 300,000 to 934,786 as the Indians went 87-75, their first winning season since 1959, to finish fifth.

On August 13, 1966 Vernon Stouffer, part owner since 1962, paid Daley $8.2 million to become majority owner. Head of an empire built on restaurants and frozen foods, Stouffer was the sugar daddy the Indians so desperately needed.

Hank Peters, hired by Paul in 1966 as farm director, began to rebuild. Under manager Alvin Dark, the Indians finished third in 1968 with an 86–75 record. It was the year of the pitcher. Tiant was 21–9 and led the league with a 1.60 ERA and nine shutouts. McDowell was second in ERA at 1.81. The Indians led the league with a 2.66 ERA, 23 shutouts, and 1,157 strikeouts.

In 1969, the first year of divisional play, the Indians were back in a more familiar neighborhood — last place in the six-team AL East. They lost 99 games, the most by a Tribe team since 1914. Tiant's right arm hurt, and he went 9–20 after going 21–9 the year before.

In the front office, Stouffer suggested that Dark become both manager and general manager after his third-place debut in 1968. Dark readily agreed, and Paul was pushed to the side. Dark couldn't handle the move, and after a fifth place finish in 1970, he was fired during the 1971 season, and Paul resumed control. For all the front office maneuvering, the Indians still lost 102 games.

After the 1970 season, Stouffer ordered $1 million in player development cuts. The farm system was trimmed and several scouts were fired. Peters quit one year later.

The Sleepy Seventies

The well-meaning but whimsical Stouffer continued to steer an erratic course. Once again it appeared the Indians were headed out of town. During the summer of 1971, he met with officials from New Orleans and hatched a plan where the Indians would play 27 to 33 regular season games in 1974 in the yet-to-be constructed SuperDome. The response of the rest of the league was lukewarm.

In 1972 Stouffer did sell the club. The buyer was smooth-talking Nick Mileti and his many partners. Mileti already owned the Cleveland Barons (a minor league hockey team) and the Cleveland Cavaliers of the NBA.

"Mileti bought the team with green stamps and promises," complained Paul, who remained as general manager.

George Steinbrenner, backed by real money instead of green stamps, purchased the Yankees on January 3, 1973. Previously rebuffed by Stouffer in an attempt to buy the Indians, Steinbrenner brought Paul to New York as general manager and president, and he took Steve O'Neill, one of the Indians' biggest stockholders. While the Yankees would win three pennants and two World Series titles in 1976–78, the Indians would continue to live hand to mouth.

The living was made a bit easier on November 29, 1971 when Paul sent the hard-throwing, and harder-to-handle, McDowell to San Francisco for Gaylord Perry and shortstop Frank Duffy. Starting in 1972, Gaylord The Great went 24–16, 19–19 and 21–13. His 24 wins in 1972 — on a team that won 72 games overall — was enough to win him the Cy Young Award.

The Indians, with Phil Seghi as general manager and Ken Aspromonte as manager, were in the 1974 race until early September before finishing fourth at 77–85. Gaylord and Jim Perry combined for 38 wins and righthander Tom Buskey saved 17 games. Outfielder Charlie Spikes hit 22 homers followed by George Hendrick and Oscar Gamble with 19 each. It was the first season since 1959 that over 1 million fans watched the team.

The 1974 season was memorable for another reason. The Indians were forced to forfeit a game against Texas on June 4 when thousands of fans among a Cleveland Stadium crowd of 25,135 stormed the field after fueling themselves on a '10 cent beer night' promotion. Umpire Nestor Chylak called the game in the ninth inning after the Indians had pulled into a 5–5 tie.

Ted Bonda, who took control of the team from the financially strapped Mileti in 1973, hired Frank Robinson on October 3, 1974. The first black manager in the big leagues captured the city's imagination by hitting a home run in his first at-bat in the Tribe's season opener.

Robinson, blunt and demanding with his players, went 79–80 in 1975 and had a record of 81–78 in 1976. But his fuse was short and he argued with umpires, players, and Seghi.

The Indians seemed to be building a core of young players in Buddy Bell, Rick Manning, Spikes, Duane Kuiper and pitchers Dennis Eckersley and Jim Kern. Bonda and Seghi took a plunge into the free agent market in 1977. They signed 20–game winner Wayne Garland to what was then considered a huge contract — $2.3 million for 10 years. But Garland tore his rotator cuff that spring and was never the same. Robinson didn't make it through the season as the Tribe lost 90 games. On May 11, Seghi traded reliever Dave LaRoche to California for two players and $250,000 to keep the team afloat.

The Indians' treadmill to nowhere, as usual, was running at full speed. Jeff Torborg, the Tribe's fifth manager in the 1970s, led the team to another 90-loss season in 1978. He did so while working under a new owner and president. Steve O'Neill, the money man who accompanied Paul and Steinbrenner to New York in 1973, agreed to buy the club at Bonda's request with one stipulation: Paul must return as president.

Paul, who helped turn the wealthy Yankees into a winner, returned to the city he called a "sleeping giant" for his last stand. It would be a painful one.

Before the season even started, Eckersley was traded to Boston in a deal that would haunt the team for years. They received catcher Bo Diaz, third baseman Ted Cox, and pitchers Rick Wise and Mike Paxton. The four newcomers made fleeting contributions. Eckersley is headed to the Hall of Fame.

Bell, another one of the team's young players, was dealt to Texas for Toby Harrah after the season. There Bell won six Gold Gloves at third base and went to four All-Star games.

Paul's second run with the Indians lasted seven years, 1978–84. In that time, the sleeping giant never stirred. The Indians finished sixth six times and seventh once. The closest they came to first place, excluding the strike season of 1981, was 17 games in 1982.

Dave Garcia replaced Torborg during the 1979 season. First baseman Mike Hargrove joined the team that year in a trade with San Diego. He hit .325 in 100 games and became known as The Human Rain Delay for his gyrations between pitches.

Take My Club, Please

Paul, with Seghi serving as general manager, supplied Garcia with a good pitching staff in 1980. Len Barker, John Denny, Dan Spillner, Rick Waits, and the persistent but injured Garland, were at the manager's disposal. Offensively, Joe Charboneau, who could drink beer through a straw in his nose, won the Rookie of the Year Award for hitting .289 with 23 homers and 87 RBI. Miguel Dilone showed promise as a leadoff hitter by hitting .341 and stealing 61 bases.

That offensive potential never blossomed. Charboneau injured his back and was out of the majors by 1983.

Dilone would play 12 years in the big leagues but never approach those kind of numbers again.

That seemed to be the Indians' pattern through the mid-1980s — good pitching and weak hitting. In 1982 they opened the season with a staff of Bert Blyleven, Rick Sutcliffe, Lary Sorenson, Denny, Barker, Waits, and the versatile Spillner. But when Blyleven injured his right elbow — the result of coming back too soon after the 1981 strike — and missed the rest of the season, the staff never recovered. Barker, who threw a perfect game against Toronto in 1981, was the top winner at 15–11. Sutcliffe and Denny would go on to win Cy Young Awards in the National League.

The Indians were brutal in 1983. They scored the fewest runs and had the highest ERA in the league. Manager Mike Ferraro, replaced by Pat Corrales after 100 games, got off one good line while coping with cancer and a bad ballclub. Broderick Perkins, unhappy with his lack of playing time, hung a paper plate on his locker and marked the days that had gone by since he last played.

"If he keeps that up," cracked Ferraro, "he's going to have to hang a pizza pie pan on his locker to keep track of the days."

Steve O'Neill died during the 1983 season, and once again rumors of the club leaving town surfaced. His nephew, Pat O'Neill, was charged with finding a buyer.

Corrales offered no magic potion for the on-the-field problems. The Indians combined for 189 losses in 1984 and 1985. But the hard-nosed Corrales, of Mexican and Arapaho Indian descent, was entertaining. In 1984 he coaxed 23 saves out of Ernie Camacho by sheer will.

Camacho could throw between 92–95 mph, but wanted to trick people with breaking pitches. By making him a closer, Corrales forced Camacho to throw nothing but fastballs. If he disobeyed orders, Corrales would sprint to the mound, pound Camacho on the chest and say, "No tricks, Ernie. No tricks."

Peter Bavasi, who grew up watching his father, Buzzie, work for the Dodgers and San Diego Padres, succeeded Paul as president when the latter retired after the 1984 season. Bavasi immediately set a thousand brushfires to distract the public from the Tribe's poor play. He closed the stadium bleachers, fired farm director Bob Quinn, forced Seghi to retire, and axed several secretaries and department heads.

He hired veteran executive Dan O'Brien to handle the business end of the team, and Joe Klein to run the baseball operations. One thing he couldn't do was make the Indians win. They lost 102 games in 1985, but Bavasi's sense of timing was perfect. Because of a series of trades by Seghi and Paul, the Indians erupted into the best hitting team in baseball in 1986. Brett Butler, Joe Carter, Mel Hall, Julio Franco, Tony Bernazard, Brook Jacoby, and Pat Tabler, all acquired through deals, feasted on opposing pitchers. When Andre Thornton, the lone power hitter in the Tribe's lineup for most of the decade, and No. 1 draft pick Cory Snyder were added to that mix, the Indians were a force. Carter led the league with 121 RBI.

The one thing missing from the 1986 Indians was the kind of pitching they had in the early 1980s. Still, the Tribe's 84–78 finish was impressive, especially because they drew 1.4 million fans to the Stadium. It was their largest attendance since 1959.

Pat O'Neill kept the good vibes going by finally finding a buyer for his uncle's team in Richard and David Jacobs. The Jacobs brothers purchased complete control of the team for $35 million on December 9, 1986. The Indians were in good hands. The winning would come later.

Sports Illustrated picked the Tribe to win the World Series in 1987 after its strong 1986 showing. Anyone who had seen the Indians pitch knew better.

The Indians lost 10 of their first 11 games. For the second time in a three-year span they'd lose more than 100 games. Even the scrappy Corrales couldn't survive that. He was replaced by bullpen coach Doc Edwards on July 16, 1987.

The team's ERA that year was 5.28, the highest ever by an Indians' staff. Corrales and Edwards used 21 different pitchers, and not one of them reached double figures in wins. Scott Bailes, Phil Niekro and Tom Candiotti tied for the team lead with seven wins each.

When the season ended, Dick Jacobs hired Hank Peters as president and general manager. (Bavasi had left prior to the season.) Peters, fired by Edward Bennett Williams in Baltimore, preached patience upon his return to Cleveland. He brought Tom Giordano and Dan O'Dowd from Baltimore. O'Dowd took over the farm system, while Giordano concentrated on scouting. John Hart, Peters' GM in waiting upon his retirement in 1991, joined the club in 1989 as a special assignment scout.

The pitching improved in 1988 and 1989 under Edwards, the former Tribe catcher. The club had one of its best starts ever in 1988 at 12–3. The Tribe faded at the All-Star break as Edwards rode the starters hard because of a questionable bullpen other than closer Doug Jones. Greg Swindell (18–14), Tom Candiotti (14–8), John Farrell (14–10) and Jones (37 saves) were impressive.

In 1989 the Tribe actually caught a whiff of contention. On August 4, they beat Boston, 4–3, to take over second place and pull within 1½ games of first. The Indians, 54–54, would win only 19 more games. Edwards was fired, and Hart led the club through the final 19 games of another sixth place finish.

The Indians had lost Butler to free agency (1987) and traded Franco to Texas (1988), Bernazard to Oakland (1987), Tabler to Kansas City (1988), and Hall to the Yankees (1989), while forcing Thornton to retire (1987). Carter, unhappy with the endless losing and Cleveland's crumbling stadium, was the next to go.

The Wind Shifts

Peters, in a trade that set the foundation for the current Indians, sent Carter, a year away from free agency, to San Diego for Carlos Baerga, Sandy Alomar Jr., and Chris James on December 7, 1989. Alomar paid immediate dividends by being named Rookie of the Year in 1990 for manager John McNamara. The team finished fourth.

The Indians, in the process of trimming payroll, set themselves up for a record-setting 105 losses in 1991. Candy Maldonado, their top power hitter from 1990, wasn't re-signed, while Candiotti was traded during the season and Jones was sent to the minors after a bad start. The Indians used a record 53 players, including 24 pitchers, 14 of them starters.

McNamara, bewildered by the constant coming and going of players, was fired and replaced by Hargrove on July 6, 1991. Hargrove finished his fourth full season as skipper in 1995.

Bolstered by an improving farm system — primed at Peters' urging — and good trades, the Indians started recovering from 1991 with identical 76–86 records in 1992 and 1993. Kenny Lofton, Paul Sorrento, and Jose Mesa were acquired by trades in 1992. At the same time, Charles Nagy, Albert Belle, and Jim Thome came up through the farm system. Baerga, meanwhile, was becoming one of the best hitting second baseman in the game.

In 1994, with the club moving into brand new Jacobs Field, Hart signed free agents Eddie Murray, Dennis Martinez, Jack Morris, and Tony Pena for extra juice. He also acquired slick shortstop Omar Vizquel in a trade with Seattle, and No. 1 pick Manny Ramirez won the right field job in spring training. The Indians, a real contender for the first time since 1959, were one game out of first place in the AL Central when the strike ended the season on August 12.

The Indians and White Sox became rivals again in 1994. The rivalry reached its peak when manager Gene Lamont caught Belle with a corked bat on July 15 in Comiskey Park. Belle had hit a homer on July 14, but Lamont waited until his first at-bat the next night to have the bat confiscated.

After the bat was locked in the umpire's locker room, an Indians player — sources indicate it was pitcher Jason Grimsley — climbed through a false ceiling that connected the Indians locker room and the umpire's locker room, and retrieved the bat. In its place, he left a Sorrento model.

The White Sox were livid, and demanded the Indians return the bat or they were going to press charges for breaking and entering. Acting Commissioner Bud Selig ordered the Indians to return the bat, which they did on July 16. The bat was then taken to league headquarters in New York where it was sawed in half and found to contain cork. Belle, who said he was innocent and accused the White Sox of tampering with his bats, was suspended for seven games.

In 1995 the Indians couldn't be stopped by the White Sox or corked bats. As in 1994 they had a terrific team, dedicated management, and the dazzling Jacobs Field.

The Gateway to Greatness

Pat Corrales managed the Indians for 635 games from June 31, 1983 through July 16, 1987. Cleveland Stadium, the huge, wind-swept bowl on the shores of Lake Erie, was the team's home. When Corrales walked into Jacobs Field for Game 3 of the 1995 World Series as Atlanta's first base coach, he was amazed.

"This place is beautiful," said Corrales. "Hell, you can't even spit on the floor anymore."

Jacobs Field *is* beautiful. It is green and shiny yet has the feel of a soft pair of faded jeans. For so long the Indians and the Stadium shared each other's misery. The team was always bad, but the ballpark was a mausoleum.

In Jacobs Field, the Indians have been reborn. They went 89–34 in their first two years on the corner of Carnegie and Ontario Avenues. GM John Hart uses Jacobs Field as a recruiting tool. He gives free agents tours of the facility, which can seat 42,400 during the regular season. Players such as Eddie Murray, Dennis Martinez, Orel Hershiser, and Julio Franco have been impressed enough to stay.

The fans feel the same way. The entire 1996 season is sold out. It's the first time in history a team has sold out the season before Opening Day. In 1994 and 1995, 93 of the possible 122 home dates were sellouts.

Jacobs Field's most distinctive feature is the 19-foot left field wall, which holds an out-of-town scoreboard. It's a mini-version of The Green Monster, but above the wall are bleachers and a plaza where standing-room-only customers can watch the game. The park is hitter friendly, especially to right center field. In September, however, the ball does not travel as well.

The exterior of the park is dominated by limestone and the building's iron and steel skeleton. The skeleton was left bare to blend in with the many girded bridges that cross the nearby Cuyahoga River, and to reflect the strength of a revived rust belt city.

The same could be said of the team that plays inside it.

CHAPTER 3

The Indians in Postseason Play

Frederick Ivor-Campbell

The tradition of major league postseason play traces back to 1871, the first year there was a professional league. National Association teams in the 1870s typically followed the conclusion of their championship (regularly scheduled) season with exhibition games against amateur clubs. In the 1880s nearly every major league club played a couple of weeks of postseason games, generally against major- and minor-league teams they hadn't faced during the regular season. In the twentieth century there had been (until 1994) a World Series every year for ninety years, prefaced since 1969 by League Championship Series to determine the American and National League winners. In 1995 a new round of championship play came into being, the Divisional Playoffs.

The early World Series had their beginnings in 1884. Two years earlier, the champions of the National League and the brand-new American Association played a pair of postseason contests (in which each team recorded a shutout against the other). Some would like to call these games the first World Series, but no one in 1882 saw them as more than exhibition games. In fact, because the NL didn't yet recognize the legitimacy of the AA and forbade its clubs to play those of the new league, the NL champion Chicago White Stockings had to release their players from their season contracts so they could face AA champion Cincinnati as technically independent players.

That winter the two major leagues made their peace, and although a proposed series between the 1883 NL and AA titlists was called off, the 1884 champion Providence Grays (NL) and the Metropolitan Club of New York (AA) played three games "for the championship of the United States." The winning Grays were acclaimed in the press as "champions of the world," and the World Series was born.

The brief 1884 Series set the stage for more elaborate World Series to follow. From 1885 through 1890 the NL and AA pennant-winners met in Series that ranged in length from six games to fifteen.

The demise of the AA after the 1891 season caused a one-year gap in World Series play. When the National League expanded from eight clubs to twelve the next year (by absorbing four teams from the defunct AA), it divided the regular season into two halves, with the first-half winner playing the winner of the second half for the world title. Boston defeated the Cleveland Spiders—unrelated to the Indians—in the first official World Series, but the unpopular divided season was not repeated (that is, until the strike year of 1981).

Two years later a new World Series scheme was devised when one William C. Temple offered a prize cup to the winner of a postseason series between the first- and second-place finishers in the NL. For four years these best-of-seven

Temple Cup games served as the officially recognized world championship. But by the end of four lopsided Series (only one of which was won by the pennant-winning club), fan interest—never robust—had declined so much that the trophy was returned to its donor and the series abandoned.

The upgrading of the American League from minor- to major-league status in 1901 made a return to interleague World Series play theoretically possible, but it was not until after the NL and AL had made peace in 1903 that the first modern Series was contested. The owners of NL champion Pittsburgh and AL champion Boston arranged a best-of-nine postseason Series in 1903, which proved both popular and financially successful—a firm foundation for future Series.

Key to the Statistics

The statistics in this section of *Total Indians* are standard—there is little point in applying newer analytical measures to performances that run to seven games or fewer. We do offer, however, stats that were not standard at the time, such as earned run averages for years before 1912 and runs batted in before 1920 (which were determined from box scores and play-by-plays) and saves before 1969. We present the cumulative box score for each Indians World Series in accordance with modern practice.

The length of the World Series varied from three games in 1884 all the way up to fifteen in 1887 and ten the following year. The best-of-seven format came in with the Temple Cup Series of 1894 and has been the norm for World Series ever since (excepting 1900, 1903, and 1919–1921). In recent years this format has become the norm for League Championship Series as well. The new Playoffs are best-of-five.

If a player appeared at more than one position during the Series, the number of games he played at each is noted (for example, a man who divided seven games at shortstop and third base would carry the notation *ss-4, 3b-3*). Other abbreviations are as follows:

POS	Position	SB	Stolen Bases
AVG	Batting average	W	Wins
G	Games	L	Losses
AB	At bats	ERA	Earned run average
R	Runs	GS	Games started
H	Hits	CG	Complete games
2B	Doubles	SHO	Shutouts
3B	Triples	SV	Saves
HR	Home runs	IP	Innings pitched
RB	Runs batted in	ER	Earned runs
BB	Bases on Balls	SO	Strikeouts

The Indians outscored the Robins in the Series, 21 runs to 8. Yet after losing the opener in Brooklyn, the Robins fought back to take the next two, and held the Series lead as the teams traveled to Cleveland for the next four games.

Both clubs garnered five hits in Game One, but an error, walk, single, and double gave the Indians two runs in the second and a lead they never yielded, as Stan Coveleski outlasted Rube Marquard for the win. In Game Two, both clubs increased their hit totals to seven, but the Robins bunched six of theirs into three innings for three runs, while Burleigh Grimes, only once yielding two hits in an inning, shut the Indians out. The two runs Brooklyn scored in the first inning of Game Three were all Sherry Smith needed to give the Robins their second win behind his three-hit pitching. But Brooklyn scored only twice more in the Series as the Indians swept to the championship with four wins in Cleveland.

With the Indians scoring four runs in Game Four before Brooklyn put its one run on the board, Coveleski breezed to his second five-hit Series run. Jim Bagby had it even easier the next day. The Robins tagged him for 13 hits, but not until the ninth inning were they able to put them together for a run. Meanwhile Bagby and his teammates were registering a couple of Series firsts as they moved to an eight-run lead. Right fielder Elmer Smith opened the scoring in the first inning with the first World Series grand slam, and Bagby himself homered for three more in the fourth—the first pitcher to hit a Series home run.

But the 1920 Series is best remembered for second baseman Bill Wambsganss's unassisted triple play in the fifth inning. With runners on first and second going on pitcher Clarence Mitchell's liner, Wambsganss snared the ball for the first out, stepped on second to force one runner, and tagged the runner coming in from first to retire the side.

In Game Six Duster Mails, a late-season addition to the team, shut out Brooklyn on three hits in a 1–0 squeaker over Sherry Smith. Coveleski won the clincher the next day, also via the shutout, with his third five-hitter of the Series and his third Series win.

Cleveland Indians (AL), 5;
Brooklyn Robins (NL), 2

CLE (A)

PLAYER/POS	AVG	G	AB	R	H	2B	3B	HR	RB	BB	SO	SB
Jim Bagby, p	.333	2	6	1	2	0	0	1	1	3	0	0
George Burns, 1b-4	.300	5	10	1	3	1	0	0	2	3	3	0
Ray Caldwell, p	.000	1	0	0	0	0	0	0	0	0	0	0
Stan Coveleski, p	.100	3	10	2	1	0	0	0	0	0	4	0
Joe Evans, of	.308	4	13	0	4	0	0	0	0	1	0	0
Larry Gardner, 3b	.208	7	24	1	5	1	0	0	2	1	1	0
Jack Graney, of-2	.000	3	3	0	0	0	0	0	0	0	2	0
Charlie Jamieson, of-5	.333	6	15	2	5	1	0	0	1	1	0	0
Doc Johnston, 1b	.273	5	11	1	3	0	0	0	0	2	1	1
Harry Lunte, 2b	.000	1	0	0	0	0	0	0	0	0	0	0
Duster Mails, p	.000	2	5	0	0	0	0	0	0	0	1	0
Les Nunamaker, c-1	.500	2	2	0	1	0	0	0	0	0	0	0
Steve O'Neill, c	.333	7	21	1	7	3	0	0	2	4	3	0
Joe Sewell, ss	.174	7	23	0	4	0	0	0	0	2	1	0
Elmer Smith, of	.308	5	13	1	4	0	1	1	5	1	1	0
Tris Speaker, of	.320	7	25	6	8	2	1	0	1	3	1	0
Pinch Thomas, c	.000	1	0	0	0	0	0	0	0	0	0	0
George Uhle, p	.000	2	0	0	0	0	0	0	0	0	0	0
Bill Wambgsanss, 2b	.154	7	26	3	4	0	0	0	1	2	1	0
Joe Wood, of	.200	4	10	2	2	1	0	0	0	1	2	0
TOTAL	.244		217	21	53	9	2	2	17	21	21	2

PITCHER	W	L	ERA	G	GS	CG	SV	SHO	IP	H	ER	BB	SO
Jim Bagby	1	1	1.80	2	2	1	0	0	15.0	20	3	1	3
Ray Caldwell	0	1	27.00	1	1	0	0	0	0.1	2	1	1	0
Stan Coveleski	3	0	0.67	3	3	3	0	1	27.0	15	2	2	8
Duster Mails	1	0	0.00	2	1	1	0	1	15.2	6	0	6	6
George Uhle	0	0	0.00	2	0	0	0	0	3.0	1	0	0	3
TOTAL	5	2	0.89	10	7	5	0	2	61.0	44	6	10	20

BRO (N)

PLAYER/POS	AVG	G	AB	R	H	2B	3B	HR	RB	BB	SO	SB
Leon Cadore, p	.000	2	0	0	0	0	0	0	0	0	0	0
Tommy Griffith, of	.190	7	21	1	4	2	0	0	3	0	2	0
Burleigh Grimes, p	.333	3	6	1	2	0	0	0	0	0	0	0
Jimmy Johnston, 3b	.214	4	14	2	3	0	0	0	0	0	2	1
Pete Kilduff, 2b	.095	7	21	0	2	0	0	0	0	1	4	0
Ed Konetchy, 1b	.174	7	23	0	4	0	1	0	2	3	2	0
Ernie Krueger, c-3	.167	4	6	0	1	0	0	0	0	0	0	0
Bill Lamar, ph	.000	3	3	0	0	0	0	0	0	0	0	0
Al Mamaux, p	.000	3	1	0	0	0	0	0	0	0	1	0
Rube Marquard, p	.000	2	1	0	0	0	0	0	0	0	0	0
Bill McCabe, pr	.000	1	0	0	0	0	0	0	0	0	0	0
Otto Miller, c	.143	6	14	0	2	0	0	0	0	1	2	0
Clarence Mitchell, p-1	.333	2	3	0	1	0	0	0	0	0	0	0
Hy Myers, of	.231	7	26	0	6	0	0	0	1	0	1	0
Bernie Neis, of-2	.000	4	5	0	0	0	0	0	0	1	0	0
Ivy Olson, ss	.320	7	25	2	8	1	0	0	0	3	1	0
Jeff Pfeffer, p	.000	1	1	0	0	0	0	0	0	0	0	0
Ray Schmandt, ph	.000	1	1	0	0	0	0	0	0	0	0	0
Jack Sheehan, 3b	.182	3	11	0	2	0	0	0	0	0	1	0
Sherry Smith, p	.000	2	6	0	0	0	0	0	0	0	2	0
Zack Wheat, of	.333	7	27	2	9	2	0	0	2	1	2	0
TOTAL	.205		215	8	44	5	1	0	8	10	20	1

PITCHER	W	L	ERA	G	GS	CG	SV	SHO	IP	H	ER	BB	SO
Leon Cadore	0	1	9.00	2	1	0	0	0	2.0	4	2	1	1
Burleigh Grimes	1	2	4.19	3	3	1	0	1	19.1	23	9	9	4
Al Mamaux	0	0	4.50	3	0	0	0	0	4.0	2	2	0	5
Rube Marquard	0	1	1.00	2	1	0	0	0	9.0	7	1	3	6
Clarence Mitchell	0	0	0.00	1	0	0	0	0	4.2	3	0	3	1
Jeff Pfeffer	0	0	3.00	1	0	0	0	0	3.0	4	1	2	1
Sherry Smith	1	1	0.53	2	2	2	0	0	17.0	10	1	3	3
TOTAL	2	5	2.44	14	7	3	0	1	59.0	53	16	21	21

GAME 1 AT BRO OCT 5

CLE	020	100	000	3	5	0
BRO	000	000	100	1	5	1

Pitchers: COVELESKI vs MARQUARD, Mamaux (7), Cadore (9)
Attendance: 23,753

GAME 2 AT BRO OCT 6

CLE	000	000	000	0	7	1
BRO	101	010	00X	3	7	0

Pitchers: BAGBY, Uhle (7) vs GRIMES
Attendance: 22,559

GAME 3 AT BRO OCT 7

CLE	000	100	000	1	3	1
BRO	200	000	00X	2	6	1

Pitchers: CALDWELL, Mails (1), Uhle (8) vs SMITH
Attendance: 25,088

GAME 4 AT CLE OCT 9

BRO	000	100	000	1	5	1
CLE	202	001	00X	5	12	2

Pitchers: CADORE, Mamaux (2), Marquard (3), Pfeffer (6) vs COVELESKI
Attendance: 25,734

GAME 5 AT CLE OCT 10

BRO	000	000	001	1	13	1
CLE	400	310	00X	8	12	2

Pitchers: GRIMES, Mitchell (4) vs BAGBY
Home Runs: E.Smith-CLE, Bagby-CLE
Attendance: 26,884

GAME 6 AT CLE OCT 11

BRO	000	000	000	0	3	0
CLE	000	001	00X	1	7	3

Pitchers: SMITH vs MAILS
Attendance: 27,194

GAME 7 AT CLE OCT 12

BRO	000	000	000	0	5	2
CLE	000	110	10X	3	7	3

Pitchers: GRIMES, Mamaux (8) vs COVELESKI
Attendance: 27,525

Boston outpitched and outhit Cleveland, and the clubs tied in runs scored. But the Braves scored most of their runs in one game, and the Indians, spreading theirs more evenly, took the Series. Boston ace Johnny Sain dueled Bob Feller in the opener. Feller gave up only two singles, but one of them followed a walk and a sacrifice (and a controversial pickoff play at second, in which the Boston runner was ruled safe although photos later showed him clearly out) and drove in the game's only run. Both teams registered eight hits in Game Two, but Cleveland's led to four runs, while Indian hurler Bob Lemon held Boston to just one—and that was unearned.

Cleveland's rookie sensation Gene Bearden shut out the Braves on five hits in Game Three as the Series moved to Cleveland's huge Municipal Stadium. Bearden himself, after doubling in the third, scored on a Boston error what proved to be the winning run. A record 81,897 fans saw Sain face Steve Gromek in Game Four. Only five Indians hit Sain safely, but a first-inning single and double put Cleveland on the board, and Larry Doby's home run two innings later made the score 2–0. Boston's Marv Rickert homered in the seventh to narrow Cleveland's lead, but that ended the scoring.

Another attendance record was set at Game Five as 86,288 fans gathered to watch Bob Feller sew up the title for Cleveland. They went home disappointed. In a game that featured five of the Series' eight home runs, Boston jumped ahead on Bob Elliott's three-run blast in the first. Dale Mitchell opened Cleveland's half of the inning with a home run, but Elliott neutralized it in the third with his second homer. The Indians drove out Boston starter Nelson Potter with four runs in the fourth inning (three coming on Jim Hegan's homer). But Warren Spahn (who had lost Game Two) hurled one-hit shutout relief over the final five frames as his Braves tied the game on Bill Salkeld's homer in the sixth, and blew out Feller and two relievers with six runs in the seventh. The fourth Indian pitcher, Satchel Paige (in his only World Series appearance), retired two batters to end the inning, but the damage had been done.

A day later though, back in Boston, Cleveland edged the Braves 4–3 for the title. Gene Bearden's relief pitching allowed two inherited baserunners to score in the eighth, but halted Boston's rally one run short of a tie.

Cleveland Indians (AL), 4;
Boston Braves (NL), 2

CLE (A)

PLAYER/POS	AVG	G	AB	R	H	2B	3B	HR	RB	BB	SO	SB
Gene Bearden, p	.500	2	4	1	2	1	0	0	0	0	1	0
Ray Boone, ph	.000	1	1	0	0	0	0	0	0	0	1	0
Lou Boudreau, ss	.273	6	22	1	6	4	0	0	3	1	1	0
Russ Christopher, p	.000	1	0	0	0	0	0	0	0	0	0	0
Allie Clark, of	.000	1	3	0	0	0	0	0	0	0	1	0
Larry Doby, of	.318	6	22	1	7	1	0	1	2	2	4	0
Bob Feller, p	.000	2	4	0	0	0	0	0	0	0	2	0
Joe Gordon, 2b	.182	6	22	3	4	0	0	1	2	1	2	1
Steve Gromek, p	.000	1	3	0	0	0	0	0	0	0	0	0
Jim Hegan, c	.211	6	19	2	4	0	0	1	5	1	4	1
Wally Judnich, of	.077	4	13	1	1	0	0	0	1	1	4	0
Ken Keltner, 3b	.095	6	21	3	2	0	0	0	0	2	3	0
Bob Kennedy, of	.500	3	2	0	1	0	0	0	1	0	1	0
Bob Lemon, p	.000	2	7	0	0	0	0	0	0	0	0	0
Dale Mitchell, of	.174	6	23	4	4	1	0	1	1	2	0	0
Bob Muncrief, p	.000	1	0	0	0	0	0	0	0	0	0	0
Satchel Paige, p	.000	1	0	0	0	0	0	0	0	0	0	0
Hal Peck, of	.000	1	0	0	0	0	0	0	0	0	0	0
Eddie Robinson, 1b	.300	6	20	0	6	0	0	0	1	1	0	0
Al Rosen, ph	.000	1	1	0	0	0	0	0	0	0	0	0
Joe Tipton, ph	.000	1	1	0	0	0	0	0	0	0	1	0
Thurman Tucker, of	.333	1	3	1	1	0	0	0	0	1	0	0
TOTAL	.199		191	17	38	7	0	4	16	12	26	2

PITCHER	W	L	ERA	G	GS	CG	SV	SHO	IP	H	ER	BB	SO
Gene Bearden	1	0	0.00	2	1	1	1	1	10.2	6	0	1	4
Russ Christopher	0	0	INF	1	0	0	0	0	0.0	2	1	0	0
Bob Feller	0	2	5.02	2	2	1	0	0	14.1	10	8	5	7
Steve Gromek	1	0	1.00	1	1	1	0	0	9.0	7	1	1	2
Ed Klieman	0	0	INF	1	0	0	0	0	0.0	3	2	0	0
Bob Lemon	2	0	1.65	2	2	1	0	0	16.1	16	3	7	6
Bob Muncrief	0	0	0.00	1	0	0	0	0	2.0	1	0	0	0
Satchel Paige	0	0	0.00	1	0	0	0	0	0.2	0	0	0	0
TOTAL	4	2	2.72	11	6	4	1	1	53.0	43	16	16	19

BOS (N)

PLAYER/POS	AVG	G	AB	R	H	2B	3B	HR	RB	BB	SO	SB
Red Barrett, p	.000	2	0	0	0	0	0	0	0	0	0	0
Vern Bickford, p	.000	1	0	0	0	0	0	0	0	0	0	0
Clint Conatser, of	.000	2	4	0	0	0	0	0	1	0	0	0
Alvin Dark, ss	.167	6	24	2	4	1	0	0	0	0	2	0
Bob Elliott, 3b	.333	6	21	4	7	0	0	2	5	2	2	0
Tommy Holmes, of	.192	6	26	3	5	0	0	0	1	0	0	0
Phil Masi, c	.125	5	8	1	1	1	0	0	1	1	0	0
Frank McCormick, 1b-1	.200	3	5	0	1	0	0	0	0	0	2	0
Mike McCormick, of	.261	6	23	1	6	0	0	0	2	0	4	0
Nelson Potter, p	.500	2	2	0	1	0	0	0	0	0	1	0
Marv Rickert, of	.211	5	19	2	4	0	0	1	2	0	4	0
Connie Ryan, ph	.000	2	1	0	0	0	0	0	0	0	1	0
Johnny Sain, p	.200	2	5	0	1	0	0	0	0	0	0	0
Bill Salkeld, c	.222	5	9	2	2	0	0	1	1	5	1	0
Ray Sanders, ph	.000	1	1	0	0	0	0	0	0	0	0	0
Sibby Sisti, 2b	.000	2	1	0	0	0	0	0	0	0	0	0
Warren Spahn, p	.000	3	4	0	0	0	0	0	1	0	0	0
Eddie Stanky, 2b	.286	6	14	0	4	1	0	0	1	7	1	0
Earl Torgeson, 1b	.389	5	18	2	7	3	0	0	1	2	1	1
Bill Voiselle, p	.000	2	2	0	0	0	0	0	0	0	0	0
TOTAL	.230		187	17	43	6	0	4	16	16	19	1

PITCHER	W	L	ERA	G	GS	CG	SV	SHO	IP	H	ER	BB	SO
Red Barrett	0	0	0.00	2	0	0	0	0	3.2	1	0	0	1
Vern Bickford	0	1	2.70	1	1	0	0	0	3.1	4	1	5	1
Nelson Potter	0	0	8.44	2	1	0	0	0	5.1	6	5	2	1
Johnny Sain	1	1	1.06	2	2	2	0	1	17.0	9	2	0	9
Warren Spahn	1	1	3.00	3	1	0	0	0	12.0	10	4	3	12
Bill Voiselle	0	1	2.53	2	1	0	0	1	10.2	8	3	2	2
TOTAL	2	4	2.60	12	6	2	0	1	52.0	38	15	12	26

GAME 1 AT BOS OCT 6

CLE	000	000	000	0	4	0
BOS	000	000	01X	1	2	2

Pitchers: FELLER vs SAIN
Attendance: 40,135

GAME 2 AT BOS OCT 7

CLE	000	210	001	4	8	1
BOS	100	000	000	1	8	3

Pitchers: LEMON vs SPAHN,
  Barrett (5), Potter (8)
Attendance: 39,633

GAME 3 AT CLE OCT 8

BOS	000	000	000	0	5	1
CLE	001	100	00X	2	5	0

Pitchers: BICKFORD, Voiselle (4),
  Barrett (8) vs BEARDEN
Attendance: 70,306

GAME 4 AT CLE OCT 9

BOS	000	000	100	1	7	0
CLE	101	000	00X	2	5	0

Pitchers: SAIN vs GROMEK
Home Runs: Doby-CLE, Rickert-BOS
Attendance: 81,897

GAME 5 AT CLE OCT 10

BOS	301	001	600	11	12	0
CLE	100	400	000	5	6	2

Pitchers: Potter, SPAHN (4) vs FELLER,
  Klieman (7), Christopher (7), Paige (7),
  Muncrief (8)
Home Runs: Elliott-BOS (2),
  Mitchell-CLE, Hegan-CLE,
  Salkeld-BOS
Attendance: 86,288

GAME 6 AT BOS OCT 11

CLE	001	002	010	4	10	0
BOS	000	100	020	3	9	0

Pitchers: LEMON, Bearden (8) vs
  VOISELLE, Spahn (8)
Home Runs: Gordon-CLE
Attendance: 40,103

The Indians, who had won a league-record 111 games to break the American League domination of the New York Yankees, entered the World Series as strong favorites to humble the Giants. It was not to be.

Cleveland would have won the opener had it not been played in New York's Polo Grounds, with their short foul lines and deep center field. Most of the game was a pitchers' duel. Vic Wertz (the only Indian to hit safely in all four games) tripled off Sal Maglie to give Cleveland a two-run lead in the top of the first, but three Giant singles and a walk in the third off Bob Lemon tied the score. Lemon then settled down to hold New York scoreless through the ninth. Cleveland threatened in the eighth when the first two batters reached base, bringing Wertz to the plate. As he had already hit Maglie safely three times, Don Liddle was brought in to pitch to him. Wertz responded with a fly to deep center that would have been a home run in Cleveland, but in New York turned into the most famous catch in World Series history as Willie Mays raced out and tracked down the ball about 425 feet from the plate. Marv Grissom replaced Liddle on the mound and issued a walk to load the bases, but he retired the next two batters and (despite Wertz's double in the top of the tenth) held Cleveland scoreless the rest of the way. In the last of the tenth, Lemon retired the first batter, but Mays walked and stole second, and Hank Thompson was walked intentionally to set up the double play. Pinch hitter Dusty Rhodes then entered the hall of heroes with a short fly to right that—though it would have been an out in Cleveland—fell into the Polo Grounds stands for three runs and a Giant victory.

The rest of the Series was anticlimax. In the second game Rhodes, with half the Giants' four hits, drove in two runs on a single and another homer, providing the margin of victory for Giant ace Johnny Antonelli, who allowed only one of Cleveland's 14 baserunners to score. Game Three was no contest. New York had scored all six of its runs before the Indians managed to come up with single runs in both the seventh and eighth. Pinch hitter Hank Majeski's three-run homer put Cleveland on the board in the fifth inning of Game Four. But as New York had already scored seven times, even a fourth Cleveland run in the seventh proved too little to prevent a Giant sweep.

New York Giants (NL), 4; Cleveland Indians (AL), 0

NY (N)

PLAYER/POS	AVG	G	AB	R	H	2B	3B	HR	RB	BB	SO	SB
Johnny Antonelli, p	.000	2	3	0	0	0	0	0	0	1	0	0
Alvin Dark, ss	.412	4	17	2	7	0	0	0	0	1	1	0
Ruben Gomez, p	.000	1	4	0	0	0	0	0	0	0	2	0
Marv Grissom, p	.000	1	1	0	0	0	0	0	0	0	1	0
Monte Irvin, of	.222	4	9	1	2	1	0	0	2	0	3	0
Don Liddle, p	.000	2	3	0	0	0	0	0	0	0	2	0
Whitey Lockman, 1b	.111	4	18	2	2	0	0	0	0	1	2	0
Sal Maglie, p	.000	1	3	0	0	0	0	0	0	0	2	0
Willie Mays, of	.286	4	14	4	4	1	0	0	3	4	1	1
Don Mueller, of	.389	4	18	4	7	0	0	0	1	0	1	0
Dusty Rhodes, of-2	.667	3	6	2	4	0	0	2	7	1	2	0
Hank Thompson, 3b	.364	4	11	6	4	1	0	0	2	7	1	0
Wes Westrum, c	.273	4	11	0	3	0	0	0	3	1	3	0
Hoyt Wilhelm, p	.000	2	1	0	0	0	0	0	0	0	1	0
Davey Williams, 2b	.000	4	11	0	0	0	0	0	0	1	2	0
TOTAL	.254		130	21	33	3	0	2	20	17	24	1

PITCHER	W	L	ERA	G	GS	CG	SV	SHO	IP	H	ER	BB	SO
Johnny Antonelli	1	0	0.84	2	1	1	1	0	10.2	8	1	7	12
Ruben Gomez	1	0	2.45	1	1	0	0	0	7.1	4	2	3	2
Marv Grissom	1	0	0.00	1	0	0	0	0	2.2	1	0	3	2
Don Liddle	1	0	1.29	2	1	0	0	0	7.0	5	1	1	2
Sal Maglie	0	0	2.57	1	1	0	0	0	7.0	7	2	2	2
Hoyt Wilhelm	0	0	0.00	2	0	0	1	0	2.1	1	0	0	3
TOTAL	4	0	1.46	9	4	1	2	0	37.0	26	6	16	23

CLE (A)

PLAYER/POS	AVG	G	AB	R	H	2B	3B	HR	RB	BB	SO	SB
Bobby Avila, 2b	.133	4	15	1	2	0	0	0	0	0	2	1	0
Sam Dente, ss	.000	3	3	1	0	0	0	0	0	1	0	0
Larry Doby, of	.125	4	16	0	2	0	0	0	0	2	4	0
Mike Garcia, p	.000	2	0	0	0	0	0	0	0	0	0	0
Bill Glynn, 1b-1	.500	2	2	1	1	1	0	0	0	0	1	0
Mickey Grasso, c	.000	1	0	0	0	0	0	0	0	0	0	0
Jim Hegan, c	.154	4	13	1	2	1	0	0	0	1	1	0
Art Houtteman, p	.000	1	0	0	0	0	0	0	0	0	0	0
Bob Lemon, p-2	.000	3	6	0	0	0	0	0	0	1	1	0
Hank Majeski, 3b-1	.167	4	6	1	1	0	0	1	3	0	1	0
Dale Mitchell, ph	.000	3	2	0	0	0	0	0	0	1	0	0
Don Mossi, p	.000	3	0	0	0	0	0	0	0	0	0	0
Hal Naragon, c	.000	1	0	0	0	0	0	0	0	0	0	0
Ray Narleski, p	.000	2	0	0	0	0	0	0	0	0	0	0
Hal Newhouser, p	.000	1	0	0	0	0	0	0	0	0	0	0
Dave Philley, of-2	.125	4	8	0	1	0	0	0	0	1	3	0
Dave Pope, of-2	.000	3	3	0	0	0	0	0	0	1	1	0
Rudy Regalado, 3b-1	.333	4	3	0	1	0	0	0	1	0	0	0
Al Rosen, 3b	.250	3	12	0	3	0	0	0	0	1	0	0
Al Smith, of	.214	4	14	2	3	0	0	1	2	2	2	0
George Strickland, ss	.000	3	9	0	0	0	0	0	0	0	2	0
Vic Wertz, 1b	.500	4	16	2	8	2	1	1	3	2	2	0
Wally Westlake, of	.143	2	7	0	1	0	0	0	0	1	3	0
Early Wynn, p	.500	1	2	0	1	0	0	0	0	0	1	0
TOTAL	.190		137	9	26	5	1	3	9	16	23	0

PITCHER	W	L	ERA	G	GS	CG	SV	SHO	IP	H	ER	BB	SO
Mike Garcia	0	1	5.40	2	1	0	0	0	5.0	6	3	4	4
Art Houtteman	0	0	4.50	1	0	0	0	0	2.0	2	1	1	1
Bob Lemon	0	2	6.75	2	2	1	0	0	13.1	16	10	8	11
Don Mossi	0	0	0.00	3	0	0	0	0	4.0	3	0	0	1
Ray Narleski	0	0	2.25	2	0	0	0	0	4.0	1	1	1	2
Hal Newhouser	0	0	∞	1	0	0	0	0	0.0	1	1	1	0
Early Wynn	0	1	3.86	1	1	0	0	0	7.0	4	3	2	5
TOTAL	0	4	4.84	12	4	1	0	0	35.1	33	19	17	24

The Cleveland Indians had enjoyed a 100–44 record in the strike-shortened 1995 season and captured the AL's new Central Division by a record 30 games. Not surprisingly, they were heavily favored against the AL East champion Red Sox. And not surprisingly, the Curse of Rocky Colavito fell in three straight to the Curse of the Bambino—in other words, the Tribe won.

Yet there were moments of high drama in the series. Game One was a titanic struggle that had nearly everything: two rain delays (39 minutes at the start and 23 minutes in the eighth), three extra inning homers, and a controversial piece of lumber. The five hour and one minute game ended at 2:08 AM the next day. But no one in Cleveland was complaining.

Boston jumped off to a 2–0 lead on John Valentin's two-run homer, but Red Sox starter Roger Clemens surrendered three runs in the sixth. Boston's Luis Alicea evened the score up with a leadoff homer in the eighth.

In the top of the eleventh, Tim Naehring homered to give the Sox the lead, but Albert Belle retaliated in the bottom of the frame with a homer of his own. The next move was Boston's, which contended Belle's bat was corked. AL authorities confiscated it and sawed it in half but found no cork.

In the twelfth the Indians loaded the bases with one out but did not score. In the thirteenth former Red Sox catcher Tony Pena ended it all with an improbable homer off a 3–0 pitch from Zane Smith.

Game Two was a much easier Indian win as veteran Orel Hershiser faced Boston's Erik Hanson. Flashy Indian shortstop Omar Vizquel doubled in two runs in the fifth. Eddie Murray added a two-run homer off Hanson in the eighth. That was more than Hershiser needed as he struck out seven in 7⅓ innings while walking just two and allowing a mere three hits. In the eighth, Hershiser even managed himself, having Tribe pilot Mike Hargrove remove him after his 37-year-old back stiffened up. Key to the Indians' success was holding Boston sluggers Mo Vaughn and Jose Canseco in check. In Game Two they were hitless in eight at-bats, making them a combined 0-for-20 in the series' first two games.

Game Three moved from Jacobs Field to Fenway Park, but the home field proved to be no advantage. Red Sox knuckleballer Tim Wakefield surrendered seven runs in 5⅓ innings as the Indians, behind Charles Nagy, eliminated Boston with an 8–2 win. Vaughn and Canseco went hitless again in seven at-bats, running their record to 0–for–27, with nine strikeouts. But

Boston's defeat was not the duo's fault entirely. Overall, Sox batters were 2–for–28 with runners in scoring position during the series. Neither of those hits—both singles—scored a run.

The Red Sox not only went home for the winter but were saddled with a 13-game postseason losing streak, the major league record. Cleveland would now face the surprising but virtually exhausted Seattle Mariners.

Cleveland Indians (Central), 3; Boston Red Sox (East), 0

CLE (E)

PLAYER/POS	AVG	G	AB	R	H	2B	3B	HR	RBI	BB	SO	SB
Sandy Alomar, c	.182	3	11	1	2	1	0	0	0	1	0	1	0
Paul Assenmacher, p	.000	3	0	0	0	0	0	0	0	0	0	0
Carlos Baerga, 2b	.286	3	14	2	4	1	0	0	1	0	1	0
Albert Belle, of	.273	3	11	3	3	1	0	1	3	4	3	0
Alvaro Espinoza, 3b	.000	1	1	0	0	0	0	0	0	0	0	0
Orel Hershiser, p	.000	1	0	0	0	0	0	0	0	0	0	0
Ken Hill, p	.000	1	0	0	0	0	0	0	0	0	0	0
Wayne Kirby, of-1	1.000	2	1	0	1	0	0	0	0	0	0	0
Kenny Lofton, of	.154	3	13	1	2	0	0	0	0	1	3	0
Dennis Martinez, p	.000	1	0	0	0	0	0	0	0	0	0	0
Jose Mesa, p	.000	2	0	0	0	0	0	0	0	0	0	0
Eddie Murray, dh	.385	3	13	3	5	0	1	1	3	2	1	0
Charles Nagy, p	.000	1	0	0	0	0	0	0	0	0	0	0
Tony Pena, c	.500	2	2	1	1	0	0	1	1	0	0	0
Herb Perry, ph	.000	1	1	0	0	0	0	0	0	0	0	0
Eric Plunk, p	.000	1	0	0	0	0	0	0	0	0	0	0
Jim Poole, p	.000	1	0	0	0	0	0	0	0	0	0	0
Manny Ramirez, of	.000	3	12	1	0	0	0	0	0	1	2	0
Paul Sorrento, 1b	.300	3	10	2	3	0	0	0	1	2	3	0
Julian Tavarez, p	.000	3	0	0	0	0	0	0	0	0	0	0
Jim Thome, 3b	.154	3	13	1	2	0	0	1	3	1	6	0
Omar Vizquel, ss	.167	3	12	2	2	1	0	0	4	2	2	1
TOTAL	.219		114	17	25	4	1	4	17	13	22	1

PITCHER	W	L	ERA	G	GS	CG	SV	SHO	IP	H	ER	BB	SO
Paul Assenmacher	0	0	0.00	3	0	0	0	0	1.2	0	0	0	3
Orel Hershiser	1	0	0.00	1	1	0	0	0	7.1	3	0	2	7
Ken Hill	1	0	0.00	1	0	0	0	0	1.1	1	0	0	2
Dennis Martinez	0	0	3.00	1	1	0	0	0	6.0	5	2	0	2
Jose Mesa	0	0	0.00	2	0	0	1	0	2.0	0	0	2	0
Charles Nagy	1	0	1.29	1	1	0	0	0	7.0	4	1	5	6
Eric Plunk	0	0	0.00	1	0	0	0	0	1.1	1	0	1	1
Jim Poole	0	0	5.40	1	0	0	0	0	1.2	2	1	1	2
Julian Tavarez	0	0	6.75	3	0	0	0	0	2.2	5	2	0	3
TOTAL	3	0	1.74	14	3	0	1	0	31.0	21	6	11	26

BOS (E)

PLAYER/POS	AVG	G	AB	R	H	2B	3B	HR	RBI	BB	SO	SB
Rick Aguilera, p	.000	1	0	0	0	0	0	0	0	0	0	0
Luis Alicea, 2b	.600	3	10	1	6	1	0	1	1	2	2	1
Stan Belinda, p	.000	1	0	0	0	0	0	0	0	0	0	0
Jose Canseco, dh-2,of-1	.000	3	13	0	0	0	0	0	0	2	2	0
Roger Clemens, p	.000	1	0	0	0	0	0	0	0	0	0	0
Rheal Cormier, p	.000	2	0	0	0	0	0	0	0	0	0	0
Mike Greenwell, of	.200	3	15	0	3	0	0	0	0	0	1	0
Erik Hanson, p	.000	1	0	0	0	0	0	0	0	0	0	0
Bill Haselman, c	.000	1	2	0	0	0	0	0	0	0	0	0
Dwayne Hosey, of	.000	3	12	1	0	0	0	0	0	2	3	1
Joe Hudson, p	.000	1	0	0	0	0	0	0	0	0	0	0
Reggie Jefferson, dh	.250	1	4	1	1	0	0	0	0	0	1	0
Mike Macfarlane, c	.333	3	9	0	3	0	0	0	1	0	3	0
Mike Maddux, p	.000	2	0	0	0	0	0	0	0	0	0	0
Willie McGee, of	.250	2	4	0	1	0	0	0	1	0	2	0
Tim Naehring, 3b	.308	3	13	2	4	0	0	1	1	0	1	0
Zane Smith, p	.000	1	0	0	0	0	0	0	0	0	0	0
Matt Stairs, ph	.000	1	1	0	0	0	0	0	0	0	1	0
Mike Stanton, p	.000	1	0	0	0	0	0	0	0	0	0	0
Lee Tinsley, of	.000	1	5	0	0	0	0	0	0	1	2	0
John Valentin, ss	.250	3	12	1	3	1	0	1	2	3	1	0
Mo Vaughn, 1b	.000	3	14	0	0	0	0	0	0	1	7	0
Tim Wakefield, p	.000	1	0	0	0	0	0	0	0	0	0	0
TOTAL	.184		114	6	21	2	0	3	6	11	26	2

PITCHER	W	L	ERA	G	GS	CG	SV	SHO	IP	H	ER	BB	SO
Rick Aguilera	0	0	13.50	1	0	0	0	0	0.2	3	1	0	1
Stan Belinda	0	0	0.00	1	0	0	0	0	0.1	0	0	0	0
Roger Clemens	0	0	3.86	1	1	0	0	0	7.0	5	3	1	5
Rheal Cormier	0	0	13.50	2	0	0	0	0	0.2	2	1	1	2
Erik Hanson	0	1	4.50	1	1	1	0	0	8.0	4	4	4	5
Joe Hudson	0	0	0.00	1	0	0	0	0	1.0	2	0	1	0
Mike Maddux	0	0	0.00	2	0	0	0	0	3.0	2	0	1	1
Zane Smith	0	1	6.75	1	0	0	0	0	1.1	1	1	0	0
Mike Stanton	0	0	0.00	1	0	0	0	0	2.1	1	0	0	4
Tim Wakefield	0	1	11.81	1	1	0	0	0	5.1	5	7	5	4
TOTAL	0	3	5.16	12	3	1	0	0	29.2	25	17	13	22

GAME 1 AT CLE OCT 3

```
BOS    002 000 010 010 0   4 11 2
CLE    000 003 000 010 1   5 10 2
```

Pitchers: Clemens, Cormier (8), Belinda (8), Stanton (8), Aguilera (11), Maddux (11), SMITH (12) vs Martinez, Tavarez (7), Assenmacher (8), Plunk (8), Mesa (10), Poole (11), HILL (12)
Home Runs: Valentin-BOS, Alicea-BOS, Naehring-BOS, Belle-CLE, Pena-CLE
Attendance: 44,218

GAME 2 AT CLE OCT 4

```
BOS    000 000 000   0 3 1
CLE    000 020 02X   4 4 2
```

Pitchers: HANSON vs HERSHISER, Tavarez (8), Assenmacher (8), Mesa (9)
Home Runs: Murray-CLE
Attendance: 44,264

GAME 3 AT BOS OCT 6

```
CLE    021 005 000   8 11 2
BOS    000 100 010   2 7 1
```

Pitchers: NAGY, Tavarez (8), Assenmacher (9) vs WAKEFIELD, Cormier (6), Maddux (6), Hudson (9)
Home Runs: Thome-CLE
Attendance: 34,211

The Indians and Mariners faced each other after vastly different experiences in the first round of MLB's new postseason format.

Cleveland had romped against Boston, sweeping them 3–0. Seattle had engaged in a thrilling, exhausting series against New York, fraying their pitching—and probably their nerves—in the process.

Most observers expected the Tribe to take Game One. Seattle's rotation had been decimated in defeating the Yankees, and Mariners' manager Lou Piniella had to start rookie Bob Wolcott rather than ace Randy Johnson. Wolcott gave up a game-tying seventh inning homer to Albert Belle, but otherwise Piniella had nothing to complain about. Seattle scored in the bottom of that frame and made the run hold up.

Cleveland stranded ten runners in Game Two (making a total of 22 left on in the first two contests) but still triumphed 5–2. Manny Ramirez came into the game mired in a 1-for-16 postseason slump but went 4-for-4 with solo homers in the sixth and eighth innings.

Randy Johnson finally appeared in the series in Game Three but wasn't around for a decision in the eleven inning contest. The Mariners jumped off to a 2–0 lead thanks to two Indian errors, but at the end of eight the score was tied. In the top of the eleventh an intentional walk to Tino Martinez backfired as Jay Buhner followed with a three-run homer.

In Game Four Cleveland evened the series with a 7–0 triumph against an ineffective Andy Benes, aided by Eddie Murray's two-run first inning homer, Jim Thome's two-run third inning homer, and Omar Vizquel's run-scoring sixth inning double.

In Game Five 37-year-old Orel Hershiser ran his career postseason record to 7–0 as he struck out eight and walked only two. He needed help, however, leaving the game with a 3–2 lead which Paul Assenmacher and Jose Mesa skillfully protected, much to the delight of 43,607 Tribe fans.

In the final game, the Indians' Dennis Martinez defeated Randy Johnson 4–0. Through eight innings only one run had scored (an unearned one by Cleveland), but in that inning Mariners hopes unraveled. Johnson surrendered a leadoff double to Tony Pena, then an infield single to Kenny Lofton, who stole second.

Next came a wild pitch. Ruben Amaro (running for Pena) scored, but so did Lofton, motoring all the way past second, embarrassing Mariners catcher Dan Wilson. That play sealed the Mariners' doom. Carlos Baerga then homered, but it was an anticlimactic blow.

After the game Cleveland celebrated and contemplated its first

World Series appearance since 1954 . . . but the nation watched the Seattle dugout, where Mariners second baseman Joey Cora wept uncontrollably.

Cleveland Indians (Central), 4; Seattle Mariners (West), 2

CLE (E)

PLAYER/POS	AVG	G	AB	R	H	2B	3B	HR	RB	BB	SO	SB
Sandy Alomar, c	.267	5	15	0	4	1	1	0	1	1	1	0
Ruben Amaro, dh-1	.000	3	1	1	0	0	0	0	0	0	0	0
Paul Assenmacher, p	.000	3	0	0	0	0	0	0	0	0	0	0
Carlos Baerga, 2b	.400	6	25	3	10	1	0	1	4	2	3	0
Albert Belle, of	.222	5	18	1	4	1	0	1	1	1	3	5	0
Alan Embree, p	.000	1	0	0	0	0	0	0	0	0	0	0
Alvaro Espinoza, 3b	.125	4	8	1	1	0	0	0	0	0	3	0
Orel Hershiser, p	.000	2	0	0	0	0	0	0	0	0	0	0
Ken Hill, p	.000	1	0	0	0	0	0	0	0	0	0	0
Wayne Kirby, of	.200	5	5	2	1	0	0	0	0	0	0	1
Kenny Lofton, of	.458	6	24	4	11	0	2	0	3	4	6	5
Dennis Martinez, p	.000	2	0	0	0	0	0	0	0	0	0	0
Jose Mesa, p	.000	4	0	0	0	0	0	0	0	0	0	0
Eddie Murray, dh	.250	6	24	2	6	1	0	1	3	2	3	0
Charles Nagy, p	.000	1	0	0	0	0	0	0	0	0	0	0
Chad Ogea, p	.000	1	0	0	0	0	0	0	0	0	0	0
Tony Pena, c	.333	4	6	1	2	1	0	0	0	1	0	0
Herb Perry, 1b	.000	3	8	0	0	0	0	0	0	1	3	0
Eric Plunk, p	.000	3	0	0	0	0	0	0	0	0	0	0
Jim Poole, p	.000	1	0	0	0	0	0	0	0	0	0	0
Manny Ramirez, of	.286	6	21	2	6	0	0	2	2	2	5	0
Paul Sorrento, 1b	.154	4	13	2	2	1	0	0	0	2	3	0
Julian Tavarez, p	.000	4	0	0	0	0	0	0	0	0	0	0
Jim Thome, 3b	.267	5	15	2	4	0	0	2	5	2	3	0
Omar Vizquel, ss	.087	6	23	2	2	1	0	0	2	5	2	3
TOTAL	.257		206	23	53	6	3	7	21	25	37	9

PITCHER	W	L	ERA	G	GS	CG	SV	SHO	IP	H	ER	BB	SO
Paul Assenmacher	0	0	0.00	3	0	0	0	0	1.1	0	0	1	2
Alan Embree	0	0	0.00	1	0	0	0	0	0.1	0	0	0	1
Orel Hershiser	2	0	1.29	2	2	0	0	0	14.0	9	2	3	15
Ken Hill	1	0	0.00	1	1	0	0	0	7.0	5	0	3	6
Dennis Martinez	1	1	2.03	2	2	0	0	0	13.1	10	3	3	7
Jose Mesa	0	0	2.25	4	0	0	1	0	4.0	3	1	1	1
Charles Nagy	0	0	1.13	1	1	0	0	0	8.0	5	1	0	6
Chad Ogea	0	0	0.00	1	0	0	0	0	0.2	1	0	0	2
Eric Plunk	0	0	9.00	3	0	0	0	0	2.0	1	2	3	2
Jim Poole	0	0	0.00	1	0	0	0	0	1.0	0	0	0	2
Julian Tavarez	0	1	2.70	4	0	0	0	0	3.1	3	1	1	2
TOTAL	4	2	1.64	23	6	0	1	0	55.0	37	10	15	46

SEA (W)

PLAYER/POS	AVG	G	AB	R	H	2B	3B	HR	RB	BB	SO	SB
Rich Amaral, ph	.000	2	2	0	0	0	0	0	0	0	1	0
Bobby Ayala, p	.000	2	0	0	0	0	0	0	0	0	0	0
Tim Belcher, p	.000	1	0	0	0	0	0	0	0	0	0	0
Andy Benes, p	.000	1	0	0	0	0	0	0	0	0	0	0
Mike Blowers, 3b	.222	6	18	1	4	0	0	1	2	0	4	0
Chris Bosio, p	.000	1	0	0	0	0	0	0	0	0	0	0
Jay Buhner, of	.304	6	23	5	7	2	0	3	5	2	8	0
Norm Charlton, p	.000	3	0	0	0	0	0	0	0	0	0	0
Vince Coleman, of-5	.100	6	20	0	2	0	0	0	0	2	6	4
Joey Cora, 2b	.174	6	23	2	4	1	0	0	0	1	0	2
Alex Diaz, of-3	.429	4	7	0	3	1	0	0	1	1	0	0
Felix Fermin, 2b-1,ss-1	.000	2	0	0	0	0	0	0	0	0	0	0
Ken Griffey, of	.333	6	21	2	7	2	0	1	2	4	4	2
Randy Johnson, p	.000	2	0	0	0	0	0	0	0	0	0	0
Tino Martinez, 1b	.136	6	22	0	3	0	0	0	0	3	7	0
Edgar Martinez, dh	.087	6	23	0	2	0	0	0	0	2	5	1
Jeff Nelson, p	.000	3	0	0	0	0	0	0	0	0	0	0
Bill Risley, p	.000	3	0	0	0	0	0	0	0	0	0	0
Alex Rodriguez, ph	.000	1	1	0	0	0	0	0	0	0	1	0
Luis Sojo, ss	.250	6	20	2	5	2	0	0	1	0	2	0
Doug Strange, 3b-2	.000	4	4	0	0	0	0	0	0	0	2	0
Bob Wells, p	.000	1	0	0	0	0	0	0	0	0	0	0
Chris Widger, c	.000	3	1	0	0	0	0	0	0	0	1	0
Dan Wilson, c	.000	6	16	0	0	0	0	0	0	0	4	0
Bob Wolcott, p	.000	1	0	0	0	0	0	0	0	0	0	0
TOTAL	.184		201	12	37	8	0	5	10	15	46	9

PITCHER	W	L	ERA	G	GS	CG	SV	SHO	IP	H	ER	BB	SO
Bobby Ayala	0	0	2.45	2	0	0	0	0	3.2	3	1	3	3
Tim Belcher	0	1	6.35	1	1	0	0	0	5.2	9	4	2	1
Andy Benes	0	1	23.14	1	1	0	0	0	2.1	6	6	2	3
Chris Bosio	0	1	3.38	1	1	0	0	0	5.1	7	2	2	3
Norm Charlton	1	0	0.00	3	0	0	1	0	6.0	1	0	1	5
Randy Johnson	0	1	2.35	2	2	0	0	0	15.1	12	4	2	13
Jeff Nelson	0	0	0.00	3	0	0	0	0	3.0	3	0	5	3
Bill Risley	0	0	0.00	3	0	0	0	0	2.2	2	0	1	2
Bob Wells	0	0	3.00	1	0	0	0	0	3.0	2	1	2	2
Bob Wolcott	1	0	2.57	1	1	0	0	0	7.0	8	2	5	2
TOTAL	2	4	3.33	18	6	0	1	0	54.0	53	20	25	37

GAME 1 AT SEA OCT 10

CLE　001 000 100　2 10 1
SEA　020 000 10X　3 7 0

Pitchers: MARTINEZ, Tavarez (7), Assenmacher (8), Plunk (8) vs WOLCOTT, Nelson (8), Charlton (8)
Home Runs: Belle-CLE, Blowers-SEA
Attendance: 57,065

GAME 2 AT SEA OCT 11

CLE　000 022 010　5 12 0
SEA　000 001 001　2 6 1

Pitchers: HERSHISER, Mesa (9) vs BELCHER, Ayala (6), Risley (9)
Home Runs: Ramirez-CLE (2), Griffey-SEA, Buhner-SEA
Attendance: 58,144

GAME 3 AT CLE OCT 13

SEA　011 000 000 03　5 9 1
CLE　000 100 010 00　2 4 2

Pitchers: Johnson, CHARLTON (9) vs Nagy, Mesa (9), TAVAREZ (10), Assenmacher (11), Plunk (11)
Home Runs: Buhner-SEA (2)
Attendance: 43,643

GAME 4 AT CLE OCT 14

SEA　000 000 000　0 6 1
CLE　312 001 00X　7 9 0

Pitchers: BENES, Wells (3), Ayala (6), Nelson (7), Risley (8) vs HILL, Poole (8), Ogea (9), Embree (9)
Home Runs: Murray-CLE, Thome-CLE
Attendance: 43,686

GAME 5 AT CLE OCT 15

SEA　001 010 000　2 5 2
CLE　100 002 00X　3 10 4

Pitchers: BOSIO, Nelson (6), Risley (7) vs HERSHISER, Tavarez (7), Assenmacher (7), Plunk (8), Mesa (9)
Home Runs: Thome-CLE
Attendance: 43,607

GAME 6 AT SEA OCT 17

CLE　000 010 030　4 8 0
SEA　000 000 000　0 4 1

Pitchers: MARTINEZ, Tavarez (8), Mesa (9) vs JOHNSON, Charlton (8)
Home Runs: Baerga-CLE
Attendance: 58,489

The Indians and Braves met for a rematch of their tussle in the 1948 World Series, but this time the transplanted Braves went home with the honors.

Game One quickly established that Atlanta's vaunted pitching staff was no myth. Perennial Cy Young Award winner Greg Maddux used just 95 pitches in shutting down the hard-hitting Indians. Only three runners reached against him, on opposite field singles by Kenny Lofton and Jim Thome, and on 'an error by Rafael Belliard. Cleveland starter Orel Hershiser tired in the seventh and walked two, leading to the second and third Atlanta runs and his first loss after seven straight postseason victories.

In Game Two Atlanta took a 2–0 series lead as catcher Javier Lopez anticipated a Dennis Martinez fastball on the outside part of the plate. He hammered it to straight-away center field for a two-run homer, shattering a 2–2 tie and providing the Braves' with all the margin they would need for a 4–3 win. Earlier Cleveland's 39-year-old Eddie Murray garnered a two-run homer of his own off starter Tom Glavine.

The Indians' bats finally came alive in Game Three's 7–6 win. It looked like the Tribe would be facing a 3–0 deficit, as they trailed 6–5 in the bottom of the eighth. But in that inning Kenny Lofton (who reached base six times in the contest) scored the tying run on Sandy Alomar's first hit of the series. In the eleventh Eddie Murray singled off Alejandro Pena's first pitch to score pinch-runner Alvaro Espinoza with the winning run.

Atlanta's Ryan Klesko and Cleveland's Albert Belle traded solo sixth-inning homers in Game Four to set up a one-one tie going into the top of the seventh. Atlanta then scored three runs on Luis Polonia's run-scoring double and David Justice's two-out, two-RBI single to center to break the contest open and ultimately give Atlanta a 5–2 win.

The Tribe stayed alive in Game Five as Jim Thome singled in the go-ahead run in the sixth and provided a crucial insurance run with an eighth inning homer. Ryan Klesko nicked Jose Mesa for a two-run homer in the ninth—the third straight game in which he'd homered—but it wasn't enough.

With a 3–2 lead in the Series and Greg Maddux waiting to pitch Game Seven, the Braves had little to worry about in Game Six. Key to their victory were two players with something to prove: Tom Glavine, who had survived Atlanta's horrible days in the late 1980s, and David Justice, who was taking heat for comments he had made about

Atlanta fans' lack of spirit. Glavine allowed only a sixth inning single to Tony Pena, walked three and struck out eight. Justice brought home the game's only run with a sixth inning homer off reliever Jim Poole.

The Braves now had their first World Championship since 1957 and had become the first franchise to win the crown in three different cities—Boston, Milwaukee, and Atlanta.

Atlanta Braves (NL), 4; Cleveland Indians (AL), 2

ATL (N)

PLAYER/POS	AVG	G	AB	R	H	2B	3B	HR	RB	BB	SO	SB
Steve Avery, p	.000	1	0	0	0	0	0	0	0	0	0	0
Rafael Belliard, ss	.000	6	16	0	0	0	0	0	1	0	4	0
Pedro Borbon, p	.000	1	0	0	0	0	0	0	0	0	0	0
Brad Clontz, p	.000	2	0	0	0	0	0	0	0	0	0	0
Mike Devereaux, of-4,dh-1	.250	5	4	0	1	0	0	0	1	2	1	0
Tom Glavine, p	.000	2	4	0	0	0	0	0	0	1	2	0
Marquis Grissom, of	.360	6	25	3	9	1	0	0	1	1	3	3
Chipper Jones, 3b	.286	6	21	3	6	3	0	0	1	4	5	0
David Justice, of	.250	6	20	3	5	1	0	1	5	5	1	0
Ryan Klesko, of-3,dh-3	.313	6	16	4	5	0	0	3	4	3	4	0
Mark Lemke, 2b	.273	6	22	1	6	0	0	0	0	3	2	0
Javy Lopez, c	.176	6	17	1	3	2	0	1	3	1	1	0
Greg Maddux, p	.000	2	3	0	0	0	0	0	0	0	1	0
Fred McGriff, 1b	.261	6	23	5	6	2	0	2	3	3	5	1
Greg McMichael, p	.000	3	0	0	0	0	0	0	0	0	0	0
Kent Mercker, p	.000	1	0	0	0	0	0	0	0	0	0	0
Mike Mordecai, ss-2,dh-1	.333	3	3	0	1	0	0	0	0	0	1	0
Charlie O'Brien, c	.000	2	3	0	0	0	0	0	0	0	1	0
Alejandro Pena, p	.000	2	0	0	0	0	0	0	0	0	0	0
Luis Polonia, of-4	.286	6	14	3	4	1	0	1	4	1	3	1
Dwight Smith, ph	.500	3	2	0	1	0	0	0	0	1	0	0
John Smoltz, p	.000	1	0	0	0	0	0	0	0	0	0	0
Mark Wohlers, p	.000	4	0	0	0	0	0	0	0	0	0	0
TOTAL	.244		193	23	47	10	0	8	23	25	34	5

PITCHER	W	L	ERA	G	GS	CG	SV	SHO	IP	H	ER	BB	SO
Steve Avery	1	0	1.50	1	1	0	0	0	6.0	3	1	5	3
Pedro Borbon	0	0	0.00	1	0	0	1	0	1.0	0	0	0	2
Brad Clontz	0	0	2.70	2	0	0	0	0	3.1	2	1	0	2
Tom Glavine	2	0	1.29	2	2	0	0	0	14.0	4	2	6	11
Greg Maddux	1	1	2.25	2	2	1	0	0	16.0	9	4	3	8
Greg McMichael	0	0	2.70	3	0	0	0	0	3.1	3	1	2	2
Kent Mercker	0	0	4.50	1	0	0	0	0	2.0	1	1	2	2
Alejandro Pena	0	1	9.00	2	0	0	0	0	1.0	3	1	2	0
John Smoltz	0	0	15.43	1	1	0	0	0	2.1	6	4	2	4
Mark Wohlers	0	0	1.80	4	0	0	2	0	5.0	4	1	3	3
TOTAL	4	2	2.67	19	6	1	3	0	54.0	35	16	25	37

CLE (A)

PLAYER/POS	AVG	G	AB	R	H	2B	3B	HR	RB	BB	SO	SB
Sandy Alomar, c	.200	5	15	0	3	2	0	0	1	0	2	0
Ruben Amaro, of-1	.000	2	2	0	0	0	0	0	0	0	1	0
Paul Assenmacher, p	.000	4	0	0	0	0	0	0	0	0	0	0
Carlos Baerga, 2b	.192	6	26	1	5	2	0	0	4	1	1	0
Albert Belle, of	.235	6	17	4	4	0	0	2	4	7	5	0
Alan Embree, p	.000	4	0	0	0	0	0	0	0	0	0	0
Alvaro Espinoza, 3b-1	.500	2	2	1	1	0	0	0	0	0	0	0
Orel Hershiser, p	.000	2	2	0	0	0	0	0	0	0	0	0
Ken Hill, p	.000	2	2	0	0	0	0	0	0	0	0	0
Wayne Kirby, of-2	.000	3	1	0	0	0	0	0	0	0	1	0
Kenny Lofton, of	.200	6	25	6	5	1	0	0	0	3	1	6
Dennis Martinez, p	.000	2	3	0	0	0	0	0	0	0	1	0
Jose Mesa, p	.000	2	0	0	0	0	0	0	0	0	0	0
Eddie Murray, 1b-3,dh-3	.105	6	19	1	2	0	0	1	3	5	4	0
Charles Nagy, p	.000	1	0	0	0	0	0	0	0	0	0	0
Tony Pena, c	.167	2	6	0	1	0	0	0	0	0	0	0
Herb Perry, 1b	.000	3	5	0	0	0	0	0	0	0	2	0
Jim Poole, p	.000	2	1	0	0	0	0	0	0	0	0	0
Manny Ramirez, of	.222	6	18	2	4	0	0	1	2	4	5	1
Paul Sorrento, 1b-2	.182	5	11	0	2	1	0	0	0	0	4	0
Julian Tavarez, p	.000	5	0	0	0	0	0	0	0	0	0	0
Jim Thome, 3b	.211	6	19	4	4	1	0	1	2	2	5	0
Omar Vizquel, ss	.174	6	23	3	4	0	1	0	1	3	5	1
TOTAL	.179		195	19	35	7	1	5	17	25	37	8

PITCHER	W	L	ERA	G	GS	CG	SV	SHO	IP	H	ER	BB	SO
Paul Assenmacher	0	0	6.75	4	0	0	0	0	1.1	1	1	3	3
Alan Embree	0	0	2.70	4	0	0	0	0	3.1	2	1	2	2
Orel Hershiser	1	1	2.57	2	2	0	0	0	14.0	8	4	4	13
Ken Hill	0	1	4.26	2	1	0	0	0	6.1	7	3	4	1
Dennis Martinez	0	1	3.48	2	2	0	0	0	10.1	12	4	8	5
Jose Mesa	1	0	4.50	2	0	0	1	0	4.0	5	2	1	4
Charles Nagy	0	0	6.43	1	1	0	0	0	7.0	8	5	1	4
Jim Poole	0	1	3.86	2	0	0	0	0	2.1	1	1	0	1
Julian Tavarez	0	0	0.00	5	0	0	0	0	4.1	3	0	2	1
TOTAL	2	4	3.57	24	6	0	1	0	53.0	47	21	25	34

GAME 1 AT ATL OCT 21

CLE	100 000 001	2	2	0
ATL	010 000 20X	3	3	2

Pitchers: HERSHISER, Assenmacher (7), Tavarez (7), Embree (8) vs MADDUX
Home Runs: McGriff-ATL
Attendance: 51,876

GAME 2 AT ATL OCT 22

CLE	020 000 100	3	6	2
ATL	002 002 00X	4	8	2

Pitchers: MARTINEZ, Embree (6), Poole (7), Tavarez (8) vs GLAVINE, McMichael (8), Pena (9), Wohlers (9)
Home Runs: Murray-CLE, Lopez-ATL
Attendance: 51,877

GAME 3 AT CLE OCT 24

ATL	100 001 130 00	6	12	1
CLE	202 000 110 01	7	12	2

Pitchers: Smoltz, Clontz (3), Mercker (5), McMichael (7), Wohlers (8), PENA (11) vs Nagy, Assenmacher (8), Tavarez (8), MESA (9)
Home Runs: McGriff-ATL, Klesko-ATL
Attendance: 43,584

GAME 4 AT CLE OCT 25

ATL	000 001 301	5	11	1
CLE	000 001 001	2	6	0

Pitchers: AVERY, McMichael (7), Wohlers (9), Borbon (9) vs HILL, Assenmacher (7), Tavarez (8), Embree (8)
Home Runs: Belle-CLE, Ramirez-CLE, Klesko-ATL
Attendance: 43,578

GAME 5 AT CLE OCT 26

ATL	000 110 002	4	7	0
CLE	200 002 01X	5	8	1

Pitchers: MADDUX, Clontz (8) vs HERSHISER, Mesa (9)
Home Runs: Belle-CLE, Thome-CLE, Polonia-ATL, Klesko-ATL
Attendance: 43,595

GAME 6 AT ATL OCT 28

CLE	000 000 000	0	1	1
ATL	000 001 00X	1	6	0

Pitchers: Martinez, POOLE (5), Hill (7), Embree (7), Tavarez (8), Assenmacher (8) vs GLAVINE, Wohlers (9)
Home Runs: Justice-ATL
Attendance: 51,875

CHAPTER 4

Baseball in Cleveland

David Pietrusza

The very first professional league game involved a Cleveland team, the Forest City club of the old National Association, the first major league. On May 4, 1871, Forest City traveled to Fort Wayne, Indiana. On that day Cleveland baseball recorded its first loss, 2–0, to the local Kekiongas.

Cleveland leadoff hitter James "Deacon" White scored several firsts: the first big league at-bat, the first hit, the first extra-base hit (a double) and the first grounded-into-double-play. Some said he was the first catcher to play close to the batter. His manager, Charlie Pabor, on the other hand, was one of the last to believe catchers should bat leadoff.

The Forest Citys finished seventh (10–19) in 1871, and collapsed midway through the 1872 season after limping along to a 6–16 record. The National Association continued, without a Cleveland representative, through the 1875 season, until it too collapsed.

Big league play returned to Cleveland in 1879 with a National League team called—of all things—the Forest Citys. The club changed its names to the Blues in 1882, in honor of their new uniforms. Perhaps the bluest Blue that season was pitcher Dave Rowe. On July 24 he surrendered 35 runs (only twelve of which were earned), still the major league record for a pitcher in one game.

The Blues' best pitcher was righthanded workhorse Jim McCormick. In 1880 he led the NL with 45 wins, 72 complete games, and 657⅔ innings pitched. In 1882 he paced it with 36 wins, 65 complete games, and 595⅔ innings pitched. Overhand pitching was not yet legal, but his endurance is nonetheless astounding.

In 1884 the club finished seventh (many of its players, including McCormick, jumped to the rival Union Association), and at season's end was sold to St. Louis Maroons owner Henry V. Lucas. Lucas thought he had obtained the Blues' player contracts in the deal, but he was wrong. All the players Lucas wanted to sign went instead to the Brooklyn Bridegrooms. Thus, as St. Louis and Brooklyn picked over the remains of the franchise, ended Cleveland's first foray into National League baseball.

In 1887 the city landed a club in the American Association, another early rival to the National League, that was known both to its detractors and to its thirsty partisans as the "Beer and Whisky League" for its lenient policy on alcohol sales. The club, again called the Blues, finished eighth and then sixth, before transferring to the National League in 1889.

The following year saw Cleveland—for the only season in its history—with two major league franchises. In 1890 dissatisfied players jumped the National League in droves and formed their own circuit, the Players League. Cleveland's PL franchise, the Infants, was financed by local street car magnate Albert L. Johnson, brother of the city's famed reform mayor, Tom Johnson. Johnson was violently opposed to the reserve clause and stated: "If the League can hold a man on a contract for any or all time it may desire when it simply guarantees him ten days' pay (for that is everything in the world it does for players), why, then the laws of our land are worse than those of any other nation on earth, and instead of progressing, as we suppose that every civilized country is trying to do, the sooner we turn back the better."

That was Johnson's idealistic side. But he had other motivation, including a desire to have his trolleys transport fans to and from the games.

Johnson's Infants boasted some impressive names: American Association slugger Pete "The Gladiator" Browning (who led the PL with a .373 average), future Hall of Famer Big Ed Delahanty, and infielder George "Patsy" Tebeau. Still the club finished seventh. The league itself folded at season's end.

Cleveland's National League club, now known as the Spiders, survived the Infants' challenge and would spend twelve seasons in the circuit. Most were fairly respectable, but one—the last—would be the worst in major league history.

In 1891, however, the Spiders would move into a new home. Like Albert Johnson, Spiders owner Frank DeHaas Robison was also a trolley magnate. In 1887 he had built Spiders Park near his *own* line. In 1890 when lightning destroyed the park, Robison replaced it with League Park. League Park, which would host Cleveland major league baseball until 1946, was again just steps from Robison's Lexington Avenue line trolley tracks.

In 1892 the National League contained twelve teams, and rather than split into two divisions, it split its season. The Spiders (featuring 36-game winner Cy Young) finished fifth in the first half but won the NL second-half flag. The Spiders lost the postseason series against first-half winner Boston 5–0. The best Cleveland could manage was an eleven inning scoreless tie in the opener when its ace Cy Young battled Boston's Jack Stivetts to a standstill.

Cy (for "Cyclone") Young was a mainstay of the franchise. When League Park opened on May 1, 1891, it was Cy Young who took the mound for the home team. Each year from 1891 through 1898 he won at least 21 games for the Spiders. Twice he captured 30 wins (34 in 1893 and 35 in 1895). He would go on to record 511 wins, the all-time major league record.

The NL junked the split-season idea after the 1892 season, but beginning with 1894 instituted the idea of postseason play, the Temple Cup Series, featuring its first and second place teams. In both 1895 and 1896 Baltimore and Cleveland finished one-two.

Managing the Spiders in those years was Patsy Tebeau,

a rough-and-ready character whose aggressiveness was more than a match for Baltimore's boisterous Orioles. On the team from 1894 to 1898 was future Hall of Fame shortstop Bobby Wallace. Wallace, however, started as a pitcher, then moved over to third base before settling in at short in his last year with the team.

In 1895 Tebeau's Spiders bested the Orioles in Temple Cup play 4–1 as Young went 3–0 and Hall of Fame outfielder Jesse "The Crab" Burkett batted .450. Baltimore's partisans were sore losers and rioted after losing Game Four, pelting the Spiders with rocks, bricks, eggs, and fruit and vegetables. Cleveland second baseman Cupid Childs was hit on the back of the head with a large rock. "The wonder now," noted the *Cleveland Plain Dealer,* "is that the Cleveland players are alive and able to tell the story and not in the hospital or the morgue."

Only a massive police presence prevented a repeat of such hooliganism after Game Five—although Orioles third baseman John "Muggsy" McGraw satisfied his personal bloodlust by splitting Patsy Tebeau's lip with a hard tag.

Baltimore and Cleveland faced off again the following October, with the Orioles sweeping the Spiders 4–0. The die was cast for Cleveland in the first two innings of Game One. In the first frame Cy Young was hit on his right wrist by a line drive. In the second Patsy Tebeau threw his back out. The Spiders never had a chance after that.

The next year saw the Spiders feature the Penobscot Indian phenom, Louis Sockalexis. Sockalexis eventually drank himself out of the league, but his brief tenure was so brilliant and well-remembered that two decades later Cleveland's American League franchise would be renamed in his honor: the Indians. (Some have thought that Sockalexis was the first American Indian to perform in the majors. He was not, but the first also played for Cleveland: utility player James Toy debuted for the old Blues back in 1887.)

As the 1897 season progressed, however, Spider fans stopped coming out to the Cleveland's League Park—and so did the Spiders. Owner Robison had responded to low attendance by rescheduling his remaining games to the road.

That was bad enough, but the next year things got *worse.* Robison also owned the St. Louis Browns (such dual ownership, called "syndicate baseball" was then legal) and shipped all the talented Spiders—Young, Tebeau, Burkett, Wallace, Childs, pitcher Jack Powell and outfielder Harry Blake—to St. Louis. What was left of the Spiders was just awful—combining for a gruesome 20–134 record, an all-time low .120 won-lost percentage. Spiders no more, the team bore such labels as "Misfits" and "Leftovers."

At season's end the National League bought out the franchise for $25,000. It was worth it to get the "Misfits"out of the league. But nature abhors a vacuum, and Ban Johnson's minor league circuit, the American League, moved its Grand Rapids franchise to Cleveland in 1900. The reborn Spiders finished sixth (63–73). The following year the American League achieved major status. Cleveland, now known as the Blues or the Bronchos, played the first game in American League big league history, losing to the White Sox on April 24, 1901.

In 1912 another prospective major league showed up in Cleveland–but it was no American League. The United States League's Forest City club played at Luna Park, a local amusement park located four miles from downtown. Its 4,600 seat grandstand cost $15,000. Patrons purchasing either a twenty-five or fifty cent ticket to the ballgame would be admitted free to the rest of the amusements. Quite a bargain, but the USL featured little in terms of playing talent and folded by Memorial Day.

The next league to challenge Organized Baseball, the Federal League, started as an outlaw *minor* league in 1913. One of its six franchises was in Cleveland. There was a sense of *deja vu* about the experience. The Green Sox or "Youngsters" played at Luna Park (not surprisingly since the amusement park's owner, M. R. Bromley, also owned the Green Sox); their manager was none other than Cy Young. Under Young the team finished second with a 63–54 record, but when the Federal League advanced to major league status in 1914, Cleveland was not one of its franchises.

To block a Federal invasion, Indians owner Charles W. Somers brought the minor league American Association Mud Hens to play at Cleveland's League Park for the 1914 and 1915 seasons. Players shuttled back and forth between the Indians and the Mud Hens, but without any noticeable effect on the American Association club's quality. It finished fifth (82–81) in 1914 and seventh (67–82) in 1915.

Semipro baseball was also proving popular in Cleveland. In 1915 at the city's Brookside Stadium, over 100,000 fans watched the White Autos defeat the Omaha Luxers 11–6 for the National Baseball Federation Championship. (Eight years earlier, female baseball phenom Alta Weiss had pitched a game for the Vermilion Independents before thousands of appreciative fans at League Park.)

There was another sort of baseball being played in Cleveland: black ball. Cleveland had a rich tradition of Negro Leagues competition. The best known club was the Cleveland Buckeyes, which played in the Negro American League from 1943 to 1948 and again in 1950, but the city also featured the Bears (Negro American League, 1939–40), Browns (Negro National League, 1924), Cubs (NNL, 1931), Elites (NNL, 1926), Giants (NNL, 1933), Hornets (NNL, 1927), Red Sox (NNL, 1934), Stars (East-West League, 1932), Tate Stars (NNL, 1922), and Tigers (NNL, 1928). Sol White, author of the groundbreaking *History of Colored Baseball,* managed the 1924 Browns. Satchel Paige and Sam "Lefty" Streeter pitched for the 1931 edition of the Cleveland Cubs. Cuban-born star Cristobel Torrienti closed out his career with the Cubs the following season.

Cleveland's black teams performed at such sites as Tate Park (named after Tate Stars owner George Tate), Hooper Field, Cubs Stadium (just across the street from League Park), Hardware Field, Luna Park, and even at League Park itself.

The 1945 Buckeyes, led by player-manager Quincy Trouppe, captured both halves of the NAL season and then went on to sweep the Homestead Grays 4–0 in the Negro World Series. With Trouppe still at the helm, the Buckeyes won again in 1947. Perhaps the Buckeyes' greatest star was fleet outfielder Sam "The Jet" Jethroe, in 1950 the National League Rookie of the Year.

Satchel Paige, by the way, was not the only former Negro Leaguer to perform for the Indians. Five former Buckeyes (Trouppe, Sam Jones, Al Smith, Dave Hoskins, and Joe Caffie) also later played for the Tribe.

CHAPTER 5

Indians Greats

Michael Gershman

Johnny Allen

Tempestuous, hard-throwing righthander Johnny Allen got his start with the Yankees thanks to the fans — not fans in the stands, but the ones he brought to Bronx superscout Paul Krichell to cool off a sweltering hotel room while Allen worked as a bellhop. The young pitcher confided to the former catcher that he was a pitcher of sorts, and Krichell gave him a tryout.

Krichell's faith paid off in 1932 when Allen posted a 17-4 rookie record. But the Yankees soon tired of Allen, who was one of the first pitchers to throw the slider. He habitually held out for more money, and when a sore arm threatened to end his career, they packed him off to Cleveland in 1936.

The trade was a mistake for the Yankees. Despite a slow start, Allen won 20 for the Tribe and followed that up in 1937 by winning his first 15 decisions. He came close to tying the American League mark for consecutive victories set by Walter Johnson in 1912, but lost 1-0 on an error by teammate Odell "Bad News" Hale. Ever the gentleman, Allen nearly punched out Hale. Nevertheless his 15-1 season mark was the major league record for won-lost percentage until Elroy Face's 18-1 performance in 1959 for the Pirates, and remains the American League standard.

In 1938 Allen won his first 12 decisions but suffered a mysterious injury during the All-Star break. Some contend that he slipped on a bar of soap in a hotel room shower. Whatever the reason, he soon went into a serious decline. After a brief stay with the Browns, he revived his career in the National League with the Dodgers and Giants before retiring after the 1944 season.

Ironically, despite Allen's notorious temper and his numerous run-ins with umpires, he went on to become umpire-in-chief of the Carolina League. He died of a heart attack on March 29, 1959.

Sandy Alomar Jr.

Sandy Alomar Jr. inherited several traits from his father, Sandy Alomar Sr., who played 15 years in the major leagues. The Cleveland catcher just hopes that longevity is one of them.

His younger brother, Roberto Alomar, now with the Baltimore Orioles, has started the last six All-Star Games at second base, has been a member of two world championship Toronto Blue Jay teams, and has played in as many as 161 games is a season, avoiding the disabled list.

The DL, though, has been the bane of Sandy Alomar Jr. Excluding his rookie season, when he played in 132 games and became the first rookie catcher to start the All-Star game, Sandy Jr. has not played more than 89 games or batted more than 300 times in a season. After missing most of the first half of the 1995 season, though, he bounced back to hit .300 with 10 home runs in 66 games for the American League champions.

Unlike his brother's quick trip to the major leagues (making the San Diego Padres at age 20), his elder brother has had a more difficult road. Sandy struggled his first three seasons in the minor leagues. When he finally blossomed and was ready for the big leagues in 1989, he was stuck behind Benito Santiago, the Rookie of the Year two years earlier and a man considered to be the best catcher in the National League, if not the majors. Alomar would have to wait — in the minors.

"I was mad that year they sent me down and didn't trade me," he says. "I know they have a job to do, but I was the one who was penalized. Maybe it was for my own good. Maybe I'm more prepared now than I would have been then."

His two years in Las Vegas with the Padres' AAA affiliate were two more years than he would spend in San Diego, but he certainly made the most of it. Alomar shared Most Valuable Player honors in 1988 with a .297 average, 16 home runs and 71 runs batted in, and bettered those stats (.301, 13, 101) to keep the award all to himself in 1989.

He was traded to the Indians along with Carlos Baerga for Joe Carter, who would ironically be packaged off to Toronto with Roberto Alomar the following year. Both Roberto and Sandy have since gone to the World Series, while the highest the Padres have gone is third place.

Despite the fact that the Padres had two generations of Alomars (their father was also a coach with the team), the family was only together for 47 games over two seasons. "I had two feelings when the trade was made," Sandy says. "The first that I was happy because I finally would have my chance. The second was that it was sad that the family was being broken up." Given the chance he needed, Sandy was chosen Rookie of the Year in 1990. Five years later he helped end a 41-year drought between World Series appearances and make the city synonymous once again with excellent baseball.

It was the culmination of a lifetime of hard work by the 29-year-old Sandy Alomar Jr. He received his first set of catching gear at the age of 7, spent every summer at the ballpark as his father played in seven different stadiums, and grew up in a family where baseball was the family business.

Note: The names of Hall of Fame members are set off by stars (★).

"I wasn't the best guy — not in little leagues, not in any league I played in," he says. "I played good. I did things right. I did what I was supposed to do to help us win. But I worked harder than the other guys. The other guys were staying steady; I was getting better. When I signed, there were much better players in Puerto Rico than me. Other guys were wondering, 'If he's already signed, when are they going to sign me?' "

His hard work and patience has paid off, but the reflective Sandy Jr. was always a little different than his brother who wanted desperately to be a baseball player. Sandy did not really know until he signed on the dotted line that he wanted to be a baseball player. What he has had to endure in the game, first with the Padres and then during his stints on the disabled list, has never let him forget that, in the end, baseball is a game.

★ Earl Averill ★

Along with Lou Boudreau, Mel Harder, and Bob Feller, Earl Averill one of only four Tribesmen to have his uniform (3) retired. (Boudreau is #3, Harder 18, and Feller 19.)

For a batter and all-around player of his stature, Averill's most publicized at bat ironically wasn't a hit. It came during the 1937 All-Star Game when he smashed a drive that caromed off pitcher Dizzy Dean's toe. Averill was thrown out, but the hit broke Dean's toe. When Diz returned to pitching (before it had completely healed), he altered his motion to favor the foot, eventually ruining his arm.

In a peculiar twist of fate, Averill's own career ended in a similar fashion, also in 1937. In the dugout one day, Averill suddenly found himself paralyzed from the waist down. The paralysis was temporary, but an examination revealed a congenital spinal problem, and that forced him to alter his swing. Although he played for four more seasons, Averill's batting average and power declined.

Averill had begun playing on amateur teams around Snohomish, Washington, in the early 1920s. He was jobless at the time, supporting a wife and young child. His friends and neighbors chipped in to send him to try out with Seattle of the Pacific Coast League. He flunked the tryout, but rather than return home, he hooked up with a semipro club in Bellingham, Washington, which eventually led to a full-time job with the PCL's San Francisco Seals.

For three seasons he feasted on Coast League pitching, but the major leagues didn't pay much attention. Finally, when Cleveland Indians general manager Billy Evans came west in 1928 to look at Averill's teammate, outfielder Roy Johnson, it was Averill who caught Evans's eye. "There was something about the nonchalant Averill that won you over," Evans later explained. "I guess it was the easy, steady manner in which he did his work, without any great show." Evans learned the Tigers had already offered $65,000 and two players for Johnson; Averill was available for a flat $50,000, and that made up Evans's mind.

On April 16, 1929, the left-handed-batting Averill stepped up for his first major league at bat. On the mound stood Detroit's ace, lefty Earl Whitehill. A moment later,

Averill circled the bases with his first home run. No other American League rookie had ever homered in his first at bat, and only two had done it in the National League. Averill remains one of only two members of the Baseball Hall of Fame, along with relief pitcher Hoyt Wilhelm, to have performed the feat.

Off to a roaring start, Averill had a monster year, batting .332 with 96 RBI and 18 homers. Vowing to do better in 1930, he raised his batting average to .339 and his RBI total to 119, but by September 17 he had hit only 14 home runs. Reminded that he was still short of the previous year's mark, he said, "Well, I'd better step on it." That day he smashed four home runs in a doubleheader, three in one game. Another drive into the seats went foul at the last moment. He amassed 11 RBIs for the afternoon. On the final day of the season he hit his nineteenth homer to make good on his promise. In each of the next two seasons he upped his homer total to 32.

At just over 5-foot-9 and 172 pounds Averill was no physical giant, but he generated excellent power and pulled the ball consistently, a necessary skill as he played half his games in Cleveland's League Park with its inviting right field fence (290 feet from the plate). Although his arm was ordinary at best, he patrolled center field with a special loping grace that made him appear perpetually relaxed.

The Cleveland fans, spoiled by the presence of the fabled Tris Speaker in center only a few years before, nevertheless deemed Averill a worthy successor. He was easily the most popular player in town, earning numerous affectionate nicknames. "the Earl of Snohomish" being his usual sobriquet on the sports pages.

Beginning in 1931 the exceptionally durable Averill played in 673 straight games. Although that figure pales alongside the marks of Lou Gehrig and Cal Ripken Jr., it was the fourth-longest consecutive game streak on record at the time.

In both 1931 and 1932 the *Sporting News* named him to the outfield on its All-Star Fielding Team. When Major League Baseball played its first All-Star Game, in Chicago, Averill was the starting center fielder for the American League. He went on to become the only AL outfielder named to the first six All-Star Games. But in 1935, when a firecracker went off in his hand, he missed the All-Star Game and ended his consecutive game streak. The injury was responsible for his first sub-.300 season, but he still hit .288, with 19 homers.

Averill bounced back in 1936 at age 34 with one of his finest years. His career-high .378 batting average was only 10 points behind league leader Luke Appling's mark. Averill led the league with 232 hits and 15 triples, while hitting 28 homers, scoring 136 runs, and driving in 126.

The following season, after his spine problem was diagnosed, his power nearly disappeared, and he missed hitting .300 that year by .001. In 1938 he hit only 14 home runs but still managed a .330 batting average. On Earl Averill Day that season, the fans showered him with gifts. During his 10 years in Cleveland he'd averaged 189 hits, 37 doubles, 12 triples, 23 home runs, 115 runs scored, 108 RBI, and a slugging percentage of .534.

His back problem worsened and early in June 1939 the Indians traded him to Detroit for a second-string pitcher and a cash payment. The Cleveland fans were up in arms, but the trade gave Averill his only chance to play on a pennant winner when the Tigers won the 1940 flag. In the World Series the Tigers lost to the Cincinnati Reds, and Averill went hitless in three tries as a pinch hitter.

After playing eight games for the Braves in 1941, Boston released him, and Averill finished the season in Seattle before returning home to Snohomish. His son, Earl Douglas Averill, grew up and spent seven years in the major leagues himself while his father awaited a call to Cooperstown. In 1975, 34 years after his retirement, the Veterans Committee named the Earl of Snohomish to the Hall of Fame. He died in 1983.

Bobby Avila

Although he was overshadowed by teammates Bob Lemon, Al Rosen, and Bob Feller, Mexico's Bobby Avila was one of the Cleveland Indians' stars of the 1950s.

Originally a professional soccer player, Avila also dreamed of being a bullfighter; however, his father wasn't impressed with either occupation, or with baseball, which Avila had learned from a how-to book authored by former big league hurler Jack Coombs.

Avila signed a contract to play in a winter league called the Vera Cruz State League and then played for Puebla of the Mexican League. He gained exposure to American ballplayers when in 1946 Mexican League magnate Jorge Pasquel attempted to convert his circuit into a rival of the major leagues and lured down such North Americans as Sal Maglie, Vern Stephens, and Mickey Owen.

In 1946 and 1947 Avila played winter ball in Cuba. The Dodgers were interested in him and offered $10,000, but the Indians signed him for $17,500. Avila then spent the 1948 season with Baltimore, where he hit .220. Bonus rules at the time mandated that Cleveland bring him up in 1949, but Avila merely warmed the bench for the Indians and spent his spare time trying to learn English from pitcher Mike Garcia, a teammate of Mexican extraction. Once Avila became a regular, though, he was a hitting machine, capturing the American League batting championship in 1954 with a .341 mark. (Ted Williams had a higher batting average but failed to reach the minimum 400 at bats.)

Avila was traded from Cleveland after the 1958 season, his tenth with the Indians and spent the remainder of his career with the Orioles, Red Sox, and Braves. After retiring in 1959 Avila pursued a variety of business interests in Mexico including ownership of the Vera Cruz Eagles and the presidency of the Mexican League. Eventually he was elected mayor of Vera Cruz.

Carlos Baerga

What's wrong with Carlos Baerga? In an era where the strikeout is a accepted byproduct of power, the second baseman for the Cleveland Indians is rocking the boat — and finding the power alleys.

Baerga is a career .305 hitter who's averaged 162 hits per year — a total that includes three less-than-full sea-

sons with only 108 games played as a rookie in 1990 and with 68 games eliminated because of the baseball strike in 1994-95.

Incredibly, while his average has increased almost every season, his strikeout numbers have gone down. When Baerga broke into the majors, he struck out once every 5.9 plate appearances. In 1991 that number was 8.9, in '92 it was 9.4, in '93 it was 10.0, in '94 it was 10.4, and it was up to 17.9 at bats between strikeouts in '95. In fact, he went "whiff-less" his first 96 at bats with the Indians last year.

Baerga started off the year at a .396 clip but cooled down to .314, good for a ninth place tie in the American League batting race, and 90 RBI. Baerga was hitting in front of Albert Belle, the first player in history to surpass 50 home runs and 50 doubles in the same season, and saw a lot of strikes. He walked only 35 times all year, but struck out even less — just 31 times in 546 at bats.

A native of San Juan, Puerto Rico, Baerga returns to his homeland to play winter ball, but he's been back to San Diego, his first major league organization, only once — and that was to play in the 1992 All-Star game. Two years earlier, he was the "promising infielder" in a deal with the Padres that sent Baerga, fellow countryman Sandy Alomar Jr., and outfielder Chris James to Cleveland in exchange for Joe Carter.

In 1992-93, Baerga put together back-to-back 20-homer, 100-RBI, 200-hit seasons, while batting .312 in '92 and .321 in '93. He drove in 105 runs in '92 and followed with 114 RBI the following year. Oddly, his hitting really picked up after the Indians stopped shifting him from shortstop to third base. Between Baerga and first baseman Paul Sorrento, the right side of the infield was solid as Baerga became more comfortable with the position. It was the left side of the infield that was in flux until Omar Vizquel (arguably the best fielding shortstop in the league) arrived from Seattle in 1994 and Jim Thome, who tied with Baerga for ninth in the '95 batting race, started playing every day.

In between, there was some ugly baseball.

"Boy, there are times when we get frustrated because a guy doesn't pick up a ball or throws to the wrong base," fifth-year Tribe manager Mike Hargrove said during the 1992 campaign, 76-86 season. "Then you realize how young these guys really are and it helps you pull your horns back in, stop for a moment, then realize where this team is, and just how good this ballclub can become."

The Indians went 100-44 during the '95 regular season, a remarkable .694 winning percentage, swept the Boston Red Sox in the divisional playoff, then beat the tenacious Seattle Mariners in six games in the ALCS to earn a trip to the team's first World Series in 41 years. The Indians lost the first two games in Atlanta by one run while getting only eight hits.

Baerga, who was 0-for-8 the first two games and injured his ankle, had three hits and drove in three runs during the classic extra-inning affair in Game 3. Baerga even started the decisive rally, lining a double off the wall in center field to start the eleventh inning before leaving for pinch runner Alvaro Espinoza. Eddie Murray then singled home Espinoza with the winning run in the first World Series game ever played at Jacobs Field.

Jim Bagby

Jim Bagby Sr. won 127 games in a nine-year career and was the pitching star of the 1920 regular season, winning 31 games for the world champion Indians, many of them in clutch situations..

He won his 30th on September 28 to give the Indians a one-game lead over the White Sox and clinched the pennant on October 2, beating Detroit, 10-1, and helping himself by hitting a bases-loaded triple.

Bagby's professional baseball career began with Augusta of the South Atlantic League in 1911. In 1912 he appeared briefly with Garry Herrmann's Cincinnati Reds before returning to the Southern Association and getting what turned out to be, literally, a lucky break. While subbing in the outfield "Sarge" Bagby collided with a fellow outfielder and fractured his forearm. Oddly enough, the injury improved his curveball.

The Indians purchased his contract in 1916, and Bagby responded with seasons of 16-16, 23-13, 17-16, and 17-11. Then came the Indians' magic year of 1920. They won their first American League pennant, edging out the New York Yankees and the rapidly unraveling "Black Sox," as Bagby had the year of his life. Pitching 339 innings, he went 31-12. As icing on the cake the Indians defeated the Brooklyn Robins, 5-2, in the World Series, and Bagby did his part.

He was 1-1 in the Series with a 1.80 ERA, and his win in Game 5 was assisted by one of the most memorable moments in Series history — Bill Wambsganss's unassisted triple play. With runners on first and second and none out, Brooklyn pitcher Clarence Mitchell lined a ball to Wambsganss. He stepped on second base to double Pete Kilduff for the second out and then tagged Otto Miller, who was running toward second.

Bagby retired as a player in 1923. His son, Jim Bagby Jr., became a respectable American League pitcher in his own right; he is best known for halting Joe DiMaggio's 56-game hitting streak in 1941.

Buddy Bell

Although Buddy Bell posted a solid .279 lifetime batting average with 201 homers, the son of former big league outfielder Gus Bell is best remembered for his fielding.

He won Gold Glove Awards and made the *Sporting News* All-Star Fielding Team in every year from 1979 to 1984, and he also led American League third basemen in total chances in 1978, 1981, 1982, and 1983. He paced the AL in assists in 1979 and 1981 and in double plays and putouts in 1973. At Bell's peak, Brooks Robinson said of him: "Might be the top player in the league. He plays every day — just write his name in the lineup. A top clutch hitter."

Selected by the Cleveland Indians in the sixteenth round of the June 5, 1969, free-agent draft, Bell started his minor league career at second base but was switched to third while with Sumter of the Western Carolinas League. He came up to Cleveland in 1972 and had a solid if unspectacular freshman year. By the next season he was representing the Tribe at the All-Star Game, the first of five appearances in the Midsummer Classic.

Bell was traded to Texas in December 1978 in a swap for fellow third baseman Toby Harrah, later played for the Reds and Padres, and retired as a Ranger in 1989. After serving as an Indians coach in 1994, Bell took over as manager of the Detroit Tigers prior to the 1995 season.

Albert Belle

Albert Belle apparently is a conscientious practitioner of the old axiom, "If you haven't got anything nice to say, don't say anything at all." He lets his bat do the talking — most of the time.

The Cleveland Indians' left fielder became only the 12th player to hit 50 home runs in a season when he drilled a pitch 405 feet on the second to last day of the 1995 season. He also became the first player in history to have 50 homers and 50 doubles in the same year, and, it was in a shortened 144-game season at that.

What was even more shocking was that Belle, who has been as hostile with reporters as he has been with opposing pitchers, decided to hold a press conference. "It's been a Cinderella storybook season," he said after becoming the first member of this 50-50 club. "But hitting a home run in the ninth inning of the seventh game of the World Series would be the perfect ending."

Not...exactly.

Belle did lead all Indian regulars in hitting and home runs in the World Series, but that was only a .235 average and two home runs. Cleveland, which had a record of 100-44 in the regular season, lost the Series in six games to the Atlanta Braves while batting .179 as a team.

Belle's regular season numbers were undeniably great. He led the league in slugging percentage (.690), doubles (52), home runs (50), total bases (377), and tied with Boston's Mo Vaughn for the lead in runs batted in (126) and with Seattle's Edgar Martinez for most runs scored (121). He also hit .317 and had a .401 on base percentage. Yet when the MVP votes were tallied, Vaughn was the winner.

Back when Albert Belle was known as Joey Belle, he had a drinking problem. He went through treatment and was trying to start over again, using his real first name, Albert. On May 10, 1991, a fan named Jeff Pillar yelled to him from a seat down the left field line, "Hey Joey, keg party at my house after the game. C'mon over." Belle picked up a ball and fired it into Pillar's chest at a distance of less than 20 feet. Belle was suspended for seven days.

It turned out to be his breakthrough year, for lack of a better term. He hit 28 home runs and drove in 95 runs for the last place Tribe in '91. Belle upped those numbers to 34 homers and 112 RBI in 1992, finishing tied for fourth in both categories, as the Indians tied for fourth in the seven-team AL East. Belle took over the league lead in RBI in '93 with 129 and was fourth in homers with 38. The Indians, meanwhile, slipped to sixth place.

The American League split into three divisions in 1994 and the Indians were only one game out of first place in the Central Division by the middle of August. Belle was only two points off the league lead in batting (.357), was first in total bases (294), second in slugging percentage

(.714), and third in home runs (36) and on base percentage (.442).

Neither the Indians nor Belle got to find out how good they could be because of the strike. And one day in Chicago, Belle's bat was confiscated — later stolen out of the umpire's room, but replaced intact — and found to have cork in it. The embarrassed Belle was suspended for six games.

In 1995, baseball was back, and nothing could stop Belle or the Indians. The Cleveland slugger proved that he needed no cork to send the ball into the seats. "Albert doesn't hit singles anymore," Indians manager Mike Hargrove says. "Albert only hits bombs." After he hit his 50th homer, teammate Carlos Baerga said, "After he did it, he was actually smiling. Albert doesn't do that very much, you know."

Perhaps that was the old Albert Belle, not the new man who sent a poetic Christmas card to the fans, through, of all things, a newspaper. It read, in part:

I hope Santa will come and leave for you all,
Lots of baseball spirit to last through the fall,
Thanks to my friends and fans of such faith,
Your cheers inspired heights that alone I'd not make.

★ Lou Boudreau ★

In relative fielding average, as measured in *Total Baseball*, Lou Boudreau ranks as the best defensive shortstop of all time. But he was also a sensational hitter at a position which is almost exclusively manned by expert fielders; he ranks seventh among all shortstops in lifetime batting average and on-base percentage and is eighth in slugging percentage. A confident and creative manager, he is credited with inventing the "Williams Shift" (originally called the "Boudreau Shift") to thwart the slugging of Ted Williams.

Born to a father who was a semipro baseball player, Boudreau captained his high school basketball team to the Illinois state championship and was the captain of the University of Illinois basketball team as a junior. While still in school, Boudreau accepted money from Cleveland General Manager Cy Slapnicka with the promise that he would sign with the Indians upon graduation. Boudreau's jealous stepfather complained to the Big Ten, and Boudreau was ruled ineligible to play college sports.

He arrived in Cleveland in 1939 as a third baseman, but veteran Ken Keltner had a lock on the position, so Manager Ossie Vitt shifted the rookie to shortstop. While that move eventually made Vitt look like a genius, other members of the Indians had little respect for their manager.

The following year, veteran players, led by Hal Trosky, Ben Chapman, and Rollie Hemsley, organized other players in an open revolt against Vitt. Almost instantly; the Indians became the "Crybabies" and lost the 1940 pennant by one game. Not part of the controversy, Boudreau had a banner sophomore season with a .295 average, 101 RBI, 46 doubles, and 10 triples. He was also named to the All-Star team for the first of seven times.

In 1941, a new manager, Roger Peckinpaugh, didn't help the Indians. Boudreau's average tumbled to .257, but his 45 doubles led the league, and he hit 10 homers to go

with his eight triples. The team ended up fourth, Cy Slapnicka retired, and Peckinpaugh replaced him as general manager.

The confident young Boudreau decided to write to Indians's owner Alva Bradley about the manager's job. Player-managers were not uncommon at the time, and Boudreau felt his experience as captain of his college team would be a plus. In his autobiography he reveals that he had second thoughts about the letter and worried that his brashness might upset the management. One friend counseled, "Don't worry. Bradley'll probably just throw your letter in the wastebasket anyway."

When he was called in for an interview, Boudreau figured it was a courtesy call. He was grilled for two hours before the Indians' staff took a vote. The count went against him, 11-1, but his one supporter, George Martin, president of the Sherwin-Williams paint company, persuaded the others that Boudreau's youthful perspective, if surrounded by experienced coaches, could be just what the team needed.

One Cleveland sportswriter was appalled and wrote, "Great! The Indians get a Baby Snooks for a manager and ruin the best shortstop in baseball." But Boudreau quickly hired three experienced baseball men, Burt Shotton, Oscar Melillo, and George Susce, to help him run the team. When the 1942 season opened, Boudreau was, at age 24, the youngest person to start a major league season as a manager.

In that first year as Cleveland's skipper, Boudreau's Indians matched their record of the year before, finishing 75-79. In 1944 they tied for fifth, but Boudreau hit and fielded well. His .327 batting average in 1944 led the league, and he set a record for shortstops with a .978 fielding percentage and 134 double plays. He also cracked 45 doubles to lead the league.

In August 1945, the day before the Japanese surrendered to end World War II, a hard slide by Dolph Camilli broke the shortstop's ankle, and his season was over.

In June 1946, with his team in fifth place, Boudreau and all of Cleveland were shocked to learn that Bill Veeck had purchased the team. Veeck made it clear to Boudreau that while he had the greatest respect for him as a player, he doubted his ability to manage. The Indians were struggling, and no one was treating them any worse than Red Sox slugger Ted Williams, who'd just returned from the service.

On July 14 the Indians were in Boston for a doubleheader. In the first game Boudreau had four doubles and a homer, making him the only American Leaguer to ring up five extra-base hits in one game, a record, but Williams went four-for-five, and his three homers drove in eight runs. The Indians lost, 11-10, and Boudreau was boiling.

Knowing that the charts the Indians kept indicated that Williams hit to right 95 percent of the time, Boudreau stationed seven of his players to the right of second base, leaving only left fielder George Case on the left side, playing a very deep shortstop. (Boudreau probably didn't know that the same strategy had been tried against Williams in 1941 by White Sox Manager Jimmy Dykes.) The "Boudreau" shift had its desired effect only once during that game, as Boudreau threw out Williams on a grounder to the right side. Williams still walked twice and doubled, scoring two runs in Boston's 6-4 victory, but Boudreau had established himself as a creative thinker. Over the years his charts indicated that his team was 37 percent more successful against Williams while using the shift. "A psychological, if not always a tactical, victory," he said.

During the same season, Boudreau also moved Bob Lemon from the outfield to the pitcher's mound; Lemon went on to win 207 games during his career and was a seven-time All-Star. But in 1946 the Indians still finished 36 games out of first, and Boudreau was sure his job was in jeopardy.

Veeck was at work on other fronts. Before the 1947 season he traded Allie Reynolds to the Yankees to acquire second baseman Joe Gordon. Of Gordon, Boudreau would later say, "He made me as a fielder." Boudreau had a great year at bat and in the field, hitting .307, leading the league with 45 doubles once again, and also leading the league in fielding percentage. But the Yankees were invincible that year, blowing away Detroit by 12 games. The Indians finished fourth, 17 games back.

During the 1947 World Series word got out about Veeck's interest in swapping Boudreau for Vern Stephens of the St. Louis Browns and several other players. Cleveland fans were outraged. Veeck received more than 4,000 letters demanding that he keep Boudreau. When the *Cleveland News* ran a front-page ballot to elicit the fans' opinions, 100,000 responded, voting to retain Boudreau by a 10-1 margin; Veeck backed down and gave Boudreau a two-year contract.

Before the 1948 season, Boudreau said that he had never felt such pressure to win the pennant. He turned knuckleball-throwing lefthander Gene Bearden into a starter, and he responded with 20 wins. Bill Veeck signed Satchel Paige, and he rang up a 6-1 record. Larry Doby was made the regular center fielder; he hit .301, with 14 home runs. Lemon matched Bearden with 20 wins, while Feller won 19.

But the real star was the player-manager himself. Boudreau hit .355, had an on-base percentage of .453, and slugged .534. He hit 18 homers, drove in 106 runs, and scored 116. He also led American League shortstops in fielding percentage for the eighth time in nine years and was the club's emotional leader, too.

All of this happened despite a hard collision at second base in early August that left Boudreau with a shoulder contusion, a bruised right knee, a sore right thumb, and a sprained left ankle. Icing his wounds, he was on the bench, managing, during an August 8 doubleheader against the Yanks, with whom the Indians were tied for first place. Down, 6-1, in the seventh inning of the first game, the Indians put three runs on the board, then loaded the bases. Lefty relief pitcher Joe Page came in, and Boudreau put himself up as a pinch hitter. The 73,484 fans in Municipal Stadium cut loose. The manager singled to right, tying the score. The Indians won both games.

The season ended with the Indians and the Red Sox in a tie for first. With the toss of a coin, Boston won the right to host the first postseason playoff in AL history. Boudreau kept the identity of his starting pitcher a secret, then brought out Gene Bearden on only two days' rest. Bearden, who had been the Indians' best pitcher down the

stretch, pitched a five-hitter, and the Indians won, 8-3. Boudreau, to no one's surprise, hit two singles and two home runs. To cap his already incredible MVP season, he stroked four doubles, and Lemon won two games as the Indians defeated the Boston Braves in the World Series.

In 1949 and 1950 the Yankees reasserted themselves and the Indians fell to third, then fourth. In 1951, after nine years as player-manager, Boudreau left the team to join the Red Sox, ending his playing career there as a part-timer in 1952. He managed the Sox through 1954, then managed Kansas City from 1955 through 1957.

After that Boudreau became the Cubs' broadcaster. In 1960, in a novel swap, he was hired to manage the team, replacing Charlie Grimm, who took Boudreau's place in the radio booth. But after one season, Boudreau was back in the booth and remained a WGN broadcaster until 1989.

Today at age 79, Lou Boudreau is still a hero to Indians fans. As a token of their regard, the street next to Cleveland Stadium was renamed Boudreau Boulevard in his honor, and his uniform number (5) was retired.

George Burns

In a career marked by more ups and downs than a San Francisco cable car, Indians' first baseman George H. "Tioga George" Burns captured the 1926 American League Most Valuable Player Award and posted a lifetime .307 average.

Burns got his start in 1913 at Burlington in the Class D Central Association. He graduated to the Western League later that year, and in 1914 he made the jump to Detroit. In his rookie year with the Tigers, Burns hit .291, but it was his glove work that really set him apart. As a fielder, he was good news and bad news: George led the American League in putouts with 1,576 (a mark he would never again match in the majors); but he also committed 30 errors — the first of four times he would lead the American League in miscues.

When he had an off year in 1917, batting just .226, the Tigers shipped him to New York, who traded him to Connie Mack's A's for outfielder Ping Bodie. Since there was a National League outfielder named George Burns, too, when Burns settled in on Tioga Street in Philadelphia, he became known as "Tioga George."

In addition to getting a nickname, Burns recovered his batting eye with the A's; in a season shortened by World War I and a possible shutdown of professional baseball, Burns led the league in hits, with 178, and also had 70 RBI.

In May 1920 Mack sold the again slumping Burns to the Indians. He arrived just in time to help the team win its first pennant. Perhaps his most important contribution to that club was his influence on rookie shortstop Joe Sewell. As Sewell prepared for his first game, Burns reached into his locker and handed the rookie one of his own 44-ounce black bats. "Here, take this. It's a good bat. Make sure you take care of it," said the veteran. It served Sewell so well that he became the hardest batter to fan in the game's history.

In the 1920 World Series Burns hit .300, and with his sixth-inning double he drove in the only run in "Duster" Mails's 1-0 Game 6 victory. Burns hit .361 in part-time action for the Tribe in 1921, but he was traded in 1922 with outfielders Elmer Smith and Joe Harris to the Red Sox for first baseman Stuffy McInnis.

Boston was a rotten team, but Burns was given a chance to play full time again and responded to the challenge by hitting a career-high 12 homers in 1922. He also got revenge on Cleveland for trading him. Playing first base on September 14, 1923, he snagged the Indians' Frank Brower's line drive, tagged Rube Lutzke off first, and ran to second base to nail Riggs Stephenson for an unassisted triple play.

The Indians reacquired Burns in January 1924, and it was with Cleveland in 1926 that Burns set a major league record for doubles with 64, a mark that lasted until Earl Webb hit 67 in 1931. He also batted .358 and drove in 114 runs. In the MVP race Burns received 63 votes to runner-up Johnny Mostil's 33. It must be noted, that, under the rules in effect at the time, previous recipients were ineligible, so Babe Ruth, George Sisler, and Walter Johnson were not on the list. Still, it was a career year for Burns.

Just two years later, Cleveland released him. He made brief stops with the Yankees and A's, where he finished his major league career in 1929. From 1932 to 1934 he was a player-manager for Seattle in the Pacific Coast League and led in RBI with 140 in 1932. He also managed Portland from the bench in 1935.

Ray Chapman

On August 17, 1920, popular Cleveland shortstop Ray Chapman stepped to the plate at New York's Polo Grounds against the Yankees' Carl Mays. A pitch barely outside the strike zone struck Chapman on the left temple and he was carried from the field on a stretcher. He never regained consciousness, dying 12 hours later in a New York City hospital, one of only two major leaguers (the other was Mike Powers) to die as the result of an on-field accident.

Chapman's unfortunate death eventually had far-reaching implications for baseball. Some baseball scholars feel that this incident had perhaps as much influence in sparking the batting revolution of the 1920s as did Babe Ruth and the introduction of the "lively ball."

Prior to 1912, baseballs hit into the stands were thrown back into play, and it was not unusual to use a single ball for an entire game. Even after 1912 it was still rare to discard a scuffed or worn-out ball. This naturally gave an advantage to pitchers. Owners didn't allow fans to keep balls hit into the stands until April 29, 1916, when Cubs owner "Lucky Charlie" Weeghman set precedent by letting fans have the balls as souvenirs.

The spitball, shineball, and all other dubious pitches had been outlawed on February 9, 1920, six months before Chapman's death. After that time balls hit into the stands stayed there, and umpires tossed out nicked or scuffed balls with greater frequency. In 1919 the National League went through 22,095 baseballs; in 1924 that figure had grown to 54,030. Batters now got to swing at baseballs that were more visible and less apt to "sail," and batting averages rose accordingly.

One change that surprisingly did not occur for another three decades was the introduction of batting helmets.

The *Spalding Guide* advocated their use immediately after the Chapman tragedy, saying, "A head helmet for the batter is not to be despised. There is nothing 'sissy' about it." Yet nothing was done until the Pittsburgh Pirates introduced protective headgear in the early 1950s.

Chapman was born on January 15, 1891, on his father's small farm in Kentucky; the family moved to Herrin, Illinois, when Ray was 14. He began working in the mines soon thereafter and held a United Mine Workers card for the rest of his life.

He also played semipro ball, and in the spring of 1910 "Sinister Dick" Kinsella, a famous scout and minor league club owner, signed him for his Springfield franchise in the III League. Chapman played little but ingratiated himself wherever he went. His manager, Dick Smith, told him, "You know, kid, even if you never played a game, you'd earn your pay just by sitting on the bench and being such a cheerleader."

In 1911 Kinsella sold Chapman to Davenport, Iowa, and the shortstop responded with a .293 average and 75 stolen bases. Spotted by Bill Armour, who'd discovered Ty Cobb, Chapman was sold to Armour's Toledo Mud Hens and became a star. "Chappie" hit .310 with 49 stolen bases and 101 runs scored and was called up to Cleveland. He became a solid player with the Indians, and his 52 stolen bases in 1917 remained a club record until broken by Miguel Dilone's 61 in 1980.

The 1920 Indians, who featured seven .300 hitters, were engaged in a three-way pennant race with the Yankees and the defending league champion White Sox. When Chapman came to the plate on August 17 he faced Carl Mays, who had a reputation as a headhunter who scuffed the ball. (In 1917 Mays led the American League with 14 hit batsmen.)

As was his custom, Chapman was crouching toward the plate. Catcher Herold "Muddy" Ruel had trouble seeing the ball, which was headed straight at the batting shortstop. One witness said Chapman seemed "hypnotized." There was an "explosive sound" and the ball came bounding back at Mays, who fielded it and flipped it to first baseman Wally Pipp for what he thought was the inning's first out. Pipp caught the ball and started to toss it around the infield, when suddenly he became aware that something was wrong with Chapman.

"We need a doctor," home plate umpire Tom Connolly shouted. "Is there a doctor in the house?" The Indians gathered around Chapman, who at first could not speak, as the Yankees team physician applied ice to his injury. After a few minutes Chapman was able to stand, to the immense relief of the crowd. With the assistance of two teammates Chapman began walking off the field toward the center field clubhouse. At second base he crumpled to the ground; he died 12 hours later at St. Lawrence Hospital.

Mays pitched the rest of that game, losing to Stanley Coveleski, 4-0. The public reaction was one of sadness mixed with shock and anger. An incensed Browns club voted unanimously that Mays "must be removed from baseball," and a widespread player boycott of the pitcher was rumored.

In response Mays said, "It is terrible to consider the case at all, but when any man, however ignorant, illiterate or malicious, even hints that a white man in his normal mind would stand out there on the field of sport and try to kill another, the man making the assertion is inhuman, uncivilized, bestial."

Other fingers were pointed at American League umpires, citing their failure to toss out scuffed balls. Umpires Billy Evans and Bill Dinneen issued a statement that blamed Mays and that read in part: "No pitcher in the American League resorted more to trickery than Carl Mays in attempting to rough a ball to get a break on it."

Evans and Dinneen also addressed the issue of throwing balls out of a game, and placed the blame squarely on team owners. "A short time ago," they alleged, "the club owners complained to President Ban Johnson that too many balls were being thrown out. President Johnson sent out a bulletin telling the umpires to keep the balls in the games as much as possible except those which were dangerous."

Ray Chapman was buried at Cleveland's St. John's Cathedral on August 20, 1920. His place at shortstop was taken by a rookie named Joe Sewell who would wind up in the Hall of Fame. The 1920 Indians went on to win the pennant after the eight "Black Sox" were suspended, and they subsequently defeated the Brooklyn Robins in the World Series.

Rocky Colavito

When Cleveland General Manager Frank "Trader" Lane sent Indians idol and American League home run champ Rocky Colavito to the Detroit Tigers for AL batting champion Harvey Kuenn, he had no idea what a firestorm of protest he would unleash.

"They wanted to lynch me," said Lane. "I went back to my hotel that day and there was this dummy hanging in effigy from a lamp post. 'Frank Lane,' it said on the dummy. They must have thought, 'here's our handsome Rocky gone and all we've got is an ugly slob of a general manager.'"

Hordes of fans, many of them young girls who adored the personable young slugger, picketed Cleveland Stadium, carrying signs with such slogans as, "Don't Knock the Rock," "We love you, Rocky," and "You'll always be ours, Rocky." Rarely has a trade generated such genuine outrage, and Lane added fuel to the fire when he asked, "What's all the fuss about? All I did was trade hamburger for steak."

It's difficult to imagine now how popular Colavito was in Cleveland. Aside from his slugging abilities and good looks, Indians fans had a personal love affair with this Bronx import and overlooked his lack of speed and ungainliness. (He was literally flat-footed.) But Colavito never stopped hustling, and his right arm was like a rocket launcher, the strongest of any AL outfielder. In 1958 he led the league's outfielders by participating in six double plays, and at one point he put together a streak of 241 errorless games.

The clean-living right fielder always had time for his public. Hundreds of fans would gather at the stadium gates after each game for his autograph, and Colavito would oblige them all. "I'll tell you what," he would shout to each day's crowd, "if you'll do me a favor and line up, I'll sign for all of you." The fans knew Colavito would keep his word, even if it took hours.

Colavito grew up in the Crotona Park section of the Bronx and had himself been a kid waiting outside the ballpark with pencil in hand. "I made up my mind that if I ever became a big league player I'd never pass the kids by," he recalled.

Colavito had resolved to be a big leaguer from the beginning. By the age of 9 he was playing on local semipro clubs, and at age 16 he dropped out of Theodore Roosevelt High School to concentrate on baseball. Because of a rule stipulating that a player could not be signed before his high school class graduated, it took a special appeal to the Commissioner's Office plus a year's waiting period before Colavito was eligible to sign.

He worshipped the Yankees' Joe DiMaggio and would have preferred to go with New York; however, the Yankees had little interest in him and offered Colavito a mere $500 bonus — but only if he survived spring training. The Philadelphia Athletics were more interested, offering a first-year salary of $5,000 plus a $6,000 bonus. But at the last minute they backed off, crying poverty. In fact, they had just mortgaged Shibe Park to meet expenses.

That left the Indians. They offered Colavito $1,000 on signing, $1,000 more if he lasted 30 days, and an additional $1,000 if he survived 30 days after that. His base salary was to be $150 per month. There was some haggling over whether the $3,000 should be paid all at once, but then Rocco Domenico Colavito Sr. put his foot down, telling his son in Italian, "Sign before you don't get nothing." The next morning the Colavitos received a call from the Phillies, who were interested in topping the Indians' bid, but it was too late.

When Colavito reported to the Indians' spring training camp in 1950 he reminded everyone of DiMaggio, and he reinforced the comparison by altering the "255" on his uniform to read just "5" — DiMaggio's number. As he moved up through the Indians' system, however, Colavito's DiMaggio fixation became a hindrance. Manager after manager warned the outfielder to be himself and not try to be just a poor copy of someone else.

In 1956 Colavito thought he had made the club, but Cleveland Manager Al Lopez instead shipped him to San Diego in the Pacific Coast League. Colavito hit .368 and amused himself with showcasing his strong arm by standing at home plate and firing the ball over the center field fence. His longest throw was 436 feet — just shy of the all-time mark of 443 set by Chattanooga's Don Grate in 1953.

Five weeks and several phone calls to Indians General Manager Hank Greenberg later, Colavito was back in Cleveland. He made no real progress until 1958 when he hit 41 homers, losing the AL title by just one home run to Mickey Mantle. On June 10, 1959, Colavito hit four homers in one game, and did it in consecutive at bats, a feat accomplished only three times before in history.

After being traded to Detroit in April 1960 Colavito had a poor season, but in 1961 he came through with 45 homers and 140 RBI. Frank Lane's remarks about Colavito being hamburger seemed a poor choice of words in retrospect. "I like hamburger," chortled Tiger General Manager Bill DeWitt.

But Detroit did not take to Colavito as Cleveland had.

In fact, many Tiger fans resented his replacing the solid, if less spectacular, Harvey Kuenn. Once Colavito got so angry at the razzing he was receiving from the right field stands that he threw a ball over the Briggs Stadium roof.

After Colavito's banner 1961 season he held out for more money than the Tigers were paying established local hero Al Kaline (Kaline was getting $52,000; Colavito wanted $57,500). Again publicity was negative. Colavito went to the A's in November 1963, then returned to the Indians in January 1965, where he led the AL in RBIs that year. He ended his career with the Yankees, the team he had once longed to play for.

In 1976 Colavito was voted the most memorable personality in Cleveland Indians history, and in 1983 he became a hitting coach for the Kansas City Royals.

★ Stan Coveleski ★

Most players start at the bottom and work their way up. Stan Coveleski went one step further; he started from the bottom of a mine.

A Pennsylvania coal miner at age 12, Coveleski escaped from the mines to become a Hall of Fame pitcher with legendary control. Starting from 32 to 45 games for 11 years, he never walked as many as 100 men a season. In the 1920 World Series, he reached his high mark, pitching three brilliant complete-game victories for the Indians.

Coveleski, whose real name was Stanislaus Kowaleski, came from a family of ballplaying brothers. Frank played for the outlaw Union League before rheumatism ended his career. John, a minor league third baseman and outfielder, tried out for the A's but lost out to Eddie Collins. Harry won 20 games in the majors three consecutive seasons, and, in 1908, he helped derail John McGraw's pennant hopes by defeating the Giants three times the last week of the season.

Harry and Stanley Coveleski never pitched against each other in the majors — and only once in their professional careers, in an exhibition game. "Harry refused to pitch against me in the majors," Stan once said. He told the Detroit manager never to use him when I was pitching. He explained to me, 'Win or lose, it would take something away from us. If I lose, they'll say I was laying down on purpose so you could win. If I win, they'll say you were laying down.' "

As a youngster, Stanley Coveleski didn't have much time to play baseball. "There was nothing strange in those days," Coveleski said, "about a 12-year-old Polish kid in the mines for 72 hours a week at a nickel an hour. What was strange was that I ever got out."

His only form of recreation was throwing stones at tin cans. He would tie cans to tree limbs and just fire away until dark. After a few years of this he "could hit one of those things blindfolded," he said.

The local semipro team, the Shamokin club of the independent Atlantic League, heard about his talent and offered him a tryout. Before long he was signed to a contract with Lancaster of the Class B Tri-State League. In September 1912 Coveleski was given a trial by the Philadelphia Athletics; he pitched a three-hitter in his major league debut, but that wasn't good enough to crack Connie Mack's ace staff. Back he went to the minors, this time to Spokane, where he lost a league-leading 20 games in 1913, and to Portland.

At Portland in 1915 Coveleski wondered if he would "ever make it to the big leagues." But he picked up a new weapon — the spitball. He saw another pitcher working on the pitch and thought he too would experiment with it. "I started working on the spitter," he told Lawrence Ritter, "and before long I had that thing down pat. Had never thrown it before in my life. But before that season was over it was my main pitch . . . I got so I had as good control over the spitter as I did over my other pitches. I could make it break any of three ways: down, out, or down and out."

The pitch got Coveleski back to the majors; Cleveland bought his contract after the 1915 season, and he immediately became a consistent winner for Cleveland, going 15-12 his rookie year. From 1918 to 1921 he won at least 22 games a year. In 1920 he walked an average of less than two batters per nine innings. In one extraordinary performance, he went the first seven innings without throwing a single ball.

That 1920 season was Coveleski's best. He went 24-14 for the world champion Indians and led the American League with 133 strikeouts. In the World Series against Brooklyn, he pitched five-hit complete game victories in Games 1, 4, and 7. The last game was a 3-0 shutout, and he finished the Series with a remarkable 0.67 ERA. "I figured it was my job and I done it and that's all," said the man often referred to as the "Silent Pole."

In 1921 Coveleski won 23 games, in 1922 he was 17-14, and in 1923 he led the AL with a 2.76 ERA. The Indians traded Coveleski to the Washington Senators in December 1924, and he pitched in the 1925 World Series, losing two games to Pittsburgh. He was unconditionally released by Washington on June 12, 1927, but signed on with the Yankees that December.

Coveleski appeared in only 12 games for the Yankees, recording a 5-1 record. He retired at the end of the season with 215 career victories and a lifetime ERA of 2.88. He settled in South Bend, Indiana, where his gas station became a gathering point for baseball-loving youngsters and earned him the nickname "the Pied Piper of South Bend." He was elected to the Hall of Fame in 1969 and received another honor when Stanley Coveleski Regional Stadium, home to a Midwest League franchise in South Bend, was dedicated in 1987.

Larry Doby

Larry Doby broke the color barrier in the American League on July 5, 1947 — in the same season that Jackie Robinson became the first black player in the National League. A seven-time AL All-Star, Doby averaged 27 homers and 77 RBIs in 9½ seasons with the Indians and led the league twice in homers and once in RBIs.

On the road, Doby was often denied entrance to hotels and restaurants that catered to whites only; on the field, opposing players were sometimes downright hostile. "Once, as I slid into second base, the guy playing shortstop spit on me. But I walked away from it," Doby related. "I knew the racial remarks were from people who were prejudiced or who wanted to disturb me. I wasn't going to let them upset my play, so I didn't think too much about them."

Born in South Carolina and raised in Paterson, New Jersey, Doby was an excellent all-around athlete. As a standout running back he led his East Side High team to the state football championship. The team was then invited to play a bowl game in Florida, but only on the condition that Doby not participate. The team voted not to go at all.

From 1942 through part of the 1947 Doby played second base for the Negro League Newark Eagles until Cleveland Indians owner Bill Veeck bought his contract for $15,000 in July 1947 and made him a major league outfielder.

The Indians had planned to introduce him in Cleveland after the All-Star break; instead, the story leaked, and, on less than a week's notice, Doby became the American League's first black player with no minor league training or emotional preparation. Limited to pinch hitting, Doby spent the off-season playing with the American Basketball League's Paterson Crescents and reading *How to Play the Outfield* by Tommy Henrich.

When spring training began in 1948, Doby was one of eight Indian outfielders; however, Hank Greenberg helped him with his hitting, Tris Speaker worked on his fielding, and Doby played right field on Opening Day. He hit .396 in the last 20 games of the season to help the Indians win the pennant and homered in the World Series against Johnny Sain to give the champion Indians a 2-1 win in Game 4.

In 1949 he, Robinson, Roy Campanella, and Don Newcombe became the first blacks to play in an All-Star Game. In 1950 he played all 14 innings of the Midsummer Classic, got two hits, and stayed in center field when Dom DiMaggio took over in left and Joe DiMaggio took over in right. He ended the season at .326 with 25 homers and was named to the *Sporting News* All-Star team; two years later, he led the American League in homers (32) and runs scored (104) and the majors in slugging percentage (.541).

In July 1954 Doby made a catch that many still remember as one of the greatest in Indian's history. He was playing shallow when Washington's Tommy Umphlett connected; Doby raced back, placed his bare hand on the top of the fence at Municipal Stadium to get added height, caught the ball, and held it after hitting the bullpen bench. Dizzy Dean called it "the greatest catch I ever saw," and Indian pitcher Art Houtteman told Doby, "As long as I live, I'll never forget the greatness of that play."

That year was the high point of Doby's career in every way. He led the league in home runs (32) and RBIs (126) and supplied most of the power for an Indian team that won 111 games. He made only two errors in 427 chances, led the league's outfielders in double plays, and finished second to Yogi Berra in MVP voting.

After Doby set a record, later broken, by going 166 games without an error in 1955, he was traded for White Sox Jim Busby and Chico Carrasquel. He returned to Cleveland in 1958 and played briefly with the Tigers and White Sox before retiring in 1959.

Doby later played for the Chunichi Dragons in Japan, taught hitting for the Expos and Indians. Many thought he would be named Major League Baseball's first black manager, but that distinction went to Frank Robinson instead. Doby did manage the Chicago White Sox briefly when he replaced Bob Lemon in the middle of the 1978 season, but Don Kessinger took over the following season.

Doby later became director of community affairs for the New Jersey Nets and has spent the last several years working in the Office of the Commissioner of Major League Baseball.

Luke Easter

Lucious "Luke" Easter was known for his tape-measure home runs with the Indians and wherever he played, whether it was the Negro Leagues, the majors, or during his lengthy minor league career. While others were impressed, he was nonchalant and once commented, "I just hit 'em and forget 'em."

Easter played for the Negro League Cincinnati Crescents in 1946 and the Homestead Grays in 1947-48. (It is estimated that in 1947 he hit 75 homers.) He also performed in the Puerto Rican Winter League in 1948, and, following the 1948 season, the Grays sold Easter's contract to Cleveland for $5,000.

In a brief career with Cleveland, he hit a career-high 31 homers in 1952 and twice drove in more than 100 runs in a season. On June 23, 1950, Easter hit a ball 477 feet into the upper deck at Municipal Stadium.

Bad knees cut short his major league stay, but starting with Indianapolis in 1952 Easter began the third phase of his career — minor league legend. In 1956, Buffalo of the International League acquired Easter for $7,500 from Charleston, and he soon became noted in upstate New York for his enormous shots.

In 1956 he led the International League in homers (35) and RBIs (106). On August 6 Easter hit a 550-foot blast that not only went over the street next to Buffalo's Offermann Stadium — it landed in the next street. In 1957 he led the International League in homers (40), total bases (300) and RBIs (128).

Released by Buffalo in May 1959, he spent six more seasons with Rochester in the International League as a player and a coach where he enjoyed a renewed popularity akin to what he had enjoyed in Buffalo.

Easter's life ended tragically. After leaving baseball he found employment at TRW, Inc. in Cleveland, where he became a shop steward. He was in the habit of taking his fellow workers' checks each payday and cashing them at a local bank. On March 29, 1979, as Easter was leaving the bank he was accosted by two men who demanded the cash. He refused to give it up and was killed by a shotgun blast.

★ Bob Feller ★

There is no greater Indian legend than Bob Feller.

In the gathering gloom of one late afternoon game, Feller took the mound against Vernon "Lefty" Gomez. Gomez walked up to the plate and lit a match. "D'yuh think that match'll help you see Feller's fastball?" sneered the umpire. "No," said Lefty. "I just want to make sure he can see me!"

Bob Feller's fastball was the stuff of legends, and stories about its speed have become part of the folklore of the game. Some are recycled tales told about earlier fireballers, such as the time a batter was called out on strikes, turned to the umpire, and said, "That last one sounded high."

While some of these yarns may be apocryphal, Feller's fastball was not. Observers said Feller was faster than Walter Johnson, Lefty Grove, or anyone who ever lived. After World War II the Army studied his fastball with a device that supposedly measured the speed of a moving projectile. The result, 98.6 mph, disappointed a few people. But the experiment was conducted just after Feller had spent nearly four years in the Navy, and he probably wasn't throwing as fast as he had been before the war.

Since then, several pitchers' fastballs, notably Nolan Ryan's, have been calibrated as faster, and the fastballs of old-timers such as Johnson and Grove were never measured with modern devices. But comparisons between one era and the next are pointless. Suffice it to say that Bob Feller was probably the fastest pitcher of his time.

He was certainly the most frightening. In his windup he pivoted away, turned his back on the batter, then exploded toward the plate. If the batter was lucky the ball zipped through the strike zone in a third of a second. But Feller could be wild, "pleasingly wild," as Hall of Famer Wilbert Robinson once said. Feller could never guarantee that his next pitch wouldn't drill the batter right in the side of his head. Batters went up against Feller with their hearts already safely back on the bench.

Robert William Andrew Feller was born in 1918 and grew up on a farm just west of Des Moines, Iowa, in a small town named Van Meter. Farm chores made him strong, and his father made him a pitcher. According to Feller, his father "made a home plate in the yard, and I'd throw to him over it. He even built me a pitching rubber. When I was 12, we built a ballfield on our farm. We fenced the pasture, put up the chicken wire and the benches and even a little grandstand behind first base. We formed our own team and played other teams from around the community on weekends."

Feller pitched five no-hitters at Van Meter High School. The Cleveland Indians took note and signed him to a contract with Fargo-Moorehead of the Northern League. But major league teams were forbidden to sign free agents still in high school, a condition the Indians had violated. Feller was advised to retire voluntarily in 1936 while his contract was transferred to New Orleans of the Southern Association.

When these contract maneuvers came to light, Commissioner Kenesaw Mountain Landis declared Feller a free agent. Feller and his parents then insisted that the young prospect preferred Cleveland, and he was allowed to sign again with the Indians, who paid a $7,500 fine.

In July 1936 the 17-year-old Feller made his debut for Cleveland in an exhibition game, striking out eight St. Louis Cardinals in three innings. From that moment on, he was major league news. After several relief appearances, he made his first start in mid-August and struck out 15 St. Louis Browns in a 4-1 victory. In September he struck out 17 Philadelphia Athletics, tying the major

league mark and setting a new American League record. In 14 appearances in 1936, Feller completed five of eight starts, won five of eight, and struck out 76 batters in 62 innings. Then he went home to finish high school.

The right-handed Feller stood 6 feet tall and weighed 185 pounds. His windup, featuring a high leg kick and a unique pivot, launched the ball with tremendous speed. Comparisons with Johnson and other legendary fireballers began after his first appearance on a big league mound. Yet many felt that his most devastating pitch was his big, fast-breaking curve. After two or three Feller fastballs, few batters could adjust to the bender.

In 1937, still only 18 years old, "Rapid Robert" went 9-7 for the Indians, with 150 strikeouts in 149 innings. The next year he was named to the AL All-Star team for the first of eight times. He won 17 games and led the AL with 240 strikeouts. On the last day of the season he struck out 18 Detroit Tigers, a major league record at the time. But he was also wild, walking 208 batters in 278 innings.

Starting in 1939 he won a total of 76 games during the next three seasons. He led the league in victories, innings pitched, and strikeouts all three years, in complete games and shutouts twice, and in earned run average once. Yet despite finishing 24-9 in 1939 with 246 strikeouts, he couldn't lift Cleveland out of third place.

On Opening Day, April 16, 1940, Feller hurled a 1-0 no-hitter against the Chicago White Sox, the first Opening Day no-hitter in baseball history. The Indians were steadily improving and now boasted the crackerjack double play combination of Lou Boudreau and Ray Mack and a couple of sluggers in Hal Trosky and Jeff Heath.

The Yankees limped out of the blocks, and by midsummer the pennant race was between Cleveland and Detroit despite the distraction of the "crybabies." (See Lou Boudreau.) On the season's final weekend Detroit played a three-game series in Cleveland. In need of a sweep, the Indians started 27-game winner Feller in the first game. The Tigers' staff was tired. Floyd Giebell was their sacrificial lamb and made only his second appearance of the season. Feller pitched brilliantly and made only one mistake, giving up a home run to Rudy York with a runner on base. But Giebell pitched a shutout to clinch the pennant for Detroit. Ironically, he never won another major league game.

In 1941 Feller went 25-13 with 260 strikeouts but missed more than a month of the season. The day after Japan bombed Pearl Harbor he enlisted in the Navy. While some baseball stars spent the war playing exhibition baseball games to build the troops' morale, Feller served as a chief specialist on the battleship *Alabama*, winning five campaign ribbons and eight battle stars.

Feller, now 27 years old, was mustered out of the service late in 1945. He was 5-3 in nine late season appearances, but no one really knew how much he might have lost because of the layoff. As it turned out, Feller was better than ever. He learned to throw a slider, which, when added to his fastball and curve, made him even harder to hit than before. On April 30, 1946, he fired his second no-hitter, beating the Yankees, 1-0. He went on to win 26 games for the sixth-place Indians. Ten of his victories were shutouts.

Even more impressive was Feller's torrid strikeout

pace. The Wheaties cereal company offered him $5,000 if he broke the existing strikeout record. Feller learned that the record was 343, set by Rube Waddell. Feller finished the season with 348 strikeouts, then was told that Waddell's record was actually 349. Had he known the correct figure, he would doubtless have pitched another inning or two to pick up a few more whiffs.

In 1947 he led the league with 20 wins, 299 innings pitched, five shutouts, and 196 strikeouts. His total income, including his salary, endorsements, and a postseason barnstorming tour with other major leaguers against black all-stars, was estimated at $150,000, an enormous figure at the time.

The Indians made a strong run at the pennant. Feller, who got off to a slow start, got hot during the second half of the season and finished 19-15, nailing down his seventh strikeout crown. Meanwhile, Bob Lemon and Gene Bearden each won 20 games for the Tribe. They beat the Red Sox, 8-3, in a one-game playoff, and Cleveland won its first pennant since 1920.

Feller opposed the Braves' Johnny Sain in Boston to open the World Series. Coming into the bottom of the eighth, Feller had just allowed a single to Marv Rickert. He walked Bill Salkeld, and Phil Masi came in as a pinch runner and was sacrificed to second. Then, in the most controversial play of the Series, Feller seemed to pick Boston's Phil Masi off second base. Later, photos clearly showed that Masi was out, but umpire Bill Stewart called him safe. Tommy Holmes followed with only the second Boston hit of the day and drove the run home. Feller lost a two-hitter, 1-0. He started Game 5 but was battered for eight hits and seven runs. Ironically, those were the only games Cleveland lost in the Series.

Although he no longer possessed a 98 mph fastball, Feller won 31 games in the next two seasons. In 1951 he compiled a 22-8 record, again led the league in wins, and, for the first time, also led in winning percentage. On July 1, against Detroit, he threw his third no-hitter, winning 2-1. At the time he was one of only three pitchers to throw three no-hitters. Cy Young and Larry Corcoran were the others. (Sandy Koufax, with four, and Nolan Ryan, with seven, have since surpassed Feller.)

In the mid-1950s Feller became a spot starter for Cleveland. He was 13-3 for the pennant-winning 1954 team but didn't pitch as the Tribe lost the World Series to the New York Giants in four straight. He retired after the 1956 season, working in the insurance business and as an unofficial baseball ambassador who never feared to speak his mind.

In 18 seasons Feller compiled a 266-162 record, with 44 shutouts. In addition to his three no-hitters, he threw 12 one-hitters. His career earned run average was 3.25. In 3,827 innings he struck out 2,581 batters and walked a record 1,764, since broken. He undoubtedly would have won 300 games had he not lost nearly four seasons to military service. Feller, who estimated that he lost some 100 wins and 1,200 strikeouts during the hiatus, never regretted his time in the service. "I did what I thought was right," he said.

Feller was named to the Hall of Fame in 1962, his first year of eligibility.

Wes Ferrell

Unlike his brother, Rick, Wes Ferrell never was elected to the Hall of Fame. But in his day, Wes was the bigger star. He won 20 or more games in each of his first four big league seasons, had 52 hits in 1935 to tie George Uhle's season record for pitchers, and hit more home runs than any pitcher in major league history.

Ferrell was one of seven brothers, most of them athletes. Rick was a major league catcher from 1929 through 1947. George and Marvin played minor league ball. (George, an outfielder, had a career batting average of .321 during 20 seasons.) Ewell was headed for professional basketball when he was fatally shot in the 1930s. In 1921 the family virtually fielded its own team and won the baseball championship of Guilford County, North Carolina.

After graduating from high school Wes attended Oak Ridge Military Academy and played semipro ball in Massachusetts's Blackstone Valley League. In 1927 his play caught the attention of Cleveland scout Bill Rapp, who wrote to Ferrell, asking if he would be interested in a contract. Ferrell, who at the time was earning $300 per month plus room and board, wrote back stating his terms: $800 per month plus a $3,000 bonus. "Why not lay it on real fancy," he thought. He was invited to Cleveland to meet personally with club President Ernest S. Barnard.

Ferrell was already feeling a little nervous when Barnard made his pitch. "Son," Barnard said calmly, pointing to the field, "look down there. See that center fielder? He's a regular on our ballclub, and he's not making $800 a month. Now I don't know if you're good enough to make this club or that we even want you. But I'll tell you what I'll do. I'll give you $3,000 to sign a contract and $500 a month, for two years. And if after that time we retain you, I'll give you an additional $3,000 bonus." It didn't take Ferrell long to say, "I'll take it."

Ferrell started the 1928 season with Cleveland, but except for two appearances, all he did was pitch batting practice. One day, he'd had enough and didn't take his accustomed pregame position. Someone shouted at him to get to the mound. "The hell with you," the brash youngster responded. "I didn't come up here for that." His outburst got him quickly demoted to Terre Haute in the 3-I League. Ferrell made the most of it by going 20-8 with a 2.74 ERA.

By 1929 Ferrell was back in Cleveland, where he started his string of four straight 20-game seasons. Soon he was back at Barnard's door, and this time he got what he wanted — a new $10,000 per year contract. Ferrell's pitching improved along with his salary, and in 1931 he won 13 straight games.

But in 1934, with the Cleveland club short of cash, Ferrell was sent to the Red Sox, along with outfielder Dick Porter, for pitcher Bob Weiland, outfielder Bob Seeds, and $25,000. There he was united with his brother, Rick, whom Boston had acquired in 1933 from the St. Louis Browns.

The two brothers had previously shared one memorable moment as opponents. On April 29, 1931, at League Park, Wes had hurled a no-hitter against Rick's Browns, striking out eight and walking three. The Brown who had come closest to getting a hit was Rick, who rapped a ball to shortstop Bill Hunneford that was ruled an error.

As batterymates, the Ferrell brothers worked well together. Although they did not always see eye-to-eye on pitch selection, Wes gave Rick high marks as a receiver. "You never saw him lunge for the ball," said Wes. "He never took a strike away from you."

Perhaps the greatest difference between the two brothers was their temperament. Rick was low-key and quiet; Wes was volatile and combative. In 1932 Cleveland Manager Roger Peckinpaugh fined Wes for refusing to leave the mound. In 1936 Red Sox player-manager Joe Cronin fined him for leaving a game without permission.

Ferrell won a league-high 25 games for the Red Sox in 1935, leading the AL in games started, complete games, and innings pitched. He was a 20-game winner the next season, tossing an AL-high 28 complete games.

But arm trouble eventually took its toll, and Ferrell, a power pitcher early in his career, had to become a junkballer. He continued to be a dangerous hitter, though. His lifetime batting average was .280, and he holds records for most home runs by a pitcher in a season, with 9, and in a career, with 37. He hit one more as a pinch hitter and slammed two homers in a game five times. His 38 homers are 10 more than brother Rick hit in his career.

In June 1937 both Rick and Wes were traded to Washington in a deal involving colorful pitcher Bobo Newsom. In August 1938 Wes was given his unconditional release, despite a 13-8 record. During the next three seasons he had brief stints with the Yankees, Dodgers, and Braves before leaving the majors.

He wasn't ready to leave baseball, however. In 1941 Ferrell managed Leaksville-Spray-Draper to a pennant in the Class D Bi-State League, played the outfield, and hit .332. The following season he managed Lynchburgh of the Class C Virginia League while playing second base and the outfield, and he led the league in batting with a .361 mark.

Six years later, while piloting Marion of the Class D Western Carolinas League, he batted a league-best .425 in 104 games. For good measure, Ferrell also hit 25 homers and drove in 119 runs. He was 40 years old at the time.

★ Elmer Flick ★

Fans today may find it amusing, but when Detroit Manager Hughie Jennings offered to swap Ty Cobb to Cleveland for Elmer Flick after the 1907 season, the deal made sense.

Although Cobb, at 22, was nine years younger than Flick and fresh from a batting championship for the pennant-winning Tigers, he was an erratic outfielder, despised by his teammates, and a negative factor in the clubhouse. Moreover, with his no-holds-barred playing style, he seemed destined for a short career.

Flick was everything that Cobb wasn't. He was modest, a team player, and well liked by both teammates and opponents. His fielding was smooth and sure. Cobb was the reigning basestealing champ with 49 thefts, but Flick had won the title twice before. And his 41 steals in 1907 ranked second only to Cobb's 49. Although Flick's 1907 batting average of .302 was well below Cobb's .350, the

Cleveland outfielder was a consistent .300 hitter. After much deliberation Cleveland owner Charles Somers decided Cobb was too much of a risk. Flick stayed in Cleveland.

Cobb went on to win batting and basestealing titles for another two decades, but in the spring of 1908 Flick developed a mysterious stomach ailment that caused him to retire soon after. The trade that never was helped Detroit win two more pennants and kept Cleveland out of the winner's circle until 1920.

Elmer Flick was born in Bedford, Ohio, in 1876 and became a semipro ballplayer literally by accident. A large crowd turned out one day at the Bedford railroad station to see the local team off to a game. At the last minute team members discovered that one of the players was missing. In desperation the team captain asked 15-year-old Flick to join the team. The barefoot lad happily climbed aboard.

After several years of semipro ball the young Flick joined Youngstown of the Inter-State League as an outfielder in 1896 and hit an amazing .438 in 31 games. The following year, in a full season with Dayton of the International League, he hit .386 and attracted the attention of the Phillies.

Unfortunately Philadelphia, with an All-Star outfield of Ed Delahanty, Duff Cooley, and Sam Thompson, had little room for Flick. And it looked as though Flick, if nothing else, would provide comic relief when he showed up at spring training carrying a canvas suitcase and a thick-handled bat he'd turned on a lathe himself. The Phillies veterans snickered at the hayseed until he started knocking the ball all over the park with his odd bat.

At 5-foot-9 and 168 pounds, Flick was built for speed rather than power. Pitchers tried to jam him inside, but his thick bat handle allowed him to get good wood on inside pitches and drive them over the infield. One reporter described the new kid as "the fastest and most promising youngster the Phillies ever had."

Promising as he was, Flick rode the bench as the season opened. But when Thompson developed back trouble, Flick entered the lineup and began hitting. He finished the season with a .302 average, 81 RBIs, and 84 runs scored.

Flick kept improving. In 1899 he upped his average to .342 with 98 RBIs and the same number of runs scored. One day in Pittsburgh he made a leaping, one-handed grab that the local press called the most spectacular ever seen in the city. The bleacher fans were so taken with the likable Flick that they showered him with silver — even after he robbed a Pirate of extra bases.

In 1900, Flick's best season, his .367 batting average was second only to Honus Wagner's. That year he scored 106 runs, led the National League with 110 RBIs, and was third in the league with 32 doubles, fifth with 16 triples, and second with 11 home runs.

In 1901 the NL was at war with the upstart American League, which had declared itself a major league. Several of Flick's teammates, including the great Napoleon Lajoie, jumped to the new league for higher wages. But Flick and left fielder Ed Delahanty stayed on, and their hitting lifted the Phillies to second place in the NL.

The money was too tempting, however, and in 1902 Delahanty jumped to Washington and Flick to Connie Mack's Philadelphia Athletics. Flick played only 11 games with the A's before the Phillies secured an injunction preventing him from playing baseball in Pennsylvania for anyone but the NL team. They had used the same strategy with Lajoie the previous year. In order to keep these valuable players in the AL, Connie Mack sold both to Cleveland.

For the next six years Lajoie and Flick gave the Indians a potent one-two batting punch. In 1905 Flick was the AL's leading hitter with a .308 mark, the lowest for a batting champion until Carl Yastrzemski's .301 in 1968. His .302 mark in 1907 was 48 points below Cobb's average, but was still the fourth highest in the league.

Flick led the league in runs scored in 1906 with 98, but his real talent was hitting triples. Shortly after his arrival in Cleveland he hit three in one game. From 1905 through 1907 he led the AL in triples each season, smacking 18, 22, and then 18 again.

At spring training in New Orleans in 1908, Flick developed an unexplained stomach problem. Some suspected contaminated water, but no other players had been affected. His weight dropped to 135 pounds, and he appeared in only nine games all season. When he tried to come back in 1909 he was only a shadow of his former self. After playing 24 games for Cleveland in 1910 he left the major leagues. During the next two seasons he attempted a comeback with Toledo in the American Association but failed. In 13 major league seasons he hit .313, collected 1,752 hits, scored 948 runs, and drove in 756 runners.

After retiring from baseball Flick became a builder, raised trotting horses in northern Ohio, and was virtually forgotten. In the flood of stories and anecdotes precipitated by Ty Cobb's death in 1961, the tale of Cobb's near-trade for Flick came up often. That probably led the Hall of Fame's Veterans Committee to reexamine Flick's career, and he was named to the Hall in 1963. At his induction ceremony the 87-year-old Flick said, "This is a bigger day than I've ever had before." He died in 1971.

Ray Fosse

One of the defining moments in Cleveland catcher Ray Fosse's career came in prime time, but, at the worst possible time for a catcher who was on his way to stardom.

In the bottom of the twelfth inning of the 1970 All-Star Game, with the crowd at Cincinnati's Riverfront Stadium screaming as local hero Pete Rose tore around third base with the potential winning run, a one-bounce throw to Fosse arrived just as Rose got to the plate and delivered a brutal, jarring collision. The ball squirted loose and the crowd roared even louder. After the collision that night, his arm was never the same.

Born in Marion, Illinois in 1947, Fosse was a top prospect coming out of high school, the Indians' number-one draft choice in the very first amateur draft in 1965. He played seven games with the Indians at the end of 1967 and one game in 1968, then hit .172 in 37 games in 1969.

He got his chance to be the regular catcher in 1970 and was an immediate hit. In fact, Fosse made the All-Star team as a backup catcher instead of Thurman Munson. Munson would go on to be the Rookie of the Year in 1970, after Fosse's injury in the All-Star Game cut his produc-

tion dramatically. Fosse, however, was the Gold Glove winner that year, and again in 1971.

The night before that fateful game, Rose had entertained Fosse and Sam McDowell, his Indians batterymate, at dinner. The next night, in the twelfth inning, the score was tied, 4-4. Rose was on second with two out, and Clyde Wright of the Angels was pitching. Jim Hickman of the Cubs singled, and the rest is history. "When I got back to Cleveland to start the second half I could not lift my left arm above my head," said Fosse, who never went on the disabled list that season. "It limited my power. I got my strength back in my shoulder but I never regained my home run power. My swing had changed."

Rose's take on the crash at the plate was predictable: "Fosse was playing to win and so was I. He stood up there and tried to make a tough tag, tried to make a good play, and I suppose I just made a better play, and that's the way it is."

Fosse ended up hitting a career-high .307 that season with a career-high 18 home runs. He hit .276 the next season, with 12 homers and 62 RBIs, and was traded to Oakland after falling to .241 in 1972 with 41 RBIs in 457 at-bats. He was a regular catcher for one more year, but after 1973 he was a platoon player who kept getting injured. He was traded back to Cleveland in 1976 and hit .301 in 90 games, but he spent all of 1978 on the disabled list and retired after hitting .231 in 19 games for the Brewers in 1979.

Fosse returned to Oakland in 1984 in a dual capacity — working in the front office and in the booth as part of the A's radio broadcast team. He went into broadcasting full-time in 1988, working both radio and TV.

Mike Garcia

Mike Garcia, "the Big Bear," was an integral part of the 1954 Cleveland Indians pitching staff, regarded as one of baseball's finest rotations.

Garcia, Bob Lemon, Early Wynn, Ray Narleski, and Bob Feller propelled the Indians to an American League-record 111 victories and a trip to the World Series. The Big Bear won 19 games that season, his fourth consecutive year with at least 18 wins. He also led the AL in ERA in 1954 and twice paced the circuit in shutouts.

Garcia's professional career started in 1942 with Appleton of the Class D Wisconsin State League, where he went 10-10 with a 3.91 ERA. After spending 1943 through 1945 in the service, he returned to baseball in 1946 with Bakersfield of the California League. That season he led the league in games and earned run average.

The following year was spent with the Wilkes-Barre Barons of the Eastern League. Garcia's 17 victories tied for the league lead, and he led all pitchers in innings pitched and hits allowed. He spent most of 1948 at Oklahoma City of the Texas League, where he was 19-16, with a 3.09 ERA. Late in the season he was called up to Cleveland.

"From the beginning Mike was a sneaky quick pitcher," said Feller. "For a big guy 6-foot-1, 200 pounds he was certainly mobile."

Garcia went 14-5 with five shutouts during his 1949 rookie season. He posted back-to-back 20-win seasons in

1951 and 1952 and followed with 18 victories in 1953 and 19 in 1954. He was not as successful in his one postseason appearance — Garcia started Game 3 of the 1954 World Series but lasted only three innings, surrendering four runs. He was a victim of the New York Giants' four-game sweep of the Tribe.

"Sure, we were disappointed," said Garcia. "We figured we'd win, but the Giants were too strong. We were a team. We shared the credit and the blame equally."

Garcia had a winning record only once in the next five years with the Indians. He played in 1960 with the Chicago White Sox and 1961 with the Washington Senators, but won only one game his final two seasons.

After retiring in 1961, Garcia operated a dry cleaning establishment in Parma, Ohio. "I love Cleveland," he said at the time. "I'm going to stay here the rest of my life." In the 1970s Garcia became disabled from diabetes and kidney failure and required frequent dialysis treatments. He was forced to sell his business to pay his mounting medical bills.

Just a month before his death, in January 1986, his former teammates organized a benefit to help Garcia. "He did more than his share," said Lemon, "and I hope the Cleveland fans remember that."

Joe Gordon

Joe "Flash" Gordon was a slick-fielding second baseman with home run power, a rare combination in baseball. He also had another claim to fame. In 1960, while managing the Indians, Gordon was traded for Jimmy Dykes, who was managing the Tigers. Two managers had never been traded for one another before, and it's never happened since.

Of course, Gordon is remembered first and foremost for his skills as a player. "The greatest all-around ballplayer I ever saw, and I don't bar any of them, is Joe Gordon," Joe McCarthy remarked after Gordon's spectacular performance in the 1941 World Series. And in 1942, the year that Ted Williams won the Triple Crown, Gordon was the American League's Most Valuable Player.

The *Sporting News* named Gordon to its All-Star team six times, from 1939-42, as well as 1947 and 1948. He holds the AL single-season record for most home runs by a second baseman with 32 for Cleveland in 1948, and still owns the Yankee record for most homers by a second baseman, with 30 in 1940. His 246 career homers are an AL record for a second baseman.

But batting was not his favorite pastime. "Hitting? What is there to it?" he once said. "You swing, and if you hit the ball, there it goes. Ah, but fielding. There's rhythm, finesse, teamwork, and balance! I love it!"

While a student at the University of Oregon, Gordon not only played baseball, but also he was a fine gymnast, long jumper, soccer player, and halfback. He even played the violin. "He played in the school orchestra when he wasn't on an athletic field," recalled boyhood friend Bobby Grayson, a three-time All-American in football, "and, later, when he managed Sacramento after World War II, he and Tommy Heath used to get together in a combo."

After hitting .418 as a sophomore at Oregon, Gordon was signed by Yankee scout Bill Essick, who had summed the kid up this way in a report back to the Bronx: "At his best when it meant the most and the going was toughest."

In 1937 Gordon played second base with the legendary 1937 Newark Bears, according to most observers, the greatest minor league team of all time. Gordon hit only .280 at Newark but professed not to be concerned. "I hit a lot of hard luck," he said, "and with a little better fortune, I might even increase those figures in the American League."

He made it across the Hudson in 1938 and was an immediate success, hitting 25 home runs and 97 RBIs in his rookie season. He averaged 25 homers and 101 RBIs during the next four seasons. Following an off-year in 1943, he spent the next two years in the military. After a dreadful season in 1946 —.210, 11 homers, and 47 RBIs — he was traded to Cleveland for Allie Reynolds.

The Yankees may have gotten the best of that deal, as Reynolds was a cornerstone of their pitching staff for the next eight years. But Gordon revived his career in Cleveland. He hit 29 homers and drove in 93 during his first season there and followed that with 32 homers and 124 RBIs for the 1948 world champs. That was his last big season, and his next stop was Sacramento in the PCL, where he managed in 1951 and 1952.

From 1953 through July 1956, Gordon served as a scout for Detroit. At that point he became manager of the Pacific Coast League's San Francisco Seals. He directed them to a first-place showing in 1957, San Francisco's last year in the minors, and he was then hired to manage Cleveland.

It wasn't a happy marriage. Shortly after Gordon was hired, Cleveland installed Frank "Trader" Lane as its new general manager. Gordon and Lane did not get along, and late in the 1959 season their feud heated up. Gordon was annoyed by Lane publicly questioning his strategy, and on September 18, 1959, Gordon announced he would not return in 1960. The next day Lane went to Pittsburgh to ask Leo Durocher, then an NBC broadcaster, if he would be interested in taking over the Tribe.

Lane also announced that Gordon would be terminated as soon as the club was mathematically eliminated from the pennant race. When Al Lopez's White Sox clinched the pennant on September 22, Lane said that Gordon was out "as of now," and that pitching coach Mel Harder would be taking over the club.

The next day Lane backpedaled. Suddenly disenchanted with Durocher and his conditions, Lane announced not only that Gordon was back, but also that he had a two-year contract and a raise. "I made a mistake," said Lane, "and I decided I didn't have to live with it, so I tried to correct it."

Yet relations between and Lane and Gordon did not improve, so when Detroit General Manager Bill DeWitt said to Lane, "We've been trading players, why don't we trade managers?" Lane pulled the trigger. On August 3, 1960, Gordon was swapped for Tigers Manager Jimmy Dykes.

Gordon was probably relieved to finally be free of Lane and graciously remarked, "I have always been appreciative of the Cleveland club for hiring me in the first place." He lasted only two months with Detroit. Wrote sportswriter Joe Falls, "Gordon took one long look at the Tigers and shook his head. When the remainder of the season was over, he barricaded himself in his apartment and refused to talk to anyone. He quit."

On October 5, 1960, Gordon was hired as manager by new Kansas City owner Charles O. Finley. He was fired in midseason and then worked as a scout and minor league batting instructor for the Angels from October 1961 through 1968.

In 1969 Gordon became the first manager of the expansion Kansas City Royals. Finishing fourth, he was let go after the season. After leaving baseball, Gordon sold real estate. He died of a heart attack in 1978.

Jack Graney

A weak-hitting, fair-fielding outfielder, Jack Graney had a 14-year career, all with the Indians, and is credited with several important firsts in big league history.

In 1914 he was the first man to bat against, get a hit off, and score a run against rookie Red Sox pitcher Babe Ruth. Two years later Graney became the first player to wear a uniform number, a small insignia attached to his sleeve. He was also the first former ballplayer to become a broadcaster, and because of his lifelong connection with Cleveland baseball, he was the first ballplayer to have a Society for American Baseball Research regional organization named after him.

The ebullient Graney was always one to tell a joke or sing a song. A hard-nosed, consistent player, he got the most from his limited talent by smart hitting and walking and playing a solid left field with a strong arm. He led the American League in walks twice and in doubles once.

He showed up at Cleveland's spring camp in Macon, Georgia, in 1908 convinced he was a pitcher. Facing the legendary Nap Lajoie, who was also the team's manager, Graney decided to prove he could be tough. He beaned Lajoie on his first pitch. Shortly thereafter he received a note from the skipper: "All wild men belong in the wild west. So you're going to Portland, Oregon."

Graney became an outfielder in the minors, returned to the majors in 1910 as a leadoff hitter and left fielder, and offset his mediocre batting skills by working pitchers for bases on balls. His propensity for not swinging earned him the nickname "Three-and-Two Jack."

After batting a barely acceptable .269 in 146 games in the 1911 season, he had a miserable year in 1912. He got ptomaine poisoning in Boston, and he broke his right collarbone in Detroit while catching a line drive. Graney decided he needed a good luck charm for the 1913 season, so he brought a bull terrier named "Tige" to spring training that year. Within days, the team had adopted the playful pup as its mascot and rechristened it "Larry."

Mascot Larry was a familiar sight wherever the Naps were found for the next five years. His antics, which included catching baseballs, jumping through a hoop of Graney's arms, and chasing other animals and unsavory people, entertained the fans before games. Larry was introduced along with the team to President Woodrow Wilson at the White House. When umpire Charles Ferguson tossed Nap Manager Joe Birmingham from the game, the Naps tried to replace Birmingham with Larry in the coaching box, but the dog was ordered off the field. When Larry contracted an illness and died in 1917, his death was "a cause of great mourning throughout the league," historian Mike Sowell said.

Graney was also a close friend and roommate of second baseman Ray Chapman. The two sang together in a group made up of Cleveland players. When Chapman was fatally injured by a Carl Mays pitch in 1920, Graney helped his injured friend off the field and then continued to play in a daze.

The year Chapman lost his life Graney lost his job as the regular left fielder. The younger and harder-hitting Charlie Jamieson was ready to step into Graney's spot in the lineup when Graney caught tonsillitis. Jamieson replaced him for good on Memorial Day. Graney had only three at bats in Cleveland's 1920 World Series victory over Brooklyn.

Graney batted just 167 times during the next two years before leaving baseball. He stayed in Cleveland and sold cars, but, when Ford closed down for a year to retool the Model T into the Model A, Graney was out of work. He lived on his stock market investments until the crash of 1929 all but wiped him out.

Stuck for a radio announcer in 1932, the Indians asked Graney to try out, and he became an immediate success. His enthusiastic style, clear voice, and logical sentences made him a favorite, even when he was forced to re-create the games from ticker-tape reports. Jimmy Dudley, Graney's sixth and last partner in 25 years behind the mike, said that Graney had "an extremely high-pitched voice which generated more excitement than anyone else's."

The former major leaguer's final broadcasting job was calling the Giants' 1954 World Series sweep of the Indians. Graney died in 1978.

Mel Harder

In the 1930s, when every team had a gang of great hitters, Mel Harder was a dependable pitcher who was afraid of no one.

The quiet, bespectacled righthander from Beemer, Nebraska, set longevity records for Cleveland pitchers, appearing in 582 games in 20 seasons and compiling a lifetime record of 223-186. Only Bob Feller won more games with the Indians, and only Walter Johnson and Ted Lyons had longer pitching careers with one team than Harder.

In 1927, his first season in the minors, the 18-year-old won 17 games with two teams. Harder saw action in 23 games in 1928 with Cleveland. Sent back to New Orleans for further seasoning, he returned in 1930 to take his spot as fourth starter in a rotation that included Wes Ferrell, Willis Hudlin, and Clint Brown. Harder, at age 20, won 11 and lost 10 for the fourth-place Tribe. His ERA was 4.22 — but this was 1930, after all, when the league ERA was 4.65.

Harder quietly improved his win totals to 13 in 1931 and 15 in both 1932 and 1933. He pitched the first game ever played in Cleveland's Municipal Stadium, on July 31, 1932, losing, 1-0, to Lefty Grove and the A's in front of 76,979 fans.

From 1932 through 1935, Harder was among the top

pitchers in the American League. His ERA in 1933 was the lowest in the AL; the following season he tied Lefty Gomez for most shutouts in the League, with six. He ranked among the AL's top five pitchers in fewest walks per game every season from 1932 to 1935; in ERA in 1933 and 1934; in opponents' on-base average in 1933, 1934, and 1935; in innings pitched in 1935; and in wins in both 1934 and 1935. He even hit two home runs in one game, on July 31, 1935.

In 1934 Harder was the winning pitcher in the second All-Star Game, although most baseball fans remember only Carl Hubbell's feat of striking out five in a row of the game's greatest sluggers. Harder pitched in the 1935 All-Star Game (at home in Cleveland) and again in 1936 and 1937. He is the only pitcher never to have allowed a run in more than 10 innings of All-Star Game competition.

After consecutive 20-win seasons in 1934 and 1935, Harder had shoulder and elbow problems, but he gamely delivered more than 220 innings in each of the next two years. Despite having ERAs that were a run or more higher than any of his past five seasons, he was able to win 15 games each year. He then posted a 17-victory season in 1938 and a 15-9 record in 1939.

On June 12, 1940, Harder was knocked from a game against the Red Sox in Boston. As he approached the bench his manager, Ossie Vitt, challenged him: "It's about time you won one, with all the money you're making." The soft-spoken, sore-armed Harder answered truthfully, "I gave you the best I had."

The remark was just another example of Vitt's crude and insensitive managerial style. The team rebelled. The cautious, conservative Harder led a group of players who met with owner Alva Bradley to complain about Vitt's behavior. But word leaked out about their meeting, and they were branded "the Cleveland Crybabies" throughout the AL. They would find diapers hanging over their dugout. Baby bottles were thrown at them. Vitt calmed down, and the Tribe actually came within one game of winning the AL pennant.

But that was as close as Harder came to appearing in the postseason. Only five men played more seasons than Harder without appearing in a World Series.

The Indians released Harder in 1941 but gave him a second chance the next year after he responded well to elbow surgery. Using his experience and smarts, he continued as a member of the Tribe staff through 1947, winning 13 games in 1942 and 12 in 1944. When his playing career was over, he was hired as the team's first base coach, but he quickly became entrusted solely with the task of working with the pitchers. He was one of baseball's first pitching coaches.

He coached in Cleveland for 16 years, and many Indian hurlers gave him credit for improving their games. Early Wynn had been a hard thrower for Washington before going to Cleveland, but Harder taught him a breaking ball and changeup. Wynn won 300 games in the majors. Herb Score said Harder showed him how to throw a good curve. Even Bob Feller went to school with Harder. It was said that Harder "had a camera in his head, and could spot any pitching flaw immediately."

After leaving the Indians, Harder spent several more seasons with the Mets, Cubs, Reds, and Royals.

Jeff Heath

Jeff Heath was a Canadian-born, power-hitting outfielder who made his mark in the United States with Cleveland during the '30s and '40s.

In 1938, his first full season as a starter, the outfielder got the baseball world's attention. Heath put on a dazzling offensive show, smashing 21 home runs, 31 doubles, a league-leading 18 triples, 112 RBI, and an eye-popping .343 batting average, second only to American League Most Valuable Player Jimmie Foxx, who hit .349. Heath's slugging percentage was .602, third in the league behind Hall of Famers Foxx and Hank Greenberg and ahead of Joe DiMaggio.

Although Heath never again matched his awesome numbers of 1938, he went on to have a solid major league career. He spent 10 years with the Indians before playing for the Washington Senators, St. Louis Browns and Boston Braves.

During the 1948 season, Heath suffered a broken ankle that forced him to miss the World Series and end his career the following season. He finished with 194 home runs, 102 triples, 279 doubles and 887 RBIs. His lifetime batting average during 14 seasons was a robust .293.

Jim Hegan

Jim Hegan was a major league catcher for more than 16 seasons and, in the course of a 14-year stretch with the Indians, helped the development of pitchers such as Mike Garcia, Bob Lemon, and Herb Score. Hegan never hit over .250, but as Hall of Fame catcher Bill Dickey once said, "When you can catch like Hegan you don't have to hit."

The father of outfielder-first baseman Mike Hegan, he was born in 1920 in Lynn, Massachusetts. He started playing professional ball for Springfield in the Class C Middle Atlantic League in 1938, hit .194 in 68 games as a rookie for the Indians in 1942, and spent the next three years in the service.

He took over the Indians' regular catching job in 1947, when he hit a career-high .249, kept the job for the next 10 years, and made five All-Star teams. For much of that time he was catching one of the best starting staffs the majors has ever seen — Hall of Famers Bob Feller, Early Wynn, Lemon, and Garcia.

In 1949, the durable Hegan caught 152 games. His most productive seasons with the bat were 1948, when hit .248 with 14 homers and 61 RBIs, and 1950, when he hit .219 with 14 homers and 58 RBIs.

Blessed with an outstanding arm, he led American League catchers in double plays four times, in putouts three times, in assists twice, and in fielding percentage three times. He also caught three no-hitters: Don Black in 1947, Lemon in 1948, and Feller in 1951. Feller said, "Jim Hegan became the best catcher I ever had. He didn't hit as well as the others, but nobody was his equal as a catcher, especially with his arm."

After catching 118 games in 1956 at age 36, he became a backup in 1957 before making the rounds: he played for the Tigers, Phillies, Giants, and Cubs the next three seasons before retiring in 1960. He coached with the Yankees, Tigers, and then the Yankees again for 20 years and died in 1984.

Orel Hershiser

It's hard to believe that Orel Hershiser IV had only one winning season in the six years before he arrived in Cleveland in 1995, but the right-hander's record since his "all-everything" season in 1988 was a surprising, and a mediocre, 51-53, including a season reduced to only four starts by a rotator cuff injury. When he changed leagues in 1995, his luck changed, too.

Dodger Hall of Fame pitcher Sandy Koufax, who was not even in the major leagues the last time Cleveland went to the Series, says that Hershiser is the type of person who could do whatever he sets out to do. "The key to Orel's success is his constant striving for perfection," Koufax says. "Perfectionists are usually given a bad name, but there's nothing wrong with trying to be better than you are, the best you can be."

Raised outside Philadelphia, Hershiser pitched for Cherry Hills East High School in New Jersey, and, undrafted, attended Bowling Green University, winning All-Metro Athletic Conference honors and hurling for the All-American Amateur Baseball Association national champions in the summer of 1979. A gifted athlete — although he looks more like an accountant than a Cy Young Award winner — Hershiser excelled in many sports growing up as he moved from city to city because of his father's printing business. "He could play anything," says his dad, Orel Hershiser III, "but it was baseball he loved."

He liked hockey, though. He learned the sport in Toronto as a youngster and was good enough to play for the Philadelphia Flyers' Junior A hockey team. Hershiser decided to go to Bowling Green University, which had good programs in both baseball and hockey. His baseball coach discouraged him from playing hockey, and Hershiser became discouraged himself when he didn't make the traveling team as a freshman. He was also having trouble academically and left school in the middle of a semester to visit high school friends for a couple of days. After hitchhiking back, he was a new man.

Not only was Hershiser doing better in school, he was also growing. He grew three inches his sophomore year and added five miles an hour to his fastball. He not only made the traveling team, he was drafted in the seventeenth round after his junior year. He quickly moved through the Dodger farm system, working mostly as a reliever.

Hershiser caught the eye of manager Tommy Lasorda and the Dodger brass in spring training of 1983, winning the Jim and Dearie Mulvey Award as the outstanding rookie in Dodgertown. He was sent back to AAA Albuquerque, but was called up to Los Angeles at the end of the year and never left. He did leave the bullpen, though, starting 20 games and tying for the National League lead in shutouts (4) with teammate Alejandro Pena, a starter who went on to become a top reliever.

He led the league in one category or another for four of the next five years. In 1985 it was winning percentage (.864 to go with a gaudy 19-3 record); in '87 it was innings (264); it was innings again (256) in '89. What about '88? Hershiser tied with Cincinnati's Danny Jackson for the lead in wins (23) and complete games (15), but led outright in shutouts (8) and innings pitched (267) to breeze to the Cy Young.

Surprisingly, his 2.26 earned run average was third in the league; it's surprising because Hershiser ended the season by breaking former Dodger Don Drysdale's once seemingly unbreakable record of 58 consecutive scoreless innings. Hershiser began his streak in the final four innings of an August 30 win at Montreal. He then pitched five straight shutout victories, and went 10 scoreless innings in his final regular season start at San Diego on September 28. During the streak, he allowed 31 hits, walked only 11, and fanned 38.

In the postseason, nothing could stop "the Bulldog," as Dodger manager Tommy Lasorda dubbed him. Hershiser started three games, got a save in another and tossed a shutout in the seventh game as the underdog Dodgers defeated the New York Mets for the pennant.

Against the favored Athletics in the 1988 World Series, Hershiser tossed a three-hit shutout, fanning eight, in Game 2. In Game 5, he completed the upset with a four-hitter, fanning nine in a 5-2 win, to collect the MVP hardware. During the game, to control his nerves, Hershiser sang the Doxology, a hymn, and, after the final out, kneeled on the mound for a moment of prayer before leaping into catcher Rick Dempsey's arms. For the 1988 postseason, he pitched 42 2/3 innings, going 3-0 with two shutouts, 32 strikeouts, 13 walks, and a 1.05 ERA, plus a .250 batting average with two doubles and two RBI.

Seven years later, Greg Maddux was having the same kind of magic year, and it was Hershiser's bulldog tenacity that led Cleveland manager Mike Hargrove to pencil him in to face Maddux in the first game of the 1995 World Series.

By then, Hershiser was 7-0 in the postseason and had pitched a three-hitter for six innings against the Braves in Game 1 before removing himself from a tie game in the seventh. "It was neither physical nor mental fatigue," Hershiser says. "I just lost my release point." The Indians lost the game, 3-2, as Maddux threw a two-hitter.

By Game 5, the Tribe was down three games to one. "If you have to go into a game like this," Hargrove said before the fifth game, "Orel Hershiser definitely fills the bill." Hershiser went eight innings, allowed only five hits and one earned run to improve his postseason record to 8-1 and made the play of the game by spearing a would-be basehit and turning it into a double play.

The Indians lost the Series in six games, but after a strong postseason — not to mention a 16-6, 3.87 ERA regular season — there was no doubt that the Bulldog was back. He not only beat Maddux (something that had happened only twice in the regular season), he also stared him down following a brushback incident in Game 5.

"I don't let my on-field emotions affect my off-field and everyday life," he says. "I build a crescendo and then can release it in the three hours during the game. I can change my emotions when I take off my uniform."

Shoeless Joe Jackson

Although his name was stained during the Black Sox scandal, "Shoeless Joe" Jackson spent five and a half years with the Indians, and his lowest batting average was .327.

Jackson became an Indian in 1910 when Connie Mack traded him from the A's for outfielder Bris Lord. In 1911 he batted .408, but incredibly did not win the batting title as Ty Cobb registered a .420 average. Jackson, as it turned out, did not win any batting titles during his career. Following the 1912 season he complained to Cobb, "What a hell of a league this is. I hit .387, .408, and .395 the last three years and I ain't won nothin' yet!"

Even though he didn't win any batting titles, he won respect from the American League pitchers. "I consider Joe Jackson the greatest natural ballplayer I've ever seen," said legendary hurler Walter Johnson. And Babe Ruth told a reporter that the only batter he had patterned himself after was "Joe Jackson."

In August 1915 Jackson was traded to the White Sox for three players and $31,500. The White Sox won the world championship in 1917 and the AL pennant in 1919. A heavy favorite to beat Cincinnati, they lost the best-of-nine World Series in eight games under extremely suspicious circumstances.

Rumors of a fix floated openly, and, as the 1920 season drew to a close the scandal burst wide open. Faced with evidence of a fix, Jackson and pitcher Eddie Cicotte confessed. Appearing before a Chicago grand jury, Jackson acknowledged having been promised $20,000 to help throw the Series but contended that he had received only $5,000 of that amount.

Jackson had batted .375 during the 1919 Series, but admitted he had failed to hustle after balls hit to left field, had made several weak throws, and had struck out in key situations. "I got a big load off my chest!" he concluded.

Jackson, Risberg, Gandil, Williams, Cicotte, Felsch, Buck Weaver, and Fred McMullin were suspended from the game and in June 1921, with the exception of McMullin, were brought to trial regarding the fix. The trial ended on August 2, and within a few hours the jury brought back acquittals for all defendants.

It was a hollow victory. The next day, newly installed Commissioner Kenesaw Mountain Landis ruled that "Regardless of the verdict of juries, no player that throws a ballgame will ever play professional baseball." Jackson, who recorded a lifetime .356 batting average, twice led the American League in hits and three times led the league in triples, was banned from baseball for life.

In February 1951 the South Carolina Legislature petitioned for Jackson's reinstatement, but its request was ignored. In December 1951 Jackson suffered his fourth heart attack and died at age 62.

★ Addie Joss ★

Of all the clutch pitching performances in the history of baseball, none measure up to the one Addie Joss turned in on October 2, 1908.

With a week left in the season, three American League teams — the Detroit Tigers, Chicago White Sox, and Indians (then called the Naps after second baseman Nap Lajoie) — were separated by only a game and a half. Some 11,000 fans filed into Cleveland's League Park expecting a well-pitched game from Joss, seeking his twenty-fourth win of the season for the Indians. But his opponent, "Big Ed" Walsh of the White Sox, had been almost unstoppable. Walsh, master of the spitball, eventually won 40 games that season and pitched 464 innings.

The first two innings passed uneventfully. In the bottom of the third, Cleveland's Joe Birmingham singled, one of only four hits Walsh surrendered all day. Moments later Birmingham stole second, and when the catcher's throw hit him in the shoulder and bounced away, he raced to third. Walsh eyed him at third and then threw a spitball that broke more than usual. Birmingham scored on the wild pitch. The unearned run was Cleveland's only score of the day as Walsh frustrated the Nap batters with his spitter, striking out 15.

As the innings rolled by, though the fans finally noticed that Joss not only had held the White Sox scoreless, but also that not a single Chicago player had set foot on base. Second baseman Lajoie made several nice plays on slow grounders. In the seventh, Chicago's Fielder Jones worked the count to 3-2. On the next pitch he dropped his bat and trotted toward first base, only to hear umpire Tom Connolly boom, "Strike three!" In the eighth, the Sox's Pat Dougherty got the first hard hit of the day off Joss, but Lajoie glided gracefully in front of the ball and threw him out.

Chicago sent three pinch hitters in a row to the plate in the ninth. The first grounded harmlessly to Lajoie. The second batter went down on strikes. A hush fell over the crowd. According to one reporter, "A mouse working his way along the grandstand floor would have sounded like a shovel scraping over concrete."

Powerful John Anderson dug in for the Sox. He lined the first pitch to left — foul. He smashed the second pitch toward third, where Bill Bradley had not had a fielding chance all day. Bradley flagged the ball down and hurried his throw. Fortunately for Joss, Anderson was a slow runner, and Bradley's low throw was dug out of the dirt by first baseman George Stovall just in time to make the out. In the heat of a torrid pennant race, against one of the game's best pitchers having his greatest season, Joss had pitched a perfect game.

It didn't bring the pennant to Cleveland, who finished a half game behind Detroit, but that didn't take any luster off Joss's effort. In 1955 Arthur Daley of the *New York Times* called it "the most astonishing clutch job baseball has had." Certainly, it was the supreme moment of a glittering but tragically short career.

Adrian Joss was born in Woodland, Wisconsin, in 1880. He pitched semipro ball as a teenager and later hurled for the University of Wisconsin. He was playing for a semipro team in Sheboygan when he was scouted and signed by Toledo of the Inter-State League in 1900. He went 19-16 in his first year and 25-15 in 1901 to draw the attention of several major league teams, including Cleveland. The Toledo owner tried to trick him into signing on for a third year, but when Joss discovered the subterfuge, he immediately joined Cleveland.

Tall and gangly at 6-foot-3 and 185 pounds, Joss

pitched with an exaggerated pinwheel motion that earned him the nickname "the Human Hairpin."He threw a good fastball and a fast-breaking curve with exceptional control. During his career he averaged only 1.43 walks per game, the third-best ratio in major league history.

On April 26, 1902, Joss made a memorable debut with Cleveland. Pitching against the St. Louis Browns, Joss pitched a one-hitter, a disputed line drive by Jesse Burkett, and won, 3-0. Cleveland's right fielder claimed he'd caught Burkett's drive 3 inches off the ground, and most of his teammates agreed. Umpire Bill Carruthers, with the only vote that counted, ruled the catch a trap.

Joss won 17 games, including a league-leading five shutouts, in his rookie year, then followed with 18 victories in 1903. He slumped to 14 wins in 1904 but led the AL with a 1.59 earned run average. From 1905 through 1908, his numbers were 20-12 with a 2.01 ERA, 21-9 with a 1.72 ERA, 27-11 with a 1.83 ERA, and 24-11 with a 1.16 ERA. His 1908 ERA led the league, as did his 27 victories in 1907, when he won 10 straight.

During the off-season Joss was a sportswriter for the *Toledo News-Bee*. Another Toledo newspaper, the *Blade*, later said of him: "Baseball was a profession, as severe as that of any other. . . . In taking his vocation seriously he was, in return, taken seriously by the people, who recognized in him a man of more than usual intelligence and one who would have adorned any profession in which he had elected to engage."

Joss was often either ill or injured. In 1903 he missed the last month of the season with a high fever. He suffered with malaria in 1904. Then in 1905 he was sidelined for a while with a back problem. In 1909 his won-lost record slipped to 14-13, and his strikeout total fell to only half that of the previous season. Nevertheless, his 1.71 ERA certainly did not signal any loss of ability.

Joss began the 1910 season with four straight victories. On April 20 he threw his second no-hitter against the White Sox, but it was a questionable call. Early in the game, the Sox's Freddy Parent beat out a slow roller to Bill Bradley at third. Most writers scoring the game marked it as a hit, but as the hitless innings piled up they began to have second thoughts.

Some of them sought out the official scorekeeper, only to discover that the penny-wise White Sox owner, Charles Comiskey, had not bothered to hire one. That left the decision up to the writers. They spoke with Bradley, who said he should have had the ball. When Joss went the rest of the way without allowing a hit, the writers agreed to change Parent's hit to an error on Bradley and give Joss his second no-hitter.

When Joss developed a sore arm his record slipped to 5-5, and he was sent home for the rest of the season. The layoff seemed to work. He pitched six innings in a postseason exhibition, with encouraging results. The following spring he seemed ready for a comeback, although several teammates noted he had lost considerable weight. During an exhibition game at Chattanooga, Tennessee, he fainted on the bench. Although he dismissed it as nothing, by the time the team reached Cincinnati he was obviously ill.

Diagnosed with pleurisy, he was ordered to return home to Toledo. On April 14, two days after the season began, Joss died of tubercular meningitis. He was 31 years old. His funeral, presided over by Billy Sunday, the ballplayer-turned-evangelist, drew a huge crowd of people. Later that summer, American Leaguers played an all-star game to raise money for Joss's family. Cy Young, who pitched for one side, said, "He was a great man. I feel sure he never made an enemy."

Joss played in the major leagues for only nine seasons, with a record of 160-97. His career ERA of 1.88 is the second lowest of all time. He completed 90 percent of his starts and threw 46 shutouts. He gave up only 19 home runs, and Ty Cobb batted just .071 in 28 at bats against him. He allowed fewer baserunners per nine innings (8.73) than any pitcher in major league history.

In 1978 the Veterans Committee decided to bend its 10-year rule and elected Joss to the Hall of Fame.

Ken Keltner

Sometimes a single magnificent moment can overshadow a player's career and cause fans to forget his other accomplishments. On the night of July 17, 1941, Ken Keltner, the Indians' third baseman, took the field in front of more than 67,000 Cleveland fans for a game that would forever etch his name in baseball history.

The man of the moment was New York Yankees star Joe DiMaggio, who had hit safely in a record 56 straight games, 12 games more than anyone else in history. Everyone wondered if he could keep the streak alive. His adversary on the mound was Cleveland lefthander Al Smith, who had won 15 games for the Tribe the year before.

For a moment in the first inning it looked as if the streak would continue. DiMaggio hit a rocket down the third base line, but Keltner, playing deep, lunged for the bouncing ball and gloved it. His momentum sent him into foul territory, but he recovered, threw perfectly to first, and retired DiMaggio.

"The Yankee Clipper" walked in the fourth inning, and in the seventh he sent another screaming drive down the third base line; Keltner executed an instant replay and again threw DiMaggio out. When reliever Al Milnar got DiMaggio to hit a bouncer to shortstop with the bases loaded in the eighth, starting a double play, his streak was history. Keltner, despite his many other accomplishments, became forever known as the man who stopped DiMaggio's streak.

Installed as the Indians' regular third baseman in 1938, Keltner hit 26 home runs with 113 RBIs as a rookie. In 1939 his RBI total slipped to 97 and his homers dropped to 13, but he batted a career-high .325 and led American League third basemen in fielding for the first time. Although Keltner's offensive numbers continued to fall in 1940, he was chosen for his first All-Star Game.

While his plays against DiMaggio earned him more headlines in 1941, Keltner had one of his best all-around years, cracking 23 homers and again leading the league in fielding. He made his second All-Star Game appearance, collecting a scratch single in the ninth inning that set up Ted Williams's game-winning home run. Selected to five more All-Star teams, Keltner led the AL once in putouts, three times in fielding, four times in assists, and five times in double plays.

In 1948 the Tribe won its first pennant in 28 years, and

Keltner, along with several other Indians, had a career year. He hit .297, with 31 home runs and 119 RBI. In the playoff made necessary after Cleveland and Boston ended the season tied for first, Keltner hit a towering three-run homer over Fenway Park's Green Monster in the fourth inning to put the Indians ahead to stay. The Tribe went on to win the World Series over the Boston Braves, four games to two.

Injuries limited Keltner to 80 games in 1949, and he played briefly for the Red Sox in 1950 before retiring. He was chosen by Cleveland fans as the Indians' all-time third baseman in 1969, but the efforts of fans in his native Milwaukee to get him elected to the Baseball Hall of Fame failed. However, he was later named to both the Ohio State Baseball Hall of Fame and the Wisconsin Athletic Hall of Fame.

★ Napoleon Lajoie ★

Cleveland fans loved Napoleon Lajoie so much that they adopted his nickname, "Nap," as the team name from 1903 to 1911.

When fans debate the question of who was baseball's best player in the first decade of this century, the two names most often mentioned are Lajoie and Honus Wagner.

Fellow Hall of Famer Kid Nichols called Lajoie "the hardest hitter I ever pitched to." A career .338 batsman, Lajoie amassed 3,242 hits, three batting titles, four 200-hit seasons, and four 100-RBI seasons. He led the American League in double plays and putouts five times each. He was tops in fielding seven times, and he paced the league in chances per game six times, the best gauge of range. Despite his 6-foot-1, 200-pound frame, Lajoie was an artist at second base — smooth, with sure hands. The word most often used to describe Lajoie is "graceful." It even appears on his Hall of Fame plaque.

Working as a teamster for City Lumber in Woonsocket, Rhode Island, the 21-year-old Lajoie was making $7.50 a week in 1895 when the Fall River, Massachusetts, team of the New England League fell short a player. Lajoie responded to a telegram asking about his interest in pro ball with six words: "I am out for the stuff." He signed for $100 a month and played his first game on May 1.

Before long, word of his talent had spread, and, in 1896, several big league clubs began bidding for him. Boston, Chicago, Pittsburgh, and New York all had discussions with Fall River's management. When Philadelphia made an offer for Lajoie's teammate Phil Geier, Fall City Manager Charlie Marston asked for $1,500, and the Phils refused. Marston then offered to include Lajoie in the deal, and the trade was made. Lajoie was quickly promoted to the majors.

He started his career at first base and hit .326 in 39 games. Although the Phils finished 32½ games out of first place in 1897, Lajoie led the league with a .569 slugging percentage, 40 doubles, and 23 triples. He hit .361 and set a record for total bases in a game, with 13. The next season Phillies Manager George Stallings moved Lajoie to second base. He batted .324 and led the National League in doubles and RBIs.

In July 1899 Lajoie was involved in a vicious collision at second base with the Reds' Harry Steinfeldt. Steinfeldt was knocked unconscious, and Lajoie was sidelined for two months. Except for a handful of pinch-hitting appearances Lajoie didn't play until the last five games of the season. He still hit .378 with 70 RBIs — in only 312 at bats.

Lajoie injured himself again in 1900, but it didn't happen on the field. In late May, with the Phils in first place, Lajoie and teammate Elmer Flick got into a fight, supposedly over a bat. The most damaging punch was one that missed its mark. Lajoie threw it, Flick ducked, and Lajoie's fist hit a concrete wall. His thumb was broken, and he missed five weeks of play.

That year the NL had reduced its membership from twelve to eight teams by expelling four of the poorer-drawing franchises from the league. That gave Ban Johnson, commissioner of the Western League, the impetus to oppose the NL, going into cities the NL had vacated including Cleveland, and he began to solicit players to join his new organization, now called the American League. Lajoie was one of the first to "go for the stuff."

By then Lajoie had been recognized as one of the top talents in the game, and he was making the maximum salary for a player, $2,400. The average salary was $525. Under-the-table payments raised that by another $200 or so, but the proud Lajoie wanted to make as much as his roommate, Ed Delahanty. Lajoie had seen checks written to Delahanty for $600 extra, so when Connie Mack offered $24,000 for four years, Lajoie became an American Leaguer. When the Phils' owner learned of the signing, he offered Lajoie $25,000 for two years, but the player refused it.

In the new league, where talent was thin, Lajoie dominated. In 1901 he led in slugging average, hits, doubles, homers, runs scored, and RBIs. His league-leading batting average of .422 is the second-highest recorded in this century. In the Dead Ball Era, when 7 or 8 homers might top the league, he belted 14, the third-highest total of the century's first decade.

A lawsuit had been filed to keep Lajoie from leaving the NL, and a lower court had rejected it. In February 1902 an appeal was finally heard before the Pennsylvania Supreme Court. Lajoie became, in effect, the first person to challenge baseball's reserve clause. He testified that he had not damaged the Phils by leaving, and that they could easily find someone to replace him because his services were "not of a unique or extraordinary character." The judges disagreed, ruling that he be prohibited from playing for any club other than the Phils for the term of his contract — in other words, forever.

The decision threw Organized Baseball into a frenzy. The hopes for a peaceful resolution of the conflict between the two leagues seemed shattered. The Athletics defiantly began the season with Lajoie at second base against Baltimore; however, in the ninth inning, Mack received a telegram informing him of a temporary injunction forbidding Lajoie to play.

For two months Lajoie was inactive while lawyers and club owners tried to come up with the next step. Someone suggested that the injunction was effective only in Pennsylvania, so the AL devised a solution. Although Mack would have preferred otherwise, he sent Lajoie to Cleveland because the sagging franchise there was in deep trouble. Owner Charles Somers had been a financial bulwark in the first years of the new league, even putting money in Mack's pocket when necessary. Thus Lajoie became a member of the Blues (Indians), but, whenever his team played in Philadelphia, he was nowhere to be found.

Lajoie was an immediate hit in Cleveland. On June 4 10,000 fans turned out to see him make his debut. His presence and play rescued the club, which otherwise might have moved to Pittsburgh or Cincinnati. Lajoie hit .378, two points higher than Delahanty, but his court-enforced vacation and his later absence from games in the City of Brotherly Love cost him the at bats needed for the slugging title.

During spring training in 1903 Cleveland newspapers ran a contest to find the team a better name than the Blues. The winning moniker was the Naps, after the team's new captain. (Only two other teams have been named after a player: the Brooklyn Robins, after their manager, Wilbert Robinson, and Cleveland again, in 1915, when it took on the Indians name in tribute to its Roman candle superstar, Penobscot Indian Louis "Chief" Sockalexis.)

Lajoie responded to the honor by leading the league in batting and slugging averages. Late in the 1904 season, with the Naps struggling, Manager Bill Armour resigned. Lajoie, at age 30, took Armour's place and kept the job for five years. Later Lajoie would say that trying to manage and play was too much for him. While he managed, his offensive stats never reached the figures he had set in previous years.

Blood poisoning ruined his 1905 season. A spike wound became infected by the dye in his socks, and Lajoie played in only 65 games. His team, nine games in front at the time of the injury, was nine games behind when he returned. Because of Lajoie's experience, the players began to wear white "sanitary" socks with colored stirrups over them.

The Naps finished third in 1906, with Lajoie leading the league in hits and doubles. During 1907 spring training the Tigers made an offer the Naps decided to refuse: noisy newcomer Ty Cobb for Flick, who had won the batting title for the Naps in 1905. Despite his earlier confrontation with Flick, Lajoie spoke out against Cobb, whose ill-tempered disposition was already legendary.

Another spiking injury cost Lajoie five weeks in 1907, and that same season George Stovall hit Lajoie over the head with a chair to show his displeasure about being lowered in the batting order. Cleveland contended for the pennant in 1908. After a July swoon that dropped the Naps nine games back, they won 15 of 18. By September 21 Detroit, Cleveland, and Chicago were only one game apart.

The Naps were half a game back when they hosted the White Sox on October 3. Lajoie should have stayed in bed. He committed an error that led to two runs, and he took an Ed Walsh fastball down the middle for a third strike with two outs and the bases loaded in the seventh. The Naps lost and trailed by 1½ games going into the season's final series.

Again, Lajoie failed. Cleveland and St. Louis played a tie in the first game, and in the sixth inning of the second game Lajoie's error led to the winning run. Lajoie later said, "I honestly believe that the 1908 race took more out of me than three ordinary seasons." He never had a lower batting average (.289) or slugging average (.375) in a full season of play.

That disappointing finish did nothing to quell the grousers on his team. Dissension raged into the 1909 season, and Lajoie decided he'd had enough. With the Naps in third place, at 57-57, he quit as manager. The fans were happy with his decision, but when the *Cleveland Press* immediately ran another contest to rename the team, the Naps won again. The Cleveland fans were glad to have him back, just as a player, and he ended the season with a .324 average.

The Tigers, led by Cobb, had won their third straight pennant in 1909, but the next year a hot young Philadelphia team took the lead early and held it. With no pennant race Cleveland fans focused on the battle for the 1910 batting title between Cobb and Lajoie. It became the most scandalous batting race in baseball history.

The champion was due to receive a sparkling new Chalmers 30 automobile, so the fans came to call the contest "the automobile race." At the end of August Lajoie and Cobb were only three points apart. "Adding to the excitement and the frustration," Jim Murphy wrote, "was the fact that there was no unanimity on exactly what the averages were at any one time. There were repeated statements about 'official' and 'unofficial' figures." On October 6 one set of numbers said Cobb had an eight-point lead; another claimed Lajoie was out front, but only by a point or so.

Cobb, believing he'd already won the car, sat out his team's last two games. Lajoie, meanwhile, prepared to face the Browns in a doubleheader to close the season. No one wanted the snarling Cobb to win; Lajoie, meanwhile, was well respected, even adored. In his final two games Lajoie went a tainted eight-for-eight.

After Lajoie had tripled his first time up, Browns Manager "Peach Pie" Jack O'Connor "recommended" that his rookie third baseman play deep, ostensibly to avoid being hurt by one of Lajoie's wicked line drives.

Lajoie bunted to the left side six straight times for hits. The seventh time he tried it, a play was made on a runner going to third, so he was given a sacrifice instead of an official at bat. (He later asked the official scorer why he hadn't been given a hit then, too.) His final time up, he grounded to short, and Bobby Wallace threw wildly to first. The official scorer decided that Lajoie would have beaten the play anyway and awarded him a hit.

When pressed by his owner, O'Connor said, "Lajoie outguessed us." O'Connor was promptly fired. And, after all the collusion Cobb won the title, .385 to .384. Chalmers decided to give cars to both men, but the fiasco prompted a policy change for awarding cars and prizes to battling titleholders.

In a strange twist of fate more than 70 years later, *Sporting News* historian Paul MacFarlane discovered that two hits were mistakenly credited to Cobb. An attempt to have the "official" data changed and the title given to Lajoie, thereby breaking Cobb's incredible string of nine consecutive batting titles, was taken to Commissioner Bowie Kuhn. But he ruled against Lajoie, and the records stood.

Losing the batting title didn't diminish Lajoie's popularity. In 1912 Cleveland threw a "Nap Lajoie Day" that featured a 9-foot floral horseshoe decorated with 1,009 silver dollars. In 1914 Lajoie became the third ballplayer to reach 3,000 hits, joining Cap Anson and Honus Wagner. But he was having problems with his new manager, Joe Birmingham, and was sold to the A's before the 1915 season.

In 1915 he set the AL record for most errors by a second baseman in a game, with five, and left the majors after hitting .246 in 113 games in 1916. At age 42 he became player-manager for the Toronto Maple Leafs and hit .380 to lead the league. He was managing the Indianapolis club in the American Association when World War I forced the league to close down for the season. Lajoie left baseball for good.

Lajoie was elected into the Hall of Fame in 1937. He died in 1959. His records speak volumes, and he was immensely popular. As Tommy Leach said, "Even when the sonofagun was blocking you off the base, he was smiling and kidding with you."

★ Bob Lemon ★

Righthander Bob Lemon set a baseball record that may never be equaled: he appeared tireless at his own induction into the Hall of Fame.

An independent thinker, Lemon was responsible for creating two pearls of baseball wisdom. He declared that "baseball is a kids' game adults just screw up," and also noted, more personally, that "I had my bad days on the field, but I didn't take them home with me. I left them in a bar along the way."

Although he never meant to be a pitcher, he became a 20-game winner seven times and led or tied for the league lead in wins three times. On a pitching staff that featured such ace moundsmen as Bob Feller, Mike Garcia, and Early Wynn, Lemon led the league numerous times in starts, innings pitched, and complete games. An all-around talent, his 37 career homers rank him second, behind only Wes Ferrell, on the all-time list for pitchers.

Lemon, whose father had played in the Pacific Coast League, got his start as an infielder with an American Legion team managed by the father of teammate Vern Stephens. Scout John Engel signed Lemon, at age 17, to a $100-a-month Indians contract. The young prospect advanced steadily through the Indians' system, leading the Eastern League in runs scored and tying for the lead in hits at Wilkes-Barre in 1941.

In 1943 Lemon entered the Navy and joined a service team in Aiea, Hawaii. When pitchers Fred Hutchinson and Lou Ciola became injured, Manager Billy Herman, aware that Lemon had a pretty good curve, started him. He did well enough to make an American League-National All-Star series in Hawaii.

After the war Lemon got off to a shaky start. He was shifted to the outfield and was on the verge of being farmed out when the comments of his fellow war veterans saved him. Detroit catcher Birdie Tebbetts said, "You may think he's a third baseman, but I know he's a pitcher. I hit against him during the war in the Pacific, and if I never have to bat against him again it will be too soon."

Aware that Ted Williams, Johnny Pesky, and Bill Dickey felt the same way, Indians Manager Lou Boudreau decided it was worth a shot. Lemon, convinced he was a major league hitter, fought the change every step of the way. For his first two seasons as a member of the Indians he refused to wear a toeplate, thinking he would return to being a position player at any time.

It took a no-hitter to make Lemon invest in the toeplate. On the night of June 30, 1948, he no-hit the Detroit Tigers before 49,628 fans. That year he was named to the AL All-Star team for the first of seven straight years and also won Games 2 and 6 of the World Series against the Braves.

Lemon and company helped the Indians to another pennant in 1954, with the Indians winning a record 111 regular-season games. In the World Series, however, they were swept by Leo Durocher's Giants. Lemon lost Game 1 on pinch hitter Dusty Rhodes's cheap tenth-inning homer. He lost Game 4 as well.

After injuring his leg in 1957, Lemon ended his playing days in the minors with San Diego the following year. When he retired, Ted Williams said, "Along with Hal Newhouser and Spud Chandler, he was one of the three toughest pitchers I ever faced."

He went on to scout for the Indians, Royals, and Yankees, manage in the International and Pacific Coast Leagues, serve as a pitching coach in the majors, and manage the Royals, White Sox, and Yankees.

In July 1978 he replaced Billy Martin as manager of the dissension-ridden Yankees and led the rattled Yankees to a victory with his patented low-key style. The Yanks beat Boston in a one-game playoff to win the Eastern Division and, after sweeping Kansas City in the ALCS, won the World Series that year against Los Angeles.

Replaced in June 1979 by Martin, he was brought in to manage the Yankees again in September 1981 and delivered a league championship, but the Yankees lost to the Dodgers in a six-game Series when Yankee reliever George Frazier lost three games. Lemon told reporters, "I've come to realize that the two most important things in life are good friends and a strong bullpen."

After being promised another full season, "win or lose," he was dismissed on April 25 and has been out of baseball since.

Kenny Lofton

Kenny Lofton has won four straight stolen base titles since 1992 — 253 swipes in five years — and the more he steals, the easier it gets.

He stands at first base, motionless, staring innocently. There's no ego to the lead Kenny Lofton takes at first base — that is, he doesn't wander so far off the base that it becomes an insult. Instead, Lofton simply waits. He knows he's quicker than any delivery to the plate, quicker than any catcher's throw to second. Sooner or later, Lofton will defeat you.

As Indians' manager Mike Hargrove put it, "Kenny is one of the few guys I've seen in a baseball uniform who can dominate a game with his speed, distort a game with his speed." He's the '90s version of Henderson, Vince Coleman with muscles, Devon White with the ability to hit line drives.

And beyond any of these attributes, Lofton has an

excellence for subduing fly balls in the gap. It's more than an instinct, it's a gift from the baseball gods. Hitting can be taught. Power can be acquired. Even running speed can be improved, to a degree. But there's no teacher who can make you better at the warning track, where your feet, your hands and timing must be one.

Working the wall is Lofton's real passion. Despite hitting over .300 three straight years — including a .349 average in 1994 that almost won him a batting title — it's the defense that still means the most to Lofton.

"It's great stealing all those bases, and the home runs were nice, but to me, the biggest thing I can do to frustrate the other team is to make a great catch — a diving catch, or one at the wall. That can change a game all by itself," Lofton said.

"The timing is what great defense is all about," he told *Bergen Record* reporter Bob Klapisch. "You got to have a great jump, and running fast helps, but at the last second, it's about timing. And that's something that can't really be taught to you. You have to have it on your own."

Incredibly, Lofton discovered these instincts only after his junior year of college. Lofton declined to try out for Arizona's baseball team in his freshman and sophomore years, then played just five games in his junior year. Until then, Lofton's world revolved around basketball; he was a point guard for a Wildcats team that made it to the Final Four in 1988 and was ranked No. 1 in the nation for much of 1989.

A native of East Chicago, Indiana, Lofton learned about will power and discipline from his grandmother, Rosie Person. She raised Lofton and six other children, despite losing her eyesight in the early 1970s. Totally blind by the time Lofton reached his teens, Person nevertheless ran an efficient home. Lofton recalls, "she could cook with her eyes closed anyway, so being blind wasn't that big of a deal."

Lofton grew into a fine high school athlete, particularly in baseball, although he was ultimately seduced by basketball. The reason for that, Lofton said, was "Indiana is big basketball country, where all the hype goes towards basketball. My heart belonged to baseball, but I got caught up in the basketball hype."

He was recruited heavily, finally chose Arizona, and projected himself four years hence into the NBA. But Lofton found his dream didn't equal his reality, or as he put it, "I wasn't treated the way I should have been. I was playing someone else's game."

The college offense, at least Arizona's, was more structured than Lofton anticipated, smothering his raw athletic skills. Running well-rehearsed plays were more important than running the game Lofton learned in the street. In fact, Lofton is probably best remembered for a dunk that made Dick Vitale's all-time list, a dunk that Lofton himself described as, "doing a 180, cocking the ball between my legs and then throwing it down backwards over my shoulder."

Eventually, though, Lofton turned back to baseball. He walked on and made Arizona's varsity team late as a junior, and, even though he hardly played, the Astros gambled, taking him in the 17th round of the 1988 draft.

Lofton was rusty as a first-year pro, batting only .214 at Class-A Auburn. He wasn't sure where his baseball career was headed, so he returned to Arizona in 1989 to finish playing hoops. By then the NBA dream had evaporated, but Lofton believes he might have played pro basketball had he attended a different school. Now baseball was all he had.

In 1989, he was quickly promoted to the South Atlantic League, batting .329 after his arrival. In 1990 at Class-A Osceola, Lofton batted .331 with 62 stolen bases. A year later, he jumped all the way to AAA Tucson, and again outhit and outran everyone in his path. By September — when Lofton was hitting .331, leading his team with 17 triples, and leading the entire Pacific Coast League with 168 hits — the Astros were curious enough to summon Lofton to the big leagues.

He hit only .203 in 20 games, striking out 19 times in 74 at bats — at 24, a victim of nerves and inexperience. The Astros considered Lofton too unfinished for an immediate promotion to the bigs, and besides they already had Steve Finley in center. And it was a certainty in Houston's hierarchy, that, in then-GM Bob Watson's words, "Kenny Lofton was not going to beat out Steve Finley."

What the Astros needed, more than another center fielder, was a catcher. Enter Cleveland, which had Eddie Taubensee to offer Houston, and was looking for a center fielder. Even though the Indians were less than impressed with Lofton in his September call-up — GM John Hart conceded Lofton was "terrible" in those 74 at-bats — they were intrigued by the longer-range projections.

Scouts gave Lofton an eight (a scout's highest rating) in speed, but a two in arm-strength. The one description that kept popping up in Lofton's dossier was "crude." Yet, the Indians sought him, and Lofton immediately became the Rookie of the Year in his first summer in Cleveland. He also became the first rookie to lead the league in steals since Luis Aparicio swiped 21 bases in 1956.

How far can Lofton's legs take him? He's only 28, young enough to chase the game's greatest thief, Rickey Henderson, and pass him, looking innocent all the while.

★ Al Lopez ★

One of the most successful and revered managers ever, Al Lopez also held the career mark for games caught for four decades.

Lopez's 1954 Indians and his 1959 White Sox were the only teams to interrupt the Yankees' string of American League dominance from 1949 through 1964, and during his first nine years as a manager, Lopez finished no lower than second place.

He never finished last, defying Leo Durocher's old saw about nice guys because Lopez was universally liked in the baseball world. After his retirement in 1969, baseball insiders made it their business to stop in on "Senor Tampa" during their citrus circuit rounds. His serene wisdom earned him a guru-like status among those in the know.

Lopez ranks eighteenth on the all-time managerial win list with a 1,410-1,004 mark in 17 seasons. Among managers with at least 1,000 wins, only John McGraw, his direct ancestor on the managerial family tree, Joe McCarthy, and Frank Selee have a better winning percentage than Lopez's .584 mark.

Lopez was the son of Spanish immigrants who came to Tampa's Ybor City section from Madrid to work in the area's cigar factories. Young Lopez also worked in the factories during school vacations. Many scouts dismissed him as a catching prospect because he carried only 165 pounds on his 5-foot-11 frame. But while the Washington Senators were training in Tampa in 1925, Manager Bucky Harris let Lopez catch batting practice and warm up pitchers, including Walter Johnson, an experience Lopez never forgot. That taste of the big leagues also won Lopez an opportunity to catch for Tampa's team in the Florida State League.

He played there two years, was promoted to Jacksonville in the Southeastern League, and was purchased by the Dodgers in 1928 for $10,000. Dodgers Manager Wilbert Robertson, a former catcher, was impressed after Lopez collected a couple of hits off Dazzy Vance in an exhibition game. He also liked Lopez's catching ability; Lopez had a good glove and strong arm, but his biggest asset as a catcher was his ability to handle pitchers with his gentle, soothing personality. He was persuasive but also comforting, the same qualities that helped him succeed as a manager.

The Dodgers farmed Lopez to Macon in the South Atlantic League in 1928, and brought him to the majors late that September. After a year with Atlanta in the Southern League, Lopez came to Brooklyn for good in 1930.

In his first full season in the majors, Lopez hit .309 and knocked in 57 runs, which would prove to be career highs. Lopez played in the 1934 and 1941 All-Star Games mainly on the strength of his fielding. The Dodgers sent him to the Boston Bees in December 1935, where Lopez twice reached a career-best eight homers. In June 1940 Boston traded him to the Pittsburgh Pirates, where he played until 1946. Prior to the 1947 season, Lopez was traded to Cleveland, where he played 61 games and hit .262.

Lopez led NL catchers in fielding four times and tied the NL record by allowing no passed balls in 114 games in 1941. In 1946 he broke the career games caught record of Rick Ferrell and retired with a career total of 1,918 games behind the plate, including a record 1,861 in the National League. Bob Boone broke Lopez's major league mark in 1987, and Gary Carter topped his NL mark in 1991. Lopez now ranks fifth on the career catching list, and his 12 seasons of catching at least 100 games ranks second to only Johnny Bench's 13.

Lopez's playing career prepared him for managing not just through his own experiences but through exposure to many of the great managers of his time. In Brooklyn he apprenticed under McGraw lieutenant Robertson, then Max Carey, Robertson's hand-picked successor, and Casey Stengel, who became a devoted admirer of Lopez. In Boston Lopez learned pitching philosophy from Bill McKechnie, and after another couple of years with Stengel, he played under another McGraw disciple, Frankie Frisch, in Pittsburgh.

After finishing his playing career with Cleveland in 1947, Lopez accepted a managing job at Indianapolis, Cleveland's top farm club. He won the pennant in 1948 and finished second the next two years. In 1951 he took over as manager of the Indians after Lou Boudreau was traded to Boston. There Lopez began his decade-long rivalry with former mentor Stengel.

In the 1951 race, Lopez's Indians had the best pitching in the league, tied the Yankees for the league lead in home runs, and briefly overtook the Bombers in mid-September before finishing five games out. They led the league in homers again in 1952 and would through 1955, featuring sluggers Larry Doby, Al Rosen, and Luke Easter. The Yankees took an early lead in 1953 and were never challenged, but Lopez turned the tables in 1954, directing the Indians to an AL-record 111 wins. That team featured the great pitching staff of Mike Garcia, Early Wynn, and Bob Lemon.

Lopez deserves credit for developing the bullpen duo of righty Ray Narleski and lefty Don Mossi. Lopez and Leo Durocher of the New York Giants, his opponent in the 1954 World Series, pioneered the use of two late-inning specialists. Lopez primarily went by the book, but Durocher — with two righthanders, one a knuckleballer — had to rely on hunches. In the Series the Giants upset the heavily favored Indians in four games, thanks to the bat of pinchhitter Dusty Rhodes and the glove of center fielder Willie Mays.

After two more second-place finishes, Lopez moved to the Chicago White Sox. In Chicago his light-hitting personnel and the spacious ballpark made home runs scarce, so Lopez changed tactics. Yet his success continued, just as McGraw's had when he adapted from the dead ball to the Babe Ruth era. Lopez's White Sox, with Luis Aparicio and Jim Rivera, became the first team in the 1950s and the first AL team since 1945 to steal 100 bases. He juggled a lot of live arms and finished second to the Yankees before winning the pennant in 1959. In the World Series they ran into a hot reliever, Larry Sherry of the Dodgers, and lost in six games.

A series of wrongheaded trades by owner Bill Veeck left the Sox full of holes after that pennant-winning season, and in 1960 Lopez finished third for the first time in his career. He posted three more second-place finishes in 1963, 1964 by only one game, and 1965, before retiring. He returned to the White Sox as a favor to the ownership in 1968, replacing the fiery Eddie Stanky, who had burned out in the middle of the season. Lopez stayed on a few weeks of 1969, posting the only losing records of his managerial tenure.

Lopez was inducted into the Hall of Fame in 1977 and proved that McGraw's managerial heritage could prosper in kinder, gentler hands, without bluster, self-promotion, and all the yelling. The use of the running game and percentage use of relievers, as well as motivating players through something other than fear, were elements of Lopez's style that became standard in baseball during the 1960s. Most importantly, Lopez managed according to his personnel, recognizing their abilities and limitations.

Dennis Martinez

After seven full seasons of major league baseball, Dennis Martinez was a world champion, an 89-game winner, and a 28-year-old drunk.

Martinez's skill and stamina on the mound — five seasons with 14 or more wins, leading the American

League in both complete games (18) and innings (292) in 1979 — was matched only by his ability to drink all night. His native Nicaragua was in constant strife, and so was Martinez's life.

The Orioles won the World Series in 1983, but Martinez didn't make a single appearance on the mound. He had gone from a 16-game winner in 1982 and a league-leading 14 wins in the strike-shortened '81 season to a 16-game loser with world champion Baltimore, a team that won 98 regular season games.

Martinez has not had a drink since. In the meantime, he has won 142 games for three clubs, pitched in three All-Star games, thrown a perfect game and become a grandfather; yet it took 12 years for Martinez to make it to the World Series again.

It was all part of a plan. "The reason we signed Dennis," says Cleveland Indians general manager John Hart, "was that if we ever got to the postseason, this was a guy we could trust with a big game."

With the Indians facing elimination in Game 6 of the 1995 World Series, Martinez struggled through 4⅔ innings, allowing nine base runners — and no runs. The Tribe would have to be nearly perfect that day to beat Tom Glavine and the Atlanta Braves. The home run surrendered by Martinez's replacement, Jim Poole, was the difference in the 1-0 game that decided the Series.

Despite pitching most of 1995 with a torn ligament in his knee, Martinez won his first eight decisions of the year and finished with the third-lowest ERA in the league (3.08). He is still a workhorse, leading the staff with 187 innings and tossing two shutouts. Offseason arthroscopic surgery has made Martinez feel like a new man. (He finished first in a popularity poll in his native Nicaragua last year and many want him to run for president.)

His career might have been over a decade ago if the Orioles hadn't traded him to the Montreal Expos in 1987 for Rene Gonzalez, who hit .221 over his four-year career in Baltimore. Martinez's ERA, which had been on the bad side of 5.00 his last three seasons with the O's, dropped like the temperature on a winter night in Quebec.

His ERA in Montreal was 3.18 or below for all but two of his eight seasons there, hitting a major league low 2.39 in 1991. He led the National League with nine complete games and five shutouts that year, culminating with his perfect game in Dodger Stadium on July 28, 1991. In all, Martinez won in double digits seven times and hurled 220 innings or more six straight years with the Expos.

Now, all the resurrected Martinez wants is a fourth trip to the World Series. "I am not too old yet, but I like it when people say you can't do something because you're too old," says the 40-year-old hurler. "Every once in a while, you need a tire replacement and then you feel like a new car again."

Sam McDowell

For six years in the late 1960s, "Sudden Sam" McDowell was one of the game's dominant pitchers.

At 6-foot-5 he was big and strong, and he had an intimidating fastball, a tricky curve, and an elusive changeup. From 1965 through 1970 he averaged 275 strikeouts a year, more than one an inning, earning him the nickname, "the American League Sandy Koufax."

With his classic over-the-top delivery reminiscent of Koufax and Warren Spahn, he averaged less than seven hits allowed per nine innings during his career. But his skills disappeared abruptly. Three years after he led the AL with 304 strikeouts and 305 innings pitched in 1970, he was 6-10 in 135 innings with two teams. Two years later he was reduced to 34 innings of mop-up work in his final major league season.

McDowell was always trying to outdo himself. In his first big league appearance, he was sailing along with a three-hit shutout (five strikeouts, five walks) in the seventh inning when he threw a pitch so hard he fractured two of his ribs. McDowell was often criticized for trying to outsmart hitters when he didn't need to. He admitted as much himself. "It's not fun throwing fastballs to guys who can't hit them. The real challenge is getting them out on stuff they can hit," he once said.

Raised by a demanding, sports-obsessed father, McDowell couldn't deal with the pressure of professional competition, and eventually became an alcoholic. Now in recovery, he consults with numerous major league teams every year, assisting players who have similar problems with the bottle. McDowell doesn't want to see other players' careers ended by alcoholism in the same way that his was.

"Baseball is the greatest and worst thing that ever happened to me," he once said. "Not because people asked too much of me, but because I asked too much of myself. As it turned out, my talent was a curse. The curse was the way I handled it and didn't handle it. . . . I was the biggest, most hopeless, and most violent drunk in baseball."

Major league hurler Dick Radatz recalled, "We thought he was just stupid. It turned out he was never sober." But Radatz added, "I was always in awe of the arm that McDowell had, despite the drinking problem. He had one of the best arms of all time, a command of all the pitches, but he always wanted to trick people with his changeup or something else."

In 1960 McDowell was signed straight out of Central Catholic High School in Pittsburgh to a Cleveland contract for a $75,000 bonus. He was not yet 18 years old. In addition to his baseball skills he also excelled at basketball, football, swimming, tennis, and track. In his first year in the minors he fanned 100 batters in 105 innings. In 1961, with Salt Lake City of the Pacific Coast League, he struck out 156 but walked 152. That performance earned him a trip to the majors — where he promptly broke his ribs.

During the next three years he made brief visits to the majors, until 1964 when he put together an 11-6 record and an impressive 177 strikeouts in 173 innings. The next season he was absolutely overpowering. He recorded a league-leading 2.18 ERA and struck out 325 men, the fourth-best season strikeout total ever, in only 273 innings. McDowell had become only the third AL pitcher ever to pass the 300K mark. The league batted only .185 against him, a league low. Unfortunately, there was only one Cy Young Award given in 1965, and it went to Sandy Koufax.

In 1966 a sore arm reduced McDowell's innings pitched by 80. But he still put together back-to-back one-hitters and led the AL in strikeouts and shutouts. In 1967

Jim Lonborg fanned 10 more men than McDowell to keep him from winning his third consecutive strikeout crown. That year Indians pitchers sent 1,189 batters down on strikes, setting a record later broken by Houston.

During the "Year of the Pitcher" in 1968, McDowell brought his ERA down by two runs per game, to 1.81. On May 1 McDowell struck out 16 Oakland A's. On July 12, again against Oakland, he fanned 15 batters. For the second straight year the Indians led the league in batters fanned. In fact, the 1968 Cleveland staff is the only pitching crew in history to strike out more batters than it allowed hits to. The Tribe finished in third place, their best showing in nearly 10 years.

The following season was more of the same for the talented, if erratic, fireballer. With a league-leading 279 strikeouts and four shutouts, he won more games than he ever had before, with 18. But his team didn't fare as well as they had the previous year. McDowell was the only pitcher with more than six decisions to post a winning record, and the Indians lost 99 times, finishing 46½ games behind Baltimore.

He had his first and only 20-win season in 1970, leading the AL both in innings pitched and strikeouts. On May 6 he fanned 15 Chicago White Sox. Exactly two months later he struck out 15 Washington Senators. His 304 strikeouts were 74 more than runner-up Mickey Lolich's, total and the *Sporting News* named him Pitcher of the Year.

McDowell wanted a large salary increase for 1971. Alvin Dark, then both the Cleveland field and general manager, balked at the $100,000 salary McDowell was asking for. Together they worked out a complicated pact based largely on incentives for specific performance levels; if McDowell reached the stated performance goals he could earn as much as $92,000.

Commissioner Bowie Kuhn voided the contract because at the time performance bonuses were against the rules. Kuhn fined Cleveland $5,000 for the mistake. McDowell was outraged; he left the team and demanded that he be declared a free agent. For that move, the Indians suspended him.

He returned after a few days and signed a new contract, but spent most of the summer sulking. His stats dropped precipitously: from 304 to 192 strikeouts, from 305 to 215 innings pitched, and an ERA increase of nearly half a run. He again led the league in walks, but with 22 more than the previous season, and in 91 fewer innings. His 153 free passes were 32 more than the AL's next-wildest pitcher that year.

The Indians and McDowell were ready to part company. In November 1971 McDowell was sent to San Francisco along with Frank Duffy for Gaylord Perry. Perry was four years older than McDowell, but the deal was a steal for the Indians. Perry's 24 victories the next year were more than McDowell would win in the remaining four years of his career.

A 1972 10-win season in San Francisco wasn't impressive enough to keep McDowell from being sold to the Yankees the following June, where he went 5-8 in 1973 and 1-6 in 1974, after moving to the bullpen. The Yanks released him, and his hometown Pirates picked him up for the 1975 season, during which he appeared in only 14 games, finishing 2-1.

During his career, the pitcher that Reggie Jackson called "Instant Heat" struck out 10 or more batters 74 times, fourth lifetime behind Nolan Ryan, Sandy Koufax, and Steve Carlton. His career average of 8.86 strikeouts per game is topped only by Ryan and Koufax.

Dale Mitchell

Dale Mitchell, the eighth-toughest man to strike out in major league history, is best remembered for a strikeout. It came in his next-to-last major league at bat, as a member of the Brooklyn Dodgers, concluding an 11-year career in which all but two and a half months were spent with the Cleveland Indians.

Mitchell pinch hit for Sal Maglie in Game 5 of the 1956 World Series and was called out on a 1-2 pitch by umpire Babe Pinelli, working his last major league game behind the plate. Mitchell's strikeout was the final out of Don Larsen's perfect game.

Mitchell contended to his death, and films seem to confirm, that the pitch was outside. In fairness to Pinelli, he'd seen a lot more strikeouts up close than Mitchell, who fanned only 119 times in 3,984 regular-season at bats, or once in every 33.5 at bats. In post-1942 records, Mitchell also owns the fourth- and sixth-best single-season marks for avoiding the whiff, fanning once in every 58.2 at bats in 1949 and once in every 56.8 at bats in 1952.

A left-handed leadoff man and left fielder, Mitchell came up with the Indians in September 1946 and hit .432. A pure contact hitter, Mitchell walked nearly three times as often as he struck out during his 11-year career, yet never more than 67 times in a season. He hit singles, 973 of them among his 1,244 hits, and reached double figures in homers only twice, with a career high of 13 in 1953.

During his official rookie year Mitchell batted .316, fifth best in the American League and the first of six .300 marks in his first seven years in the big leagues. For the 1948 world champion Indians, Mitchell reached career highs with 204 hits, a .336 batting average, 30 doubles, a 21-game hitting streak (which he matched in 1951), and 13 steals. He finished his career with 45 steals but was caught stealing 47 times.

He went one-for-five in the Tribe's pennant playoff game against the Boston Red Sox in 1948. In the World Series against the Boston Braves he went hitless in his first six at bats before singling to lead off the fifth inning of Game 2. He eventually scored on Lou Boudreau's single that knocked out Warren Spahn in Cleveland's 4-1 win, which evened the Series.

Cleveland won Game 3, 2-0, and after the Braves scored three runs in the top of the first in Game 4 against Bob Feller, Mitchell did the unlikely. He led off the bottom of the first with a home run, igniting a Cleveland comeback that eventually put the Indians up, 5-4. However, Feller and the bullpen collapsed, and Boston won by a count of 11-5.

In Game 6 Mitchell led off the third with an opposite-field double and scored on another Boudreau hit, giving the Tribe a 1-0 lead. With Cleveland ahead, 4-3, and the tying run on third in the eighth, Bob Kennedy and his better arm replaced Mitchell in left, even though Mitchell led AL outfielders in fielding percentage in 1948 and

1949. Cleveland held on to win the game and the Series.

In 1949 Mitchell had his best all-around season, leading the AL with 203 hits and 23 triples. His .317 batting average and 274 total bases ranked fourth best in the league, and he had his best year on the basepaths, with 10 steals in 13 attempts. In the All-Star Game, as a late-inning replacement for Ted Williams, Mitchell knocked in the final run with a double in the AL's 11-7 win.

In the 1952 All-Star Game, Mitchell was one of three starters from the Indians, but he went hitless in his only at bat of the rain-shortened contest. He finished the 1952 season batting .323, second to Philadelphia's Ferris Fain in the batting race, and hit .300 in 1953, his final year as a regular.

Al Smith replaced Mitchell as the Tribe's leadoff hitter and left fielder in 1954, and Cleveland won 111 games. Mitchell played only seven times in the field and went 14-for-44 as a pinch hitter, a .318 clip. Mitchell made three pinch-hit appearances in the World Series against the New York Giants that season. In the opener he drew a walk batting for Hank Majeski, who had been announced for Dave Philley, right after Willie Mays caught Vic Wertz's 460-foot drive.

Mitchell led the AL in pinch-hit at bats in 1955, going 13-for-45 for a .289 average, and he played eight games at first base and three in the outfield. After Mitchell went 3-for-22 as a pinch hitter and 4-for-30 overall in 1956, the Indians sold him to Brooklyn on July 29. He went 7-for-24 with the Dodgers and appeared in his third World Series. Mitchell failed to deliver in four pinch-hit appearances, including his famous strikeout, and he grounded out to short in his final major league at bat leading off the sixth inning of Game 7.

He retired with a career average of .312 and died in Tulsa, Oklahoma, on January 5, 1987.

Eddie Murray

Eddie Murray produces under pressure.

In the divisional playoff opener, with the Indians trailing Boston, 2-0, he singled in the first run, tripled and hit a two-run homer in Game 2, and started the clinching five-run rally in Game 3 with a single. He hit a two-run homer off Andy Benes in Game 4 of the ALCS, homered in Game 2 of the World Series against Series MVP Tom Glavine, and won Game 3 with a single in the bottom of the twelfth inning in Cleveland's first World Series game in forty-six years.

Murray produces on the field and keeps to himself off it. Eddie Murray is not interested in your questions or your company. He is about hitting, not about baseball politics. If Murray, one of the greatest hitters of our time, remains unnoticed until the day he retires, well, that'll be just fine with him

At the age of 39, Murray is a sure-bet Hall of Famer, already having passed 3000 hits, and he is edging closer to 500 career home runs. There are only two players in major league history who've accomplished that feat, Hank Aaron and Willie Mays. That's breathtaking company, and Murray has joined these legends without so much as an ounce of help from hype.

For reasons that date back to 1979 — when New York

Daily News columnist Dick Young wrote harshly about Murray's family — Eddie has deliberately kept his distance from the press. As a consequence, Murray has kept fans from knowing what makes this hitting machine tick. Teammates say he is an unrivaled, positive influence in the clubhouse, and none other than Cal Ripken credited Murray with having instilled in him the importance of being durable.

In the span of his 19-year career with the Orioles, Dodgers, Mets, and Indians, Murray has played in 96 per cent of his teams' games and been on the disabled list only once. That occurred in 1986 when he missed 25 games because of a pulled hamstring. When Ripken broke Lou Gehrig's consecutive games streak last summer, he bluntly said, "Eddie was one of the biggest influences on my career early on. From Eddie, I understood how important it was to the team to be in the lineup every day."

The beauty of Murray's long career has been his consistency, both in the lineup and in his production. He has driven in more runs than Reggie Jackson, hit more doubles than Babe Ruth, and racked up more total bases than Ted Williams. Yet, for all his accomplishments, despite his 479 career home runs, Murray has never hit 35 home runs in any year, never led the league in any offensive category over a full season, and never won an MVP award. He's had fewer 100-RBI seasons (six) than Gil Hodges and will have the lowest personal best for hits in a year (186) of any of the 20 players to reach 3000 hits.

What those numbers means is that Eddie Murray has been very good for a very long time. He's certainly an intelligent hitter, with an uncanny ability to perform in late innings with runners in scoring position. The Indians were quick to re-sign him for 1996 after his two-year contract expired, and it appears Murray's career will now proceed on a year-by-year basis. While his power numbers have diminished from a decade ago — except for the strike-shortened 1981 season, Murray hit at least 29 homers and drove in at least 100 runs every year between 1980 and 1985 — he's still dangerous.

While the Indians were winning the pennant last year, Murray hit an impressive .323 with 21 homers and 82 RBI. His finest moment came on June 30, when Murray reached the 3000-hit plateau. He did so against the Twins in the Metrodome, and even though the opposing team respectfully played a 60-second tribute to Murray's career on its DiamondVision screen, and a crowd of 27,416 cheered enthusiastically, Murray responded to the moment with typical detachment. He waved briefly and offered a smile, but there wasn't much in the way of celebration from Murray. And he sure didn't gloat.

He later told a press conference, "It was a nice number to reach, but it's nice to get it over with, too." All along, Murray had downplayed the significance of the mark, as far back as 1984, when Ripken asked him, "You ever think about getting to 3000 hits?" Ripken said Murray's reply was, "Doesn't matter."

"Murray didn't blink an eye," Ripken said. "I said, 'You'll get them easy.' But he just wouldn't respond."

Murray was part of a difficult, losing season in New York in 1992, and his aloofness kept his stay with the Mets to two quick years. But in '92, when the Mets wanted to nominate Murray for the Roberto Clemente Award, which baseball bestows upon players with notable efforts in public service, Murray refused to provide a list of his charitable involvements. When the Mets obtained them from his agent, Ron Shapiro, he became upset. Murray simply didn't want anyone to know how and where he helped the needy.

It's not that Murray is unfeeling: he's simply a self-contained man. Former Orioles catcher Rick Dempsey recounted a story from the early 1980s, when the Birds were touring in Japan, facing a team whose pitcher was notorious for knocking down home run hitters. Murray was an obvious target, and he was immediately decked on the first pitch.

Instead of getting angry, Murray calmly dusted himself off and stepped into the batter's box. As the pitch was being delivered, he stepped out and watched it cut the plate in half. That was strike one. Murray then stepped back in, and again backed out just as the pitch was being delivered. Called strike two. As the third and seemingly final pitch was being delivered, Murray pretended to back out, then stepped in and so dramatically crushed the ball, it left the stadium and landed in an adjacent lake.

Dempsey said, "It was the longest home run I've ever seen. No doubt. And I don't think I'll ever see one like it. I felt like we were watching Babe Ruth's called shot in the (1932) World Series."

Former Orioles righthander Mike Boddicker said, "You should've seen the reaction of the Japanese players. And the noise of the crowd was something else." Of course, Murray never said a word to the Japanese pitcher. But his message was delivered nonetheless. That's Murray's way, a hitting scientist who'll never share his secrets. When he does make it to the Hall of Fame, he'll be as much of a mystery then as he is now.

★ Satchel Paige ★

Baseball historians may debate whether Leroy "Satchel" Paige was the finest pitcher the Negro League ever produced, but Bob Feller called him unequivocally "the best pitcher I ever saw."

Whether the discussion centers around his fabulous control or the mystery of his age, Paige remains one of the most fascinating figures in baseball history.

And it wasn't easy for him to play white baseball. When the 40ish Paige came to the major leagues in 1948, the *Sporting News* publisher, J. G. Taylor Spink, was infuriated. "To bring in a pitching rookie of Paige's age is to demean the standards of baseball," Spink wrote.

"I demeaned the big leagues considerable that year," Paige later replied. "I win six and lose one."

Paige was born in Mobile, Alabama, the seventh of 11 children, at some point around the turn of the century. The official date is 1906, but 1903 and 1908 have also been suggested. He was a scrappy youth, and in school he was involved in numerous battles. He was sent to the Industrial School for Negro Children at Mount Meigs, Alabama, for truancy, breaking windows, and fighting. He was not released until he was 17. Even then his ability to throw a baseball attracted attention.

Paige signed on with a local black semipro team, the Mobile Tigers. In 1924 he won roughly 30 games and lost only 1. He pitched with the Tigers until 1926, when the Chattanooga Black Lookouts of the Negro Southern League offered him $50 a month to pitch for them.

Paige's mother, mindful of the trouble he had once found himself in, was concerned about her boy leaving the Mobile area. But team owner Alex Herman promised Mrs. Paige he would take exceedingly good care of her son—and for the first season he did, making the youth keep regular hours and even doubling Paige's salary after the first month.

From the beginning, Paige amazed all observers with his fastball and control. Soon he was a celebrity in the world of southern black baseball. He had his own roadster, played guitar with Louis Armstrong's orchestra, and supped with Jelly Roll Morton.

Although record-keeping was lax at the time, it was estimated that he was winning 60 games a year and striking out 10 to 18 batters per contest. Finally, in 1931 Paige went north to one of the finest Black teams around, Gus Greenlee's Pittsburgh Crawfords. His salary was $200 a month.

With the Crawfords, Paige teamed with Josh Gibson to form one of baseball's most impressive batteries. Gibson hit gargantuan home runs and Paige provided the pitching; in a three-year period, Paige won an estimated 105 games, while losing only 37.

Paige was overwhelming, but he was also constantly on the road. "One day I pitched a no-hitter for the Crawfords against the Homestead Grays" in Washington, recalled Paige. "That was on July 4; I remember because somebody kept shooting off firecrackers every time I got another batter out. Those firecrackers were still popping when I ran out of the park, hopped in my car, and drove all night to Chicago. I got there just in time to beat Jim Trent and the Chicago American Giants, 1-0, in 12 innings. And the same day, somebody said I was supposed to be in Cleveland. Can you beat that?"

While in Pittsburgh, Paige met a young waitress at Greenlee's Crawford Grill. Her name was Janet Howard, and they later married. Family responsibilities gave Paige a desire to earn bigger salaries than Greenlee was paying (now up to $700 a month), so in 1934 Paige pulled up what little stakes he had and signed with a semipro team in Bismarck, North Dakota.

When he arrived in Bismarck, Paige set out to prove that he was as good as his reputation. He set up a matchstick on a stick beside home plate and knocked it off in 13 of 20 tries. Then he let loose with his fastball. He was so fast and his ball moved in such a way that the Bismarck catcher wouldn't warm him up without wearing shin guards and a chest protector.

Throughout the 1930s, Paige crisscrossed the country. In 1934 he also pitched for the Cuban House of David team, at one point even donning a false beard. To while away winters, he put together the Satchel Paige All-Stars. In one three-season span, the team won 128 games (including 40 against squads featuring big leaguers) and lost only 23.

Paige engaged major league opposition numerous times during his career. No batter who faced him ever downplayed his ability. "Paige was the best pitcher I ever saw," said Bob Feller. "I'm judging him on the way he overpowered or outwitted some of the best major league hitters of his day."

Cardinals pitcher Dizzy Dean once remarked, "If me and Satch were together in St. Louis, we would clinch the pennant by July and go fishing from then until World Series time." In one 13-inning matchup in 1934, Paige bested Dean, 1-0, and struck out 17.

In 1935 Paige again pitched for Bismarck and the House of David, but he soon found himself on the road to a far more exotic destination, the Dominican Republic. Dominican dictator Rafael L. Trujillo was recruiting a baseball team and sent an emissary to the United States with $30,000 and orders to recruit the best team he could find. He assembled a good team, featuring future Hall of Famers Paige, Gibson, and James "Cool Papa" Bell.

After arriving in Santo Domingo, the Negro Leaguers saw that this game was genuine hardball. Heavily-armed soldiers ringed the ballparks. It was win — or else. "You could see Trujillo lining up his army. They began to look like a firing squad," said Paige. Against the Estrellas de Oriente team, the nervous Americans lost the first three games, then bore down and won the final four contests. "You never saw ol' Satch throw harder," Paige admitted.

Greenlee offered Paige $450 to return to the Crawfords. "I wouldn't throw ice cubes for that amount of money," sniffed Paige. When Greenlee sold the pitcher's contract to the Newark Eagles, Paige couldn't have cared less; he packed his bags and headed for Mexico. While playing in Mexico in 1938, he seriously damaged his arm, and his pitching future seemed doubtful.

J. L. Wilkinson of the Kansas City Monarchs bought Paige's contract from Newark, figuring he would use the hurler as a draw for a sort of junior varsity version of the club. Paige would play first and pitch occasionally. Wilkinson got one of the biggest bargains in pitching history. Soon Paige was better than ever, and he helped lead the Monarchs to Negro American League titles every year from 1939 to 1942.

Scheduled to pitch in the 1942 Negro World Series, Paige, now with the Kansas City Monarchs, was stopped for speeding and was delayed from getting to Shibe Park to pitch against the Grays. He didn't arrive until the third inning. The Grays were ahead, 4-3, and had a runner on first. Paige, with no time to loosen up, was inserted into the game. He proceeded to warm up by trying to pick the runner off first. Once he was loose, he pitched to the batter and did just fine, handling the Grays easily for the rest of the game. The Monarchs won, 9-5. It was Paige's third win of the Series.

Paige was the winning pitcher in the 1943 East-West Game (the Negro Leagues' version of the All-Star contest), making him the only pitcher to win two of them. In 1944 he boycotted the game because of management's failure to donate receipts to the war effort.

In 1946 Branch Rickey broke baseball's color barrier when he signed Jackie Robinson. "Somehow I'd always figured it would be me," said Paige. "Maybe it had happened too late, and everybody figured I was too old. Maybe that was why it was Jackie and not me."

Actually, he *was* too old — too old if he were anybody but Satchel Paige. He continued to pitch well against big leaguers in postseason exhibitions (particularly against one squad led by Bob Feller after the 1947 season) and in Negro League competition, but as the 1948 season opened he was still on the Monarchs roster.

Colorful Cleveland Indians owner Bill Veeck decided to give Paige a chance. Despite cries that the Paige signing was just another Veeck publicity stunt, Paige pitched well for the Indians in 1948, giving major league audiences a hint at what a great hurler he still was. After Veeck sold the Indians in 1949, however, Paige was released and went back to barnstorming. But when Veeck acquired the St. Louis Browns, Paige returned to the big leagues.

In 1952 Paige was 12-10 for the Browns, and he pitched a league-leading eight wins in relief and 10 saves. The following season he saved 11 games although his record was only 3-9. He was no wizard with the bat: in 124 major league at bats, Paige had only 12 hits for a batting average of .097.

After leaving the majors, Paige continued to pitch. He barnstormed in 1954 and rejoined the Monarchs in 1955. In 1956 he signed up again with Veeck, who was operating the Miami Marlins in the International League. On August 7, 1956, 51,713 fans saw Paige pitch at the Orange Bowl. He finished the year 11-4 with a 1.86 ERA. In 1957 he was 10-8 and 2.42; in 1958, 10-10 and 2.95. Relations between Paige and Miami management deteriorated, however, and that was his last season with the club.

Paige briefly popped up again with Portland of the Pacific Coast League in 1961 and posted a 2.88 ERA. He later barnstormed with the Indianapolis Clowns. In 1965 Charles Finley brought him back for one more game in Kansas City, and he pitched three shutout innings against the Boston Red Sox. Only Carl Yastrzemski reached him for a hit. In 1968 it was discovered that Paige was only 158 major league days short of qualifying for a $7,000-a-year pension, and he was placed on the Atlanta Braves roster as a coach.

In 1971 Paige was inducted to the Baseball Hall of Fame by the Committee on Negro Leagues. He died in 1982.

★ Gaylord Perry ★

Rule 8.02 of the Official Baseball Rules specifically prohibits a pitcher from either defacing the baseball or applying any foreign substance to it. Section E states that "the umpire shall be the sole judge on whether any portion of this rule has been violated." In other words, don't get caught.

Gaylord Perry openly flaunted this rule for most of his career and was seldom caught. Although the spitball was banned in 1920 and last thrown legally in 1934 by pitcher Burleigh Grimes, who was allowed to use the pitch until his retirement, Perry may have been the most successful spitballer in the history of baseball.

On November 29, 1971, he was traded to the Indians with shortstop Frank Duffy for "Sudden Sam" McDowell. He responded by winning 24 games — and the Cy Young Award — in his first season. In three and a half years with the Tribe Perry won 70 games and would win 314 in a 22-year big league career.

Perry grew up on a small tenant farm in eastern North Carolina. His father was a successful semipro pitcher and taught both Gaylord and his older brother, Jim, the ins and outs of pitching. Both boys were excellent pitchers and basketball players at Williamston High School, and both turned down scholarship offers to play college basketball in favor of professional baseball. Gaylord signed with the New York Giants for a team-record $73,500 in 1958.

Although a crony of his father's had shown Perry how to throw a spitball while the youth was still in high school, the illegal pitch was not yet part of his repertoire; he depended on a good fastball, curve, and changeup. Like brother Jim, Gaylord Perry moved through the minor leagues quickly. After leading the Pacific Coast League with 16 wins for Tacoma in 1961, he was called up to the Giants, who had moved to San Francisco in 1959. Perry then bounced back and forth between San Francisco and Tacoma for several seasons, pitching well in Class AAA but getting roughed up at the major league level.

That all changed in 1964. Disappointed with his performance and impatient with the development of his slider, Perry noticed veteran pitcher Bob Shaw throwing a curious pitch that came in thigh-high, then broke sharply down to the hitter's ankles. Perry asked Shaw to teach him the pitch. It was the spitball, and Perry's future life of crime was assured.

Although Perry took several seasons to learn to control the pitch effectively, it made an immediate difference, and he pitched his way into the Giants starting rotation in 1964. The rules at the time made it easy to get away with using the spitball. Pitchers were allowed to put their fingers to their mouth on the mound. They were supposed to wipe them dry, but a phantom wipe was easy to learn. Some have since claimed that at least 25 percent of major league pitchers were using the pitch in the mid-1960s.

Unlike a fastball, which is released with backspin, the spitball tumbles forward, making a sudden, sharp drop as it approaches the plate. Saliva on the first two fingers of the pitching hand allows the pitcher to "squeeze" the ball at the point of release and impart a forward spin.

Perry put it all together in 1966. With both his spitball and slider under control, he was nearly unbeatable and became an overnight sensation in his eighth year of pro ball. He won 21 games and was the winning pitcher in the All-Star Game. On July 22 he struck out 15 batters in a game against the Phillies. He finished the season with 201 strikeouts and walked only 40.

He pitched even better in 1967, lowering his ERA from 2.99 to 2.61. During one stretch he hurled 40 consecutive scoreless innings. But he lost 10 one-run decisions and finished the season with a record of 15-17. The spitball suddenly became a hot topic. As long as no one pitcher was too effective with it, few people complained. But Perry's success was out of the ordinary. Before the 1968 season, Rule 8.02 was amended to forbid the pitcher to put his hand to his mouth.

Perry adapted. All winter he practiced throwing a similar pitch using grease instead of saliva. He stood before a mirror practicing the artful transfer of grease from his belt or another part of his uniform to his hands. In his first few spring outings Perry was shelled, but he mastered the new pitch just as the season began and resumed his winning ways.

Everyone knew he was throwing the pitch, but no one could quite figure out how he was loading the ball. Perry became a master at decoying the batter and using the spitball as a psychological weapon. His pitching hand went to his cap and his neck, and then he'd adjust his belt,

wipe his hand on his shirt, return to his cap, and appear to be delivering a speech in sign language before finally releasing the ball. By that time the batter was either overanxious or convinced Perry was throwing a spitter.

When asked about his success, Perry just smiled and gave the credit to his "super-slider." Nobody was fooled, but nobody could catch him in the act either. Perry pitched a no-hitter against Bob Gibson and St. Louis on September 17, 1968.

In 1970 Perry won 23 games and finished second in the Cy Young voting to Gibson. His brother, Jim, won 24 games for the Twins and won the American League's Cy Young Award. They were the first brothers to win 20 games in the same season.

San Francisco traded Perry to Cleveland in 1971, and he responded with the best season of his career, winning the Cy Young Award with a sparkling 1.92 ERA and leading the AL with 24 wins. The trade set a pattern for the remainder of his career. After several successful seasons, he'd be traded to a team that believed his presence would either help them to a pennant or put fans in the park. The club usually failed to match Perry's performance, and the pattern would be repeated.

The Perry brothers were united in Cleveland in 1974 and the first half of 1975. Gaylord won 21 games, including 15 straight, one shy of the AL record, and Jim added 17 victories in 1974. But on May 20, 1975, Jim was traded to the A's for Blue Moon Odom. Less than a month later Gaylord was dealt to Texas for Jim Bibby, Jackie Brown, Rick Waits, and $100,000.

After winning 15 games in both 1976 and 1977, the Rangers traded Perry to San Diego in January 1978. He won 21 games for the Padres that season and his second Cy Young Award. He remains the only major league pitcher to win a Cy Young Award in each league.

Perry then signed with Texas again and the Rangers traded him at midseason to the Yankees. He played with Atlanta in 1981, Seattle in 1982, and Kansas City in 1983.

Perry won his 300th game with Seattle in 1982 and retired after the 1983 season with 314 wins. The 529 victories by the Perry brothers are second only to the Niekros' 539. One of the few negatives of Gaylord Perry's career is that, in 22 seasons of major league service, he never appeared in a World Series. Only Phil Niekro played longer, 24 seasons, without appearing in a Fall Classic.

Perry published an entertaining biography, *Me and the Spitter*, in 1974. After he retired, Perry returned to North Carolina and became a farmer. He was inducted into the Baseball Hall of Fame on his third try, in 1991.

Jim Perry

James Evan Perry was the older half of the best strikeout-hurling brother combination ever to pitch in the major leagues.

Perry entered the American League in 1959 with the Indians. He whiffed 79 batters in 153 innings and won 12 games, posting a 2.65 ERA and taking second place in Rookie of the Year balloting. The following year he led the AL in wins, with 18, and hurled a circuit-topping four shutouts. In his third year, as Gaylord Perry was being readied for his major league debut, Jim Perry was named to the AL All-Star team.

Early in the 1963 season the Indians traded Perry to the Minnesota Twins. In 1970, his eighth year with the Minnesota Twins, he led the AL in wins, with 24, and won his league's Cy Young Award. That same year, the Perry brothers became the first sibling pitchers to face each other in the All-Star Game.

Jim Perry had four more great seasons. In 1974, his last great year, he and Gaylord pitched together on the Indians. Jim hurled 17 wins, with a 2.96 ERA. He retired following the 1975 season, after being traded to Oakland with Dick Bosman for Blue Moon Odom and cash. He finished with 215 wins and 1,576 strikeouts in 3,285⅔ innings.

Vic Power

Vic Power was the first Indian to win a Gold Glove, and he took home the first seven that were awarded to American League first basemen, four of them while wearing the Tribe's colors.

The man also had style with a capital "S." Until he came along there was an unwritten rule about fielding: catch the ball with two hands. Power's legacy to baseball is the one-handed catch.

Power originally wanted to be an artist, but his ambitions changed at age 13, when his father died from tetanus after an industrial accident. Young Power decided to be a lawyer so he could bring suit against his father's former employers. But in 1947 he dropped that idea and signed with Caguas of the Puerto Rican winter league for $250 per month. The next winter his salary doubled, and he was able to afford a house in San Juan for his family.

In 1949 former Negro League catcher Quincy Trouppe brought Power to Canada to play with Drummondville in Quebec's outlaw Provincial League, a circuit that featured many of the former Mexican League jumpers. He hit .341. In 1950 the Provincial League joined Major League Baseball, and Power batted .334, with 105 RBIs.

Yankee scout Tom Greenwade, who had signed Mickey Mantle, Elston Howard, and Bobby Murcer, traveled north to check out Power. While Greenwade watched, Power committed an error, and Greenwade reported that he was a poor fielder. However, the scout liked him as a hitter, and the Yankees paid $7,500 for him.

In Drummondville, Power became Power. The first baseman had actually been named Victor Pellot. However, "pellot" had unfortunate sexual connotations in French, and Quebec was largely a French-speaking culture. He took his mother's maiden name.

Power reached the high minors quickly. In 1951 he was sent to Syracuse, where he batted .291. With Kansas City in 1952 he batted .331 and led the Triple A American Association in doubles, with 40, and triples, with 17. Rumors circulated widely that Power would become the first black Yankee.

The Yankees, however, wanted a more tractable man than Vic Power, who was mystified by American racial mores and was forever either challenging them or running afoul of them. Once in spring training with the Yankees, the team bus passed through Georgia and halted for a rest room stop. "They called the sheriff," Power recalled. "He arrested me, and only after the Yankees begged him did he agree to a $500 bond. I never went back for the trial and I guess they're still looking for me.

"But things like that were always happening. I wasn't allowed to go to the white hotel. I stayed in the best house in the colored section, and that was usually a funeral parlor. I slept with dead people at night. Or let's say I tried to sleep. I was too scared most of the time. Puerto Ricans are a very superstitious people. Yet the worst thing about all this was that I had to compete with well-rested guys. Maybe that's why I didn't make the Yankees."

In Kansas City, Power compounded the Yankees' displeasure by keeping company with white women, hardly the image the conservative George Weiss wished to project. He kept Power at Kansas City again in 1953, and the first baseman led the American Association in hits, with 217, for a .349 average. At season's end, Power was finally placed on New York's 40-man roster.

Now it seemed certain that Power would finally make the Yankees, but it was not to be. In December 1953, Power and five others were sent to the Philadelphia Athletics in exchange for five players. The first black Yankee turned out to be Power's Kansas City roommate, Elston Howard.

The A's were a poor team, but Power soon established himself as the slickest first baseman in baseball despite Yankee owner Dan Topping's parting comment that he was a "poor fielder." Power won a Gold Glove in each of the first seven years it was awarded to a first baseman. One statistic is telling. He led American League first basemen in assists six times, even though he was righthanded at a position that gives a lefty a huge edge.

It wasn't just that he was competent or even brilliant. He was *flashy*, and although he hated to hear it, he *was* a showboat—and probably the best-fielding first baseman between Hal Chase and Keith Hernandez.

In an age when fielders were cautioned to make all catches with both hands, Power flagrantly used only one and used it better than anyone else used two. "If the guy who invented the game wanted players to catch with two hands, he'd have put two gloves on 'em," he jibed. And when Vic Power said it, somehow it made sense.

Power was also a relatively good hitter. He finished with a .284 lifetime batting average, including five seasons above .300.

In June 1958 the Athletics, now in Kansas City, traded Power and Woodie Held to Cleveland for Roger Maris and two other players. With the Indians that year Power stole home twice in one game. In the eighth inning he did it again to tie the score. In the ninth he did it once more to win the game.

In April 1962 he was traded to Minnesota and there took young Tony Oliva under his wing. Oliva was impressionable. Once, Power told him that Ted Williams credited shoveling snow for his great hitting ability. All winter Oliva kept busy shoveling out Power's sidewalk and driveway.

Power was sent to the Angels in a three-way trade involving Cleveland in June 1964. With that club Power would amuse himself, singing Spanish songs with owner Gene Autry and indulging in less innocent amusements elsewhere. The Angels sold Power to the Phillies in September 1964, as Gene Mauch's club desperately tried to shore up its defense and win a pennant.

In November, Power was sold back to the Angels. At season's end he had a chance to play in Japan but turned it down thinking he would pursue a career in pictures. His only role was as a bit player in a Western.

Power retired after the 1965 season and returned to Puerto Rico in 1967, where he managed an amateur team and ran instructional clinics for children. He also secured a government position involving sports and scouted for the Angels. When his obituary is written one day in the future, Vic Power will be remembered as the player who taught the rest of baseball that they could catch the ball with one hand.

Allie Reynolds

Along with Roger Maris and Graig Nettles, Allie Reynolds forms a trio of Indians who went on to greater fame with the Yankees.

Known as "Superchief" because of his partly Native American ancestry, Reynolds had a commanding presence on the mound. At his best when the stakes were at their highest, Reynolds was a Yankee for eight seasons, and while he was there the Bronx Bombers went to the World Series six times.

An Oklahoma native, Reynolds attended the university now known as Oklahoma State on a track scholarship. He could run the 100-yard dash in 9.8 seconds, and he was also a star running back on the football team. Baseball? He wasn't interested until a knee injury his sophomore year kept him from running track, and he started pitching in the intramural league. Hank Iba, who coached baseball and basketball at the university, saw Reynolds play and asked him to pitch batting practice.

"I tried it because I didn't have anything else to do except piddle around with intramural ball," Reynolds said. "But it wasn't a good idea. I struck everybody out." He stopped piddling around with intramurals and joined the team as a pitcher. After he graduated, the football Giants offered Reynolds $100 a game. "I went to Mr. Iba for advice because I didn't know anything about professional sports and he told me, 'If I were you, I'd consider baseball before football.' It was a fine suggestion."

Reynolds signed with the Indians in 1939 for $1,000 and reported to Springfield in the Middle Atlantic League. After going 18-7 with Wilkes-Barre in 1942 and leading the league in ERA and strikeouts, he was ready for the big time.

He was 11-12 in 1943 and led the American League in strikeouts with 151, bur he also walked 109 batters in 199 innings. Possessed of a great fastball and a wicked curve, Reynolds still had a lot to learn about pitching. He was 18-12 in 1945 against aging veterans and secondary players and led the AL with 130 walks in 247 innings; he got a cold dose of reality in 1946 when he fell to 11-15 as regulars returned from the war.

Then Reynolds's career took a dramatic turn.

Yankee General Manager Larry MacPhail was looking to dump what he considered to be an aging Joe Gordon, and the Indians needed a second baseman and were offering a pitcher in return. The newly hired Yankee manager,

Bucky Harris, asked seasoned Yankee outfielders Joe DiMaggio and Tommy Henrich for some advice. The message from both was the same: get Reynolds.

At this point, Reynolds was age 30 and had only a 51-47 career record despite his great stuff. He started slowly with the Yankees. Then he got some advice from 40-year-old Spud Chandler, who was in his last year in the majors.

"Don't just throw the ball," Chandler told him. "Think about what you're doing. Change speeds. Set hitters up. Think, think, think." Reynolds listened. Over the next six seasons he averaged 19 wins and only 8 losses. And in 1947, his first year in pinstripes, he went 19-8 and led the AL in winning percentage with .704.

In 1951, Reynolds became only the second major leaguer, with Johnny Vander Meer, to pitch two no-hitters in the same season. The first was against Cleveland in midseason, a 1-0 game decided on Gene Woodling's home run in the eighth inning. The second came on September 28 in the middle of a wild pennant race against the Red Sox. This was an 8-0 laugher — until there were two out in the ninth. The batter was Ted Williams. He lifted a towering pop foul that Yogi Berra drifted under — and dropped. Williams then popped the next pitch to almost the same exact spot. This time Berra caught it.

Reynolds's last great season was 1952 when he went 20-8, his only 20-win season, with a league-leading 2.06 ERA. He also led the AL in strikeouts with 160 and in shutouts with six while completing 24 of 29 starts. For good measure, he saved six games. But his back was injured the next year when the Yankee team bus was in an accident, and although he went 26-11 with 20 saves over the next two seasons, the end was near. He retired after the 1954 season with a 182-107 lifetime record.

★ Frank Robinson ★

Few ballplayers in major league history have had as much impact on the game as Frank Robinson.

He's the only player to win the Most Valuable Player Award in both the American and National Leagues, with Cincinnati in 1961 and Baltimore in 1966. In 1975 he brought the same fire and intensity to his job in Cleveland as the first black major league manager, and, in 1982, his first year of eligibility, he was voted into the Baseball Hall of Fame, capturing 89 percent of the writers' ballots.

Robinson's 586 career home runs place him fourth on the all-time list. He holds the major league record for hitting home runs in the greatest number of ballparks, having cleared the fences in 33 different locations. But he was far more than just a slugger, finishing his career as a .294 hitter with 204 stolen bases in 281 attempts. Robinson also ranks third lifetime in most times hit by a pitch, with 204, a testimony to his aggressive style.

Although Robinson played for five teams during his 21-year career, his main achievements came with the Cincinnati Reds from 1956 through 1965 and with the Baltimore Orioles from 1966 through 1972. He was voted NL Rookie of the Year in 1956, and his 38 home runs tied Wally Berger's NL rookie record, and he led the league with 122 runs scored. In 1957 he made the first of 11 All-Star Game appearances as a player.

At the end of the 1965 season, though, Cincinnati

general manager William DeWitt traded Robinson to the Orioles for pitchers Milt Pappas and Jack Baldschun and outfielder Joe Simpson. Robinson sparked the Orioles to four pennants and two World Series titles in the next six years. In his first season in Baltimore he led the Orioles to an AL pennant and a World Series sweep of the Los Angeles Dodgers. He won the Triple Crown with 49 home runs, 122 RBIs, and a .316 average, and was named AL MVP.

He was traded to Cleveland in 1974 and hit only .200 in 15 games, but he was named the Indians' player-manager for the following season. On Opening Day 1975 Robinson became the first black to manage in the majors. He also homered to help the Indians win.

In 1976 Robinson led the Indians to an 81-78 record, only their third winning season since 1959. But after a slow start in 1977, Robinson became the first black manager to be fired. The following year he accepted the position as manager of the Orioles' International League affiliate in Rochester, New York, before returning to Baltimore as a coach, manager, and assistant general manager until 1995.

Al Rosen

After Al "Flip" Rosen spent several seasons waiting to crack the Cleveland Indians lineup, he became the dominant power-hitting third baseman in the game.

Nicknamed "Flip" for his softball pitching motion, Rosen left the field at age 32 under unusual circumstances and returned 20 years later to become a success in the front offices of the Yankees, Astros, and Giants.

Rosen attended college both before and after his military stint in the Navy during World War II. A noted tough guy, he spent time as an amateur boxer and had his nose broken 11 times. He signed a contract with the Indians, but his reputation as a poor fielder kept him in the minors, particularly because smooth glove man and fan favorite Ken Keltner was entrenched at third. In 1949 the 32-year-old Keltner hit only .232, and he was released before the 1950 season. The Indians gave the job to Rosen.

Rosen, 26 at the time, broke in with a bang. He slugged 37 homers, which led the American League and set an AL rookie record that stood until Mark McGwire broke it 37 years later. Rosen scored 100 runs and drove in 116. His totals dropped off to 24 homers and 102 RBI the following season, but no other third baseman in the game supplied anywhere near as much offense.

In 1952 Rosen led the league in RBI with 105, hit 28 homers, and scored 101 runs. Those were nothing compared to his 1953 numbers. Not only were Rosen's 115 runs scored and .613 slugging average league bests, but he also led the AL with 43 home runs and 145 RBIs. He lost the batting title to Washington's Mickey Vernon by one point. Needing a hit in his final at bat to win the Triple Crown, Rosen chopped a roller to third base and was out by half a step.

Nevertheless, Rosen set single-season records for third basemen in RBI and total bases. He was a unanimous choice for Most Valuable Player. Rosen's confidence at the plate extended into the field. A mediocre defender when he arrived at the majors, he led AL third basemen in assists in 1950, and in assists, double plays, and total chances per game in 1953.

Chosen as the AL third baseman for the All-Star Game in 1954, he put on a show for his hometown fans in Cleveland's Municipal Stadium, slugging two homers and adding a single for five RBI. And although he broke a finger during the season, he still managed 102 RBI and 24 home runs.

The Indians won an AL-record 111 games and the pennant in 1954, but Rosen and the rest of his teammates barely had a chance to enjoy being in the World Series. The Giants engineered a four-game sweep, as Cleveland was outscored, 20-9, in the Series. Rosen had just three hits, all singles, in 12 at bats.

An off-season auto accident landed Rosen in the hospital with whiplash, and the injury dogged him during the 1955 season. Meanwhile, he and club management were at odds over his salary. When his performance didn't match his previous season's numbers, the Indian fans started booing Rosen. A disgusted Rosen quit after the next season. He had a successful business as a stockbroker, so he didn't need the money.

Almost two decades later, in 1978, after Gabe Paul was forced out as Yankee president by volatile owner George Steinbrenner, Rosen was hired as Paul's replacement. That November, acting on a tip from a scout, Rosen went after Texas farmhand Dave Righetti and landed him, though it took a complicated 10-player-plus-cash swap to pull it off. Righetti became a key man on the New York pitching staff for 10 years, and Rosen quickly developed a reputation as a tough negotiator.

Steinbrenner's constant meddling didn't sit well with Rosen, however, and he quit the team during the 1979 All-Star break. He sent a note to Steinbrenner, saying, "I'll always love you as a friend. I just can't work for you." Bally's Hotel and Casino in Atlantic City offered him a position, and he accepted.

While at Bally's, Al Rosen hired Willie Mays as a greeter and public relations man. Commissioner Bowie Kuhn promptly notified Mays that he could not work as a scout and coach for the Giants if he also worked for a casino. Kuhn applied the same sanctions to Mickey Mantle four years later.

Baseball beckoned again in 1980 when mercurial Houston owner John McMullen fired popular General Manager Tal Smith and replaced him with Rosen. As Astro general manager for six years, Rosen helped build a young team that was always close but seldom on top.

In 1980 the Astros won the NL West in a playoff with the Dodgers but fell to the Phillies in the National League Championship Series. They won the second half of the split season of 1981 but dropped the first round of postseason play to Los Angeles. A tumble to fifth in 1982 was followed by third- and second-place finishes the next two years.

Among Rosen's more valuable acquisitions in Houston were Dickie Thon, Ray Knight, and Mike LaCoss, along with the remarkable theft of Mike Scott from the Mets for Danny Heep.

Giants owner Bob Lurie lured Rosen away from Houston in 1985. Rosen saw to it that Roger Craig was named manager, and they brought the Giants back from mediocrity to NL champions.

Rosen landed Kevin Mitchell, Dave Dravecky, and Craig Lefferts in the same deal to provide punch and pitching. The rise of talented youngsters Will Clark and Robby Thompson through the farm system solidified the infield. The Giants returned to the World Series in 1989 for the first time in 27 years.

Herb Score

Herb Score is one of baseball's might-have-beens. The Cleveland Indian lefthander was seemingly on his way to the Hall of Fame — until a line drive off the bat of Yankee Gil McDougald ruined his career in 1957.

Score was a high school sensation, and scouts from 14 of the 16 major league clubs were camping on his doorstep. Four clubs promised to top his best offer. Score received a concrete offer of $80,000 from one club, but he signed with Cleveland for only $60,000. He made that decision based on the friendship he had established with Cy Slapnicka, the scout who also had signed pitcher Bob Feller.

The Indians sent Score to their Indianapolis club in 1952, but he was pitching wildly, and they demoted him to Reading in 1953. The next year Score returned to Indianapolis and set the American Association on fire, leading in innings pitched at 251, with 22 wins, a league-record 330 strikeouts, 140 walks, and a 2.62 ERA. The *Sporting News* named him Minor League Player of the Year.

As a rookie with Cleveland in 1955 he went 16-10, with a league-leading 245 strikeouts in 227⅓ innings, still an American League rookie record. It was also the highest strikeout total by a big leaguer since Feller set the top major league mark of 348 in 1946. Sixteen of Score's strikeouts came against the Red Sox on May 1, including nine in the first three innings. Score's 2.85 ERA was also the fourth best in the league. To no one's surprise, the Baseball Writers Association of America elected him AL Rookie of the Year.

Score was even better in 1956. He went 20-9 and led the league with five shutouts and 263 strikeouts in 249 1/3 innings. He struck out 15 Senators on May 19 and started in the All-Star Game. He was 23 years old.

"He made perfect seem second-rate," Rocky Colavito said. "He had a burning desire to excel. In warm-ups he didn't jog, he ran. In playing catch along the sidelines, he didn't lob, he threw. Even after he won a game, he talked to me for hours about how he might have played better. He wouldn't accept an average performance."

Score started 1957 strongly, and Red Sox owner Tom Yawkey offered Cleveland $1 million in cash for him. The Indians turned it down. On May 7, the night his life changed drastically, Score faced the Yankees at Cleveland's Municipal Stadium

He retired the leadoff batter, Hank Bauer. McDougald was next and he lined one back through the box. Score could see it coming straight at his eye, but there was nothing he could do. He bled profusely and his teammates stuffed a towel around his mouth and nose. "Hey, get the towel out, you're going to choke me!" he shouted. "I was conscious the whole time and lucid and calm. I think I was the calmest one there," he recalled.

When they got him back to the clubhouse, Score realized he couldn't see anything out of his damaged eye. "Do I still have an eye?" he asked the team physician. He did, but he had to spend eight days in a Cleveland hospital, motionless, in total darkness.

When he came back he was never the same. He hung on for six years, trying to reclaim his brilliance. Instead, he won 19 games and lost 27.

"You know, people think what happened to me that night cost me my career," Score said years later. "But they're wrong. That had nothing to do with my losing my effectiveness. The following spring I was pitching as well as I ever did. Then I was pitching in Washington. In the third or fourth inning my arm started to bother me. I didn't say anything. I figured it would work out. These are the mistakes you make when you're young."

In 1960 Score was traded to the White Sox for pitcher Barry Latman. Chicago asked him to go down to the San Diego farm club. He complied, but he was still ineffective. His last stop was Indianapolis, where the results were the same.

"Some people asked me why I went back to the minor leagues," Score said. "They felt I was humiliating myself. But I never felt humiliated. There was no disgrace in what I was doing. The disgrace would have been in not trying." Score retired as a player in 1962 and has broadcast Cleveland baseball for the past 30 years.

★ Joe Sewell ★

Shortstop Joe Sewell was not only a smooth fielder and a lifetime .312 hitter. He was, without question, the hardest man in the history of the game to strike out.

Even considering the standards of his day, his bat control was remarkable, and, by contemporary standards, his strikeout ratio is unbelievable. Sewell fanned only once in every 62.6 at bats. Second on the all-time list is Lloyd Waner at 44.9. As a point of comparison, one of the very best of the post-expansion era is Felix Millan — at 23.9.

His ability to make contact resulted in seasons when Sewell struck out just three or four times. In one year, during which Sewell struck out only four times, three of them occurred on called strikes. In only one case did Sewell swing and miss. And at least one of the called third strikes was highly questionable.

"The ball was right at the bill of my cap," recalled Sewell. Umpire Bill McGowan said, 'Strike three, you're out. Oh my God, I missed it, Joe.' But I didn't say a word. I just walked back to the bench. And the next day he came out and apologized and I said, 'Bill, don't worry about it. You were honest about it.' "

Sewell felt there were three key factors in batting: knowing the strike zone, making allowances for the umpire behind the plate, and keeping your eye on the ball. "I hit the ball just about every time I swung at it," he contended late in life. "I could see a ball leave my bat. A lot of people don't believe that's possible. But it sure is.

"All you have to do is watch it. It doesn't disappear when you put the bat on it. I watched a big league game not long ago and I saw some boys striking at balls that I swear they missed by a foot. They couldn't have been looking at those balls. You just know they couldn't."

Alabama-born Joseph Wheeler Sewell, named for a Confederate cavalry officer, was the son of a country doctor. The elder Sewell encouraged sons Joe, Luke, and Tommy to attend the University of Alabama. All did, and all became major league ballplayers. Luke was an American League catcher for 20 seasons, but Tommy had only one at bat in the majors, with the Cubs during the 1927 season.

"When I came to the University it was the best break I ever had in my life," contended Joe Sewell. "We had a football coach who came in here from Cleveland named Zinn Scott. He also wrote for the *Cleveland Plain Dealer*. He recommended me and Luke and Riggs Stephenson to the Cleveland Indians. There were seven of us from our baseball team that went off to the major leagues and made it."

After graduating from Alabama in 1920, Sewell signed with the New Orleans Pelicans of the Southern Association. He had only been there for 92 pro games and was hitting .289 when he was ordered to report to the Cleveland Indians.

The Indians were battling the Yankees and the White Sox for the pennant and desperately needed a shortstop. The popular and talented Ray Chapman had been killed by a Carl Mays pitch at New York's Polo Grounds on August 16, 1920, and had been replaced by light-hitting Harry Lunte. Lunte soon pulled a hamstring and was out of action.

That's when the Indians called on the inexperienced Sewell. It would have been easy for him to fail, coming aboard during the pressure of a tremendous pennant race, and he was filling in under the most tragic of circumstances. For one game, he sat on the Cleveland bench and thought, "I ain't supposed to be here."

Then Manager Tris Speaker inserted him into the lineup against the A's, and first baseman "Tioga George" Burns made the rookie feel right at home. Burns reached into his locker and handed the rookie one of his own 44-ounce black bats. "Here, take this. It's a good bat. Make sure you take care of it," said the veteran.

And Sewell did take care of it. He named the bat "Black Betsy," and it lasted him throughout his career "That was my Sunday bat, my best bat," Sewell would remark decades later. "I used that bat for 14 years in the major leagues and never broke it."

Armed with this wondrous weapon, Sewell lined a hard-hit ball to center his first time up, but it was caught. In his second at bat he hit a pitch over third and into the left field corner where it rattled around and enabled Sewell to reach third base. "Boy, I went around those bases just like I was flying. Not even my toes seemed to touch the ground. When I got to third base I said to myself, 'Shucks, this ain't so tough up here.' And, from that day on, I was never nervous again."

In the 1920 World Series Burns hit .300, and with his sixth-inning double he drove in the only run in "Duster" Mails's 1-0 Game 6 victory. Burns hit .361 in part-time action for the Tribe in 1921, but he was traded in 1922 with outfielders Elmer Smith and Joe Harris to the Red Sox for first baseman Stuffy McInnis.

In 1920 Sewell hit .329 as Cleveland captured the pennant. In the World Series, however, he hit only .174 and committed six errors at short. Despite Sewell's poor performance, the Indians won the Series, defeating the Dodgers in seven games.

For a man of his size, Sewell was a remarkably durable player. He had run up a streak of "460 or so consecutive games" when he was spiked by St. Louis Browns pitcher Elam Van Gilder and missed the next game. He then proceeded to put together another streak of 1,103 straight contests. "And I must have played almost a month with my shoe cut open before I was back to normal. But I played," said Sewell, who finally was put out of action again by the flu. His streak is the sixth-longest in major league history.

Sewell hit at least .315 each season from 1923 through 1929. Converted to third base in the late 1920s, Sewell was released by Cleveland in January 1931 and signed with the Yankees. In the 1932 World Series against the Cubs he hit .333. That was the Fall Classic that featured Babe Ruth's fabled "Called Shot" home run off pitcher Charlie Root. "Do I believe he really called it?" asked Sewell. "Yes sir. I was there. I saw it. I don't care what anybody says. He did it. He probably couldn't have done it again for a thousand years, but he did it that time."

After retiring as a player, Sewell coached for the Yankees in 1934 and 1935, then scouted for Cleveland for 11 seasons and the Mets for one. He coached baseball at the University of Alabama for six seasons and captured both the Southeastern Conference championship and Coach of the Year honors in 1968.

Sewell was inducted into the Hall of Fame in 1977.

Louis Sockalexis

It took Louis Sockalexis, a Penobscot Indian from Maine, only 94 big-league games and 367 at bats to become a baseball legend — so famous that almost 20 years after his brief, fleeting career, the Cleveland baseball team was named the Indians in his honor.

Sockalexis was a superb athlete, with skills that bring to mind the myth of the noble savage: the perfect physical specimen, gifted at the most basic level with bodily prowess. He was very fast, timed in full baseball gear at ten seconds in the hundred-yard dash. He had an exceptional throwing arm, "one of the first great arms in baseball," according to historian Bill Curran. And he could hit, with power such as people in the Dead-Ball Era of baseball had never seen before.

But there was something else about Sockalexis, something that inspired the creation of wild tall tales. It was as if he was playing at such a level of excellence that normal prose (and normal thinking) was unable to capture it. They say he hit a baseball 600 feet; a feat most likely impossible with the balls of mush they played with in his time. They said he threw a ball from Oak Hill on Indian Island (the Penobscot reservation in Old Town, Maine, where Sockalexis grew up) that hit the smokestack of the Jordan Lumber Mill. (It would have been a neat trick; the two spots are more than three quarters of a mile apart.) Someone claimed he was the direct descendant of Sitting Bull. It is said that Gilbert Patten, who wrote boys' baseball novels under the pen name of Burt L. Standish, based the famous Frank Merriwell character on Sockalexis.

But the reason for the Indian's incredibly short career

was a simple one. He loved to celebrate his accomplishments with firewater, and he couldn't handle it. He spent much of the final years of his brief life as a panhandler, begging for pennies to buy one more glass of whiskey. A report in 1900, just one year after he was gone from major league baseball, tells of a disheveled Sockalexis with his toes poking through the holes in his worn-out shoes, being tossed in jail for 30 days for vagrancy.

By the time he was 20, Sockalexis was already a New England legend on the baseball and football fields. Mike "Doc" Powers, a young talent himself (later to have an 11-year career as a big-league catcher) and captain of the woeful Holy Cross baseball team, spotted the Indian in 1894 during a Maine barnstorming tour, and arranged for Sockalexis to join the school as a "special" student, which meant he needed extra tutoring, since he hadn't finished high school. Sockalexis single-handedly put Holy Cross on the baseball map. His feats immediately burgeoned into legend. He stole six bases in one game, two for himself and four more as designated runner for an injured Holy Cross teammate.

When Powers transferred to Notre Dame, his protégé followed. But it was at Notre Dame that Sockalexis first fell afoul of the grape. He was there only one month before being expelled for public drunkenness. The Cleveland team snapped him up for the majors for $1,500.

He was an immediate smash. In six exhibition games he had ten assists. *Sporting Life* made mention of his physique in glowing terms: "A massive man with gigantic bones and bulging muscles." Although Sockalexis was about 5-foot-11 and weighed 185 pounds or so, he was huge for his times. As writer Luke Salisbury describes him, "He was as big as the football linemen of his day and faster than the backs."

Early in the season he made a remarkable catch to save a game; soon after a sensational throw sent tongues wagging and writers to their dictionaries in search of new adjectives. While Sockalexis was not the first Indian to pay major league baseball, he was certainly the first to be treated like one. Fans went crazy; they took to wearing Indian headdresses and screaming war whoops every time Sockalexis came to bat.

The stolid, college-educated Indian claimed the fan rudeness didn't bother him. But his excellence quickly quieted the Indian wildness. In his first appearance in New York, against acclaimed fireballer Amos Rusie, the war whoops were silenced when he smashed a line drive homer. In Cleveland his exploits were greeted with uproarious cheers.

In the four games before July 4, 1897, Sockalexis was eleven for twenty-one. Only twice that season had he gone without a hit in two consecutive games. His batting average was .335. But the Fourth of July celebration was to much for him. The facts blur here, but Sockalexis missed several games afterward. It was clear he had gone on a drinking tear and had hurt his ankle; some say when he tried to sneak out of a second floor hotel room where he was being guarded by teammates to keep him from drinking any more. The newspapers of the time referred to "a tryst with a pale-faced maiden and a dalliance with the grape."

Whatever the cause, he was hurt. When he returned he went nine for eighteen, but his fielding was atrocious. He might have been drunk, or just severely hung over, but everyone noticed it. The *Cleveland Plain Dealer* of July 13, under the headline "A Wooden Indian," commented, "Sockalexis acted as if he had disposed of too many mint juleps previous to the game . . . Sockalexis . . . was directly responsible for all but one of Boston's runs. A lame foot is the Indian's excuse, but a Turkish bath and a good rest might be an excellent remedy."

Sporting Life opined, "Too much popularity has ruined Sockalexis by all accounts. It is no longer a secret that Cleveland management can no longer control him." Manager Patsy Tebeau had taken all he could; from July 25 to September 12 Sockalexis played only once. In his final game that year he made two errors, although he finished the season with a .338 average, three homers, 42 RBIs in 66 games, and 16 stolen bases.

It seems likely that the alcohol and the injury combined to cause the Indian's downfall. When he was playing every day, it was easier for him to keep his tendency toward drunkenness under control. But sitting on the bench offered no such automatic check on his behavior. The team put up with him for just 21 games in 1898 and seven more in 1899 before they let him go. Out of baseball by 1903, he worked as a laborer when he wasn't on a binge throughout New England, and died of alcoholism in 1913. Cleveland renamed itself the Indians in his honor in 1915.

★ Tris Speaker ★

Most baseball fans know that Tris Speaker played unusually shallow in center field, so shallow that he recorded 448 assists, more than any other outfielder in baseball history. In 1909 and 1912 he set the American League record with 35 assists in a season. In 1918 he played so close to second base that he made two unassisted double plays.

It's easy to look upon Speaker's defensive mastery merely as a byproduct of the Dead Ball Era, when flyballs to deep center field were rare. The argument is that Speaker could risk the chance of one or two flyballs a week sailing over his head because of the number of soft drives he'd catch by playing so shallow, a luxury that modern outfielders can't afford. Even Speaker, some say, would have to play much deeper today.

But the evidence is to the contrary. Speaker played the last nine years of his 22-year major league career after the lively ball was introduced in 1920. He continued to play within spitting distance of second base, and he continued to get away with it. His secret was a seemingly prescient ability to get a jump on a batted ball.

Joe Sewell, who patrolled shortstop for Speaker's Cleveland Indians starting in 1920, said, "I played seven years with him right behind me in shallow center field. You know how an infielder gets down for the pitch? Well, you'd get down and the ball would be hit — a shot. You'd turn, and in all that time I never did see him turn. He'd be turned and gone with his back to the plate, the ball, the infield, and when he'd turn around again, there would be the ball."

Perhaps the single greatest proof of his mastery of the outfield is that Speaker is remembered for his fielding even though he was one of the greatest hitters in baseball history. His career marks include a .345 batting average, fifth best overall, as well as 3,514 hits, 1,882 runs scored, 1,529 RBIs, and 434 stolen bases.

Tristram E. Speaker was born in Hubbard, Texas, in 1888. An outstanding high school athlete, he worked as a telegraph linesman and cowpuncher before joining Cleburne of the North Texas League in 1906 as a left-handed pitcher for $50 a month. He saw little action and less success on the mound. After the young recruit lost six consecutive starts, Cleburne lost its regular right fielder to injury. Speaker told the manager he could play the position and soon became an outfielder. He batted only .268 his first year but hit .314 with Houston the following season.

When Pittsburgh owner Barney Dreyfuss heard about the young hitter he was intrigued, until he learned that Speaker smoked cigarettes. (Dreyfuss thought it a nasty habit.) The Boston Red Sox showed more interest, bringing him up for seven games in September but writing him off when he batted only .158.

The Red Sox didn't send him a contract for 1908, so Speaker paid his own way to Marlin, Texas, where the New York Giants were training, and offered his services to Manager John McGraw. Unimpressed, McGraw said there was a "No Vacancy" sign on his outfield and didn't even give him a tryout.

Speaker moved on to the Red Sox training camp in Little Rock, Arkansas. Although not welcomed with open arms, he was allowed to train with the team. When it was time to head north the Red Sox gave Speaker to the Little Rock ballclub in payment for the use of the facilities, retaining an option to buy him back at a nominal sum. After the youngster hit .350 to lead the Southern Association, Boston exercised its option, but Speaker hit only .220 in 31 games at the end of the season.

During this period Cy Young, the great pitcher, turned Speaker into a great outfielder. "Cy used to hit fungoes to me every day when I joined the Red Sox," Speaker later explained. "He always tried to hit the ball just one step beyond me so that I couldn't catch it unless I hustled. I watched him, and in a few days I knew just by the way he swung whether the ball would go to my right or left. Then I figured that if I could do that with a fungo hitter, I could do it in a ball game. I asked our pitchers how they pitched to each batter. I also studied the batter and when he started his swing, I knew if he would hit to my left or right and I was on my way."

Speaker won the center field job in 1909 and hit .309. Nearly 6 feet tall and a solid 193 pounds, the left-handed hitter sprayed the ball to all fields. He was never a big home run hitter. Of the four times he reached double figures in homers, three came in the 1920s after the lively ball arrived. His specialty was the line drive, and when coupled with his speed, a single often became a double or triple. His 222 career three-base hits are the sixth-highest total ever; his 792 doubles are an all-time record. Speaker led the AL in two-base hits eight times, topping 50 on five different occasions.

Speaker picked up the nickname "Spoke" from some dugout wag with an affinity for the past tense. But Speaker acted more like his other namesake, "the Grey Eagle," on the ballfield, even when he was pushing 40. He

played in 100 or more games for 19 consecutive seasons and hit better than .300 in all but one.

When the Red Sox won the pennant in 1912, they did it behind the strength of "Smoky Joe" Wood's arm and one of the best outfields ever assembled. Wood, Speaker's roommate, went 34-5. Flanking Speaker was left fielder Duffy Lewis, who drove in 109 runs, and right fielder Harry Hooper, who scored 98.

That year Speaker won the Chalmers Award, a forerunner of the Most Valuable Player Award. He hit .383, scored 136 runs and drove in 90, led the league in doubles, with 53, and in home runs, with 10, and stole 52 bases. He finished off a good year's work by hitting .300 to lead the Red Sox to a World Series victory over the New York Giants. In 1915 Boston finished first again; Speaker hit .322 for the season and .294 in the Sox's World Series win over Philadelphia.

Speaker was an incorrigible practical joker, and practical jokes are seldom funny to their victims. One time he pulled off Duffy Lewis's cap and showed the crowd Lewis's glistening bald pate. Lewis, who had shaved his head because of the heat and was worried that the fuzz wouldn't return, was not amused. He threw a bat against Speaker's shins, and the center fielder didn't walk much for a couple of days.

The Federal League was formed in 1914 and tried to lure established stars away from the majors with big salaries. Naturally, Speaker was high on the FL's list. To keep him happy in Fenway Park, the Red Sox increased his wages to $18,000 a year, one of the highest salaries in baseball.

But when the Feds went belly up after the 1915 season, Red Sox owner Joe Lannin saw no reason to pay a king's ransom for a center fielder whose only other option was to return to Texas and punch cows. He tried to cut Speaker's salary by half. Speaker proposed that Lannin take a flying leap. When neither side budged, Lannin traded Speaker to Cleveland in April 1916 for pitcher "Sad Sam" Jones, third baseman Fred Thomas, and $50,000.

The Red Sox still managed to win the 1916 pennant. Speaker won the AL batting crown with a .386 average and led the league with 211 hits, 41 doubles, a .470 on-base percentage, and a .502 slugging average.

He continued to star for the Indians. In 1919 Manager Lee Fohl was fired and replaced by Speaker. Although the team began winning under him, his own performance suffered, and Speaker finished with a .296 average, the first and only time he ever hit below .300 while playing regularly.

In 1920 he was brilliant. He coaxed outstanding years out of his pitchers, platooned half his lineup, and when star shortstop Ray Chapman was killed by a pitched ball Speaker plugged in rookie Joe Sewell. Speaker was also fortunate to have a superb center fielder named Speaker, who hit .388 with 107 RBI. Cleveland edged the White Sox and Yankees for its first pennant. Then, in a World Series that produced the first Series grand slam, the first Series home run by a pitcher, and the first unassisted triple play in a Series, the Tribe downed Brooklyn to become world champions.

Speaker continued to manage Cleveland through 1926. Although he didn't win another pennant, he had only two losing seasons. Several of his best seasons with a bat came during this period. In 1923 at age 35 he hit .380 with a career-high 130 RBIs. In 1925 he recorded a career-best .389 average.

Following the 1926 season a disgruntled former teammate accused Speaker and Ty Cobb of fixing a game back in 1919, the year of the "Black Sox" game-throwing scandal. Commissioner Judge Kenesaw Mountain Landis investigated and gave both men a clean bill of health; but in the meantime Speaker had been fired and Cobb released by Detroit. Speaker signed with Washington and hit .327 in 1927. He finished his career as a sub on Connie Mack's Philadelphia Athletics in 1928.

Speaker managed for a couple of seasons in the minors, and then became a broadcaster in Kansas City. After World War II he coached for Cleveland. His special project was Larry Doby, who played second base in the Negro Leagues. With Speaker's help, Doby became one of the top center fielders in the AL.

Speaker was elected to the Hall of Fame in 1937. His plaque states that he was "the greatest center fielder of his day." Many would change the last three words to "ever."

Andre Thornton

Hard-hitting first baseman Andre Thornton hit more home runs in Cleveland Stadium than any other Indian — 119— to Rocky Colavito's 113 (98 of them as an Indian), Larry Doby's 103, and Al Rosen's 102.

Thornton was in both the Braves' and Phillies' organizations before he made the majors and didn't really settle into a spot with the Cubs or Expos either. But, on December 10, 1976, Cleveland made one of the all-time great steals, obtaining Thornton from Montreal for Jackie Brown.

The proud but unassuming Thornton was a deeply religious man who engendered respect on the field with his powerful bat and off it with his sincere devotion to Christian beliefs. He twice slugged more than 30 homers in a season and drove in more than 100 runs in an Indian uniform.

During his eleven years in Cleveland, he led the Tribe in home runs seven times, including four seasons in a row. Only a succession of nagging injuries kept him from becoming the all-time Indian home run leader; he finished his career with 214, just 14 behind Hal Trosky.

Luis Tiant

Luis Tiant, probably most famous for his pirouette pitching motion and his postgame cigars, was an outstanding moundsman for the Cleveland Indians and the Boston Red Sox during the 1960s and 1970s.

"Tiant is the Fred Astaire of baseball," Reggie Jackson once said. Broadcaster Curt Gowdy added that Tiant's pitches seemed to come "from everywhere except between his legs." Tiant won 229 games during his big league career, posted four 20-win seasons, and led the American League in shutouts and ERA twice each.

Born in Cuba on November 23, 1940, Tiant was the son of Luis Eleuterio Tiant, a great Cuban pitcher who could not play in the major leagues because he was black.

"When I was 17," the younger Tiant once said, "I told my mother and father I wanted to be a ballplayer. My father said no because he felt there was no place in baseball for a black man. But my mother finally got him to let me try."

Tiant failed a tryout with the Havana Sugar Kings of the International League. In February 1959 former All-Star Bobby Avila signed him to the Mexico City Tigers of the Mexican League. After the 1961 season, the Indians purchased Tiant's contract from Mexico City for $35,000.

In the minors Tiant pitched for Jacksonville of the International League, Charleston of the Eastern League, Burlington of the Carolina League, and Portland of the Pacific Coast League. In 1963 he pitched a no-hitter for Burlington. In 1964 he went 15-1 for Portland and was the PCL Player of the Year.

During the 1964 season the Indians called up Tiant. He started 16 games for Cleveland, won 10 of them, and lost 4. He also pitched three shutouts and posted a 2.83 ERA. In 1966 he pitched four consecutive shutouts and led the American League with five for the season. In 1968 he won 21 games and led the league with a 1.60 ERA, but Detroit hurler Denny McLain's 31 wins overshadowed his performance.

That year the Cleveland starter began using his famous herky-jerky pitching motion. "The first time I do it was against California," recalled Tiant, who spoke Spanish as his first language and developed some unique speech patterns as he learned English. "I forget who was batting, but I know it bother him . . . The motion depends on how I feel, how I think the batter is thinking. Sometimes I do nothing but throw the ball. You can't use the motions too much or they will get used to it."

Tiant had been a regular in winter ball, but after his 1968 season the Indians ordered him to take the winter off. That strategy backfired and Tiant lost his sharpness in the 1969 season. He led the league in defeats, with 20, and Cleveland traded him during the off-season to Minnesota in a six-player deal that brought Graig Nettles to the Indians.

In 1970 Tiant was off to a 6-0 start for the Twins when he fractured a shoulder blade. "The doctor tell me he only saw it happen before with a javelin thrower," Tiant said. "But the doctor tell me that rest will heal it."

The Twins, however, couldn't wait and after his poor performance during spring training in 1971, they gave Tiant his release. "It was the most forlorn experience I ever had in baseball," recalled the club's public relations director, Tom Mee. "One by one, everyone on the team walked over to Luis and shook his hand before getting on the bus. Then we left him there, practically in tears, standing by himself in the hotel lobby. It was awful."

In April the Braves signed Tiant to a minor league contract and then released him in May. The Red Sox signed him and sent him to Louisville of the International League. Only 20 days later he was called up to Boston. He was only 1-7 for the Red Sox that season, but in 1972 he went 15-6 with six shutouts and a league-leading 1.91 ERA and was named Comeback Player of the Year by the *Sporting News*.

Tiant won 20 games or more for the Sox three times during the next four years. In the Red Sox's pennant-winning 1975 season, he defeated the Oakland A's on a three-hitter in Game 1 of the American League Championship Series. In the Fall Classic he beat the Reds in both Game 1, on a 6-0 shutout, and Game 4. He also started the historic Game 6, a contest Boston won on Carlton Fisk's twelfth-inning homer, but Tiant was not involved in the decision.

That year he finally got together with his father, whom he had not seen since 1961. In 1976 Tiant won 21 games for the Red Sox, but he got into a contract squabble with the new team ownership over a verbal agreement that the late owner Tom Yawkey had made with him guaranteeing his salary for 1977. In December his parents died within three days of each other. After a 13-8 season in 1978, Tiant became a free agent and signed with the Yankees. He won 13 games for New York in 1979 and 8 in 1980.

He finished his career seeing limited action in Pittsburgh in 1981 and in California in 1982. Tiant now lives in Canton, Massachusetts, where he works for Northeastern University as part of Project Teamwork, a program sponsored by Reebok International Limited in which athletes speak to high school students to urge them to stay in school.

Hal Trosky

Hal Trosky originally wanted to be a pitcher, but it just didn't work out for him. Instead, he became a first baseman and led the American League in putouts twice and assists, fielding range, and double plays once. He was a lifetime .302 hitter and drove in more than 100 runs in six straight seasons.

Trosky started his professional career with Cedar Rapids and Dubuque of the Mississippi Valley League in 1931, did some pitching, and batted .302. He also played with Quincy of the Ill League, Burlington of the Mississippi Valley League, and Toledo of the American Association, hitting .300 wherever he played.

Brought up to Cleveland in the waning moments of the 1933 season, he became the Indians' starting first baseman in 1934 and enjoyed one of the finest rookie campaigns in major league history. He hit three homers in a game on May 30, 1934, and finished the season with a .330 batting average, 35 home runs, and 142 RBI. Only two rookies in American League history, Mark McGwire and Al Rosen, have hit more homers, and Ted Williams and Walt Dropo are the only AL rookies to drive in more runs in a season.

In 1936 Trosky led the league with 162 RBI and had a 28-game hitting streak. He also belted 42 home runs and batted .343, joining a short list of major leaguers who have hit 40 homers and registered 200 base hits in the same season. The only other players to accomplish it in AL history are Babe Ruth, Jimmie Foxx, Lou Gehrig, Joe DiMaggio, Al Rosen, Hank Greenberg, and Jim Rice.

Four years later Trosky was one of the "Cry Baby" Indians who demanded that Cleveland owner Alva Bradley remove Manager Oscar Vitt. Pitcher Mel Harder was the first player to complain to Bradley, but Trosky phoned Bradley shortly thereafter and said, "I just want to tell you that I'm 100 percent in favor of the story you're now hearing. Those are my sentiments without reservation."

The 1940 season was Trosky's last productive campaign. He batted .295, hit 25 homers, and drove in 93

runs. After appearing in only 89 games he announced his retirement after the 1941 season because of migraine headaches. Trosky returned to farming in Iowa, decided he wanted to return as a player, and his contract was sold to the Chicago White Sox in November 1943. He hit 10 homers in 1944, sat out again in 1945, then returned in 1946 to slug the last 2 of his 228 lifetime round-trippers.

Trosky later scouted for the White Sox. His son, Hal Trosky Jr., achieved what his father never could —he became a major league pitcher, although he had a short career. Trosky made two appearances for the White Sox in 1958, going 1-0 with a 6.00 ERA. He never pitched in another big league game.

★ Bill Veeck ★

Bill Veeck promoted baseball better than anyone before or since.

He was baseball's promotional genius and, perhaps, its only populist owner. His many memorable innovations included planting the ivy at Wrigley Field in Chicago, inventing the exploding scoreboard, letting fans manage his teams, putting a shower in the bleachers, integrating the American League by signing Larry Doby and Satchel Paige, and opening a day-care center in Cleveland Stadium. Veeck also brought pennants to two teams that had gone a combined 68 years without any.

During his stints as owner of the Cleveland Indians, the Chicago White Sox (twice), the St. Louis Browns, and two minor league teams, Veeck was part shaman, part sham. He believed that any team that relied solely on true baseball fans for its patronage would "go out of business by Mother's Day." With this in mind, Veeck the baseball purist became the game's P. T. Barnum, a characterization he hated. He preferred to be called a hustler and literally wrote the book on the art — *The Hustler's Handbook*.

Veeck was driven to be different, and his drive changed the face of baseball. Associates swear that his mind worked twice as fast as everyone else's, and he exploited that advantage throughout his career. Veeck never wore ties, not even to his weddings, and he was known in Chicago as "Sportshirt Bill." It was great public relations for his common-man image and great relief for a man with chronic skin irritation and asthma.

The unconventional Veeck couldn't resist knocking the baseball establishment. "My dad would walk into a room, look for the three biggest stuffed shirts, pull out a verbal pin, and go at them," recalls Veeck's son Mike, who now runs minor league clubs. The New York Yankees were Veeck's favorite target, particularly their humorless, portly general manager, George Weiss, architect of the final Yankee dynasty. Veeck addressed him as "Old Pus Bag" and stomped on Weiss's fedora at one memorable league meeting.

But even Veeck's image as baseball's great maverick outsider was a hustle. Professing utter disdain for the baseball establishment, Veeck was in fact born into it. His father, William Louis Veeck Sr., was a *Chicago American* columnist, man-about-town, and relentless critic of the Cubs. In 1918 Cubs owner William Wrigley challenged the older Veeck, "If you're so smart, why don't you see if you can do a better job?" Veeck accepted, becoming the Cubs' vice president and treasurer, and a year later, team president.

At age 11 Bill Veeck took his first job in baseball as a Wrigley Field vendor and office boy. "I'm the only human being ever raised at a ballpark," Veeck loved to say. Much later, several of his nine children could say the same thing, as Veeck and his second wife Mary Frances resided in an apartment at Sportsman's Park while he owned the Browns. The young Veeck left Wrigley Field to attend two of the nation's most prestigious prep schools, Andover and the Ranch School in Los Alamos, New Mexico. The tall, solidly built, sandy-haired teen obtained a diploma from neither, although he entered Kenyon College in 1932 and played football there.

Veeck left school to work for the Chicago Cubs in 1933 after his father died. During an unusual second-generation collaboration with club owner and chewing gum heir William Wrigley, Veeck ran tryouts, wrote advertisements, and kept books. At the same time he was attending night school, studying business, accounting, and engineering at Northwestern University. In 1940 he was named club treasurer and assistant secretary, but he was convinced that he would rise no further.

The Cubs always held a special place in his heart, and many who knew Veeck contended that he dreamed to his final days of owning the team. He spent his final seasons with the Cub establishment at the ballpark in the Wrigley Field bleachers, between the ivy he'd planted in 1938 and the scoreboard he'd built. He left the organization when the Cubs began selling bleacher seats in advance, a practice Veeck decried as an affront to regular fans. When Veeck left the Cubs in 1941 he cited conflicts between "baseball men" and "gum men."

At age 27, with former Cub Charlie Grimm as a partner, Veeck bought the Milwaukee Brewers of the American Association and unleashed his promotional talents on the baseball world. Every Brewers game became an unpredictable event as Veeck staged most of his promotions unannounced. A visit to the ballpark meant live music, surprise giveaways of everything from live lobsters and guinea pigs to nails, plus a chance to talk directly to Veeck as he mingled with spectators. "I think people look at it as quaint, Dad sitting in the stands," Mike Veeck once said. "It was just his way of doing market research."

Complaints from graveyard-shift workers who couldn't attend night games prompted Bill Veeck to stage 8:30 a.m. starts. At the first morning game Veeck himself served fans coffee and corn flakes, attracting national attention. Veeck also spruced up the ballpark, making it as clean and comfortable as possible. To help his team on the field, Veeck wasn't above doctoring the infield, moving fences between seasons or even between innings, or staging a timely lighting-system failure.

Following a three-year stint in the Marines that cost Veeck his right leg (his medical record lists 36 lifetime operations) he sold the Brewers. In 1943 Veeck schemed to buy the Phillies with the intention of stocking the National League team with black stars, but Commissioner Kenesaw Mountain Landis derailed the plan. In 1946 Veeck purchased the American League's Cleveland Indians as part of a 10-member syndicate that included celebrity and Cleveland resident Bob Hope.

In the Indians he saw a team that was nearly profitable without really trying, and he had plenty of ideas to try. Longtime Veeck associate Rudie Schaffer said, "Back before Bill stirred up the pot, the biggest promotion in the major leagues was to open the gates and say we're playing at three." Aside from promotions, Veeck also took some practical steps, such as getting Indians games broadcast on radio by giving away the rights, moving the team from decaying League Park to larger Municipal/Cleveland Stadium, and hiring public relations people to help him promote the team.

As if Veeck needed help. He was an instant hit in Cleveland, carousing with the city's elite until the wee hours, then heading for an all-night truck stop to swap stories and hand out tickets. When Cleveland got too quiet he flew to New York's Copacabana Club after night games to listen to jazz and play charades, catching the first morning flight home. Roland Hemond, White Sox general manager under Veeck, said, "Working 5 years with Bill was like working 10 years with anybody else because you slept so little, but every minute was to be treasured."

The Indians' 1948 world championship, the Tribe's first since 1920, was Veeck's finest moment. That year the team drew an unprecedented 2,620,627 fans — a record that stood for three decades — and won their one-game pennant playoff against the Boston Red Sox. Pitching for Cleveland was Gene Bearden, a rookie knuckleballer acquired from the hated Yankees on the recommendation of Casey Stengel, formerly one of Veeck's managers in Milwaukee. Bearden also won his only World Series start and saved the finale of the Tribe's six-game Series win over the Boston Braves. "Lost in a lot of the showmanship was a tremendously sound baseball mind," Mike Veeck commented.

In 1949 Veeck sold the Indians, partly to offset the financial fallout from the end of his first marriage and partly because he needed a new challenge. He found it with the St. Louis Browns, a team whose 1944 wartime pennant was the only bright spot in a half-century of futility. In 1935 the Browns drew only 80,972 fans for the season, fewer than Veeck's Indians had drawn in a single game. Veeck bought the Browns in 1951, but he was never able to match his Cleveland success on the field or at the gate.

The Browns did provide the setting for what became Veeck 's most famous stunt: he sent 3-foot-7, 65-pound Eddie Gaedel to bat on August 19, 1951. Veeck claimed he had not read Ring Lardner's short story, "You Could Look It Up," in which a pinch-hitting little person is induced to swing at a fat pitch and grounds out. Veeck warned Gaedel, "I've got a man up in the stands with a high-powered rifle, and if you swing at any pitch, he'll fire."

"For a minute, I felt like Babe Ruth," Gaedel said, after drawing a walk. Veeck contended that putting Gaedel in the batting order, like his other stunts, was "a practical idea, too." He planned to use Gaedel again, with the bases loaded, but AL President Will Harridge was outraged and barred little people from Major League Baseball.

Veeck was forced to sell the Browns after the 1953 season but returned to baseball in March 1959, in purchasing a majority stake in the White Sox. Aided by the midseason acquisition of slugger Ted Kluszewski, the White Sox won the pennant in 1959, their first in 40 years, but lost to the Dodgers in the World Series.

In June 1961 he sold the Sox and moved to Maryland's eastern shore, suffering from reduced blood flow to the brain and a chronic cough.

He recovered his health, wrote the autobiography *Veeck — As in Wreck* with Ed Linn, and finally got back into baseball when he bought the Chicago White Sox again in December 1975 to prevent them from moving from Chicago. Veeck's innovations with his final major league team included planting a public address microphone in the broadcast booth to catch Harry Caray's rendition of "Take Me Out to the Ballgame", beginning a Chicago ballpark tradition, but failing health and finances forced Veeck to sell the club in 1980.

When Veeck died in 1986, Minnie Minoso attended his funeral wearing a White Sox uniform. Veeck was elected to the Hall of Fame in 1991.

Joe Vosmik

Joe Vosmik's skills began to erode when he was only 29, but he had already had quite a run. Vosmik, a left fielder, hit better than .300 in six of his first eight seasons—twice bettering .340—while averaging 91 RBIs.

Born in Cleveland in 1910, Vosmik signed with his hometown Indians in 1929. According to one account, Cleveland General Manager Billy Evans needed to sign one more kid at a tryout camp and asked his wife's opinion. Allegedly she chose "the good-looking blond boy."

Vosmik hit .381 and .397 during his two seasons in the minors and took over left field for the Indians in 1931, batting .320 with a career-high 117 RBI while striking out only 30 times in 591 at bats. Vosmik never did strike out much — only 272 times in 5472 at bats, or one every 20 at bats.)

He batted .312 with a career-high 10 homers and 97 RBIs the next season before slumping badly in 1933, when he hit .263 with 56 RBIs. After batting .341 in 104 games in 1934, he had his career season in 1935, leading the American League in hits (216), doubles (47) and triples (20) while driving in 110 runs and finishing one point behind Senators second baseman Buddy Myer in the batting race.

After Vosmik's average dropped to .287 in 1936, he was traded to the Browns. He hit .325 the next season, with 93 RBIs. Sent to the Red Sox, in 1938, he batting .324, with a league-leading 201 hits.

The decline began in 1939, when he hit .276. He was promptly sold to the Dodgers. Vosmik played season as a regular, was released by the Dodgers in 1941 and resurfaced for 36 at bats (and seven hits) as a Senator in 1944. He finished with a .307 career average and 1,682 hits.

Vosmik died in 1962.

Bill Wambsganss

In 1920 Cleveland second baseman Bill Wambsganss secured a place in baseball history by pulling off one of the most spectacular plays ever — an unassisted triple play in the World Series. The feat had never been done before, and it hasn't been done since.

As a young man Wambsganss, the son of a Lutheran minister, was preparing to follow in his father's footsteps by entering a theological seminary in St. Louis. He was simply not cut out for the job, however, because he was absolutely terrified of public speaking. As he later recalled, "Unfortunately, nobody there was willing to take the bull by the horns and say right out that this kid just wouldn't make a good minister. So I went through. It's a joke, but I did."

It is said that the Creator works in mysterious ways. At the seminary was another student who had played professional baseball. In 1913 the manager of the Cedar Rapids club wrote to him, asking if he knew of any good shortstops. He recommended Wambsganss.

Wambsganss played for Cedar Rapids that season and part of the next, and in August 1914 he was sold to the Cleveland Indians. At Cleveland he was converted into a second baseman and combined with shortstop Ray Chapman for a smooth keystone combo.

Despite Chapman's death from a beaning during the 1920 season, the Indians won the American League pennant and played the Brooklyn Robins in the World Series that fall. With the Series knotted at two games apiece, the teams squared off for Game 5 on Sunday, October 10.

The Indians broke through early, scoring four runs in the first inning on right fielder Elmer Smith's grand slam, the first bases-loaded homer in Series history. In the fourth inning Cleveland starter Jim Bagby made it 7-0 when he smacked a three-run homer into the center field bleachers, the first World Series homer ever by a pitcher.

In the fifth inning Brooklyn second baseman Pete Kilduff led off with a single against Bagby, followed by another single from catcher Otto Miller. Suddenly, the Robins had runners on first and second with none out. Next up was Clarence Mitchell, a good-hitting pitcher who had relieved starter Burleigh Grimes. Brooklyn Manager Wilbert "Uncle Robbie" Robinson signaled for a hit-and-run.

Kilduff and Miller took off, and Mitchell sent a screaming line drive in the direction of second base. Wambsganss hadn't been near the bag when the pitch was thrown, but he ran frantically and dove for the ball, coming up with a beautiful one-handed grab for the first out.

By now Kilduff had almost reached third, and it took little effort for Wambsganss to scramble to his feet and touch second base for a double play. In the next moment, Wambsganss seemed about to throw the ball to first for an easy third out, but Cleveland shortstop Joe Sewell yelled, "Tag him! Tag him!"

"You see," Sewell recalled, "Bill had run to the bag, made sure he touched it, but hadn't yet looked toward first base. He had his arm cocked to throw, but when he looked around there was Otto Miller, running right toward him. Bill just went up to him and touched him on the chest with the ball, just as easy as saying hello. I think that was the first that Otto Miller realized the ball had been caught. When Bill touched him, Miller stopped in his tracks with the most dumbfounded look on his face."

The 26,884 fans at Cleveland's League Park weren't quite sure what they had witnessed. "So there was dead silence for a few seconds," recalled Wambsganss. "Then as I approached the dugout, it began to dawn on them what they had just seen, and the cheering started and got quickly louder and louder and louder. By the time I got back to the bench it was bedlam, straw hats flying onto the field, people yelling themselves hoarse, my teammates pounding me on the back."

Wambsganss died in 1985 at the age of 91. In 13 years in the big leagues he amassed 1,359 hits in 1,492 games and recorded 3,411 putouts and 4,262 assists, but he will always be remembered as the man who pulled off the unassisted triple play in the 1920 World Series.

Vic Wertz

Vic Wertz made the most famous out in Indians history, "the Catch," the towering flyball that he powered well over 400 feet in the 1954 World Series — only to have it snagged by Willie Mays in a breathtaking act of defensive artistry. Mays then made an equally sensational throw to allow only a single-base advance by one of the two baserunners.

It became part of baseball history because it happened during a World Series, was on national television, and because it broke the spirit of the Indians completely. Wertz had his own view. He said, "If it had been a home run or a triple, would people have remembered it? Not likely."

Wertz had already reached Giants pitcher Sal Maglie for three hits, including a two-run triple in the first inning that had given Cleveland the lead. But when Wertz came to bat in the eighth with Larry Doby and Al Rosen on base, Leo Durocher replaced Maglie with lefty Don Liddle.

When left fielder Monte Irvin saw the ball hit he ran toward it. "I was hoping to play the rebound and hold it to a triple," he recalled. When asked about the catch afterwards, Durocher said it was routine. "Routine!" the reporters protested. "Routine for Willie Mays, I mean," Leo replied.

The Giants won the game in the last of the ninth on Dusty Rhodes's pinch homer, and the Indians were swept. Wertz hit .500 in that Series, twice the average of any other Cleveland regular, and led both teams with eight hits. It was his only postseason appearance during his 17-year career.

He first played professional baseball at age 17, hitting .239 for Winston-Salem of the Piedmont League. With Buffalo in 1946 he hit .301, slugged 19 homers, and drove in 91 runs. The impressed Tigers promoted the powerful young left-handed hitter, and in his rookie year he banged 22 doubles, the first of eight times in his career that he would reach that mark. In 1949 Wertz was installed as the Tigers' regular left fielder and became an All-Star, collecting 20 homers, 133 RBI, and a .304 average for the season.

He drove in 123 runs in 1950 and 94 in 1951, but in August 1952 the Tigers sent Wertz, Dick Littlefield, and two others to the St. Louis Browns for Ned Garver and three additional players. Wertz hit 23 homers that season for the two teams. He hit 19 the following year for the Browns, but was swapped to Cleveland on June 1, 1954.

After three years of split duty in the outfield and at first base, Wertz was installed as the Indians' permanent first baseman in 1955. In August of that year Wertz was stricken by a non-paralytic form of polio, but he made a remarkably quick recovery and in 1956 had the best home run year of his career, slamming 32 dingers while driving in 106 runs. He continued his power surge in 1957 with 28 homers and 105 RBI.

A leg injury kept him out of all but 25 games in 1958, and the Indians swapped Wertz and Gary Geiger to the Red Sox in December for Jimmy Piersall. As a 35-year-old in Boston in 1960, Wertz hit 19 homers with 103 RBIs, the fifth 100-plus RBI season of his career.

Late in the 1961 season Wertz was released to the Tigers on waivers. In 1962 he hit .324 for Detroit in 74 games, including a league-leading 17 pinch hits, but his power stroke was gone — only five of his hits had left the park. When the Tigers cut him in early 1963 he played 35 games with the Minnesota Twins before retiring.

A successful operator of a beer distributorship in Detroit, Wertz also scouted for the Tigers. Historian Bill James says that "with Hodges and Kluszewski, Wertz ranks as the best first baseman of the 1950s."

★ Early Wynn ★

Mickey Mantle once said that pitcher Early Wynn was "so mean he'd knock you down in the dugout."

The overpowering righthander had five 20-win seasons, 300 career victories, and is in the Hall of Fame. Opposing hitters remember Wynn for the way he established himself with inside fastballs. Once when Ted Williams refused Wynn's invitation to go fishing in the Everglades, Wynn said, "Admit it. You're afraid to go into the Everglades with me." Williams replied, "No hitter ever would go into the Everglades with a pitcher like you. His body might never be found."

Wynn would have won even more games had he not pitched more than six full seasons for the weak-hitting Washington Senators. He suffered 45 shutout defeats — many of them with the Senators — which accounted for nearly one-fifth of his career 244 losses. As it was, some of his best run support came from his own bat. The switch-hitting Wynn compiled a .214 batting average with 17 homers and 173 RBIs. Called upon to pinch hit 90 times in his career, he is one of only five pitchers to stroke a pinch-hit grand slam, turning the trick against Detroit's Johnny Gorsica on September 15, 1946.

In 1936, at age 16, Wynn tried out with the Senators in Florida and impressed Clyde Milan, who signed him. Wynn played for Sanford and Charlotte before he broke in with Washington late in 1939. He made three appearances with the Senators in 1939 and five more in 1942, when he went 3-1 with a 1.58 ERA.

Washington finished in second place in the American League in 1943, and Wynn won 18 games with a 2.91 ERA. But the following season Washington was terrible, losing 90 games and finishing in the cellar. The Senators were last in the league in errors and next-to-last in home runs and afforded Wynn little offensive support. Despite a respectable ERA of 3.38, Wynn lost a league-leading 17 games including 11 straight.

Wynn spent all of 1945 in the armed services and returned for part of the 1946 season. In 1947 he won 17 games, but he finished 8-19 in 1948 and was traded with Mickey Vernon to Cleveland in December for three players. Wynn said Cleveland pitching coach Mel Harder made him a consistent winner. "He showed me how to improve my grip and delivery of the curveball and also encouraged me to throw a knuckleball," Wynn said.

Nicknamed "Gus," short for "Gloomy Gus," Wynn had his first big year as an Indian in 1950, going 18-8 and leading the league with a 3.20 ERA. He was one of three Indians to win 20 games in 1951, joining Bob Feller (22) and Mike Garcia (20). The Indians remained in the pennant race until the final two weeks, before finishing in second place, five games behind the Yankees.

Cleveland got off to a blazing start in 1952, while the Yankees were just 18-17 by the end of May. When Labor Day arrived, New York was 2½ games behind Cleveland, but was faced with 18 of its last 21 games on the road. The Indians, meanwhile, had 20 of their last 22 at home. The two clubs met in mid-September before more than 73,000 fans and the Yankees beat Garcia, 7-1. Cleveland finished the season two games back, despite Wynn's 23 victories.

In 1954 Wynn and teammate Bob Lemon topped the league with 23 victories apiece, and the Indians ran away with the pennant, winning 111 games. Lemon started Game 1 of the World Series for the Indians against the Giants, the game which featured the immortal Willie Mays catch. Wynn started Game 2 and had a 1-0 lead entering the bottom of the fifth. But New York scored twice in the inning and added an insurance run in the seventh. Wynn allowed only four hits in seven innings, but he was a tough-luck loser. The Giants went on to sweep the Indians in four games.

In 1955 rookie Herb Score made his major league debut for the Tribe, going 16-10 with a league-leading 245 strikeouts. Wynn won 17 games and Lemon added 18 victories, but the Indians finished three games back of the Yankees. Wynn, Score, and Lemon each won 20 games in 1956, but New York cruised to its seventh pennant in eight years. During one game, Wynn was hit in the jaw by a line drive off the bat of Jose Valdivielso. He refused to come out of the game immediately. When he finally did leave, he required 16 stitches and lost seven lower teeth.

The following season was a nightmare for both Wynn and the Indians. Despite leading the league in strikeouts, Wynn posted a 14-17 record, and his 4.31 ERA was his highest since 1948. On May 7 Score was struck in the eye by a line drive by New York's Gil McDougald, an injury that all but ended his career. Cleveland finished in sixth place, and on December 4 Wynn was traded to the White Sox along with Al Smith for Minnie Minoso and Fred Hatfield.

Wynn led the AL in strikeouts again in 1958, and he picked up the win in the All-Star Game, ironically on a pinch-hit single by McDougald. In 1959, at age 39, Wynn had his greatest season. He led the league in starts and innings pitched (for the third time), won 22 games, started the first 1959 All-Star Game, was named the Cy Young Award winner, and pitched the "Go-Go" Sox to a 1959 pennant. He shut out the Dodgers, 11-0, in the Series opener but was ineffective in Game 4, as the White Sox committed three errors in one inning. Facing a must-win

situation in Game 6, Wynn was bombed in three innings, and Los Angeles breezed to a 9-3 win and a world championship.

When the 1962 season started, Wynn had 292 career wins. He went 7-15, leaving him one victory short of the 300 mark. He was not signed by the Sox the next season but was picked up in June by the Indians. "I was out of shape, but I immediately reported to Cleveland and worked out twice a day . . . Fifteen days later I was ready," Wynn said.

He lasted only five innings against Kansas City on July 13, but he posted his 300th win. "I never slept the night before. The gout was killing me . . . It was so nice to win 300 though. I felt I had it coming to me after pitching so well for so long and losing so many tough ones," Wynn said.

Wynn, who pitched in four decades, was the major league's all-time leader in walks until Nolan Ryan surpassed him. He later became a pitching coach with the Indians and Twins and a manager in the Twins' farm system. After retiring from coaching, Wynn became a broadcaster for the Toronto Blue Jays and the Chicago White Sox. He was named to the Hall of Fame in 1972.

★ Cy Young ★

One question that never can be answered is, "How many Cy Youngs would Cy Young have won if there had been a Cy Young Award when he pitched?"

Various historians and statisticians have given estimates of four to six, but such assertions are based solely on numbers and ignore the human factor. Because Cy Young was well-liked, he might have been voted the award a couple of times when he wasn't statistically the best pitcher in his league.

Young is significant not only because of how many seasons he was the best pitcher in the league but also because of his consistency. While other pitchers came and went, Young turned in one very good year after another. In several single seasons he was probably the best pitcher in baseball, but for nearly two decades he was always one of the best. He won 30 or more games 5 times, 25 or more 12 times, and 20 or more 15 times.

When Young first arrived in the major leagues in 1890, John Clarkson, Tim Keefe, and Old Hoss Radbourn were still star pitchers. When he retired, Walter Johnson and Christy Mathewson were well into their careers. Amos Rusie and Kid Nichols were among Young's contemporaries, yet Young was still pitching years after they retired. By the time he called it quits at age 44, Young had compiled a record that will never be matched, and for this reason his name is on the modern award signifying pitching excellence.

Denton True Young was born on an Ohio farm in 1867. In his prime he stood 6-foot-2 and weighed 210 pounds. He always credited his durability to hard work on the farm as a youth. Yet most ballplayers of his era came from a similar background. In 1889, when Young was still called "Dent," he played third base for the Tuscarawas County semipro team in Ohio. The next year he turned professional as a pitcher with Canton of the Tri-State League.

Young was 15-15 in August when the Cleveland Spiders of the National League acquired him. In one version of the deal, the Canton manager owed a debt to Cleveland, which he repaid with Young. In another, the Cleveland manager bought Young for $300 and a suit of clothes for the Canton manager. Still other reports set the sale price at $500, with the new suit going to Young, who had arrived in Cleveland looking like a country bumpkin. Once the deal was done, the burly righthander went 9-6 for the seventh-place Spiders.

He picked up the nickname "Cy" early in his career. Some say the name was short for "Cyclone," because of the speed of his pitches. A more common suggestion is that "Cy" was a common name for a rube.

A story in *Sporting Life* appears to support both contentions. "As the players came from the clubhouse for practice an uncouth figure that brought a titter from the stands, shambled along behind them. It was Denton T. Young, the new 'phenom.' Darius Green, the Pied Piper, and other noted characters of fact and fiction had nothing on Young for weirdness of appearance. The baseball knickerbockers he wore had been made for a man many inches shorter and served the recruit little better than a bluff. His jersey shirt stretched across his massive body like a drumhead, and his arms dangled through its sleeves almost to the shoulder. He dragged himself across the field bashfully, every angle of his great frame exaggerated and emphasized, and the stands tittered again.

"The great (Cap) Anson saw Young. 'Is that the phenom?' he asked with a sneer." As the story goes, the Chicago players all laughed when they saw Young. *Sporting Life* continued, "The gaunt figure lost its uncouthness as he warmed to his work, and the ball shot to the catcher's thin glove with a crack that betokened even greater speed than the flash of the sphere in the sunlight . . . The game began and the Chicago batters strode to the plate arrogant and confident. One after the other they threw down their bats and returned to the bench puzzled and baffled . . . Young grew even more effective as the innings passed and Chicago left the field beaten and blind with rage. Then the crowd which had laughed at the unique figure of the new pitcher arose in a mass and gave him an ovation." After the game Anson offered Cleveland $1,000 for the young pitcher. He was laughed out of town.

Cleveland raised the phenom's salary from $300 to $1,400 in 1891. Young came through with a 27-22 record in 423 innings pitched. He was still a bit wild and walked 140 batters, but in the next decade his control improved steadily. When the pitching distance was moved back to 60-plus feet in 1893, many pitchers experienced control problems. Not Young. Eventually he became one of baseball's "control artists," walking only slightly more than one batter per game. According to historian Lee Allen, "There have been faster pitchers . . . but his control was so unerring and he was so tireless that he just kept throwing as if he were systematically chopping down a tree."

The old American Association went under after the 1891 season. Hoping to create a postseason moneymaker, the National League divided the 1892 season into two halves, with the winner of the first half meeting the second-half winner in a so-called "World Series." Boston won the opening half, and Cleveland took the second part of the season behind Young. He finished 36-11, leading the league with a .766 winning percentage, nine shutouts,

and an earned run average of 1.93. Young opened the postseason by pitching an 11-inning scoreless tie against Boston's Jack Stivetts, but Boston won the next five games to take the Series.

Often praised for his sportsmanship, Young was considered one of the NL's gentlemen during the 1890s. Perhaps he stood out because his Spider teammates were generally regarded as a bunch of thugs. The Baltimore Orioles, who won pennants from 1894 through 1896, are better known today for their notorious behavior. But according to Lee Allen, "the Spiders could hold their own with the Orioles when it came to umpire-baiting, tricky play, and general cussedness. Their field captain and manager, Patsy Tebeau, was the prototype of hooligans, and his players cheerfully followed his example."

The great hitter Jesse Burkett, one of the Spider outfielders, ranked second only to Tebeau in his ability to intimidate an opponent with fists, spikes, or brutal profanity. When the Orioles and Spiders faced each other there was likely to be blood on the field and blue air above it.

In 1895 the Spiders and Orioles faced off in "the Temple Cup Series," another NL attempt to create a postseason draw. The Orioles didn't take the contest seriously and lost to the Spiders in five games. Young, a 35-game winner in the regular season, won three of the five postseason games. When the two teams met the next year in another Cup series, the Orioles, stung by criticism of their 1895 performance, swept the Spiders in four games.

On September 18, 1897, Young pitched a 6-0 no-hitter against Cincinnati. But that was a fleeting success. Despite his pitching, Burkett's hitting, and Tebeau's reign of terror, the Spiders began to slip. Attendance fell, and Cleveland owners Frank and Stanley Robison acquired the St. Louis franchise as well. In 1899 they moved their best players, including Young, to St. Louis and left Cleveland with the dregs. Young hated the heat in St. Louis. Nor was he particularly fond of the $2,400 cap the NL had placed on salaries.

When Ban Johnson offered him $3,000 to pitch for Boston in the new AL, Young jumped. His first three years in Boston were three of his very best. Young led the new AL in victories all three seasons while compiling a 93-30 mark.

By the time Boston won the pennant in 1903, relations with the NL had improved to the point that a real World Series was staged between Boston and Pittsburgh. In the best-of-nine affair Young's teammate Bill Dinneen emerged as Boston's pitching star with three wins, including the final game. Young lost the opening game, then pitched seven innings of relief in another Boston loss in Game 3. He pulled double duty in that contest, taking tickets before the game when Boston's overflow crowd swamped the gates. But he came back to beat Pittsburgh, 11-2 and 7-3, in Games 5 and 7.

Young helped pitch Boston to another pennant in 1904, but the NL champion New York Giants refused to take part in a World Series. His 26-16 mark included a league-leading 10 shutouts. In one early-season stretch he threw 44 consecutive scoreless innings. During the streak, on May 5 against Philadelphia, he tossed a perfect game to win, 3-0.

When Boston slipped to fourth place the following year, Young suffered the first losing season of his career.

Still, he completed 32 of 33 starts, lowered his ERA to 1.82, and struck out a personal-best 208 batters. In 1906, however, Young did not meet his usual standards. His record dropped to 13-21, and his ERA ballooned to 3.19. Some people wondered if Young, by then 39 years old, was nearing the end of his career.

In 1907, the year Boston's team was renamed the Red Sox, Manager Chick Stahl committed suicide during spring training. Young was named to take over, even though he didn't want the job. Young told team owner John I. Taylor that he would run the club only until someone else could be found. He opened the season as the first Red Sox manager and went 3-3 before Taylor produced a replacement. Young gladly resumed his pitching duties and went 22-15 with a 1.99 ERA for the seventh-place Sox.

On June 30, 1908, at age 41, he pitched his third no-hitter, an 8-0 win over New York, and went on to compile his last 20-win season. On August 13 the *Boston Post* sponsored Cy Young Day, and an all-star team played the Red Sox. A crowd of 20,000 jammed the Huntington Avenue Grounds, and another 10,000 fans were turned away. Young received a leather traveling bag from the umpires, a silver cup from the players, numerous floral tributes, and $6,000. He was so overcome with emotion that he couldn't speak.

In 1909 Young was sold to the Cleveland Indians for $12,500, and he went 19-15. In 1911 he split his final season between Cleveland and the Boston Braves, finishing 7-9. His arm was still sound, but Young complained that he was too fat to field bunts.

In 1937 Young was the third pitcher named to the Hall of Fame, after Walter Johnson and Christy Mathewson. He retired to his farm in Ohio but lost a fortune in the stock market and was forced to board with neighbors. He remained active until his final years. The aging Young often sat in his favorite armchair, looking over the familiar Ohio landscape, proud of his victory total. He once told a visitor, "Far as I can see, these modern pitchers aren't going to catch me." Young was 88 when he died in 1955. The next year the award bearing his name was given for the first time.

Cy Young compiled an astonishing record. He won 511 games and lost 316, more than any other pitcher. His statistics include at least three other firsts, with 815 starts, 749 complete games, and 7,354⅓ innings pitched. His 2,800 strikeouts, 75 shutouts, and 2.63 earned run average are among the best ever. In 1993 Young was given permanent recognition in Boston when Northeastern University erected a statue of him approximately where the pitcher's mound at the Huntington Avenue Grounds once was.

The Indians Index

CHAPTER 7

The Player Register

The Indians Player Register consists of the central batting, baserunning, and fielding statistics of every man who has batted for the team since 1901, excepting those men who were primarily pitchers. A pitcher's complete batting record, however, is included for those pitchers who also, over the course of their careers, played in 100 or more games at another position—including pinch hitter—or played in more than half of their total major league games at a position other than pitcher, or played more games at a position other than pitcher in at least one year. (Pitcher batting is also expressed in Batting Wins in the Pitcher Batting column of the Indians Pitcher Register.)

The players are listed alphabetically by surname and, when more than one player bears the name, alphabetically by *given* name—not by "use name," by which we mean the name that may have been applied to him during his playing career. This is the standard method of alphabetizing used in other biographical reference works, and in the case of baseball it makes it easier to find a lesser-known player with a common surname like Smith or Johnson. On the whole, we have been conservative in ascribing nicknames, doing so only when the player was in fact known by that name during his playing days.

Each page of the Player Register is topped at the corner by a finding aid: in capital letters, the surname of, first, the player whose entry heads up the page and, second, the player whose entry concludes it. Another finding aid is the use of boldface numerals to indicate a league-leading total in those categories in which a player is truly attempting to excel (no boldface is given to the "leaders" in batter strikeouts, times caught stealing, at bats, or games played). An additional finding aid is an asterisk alongside the team for which a player appeared in postseason competition, thus making for easy cross-reference to the earlier section on postseason play. Additional symbols denote All Star Game selection and/or play; these appear to the right of the team/league column. Condensed type appears occasionally throughout this section; it has no special significance but is designed simply to accommodate unusually wide figures, such as the 4.000 slugging average of a man who, in his only at bat of the year, hit a home run.

The record for each man who played in more than one season as an Indian is given in a line for each season, plus a career total line and an Indians total line. Refer to the preceding Player Index, and ultimately to *Total Baseball*, for complete seasonal data for Indians when they wore the uniforms of other clubs. If a man played for another team in addition to the Indians, only his total for the Indians is shown in a given year. And a man who played in only one year will have no additional career total line, since it would be identical to his seasonal listing.

Gaps remain in the official record of baseball and in the ongoing process of sabermetric reconstruction. The reader will note occasional blank elements in biographical lines, or in single-season columns; these are not typographical lapses but signs that the information does not exist or has not yet been found. In the totals lines of many players, an underlined figure indicates that the total reflects partial data, such as caught stealing for a man whose career covers the National League of 1918–1930 (during which this data was available only for 1920–1925), or batter strikeouts for a man whose career spanned both sides of the year 1909.

For a discussion of which data is missing for particular years, see "The History of Major League Baseball Statistics" in *Total Baseball*. Here is a quick summation of the data missing from *Total Indians*:

Hit batters, 1897–1908 NL/AL, 5 percent missing;
Caught stealing, 1886–1914, 1916 for players with fewer than 20 stolen bases, 1917–1919, 1926–1950 NL; 1886–1891 AA; 1890 PL; 1901–1913, 1916 for players with fewer than 20 stolen bases, 1917–1919 AL (1927 data, missing from the first edition, is now 90 percent complete); 1914–15 FL;
Sacrifice hit, 1908–1930, 1939 (in these years fly balls scoring runners counted as sacrifice hits, and in 1927–1930 fly balls advancing runners to any base counted as sacrifices);
Sacrifice fly, 1908–1930, 1939 (counted but inseparable from sacrifice hits), 1940–1953 (not counted);

For a key to the team and league abbreviations used in the Player Register, flip to the last page of this volume. For a guide to the other procedures and abbreviations employed in the Player Register, review the comments on the prodigiously extended playing record on the next page.

Looking at the biographical line for any player, we see first his use name in full capitals, then his given name and nickname (and any other name he may have used or been born with, such as the matronymic of a Latin American player). His date and place of birth follow "b" and his date and place of death follow "d." Years through 1900 are expressed fully, in four digits, and years after 1900 are expressed in their last two digits.

Then comes the player's manner of batting and throwing, abbreviated for a lefthanded batter who throws right as BL/TR (a switch-hitter would be shown as BB for "bats both" and a switch thrower as TB for "throws both").

Next, and for most players last, is the player's debut date in the major leagues.

Some players continue in major league baseball after their playing days are through, as managers, coaches, or even umpires. A player whose biographical line concludes with an M served as a major league manager, not necessarily with the Indians; one whose line bears a C served as a major league coach; and one with a U served as a umpire. (In the last case we have placed a U on the biographical line only for those players who umpired in at

YEAR	TM/L	G	AB	R	H	2B	3B	HR	RBI	BB	SO	AVG	OBP	SLG	PRO+	BR/A	SB	CS	SBR	FA	FR	G/POS	TPR
■ KID DE LEON		Ponce de Leon, Juan "Castilian Kid" (also played in 1874 as Kid Madrid)																					
		b: 3/13/1460, Madrid, Spain d: 2/25/1968, St. Augustine, Fl. BR/TR, 5'11", 173 lbs. Deb: 5/21/01 FMUCH																					
1901	Cle-A	52	277	73	94	7	4	1	14	2		.339	.342	.400	111	4						*2-52	0.2
1902	Cle-A	2	3	1	1	0	0	0	0	0		.333	.333	.333	95	0						/S-2	0.0
1905	Cle-A	28	121	12	33	2	1	1	10	8		.273	.318	.331	101	2				.901	0	C-16,O-10/S	0.0
1906	Cle-A	87	375	76	108	12	5	2	40	11		.288	.309	.358	128	-0	0			.914	0	1-63,O-15/C	0.9
1907	Cle-A	1	1	1	0	0	0	0	0	0		—	—	—			0	0		.000	0	/2-1	0.0
1908	Cle-A	9	31	5	9	3	0	0	2	0		.290	.290	.387	113	0	0			.899	-1	/3-8	0.0
1909	Cle-A	148	541	73	165	27	19	4	85	26		.305	.343	.447	146	26	20			.920	-5	*3-141	3.0
1910	Cle-A	146	561	83	159	25	15	2	75	34		.283	.329	.392	123	13	21			.934	3	*3-144	2.4
1911	Cle-A	148	592	96	198	40	4	11	115	50		.334	.379	.505	157	38	38			.912	-8	*3-147	3.3
1912	Cle-A	149	577	116	200	40	21	10	130	50		.347	.404	.541	171	50	40			.930	9	*3-149	5.4
1913	Cle-A	149	564	116	190	34	9	12	117	63	31	.337	.413	.493	171	48	34			.927	7	*3-148	6.1
1916	Cle-A	100	360	46	97	23	2	10	52	36	30	.269	.344	.428	130	12	15			.931	3	3-98	2.1
1917	Cle-A	146	553	57	156	24	2	6	71	48	27	.282	.345	.365	109	6	18			.940	11	*3-145	2.7
1918	Cle-A	126	504	65	154	24	5	6	62	38	13	.306	.357	.409	138	20	8			.943	11	*3-122	3.4
1956	*Cle-A☆	141	567	70	166	22	1	10	83	44	18	.293	.346	.388	100	-0	13	6	0	.944	-2	*3-140	0.9
1957	*Cle-A★	94	330	46	97	16	2	9	71	26	12	.294	.353	.436	98	-2	8	5	-1	.955	13	3-92	1.6
1966	*Cle-A†	69	234	30	65	12	3	7	36	15	14	.278	.327	.444	98	-2	1	3	-2	.940	-8	3-67	-0.4
Total	21	1694	6489	981	1983	329	100	100	992	502	184	.306	.354	.446	130	246	235	34		.938	41	*3-1409,1-126/CSO2R	35.6
Team	17	1541	5911	892	1797	304	89	90	949	449	145	.304	.353	.448	132	210	216	14		.937	32	*3-1257,1-126/CSO2R	31.4

least six games in a year.) The select few who have been enshrined in the Baseball Hall of Fame at Cooperstown, NY, are noted with an H. Also on this line is an F to denote family connection—father-son-grandson or brother.

The explanations for the statistical column heads follow; for more technical information about formulas and calculations, see the next-to-last page. The vertical rules in the column-header line separate the stats into seven logical groupings: year, team, league; fundamental counting stats for batters; hits and plate appearances broken out into their component counting stats; basic calculated averages; sabermetric figures of more complex calculation; baserunning stats; fielding stats and Total Player Rating.

Newly found hit-by-pitch data for batters in the 1897-1908 period is reflected in their on base percentages. We have also made an upward adjustment to overall league performance in the Federal League of 1914-15 (thus lowering individual ratings), because while that league is regarded as a major league, there can be no doubt that its caliber of play was not equivalent to that in the rival leagues of those years. Suffice it to say here that league at bats were reduced to 90 percent for the FL. Few Indians extended their careers into the FL.

YEAR Year of play

* Denotes postseason play, World Series or League Championship Series

TM/L Team and League

★ Named to All Star Game, played

☆ Named to All Star Game, did not play

† Named to All Star Game, replaced because of injury

G Games

AB At-bats

R Runs

H Hits

2B Doubles

3B Triples

HR Home Runs

RBI Runs Batted In

BB Bases on Balls

SO Strikeouts

AVG Batting Average (Figured as hits over at-bats; mathematically meaningless averages created through a division by zero are rendered as dashes; see Kid De Leon's entry for 1908. League leaders in this category, as in others in the Player Register, are noted by bold type. However, some bold-face leaders in batting average will have lower marks than other batters who are not credited with having won a championship; for a full explanation of the reasoning for this anomaly, see "The History of Major League Baseball Statistics" in *Total Baseball*.

OBP On Base Percentage (See comments for AVG)

SLG Slugging Average (See comments for AVG)

PRO+ Production Plus, or Adjusted Production (On Base Percentage plus Slugging Average, normalized to league average and adjusted for home-park factor.) See comments for /A.

BR/A Batting Runs (Linear Weights measure of runs contributed beyond what a league-average batter or team might have contributed, defined as zero. Occasionally the curious figure of -0 will appear in this column, or in the columns of other Linear Weights measures of batting, baserunning, fielding, and the TPR. This "negative zero" figure signifies a run contribution that falls below the league average, but to so small a degree that it cannot be said to have cost the team a run. The "/A" signifies that the measure has been adjusted for home-park factor and normalized to league average. A mark of 100 is a league-average performance. Pitcher batting is removed from all league batting statistics before normalization, for a variety of reasons. Three-year averages are employed for batting park factors. If a team moved or the park changed dramatically, then two-year averages are employed; if the park was used for only one year, then of course only that run-scoring data is used.)

SB   Stolen Bases

CS   Caught Stealing (Available 1915, 1916 for players with 20 or more stolen bases, 1920–1925, 1951–date NL; 1914–1915, 1916 for players with 20 or more stolen bases, 1920 to date AL with scattered data still missing from 1927.)

SBA   Stolen Base Average (Stolen bases divided by attempts; availability dependent upon CS as shown above.)

SBR   Stolen Base Runs (This is a Linear Weights measure of runs contributed *beyond* what a league-average base stealer might have gained, defined as zero and calculated on the basis of a 66.7 percent success rate, which computer simulations have shown to be the break-even point beyond which stolen bases have positive run value to the team. The presence of a figure in the SBR column in the Player Register is dependent upon the availability of CS as shown above. Lifetime Stolen Base Runs are not totaled where data is incomplete, but seasonal SBRs are reflected in the seasonal Total Player Ratings, which in turn are added to form the lifetime Total Player Rating.)

FA   Fielding Average, often called Fielding Percentage as well (putouts plus assists divided by putouts plus assists plus errors, here calculated only for the position at which a man played the most games in a season or career.)

FR   Fielding Runs (The Linear Weights measure of runs saved *beyond* what a league-average player at that position might have saved, defined as zero; this stat is calculated to take account of the particular demands of the different positions; see next-to-last page for formulas.)

G/POS   Positions played (This is a ranking from left to right by frequency of the positions played in the field or at designated hitter. An asterisk to the left of the position indicates, generally, that in a given year the man played two-thirds of his team's scheduled games at that position. When a slash separates positions, the man played those positions listed to the left of the slash in 10 or more games and the positions to the right of the slash in fewer than 10 games. If there is no slash, he played all positions listed in 10 or more games. For the lifetime line, the asterisk signifies 1,000 games and the slash marks a dividing point of 100 games. A player's POS column will list him as a pinch runner or pinch hitter in only those years in which he appeared at no other position. New to this edition are listings of the number of games played at the individual's two most common positions. The positions and their abbreviations are)

1:	First base	P:	Pitcher
2:	Second base	D:	Designated hitter
S:	Shortstop	R:	Runner (pinch)
3:	Third base	H:	Hitter (pinch)
O:	Outfield	M:	Manager (playing)
C:	Catcher		

TPR   Total Player Rating (This is the sum of a player's Adjusted Batting Runs, Fielding Runs, and Base Stealing Runs, minus his positional adjustment, all divided by the Runs Per Win factor for that year—generally around 10, historically in the 9–11 range. In the lifetime line, the TPR is the sum of the seasonal TPRs. For men who were primarily pitchers but whose extent of play at other positions warrants a listing in the Player Register as well as the Pitcher Register, the TPR may be listed as 0.0; this signifies that their batting records are summed up in the Total Pitcher Index [TPI] column of the Pitcher Register.) A broader and more sophisticated computation of the positional adjustment to Batting Runs has improved the accuracy and reasonableness of the method, by which the TPR of those who play skill positions like shortstop and second base tend to be boosted and the TPR of the sluggers who customarily play first base and left field are generally diminished. Because games in left, center, and right fields are now available for all outfielders, center fielders no longer need be compared to an average of the regular center fielders and now may be set against all the men who played center, thus tending to elevate their Fielding Runs. Because Hit Batsmen data is now available for the 1903–1908 period, plus considerable data for the years 1897–1902, men like Frank Chance, who was hit over 100 times in his career, increase their Batter Ratings perceptibly. And for players who were both batters and pitchers, the method of allocating Wins between TPR and TPI (Total Pitcher Index) was improved. Previously, if a pitcher pitched in over half his games, all his batting was included with his pitcher rating (TPI); if he pitched in less than half his games, his Batting Wins were thrown over to his batter rating (TPR), with his TPI including only his Pitching Wins and Pitcher Defense. The new method prorates batting proportionally with the number of games pitched. In addition, fielding ratings at nonpitching positions for players who pitched in over half their games, previously omitted, are now part of the Total Baseball Ranking.

Total   The lifetime record is shown alongside the notation "Total x," where *x* stands for the number of years totaled. Note the underlined entries in the record for Kid De Leon, reflecting the partial data for batter strikeouts, and times caught stealing.

Team   The totals for a player while he was an Indian, from 1901 onward.

■ FRED ABBOTT
Abbott, Harry Frederick (b: Harry Frederick Winbigler)
b: 10/22/1874, Versailles, Ohio d: 6/11/35, Los Angeles, Cal. BR/TR, 5'10", 180 lbs. Deb: 4/25/03

YEAR	TM/L	G	AB	R	H	2B	3B	HR	RBI	BB	SO	AVG	OBP	SLG	PRO+	BR/A	SB	CS	SBR	FA	FR	G/POS	TPR
1903	Cle-A	77	255	25	60	11	3	1	25	7		.235	.270	.314	76	-8	8			.958	9	C-71/1-3	0.8
1904	Cle-A	41	130	14	22	4	2	0	12	6		.169	.206	.231	38	-9	2			.953	-3	C-33/1-7	-0.9
Total	3	160	513	48	107	21	6	1	49	19		.209	.248	.279	61	-24	14			.956	6	C-138/1-15	-0.6
Team	2	118	385	39	82	15	5	1	37	13		.213	.248	.286	64	-17	10			.956	6	C-104/1-10	-0.1

■ BERT ADAMS
Adams, John Bertram b: 6/21/1891, Wharton, Tex. d: 6/24/40, Los Angeles, Cal. BB/TR, 6'1", 185 lbs. Deb: 8/30/10

YEAR	TM/L	G	AB	R	H	2B	3B	HR	RBI	BB	SO	AVG	OBP	SLG	PRO+	BR/A	SB	CS	SBR	FA	FR	G/POS	TPR
1910	Cle-A	5	13	1	3	0	0	0	0	0		.231	.231	.231	44	-1	0			.964	3	/C-5	0.3
1911	Cle-A	2	5	0	1	0	0	0	0	1		.200	.333	.200	50	-0	0			.900	-1	/C-2	-0.1
1912	Cle-A	20	54	5	11	2	1	0	6	4		.204	.259	.278	52	-4	0			.942	2	C-20	0.0
Total	8	267	678	37	137	17	4	2	45	23		.202	.229	.248	42	-48	9			.970	-2	C-248/1-3	-3.7
Team	3	27	72	6	15	2	1	0	6	5		.208	.260	.264	50	-5	0			.943	4	/C-27	0.2

■ JOE ADCOCK
Adcock, Joseph Wilbur b: 10/30/27, Coushatta, La. BR/TR, 6'4", 220 lbs. Deb: 4/23/50 M

YEAR	TM/L	G	AB	R	H	2B	3B	HR	RBI	BB	SO	AVG	OBP	SLG	PRO+	BR/A	SB	CS	SBR	FA	FR	G/POS	TPR
1963	Cle-A	97	283	28	71	7	1	13	49	30	53	.251	.323	.420	107	3	1	2	-1	.995	-4	1-78	-0.6
Total	17	1959	6606	823	1832	295	35	336	1122	594	1059	.277	.339	.485	125	210	20	25		.994	-28	*1-1501,O-310	7.3

■ TOMMIE AGEE
Agee, Tommie Lee b: 8/9/42, Magnolia, Ala. BR/TR, 5'11", 195 lbs. Deb: 9/14/62

YEAR	TM/L	G	AB	R	H	2B	3B	HR	RBI	BB	SO	AVG	OBP	SLG	PRO+	BR/A	SB	CS	SBR	FA	FR	G/POS	TPR
1962	Cle-A	5	14	0	3	0	0	0	2	0	4	.214	.214	.214	16	-2	0	0	0	1.000	-0	/O-3	-0.2
1963	Cle-A	13	27	3	4	1	0	1	3	2	9	.148	.207	.296	39	-2	0	0	0	1.000	-1	O-13	-0.4
1964	Cle-A	13	12	0	2	0	0	0	0	0	3	.167	.167	.167	-7	-2	0	0	0	1.000	-4	O-12	-0.6
Total	12	1129	3912	558	999	170	27	130	433	342	918	.255	.321	.412	108	35	167	81	2	.975	22	*O-1073	0.2
Team	3	31	53	3	9	1	0	1	5	2	16	.170	.200	.245	23	-6	0	0	0	1.000	-6	/O-28	-1.2

■ LUIS AGUAYO
Aguayo, Luis (Muriel) b: 3/13/59, Vega Baja, P.R. BR/TR, 5'9", 185 lbs. Deb: 4/19/80

YEAR	TM/L	G	AB	R	H	2B	3B	HR	RBI	BB	SO	AVG	OBP	SLG	PRO+	BR/A	SB	CS	SBR	FA	FR	G/POS	TPR
1989	Cle-A	47	97	7	17	4	1	1	8	7	19	.175	.245	.268	44	-7	0	0	0	.950	5	3-19,S-15,2/D	-0.1
Total	10	568	1104	142	260	43	10	37	109	94	220	.236	.307	.393	91	-16	7	5	-1	.960	-2	S-259,2-147/3D	-0.0

■ MIKE ALDRETE
Aldrete, Michael Peter b: 1/29/61, Carmel, Cal. BL/TL, 5'11", 185 lbs. Deb: 5/28/86

YEAR	TM/L	G	AB	R	H	2B	3B	HR	RBI	BB	SO	AVG	OBP	SLG	PRO+	BR/A	SB	CS	SBR	FA	FR	G/POS	TPR
1991	Cle-A	85	183	22	48	6	1	1	19	36	37	.262	.384	.322	97	1	1	2	-1	.994	-3	1-47,O-16/D	-0.5
Total	9	867	2039	261	542	98	9	35	251	300	362	.266	.361	.374	106	24	19	17	-5	.984	-31	O-394,1-277/D	-3.6

■ GARY ALEXANDER
Alexander, Gary Wayne b: 3/27/53, Los Angeles, Cal. BR/TR, 6'2", 200 lbs. Deb: 9/12/75

YEAR	TM/L	G	AB	R	H	2B	3B	HR	RBI	BB	SO	AVG	OBP	SLG	PRO+	BR/A	SB	CS	SBR	FA	FR	G/POS	TPR
1978	Cle-A	90	324	39	76	14	3	17	62	35	100	.235	.311	.454	114	5	0	2	-1	.983	-9	C-66,D-25	-0.5
1979	Cle-A	110	358	54	82	9	2	15	54	46	100	.229	.319	.391	90	-5	4	2	0	.961	-20	C-91,D-13/O	-2.2
1980	Cle-A	76	178	22	40	7	1	5	31	17	52	.225	.292	.360	77	-6	0	4	-2	.971	-2	D-40,C-13/O	-1.1
Total	7	432	1276	169	293	45	11	55	202	154	381	.230	.315	.411	99	-3	8	12	-5	.969	-42	C-229,D-123/O1	-4.8
Team	3	276	860	115	198	30	6	37	147	98	252	.230	.310	.408	96	-6	4	8	-4	.970	-31	C-170/D-78,O	-3.8

■ HUGH ALEXANDER
Alexander, Hugh b: 7/10/17, Buffalo, Mo. BR/TR, 6', 190 lbs. Deb: 8/15/37

YEAR	TM/L	G	AB	R	H	2B	3B	HR	RBI	BB	SO	AVG	OBP	SLG	PRO+	BR/A	SB	CS	SBR	FA	FR	G/POS	TPR
1937	Cle-A	7	11	0	1	0	0	0	0	0	5	.091	.091	.091	-54	-3	1	0	0	.667	-2	/O-3	-0.4

■ ANDY ALLANSON
Allanson, Andrew Neal b: 12/22/61, Richmond, Va. BR/TR, 6'5", 225 lbs. Deb: 4/7/86

YEAR	TM/L	G	AB	R	H	2B	3B	HR	RBI	BB	SO	AVG	OBP	SLG	PRO+	BR/A	SB	CS	SBR	FA	FR	G/POS	TPR
1986	Cle-A	101	293	30	66	7	3	1	29	14	36	.225	.263	.280	49	-21	10	1	2	.960	-7	C-99	-2.0
1987	Cle-A	50	154	17	41	6	0	3	16	9	30	.266	.307	.364	76	-5	1	1	-0	.986	-7	C-50	-0.9
1988	Cle-A	133	434	44	114	11	0	5	50	25	63	.263	.307	.323	75	-14	5	9	-4	.986	1	*C-133	-0.8
1989	Cle-A	111	323	30	75	9	1	3	17	23	47	.232	.291	.294	64	-15	4	4	-1	.986	3	*C-111	-0.7
Total	8	512	1486	145	357	48	4	16	140	87	223	.240	.286	.310	64	-74	23	18	-4	.980	-1	C-501/1-4,D	-5.1
Team	4	395	1204	121	296	33	4	12	112	71	176	.246	.292	.310	66	-56	20	15	-3	.980	-10	C-393	-4.4

■ ROD ALLEN
Allen, Roderick Bernet b: 10/5/59, Los Angeles, Cal. BR/TR, 6'1", 185 lbs. Deb: 4/7/83

YEAR	TM/L	G	AB	R	H	2B	3B	HR	RBI	BB	SO	AVG	OBP	SLG	PRO+	BR/A	SB	CS	SBR	FA	FR	G/POS	TPR
1988	Cle-A	5	11	1	1	1	0	0	0	0	2	.091	.091	.182	-25	-2	0	0	0	.000	0	/D-4	-0.2
Total	3	31	50	8	11	2	0	0	3	2	11	.220	.264	.260	45	-4	1	0	0	1.000	-0	/D-18,O-4	-0.4

■ MILO ALLISON
Allison, Milo Henry b: 10/16/1890, Elk Rapids, Mich. d: 6/18/57, Kenosha, Wis. BL/TR, 6', 163 lbs. Deb: 9/26/13

YEAR	TM/L	G	AB	R	H	2B	3B	HR	RBI	BB	SO	AVG	OBP	SLG	PRO+	BR/A	SB	CS	SBR	FA	FR	G/POS	TPR
1916	Cle-A	14	18	10	5	0	0	0	0	6	1	.278	.458	.278	115	1	0			1.000	-1	/O-5	0.0
1917	Cle-A	32	35	4	5	0	0	0	0	9	7	.143	.318	.143	38	-2	3			1.000	-3	O-11	-0.6
Total	4	49	60	15	13	0	0	0	0	15	9	.217	.373	.217	74	-1	4			1.000	-4	/O-17	-0.6
Team	2	46	53	14	10	0	0	0	0	15	8	.189	.368	.189	65	-1	3			1.000	-4	/O-16	-0.6

■ BEAU ALLRED
Allred, Dale Le Beau b: 6/4/65, Mesa, Ariz. BL/TL, 6', 190 lbs. Deb: 9/7/89

YEAR	TM/L	G	AB	R	H	2B	3B	HR	RBI	BB	SO	AVG	OBP	SLG	PRO+	BR/A	SB	CS	SBR	FA	FR	G/POS	TPR
1989	Cle-A	13	24	0	6	3	0	0	1	2	10	.250	.308	.375	90	-0	0	0	0	1.000	1	/O-5,D-2	0.1
1990	Cle-A	4	16	2	3	1	0	1	2	2	3	.188	.278	.438	98	-0	0	0	0	.833	-1	/O-4	-0.1
1991	Cle-A	48	125	17	29	3	0	3	12	25	35	.232	.364	.328	92	-0	2	2	-1	.972	2	O-42/D-1	0.0
Total	3	65	165	19	38	7	0	4	15	29	48	.230	.349	.345	93	-1	2	2	-1	.969	2	/O-51,D-3	0.0

■ SANDY ALOMAR
Alomar, Santos Jr. (Velazquez) b: 6/18/66, Salinas, P.R. BR/TR, 6'5", 200 lbs. Deb: 9/30/88 F

YEAR	TM/L	G	AB	R	H	2B	3B	HR	RBI	BB	SO	AVG	OBP	SLG	PRO+	BR/A	SB	CS	SBR	FA	FR	G/POS	TPR
1990	Cle-A★	132	445	60	129	26	2	9	66	25	46	.290	.331	.418	109	4	4	1	1	.981	-13	*C-129	0.0
1991	Cle-A★	51	184	10	40	9	0	0	7	8	24	.217	.265	.266	47	-13	0	4	-2	.987	2	C-46/D-4	-1.1
1992	Cle-A★	89	299	22	75	16	0	2	26	13	32	.251	.293	.324	74	-11	3	3	-1	.996	-4	C-88/D-1	-1.1
1993	Cle-A	64	215	24	58	7	1	6	32	11	28	.270	.323	.395	92	-3	3	1	0	.984	-12	C-64	-1.0
1994	Cle-A	80	292	44	84	15	1	14	43	25	31	.288	.348	.490	113	5	8	4	0	.996	1	C-78	1.0
1995	*Cle-A	66	203	32	61	6	0	10	35	7	26	.300	.333	.478	108	2	3	1	0	.995	1	C-61	0.6
Total	8	490	1658	193	451	80	4	42	215	92	191	.272	.319	.401	94	-16	21	14	-2	.990	-25	C-472/D-5	-1.6
Team	6	482	1638	192	447	79	4	41	209	89	187	.273	.319	.401	94	-16	21	14	-2	.989	-24	C-466/D-5	-1.6

■ DELL ALSTON
Alston, Wendell b: 9/22/52, Valhalla, N.Y. BL/TR, 6', 180 lbs. Deb: 5/17/77

YEAR	TM/L	G	AB	R	H	2B	3B	HR	RBI	BB	SO	AVG	OBP	SLG	PRO+	BR/A	SB	CS	SBR	FA	FR	G/POS	TPR
1979	Cle-A	54	62	10	18	0	2	1	12	10	10	.290	.389	.403	114	2	4	4	-1	.969	-5	O-30/D-7	-0.5
1980	Cle-A	52	54	11	12	1	2	0	9	5	7	.222	.311	.315	72	-2	2	4	-2	.947	-4	O-26/D-6	-0.8
Total	4	189	332	48	79	7	4	3	35	28	44	.238	.301	.310	71	-13	20	21	-7	.957	-14	O-108/D-26,1	-3.8
Team	2	106	116	21	30	1	4	1	21	15	17	.259	.353	.362	94	-0	6	8	-3	.957	-9	/O-56,D-13	-1.3

■ DAVE ALTIZER
Altizer, David Tilden "Filipino" b: 11/6/1876, Pearl, Ill. d: 5/14/64, Pleasant Hill, Ill BL/TR, 5'10.5", 160 lbs. Deb: 5/29/06

YEAR	TM/L	G	AB	R	H	2B	3B	HR	RBI	BB	SO	AVG	OBP	SLG	PRO+	BR/A	SB	CS	SBR	FA	FR	G/POS	TPR
1908	Cle-A	29	89	11	19	1	2	0	5	7		.213	.278	.270	78	-2	7			.952	4	O-24/S-3	0.1
Total	6	514	1734	204	433	36	21	4	116	140		.250	.318	.302	101	6	119			.926	-22	S-221,O-107,1/23	-1.7

■ JOE ALTOBELLI
Altobelli, Joseph Salvatore b: 5/26/32, Detroit, Mich. BL/TL, 6', 185 lbs. Deb: 4/14/55 MC

YEAR	TM/L	G	AB	R	H	2B	3B	HR	RBI	BB	SO	AVG	OBP	SLG	PRO+	BR/A	SB	CS	SBR	FA	FR	G/POS	TPR
1955	Cle-A	42	75	8	15	3	0	2	5	5	14	.200	.259	.320	53	-5	0	1	-1	.992	-1	1-40	-0.8
1957	Cle-A	83	87	9	18	3	2	0	9	5	14	.207	.258	.287	49	-6	3	2	-0	.994	-0	1-56/O-7	-0.8
Total	3	166	257	27	54	8	3	5	28	23	42	.210	.280	.323	60	-15	3	3	-1	.993	-3	/1-98,O-32	-2.3
Team	2	125	162	17	33	6	2	2	14	10	28	.204	.259	.302	51	-11	3	3	-1	.992	-1	/1-96,O-7	-1.6

■ LUIS ALVARADO
Alvarado, Luis Cesar (Martinez) b: 1/15/49, Lajas, P.R. BR/TR, 5'9", 162 lbs. Deb: 9/13/68

YEAR	TM/L	G	AB	R	H	2B	3B	HR	RBI	BB	SO	AVG	OBP	SLG	PRO+	BR/A	SB	CS	SBR	FA	FR	G/POS	TPR
1974	Cle-A	61	114	12	25	2	0	0	12	6	14	.219	.258	.237	44	-8	1	1	-0	.972	11	2-46/S-7,D	0.4
Total	9	463	1160	116	248	43	4	5	84	49	160	.214	.248	.271	47	-81	11	10	-3	.957	26	S-241,2-141/3D	-3.3

YEAR	TM/L	G	AB	R	H	2B	3B	HR	RBI	BB	SO	AVG	OBP	SLG	PRO+	BR/A	SB	CS	SBR	FA	FR	G/POS	TPR
■ MAX ALVIS Alvis, Roy Maxwell b: 2/2/38, Jasper, Tex. BR/TR, 5'11", 187 lbs. Deb: 9/11/62																							
1962	Cle-A	12	51	1	11	2	0	0	3	2	13	.216	.245	.255	36	-5	3	1	0	.935	-4	3-12	-0.8
1963	Cle-A	158	602	81	165	32	7	22	67	36	109	.274	.326	.460	118	13	9	7	-2	.942	-5	*3-158	0.7
1964	Cle-A	107	381	51	96	14	3	18	53	29	77	.252	.315	.446	110	4	5	5	-2	.955	-7	*3-105	-0.6
1965	Cle-A★	159	604	88	149	24	2	21	61	47	121	.247	.311	.397	99	-2	12	8	-1	.958	-19	*3-156	-2.7
1966	Cle-A	157	596	67	146	22	3	17	55	50	98	.245	.306	.378	95	-4	4	7	-3	.958	-6	*3-157	-1.8
1967	Cle-A★	161	637	66	163	23	4	21	70	38	107	.256	.302	.403	106	3	3	10	-5	.965	-8	*3-161	-1.3
1968	Cle-A	131	452	38	101	17	3	8	37	41	91	.223	.294	.327	89	-6	5	5	-2	.960	-17	*3-128	-2.8
1969	Cle-A	66	191	13	43	6	0	1	15	14	26	.225	.278	.272	53	-12	1	1	-0	.973	-2	3-58/S-1	-1.5
Total	9	1013	3629	421	895	142	22	111	373	262	662	.247	.304	.390	97	-19	43	46	-15	.956	-64	3-971/S-1	-11.8
Team	8	951	3514	405	874	140	22	108	361	257	642	.249	.306	.393	99	-8	42	44	-14	.957	-66	3-935/S-1	-10.8
■ RUBEN AMARO Amaro, Ruben Jr. b: 2/12/65, Philadelphia, Pa. BB/TR, 5'10", 170 lbs. Deb: 6/8/91 F																							
1994	Cle-A	26	23	5	5	1	0	2	5	2	3	.217	.280	.522	100	-0	2	1	0	.909	-4	O-12/D-3	-0.4
1995	*Cle-A	28	60	5	12	3	0	1	7	4	6	.200	.273	.300	49	-5	1	3	-2	1.000	-4	O-22/D-3	-1.0
Total	5	215	528	60	120	22	8	11	54	52	71	.227	.310	.362	86	-10	14	9	-1	.987	-12	O-168/D-7,2	-2.6
Team	2	54	83	10	17	4	0	3	12	6	9	.205	.275	.361	63	-5	3	4	-2	.978	-9	/O-34,D-6	-1.4
■ DWAIN ANDERSON Anderson, Dwain Cleaven b: 11/23/47, Oakland, Cal. BR/TR, 5'11", 165 lbs. Deb: 9/3/71																							
1974	Cle-A	2	3	0	1	0	0	0	0	0	1	.333	.333	.333	93	-0	0	0	0	1.000	-1	/2-1	-0.1
Total	4	149	306	33	62	6	2	1	14	32	70	.203	.282	.245	52	-20	2	2	-1	.940	-4	/S-96,3-21,2O	-1.7
■ ALAN ASHBY Ashby, Alan Dean b: 7/8/51, Long Beach, Cal. BB/TR, 6'2", 190 lbs. Deb: 7/3/73																							
1973	Cle-A	11	29	4	5	1	0	1	3	2	11	.172	.226	.310	49	-2	0	0	0	.978	-2	C-11	-0.4
1974	Cle-A	10	7	1	1	0	0	0	0	1	2	.143	.250	.143	15	-1	0	0	0	1.000	0	/C-9	0.0
1975	Cle-A	90	254	32	57	10	1	5	32	30	42	.224	.309	.331	81	-6	3	2	-0	.990	3	C-87/1-2,3D	0.0
1976	Cle-A	89	247	26	59	5	1	4	32	27	49	.239	.314	.316	86	-4	0	2	-1	.987	6	C-86/1-2,3	0.3
Total	17	1370	4123	397	1010	183	13	90	513	461	622	.245	.323	.361	93	-37	7	10	-4	.986	-41	*C-1299/1-4,3D	-2.6
Team	4	200	537	63	122	16	2	10	67	60	104	.227	.306	.320	80	-13	3	4	-2	.988	7	C-193/1-4,3D	-0.1
■ KEN ASPROMONTE Aspromonte, Kenneth Joseph b: 9/22/31, Brooklyn, N.Y. BR/TR, 6', 180 lbs. Deb: 9/2/57 FM																							
1960	Cle-A	117	459	65	133	20	1	10	48	53	32	.290	.366	.403	111	8	4	1	1	.976	-12	2-80,3-36	0.4
1961	Cle-A	22	70	5	16	6	1	0	5	6	3	.229	.289	.343	70	-3	0	0	0	.963	-2	2-21	-0.3
1962	Cle-A	20	28	4	4	2	0	0	1	6	5	.143	.294	.214	41	-2	0	0	0	1.000	-1	/2-6,3-3	-0.3
Total	7	475	1483	171	369	69	3	19	124	179	149	.249	.332	.338	82	-33	7	5	-1	.969	-7	2-342/3-56,S10	-1.1
Team	3	159	557	74	153	28	2	10	54	65	40	.275	.353	.386	102	3	4	1	1	.975	-15	2-107/3-39	-0.2
■ CHICK AUTRY Autry, Martin Gordon b: 3/5/03, Martindale, Tex. d: 1/26/50, Savannah, Ga. BR/TR, 6', 180 lbs. Deb: 4/20/24																							
1926	Cle-A	3	7	1	1	0	0	0	0	1	0	.143	.250	.143	4	-1	0	0	0	1.000	-0	/C-3	-0.1
1927	Cle-A	16	43	5	11	4	1	0	7	0	6	.256	.256	.395	66	-2	0	0	0	.933	2	C-14	0.1
1928	Cle-A	22	60	6	18	6	1	1	9	1	7	.300	.311	.483	105	0	0	0	0	.972	0	C-18	0.2
Total	6	120	277	21	68	17	3	2	33	7	29	.245	.269	.350	59	-18	0	0	0	.965	5	/C-96	-0.5
Team	3	41	110	12	30	10	2	1	16	2	13	.273	.286	.427	83	-3	0	0	0	.956	2	/C-35	0.2
■ EARL AVERILL Averill, Earl Douglas b: 9/9/31, Cleveland, Ohio BR/TR, 5'10", 190 lbs. Deb: 4/19/56 F																							
1956	Cle-A	42	93	12	22	6	0	3	14	14	25	.237	.343	.398	93	-1	0	1	-1	.994	3	C-34	0.2
1958	Cle-A	17	55	2	10	1	0	2	7	4	7	.182	.250	.309	54	-4	1	0	0	.863	0	3-17	-0.3
Total	7	449	1031	137	249	41	0	44	159	162	220	.242	.349	.409	101	1	3	3	-1	.984	-11	C-219/O-72,321	-0.4
Team	2	59	148	14	32	7	0	5	21	18	32	.216	.310	.365	80	-5	1	1	-0	.994	3	/C-34,3-17	-0.1
■ EARL AVERILL Averill, Howard Earl "Rock" b: 5/21/02, Snohomish, Wash. d: 8/16/83, Everett, Wash. BL/TR, 5'9.5", 172 lbs. Deb: 4/16/29 FH																							
1929	Cle-A	151	597	110	198	43	13	18	96	63	53	.332	.398	.538	134	29	13	13	-4	.966	-4	*O-151	1.1
1930	Cle-A	139	534	102	181	33	8	19	119	56	48	.339	.404	.537	131	25	10	7	-1	.949	2	*O-134	1.5
1931	Cle-A	155	627	140	209	36	10	32	143	68	38	.333	.404	.576	147	41	9	9	-3	.976	0	*O-155	2.5
1932	Cle-A	153	631	116	198	37	14	32	124	75	40	.314	.392	.569	137	33	5	8	-3	.964	2	*O-153	1.9
1933	Cle-A★	151	599	83	180	39	16	11	92	54	29	.301	.363	.474	115	12	3	1	0	.971	2	*O-149	0.6
1934	Cle-A★	154	598	128	187	48	6	31	113	99	44	.313	.414	.569	149	44	5	3	-0	.970	9	*O-154	4.2
1935	Cle-A†	140	563	109	162	34	13	19	79	70	58	.288	.368	.496	119	15	8	4	0	.982	-2	*O-139	0.7
1936	Cle-A★	152	614	136	**232**	39	**15**	28	126	65	35	.378	.438	.627	159	55	3	3	-1	.969	-4	*O-150	3.9
1937	Cle-A★	156	609	121	182	33	11	21	92	88	65	.299	.387	.493	119	18	5	4	-1	.976	-8	*O-156	0.4
1938	Cle-A★	134	482	101	159	27	15	14	93	81	48	.330	.429	.535	143	34	5	2	0	.975	5	*O-131	3.2
1939	Cle-A	24	55	8	15	8	0	1	7	6	12	.273	.344	.473	111	1	0	1	-1	1.000	-2	O-11	-0.3
Total	13	1668	6353	1224	2019	401	128	238	1164	774	518	.318	.395	.534	132	296	70	57	-13	.970	-8	*O-1589	17.6
Team	11	1509	5909	1154	1903	377	121	226	1084	725	470	.322	.399	.542	135	305	66	55	-13	.970	1	*O-1483	19.7
■ BOBBY AVILA Avila, Roberto Francisco (Gonzales) b: 4/2/24, Veracruz, Mexico BR/TR, 5'10", 175 lbs. Deb: 4/30/49																							
1949	Cle-A	31	14	3	3	0	0	0	3	1	3	.214	.267	.214	29	-1	0	0	0	1.000	4	/2-5	0.2
1950	Cle-A	80	201	39	60	10	2	1	21	29	17	.299	.390	.383	102	1	5	0	2	.983	-5	2-62/S-2	0.0
1951	Cle-A	141	542	76	165	21	3	10	58	60	31	.304	.374	.410	118	14	14	8	-1	.982	-1	*2-136	1.9
1952	Cle-A★	150	597	102	179	26	**11**	7	45	67	36	.300	.371	.415	127	21	12	10	-2	.966	-18	*2-149	0.9
1953	Cle-A	141	559	85	160	22	3	8	55	58	27	.286	.355	.379	101	1	10	8	-2	**.986**	13	*2-140	2.1
1954	*Cle-A★	143	555	112	189	27	2	15	67	59	31	**.341**	.405	.477	139	30	9	7	-2	.976	8	*2-141/S-7	4.7
1955	Cle-A★	141	537	83	146	22	4	13	61	82	47	.272	.370	.400	103	4	1	4	-2	.982	-3	*2-141	1.0
1956	Cle-A	138	513	74	115	14	2	10	54	70	68	.224	.323	.318	68	-23	17	4	3	.977	-10	*2-135	-1.8
1957	Cle-A	129	463	60	124	19	3	5	48	46	47	.268	.335	.354	89	-6	2	4	-2	.983	-15	*2-107,3-16	-1.5
1958	Cle-A	113	375	54	95	21	3	5	30	55	45	.253	.350	.365	100	1	5	7	-3	.986	-21	2-82,3-33	-1.7
Total	11	1300	4620	725	1296	185	35	80	467	561	399	.281	.360	.388	104	34	78	52	-8	.979	-64	*2-1168/3-50,OS	3.6
Team	10	1207	4356	688	1236	182	33	74	442	527	352	.284	.363	.392	106	43	75	52	-9	.979	-46	*2-1098/3-49,S	5.8
■ BENNY AYALA Ayala, Benigno (Felix) b: 2/7/51, Yauco, P.R. BR/TR, 6'1", 185 lbs. Deb: 8/27/74																							
1985	Cle-A	46	76	10	19	7	0	2	15	4	17	.250	.287	.421	92	-1	0	0	0	.917	-4	O-20/D-3	-0.5
Total	10	425	865	114	217	42	1	38	145	71	136	.251	.309	.434	104	2	2	4	-2	.958	-19	O-157,D-143/1	-2.7
■ DICK AYLWARD Aylward, Richard John "Dandy" b: 6/4/25, Baltimore, Md. d: 6/11/83, Spring Valley, Cal. BR/TR, 6', 190 lbs. Deb: 5/1/53																							
1953	Cle-A	4	3	0	0	0	0	0	0	0	1	.000	.000	.000	-99	-1	0	0	0	1.000	-0	/C-4	-0.1
■ JOE AZCUE Azcue, Jose Joaquin (Lopez) b: 8/18/39, Cienfuegos, Cuba BR/TR, 6', 200 lbs. Deb: 8/3/60																							
1963	Cle-A	94	320	26	91	16	0	14	46	15	46	.284	.316	.466	117	6	1	1	-0	.992	5	C-91	1.4
1964	Cle-A	83	271	20	74	9	1	4	34	16	38	.273	.318	.358	88	-4	0	2	-1	.993	-0	C-76	-0.2
1965	Cle-A	111	335	16	77	7	0	2	35	27	54	.230	.293	.269	60	-17	2	1	0	.994	-1	*C-108	-1.3
1966	Cle-A	98	302	22	83	10	1	9	37	20	22	.275	.324	.404	108	3	0	2	-1	.989	-8	C-97	-0.1
1967	Cle-A	86	295	33	74	12	5	11	34	22	35	.251	.309	.437	117	5	0	3	-2	**.999**	5	C-86	1.5
1968	Cle-A★	115	357	23	100	10	0	4	42	28	33	.280	.332	.342	106	3	1	1	-0	**.996**	11	C-97	2.2

YEAR	TM/L	G	AB	R	H	2B	3B	HR	RBI	BB	SO	AVG	OBP	SLG	PRO+	BR/A	SB	CS	SBR	FA	FR	G/POS	TPR
1969	Cle-A	7	24	1	7	0	0	1	1	4	3	.292	.393	.417	122	1	0	0	0	.980	2	/C-6	0.3
Total	11	909	2828	201	712	94	9	50	304	207	344	.252	.307	.344	85	-58	5	12	-6	.992	25	C-868	0.7
Team	7	594	1904	141	506	64	7	45	229	132	231	.266	.317	.378	99	-3	4	10	-5	.994	13	C-561	3.8
■ **CARLOS BAERGA**	Baerga, Carlos Obed (Ortiz) b: 11/4/68, Santurce, P.R. BB/TR, 5'11", 165 lbs. Deb: 4/14/90																						
1990	Cle-A	108	312	46	81	17	2	7	47	16	57	.260	.304	.394	94	-3	0	2	-1	.944	-9	3-50,S-48/2	-1.2
1991	Cle-A	158	593	80	171	28	2	11	69	48	74	.288	.348	.398	105	4	3	2	-0	.944	11	3-89,2-75/S	1.7
1992	Cle-A★	161	657	92	205	32	1	20	105	35	76	.312	.359	.455	129	24	10	2	2	.979	8	*2-160/D-1	3.8
1993	Cle-A★	154	624	105	200	28	6	21	114	34	68	.321	.361	.486	126	21	15	4	2	.979	8	*2-150/D-4	3.4
1994	Cle-A	103	442	81	139	32	2	19	80	10	45	.314	.338	.525	118	10	8	2	1	.973	9	*2-102/D-1	2.3
1995	*Cle-A★	135	557	87	175	28	2	15	90	35	31	.314	.358	.452	109	7	11	2	2	.973	12	*2-134/D-1	2.5
Total	6	819	3185	491	971	165	15	93	505	178	351	.305	.349	.454	116	63	47	14	6	.975	39	2-629,3-139/SD	12.5
■ **FRANK BAKER**	Baker, Frank b: 1/11/44, Bartow, Fla. BL/TR, 5'10", 180 lbs. Deb: 7/27/69																						
1969	Cle-A	52	172	21	44	5	3	3	15	14	34	.256	.316	.372	89	-3	2	1	0	.950	1	O-46	-0.5
1971	Cle-A	73	181	18	38	12	1	1	23	12	34	.210	.263	.304	55	-11	1	3	-2	.985	-6	O-51	-2.3
Total	2	125	353	39	82	17	4	4	38	26	68	.232	.289	.337	71	-14	3	4	-2	.966	-6	/O-97	-2.8
■ **HOWARD BAKER**	Baker, Howard Francis b: 3/1/1888, Bridgeport, Conn. d: 1/16/64, Bridgeport, Conn. BR/TR, 5'11", 175 lbs. Deb: 8/11/12																						
1912	Cle-A	11	30	1	5	0	0	0	2	5		.167	.286	.167	29	-3	0			.964	-1	3-10	-0.4
Total	3	29	82	5	18	1	1	0	7	8		.220	.289	.256	61	-4	2			.922	-6	/3-26	-1.1
■ **NEAL BALL**	Ball, Cornelius b: 4/22/1881, Grand Haven, Mich. d: 10/15/57, Bridgeport, Conn. BR/TR, 5'7", 145 lbs. Deb: 9/12/07																						
1909	Cle-A	96	324	29	83	13	2	1	25	17		.256	.295	.318	90	-4	17			.914	-11	S-95	-1.6
1910	Cle-A	53	119	13	25	3	1	0	12	9		.210	.266	.252	61	-5	4			.927	-2	S-27/2-6,O3	-0.7
1911	Cle-A	116	412	45	122	14	9	3	45	27		.296	.339	.396	104	1	21			.945	6	2-94,3-17/S	0.5
1912	Cle-A	40	132	12	30	4	1	0	14	9		.227	.277	.273	55	-8	7			.938	0	2-37	-0.8
Total	7	501	1609	162	404	56	17	4	151	99		.251	.296	.314	83	-34	92			.902	-25	S-271,2-178/3O	-6.2
Team	4	305	987	99	260	34	13	4	96	62		.263	.308	.336	88	-17	49			.945	-7	2-137,S-123/3O	-2.6
■ **CHRIS BANDO**	Bando, Christopher Michael b: 2/4/56, Cleveland, Ohio BB/TR, 6', 195 lbs. Deb: 8/13/81 F																						
1981	Cle-A	21	47	3	10	3	0	0	6	2	2	.213	.245	.277	51	-3	0	0	0	.967	-2	C-15/D-2	-0.5
1982	Cle-A	66	184	13	39	6	1	3	16	24	30	.212	.303	.304	68	-8	0	0	0	.990	-6	C-63/3-2	-1.2
1983	Cle-A	48	121	15	31	3	0	4	15	15	19	.256	.338	.380	94	-1	0	1	-1	.995	-2	C-43	-0.2
1984	Cle-A	75	220	38	64	11	0	12	41	33	35	.291	.383	.505	141	13	1	2	-1	.982	-4	C-63/1-1,3D	1.1
1985	Cle-A	73	173	11	24	4	1	0	13	22	21	.139	.236	.173	14	-20	0	1	-1	.986	-3	C-67	-2.1
1986	Cle-A	92	254	28	68	9	0	2	26	22	49	.268	.329	.327	81	-6	0	1	-1	.990	-10	C-86	-1.2
1987	Cle-A	89	211	20	46	9	0	5	16	12	28	.218	.260	.332	55	-14	0	0	0	.990	-2	C-86	-1.1
1988	Cle-A	32	72	6	9	1	0	1	8	8	12	.125	.222	.181	14	-8	0	0	0	.979	1	C-32	-0.6
Total	9	498	1284	134	292	46	2	27	142	138	197	.227	.303	.329	73	-47	1	5	-3	.987	-28	C-457/3-3,D1	-5.7
Team	8	496	1282	134	291	46	2	27	141	138	196	.227	.303	.329	73	-48	1	5	-3	.987	-29	C-455/3-3,D1	-5.8
■ **GEORGE BANKS**	Banks, George Edward b: 9/24/38, Pacolet Mills, S.C. d: 3/1/85, Spartanburg, S.C. BR/TR, 5'11", 185 lbs. Deb: 4/15/62																						
1964	Cle-A	9	17	6	5	1	0	2	3	6	6	.294	.478	.706	226	3	0	0	0	1.000	-1	/O-3,2-1,3	0.3
1965	Cle-A	4	5	0	1	1	0	0	0	1	3	.200	.333	.400	107	0	0	1	-1	1.000	0	/3-1	0.0
1966	Cle-A	4	4	0	1	0	0	0	1	0	1	.250	.250	.250	44	-0	0	0	0	.000	0	H	0.0
Total	5	106	201	33	44	6	2	9	27	37	59	.219	.346	.403	102	1	0	1	-1	.919	-1	/3-29,O-20,2	0.0
Team	3	17	26	6	7	2	0	2	4	7	10	.269	.424	.577	179	3	0	1	-1	1.000	-0	/O-3,3-2,2	0.3
■ **ALAN BANNISTER**	Bannister, Alan b: 9/3/51, Montebello, Cal. BR/TR, 5'11", 175 lbs. Deb: 7/13/74																						
1980	Cle-A	81	262	41	86	17	4	1	32	28	25	.328	.393	.435	126	10	9	2	2	.968	-17	2-41,O-40/3S	-0.4
1981	Cle-A	68	232	36	61	11	1	1	17	16	19	.263	.310	.332	86	-4	16	2	4	.986	-14	O-35,2-30/1S	-1.4
1982	Cle-A	101	348	40	93	16	1	4	41	42	41	.267	.348	.353	94	-2	18	5	2	.991	-11	O-55,2-48/S3D	-1.0
1983	Cle-A	117	377	51	100	25	4	5	45	31	43	.265	.326	.393	93	-4	6	6	-2	.969	-14	O-91,2-27/1D	-2.1
Total	12	972	3007	430	811	143	28	19	288	292	318	.270	.337	.355	90	-35	108	37	10	.983	-138	O-396,2-256,S/D31	-14.8
Team	4	367	1219	168	340	69	10	11	135	117	128	.279	.344	.379	99	1	49	15	6	.979	-56	O-221,2-146/1SD3	-4.9
■ **WALTER BARBARE**	Barbare, Walter Lawrence "Dinty" b: 8/11/1891, Greenville, S.C. d: 10/28/65, Greenville, S.C. BR/TR, 6', 162 lbs. Deb: 9/17/14																						
1914	Cle-A	15	52	6	16	2	2	0	5	2	5	.308	.345	.423	126	1	1	4	-2	.933	0	3-14/S-1	0.0
1915	Cle-A	77	246	15	47	3	1	0	11	10	27	.191	.235	.211	33	-21	6	5	-1	.960	7	3-68/1-1	-1.3
1916	Cle-A	13	48	3	11	1	0	0	3	4	9	.229	.288	.250	58	-2	0			.977	1	3-12	-0.1
Total	8	500	1777	173	462	52	21	1	156	88	121	.260	.297	.315	71	-72	37	16		.959	-21	3-230,S-157/21	-7.2
Team	3	105	346	24	74	6	3	0	19	16	41	.214	.259	.249	51	-22	7	9		.959	9	/3-94,1-1,S	-1.4
■ **JAP BARBEAU**	Barbeau, William Joseph b: 6/10/1882, New York, N.Y. d: 9/10/69, Milwaukee, Wis. BR/TR, 5'5", 140 lbs. Deb: 9/27/05																						
1905	Cle-A	11	37	1	10	1	1	0	2	1		.270	.289	.351	102	-0	1			.905	1	2-11	0.1
1906	Cle-A	42	129	8	25	5	3	0	12	9		.194	.257	.279	69	-5	5			.830	-7	3-32/S-6	-1.2
Total	4	199	712	96	160	25	8	0	46	78		.225	.311	.282	82	-12	39			.884	-33	3-170/2-12,S	-4.5
Team	2	53	166	9	35	6	4	0	14	10		.211	.264	.295	76	-5	6			.830	-6	/3-32,2-11,S	-1.1
■ **RAY BARKER**	Barker, Raymond Herrell "Buddy" b: 3/12/36, Martinsburg, W.Va. BL/TR, 6', 192 lbs. Deb: 9/13/60																						
1965	Cle-A	11	6	0	0	0	0	0	0	2	2	.000	.250	.000	-22	-1	0	0	0	1.000	-0	/1-3	-0.1
Total	4	192	318	34	68	16	0	10	44	29	76	.214	.286	.358	84	-7	1	0		.987	12	1-124/3-3,O	0.1
■ **JOHNNY BASSLER**	Bassler, John Landis b: 6/3/1895, Mechanics Grove, Pa. d: 6/29/79, Santa Monica, Cal BL/TR, 5'9", 170 lbs. Deb: 7/11/13 C																						
1913	Cle-A	1	2	0	0	0	0	0	0	0	0	.000	.000	.000	-97	-0	0			.500	-1	/C-1	-0.2
1914	Cle-A	43	77	5	14	1	1	0	6	15	8	.182	.323	.221	61	-3	3	2	-0	.946	-1	C-25/3-1,O	-0.2
Total	9	811	2319	250	704	99	16	1	318	437	81	.304	.416	.361	104	42	13	8		.980	-1	C-756/O-1,3	7.8
Team	2	44	79	5	14	1	1	0	6	15	8	.177	.316	.215	58	-3	3	2		.940	-2	/C-26,O-1,3	-0.4
■ **RAY BATES**	Bates, Raymond b: 2/8/1890, Paterson, N.J. d: 8/15/70, Tucson, Ariz. BR/TR, 6', 165 lbs. Deb: 5/31/13																						
1913	Cle-A	27	30	4	5	0	2	0	4	3	9	.167	.265	.300	63	-1	3			.905	-0	3-12/O-2	-0.2
Total	2	154	515	51	120	20	9	2	70	24	48	.233	.277	.318	82	-13	15			.932	6	3-136/O-2	-0.6
■ **JIM BAXES**	Baxes, Dimitrios Speros b: 7/5/28, San Francisco, Cal BR/TR, 6'1", 190 lbs. Deb: 4/11/59 F																						
1959	Cle-A	77	247	35	59	11	0	15	34	21	47	.239	.299	.466	111	2	0	1	-1	.956	-13	2-48,3-22	-0.8
Total	1	88	280	39	69	12	0	17	39	25	54	.246	.310	.471	113	4	1	1		.931	-7	/2-48,3-32	0.0
■ **HARRY BAY**	Bay, Harry Elbert "Deerfoot" b: 1/17/1878, Pontiac, Ill. d: 3/20/52, Peoria, Ill. BL/TL, 5'8", 138 lbs. Deb: 7/23/01																						
1902	Cle-A	108	455	71	132	10	5	0	23	36		.290	.343	.334	92	-4	22			**.973**	4	*O-107	-0.7
1903	Cle-A	140	579	94	169	15	12	1	35	29		.292	.329	.364	110	7	**45**			.950	-3	*O-140	-0.5
1904	Cle-A	132	506	69	122	12	9	3	36	43		.241	.307	.318	99	-0	**38**			**.987**	7	*O-132	-0.1
1905	Cle-A	144	552	90	166	18	10	0	22	36		.301	.349	.370	126	16	36			.970	1	*O-144	1.1
1906	Cle-A	68	280	47	77	8	3	0	14	26		.275	.337	.325	109	3	17			.979	-3	O-68	-0.3
1907	Cle-A	34	95	14	17	1	1	0	7	10		.179	.271	.211	53	-5	7			.968	0	O-31	-0.6

YEAR	TM/L	G	AB	R	H	2B	3B	HR	RBI	BB	SO	AVG	OBP	SLG	PRO+	BR/A	SB	CS	SBR	FA	FR	G/POS	TPR
1908	Cle-A	2	0	0	0	0	0	0	0	0		—	—	—	—	0	0			.000	0	R	0.0
Total	8	675	2640	413	722	65	42	5	141	195		.273	.328	.336	103	11	169			.968	6	O-665	-2.1
Team	7	628	2467	385	683	64	40	4	137	180		.277	.330	.340	105	18	165			.970	6	O-622	-1.1

■ **JOHNNY BEALL** Beall, John Woolf b: 3/12/1882, Beltsville, Md. d: 6/14/26, Beltsville, Md. BL/TR, 6', 180 lbs. Deb: 4/17/13

YEAR	TM/L	G	AB	R	H	2B	3B	HR	RBI	BB	SO	AVG	OBP	SLG	PRO+	BR/A	SB	CS	SBR	FA	FR	G/POS	TPR
1913	Cle-A	6	6	0	1	0	0	0	1	0	2	.167	.167	.167	-2	-1	0			.000	0	H	-0.1
Total	4	58	170	18	43	4	1	3	17	11	25	.253	.306	.341	95	-1	2			.972	2	/O-51	-0.3

■ **ERVE BECK** Beck, Ervin Thomas "Dutch" b: 7/19/1878, Toledo, Ohio d: 12/23/16, Toledo, Ohio BR/TR, 5'10", 168 lbs. Deb: 9/19/1899

YEAR	TM/L	G	AB	R	H	2B	3B	HR	RBI	BB	SO	AVG	OBP	SLG	PRO+	BR/A	SB	CS	SBR	FA	FR	G/POS	TPR
1901	Cle-A	135	539	78	156	26	8	6	79	23		.289	.320	.401	103	1	7			.927	-11	*2-132	-0.4
Total	3	232	912	122	265	42	11	9	123	30		.291	.315	.390	99	-4	12			.929	-16	2-170/1-42,OS	-1.4

■ **HEINZ BECKER** Becker, Heinz Reinhard "Dutch" b: 8/26/15, Berlin, Germany d: 11/11/91, Dallas, Tex. BB/TR, 6'2", 200 lbs. Deb: 4/21/43

YEAR	TM/L	G	AB	R	H	2B	3B	HR	RBI	BB	SO	AVG	OBP	SLG	PRO+	BR/A	SB	CS	SBR	FA	FR	G/POS	TPR
1946	Cle-A	50	147	15	44	10	1	0	17	23	18	.299	.401	.381	127	6	1	0	0	.995	0	1-44	0.5
1947	Cle-A	2	2	0	0	0	0	0	0	0	1	.000	.000	.000	-99	-1	0	0	0	.000	0	H	-0.1
Total	4	152	358	45	94	18	3	2	47	50	42	.263	.359	.346	102	3	1	0		.994	0	/1-90	-0.3
Team	2	52	149	15	44	10	1	0	17	23	19	.295	.397	.376	125	6	1	0		.995	0	/1-44	0.4

■ **JOE BECKER** Becker, Joseph Edward b: 6/25/08, St.Louis, Mo. BR/TR, 6'1", 180 lbs. Deb: 5/10/36 C

YEAR	TM/L	G	AB	R	H	2B	3B	HR	RBI	BB	SO	AVG	OBP	SLG	PRO+	BR/A	SB	CS	SBR	FA	FR	G/POS	TPR
1936	Cle-A	22	50	5	9	3	1	1	11	5	4	.180	.255	.340	45	-5	0	0	0	.977	-4	C-15	-0.8
1937	Cle-A	18	33	3	11	2	1	0	2	3	4	.333	.405	.455	116	1	0	0	0	.949	-1	C-12	0.1
Total	2	40	83	8	20	5	2	1	13	8	8	.241	.315	.386	73	-4	0	0	0	.964	-5	/C-27	-0.7

■ **GENE BEDFORD** Bedford, William Eugene b: 12/2/1896, Dallas, Tex. d: 10/6/77, San Antonio, Tex. BB/TR, 5'8", 170 lbs. Deb: 6/25/25

YEAR	TM/L	G	AB	R	H	2B	3B	HR	RBI	BB	SO	AVG	OBP	SLG	PRO+	BR/A	SB	CS	SBR	FA	FR	G/POS	TPR
1925	Cle-A	2	3	1	0	0	0	0	0	0	1	.000	.000	.000	-99	-1	0	0	0	1.000	-1	/2-2	-0.2

■ **BUDDY BELL** Bell, David Gus b: 8/27/51, Pittsburgh, Pa. BR/TR, 6'2", 185 lbs. Deb: 4/15/72 FC

YEAR	TM/L	G	AB	R	H	2B	3B	HR	RBI	BB	SO	AVG	OBP	SLG	PRO+	BR/A	SB	CS	SBR	FA	FR	G/POS	TPR
1972	Cle-A	132	466	49	119	21	1	9	36	34	29	.255	.310	.363	96	-2	5	6	-2	.990	7	*O-123/3-6	-0.3
1973	Cle-A★	156	631	86	169	23	7	14	59	49	47	.268	.327	.393	100	-1	7	15	-7	.958	24	*3-154/O-2	1.6
1974	Cle-A	116	423	51	111	15	1	7	46	35	29	.262	.323	.352	95	-3	1	3	-2	.963	4	*3-115/D-1	-0.1
1975	Cle-A	153	553	66	150	20	4	10	59	51	72	.271	.334	.376	100	0	6	5	-1	.950	-3	*3-153	-0.5
1976	Cle-A	159	604	75	170	26	2	7	60	44	49	.281	.332	.366	105	4	3	8	-4	.956	5	*3-158/1-2	0.4
1977	Cle-A	129	479	64	140	23	4	11	64	45	63	.292	.354	.426	115	10	1	8	-5	.960	13	*3-118,O-11	1.6
1978	Cle-A	142	556	71	157	27	8	6	62	39	43	.282	.329	.392	103	2	1	3	-2	.970	28	*3-139/D-1	2.7
Total	18	2405	8995	1151	2514	425	56	201	1106	836	776	.279	.343	.406	108	105	55	79	-31	.964	191	*3-2183,O-136/SD12	22.9
Team	7	987	3712	462	1016	155	27	64	386	297	332	.274	.330	.382	102	10	24	48	-22	.960	79	3-843,O-136/1D	5.4

■ **DAVID BELL** Bell, David Michael b: 9/14/72, Cincinnati, Ohio BR/TR, 5'10", 170 lbs. Deb: 5/3/95 F

YEAR	TM/L	G	AB	R	H	2B	3B	HR	RBI	BB	SO	AVG	OBP	SLG	PRO+	BR/A	SB	CS	SBR	FA	FR	G/POS	TPR
1995	Cle-A	2	2	0	0	0	0	0	0	0	0	.000	.000	.000	-99	-1	0	0	0	1.000	0	/3-2	0.0
Total	1	41	146	13	36	7	2	2	19	4	25	.247	.276	.363	67	-7	1	2	-1	.900	-2	/2-37,3-5	-0.8

■ **JAY BELL** Bell, Jay Stuart b: 12/11/65, Eglin A.F.B., Fla. BR/TR, 6'1", 180 lbs. Deb: 9/29/86

YEAR	TM/L	G	AB	R	H	2B	3B	HR	RBI	BB	SO	AVG	OBP	SLG	PRO+	BR/A	SB	CS	SBR	FA	FR	G/POS	TPR
1986	Cle-A	5	14	3	5	2	0	1	4	2	3	.357	.438	.714	211	2	0	0	0	.778	-0	/2-2,D-2	0.2
1987	Cle-A	38	125	14	27	9	1	2	13	8	31	.216	.269	.352	62	-7	2	0	1	.947	3	S-38	-0.1
1988	Cle-A	73	211	23	46	5	1	2	21	21	53	.218	.292	.280	59	-11	4	2	0	.965	-13	S-72/D-1	-1.9
Total	10	1071	4002	598	1070	220	43	70	390	403	759	.267	.338	.396	101	6	58	37	-5	.973	49	*S-1062/3-3,D2	13.4
Team	3	116	350	40	78	16	2	5	38	31	87	.223	.290	.323	67	-16	6	2	1	.958	-10	S-110/D-3,2	-1.8

■ **BEAU BELL** Bell, Roy Chester b: 8/20/07, Bellville, Tex. d: 9/14/77, College Station, Tex. BR/TR, 6'2", 185 lbs. Deb: 4/16/35

YEAR	TM/L	G	AB	R	H	2B	3B	HR	RBI	BB	SO	AVG	OBP	SLG	PRO+	BR/A	SB	CS	SBR	FA	FR	G/POS	TPR
1940	Cle-A	120	444	55	124	22	2	4	58	34	41	.279	.332	.365	83	-11	2	2	-1	.971	-2	O-97,1-14	-1.9
1941	Cle-A	48	104	12	20	4	3	0	9	10	8	.192	.270	.288	50	-8	1	2	-1	1.000	-3	O-14,1-10	-1.3
Total	7	767	2718	378	806	165	32	46	437	272	239	.297	.362	.432	99	-6	11	12	-4	.976	-5	O-599/1-86,3	-4.5
Team	2	168	548	67	144	26	5	4	67	44	49	.263	.320	.350	77	-19	3	4	-2	.973	-5	O-111/1-24	-3.2

■ **ALBERT BELLE** Belle, Albert Jojuan "Joey" b: 8/25/66, Shreveport, La. BR/TR, 6'1", 190 lbs. Deb: 7/15/89

YEAR	TM/L	G	AB	R	H	2B	3B	HR	RBI	BB	SO	AVG	OBP	SLG	PRO+	BR/A	SB	CS	SBR	FA	FR	G/POS	TPR
1989	Cle-A	62	218	22	49	8	4	7	37	12	55	.225	.272	.394	84	-5	2	2	-1	.979	1	O-44,D-17	-0.7
1990	Cle-A	9	23	1	4	0	0	1	3	1	6	.174	.208	.304	42	-2	0	0	0	.000	-0	/O-1,D-6	-0.2
1991	Cle-A	123	461	60	130	31	2	28	95	25	99	.282	.326	.540	134	19	3	1	0	.952	3	O-89,D-32	1.9
1992	Cle-A	153	585	81	152	23	1	34	112	52	128	.260	.324	.477	124	16	8	2	1	.969	-4	*D-100,O-52	1.0
1993	Cle-A★	159	594	93	172	36	3	38	**129**	76	96	.290	.378	.552	147	39	23	12	-0	.986	19	*O-150/D-9	5.2
1994	Cle-A★	106	412	90	147	35	2	36	101	58	71	.357	.442	.714	191	56	9	6	-1	.973	3	*O-104/D-2	**5.0**
1995	*Cle-A★	143	546	**121**	173	**52**	1	**50**	**126**	73	80	.317	.403	**.690**	178	60	5	2	0	.981	8	*O-142/D-1	**6.0**
Total	7	755	2839	468	827	185	13	194	603	297	535	.291	.364	.571	148	183	50	25	0	.976	30	O-582,D-167	18.2

■ **HARRY BEMIS** Bemis, Harry Parker b: 2/1/1874, Farmington, N.H. d: 5/23/47, Cleveland, Ohio BR/TR, 5'6.5", 155 lbs. Deb: 4/23/02

YEAR	TM/L	G	AB	R	H	2B	3B	HR	RBI	BB	SO	AVG	OBP	SLG	PRO+	BR/A	SB	CS	SBR	FA	FR	G/POS	TPR
1902	Cle-A	93	317	42	99	12	7	1	29	19		.312	.366	.404	118	8	3			.964	7	C-87/O-2,2	2.2
1903	Cle-A	92	314	31	82	20	3	1	41	8		.261	.295	.354	96	-2	5			**.988**	-7	C-74,1-10/2	-0.2
1904	Cle-A	97	336	35	76	11	6	0	25	8		.226	.259	.295	76	-10	6			.958	-3	C-79,1-13/2	-0.4
1905	Cle-A	70	226	27	66	13	3	0	28	13		.292	.344	.376	127	7	3			.972	-5	C-58/2-4,31	0.9
1906	Cle-A	93	297	28	82	13	5	2	30	12		.276	.311	.374	116	4	8			.963	-9	C-81	0.3
1907	Cle-A	65	172	12	43	7	0	0	19	7		.250	.283	.291	82	-4	5			.957	-7	C-51/1-2	-0.8
1908	Cle-A	91	277	23	62	9	1	0	33	7		.224	.253	.264	68	-10	14			.964	-6	C-76/1-2	-1.1
1909	Cle-A	42	123	4	23	2	3	0	13	0		.187	.194	.252	39	-9	2			.971	-0	C-36	-0.7
1910	Cle-A	61	167	12	36	5	1	1	16	5		.216	.238	.275	60	-8	3			.961	-4	C-46	-0.9
Total	9	704	2229	214	569	92	29	5	234	79		.255	.292	.329	92	-24	49			.966	-36	C-588/1-28,230	-0.7

■ **STAN BENJAMIN** Benjamin, Alfred Stanley b: 5/20/14, Framingham, Mass. BR/TR, 6'2", 194 lbs. Deb: 9/16/39

YEAR	TM/L	G	AB	R	H	2B	3B	HR	RBI	BB	SO	AVG	OBP	SLG	PRO+	BR/A	SB	CS	SBR	FA	FR	G/POS	TPR
1945	Cle-A	14	21	1	7	2	0	0	3	0	0	.333	.333	.429	126	1	0	1	-1	1.000	2	/O-4	0.1
Total	5	241	770	77	176	32	11	5	41	32	115	.229	.260	.318	66	-37	23	1		.975	-5	O-168/1-23,32	-5.5

■ **BUTCH BENTON** Benton, Alfred Lee b: 8/24/57, Tampa, Fla. BR/TR, 6'1", 190 lbs. Deb: 9/14/78

YEAR	TM/L	G	AB	R	H	2B	3B	HR	RBI	BB	SO	AVG	OBP	SLG	PRO+	BR/A	SB	CS	SBR	FA	FR	G/POS	TPR
1985	Cle-A	31	67	5	12	4	0	0	7	3	9	.179	.214	.239	24	-7	0	0	0	.957	-3	C-26	-0.9
Total	4	51	99	6	16	4	0	0	10	5	14	.162	.217	.202	16	-11	0	0	0	.959	-2	/C-39	-1.2

■ **JOHNNY BERARDINO** Berardino, John "Bernie" b: 5/1/17, Los Angeles, Cal. BR/TR, 6', 180 lbs. Deb: 4/22/39

YEAR	TM/L	G	AB	R	H	2B	3B	HR	RBI	BB	SO	AVG	OBP	SLG	PRO+	BR/A	SB	CS	SBR	FA	FR	G/POS	TPR
1948	Cle-A	66	147	19	28	5	1	2	10	27	16	.190	.328	.279	64	-7	0	1	-1	.988	4	2-20,1-18,S/3	-0.3
1949	Cle-A	50	116	11	23	6	1	0	13	14	14	.198	.295	.267	50	-8	0	1	-1	.935	-1	3-25/2-8,S	-1.0
1950	Cle-A	4	5	1	2	0	0	0	3	1	0	.400	.500	.400	137	0	0	0	0	1.000	1	/2-1,3-1	0.1
1952	Cle-A	35	32	5	3	0	0	0	2	10	8	.094	.310	.094	17	-3	0	1	-1	.960	2	/2-8,S-8,31	-0.2
Total	11	912	3028	334	755	167	23	36	387	284	268	.249	.316	.355	77	-101	27	29	-9	.968	1	2-453,S-266/310	-6.4
Team	4	155	300	36	56	11	2	2	28	52	38	.187	.317	.257	55	-18	0	3	-2	.976	5	/2-37,3-33,S1	-1.4

■ **MOE BERG** Berg, Morris b: 3/2/02, New York, N.Y. d: 5/29/72, Belleville, N.J. BR/TR, 6'1", 185 lbs. Deb: 7/4/23 C

YEAR	TM/L	G	AB	R	H	2B	3B	HR	RBI	BB	SO	AVG	OBP	SLG	PRO+	BR/A	SB	CS	SBR	FA	FR	G/POS	TPR
1931	Cle-A	10	13	1	1	1	0	0	0	1	1	.077	.143	.154	-21	-2	0	0	0	.889	0	/C-8	-0.2

YEAR	TM/L	G	AB	R	H	2B	3B	HR	RBI	BB	SO	AVG	OBP	SLG	PRO+	BR/A	SB	CS	SBR	FA	FR	G/POS	TPR
1934	Cle-A	29	97	4	25	3	1	0	9	1	7	.258	.265	.309	47	-8	0	0	0	.980	5	C-28	-0.1
Total	15	663	1813	150	441	71	6	6	206	78	117	.243	.278	.299	49	-140	11	5	0	.986	29	C-529/S-84,231	-7.1
Team	2	39	110	5	26	4	1	0	9	2	8	.236	.250	.291	39	-10	0	0	0	.971	5	/C-36	-0.3
■ BOZE BERGER	Berger, Louis William b: 5/13/10, Baltimore, Md. d: 11/3/92, Bethesda, Md. BR/TR, 6'2", 180 lbs. Deb: 8/17/32																						
1932	Cle-A	1	1	0	0	0	0	0	0	0	1	.000	.000	.000	-94	-0	0	0	0	1.000	1	/S-1	0.1
1935	Cle-A	124	461	62	119	27	5	5	43	34	97	.258	.310	.371	74	-19	7	5	-1	.964	13	*2-120/S-3,13	0.2
1936	Cle-A	28	52	1	9	2	0	0	3	1	14	.173	.189	.212	-1	-8	0	0	0	.959	4	/1-8,2-8,3S	-0.4
Total	6	343	1144	146	270	51	8	13	97	94	226	.236	.296	.329	57	-77	12	7	-1	.954	9	2-173/S-84,31	-4.6
Team	3	153	514	63	128	29	5	5	46	35	112	.249	.298	.354	66	-27	7	5	-1	.962	18	2-128/1-10,3S	-0.1
■ AL BERGMAN	Bergman, Alfred Henry "Dutch" b: 9/27/1890, Peru, Ind. d: 6/20/61, Fort Wayne, Ind. BR/TR, 5'7", 155 lbs. Deb: 8/29/16																						
1916	Cle-A	8	14	2	3	0	1	0	0	2	4	.214	.313	.357	95	-0	0			.889	-2	/2-3	-0.2
■ TONY BERNAZARD	Bernazard, Antonio (Garcia) b: 8/24/56, Caguas, P.R. BB/TR, 5'9", 160 lbs. Deb: 7/13/79																						
1984	Cle-A	140	439	44	97	15	4	2	38	43	70	.221	.293	.287	60	-23	20	13	-2	.971	-11	*2-136/D-1	-3.1
1985	Cle-A	153	500	73	137	26	3	11	59	69	72	.274	.363	.404	111	9	17	9	-0	.978	-29	*2-147/S-1	-1.5
1986	Cle-A	146	562	88	169	28	4	17	73	53	77	.301	.367	.456	125	19	17	8	0	.979	1	*2-146	2.6
1987	Cle-A	79	293	39	70	12	1	11	30	25	49	.239	.301	.399	83	-8	7	4	-0	.983	-16	2-78	-1.9
Total	10	1071	3700	523	970	177	30	75	391	428	606	.262	.341	.387	100	6	113	55		.978	-48	2-1000/S-24,D	0.7
Team	4	518	1794	244	473	81	12	41	200	190	268	.264	.338	.391	98	-2	61	34		.977	-55	2-507/D-1,S	-3.9
■ KEN BERRY	Berry, Allen Kent b: 5/10/41, Kansas City, Mo. BR/TR, 5'11", 180 lbs. Deb: 9/9/62																						
1975	Cle-A	25	40	6	8	1	0	0	1	1	7	.200	.238	.225	31	-4	0	1	-1	.926	-2	O-18/D-5	-0.7
Total	14	1383	4136	422	1053	150	23	58	343	298	569	.255	.309	.344	90	-56	45	46	-14	.989	-5	*O-1311/D-18,2	-13.8
■ BOB BESCHER	Bescher, Robert Henry b: 2/25/1884, London, Ohio d: 11/29/42, London, Ohio BB/TL, 6'1", 200 lbs. Deb: 9/5/08																						
1918	Cle-A	25	60	12	20	2	1	0	6	17	5	.333	.487	.400	153	5	3			.969	-0	O-17	0.4
Total	11	1228	4536	749	1171	190	74	28	345	619	451	.258	.353	.351	109	68	428			.960	9	*O-1188	1.8
■ KURT BEVACQUA	Bevacqua, Kurt Anthony b: 1/23/47, Miami Beach, Fla. BR/TR, 6'1", 185 lbs. Deb: 6/22/71																						
1971	Cle-A	55	137	9	28	3	1	3	13	4	28	.204	.227	.307	46	-10	0	0	0	.971	-9	2-36/O-5,3S	-1.8
1972	Cle-A	19	35	2	4	0	0	1	1	3	10	.114	.184	.200	14	-4	0	0	0	.900	-1	O-11/3-1	-0.6
Total	15	970	2117	214	499	90	11	27	275	221	329	.236	.309	.327	78	-59	12	20	-8	.938	-46	3-329,2-133,1/ODS	-12.2
Team	2	74	172	11	32	3	1	4	14	7	38	.186	.218	.285	40	-14	0	0	0	.971	-10	/2-36,O-16,3S	-2.4
■ JOSH BILLINGS	Billings, John Augustus b: 11/30/1891, Grantville, Kan. d: 12/30/81, Santa Monica, Cal. BR/TR, 5'11", 165 lbs. Deb: 9/9/13																						
1913	Cle-A	1	3	0	0	0	0	0	0	0	3	.000	.000	.000	-97	-1	0			.857	0	/C-1	0.0
1914	Cle-A	11	8	2	2	1	0	0	0	1	1	.250	.333	.375	109	0	1			.813	2	/C-3	0.3
1915	Cle-A	8	21	2	4	1	0	0	0	0	6	.190	.190	.238	28	-2	1			1.000	-1	/C-7,O-1	-0.3
1916	Cle-A	22	31	2	5	0	0	0	1	2	11	.161	.212	.161	12	-3	0			.981	3	C-12	0.0
1917	Cle-A	66	129	8	23	3	2	0	9	8	21	.178	.243	.233	42	-9	2			.974	2	C-48	-0.4
1918	Cle-A	2	3	0	1	0	0	0	0	0	0	.333	.333	.333	92	-0	0			1.000	-0	/C-1	0.0
Total	11	243	488	44	106	12	5	0	29	23	73	.217	.268	.262	47	-35	5			.970	7	C-157/1-1,O	-1.6
Team	6	110	195	14	35	5	2	0	10	11	42	.179	.234	.226	37	-15	4			.967	6	/C-72,O-1	-0.4
■ STEVE BIRAS	Biras, Stephen Alexander b: 2/26/22, E.St.Louis, Ill. d: 4/21/65, St.Louis, Mo. BR/TR, 5'11", 185 lbs. Deb: 9/15/44																						
1944	Cle-A	2	2	0	2	0	0	0	2	0	0	1.000	1.000	1.000	491	1	0	0	0	.667	0	/2-1	0.1
■ JOE BIRMINGHAM	Birmingham, Joseph Leo "Dode" b: 8/6/1884, Elmira, N.Y. d: 4/24/46, Tampico, Mexico BR/TR, 5'10", 185 lbs. Deb: 9/12/06 M																						
1906	Cle-A	10	41	5	13	2	1	0	6	1		.317	.333	.415	136	1	2			1.000	1	/O-9,3-1	0.3
1907	Cle-A	136	476	55	112	10	9	1	33	16		.235	.265	.300	79	-12	23			.949	12	*O-130/S-5	-0.5
1908	Cle-A	122	413	32	88	10	1	2	38	19		.213	.253	.257	65	-16	15			.957	6	*O-121/S-1	-1.7
1909	Cle-A	100	343	29	99	10	5	1	38	19		.289	.333	.356	113	5	12			.948	4	O-98	0.6
1910	Cle-A	104	367	41	84	11	2	0	35	23		.229	.284	.270	72	-12	18			.961	14	*O-103/3-1	-0.3
1911	Cle-A	125	447	55	136	18	5	2	51	15		.304	.334	.380	98	-3	16			.973	8	*O-102,3-16	0.0
1912	Cle-A	107	369	49	94	19	3	1	45	26		.255	.311	.331	81	-10	15			.952	5	O-96/1-9M	-1.0
1913	Cle-A	47	131	16	37	9	1	0	15	8	22	.282	.324	.366	99	-1	7			.974	-3	O-36,M	-0.5
1914	Cle-A	19	47	2	6	0	0	0	4	2	5	.128	.163	.128	-12	-6	0	1	-1	1.000	-2	O-14,M	-1.1
Total	9	770	2634	284	669	89	27	7	265	129	27	.254	.295	.316	85	-53	108	1		.958	46	O-709/3-18,1S	-4.2
■ RIVINGTON BISLAND	Bisland, Rivington Martin b: 2/17/1890, New York, N.Y. d: 1/11/73, Salzburg, Austria BR/TR, 5'9", 155 lbs. Deb: 9/13/12																						
1914	Cle-A	18	57	9	6	1	0	0	2	6	2	.105	.190	.123	-5	-7	2	5	-2	.962	-0	S-15/3-1	-1.0
Total	3	31	102	12	12	1	0	0	5	8	7	.118	.189	.127	-6	-13	2	5	-2	.962	-5	/S-27,3-1	-2.1
■ OSSIE BLANCO	Blanco, Oswaldo Carlos (Diaz) b: 9/8/45, Caracas, Venez. BR/TR, 6', 185 lbs. Deb: 5/26/70																						
1974	Cle-A	18	36	1	7	0	0	0	2	7	4	.194	.326	.194	53	-2	0	3	-2	.992	-1	1-16/D-1	-0.6
Total	2	52	102	5	20	0	0	0	10	10	18	.196	.268	.196	31	-9	0	4	-2	.993	-2	/1-38,D-1,O	-1.6
■ LARVELL BLANKS	Blanks, Larvell b: 1/28/50, Del Rio, Tex. BR/TR, 5'8", 167 lbs. Deb: 7/19/72																						
1976	Cle-A	104	328	45	92	8	7	5	41	30	31	.280	.341	.393	116	6	1	2	-1	.977	-20	S-56,2-46/3D	-0.6
1977	Cle-A	105	322	43	92	10	4	6	38	19	37	.286	.327	.398	100	-1	3	0	1	.960	-25	S-66,3-18,2/D	-1.8
1978	Cle-A	70	193	19	49	10	0	2	20	10	16	.254	.291	.337	77	-6	0	0	0	.926	-10	S-43,2-17/3D	-1.0
Total	9	629	1766	203	446	57	14	20	172	132	178	.253	.306	.335	78	-51	9	7	-2	.957	-66	S-407,2-124/3D	-7.6
Team	3	279	843	107	233	28	11	13	99	59	84	.276	.324	.382	100	-0	4	2	0	.954	-55	S-165/2-75,3D	-3.4
■ BRUCE BOCHTE	Bochte, Bruce Anton b: 11/12/50, Pasadena, Cal. BL/TL, 6'3", 200 lbs. Deb: 7/19/74																						
1977	Cle-A	112	392	52	119	19	1	5	43	40	38	.304	.368	.395	112	7	3	2	-0	.966	5	O-76,1-36/D	0.7
Total	12	1538	5233	643	1478	250	21	100	658	653	662	.282	.363	.396	114	109	43	41	-12	.992	-30	*1-1008,O-429/D	-1.3
■ EDDIE BOCKMAN	Bockman, Joseph Edward b: 7/26/20, Santa Ana, Cal. BR/TR, 5'9", 175 lbs. Deb: 9/11/46																						
1947	Cle-A	46	66	8	17	2	2	1	14	5	17	.258	.310	.394	97	-1	0	0	0	.946	9	3-12/2-4,SO	0.8
Total	4	199	474	54	109	16	4	11	56	46	87	.230	.299	.350	74	-18	5	0	2	.958	24	3-135/2-10,OS	0.5
■ JOE BOLEY	Boley, John Peter (b: John Peter Bolinsky) b: 7/19/1896, Mahanoy City, Pa. d: 12/30/62, Mahanoy City, Pa. BR/TR, 5'11", 170 lbs. Deb: 4/12/27																						
1932	Cle-A	1	4	0	1	0	0	0	0	0	0	.250	.250	.250	28	-0	0	0	0	.000	0	/S-1	0.0
Total	6	540	1780	203	478	88	22	7	227	130	84	.269	.323	.354	72	-74	15	8	-0	.957	-64	S-527/2-1,3	-7.8
■ JIM BOLGER	Bolger, James Cyril "Dutch" b: 2/23/32, Cincinnati, Ohio BR/TR, 6'2", 180 lbs. Deb: 6/24/50																						
1959	Cle-A	8	7	0	0	0	0	0	0	1	1	.000	.125	.000	-65	-2	0	0	0	.000	0	H	-0.2
Total	7	312	612	65	140	14	6	6	48	32	83	.229	.274	.301	54	-40	3	4	-2	.966	-9	O-164/3-3	-5.8
■ CECIL BOLTON	Bolton, Cecil Glenford "Glenn" b: 2/13/04, Booneville, Miss. d: 8/25/93, Jackson, Miss. BL/TR, 6'4", 195 lbs. Deb: 9/21/28																						
1928	Cle-A	4	13	1	2	0	2	0	0	2	2	.154	.267	.462	87	-0	0	0	0	.955	-1	/1-4	-0.2
■ WALT BOND	Bond, Walter Franklin b: 10/19/37, Denmark, Tenn. d: 9/14/67, Houston, Tex. BL/TR, 6'7", 228 lbs. Deb: 4/19/60																						
1960	Cle-A	40	131	19	29	2	1	5	18	13	14	.221	.306	.366	84	-3	4	1	1	1.000	2	O-36	-0.2

YEAR	TM/L	G	AB	R	H	2B	3B	HR	RBI	BB	SO	AVG	OBP	SLG	PRO+	BR/A	SB	CS	SBR	FA	FR	G/POS	TPR
1961	Cle-A	38	52	7	9	1	1	2	7	6	10	.173	.271	.346	65	-3	1	0	0	1.000	-1	O-12	-0.4
1962	Cle-A	12	50	10	19	3	0	6	17	4	9	.380	.426	.800	228	9	1	0	0	1.000	-0	O-12	0.8
Total	6	365	1199	149	307	40	11	41	179	106	175	.256	.325	.410	110	14	10	4	1	.974	-11	O-172,1-150	-1.2
Team	3	90	233	36	57	6	2	13	42	23	33	.245	.323	.455	110	3	6	1	1	1.000	1	/O-60	0.2

■ **BOBBY BONDS** Bonds, Bobby Lee b: 3/15/46, Riverside, Cal. BR/TR, 6'1", 190 lbs. Deb: 6/25/68 FC

YEAR	TM/L	G	AB	R	H	2B	3B	HR	RBI	BB	SO	AVG	OBP	SLG	PRO+	BR/A	SB	CS	SBR	FA	FR	G/POS	TPR
1979	Cle-A	146	538	93	148	24	1	25	85	74	135	.275	.371	.463	123	18	34	23	-4	.979	11	*O-116,D-29	1.9
Total	14	1849	7043	1258	1886	302	66	332	1024	914	1757	.268	.356	.471	129	276	461	169	37	.977	61	*O-1736/D-81	29.5

■ **FRANK BONNER** Bonner, Frank J b: 8/20/1869, Lowell, Mass. d: 12/31/05, Kansas City, Mo. BR/TR, 5'7.5", 169 lbs. Deb: 4/26/1894

YEAR	TM/L	G	AB	R	H	2B	3B	HR	RBI	BB	SO	AVG	OBP	SLG	PRO+	BR/A	SB	CS	SBR	FA	FR	G/POS	TPR
1902	Cle-A	34	132	14	37	6	0	0	14	5		.280	.312	.326	80	-4	1			.907	-10	2-34	-1.2
Total	6	246	949	115	244	44	8	4	115	55		.257	.305	.333	73	-38	28			.931	-36	2-190/S-23,3OC	-5.6

■ **BUDDY BOOKER** Booker, Richard Lee b: 5/28/42, Lynchburg, Va. BL/TR, 5'10", 170 lbs. Deb: 6/4/66

YEAR	TM/L	G	AB	R	H	2B	3B	HR	RBI	BB	SO	AVG	OBP	SLG	PRO+	BR/A	SB	CS	SBR	FA	FR	G/POS	TPR
1966	Cle-A	18	28	6	6	1	0	2	5	2	6	.214	.267	.464	105	0	0	0	0	.964	-5	C-12	-0.5
Total	2	23	33	6	6	1	0	2	5	3	8	.182	.250	.394	83	-1	0	0	0	.967	-6	/C-15	-0.7

■ **RAY BOONE** Boone, Raymond Otis "Ike" b: 7/27/23, San Diego, Cal. BR/TR, 6'1", 188 lbs. Deb: 9/3/48 F

YEAR	TM/L	G	AB	R	H	2B	3B	HR	RBI	BB	SO	AVG	OBP	SLG	PRO+	BR/A	SB	CS	SBR	FA	FR	G/POS	TPR
1948	*Cle-A	6	5	0	2	1	0	0	1	0	1	.400	.400	.600	168	0	0	0	0	.889	1	/S-4	0.2
1949	Cle-A	86	258	39	65	4	4	4	26	38	17	.252	.352	.345	87	-5	0	2	-1	.947	2	S-76	0.1
1950	Cle-A	109	365	53	110	14	6	7	58	56	27	.301	.397	.430	116	10	4	3	-1	.945	-9	*S-102	0.7
1951	Cle-A	151	544	65	127	14	1	12	51	48	36	.233	.302	.329	75	-21	5	3	-0	.957	-7	*S-151	-1.7
1952	Cle-A	103	316	57	83	8	2	7	45	53	33	.263	.372	.367	113	7	0	1	-1	.941	-10	S-96/3-2,2	0.3
1953	Cle-A	34	112	21	27	1	2	4	21	24	21	.241	.375	.393	110	2	1	2	-1	.952	-1	S-31	0.3
Total	13	1373	4589	645	1260	162	46	151	737	608	463	.275	.363	.429	115	95	21	19	-5	.958	-46	3-510,S-464,1/2	5.3
Team	6	489	1600	235	414	42	15	34	202	219	135	.259	.352	.368	97	-5	10	11	-4	.949	-25	S-460/3-2,2	-0.1

■ **HARLEY BOSS** Boss, Elmer Harley "Lefty" b: 11/19/08, Hodge, La. d: 5/15/64, Nashville, Tenn. BL/TL, 5'11.5", 185 lbs. Deb: 7/19/28

YEAR	TM/L	G	AB	R	H	2B	3B	HR	RBI	BB	SO	AVG	OBP	SLG	PRO+	BR/A	SB	CS	SBR	FA	FR	G/POS	TPR
1933	Cle-A	112	438	54	118	17	7	1	53	25	27	.269	.310	.347	71	-19	2	5	-2	.994	6	*1-110	-2.5
Total	4	155	519	64	139	19	8	1	61	30	34	.268	.309	.341	69	-24	2	5	-2	.992	5	1-134	-3.2

■ **LOU BOUDREAU** Boudreau, Louis b: 7/17/17, Harvey, Ill. BR/TR, 5'11", 185 lbs. Deb: 9/9/38 MH

YEAR	TM/L	G	AB	R	H	2B	3B	HR	RBI	BB	SO	AVG	OBP	SLG	PRO+	BR/A	SB	CS	SBR	FA	FR	G/POS	TPR
1938	Cle-A	1	1	0	0	0	0	0	0	1	0	.000	.500	.000	36	0	0	0	0	.000	0	/3-1	0.0
1939	Cle-A	53	225	42	58	15	4	0	19	28	24	.258	.340	.360	82	-6	2	1	0	.953	8	S-53	0.6
1940	Cle-A★	155	627	97	185	46	10	9	101	73	39	.295	.370	.443	113	13	6	3	0	**.968**	12	*S-155	3.5
1941	Cle-A★	148	579	95	149	**45**	8	10	56	85	57	.257	.355	.415	108	7	9	4	0	**.966**	13	*S-147	3.1
1942	Cle-A★	147	506	57	143	18	10	2	58	75	39	.283	.379	.370	118	15	7	16	-8	**.965**	-0	*S-146,M	1.6
1943	Cle-A☆	152	539	69	154	32	7	3	67	90	31	.286	.388	.388	135	27	4	7	-3	**.970**	**28**	*S-152/C-1M	**6.7**
1944	Cle-A☆	150	584	91	191	**45**	5	3	67	73	39	**.327**	.406	.437	146	37	11	3	2	**.978**	26	*S-149/C-1M	**7.8**
1945	Cle-A†	97	345	50	106	24	1	3	48	35	20	.307	.374	.409	133	14	0	4	-2	.983	1	S-97,M	2.2
1946	Cle-A	140	515	51	151	30	6	6	62	40	14	.293	.345	.410	118	11	6	7	-2	**.970**	16	*S-139,M	3.4
1947	Cle-A★	150	538	79	165	**45**	3	4	67	67	10	.307	.388	.424	129	22	1	0	0	**.982**	17	*S-148,M	4.8
1948	*Cle-A★	152	560	116	199	34	6	18	106	98	9	.355	.453	.534	166	56	3	2	-0	**.975**	9	*S-151/C-1M	**6.9**
1949	Cle-A	134	475	53	135	20	3	4	60	70	10	.284	.381	.364	100	2	0	1	-1	.982	5	S-88,3-38/12M	1.1
1950	Cle-A	81	260	23	70	13	2	1	29	31	5	.269	.349	.346	81	-7	1	2	-1	.986	0	S-61/1-8,23M	-0.3
Total	15	1646	6029	861	1779	385	66	68	789	796	309	.295	.380	.415	121	187	51	50	-15	.973	134	*S-1539/3-57,12C	41.3
Team	13	1560	5754	823	1706	367	65	63	740	766	297	.296	.382	.416	123	190	50	50	-15	.973	135	*S-1486/3-41,12C	41.4

■ **BUDDY BRADFORD** Bradford, Charles William b: 7/25/44, Mobile, Ala. BR/TR, 5'11", 191 lbs. Deb: 9/9/66

YEAR	TM/L	G	AB	R	H	2B	3B	HR	RBI	BB	SO	AVG	OBP	SLG	PRO+	BR/A	SB	CS	SBR	FA	FR	G/POS	TPR
1970	Cle-A	75	163	25	32	6	1	7	23	21	43	.196	.292	.374	79	-5	0	1	-1	.984	-4	O-64/3-1	-1.3
1971	Cle-A	20	38	4	6	2	1	0	3	6	10	.158	.273	.263	48	-3	0	0	0	.930	-0	O-18	-0.4
Total	11	697	1605	224	363	50	8	52	175	184	411	.226	.313	.364	91	-19	36	24	-4	.971	-64	O-587/D-8,3	-11.8
Team	2	95	201	29	38	8	2	7	26	27	53	.189	.288	.353	73	-8	0	1	-1	.970	-5	/O-82,3-1	-1.7

■ **JACK BRADLEY** Bradley, John Thomas b: 9/20/1893, Denver, Colo. d: 3/18/69, Tulsa, Okla. BR/TR, 5'11", 175 lbs. Deb: 6/18/16

YEAR	TM/L	G	AB	R	H	2B	3B	HR	RBI	BB	SO	AVG	OBP	SLG	PRO+	BR/A	SB	CS	SBR	FA	FR	G/POS	TPR
1916	Cle-A	2	3	0	0	0	0	0	0	0	1	.000	.000	.000	-94	-1	0			1.000	-0	/C-1	-0.1

■ **BILL BRADLEY** Bradley, William Joseph b: 2/13/1878, Cleveland, Ohio d: 3/11/54, Cleveland, Ohio BR/TR, 6', 185 lbs. Deb: 8/26/1899 M

YEAR	TM/L	G	AB	R	H	2B	3B	HR	RBI	BB	SO	AVG	OBP	SLG	PRO+	BR/A	SB	CS	SBR	FA	FR	G/POS	TPR
1901	Cle-A	133	516	95	151	28	13	1	55	26		.293	.336	.403	109	5	15			**.930**	10	*3-133/P-1	1.5
1902	Cle-A	137	550	104	187	39	12	11	77	27		.340	.375	.515	151	35	11			.923	12	*3-137	4.4
1903	Cle-A	136	536	101	168	36	22	6	68	25		.313	.348	.496	154	33	21			.924	12	*3-136	4.7
1904	Cle-A	154	609	94	183	32	8	5	83	26		.300	.334	.404	134	22	23			**.955**	9	*3-154	3.9
1905	Cle-A	146	541	63	145	34	6	0	51	27		.268	.321	.353	112	7	22			**.945**	13	*3-146,M	2.8
1906	Cle-A	82	302	32	83	16	2	2	25	18		.275	.324	.361	116	5	13			.966	5	3-82	1.4
1907	Cle-A	139	498	48	111	20	1	0	34	35		.223	.286	.267	76	-13	20			**.938**	5	*3-139	-0.4
1908	Cle-A	148	548	70	133	24	7	1	46	29		.243	.297	.318	99	-1	18			.939	-31	*3-118,S-30	-3.1
1909	Cle-A	95	334	30	62	6	3	0	22	19		.186	.236	.222	43	-22	8			.957	-11	3-87/1-3,2	-3.4
1910	Cle-A	61	214	12	42	3	0	0	12	10		.196	.236	.210	39	-15	6			.956	-1	3-61	-1.6
Total	14	1461	5430	754	1471	275	84	33	552	290		.271	.317	.371	107	40	181			.933	29	*3-1390/S-35,12P	9.2
Team	10	1231	4648	649	1265	238	74	26	473	242		.272	.317	.372	111	56	157			.940	21	*3-1193/S-30,21P	10.2

■ **BILL BRENZEL** Brenzel, William Richard b: 3/3/10, Oakland, Cal. d: 6/12/79, Oakland, Cal. BR/TR, 5'10", 173 lbs. Deb: 4/13/32

YEAR	TM/L	G	AB	R	H	2B	3B	HR	RBI	BB	SO	AVG	OBP	SLG	PRO+	BR/A	SB	CS	SBR	FA	FR	G/POS	TPR
1934	Cle-A	15	51	4	11	3	0	0	3	2	1	.216	.245	.275	33	-5	0	0	0	1.000	3	C-15	-0.2
1935	Cle-A	52	142	12	31	5	1	0	14	6	10	.218	.250	.268	33	-14	2	2	-1	.975	-7	C-51	-1.8
Total	3	76	217	16	43	9	1	0	19	8	15	.198	.227	.249	23	-25	2	2		.985	-2	/C-75	-2.3
Team	2	67	193	16	42	8	1	0	17	8	11	.218	.249	.269	33	-19	2	2		.983	-4	/C-66	-2.0

■ **CHARLIE BREWSTER** Brewster, Charles Lawrence b: 12/27/16, Marthaville, La. BR/TR, 5'8.5", 175 lbs. Deb: 5/2/43

YEAR	TM/L	G	AB	R	H	2B	3B	HR	RBI	BB	SO	AVG	OBP	SLG	PRO+	BR/A	SB	CS	SBR	FA	FR	G/POS	TPR
1946	Cle-A	3	2	0	0	0	0	0	0	1	1	.000	.333	.000	-1	-0	0	0	0	1.000	0	/S-1	0.0
Total	3	69	213	17	47	4	0	0	14	16	28	.221	.281	.239	52	-13	1	0	0	.902	-20	/S-57,2-2	-3.1

■ **ROCKY BRIDGES** Bridges, Everett Lamar b: 8/7/27, Refugio, Tex. BR/TR, 5'8", 175 lbs. Deb: 4/17/51 C

YEAR	TM/L	G	AB	R	H	2B	3B	HR	RBI	BB	SO	AVG	OBP	SLG	PRO+	BR/A	SB	CS	SBR	FA	FR	G/POS	TPR
1960	Cle-A	10	27	1	9	0	0	0	3	1	2	.333	.357	.333	91	-0	0	0	0	1.000	3	/S-7,3-3	0.3
Total	11	919	2272	245	562	80	11	16	187	205	229	.247	.312	.313	67	-102	10	15	-6	.968	95	S-447,2-270,3/O	3.2

■ **DAN BRIGGS** Briggs, Dan Lee b: 11/18/52, Scotia, Cal. BL/TL, 6', 180 lbs. Deb: 9/10/75

YEAR	TM/L	G	AB	R	H	2B	3B	HR	RBI	BB	SO	AVG	OBP	SLG	PRO+	BR/A	SB	CS	SBR	FA	FR	G/POS	TPR
1978	Cle-A	15	49	4	8	0	1	1	1	4	9	.163	.226	.265	38	-4	0	0	0	1.000	2	O-15	-0.3
Total	7	325	688	67	134	20	6	12	53	45	133	.195	.251	.294	56	-42	2	7	-4	.989	-2	1-152,O-130/D	-6.0

■ **JACK BROHAMER** Brohamer, John Anthony b: 2/26/50, Maywood, Cal. BL/TR, 5'10", 165 lbs. Deb: 4/18/72

YEAR	TM/L	G	AB	R	H	2B	3B	HR	RBI	BB	SO	AVG	OBP	SLG	PRO+	BR/A	SB	CS	SBR	FA	FR	G/POS	TPR
1972	Cle-A	136	527	49	123	13	2	5	35	27	46	.233	.272	.294	66	-22	3	2	-0	.977	6	*2-132/3-1	-1.1
1973	Cle-A	102	300	29	66	12	1	4	29	32	23	.220	.295	.307	69	-12	0	2	-1	.971	17	2-97	0.8
1974	Cle-A	101	315	33	85	11	1	2	30	26	22	.270	.331	.330	92	-3	2	1	0	.987	-4	2-99	-0.3
1975	Cle-A	69	217	15	53	5	0	6	16	14	14	.244	.290	.350	80	-6	2	2	-1	.976	4	2-66	0.0

YEAR	TM/L	G	AB	R	H	2B	3B	HR	RBI	BB	SO	AVG	OBP	SLG	PRO+	BR/A	SB	CS	SBR	FA	FR	G/POS	TPR
1980	Cle-A	53	142	13	32	5	1	1	15	14	6	.225	.295	.296	62	-7	0	1	-1	.979	-4	2-47/D-1	-0.9
Total	9	805	2500	262	613	91	12	30	227	222	178	.245	.309	.327	79	-65	9	17	-8	.979	33	2-639,3-105/D	-0.8
Team	5	461	1501	139	359	46	5	18	125	113	111	.239	.294	.312	74	-51	7	8	-3	.978	18	2-441/D-1,3	-1.5

■ HERMAN BRONKIE Bronkie, Herman Charles "Dutch" b: 3/31/1885, S.Manchester, Conn d: 5/27/68, Somers, Conn. BR/TR, 5'9", 165 lbs. Deb: 9/20/10

YEAR	TM/L	G	AB	R	H	2B	3B	HR	RBI	BB	SO	AVG	OBP	SLG	PRO+	BR/A	SB	CS	SBR	FA	FR	G/POS	TPR
1910	Cle-A	5	9	1	2	0	0	0	0	1		.222	.300	.222	63	-0	1			.625	-1	/3-3,S-1	-0.2
1911	Cle-A	2	6	0	1	0	0	0	0	0		.167	.167	.167	-7	-1	0			1.000	-1	/3-2	-0.2
1912	Cle-A	6	16	1	0	0	0	0	0	1		.000	.059	.000	-80	-4	0			.917	2	/3-6	-0.1
Total	7	122	360	40	87	14	5	1	24	33		.242	.307	.317	75	-12	3			.931	2	/3-82,2-16,1S	-0.9
Team	3	13	31	2	3	0	0	0	0	2		.097	.152	.097	-27	-5	1			.861	0	/3-11,S-1	-0.5

■ TOM BROOKENS Brookens, Thomas Dale b: 8/10/53, Chambersburg, Pa. BR/TR, 5'10", 170 lbs. Deb: 7/10/79

YEAR	TM/L	G	AB	R	H	2B	3B	HR	RBI	BB	SO	AVG	OBP	SLG	PRO+	BR/A	SB	CS	SBR	FA	FR	G/POS	TPR
1990	Cle-A	64	154	18	41	7	2	1	20	14	25	.266	.327	.357	92	-2	0	0	0	.923	4	3-35,2-21/S1D	0.3
Total	12	1336	3865	477	950	175	40	71	431	281	605	.246	.299	.367	83	-97	86	60		.943	48	*3-1065,2-162,S/DO1C	-6.1

■ FRANK BROWER Brower, Frank Willard "Turkeyfoot" b: 3/26/1893, Gainesville, Va. d: 11/20/60, Baltimore, Md. BL/TR, 6'2", 180 lbs. Deb: 8/14/20

YEAR	TM/L	G	AB	R	H	2B	3B	HR	RBI	BB	SO	AVG	OBP	SLG	PRO+	BR/A	SB	CS	SBR	FA	FR	G/POS	TPR
1923	Cle-A	126	397	77	113	25	8	16	66	62	32	.285	.392	.509	136	21	6	5	-1	.988	-3	*1-112/O-4	1.1
1924	Cle-A	66	107	16	30	10	1	3	20	27	9	.280	.434	.477	133	6	1	1	-0	.990	-1	1-26/P-4,O	0.3
Total	5	450	1297	206	371	74	20	30	205	168	84	.286	.379	.443	117	33	17	14	-3	.952	-4	O-194,1-158/P3	0.5
Team	2	192	504	93	143	35	9	19	86	89	41	.284	.401	.502	136	27	7	6	-2	.989	-4	1-138/O-7,P	1.4

■ LARRY BROWN Brown, Larry Leslie b: 3/1/40, Shinnston, W.Va. BR/TR, 5'11", 165 lbs. Deb: 7/6/63 F

YEAR	TM/L	G	AB	R	H	2B	3B	HR	RBI	BB	SO	AVG	OBP	SLG	PRO+	BR/A	SB	CS	SBR	FA	FR	G/POS	TPR
1963	Cle-A	74	247	28	63	6	0	5	18	22	27	.255	.319	.340	85	-5	4	3	-1	.938	-8	S-46,2-27	-0.9
1964	Cle-A	115	335	33	77	12	1	12	40	24	55	.230	.285	.379	84	-8	1	2	-1	.981	11	*2-103/S-4	1.0
1965	Cle-A	124	438	52	111	22	2	8	40	38	62	.253	.316	.368	93	-4	5	7	-3	.977	3	S-95,2-26	0.5
1966	Cle-A	105	340	29	78	12	0	3	17	36	58	.229	.309	.291	73	-11	0	1	-1	.961	-4	S-90,2-10	-0.7
1967	Cle-A	152	485	38	110	16	2	7	37	53	62	.227	.311	.311	84	-9	4	4	-1	.967	1	*S-150	0.6
1968	Cle-A	154	495	43	116	18	3	6	35	43	46	.234	.302	.319	90	-6	1	1	-0	.966	-14	*S-154	-0.6
1969	Cle-A	132	469	48	112	10	2	4	24	44	43	.239	.305	.294	66	-21	5	3	-0	.959	-17	*S-101,3-29/2	-2.8
1970	Cle-A	72	155	17	40	5	2	0	15	20	14	.258	.343	.316	79	-4	1	0	0	.950	-2	S-27,3-17,2	-0.2
1971	Cle-A	13	50	4	11	1	0	0	5	3	3	.220	.278	.240	44	-4	0	0	0	.980	-6	S-13	-0.9
Total	12	1129	3449	331	803	108	13	47	254	317	414	.233	.301	.313	76	-103	22	23	-7	.964	-34	S-712,2-265,3	-6.9
Team	9	941	3014	292	718	102	12	45	231	283	370	.238	.308	.325	81	-71	21	21	-6	.964	-35	S-680,2-187/3	-4.0

■ DICK BROWN Brown, Richard Ernest b: 1/17/35, Shinnston, W.Va. d: 4/17/70, Baltimore, Md. BR/TR, 6'3", 190 lbs. Deb: 6/20/57 F

YEAR	TM/L	G	AB	R	H	2B	3B	HR	RBI	BB	SO	AVG	OBP	SLG	PRO+	BR/A	SB	CS	SBR	FA	FR	G/POS	TPR
1957	Cle-A	34	114	10	30	4	0	4	22	4	23	.263	.288	.404	88	-2	1	1	-0	.986	1	C-33	0.0
1958	Cle-A	68	173	20	41	5	0	7	20	14	27	.237	.305	.387	91	-2	1	0	0	.987	6	C-62	0.6
1959	Cle-A	48	141	15	31	7	0	5	16	11	39	.220	.290	.376	85	-3	0	0	0	.996	3	C-48	0.2
Total	9	636	1866	175	455	62	3	62	223	119	356	.244	.293	.380	83	-49	7	6	-2	.989	35	C-614	1.0
Team	3	150	428	45	102	16	0	16	58	29	89	.238	.296	.388	88	-8	2	1	0	.990	10	C-143	0.8

■ JERRY BROWNE Browne, Jerome Austin b: 2/13/66, Christiansted, V.I. BB/TR, 5'10", 170 lbs. Deb: 9/6/86

YEAR	TM/L	G	AB	R	H	2B	3B	HR	RBI	BB	SO	AVG	OBP	SLG	PRO+	BR/A	SB	CS	SBR	FA	FR	G/POS	TPR
1989	Cle-A	153	598	83	179	31	4	5	45	68	64	.299	.372	.390	113	12	14	6	1	.979	-48	*2-151/D-2	-3.1
1990	Cle-A	140	513	92	137	26	5	6	50	72	46	.267	.359	.372	105	6	12	7	-1	.985	-21	*2-139	-1.3
1991	Cle-A	107	290	28	66	5	2	1	29	27	29	.228	.296	.269	57	-16	2	4	-2	.964	-10	2-47,O-17,3/D	-2.7
Total	10	982	3190	431	866	135	25	23	288	393	325	.271	.354	.351	94	-17	73	45	-5	.977	-138	2-609,O-175,3/D1S	-14.5
Team	3	400	1401	203	382	62	11	12	124	167	139	.273	.352	.358	99	1	28	17	-2	.980	-78	2-337/O-17,3D	-7.1

■ FRITZ BUELOW Buelow, Frederick William Alexander b: 2/13/1876, Berlin, Germany d: 12/27/33, Detroit, Mich. BR/TR, 5'10.5", 170 lbs. Deb: 9/28/1899

YEAR	TM/L	G	AB	R	H	2B	3B	HR	RBI	BB	SO	AVG	OBP	SLG	PRO+	BR/A	SB	CS	SBR	FA	FR	G/POS	TPR
1904	Cle-A	42	119	11	21	4	1	0	5	11		.176	.252	.227	52	-6	2			.979	1	C-42	-0.1
1905	Cle-A	75	239	11	41	4	1	1	18	6		.172	.198	.209	29	-19	7			.963	-7	C-60/O-8,13	-2.3
1906	Cle-A	34	86	7	14	2	0	0	7	9		.163	.250	.186	38	-6	0			.938	3	C-33/1-1	-0.1
Total	9	431	1334	125	256	25	18	6	112	69		.192	.238	.251	46	-89	20			.960	1	C-402/O-11,13	-5.4
Team	3	151	444	29	76	10	2	1	30	26		.171	.224	.209	37	-31	9			.963	-4	C-135/O-8,13	-2.5

■ JOHNNY BURNETT Burnett, John Henderson b: 11/1/04, Bartow, Fla. d: 8/13/59, Tampa, Fla. BL/TR, 5'11", 175 lbs. Deb: 5/7/27

YEAR	TM/L	G	AB	R	H	2B	3B	HR	RBI	BB	SO	AVG	OBP	SLG	PRO+	BR/A	SB	CS	SBR	FA	FR	G/POS	TPR
1927	Cle-A	17	8	5	0	0	0	0	0	0	3	.000	.000	.000	-99	-2	1	0	0	.833	2	/2-2	0.0
1928	Cle-A	3	10	3	5	0	0	0	1	0	1	.500	.500	.500	162	1	0	0	0	.867	0	/S-2	0.1
1929	Cle-A	19	33	2	5	1	0	0	2	1	2	.152	.200	.182	-1	-5	0	0	0	.923	6	S-10/2-8	0.1
1930	Cle-A	54	170	28	53	13	0	0	20	17	8	.312	.378	.388	91	-2	2	2	-1	.973	-5	3-27,S-19	-0.3
1931	Cle-A	111	427	85	128	25	5	1	52	39	25	.300	.360	.389	92	-5	5	2	0	.938	-15	S-63,2-35,3/O	-1.0
1932	Cle-A	129	512	81	152	23	5	4	53	46	27	.297	.359	.385	87	-9	2	5	-2	.946	-22	*S-103,2-26	-2.2
1933	Cle-A	83	261	39	71	11	2	1	29	23	14	.272	.333	.341	76	-9	3	2	-0	.938	-5	S-41,2-17,3	-0.9
1934	Cle-A	72	208	28	61	11	2	3	30	18	11	.293	.352	.409	94	-2	1	1	-0	.981	-8	3-42/S-9,2O	-0.7
Total	9	558	1835	288	521	94	15	9	213	163	107	.284	.345	.366	81	-50	15	12	-3	.935	-53	S-265,3-133,2/O	-6.7
Team	8	488	1629	271	475	84	14	9	187	144	91	.292	.352	.377	86	-33	14	12	-3	.936	-47	S-247,3-102/2O	-4.9

■ JEROMY BURNITZ Burnitz, Jeromy Neal b: 4/15/69, Westminster, Cal. BL/TR, 6', 190 lbs. Deb: 6/21/93

YEAR	TM/L	G	AB	R	H	2B	3B	HR	RBI	BB	SO	AVG	OBP	SLG	PRO+	BR/A	SB	CS	SBR	FA	FR	G/POS	TPR
1995	Cle-A	9	7	4	4	1	0	0	0	0	0	.571	.571	.714	231	1	0	0	0	1.000	-1	/O-6,D-2	0.1
Total	3	140	413	79	102	15	6	16	53	61	111	.247	.347	.429	105	4	4	7	-3	.976	-3	O-127/D-2	-0.5

■ GEORGE BURNS Burns, George Henry "Tioga George" b: 1/31/1893, Niles, Ohio d: 1/7/78, Kirkland, Wash. BR/TR, 6'1.5", 180 lbs. Deb: 4/14/14

YEAR	TM/L	G	AB	R	H	2B	3B	HR	RBI	BB	SO	AVG	OBP	SLG	PRO+	BR/A	SB	CS	SBR	FA	FR	G/POS	TPR
1920	*Cle-A	44	56	7	15	4	1	0	13	4	3	.268	.339	.375	86	-1	1	0	0	.979	1	1-12/O-1	0.0
1921	Cle-A	84	244	52	88	21	4	0	49	13	19	.361	.398	.480	121	7	3	1	0	.990	2	1-73	0.7
1924	Cle-A	129	462	64	143	37	5	4	68	29	27	.310	.370	.437	106	3	14	5	1	.987	8	*1-127	0.5
1925	Cle-A	127	488	69	164	41	4	6	79	24	24	.336	.371	.473	112	7	16	11	-2	.989	-1	*1-126	-0.2
1926	Cle-A	151	603	97	**216**	**64**	3	4	114	28	33	.358	.394	.494	129	24	13	7	-0	.988	1	*1-151	1.5
1927	Cle-A	140	549	84	175	51	2	3	78	42	27	.319	.375	.435	109	7	13	11	-3	.990	3	*1-139	-0.2
1928	Cle-A	82	209	29	52	12	1	5	30	17	11	.249	.323	.388	85	-5	2	3	-1	.984	2	1-53	-0.8
Total	16	1866	6573	901	2018	444	72	72	951	363	433	.307	.354	.429	112	91	154	63	8	.987	0	*1-1671/O-50	0.7
Team	7	757	2611	402	853	230	20	22	431	157	144	.327	.375	.455	112	43	62	38	-4	.988	16	1-681/O-1	1.5

■ ELLIS BURTON Burton, Ellis Narrington b: 8/12/36, Los Angeles, Cal. BB/TR, 5'11", 165 lbs. Deb: 9/18/58

YEAR	TM/L	G	AB	R	H	2B	3B	HR	RBI	BB	SO	AVG	OBP	SLG	PRO+	BR/A	SB	CS	SBR	FA	FR	G/POS	TPR
1963	Cle-A	26	31	6	6	3	0	1	1	4	4	.194	.286	.387	87	-1	0	0	0	1.000	-4	O-16	-0.5
Total	5	215	556	79	120	24	4	17	59	65	117	.216	.304	.365	85	-11	11	6	-0	.981	-24	O-177	-4.6

■ JIM BUSBY Busby, James Franklin b: 1/8/27, Kenedy, Tex. BR/TR, 6'1", 175 lbs. Deb: 4/23/50 C

YEAR	TM/L	G	AB	R	H	2B	3B	HR	RBI	BB	SO	AVG	OBP	SLG	PRO+	BR/A	SB	CS	SBR	FA	FR	G/POS	TPR
1956	Cle-A	135	494	72	116	17	3	12	50	43	47	.235	.301	.354	71	-22	8	3	1	.989	5	*O-133	-2.3
1957	Cle-A	30	74	9	14	2	1	2	4	1	8	.189	.200	.324	41	-6	0	1	-1	.978	-3	O-26	-1.2
Total	13	1352	4250	541	1113	162	35	48	438	310	439	.262	.316	.350	82	-110	97	48	0	.988	22	*O-1280/C-1,3	-14.0
Team	2	165	568	81	130	19	4	14	54	44	55	.229	.289	.350	68	-28	8	4	0	.987	1	O-159	-3.5

■ HANK BUTCHER Butcher, Henry Joseph b: 7/12/1886, Chicago, Ill. d: 12/28/79, Hazel Crest, Ill. BR/TR, 5'10", 180 lbs. Deb: 7/8/11

YEAR	TM/L	G	AB	R	H	2B	3B	HR	RBI	BB	SO	AVG	OBP	SLG	PRO+	BR/A	SB	CS	SBR	FA	FR	G/POS	TPR
1911	Cle-A	38	133	21	32	7	3	1	11	11		.241	.303	.361	84	-3	9			.984	0	O-34	-0.5
1912	Cle-A	26	82	9	16	4	1	1	10	6		.195	.250	.305	57	-5	1			.920	1	O-21	-0.5
Total	2	64	215	30	48	11	4	2	21	17		.223	.283	.340	74	-8	10			.956	2	/O-55	-1.0

■ BRETT BUTLER Butler, Brett Morgan b: 6/15/57, Los Angeles, Cal. BL/TL, 5'10", 160 lbs. Deb: 8/20/81

YEAR	TM/L	G	AB	R	H	2B	3B	HR	RBI	BB	SO	AVG	OBP	SLG	PRO+	BR/A	SB	CS	SBR	FA	FR	G/POS	TPR
1984	Cle-A	159	602	108	162	25	9	3	49	86	62	.269	.364	.355	98	2	52	22	2	.991	15	*O-156	1.4
1985	Cle-A	152	591	106	184	28	14	5	50	63	42	.311	.379	.431	122	19	47	20	2	**.998**	22	*O-150/D-1	3.7
1986	Cle-A	161	587	92	163	17	**14**	4	51	70	65	.278	.359	.375	102	3	32	15	1	.993	9	*O-159	0.7
1987	Cle-A	137	522	91	154	25	8	9	41	91	55	.295	.401	.425	119	18	33	16	0	.990	15	*O-136	2.7
Total	15	2074	7706	1285	2243	268	127	54	552	1078	845	.291	.381	.380	112	166	535	244		.992	109	*O-2034/D-1	23.2
Team	4	609	2302	397	663	95	45	21	191	310	224	.288	.375	.396	110	42	164	73		.993	60	O-601/D-1	8.5

■ JOE CAFFIE Caffie, Joseph Clifford "Rabbit" b: 2/14/31, Ramer, Ala. BL/TR, 5'10.5", 180 lbs. Deb: 9/13/56

YEAR	TM/L	G	AB	R	H	2B	3B	HR	RBI	BB	SO	AVG	OBP	SLG	PRO+	BR/A	SB	CS	SBR	FA	FR	G/POS	TPR
1956	Cle-A	12	38	7	13	0	0	0	1	4	8	.342	.432	.342	104	1	3	2	-0	1.000	1	O-10	0.1
1957	Cle-A	32	89	14	24	2	1	3	10	4	11	.270	.301	.416	95	-1	0	1	-1	.976	-0	O-19	-0.3
Total	2	44	127	21	37	2	1	3	11	8	19	.291	.343	.394	99	-0	3	3	-1	.984	1	/O-29	-0.2

■ BEN CAFFYN Caffyn, Benjamin Thomas b: 2/10/1880, Peoria, Ill. d: 11/22/42, Peoria, Ill. BL/TL, Deb: 8/21/06

YEAR	TM/L	G	AB	R	H	2B	3B	HR	RBI	BB	SO	AVG	OBP	SLG	PRO+	BR/A	SB	CS	SBR	FA	FR	G/POS	TPR
1906	Cle-A	30	103	16	20	4	0	0	3	12		.194	.291	.233	65	-4	2			.909	-4	O-29	-1.0

■ WAYNE CAGE Cage, Wayne Levell b: 11/23/51, Monroe, La. BL/TL, 6'4", 205 lbs. Deb: 4/22/78

YEAR	TM/L	G	AB	R	H	2B	3B	HR	RBI	BB	SO	AVG	OBP	SLG	PRO+	BR/A	SB	CS	SBR	FA	FR	G/POS	TPR
1978	Cle-A	36	98	11	24	6	1	4	13	9	28	.245	.308	.449	112	1	1	2	-1	.988	1	D-20,1-11	0.0
1979	Cle-A	29	56	6	13	2	0	1	6	5	16	.232	.295	.321	66	-3	0	2	-1	1.000	1	/1-7,D-9	-0.3
Total	2	65	154	17	37	8	1	5	19	14	44	.240	.304	.403	94	-2	1	4	-2	.992	2	/D-29,1-18	-0.3

■ BRUCE CALDWELL Caldwell, Bruce b: 2/8/06, Ashton, R.I. d: 2/15/59, West Haven, Conn. BR/TR, 6', 195 lbs. Deb: 6/30/28

YEAR	TM/L	G	AB	R	H	2B	3B	HR	RBI	BB	SO	AVG	OBP	SLG	PRO+	BR/A	SB	CS	SBR	FA	FR	G/POS	TPR
1928	Cle-A	18	27	2	6	1	1	0	3	2	2	.222	.300	.333	66	-1	1	0	0	1.000	-2	O-10/1-1	-0.3
Total	2	25	38	4	7	1	1	0	5	4	4	.184	.279	.263	44	-3	1	0	0	.900	-3	/O-10,1-7	-0.6

■ RAY CALDWELL Caldwell, Raymond Benjamin "Rube" or "Sum" b: 4/26/1888, Corydon, Pa. d: 8/17/67, Salamanca, N.Y. BL/TR, 6'2", 190 lbs. Deb: 9/9/10

YEAR	TM/L	G	AB	R	H	2B	3B	HR	RBI	BB	SO	AVG	OBP	SLG	PRO+	BR/A	SB	CS	SBR	FA	FR	G/POS	TPR
1919	Cle-A	6	23	4	8	4	0	0	2	0	4	.348	.348	.522	134	1	0			.900	-1	/P-6	0.0
1920	*Cle-A	41	89	17	19	3	0	0	7	10	13	.213	.300	.247	45	-7	0	2	-1	.917	-3	P-34	0.0
1921	Cle-A	38	53	2	11	4	0	1	3	2	5	.208	.236	.340	45	-5	0	0	0	.930	-0	P-37	0.0
Total	12	590	1164	138	289	46	8	8	114	78	158	.248	.297	.322	78	-36	23	6		.960	-20	P-343/O-46,1	-0.7
Team	3	85	165	23	38	11	0	1	12	12	22	.230	.287	.315	57	-11	0	2		.920	-5	/P-77	0.0

■ DAVE CALLAHAN Callahan, David Joseph b: 7/20/1888, Ottawa, Ill. d: 10/28/69, Ottawa, Ill. BL/TR, 5'10", 165 lbs. Deb: 9/14/10

YEAR	TM/L	G	AB	R	H	2B	3B	HR	RBI	BB	SO	AVG	OBP	SLG	PRO+	BR/A	SB	CS	SBR	FA	FR	G/POS	TPR
1910	Cle-A	13	44	6	8	1	0	0	2	4		.182	.265	.205	47	-3	5			1.000	0	O-12	-0.3
1911	Cle-A	6	16	1	4	0	1	0	0	1		.250	.294	.375	85	-0	0			1.000	0	/O-4	0.0
Total	2	19	60	7	12	1	1	0	2	5		.200	.273	.250	58	-3	5			1.000	1	/O-16	-0.3

■ LOU CAMILLI Camilli, Louis Steven b: 9/24/46, ElPaso, Tex. BB/TR, 5'10", 170 lbs. Deb: 8/9/69

YEAR	TM/L	G	AB	R	H	2B	3B	HR	RBI	BB	SO	AVG	OBP	SLG	PRO+	BR/A	SB	CS	SBR	FA	FR	G/POS	TPR
1969	Cle-A	13	14	0	0	0	0	0	0	0	3	.000	.000	.000	-97	-4	0	0	0	1.000	3	3-13	0.0
1970	Cle-A	16	15	0	0	0	0	0	0	2	2	.000	.118	.000	-62	-3	0	0	0	1.000	-1	/S-3,2-2,3	-0.4
1971	Cle-A	39	81	5	16	2	0	0	0	8	10	.198	.270	.222	37	-6	0	0	0	.938	1	S-23,2-16	-0.4
1972	Cle-A	39	41	2	6	2	0	0	3	3	8	.146	.205	.195	19	-4	0	0	0	1.000	-2	/S-8,2-2	-0.6
Total	4	107	151	7	22	4	0	0	3	13	23	.146	.213	.172	11	-18	0	0	0	.951	2	/S-34,2-20,3	-1.4

■ BRUCE CAMPBELL Campbell, Bruce Douglas b: 10/20/09, Chicago, Ill. d: 6/17/95, BL/TR, 6'1", 185 lbs. Deb: 9/12/30

YEAR	TM/L	G	AB	R	H	2B	3B	HR	RBI	BB	SO	AVG	OBP	SLG	PRO+	BR/A	SB	CS	SBR	FA	FR	G/POS	TPR
1935	Cle-A	80	308	56	100	26	3	7	54	31	33	.325	.390	.497	126	11	2	1	0	.992	-5	O-75	0.3
1936	Cle-A	76	172	35	64	15	2	6	30	19	17	.372	.440	.587	150	14	2	1	0	.960	-4	O-47	0.7
1937	Cle-A	134	448	82	135	42	11	4	61	67	49	.301	.392	.471	116	12	4	5	-2	.978	-2	*O-123	0.4
1938	Cle-A	133	511	90	148	27	12	12	72	53	57	.290	.360	.460	106	3	11	7	-1	.967	-0	*O-122	-0.1
1939	Cle-A	130	450	84	129	23	13	8	72	67	48	.287	.383	.449	116	12	7	6	-2	.942	-3	*O-115	0.3
Total	13	1360	4762	759	1382	295	87	106	766	548	584	.290	.367	.455	108	55	53	50	-14	.956	-19	*O-1194	-3.0
Team	5	553	1889	347	576	133	41	37	289	237	204	.305	.385	.478	118	52	26	20	-4	.967	-15	O-482	1.6

■ SOUP CAMPBELL Campbell, Clarence b: 3/7/15, Sparta, Va. BL/TR, 6'1", 188 lbs. Deb: 4/21/40

YEAR	TM/L	G	AB	R	H	2B	3B	HR	RBI	BB	SO	AVG	OBP	SLG	PRO+	BR/A	SB	CS	SBR	FA	FR	G/POS	TPR
1940	Cle-A	35	62	8	14	1	0	0	2	7	12	.226	.304	.242	45	-5	0	0	0	1.000	-2	O-16	-0.7
1941	Cle-A	104	328	36	82	10	4	3	35	31	21	.250	.317	.332	75	-12	1	9	-5	.981	2	O-78	-1.9
Total	2	139	390	44	96	11	4	3	37	38	33	.246	.315	.318	70	-17	1	9	-5	.984	0	/O-94	-2.6

■ BERNIE CARBO Carbo, Bernardo b: 8/5/47, Detroit, Mich. BL/TR, 6', 175 lbs. Deb: 9/2/69

YEAR	TM/L	G	AB	R	H	2B	3B	HR	RBI	BB	SO	AVG	OBP	SLG	PRO+	BR/A	SB	CS	SBR	FA	FR	G/POS	TPR
1978	Cle-A	60	174	21	50	8	0	4	16	20	31	.287	.364	.402	117	4	1	0	0	1.000	-2	D-49/O-4	0.1
Total	12	1010	2733	372	722	140	9	96	358	538	611	.264	.389	.427	125	109	26	18	-3	.978	12	O-702,D-131/3	8.5

■ JOSE CARDENAL Cardenal, Jose Rosario Domec (b: Jose Rosario Domec (Cardenal)) b: 10/7/43, Matanzas, Cuba BR/TR, 5'10", 150 lbs. Deb: 4/14/63 C

YEAR	TM/L	G	AB	R	H	2B	3B	HR	RBI	BB	SO	AVG	OBP	SLG	PRO+	BR/A	SB	CS	SBR	FA	FR	G/POS	TPR
1968	Cle-A	157	583	78	150	21	7	7	44	39	74	.257	.306	.353	101	-0	40	18	1	.974	13	*O-153	0.6
1969	Cle-A	146	557	75	143	26	3	11	45	49	58	.257	.317	.373	89	-8	36	6	7	.982	11	*O-142/3-5	0.2
Total	18	2017	6964	936	1913	333	46	138	775	608	807	.275	.335	.395	102	16	329	139	15	.976	48	*O-1778/1-58,32S	-0.9
Team	2	303	1140	153	293	47	10	18	89	88	132	.257	.311	.363	95	-9	76	24	8	.978	24	O-295/3-5	0.8

■ LEO CARDENAS Cardenas, Leonardo Lazaro (Alfonso) "Chico" b: 12/17/38, Matanzas, Cuba BR/TR, 5'10", 163 lbs. Deb: 7/25/60

YEAR	TM/L	G	AB	R	H	2B	3B	HR	RBI	BB	SO	AVG	OBP	SLG	PRO+	BR/A	SB	CS	SBR	FA	FR	G/POS	TPR
1973	Cle-A	72	195	9	42	4	0	0	12	13	42	.215	.264	.236	41	-15	1	4	-2	.964	-8	S-67/3-5	-1.9
Total	16	1941	6707	662	1725	285	49	118	689	522	1135	.257	.313	.367	88	-107	39	48	-17	.971	-22	*S-1843/3-69,D2	2.9

■ FRED CARISCH Carisch, Frederick Behlmer b: 11/14/1881, Fountain City, Wis. d: 4/19/77, San Gabriel, Cal. BR/TR, 5'10.5", 174 lbs. Deb: 8/31/03 C

YEAR	TM/L	G	AB	R	H	2B	3B	HR	RBI	BB	SO	AVG	OBP	SLG	PRO+	BR/A	SB	CS	SBR	FA	FR	G/POS	TPR
1912	Cle-A	24	69	4	19	3	1	0	5	1		.275	.286	.348	78	-2	3			.952	6	C-23	0.6
1913	Cle-A	82	222	11	48	4	2	0	26	21	19	.216	.287	.252	56	-12	6			.971	13	C-79	0.8
1914	Cle-A	40	102	8	22	3	2	0	5	12	18	.216	.298	.284	72	-3	2	2	-1	.962	0	C-38	-0.1
Total	8	226	655	43	149	17	9	1	57	46	37	.227	.280	.285	66	-28	16	2		.968	24	C-202/1-14	1.2
Team	3	146	393	23	89	10	5	0	36	34	37	.226	.290	.277	65	-18	11	2		.966	20	C-140	1.3

■ EDDIE CARNETT Carnett, Edwin Elliott "Lefty" b: 10/21/16, Springfield, Mo. BL/TL, 6', 185 lbs. Deb: 4/19/41

YEAR	TM/L	G	AB	R	H	2B	3B	HR	RBI	BB	SO	AVG	OBP	SLG	PRO+	BR/A	SB	CS	SBR	FA	FR	G/POS	TPR
1945	Cle-A	30	73	5	16	7	0	0	7	2	9	.219	.250	.315	66	-4	0	1	-1	.971	-0	O-16/P-2	-0.6
Total	3	158	530	56	142	25	8	1	67	28	44	.268	.312	.351	91	-7	5	3	-0	.952	-8	O-104/1-25,P	-2.4

■ CHARLIE CARR Carr, Charles Carbitt b: 12/27/1876, Coatesville, Pa. d: 11/25/32, Memphis, Tenn. BR/TR, 6'2", 195 lbs. Deb: 9/15/1898

YEAR	TM/L	G	AB	R	H	2B	3B	HR	RBI	BB	SO	AVG	OBP	SLG	PRO+	BR/A	SB	CS	SBR	FA	FR	G/POS	TPR
1904	Cle-A	32	120	9	27	5	1	0	7	4		.225	.250	.283	69	-4	0			.973	-0	1-32	-0.6
1905	Cle-A	89	306	29	72	12	4	1	31	13		.235	.266	.310	82	-7	12			.991	-2	1-87	-1.3
Total	7	507	1950	185	492	68	32	6	240	71		.252	.280	.329	78	-56	49			.984	26	1-505	-4.3
Team	2	121	426	38	99	17	5	1	38	17		.232	.262	.303	78	-12	12			.986	-2	1-119	-1.9

■ CHICO CARRASQUEL Carrasquel, Alfonso (Colon) b: 1/23/28, Caracas, Venez. BR/TR, 6', 170 lbs. Deb: 4/18/50

YEAR	TM/L	G	AB	R	H	2B	3B	HR	RBI	BB	SO	AVG	OBP	SLG	PRO+	BR/A	SB	CS	SBR	FA	FR	G/POS	TPR
1956	Cle-A	141	474	60	115	15	1	7	48	52	61	.243	.325	.323	70	-20	0	4	-2	.967	-25	*S-141/3-1	-3.6
1957	Cle-A	125	392	37	108	14	1	8	57	41	53	.276	.356	.378	102	2	0	2	-1	.960	-5	*S-122	0.7
1958	Cle-A	49	156	14	40	6	0	2	21	14	12	.256	.318	.333	81	-4	0	0	0	.931	-19	S-32,3-14	-2.1
Total	10	1325	4644	568	1199	172	25	55	474	491	467	.258	.334	.342	82	-111	31	28		.969	-47	*S-1241/3-49,21	-6.8
Team	3	315	1022	111	263	35	2	17	126	107	126	.257	.336	.345	83	-22	0	6		.961	-50	S-295/3-15	-5.0

YEAR	TM/L	G	AB	R	H	2B	3B	HR	RBI	BB	SO	AVG	OBP	SLG	PRO+	BR/A	SB	CS	SBR	FA	FR	G/POS	TPR

■ CAM CARREON   Carreon, Camilo   b: 8/6/37, Colton, Cal.   d: 9/2/87, Tucson, Ariz.   BR/TR, 6', 198 lbs.   Deb: 9/27/59   F

| 1965 | Cle-A | 19 | 52 | 6 | 12 | 2 | 1 | 1 | 7 | 9 | 6 | .231 | .344 | .365 | 101 | 0 | 1 | 1 | -0 | 1.000 | 0 | C-19 | 0.1 |
| Total | 8 | 354 | 986 | 113 | 260 | 43 | 4 | 11 | 114 | 97 | 117 | .264 | .331 | .349 | 87 | -16 | 3 | 4 | -2 | .993 | 14 | C-320 | 0.8 |

■ KIT CARSON   Carson, Walter Lloyd   b: 11/15/12, Colton, Cal.   d: 6/21/83, Long Beach, Cal.   BL/TL, 6', 180 lbs.   Deb: 7/21/34

1934	Cle-A	5	18	4	5	2	1	0	1	2	3	.278	.350	.500	115	0	0	0	0	1.000	-1	/O-4	-0.1
1935	Cle-A	16	22	1	5	2	0	0	1	2	6	.227	.292	.318	57	-1	0	1	-1	1.000	-0	/O-4	-0.2
Total	2	21	40	5	10	4	1	0	2	4	9	.250	.318	.400	83	-1	0	1	-1	1.000	-2	/O-8	-0.3

■ JOE CARTER   Carter, Joseph Chris   b: 3/7/60, Oklahoma City, Okla.   BR/TR, 6'3", 215 lbs.   Deb: 7/30/83

1984	Cle-A	66	244	32	67	6	1	13	41	11	48	.275	.309	.467	109	2	2	4	-2	.956	1	O-59/1-7	-0.1
1985	Cle-A	143	489	64	128	27	0	15	59	25	74	.262	.300	.409	93	-6	24	6	4	.983	-1	*O-135,1-11/23D	-0.8
1986	Cle-A	162	663	108	200	36	9	29	**121**	32	95	.302	.339	.514	130	25	29	7	5	.976	-6	*O-104,1-70	1.5
1987	Cle-A	149	588	83	155	27	2	32	106	27	105	.264	.306	.480	103	1	31	6	6	.983	-8	1-84,O-62/D	-0.9
1988	Cle-A	157	621	85	168	36	6	27	98	35	82	.271	.317	.478	116	11	27	5	5	.985	14	*O-156	2.5
1989	Cle-A	162	651	84	158	32	4	35	105	39	112	.243	.294	.465	109	4	13	5	1	.978	-1	*O-146,1-11/D	-0.1
Total	13	1749	6797	959	1782	345	41	327	1173	419	1115	.262	.312	.469	108	53	212	57	29	.978	18	*O-1497,1-208/D32	4.4
Team	6	839	3256	456	876	164	22	151	530	169	516	.269	.312	.472	111	38	126	33	18	.978	-1	O-662,1-183/D32	2.1

■ RICO CARTY   Carty, Ricardo Adolfo Jacobo (b: Ricardo Adolfo Jacobo (Carty))   d: 9/1/39, San Pedro De Macoris, D.R.   BR/TR, 6'3", 200 lbs.   Deb: 9/15/63

1974	Cle-A	33	91	6	33	5	0	1	16	5	9	.363	.396	.451	144	5	0	0	-0	.985	-2	D-14/1-8	0.3
1975	Cle-A	118	383	57	118	19	1	18	64	45	31	.308	.384	.504	149	25	2	2	-1	.990	-1	D-72,1-26,O	2.0
1976	Cle-A	152	552	67	171	34	0	13	83	67	45	.310	.384	.442	143	31	1	1	-0	1.000	-2	*D-137,1-12/O	2.5
1977	Cle-A	127	461	50	129	23	1	15	80	56	51	.280	.358	.432	118	12	1	2	-1	1.000	1	*D-123/1-2	0.8
Total	15	1651	5606	712	1677	278	17	204	890	642	663	.299	.372	.464	132	240	21	26	-9	.970	3	O-807,D-650/1C3	17.9
Team	4	430	1487	180	451	81	2	47	243	173	136	.303	.377	.455	137	72	4	5	-2	.992	-4	D-346/1-48,O	5.6

■ GEORGE CASE   Case, George Washington   b: 11/11/15, Trenton, N.J.   d: 1/23/89, Trenton, N.J.   BR/TR, 6', 183 lbs.   Deb: 9/8/37   C

| 1946 | Cle-A | 118 | 484 | 46 | 109 | 23 | 4 | 1 | 22 | 34 | 38 | .225 | .280 | .295 | 65 | -24 | **28** | 11 | **2** | .983 | -4 | *O-118 | -3.4 |
| Total | 11 | 1226 | 5016 | 785 | 1415 | 233 | 43 | 21 | 377 | 426 | 297 | .282 | .341 | .358 | 95 | -36 | 349 | 109 | 39 | .970 | 30 | *O-1187 | -2.6 |

■ CARMEN CASTILLO   Castillo, Monte Carmelo   b: 6/8/58, San Pedro De Macoris, D.R.   BR/TR, 6'1", 190 lbs.   Deb: 7/17/82

1982	Cle-A	47	120	11	25	4	0	2	11	6	17	.208	.258	.292	51	-8	0	0	0	.978	-3	O-43/D-2	-1.2
1983	Cle-A	23	36	9	10	2	1	1	3	4	6	.278	.366	.472	124	1	1	1	-0	.929	-1	O-19/D-1	0.0
1984	Cle-A	87	211	36	55	9	2	10	36	21	32	.261	.333	.464	116	4	3	2	-2	.933	-6	O-70/D-2	-0.5
1985	Cle-A	67	184	27	45	5	1	11	25	11	40	.245	.298	.462	105	1	3	0	1	.953	-2	O-51/D-9	-0.2
1986	Cle-A	85	205	34	57	9	0	8	32	9	48	.278	.312	.439	103	0	2	1	0	.939	-2	O-37/D-35	-0.3
1987	Cle-A	89	220	27	55	17	0	11	31	16	52	.250	.301	.477	101	-0	1	1	-0	1.000	-2	D-43/O-23	-0.3
1988	Cle-A	66	176	12	48	8	0	4	14	5	31	.273	.297	.386	87	-3	6	2	1	.933	-6	O-45/D-9	-1.0
Total	10	631	1519	190	383	71	8	55	197	90	291	.252	.300	.418	93	-18	15	11	-2	.953	-30	O-380,D-154	-6.1
Team	7	464	1152	156	295	54	4	47	152	72	226	.256	.306	.432	98	-14	8	-1		.949	-21	O-288,D-101	-3.5

■ ED CERMAK   Cermak, Edward Hugo   b: 3/10/1882, Cleveland, Ohio   d: 11/22/11, Cleveland, Ohio   BR/TR, 5'11", 170 lbs.   Deb: 9/9/01

| 1901 | Cle-A | 1 | 4 | 0 | 0 | 0 | 0 | 0 | 0 | 0 | | .000 | .000 | .000 | -99 | -1 | 0 | | | 1.000 | 1 | /O-1 | 0.0 |

■ RICK CERONE   Cerone, Richard Aldo   b: 5/19/54, Newark, N.J.   BR/TR, 5'11", 192 lbs.   Deb: 8/17/75

1975	Cle-A	7	12	1	3	1	0	0	0	1	0	.250	.308	.333	81	-0	0	0	0	1.000	-1	/C-7	-0.1
1976	Cle-A	7	16	1	2	0	0	0	1	0	2	.125	.125	.125	-27	-3	0	0	0	.963	0	/C-6,D-1	-0.2
Total	18	1329	4069	393	998	190	15	59	436	320	450	.245	.304	.343	78	-123	6	22	-11	.990	-19	*C-1279/D-11,1P2O3	-10.0
Team	2	14	28	2	5	1	0	0	1	1	2	.179	.207	.214	22	-3	0	0	0	.978	-1	/C-13,D-1	-0.3

■ CHRIS CHAMBLISS   Chambliss, Carroll Christopher   b: 12/26/48, Dayton, O.   BL/TR, 6'1", 215 lbs.   Deb: 5/28/71   C

1971	Cle-A	111	415	49	114	20	4	9	48	40	83	.275	.341	.407	102	1	2	0	1	.992	-5	*1-108	-1.4
1972	Cle-A	121	466	51	136	27	2	6	44	26	63	.292	.329	.397	112	6	3	4	-2	.993	-6	*1-119	-1.3
1973	Cle-A	155	572	70	156	30	2	11	53	58	76	.273	.343	.390	104	3	4	8	-4	.991	7	*1-154	-0.6
1974	Cle-A	17	67	8	22	4	0	0	7	5	5	.328	.375	.388	121	2	0	1	-1	.982	-2	1-17	-0.2
Total	17	2175	7571	912	2109	392	42	185	972	632	926	.279	.336	.415	108	75	40	35	-9	.993	25	*1-1962/D-24	-4.0
Team	4	404	1520	178	428	81	8	26	152	129	227	.282	.340	.397	106	12	9	13	-6	.992	-6	1-398	-3.5

■ BOB CHANCE   Chance, Robert   b: 9/10/40, Statesboro, Ga.   BL/TR, 6'2", 219 lbs.   Deb: 9/4/63

1963	Cle-A	16	52	5	15	4	0	2	7	1	10	.288	.302	.481	116	1	0	1	-1	.909	-2	O-14	-0.2
1964	Cle-A	120	390	45	109	16	1	14	75	40	101	.279	.351	.433	118	9	3	3	-1	.988	-12	1-81,O-31	-0.9
Total	6	277	747	76	195	34	1	24	112	68	195	.261	.326	.406	106	5	3	5	-2	.987	-18	1-153/O-48	-2.5
Team	2	136	442	50	124	20	1	16	82	41	111	.281	.346	.439	118	10	3	4	-2	.988	-14	/1-81,O-45	-1.1

■ RAY CHAPMAN   Chapman, Raymond Johnson   b: 1/15/1891, Beaver Dam, Ky.   d: 8/17/20, New York, N.Y.   BR/TR, 5'10", 170 lbs.   Deb: 8/30/12

1912	Cle-A	31	109	29	34	6	3	0	19	10		.312	.375	.422	124	3	10			.904	-10	S-31	-0.4
1913	Cle-A	141	508	78	131	19	7	3	39	46	51	.258	.322	.341	91	-6	29			.936	-9	*S-138/O-1	-0.2
1914	Cle-A	106	375	59	103	16	10	2	42	48	48	.275	.358	.387	119	9	24	9		.913	-15	S-72,3-33	0.2
1915	Cle-A	154	570	101	154	14	17	3	67	70	82	.270	.353	.370	114	10	36	15	2	.944	9	*S-154	3.4
1916	Cle-A	109	346	50	80	10	5	0	27	50	46	.231	.330	.289	81	-7	21	14	-2	.935	13	S-52,3-36,2	0.9
1917	Cle-A	156	563	98	170	28	13	2	36	61	65	.302	.370	.409	128	18	52			.938	**24**	*S-156	5.4
1918	Cle-A	128	446	**84**	119	18	8	1	32	84	46	.267	.390	.352	113	10	30			.936	6	*S-128/O-1	2.4
1919	Cle-A	115	433	75	130	23	10	3	53	31	38	.300	.351	.420	109	4	18			.944	-0	*S-115	1.2
1920	Cle-A	111	435	97	132	27	8	3	49	52	38	.303	.380	.423	109	6	13	9	-2	.959	12	*S-111	2.5
Total	9	1051	3785	671	1053	162	81	17	364	452	414	.278	.358	.377	110	48	233	47		.939	30	S-957/2-49,3O	15.4

■ SAM CHAPMAN   Chapman, Samuel Blake   b: 4/11/16, Tiburon, Cal.   BR/TR, 6'1", 190 lbs.   Deb: 5/16/38

| 1951 | Cle-A | 94 | 246 | 24 | 56 | 9 | 1 | 6 | 36 | 27 | 32 | .228 | .304 | .346 | 80 | -8 | 3 | 0 | 1 | .985 | -18 | O-84/1-1 | -2.7 |
| Total | 11 | 1368 | 4988 | 754 | 1329 | 210 | 52 | 180 | 773 | 562 | 682 | .266 | .342 | .438 | 107 | 34 | 41 | 38 | -11 | .972 | 53 | *O-1309/1-20 | 1.3 |

■ BEN CHAPMAN   Chapman, William Benjamin   b: 12/25/08, Nashville, Tenn.   d: 7/7/93, Hoover, Ala.   BR/TR, 6', 190 lbs.   Deb: 4/15/30   MC

1939	Cle-A	149	545	101	158	31	9	6	82	87	30	.290	.390	.413	109	10	18	6	2	.971	-4	*O-146	0.3
1940	Cle-A	143	548	82	157	40	6	4	50	78	45	.286	.377	.403	105	7	13	7	-0	.964	2	*O-140	0.0
Total	15	1717	6478	1144	1958	407	107	90	977	824	556	.302	.383	.440	115	159	287	135	5	.967	50	*O-1495/3-96,2PS	14.0
Team	2	292	1093	183	315	71	15	10	132	165	75	.288	.384	.408	107	17	31	13	2	.968	-2	O-286	0.3

■ LARRY CHAPPELL   Chappell, La Verne Ashford   b: 2/19/1890, McClusky, Ill.   d: 11/8/18, San Francisco, Cal.   BL/TL, 6', 186 lbs.   Deb: 7/18/13

| 1916 | Cle-A | 3 | 2 | 1 | 0 | 0 | 0 | 0 | 0 | 1 | 0 | .000 | .333 | .000 | 1 | -0 | 1 | | | .000 | 0 | H | 0.0 |
| Total | 5 | 109 | 305 | 27 | 69 | 9 | 2 | 0 | 26 | 25 | 42 | .226 | .289 | .269 | 66 | -13 | 9 | | | .951 | -5 | /O-83 | -2.3 |

■ JOE CHARBONEAU   Charboneau, Joseph   b: 6/17/55, Belvidere, Ill.   BR/TR, 6'2", 205 lbs.   Deb: 4/11/80

1980	Cle-A	131	453	76	131	17	2	23	87	49	70	.289	.362	.488	130	18	2	4	-2	.963	1	O-67,D-57	1.3
1981	Cle-A	48	138	14	29	7	1	4	18	7	22	.210	.248	.362	75	-5	1	0	0	.963	-2	O-27,D-14	-0.8
1982	Cle-A	22	56	7	12	2	1	2	9	5	7	.214	.290	.393	86	-1	0	0	0	.955	-3	O-18/D-1	-0.5
Total	3	201	647	97	172	26	4	29	114	61	99	.266	.333	.453	115	12	3	4	-2	.962	-4	O-112/D-72	-0.0

YEAR	TM/L	G	AB	R	H	2B	3B	HR	RBI	BB	SO	AVG	OBP	SLG	PRO+	BR/A	SB	CS	SBR	FA	FR	G/POS	TPR

■ AL CIHOCKI
Cihocki, Albert Joseph b: 5/7/24, Nanticoke, Pa. BR/TR, 5'11", 185 lbs. Deb: 4/17/45

| 1945 | Cle-A | 92 | 283 | 21 | 60 | 9 | 3 | 0 | 24 | 11 | 48 | .212 | .241 | .265 | 49 | -19 | 2 | 1 | 0 | .946 | 1 | S-41,3-29,2 | -1.5 |

■ BILL CISSELL
Cissell, Chalmer William b: 1/3/04, Perryville, Mo. d: 3/15/49, Chicago, Ill. BR/TR, 5'11", 170 lbs. Deb: 4/11/28

1932	Cle-A	131	541	78	173	35	6	6	93	28	25	.320	.354	.440	98	-3	18	15	-4	.964	11	*2-129/S-6	1.1
1933	Cle-A	112	409	53	94	21	3	6	33	31	29	.230	.284	.340	62	-23	6	6	-2	.947	-7	2-62,S-46/3	-2.5
Total	9	956	3707	516	990	173	43	29	423	212	250	.267	.308	.360	73	-158	113	63	-4	.958	-14	2-483,S-439/3	-9.5
Team	2	243	950	131	267	56	9	12	126	59	54	.281	.324	.397	83	-26	24	21	-5	.959	3	2-191/S-52,3	-1.4

■ UKE CLANTON
Clanton, Eucal "Cat" b: 2/19/1898, Powell, Mo. d: 2/24/60, Antlers, Okla. BL/TL, 5'8", 165 lbs. Deb: 9/21/22

| 1922 | Cle-A | 1 | 1 | 0 | 0 | 0 | 0 | 0 | 0 | 0 | 1 | .000 | .000 | .000 | -99 | -0 | 0 | 0 | 0 | .500 | -0 | /1-1 | -0.1 |

■ ALLIE CLARK
Clark, Alfred Aloysius b: 6/16/23, S.Amboy, N.J. BR/TR, 6', 185 lbs. Deb: 8/5/47

1948	*Cle-A	81	271	43	84	5	2	9	38	23	13	.310	.364	.443	117	6	0	2	-1	.982	-6	O-65/3-5,1	-0.5
1949	Cle-A	35	74	8	13	4	0	1	9	4	7	.176	.218	.270	29	-8	0	0	0	1.000	-4	O-17/1-1	-1.3
1950	Cle-A	59	163	19	35	6	1	6	21	11	10	.215	.264	.374	64	-10	0	1	-1	.987	-3	O-41	-1.4
1951	Cle-A	3	10	3	3	2	0	1	3	1	2	.300	.364	.800	221	1	0	0	0	1.000	-1	/O-3	0.1
Total	7	358	1021	131	267	48	4	32	149	72	70	.262	.312	.410	92	-16	2	5	-2	.988	-19	O-242/3-15,1	-4.7
Team	4	178	518	73	135	17	3	17	71	39	32	.261	.312	.403	90	-11	0	3	-2	.986	-14	O-126/3-5,1	-3.1

■ DAVE CLARK
Clark, David Earl b: 9/3/62, Tupelo, Miss. BL/TR, 6'2", 200 lbs. Deb: 9/3/86

1986	Cle-A	18	58	10	16	1	0	3	9	7	11	.276	.354	.448	119	2	1	0	0	1.000	1	O-10/D-7	0.2
1987	Cle-A	29	87	11	18	5	0	3	12	2	24	.207	.225	.368	53	-6	1	0	0	1.000	0	O-13,D-12	-0.6
1988	Cle-A	63	156	11	41	4	1	3	18	17	28	.263	.335	.359	92	-1	0	2	-1	.947	-4	D-27,O-23	-0.8
1989	Cle-A	102	253	21	60	12	0	8	29	30	63	.237	.318	.379	94	-2	0	2	-1	.964	-5	D-55,O-21	-1.0
Total	10	603	1464	189	387	54	6	49	212	155	319	.264	.336	.410	99	-2	15	10	-2	.971	-24	O-324,D-102	-3.7
Team	4	212	554	53	135	22	1	17	68	56	126	.244	.313	.379	90	-8	2	4	-2	.974	-8	D-101/O-67	-2.2

■ JIM CLARK
Clark, James Edward b: 4/30/47, Kansas City, Kan. BR/TR, 6'1", 190 lbs. Deb: 7/16/71

| 1971 | Cle-A | 13 | 18 | 2 | 3 | 0 | 1 | 0 | 0 | 2 | 7 | .167 | .250 | .278 | 45 | -1 | 0 | 0 | 0 | 1.000 | 0 | /O-3,1-1 | -0.1 |

■ NIG CLARKE
Clarke, Jay Justin b: 12/15/1882, Amherstburg, Ont., Canada d: 6/15/49, River Rouge, Mich BL/TL, 5'8", 165 lbs. Deb: 4/26/05

1905	Cle-A	5	9	2	1	1	0	0	1	1		.111	.200	.222	33	-1	0			1.000	-2	/C-5	-0.2
1905	Cle-A	37	114	9	23	5	1	0	8	10		.202	.266	.263	67	-4	3			.961	-1	C-37	-0.2
1906	Cle-A	57	179	22	64	12	4	1	21	13		.358	.404	.486	181	16	3			.982	-0	C-54	2.2
1907	Cle-A	120	390	44	105	19	6	3	33	35		.269	.364	.372	124	10	3			.961	-11	*C-115	1.1
1908	Cle-A	97	290	34	70	8	6	1	27	30		.241	.315	.321	106	2	6			.969	-8	C-90	0.3
1909	Cle-A	55	164	15	45	4	2	0	14	9		.274	.316	.323	98	-1	1			.952	-3	C-44	0.1
1910	Cle-A	21	58	4	9	2	0	0	2	8		.155	.258	.190	40	-4	0			.974	3	C-17	0.0
Total	9	506	1536	157	390	64	20	6	127	138		.254	.338	.333	102	3	16			.960	-25	C-462/1-4	2.3
Team	7	392	1204	130	317	51	19	5	106	106		.263	.325	.350	114	19	13			.965	-21	C-362	3.3

■ JOSH CLARKE
Clarke, Joshua Baldwin "Pepper" b: 3/8/1879, Winfield, Kan. d: 7/2/62, Ventura, Cal. BL/TR, 5'10", 180 lbs. Deb: 6/15/1898 F

1908	Cle-A	131	492	70	119	8	4	1	21	76		.242	.348	.280	104	6	37			.963	-3	*O-131	-0.2
1909	Cle-A	4	12	1	0	0	0	0	0	2		.000	.143	.000	-52	-2	0			.600	-2	/O-4	-0.4
Total	5	223	809	118	193	18	9	5	43	135		.239	.352	.302	102	8	51			.949	-9	O-196/2-16,S	-1.1
Team	2	135	504	71	119	8	4	1	21	78		.236	.343	.274	100	4	37			.955	-4	O-135	-0.6

■ SUMPTER CLARKE
Clarke, Sumpter Mills b: 10/18/1897, Savannah, Ga. d: 3/16/62, Knoxville, Tenn. BR/TR, 5'11", 170 lbs. Deb: 9/27/20 F

1923	Cle-A	1	3	0	0	0	0	0	0	0	0	.000	.000	.000	-99	-1	0	0	0	1.000	-0	/O-1	-0.1
1924	Cle-A	35	104	17	24	6	1	0	11	6	12	.231	.273	.308	49	-8	0	0	0	1.000	-5	O-33	-1.5
Total	3	37	110	17	25	6	1	0	11	6	13	.227	.267	.300	46	-9	0	0	0	1.000	-6	/O-34,3-1	-1.6
Team	2	36	107	17	24	6	1	0	11	6	12	.224	.265	.299	45	-9	0			1.000	-5	/O-34	-1.6

■ TY CLINE
Cline, Tyrone Alexander b: 6/15/39, Hampton, S.C. BL/TL, 6'0.5", 170 lbs. Deb: 9/14/60

1960	Cle-A	7	26	2	8	1	1	0	2	0	4	.308	.308	.423	99	-0	0	0	0	1.000	2	/O-6	0.1
1961	Cle-A	12	43	9	9	2	1	0	1	6	1	.209	.333	.302	73	-1	1	0	0	1.000	-2	O-12	-0.4
1962	Cle-A	118	375	53	93	15	5	2	28	28	50	.248	.309	.331	74	-14	5	4	-1	.992	3	*O-107	-1.8
Total	12	892	1834	251	437	53	25	6	125	153	262	.238	.304	.304	72	-65	22	19	-5	.986	-38	O-548/1-62	-14.2
Team	3	137	444	64	110	18	7	2	31	34	55	.248	.311	.333	76	-15	6	4	-1	.993	2	O-125	-2.1

■ BILLY CLINGMAN
Clingman, William Frederick b: 11/21/1869, Cincinnati, Ohio d: 5/14/58, Cincinnati, Ohio BB/TR, 5'11", 150 lbs. Deb: 9/9/1890

| 1903 | Cle-A | 21 | 64 | 10 | 18 | 1 | 1 | 0 | 7 | 11 | | .281 | .387 | .328 | 118 | 2 | 2 | | | .932 | 5 | 2-11/S-7,3 | 0.3 |
| Total | 10 | 816 | 2839 | 410 | 697 | 86 | 31 | 8 | 301 | 303 | | .246 | .323 | .306 | 74 | -97 | 98 | | | .919 | 81 | 3-422,S-380/2O | 1.7 |

■ LOU CLINTON
Clinton, Lucien Louis b: 10/13/37, Ponca City, Okla. BR/TR, 6'1", 185 lbs. Deb: 4/22/60

| 1965 | Cle-A | 12 | 34 | 2 | 6 | 1 | 0 | 1 | 2 | 3 | 7 | .176 | .243 | .294 | 51 | -2 | 0 | 0 | 0 | .941 | -0 | /O-9 | -0.3 |
| Total | 8 | 691 | 2153 | 270 | 532 | 112 | 31 | 65 | 269 | 188 | 418 | .247 | .310 | .418 | 99 | -7 | 12 | 7 | | .980 | 15 | O-619 | -2.1 |

■ ROCKY COLAVITO
Colavito, Rocco Domenico b: 8/10/33, New York, N.Y. BR/TR, 6'3", 190 lbs. Deb: 9/10/55 C

1955	Cle-A	5	9	3	4	2	0	0	0	0	2	.444	.444	.667	189	1	0	0	0	1.000	2	/O-2	0.3
1956	Cle-A	101	322	55	89	11	4	21	65	49	46	.276	.375	.531	134	15	0	1	-1	.968	-1	O-98	0.9
1957	Cle-A	134	461	66	116	26	0	25	84	71	80	.252	.353	.471	124	15	1	6	-3	.962	12	*O-130	1.7
1958	Cle-A	143	489	80	148	26	3	41	113	84	89	.303	.407	.620	183	56	0	2	-1	.981	2	*O-129,1-11/P	5.0
1959	Cle-A★	154	588	90	151	24	0	42	111	71	86	.257	.337	.512	135	26	3	3	-1	.985	12	*O-154	2.9
1965	Cle-A★	162	592	92	170	25	2	26	108	93	63	.287	.387	.468	140	34	1	1	-0	1.000	4	*O-162	3.1
1966	Cle-A★	151	533	68	127	13	0	30	72	76	81	.238	.337	.432	119	14	2	1	0	.982	7	*O-146	1.5
1967	Cle-A	63	191	10	46	9	0	5	21	24	31	.241	.339	.366	104	1	2	2	-1	.962	-4	O-50	-0.6
Total	14	1841	6503	971	1730	283	21	374	1159	951	880	.266	.362	.489	132	287	19	27	-11	.980	66	*O-1774/1-11,P	25.2
Team	8	913	3185	464	851	136	9	190	574	468	478	.267	.364	.495	137	162	9	16	-7	.980	33	O-871/1-11,P	14.8

■ ALEX COLE
Cole, Alexander b: 8/17/65, Fayetteville, N.C. BL/TL, 6'2", 170 lbs. Deb: 7/27/90

1990	Cle-A	63	227	43	68	5	4	0	13	28	38	.300	.379	.357	107	3	40	9	7	.961	2	O-59/D-1	1.0
1991	Cle-A	122	387	58	114	17	3	0	21	58	47	.295	.388	.354	106	6	27	17	-2	.970	1	*O-107/D-6	0.2
1992	Cle-A	41	97	11	20	1	0	0	2	16	19	.206	.287	.216	44	-7	9	2	-2	.971	-4	O-24/D-4	-1.0
Total	6	549	1688	273	477	53	25	5	110	209	285	.283	.364	.352	92	-10	143	56	9	.971	-4	O-459/D-14	-1.4
Team	3	226	711	112	202	23	7	0	39	96	106	.284	.372	.336	98	2	76	28	6	.967	-2	O-190/D-11	0.2

■ GORDY COLEMAN
Coleman, Gordon Calvin b: 7/5/34, Rockville, Md. d: 3/12/94, Cincinnati, Ohio BL/TR, 6'2", 218 lbs. Deb: 9/19/59

| 1959 | Cle-A | 6 | 15 | 5 | 8 | 0 | 1 | 0 | 2 | 1 | 2 | .533 | .563 | .667 | 245 | 3 | 0 | 0 | 0 | .955 | 0 | /1-3 | 0.3 |
| Total | 9 | 773 | 2384 | 282 | 650 | 102 | 11 | 98 | 387 | 177 | 333 | .273 | .326 | .448 | 106 | 18 | 9 | 8 | -2 | .990 | 16 | 1-659 | -1.1 |

■ BOB COLEMAN
Coleman, Robert Hunter b: 9/26/1890, Huntingburg, Ind. d: 7/16/59, Boston, Mass. BR/TR, 6'2", 190 lbs. Deb: 6/13/13 MC

| 1916 | Cle-A | 19 | 28 | 3 | 6 | 2 | 0 | 0 | 4 | 7 | 6 | .214 | .371 | .286 | 92 | 0 | 0 | | | .972 | -3 | C-12 | -0.2 |
| Total | 3 | 116 | 228 | 19 | 55 | 8 | 1 | 0 | 27 | 29 | 46 | .241 | .327 | .298 | 87 | -3 | 3 | | | .976 | -5 | C-108 | -0.1 |

YEAR	TM/L	G	AB	R	H	2B	3B	HR	RBI	BB	SO	AVG	OBP	SLG	PRO+	BR/A	SB	CS	SBR	FA	FR	G/POS	TPR

■ MERL COMBS   Combs, Merrill Russell   b: 12/11/19, Los Angeles, Cal.   d: 7/8/81, Riverside, Cal.   BL/TR, 6', 172 lbs.   Deb: 9/12/47   C

1951	Cle-A	19	28	2	5	2	0	0	2	2	3	.179	.233	.250	32	-3	0	0	0	.960	5	S-16	0.2
1952	Cle-A	52	139	11	23	1	1	1	10	14	15	.165	.242	.209	28	-14	0	1	-1	.972	9	S-49/2-3	-0.3
Total	5	140	361	45	73	6	1	2	25	57	43	.202	.314	.241	52	-23	0	1		.968	17	/S-96,3-26,2	-0.3
Team	2	71	167	13	28	3	1	1	12	16	18	.168	.240	.216	29	-16	0	1		.970	14	/S-65,2-3	-0.1

■ BUNK CONGALTON   Congalton, William Millar   b: 1/24/1875, Guelph, Ont., Can.   d: 8/16/37, Cleveland, Ohio   BL/TL, 5'11", 190 lbs.   Deb: 4/18/02

1905	Cle-A	12	47	4	17	0	0	0	5	2		.362	.388	.362	136	2	3			.923	-1	O-12	0.0
1906	Cle-A	117	419	51	134	13	5	3	50	24		.320	.361	.396	139	18	12			.957	-9	*O-114	0.4
1907	Cle-A	9	22	2	4	0	0	0	2	4		.182	.308	.182	56	-1	0			1.000	0	/O-6	-0.1
Total	4	307	1163	115	337	27	13	6	128	57		.290	.326	.351	115	17	31			.967	-12	O-300	-1.0
Team	3	138	488	57	155	13	5	3	57	30		.318	.361	.383	135	19	15			.958	-10	O-132	0.3

■ BRUCE CONNATSER   Connatser, Broadus Milburn   b: 9/19/02, Sevierville, Tenn.   d: 1/27/71, Terre Haute, Ind.   BR/TR, 5'11.5", 170 lbs.   Deb: 9/15/31

1931	Cle-A	12	49	5	14	3	0	0	4	2	3	.286	.327	.347	73	-2	0	0	0	1.000	1	1-12	-0.2
1932	Cle-A	23	60	8	14	3	1	0	4	4	8	.233	.281	.317	51	-4	1	0	0	1.000	1	1-14	-0.4
Total	2	35	109	13	28	6	1	0	8	6	11	.257	.302	.330	61	-6	1	0	0	1.000	2	/1-26	-0.6

■ JOE CONNOLLY   Connolly, Joseph George "Coaster Joe"   b: 6/4/1896, San Francisco, Cal   d: 3/30/60, San Francisco, Cal   BR/TR, 6', 170 lbs.   Deb: 10/1/21

1922	Cle-A	12	45	6	11	2	1	0	6	5	8	.244	.320	.333	70	-2	1	0	0	.972	2	O-12	-0.1
1923	Cle-A	52	109	25	33	10	1	3	25	13	7	.303	.377	.495	129	4	1	2	-1	.957	-10	O-39	-0.8
Total	4	80	168	32	45	12	3	3	32	21	18	.268	.349	.417	100	-0	2	2	-1	.966	-9	/O-55	-1.2
Team	2	64	154	31	44	12	2	3	31	18	15	.286	.360	.448	111	2	2	2	-1	.963	-8	/O-51	-0.9

■ JOE CONNOR   Connor, Joseph Francis   b: 12/8/1874, Waterbury, Conn.   d: 11/8/57, Waterbury, Conn.   BR/TR, 6'2", 185 lbs.   Deb: 9/9/1895   F

| 1901 | Cle-A | 37 | 121 | 13 | 17 | 3 | 1 | 0 | 6 | 7 | | .140 | .200 | .182 | 7 | -15 | 2 | | | .942 | -0 | C-32/O-4,S | -1.2 |
| Total | 4 | 92 | 271 | 29 | 54 | 7 | 2 | 1 | 22 | 18 | | .199 | .257 | .251 | 43 | -21 | 8 | | | .952 | 5 | /C-75,O-5,31S2 | -0.9 |

■ JACK CONWAY   Conway, Jack Clements   b: 7/30/19, Bryan, Tex.   BR/TR, 5'11.5", 175 lbs.   Deb: 9/9/41

1941	Cle-A	2	2	0	1	0	0	0	1	0	0	.500	.500	.500	174	0	0	0	0	1.000	1	/S-2	0.1
1946	Cle-A	68	258	24	58	6	2	0	18	20	36	.225	.281	.264	56	-15	2	2	-1	.955	-7	2-50,S-14/3	-2.0
1947	Cle-A	34	50	3	9	2	0	0	5	3	8	.180	.226	.220	25	-5	0	0	0	.877	0	S-24/2-5,3	-0.5
Total	4	128	359	35	80	10	3	1	27	28	54	.223	.279	.276	57	-21	2	2	-1	.962	0	/2-68,S-46,3	-1.8
Team	3	104	310	27	68	8	2	0	24	23	44	.219	.273	.258	52	-20	2	2	-1	.956	-6	/2-55,S-40,3	-2.4

■ HERB CONYERS   Conyers, Herbert Leroy   b: 1/8/21, Cowgill, Mo.   d: 9/16/64, Cleveland, Ohio   BL/TR, 6'5", 210 lbs.   Deb: 4/18/50

| 1950 | Cle-A | 7 | 9 | 2 | 3 | 0 | 0 | 1 | 1 | 1 | 2 | .333 | .400 | .667 | 175 | 1 | 1 | 0 | 0 | 1.000 | -0 | /1-1 | 0.1 |

■ MARLAN COUGHTRY   Coughtry, James Marlan   b: 9/11/34, Hollywood, Cal.   BR/TR, 6'1", 170 lbs.   Deb: 9/2/60

| 1962 | Cle-A | 3 | 2 | 1 | 1 | 0 | 0 | 0 | 1 | 1 | 1 | .500 | .667 | .500 | 226 | 1 | 0 | 0 | 0 | .000 | 0 | H | 0.1 |
| Total | 2 | 35 | 54 | 5 | 10 | 0 | 0 | 0 | 4 | 10 | 18 | .185 | .313 | .185 | 37 | -4 | 0 | 0 | 0 | .915 | 6 | /2-15,3-9 | 0.2 |

■ TED COX   Cox, William Ted   b: 1/24/55, Oklahoma City, Okla   BR/TR, 6'3", 195 lbs.   Deb: 9/18/77

1978	Cle-A	82	227	14	53	7	0	1	19	16	30	.233	.287	.278	60	-12	0	1	-1	.980	-5	O-38,3-20,D/1S	-2.0
1979	Cle-A	78	189	17	40	6	0	4	22	14	27	.212	.273	.307	56	-12	3	4	-2	.964	0	3-52,O-16/2D	-1.3
Total	5	272	771	65	189	29	1	10	79	50	98	.245	.300	.324	71	-31	3	6	-3	.947	-11	3-166/O-54,D12S	-4.9
Team	2	160	416	31	93	13	0	5	41	30	57	.224	.281	.291	58	-24	3	5	-2	.958	-5	/3-72,O-54,D12S	-3.3

■ ROD CRAIG   Craig, Rodney Paul   b: 1/12/58, Los Angeles, Cal.   BB/TR, 6'1", 195 lbs.   Deb: 9/11/79

| 1982 | Cle-A | 49 | 65 | 7 | 15 | 2 | 0 | 1 | 4 | 6 | .231 | .275 | .262 | 49 | -5 | 3 | 1 | 0 | .966 | -4 | O-22/D-4 | -0.9 |
| Total | 4 | 145 | 367 | 49 | 94 | 25 | 2 | 3 | 27 | 24 | 48 | .256 | .305 | .360 | 80 | -10 | 7 | 8 | -3 | .977 | -9 | O-102/D-4 | -2.5 |

■ DEL CRANDALL   Crandall, Delmar Wesley   b: 3/5/30, Ontario, Cal.   BR/TR, 6'1", 195 lbs.   Deb: 6/17/49   MC

| 1966 | Cle-A | 50 | 108 | 10 | 25 | 2 | 0 | 4 | 8 | 14 | 9 | .231 | .320 | .361 | 95 | -1 | 0 | 0 | 0 | .991 | 15 | C-49 | 1.8 |
| Total | 16 | 1573 | 5026 | 585 | 1276 | 179 | 18 | 179 | 657 | 424 | 477 | .254 | .315 | .404 | 97 | -35 | 26 | 28 | -9 | .989 | 61 | *C-1479/1-14,O | 8.2 |

■ ED CROSBY   Crosby, Edward Carlton   b: 5/26/49, Long Beach, Cal.   BL/TR, 6'2", 180 lbs.   Deb: 7/12/70

1974	Cle-A	37	86	11	18	3	0	0	6	6	12	.209	.261	.244	46	-6	0	1	-1	.926	-10	3-18,S-13/2	-1.6
1975	Cle-A	61	128	12	30	3	0	0	7	13	14	.234	.305	.258	60	-6	0	4	-2	.974	4	S-30,2-19,3	-0.2
1976	Cle-A	2	2	0	1	0	0	0	0	0	0	.500	.500	.500	195	0	0	0	0	1.000	1	/3-1,D-1	0.1
Total	6	297	677	67	149	22	4	0	44	55	74	.220	.284	.264	55	-40	1	7	-4	.964	-11	S-157/2-72,3D	-4.0
Team	3	100	216	23	49	6	0	0	13	19	26	.227	.289	.255	56	-12	0	5	-3	.967	-6	/S-43,3-32,2D	-1.7

■ FRANK CROSS   Cross, Frank Atwell "Mickey"   b: 1/20/1873, Cleveland, Ohio   d: 11/2/32, Geauga Lake, Ohio   TR ,   Deb: 5/20/01   F

| 1901 | Cle-A | 1 | 5 | 0 | 3 | 0 | 0 | 0 | 0 | 0 | | .600 | .600 | .600 | 243 | 1 | 0 | | | .000 | -0 | /O-1 | 0.0 |

■ ROY CULLENBINE   Cullenbine, Roy Joseph   b: 10/18/13, Nashville, Tenn.   d: 5/28/91, Mt.Clemens, Mich.   BB/TR, 6'1", 190 lbs.   Deb: 4/19/38

1943	Cle-A	138	488	66	141	24	4	8	56	96	58	.289	.407	.404	146	33	3	4	-2	.981	3	*O-121,1-13	2.9
1944	Cle-A☆	154	571	98	162	34	5	16	80	87	49	.284	.380	.445	141	31	4	4	-1	.967	-2	*O-151	2.1
1945	Cle-A	8	13	3	1	1	0	0	0	11	0	.077	.500	.154	97	1	0	0	0	1.000	-2	/O-4,3-3	-0.1
Total	10	1181	3879	627	1072	209	32	110	599	853	399	.276	.408	.432	132	199	26	20		.969	34	O-843,1-208/3	18.1
Team	3	300	1072	167	304	59	9	24	136	194	107	.284	.395	.423	143	66	7	8		.974	-2	O-276/1-13,3	4.9

■ NICK CULLOP   Cullop, Henry Nicholas "Tomato Face" (b: Heinrich Nicholas Kolop)   b: 10/16/1900, St.Louis, Mo.   d: 12/8/78, Westerville, Ohio   BR/TR, 6', 200 lbs.   Deb: 4/14/26

| 1927 | Cle-A | 32 | 68 | 9 | 16 | 2 | 3 | 2 | 8 | 9 | 19 | .235 | .333 | .397 | 88 | -1 | 0 | 4 | -2 | .982 | 3 | O-20/P-1 | -0.2 |
| Total | 5 | 173 | 490 | 49 | 122 | 29 | 12 | 11 | 67 | 40 | 128 | .249 | .308 | .424 | 96 | -6 | 1 | 4 | -2 | .975 | 2 | O-124/1-2,P | -1.3 |

■ WIL CULMER   Culmer, Wilfred Hillard   b: 11/11/58, Nassau, Bahamas   BR/TR, 6'4", 210 lbs.   Deb: 4/12/83

| 1983 | Cle-A | 7 | 19 | 0 | 2 | 0 | 0 | 0 | 1 | 0 | 4 | .105 | .105 | .105 | -40 | -4 | 0 | 1 | -1 | 1.000 | -1 | /O-4,D-2 | -0.6 |

■ TONY CURRY   Curry, George Anthony   b: 12/22/38, Nassau, Bahamas   BL/TL, 5'11", 185 lbs.   Deb: 4/12/60

| 1966 | Cle-A | 19 | 16 | 4 | 2 | 0 | 0 | 0 | 3 | 3 | 8 | .125 | .263 | .125 | 16 | -2 | 0 | 0 | 0 | .000 | 0 | H | -0.2 |
| Total | 3 | 129 | 297 | 33 | 73 | 16 | 2 | 6 | 40 | 20 | 69 | .246 | .296 | .374 | 82 | -8 | 0 | 2 | -1 | .915 | -8 | /O-72 | -2.1 |

■ AL CYPERT   Cypert, Alfred Boyd "Cy"   b: 8/8/1889, Little Rock, Ark.   d: 1/9/73, Washington, D.C.   BR/TR, 5'10.5", 150 lbs.   Deb: 6/27/14

| 1914 | Cle-A | 1 | 1 | 0 | 0 | 0 | 0 | 0 | 0 | 0 | 1 | .000 | .000 | .000 | -96 | -0 | 0 | | | .000 | 0 | /3-1 | 0.0 |

■ PAUL DADE   Dade, Lonnie Paul   b: 12/7/51, Seattle, Wash.   BR/TR, 6', 195 lbs.   Deb: 9/12/75

1977	Cle-A	134	461	65	134	15	3	3	45	32	58	.291	.339	.356	93	-4	16	8	0	.989	-7	O-99,3-26/2D	-1.6
1978	Cle-A	93	307	37	78	12	1	3	20	34	45	.254	.332	.329	88	-4	12	9	-2	.962	2	O-81/D-9	-0.8
1979	Cle-A	44	170	22	48	4	3	0	18	12	22	.282	.330	.371	88	-3	12	6	0	.962	2	O-37/3-2,D	-0.9
Total	6	439	1313	186	355	54	7	10	107	113	193	.270	.331	.345	89	-19	57	33		.970	4	O-236,3-121/D2	-2.8
Team	3	271	938	124	260	31	5	9	83	78	125	.277	.335	.350	90	-11	40	23		.973	-4	O-217/3-28,D2	-2.6

■ PETE DALENA   Dalena, Peter Martin   b: 6/26/60, Fresno, Cal.   BL/TR, 5'11", 200 lbs.   Deb: 7/7/89

| 1989 | Cle-A | 5 | 7 | 0 | 1 | 1 | 0 | 0 | 0 | 0 | 3 | .143 | .143 | .286 | 18 | -1 | 0 | 0 | 0 | .000 | 0 | /D-1 | -0.1 |

YEAR	TM/L	G	AB	R	H	2B	3B	HR	RBI	BB	SO	AVG	OBP	SLG	PRO+	BR/A	SB	CS	SBR	FA	FR	G/POS	TPR

■ TOM DALY
Daly, Thomas Daniel   b: 12/12/1891, St.John, N.B., Can.   d: 11/7/46, Medford, Mass.   BR/TR, 5'11.5", 171 lbs.   Deb: 9/23/13   C

| | 1916 | Cle-A | 31 | 73 | 3 | 16 | 1 | 1 | 0 | 8 | 1 | 2 | .219 | .230 | .260 | 45 | -5 | 0 | | | .982 | -2 | C-25/O-1 | -0.6 |
| Total | 8 | | 244 | 540 | 49 | 129 | 17 | 3 | 0 | 55 | 25 | 43 | .239 | .274 | .281 | 59 | -29 | 5 | | | .972 | -15 | | -4.4 |

■ VIC DAVALILLO
Davalillo, Victor Jose (Romero)   b: 7/31/36, Cabimas, Venez.   BL/TL, 5'7", 155 lbs.   Deb: 4/9/63   F

1963	Cle-A	90	370	44	108	18	5	7	36	16	41	.292	.323	.424	108	3	3	3	-1	.988	17	O-89	1.5
1964	Cle-A	150	577	64	156	26	2	6	51	34	77	.270	.312	.354	85	-12	21	11	-0	.986	16	*O-143	-0.3
1965	Cle-A★	142	505	67	152	19	1	5	40	35	50	.301	.346	.372	103	2	26	7	4	.988	15	*O-134	1.6
1966	Cle-A	121	344	42	86	6	4	3	19	24	37	.250	.299	.317	77	-10	8	6	-1	.986	0	*O-108	-1.6
1967	Cle-A	139	359	47	103	17	5	2	22	10	30	.287	.308	.379	101	-1	6	7	-2	.986	-8	*O-125	-1.7
1968	Cle-A	51	180	15	43	2	3	2	13	9	19	.239	.255	.317	74	-6	8	6	-1	.967	2	O-49	-0.9
Total	16	1458	4017	509	1122	160	37	36	329	212	422	.279	.317	.364	94	-36	125	58	3	.986	19	*O-1066/1-47,DP	-6.4
Team	6	693	2335	279	648	88	20	25	181	122	254	.278	.315	.364	93	-23	72	40	-2	.986	41	O-648	-1.4

■ HOMER DAVIDSON
Davidson, Homer Hurd "Divvy"   b: 10/14/1884, Cleveland, Ohio   d: 7/26/48, Detroit, Mich.   BR/TR, 5'10.5", 155 lbs.   Deb: 4/25/08

| 1908 | Cle-A | 9 | 4 | 2 | 0 | 0 | 0 | 0 | 0 | 0 | | .000 | .000 | .000 | -99 | -1 | 1 | | | 1.000 | 2 | /C-5,O-1 | 0.1 |

■ BILL DAVIS
Davis, Arthur Willard   b: 6/6/42, Graceville, Minn.   BL/TL, 6'7", 215 lbs.   Deb: 9/16/65

1965	Cle-A	10	10	0	3	1	0	0	0	0	3	.300	.300	.400	96	-0	0	0	0	.000	0	H	0.0
1966	Cle-A	23	38	2	6	1	0	1	4	6	9	.158	.273	.263	55	-2	0	0	0	.981	0	/1-9	-0.3
Total	3	64	105	3	19	3	0	1	5	14	28	.181	.283	.238	50	-7	0	0	0	.988	-1	/1-23	-1.0
Team	2	33	48	2	9	2	0	1	4	6	10	.188	.278	.292	63	-2	0	0	0	.981	0	/1-9	-0.3

■ HARRY DAVIS
Davis, Harry H (b: Harry Davis) "Jasper"   b: 7/19/1873, Philadelphia, Pa.   d: 8/11/47, Philadelphia, Pa.   BR/TR, 5'10", 180 lbs.   Deb: 9/21/1895   M

| 1912 | Cle-A | 2 | 5 | 0 | 0 | 0 | 0 | 0 | 0 | 0 | 0 | .000 | .000 | .000 | -97 | -1 | 0 | | | .941 | 0 | /1-2,M | -0.1 |
| Total | 22 | 1755 | 6653 | 1001 | 1841 | 361 | 145 | 75 | 951 | 525 | | .277 | .335 | .408 | 119 | 135 | 285 | | | .988 | -6 | *1-1628/O-78,32S | 10.9 |

■ CHUBBY DEAN
Dean, Alfred Lovill   b: 8/24/16, Mt.Airy, N.C.   d: 12/21/70, Riverside, Cal.   BL/TL, 5'11", 181 lbs.   Deb: 4/14/36

1941	Cle-A	17	25	2	4	1	0	0	2	3	2	.160	.250	.200	21	-3	0	0	0	1.000	1	/P-8	0.0
1942	Cle-A	70	101	4	27	1	0	0	7	11	7	.267	.339	.277	79	-2	0	0	0	.939	-3	P-27	0.0
1943	Cle-A	41	46	2	9	0	0	0	5	6	2	.196	.288	.196	45	-3	0	0	0	.929	-1	P-17	0.0
Total	8	533	1047	106	287	47	7	3	128	115	65	.274	.347	.341	79	-32	5	3		.964	-5	P-162,1-157	-3.8
Team	3	128	172	8	40	2	0	0	14	20	11	.233	.313	.244	61	-8	0	0		.952	-4	/P-52	0.0

■ HANK DeBERRY
DeBerry, John Herman   b: 12/29/1894, Savannah, Tenn.   d: 9/10/51, Savannah, Tenn.   BR/TR, 5'11", 195 lbs.   Deb: 9/12/16

1916	Cle-A	15	33	7	9	4	0	0	4	6	9	.273	.385	.394	126	1	0			1.000	-3	C-14	-0.1
1917	Cle-A	25	33	3	9	2	0	0	1	2	7	.273	.333	.333	96	-0	0			.968	1	/C-9	0.1
Total	11	648	1850	170	494	81	16	11	234	148	119	.267	.323	.346	76	-65	13			.982	113	C-569	8.1
Team	2	40	66	10	18	6	0	0	5	8	16	.273	.360	.364	112	1	0			.987	-3	/C-23	0.0

■ FRANK DELAHANTY
Delahanty, Frank George "Pudgie"   b: 1/29/1883, Cleveland, Ohio   d: 7/22/66, Cleveland, Ohio   BR/TR, 5'9", 160 lbs.   Deb: 8/23/05   F

| 1907 | Cle-A | 15 | 52 | 3 | 9 | 0 | 1 | 0 | 4 | 4 | 4 | .173 | .232 | .212 | 41 | -3 | 2 | | | .917 | -0 | O-15 | -0.5 |
| Total | 6 | 287 | 986 | 109 | 223 | 22 | 22 | 5 | 94 | 66 | | .226 | .280 | .308 | 66 | -47 | 50 | | | .964 | -7 | O-265/1-5,2 | -7.1 |

■ MIKE de la HOZ
de la Hoz, Miguel Angel (Piloto)   b: 10/2/38, Havana, Cuba   BR/TR, 5'11", 175 lbs.   Deb: 7/22/60

1960	Cle-A	49	160	20	41	6	2	6	23	9	12	.256	.304	.431	98	-1	0	0	0	.950	-15	S-38/3-8	-1.3
1961	Cle-A	61	173	20	45	10	0	3	23	7	10	.260	.297	.370	79	-6	0	0	0	.969	3	2-17,S-17,3	-0.3
1962	Cle-A	12	12	0	1	0	0	0	0	0	3	.083	.083	.083	-57	-3	0	0	0	1.000	-0	/2-2	-0.3
1963	Cle-A	67	150	15	40	10	0	5	25	9	29	.267	.313	.433	107	1	0	0	0	.962	4	2-34/3-6,SO	0.9
Total	9	494	1114	116	280	42	5	25	115	56	130	.251	.292	.365	82	-29	2	3	-1	.936	-28	3-129,2-119,S/O1	-4.9
Team	4	189	495	55	127	26	2	14	71	25	54	.257	.298	.402	91	-8	0	0	0	.941	-7	/S-57,2-53,3O	-0.7

■ DON DEMETER
Demeter, Donald Lee   b: 6/25/35, Oklahoma City, Okla   BR/TR, 6'4", 190 lbs.   Deb: 9/18/56

| 1967 | Cle-A | 51 | 121 | 15 | 25 | 4 | 0 | 5 | 12 | 6 | 16 | .207 | .256 | .364 | 80 | -3 | 0 | 0 | 0 | .985 | -2 | O-35/3-1 | -0.7 |
| Total | 11 | 1109 | 3443 | 467 | 912 | 147 | 17 | 163 | 563 | 180 | 658 | .265 | .309 | .459 | 108 | 26 | 22 | 25 | -8 | .990 | -37 | O-802,3-150,1 | -5.8 |

■ STEVE DEMETER
Demeter, Stephen   b: 1/27/35, Homer City, Pa.   BR/TR, 5'9.5", 185 lbs.   Deb: 7/29/59   C

| 1960 | Cle-A | 4 | 5 | 0 | 0 | 0 | 0 | 0 | 0 | 0 | 1 | .000 | .000 | .000 | -99 | -1 | 0 | 0 | 0 | 1.000 | 0 | /3-3 | -0.1 |
| Total | 2 | 15 | 23 | 1 | 2 | 1 | 0 | 0 | 1 | 0 | 2 | .087 | .087 | .130 | -40 | -4 | 0 | 0 | 0 | .933 | 1 | /3-7 | -0.3 |

■ RICK DEMPSEY
Dempsey, John Rikard   b: 9/13/49, Fayetteville, Tenn.   BR/TR, 6', 190 lbs.   Deb: 9/23/69

| 1987 | Cle-A | 60 | 141 | 16 | 25 | 10 | 0 | 1 | 9 | 23 | 29 | .177 | .297 | .270 | 51 | -10 | 0 | 0 | 0 | .984 | 1 | C-59 | -0.5 |
| Total | 24 | 1766 | 4692 | 525 | 1093 | 223 | 12 | 96 | 471 | 592 | 736 | .233 | .321 | .347 | 88 | -72 | 20 | 19 | -5 | .988 | 59 | *C-1633/O-23,D1P3 | 4.2 |

■ OTTO DENNING
Denning, Otto George "Dutch"   b: 12/28/12, Hays, Kan.   d: 5/25/92, Chicago, Ill.   BR/TR, 6', 180 lbs.   Deb: 4/15/42

1942	Cle-A	92	214	15	45	14	0	1	19	18	14	.210	.275	.290	62	-11	0	0	0	**.992**	-2	C-78/O-2	-0.9
1943	Cle-A	37	129	8	31	6	0	0	13	5	1	.240	.269	.287	67	-6	3	1	0	.966	-3	1-34	-1.2
Total	2	129	343	23	76	20	0	1	32	23	15	.222	.272	.289	64	-17	3	1	0	.955	-6	/C-78,1-34,O	-2.1

■ SAM DENTE
Dente, Samuel Joseph "Blackie"   b: 4/26/22, Harrison, N.J.   BR/TR, 5'11", 175 lbs.   Deb: 7/10/47

1954	*Cle-A	68	169	18	45	7	1	1	19	14	4	.266	.322	.337	79	-5	0	0	0	.971	-3	S-60/2-7	-0.4
1955	Cle-A	73	105	10	27	4	0	0	10	12	8	.257	.333	.295	68	-4	0	0	0	.976	7	S-53,3-13/2	0.5
Total	9	745	2320	205	585	78	16	4	214	167	96	.252	.303	.305	62	-128	9	9	-3	.958	-5	S-563/3-88,201	-9.5
Team	2	141	274	28	72	11	1	1	29	26	12	.263	.327	.321	75	-9	0	0	0	.973	4	S-113/3-13,2	0.1

■ GENE DESAUTELS
Desautels, Eugene Abraham "Red"   b: 6/13/07, Worcester, Mass.   d: 11/5/94, Flint, Mich.   BR/TR, 5'11", 170 lbs.   Deb: 6/22/30

1941	Cle-A	66	189	20	38	5	1	1	17	14	12	.201	.260	.254	38	-17	1	0	0	.997	6	C-66	-0.6
1942	Cle-A	62	162	14	40	5	0	0	9	12	13	.247	.303	.278	68	-7	1	0	0	.975	-8	C-61	-1.1
1943	Cle-A	68	185	14	38	6	1	0	19	11	16	.205	.250	.249	49	-12	2	0	1	.982	0	C-66	-0.7
1945	Cle-A	10	9	1	1	0	0	0	0	1	1	.111	.200	.111	-9	-1	0	0	0	1.000	0	C-10	-0.1
Total	13	712	2012	211	469	73	11	3	187	232	168	.233	.315	.285	57	-122	12	6	0	.989	31	C-699	-5.1
Team	4	206	545	49	117	16	2	1	45	38	42	.215	.268	.257	50	-38	4	0	1	.987	-1	C-203	-2.5

■ GEORGE DeTORE
DeTore, George Francis   b: 11/11/06, Utica, N.Y.   d: 2/7/91, Utica, N.Y.   BR/TR, 5'8", 170 lbs.   Deb: 9/14/30   C

1930	Cle-A	3	12	0	2	1	0	0	1	0	2	.167	.167	.250	4	-2	0	0	0	.750	-2	/3-3	-0.3
1931	Cle-A	30	56	3	15	6	0	0	7	8	2	.268	.359	.375	88	-1	0	2	-1	.958	4	3-13,S-10/2	0.3
Total	2	33	68	3	17	7	0	0	8	8	4	.250	.329	.353	74	-3	0	2	-1	.929	2	/3-16,S-10,2	0.0

■ JIM DEVLIN
Devlin, James Raymond   b: 8/25/22, Plains, Pa.   BL/TR, 5'11.5", 165 lbs.   Deb: 4/27/44

| 1944 | Cle-A | 1 | 1 | 0 | 0 | 0 | 0 | 0 | 0 | 0 | 0 | .000 | .000 | .000 | -99 | -0 | 0 | 0 | 0 | 1.000 | 0 | /C-1 | 0.0 |

■ BO DIAZ
Diaz, Baudilio Jose (Seijas)   b: 3/23/53, Cua, Venezuela   d: 11/23/90, Caracas, Venez.   BR/TR, 5'11", 190 lbs.   Deb: 9/6/77

1978	Cle-A	44	127	12	30	4	0	2	11	4	17	.236	.260	.315	61	-7	0	0	0	.971	-1	C-44	-0.7
1979	Cle-A	15	32	0	5	2	0	0	1	2	6	.156	.206	.219	15	-4	0	0	0	.958	4	C-15	0.0
1980	Cle-A	76	207	15	47	11	2	3	32	7	27	.227	.252	.343	61	-12	1	0	0	.989	3	C-75	-0.6

YEAR	TM/L	G	AB	R	H	2B	3B	HR	RBI	BB	SO	AVG	OBP	SLG	PRO+	BR/A	SB	CS	SBR	FA	FR	G/POS	TPR
1981	Cle-A★	63	182	25	57	19	0	7	38	13	23	.313	.362	.533	157	13	2	2	-1	.975	-3	C-51/D-3	1.1
Total	13	993	3274	327	834	162	5	87	452	198	429	.255	.300	.387	87	-63	9	17	-8	.986	3	C-965/D-3	-2.1
Team	4	198	548	52	139	36	2	12	82	26	73	.254	.289	.392	89	-10	3	2	-0	.978	2	C-185/D-3	-0.2

■ **PAUL DICKEN** Dicken, Paul Franklin b: 10/2/43, DeLand, Fla. BR/TR, 6'5", 195 lbs. Deb: 6/7/64

YEAR	TM/L	G	AB	R	H	2B	3B	HR	RBI	BB	SO	AVG	OBP	SLG	PRO+	BR/A	SB	CS	SBR	FA	FR	G/POS	TPR
1964	Cle-A	11	11	0	0	0	0	0	0	0	5	.000	.000	.000	-99	-3	0	0	0	.000	0	H	-0.3
1966	Cle-A	2	2	0	0	0	0	0	0	0	1	.000	.000	.000	-99	-1	0	0	0	.000	0	H	-0.1
Total	2	13	13	0	0	0	0	0	0	0	6	.000	.000	.000	-99	-3	0	0	0	.000	0	-0,-0	-0.4

■ **DON DILLARD** Dillard, David Donald b: 1/8/37, Greenville, S.C. BL/TR, 6'1", 200 lbs. Deb: 4/24/59

YEAR	TM/L	G	AB	R	H	2B	3B	HR	RBI	BB	SO	AVG	OBP	SLG	PRO+	BR/A	SB	CS	SBR	FA	FR	G/POS	TPR
1959	Cle-A	10	10	0	4	0	0	0	1	0	2	.400	.400	.400	125	0	0	0	0	.000	0	H	0.0
1960	Cle-A	6	7	0	1	0	0	0	0	1	3	.143	.250	.143	9	-1	0	0	0	.000	-0	/O-1	-0.1
1961	Cle-A	74	147	27	40	5	0	7	17	15	28	.272	.340	.449	112	2	0	0	0	1.000	-4	O-39	-0.3
1962	Cle-A	95	174	22	40	5	1	5	14	11	25	.230	.276	.356	71	-8	0	1	-1	.965	-10	O-50	-2.1
Total	6	272	476	59	116	16	5	14	47	32	85	.244	.293	.387	86	-10	0	3	-2	.976	-15	O-121	-3.2
Team	4	185	338	49	85	10	1	12	32	27	58	.251	.307	.393	89	-6	0	1	-1	.984	-14	/O-90	-2.5

■ **MIGUEL DILONE** Dilone, Miguel Angel (Reyes) b: 11/1/54, Santiago, D.R. BB/TR, 6', 160 lbs. Deb: 9/2/74

YEAR	TM/L	G	AB	R	H	2B	3B	HR	RBI	BB	SO	AVG	OBP	SLG	PRO+	BR/A	SB	CS	SBR	FA	FR	G/POS	TPR
1980	Cle-A	132	528	82	180	30	9	0	40	28	45	.341	.376	.432	120	15	61	18	8	.973	-0	*O-118,D-11	1.6
1981	Cle-A	72	269	33	78	5	5	0	19	18	28	.290	.334	.346	98	-1	29	10	3	.971	6	O-56,D-11	0.6
1982	Cle-A	104	379	50	89	12	3	3	25	25	36	.235	.286	.306	63	-19	33	5	7	.964	-3	O-97/D-1	-1.8
1983	Cle-A	32	68	15	13	3	1	0	7	10	5	.191	.295	.265	53	-4	5	1	1	1.000	1	O-19	-0.3
Total	12	800	2000	314	530	67	25	6	129	142	197	.265	.316	.333	81	-51	267	78	33	.975	-16	O-539/D-36,3	-5.4
Team	4	340	1244	180	360	50	18	3	91	81	114	.289	.335	.366	94	-10	128	34	18	.972	4	O-290/D-23	0.1

■ **WALT DOANE** Doane, Walter Rudolph b: 3/12/1887, Bellevue, Idaho d: 10/19/35, W.Brandywine, Pa. BL/TR, 6', 165 lbs. Deb: 9/20/09

YEAR	TM/L	G	AB	R	H	2B	3B	HR	RBI	BB	SO	AVG	OBP	SLG	PRO+	BR/A	SB	CS	SBR	FA	FR	G/POS	TPR
1909	Cle-A	4	9	1	1	0	0	0	0	1		.111	.200	.111	-1	-1	0			.778	1	/O-2,P-1	0.0
1910	Cle-A	6	7	0	2	1	0	0	2	1		.286	.375	.429	150	0	0			.750	-1	/P-6	0.0
Total	2	10	16	1	3	1	0	0	2	2		.188	.278	.250	64	-1	0			.800	-0	/P-7,O-2	0.0

■ **LARRY DOBY** Doby, Lawrence Eugene b: 12/13/24, Camden, S.C. BL/TR, 6'1", 182 lbs. Deb: 7/5/47 MC

YEAR	TM/L	G	AB	R	H	2B	3B	HR	RBI	BB	SO	AVG	OBP	SLG	PRO+	BR/A	SB	CS	SBR	FA	FR	G/POS	TPR
1947	Cle-A	29	32	3	5	1	0	0	2	1	11	.156	.182	.188	3	-4	0	0	0	1.000	-1	/2-4,1-1,S	-0.5
1948	*Cle-A	121	439	83	132	23	9	14	66	54	77	.301	.384	.490	135	21	9	9	-3	.955	3	*O-114	1.5
1949	Cle-A★	147	547	106	153	25	3	24	85	91	90	.280	.389	.468	129	23	10	9	-2	.976	-7	*O-147	0.6
1950	Cle-A★	142	503	110	164	25	5	25	102	98	71	.326	**.442**	.545	**156**	**46**	8	6	-1	.987	-6	*O-140	3.1
1951	Cle-A★	134	447	84	132	27	5	20	69	101	81	.295	.428	.512	**163**	43	4	1	1	.977	-1	*O-132	3.6
1952	Cle-A★	140	519	**104**	143	26	8	**32**	104	90	111	.276	.383	**.541**	**166**	45	5	2	0	.986	11	*O-136	**5.1**
1953	Cle-A★	149	513	92	135	18	5	29	102	96	121	.263	.385	.487	138	29	3	2	-0	.984	-7	*O-146	1.6
1954	*Cle-A★	153	577	94	157	18	4	**32**	**126**	85	94	.272	.368	.484	130	23	3	1	0	.995	6	*O-153	2.4
1955	Cle-A☆	131	491	91	143	17	5	26	75	61	100	.291	.372	.505	129	19	2	0	1	.994	3	*O-129	1.7
1958	Cle-A	89	247	41	70	10	1	13	45	26	49	.283	.352	.490	132	10	0	2	-1	1.000	1	O-68	0.7
Total	13	1533	5348	960	1515	243	52	253	970	871	1011	.283	.387	.490	137	285	47	36	-8	.983	3	*O-1440/2-4,1S	21.2
Team	10	1235	4315	808	1234	190	45	215	776	703	805	.286	.390	.500	141	254	44	32	-6	.983	2	*O-1165/2-4,S1	19.8

■ **FRANK DOLJACK** Doljack, Frank Joseph "Dolie" b: 10/5/07, Cleveland, Ohio d: 1/23/48, Cleveland, Ohio BR/TR, 5'11", 175 lbs. Deb: 9/4/30

YEAR	TM/L	G	AB	R	H	2B	3B	HR	RBI	BB	SO	AVG	OBP	SLG	PRO+	BR/A	SB	CS	SBR	FA	FR	G/POS	TPR
1943	Cle-A	3	7	0	0	0	0	0	0	1	2	.000	.125	.000	-66	-1	0	0	0	1.000	-1	/O-2	-0.2
Total	6	192	561	68	151	31	7	9	85	47	60	.269	.329	.398	87	-12	8	10	-4	.934	-0	O-149/1-3	-2.1

■ **PAT DONAHUE** Donahue, Patrick William b: 11/8/1884, Springfield, Ohio d: 1/31/66, Springfield, Ohio BR/TR, 6', 175 lbs. Deb: 5/29/08 F

YEAR	TM/L	G	AB	R	H	2B	3B	HR	RBI	BB	SO	AVG	OBP	SLG	PRO+	BR/A	SB	CS	SBR	FA	FR	G/POS	TPR
1910	Cle-A	2	6	0	1	0	0	0	0	0		.167	.167	.167	4	-1	0			1.000	-1	/C-2,1-1	-0.1
Total	3	118	307	24	65	6	1	3	35	29		.212	.288	.267	75	-8	3			.978	1	C-107/1-4	0.2

■ **MIKE DONOVAN** Donovan, Michael Berchman b: 10/18/1881, Brooklyn, N.Y. d: 2/3/38, New York, N.Y. BR/TR, 5'8", 155 lbs. Deb: 5/29/04

YEAR	TM/L	G	AB	R	H	2B	3B	HR	RBI	BB	SO	AVG	OBP	SLG	PRO+	BR/A	SB	CS	SBR	FA	FR	G/POS	TPR
1904	Cle-A	2	2	0	0	0	0	0	0	0		.000	.000	.000	-99	-0	0			.000	0	/S-1	-0.1
Total	2	7	21	2	5	1	0	0	2	0		.238	.238	.286	69	-1	0			.926	1	/3-5,S-1	0.0

■ **TOM DONOVAN** Donovan, Thomas Joseph b: 1/1/1873, West Troy, N.Y. d: 3/25/33, Watervliet, N.Y. BR/TR, 6'2", 168 lbs. Deb: 9/10/01 F

YEAR	TM/L	G	AB	R	H	2B	3B	HR	RBI	BB	SO	AVG	OBP	SLG	PRO+	BR/A	SB	CS	SBR	FA	FR	G/POS	TPR
1901	Cle-A	18	71	9	18	3	1	0	5	0		.254	.254	.324	62	-4	1			.862	-1	O-18/P-1	-0.5

■ **BILL DORAN** Doran, William James b: 6/14/1898, San Francisco, Cal. d: 3/9/78, Santa Monica, Cal. BL/TR, 5'11.5", 175 lbs. Deb: 6/23/22

YEAR	TM/L	G	AB	R	H	2B	3B	HR	RBI	BB	SO	AVG	OBP	SLG	PRO+	BR/A	SB	CS	SBR	FA	FR	G/POS	TPR
1922	Cle-A	3	2	0	1	0	0	0	0	1	0	.500	.667	.500	206	0	0	0	0	.000	0	/3-2	0.0

■ **RED DORMAN** Dorman, Dwight Dexter "Curlie" b: 10/3/05, Jacksonville, Ill. d: 12/7/74, Anaheim, Cal. BR/TR, 5'10.5", 180 lbs. Deb: 8/21/28

YEAR	TM/L	G	AB	R	H	2B	3B	HR	RBI	BB	SO	AVG	OBP	SLG	PRO+	BR/A	SB	CS	SBR	FA	FR	G/POS	TPR
1928	Cle-A	25	77	12	28	6	0	0	11	9	6	.364	.430	.442	128	4	1	0	0	.915	-3	O-24	0.0

■ **BRIAN DORSETT** Dorsett, Brian Richard b: 4/9/61, Terre Haute, Ind. BR/TR, 6'3", 215 lbs. Deb: 9/8/87

YEAR	TM/L	G	AB	R	H	2B	3B	HR	RBI	BB	SO	AVG	OBP	SLG	PRO+	BR/A	SB	CS	SBR	FA	FR	G/POS	TPR
1987	Cle-A	5	11	2	3	0	0	1	3	0	3	.273	.333	.545	127	0	0	0	0	1.000	-2	/C-4	-0.1
Total	7	146	370	35	87	15	0	8	48	28	65	.235	.292	.341	68	-17	0	0	0	.994	-2	C-119/1-6,D	-1.2

■ **FRANK DUFFY** Duffy, Frank Thomas b: 10/14/46, Oakland, Cal. BR/TR, 6'1", 180 lbs. Deb: 9/4/70

YEAR	TM/L	G	AB	R	H	2B	3B	HR	RBI	BB	SO	AVG	OBP	SLG	PRO+	BR/A	SB	CS	SBR	FA	FR	G/POS	TPR
1972	Cle-A	130	385	23	92	16	4	3	27	31	54	.239	.297	.325	82	-8	6	2	1	.977	3	*S-126	1.2
1973	Cle-A	116	361	34	95	16	4	8	50	25	41	.263	.314	.396	97	-2	6	6	-2	**.986**	12	*S-115	2.3
1974	Cle-A	158	549	62	128	18	0	8	48	30	64	.233	.273	.310	68	-23	7	8	-3	.980	-8	*S-158	-1.5
1975	Cle-A	146	482	44	117	22	2	1	47	27	60	.243	.286	.303	66	-22	10	10	-3	.977	14	*S-145	0.4
1976	Cle-A	133	392	38	83	11	2	2	30	29	50	.212	.270	.265	58	-21	10	0	3	**.983**	11	*S-132	0.7
1977	Cle-A	122	334	30	67	13	2	4	31	21	47	.201	.248	.287	47	-25	8	3	1	.967	3	*S-121	-1.1
Total	10	915	2665	248	619	104	14	26	240	171	342	.232	.281	.311	69	-112	49	30	-3	.977	53	S-839/3-23,2D1	3.1
Team	6	805	2503	231	582	96	14	26	233	163	316	.233	.281	.313	70	-101	47	29	-3	.979	35	S-797	2.0

■ **DAVE DUNCAN** Duncan, David Edwin b: 9/26/45, Dallas, Tex. BR/TR, 6'2", 200 lbs. Deb: 5/6/64 C

YEAR	TM/L	G	AB	R	H	2B	3B	HR	RBI	BB	SO	AVG	OBP	SLG	PRO+	BR/A	SB	CS	SBR	FA	FR	G/POS	TPR
1973	Cle-A	95	344	43	80	11	1	17	43	35	86	.233	.309	.419	101	-0	3	3	-1	.988	-1	C-86/D-9	0.2
1974	Cle-A	136	425	45	85	10	1	16	46	42	91	.200	.275	.341	77	-13	0	4	-2	.976	-8	*C-134/1-3,D	-1.9
Total	11	929	2885	274	617	79	4	109	341	252	677	.214	.280	.357	85	-65	5	13	-6	.984	-32	C-885/D-10,1	-7.1
Team	2	231	769	88	165	21	2	33	89	77	177	.215	.290	.376	88	-14	3	7	-3	.982	-8	C-220/D-10,1	-1.7

■ **GEORGE DUNLOP** Dunlop, George Henry b: 7/19/1888, Meriden, Conn. d: 12/12/72, Meriden, Conn. BR/TR, 5'10", 170 lbs. Deb: 9/9/13

YEAR	TM/L	G	AB	R	H	2B	3B	HR	RBI	BB	SO	AVG	OBP	SLG	PRO+	BR/A	SB	CS	SBR	FA	FR	G/POS	TPR
1913	Cle-A	7	17	3	4	1	0	0	0	0	5	.235	.235	.294	53	-1	0			.923	1	/S-4,3-3	0.0
1914	Cle-A	1	3	0	0	0	0	0	0	1	1	.000	.250	.000	-23	-0	0			1.000	-1	/S-1	-0.2
Total	2	8	20	3	4	1	0	0	0	1	6	.200	.238	.250	42	-1	0			.929	0	/S-5,3-3	-0.2

■ **JERRY DYBZINSKI** Dybzinski, Jerome Matthew b: 7/7/55, Cleveland, Ohio BR/TR, 6'2", 180 lbs. Deb: 4/11/80

YEAR	TM/L	G	AB	R	H	2B	3B	HR	RBI	BB	SO	AVG	OBP	SLG	PRO+	BR/A	SB	CS	SBR	FA	FR	G/POS	TPR
1980	Cle-A	114	248	32	57	11	1	1	23	13	35	.230	.274	.294	55	-15	4	1	1	.971	21	S-73,2-29/3D	1.3
1981	Cle-A	48	57	10	17	0	0	0	6	5	8	.298	.355	.298	91	-0	7	1	2	.970	8	S-34/2-3,3D	1.1
1982	Cle-A	80	212	19	49	6	2	0	22	21	25	.231	.309	.278	63	-10	3	5	-2	.957	17	S-77/3-3	1.1
Total	6	468	909	108	213	32	5	3	93	70	109	.234	.296	.290	61	-47	32	13	2	.966	67	S-383/3-33,2D	4.8
Team	3	242	517	61	123	17	3	1	51	39	68	.238	.298	.288	62	-26	14	7	0	.964	46	S-184/2-32,3D	3.5

YEAR	TM/L	G	AB	R	H	2B	3B	HR	RBI	BB	SO	AVG	OBP	SLG	PRO+	BR/A	SB	CS	SBR	FA	FR	G/POS	TPR

■ JIM DYCK   Dyck, James Robert b: 2/3/22, Omaha, Neb. BR/TR, 6'2", 205 lbs. Deb: 9/27/51

| 1954 | Cle-A | 2 | 1 | 0 | 1 | 0 | 0 | 0 | 1 | 1 | 0 | 1.000 | 1.000 | 1.000 | 441 | 1 | 0 | 0 | 0 | .000 | 0 | H | 0.1 |
| Total | 6 | 330 | 983 | 139 | 242 | 52 | 5 | 26 | 114 | 131 | 140 | .246 | .339 | .389 | 98 | -2 | 4 | 6 | -2 | .982 | 3 | O-157,3-147/1 | -0.9 |

■ TRUCK EAGAN   Eagan, Charles Eugene b: 8/10/1877, San Francisco, Cal d: 3/19/49, San Francisco, Cal BR/TR, 5'11", 190 lbs. Deb: 5/1/01

| 1901 | Cle-A | 5 | 18 | 2 | 3 | 0 | 1 | 0 | 2 | 1 | | .167 | .211 | .278 | 36 | -2 | 0 | | | 1.000 | 0 | /2-5,3-1 | -0.1 |
| Total | 1 | 9 | 30 | 2 | 4 | 0 | 1 | 0 | 4 | 1 | | .133 | .161 | .200 | 2 | -4 | 1 | | | .987 | -1 | /2-5,S-3,3 | -0.4 |

■ LUKE EASTER   Easter, Luscious Luke b: 8/4/15, Jonestown, Miss. d: 3/29/79, Euclid, Ohio BL/TR, 6'4.5", 240 lbs. Deb: 8/11/49 C

1949	Cle-A	21	45	6	10	3	0	0	2	8	6	.222	.340	.289	68	-2	0	1	-1	1.000	-4	O-12	-0.7
1950	Cle-A	141	540	96	151	20	4	28	107	70	95	.280	.373	.487	123	17	0	3	-2	.991	-3	*1-128,O-13	0.8
1951	Cle-A	128	486	65	131	12	5	27	103	37	71	.270	.333	.481	125	13	0	1	-1	.988	-7	*1-125	0.0
1952	Cle-A	127	437	63	115	10	3	31	97	44	84	.263	.337	.513	144	22	1	1	-0	.983	4	*1-118	2.2
1953	Cle-A	68	211	26	64	9	0	7	31	15	35	.303	.361	.445	120	5	0	2	-1	.981	-2	1-56	0.0
1954	Cle-A	6	6	0	1	0	0	0	0	0	0	.167	.167	.167	-8	-1	0	0	0	.000	0	H	-0.1
Total	6	491	1725	256	472	54	12	93	340	174	293	.274	.350	.481	126	55	1	8	-5	.986	-12	1-427/O-25	2.2

■ TED EASTERLY   Easterly, Theodore Harrison b: 4/20/1885, Lincoln, Neb. d: 7/6/51, Clearlake Highlands, Cal. BL/TR, 5'8", 165 lbs. Deb: 4/17/09

1909	Cle-A	98	287	32	75	14	10	1	27	13		.261	.293	.390	111	2	8			.965	0	C-76	1.0
1910	Cle-A	110	363	34	111	16	6	0	55	21		.306	.344	.383	126	10	10			.964	-8	C-65,O-32	0.7
1911	Cle-A	99	287	34	93	19	5	1	37	8		.324	.345	.436	116	4	6			.910	-12	O-54,C-22	-0.8
1912	Cle-A	65	186	17	55	4	0	2	21	7		.296	.328	.387	91	-3	3			.958	-4	C-51	-0.2
Total	7	706	2020	215	607	88	38	8	261	107		.300	.338	.394	108	14	42			.965	-41	C-459/O-87	1.3
Team	4	372	1123	117	334	53	21	4	140	49		.297	.329	.393	113	13	27			.961	-24	C-214/O-86	0.7

■ EDDIE EDMONSON   Edmonson, Earl Edward b: 11/20/1889, Hopewell, Pa. d: 5/10/71, Leesburg, Fla. BL/TR, 6', 175 lbs. Deb: 10/4/13

| 1913 | Cle-A | 2 | 5 | 0 | 0 | 0 | 0 | 0 | 0 | 0 | 0 | .000 | .000 | .000 | -97 | -1 | 0 | | | 1.000 | -1 | /1-1,O-1 | -0.2 |

■ HANK EDWARDS   Edwards, Henry Albert b: 1/29/19, Elmwood Place, O. d: 6/22/88, Santa Ana, Cal. BL/TL, 6', 190 lbs. Deb: 9/10/41

1941	Cle-A	16	68	10	15	1	1	1	6	2	4	.221	.243	.309	47	-5	0	0	0	.929	-1	O-16	-0.7
1942	Cle-A	13	48	6	12	2	1	0	7	5	8	.250	.321	.333	89	-1	2	1	0	.968	-1	O-12	-0.3
1943	Cle-A	92	297	38	82	18	6	3	28	30	34	.276	.343	.407	127	9	4	8	-4	.983	-5	O-74	-0.3
1946	Cle-A	124	458	62	138	33	**16**	10	54	43	48	.301	.361	.509	151	28	1	3	-2	.968	1	*O-123	2.3
1947	Cle-A	108	393	54	102	12	3	15	59	31	55	.260	.313	.420	106	1	1	3	-2	.990	-7	*O-100	-1.3
1948	Cle-A	55	160	27	43	9	2	3	18	18	18	.269	.346	.406	102	0	1	1	-0	.987	-3	O-41	-0.5
1949	Cle-A	5	15	3	4	0	0	1	1	1	2	.267	.313	.467	107	-0	0	0	0	1.000	-1	/O-5	-0.1
Total	11	735	2191	285	613	116	41	51	276	208	264	.280	.343	.440	119	48	9	22	-11	.981	-31	O-560	-1.8
Team	7	413	1439	200	396	75	29	33	173	130	169	.275	.336	.436	120	32	9	16	-7	.978	-16	O-371	-0.9

■ DOC EDWARDS   Edwards, Howard Rodney b: 12/10/36, Red Jacket, W.Va. BR/TR, 6'2", 215 lbs. Deb: 4/21/62 MC

1962	Cle-A	53	143	13	39	6	0	3	9	9	14	.273	.325	.378	91	-2	0	0	0	.992	9	C-39	0.8
1963	Cle-A	10	31	6	8	2	0	0	2	6		.258	.303	.323	76	-1	0	0	0	.988	5	C-10	0.4
Total	5	317	906	69	216	33	0	15	87	53	109	.238	.287	.325	68	-39	1	4	-2	.986	17	C-274/1-7	-1.6
Team	2	63	174	19	47	8	0	3	9	11	20	.270	.321	.368	88	-3	0	0	0	.991	13	/C-49	1.2

■ BEN EGAN   Egan, Arthur Augustus b: 11/20/1883, Augusta, N.Y. d: 2/18/68, Sherrill, N.Y. BR/TR, 6', 195 lbs. Deb: 9/29/08 C

1914	Cle-A	29	88	7	20	2	1	0	11	3	20	.227	.277	.273	63	-4	0	1	-1	.975	4	C-27	0.2
1915	Cle-A	42	120	4	13	3	0	0	6	8	14	.108	.164	.133	-11	-16	0			.970	8	C-40	-0.6
Total	4	122	352	21	58	9	5	0	30	18	34	.165	.212	.219	27	-33	3	1		.966	16	C-115	-0.9
Team	2	71	208	11	33	5	1	0	17	11	34	.159	.212	.192	21	-21	0	1		.972	12	/C-67	-0.4

■ HACK EIBEL   Eibel, Henry Hack b: 12/6/1893, Brooklyn, N.Y. d: 10/16/45, Macon, Ga. BL/TL, 5'11", 220 lbs. Deb: 6/13/12

| 1912 | Cle-A | 1 | 3 | 0 | 0 | 0 | 0 | 0 | 0 | 0 | | .000 | .000 | .000 | -97 | -1 | 0 | | | .000 | -0 | /O-1 | -0.1 |
| Total | 2 | 30 | 46 | 4 | 8 | 2 | 0 | 0 | 6 | 3 | | .174 | .224 | .217 | 19 | -5 | 1 | | | .800 | -2 | /O-6,P-3,1 | -0.7 |

■ IKE EICHRODT   Eichrodt, Frederick George b: 1/6/03, Chicago, Ill. d: 7/14/65, Indianapolis, Ind BR/TR, 5'11.5", 167 lbs. Deb: 9/7/25

1925	Cle-A	15	52	4	12	3	1	0	4	2	7	.231	.259	.327	48	-4	0	0	0	.938	-2	O-13	-0.7
1926	Cle-A	37	80	14	25	7	1	0	7	2	11	.313	.329	.425	95	-1	1	0	0	.976	-4	O-27	-0.5
1927	Cle-A	85	267	24	59	19	2	0	25	16	25	.221	.265	.307	48	-21	2	3	-1	.979	1	O-81	-2.5
Total	4	171	516	51	121	34	4	0	51	21	51	.234	.264	.320	52	-39	3	3	-1	.979	-9	O-153	-5.5
Team	3	137	399	42	96	29	4	0	36	20	43	.241	.277	.333	57	-27	3	3	-1	.973	-4	O-121	-3.7

■ FRANK ELLERBE   Ellerbe, Francis Rogers "Governor" b: 12/25/1895, Marion Co., S.C. d: 7/8/88, Latta, S.C. BR/TR, 5'10.5", 165 lbs. Deb: 8/28/19

| 1924 | Cle-A | 46 | 120 | 7 | 31 | 1 | 3 | 1 | 14 | 1 | 10 | .258 | .270 | .342 | 56 | -8 | 0 | 0 | 0 | .975 | 5 | 3-39/2-2 | -0.1 |
| Total | 6 | 420 | 1453 | 179 | 389 | 58 | 22 | 4 | 152 | 72 | 136 | .268 | .306 | .346 | 68 | -70 | 12 | 13 | -4 | .952 | 14 | 3-345/S-47,2O | -3.7 |

■ JOHN ELLIS   Ellis, John Charles b: 8/21/48, New London, Conn. BR/TR, 6'2.5", 225 lbs. Deb: 5/17/69

1973	Cle-A	127	437	59	118	12	2	14	68	46	57	.270	.344	.403	108	5	0	0	0	.980	-18	C-72,D-38,1	-1.2
1974	Cle-A	128	477	58	136	23	6	10	64	32	52	.285	.331	.421	116	9	1	2	-1	.992	-8	1-69,C-42,D	-0.4
1975	Cle-A	92	296	22	68	11	1	7	32	14	33	.230	.269	.345	72	-12	0	1	-1	.976	-8	C-84/1-2,D	-1.7
Total	13	883	2672	259	699	116	13	69	391	190	403	.262	.315	.392	99	-10	6	10	-4	.989	-45	1-304,C-297,D/3	-7.5
Team	3	347	1210	139	322	46	9	31	164	92	143	.266	.321	.396	103	2	1	3	-2	.979	-33	C-198/1-83,D	-3.3

■ CLYDE ENGLE   Engle, Arthur Clyde "Hack" b: 3/19/1884, Dayton, Ohio d: 12/26/39, Boston, Mass. BR/TR, 5'10", 190 lbs. Deb: 4/12/09

| 1916 | Cle-A | 11 | 26 | 1 | 4 | 0 | 0 | 0 | 1 | 0 | 6 | .154 | .154 | .154 | -7 | -3 | 0 | | | .810 | -2 | /3-7,1-2,O | -0.6 |
| Total | 8 | 836 | 2822 | 373 | 748 | 101 | 39 | 12 | 318 | 271 | 119 | .265 | .335 | .341 | 95 | -19 | 128 | | | .959 | -21 | O-276,1-255,3/2S | -5.9 |

■ JIM ESCHEN   Eschen, James Godrich b: 8/21/1891, Brooklyn, N.Y. d: 9/27/60, Sloatsburg, N.Y. BR/TR, 5'10.5", 160 lbs. Deb: 7/10/15 F

| 1915 | Cle-A | 15 | 42 | 11 | 10 | 1 | 0 | 0 | 2 | 5 | | .238 | .319 | .262 | 73 | -1 | 0 | 1 | -1 | .968 | 1 | O-10 | -0.1 |

■ JOSE ESCOBAR   Escobar, Jose Elias (Sanchez) b: 10/30/60, Las Flores, Venez. BR/TR, 5'10", 140 lbs. Deb: 4/13/91

| 1991 | Cle-A | 10 | 15 | 0 | 3 | 0 | 0 | 0 | 0 | 0 | 1 | .200 | .250 | .200 | 26 | -1 | 0 | 0 | 0 | 1.000 | 2 | /S-5,2-4,3 | 0.0 |

■ ALVARO ESPINOZA   Espinoza, Alvaro Alberto b: 2/19/62, Valencia, Venez. BR/TR, 6', 170 lbs. Deb: 9/14/84

1993	Cle-A	129	263	34	73	15	0	4	27	8	36	.278	.301	.380	82	-7	2	2	-1	.937	1	3-99,S-35/2	-0.5
1994	Cle-A	90	231	27	55	13	0	1	19	6	33	.238	.261	.307	46	-19	1	3	-2	.915	24	3-37,S-36,2/1	0.7
1995	*Cle-A	66	143	15	36	4	0	2	17	2	16	.252	.267	.322	52	-10	0	2	-1	.966	9	2-22,3-22,S/1D	-0.1
Total	10	802	2160	218	551	93	5	14	167	64	275	.255	.280	.322	65	-107	11	15	-6	.971	106	S-584,3-160/21DP	3.5
Team	3	285	637	76	164	32	0	7	63	16	85	.257	.279	.341	62	-36	3	7	-3	.939	35	3-158/S-90,21D	0.1

■ CHUCK ESSEGIAN   Essegian, Charles Abraham b: 8/9/31, Boston, Mass. BR/TR, 5'11", 202 lbs. Deb: 4/15/58

1961	Cle-A	60	166	25	48	7	1	12	35	10	33	.289	.333	.560	138	8	0	0	0	.968	-2	O-49	0.4
1962	Cle-A	106	336	59	92	12	0	21	50	42	68	.274	.366	.497	134	16	0	0	0	.994	-4	O-90	0.7
Total	6	404	1018	139	260	45	4	47	150	97	233	.255	.326	.446	106	8	0	0	0	.981	-7	O-260	-1.3
Team	2	166	502	84	140	19	1	33	85	52	101	.279	.356	.518	135	24	0	0	0	.984	-5	O-139	1.1

YEAR	TM/L	G	AB	R	H	2B	3B	HR	RBI	BB	SO	AVG	OBP	SLG	PRO+	BR/A	SB	CS	SBR	FA	FR	G/POS	TPR

■ **JIM ESSIAN**   Essian, James Sarkis   b: 1/2/51, Detroit, Mich.   BR/TR, 6'2", 195 lbs.   Deb: 9/15/73   M

| 1983 | Cle-A | 48 | 93 | 11 | 19 | 4 | 0 | 2 | 11 | 16 | 8 | .204 | .321 | .312 | 72 | -3 | 0 | 1 | -1 | .989 | 3 | C-47/3-1 | 0.1 |
| Total | 12 | 710 | 1855 | 194 | 453 | 85 | 3 | 33 | 207 | 231 | 171 | .244 | .330 | .347 | 90 | -22 | 9 | 13 | -5 | .984 | 63 | C-642/3-18,D102 | 5.3 |

■ **FRED EUNICK**   Eunick, Fernandas Bowen   b: 4/22/1892, Baltimore, Md.   d: 12/9/59, Baltimore, Md.   BR/TR, 5'6", 148 lbs.   Deb: 8/29/17

| 1917 | Cle-A | 1 | 2 | 0 | 0 | 0 | 0 | 0 | 0 | 0 | 0 | .000 | .000 | .000 | -93 | -0 | 0 | | | 1.000 | -0 | /3-1 | -0.1 |

■ **JOE EVANS**   Evans, Joseph Patton "Doc"   b: 5/15/1895, Meridian, Miss.   d: 8/9/53, Gulfport, Miss.   BR/TR, 5'9", 160 lbs.   Deb: 7/3/15

1915	Cle-A	42	109	17	28	4	2	0	11	22	18	.257	.382	.330	111	2	6	1	1	.885	-0	3-30/2-2	0.5
1916	Cle-A	33	82	4	12	1	0	0	1	7	12	.146	.213	.159	11	-9	4			.915	4	3-28	-0.5
1917	Cle-A	132	385	36	73	4	5	2	33	42	44	.190	.271	.227	53	-22	12			.939	3	*3-127	-1.9
1918	Cle-A	79	243	38	64	6	7	1	22	30	29	.263	.344	.358	102	1	7			.932	4	3-74	0.7
1919	Cle-A	21	14	9	1	0	0	0	0	2	1	.071	.188	.071	-24	-2	1			.923	4	/S-6	0.1
1920	*Cle-A	56	172	32	60	9	9	0	23	15	3	.349	.404	.506	136	9	6	2	1	.966	-3	O-43/S-6	0.4
1921	Cle-A	57	153	36	51	11	0	0	21	19	5	.333	.410	.405	107	3	4	1	1	.933	-1	O-47	0.0
1922	Cle-A	75	145	35	39	6	2	0	22	8	4	.269	.307	.338	67	-7	11	2	2	.969	-7	O-49	-1.4
Total	11	733	2043	306	529	71	31	3	210	212	152	.259	.329	.328	79	-57	67	16		.971	0	O-307,3-280/S12	-6.4
Team	8	495	1303	207	328	41	25	3	133	145	116	.252	.328	.328	83	-26	51	6		.928	3	3-259,O-139/S2	-2.1

■ **HOOT EVERS**   Evers, Walter Arthur   b: 2/8/21, St.Louis, Mo.   d: 1/25/91, Houston, Tex.   BR/TR, 6'2", 185 lbs.   Deb: 9/16/41   C

1955	Cle-A	39	66	10	19	7	1	2	9	3	12	.288	.319	.515	117	1	0	1	-1	1.000	-4	O-25	-0.4
1956	Cle-A	3	0	1	0	0	0	0	0	1	0	—	1.000	—	180	0	0	0	0	.000	0	H	0.0
Total	12	1142	3801	556	1055	187	41	98	565	415	420	.278	.353	.426	106	27	45	36	-8	.983	-4	*O-1051	-3.4
Team	2	42	66	11	19	7	1	2	9	4	12	.288	.329	.515	120	1	0	1	-1	1.000	-4	/O-25	-0.4

■ **FERRIS FAIN**   Fain, Ferris Roy "Burrhead"   b: 5/29/21, San Antonio, Tex.   BL/TL, 5'11", 186 lbs.   Deb: 4/15/47

| 1955 | Cle-A | 56 | 118 | 9 | 30 | 3 | 0 | 0 | 8 | 42 | 13 | .254 | .453 | .280 | 97 | 3 | 3 | 0 | 1 | .992 | 3 | 1-51 | 0.5 |
| Total | 9 | 1151 | 3930 | 595 | 1139 | 213 | 30 | 48 | 570 | 904 | 261 | .290 | .425 | .396 | 120 | 160 | 46 | 28 | -3 | .987 | 59 | *1-1116/O-11 | 17.8 |

■ **BIBB FALK**   Falk, Bibb August "Jockey"   b: 1/27/1899, Austin, Tex.   d: 6/8/89, Austin, Tex.   BL/TL, 6', 175 lbs.   Deb: 9/17/20   FMC

1929	Cle-A	125	426	65	133	30	7	13	93	42	14	.312	.374	.507	120	12	4	1	-1	.943	-4	*O-120	-0.1
1930	Cle-A	82	191	34	62	12	1	4	36	23	8	.325	.397	.461	113	4	2	0	1	.967	1	O-42	0.3
1931	Cle-A	79	161	30	49	13	1	2	28	17	13	.304	.371	.435	105	1	1	1	0	.949	-3	O-33	-0.4
Total	12	1353	4652	655	1463	300	59	69	784	412	279	.314	.372	.449	113	82	47	49	-15	.967	1	*O-1222	-1.8
Team	3	286	778	129	244	55	9	19	157	82	35	.314	.379	.481	115	17	7	5	-1	.949	-6	O-195	-0.2

■ **JACK FARMER**   Farmer, Floyd Haskell   b: 7/14/1892, Granville, Tenn.   d: 5/21/70, Columbia, La.   BR/TR, 6', 180 lbs.   Deb: 7/8/16

| 1918 | Cle-A | 7 | 9 | 1 | 2 | 0 | 0 | 0 | 1 | 0 | 3 | .222 | .300 | .222 | 53 | -0 | 2 | | | .429 | -2 | /O-3 | -0.3 |
| Total | 2 | 62 | 175 | 11 | 47 | 6 | 4 | 0 | 15 | 7 | 27 | .269 | .308 | .349 | 100 | -0 | 3 | | | .829 | -11 | /2-31,O-18,S3 | -1.3 |

■ **FELIX FERMIN**   Fermin, Felix Jose (Minaya)   b: 10/9/63, Mao Valverde, D.R.   BR/TR, 5'11", 179 lbs.   Deb: 7/8/87

1989	Cle-A	156	484	50	115	9	1	0	21	41	27	.238	.302	.260	59	-25	6	4	-1	.967	18	*S-153/2-2	0.4
1990	Cle-A	148	414	47	106	13	2	1	40	26	22	.256	.300	.304	70	-17	3	3	-1	.975	4	*S-147/2-1	-0.2
1991	Cle-A	129	424	30	111	13	2	0	31	26	27	.262	.309	.302	69	-17	5	4	-1	.980	1	*S-129	-0.7
1992	Cle-A	79	215	27	58	7	2	0	13	18	10	.270	.329	.321	84	-4	0	0	0	.971	-5	S-55,3-17/21	-0.6
1993	Cle-A	140	480	48	126	16	2	2	45	24	14	.262	.303	.317	67	-22	4	5	-2	.960	-29	*S-140	-4.1
Total	9	892	2751	290	716	85	11	4	206	164	147	.260	.308	.304	67	-122	27	21		.971	-9	S-813/2-64,31	-7.1
Team	5	652	2017	202	516	58	9	3	150	135	100	.256	.306	.298	68	-85	18	16		.971	-11	S-624/3-17,21	-5.2

■ **WES FERRELL**   Ferrell, Wesley Cheek   b: 2/2/08, Greensboro, N.C.   d: 12/9/76, Sarasota, Fla.   BR/TR, 6'2", 195 lbs.   Deb: 9/9/27   F

1927	Cle-A	1	0	0	0	0	0	0	0	0	0	—	—	—	0	0	0	0	.000	-0	/P-1	0.0
1928	Cle-A	2	4	0	1	0	1	0	0	0	0	.250	.250	.750	152	0	0	0	0	1.000	0	/P-2	0.0
1929	Cle-A	47	93	12	22	5	3	1	12	6	28	.237	.283	.387	68	-5	1	0	0	.973	9	P-43	0.0
1930	Cle-A	53	118	19	35	8	3	0	14	12	15	.297	.362	.415	93	-1	0	0	0	.967	-3	P-43	0.0
1931	Cle-A	48	116	24	37	6	1	9	30	10	21	.319	.373	.621	149	7	0	0	0	.969	5	P-40	0.0
1932	Cle-A	55	128	14	31	5	2	2	18	6	21	.242	.276	.359	59	-8	0	0	0	.986	1	P-38	0.0
1933	Cle-A☆	61	140	26	38	7	0	7	26	20	22	.271	.363	.471	114	3	0	0	0	1.000	2	P-28,O-13	0.1
Total	15	548	1176	175	329	57	12	38	208	129	185	.280	.351	.446	99	-5	2	0	0	.975	7	P-374/O-13	0.1
Team	7	267	599	95	164	31	10	19	100	54	107	.274	.334	.454	98	-4	1	0	0	.978	8	P-195/O-13	0.1

■ **CHICK FEWSTER**   Fewster, Wilson Lloyd   b: 11/10/1895, Baltimore, Md.   d: 4/16/45, Baltimore, Md.   BR/TR, 5'11", 160 lbs.   Deb: 9/19/17

1924	Cle-A	101	322	36	86	12	2	0	36	24	36	.267	.324	.317	65	-17	12	12	-4	.961	-22	2-94/3-5	-4.0
1925	Cle-A	93	294	39	73	16	1	1	38	36	25	.248	.330	.320	65	-15	6	9	-4	.939	-9	2-83,3-10/O	-2.5
Total	11	644	1963	282	506	91	12	6	167	240	264	.258	.346	.326	77	-59	57	47	-11	.945	-43	2-366,O-123/S3	-10.9
Team	2	194	616	75	159	28	3	1	74	60	61	.258	.327	.318	65	-32	18	21	-7	.949	-31	2-177/3-15,O	-6.5

■ **DAN FIROVA**   Firova, Daniel Michael   b: 10/16/56, Refugio, Tex.   BR/TR, 6', 185 lbs.   Deb: 9/1/81

| 1988 | Cle-A | 1 | 0 | 0 | 0 | 0 | 0 | 0 | 0 | 0 | 0 | — | — | — | 0 | 0 | 0 | 0 | .000 | 0 | /C-1 | 0.0 |
| Total | 3 | 17 | 7 | 0 | 0 | 0 | 0 | 0 | 0 | 0 | 1 | .000 | .000 | .000 | -97 | -2 | 0 | 0 | 0 | .944 | 1 | /C-17 | -0.1 |

■ **MIKE FISCHLIN**   Fischlin, Michael Thomas   b: 9/13/55, Sacramento, Cal.   BR/TR, 6'1", 165 lbs.   Deb: 9/3/77

1981	Cle-A	22	43	3	10	1	0	0	5	3	6	.233	.283	.256	57	-2	3	2	-0	.955	-0	S-19/2-1	-0.2
1982	Cle-A	112	276	34	74	12	1	0	21	34	36	.268	.353	.319	86	-4	9	5	-0	.970	-7	*S-101/3-8,2C	-0.3
1983	Cle-A	95	225	31	47	5	2	2	23	26	32	.209	.296	.276	56	-13	9	2	2	.965	21	2-71,S-15/3D	1.3
1984	Cle-A	85	133	17	30	4	2	1	14	12	20	.226	.290	.308	64	-6	2	2	-1	.981	18	2-55,3-17,S	1.3
1985	Cle-A	73	60	12	12	4	1	0	2	5	7	.200	.262	.300	54	-4	0	1	-1	.990	27	2-31,S-22/13D	2.3
Total	10	517	941	109	207	29	6	3	68	92	142	.220	.293	.273	57	-54	24	13	-1	.959	63	S-268,2-191/31DC	2.7
Team	5	387	737	97	173	26	6	3	65	80	101	.235	.313	.299	69	-29	23	12	-0	.964	59	S-172,2-164/31DC	4.4

■ **GUS FISHER**   Fisher, August Harris   b: 10/21/1885, Pottsboro, Tex.   d: 4/8/72, Portland, Ore.   BL/TR, 5'10", 175 lbs.   Deb: 4/18/11

| 1911 | Cle-A | 70 | 203 | 20 | 53 | 6 | 3 | 0 | 12 | 7 | | .261 | .302 | .320 | 73 | -8 | 6 | | | .956 | 8 | C-58/1-1 | 0.5 |
| Total | 2 | 74 | 213 | 21 | 54 | 6 | 3 | 0 | 12 | 7 | | .254 | .293 | .310 | 68 | -10 | 6 | | | .958 | 8 | /C-62,1-1 | 0.4 |

■ **ED FITZ GERALD**   Fitz Gerald, Edward Raymond   b: 5/21/24, Santa Ynez, Cal.   BR/TR, 6', 180 lbs.   Deb: 4/19/48   C

| 1959 | Cle-A | 49 | 129 | 12 | 35 | 6 | 1 | 4 | 12 | 14 | | .271 | .343 | .357 | 96 | -1 | 0 | 0 | 0 | .978 | 1 | C-45 | 0.2 |
| Total | 12 | 807 | 2086 | 199 | 542 | 82 | 10 | 19 | 217 | 185 | 235 | .260 | .324 | .336 | 80 | -56 | 9 | 6 | | .975 | -48 | C-651/1-5,3 | -8.2 |

■ **LES FLEMING**   Fleming, Leslie Harvey "Moe"   b: 8/7/15, Singleton, Tex.   d: 3/5/80, Cleveland, Tex.   BL/TL, 5'10", 185 lbs.   Deb: 4/22/39

1941	Cle-A	2	8	0	2	1	0	0	0	0	0	.250	.250	.375	67	-0	0	0	0	1.000	-0	/1-2	-0.1
1942	Cle-A	156	548	71	160	27	4	14	82	106	57	.292	.412	.432	146	38	6	8	-3	.993	-9	*1-156	1.7
1945	Cle-A	42	140	18	46	10	2	3	21	17	17	.329	.382	.493	160	10	0	0	0	.938	-2	O-33/1-5	0.6
1946	Cle-A	99	306	40	85	17	5	8	42	50	42	.278	.383	.444	140	17	1	0	0	.984	6	1-80/O-1	1.6
1947	Cle-A	103	281	39	68	14	2	4	46	53	14	.242	.362	.349	101	2	0	0	0	.989	6	1-77	0.3
Total	7	434	1330	168	369	69	15	29	199	226	152	.277	.386	.417	131	63	7	8	-3	.990	-6	1-325/O-37	3.6
Team	5	402	1283	168	361	69	13	29	191	220	146	.281	.390	.423	135	67	7	8	-3	.990	-5	1-320/O-34	4.1

YEAR	TM/L	G	AB	R	H	2B	3B	HR	RBI	BB	SO	AVG	OBP	SLG	PRO+	BR/A	SB	CS	SBR	FA	FR	G/POS	TPR

■ ELMER FLICK
Flick, Elmer Harrison b: 1/11/1876, Bedford, Ohio d: 1/9/71, Bedford, Ohio BL/TR, 5'9", 168 lbs. Deb: 5/2/1898 H

1902	Cle-A	110	424	70	126	19	11	2	61		47	.297	.371	.408	121	13	20			.929	-4	*O-110	0.1
1903	Cle-A	140	523	81	155	23	16	2	51	51		.296	.368	.413	136	24	24			.955	1	*O-140	1.7
1904	Cle-A	150	579	97	177	31	17	6	56	51		.306	.371	.449	160	40	**38**			.955	10	*O-145/2-6	4.5
1905	Cle-A	132	500	72	154	29	**18**	4	64	53		.308	.383	**.462**	**165**	37	35			.938	0	*O-131/2-1	3.3
1906	Cle-A	157	624	**98**	194	34	**22**	1	62	54		.311	.372	.441	156	40	**39**			.981	-11	*O-150/2-8	2.3
1907	Cle-A	147	549	80	166	15	**18**	3	58	64		.302	.386	.412	153	35	41			.956	1	*O-147	3.3
1908	Cle-A	9	35	4	8	1	1	0	2	3		.229	.289	.314	96	-0	0			1.000	-0	/O-9	-0.1
1909	Cle-A	66	235	28	60	10	2	0	15	22		.255	.322	.315	97	-0	9			.958	-4	O-61	-0.7
1910	Cle-A	24	68	5	18	2	1	1	7	10		.265	.359	.368	126	2	1			.955	-3	O-18	-0.2
Total	13	1483	5597	950	1752	268	164	48	756	597		.313	.389	.445	149	353	330			.947	23	*O-1456/2-15	28.7
Team	9	935	3537	535	1058	164	106	19	376	355		.299	.371	.422	145	191	207			.955	-11	O-911/2-15	14.2

■ HANK FOILES
Foiles, Henry Lee b: 6/10/29, Richmond, Va. BR/TR, 6', 195 lbs. Deb: 4/21/53

1953	Cle-A	7	7	2	1	0	0	0	0	1	1	.143	.250	.143	9	-1	0	0	0	.933	1	/C-7	0.0
1955	Cle-A	62	111	13	29	9	0	1	7	17	18	.261	.359	.369	93	-1	0	0	0	.988	14	C-41	1.4
1956	Cle-A	1	0	0	0	0	0	0	0	0	0	—	—	—	—	0	0	0	0	.000	0	/C-1	0.0
1960	Cle-A	24	68	9	19	1	0	1	6	7	5	.279	.347	.338	89	-1	0	0	0	.982	0	C-22	0.1
Total	11	608	1455	171	353	59	10	46	166	170	295	.243	.323	.392	92	-17	3	7		.986	35	C-544	3.6
Team	4	94	186	24	49	10	0	2	13	25	24	.263	.351	.349	88	-3	0	0̄		.984	16	/C-71	1.5

■ LEW FONSECA
Fonseca, Lewis Albert b: 1/21/1899, Oakland, Cal. d: 11/26/89, Ely, Iowa BR/TR, 5'10.5", 180 lbs. Deb: 4/13/21 M

1927	Cle-A	112	428	60	133	20	7	2	40	12	17	.311	.333	.404	90	-8	12	4	1	.973	-6	2-96,1-13	-0.9
1928	Cle-A	75	263	38	86	19	4	3	36	13	17	.327	.361	.464	114	5	4	2	0	1.000	5	1-56,3-15/S2	0.5
1929	Cle-A	148	566	97	209	44	15	6	103	50	23	**.369**	.427	.532	140	34	19	11	-1	.995	6	*1-147	2.3
1930	Cle-A	40	129	20	36	9	2	0	17	7	7	.279	.316	.380	73	-6	1	0	0	.980	2	1-28/3-6	-0.5
1931	Cle-A	26	108	21	40	9	1	1	14	8	7	.370	.419	.500	133	5	3	2	-0	.993	1	1-26	0.3
Total	12	937	3404	518	1075	203	50	31	485	186	199	.316	.355	.432	103	8	64	36	-2	.994	-3	1-375,2-363,0/3SP	-2.5
Team	5	401	1494	236	504	101	29	12	210	90	71	.337	.379	.468	115	31	39	19	0	.994	8	1-270/2-97,3S	1.7

■ TED FORD
Ford, Theodore Henry b: 2/7/47, Vineland, N.J. BR/TR, 5'10", 180 lbs. Deb: 4/7/70

1970	Cle-A	26	46	5	8	1	0	1	3	13		.174	.224	.261	32	-4	0	0	0	1.000	1	O-12	-0.4
1971	Cle-A	74	196	15	38	6	0	2	14	9	34	.194	.229	.255	34	-17	2	2	-1	1.000	-1	O-55	-2.2
1973	Cle-A	11	40	3	9	0	1	0	3	2	7	.225	.262	.275	50	-3	1	0	0	1.000	-4	O-10	-0.7
Total	4	240	711	66	156	26	2	17	68	51	134	.219	.275	.333	76	-22	7	5	-1	.985	6	O-196	-2.7
Team	3	111	282	23	55	7	1	3	18	14	54	.195	.233	.259	36	-24	3	2	-0	1.000	-3	/O-77	-3.3

■ RAY FOSSE
Fosse, Raymond Earl b: 4/4/47, Marion, Ill. BR/TR, 6'2", 215 lbs. Deb: 9/8/67

1967	Cle-A	7	16	1	1	0	0	0	0	0	5	.063	.063	.063	-62	-3	0	0	0	1.000	5	/C-7	0.2
1968	Cle-A	1	0	0	0	0	0	0	0	0	0	—	—	—	—	0	0	0	0	1.000	-0	/C-1	0.0
1969	Cle-A	37	116	11	20	3	0	2	9	8	29	.172	.224	.250	34	-10	1	0	0	.977	3	C-37	-0.5
1970	Cle-A★	120	450	62	138	17	1	18	61	39	55	.307	.363	.469	122	13	1	5	-3	.989	6	*C-120	2.3
1971	Cle-A†	133	486	53	134	21	1	12	62	36	62	.276	.331	.397	97	-2	4	1	1	.988	-3	*C-126/1-4	-0.1
1972	Cle-A	134	457	42	110	20	1	10	41	45	46	.241	.313	.354	95	-3	5	1	1	.985	6	*C-124/1-3	1.0
1976	Cle-A	90	276	26	83	9	1	2	30	20	26	.301	.348	.362	109	3	1	2	-1	.987	1	C-85/1-3,D	0.6
1977	Cle-A	78	238	25	63	7	1	6	27	7	26	.265	.294	.378	84	-6	0	5	-3	.983	6	C-77/1-1,D	0.2
Total	12	924	2957	299	758	117	13	61	324	203	363	.256	.308	.367	90	-46	15	19	-7	.985	28	C-889/1-13,D2	1.0
Team	8	600	2039	219	549	77	5	50	230	155	243	.269	.325	.385	98	-8	12	14	-5	.986	26	C-577/1-11,D	3.7

■ ROY FOSTER
Foster, Roy b: 7/29/45, Bixby, Okla. BR/TR, 6', 185 lbs. Deb: 4/7/70

1970	Cle-A	139	477	66	128	26	0	23	60	54	75	.268	.357	.468	120	13	3	3	-1	.965	-3	*O-131	0.2
1971	Cle-A	125	396	51	97	21	1	18	45	35	48	.245	.316	.439	103	0	6	1	1	.968	-1	*O-107	-0.5
1972	Cle-A	73	143	19	32	4	0	4	13	21	23	.224	.331	.336	96	-0	0	2	-1	.966	-6	O-45	-1.1
Total	3	337	1016	136	257	51	1	45	118	110	146	.253	.338	.438	110	13	9	6	-1	.967	-11	O-283	-1.4

■ JULIO FRANCO
Franco, Julio Cesar (b: Julio Cesar Robles (Franco)) b: 8/23/58, Hato Mayor, D.R. BR/TR, 6', 175 lbs. Deb: 4/23/82

1983	Cle-A	149	560	68	153	24	8	8	80	27	50	.273	.309	.387	87	-11	32	12	2	.961	-7	*S-149	-0.1
1984	Cle-A	160	658	82	188	22	5	3	79	43	68	.286	.335	.348	88	-10	19	10	-0	.955	-1	*S-159/D-1	0.5
1985	Cle-A	160	636	97	183	33	4	6	90	54	74	.288	.347	.381	100	1	13	9	-2	.949	-22	*S-151/2-8,D	-0.7
1986	Cle-A	149	599	80	183	30	5	10	74	32	66	.306	.341	.422	108	6	10	7	-1	.971	-5	*S-134,2-13/D	1.2
1987	Cle-A	128	495	86	158	24	3	8	52	57	56	.319	.393	.428	117	14	32	9	4	.963	-24	*S-111/2-9,D	0.4
1988	Cle-A	152	613	88	186	23	6	10	54	56	72	.303	.364	.409	113	11	25	11	1	.982	-10	*2-151/S-1	0.9
Total	13	1658	6381	964	1922	299	45	120	861	623	807	.301	.366	.419	114	136	237	87	19	.960	-115	S-715,2-628,D/103	11.2
Team	6	898	3561	501	1051	156	31	45	429	269	386	.295	.348	.394	102	12	131	58	5	.959	-69	S-704,2-181/D	2.2

■ TITO FRANCONA
Francona, John Patsy b: 11/4/33, Aliquippa, Pa. BL/TL, 5'11", 190 lbs. Deb: 4/17/56 F

1959	Cle-A	122	399	68	145	17	2	20	79	35	42	.363	.419	.566	174	**40**	2	0	1	.972	-4	O-64,1-35	3.1
1960	Cle-A	147	544	84	159	**36**	2	17	79	67	67	.292	.375	.460	128	22	4	1	1	.989	5	*O-138,1-13	2.0
1961	Cle-A☆	155	592	87	178	30	8	16	85	56	52	.301	.365	.459	122	18	2	1	0	.987	4	*O-138,1-14	1.3
1962	Cle-A	158	621	82	169	28	5	14	70	47	74	.272	.330	.401	99	-2	3	2	-0	.986	2	*1-158	-1.1
1963	Cle-A	142	500	57	114	29	0	10	41	47	77	.228	.297	.346	80	-13	9	1	2	.986	-2	*O-122,1-11	-2.2
1964	Cle-A	111	270	35	67	13	2	8	24	44	46	.248	.362	.400	113	6	1	3	-2	.985	-12	O-69,1-17	-1.2
Total	15	1719	5121	650	1395	224	34	125	656	544	694	.272	.346	.403	108	56	46	21	1	.984	-49	O-911,1-475	-7.0
Team	6	835	2926	413	832	153	19	85	378	296	358	.284	.355	.437	117	71	21	8	2	.985	-8	O-531,1-248	1.9

■ TERRY FRANCONA
Francona, Terry Jon b: 4/22/59, Aberdeen, S.D. BL/TL, 6'1", 190 lbs. Deb: 8/19/81 F

| 1988 | Cle-A | 62 | 212 | 24 | 66 | 8 | 0 | 1 | 12 | 5 | 18 | .311 | .327 | .363 | 91 | -3 | 0 | 0 | 0 | .977 | 0 | D-38/1-5,O | -0.4 |
| Total | 10 | 708 | 1731 | 163 | 474 | 74 | 6 | 16 | 143 | 65 | 119 | .274 | .302 | .351 | 81 | -46 | 12 | 12 | -4 | .992 | -4 | 1-304,O-203/DP3 | -7.7 |

■ JOE FRAZIER
Frazier, Joseph Filmore b: 10/6/22, Liberty, N.C. BL/TR, 6', 180 lbs. Deb: 8/31/47 M

| 1947 | Cle-A | 9 | 14 | 1 | 1 | 1 | 0 | 0 | 1 | 1 | 1 | .071 | .133 | .143 | -24 | -2 | 0 | 0 | 0 | .857 | -1 | /O-5 | -0.4 |
| Total | 4 | 217 | 282 | 31 | 68 | 15 | 2 | 10 | 45 | 35 | 46 | .241 | .331 | .415 | 97 | -1 | 0 | 1 | -1 | .961 | -7 | /O-56,1-1 | -1.0 |

■ VERN FREIBURGER
Freiburger, Vern Donald b: 12/19/23, Detroit, Mich. BR/TL, 6'1", 170 lbs. Deb: 9/6/41

| 1941 | Cle-A | 2 | 8 | 0 | 1 | 0 | 0 | 0 | 1 | 0 | 2 | .125 | .125 | .125 | -35 | -2 | 0 | 0 | 0 | .947 | 1 | /1-2 | -0.1 |

■ JIM FRIDLEY
Fridley, James Riley "Big Jim" b: 9/6/24, Philippi, W.Va. BR/TR, 6'2", 205 lbs. Deb: 4/15/52

| 1952 | Cle-A | 62 | 175 | 23 | 44 | 2 | 0 | 4 | 16 | 14 | 40 | .251 | .311 | .331 | 84 | -4 | 3 | 3 | -1 | .978 | -5 | O-54 | -1.3 |
| Total | 3 | 152 | 424 | 50 | 105 | 12 | 5 | 8 | 53 | 35 | 83 | .248 | .310 | .356 | 89 | -8 | 3 | 4 | -2 | .982 | -7 | O-123 | -2.2 |

■ OWEN FRIEND
Friend, Owen Lacey "Red" b: 3/21/27, Granite City, Ill. BR/TR, 6'1", 180 lbs. Deb: 10/2/49 C

| 1953 | Cle-A | 34 | 68 | 7 | 16 | 2 | 0 | 2 | 13 | 5 | 16 | .235 | .288 | .353 | 74 | -3 | 0 | 0 | 0 | 1.000 | 6 | 2-19/S-8,3 | 0.4 |
| Total | 5 | 208 | 598 | 69 | 136 | 24 | 6 | 13 | 76 | 55 | 109 | .227 | .295 | .339 | 63 | -34 | 2 | 2 | -1 | .963 | 23 | 2-141/3-27,S | -0.6 |

YEAR	TM/L	G	AB	R	H	2B	3B	HR	RBI	BB	SO	AVG	OBP	SLG	PRO+	BR/A	SB	CS	SBR	FA	FR	G/POS	TPR

■ BUCK FRIERSON
Frierson, Robert Lawrence b: 7/29/17, Chicota, Tex. BR/TR, 6'3", 195 lbs. Deb: 9/9/41

| 1941 | Cle-A | 5 | 11 | 2 | 3 | 1 | 0 | 0 | 2 | 1 | 1 | .273 | .333 | .364 | 89 | -0 | 0 | 0 | 0 | 1.000 | -1 | /O-3 | -0.1 |

■ DOUG FROBEL
Frobel, Douglas Steven b: 6/6/59, Ottawa, Ont., Can. BL/TR, 6'4", 196 lbs. Deb: 9/5/82

| 1987 | Cle-A | 29 | 40 | 5 | 4 | 0 | 0 | 2 | 5 | 5 | 13 | .100 | .200 | .250 | 18 | -5 | 0 | 0 | 0 | 1.000 | -3 | O-12/D-5 | -0.8 |
| Total | 5 | 268 | 542 | 70 | 109 | 21 | 4 | 20 | 58 | 55 | 155 | .201 | .277 | .365 | 78 | -18 | 13 | 10 | -2 | .957 | -10 | O-202/D-5 | -3.6 |

■ VERN FULLER
Fuller, Vernon Gordon b: 3/1/44, Menomonie, Wis. BR/TR, 6'1", 170 lbs. Deb: 9/5/64

1964	Cle-A	2	1	0	0	0	0	0	0	0	0	.000	.000	.000	-99	-0	0	0	0	.000	0	H	0.0
1966	Cle-A	16	47	7	11	2	1	2	2	7	6	.234	.357	.447	129	2	0	0	0	1.000	-4	2-16	-0.1
1967	Cle-A	73	206	18	46	10	0	7	21	19	55	.223	.301	.374	98	-1	2	3	-1	.986	0	2-64/S-2	0.2
1968	Cle-A	97	244	14	59	8	2	0	18	24	49	.242	.320	.291	87	-3	2	2	-1	.988	-12	2-73,3-23/S	-1.4
1969	Cle-A	108	254	25	60	11	1	4	22	20	53	.236	.297	.335	74	-9	2	1	0	.978	9	*2-102/3-7	0.6
1970	Cle-A	29	33	3	6	2	0	1	2	3	9	.182	.250	.333	57	-2	0	0	0	.919	3	2-16/3-4,1	0.1
Total	6	325	785	67	182	33	4	14	65	73	172	.232	.307	.338	87	-13	6	6	-2	.982	-4	2-271/3-34,S1	-0.6

■ FABIAN GAFFKE
Gaffke, Fabian Sebastian b: 8/5/13, Milwaukee, Wis. d: 2/8/92, Milwaukee, Wis. BR/TR, 5'10", 185 lbs. Deb: 9/9/36

1941	Cle-A	4	4	0	1	0	0	0	2	2		.250	.500	.250	109	0	0	0	0	1.000	-1	/O-2	0.0
1942	Cle-A	40	67	4	11	2	0	0	3	6	13	.164	.243	.194	25	-7	1	0	0	1.000	-2	O-16	-0.9
Total	6	129	321	43	73	14	4	7	42	30	47	.227	.297	.361	67	-17	2	2	-1	.979	-9	/O-85,C-1	-2.8
Team	2	44	71	4	12	2	0	0	3	8	15	.169	.262	.197	32	-6	1	0	0	1.000	-3	/O-18	-0.9

■ RALPH GAGLIANO
Gagliano, Ralph Michael b: 10/8/46, Memphis, Tenn. BL/TR, 5'11", 170 lbs. Deb: 9/21/65 F

| 1965 | Cle-A | 1 | 0 | 0 | 0 | 0 | 0 | 0 | 0 | 0 | 0 | — | — | — | — | 0 | 0 | 0 | 0 | .000 | 0 | R | 0.0 |

■ MILT GALATZER
Galatzer, Milton b: 5/4/07, Chicago, Ill. d: 1/29/76, San Francisco, Cal BL/TL, 5'10", 168 lbs. Deb: 6/25/33

1933	Cle-A	57	160	19	38	2	1	1	17	23	21	.237	.333	.281	61	-8	2	3	-1	.975	-0	O-40/1-5	-1.2
1934	Cle-A	49	196	29	53	10	2	0	15	21	8	.270	.344	.342	76	-7	3	2	-0	.980	3	O-49	-0.6
1935	Cle-A	93	259	45	78	9	3	0	19	35	8	.301	.389	.359	93	-1	4	5	-2	.934	-8	O-81	-1.3
1936	Cle-A	49	97	12	23	4	1	0	6	13	8	.237	.333	.299	57	-6	1	2	-1	.964	-8	O-42/P-1,1	-1.4
Total	5	251	717	105	192	25	7	1	57	92	46	.268	.354	.326	75	-24	10	12	-4	.959	-14	O-212/1-8,P	-4.7
Team	4	248	712	105	192	25	7	1	57	92	45	.270	.356	.329	76	-22	10	12	-4	.959	-14	O-212/1-6,P	-4.5

■ SHORTY GALLAGHER
Gallagher, Charles William b: 4/30/1872, Detroit, Mich. d: 6/23/24, Detroit, Mich. Deb: 8/13/01

| 1901 | Cle-A | 2 | 4 | 0 | 0 | 0 | 0 | 0 | 0 | 0 | | .000 | .000 | .000 | -99 | -1 | 0 | | | .667 | -1 | /O-2 | -0.2 |

■ DAVE GALLAGHER
Gallagher, David Thomas b: 9/20/60, Trenton, N.J. BR/TR, 6', 180 lbs. Deb: 4/12/87

| 1987 | Cle-A | 15 | 36 | 2 | 4 | 1 | 1 | 0 | 1 | 2 | 5 | .111 | .158 | .194 | -7 | -6 | 2 | 0 | 1 | .972 | 1 | O-14 | -0.4 |
| Total | 9 | 794 | 2081 | 273 | 564 | 100 | 10 | 17 | 190 | 187 | 251 | .271 | .333 | .353 | 90 | -26 | 20 | 24 | -8 | .993 | -30 | O-699/D-12,1 | -8.0 |

■ JACKIE GALLAGHER
Gallagher, John Laurence b: 1/28/02, Providence, R.I. d: 9/10/84, Gladwyne, Pa. BL/TR, 5'10", 175 lbs. Deb: 8/24/23

| 1923 | Cle-A | 1 | 1 | 0 | 1 | 0 | 0 | 0 | 0 | 0 | 0 | 1.000 | 1.000 | 1.000 | 428 | 0 | 0 | 0 | 0 | .000 | -1 | /O-1 | 0.0 |

■ OSCAR GAMBLE
Gamble, Oscar Charles b: 12/20/49, Ramer, Ala. BL/TR, 5'11", 165 lbs. Deb: 8/27/69

1973	Cle-A	113	390	56	104	11	3	20	44	34	37	.267	.330	.464	120	9	3	4	-2	.971	-1	D-70,O-37	0.3
1974	Cle-A	135	454	74	132	16	4	19	59	48	51	.291	.365	.469	140	23	5	6	-2	1.000	-1	*D-115,O-13	1.7
1975	Cle-A	121	348	60	91	16	3	15	45	53	39	.261	.362	.454	130	14	11	5	0	.987	1	O-82,D-29	1.2
Total	17	1584	4502	656	1195	188	31	200	666	610	546	.265	.358	.454	127	168	47	37	-8	.977	-15	O-818,D-561/1	9.5
Team	3	369	1192	190	327	43	10	54	148	135	127	.274	.354	.463	130	46	19	15	-3	.984	-1	D-214,O-132	3.2

■ CHICK GANDIL
Gandil, Arnold b: 1/19/1887, St.Paul, Minn. d: 12/13/70, Calistoga, Cal. BR/TR, 6'1.5", 190 lbs. Deb: 4/14/10

| 1916 | Cle-A | 146 | 533 | 51 | 138 | 26 | 9 | 0 | 72 | 36 | 48 | .259 | .312 | .341 | 91 | -7 | 13 | | | **.995** | 8 | *1-145 | -0.5 |
| Total | 9 | 1147 | 4245 | 449 | 1176 | 173 | 78 | 11 | 557 | 273 | 233 | .277 | .327 | .362 | 103 | 3 | 153 | | | .992 | 36 | *1-1138/O-2 | 0.3 |

■ BOB GARBARK
Garbark, Robert Michael (b: Robert Michael Garbach) b: 11/13/09, Houston, Tex. d: 8/15/90, Meadville, Pa. BR/TR, 5'11", 178 lbs. Deb: 9/3/34 F

1934	Cle-A	5	11	1	0	0	0	0	0	1	3	.000	.083	.000	-76	-3	0	0	0	1.000	-2	/C-5	-0.4
1935	Cle-A	6	18	4	6	1	0	0	4	5	1	.333	.478	.389	124	1	0	0	0	1.000	2	/C-6	0.3
Total	7	145	327	31	81	9	0	0	28	26	17	.248	.307	.275	64	-15	0	1	-1	.996	-2	C-134/1-1	-1.2
Team	2	11	29	5	6	1	0	0	4	6	4	.207	.343	.241	52	-2	0	0	0	1.000	-0	/C-11	-0.1

■ RAY GARDNER
Gardner, Raymond Vincent b: 10/25/01, Frederick, Md. d: 5/3/68, Frederick, Md. BR/TR, 5'8", 145 lbs. Deb: 4/16/29

1929	Cle-A	82	256	28	67	3	2	1	24	29	16	.262	.337	.301	63	-13	10	13	-5	.952	8	S-82	-0.1
1930	Cle-A	33	13	7	1	0	0	0	1	0	0	.077	.077	.077	-59	-3	0	1	-1	.861	8	S-22/2-5,3	0.4
Total	2	115	269	35	68	3	2	1	25	29	16	.253	.326	.290	57	-16	10	14	-5	.945	16	S-104/2-5,3	0.3

■ LARRY GARDNER
Gardner, William Lawrence b: 5/13/1886, Enosburg Falls, Vt d: 3/11/76, St.George, Vt. BL/TR, 5'8", 165 lbs. Deb: 6/25/08

1919	Cle-A	139	524	67	157	29	7	2	79	39	29	.300	.352	.393	103	1	7			.946	-6	*3-139	0.1
1920	*Cle-A	154	597	72	185	31	11	3	118	53	25	.310	.367	.414	103	3	3	20	-11	**.976**	-2	*3-154	-0.2
1921	Cle-A	153	586	101	187	32	14	3	120	65	16	.319	.391	.437	109	9	3	3	-1	.950	-1	*3-152	1.7
1922	Cle-A	137	470	74	134	31	3	2	68	49	21	.285	.355	.377	90	-6	9	8	-2	.951	-5	*3-128	-0.4
1923	Cle-A	52	79	4	20	5	1	0	12	12	7	.253	.352	.342	83	-2	0	1	-1	.962	3	3-19	0.1
1924	Cle-A	38	50	3	10	0	0	0	4	5	1	.200	.273	.200	23	-6	0	1	-1	.875	-4	/3-8,2-6	-0.9
Total	17	1923	6688	866	1931	301	129	27	934	654	282	.289	.355	.384	109	75	165	68		.948	-40	*3-1656,2-181/S	6.3
Team	6	673	2306	321	693	128	36	10	401	223	99	.301	.365	.400	100	-0	22	33		.956	-16	3-600/2-6	0.4

■ GARY GEIGER
Geiger, Gary Merle b: 4/4/37, Sand Ridge, Ill. BL/TR, 6', 168 lbs. Deb: 4/15/58

| 1958 | Cle-A | 91 | 195 | 28 | 45 | 3 | 1 | 6 | 18 | 23 | 48 | .231 | .318 | .272 | 70 | -7 | 2 | 2 | -1 | .986 | 4 | O-53/3-2,P | -0.6 |
| Total | 12 | 954 | 2569 | 388 | 633 | 91 | 29 | 77 | 283 | 341 | 466 | .246 | .339 | .394 | 98 | -6 | 62 | 29 | 1 | .986 | 8 | O-749/1-6,3P | -3.5 |

■ FRANK GENINS
Genins, C. Frank "Frenchy" b: 11/2/1866, St.Louis, Mo. d: 9/30/22, St.Louis, Mo. TR, Deb: 7/5/1892

| 1901 | Cle-A | 26 | 101 | 15 | 23 | 1 | 0 | 0 | 9 | 8 | | .228 | .284 | .277 | 58 | -6 | 3 | | | .940 | 1 | O-26 | -0.6 |
| Total | 3 | 149 | 514 | 75 | 116 | 18 | 0 | 2 | 44 | 43 | | .226 | .288 | .272 | 56 | -30 | 32 | | | .934 | -10 | /O-70,S-39,321 | -3.7 |

■ JIM GENTILE
Gentile, James Edward "Diamond Jim" b: 6/3/34, San Francisco, Cal. BL/TL, 6'4", 215 lbs. Deb: 9/10/57

| 1966 | Cle-A | 33 | 47 | 2 | 6 | 1 | 0 | 4 | 5 | 18 | | .128 | .212 | .277 | 39 | -4 | 0 | 0 | 0 | .944 | -0 | /1-9 | -0.5 |
| Total | 9 | 936 | 2922 | 434 | 759 | 113 | 6 | 179 | 549 | 475 | 663 | .260 | .372 | .486 | 137 | 157 | 3 | 1 | | .990 | 10 | 1-854 | 11.7 |

■ GREEK GEORGE
George, Charles Peter b: 12/25/12, Waycross, Ga. BR/TR, 6'2", 200 lbs. Deb: 6/30/35

1935	Cle-A	2	0	0	0	0	0	0	0	0		—	—	—	—	0	0	0	0	1.000	0	/C-1	0.0
1936	Cle-A	23	77	3	15	3	0	0	5	9	16	.195	.279	.234	28	-9	0	0	0	.994	16	/C-22	0.7
Total	5	118	299	15	53	9	2	0	24	28	59	.177	.248	.221	29	-29	0	0	0	.983	14	/C-94	-1.3
Team	2	25	77	3	15	3	0	0	5	9	16	.195	.279	.234	28	-9	0	0	0	.995	16	/C-23	0.7

■ GEORGE GERKEN
Gerken, George Herbert "Pickles" b: 7/28/03, Chicago, Ill. d: 10/23/77, Arcadia, Cal. BR/TR, 5'11.5", 175 lbs. Deb: 4/19/27

1927	Cle-A	6	14	1	3	0	0	0	2	1	3	.214	.267	.214	26	-1	0	0	0	.917	0	O-5	-0.2
1928	Cle-A	38	115	16	26	7	2	0	9	12	22	.226	.305	.322	64	-6	3	3	-1	.940	-1	/O-34	-1.0
Total	2	44	129	17	29	7	2	0	11	13	25	.225	.301	.310	60	-8	3	3	-1	.937	-1	/O-39	-1.2

YEAR	TM/L	G	AB	R	H	2B	3B	HR	RBI	BB	SO	AVG	OBP	SLG	PRO+	BR/A	SB	CS	SBR	FA	FR	G/POS	TPR
■ **GUS GETZ**					Getz, Gustave "Gee-Gee"		b: 8/3/1889, Pittsburgh, Pa.			d: 5/28/69, Keansburg, N.J.		BR/TR, 5'11", 165 lbs.		Deb: 8/15/09									
1918	Cle-A	6	15	2	2	1	0	0	4	1		.133	.350	.200	60	-0	0			.941	-0	/3-5	-0.1
Total	7	339	1114	85	265	22	9	2	93	24	46	.238	.257	.279	60	-56	41			.942	18	3-271/2-19,SO1	-3.5
■ **GUS GIL**					Gil, Tomas Gustavo (Guillen)		b: 4/19/39, Caracas, Venez.			BR/TR, 5'10", 180 lbs.		Deb: 4/11/67											
1967	Cle-A	51	96	11	11	4	0	0	5	9	18	.115	.198	.156	6	-11	0	0	0	1.000	2	2-49/1-1	-0.8
Total	4	221	468	46	87	16	0	1	37	56	63	.186	.274	.226	43	-34	5	0	2	.987	7	2-113/3-58,S1	-2.1
■ **BRIAN GILES**					Giles, Brian Stephen		b: 1/21/71, ElCajon, Cal.			BL/TL, 5'11", 195 lbs.		Deb: 9/16/95										
1995	Cle-A	6	9	6	5	0	0	1	3	0	1	.556	.556	.889	268	2	0	0	0	1.000	0	/O-3,D-1	0.2
■ **JOHNNY GILL**					Gill, John Wesley "Patcheye"		b: 3/27/05, Nashville, Tenn.			d: 12/26/84, Nashville, Tenn.		BL/TR, 6'2", 190 lbs.		Deb: 8/28/27								
1927	Cle-A	21	60	8	13	3	0	1	4	7	13	.217	.319	.317	65	-3	1	1	-0	1.000	-2	O-17	-0.6
1928	Cle-A	2	2	0	0	0	0	0	0	0	1	.000	.000	.000	-99	-1	0	0	0	.000	0	H	-0.1
Total	6	118	322	39	79	17	1	10	45	23	43	.245	.306	.398	84	-8	1	2	-1	.968	-2	/O-79	-1.5
Team	2	23	62	8	13	3	0	1	4	7	14	.210	.310	.306	60	-4	1	1	-0	1.000	-2	/O-17	-0.7
■ **TINSLEY GINN**					Ginn, Tinsley Rucker		b: 9/26/1891, Royston, Ga.			d: 8/30/31, Atlanta, Ga.		BL/TR, 5'9", 180 lbs.		Deb: 6/27/14								
1914	Cle-A	2	1	0	0	0	0	0	0	0	0	.000	.000	.000	-96	-0	0			.000	0	/O-2	0.0
■ **JOE GINSBERG**					Ginsberg, Myron Nathan		b: 10/11/26, New York, N.Y.			BL/TR, 5'11", 180 lbs.		Deb: 9/15/48									
1953	Cle-A	46	109	10	31	4	0	0	10	14	4	.284	.371	.321	91	-1	0	0	0	.966	-5	C-39	-0.4
1954	Cle-A	3	2	0	1	0	1	0	1	0	0	.500	.667	1.500	473	1	0	0	0	1.000	-0	/C-1	0.1
Total	13	695	1716	168	414	59	8	20	182	226	135	.241	.334	.320	79	-47	7	5		.983	-17	C-574	-3.9
Team	2	49	111	10	32	4	1	0	11	14	4	.288	.378	.342	98	0	0	0	0	.966	-5	/C-40	-0.3
■ **JIM GLEESON**					Gleeson, James Joseph "Gee Gee"		b: 3/5/12, Kansas City, Mo.			BB/TR, 6'1", 191 lbs.		Deb: 4/25/36		C						
1936	Cle-A	41	139	26	36	9	4	2	12	18	17	.259	.344	.439	91	-2	2	1	0	.958	-2	O-33	-0.5
Total	5	392	1277	195	336	77	19	16	154	158	147	.263	.350	.391	101	5	20	1	5	.972	-11	O-336	-2.4
■ **BILL GLYNN**					Glynn, William Vincent		b: 7/30/25, Sussex, N.J.			BL/TL, 6', 190 lbs.		Deb: 9/16/49									
1952	Cle-A	44	92	15	25	5	0	2	7	5	16	.272	.309	.391	101	-0	1	0		.973	-0	1-32	-0.1
1953	Cle-A	147	411	60	100	14	2	3	30	44	65	.243	.324	.309	74	-14	1	3	-2	.993	6	*1-135/O-2	-1.5
1954	*Cle-A	111	171	19	43	3	2	5	18	12	21	.251	.301	.380	84	-4	3	2	-0	.987	3	1-96/O-1	-0.4
Total	4	310	684	94	170	22	4	10	56	61	105	.249	.315	.336	79	-21	5	5	-2	.989	9	1-264/O-3	-2.1
Team	3	302	674	94	168	22	4	10	55	61	102	.249	.316	.338	80	-19	5	5	-2	.989	9	1-263/O-3	-2.0
■ **JOHN GOCHNAUER**					Gochnauer, John Peter		b: 9/12/1875, Altoona, Pa.			d: 9/27/29, Altoona, Pa.		BR/TR, 5'9", 160 lbs.		Deb: 9/29/01								
1902	Cle-A	127	459	45	85	16	4	0	37	38		.185	.247	.237	36	-39	7			.933	-3	*S-127	-3.3
1903	Cle-A	134	438	48	81	16	4	0	48	48		.185	.265	.240	53	-24	10			.867	-22	*S-134	-4.2
Total	3	264	908	94	170	32	8	0	87	87		.187	.258	.240	45	-63	18			.901	-26	S-264	-7.5
Team	2	261	897	93	166	32	8	0	85	86		.185	.256	.239	44	-63	17			.900	-25	S-261	-7.5
■ **JONAH GOLDMAN**					Goldman, Jonah John		b: 8/29/06, New York, N.Y.			d: 8/17/80, Palm Beach, Fla.		BR/TR, 5'7", 170 lbs.		Deb: 9/22/28								
1928	Cle-A	7	21	1	5	1	0	0	2	3	0	.238	.333	.286	63	-1	0	0	0	.878	0	/S-7	0.0
1930	Cle-A	111	306	32	74	18	0	1	44	28	25	.242	.312	.310	56	-20	3	5	-2	.945	21	S-93,3-20	0.7
1931	Cle-A	30	62	0	8	1	0	0	3	4	6	.129	.182	.145	-12	-10	1	1	-0	.947	14	S-30	0.5
Total	3	148	389	33	87	20	0	1	49	35	31	.224	.293	.283	46	-31	4	6	-2	.941	35	S-130/3-20	1.2
■ **RENE GONZALES**					Gonzales, Rene Adrian		b: 9/3/60, Austin, Tex.			BR/TR, 6'3", 191 lbs.		Deb: 7/27/84									
1994	Cle-A	22	23	6	8	1	1	1	5	5	3	.348	.464	.609	173	3	2	0	1	.952	3	3-13/1-4,S2	0.6
Total	11	652	1445	166	347	55	4	17	130	151	219	.240	.318	.319	76	-45	23	16	-3	.956	49	3-336,2-181/S,1OP	0.5
■ **DENNY GONZALEZ**					Gonzalez, Denio Mariano (Manzueta)		b: 7/22/63, Sabana Grande Boya, D.R.			BR/TR, 5'11", 185 lbs.		Deb: 8/6/84								
1989	Cle-A	8	17	3	5	1	0	0	1	0	4	.294	.333	.353	92	-0	0	0	0	.000	-0	/3-1,D-6	-0.1
Total	5	98	262	29	54	9	1	4	18	27	64	.206	.283	.294	62	-13	3	5	-2	.925	-4	/3-35,S-25,O2D	-1.9
■ **JOSE GONZALEZ**					Gonzalez, Jose Rafael (Gutierrez)		b: 11/23/64, Puerto Plata, D.R.			BR/TR, 6'2", 196 lbs.		Deb: 9/2/85								
1991	Cle-A	33	69	10	11	2	1	2	4	11	27	.159	.284	.261	51	-4	8	0	2	.981	-3	O-32	-0.6
Total	8	461	676	95	144	30	7	9	42	60	186	.213	.279	.318	69	-29	33	9	5	.972	-62	O-378/D-1	-9.6
■ **ORLANDO GONZALEZ**					Gonzalez, Orlando Eugene		b: 11/15/51, Havana, Cuba			BL/TL, 6'2", 180 lbs.		Deb: 6/7/76								
1976	Cle-A	28	68	5	17	2	0	0	4	5	7	.250	.301	.279	72	-2	1	2	-1	.992	-2	1-15/O-7,D	-0.7
Total	3	79	164	16	39	2	0	0	5	15	16	.238	.302	.250	59	-8	1	4	-2	.991	-3	/1-29,O-20,D	-1.7
■ **PEDRO GONZALEZ**					Gonzalez, Pedro (Olivares)		b: 12/12/37, San Pedro De Macoris, D.R.			BR/TR, 6', 176 lbs.		Deb: 4/11/63								
1965	Cle-A	116	400	38	101	14	3	5	39	18	57	.253	.290	.340	78	-12	7	4	-0	.980	8	*2-112/O-3,3	0.6
1966	Cle-A	110	352	21	82	9	2	2	17	15	54	.233	.268	.287	60	-18	8	5	-1	.984	11	*2-104/3-1,O	-0.1
1967	Cle-A	80	189	19	43	6	0	1	8	12	36	.228	.277	.275	63	-9	4	6	-2	.971	-5	2-64/1-4,3S	-1.4
Total	5	407	1084	99	264	39	6	8	70	52	176	.244	.283	.313	70	-43	22	20	-5	.980	14	2-293/1-35,O3S	-1.4
Team	3	306	941	78	226	29	5	8	64	45	147	.240	.279	.307	68	-39	19	15	-3	.980	14	2-280/3-7,O1S	-0.9
■ **LEE GOOCH**					Gooch, Lee Currin		b: 2/23/1890, Oxford, N.C.			d: 5/18/66, Raleigh, N.C.		BR/TR, 6', 190 lbs.		Deb: 8/17/15								
1915	Cle-A	2	2	0	1	0	0	0	0	0	0	.500	.500	.500	196	0	0			.000	0	H	0.0
Total	2	19	61	4	18	2	0	1	8	4	10	.295	.338	.377	120	1	0			.973	-2	/O-16	-0.2
■ **WILBUR GOOD**					Good, Wilbur David "Lefty"		b: 9/28/1885, Punxsutawney, Pa.			d: 12/30/63, Brooksville, Fla.		BL/TL, 5'6", 165 lbs.		Deb: 8/18/05							
1908	Cle-A	46	154	23	43	1	3	1	14	13		.279	.351	.344	126	5	7			.845	-8	O-42	-0.6
1909	Cle-A	94	318	33	68	6	5	0	17	28		.214	.296	.264	74	-9	13			.953	2	O-80	-1.1
Total	11	749	2364	324	609	84	44	9	187	190		.258	.322	.342	98	-7	104			.942	-8	O-624/P-5	-5.3
Team	2	140	472	56	111	7	8	1	31	41		.235	.314	.290	90	-4	20			.915	-6	O-122	-1.7
■ **JOE GORDON**					Gordon, Joseph Lowell "Flash"		b: 2/18/15, Los Angeles, Cal.			d: 4/14/78, Sacramento, Cal.		BR/TR, 5'10", 180 lbs.		Deb: 4/18/38		MC				
1947	Cle-A★	155	562	89	153	27	6	29	93	62	49	.272	.346	.496	136	24	7	3	0	.978	-4	*2-155	3.1
1948	*Cle-A★	144	550	96	154	21	4	32	124	77	68	.280	.371	.507	136	26	5	2	0	.971	-7	*2-144/S-2	2.7
1949	Cle-A★	148	541	74	136	18	3	20	84	83	33	.251	.355	.407	103	2	5	6	-2	.980	-18	*2-145	-1.1
1950	Cle-A	119	368	59	87	12	1	19	57	56	44	.236	.340	.429	99	-2	4	1	0	.969	-18	*2-105	-1.4
Total	11	1566	5707	914	1530	264	52	253	975	759	702	.268	.357	.466	121	153	89	60		.970	54	*2-1519/1-30,S	28.2
Team	4	566	2021	318	530	78	14	100	358	278	194	.262	.354	.463	120	50	21	12		.975	-47	2-549/S-2	3.3
■ **ROD GRABER**					Graber, Rodney Blaine		b: 6/20/30, Massillon, Ohio			BL/TL, 5'11", 175 lbs.		Deb: 9/9/58								
1958	Cle-A	4	8	0	1	0	0	0	0	0	2	.125	.222	.125	-2	-1	0	0	0	1.000	-0	/O-2	-0.1
■ **PEACHES GRAHAM**					Graham, George Frederick		b: 3/23/1877, Aledo, Ill.			d: 7/25/39, Long Beach, Cal.		BR/TR, 5'9", 180 lbs.		Deb: 9/14/02		F				
1902	Cle-A	2	6	0	2	0	0	0	1	1		.333	.429	.333	118	0	0			1.000	0	/2-1	0.0
Total	7	373	999	99	265	34	6	1	85	114		.265	.347	.314	95	-3	21			.953	-25	C-298/O-7,231SP	-0.2

YEAR	TM/L	G	AB	R	H	2B	3B	HR	RBI	BB	SO	AVG	OBP	SLG	PRO+	BR/A	SB	CS	SBR	FA	FR	G/POS	TPR
■ JACK GRANEY	Graney, John Gladstone b: 6/10/1886, St.Thomas, Ont., Can. d: 4/20/78, Louisiana, Mo. BL/TL, 5'9", 180 lbs. Deb: 4/30/08																						
1908	Cle-A	2	0	0	0	0	0	0	0	0		—	—	—	—	0	0			.000	-0	/P-2	0.0
1910	Cle-A	116	454	62	107	13	9	1	31	37		.236	.293	.311	88	-7	18			.949	1	*O-114	-1.3
1911	Cle-A	146	527	84	142	25	5	1	45	66		.269	.363	.342	96	-1	21			.927	2	*O-142	-0.7
1912	Cle-A	78	264	44	64	13	2	0	20	50		.242	.367	.307	90	-1	9			.958	4	O-75	-0.1
1913	Cle-A	148	517	56	138	18	12	3	68	48	55	.267	.335	.366	102	1	27			.970	2	*O-148	-0.5
1914	Cle-A	130	460	63	122	17	10	1	39	67	46	.265	.362	.352	111	8	20	18	-5	.935	5	*O-127	0.2
1915	Cle-A	116	404	42	105	20	7	1	56	59	29	.260	.357	.351	110	6	12	15	-5	.972	5	*O-115	0.0
1916	Cle-A	155	589	106	142	**41**	14	5	54	102	72	.241	.355	.384	115	12	10			.959	3	*O-154	0.7
1917	Cle-A	146	535	87	122	29	7	3	35	**94**	49	.228	.348	.325	98	1	16			.959	-7	*O-145	-1.6
1918	Cle-A	70	177	27	42	7	4	0	9	28	13	.237	.351	.322	94	-0	3			.975	-6	O-45	-1.0
1919	Cle-A	128	461	79	108	22	8	1	30	**105**	39	.234	.380	.323	93	0	7			.961	6	*O-125	-0.3
1920	*Cle-A	62	152	31	45	11	1	0	13	27	21	.296	.412	.382	108	3	4	2	0	.941	-6	O-47	-0.6
1921	Cle-A	68	107	19	32	3	0	2	18	20	9	.299	.414	.383	103	2	1	1	-0	.933	-9	O-32	-0.9
1922	Cle-A	37	58	6	9	0	0	0	2	9	12	.155	.279	.155	16	-7	0	0	0	.862	-1	O-13	-0.9
Total	14	1402	4705	706	1178	219	79	18	420	712	345	.250	.354	.342	100	16	148	36		.953	-3	*O-1282/P-2	-7.0
■ EDDIE GRANT	Grant, Edward Leslie "Harvard Eddie" b: 5/21/1883, Franklin, Mass. d: 10/5/18, Argonne Forest, France BL/TR, 5'11.5", 168 lbs. Deb: 8/4/05																						
1905	Cle-A	2	8	1	3	0	0	0	0	0		.375	.375	.375	136	0	0			.833	-2	/2-2	-0.2
Total	10	990	3385	399	844	79	30	5	277	233		.249	.300	.295	78	-95	153			.942	-26	3-769,S-103/21	-10.1
■ JIMMY GRANT	Grant, James Charles b: 10/6/18, Racine, Wis. d: 7/8/70, Rochester, Minn. BL/TR, 5'8", 166 lbs. Deb: 9/8/42																						
1943	Cle-A	15	22	3	3	2	0	0	1	4	7	.136	.269	.227	49	-1	0	0	0	.941	2	/3-5	0.0
1944	Cle-A	61	99	12	27	4	3	1	12	11	20	.273	.357	.404	122	3	1	0	0	.926	-4	2-20/3-4	0.1
Total	3	146	354	38	87	16	6	5	36	38	67	.246	.322	.367	101	-0	5	3		.907	-0	/3-70,2-20	0.1
Team	2	76	121	15	30	6	3	1	13	15	27	.248	.341	.372	109	1	1	0		.958	-2	/2-20,3-9	0.1
■ MICKEY GRASSO	Grasso, Newton Michael b: 5/10/20, Newark, N.J. d: 10/15/75, Miami, Fla. BR/TR, 6', 195 lbs. Deb: 9/18/46																						
1954	*Cle-A	4	6	1	2	0	0	1	1	1	1	.333	.500	.833	256	1	0	0	0	.833	-1	/C-4	0.1
Total	7	322	957	78	216	23	1	5	87	81	108	.226	.291	.268	53	-62	2	1	0	.964	9	C-310	-4.0
■ GARY GRAY	Gray, Gary George b: 9/21/52, New Orleans, La. BR/TR, 6', 203 lbs. Deb: 6/23/77																						
1980	Cle-A	28	54	4	8	1	0	2	4	3	13	.148	.193	.278	27	-6	0	0	0	1.000	-2	/1-6,O-6,D	-0.8
Total	6	211	625	65	150	23	3	24	71	34	137	.240	.281	.402	86	-14	5	2	0	.988	-7	1-100/D-62,O	-2.8
■ GENE GREEN	Green, Gene Leroy b: 6/26/33, Los Angeles, Cal. d: 5/23/81, St.Louis, Mo. BR/TR, 6'2", 205 lbs. Deb: 9/10/57																						
1962	Cle-A	66	143	16	40	4	1	11	28	8	21	.280	.318	.552	133	6	0	0	0	.964	-2	O-33/1-2	0.2
1963	Cle-A	43	78	4	16	3	0	2	7	4	22	.205	.262	.321	63	-4	0	0	0	1.000	-3	O-18	-0.8
Total	7	408	1151	130	307	49	7	46	160	89	185	.267	.322	.441	101	-0	2	3	-1	.963	-16	O-170,C-146/1	-1.9
Team	2	109	221	20	56	7	1	13	35	12	43	.253	.298	.471	108	2	0	0	0	.972	-5	/O-51,1-2	-0.6
■ ALFREDO GRIFFIN	Griffin, Alfredo Claudino (b: Alfredo Claudino Baptist (Griffin)) b: 10/6/57, Santo Domingo, D.R. BB/TR, 5'11", 165 lbs. Deb: 9/4/76																						
1976	Cle-A	12	4	0	1	0	0	0	0	0	2	.250	.250	.250	47	-0	0	1	-1	.750	0	/S-6,D-4	0.0
1977	Cle-A	14	41	5	6	1	0	0	3	3	5	.146	.205	.171	4	-5	2	2	-1	.940	-1	S-13/D-1	-0.6
1978	Cle-A	5	4	1	2	1	0	0	0	2	1	.500	.667	.750	301	1	0	0	0	.917	3	/S-2	0.4
Total	18	1962	6780	759	1688	245	78	24	527	338	664	.249	.287	.319	67	-306	192	134	-23	.961	-10	*S-1861/2-55,D3	-17.6
Team	3	31	49	6	9	2	0	0	3	5	8	.184	.259	.224	35	-4	2	3	-1	.924	2	/S-21,D-5	-0.2
■ ART GRIGGS	Griggs, Arthur Carle b: 12/10/1883, Topeka, Kan. d: 12/19/38, Los Angeles, Cal. BR/TR, 5'11", 185 lbs. Deb: 5/2/09																						
1911	Cle-A	27	68	7	17	3	2	1	7	5		.250	.301	.397	93	-1	1			.949	-2	2-11/O-4,31	-0.3
1912	Cle-A	89	273	29	83	16	7	0	39	33		.304	.381	.414	123	9	10			.986	1	1-71	0.8
Total	7	442	1370	127	379	73	20	5	152	105		.277	.332	.370	114	19	36			.983	-13	1-195/O-96,23S	-0.3
Team	2	116	341	36	100	19	9	1	46	38		.293	.366	.411	118	8	11			.986	-1	/1-72,2-11,O3	0.5
■ OSCAR GRIMES	Grimes, Oscar Ray Jr. b: 4/13/15, Minerva, Ohio d: 5/19/93, Westlake, Ohio BR/TR, 5'11", 178 lbs. Deb: 9/28/38 F																						
1938	Cle-A	4	10	2	2	0	1	0	2	2	0	.200	.333	.400	85	-0	0	0	0	1.000	-1	/2-2,1-1	-0.1
1939	Cle-A	119	364	51	98	20	5	4	56	56	61	.269	.368	.385	96	-1	8	3	1	.968	-11	2-48,1-43,S/3	-1.0
1940	Cle-A	11	13	3	0	0	0	0	0	0	5	.000	.000	.000	-99	-4	0	0	0	.958	2	/1-4,3-1	-0.2
1941	Cle-A	77	244	28	58	9	3	4	24	39	47	.238	.345	.348	88	-4	4	0	1	.995	-5	1-62,2-13/3	-1.1
1942	Cle-A	51	84	10	15	2	0	0	2	13	17	.179	.289	.202	42	-6	3	2	-0	.944	-3	2-24/3-8,1S	-0.9
Total	9	602	1832	235	469	73	24	18	200	297	303	.256	.363	.352	98	1	30	12	2	.940	-39	3-257,2-135,1/S	-2.7
Team	5	262	715	94	173	31	9	8	84	110	130	.242	.345	.344	84	-15	15	5	2	.992	-19	1-111/2-87,S3	-3.3
■ HARVEY GRUBB	Grubb, Harvey Harrison b: 9/18/1890, Lexington, N.C. d: 1/25/70, Corpus Christi, Tex. BR/TR, 6', 165 lbs. Deb: 9/27/12																						
1912	Cle-A	1	0	0	0	0	0	0	0	0		—	1.000	—	187	0	0			1.000	0	/3-1	0.0
■ JOHNNY GRUBB	Grubb, John Maywood b: 8/4/48, Richmond, Va. BL/TR, 6'3", 188 lbs. Deb: 9/10/72																						
1977	Cle-A	34	93	8	28	3	3	2	14	19	18	.301	.425	.462	146	7	0	3	-2	1.000	-0	O-28/D-4	0.4
1978	Cle-A	113	378	54	100	16	6	14	61	59	60	.265	.367	.450	130	16	5	1	1	.973	5	*O-110	1.8
Total	16	1424	4154	553	1153	207	29	99	475	566	558	.278	.369	.413	121	130	27	33		.981	-31	*O-1042,D-185/13	4.7
Team	2	147	471	62	128	19	9	16	75	78	78	.272	.379	.452	133	23	5	4		.978	5	O-138/D-4	2.2
■ LOU GUISTO	Guisto, Louis Joseph b: 1/16/1895, Napa, Cal. d: 10/15/89, Napa, Cal. BR/TR, 5'11", 193 lbs. Deb: 9/10/16																						
1916	Cle-A	6	19	2	3	0	0	0	2	4	3	.158	.304	.158	37	-1	1			1.000	0	/1-6	-0.2
1917	Cle-A	73	200	9	37	4	2	0	29	25	18	.185	.282	.225	51	-11	3			.989	-1	1-59	-1.6
1921	Cle-A	2	2	0	1	0	0	0	1	0	1	.500	.500	.500	153	0	0	0	0	1.000	0	/1-1	0.0
1922	Cle-A	35	84	7	21	10	1	0	9	2	7	.250	.276	.393	72	-4	0	0	0	.995	1	1-24	-0.4
1923	Cle-A	40	144	17	26	5	0	0	18	15	15	.181	.262	.215	27	-15	1	1	-0	.988	1	1-40	-1.6
Total	5	156	449	35	88	19	3	0	59	46	44	.196	.277	.252	47	-31	5	1		.990	1	1-130	-3.8
■ TOM GULLEY	Gulley, Thomas Jefferson b: 12/25/1899, Garner, N.C. d: 11/24/66, St.Charles, Ark. BL/TR, 5'11", 178 lbs. Deb: 8/24/23																						
1923	Cle-A	2	3	1	1	1	0	0	0	0	0	.333	.333	.667	159	0	0	0	0	1.000	-0	/O-1	0.0
1924	Cle-A	8	20	4	3	0	1	0	1	3	2	.150	.261	.250	32	-2	0	0	0	.933	0	/O-5	-0.2
Total	3	26	58	10	12	4	2	0	9	8	4	.207	.303	.345	69	-3	0	0	0	.971	-2	/O-18	-0.5
Team	2	10	23	5	4	1	1	0	1	3	2	.174	.269	.304	48	-2	0	0	0	.938	-0	/O-6	-0.2
■ ODELL HALE	Hale, Arvel Odell "Bad News" b: 8/10/08, Hosston, La. d: 6/9/80, ElDorado, Ark. BR/TR, 5'10", 175 lbs. Deb: 8/1/31																						
1931	Cle-A	25	92	14	26	2	4	1	5	8	8	.283	.340	.424	94	-1	2	0	1	.918	-4	3-15,2-10/S	-0.3
1933	Cle-A	98	351	49	97	19	8	10	64	30	37	.276	.333	.462	104	0	2	3	-1	.954	3	2-73,3-21	0.8
1934	Cle-A	143	563	82	170	44	6	13	101	48	50	.302	.357	.471	110	7	8	12	-5	.956	**26**	*2-137/3-5	3.3
1935	Cle-A	150	589	80	179	37	11	16	101	52	55	.304	.361	.486	115	11	15	13	-3	.938	7	*3-149/2-1	1.9
1936	Cle-A	153	620	126	196	50	13	14	87	64	43	.316	.380	.506	116	14	8	5	-1	.946	17	*3-148/2-3	3.1
1937	Cle-A	154	561	74	150	32	4	6	82	56	41	.267	.335	.371	77	-20	9	6	-1	.964	26	3-90,2-64	1.1
1938	Cle-A	130	496	69	138	32	2	8	69	44	39	.278	.338	.399	86	-12	8	1	2	.963	-13	*2-127	-1.4
1939	Cle-A	108	253	36	79	16	2	4	48	25	18	.312	.374	.439	111	4	4	5	-2	.966	-16	2-73/3-2	-0.9

YEAR TM/L	G	AB	R	H	2B	3B	HR	RBI	BB	SO	AVG	OBP	SLG	PRO+	BR/A	SB	CS	SBR	FA	FR	G/POS	TPR
1940 Cle-A	48	50	3	11	3	1	0	6	5	7	.220	.291	.320	60	-3	0	0	0	.700	-1	/3-3	-0.4
Total 10	1062	3701	551	1071	240	51	73	573	353	315	.289	.352	.441	100	-6	57	45	-10	.959	42	2-518,3-439/S	6.5
Team 9	1009	3575	533	1046	235	51	72	563	332	298	.293	.353	.447	102	1	56	45	-10	.959	44	2-488,3-433/S	7.2
■ BOB HALE Hale, Robert Houston b: 11/7/33, Sarasota, Fla. BL/TL, 5'10", 195 lbs. Deb: 7/4/55																						
1960 Cle-A	70	70	2	21	7	0	0	12	3	6	.300	.329	.400	99	-0	0	0	0	.944	0	/1-5	0.0
1961 Cle-A	42	36	0	6	0	0	0	6	1	7	.167	.211	.167	2	-5	0	0	0	.000	0	H	-0.5
Total 7	376	626	41	171	29	2	2	89	26	51	.273	.305	.335	76	-22	0	4	-2	.977	2	1-120	-2.9
Team 2	112	106	2	27	7	0	0	18	4	13	.255	.288	.321	66	-5	0	0	0	.944	0	/1-5	-0.5
■ JIMMIE HALL Hall, Jimmie Randolph b: 3/17/38, Mt.Holly, N.C. BL/TR, 6', 175 lbs. Deb: 4/9/63																						
1968 Cle-A	53	111	4	22	4	0	1	8	10	19	.198	.264	.261	61	-5	1	0	0	.983	2	O-29	-0.5
1969 Cle-A	4	10	1	0	0	0	0	0	2	3	.000	.167	.000	-48	-2	1	0	0	1.000	-0	/O-3	-0.2
Total 8	963	2848	387	724	100	24	121	391	287	529	.254	.323	.434	112	40	38	18	1	.982	-17	O-806/1-7	-1.5
Team 2	57	121	5	22	4	0	1	8	12	22	.182	.256	.240	50	-7	2	0	1	.984	1	/O-32	-0.7
■ MEL HALL Hall, Melvin b: 9/16/60, Lyons, N.Y. BL/TL, 6'1", 205 lbs. Deb: 9/3/81																						
1984 Cle-A	83	257	43	66	13	1	7	30	35	55	.257	.350	.397	104	2	1	1	-0	.993	0	O-69/D-9	0.0
1985 Cle-A	23	66	7	21	6	0	0	12	8	12	.318	.392	.409	121	2	0	1	-1	1.000	-3	O-15/D-5	-0.2
1986 Cle-A	140	442	68	131	29	2	18	77	33	65	.296	.348	.493	128	16	6	2	1	.972	-7	*O-126/D-7	0.6
1987 Cle-A	142	485	57	136	21	1	18	76	20	68	.280	.310	.439	95	-5	5	4	-1	.989	6	*O-122,D-14	-0.4
1988 Cle-A	150	515	69	144	32	4	6	71	28	50	.280	.317	.392	95	-4	7	3	0	.967	-3	*O-141/D-6	-1.1
Total 12	1251	4212	565	1168	229	25	134	615	266	571	.277	.323	.439	107	31	31	22	-4	.981	-12	*O-1037,D-150	-1.7
Team 5	538	1765	244	498	101	8	49	266	124	250	.282	.331	.432	106	12	19	11	-1	.979	-7	O-473/D-41	-1.1
■ RUSS HALL Hall, Robert Russell b: 9/29/1871, Shelbyville, Ky. d: 7/1/37, Los Angeles, Cal. TL, 5'10", 170 lbs. Deb: 4/15/1898																						
1901 Cle-A	1	4	2	2	0	0	0	0	0		.500	.500	.500	185	0	0			.500	-1	/S-1	-0.1
Total 2	40	147	15	37	2	1	0	10	7		.252	.290	.279	62	-7	1			.824	-16	/S-36,3-3,O	-2.1
■ BILL HALLMAN Hallman, William Wilson b: 3/31/1867, Pittsburgh, Pa. d: 9/11/20, Philadelphia, Pa. BR/TR, 5'8", 160 lbs. Deb: 4/23/1888 M																						
1901 Cle-A	5	19	2	4	0	0	0	3	2		.211	.286	.211	41	-1	0			.815	-3	/S-5	-0.4
Total 14	1503	6012	937	1634	234	81	21	769	425		.272	.325	.348	84	-136	200			.940	-88	*2-1135,3-145,S/OC1P	-14.9
■ AL HALT Halt, Alva William b: 11/23/1890, Sandusky, Ohio d: 1/22/73, Sandusky, Ohio BR/TR, 6', 180 lbs. Deb: 5/29/14																						
1918 Cle-A	26	69	9	12	2	0	0	1	9	12	.174	.269	.203	39	-5	4			.971	-1	3-14/2-4,S1	-0.6
Total 3	257	854	76	204	30	9	6	90	61	130	.239	.293	.316	63	-47	35			.933	-9	3-125,S-115/210	-4.5
■ JACK HAMMOND Hammond, Walter Charles "Wobby" b: 2/26/1891, Amsterdam, N.Y. d: 3/4/42, Kenosha, Wis. BR/TR, 5'11", 170 lbs. Deb: 4/15/15																						
1915 Cle-A	35	84	9	18	2	1	0	4	1	19	.214	.224	.262	44	-6	0	1	-1	.957	-8	2-19	-1.6
1922 Cle-A	1	4	1	1	0	0	0	0	0	0	.250	.250	.250	30	-0	0	0	0	.333	-2	/2-1	-0.2
Total 2	45	99	13	22	2	1	0	4	2	19	.222	.238	.263	45	-7	0	1	-1	.943	-8	/2-24	-1.7
Team 2	36	88	10	19	2	1	0	4	1	19	.216	.225	.261	44	-7	0	1	-1	.931	-9	/2-20	-1.8
■ GRANNY HAMNER Hamner, Granville Wilbur b: 4/26/27, Richmond, Va. d: 9/12/93, Philadelphia, Pa. BR/TR, 5'10", 163 lbs. Deb: 9/14/44 F																						
1959 Cle-A	27	67	4	11	1	1	1	3	1	8	.164	.176	.254	17	-8	0	0	0	.960	-2	S-10/2-7,3	-0.9
Total 17	1531	5839	711	1529	272	62	104	708	351	432	.262	.304	.383	84	-149	35	14	2	.946	-139	S-934,2-568/3P	-18.8
■ DOUG HANSEN Hansen, Douglas William b: 12/16/28, Los Angeles, Cal. BR/TR, 6', 180 lbs. Deb: 9/4/51																						
1951 Cle-A	3	0	2	0	0	0	0	0	0	0	—	—	—	—	0	0	0	0	.000	0	R	0.0
■ CARROLL HARDY Hardy, Carroll William b: 5/18/33, Sturgis, S.Dak. BR/TR, 6', 185 lbs. Deb: 4/15/58																						
1958 Cle-A	27	49	10	10	3	0	1	6	6	14	.204	.304	.327	75	-2	1	2	-1	1.000	1	O-17	-0.3
1959 Cle-A	32	53	12	11	1	0	0	2	3	7	.208	.250	.226	33	-5	1	1	-0	1.000	1	O-15	-0.5
1960 Cle-A	29	18	7	2	1	0	0	1	2	2	.111	.200	.167	0	-3	0	0	0	1.000	-4	O-17	-0.7
Total 8	433	1117	172	251	47	10	17	113	120	222	.225	.304	.330	72	-45	13	14	-5	.981	-5	O-344	-7.1
Team 3	88	120	29	23	5	0	1	9	11	23	.192	.265	.258	46	-9	2	3	-1	1.000	-3	/O-49	-1.5
■ JACK HARDY Hardy, John Doolittle b: 6/23/1877, Cleveland, Ohio d: 10/20/21, Cleveland, Ohio BR/TR, 6', 185 lbs. Deb: 8/29/03																						
1903 Cle-A	5	19	1	3	1	0	0	1	1		.158	.200	.211	24	-2	1			1.000	-1	/O-5	-0.3
Total 4	23	55	5	10	1	0	0	5	2		.182	.211	.200	28	-5	1			.953	-2	/C-14,O-6,2	-0.7
■ MIKE HARGROVE Hargrove, Dudley Michael b: 10/26/49, Perryton, Tex. BL/TL, 6', 195 lbs. Deb: 4/7/74 MC																						
1979 Cle-A	100	338	60	110	21	4	10	56	63	40	.325	.438	.500	152	28	2	3	-1	.993	0	O-65,1-28/D	2.2
1980 Cle-A	160	589	86	179	22	2	11	85	111	36	.304	.421	.404	127	28	4	2	0	.993	-5	*1-160	1.3
1981 Cle-A	94	322	43	102	21	0	2	49	60	16	.317	**.432**	.401	143	22	5	4	-1	.989	6	1-88/D-4	2.3
1982 Cle-A	160	591	67	160	26	1	4	65	101	58	.271	.380	.338	100	5	2	2	-1	.996	11	*1-153/D-5	0.7
1983 Cle-A	134	469	57	134	21	4	3	57	78	40	.286	.393	.367	107	8	0	6	-4	.994	12	*1-131/D-1	0.9
1984 Cle-A	133	352	44	94	14	2	2	44	53	38	.267	.363	.335	93	-1	0	2	-1	.991	6	*1-124	-0.3
1985 Cle-A	107	284	31	81	14	1	1	27	39	29	.285	.372	.352	100	2	1	0	0	.991	5	1-85	0.2
Total 12	1666	5564	783	1614	266	28	80	686	965	550	.290	.400	.391	121	205	24	37		.991	52	*1-1378,O-167/D	15.7
Team 7	888	2945	388	860	139	14	33	383	505	257	.292	.400	.382	116	91	14	19		.993	34	1-769/O-65,D	7.3
■ TOMMY HARPER Harper, Tommy b: 10/14/40, Oak Grove, La. BR/TR, 5'10", 168 lbs. Deb: 4/9/62 C																						
1968 Cle-A	130	235	26	51	15	2	6	26	26	56	.217	.298	.374	104	1	11	7	-1	.984	-16	*O-115/2-2	-2.3
Total 15	1810	6269	972	1609	256	36	146	567	753	1080	.257	.340	.379	100	15	408	116	53	.986	-47	*O-1227,3-270,D/21	-4.0
■ TOBY HARRAH Harrah, Colbert Dale b: 10/26/48, Sissonville, W.Va. BR/TR, 6', 180 lbs. Deb: 9/5/69 MC																						
1979 Cle-A	149	527	99	147	25	1	20	77	89	60	.279	.391	.444	124	21	20	9	1	.940	-48	*3-127,S-33/D	-2.5
1980 Cle-A	160	561	100	150	22	4	11	72	98	60	.267	.383	.380	109	11	17	2	4	.971	2	*3-156/S-2,D	1.5
1981 Cle-A	103	361	64	105	12	4	5	44	57	44	.291	.389	.388	126	15	12	1	3	.949	-12	*3-101/S-3,D	0.4
1982 Cle-A☆	162	602	100	183	29	4	25	78	84	52	.304	.400	.490	144	39	17	3	3	.971	-19	*3-159/2-3,S	1.9
1983 Cle-A	138	526	81	140	23	1	9	53	75	49	.266	.365	.365	98	1	16	10	-1	**.971**	-11	*3-137/2-1,D	-1.3
Total 17	2155	7402	1115	1954	307	40	195	918	1153	868	.264	.368	.395	114	171	238	94	15	.963	-166	*3-1099,S-813,2/DO	11.3
Team 5	712	2577	444	725	111	14	70	324	403	265	.281	.386	.417	120	87	82	25	10	.963	-87	3-680/S-40,D2	0.0
■ BILLY HARRELL Harrell, William b: 7/18/28, Norristown, Pa. BR/TR, 6'1.5", 180 lbs. Deb: 9/2/55																						
1955 Cle-A	13	19	2	8	0	0	0	1	3	3	.421	.500	.421	144	1	1	0	0	.926	-0	S-11	0.2
1957 Cle-A	22	57	6	15	1	1	1	5	4	7	.263	.311	.368	86	-1	3	1	0	.893	-4	S-14/3-6,2	-0.4
1958 Cle-A	101	229	36	50	4	0	7	19	15	36	.218	.272	.328	66	-11	12	2	2	.986	-7	3-46,S-45/2O	-1.2
Total 4	173	342	54	79	7	1	8	26	23	54	.231	.283	.327	68	-16	17	3	3	.933	-5	/S-77,3-62,2lO	-1.2
Team 3	136	305	44	73	5	1	8	25	22	46	.239	.295	.341	75	-11	16	3	3	.937	-11	/S-70,3-52,2O	-1.4
■ KEN HARRELSON Harrelson, Kenneth Smith "Hawk" b: 9/4/41, Woodruff, S.C. BR/TR, 6'2", 190 lbs. Deb: 6/9/63																						
1969 Cle-A	149	519	83	115	13	4	27	84	95	96	.222	.344	.418	109	7	17	8	0	.985	5	*O-144,1-16	0.3
1970 Cle-A	17	39	3	11	1	0	1	1	6	4	.282	.378	.385	106	0	0	0	0	1.000	1	1-13	0.0

YEAR	TM/L	G	AB	R	H	2B	3B	HR	RBI	BB	SO	AVG	OBP	SLG	PRO+	BR/A	SB	CS	SBR	FA	FR	G/POS	TPR
1971	Cle-A	52	161	20	32	2	0	5	14	24	21	.199	.303	.304	66	-7	1	0	0	.988	-1	1-40/O-7	-1.3
Total	9	900	2941	374	703	94	14	131	421	382	577	.239	.328	.414	109	35	53	30	-2	.990	2	1-469,O-365	-1.3
Team	3	218	719	106	158	16	4	33	99	125	121	.220	.337	.391	99	0	18	8	1	.986	4	O-151/1-69	-1.0
■ **BILLY HARRIS** Harris, James William b: 11/24/43, Hamlet, N.C. BL/TR, 6', 175 lbs. Deb: 6/16/68																							
1968	Cle-A	38	94	10	20	5	1	0	3	8	22	.213	.275	.287	71	-3	2	0	1	.970	-1	2-27,3-10/S	-0.3
Total	2	43	101	11	22	6	1	0	3	8	23	.218	.275	.297	73	-3	2	0	1	.971	-1	/2-28,3-10,S	-0.3
■ **JOE HARRIS** Harris, Joseph "Moon" b: 5/20/1891, Coulters, Pa. d: 12/10/59, Renton, Pa. BR/TR, 5'9", 170 lbs. Deb: 6/9/14																							
1917	Cle-A	112	369	40	112	22	4	0	65	55	32	.304	.398	.385	129	15	11			.985	10	1-95/O-5,3	2.3
1919	Cle-A	62	184	30	69	16	1	1	46	33	21	.375	.472	.489	160	17	2			.988	2	1-46/S-4	1.8
Total	10	970	3035	461	963	201	64	47	517	413	188	.317	.404	.472	131	140	36			.989	20	1-522,O-319/S3	10.8
Team	2	174	553	70	181	38	5	1	111	88	53	.327	.423	.420	140	31	13			.986	12	1-141/O-5,S3	4.1
■ **JACK HARSHMAN** Harshman, John Elvin b: 7/12/27, San Diego, Cal. BL/TL, 6'2", 185 lbs. Deb: 9/16/48																							
1959	Cle-A	21	34	3	7	1	0	0	5	5	4	.206	.308	.235	53	-2	0	0	0	1.000	-0	P-13	0.0
1960	Cle-A	15	17	0	3	1	0	0	1	0	4	.176	.176	.235	11	-2	0	0	0	1.000	-1	P-15	0.0
Total	10	258	424	46	76	7	0	21	65	72	119	.179	.298	.344	74	-16	0	0		.962	-5	P-217/1-13,O	-0.3
Team	2	36	51	3	10	2	0	0	6	5	8	.196	.268	.235	40	-4	0	0		1.000	-1	/P-28	0.0
■ **BRUCE HARTFORD** Hartford, Bruce Daniel b: 5/14/1892, Chicago, Ill. d: 5/25/75, Los Angeles, Cal. BR/TR, 6'0.5", 190 lbs. Deb: 6/3/14																							
1914	Cle-A	8	22	5	4	1	0	0	0	4	9	.182	.308	.227	59	-1	0			.913	-3	/S-8	-0.4
■ **GROVER HARTLEY** Hartley, Grover Allen "Slick" b: 7/2/1888, Osgood, Ind. d: 10/19/64, Daytona Beach, Fla BR/TR, 5'11", 175 lbs. Deb: 5/13/11 C																							
1929	Cle-A	24	33	2	9	0	1	0	8	2	1	.273	.314	.333	64	-2	0	0	0	1.000	-3	C-13	-0.4
1930	Cle-A	1	4	0	3	0	0	0	1	0	0	.750	.750	.750	271	1	0	0	0	.750	-0	/C-1	0.1
Total	14	569	1319	135	353	60	11	3	144	127	97	.268	.339	.337	81	-33	29	0		.968	-19	C-435/1-19,23OS	-2.5
Team	2	25	37	2	12	0	1	0	9	2	1	.324	.359	.378	87	-1	0	0		.950	-3	/C-14	-0.3
■ **LUTHER HARVEL** Harvel, Luther Raymond "Red" b: 9/30/05, Cambria, Ill. d: 4/10/86, Kansas City, Mo. BR/TR, 5'11", 180 lbs. Deb: 7/31/28																							
1928	Cle-A	40	136	12	30	6	1	0	12	4	17	.221	.264	.279	42	-11	1	1	-0	.948	-2	O-39	-1.5
■ **ERWIN HARVEY** Harvey, Ervin King "Zaza" b: 1/5/1879, Saratoga, Cal. d: 6/3/54, Santa Monica, Cal. BL/TL, 6', 190 lbs. Deb: 5/3/00																							
1901	Cle-A	45	170	21	60	5	5	1	24	9		.353	.392	.459	141	9	15			.890	2	O-45	0.7
1902	Cle-A	12	46	5	16	2	0	0	5	3		.348	.388	.391	121	1	1			1.000	0	O-12	0.1
Total	3	76	259	37	86	10	6	1	32	14		.332	.373	.429	127	9	17			.907	4	/O-57,P-17	0.8
Team	2	57	216	26	76	7	5	1	29	12		.352	.391	.444	137	11	16			.907	2	/O-57	0.8
■ **RON HASSEY** Hassey, Ronald William b: 2/27/53, Tucson, Ariz. BL/TR, 6'2", 200 lbs. Deb: 4/23/78 C																							
1978	Cle-A	25	74	5	15	0	0	2	9	5	7	.203	.262	.284	54	-5	2	0	1	.993	5	C-24	0.2
1979	Cle-A	75	223	20	64	14	0	4	32	19	19	.287	.343	.404	100	0	1	0	0	.992	6	C-68/1-2,D	0.9
1980	Cle-A	130	390	43	124	18	4	8	65	49	51	.318	.395	.446	130	17	0	2	-1	.993	-7	*C-113/1-3,D	1.3
1981	Cle-A	61	190	8	44	4	0	1	25	17	11	.232	.301	.268	66	-8	0	1	-1	.991	8	C-56/1-5,D	0.2
1982	Cle-A	113	323	33	81	18	0	5	34	53	32	.251	.358	.353	97	0	3	2	-0	.993	8	*C-105/1-2,D	1.2
1983	Cle-A	117	341	48	92	21	0	6	42	38	35	.270	.346	.384	97	-1	2	2	-1	.995	-3	*C-113/D-1	0.0
1984	Cle-A	48	149	11	38	5	1	0	19	15	26	.255	.323	.302	73	-5	1	0	0	1.000	-1	C-44/1-1,D	-0.4
Total	14	1192	3440	348	914	172	7	71	438	385	378	.266	.343	.382	100	7	14	10	-2	.993	9	C-946/D-96,1	5.2
Team	7	569	1690	168	458	80	5	26	226	196	181	.271	.349	.370	98	-1	9	7	-2	.994	17	C-523/D-13,1	3.4
■ **FRED HATFIELD** Hatfield, Fred James b: 3/18/25, Lanett, Ala. BL/TR, 6'1", 171 lbs. Deb: 8/31/50 C																							
1958	Cle-A	3	8	0	1	0	0	0	1	1	1	.125	.222	.125	-2	-1	0	0	0	1.000	1	/3-2	0.0
Total	9	722	2039	259	493	67	10	25	165	248	247	.242	.334	.321	78	-57	15	14	-4	.962	43	3-408,2-179/S	-0.8
■ **ARTHUR HAUGER** Hauger, John Arthur b: 11/18/1893, Delhi, Ohio d: 8/2/44, Redwood City, Cal BL/TR, 5'11", 168 lbs. Deb: 7/17/12																							
1912	Cle-A	15	18	0	1	0	0	0	0	1		.056	.105	.056	-52	-4	0			1.000	-2	/O-5	-0.5
■ **JOE HAUSER** Hauser, Joseph John "Unser Choe" b: 1/12/1899, Milwaukee, Wis. BL/TL, 5'10.5", 175 lbs. Deb: 4/18/22																							
1929	Cle-A	37	48	8	12	1	1	3	9	4	8	.250	.321	.500	104	0	0	0	0	.986	1	/1-8	0.0
Total	6	629	2044	351	580	103	28	80	356	250	229	.284	.368	.479	117	46	19	19		.990	-14	1-547	-0.6
■ **HOWIE HAWORTH** Haworth, Homer Howard "Cully" b: 8/27/1893, Newberg, Ore. d: 1/28/53, Troutdale, Ore. BL/TR, 5'10.5", 165 lbs. Deb: 8/14/15																							
1915	Cle-A	7	7	0	1	0	0	0	1	2	2	.143	.333	.143	42	-0	0			.917	-1	/C-5	-0.1
■ **FRANKIE HAYES** Hayes, Frank Witman "Blimp" b: 10/13/14, Jamesburg, N.J. d: 6/22/55, Point Pleasant, N.J. BR/TR, 6', 185 lbs. Deb: 9/21/33																							
1945	Cle-A†	119	385	39	91	15	6	6	43	53	52	.236	.335	.353	104	2	1	1	-0	.988	2	*C-119	1.2
1946	Cle-A★	51	156	11	40	12	0	3	18	21	26	.256	.345	.391	112	3	1	3	-2	.981	-1	C-50	0.3
Total	14	1364	4493	545	1164	213	32	119	628	564	627	.259	.343	.400	100	1	30	20		.977	-106	*C-1311/1-4	-2.6
Team	2	170	541	50	131	27	6	9	61	74	78	.242	.338	.364	107	5	2	4		.986	1	C-169	1.5
■ **VON HAYES** Hayes, Von Francis b: 8/31/58, Stockton, Cal. BL/TR, 6'5", 185 lbs. Deb: 4/14/81																							
1981	Cle-A	43	109	21	28	8	2	1	17	14	10	.257	.352	.394	116	3	8	1	2	.939	1	D-21,O-13/3	0.4
1982	Cle-A	150	527	65	132	25	3	14	82	42	63	.250	.311	.389	91	-7	32	13	2	.981	6	*O-139/3-5,1	-0.3
Total	12	1495	5249	767	1402	282	36	143	696	712	804	.267	.357	.416	113	101	253	97	18	.983	-20	*O-1040,1-401/D3	4.3
Team	2	193	636	86	160	33	5	15	99	56	73	.252	.318	.390	95	-4	40	14	4	.977	7	O-152/D-21,31	0.1
■ **JEFF HEATH** Heath, John Geoffrey b: 4/1/15, Ft.William, Ont., Canada d: 12/9/75, Seattle, Wash. BL/TR, 5'11.5", 200 lbs. Deb: 9/13/36																							
1936	Cle-A	12	41	6	14	3	3	1	8	3	4	.341	.386	.634	147	3	1	0	0	1.000	-3	O-12	0.0
1937	Cle-A	20	61	8	14	1	4	0	8	0	9	.230	.230	.377	50	-5	0	1	-1	1.000	-1	O-14	-0.6
1938	Cle-A	126	502	104	172	31	**18**	21	112	33	55	.343	.383	.602	146	32	3	1	0	.974	1	*O-122	2.6
1939	Cle-A	121	431	64	126	31	7	14	69	41	64	.292	.354	.494	119	10	8	4	0	.964	6	*O-108	1.1
1940	Cle-A	100	356	55	78	16	3	14	50	40	62	.219	.298	.399	81	-11	5	3	-0	.971	2	O-90	-1.4
1941	Cle-A★	151	585	89	199	32	**20**	24	123	50	69	.340	.396	.586	165	51	18	12	-2	.949	-4	*O-151	3.4
1942	Cle-A	147	568	82	158	37	13	10	76	62	66	.278	.350	.442	130	20	9	9	-3	.980	2	*O-146	1.2
1943	Cle-A★	118	424	58	116	22	6	18	79	63	58	.274	.369	.481	157	30	5	8	-3	.968	-4	*O-111	1.8
1944	Cle-A†	60	151	20	50	5	2	5	33	18	12	.331	.402	.490	160	12	0	1	-1	.952	-1	O-37	0.9
1945	Cle-A	102	370	60	113	16	7	15	61	56	39	.305	.398	.508	169	33	3	1	0	.973	-4	*O-101	2.5
Total	14	1383	4937	777	1447	279	102	194	887	593	670	.293	.370	.509	140	262	56	47	-11	.972	-20	*O-1299	16.4
Team	10	957	3489	546	1040	194	83	122	619	366	438	.298	.366	.506	139	173	52	40	-8	.968	-5	O-892	11.5
■ **JIM HEGAN** Hegan, James Edward b: 8/3/20, Lynn, Mass. d: 6/17/84, Swampscott, Mass. BR/TR, 6'2", 195 lbs. Deb: 9/9/41 FC																							
1941	Cle-A	16	47	4	15	2	0	1	5	4	7	.319	.373	.426	116	1	0	0	0	.973	-0	C-16	0.2
1942	Cle-A	68	170	10	33	5	0	0	11	11	31	.194	.243	.224	34	-15	1	3	-2	.977	8	C-66	-0.5
1946	Cle-A	88	271	29	64	11	5	0	17	17	44	.236	.284	.314	71	-11	1	4	-2	.991	9	C-87	0.0
1947	Cle-A☆	135	378	38	94	14	5	4	42	41	49	.249	.324	.344	88	-6	3	1	0	.989	7	*C-133	0.9
1948	*Cle-A	144	472	60	117	21	6	14	61	48	74	.248	.317	.407	94	-7	6	3	0	.990	21	*C-142	2.3
1949	Cle-A☆	152	468	54	105	19	5	8	55	49	89	.224	.298	.338	69	-23	1	0	0	.990	10	*C-152	-0.3

YEAR	TM/L	G	AB	R	H	2B	3B	HR	RBI	BB	SO	AVG	OBP	SLG	PRO+	BR/A	SB	CS	SBR	FA	FR	G/POS	TPR
1950	Cle-A★	131	415	53	91	16	5	14	58	42	52	.219	.291	.383	74	-19	1	0	0	.993	24	*C-129	1.0
1951	Cle-A★	133	416	60	99	17	5	6	43	38	72	.238	.302	.346	79	-13	0	3	-2	.991	11	*C-129	0.1
1952	Cle-A☆	112	333	39	75	17	2	4	41	29	47	.225	.287	.324	75	-13	0	2	-1	.987	7	*C-107	-0.2
1953	Cle-A	112	299	37	65	10	1	9	37	25	41	.217	.280	.348	71	-13	1	2	-1	.976	3	*C-106	-0.7
1954	*Cle-A	139	423	56	99	12	7	11	40	34	48	.234	.291	.374	80	-13	0	1	-1	**.994**	13	*C-137	0.5
1955	Cle-A	116	304	30	67	5	2	9	40	34	33	.220	.299	.339	69	-14	0	1	-1	**.997**	7	*C-111	-0.4
1956	Cle-A	122	315	42	70	15	2	6	34	49	54	.222	.327	.340	75	-11	1	1	-0	.985	16	*C-118	0.8
1957	Cle-A	58	148	14	32	7	0	4	15	16	23	.216	.293	.345	74	-5	0	1	-1	1.000	3	C-58	-0.2
Total	17	1666	4772	550	1087	187	46	92	525	456	742	.228	.296	.344	74	-191	15	24	-10	.990	149	*C-1629	2.4
Team	14	1526	4459	526	1026	171	45	90	499	437	664	.230	.299	.349	76	-164	15	22	-9	.990	137	*C-1491	3.5

■ JACK HEIDEMANN

Heidemann, Jack Seale b: 7/11/49, Brenham, Tex. BR/TR, 6', 178 lbs. Deb: 5/2/69

YEAR	TM/L	G	AB	R	H	2B	3B	HR	RBI	BB	SO	AVG	OBP	SLG	PRO+	BR/A	SB	CS	SBR	FA	FR	G/POS	TPR
1969	Cle-A	3	3	0	0	0	0	0	0	0	2	.000	.250	.000	-24	-0	0	0	0	1.000	1	/S-3	0.0
1970	Cle-A	133	445	44	94	14	2	6	37	34	88	.211	.270	.292	52	-29	2	4	-2	.961	-2	*S-132	-1.9
1971	Cle-A	81	240	16	50	7	0	0	9	12	46	.208	.252	.237	36	-20	1	3	-2	.977	-9	S-81	-2.4
1972	Cle-A	10	20	0	3	0	0	0	0	2	3	.150	.261	.150	24	-2	0	0	0	.964	-1	S-10	-0.3
1974	Cle-A	12	11	2	1	0	0	0	0	0	2	.091	.091	.091	-48	-2	0	0	0	1.000	-1	/3-6,S-4,12	-0.3
Total	8	426	1093	94	231	27	4	9	75	78	203	.211	.268	.268	49	-73	5	10	-5	.965	-42	S-322/3-51,2D1	-9.3
Team	5	239	719	62	148	21	2	6	46	48	141	.206	.261	.266	45	-53	3	7	-3	.967	-13	S-230/3-6,21	-4.9

■ WOODIE HELD

Held, Woodson George b: 3/25/32, Sacramento, Cal. BR/TR, 5'11", 180 lbs. Deb: 9/5/54

YEAR	TM/L	G	AB	R	H	2B	3B	HR	RBI	BB	SO	AVG	OBP	SLG	PRO+	BR/A	SB	CS	SBR	FA	FR	G/POS	TPR
1958	Cle-A	67	144	12	28	4	1	3	17	15	36	.194	.288	.299	63	-7	1	2	-1	.966	-0	O-43,S-14/3	-0.9
1959	Cle-A	143	525	82	132	19	3	29	71	46	118	.251	.314	.465	115	8	1	2	-1	.962	-9	*S-103,3-40/O2	0.7
1960	Cle-A	109	376	45	97	15	1	21	67	44	73	.258	.344	.471	122	11	0	1	-1	.967	9	*S-109	2.7
1961	Cle-A	146	509	67	136	23	5	23	78	69	111	.267	.358	.468	122	16	0	0	0	.960	-14	*S-144	1.4
1962	Cle-A	139	466	55	116	12	2	19	58	73	107	.249	.364	.406	110	8	5	1	1	.956	-14	*S-133/3-5,O	0.7
1963	Cle-A	133	416	61	103	19	4	17	61	61	96	.248	.355	.435	121	13	2	2	-1	.982	-3	2-96,O-35/S3	1.7
1964	Cle-A	118	364	50	86	13	0	18	49	43	88	.236	.329	.420	107	4	1	0	0	.966	0	2-52,O-41,3	0.6
Total	14	1390	4019	524	963	150	22	179	559	508	944	.240	.333	.421	109	48	14	11	-2	.960	-56	S-539,O-448,23	2.2
Team	7	855	2800	372	698	105	16	130	401	351	629	.249	.341	.438	114	53	10	8	-2	.960	-31	S-508,2-151,O/3	6.9

■ HANK HELF

Helf, Henry Hartz b: 8/26/13, Austin, Tex. d: 10/27/84, Austin, Tex. BR/TR, 6'1", 196 lbs. Deb: 5/5/38

YEAR	TM/L	G	AB	R	H	2B	3B	HR	RBI	BB	SO	AVG	OBP	SLG	PRO+	BR/A	SB	CS	SBR	FA	FR	G/POS	TPR
1938	Cle-A	6	13	1	1	0	0	0	1	1	1	.077	.143	.077	-44	-3	0	0	0	.947	0	/C-5	-0.2
1940	Cle-A	1	1	0	0	0	0	0	0	0	0	.000	.000	.000	-99	-0	0	0	0	1.000	-0	/C-1	0.0
Total	3	78	196	18	36	11	0	6	22	10	41	.184	.227	.332	51	-14	0	1	-1	.964	12	/C-75	0.2
Team	2	7	14	1	1	0	0	0	1	1	1	.071	.133	.071	-48	-3	0	0	0	.950	0	/C-6	-0.2

■ CHARLIE HEMPHILL

Hemphill, Charles Judson "Eagle Eye" b: 4/20/1876, Greenville, Mich. d: 6/22/53, Detroit, Mich. BL/TL, 5'9", 160 lbs. Deb: 6/27/1899 F

YEAR	TM/L	G	AB	R	H	2B	3B	HR	RBI	BB	SO	AVG	OBP	SLG	PRO+	BR/A	SB	CS	SBR	FA	FR	G/POS	TPR
1902	Cle-A	25	94	14	25	2	0	0	11	5		.266	.303	.287	67	-4	4			.860	-1	O-19	-0.6
Total	11	1242	4541	580	1230	117	68	22	421	435		.271	.337	.341	106	37	207			.944	-29	*O-1175/2-3	-5.2

■ ROLLIE HEMSLEY

Hemsley, Ralston Burdett b: 6/24/07, Syracuse, Ohio d: 7/31/72, Washington, D.C. BR/TR, 5'10", 170 lbs. Deb: 4/13/28 C

YEAR	TM/L	G	AB	R	H	2B	3B	HR	RBI	BB	SO	AVG	OBP	SLG	PRO+	BR/A	SB	CS	SBR	FA	FR	G/POS	TPR
1938	Cle-A	66	203	27	60	11	3	2	28	23	14	.296	.367	.409	96	-1	1	1	-0	.980	15	C-58	1.4
1939	Cle-A☆	107	395	58	104	17	4	2	36	26	26	.263	.309	.342	69	-19	2	4	-2	.984	6	*C-106	-0.8
1940	Cle-A★	119	416	46	111	20	5	4	42	22	25	.267	.304	.368	75	-16	1	3	-2	**.994**	9	*C-117	0.0
1941	Cle-A	98	288	29	69	10	5	2	24	18	19	.240	.284	.330	65	-15	2	0	1	.980	-2	C-96	-0.9
Total	19	1593	5047	562	1321	257	72	31	555	357	395	.262	.311	.360	74	-205	29	18		.978	90	*C-1482/O-7,1	-2.8
Team	4	390	1302	160	344	58	17	10	130	89	84	.264	.311	.358	75	-52	6	8		.986	28	C-377	-0.3

■ GEORGE HENDRICK

Hendrick, George Andrew b: 10/18/49, Los Angeles, Cal. BR/TR, 6'3", 195 lbs. Deb: 6/4/71

YEAR	TM/L	G	AB	R	H	2B	3B	HR	RBI	BB	SO	AVG	OBP	SLG	PRO+	BR/A	SB	CS	SBR	FA	FR	G/POS	TPR
1973	Cle-A	113	440	64	118	18	0	21	61	25	71	.268	.310	.452	111	4	7	6	-2	.988	-3	*O-110	-0.6
1974	Cle-A★	139	495	65	138	23	1	19	67	33	73	.279	.325	.444	121	11	6	4	-1	.989	3	*O-133/D-1	0.8
1975	Cle-A★	145	561	82	145	21	2	24	86	40	78	.258	.308	.431	107	3	6	7	-2	.983	1	*O-143	-0.5
1976	Cle-A	149	551	72	146	20	3	25	81	51	82	.265	.327	.448	127	17	4	4	-1	.987	3	*O-146/D-3	1.3
Total	18	2048	7129	941	1980	343	27	267	1111	567	1013	.278	.333	.446	117	144	59	47	-11	.985	-17	*O-1813,1-121/D	4.3
Team	4	546	2047	283	547	82	6	89	295	149	304	.267	.318	.444	116	35	23	21	-6	.987	4	O-532/D-4	1.0

■ HARVEY HENDRICK

Hendrick, Harvey "Gink" b: 11/9/1897, Mason, Tenn. d: 10/29/41, Covington, Tenn. BL/TR, 6'2", 190 lbs. Deb: 4/20/23

YEAR	TM/L	G	AB	R	H	2B	3B	HR	RBI	BB	SO	AVG	OBP	SLG	PRO+	BR/A	SB	CS	SBR	FA	FR	G/POS	TPR
1925	Cle-A	25	28	2	8	1	2	0	9	3	5	.286	.355	.464	106	0	0	0	0	1.000	0	/1-3	0.0
Total	11	922	2910	434	896	157	46	48	413	239	243	.308	.364	.443	113	53	75	0	23	.986	-32	1-378,O-220,3/S2	-1.8

■ TIM HENDRYX

Hendryx, Timothy Green b: 1/31/1891, LeRoy, Ill. d: 8/14/57, Corpus Christi, Tex. BR/TR, 5'9", 170 lbs. Deb: 9/4/11

YEAR	TM/L	G	AB	R	H	2B	3B	HR	RBI	BB	SO	AVG	OBP	SLG	PRO+	BR/A	SB	CS	SBR	FA	FR	G/POS	TPR
1911	Cle-A	4	7	0	2	0	0	0	0	0		.286	.286	.286	59	-0	0			1.000	-1	/3-3	-0.1
1912	Cle-A	23	70	9	17	2	4	1	14	8		.243	.329	.429	113	1	3			1.000	-2	O-22	-0.2
Total	8	416	1291	152	356	68	22	6	192	185		.276	.372	.376	115	31	26			.966	-22	O-360/3-3	-1.5
Team	2	27	77	9	19	2	4	1	14	8		.247	.326	.416	108	0	3			1.000	-3	/O-22,3-3	-0.3

■ DAVE HENGEL

Hengel, David Lee b: 12/18/61, Oakland, Cal. BR/TR, 6', 185 lbs. Deb: 9/3/86

YEAR	TM/L	G	AB	R	H	2B	3B	HR	RBI	BB	SO	AVG	OBP	SLG	PRO+	BR/A	SB	CS	SBR	FA	FR	G/POS	TPR
1989	Cle-A	12	25	2	3	1	0	0	1	2	4	.120	.185	.160	-2	-3	0	0	0	1.000	-1	/O-9,D-3	-0.4
Total	4	69	167	10	31	3	0	4	18	4	36	.186	.209	.275	31	-16	0	0		.962	-5	/O-36,D-27	-2.1

■ REMY HERMOSO

Hermoso, Angel Remigio b: 10/1/46, Carabobo, Venezuela BR/TR, 5'8", 155 lbs. Deb: 9/14/67

YEAR	TM/L	G	AB	R	H	2B	3B	HR	RBI	BB	SO	AVG	OBP	SLG	PRO+	BR/A	SB	CS	SBR	FA	FR	G/POS	TPR
1974	Cle-A	48	122	15	27	3	1	0	5	7	7	.221	.264	.262	52	-8	2	2	-1	.967	7	2-45	0.1
Total	4	91	223	25	47	3	1	0	8	14	21	.211	.261	.233	42	-17	6	3	0	.968	12	/2-66,S-15,3	-0.0

■ JOSE HERNANDEZ

Hernandez, Jose Antonio (Figueroa) b: 7/14/69, Rio Piedras, P.R. BR/TR, 6'1", 180 lbs. Deb: 8/9/91

YEAR	TM/L	G	AB	R	H	2B	3B	HR	RBI	BB	SO	AVG	OBP	SLG	PRO+	BR/A	SB	CS	SBR	FA	FR	G/POS	TPR
1992	Cle-A	3	4	0	0	0	0	0	0	0	2	.000	.000	.000	-99	-1	0	0	0	.857	-0	/S-3	-0.1
Total	4	197	479	63	110	15	8	14	53	24	131	.230	.268	.382	72	-21	3	3	-1	.968	19	S-111/3-49,2O	0.5

■ KEITH HERNANDEZ

Hernandez, Keith b: 10/20/53, San Francisco, Cal. BL/TL, 6', 195 lbs. Deb: 8/30/74

YEAR	TM/L	G	AB	R	H	2B	3B	HR	RBI	BB	SO	AVG	OBP	SLG	PRO+	BR/A	SB	CS	SBR	FA	FR	G/POS	TPR
1990	Cle-A	43	130	7	26	2	0	1	8	14	17	.200	.283	.238	47	-9	0	0	0	.994	-2	1-42	-1.4
Total	17	2088	7370	1124	2182	426	60	162	1071	1070	1012	.296	.388	.436	129	320	98	63	-8	.994	148	*1-2014/O-7	34.4

■ OTTO HESS

Hess, Otto C. b: 10/10/1878, Bern, Switzerland d: 2/25/26, Tucson, Ariz. BL/TL, 6'1", 170 lbs. Deb: 8/3/02

YEAR	TM/L	G	AB	R	H	2B	3B	HR	RBI	BB	SO	AVG	OBP	SLG	PRO+	BR/A	SB	CS	SBR	FA	FR	G/POS	TPR
1902	Cle-A	7	14	2	1	0	0	0	1	2		.071	.188	.071	-27	-2	0			.870	1	/P-7	0.0
1904	Cle-A	34	100	4	12	2	1	0	5	3		.120	.146	.160	-3	-12	0			.951	-1	P-21,O-12	-0.5
1905	Cle-A	54	173	15	44	8	1	2	13	7		.254	.291	.347	101	-0	2			.950	3	O-28,P-26	0.1
1906	Cle-A	53	154	13	31	5	2	0	11	2		.201	.212	.260	48	-10	1			.949	-3	P-43/O-5	-0.2
1907	Cle-A	19	30	4	4	0	0	0	0	4		.133	.278	.133	32	-2	1			.941	-1	P-17/O-2	-0.1
1908	Cle-A	9	14	0	0	0	0	0	0	1		.000	.067	.000	-78	-3	0			1.000	-1	/P-4,O-4	-0.4
Total	10	280	714	63	154	21	9	5	58	27		.216	.248	.291	64	-33	4			.941	-3	P-198/O-51,1	-1.2
Team	6	176	485	38	92	15	4	2	30	19		.190	.226	.249	50	-29	4			.939	-2	P-118/O-51	-1.1

■ CHARLIE HICKMAN

Hickman, Charles Taylor "Cheerful Charlie" or "Piano Legs"
b: 3/4/1876, Taylortown, Dunkard Township, Pa. d: 4/19/34, Morgantown, W.Va. BR/TR, 5'11.5", 215 lbs. Deb: 9/8/1897

YEAR	TM/L	G	AB	R	H	2B	3B	HR	RBI	BB	SO	AVG	OBP	SLG	PRO+	BR/A	SB	CS	SBR	FA	FR	G/POS	TPR
1902	Cle-A	102	426	61	161	31	11	8	94	12		.378	.399	.559	170	37	8			.966	-7	1-98/2-3,P	2.7

YEAR	TM/L	G	AB	R	H	2B	3B	HR	RBI	BB	SO	AVG	OBP	SLG	PRO+	BR/A	SB	CS	SBR	FA	FR	G/POS	TPR
1903	Cle-A	131	522	64	154	31	11	12	97	17		.295	.325	.466	137	21	14			.972	-7	*1-125/2-7	1.3
1904	Cle-A	86	337	34	97	22	10	4	45	13		.288	.318	.448	142	14	9			.943	-0	2-45,1-40/O	1.6
1908	Cle-A	65	197	16	46	6	1	2	16	9		.234	.271	.305	86	-3	2			.907	-0	O-28,1-20/2	-0.6
Total	12	1081	3982	478	1176	217	91	59	614	153		.295	.331	.440	133	145	72			.968	-26	1-394,O-290,23/PS	9.8
Team	4	384	1482	175	458	90	33	26	252	51		.309	.337	.467	142	70	33			.969	-14	1-283/2-56,OP	5.0

■ MARK HIGGINS
Higgins, Mark Douglas b: 7/9/63, Miami, Fla. BR/TR, 6'2", 210 lbs. Deb: 9/7/89

YEAR	TM/L	G	AB	R	H	2B	3B	HR	RBI	BB	SO	AVG	OBP	SLG	PRO+	BR/A	SB	CS	SBR	FA	FR	G/POS	TPR
1989	Cle-A	6	10	1	1	0	0	0	0	1	6	.100	.182	.100	-18	-2	0	0	0	1.000	1	/1-5	-0.1

■ BOB HIGGINS
Higgins, Robert Stone b: 9/23/1886, Fayetteville, Tenn. d: 5/25/41, Chattanooga, Tenn. BR/TR, 5'8", 176 lbs. Deb: 9/13/09

YEAR	TM/L	G	AB	R	H	2B	3B	HR	RBI	BB	SO	AVG	OBP	SLG	PRO+	BR/A	SB	CS	SBR	FA	FR	G/POS	TPR
1909	Cle-A	8	23	0	2	0	0	0	0	0		.087	.087	.087	-43	-4	0			1.000	3	/C-8	0.0
Total	3	13	35	1	5	0	0	0	2	1		.143	.167	.143	-6	-4	1			.970	3	/C-11,3-1	-0.1

■ GLENALLEN HILL
Hill, Glenallen b: 3/22/65, Santa Cruz, Cal. BR/TR, 6'3", 210 lbs. Deb: 9/1/89

YEAR	TM/L	G	AB	R	H	2B	3B	HR	RBI	BB	SO	AVG	OBP	SLG	PRO+	BR/A	SB	CS	SBR	FA	FR	G/POS	TPR
1991	Cle-A	37	122	15	32	3	0	5	14	16	30	.262	.348	.410	108	1	4	2	0	.978	-1	O-33/D-1	0.0
1992	Cle-A	102	369	38	89	16	1	18	49	20	73	.241	.288	.436	102	-1	9	6	-1	.956	2	O-59,D-34	-0.2
1993	Cle-A	66	174	19	39	7	2	5	25	11	50	.224	.274	.374	73	-7	7	3	0	.940	-4	O-39,D-18	-1.2
Total	7	595	1929	270	501	90	13	88	284	149	427	.260	.315	.457	107	13	77	28		.967	-10	O-444/D-92	-0.3
Team	3	205	665	72	160	26	3	28	88	47	153	.241	.296	.415	95	-7	20	11		.959	-3	O-131/D-53	-1.4

■ HUGH HILL
Hill, Hugh Ellis b: 7/21/1879, Ringgold, Ga. d: 9/6/58, Cincinnati, Ohio BL/TR, 5'11.5", 168 lbs. Deb: 5/1/03 F

YEAR	TM/L	G	AB	R	H	2B	3B	HR	RBI	BB	SO	AVG	OBP	SLG	PRO+	BR/A	SB	CS	SBR	FA	FR	G/POS	TPR
1903	Cle-A	1	1	0	0	0	0	0	0	0		.000	.000	.000	-99	-0	0			.000	0	H	0.0
Total	2	24	94	13	21	2	1	3	4	2		.223	.240	.362	89	-2	3			1.000	0	/O-23	-0.3

■ HARRY HINCHMAN
Hinchman, Harry Sibley b: 8/4/1878, Philadelphia, Pa. d: 1/19/33, Toledo, Ohio BB/TR, 5'11", 165 lbs. Deb: 7/29/07 F

YEAR	TM/L	G	AB	R	H	2B	3B	HR	RBI	BB	SO	AVG	OBP	SLG	PRO+	BR/A	SB	CS	SBR	FA	FR	G/POS	TPR
1907	Cle-A	15	51	3	11	3	1	0	9	5		.216	.286	.314	90	-1	2			.904	4	2-15	0.3

■ BILL HINCHMAN
Hinchman, William White b: 4/4/1883, Philadelphia, Pa. d: 2/20/63, Columbus, Ohio BR/TR, 5'11", 190 lbs. Deb: 9/24/05 FC

YEAR	TM/L	G	AB	R	H	2B	3B	HR	RBI	BB	SO	AVG	OBP	SLG	PRO+	BR/A	SB	CS	SBR	FA	FR	G/POS	TPR
1907	Cle-A	152	514	62	117	19	9	1	50	47		.228	.311	.305	96	-1	15			.958	-5	*O-148/1-4,2	-1.3
1908	Cle-A	137	464	55	107	23	8	6	59	38		.231	.301	.353	112	6	9			.975	-6	O-75,S-51/1	-0.3
1909	Cle-A	139	457	57	118	20	13	2	53	41		.258	.331	.372	117	9	22			.918	1	*O-131/S-6	0.6
Total	10	908	3043	364	793	128	69	20	369	298		.261	.336	.368	118	66	85			.954	-17	O-750/1-63,S32	1.2
Team	3	428	1435	174	342	62	30	9	162	126		.238	.314	.342	108	14	46			.944	-10	O-354/S-57,12	-1.0

■ CHUCK HINTON
Hinton, Charles Edward b: 5/3/34, Rocky Mount, N.C. BR/TR, 6'1", 197 lbs. Deb: 5/14/61

YEAR	TM/L	G	AB	R	H	2B	3B	HR	RBI	BB	SO	AVG	OBP	SLG	PRO+	BR/A	SB	CS	SBR	FA	FR	G/POS	TPR
1965	Cle-A	133	431	59	110	17	6	18	54	53	65	.255	.338	.448	120	11	17	3	3	.966	-9	O-72,1-40,2/3	0.3
1966	Cle-A	123	348	46	89	9	3	12	50	35	66	.256	.326	.402	108	3	10	6	-1	.973	-8	*O-104/1-6,2	-1.0
1967	Cle-A	147	498	55	122	19	3	10	37	43	100	.245	.306	.355	94	-4	6	8	-3	.976	-13	*O-136/2-5	-2.8
1969	Cle-A	94	121	18	31	3	2	3	19	8	22	.256	.308	.388	91	-2	2	0	1	.941	-10	O-40,3-14	-1.2
1970	Cle-A	107	195	24	62	4	0	9	29	25	34	.318	.395	.477	133	9	0	2	-1	.994	-6	1-40,O-35/C23	-0.1
1971	Cle-A	88	147	13	33	7	0	5	14	20	34	.224	.317	.374	87	-2	0	0	0	1.000	-7	1-20,O-20/C	-1.2
Total	11	1353	3968	518	1048	152	47	113	443	416	685	.264	.335	.412	108	44	130	50		.979	-59	O-928,1-160/23CS	-5.8
Team	6	692	1740	215	447	59	14	57	203	184	321	.257	.329	.405	107	16	35	19		.972	-53	O-407,1-106/23C	-6.0

■ TOMMY HINZO
Hinzo, Thomas Lee b: 6/18/64, San Diego, Cal. BB/TR, 5'10", 170 lbs. Deb: 7/16/87

YEAR	TM/L	G	AB	R	H	2B	3B	HR	RBI	BB	SO	AVG	OBP	SLG	PRO+	BR/A	SB	CS	SBR	FA	FR	G/POS	TPR
1987	Cle-A	67	257	31	68	9	3	3	21	10	47	.265	.297	.358	72	-10	9	4	0	.973	-4	2-67	-1.0
1989	Cle-A	18	17	4	0	0	0	0	0	2	6	.000	.105	.000	-67	-4	1	2	-1	.867	0	/2-6,S-1,D	-0.4
Total	2	85	274	35	68	9	3	3	21	12	53	.248	.285	.336	64	-14	10	6	-1	.968	-4	/2-73,D-1,S	-1.4

■ MYRIL HOAG
Hoag, Myril Oliver b: 3/9/08, Davis, Cal. d: 7/28/71, High Springs, Fla BR/TR, 5'11", 180 lbs. Deb: 4/15/31

YEAR	TM/L	G	AB	R	H	2B	3B	HR	RBI	BB	SO	AVG	OBP	SLG	PRO+	BR/A	SB	CS	SBR	FA	FR	G/POS	TPR
1944	Cle-A	67	277	33	79	9	3	1	27	25	23	.285	.347	.350	103	1	6	4	-1	.947	-1	O-66	-0.4
1945	Cle-A	40	128	10	27	5	3	0	3	11	18	.211	.279	.297	70	-5	1	2	-1	.987	0	O-33/P-2	-0.8
Total	13	1020	3147	384	854	141	33	28	401	252	298	.271	.328	.364	83	-80	59	49	-12	.965	-67	O-876/P-3,31	-18.7
Team	2	107	405	43	106	14	6	1	30	36	41	.262	.325	.333	93	-4	7	6	-2	.959	-1	/O-99,P-2	-1.2

■ ORIS HOCKETT
Hockett, Oris Leon "Brown" b: 9/29/09, Amboy, Ind. d: 3/23/69, Torrance, Cal. BL/TR, 5'9", 182 lbs. Deb: 9/4/38

YEAR	TM/L	G	AB	R	H	2B	3B	HR	RBI	BB	SO	AVG	OBP	SLG	PRO+	BR/A	SB	CS	SBR	FA	FR	G/POS	TPR
1941	Cle-A	2	6	0	2	0	0	0	1	2	0	.333	.500	.333	131	0	0	0	0	1.000	-1	/O-2	0.0
1942	Cle-A	148	601	85	150	22	7	7	48	45	45	.250	.305	.344	88	-12	12	12	-4	.980	-2	*O-145	-2.6
1943	Cle-A	141	601	70	166	33	4	2	51	45	45	.276	.331	.354	107	4	13	18	-7	.960	1	*O-139	-1.0
1944	Cle-A☆	124	457	47	132	29	5	1	50	35	27	.289	.339	.381	110	5	8	9	-3	.986	-4	*O-110	-0.8
Total	7	551	2165	259	598	112	21	13	214	159	157	.276	.329	.365	103	3	43	48	-16	.974	-6	O-520	-4.8
Team	4	415	1665	202	450	84	16	10	150	127	117	.270	.325	.358	101	-3	33	39	-14	.974	-4	O-396	-4.4

■ JOHNNY HODAPP
Hodapp, Urban John b: 9/26/05, Cincinnati, Ohio d: 6/14/80, Cincinnati, Ohio BR/TR, 6', 185 lbs. Deb: 8/19/25

YEAR	TM/L	G	AB	R	H	2B	3B	HR	RBI	BB	SO	AVG	OBP	SLG	PRO+	BR/A	SB	CS	SBR	FA	FR	G/POS	TPR
1925	Cle-A	37	130	12	31	5	1	0	14	11	7	.238	.298	.292	50	-10	2	3	-1	.960	3	3-37	-0.5
1926	Cle-A	3	5	0	1	0	0	0	0	0	1	.200	.200	.200	4	-1	0	0	0	.750	-1	/3-3	-0.1
1927	Cle-A	79	240	25	73	15	3	5	40	14	23	.304	.343	.454	105	1	2	2	-1	.935	1	3-67/1-4	0.3
1928	Cle-A	116	449	51	145	31	6	2	73	20	20	.323	.352	.432	104	2	2	1	0	.944	-2	*3-101,1-13	0.4
1929	Cle-A	90	294	30	96	12	7	4	51	15	14	.327	.361	.456	105	2	3	3	-1	.977	5	2-72	0.8
1930	Cle-A	154	635	111	**225**	**51**	8	9	121	32	29	.354	.386	.502	119	17	6	5	-1	.970	12	*2-154	3.2
1931	Cle-A	122	468	71	138	19	4	2	56	27	23	.295	.336	.365	80	-14	1	5	-3	.969	16	*2-121	0.7
1932	Cle-A	7	16	2	2	1	0	0	0	0	2	.125	.125	.188	-19	-3	0	0	0	1.000	-2	/2-7	-0.4
Total	9	791	2826	378	880	169	34	28	429	163	136	.311	.350	.425	98	-13	18	20	-7	.967	30	2-460,3-212/O1	3.9
Team	8	608	2237	302	711	134	29	22	355	119	119	.318	.353	.433	99	-7	16	19	-7	.971	32	2-354,3-208/1	4.4

■ GOMER HODGE
Hodge, Harold Morris b: 4/3/44, Rutherfordton, N.C. BB/TR, 6'2", 185 lbs. Deb: 4/6/71

YEAR	TM/L	G	AB	R	H	2B	3B	HR	RBI	BB	SO	AVG	OBP	SLG	PRO+	BR/A	SB	CS	SBR	FA	FR	G/POS	TPR
1971	Cle-A	80	83	3	17	3	0	1	9	4	19	.205	.258	.277	47	-6	0	0	0	1.000	-2	/1-3,3-3,2	-0.8

■ TEX HOFFMAN
Hoffman, Edward Adolph b: 11/30/1893, San Antonio, Tex. d: 5/19/47, New Orleans, La. BL/TR, 5'9", 195 lbs. Deb: 7/11/15

YEAR	TM/L	G	AB	R	H	2B	3B	HR	RBI	BB	SO	AVG	OBP	SLG	PRO+	BR/A	SB	CS	SBR	FA	FR	G/POS	TPR
1915	Cle-A	9	13	1	2	0	0	0	2	1	5	.154	.214	.154	10	-1	0			.750	-2	/3-3	-0.3

■ HARRY HOGAN
Hogan, Harry S. b: 11/1/1875, Syracuse, N.Y. d: 1/24/34, Syracuse, N.Y. Deb: 8/13/01

YEAR	TM/L	G	AB	R	H	2B	3B	HR	RBI	BB	SO	AVG	OBP	SLG	PRO+	BR/A	SB	CS	SBR	FA	FR	G/POS	TPR
1901	Cle-A	1	4	0	0	0	0	0	0	0		.000	.000	.000	-99	-1	0			.000	-0	/O-1	-0.1

■ KENNY HOGAN
Hogan, Kenneth Sylvester b: 10/9/02, Cleveland, Ohio d: 1/2/80, Cleveland, Ohio BL/TR, 5'9", 145 lbs. Deb: 10/2/21

YEAR	TM/L	G	AB	R	H	2B	3B	HR	RBI	BB	SO	AVG	OBP	SLG	PRO+	BR/A	SB	CS	SBR	FA	FR	G/POS	TPR
1923	Cle-A	1	0	0	0	0	0	0	0	0	0	—	—	—	—	0	0	0	0	.000	0	R	0.0
1924	Cle-A	2	1	0	0	0	0	0	0	0	0	.000	.000	.000	-99	-0	0	0	0	.000	0	H	0.0
Total	3	4	3	0	0	0	0	0	0	0	1	.000	.000	.000	-99	-1	0	0		.985	-1	/O-1	-0.1
Team	2	3	1	0	0	0	0	0	0	0	0	.000	.000	.000	-99	-0	0	0		.000	0	H	0.0

■ EDDIE HOHNHORST
Hohnhorst, Edward Hicks b: 1/31/1885, Kentucky d: 3/28/16, Covington, Ky. BL/TL, 6'1", 175 lbs. Deb: 9/10/10

YEAR	TM/L	G	AB	R	H	2B	3B	HR	RBI	BB	SO	AVG	OBP	SLG	PRO+	BR/A	SB	CS	SBR	FA	FR	G/POS	TPR
1910	Cle-A	18	63	8	20	3	1	0	6	4		.317	.358	.397	135	2	3			.972	-1	1-18	0.1
1912	Cle-A	15	54	5	11	1	0	0	2	2		.204	.232	.222	29	-5	5			.963	-1	1-15	-0.6
Total	2	33	117	13	31	4	1	0	8	6		.265	.301	.316	83	-3	8			.968	-2	/1-33	-0.5

YEAR	TM/L	G	AB	R	H	2B	3B	HR	RBI	BB	SO	AVG	OBP	SLG	PRO+	BR/A	SB	CS	SBR	FA	FR	G/POS	TPR

■ DUTCH HOLLAND Holland, Robert Clyde b: 10/12/03, Middlesex, N.C. d: 6/16/67, Lumberton, N.C. BR/TR, 6'1", 190 lbs. Deb: 8/16/32

| 1934 | Cle-A | 50 | 128 | 19 | 32 | 12 | 1 | 2 | 13 | 13 | 11 | .250 | .319 | .406 | 85 | -3 | 0 | 0 | 0 | .957 | -4 | O-31 | -0.8 |
| Total | 3 | 102 | 315 | 37 | 86 | 26 | 2 | 3 | 34 | 28 | 39 | .273 | .332 | .397 | 95 | -3 | 1 | 0 | | .969 | -3 | /O-77 | -1.0 |

■ SAM HORN Horn, Samuel Lee b: 11/2/63, Dallas, Tex. BL/TL, 6'5", 250 lbs. Deb: 7/25/87

| 1993 | Cle-A | 12 | 33 | 8 | 15 | 1 | 0 | 4 | 8 | 1 | 5 | .455 | .486 | .848 | 252 | 7 | 0 | 0 | 0 | .000 | 0 | D-11 | 0.6 |
| Total | 8 | 389 | 1040 | 132 | 250 | 49 | 1 | 62 | 179 | 132 | 323 | .240 | .330 | .468 | 118 | 25 | 0 | 1 | -1 | .972 | -0 | D-293/1-12 | 1.1 |

■ TONY HORTON Horton, Anthony Darrin b: 12/6/44, Santa Monica, Cal. BR/TR, 6'3", 210 lbs. Deb: 7/31/64

1967	Cle-A	106	363	35	102	13	4	10	44	18	52	.281	.322	.421	117	7	3	0	1	.991	-6	1-94	-0.4
1968	Cle-A	133	477	57	119	29	3	14	59	34	56	.249	.304	.411	117	8	3	1	0	.992	-4	*1-128	-0.6
1969	Cle-A	159	625	77	174	25	4	27	93	37	91	.278	.321	.461	113	8	3	3	-1	.989	-0	*1-157	-0.6
1970	Cle-A	115	413	48	111	19	3	17	59	30	54	.269	.324	.453	107	3	3	2	-0	.994	3	*1-112	-0.4
Total	7	636	2228	251	597	102	15	76	297	140	319	.268	.315	.430	109	18	12	8	-1	.990	-7	1-555/O-24	-3.4
Team	4	513	1878	217	506	86	14	68	255	119	253	.269	.317	.439	113	25	12	6	0	.992	-7	1-491	-2.0

■ WILLIE HORTON Horton, Willie Watterson b: 10/18/42, Arno, Va. BR/TR, 5'11", 209 lbs. Deb: 9/10/63 C

| 1978 | Cle-A | 50 | 169 | 15 | 42 | 7 | 0 | 5 | 22 | 15 | 25 | .249 | .314 | .379 | 95 | -1 | 3 | 0 | 1 | .000 | 0 | D-48 | -0.2 |
| Total | 18 | 2028 | 7298 | 873 | 1993 | 284 | 40 | 325 | 1163 | 620 | 1313 | .273 | .335 | .457 | 119 | 166 | 20 | 38 | -17 | .972 | -24 | *O-1190,D-753/3 | 5.2 |

■ DOUG HOWARD Howard, Douglas Lynn b: 2/6/48, Salt Lake City, Utah BR/TR, 6'3", 185 lbs. Deb: 9/6/72

| 1976 | Cle-A | 39 | 90 | 7 | 19 | 4 | 0 | 0 | 13 | 3 | 13 | .211 | .245 | .256 | 47 | -6 | 1 | 1 | -0 | .991 | 1 | 1-32/O-2,D | -0.7 |
| Total | 5 | 97 | 217 | 19 | 46 | 5 | 1 | 1 | 22 | 7 | 30 | .212 | .243 | .258 | 46 | -15 | 2 | 1 | 0 | .994 | -1 | /1-46,O-24,D3 | -1.9 |

■ IVON HOWARD Howard, Ivon Chester b: 10/12/1882, Kenney, Ill. d: 3/30/67, Medford, Ore. BB/TR, 5'10", 170 lbs. Deb: 4/25/14 F

1916	Cle-A	81	246	20	46	11	5	0	23	30	34	.187	.298	.272	68	-9	9			.970	7	2-65/1-7	-0.1
1917	Cle-A	27	39	7	4	0	0	0	3	3	5	.103	.167	.103	-17	-5	1			.833	2	/3-6,2-4,O	-0.4
Total	4	302	818	91	191	27	14	2	86	104	129	.233	.331	.308	92	-4	53			.990	6	/1-83,2-71,3OS	0.2
Team	2	108	285	27	50	11	5	0	23	33	39	.175	.281	.249	56	-15	10			.969	9	/2-69,1-7,3O	-0.5

■ THOMAS HOWARD Howard, Thomas Sylvester b: 12/11/64, Middletown, Ohio BB/TR, 6'2", 200 lbs. Deb: 7/3/90

1992	Cle-A	117	358	36	99	15	2	2	32	17	60	.277	.309	.346	85	-8	15	8	-0	.990	-7	O-97/D-2	-1.7
1993	Cle-A	74	178	26	42	7	0	3	23	12	42	.236	.284	.326	64	-9	5	1	1	.977	-3	O-47/D-7	-1.2
Total	6	556	1464	185	395	70	10	21	140	95	258	.270	.315	.374	87	-28	56	33		.985	-20	O-419/D-9	-5.9
Team	2	191	536	62	141	22	2	5	55	29	102	.263	.301	.340	78	-17	20	9		.986	-10	O-144/D-9	-2.9

■ RED HOWELL Howell, Murray Donald "Porky" b: 1/29/09, Atlanta, Ga. d: 10/1/50, Travelers Rest, S.C BR/TR, 6', 215 lbs. Deb: 4/24/41

| 1941 | Cle-A | 11 | 7 | 0 | 2 | 0 | 0 | 0 | 2 | 4 | 2 | .286 | .545 | .286 | 132 | 1 | 0 | 0 | 0 | .000 | 0 | H | 0.1 |

■ DICK HOWSER Howser, Richard Dalton b: 5/14/36, Miami, Fla. d: 6/17/87, Kansas City, Mo. BR/TR, 5'8", 155 lbs. Deb: 4/11/61 MC

1963	Cle-A	49	162	25	40	5	0	1	10	22	18	.247	.337	.296	80	-4	9	3	1	.950	-17	S-44	-1.7
1964	Cle-A	162	637	101	163	23	4	3	52	76	39	.256	.337	.319	84	-11	20	7	2	.974	3	*S-162	0.6
1965	Cle-A	107	307	47	72	8	2	1	6	57	25	.235	.356	.283	83	-4	17	4	3	.977	-6	S-73,2-17	-0.1
1966	Cle-A	67	140	18	32	9	1	2	4	15	23	.229	.303	.350	87	-2	2	4	-2	.986	-7	2-26,S-26	-0.8
Total	8	789	2483	398	617	90	17	16	165	367	186	.248	.348	.318	86	-34	105	34	11	.963	-56	S-548/2-94,3	-3.2
Team	4	385	1246	191	307	45	7	7	72	170	105	.246	.338	.311	84	-21	48	18	4	.970	-26	S-305/2-43	-2.0

■ MIKE HUFF Huff, Michael Kale b: 8/11/63, Honolulu, Hawaii BR/TR, 6'1", 180 lbs. Deb: 8/7/89

| 1991 | Cle-A | 51 | 146 | 28 | 35 | 6 | 1 | 2 | 10 | 25 | 30 | .240 | .366 | .336 | 95 | 0 | 11 | 2 | 2 | .990 | -3 | O-48/2-2 | -0.2 |
| Total | 6 | 358 | 772 | 108 | 193 | 42 | 6 | 9 | 75 | 108 | 141 | .250 | .352 | .355 | 91 | -7 | 19 | 9 | 0 | .991 | -47 | O-335/2-4,D | -5.8 |

■ ROY HUGHES Hughes, Roy John "Jeep" or "Sage" b: 1/11/11, Cincinnati, Ohio d: 3/5/95, Asheville, N.C. BR/TR, 5'10.5", 167 lbs. Deb: 4/16/35

1935	Cle-A	82	266	40	78	15	3	0	14	18	17	.293	.340	.372	83	-7	13	3	2	.987	-1	2-40,S-29/3	-0.1
1936	Cle-A	152	638	112	188	35	9	0	63	57	40	.295	.356	.378	81	-19	20	9	1	.973	5	*2-152	-0.2
1937	Cle-A	104	346	57	96	12	6	1	40	40	22	.277	.352	.355	78	-11	11	6	-0	.939	12	3-58,2-32	0.4
Total	9	763	2582	396	705	105	27	5	205	222	175	.273	.332	.340	78	-83	44	18	13	.980	2	2-345,3-170,S/1	-3.4
Team	3	338	1250	209	362	62	18	1	117	115	79	.290	.352	.370	80	-37	44	18	2	.979	16	2-224/3-59,S	0.1

■ BILL HUNNEFIELD Hunnefield, William Fenton "Wild Bill" b: 1/5/1899, Dedham, Mass. d: 8/28/76, Nantucket, Mass. BB/TR, 5'10", 165 lbs. Deb: 4/17/26

| 1931 | Cle-A | 21 | 71 | 13 | 17 | 4 | 1 | 0 | 4 | 9 | 4 | .239 | .325 | .324 | 67 | -3 | 3 | 1 | 0 | .853 | -10 | S-21/2-1 | -1.0 |
| Total | 6 | 511 | 1664 | 230 | 452 | 75 | 9 | 9 | 144 | 117 | 111 | .272 | .322 | .344 | 76 | -60 | 67 | 32 | 1 | .925 | -67 | S-230,2-204/31 | -9.4 |

■ BILLY HUNTER Hunter, Gordon William b: 6/4/28, Punxsutawney, Pa. BR/TR, 6', 180 lbs. Deb: 4/14/53 MC

| 1958 | Cle-A | 76 | 190 | 21 | 37 | 10 | 2 | 0 | 9 | 17 | 37 | .195 | .264 | .268 | 48 | -14 | 4 | 1 | 1 | .948 | 1 | S-75/3-2 | -0.7 |
| Total | 6 | 630 | 1875 | 166 | 410 | 58 | 18 | 16 | 144 | 111 | 192 | .219 | .265 | .294 | 53 | -126 | 23 | 12 | -0 | .958 | 19 | S-528/2-72,3 | -6.7 |

■ BILL HUNTER Hunter, William Ellsworth b: 7/8/1887, Buffalo, N.Y. d: 4/10/34, Buffalo, N.Y. BL/TL, 5'7.5", 155 lbs. Deb: 8/6/12 F

| 1912 | Cle-A | 21 | 55 | 6 | 9 | 2 | 0 | 0 | 2 | 1 | | .164 | .303 | .200 | 43 | -4 | 0 | | | 1.000 | -0 | O-16 | -0.5 |

■ HAPPY IOTT Iott, Frederick "Happy Jack" or "Biddo" (b: Frederick Hoyot) b: 7/7/1876, Houlton, Me. d: 2/17/41, Island Falls, Me. BR/TR, 5'10", 175 lbs. Deb: 9/16/03

| 1903 | Cle-A | 3 | 10 | 1 | 2 | 0 | 0 | 0 | 2 | | | .200 | .333 | .200 | 64 | -0 | 1 | | | .875 | -0 | /O-3 | -0.1 |

■ TOMMY IRWIN Irwin, Thomas Andrew b: 12/20/12, Altoona, Pa. BR/TR, 5'11", 165 lbs. Deb: 10/1/38

| 1938 | Cle-A | 3 | 9 | 1 | 1 | 0 | 0 | 0 | 0 | 3 | 1 | .111 | .333 | .111 | 16 | -1 | 0 | 0 | 0 | 1.000 | 0 | /S-3 | -0.1 |

■ JIM JACKSON Jackson, James Benner b: 11/28/1877, Philadelphia, Pa. d: 10/9/55, Philadelphia, Pa. BR/TR, Deb: 4/26/01

1905	Cle-A	109	426	59	109	12	4	0	31	34		.256	.317	.317	100	0	15			.950	4	*O-106/3-3	-0.1
1906	Cle-A	105	374	44	80	13	2	0	38	38		.214	.290	.259	73	-10	25			.975	-6	*O-104	-2.3
Total	4	348	1274	159	300	47	10	4	132	107		.235	.298	.297	80	-31	57			.959	-1	O-340/3-3	-5.3
Team	2	214	800	103	189	25	6	2	69	72		.236	.304	.290	87	-10	40			.962	-2	O-210/3-3	-2.4

■ JOE JACKSON Jackson, Joseph Jefferson "Shoeless Joe" b: 7/16/1889, Pickens Co.,S.C. d: 12/5/51, Greenville, S.C. BL/TR, 6'1", 200 lbs. Deb: 8/25/08

1910	Cle-A	20	75	15	29	2	5	1	11	8		.387	.446	.587	220	10	4			.977	0	O-20	1.0
1911	Cle-A	147	571	126	233	45	19	7	83	56		.408	.468	.590	192	70	41			.958	8	*O-147	6.8
1912	Cle-A	154	572	121	226	44	26	3	90	54		.395	.458	.579	190	66	35			.950	13	*O-150	6.9
1913	Cle-A	148	528	109	197	39	17	7	71	80	26	.373	.460	.551	190	62	26			.930	2	*O-148	6.0
1914	Cle-A	122	453	61	153	22	13	3	53	41	34	.338	.399	.464	153	28	22	15	-2	.967	2	*O-119	2.4
1915	Cle-A	83	303	42	99	16	9	3	45	28	11	.327	.389	.469	154	19	10	10	-3	.961	-3	O-49,1-30	1.0
Total	13	1332	4981	873	1772	307	168	54	785	519	158	.356	.423	.517	169	433	202	61		.962	23	*O-1289/1-30	37.4
Team	6	674	2502	474	937	168	89	24	353	267	71	.375	.441	.542	181	255	138	25		.952	22	O-633/1-30	24.1

■ RANDY JACKSON Jackson, Ransom Joseph "Handsome Ransom" b: 2/10/26, Little Rock, Ark. BR/TR, 6'1.5", 180 lbs. Deb: 5/2/50

1958	Cle-A	29	91	7	22	3	1	4	13	6	18	.242	.266	.429	90	-2	0	0	0	.901	5	3-24	0.4
1959	Cle-A	3	7	0	1	0	0	0	0	0	1	.143	.143	.143	-22	-1	0	0	0	1.000	-1	/3-2	-0.2
Total	10	955	3203	412	835	115	44	103	415	281	382	.261	.322	.421	94	-31	36	16	1	.955	18	3-844/O-2	-2.1
Team	2	32	98	7	23	3	1	4	13	6	19	.235	.257	.408	82	-3	0	0	0	.903	5	/3-26	0.2

YEAR	TM/L	G	AB	R	H	2B	3B	HR	RBI	BB	SO	AVG	OBP	SLG	PRO+	BR/A	SB	CS	SBR	FA	FR	G/POS	TPR

■ BABY DOLL JACOBSON
Jacobson, William Chester   b: 8/16/1890, Cable, Ill.   d: 1/16/77, Orion, Ill.   BR/TR, 6'3", 215 lbs.   Deb: 4/14/15

1927	Cle-A	32	103	13	26	5	0	0	13	6	4	.252	.300	.301	56	-7	0	0	0	.932	-1	O-31	-0.9
Total	11	1472	5507	787	1714	328	94	83	819	355	410	.311	.357	.450	111	63	86	54	-7	.973	31	*O-1378/1-48	-1.4

■ BROOK JACOBY
Jacoby, Brook Wallace   b: 11/23/59, Philadelphia, Pa.   BR/TR, 5'11", 195 lbs.   Deb: 9/13/81

1984	Cle-A	126	439	64	116	19	3	7	40	32	73	.264	.319	.369	88	-7	3	2	-0	.951	-20	*3-126/S-1	-2.9
1985	Cle-A	161	606	72	166	26	3	20	87	48	120	.274	.327	.426	105	3	2	3	-1	.958	-7	*3-161/2-1	-0.7
1986	Cle-A★	158	583	83	168	30	4	17	80	56	137	.288	.351	.441	116	13	2	1	0	.941	-13	*3-158	-0.3
1987	Cle-A	155	540	73	162	26	4	32	69	75	73	.300	.388	.541	142	33	2	3	-1	.946	-7	*3-144/1-7,D	2.1
1988	Cle-A	152	552	59	133	25	0	9	49	48	101	.241	.303	.335	76	-17	2	3	-1	.975	1	*3-151	-1.9
1989	Cle-A	147	519	49	141	26	5	13	64	62	90	.272	.353	.416	114	10	2	5	-2	.955	-10	*3-144/D-3	-0.1
1990	Cle-A★	155	553	77	162	24	4	14	75	63	58	.293	.367	.427	122	17	1	4	-2	.981	-12	3-99,1-78	-0.2
1991	Cle-A	66	231	14	54	9	1	4	24	16	32	.234	.289	.333	71	-9	0	1	-1	.988	-0	1-55,3-15	-1.3
1992	Cle-A	120	291	30	76	7	0	4	36	28	54	.261	.328	.326	85	-5	0	3	-2	.957	3	*3-111,1-10	-0.5
Total	11	1311	4520	535	1220	204	24	120	545	439	764	.270	.337	.405	104	22	16	25	-10	.958	-71	*3-1166,1-153/D2S	-8.1
Team	9	1240	4314	521	1178	192	24	120	524	428	738	.273	.341	.412	106	38	14	25	-11	.957	-65	*3-1109,1-150/D2S	-5.8

■ DION JAMES
James, Dion   b: 11/9/62, Philadelphia, Pa.   BL/TL, 6'1", 170 lbs.   Deb: 9/16/83

1989	Cle-A	71	245	26	75	11	0	4	29	24	26	.306	.368	.400	114	5	1	4	-2	.976	0	O-37,D-27/1	0.2
1990	Cle-A	87	248	28	68	15	2	1	22	27	23	.274	.348	.363	99	0	5	3	-0	.996	-5	1-35,O-33,D	-0.8
Total	10	911	2696	361	779	142	21	32	266	317	305	.289	.366	.393	108	37	42	38	-10	.986	-50	O-678,D-75,1	-4.8
Team	2	158	493	54	143	26	2	5	51	51	49	.290	.358	.381	107	5	6	7	-2	.965	-4	/O-70,1-37,D	-0.6

■ CHRIS JAMES
James, Donald Chris   b: 10/4/62, Rusk, Tex.   BR/TR, 6'1", 195 lbs.   Deb: 4/23/86

1990	Cle-A	140	528	62	158	32	4	12	70	31	71	.299	.343	.443	119	12	4	3	-1	1.000	0	*D-124,O-14	0.7
1991	Cle-A	115	437	31	104	16	2	5	41	18	61	.238	.275	.318	63	-22	3	4	-2	1.000	0	D-60,O-39,1	-2.8
Total	10	946	3040	343	794	145	24	90	386	193	490	.261	.310	.413	99	-13	27	17	-2	.987	-12	O-568,D-204/312	-5.3
Team	2	255	965	93	262	48	6	17	111	49	132	.272	.312	.387	93	-10	7	7	-2	1.000	0	D-184/O-53,1	-2.1

■ CHARLIE JAMIESON
Jamieson, Charles Devine "Cuckoo"   b: 2/7/1893, Paterson, N.J.   d: 10/27/69, Paterson, N.J.   BL/TL, 5'8.5", 165 lbs.   Deb: 9/20/15

1919	Cle-A	26	17	3	6	2	1	0	2	0	4	.353	.353	.588	153	1	2			.750	-1	/P-4,O-3	0.0
1920	*Cle-A	108	370	69	118	17	7	1	40	41	26	.319	.388	.411	108	5	2	9	-5	.966	-2	O-98/1-4	-0.8
1921	Cle-A	140	536	94	166	33	10	1	46	67	27	.310	.387	.414	103	4	8	4	0	.974	-6	*O-137	-1.1
1922	Cle-A	145	567	87	183	29	11	3	57	54	22	.323	.388	.429	112	11	15	9	-1	.978	-2	*O-144/P-2	-0.2
1923	Cle-A	152	644	130	**222**	36	12	2	51	80	37	.345	.422	.447	129	30	18	14	-3	.974	7	*O-152	2.3
1924	Cle-A	143	594	98	213	34	8	3	54	47	15	.359	.407	.458	121	19	21	12	-1	.974	4	*O-139	1.2
1925	Cle-A	138	557	109	165	24	5	4	42	72	26	.296	.380	.379	92	-5	14	18	-7	.955	7	*O-135	-1.2
1926	Cle-A	143	555	89	166	33	7	2	45	53	22	.299	.361	.395	96	-3	9	7	-2	.960	-3	*O-143	-1.4
1927	Cle-A	127	489	73	151	23	6	0	36	64	14	.309	.394	.380	101	4	7	9	-3	.969	5	*O-127	-0.3
1928	Cle-A	112	433	63	133	18	4	1	37	56	20	.307	.388	.374	100	2	3	12	-6	.984	20	*O-111	0.8
1929	Cle-A	102	364	56	106	22	1	0	26	50	12	.291	.378	.357	87	-5	2	13	-7	.980	-2	O-93	-1.9
1930	Cle-A	103	366	64	110	22	1	1	52	36	20	.301	.368	.374	85	-7	5	2	-0	.955	-5	O-95	-1.7
1931	Cle-A	28	43	7	13	2	1	0	4	5	1	.302	.375	.395	97	-0	1	1	-0	.833	-2	/O-7	-0.2
1932	Cle-A	16	16	0	1	1	0	0	2	0	3	.063	.211	.125	-10	-3	0	0	0	1.000	1	/O-2	-0.2
Total	18	1779	6560	1062	1990	322	80	18	552	748	345	.303	.388	.385	101	31	131	110		.967	18	*O-1638/P-13,1	-9.1
Team	14	1483	5551	942	1753	296	74	18	492	627	247	.316	.388	.406	104	54	107	110		.970	23	*O-1386/P-6,1	-4.7

■ TEX JEANES
Jeanes, Ernest Lee   b: 12/19/1900, Maypearl, Tex.   d: 4/5/73, Longview, Tex.   BR/TR, 6', 176 lbs.   Deb: 4/20/21

1921	Cle-A	5	3	2	2	1	0	0	4	1	0	.667	.750	1.000	338	1	0	0	0	1.000	-1	/O-5	0.0
1922	Cle-A	1	1	0	0	0	0	0	0	1	0	.000	.500	.000	39	0	0	0	0	.000	-1	/P-1,O-1	0.0
Total	5	53	73	15	20	4	0	1	11	7	7	.274	.338	.370	85	-2	1	0	0	1.000	-9	/O-39,P-2	-1.1
Team	2	6	4	2	2	1	0	0	4	2	0	.500	.667	.750	260	1	0	0	0	1.000	-2	/O-6,P-1	0.0

■ REGGIE JEFFERSON
Jefferson, Reginald Jirod   b: 9/25/68, Tallahassee, Fla.   BB/TL, 6'4", 210 lbs.   Deb: 5/18/91

1991	Cle-A	26	101	10	20	3	0	2	12	3	22	.198	.221	.287	39	-8	0	0	0	.993	2	1-26	-0.8
1992	Cle-A	24	89	8	30	6	2	1	6	1	17	.337	.352	.483	134	4	0	0	0	.993	1	1-15/D-7	0.3
1993	Cle-A	113	366	35	91	11	2	10	34	28	78	.249	.311	.372	83	-9	1	3	-2	.976	-0	D-88,1-15	-1.6
Total	5	277	846	99	230	39	4	27	111	59	175	.272	.325	.423	98	-4	1	3	-2	.988	2	D-159/1-78,O	-1.6
Team	3	163	556	53	141	20	4	13	52	32	117	.254	.301	.374	83	-14	1	3	-2	.989	2	/D-95,1-56	-2.1

■ STAN JEFFERSON
Jefferson, Stanley   b: 12/4/62, New York, N.Y.   BB/TR, 5'11", 175 lbs.   Deb: 9/7/86

1990	Cle-A	49	98	21	27	8	0	2	10	8	18	.276	.343	.418	112	2	8	4	0	.985	0	O-34/D-5	0.1
Total	6	296	832	125	180	25	9	16	67	65	177	.216	.279	.326	66	-40	60	20	6	.990	-20	O-235/D-9	-6.1

■ DAN JESSEE
Jessee, Daniel Edward   b: 2/22/01, Olive Hill, Ky.   d: 4/30/70, Venice, Fla.   BL/TR, 5'10", 165 lbs.   Deb: 8/14/29

1929	Cle-A	1	0	0	0	0	0	0	0	0	0	—	—	—		0	0	0	0	.000	0	R	0.0

■ JOHNNY JETER
Jeter, John   b: 10/24/44, Shreveport, La.   BR/TR, 6'1", 180 lbs.   Deb: 6/14/69 F

1974	Cle-A	6	17	3	6	1	0	0	1	1	6	.353	.389	.412	132	1	1	2	-1	.833	-2	/O-6	-0.2
Total	6	336	873	108	213	27	10	18	69	46	237	.244	.284	.360	82	-24	28	16	-1	.975	-11	O-262/D-3	-4.8

■ HOUSTON JIMENEZ
Jimenez, Alfonso (Gonzalez)   b: 10/30/57, Navojoa, Mexico   BR/TR, 5'8", 144 lbs.   Deb: 6/13/83

1988	Cle-A	9	21	1	1	0	0	0	1	0	2	.048	.048	.048	-71	-5	0	0	0	.973	6	/2-7,S-2	0.1
Total	4	158	411	34	76	16	2	0	29	20	49	.185	.223	.234	25	-42	0	2	-1	.962	7	S-147/2-9	-2.6

■ ALEX JOHNSON
Johnson, Alexander   b: 12/7/42, Helena, Ark.   BR/TR, 6', 205 lbs.   Deb: 7/25/64

1972	Cle-A	108	356	31	85	10	1	8	37	22	40	.239	.285	.340	83	-8	6	8	-3	.955	-5	O-95	-2.4
Total	13	1322	4623	550	1331	180	33	78	525	244	626	.288	.329	.392	105	22	113	63	-4	.953	-5	O-1000,D-199	-4.2

■ CLIFF JOHNSON
Johnson, Clifford   b: 7/22/47, San Antonio, Tex.   BR/TR, 6'4", 225 lbs.   Deb: 9/13/72

1979	Cle-A	72	240	37	65	10	0	18	61	24	39	.271	.349	.538	135	11	2	0	1	.000	-0	D-62/C-1	0.9
1980	Cle-A	54	174	25	40	3	1	6	28	25	30	.230	.327	.362	88	-3	0	1	-1	.000	0	D-45	-0.5
Total	15	1369	3945	539	1016	188	10	196	699	568	719	.258	.358	.459	125	141	9	12	-5	.993	-33	D-746,1-189,C/O	7.4
Team	2	126	414	62	105	13	1	24	89	49	69	.254	.340	.464	115	8	2	1	0	.000	-0	D-107/C-1	0.4

■ LARRY JOHNSON
Johnson, Larry Doby   b: 8/17/50, Cleveland, Ohio   BR/TR, 6', 185 lbs.   Deb: 10/3/72

1972	Cle-A	1	2	0	1	0	0	0	0	0	0	.500	.500	.500	192	0	0	0	0	1.000	0	/C-1	0.1
1974	Cle-A	1	0	1	0	0	0	0	0	0	0	—	—	—		0	0	0	0	.000	0	R	0.0
Total	5	12	26	1	5	0	0	0	1	0	2	.192	.250	.269	46	-2	0	0	0	.975	1	/C-9,D-1	-0.2
Team	2	2	2	1	1	0	0	0	0	0	0	.500	.500	.500	192	0	0	0	0	1.000	0	/C-1	0.1

■ LOU JOHNSON
Johnson, Louis Brown "Slick"   b: 9/22/34, Lexington, Ky.   BR/TR, 5'11", 175 lbs.   Deb: 4/17/60

1968	Cle-A	65	202	25	52	11	1	5	23	9	24	.257	.302	.396	112	2	6	1	1	.989	1	O-57	0.2
Total	8	677	2049	244	529	97	14	48	232	110	320	.258	.313	.389	103	5	50	24	1	.981	-19	O-606	-4.2

YEAR	TM/L	G	AB	R	H	2B	3B	HR	RBI	BB	SO	AVG	OBP	SLG	PRO+	BR/A	SB	CS	SBR	FA	FR	G/POS	TPR

■ DOC JOHNSTON Johnston, Wheeler Roger b: 9/9/1887, Cleveland, Tenn. d: 2/17/61, Chattanooga, Tenn. BL/TL, 6', 170 lbs. Deb: 10/3/09 F

1912	Cle-A	43	164	22	46	7	4	1	11	11		.280	.326	.390	101	-0	8			.991	-2	1-41	-0.3
1913	Cle-A	133	530	74	135	19	12	2	39	35	65	.255	.309	.347	89	-8	19			.989	-1	*1-133	-1.2
1914	Cle-A	103	340	43	83	15	1	0	23	28	46	.244	.311	.294	79	-9	14	9	-1	.987	-7	1-90/O-2	-2.1
1918	Cle-A	74	273	30	62	12	2	0	25	26	19	.227	.301	.286	70	-10	12			.989	-3	1-73	-1.8
1919	Cle-A	102	331	42	101	17	3	1	33	25	18	.305	.359	.384	102	1	21			.984	-3	1-98	-0.6
1920	*Cle-A	147	535	68	156	24	10	2	71	28	32	.292	.333	.385	87	-11	13	7	-0	.992	-1	*1-147	-1.5
1921	Cle-A	118	384	53	114	20	7	2	46	29	15	.297	.353	.401	90	-6	2	9	-5	.988	-1	*1-116	-1.3
Total	11	1055	3774	478	992	154	68	14	381	264	292	.263	.319	.351	88	-63	139	48		.989	-37	*1-1023/O-2	-14.6
Team	7	720	2557	332	697	114	39	8	248	182	195	.273	.328	.357	88	-43	89	25		.989	-18	1-698/O-2	-8.8

■ HAL JONES Jones, Harold Marion b: 4/9/36, Louisiana, Mo. BR/TR, 6'2", 194 lbs. Deb: 4/25/61

1961	Cle-A	12	35	2	6	0	0	2	4	2	12	.171	.216	.314	48	-3	0	0	0	.974	-2	1-10	-0.5
1962	Cle-A	5	16	2	5	1	0	0	1	0	4	.313	.353	.375	99	-0	0	0	0	.969	0	/1-4	0.0
Total	2	17	51	4	11	1	0	2	5	2	16	.216	.259	.353	64	-3	0	0	0	.973	-2	/1-14	-0.5

■ WILLIE JONES Jones, Willie Edward "Puddin' Head" b: 8/16/25, Dillon, S.C. d: 10/18/83, Cincinnati, Ohio BR/TR, 6'1", 192 lbs. Deb: 9/10/47

| 1959 | Cle-A | 11 | 18 | 1 | 4 | 1 | 0 | 0 | 1 | 1 | 3 | .222 | .263 | .278 | 51 | -1 | 0 | 0 | 0 | .929 | 2 | /3-4 | 0.0 |
| Total | 15 | 1691 | 5826 | 786 | 1502 | 252 | 33 | 190 | 812 | 755 | 541 | .258 | .345 | .410 | 102 | 20 | 40 | 17 | 2 | .963 | -55 | *3-1614/2-1,1 | -4.9 |

■ SCOTT JORDAN Jordan, Scott Allan b: 5/27/63, Waco, Tex. BR/TR, 6', 175 lbs. Deb: 9/2/88

| 1988 | Cle-A | 7 | 9 | 0 | 1 | 0 | 0 | 0 | 1 | 0 | 3 | .111 | .111 | .111 | -37 | -2 | 0 | 0 | 0 | 1.000 | -1 | /O-6 | -0.3 |

■ TOM JORDAN Jordan, Thomas Jefferson b: 9/5/19, Lawton, Okla. BR/TR, 6'1.5", 195 lbs. Deb: 9/4/44

| 1946 | Cle-A | 14 | 35 | 2 | 7 | 1 | 0 | 1 | 3 | 3 | 1 | .200 | .263 | .314 | 65 | -2 | 1 | 1 | -0 | .974 | -6 | C-13 | -0.8 |
| Total | 3 | 39 | 96 | 5 | 23 | 4 | 2 | 1 | 6 | 4 | 2 | .240 | .270 | .354 | 78 | -3 | 1 | 1 | -0 | .963 | -6 | /C-29 | -0.9 |

■ WALLY JUDNICH Judnich, Walter Franklin b: 1/24/17, San Francisco, Cal. d: 7/12/71, Glendale, Cal. BL/TL, 6'1", 205 lbs. Deb: 4/16/40

| 1948 | *Cle-A | 79 | 218 | 36 | 56 | 13 | 3 | 2 | 29 | 56 | 23 | .257 | .411 | .372 | 112 | 7 | 2 | 3 | -1 | .970 | -8 | O-49,1-20 | -0.5 |
| Total | 7 | 790 | 2786 | 424 | 782 | 150 | 29 | 90 | 420 | 385 | 298 | .281 | .369 | .452 | 119 | 75 | 20 | 24 | -8 | .988 | -2 | O-604,1-149 | 2.8 |

■ IKE KAHDOT Kahdot, Isaac Leonard "Chief" b: 10/22/01, Georgetown, Okla. BR/TR, 5'5.5", 145 lbs. Deb: 9/5/22

| 1922 | Cle-A | 4 | 2 | 0 | 0 | 0 | 0 | 0 | 0 | 0 | 1 | .000 | .000 | .000 | -99 | -1 | 0 | 0 | 0 | 1.000 | 1 | /3-2 | 0.0 |

■ NICK KAHL Kahl, Nicholas Alexander b: 4/10/1879, Coulterville, Ill. d: 7/13/59, Sparta, Ill. BR/TR, 5'9", 185 lbs. Deb: 5/2/05

| 1905 | Cle-A | 40 | 135 | 16 | 29 | 4 | 1 | 0 | 21 | 4 | | .215 | .248 | .259 | 60 | -6 | 1 | | | .948 | 0 | 2-32/S-1,O | -0.6 |

■ WILLIE KAMM Kamm, William Edward b: 2/2/1900, San Francisco, Cal. d: 12/21/88, Belmont, Cal. BR/TR, 5'10.5", 170 lbs. Deb: 4/18/23

1931	Cle-A	114	410	68	121	31	4	0	66	64	13	.295	.392	.390	100	2	13	9	-2	.947	1	*3-114	0.8
1932	Cle-A	148	524	76	150	34	9	3	83	75	36	.286	.379	.381	96	-2	6	3	0	.967	7	*3-148	1.4
1933	Cle-A	133	447	59	126	17	2	1	47	54	27	.282	.359	.336	81	-10	6	3	0	.984	1	*3-131	-0.2
1934	Cle-A	121	386	52	104	23	3	0	42	62	38	.269	.372	.345	84	-7	7	1	0	.978	11	*3-118	1.0
1935	Cle-A	6	18	2	6	0	0	0	1	0	1	.333	.333	.333	72	-1	0	1	-1	.875	-2	/3-4	-0.3
Total	13	1693	5851	802	1643	348	85	29	826	824	405	.281	.372	.384	97	-8	126	84		.967	66	*3-1674	13.6
Team	5	522	1785	257	507	105	18	4	239	255	115	.284	.375	.370	91	-17	32	17		.969	18	3-515	2.7

■ MARTY KAVANAGH Kavanagh, Martin Joseph b: 6/13/1891, Harrison, N.J. d: 7/28/60, Eloise, Mich. BR/TR, 6', 187 lbs. Deb: 4/18/14

1916	Cle-A	19	44	4	11	2	1	1	10	2	5	.250	.283	.409	102	-0				.894	-0	/2-9,1-1,3	0.0
1917	Cle-A	14	14	1	0	0	0	0	0	3	2	.000	.176	.000	-43	-2	0			1.000	0	/O-2	-0.2
1918	Cle-A	13	38	4	8	2	0	0	6	7	7	.211	.348	.263	77	-1	1			.967	-1	1-12	-0.3
Total	5	370	1033	138	257	47	20	10	122	118	122	.249	.330	.362	104	4	26			.926	-26	2-172/1-73,03S	-3.4
Team	3	46	96	9	19	4	1	1	16	12	14	.198	.294	.292	71	-3	1			.968	-1	/1-13,2-9,O3	-0.5

■ PAT KEEDY Keedy, Charles Patrick b: 1/10/58, Birmingham, Ala. BR/TR, 6'4", 205 lbs. Deb: 9/10/85

| 1989 | Cle-A | 9 | 14 | 3 | 3 | 2 | 0 | 0 | 1 | 2 | 5 | .214 | .313 | .357 | 87 | -0 | 0 | 0 | 0 | 1.000 | -0 | /O-3,3-2,1SD | 0.0 |
| Total | 3 | 29 | 59 | 10 | 12 | 4 | 0 | 3 | 4 | 4 | 19 | .203 | .254 | .424 | 77 | -2 | 1 | 1 | | .929 | 3 | /3-15,O-5,1DS2 | 0.2 |

■ PAT KELLY Kelly, Harold Patrick b: 7/30/44, Philadelphia, Pa. BL/TL, 6'1", 185 lbs. Deb: 9/6/67

| 1981 | Cle-A | 48 | 75 | 8 | 16 | 4 | 0 | 1 | 16 | 14 | 9 | .213 | .337 | .307 | 88 | -1 | 2 | 4 | -2 | 1.000 | -2 | D-18/O-8 | -0.6 |
| Total | 15 | 1385 | 4338 | 620 | 1147 | 189 | 35 | 76 | 418 | 588 | 768 | .264 | .356 | .377 | 107 | 54 | 250 | 118 | 4 | .978 | -15 | O-997,D-214 | -0.5 |

■ KEN KELTNER Keltner, Kenneth Frederick "Butch" b: 10/31/16, Milwaukee, Wis. d: 12/12/91, New Berlin, Wis. BR/TR, 6', 190 lbs. Deb: 10/2/37

1937	Cle-A	1	1	0	0	0	0	0	0	0	0	.000	.000	.000	-99	-0	0	0	0	1.000	0	/3-1	0.0
1938	Cle-A	149	576	86	159	31	9	26	113	33	75	.276	.319	.497	103	-2	4	3	-1	.956	-10	*3-149	-0.9
1939	Cle-A	154	587	84	191	35	11	13	97	51	41	.325	.379	.489	125	20	6	6	-2	.974	6	*3-154	2.4
1940	Cle-A★	149	543	67	138	24	10	15	77	51	56	.254	.322	.418	93	-7	10	5	0	.953	-6	*3-148	-0.9
1941	Cle-A★	149	581	83	156	31	13	23	84	51	56	.269	.330	.485	119	12	2	2	-1	.971	23	*3-149	3.5
1942	Cle-A★	152	624	72	179	34	4	6	78	20	36	.287	.312	.383	101	-3	4	3	-1	.945	16	*3-151	1.4
1943	Cle-A★	110	427	47	111	31	3	4	39	36	20	.260	.317	.375	109	3	2	4	-1	.969	6	*3-107	1.0
1944	Cle-A★	149	573	74	169	41	9	13	91	53	29	.295	.355	.466	139	26	4	3	-1	.968	15	*3-149	4.4
1946	Cle-A★	116	398	47	96	17	1	13	45	54	38	.241	.294	.387	95	-5	0	3	-2	.965	-2	*3-112	-0.7
1947	Cle-A	151	541	49	139	29	3	11	76	59	45	.257	.331	.383	101	0	5	4	-1	.972	-9	*3-150	-1.0
1948	*Cle-A★	153	558	91	166	24	4	31	119	89	52	.297	.395	.522	146	36	2	1	0	.969	-0	*3-153	3.3
1949	Cle-A	80	246	35	57	9	2	8	30	38	26	.232	.335	.382	91	-4	0	1	-1	.980	-1	3-69	-0.7
Total	13	1526	5683	737	1570	308	69	163	852	514	480	.276	.338	.441	113	75	39	33	-8	.965	36	*3-1500/1-1	11.6
Team	12	1513	5655	735	1561	306	69	163	848	501	474	.276	.337	.441	113	76	39	33	-8	.965	37	*3-1492	11.8

■ FRED KENDALL Kendall, Fred Lyn b: 1/31/49, Torrance, Cal. BR/TR, 6'1", 190 lbs. Deb: 9/8/69

| 1977 | Cle-A | 103 | 317 | 18 | 79 | 13 | 1 | 3 | 39 | 16 | 27 | .249 | .287 | .325 | 69 | -14 | 0 | 1 | -1 | .991 | -13 | *C-102/D-1 | -2.5 |
| Total | 12 | 877 | 2576 | 170 | 603 | 86 | 11 | 31 | 244 | 189 | 240 | .234 | .288 | .312 | 72 | -102 | 5 | 5 | -2 | .987 | -71 | C-795/1-19,D30 | -15.6 |

■ BOB KENNEDY Kennedy, Robert Daniel b: 8/18/20, Chicago, Ill. BR/TR, 6'2", 193 lbs. Deb: 9/14/39 FMC

1948	*Cle-A	66	73	10	22	3	2	0	5	4	6	.301	.338	.397	98	-1	0	0	0	1.000	-13	O-50/2-2,1	-1.4
1949	Cle-A	121	424	49	117	23	5	9	57	37	40	.276	.334	.417	100	-2	5	5	-2	.990	3	O-98,3-21	-0.6
1950	Cle-A	146	540	70	157	27	5	9	54	53	31	.291	.355	.409	99	-2	3	4	-2	.987	-1	*O-144	-0.8
1951	Cle-A	108	321	30	79	15	4	7	29	34	33	.246	.320	.383	95	-3	4	2	0	.968	-1	O-106	-0.7
1952	Cle-A	22	40	6	12	3	1	0	12	9	5	.300	.429	.425	148	3	1	0	0	1.000	0	O-13/3-3	0.3
1953	Cle-A	100	161	22	38	5	0	3	22	19	11	.236	.320	.323	76	-5	0	2	-1	1.000	-21	O-89	-3.0
1954	Cle-A	1	0	0	0	0	0	0	0	0	0	.000									-0	/O-1	0.0
Total	16	1483	4624	514	1176	196	41	63	514	364	443	.254	.310	.355	80	-142	45	50	-17	.978	-55	O-821,3-540/12	-23.9
Team	7	564	1559	196	425	76	17	28	179	156	126	.273	.340	.397	97	-11	13	13	-4	.986	-32	O-501/3-24,21	-6.2

■ JERRY KENNEY Kenney, Gerald T b: 6/30/45, St.Louis, Mo. BL/TR, 6'1", 170 lbs. Deb: 9/5/67

| 1973 | Cle-A | 5 | 16 | 0 | 4 | 0 | 1 | 0 | 2 | 2 | 0 | .250 | .333 | .375 | 97 | -0 | 0 | 0 | 0 | 1.000 | -2 | /2-5 | -0.1 |
| Total | 6 | 465 | 1369 | 165 | 325 | 38 | 13 | 7 | 103 | 184 | 139 | .237 | .329 | .299 | 82 | -30 | 59 | 29 | | .962 | 36 | 3-328/S-78,021 | 1.4 |

YEAR	TM/L	G	AB	R	H	2B	3B	HR	RBI	BB	SO	AVG	OBP	SLG	PRO+	BR/A	SB	CS	SBR	FA	FR	G/POS	TPR
■ MARTY KEOUGH Keough, Richard Martin b: 4/14/35, Oakland, Cal. BL/TL, 6', 180 lbs. Deb: 4/21/56 F																							
1960	Cle-A	65	149	19	37	5	0	3	11	9	23	.248	.296	.342	74	-6	2	3	-1	.986	-4	O-42	-1.3
Total	11	841	1796	256	434	71	23	43	176	164	318	.242	.311	.379	86	-35	26	19	-4	.984	-25	O-464,1-130	-9.0
■ JACK KIBBLE Kibble, John Westly "Happy" b: 1/2/1892, Seatonville, Ill. d: 12/13/69, Roundup, Mont. BB/TR, 5'9.5", 154 lbs. Deb: 9/10/12																							
1912	Cle-A	5	8	1	0	0	0	0	0	0		.000	.111	.000	-65	-2	0			1.000	4	/3-4,2-1	0.2
■ JERRY KINDALL Kindall, Gerald Donald "Slim" b: 5/27/35, St.Paul, Minn. BR/TR, 6'2.5", 175 lbs. Deb: 7/1/56																							
1962	Cle-A	154	530	51	123	21	1	13	55	45	107	.232	.292	.349	74	-20	4	3	-1	.978	21	*2-154	1.6
1963	Cle-A	86	234	27	48	4	1	5	20	18	71	.205	.268	.295	58	-13	3	1	0	.958	3	S-46,2-37/1	-0.5
1964	Cle-A	23	25	5	9	1	0	2	2	2	7	.360	.407	.640	188	3	0	0	0	.989	3	1-23	0.6
Total	9	742	2057	211	439	83	9	44	198	145	535	.213	.268	.327	62	-111	17	11		.967	50	2-511,S-136/31	-1.3
Team	3	263	789	83	180	26	2	20	77	65	185	.228	.289	.342	73	-31	7	4		.980	26	2-191/S-46,1	1.7
■ RALPH KINER Kiner, Ralph McPherran b: 10/27/22, Santa Rita, N.Mex. BR/TR, 6'2", 195 lbs. Deb: 4/16/46 H																							
1955	Cle-A	113	321	56	78	13	0	18	54	65	46	.243	.370	.452	116	8	0	0	0	.986	-5	O-87	-0.1
Total	10	1472	5205	971	1451	216	39	369	1015	1011	749	.279	.398	.548	148	363	22	2	5	.974	-2	*O-1382/1-58	28.9
■ JIM KING King, James Hubert b: 8/27/32, Elkins, Ark. BL/TR, 6', 185 lbs. Deb: 4/17/55																							
1967	Cle-A	19	21	2	3	0	0	0	0	1	2	.143	.182	.143	-3	-3	0	0	0	1.000	-0	/O-1	-0.3
Total	11	1125	2918	374	699	112	19	117	401	363	401	.240	.328	.411	104	15	23	8	2	.984	13	O-851/C-2	-0.6
■ WAYNE KIRBY Kirby, Wayne Leonard b: 1/22/64, Williamsburg, Va. BL/TR, 5'10", 185 lbs. Deb: 9/12/91																							
1991	Cle-A	21	43	4	9	2	0	0	5	2	6	.209	.244	.256	38	-4	1	2	-1	1.000	-1	O-21	-0.6
1992	Cle-A	21	18	9	3	1	0	1	1	3	2	.167	.286	.389	89	-0	0	3	-2	1.000	-0	/O-2,D-4	-0.2
1993	Cle-A	131	458	71	123	19	5	6	60	37	58	.269	.327	.371	88	-8	17	5	2	.983	13	*O-123/D-5	0.4
1994	Cle-A	78	191	33	56	6	0	5	23	13	30	.293	.341	.403	91	-3	11	4	1	.959	-11	O-68/D-2	-1.3
1995	*Cle-A	101	188	29	39	10	2	1	14	13	32	.207	.262	.298	45	-15	10	3	1	.990	-10	O-68/D-7	-2.4
Total	5	352	898	146	230	38	7	13	103	68	128	.256	.312	.357	77	-30	39	17	2	.981	-9	O-282/D-18	-4.1
■ JAY KIRKE Kirke, Judson Fabian b: 6/16/1888, Fleischmanns, N.Y d: 8/31/68, New Orleans, La. BL/TR, 6', 195 lbs. Deb: 9/28/10																							
1914	Cle-A	67	242	18	66	10	2	1	25	7	30	.273	.296	.343	89	-4	5	10	-5	.974	0	O-42,1-18	-1.2
1915	Cle-A	87	339	35	105	19	2	2	40	14	21	.310	.346	.395	120	6	5	6	-2	.986	-1	1-87	0.1
Total	7	320	1148	122	346	49	13	7	148	35	112	.301	.328	.385	103	-0	21	16	-3	.927	-4	O-142,1-125/32S	-2.1
Team	2	154	581	53	171	29	4	3	65	21	51	.294	.326	.373	107	2	10	16	-7	.987	-1	1-105/O-42	-1.1
■ WILLIE KIRKLAND Kirkland, Willie Charles b: 2/17/34, Siluria, Ala. BL/TR, 6'1", 206 lbs. Deb: 4/15/58																							
1961	Cle-A	146	525	84	136	22	5	27	95	48	77	.259	.322	.474	113	7	7	0	2	.974	8	*O-138	1.0
1962	Cle-A	137	419	56	84	9	1	21	72	43	62	.200	.275	.377	76	-16	9	1	2	.972	0	*O-125	-2.0
1963	Cle-A	127	427	51	98	13	2	15	47	45	99	.230	.304	.375	90	-6	8	2	1	.984	7	*O-112	-0.4
Total	9	1149	3494	443	837	134	29	148	509	323	648	.240	.307	.422	99	-15	52	19	4	.974	-2	O-995	-6.3
Team	3	410	1371	191	318	44	8	63	214	136	238	.232	.302	.414	94	-15	24	3	5	.977	16	O-375	-1.4
■ RON KITTLE Kittle, Ronald Dale b: 1/5/58, Gary, Indiana BR/TR, 6'4", 220 lbs. Deb: 9/2/82																							
1988	Cle-A	75	225	31	58	8	0	18	43	16	65	.258	.329	.533	134	9	0	0	0	.000	0	D-63	0.8
Total	10	843	2708	356	648	100	3	176	460	236	744	.239	.309	.473	110	28	16	16	-5	.974	-17	O-353,D-351/1	-1.9
■ MALACHI KITTRIDGE Kittridge, Malachi Jeddidah "Jeddidah" b: 10/12/1869, Clinton, Mass. d: 6/23/28, Gary, Ind. BR/TR, 5'7", 170 lbs. Deb: 4/19/1890 M																							
1906	Cle-A	5	10	0	1	0	0	0	0	0		.100	.100	.100	-38	-2	0			.938	-1	/C-5	-0.2
Total	16	1215	4027	375	882	108	31	17	390	314		.219	.277	.274	56	-236	64			.961	47	*C-1196/P-1	-6.7
■ LOU KLEIN Klein, Louis Frank b: 10/22/18, New Orleans, La. d: 6/20/76, Metairie, La. BR/TR, 5'11", 170 lbs. Deb: 4/21/43 MC																							
1951	Cle-A	2	2	0	0	0	0	0	0	0	1	.000	.000	.000	-99	-1	0	0	0	.000	0	H	-0.1
Total	5	305	1037	162	269	48	15	16	101	105	119	.259	.330	.381	97	-6	10	0		.975	-30	2-202/S-79,3O	-2.2
■ LOU KLIMCHOCK Klimchock, Louis Stephen b: 10/15/39, Hostetter, Pa. BL/TR, 5'11", 180 lbs. Deb: 9/27/58																							
1968	Cle-A	11	15	0	2	0	0	0	3	1	0	.133	.188	.133	-2	-2	0	0	0	.500	-3	/3-4,1-1,2	-0.5
1969	Cle-A	90	258	26	74	13	2	6	26	18	14	.287	.333	.422	107	2	0	0	0	.934	-16	3-56,2-21/C	-1.3
1970	Cle-A	41	56	5	9	0	0	1	2	3	9	.161	.217	.214	18	-6	0	0	0	1.000	-1	/1-5,2-5	-0.7
Total	12	318	669	64	155	21	3	13	69	31	71	.232	.267	.330	63	-35	0	1	-1	.906	-30	/3-70,2-52,1OC	-6.6
Team	3	142	329	31	85	13	2	7	31	22	23	.258	.307	.374	87	-6	0	0	0	.922	-19	/3-60,2-27,1C	-2.5
■ JOE KLUGMANN Klugmann, Joe b: 3/26/1895, St.Louis, Mo. d: 7/18/51, Moberly, Mo. BR/TR, 5'11", 175 lbs. Deb: 9/23/21																							
1925	Cle-A	38	85	12	28	9	2	0	12	8	4	.329	.387	.482	119	2	3	1	0	.959	-3	2-29/1-4,3	0.0
Total	4	77	187	22	47	11	3	0	17	11	15	.251	.296	.342	67	-10	3	2	-0	.947	-3	/2-64,1-4,3S	-1.3
■ COTTON KNAUPP Knaupp, Henry Antone b: 8/13/1889, San Antonio, Tex. d: 7/6/67, New Orleans, La. BR/TR, 5'9", 165 lbs. Deb: 8/30/10																							
1910	Cle-A	18	59	3	14	3	1	0	11	8		.237	.338	.322	105	1	1			.884	-8	S-18	-0.8
1911	Cle-A	13	39	2	4	1	0	0	0	0		.103	.103	.128	-35	-7	3			.964	2	S-13	-0.5
Total	2	31	98	5	18	4	1	0	11	8		.184	.252	.245	48	-6	4			.913	-6	/S-31	-1.3
■ BILL KNICKERBOCKER Knickerbocker, William Hart b: 12/29/11, Los Angeles, Cal. d: 9/8/63, Sebastopol, Cal. BR/TR, 5'11", 170 lbs. Deb: 4/12/33																							
1933	Cle-A	80	279	20	63	16	3	2	32	11	30	.226	.255	.326	51	-21	1	4	-2	.939	2	S-80	-1.5
1934	Cle-A	146	593	82	188	32	5	4	67	25	40	.317	.347	.408	93	-8	6	6	-2	.962	-7	*S-146	-0.7
1935	Cle-A	132	540	77	161	34	5	0	55	27	31	.298	.332	.380	82	-15	2	12	-7	.956	9	*S-128	-0.5
1936	Cle-A	155	618	81	182	35	3	8	73	56	30	.294	.354	.400	85	-15	5	14	-7	.952	-1	*S-155	-1.1
Total	10	907	3418	423	943	198	27	28	368	244	238	.276	.326	.374	79	-109	25	46	-20	.955	-42	S-649,2-211/3	-11.0
Team	4	513	2030	260	594	117	16	14	227	119	131	.293	.333	.387	82	-58	14	36	-17	.954	3	S-509	-3.8
■ RAY KNODE Knode, Robert Troxell "Bob" b: 1/28/01, Westminster, Md. d: 4/13/82, Battle Creek, Mich BL/TL, 5'10", 160 lbs. Deb: 6/30/23 F																							
1923	Cle-A	22	38	7	11	0	0	2	4	2	4	.289	.325	.447	102	-0	1	0	0	.992	0	1-21	0.0
1924	Cle-A	11	37	6	9	1	0	0	4	3	0	.243	.300	.270	47	-3	2	1	0	.992	1	1-10	-0.2
1925	Cle-A	45	108	13	27	5	0	0	11	10	4	.250	.314	.296	55	-7	3	3	-1	.990	1	1-34	-0.9
1926	Cle-A	31	24	6	8	1	1	0	4	3	4	.333	.407	.458	124	1	0	0	0	.984	1	1-11	0.1
Total	4	109	207	32	55	7	1	2	23	18	12	.266	.324	.338	70	-9	6	4	-1	.990	2	/1-76	-1.0
■ BRAD KOMMINSK Komminsk, Brad Lynn b: 4/4/61, Lima, Ohio BR/TR, 6'2", 205 lbs. Deb: 8/14/83																							
1989	Cle-A	71	198	27	47	8	2	8	33	24	55	.237	.323	.419	106	1	8	2	1	.995	3	O-68	0.4
Total	8	376	986	140	215	37	5	23	105	114	258	.218	.303	.336	75	-31	39	20	-0	.984	-17	O-329/D-3,3	-6.0
■ LARRY KOPF Kopf, William Lorenz (a.k.a. Fred Brady In 1913) b: 11/3/1890, Bristol, Conn. d: 10/15/86, Anderson Twp., O. BB/TR, 5'9", 160 lbs. Deb: 9/2/13 F																							
1913	Cle-A	6	10	2	3	1	0	0	1	0	0	.300	.300	.400	102	-0	0			.923	2	/2-4,3-1	0.2
Total	10	853	3010	349	750	84	30	5	266	242	214	.249	.312	.302	78	-82	72			.928	-122	S-664/2-99,3O	-17.8
■ JOHN KRONER Kroner, John Harold b: 11/13/08, St.Louis, Mo. d: 8/26/68, St.Louis, Mo. BR/TR, 6', 185 lbs. Deb: 9/29/35																							
1937	Cle-A	86	283	29	67	14	1	2	26	22	25	.237	.292	.314	52	-21	1	1	-0	.969	-3	2-64,3-11	-1.9

YEAR	TM/L	G	AB	R	H	2B	3B	HR	RBI	BB	SO	AVG	OBP	SLG	PRO+	BR/A	SB	CS	SBR	FA	FR	G/POS	TPR
1938	Cle-A	51	117	13	29	16	0	1	17	19	6	.248	.353	.410	92	-1	0	1	-1	.974	12	2-31/1-7,3S	1.0
Total	4	223	702	83	184	47	9	7	105	68	56	.262	.327	.385	75	-29	3	5		.968	6	2-133/3-44,S10	-1.4
Team	2	137	400	42	96	30	1	3	43	41	31	.240	.311	.343	64	-22	1	2		.970	9	/2-95,3-14,1S	-0.9
■ ERNIE KRUEGER	Krueger, Ernest George b: 12/27/1890, Chicago, Ill. d: 4/22/76, Waukegan, Ill. BR/TR, 5'10.5", 185 lbs. Deb: 8/4/13																						
1913	Cle-A	5	6	0	0	0	0	0	0	0	2	.000	.000	.000	-97	-1	0			1.000	-0	/C-4	-0.2
Total	8	318	836	87	220	33	14	11	93	64	85	.263	.319	.376	97	-4	12			.964	-3	C-257	1.0
■ ART KRUGER	Kruger, Arthur T. b: 3/16/1881, San Antonio, Tex. d: 11/28/49, Honda, Cal. BR/TR, 6', 185 lbs. Deb: 4/11/07																						
1910	Cle-A	47	168	14	26	4	2	0	10	15		.155	.237	.202	37	-12	10			.947	2	O-47	-1.4
1910	Cle-A	15	55	5	12	2	1	0	4	5		.218	.295	.291	82	-1	2			.974	2	O-15	0.0
Total	4	365	1222	113	283	49	21	6	115	73		.232	.281	.321	70	-52	38			.968	-2	O-344	-7.5
Team	2	62	223	19	38	6	3	0	14	20		.170	.251	.224	48	-13	12			.955	4	/O-62	-1.4
■ JACK KUBISZYN	Kubiszyn, John Henry b: 12/19/36, Buffalo, N.Y. BR/TR, 5'11", 170 lbs. Deb: 4/23/61																						
1961	Cle-A	25	42	4	9	0	0	0	0	2	5	.214	.250	.214	26	-4	0	0	0	1.000	3	/3-8,S-7,2	-0.1
1962	Cle-A	25	59	3	10	2	0	1	2	5	7	.169	.234	.254	32	-6	0	0	0	.964	2	S-18/3-1	-0.2
Total	2	50	101	7	19	2	0	1	2	7	12	.188	.241	.238	30	-10	0	0	0	.969	5	/S-25,3-9,2	-0.3
■ HARVEY KUENN	Kuenn, Harvey Edward b: 12/4/30, W.Allis, Wis. d: 2/28/88, Peoria, Ariz. BR/TR, 6'2", 190 lbs. Deb: 9/6/52 MC																						
1960	Cle-A★	126	474	65	146	24	0	9	54	55	25	.308	.381	.416	119	14	3	0	1	.966	1	*O-119/3-5	1.0
Total	15	1833	6913	951	2092	356	56	87	671	594	404	.303	.359	.408	108	80	68	56	-13	.978	-163	O-826,S-748,3/1	-8.3
■ KENNY KUHN	Kuhn, Kenneth Harold b: 3/20/37, Louisville, Ky. BL/TR, 5'10.5", 175 lbs. Deb: 7/7/55																						
1955	Cle-A	4	6	0	2	0	0	0	0	1	0	.333	.429	.333	103	0	1	0	0	1.000	-2	/S-4	-0.1
1956	Cle-A	27	22	7	6	1	0	0	2	0	4	.273	.273	.318	54	-1	0	1	-1	1.000	2	S-17/2-5	0.0
1957	Cle-A	40	53	5	9	0	0	0	5	4	9	.170	.228	.170	10	-6	0	0	0	.974	-3	2-14/3-2,S	-0.9
Total	3	71	81	12	17	1	0	0	7	5	13	.210	.256	.222	30	-8	1	1	-0	.963	-3	/S-22,2-19,3	-1.0
■ DUANE KUIPER	Kuiper, Duane Eugene b: 6/19/50, Racine, Wis. BL/TR, 6', 175 lbs. Deb: 9/9/74																						
1974	Cle-A	10	22	7	11	2	0	0	4	2	2	.500	.542	.591	228	4	1	1	-0	1.000	1	/2-8	0.5
1975	Cle-A	90	346	42	101	11	1	0	25	30	26	.292	.362	.329	97	-0	19	18	-5	.972	-14	2-87/D-1	-1.5
1976	Cle-A	135	506	47	133	13	6	0	37	30	42	.263	.305	.312	82	-12	10	17	-7	**.987**	20	*2-128/1-5,D	0.9
1977	Cle-A	148	610	62	169	15	8	1	50	37	55	.277	.326	.333	83	-14	11	11	-3	.985	2	*2-148	-0.5
1978	Cle-A	149	547	52	155	18	6	0	43	19	35	.283	.312	.338	84	-12	4	9	-4	.979	-19	*2-149	-2.5
1979	Cle-A	140	479	46	122	9	5	0	39	37	27	.255	.313	.294	65	-23	4	9	-4	**.988**	-4	*2-140	-2.1
1980	Cle-A	42	149	10	42	5	0	0	9	13	8	.282	.340	.315	80	-4	0	1	-1	.995	-8	2-42	-0.9
1981	Cle-A	72	206	15	53	6	0	0	14	8	13	.257	.285	.286	66	-9	1	1	-0	.983	-5	2-72	-1.1
Total	12	1057	3379	329	917	91	29	1	263	248	255	.271	.326	.316	81	-79	52	71	-27	.983	-36	2-920/1-6,D	-8.8
Team	8	786	2865	281	786	79	26	1	221	176	208	.274	.322	.321	81	-70	50	67	-25	.984	-27	2-774/1-5,D	-7.2
■ CANDY LaCHANCE	LaChance, George Joseph b: 2/15/1870, Putnam, Conn. d: 8/18/32, Waterville, Conn. BB/TR, 6'1", 183 lbs. Deb: 8/15/1893																						
1901	Cle-A	133	548	81	166	22	9	1	75	7		.303	.314	.381	96	-5	11			.979	-3	*1-133	-0.8
Total	12	1263	4919	678	1377	197	86	39	690	219		.280	.318	.379	93	-49	192			.984	-93	*1-1176/S-48,OC	-14.6
■ GUY LACY	Lacy, Osceola Guy b: 6/12/1897, Cleveland, Tenn. d: 11/19/53, Cleveland, Tenn. BR/TR, 5'11.5", 170 lbs. Deb: 5/7/26																						
1926	Cle-A	13	24	2	4	0	0	1	2	2	2	.167	.259	.292	43	-2	0	0	0	.976	1	2-11/3-2	-0.1
■ NAP LAJOIE	Lajoie, Napoleon "Larry" b: 9/5/1874, Woonsocket, R.I. d: 2/7/59, Daytona Beach, Fla. BR/TR, 6'1", 195 lbs. Deb: 8/12/1896 MH																						
1902	Cle-A	86	348	81	132	35	5	7	64	19		.379	.421	.569	180	36	19			.974	30	2-86	6.3
1903	Cle-A	125	485	90	167	41	11	7	93	24		**.344**	.379	**.518**	**170**	**39**	21			.955	**40**	*2-122/1-1,3	**8.4**
1904	Cle-A	140	553	92	**208**	**49**	15	6	**102**	27		**.376**	**.413**	**.552**	**205**	**64**	29			.962	-1	2-95,S-44/1	**7.2**
1905	Cle-A	65	249	29	82	12	2	2	41	17		.329	.377	.418	150	14	11			.991	9	2-59/1-5M	2.5
1906	Cle-A	152	602	88	**214**	**48**	9	0	91	30		.355	.392	.465	170	46	20			**.973**	32	*2-130,3-15/SM	**8.5**
1907	Cle-A	137	509	53	152	30	6	2	63	30		.299	.345	.393	134	18	24			**.969**	**45**	*2-128/1-9M	**6.6**
1908	Cle-A	157	581	77	168	32	6	2	74	47		.289	.352	.375	136	23	15			**.964**	**49**	*2-156/1-1M	**7.8**
1909	Cle-A	128	469	56	152	33	7	1	47	35		.324	.378	.431	149	26	13			.959	19	*2-120/1-8M	4.6
1910	Cle-A	159	591	94	**227**	**51**	7	4	76	60		**.384**	.445	.514	198	**66**	26			.966	15	*2-149,1-10	**8.5**
1911	Cle-A	90	315	36	115	20	1	2	60	26		.365	.420	.454	142	18	13			.990	-7	1-41,2-37	1.0
1912	Cle-A	117	448	66	165	34	4	0	90	28		.368	.414	.462	146	26	18			.959	5	2-97,1-20	2.7
1913	Cle-A	137	465	66	156	25	2	1	68	33	17	.335	.398	.404	131	19	17			**.970**	9	*2-126	2.8
1914	Cle-A	121	419	37	108	14	3	0	50	32	15	.258	.313	.305	83	-9	14	15	-5	.959	6	2-80,1-31	-1.0
Total	21	2480	9589	1504	3242	657	163	83	1599	516	85	.338	.380	.467	150	559	380	21		.963	367	*2-2035,1-286/SO3	94.2
Team	13	1614	6034	865	2046	424	78	34	919	408	32	.339	.388	.452	155	387	240	15		.965	252	*2-1385,1-128/S3	65.9
■ TOM LAMPKIN	Lampkin, Thomas Michael b: 3/4/64, Cincinnati, Ohio BL/TR, 5'11", 180 lbs. Deb: 9/10/88																						
1988	Cle-A	4	4	0	0	0	0	0	0	1	0	.000	.200	.000	-38	-1	0	0	0	1.000	-1	/C-3	-0.2
Total	6	215	380	41	82	13	2	6	41	43	53	.216	.299	.308	65	-18	11	4	1	.983	-7	C-118/O-10,D	-1.9
■ GROVER LAND	Land, Grover Cleveland b: 9/22/1884, Frankfort, Ky. d: 7/22/58, Phoenix, Ariz. BR/TR, 6', 190 lbs. Deb: 9/2/08 C																						
1908	Cle-A	8	16	1	3	0	0	0	2	0		.188	.188	.188	22	-1	0			.955	-1	/C-8	-0.3
1909	Cle-A	1	4	0	2	0	0	0	1	0		.500	.500	.500	207	0	0			1.000	0	/C-1	0.1
1910	Cle-A	34	111	4	23	0	0	0	7	2		.207	.228	.207	36	-8	1			.982	5	C-33	-0.1
1911	Cle-A	35	107	5	15	1	2	0	10	3		.140	.164	.187	-2	-15	2			.961	1	C-34/1-1	-1.1
1913	Cle-A	17	47	3	11	1	0	0	9	4	1	.234	.321	.255	67	-2	1			.924	1	C-17	0.0
Total	7	293	910	62	221	21	6	0	80	27	44	.243	.271	.279	50	-64	14			.964	-2	C-271/1-1	-4.6
Team	5	95	285	13	54	2	2	0	29	9	1	.189	.222	.211	28	-26	4			.961	5	/C-93,1-1	-1.4
■ JIM LANDIS	Landis, James Henry b: 3/9/34, Fresno, Cal. BR/TR, 6'1", 180 lbs. Deb: 4/16/57																						
1966	Cle-A	85	158	23	35	5	1	3	14	20	25	.222	.317	.323	84	-3	2	1	0	1.000	-11	O-61	-1.7
Total	11	1346	4288	625	1061	169	50	93	467	588	767	.247	.346	.375	100	10	139	51		.989	58	*O-1265	1.1
■ SAM LANGFORD	Langford, Elton b: 5/21/1899, Briggs, Tex. d: 7/31/93, Plainview, Tex. BL/TR, 6', 180 lbs. Deb: 4/13/26																						
1927	Cle-A	20	67	10	18	5	0	1	7	5	7	.269	.347	.388	90	-1	0	1	-1	1.000	-2	O-20	-0.5
1928	Cle-A	110	427	50	118	17	8	4	50	21	35	.276	.312	.382	81	-13	3	7	-3	.972	-8	*O-107	-3.1
Total	3	131	495	61	136	22	8	5	57	26	42	.275	.316	.382	81	-14	3	8	-4	.976	-11	O-127	-3.6
Team	2	130	494	60	136	22	8	5	57	26	42	.275	.317	.383	82	-14	3	8	-4	.976	-11	O-127	-3.6
■ LYN LARY	Lary, Lynford Hobart "Broadway" b: 1/28/06, Armona, Cal. d: 1/9/73, Downey, Cal. BR/TR, 6', 165 lbs. Deb: 5/11/29																						
1937	Cle-A	156	644	110	187	46	7	8	77	88	64	.290	.378	.421	100	2	18	8	1	.963	6	*S-156	1.7
1938	Cle-A	141	568	94	152	36	4	3	51	88	65	.268	.366	.361	84	-12	23	6	3	.964	-0	*S-141	0.2
1939	Cle-A	3	2	0	0	0	0	0	0	0	1	.000	.000	.000	-99	-1	0	0	0	.000	-1	/S-2	-0.1
Total	12	1302	4603	805	1239	247	56	38	526	705	470	.269	.369	.372	90	-47	162	49	19	.956	11	*S-1138/3-95,12O	6.5
Team	3	300	1214	204	339	82	11	11	128	176	130	.279	.372	.392	93	-11	41	14	4	.963	5	S-299	1.8

■ **JIM LAWRENCE** Lawrence, James Ross b: 2/12/39, Hamilton, Ont., Can. BL/TR, 6'1", 185 lbs. Deb: 5/30/63

YEAR	TM/L	G	AB	R	H	2B	3B	HR	RBI	BB	SO	AVG	OBP	SLG	PRO+	BR/A	SB	CS	SBR	FA	FR	G/POS	TPR
1963	Cle-A	2	0	0	0	0	0	0	0	0	0	—	—	—	—	0	0	0	0	.750	0	/C-2	0.0

■ **EMIL LEBER** Leber, Emil Bohmiel b: 5/15/1881, Cleveland, Ohio d: 11/6/24, Cleveland, Ohio BR/TR, 5'11", 170 lbs. Deb: 9/2/05

YEAR	TM/L	G	AB	R	H	2B	3B	HR	RBI	BB	SO	AVG	OBP	SLG	PRO+	BR/A	SB	CS	SBR	FA	FR	G/POS	TPR
1905	Cle-A	2	6	1	0	0	0	0	0	1		.000	.143	.000	-53	-1	0			1.000	-0	/3-2	-0.1

■ **CLIFF LEE** Lee, Clifford Walker b: 8/4/1896, Lexington, Neb. d: 8/25/80, Denver, Colo. BR/TR, 6'1", 175 lbs. Deb: 5/15/19

YEAR	TM/L	G	AB	R	H	2B	3B	HR	RBI	BB	SO	AVG	OBP	SLG	PRO+	BR/A	SB	CS	SBR	FA	FR	G/POS	TPR
1925	Cle-A	77	230	43	74	15	6	4	42	21	33	.322	.378	.491	118	6	2	1	0	.951	-3	O-70	-0.1
1926	Cle-A	21	40	4	7	1	0	1	2	6	8	.175	.283	.275	45	-3	0	0	0	1.000	0	/O-9,C-3	-0.4
Total	8	521	1583	216	475	87	28	38	216	104	186	.300	.344	.462	103	2	14	11		.960	-36	O-300/1-86,C3	-5.5
Team	2	98	270	47	81	16	6	5	44	27	41	.300	.364	.459	108	2	2	1		.958	-3	/O-79,C-3	-0.5

■ **LERON LEE** Lee, Leron b: 3/4/48, Bakersfield, Cal. BL/TR, 6', 196 lbs. Deb: 9/5/69

YEAR	TM/L	G	AB	R	H	2B	3B	HR	RBI	BB	SO	AVG	OBP	SLG	PRO+	BR/A	SB	CS	SBR	FA	FR	G/POS	TPR
1974	Cle-A	79	232	18	54	13	0	5	25	15	42	.233	.279	.353	82	-6	3	2	-0	.958	4	O-62/D-2	-0.6
1975	Cle-A	13	23	3	3	1	0	0	0	2	5	.130	.231	.174	16	-3	1	0	0	1.000	-1	/O-5,D-3	-0.3
Total	8	614	1617	173	404	83	13	31	152	133	315	.250	.309	.375	95	-15	19	14	-3	.962	-5	O-421/D-5	-4.2
Team	2	92	255	21	57	14	0	5	25	17	47	.224	.275	.337	76	-9	4	2	0	.960	3	/O-67,D-5	-0.9

■ **GENE LEEK** Leek, Eugene Harold b: 7/15/36, San Diego, Cal. BR/TR, 6', 185 lbs. Deb: 4/22/59

YEAR	TM/L	G	AB	R	H	2B	3B	HR	RBI	BB	SO	AVG	OBP	SLG	PRO+	BR/A	SB	CS	SBR	FA	FR	G/POS	TPR
1959	Cle-A	13	36	7	8	3	0	1	5	2	7	.222	.263	.389	80	-1	0	0	0	.955	-2	3-13/S-1	-0.3
Total	3	77	249	23	55	12	1	6	25	9	67	.221	.254	.349	55	-16	0	1	-1	.959	16	/3-66,S-8,O	0.1

■ **PAUL LEHNER** Lehner, Paul Eugene "Peanuts" or "Gulliver" b: 7/1/20, Dolomite, Ala. d: 12/27/67, Birmingham, Ala. BL/TL, 5'9", 165 lbs. Deb: 9/10/46

YEAR	TM/L	G	AB	R	H	2B	3B	HR	RBI	BB	SO	AVG	OBP	SLG	PRO+	BR/A	SB	CS	SBR	FA	FR	G/POS	TPR
1951	Cle-A	12	13	2	3	0	0	0	1	1	2	.231	.286	.231	43	-1	0	0	0	1.000	-0	/O-1	-0.1
Total	7	540	1768	175	455	80	21	22	197	127	118	.257	.309	.364	78	-60	6	11	-5	.981	-11	O-432/1-20	-9.7

■ **NEMO LEIBOLD** Leibold, Harry Loran b: 2/17/1892, Butler, Ind. d: 2/4/77, Detroit, Mich. BL/TR, 5'6.5", 157 lbs. Deb: 4/12/13

YEAR	TM/L	G	AB	R	H	2B	3B	HR	RBI	BB	SO	AVG	OBP	SLG	PRO+	BR/A	SB	CS	SBR	FA	FR	G/POS	TPR
1913	Cle-A	93	286	37	74	11	6	0	12	21	43	.259	.309	.339	87	-5	16			.945	-0	O-74	-1.0
1914	Cle-A	115	402	46	106	13	3	0	32	54	56	.264	.354	.311	96	-0	12	14	-5	.931	9	*O-107	-0.1
1915	Cle-A	57	207	28	53	5	4	0	4	24	16	.256	.339	.319	95	-1	5	3	-0	.969	9	O-52	0.6
Total	13	1268	4167	638	1109	145	49	3	284	571	335	.266	.357	.327	91	-30	134	60		.961	37	*O-1120/3-1	-7.8
Team	3	265	895	111	233	29	13	0	48	99	115	.260	.337	.322	93	-6	33	17		.945	18	O-233	-0.5

■ **JACK LELIVELT** Lelivelt, John Frank b: 11/14/1885, Chicago, Ill. d: 1/20/41, Seattle, Wash. BL/TL, 5'11", 175 lbs. Deb: 6/24/09 F

YEAR	TM/L	G	AB	R	H	2B	3B	HR	RBI	BB	SO	AVG	OBP	SLG	PRO+	BR/A	SB	CS	SBR	FA	FR	G/POS	TPR
1913	Cle-A	23	23	0	9	2	0	0	7	0	3	.391	.391	.478	150	1	1			.000	-1	/O-1	0.1
1914	Cle-A	34	64	6	21	5	1	0	13	2	10	.328	.348	.438	131	2	2	3	-1	.933	-3	O-13/1-1	-0.3
Total	6	384	1154	114	347	43	22	2	126	89	15	.301	.353	.381	124	31	46	3		.962	13	O-281/1-15	3.1
Team	2	57	87	6	30	7	1	0	20	2	13	.345	.360	.448	136	3	3	3		.933	-3	/O-14,1-1	-0.2

■ **JOHNNIE LeMASTER** LeMaster, Johnnie Lee b: 6/19/54, Portsmouth, Ohio BR/TR, 6'2", 167 lbs. Deb: 9/2/75

YEAR	TM/L	G	AB	R	H	2B	3B	HR	RBI	BB	SO	AVG	OBP	SLG	PRO+	BR/A	SB	CS	SBR	FA	FR	G/POS	TPR
1985	Cle-A	11	20	0	3	0	0	0	2	0	6	.150	.150	.150	-18	-3	0	1	-1	.949	3	S-10	0.0
Total	12	1039	3191	320	709	109	19	22	229	241	564	.222	.278	.289	60	-174	94	51	-2	.961	-9	S-992/3-10,2D	-9.7

■ **JIM LEMON** Lemon, James Robert b: 3/23/28, Covington, Va. BR/TR, 6'4", 200 lbs. Deb: 8/20/50 MC

YEAR	TM/L	G	AB	R	H	2B	3B	HR	RBI	BB	SO	AVG	OBP	SLG	PRO+	BR/A	SB	CS	SBR	FA	FR	G/POS	TPR
1950	Cle-A	12	34	4	6	1	0	1	1	3	12	.176	.243	.294	38	-3	0	0	0	.824	-2	O-10	-0.5
1953	Cle-A	16	46	5	8	1	0	1	5	3	15	.174	.224	.261	32	-5	0	0	0	.913	-1	O-11/1-2	-0.6
Total	12	1010	3445	446	901	121	35	164	529	363	787	.262	.335	.460	114	57	13	18	-7	.961	-12	O-901/1-30	-1.0
Team	2	28	80	9	14	2	0	2	6	6	27	.175	.233	.275	34	-8	0	0	0	.875	-2	/O-21,1-2	-1.1

■ **BOB LEMON** Lemon, Robert Granville b: 9/22/20, San Bernardino, Cal. BL/TR, 6', 185 lbs. Deb: 9/9/41 MCH

YEAR	TM/L	G	AB	R	H	2B	3B	HR	RBI	BB	SO	AVG	OBP	SLG	PRO+	BR/A	SB	CS	SBR	FA	FR	G/POS	TPR
1941	Cle-A	5	4	0	1	0	0	0	0	0	1	.250	.250	.250	34	-0	0	0	0	1.000	0	/3-1	0.0
1942	Cle-A	5	5	0	0	0	0	0	0	0	3	.000	.000	.000	-99	-1	0	0	0	.500	0	/3-1	-0.1
1946	Cle-A	55	89	9	16	3	0	1	4	7	18	.180	.240	.247	39	-8	0	1	-1	.976	6	P-32,O-12	-0.3
1947	Cle-A	47	56	11	18	4	3	2	5	6	9	.321	.387	.607	179	5	0	0	0	.983	4	P-37/O-2	-0.1
1948	*Cle-A☆	52	119	20	34	9	0	5	21	8	23	.286	.331	.487	119	2	0	0	0	.965	8	P-43	0.0
1949	Cle-A☆	46	108	17	29	6	2	7	19	10	20	.269	.331	.556	135	4	0	0	0	.963	6	P-37	0.0
1950	Cle-A★	72	136	21	37	9	1	6	26	13	25	.272	.340	.485	113	2	0	0	0	.957	5	P-44	0.0
1951	Cle-A★	56	102	11	21	4	1	3	13	9	22	.206	.270	.353	72	-5	0	0	0	.976	4	P-42	0.0
1952	Cle-A★	54	124	14	28	5	0	2	9	4	21	.226	.250	.315	60	-7	0	0	0	.982	7	P-42	0.0
1953	Cle-A☆	51	112	12	26	9	1	2	17	7	20	.232	.277	.384	79	-4	2	0	1	.972	8	P-41	0.0
1954	*Cle-A★	40	98	11	21	4	1	2	10	6	24	.214	.260	.337	61	-6	0	0	0	.963	4	P-36	0.0
1955	Cle-A	49	78	11	19	0	0	1	9	13	16	.244	.352	.282	69	-3	0	0	0	.983	2	P-35	0.0
1956	Cle-A	43	93	8	18	0	0	5	12	9	21	.194	.272	.355	63	-5	0	0	0	.934	4	P-39	0.0
1957	Cle-A	25	46	2	3	1	0	1	1	0	14	.065	.065	.152	-43	-9	0	0	0	1.000	3	P-21	0.0
1958	Cle-A	15	13	1	3	0	0	0	1	1	4	.231	.286	.231	45	-1	0	0	0	1.000	1	P-11	0.0
Total	15	615	1183	148	274	54	9	37	147	93	241	.232	.289	.386	82	-36	2	1	0	.969	62	P-460/O-14,3	-0.5

■ **EDDIE LEON** Leon, Eduardo Antonio b: 8/11/46, Tucson, Ariz. BR/TR, 6', 175 lbs. Deb: 9/9/68

YEAR	TM/L	G	AB	R	H	2B	3B	HR	RBI	BB	SO	AVG	OBP	SLG	PRO+	BR/A	SB	CS	SBR	FA	FR	G/POS	TPR
1968	Cle-A	6	1	0	0	0	0	0	0	0	1	.000	.000	.000	-99	-0	0	0	0	1.000	3	/S-6	0.3
1969	Cle-A	64	213	20	51	6	0	3	19	19	37	.239	.302	.310	69	-9	2	2	-1	.952	9	S-64	0.6
1970	Cle-A	152	549	58	136	20	4	10	56	47	89	.248	.309	.353	78	-16	1	2	-1	.982	8	*2-141,S-23/3	0.5
1971	Cle-A	131	429	35	112	12	2	4	35	34	69	.261	.317	.326	76	-13	3	5	-2	.983	0	*2-107,S-24	-0.4
1972	Cle-A	89	225	14	45	2	1	4	16	20	47	.200	.268	.271	59	-11	0	2	-1	.993	-1	2-36,S-35	-0.8
Total	8	601	1862	165	440	51	10	24	159	156	358	.236	.298	.313	69	-76	7	16	-8	.963	25	S-296,2-294/3D	-0.4
Team	5	442	1417	127	344	40	7	21	126	120	243	.243	.304	.325	73	-50	6	11	-5	.983	19	2-284,S-152/3	0.2

■ **JOE LEONARD** Leonard, Joseph Howard b: 11/15/1894, W.Chicago, Ill. d: 5/1/20, Washington, D.C. BL/TR, 5'7.5", 156 lbs. Deb: 5/7/14

YEAR	TM/L	G	AB	R	H	2B	3B	HR	RBI	BB	SO	AVG	OBP	SLG	PRO+	BR/A	SB	CS	SBR	FA	FR	G/POS	TPR
1916	Cle-A	3	2	1	0	0	0	0	0	0	1	.000	.000	.000	-94	-0	0			1.000	0	/2-1	0.0
Total	5	269	791	94	179	23	12	2	61	99	113	.226	.315	.293	82	-16	17			.937	-27	3-173/2-29,1OS	-4.2

■ **JESSE LEVIS** Levis, Jesse b: 4/14/68, Philadelphia, Pa. BL/TR, 5'9", 180 lbs. Deb: 4/24/92

YEAR	TM/L	G	AB	R	H	2B	3B	HR	RBI	BB	SO	AVG	OBP	SLG	PRO+	BR/A	SB	CS	SBR	FA	FR	G/POS	TPR
1992	Cle-A	28	43	2	12	4	0	1	3	0	5	.279	.279	.442	101	-0	0	0	0	.985	1	C-21/D-1	0.1
1993	Cle-A	31	63	7	11	2	0	0	4	2	10	.175	.200	.206	9	-8	0	0	0	.991	1	C-29	-0.6
1994	Cle-A	1	1	0	1	0	0	0	0	0	0	1.000	1.000	1.000	417	0	0	0	0	.000	0	/H	0.0
1995	Cle-A	12	18	1	6	2	0	0	3	1	0	.333	.368	.444	110	0	0	0	0	1.000	0	C-12	0.1
Total	4	72	125	10	30	8	0	1	10	3	15	.240	.258	.328	58	-8	0	0	0	.991	2	/C-62,D-1	-0.4

■ **MARK LEWIS** Lewis, Mark David b: 11/30/69, Hamilton, Ohio BR/TR, 6'1", 190 lbs. Deb: 4/26/91

YEAR	TM/L	G	AB	R	H	2B	3B	HR	RBI	BB	SO	AVG	OBP	SLG	PRO+	BR/A	SB	CS	SBR	FA	FR	G/POS	TPR
1991	Cle-A	84	314	29	83	15	1	0	30	15	45	.264	.298	.318	70	-13	2	2	-1	.966	-14	2-50,S-36	-2.4
1992	Cle-A	122	413	44	109	21	0	5	30	25	69	.264	.311	.351	87	-8	4	5	-2	.954	-9	*S-121/3-1	-1.1
1993	Cle-A	14	52	6	13	2	0	1	5	0	7	.250	.250	.346	59	-3	3	0	1	.964	-3	S-13	-0.4
1994	Cle-A	20	73	6	15	5	0	1	8	2	13	.205	.227	.315	38	-7	1	0	0	.902	-7	S-13/3-6,2	-1.2
Total	5	321	1023	110	278	56	2	10	103	63	167	.272	.316	.360	85	-21	10	10	-3	.958	-32	S-185/3-79,2	-4.2
Team	4	240	852	85	220	43	1	7	73	42	134	.258	.295	.336	74	-31	10	7	-1	.958	-34	S-183/2-51,3	-5.1

YEAR	TM/L	G	AB	R	H	2B	3B	HR	RBI	BB	SO	AVG	OBP	SLG	PRO+	BR/A	SB	CS	SBR	FA	FR	G/POS	TPR

■ CARL LIND   Lind, Henry Carl "Hooks" b: 9/19/03, New Orleans, La. d: 8/2/46, New York, N.Y. BR/TR, 6', 160 lbs. Deb: 9/14/27

1927	Cle-A	12	37	2	5	0	0	0	1	5	7	.135	.256	.135	4	-5	1	0	0	.969	2	2-11/S-1	-0.3
1928	Cle-A	154	650	102	191	42	4	1	54	36	48	.294	.331	.375	84	-15	8	5	-1	.960	4	*2-154	-0.7
1929	Cle-A	66	225	19	54	8	1	0	13	13	17	.240	.282	.284	44	-19	0	2	-1	.957	16	2-64/3-1	-0.1
1930	Cle-A	24	69	8	17	3	0	0	6	3	7	.246	.278	.290	43	-6	0	1	-1	.940	11	S-22/2-2	0.5
Total	4	256	981	131	267	53	5	1	74	57	79	.272	.313	.339	69	-45	9	8	-2	.960	33	2-231/S-23,3	-0.6

■ BILL LINDSAY   Lindsay, William Gibbons b: 2/24/1881, Madison, N.C. d: 7/14/63, Greensboro, N.C. BL/TR, 5'10.5", 165 lbs. Deb: 6/21/11

| 1911 | Cle-A | 19 | 66 | 6 | 16 | 2 | 0 | 0 | 5 | 1 | | .242 | .265 | .273 | 49 | -5 | 2 | | | .883 | 2 | 3-15/2-1 | -0.2 |

■ LARRY LINTZ   Lintz, Larry b: 10/10/49, Martinez, Cal. BB/TR, 5'9", 150 lbs. Deb: 7/14/73

| 1978 | Cle-A | 3 | 0 | 1 | 0 | 0 | 0 | 0 | 0 | 0 | 0 | — | — | — | — | 0 | 1 | 2 | -1 | .000 | 0 | R | -0.1 |
| Total | 6 | 350 | 616 | 137 | 140 | 13 | 1 | 0 | 27 | 97 | 101 | .227 | .336 | .252 | 63 | -27 | 128 | 38 | | .962 | 3 | 2-179/S-56,DO3 | 0.2 |

■ BOB LIPSKI   Lipski, Robert Peter b: 7/7/38, Scranton, Pa. BL/TR, 6'1", 180 lbs. Deb: 4/28/63

| 1963 | Cle-A | 2 | 1 | 0 | 0 | 0 | 0 | 0 | 0 | 0 | 1 | .000 | .000 | .000 | -99 | -0 | 0 | 0 | 0 | 1.000 | 0 | /C-2 | 0.0 |

■ JOE LIS   Lis, Joseph Anthony b: 8/15/46, Somerville, N.J. BR/TR, 6', 195 lbs. Deb: 9/5/70

1974	Cle-A	57	109	15	22	3	0	6	16	14	30	.202	.293	.394	97	-1	1	0	0	1.000	-0	1-31/3-9,OD	-0.2
1975	Cle-A	9	13	4	4	2	0	2	8	3	3	.308	.471	.923	286	3	0	0	0	1.000	-0	/1-8,D-1	0.3
1976	Cle-A	20	51	4	16	1	0	2	7	8	8	.314	.407	.451	153	4	0	0	0	1.000	-0	1-17/D-1	0.4
Total	8	356	780	96	182	31	1	32	92	110	209	.233	.334	.399	105	6	1	3	-2	.992	-1	1-204/O-59,D3C	-1.0
Team	3	86	173	23	42	6	0	10	31	25	41	.243	.342	.451	128	6	1	0	0	1.000	-1	/1-56,D-11,3O	0.4

■ PETE LISTER   Lister, Morris Elmer b: 7/21/1881, Savanna, Ill. d: 3/27/47, St.Petersburg, Fla BR/TR, Deb: 9/14/07

| 1907 | Cle-A | 22 | 65 | 5 | 18 | 2 | 0 | 0 | 4 | 3 | | .277 | .319 | .308 | 99 | -0 | 2 | | | .974 | -1 | 1-22 | -0.2 |

■ LARRY LITTLETON   Littleton, Larry Marvin b: 4/3/54, Charlotte, N.C. BR/TR, 6'1", 185 lbs. Deb: 4/12/81

| 1981 | Cle-A | 26 | 23 | 2 | 0 | 0 | 0 | 0 | 1 | 3 | 6 | .000 | .115 | .000 | -65 | -5 | 0 | 0 | 0 | 1.000 | -10 | O-24 | -1.6 |

■ PADDY LIVINGSTON   Livingston, Patrick Joseph b: 1/14/1880, Cleveland, Ohio d: 9/19/77, Cleveland, Ohio BR/TR, 5'8", 197 lbs. Deb: 9/2/01 C

1901	Cle-A	1	2	0	0	0	0	0	0	0		.000	.333	.000	-2	-0	0			1.000	-1	/C-1	-0.1
1912	Cle-A	20	47	5	11	2	1	0	3	1		.234	.280	.319	69	-2	0			.976	0	C-14	-0.1
Total	7	206	574	48	120	17	12	0	45	41		.209	.287	.280	73	-18	9			.969	21	C-195	2.1
Team	2	21	49	5	11	2	1	0	3	1		.224	.283	.306	66	-2	0			.976	-1	/C-15	-0.2

■ STU LOCKLIN   Locklin, Stuart Carlton b: 7/22/28, Appleton, Wis. BL/TL, 6'1.5", 190 lbs. Deb: 6/23/55

1955	Cle-A	16	18	4	3	1	0	0	0	3	4	.167	.286	.222	37	-2	0	0	0	1.000	-3	/O-7	-0.4
1956	Cle-A	9	6	0	1	0	0	0	0	0	1	.167	.167	.167	-12	-1	0	0	0	1.000	-0	/O-1	-0.1
Total	2	25	24	4	4	1	0	0	0	3	5	.167	.259	.208	26	-3	0	0	0	1.000	-3	/O-8	-0.5

■ KENNY LOFTON   Lofton, Kenneth b: 5/31/67, E.Chicago, Ind. BL/TL, 6', 180 lbs. Deb: 9/14/91

1992	Cle-A	148	576	96	164	15	8	5	42	68	54	.285	.362	.365	106	6	**66**	12	**13**	.982	17	*O-143	3.3
1993	Cle-A	148	569	116	185	28	8	1	42	81	83	.325	.410	.408	121	21	**70**	14	**13**	.979	13	*O-146	4.1
1994	Cle-A★	112	459	105	**160**	32	9	12	57	52	56	.349	.417	.536	143	30	**60**	12	**11**	.993	8	*O-112	4.2
1995	*Cle-A★	118	481	93	149	22	13	7	53	40	49	.310	.362	.453	111	7	**54**	15	7	.970	1	*O-114/D-2	1.2
Total	5	546	2159	419	673	98	38	25	194	246	261	.312	.384	.427	117	59	252	54	43	.981	39	O-535/D-2	12.1
Team	4	526	2085	410	658	97	38	25	194	241	242	.316	.388	.435	120	65	250	53	43	.981	39	O-515/D-2	12.8

■ HOWARD LOHR   Lohr, Howard Sylvester b: 6/3/1892, Philadelphia, Pa. d: 6/9/77, Philadelphia, Pa. BR/TR, 6', 165 lbs. Deb: 6/17/14

| 1916 | Cle-A | 3 | 7 | 0 | 1 | 0 | 0 | 0 | 1 | 0 | 1 | .143 | .143 | .143 | -13 | -1 | 1 | | | 1.000 | -1 | /O-3 | -0.2 |
| Total | 2 | 21 | 54 | 6 | 11 | 1 | 1 | 0 | 8 | 0 | 9 | .204 | .204 | .259 | 36 | -4 | 3 | | | .933 | -4 | /O-20 | -1.0 |

■ RON LOLICH   Lolich, Ronald John b: 9/19/46, Portland, Ore. BR/TR, 6'1", 185 lbs. Deb: 7/18/71

1972	Cle-A	24	80	4	15	1	0	2	8	4	20	.188	.226	.275	47	-5	0	0	0	1.000	-1	O-22	-0.8
1973	Cle-A	61	140	16	32	7	0	2	15	7	27	.229	.265	.321	63	-7	0	2	-1	.909	-4	O-32,D-12	-1.4
Total	3	87	228	20	48	9	0	4	23	11	49	.211	.247	.303	56	-13	0	2		.953	-5	/O-56,D-12	-2.4
Team	2	85	220	20	47	8	0	4	23	11	47	.214	.251	.305	58	-12	0	2		.952	-5	/O-54,D-12	-2.2

■ SHERM LOLLAR   Lollar, John Sherman b: 8/23/24, Durham, Ark. d: 9/24/77, Springfield, Mo. BR/TR, 6'1", 185 lbs. Deb: 4/20/46 C

| 1946 | Cle-A | 28 | 62 | 7 | 15 | 6 | 0 | 1 | 9 | 5 | 9 | .242 | .299 | .387 | 97 | -1 | 0 | 1 | -1 | .990 | -3 | C-24 | -0.4 |
| Total | 18 | 1752 | 5351 | 623 | 1415 | 244 | 14 | 155 | 808 | 671 | 453 | .264 | .359 | .402 | 104 | 40 | 20 | 10 | 0 | .992 | -16 | *C-1571/1-27,3 | 9.2 |

■ AL LOPEZ   Lopez, Alfonso Ramon b: 8/20/08, Tampa, Fla. BR/TR, 5'11", 165 lbs. Deb: 9/27/28 MH

| 1947 | Cle-A | 61 | 126 | 9 | 33 | 1 | 0 | 0 | 14 | 9 | 13 | .262 | .311 | .270 | 64 | -6 | 1 | 1 | -0 | 1.000 | 0 | C-57 | -0.4 |
| Total | 19 | 1950 | 5916 | 613 | 1547 | 206 | 43 | 51 | 652 | 556 | 538 | .261 | .326 | .337 | 83 | -133 | 46 | 1 | 13 | .985 | 67 | *C-1918/3-3,21 | 4.6 |

■ LUIS LOPEZ   Lopez, Luis Antonio b: 9/1/64, Brooklyn, N.Y. BR/TR, 6'1", 190 lbs. Deb: 9/14/90

| 1991 | Cle-A | 35 | 82 | 7 | 18 | 4 | 1 | 0 | 7 | 4 | 7 | .220 | .264 | .293 | 54 | -5 | 0 | 0 | 0 | 1.000 | -2 | C-12,1-10/3OD | -0.8 |
| Total | 2 | 41 | 88 | 7 | 18 | 4 | 1 | 0 | 7 | 4 | 9 | .205 | .247 | .273 | 43 | -7 | 0 | 0 | 0 | .977 | -2 | /C-12,1-11,DO3 | -1.0 |

■ BRIS LORD   Lord, Bristol Robotham "The Human Eyeball" b: 9/21/1883, Upland, Pa. d: 11/13/64, Annapolis, Md. BR/TR, 5'9", 185 lbs. Deb: 4/21/05

1909	Cle-A	69	249	26	67	7	3	1	25	8		.269	.295	.333	94	-2	10			.992	6	O-67	0.1
1910	Cle-A	58	210	23	46	8	7	0	17	12		.219	.264	.324	84	-5	4			.958	4	O-56	-0.4
Total	8	742	2767	379	707	119	49	13	236	175		.256	.304	.348	95	-22	74			.957	8	O-713/P-1	-5.3
Team	2	127	459	49	113	15	10	1	42	20		.246	.282	.329	90	-7	14			.977	10	O-123	-0.3

■ JOHN LOWENSTEIN   Lowenstein, John Lee b: 1/27/47, Wolf Point, Mont. BL/TR, 6', 175 lbs. Deb: 9/2/70

1970	Cle-A	17	43	5	11	3	1	1	6	1	9	.256	.273	.442	89	-1	1	0	0	1.000	4	2-10/3-2,OS	0.4
1971	Cle-A	58	140	15	26	5	0	4	9	16	28	.186	.269	.307	58	-8	1	5	-3	.986	-6	2-29,O-18/S	-1.6
1972	Cle-A	68	151	16	32	8	1	6	21	20	43	.212	.304	.397	104	1	2	4	-2	1.000	-2	O-58/1-2	-0.6
1973	Cle-A	98	305	42	89	16	1	6	40	23	41	.292	.341	.410	109	3	5	3	-0	.931	-10	O-51,2-25/31D	-0.7
1974	Cle-A	140	508	65	123	14	2	8	48	53	85	.242	.316	.325	85	-9	36	17	1	.986	-1	*O-100,3-28,1/2	-1.5
1975	Cle-A	91	265	37	64	5	1	12	33	28	28	.242	.304	.404	102	0	15	10	-2	.983	-5	O-36,D-31/32	-0.9
1976	Cle-A	93	229	33	47	8	2	2	14	25	35	.205	.283	.284	67	-9	11	8	-2	.972	-5	O-61,D-11/1	-2.0
1977	Cle-A	81	149	24	36	6	1	4	12	21	29	.242	.335	.376	97	-0	1	8	-5	1.000	-3	O-39,D-19/1	-1.0
Total	16	1368	3476	510	881	137	18	116	441	446	596	.253	.344	.403	108	43	128	78	-8	.984	-96	O-906,D-125/321S	-9.2
Team	8	646	1790	237	428	65	9	43	183	187	298	.239	.312	.358	90	-23	72	55	-11	.979	-28	O-365/2-70,D31S	-7.9

■ GORDY LUND   Lund, Gordon Thomas b: 2/23/41, Iron Mountain, Mich BR/TR, 5'11", 170 lbs. Deb: 8/1/67

| 1967 | Cle-A | 3 | 8 | 1 | 2 | 1 | 0 | 0 | 0 | 0 | 2 | .250 | .250 | .375 | 82 | -0 | 0 | 0 | 0 | .667 | -2 | /S-2 | -0.2 |
| Total | 2 | 23 | 46 | 5 | 12 | 1 | 0 | 0 | 1 | 5 | 9 | .261 | .333 | .283 | 76 | -1 | 1 | 1 | -0 | .902 | -2 | /S-19,3-1,2 | -0.3 |

■ HARRY LUNTE   Lunte, Harry August b: 9/15/1892, St.Louis, Mo. d: 7/27/65, St.Louis, Mo. BR/TR, 5'11.5", 165 lbs. Deb: 5/19/19

1919	Cle-A	26	77	2	15	2	0	0	2	1		.195	.215	.221	21	-8	0			.935	-2	S-24	-1.0
1920	*Cle-A	23	71	6	14	0	0	0	7	5	6	.197	.250	.197	19	-8	0	1	-1	.979	3	S-21/2-2	-0.4
Total	2	49	148	8	29	2	0	0	9	6	13	.196	.232	.209	20	-16	0	1		.955	1	/S-45,2-2	-1.4

■ AL LUPLOW
Luplow, Alvin David b: 3/13/39, Saginaw, Mich. BL/TR, 5'11", 180 lbs. Deb: 9/16/61

YEAR	TM/L	G	AB	R	H	2B	3B	HR	RBI	BB	SO	AVG	OBP	SLG	PRO+	BR/A	SB	CS	SBR	FA	FR	G/POS	TPR
1961	Cle-A	5	18	0	1	0	0	0	0	2	6	.056	.150	.056	-44	-4	0	0	0	1.000	2	/O-5	-0.3
1962	Cle-A	97	318	54	88	15	3	14	45	36	44	.277	.361	.475	127	12	1	0	0	.960	-3	O-86	0.5
1963	Cle-A	100	295	34	69	6	2	7	27	33	62	.234	.317	.339	85	-6	4	4	-1	.994	3	O-85	-0.8
1964	Cle-A	19	18	1	2	0	0	0	1	1	8	.111	.158	.111	-24	-3	0	0	0	1.000	-1	/O-5	-0.4
1965	Cle-A	53	45	3	6	2	0	1	4	3	14	.133	.188	.244	22	-5	0	1	-1	1.000	-2	/O-6	-0.7
Total	7	481	1243	147	292	34	6	33	125	127	213	.235	.312	.352	85	-23	8	11	-4	.977	-14	O-346	-6.1
Team	5	274	694	92	166	23	5	22	77	75	134	.239	.321	.382	94	-5	5	5	-2	.978	-1	O-187	-1.7

■ BILLY LUSH
Lush, William Lucas b: 11/10/1873, Bridgeport, Conn. d: 8/28/51, Hawthorne, N.Y. BB/TR, 5'8", 165 lbs. Deb: 9/3/1895 F

YEAR	TM/L	G	AB	R	H	2B	3B	HR	RBI	BB	SO	AVG	OBP	SLG	PRO+	BR/A	SB	CS	SBR	FA	FR	G/POS	TPR
1904	Cle-A	138	477	76	123	13	8	1	50	72		.258	.359	.325	118	13	12			.959	3	*O-138	0.9
Total	7	489	1722	294	429	49	35	8	152	291		.249	.360	.332	107	27	84			.943	24	O-461/3-13,2S	2.6

■ RUBE LUTZKE
Lutzke, Walter John b: 11/17/1897, Milwaukee, Wis. d: 3/6/38, Granville, Wis. BR/TR, 5'11", 175 lbs. Deb: 4/18/23

YEAR	TM/L	G	AB	R	H	2B	3B	HR	RBI	BB	SO	AVG	OBP	SLG	PRO+	BR/A	SB	CS	SBR	FA	FR	G/POS	TPR
1923	Cle-A	143	511	71	131	20	6	3	65	59	57	.256	.338	.337	78	-16	9	6	-1	.939	17	*3-141/S-2	1.3
1924	Cle-A	106	341	37	83	18	3	0	42	38	46	.243	.328	.314	65	-17	4	0	1	.947	19	*3-103/2-3	1.0
1925	Cle-A	81	238	31	52	9	0	1	16	26	29	.218	.295	.269	44	-20	2	4	-2	.936	-0	3-69,2-10	-1.7
1926	Cle-A	142	475	42	124	28	6	0	59	34	35	.261	.313	.345	71	-21	6	3	0	.960	-1	*3-142	-1.2
1927	Cle-A	100	311	35	78	12	3	0	41	22	29	.251	.307	.309	60	-19	2	1	0	.938	6	3-98	-0.8
Total	5	572	1876	216	468	87	18	4	223	179	196	.249	.319	.321	66	-93	23	14	-2	.945	42	3-553/2-13,S	-1.4

■ RUSS LYON
Lyon, Russell Mayo b: 6/26/13, Ball Ground, Ga. d: 12/24/75, Charleston, S.C. BR/TR, 6'1", 230 lbs. Deb: 4/21/44

YEAR	TM/L	G	AB	R	H	2B	3B	HR	RBI	BB	SO	AVG	OBP	SLG	PRO+	BR/A	SB	CS	SBR	FA	FR	G/POS	TPR
1944	Cle-A	7	11	1	2	0	0	0	0	1	1	.182	.250	.182	25	-1	0	0	0	.909	0	/C-3	-0.1

■ RAY MACK
Mack, Raymond James (b: Raymond James Mlckovsky) b: 8/31/16, Cleveland, Ohio d: 5/7/69, Bucyrus, Ohio BR/TR, 6', 200 lbs. Deb: 9/9/38

YEAR	TM/L	G	AB	R	H	2B	3B	HR	RBI	BB	SO	AVG	OBP	SLG	PRO+	BR/A	SB	CS	SBR	FA	FR	G/POS	TPR
1938	Cle-A	2	6	2	2	0	1	0	2	0	1	.333	.333	.667	147	0	0	0	0	1.000	2	/2-2	0.2
1939	Cle-A	36	112	12	17	4	1	1	6	12	19	.152	.240	.232	22	-14	0	2	-1	.976	2	2-34/3-1	-1.0
1940	Cle-A★	146	530	60	150	21	5	12	69	51	77	.283	.346	.409	98	-2	4	2	0	.965	-9	*2-146	-0.1
1941	Cle-A	145	500	54	114	22	4	9	44	54	69	.228	.303	.342	74	-20	8	4	0	.970	-5	*2-145	-1.4
1942	Cle-A	143	481	43	108	14	6	2	45	41	51	.225	.288	.291	67	-22	9	3	1	.969	-4	*2-143	-1.7
1943	Cle-A	153	545	56	120	25	2	7	62	47	61	.220	.285	.312	79	-16	8	3	1	.967	-2	*2-153	-1.0
1944	Cle-A	83	284	24	66	15	3	0	29	28	45	.232	.301	.306	77	-9	4	1	1	.951	10	2-83	0.7
1946	Cle-A	61	171	13	35	6	2	1	9	23	27	.205	.299	.281	67	-8	2	2	-1	.970	1	2-61	-0.4
Total	9	791	2707	273	629	113	24	34	278	261	365	.232	.301	.330	76	-93	35	17	0	.966	3	2-788/3-1	-4.2
Team	8	769	2629	264	612	107	24	32	266	256	350	.233	.302	.328	77	-89	35	17	0	.966	-4	2-767/3-1	-4.7

■ FELIX MACKIEWICZ
Mackiewicz, Felix Thaddeus b: 11/20/17, Chicago, Ill. d: 12/20/93, Olivette, Mo. BR/TR, 6'2", 195 lbs. Deb: 9/7/41

YEAR	TM/L	G	AB	R	H	2B	3B	HR	RBI	BB	SO	AVG	OBP	SLG	PRO+	BR/A	SB	CS	SBR	FA	FR	G/POS	TPR
1945	Cle-A	120	359	42	98	14	7	2	37	44	41	.273	.356	.368	115	7	5	5	-2	.987	5	*O-112	0.6
1946	Cle-A	78	258	35	67	15	4	0	16	16	32	.260	.305	.349	88	-5	5	1	1	.983	-2	O-72	-1.0
1947	Cle-A	2	5	0	0	0	0	0	0	0	2	.000	.000	.000	-99	-1	0	0	0	1.000	-0	/O-2	-0.2
Total	6	223	672	85	174	32	12	2	55	63	88	.259	.325	.351	97	-3	10	6	-1	.986	2	O-198	-1.3
Team	3	200	622	77	165	29	11	2	53	60	75	.265	.333	.357	102	1	10	6	-1	.986	3	O-186	-0.6

■ CLARENCE MADDERN
Maddern, Clarence James b: 9/26/21, Bisbee, Ariz. d: 8/9/86, Tucson, Ariz. BR/TR, 6'1", 185 lbs. Deb: 9/19/46

YEAR	TM/L	G	AB	R	H	2B	3B	HR	RBI	BB	SO	AVG	OBP	SLG	PRO+	BR/A	SB	CS	SBR	FA	FR	G/POS	TPR
1951	Cle-A	11	12	0	2	0	0	0	0	0	1	.167	.167	.167	-10	-2	0	0	0	.667	-0	/O-1	-0.2
Total	4	104	238	17	59	12	1	5	29	12	26	.248	.301	.370	84	-6	0	0	0	.973	-2	/O-58,1-1	-1.1

■ EVER MAGALLANES
Magallanes, Everado (Espinoza) b: 11/6/65, Chihuahua, Mexico BL/TR, 5'10", 165 lbs. Deb: 5/17/91

YEAR	TM/L	G	AB	R	H	2B	3B	HR	RBI	BB	SO	AVG	OBP	SLG	PRO+	BR/A	SB	CS	SBR	FA	FR	G/POS	TPR
1991	Cle-A	3	2	0	0	0	0	0	0	1	1	.000	.333	.000	1	-0	0	0	0	1.000	-1	/S-2	-0.1

■ TOM MAGRANN
Magrann, Thomas Joseph b: 12/9/63, Hollywood, Fla. BR/TR, 6'3", 177 lbs. Deb: 9/7/89

YEAR	TM/L	G	AB	R	H	2B	3B	HR	RBI	BB	SO	AVG	OBP	SLG	PRO+	BR/A	SB	CS	SBR	FA	FR	G/POS	TPR
1989	Cle-A	9	10	0	0	0	0	0	0	0	4	.000	.000	.000	-98	-3	0	0	0	1.000	3	/C-9	0.1

■ JIM MAHONEY
Mahoney, James Thomas "Moe" b: 5/26/34, Englewood, N.J. BR/TR, 6', 175 lbs. Deb: 7/28/59 C

YEAR	TM/L	G	AB	R	H	2B	3B	HR	RBI	BB	SO	AVG	OBP	SLG	PRO+	BR/A	SB	CS	SBR	FA	FR	G/POS	TPR
1962	Cle-A	41	74	12	18	4	0	3	5	3	14	.243	.273	.419	86	-2	0	0	0	.964	8	S-23/2-8,3	0.8
Total	4	120	210	32	48	4	1	4	15	11	47	.229	.267	.314	57	-13	1	2	-1	.962	31	/S-89,2-10,3	2.1

■ HANK MAJESKI
Majeski, Henry "Heeney" b: 12/13/16, Staten Island, N.Y d: 8/9/91, Staten Island, N.Y. BR/TR, 5'9", 180 lbs. Deb: 5/17/39

YEAR	TM/L	G	AB	R	H	2B	3B	HR	RBI	BB	SO	AVG	OBP	SLG	PRO+	BR/A	SB	CS	SBR	FA	FR	G/POS	TPR
1952	Cle-A	36	54	7	16	2	0	0	9	7	7	.296	.377	.333	106	1	0	0	0	.913	-0	3-11/2-3	0.0
1953	Cle-A	50	50	6	15	1	0	2	12	3	8	.300	.352	.440	116	1	0	0	0	1.000	-2	2-10/3-7,O	-0.1
1954	*Cle-A	57	121	10	34	4	0	3	17	7	14	.281	.320	.388	92	-2	0	0	0	.990	4	2-25,3-10	0.4
1955	Cle-A	36	48	3	9	2	0	2	6	8	3	.188	.328	.354	80	-1	0	0	0	1.000	-2	/3-9,2-4	-0.3
Total	13	1069	3421	404	956	181	27	57	501	299	260	.279	.342	.398	100	-9	10	11	-4	.968	49	3-861/2-48,SO	3.2
Team	4	179	273	26	74	9	0	7	44	25	32	.271	.339	.381	97	-1	0	0	0	.993	0	/2-42,3-37,O	0.0

■ CANDY MALDONADO
Maldonado, Candido (Guadarrama) b: 9/5/60, Humacao, P.R. BR/TR, 6', 190 lbs. Deb: 9/7/81

YEAR	TM/L	G	AB	R	H	2B	3B	HR	RBI	BB	SO	AVG	OBP	SLG	PRO+	BR/A	SB	CS	SBR	FA	FR	G/POS	TPR
1990	Cle-A	155	590	76	161	32	2	22	95	49	134	.273	.334	.446	117	12	3	5	-2	.993	7	*O-134,D-20	1.3
1993	Cle-A	28	81	11	20	2	0	5	20	11	18	.247	.337	.457	112	1	0	1	-1	.976	-3	O-26/D-2	-0.3
1994	Cle-A	42	92	14	18	5	1	5	12	19	31	.196	.333	.435	96	-1	1	1	-0	1.000	-1	D-25/O-5	-0.3
Total	15	1410	4106	498	1042	227	17	146	618	391	864	.254	.325	.424	107	31	34	33	-10	.977	-74	*O-1215/D-61,3	-8.6
Team	3	225	763	101	199	39	3	32	127	79	183	.261	.334	.446	113	12	4	7	-3	.991	3	O-165/D-47	0.7

■ RICK MANNING
Manning, Richard Eugene b: 9/2/54, Niagara Falls, N.Y. BL/TR, 6'1", 180 lbs. Deb: 5/23/75

YEAR	TM/L	G	AB	R	H	2B	3B	HR	RBI	BB	SO	AVG	OBP	SLG	PRO+	BR/A	SB	CS	SBR	FA	FR	G/POS	TPR
1975	Cle-A	120	480	69	137	16	5	3	35	44	62	.285	.348	.358	100	1	19	11	-1	.974	13	*O-118/D-1	0.8
1976	Cle-A	138	552	73	161	24	7	6	43	41	75	.292	.341	.393	116	10	16	10	-1	.987	8	*O-136	1.2
1977	Cle-A	68	252	33	57	7	3	5	18	21	35	.226	.286	.337	71	-10	9	5	-0	.990	5	O-68	-0.8
1978	Cle-A	148	566	65	149	27	3	3	50	38	62	.263	.311	.337	83	-13	12	12	-4	.995	5	*O-144	-1.8
1979	Cle-A	144	560	67	145	12	2	3	51	55	48	.259	.326	.304	71	-21	30	8	4	.986	15	*O-141/D-1	-0.8
1980	Cle-A	140	471	55	110	17	4	3	52	63	66	.234	.326	.306	74	-15	12	6	0	.990	8	*O-139	-1.3
1981	Cle-A	103	360	47	88	15	3	4	33	40	57	.244	.320	.336	90	-4	25	3	6	.987	13	*O-103	1.2
1982	Cle-A	152	562	71	152	18	2	8	44	54	60	.270	.334	.352	89	-7	12	8	-1	.978	6	*O-152	-0.7
1983	Cle-A	50	194	20	54	6	0	1	10	12	22	.278	.320	.325	75	-6	7	3	0	.987	3	O-50	-0.4
Total	13	1555	5248	664	1349	189	43	56	458	471	616	.257	.319	.341	84	-108	168	78	4	.985	40	*O-1508/D-12	-11.3
Team	9	1063	3997	500	1053	142	29	36	336	368	487	.263	.326	.341	87	-66	142	66	3	.986	77	*O-1051/D-2	-2.6

■ JEFF MANTO
Manto, Jeffrey Paul b: 8/23/64, Bristol, Pa. BR/TR, 6'3", 210 lbs. Deb: 6/7/90

YEAR	TM/L	G	AB	R	H	2B	3B	HR	RBI	BB	SO	AVG	OBP	SLG	PRO+	BR/A	SB	CS	SBR	FA	FR	G/POS	TPR
1990	Cle-A	30	76	12	17	5	1	2	14	21	18	.224	.392	.395	121	3	0	1	-1	.990	1	1-25/3-5	0.2
1991	Cle-A	47	128	15	27	7	0	2	13	14	22	.211	.308	.313	72	-5	2	0	1	.929	1	3-32,1-14/CO	-0.3
Total	4	174	476	58	110	21	1	21	65	59	112	.231	.325	.412	93	-5	2	4	-2	.953	1	3-112/1-43,DCSO	-0.9
Team	2	77	204	27	44	12	1	4	27	35	40	.216	.342	.343	91	-2	2	1	0	.986	3	/1-39,3-37,CO	-0.1

■ ROGER MARIS
Maris, Roger Eugene (b: Roger Eugene Maras) b: 9/10/34, Hibbing, Minn. d: 12/14/85, Houston, Tex. BL/TR, 6', 204 lbs. Deb: 4/16/57

YEAR	TM/L	G	AB	R	H	2B	3B	HR	RBI	BB	SO	AVG	OBP	SLG	PRO+	BR/A	SB	CS	SBR	FA	FR	G/POS	TPR
1957	Cle-A	116	358	61	84	9	5	14	51	60	79	.235	.346	.405	106	3	8	4	0	.975	5	*O-112	0.3
1958	Cle-A	51	182	26	41	5	1	9	27	17	33	.225	.291	.412	94	-2	4	2	0	.967	5	O-47	0.0
Total	12	1463	5101	826	1325	195	42	275	851	652	733	.260	.348	.476	128	191	21	9	1	.982	-3	*O-1383	11.7
Team	2	167	540	87	125	14	6	23	78	77	112	.231	.328	.407	102	1	12	6	0	.973	10	O-159	0.3

YEAR	TM/L	G	AB	R	H	2B	3B	HR	RBI	BB	SO	AVG	OBP	SLG	PRO+	BR/A	SB	CS	SBR	FA	FR	G/POS	TPR
■ FRED MARSH Marsh, Fred Francis b: 1/5/24, Valley Falls, Kan. BR/TR, 5'10", 180 lbs. Deb: 4/19/49																							
1949	Cle-A	1	0	0	0	0	0	0	0	0	0	—	—	—	—	0	0	0	0	.000	0	R	0.0
Total	7	465	1236	148	296	43	8	10	96	125	171	.239	.310	.311	69	-54	13	14	-5	.928	-2	3-232,S-107/21O	-5.3
■ BILLY MARTIN Martin, Alfred Manuel b: 5/16/28, Berkeley, Cal. d: 12/25/89, Johnson City, N.Y. BR/TR, 5'11.5", 165 lbs. Deb: 4/18/50 MC																							
1959	Cle-A	73	242	37	63	7	0	9	24	8	18	.260	.292	.401	92	-4	0	2	-1	.997	-11	2-67/3-4	-1.1
Total	11	1021	3419	425	877	137	28	64	333	188	355	.257	.301	.369	81	-96	34	29	-7	.980	-61	2-767,S-118/3O	-10.5
■ CARLOS MARTINEZ Martinez, Carlos Alberto Escobar (b: Carlos Alberto Escobar (Martinez)) b: 8/11/64, LaGuaira, Venez. BR/TR, 6'5", 175 lbs. Deb: 9/2/88																							
1991	Cle-A	72	257	22	73	14	0	5	30	10	43	.284	.316	.397	95	-2	3	2	-0	.968	-4	D-41,1-31	-1.0
1992	Cle-A	69	228	23	60	9	1	5	35	7	21	.263	.288	.377	87	-5	1	2	-1	.996	-5	1-37,3-28/D	-1.3
1993	Cle-A	80	262	26	64	10	0	5	31	20	29	.244	.298	.340	71	-11	1	1	-0	.934	-9	3-35,1-22,D	-2.2
Total	7	465	1485	145	383	63	6	25	161	74	209	.258	.295	.359	81	-41	10	10	-3	.986	-25	1-210,3-162/DO	-8.5
Team	3	221	747	71	197	33	1	15	96	37	93	.264	.301	.371	84	-18	5	5	-2	.981	-18	/1-90,D-64,3	-4.5
■ TONY MARTINEZ Martinez, Gabriel Antonio (Diaz) b: 3/18/40, Perico, Cuba d: 8/24/91, Miami, Fla. BR/TR, 5'10", 165 lbs. Deb: 4/9/63																							
1963	Cle-A	43	141	10	22	4	0	0	8	5	18	.156	.185	.184	4	-18	1	1	-0	.961	-6	S-41	-2.4
1964	Cle-A	9	14	1	3	1	0	0	2	0	2	.214	.214	.286	38	-1	0	1	-1	1.000	4	/2-4,S-1	0.2
1965	Cle-A	4	3	0	0	0	0	0	0	0	0	.000	.000	.000	-99	-1	0	0	0	.000	0	H	-0.1
1966	Cle-A	17	17	2	5	0	0	0	0	1	6	.294	.333	.294	82	-0	1	1	-0	.833	1	/S-5,2-4	0.1
Total	4	73	175	13	30	5	0	0	10	6	26	.171	.199	.200	13	-20	2	3	-1	.958	-1	/S-47,2-8	-2.2
■ LEE MAYE Maye, Arthur Lee b: 12/11/34, Tuscaloosa, Ala. BL/TR, 6'2", 190 lbs. Deb: 7/17/59																							
1967	Cle-A	115	297	43	77	20	4	9	27	26	47	.259	.321	.444	123	8	3	3	-1	.981	-10	O-77/2-1	-0.7
1968	Cle-A	109	299	20	84	13	2	4	26	15	24	.281	.317	.378	112	3	0	0	0	.984	1	O-80/1-1	0.0
1969	Cle-A	43	108	9	27	5	0	1	15	8	15	.250	.308	.324	74	-4	1	0	0	.982	1	O-28	-0.4
Total	13	1288	4048	533	1109	190	39	94	419	282	481	.274	.324	.410	108	32	59	34	-3	.970	-31	*O-1040/3-6,12	-5.7
Team	3	267	704	72	188	38	6	14	68	49	86	.267	.317	.398	110	7	4	3	-1	.983	-8	O-185/1-1,2	-1.1
■ JIMMY McALEER McAleer, James Robert "Loafer" b: 7/10/1864, Youngstown, Ohio d: 4/29/31, Youngstown, Ohio BR/TR, 6', 175 lbs. Deb: 4/24/1889 M																							
1901	Cle-A	3	7	0	1	0	0	0	0	0		.143	.143	.143	-22	-1	0			1.000	-1	/O-2,P-1,3M	-0.2
Total	13	1020	3977	619	1006	114	39	12	469	365		.253	.322	.310	72	-154	262			.944	54	*O-1015/2-2,3P	-13.3
■ BAKE McBRIDE McBride, Arnold Ray b: 2/3/49, Fulton, Mo. BL/TR, 6'2", 190 lbs. Deb: 7/26/73																							
1982	Cle-A	27	85	8	31	3	3	0	13	2	12	.365	.379	.471	132	4	2	2	-1	1.000	-2	O-22	0.0
1983	Cle-A	70	230	21	67	8	1	1	18	9	26	.291	.321	.348	81	-6	8	2	1	.977	0	O-46,D-15	-0.7
Total	11	1071	3853	548	1153	167	55	63	430	248	457	.299	.348	.420	109	45	183	63		.989	46	O-963/D-15	7.0
Team	2	97	315	29	98	11	4	1	31	11	38	.311	.336	.381	94	-2	10	4		.984	-2	/O-68,D-15	-0.7
■ JACK McCARTHY McCarthy, John Arthur b: 3/26/1869, Gilbertville, Mass d: 9/11/31, Chicago, Ill. BL/TL, 5'9", 155 lbs. Deb: 8/3/1893																							
1901	Cle-A	86	343	60	110	14	7	0	32	30		.321	.382	.402	123	12	9			.949	-1	O-86	0.4
1902	Cle-A	95	359	45	102	31	5	0	41	24		.284	.329	.398	105	2	12			.944	-5	O-95	-0.9
1903	Cle-A	108	415	47	110	20	8	0	43	19		.265	.299	.352	96	-2	15			.964	-3	*O-108	-1.3
Total	12	1091	4195	550	1203	171	66	7	474	268		.287	.333	.364	100	-3	145			.946	-17	*O-1046/1-23	-8.8
Team	3	289	1117	152	322	65	20	0	116	73		.288	.335	.382	108	11	36			.952	-8	O-289	-1.8
■ BARNEY McCOSKY McCosky, William Barney b: 4/11/17, Coal Run, Pa. BL/TR, 6'1", 184 lbs. Deb: 4/18/39																							
1951	Cle-A	31	61	8	13	3	0	0	2	8	5	.213	.304	.262	57	-4	1	0	0	1.000	-1	O-16	-0.5
1952	Cle-A	54	80	14	17	4	1	1	6	8	5	.213	.284	.325	74	-3	1	1	-0	.944	-5	O-19	-1.0
1953	Cle-A	22	21	3	4	3	0	0	3	1	4	.190	.227	.333	51	-2	0	0	0	.000	0	H	-0.2
Total	11	1170	4172	664	1301	214	71	24	397	497	261	.312	.386	.414	109	62	58	31		.984	-1	*O-1036	0.6
Team	3	107	162	25	34	10	1	1	11	17	14	.210	.285	.302	65	-8	2	1		.978	-7	/O-35	-1.7
■ TOMMY McCRAW McCraw, Tommy Lee b: 11/21/40, Malvern, Ark. BL/TL, 6', 183 lbs. Deb: 6/4/63 C																							
1972	Cle-A	129	391	43	101	13	5	7	33	41	47	.258	.335	.371	106	4	12	10	-2	1.000	-1	O-84,1-38	-0.7
1974	Cle-A	45	112	17	34	8	0	3	17	5	11	.304	.339	.455	128	4	0	1	-1	.990	2	1-38/O-1	0.3
1975	Cle-A	23	51	7	14	1	1	2	5	7	7	.275	.362	.451	129	2	4	1	1	1.000	-2	1-16/O-3	0.0
Total	13	1468	3956	484	972	150	42	75	404	332	544	.246	.311	.362	94	-33	143	68	2	.991	-22	1-911,O-431/D	-12.2
Team	3	197	554	67	149	22	6	12	55	53	65	.269	.338	.395	113	9	16	12	-2	.993	-1	/1-92,O-88	-0.4
■ FRANK McCREA McCrea, Francis William b: 9/6/1896, Jersey City, N.J. d: 2/25/81, Dover, N.J. BR/TR, 5'9", 155 lbs. Deb: 9/26/25																							
1925	Cle-A	1	5	1	1	0	0	0	0	0	0	.200	.200	.200	2	-1	0	0	0	1.000	-1	/C-1	-0.1
■ JIM McDONNELL McDonnell, James William "Mack" b: 8/15/22, Gagetown, Mich. BL/TR, 5'11", 165 lbs. Deb: 9/23/43																							
1943	Cle-A	2	1	1	0	0	0	0	0	2	1	.000	.667	.000	108	0	0	0	0	1.000	-0	/C-1	0.0
1944	Cle-A	20	43	5	10	0	0	0	4	4	3	.233	.298	.233	55	-2	0	0	0	.900	-2	C-13	-0.4
1945	Cle-A	28	51	3	10	2	0	0	8	2	4	.196	.226	.235	36	-4	0	0	0	.980	8	C-23	0.5
Total	3	50	95	9	20	2	0	0	12	8	8	.211	.272	.232	48	-6	0	0	0	.953	6	/C-37	0.1
■ ODDIBE McDOWELL McDowell, Oddibe b: 8/25/62, Hollywood, Fla. BL/TL, 5'9", 165 lbs. Deb: 5/19/85																							
1989	Cle-A	69	239	33	53	5	2	3	22	25	36	.222	.298	.297	67	-10	12	5	1	.992	2	O-64/D-2	-1.0
Total	7	830	2829	458	715	125	28	74	266	294	550	.253	.325	.395	94	-23	169	53	19	.987	5	O-746/D-12	-2.1
■ JIM McGUIRE McGuire, James A. b: 2/4/1875, Dunkirk, N.Y. d: 1/26/17, Buffalo, N.Y. TR, Deb: 9/10/01																							
1901	Cle-A	18	69	4	16	2	0	0	3	0		.232	.232	.261	38	-6	0			.913	1	S-18	-0.3
■ DEACON McGUIRE McGuire, James Thomas b: 11/18/1863, Youngstown, Ohio d: 10/31/36, Duck Lake, Mich. BR/TR, 6'1", 185 lbs. Deb: 6/21/1884 MC																							
1908	Cle-A	1	4	0	1	1	0	0	2	0		.250	.250	.500	142	0	0			1.000	-0	/1-1	0.0
1910	Cle-A	1	3	0	1	0	0	0	0	0		.333	.500	.333	159	0	0			1.000	-1	/C-1,M	-0.1
Total	26	1781	6290	770	1749	300	79	45	787	515		.278	.341	.372	101	15	117			.938	-16	*C-1611/1-94,O3SP	12.6
Team	2	2	7	0	2	1	0	0	2	0		.286	.375	.429	150	0	0			1.000	-1	/C-1,1-1	-0.1
■ STUFFY McINNIS McInnis, John Phalen "Jack" b: 9/19/1890, Gloucester, Mass. d: 2/16/60, Ipswich, Mass. BR/TR, 5'9.5", 162 lbs. Deb: 4/12/09 M																							
1922	Cle-A	142	537	58	164	28	7	1	78	15	5	.305	.325	.389	85	-13	1	5	-3	**.997**	-5	*1-140	-2.6
Total	19	2128	7822	872	2405	312	101	20	1062	380	189	.307	.343	.381	106	35	172	59		.993	17	*1-1995/S-55,32O	-2.5
■ MARK McLEMORE McLemore, Mark Tremell b: 10/4/64, San Diego, Cal. BB/TR, 5'11", 195 lbs. Deb: 9/13/86																							
1990	Cle-A	8	12	2	2	0	0	0	0	0	6	.167	.167	.167	-7	-2	0	0	0	1.000	3	/3-4,2-3,D	0.1
Total	10	783	2513	361	632	95	19	17	244	286	388	.251	.329	.325	75	-83	118	54	3	.980	27	2-511,O-204/DS3	-3.8
■ PAT McNULTY McNulty, Patrick Howard b: 2/27/1899, Cleveland, Ohio d: 5/4/63, Hollywood, Cal. BL/TR, 5'11", 160 lbs. Deb: 9/5/22																							
1922	Cle-A	22	59	10	16	2	1	0	5	9	5	.271	.368	.339	85	-1	4	1	1	.956	-3	O-22	-0.5
1924	Cle-A	101	291	46	78	13	5	0	26	33	22	.268	.347	.347	78	-9	10	7	-1	.961	-4	O-75	-1.8
1925	Cle-A	118	373	70	117	18	2	6	43	47	23	.314	.392	.421	105	4	7	7	-2	.965	-2	*O-111	-0.5
1926	Cle-A	48	56	3	14	2	1	0	6	5	9	.250	.311	.321	65	-3	0	1	-1	.909	-2	/O-9	-0.5

YEAR	TM/L	G	AB	R	H	2B	3B	HR	RBI	BB	SO	AVG	OBP	SLG	PRO+	BR/A	SB	CS	SBR	FA	FR	G/POS	TPR
1927	Cle-A	19	41	3	13	1	0	0	4	4	3	.317	.378	.341	87	-1	1	2	-1	.906	-1	O-12	-0.2
Total	5	308	820	132	238	36	9	6	84	98	62	.290	.368	.378	91	-10	22	18	-4	.957	-11	O-229	-3.5
■ **LUIS MEDINA**	Medina, Luis Main b: 3/26/63, Santa Monica, Cal. BR/TL, 6'4", 200 lbs. Deb: 9/2/88																						
1988	Cle-A	16	51	10	13	0	0	6	8	2	18	.255	.309	.608	146	3	0	0	0	1.000	-0	1-16	0.1
1989	Cle-A	30	83	8	17	1	0	4	8	6	35	.205	.258	.361	72	-3	0	1	-1	.500	-1	D-25/O-3,1	-0.6
1991	Cle-A	5	16	0	1	0	0	0	0	1	7	.063	.118	.063	-48	-3	0	0	0	.000	0	/D-5	-0.4
Total	3	51	150	18	31	1	0	10	16	9	60	.207	.261	.413	85	-4	0	1	-1	1.000	-2	/D-30,1-17,O	-0.9
■ **MOXIE MEIXELL**	Meixell, Merton Merrill b: 10/18/1887, Lake Crystal, Minn d: 8/17/82, Los Angeles, Cal. BL/TR, 5'10", 168 lbs. Deb: 7/7/12																						
1912	Cle-A	3	2	0	1	0	0	0	0	0		.500	.500	.500	181	0	0			.000	0	/O-1	0.0
■ **SAM MELE**	Mele, Sabath Anthony b: 1/21/23, Astoria, N.Y. BR/TR, 6'1", 187 lbs. Deb: 4/15/47 MC																						
1956	Cle-A	57	114	17	29	7	0	4	20	12	20	.254	.325	.421	94	-1	0	1	-1	.969	-0	O-20/1-8	-0.3
Total	10	1046	3437	406	916	168	39	80	544	311	342	.267	.329	.408	97	-26	15	14		.985	-39	O-840/1-79	-10.7
■ **BILL MELTON**	Melton, William Edwin b: 7/7/45, Gulfport, Miss. BR/TR, 6'2", 200 lbs. Deb: 5/4/68																						
1977	Cle-A	50	133	17	32	11	0	0	14	17	21	.241	.336	.323	83	-3	1	3	-2	1.000	1	1-15,D-14,3	-0.5
Total	10	1144	3971	496	1004	162	9	160	591	479	669	.253	.340	.419	112	61	23	24	-8	.949	57	3-901/D-88,O1	10.2
■ **MATT MERULLO**	Merullo, Matthew Bates b: 8/4/65, Winchester, Mass. BL/TR, 6'2", 200 lbs. Deb: 4/12/89 F																						
1994	Cle-A	4	10	1	1	0	0	0	0	2	1	.100	.250	.100	-5	-2	0	0	0	.957	-0	/C-4	-0.1
Total	6	223	496	37	116	17	2	7	59	32	69	.234	.286	.319	64	-25	0	2	-1	.981	-14	C-120/D-27,1	-3.5
■ **CATFISH METKOVICH**	Metkovich, George Michael b: 10/8/20, Angels Camp, Cal. d: 5/17/95, Costa Mesa, Cal. BL/TL, 6'1", 185 lbs. Deb: 7/16/43																						
1947	Cle-A	126	473	68	120	22	7	5	40	32	51	.254	.302	.362	86	-11	5	3	-0	.989	1	*O-119/1-1	-1.7
Total	10	1055	3585	476	934	167	36	47	373	307	359	.261	.323	.367	91	-49	61	28	2	.976	-28	O-644,1-289	-12.5
■ **DUTCH MEYER**	Meyer, Lambert Dalton b: 10/6/15, Waco, Tex. BR/TR, 5'10.5", 181 lbs. Deb: 6/23/37																						
1945	Cle-A	130	524	71	153	29	8	7	48	40	32	.292	.342	.418	125	15	2	4	-2	.978	-32	*2-130	-1.2
1946	Cle-A	72	207	13	48	5	3	0	16	26	16	.232	.321	.285	75	-7	0	1	-1	.977	-13	2-64	-1.8
Total	6	286	994	113	262	49	12	10	93	82	75	.264	.322	.367	94	-9	5	7	-3	.977	-32	2-269	-3.0
Team	2	202	731	84	201	34	11	7	64	66	48	.275	.336	.380	111	8	2	5	-2	.978	-45	2-194	-3.0
■ **LARRY MILBOURNE**	Milbourne, Lawrence William b: 2/14/51, Port Norris, N.J. BB/TR, 6', 165 lbs. Deb: 4/6/74																						
1982	Cle-A	82	291	29	80	11	4	2	25	12	20	.275	.308	.361	83	-7	2	5	-2	.981	-6	2-63,S-21/3D	-1.1
Total	11	989	2448	290	623	71	24	11	184	133	176	.254	.295	.317	70	-101	41	33	-8	.974	1	2-471,S-280,3/DO	-6.7
■ **ED MILLER**	Miller, Edwin J. "Big Ed" b: 11/24/1888, Annville, Pa. d: 4/17/80, S.Lebanon Twsp, Pa BR/TR, 6', 180 lbs. Deb: 6/29/12																						
1918	Cle-A	32	96	9	22	4	3	0	3	12	10	.229	.321	.333	89	-1	2			.977	1	1-22/O-4	-0.2
Total	3	86	200	21	39	5	4	0	12	18	23	.195	.275	.260	58	-11	4			.972	-5	/1-38,O-9,2S3	-2.0
■ **RAY MILLER**	Miller, Raymond Peter b: 2/12/1888, Pittsburgh, Pa. d: 4/7/27, Pittsburgh, Pa. BL/TL, 5'10", 168 lbs. Deb: 4/14/17																						
1917	Cle-A	19	21	1	4	1	0	0	2	8	3	.190	.414	.238	92	0	0			1.000	1	/1-4	0.2
Total	1	25	48	2	8	2	0	0	2	10	6	.167	.310	.208	56	-2	0			1.000	2	/1-10	-0.1
■ **RANDY MILLIGAN**	Milligan, Randy Andre b: 11/27/61, San Diego, Cal. BR/TR, 6'2", 230 lbs. Deb: 9/12/87																						
1993	Cle-A	19	47	7	20	7	0	0	7	14	4	.426	.557	.574	206	8	0	0	0	1.000	-1	1-18/D-1	0.6
Total	8	703	2118	305	553	106	10	70	284	447	431	.261	.393	.420	127	97	16	18		.992	9	1-587/D-42,O	5.7
■ **JACK MILLS**	Mills, Abbott Paige b: 10/23/1889, S.Williamstown, Mass. d: 6/3/73, Washington, D.C. BL/TR, 6', 165 lbs. Deb: 7/1/11																						
1911	Cle-A	13	17	5	5	0	0	0	1	1		.294	.368	.294	85	-0	1			1.000	2	/3-7	0.1
■ **BUSTER MILLS**	Mills, Colonel Buster "Bus" b: 9/16/08, Ranger, Tex. d: 12/1/91, Arlington, Tex. BR/TR, 5'11.5", 195 lbs. Deb: 4/18/34 MC																						
1942	Cle-A	80	195	19	54	4	2	1	26	23	18	.277	.353	.333	99	0	5	4	-1	.973	2	O-53	-0.1
1946	Cle-A	9	22	1	6	0	0	0	3	3	5	.273	.360	.273	84	-0	0	1	-1	1.000	-0	/O-6	-0.2
Total	7	415	1379	200	396	62	19	14	163	131	137	.287	.355	.390	91	-17	23	21		.964	-5	O-341	-3.7
Team	2	89	217	20	60	4	2	1	29	26	23	.276	.354	.327	98	-0	5	5		.975	1	/O-59	-0.3
■ **FRANK MILLS**	Mills, Frank Le Moyne b: 5/13/1895, Knoxville, Ohio d: 8/31/83, Youngstown, Ohio BL/TR, 6', 180 lbs. Deb: 9/22/14																						
1914	Cle-A	4	8	0	1	0	0	0	0	1	2	.125	.222	.125	4	-1	0			.900	-1	/C-2	-0.2
■ **MINNIE MINOSO**	Minoso, Saturnino Orestes Armas (Arrieta) b: 11/29/22, Havana, Cuba BR/TR, 5'10", 175 lbs. Deb: 4/19/49 C																						
1949	Cle-A	9	16	2	3	0	0	1	1	2	2	.188	.350	.375	94	-0	0	1	-1	1.000	-1	/O-7	-0.2
1951	Cle-A	8	14	3	6	2	0	0	2	1	1	.429	.529	.571	209	2	0	0	0	.952	-0	/1-7	0.2
1958	Cle-A	149	556	94	168	25	2	24	80	59	53	.302	.384	.484	141	32	14	14	-4	.975	13	*O-147/3-1	3.3
1959	Cle-A★	148	570	92	172	32	0	21	92	54	46	.302	.379	.468	136	29	8	10	-4	.985	16	*O-148	3.4
Total	17	1835	6579	1136	1963	336	83	186	1023	814	584	.298	.391	.459	130	297	205	130	-16	.974	62	*O-1665,3-116/1DS	26.0
Team	4	314	1156	191	349	59	2	46	175	116	102	.302	.383	.476	139	63	22	25	-8	.980	29	O-302/1-7,3	6.7
■ **DALE MITCHELL**	Mitchell, Loren Dale b: 8/23/21, Colony, Okla. d: 1/5/87, Tulsa, Okla. BL/TL, 6'1", 195 lbs. Deb: 9/15/46																						
1946	Cle-A	11	44	7	19	3	0	0	5	1	2	.432	.444	.500	175	4	1	0	0	1.000	-0	O-11	0.4
1947	Cle-A	123	493	69	156	16	10	1	34	23	14	.316	.347	.396	109	4	2	5	-2	.977	-9	*O-115	-1.4
1948	*Cle-A	141	608	82	204	30	8	4	56	45	17	.336	.383	.431	119	16	13	18	-7	**.991**	4	*O-140	0.4
1949	Cle-A★	149	640	81	**203**	16	**23**	3	56	43	11	.317	.360	.428	110	7	10	3	1	**.994**	3	*O-149	0.3
1950	Cle-A	130	506	81	156	27	5	3	49	67	21	.308	.390	.399	106	6	3	7	-3	.972	-11	*O-127	-1.3
1951	Cle-A	134	510	83	148	21	7	11	62	53	16	.290	.358	.424	117	11	7	7	-2	.992	-6	*O-124	-0.1
1952	Cle-A★	134	511	61	165	26	3	5	58	52	9	.323	.387	.415	132	22	6	6	-2	.992	-5	*O-128	1.0
1953	Cle-A	134	500	76	150	26	4	13	60	42	20	.300	.354	.446	118	11	3	1	0	.970	-6	*O-125	0.1
1954	*Cle-A	53	60	6	17	1	0	1	6	9	1	.283	.377	.350	98	0	0	0	0	.889	-1	/O-6,1-1	-0.1
1955	Cle-A	61	58	4	15	2	1	0	10	4	3	.259	.306	.328	68	-3	0	0	0	1.000	-1	/1-8,O-3	-0.4
1956	Cle-A	38	30	2	4	0	0	0	6	7	2	.133	.297	.133	17	-3	0	0	0	.000	-0	/O-1	-0.4
Total	11	1127	3984	555	1244	169	61	41	403	346	119	.312	.368	.416	114	74	45	47	-15	.985	-32	O-931/1-9	-1.7
Team	11	1108	3960	552	1237	168	61	41	402	346	116	.312	.368	.417	114	75	45	47	-15	.985	-32	O-929/1-9	-1.5
■ **DANNY MOELLER**	Moeller, Daniel Edward b: 3/23/1885, DeWitt, Iowa d: 4/14/51, Florence, Ala. BB/TR, 5'11", 165 lbs. Deb: 9/24/07																						
1916	Cle-A	25	30	5	2	0	0	0	1	5	6	.067	.200	.067	-19	-4	2			1.000	-2	/O-8,2-1	-0.7
Total	7	704	2538	379	618	83	43	15	192	302	296	.243	.328	.328	93	-20	171			.938	5	O-660/2-1	-5.7
■ **BLAS MONACO**	Monaco, Blas b: 11/16/15, San Antonio, Tex. BB/TR, 5'11", 170 lbs. Deb: 8/18/37																						
1937	Cle-A	5	7	0	2	0	1	0	2	0	2	.286	.375	.571	134	0	0	0	0	1.000	0	/2-3	0.1
1946	Cle-A	12	6	2	0	0	0	0	0	1	1	.000	.143	.000	-62	-1	0	0	0	.000	0	H	-0.1
Total	2	17	13	2	2	0	1	0	2	1	3	.154	.267	.308	53	-1	0	0	0	1.000	0	/2-3	0.0
■ **ED MONTAGUE**	Montague, Edward Francis b: 7/24/05, San Francisco, Cal. d: 6/17/88, Daly City, Cal. BR/TR, 5'10", 165 lbs. Deb: 5/14/28																						
1928	Cle-A	32	51	12	12	0	1	0	3	6	7	.235	.339	.275	62	-3	0	0	0	.914	5	S-15/3-9	0.4
1930	Cle-A	58	179	37	47	5	2	1	16	37	38	.263	.392	.330	82	-3	1	5	-3	.917	-15	S-46,3-13	-1.4

YEAR	TM/L	G	AB	R	H	2B	3B	HR	RBI	BB	SO	AVG	OBP	SLG	PRO+	BR/A	SB	CS	SBR	FA	FR	G/POS	TPR
1931	Cle-A	64	193	27	55	8	3	1	26	21	22	.285	.358	.373	87	-3	3	4	-2	.924	16	S-64	1.5
1932	Cle-A	66	192	29	47	5	1	0	24	21	24	.245	.326	.281	55	-12	3	3	-1	.891	-13	S-57,3-11	-2.1
Total	4	220	615	105	161	18	7	2	69	85	91	.262	.357	.324	74	-21	7	12	-5	.912	-7	S-182/3-33	-1.6
■ EDDIE MOORE Moore, Graham Edward b: 1/18/1899, Barlow, Ky. d: 2/10/76, Ft.Myers, Fla. BR/TR, 5'7", 165 lbs. Deb: 9/25/23																							
1934	Cle-A	27	65	4	10	2	0	0	8	10	4	.154	.267	.185	18	-8	0	0	0	.932	1	2-18/3-3,S	-0.6
Total	10	748	2474	360	706	108	26	13	257	272	121	.285	.359	.366	89	-37	52	14	7	.956	-29	2-349,O-145/S3	-4.9
■ ANDRES MORA Mora, Andres (Ibarra) b: 5/25/55, Rio Bravo, Mex. BR/TR, 6', 180 lbs. Deb: 4/13/76																							
1980	Cle-A	9	18	0	2	0	0	0	0	0	0	.111	.111	.111	-39	-3	0	0	0	1.000	0	/O-3	-0.4
Total	4	235	700	71	156	27	2	27	83	31	149	.223	.258	.383	83	-19	1	1	-0	.978	-10	O-160/D-40,3	-3.8
■ BILLY MORAN Moran, William Nelson b: 11/27/33, Montgomery, Ala. BR/TR, 5'11", 185 lbs. Deb: 4/15/58																							
1958	Cle-A	115	257	26	58	11	0	1	18	13	23	.226	.263	.280	51	-17	3	2	-0	.960	13	2-74,S-38	0.0
1959	Cle-A	11	17	1	5	0	0	0	2	0	1	.294	.294	.294	64	-1	0	0	0	1.000	-1	/2-6,S-5	-0.1
1964	Cle-A	69	151	14	31	6	0	1	10	18	16	.205	.294	.265	57	-8	0	1	-1	.972	3	3-42,2-15/1	-0.6
1965	Cle-A	22	24	1	3	0	0	0	0	2	5	.125	.222	.125	1	-3	0	0	0	1.000	1	/2-7,S-1	-0.2
Total	7	634	2076	242	545	88	10	28	202	133	218	.263	.310	.355	85	-45	10	8	-2	.976	39	2-467/3-89,S1	3.3
Team	4	217	449	42	97	17	0	2	30	33	45	.216	.273	.267	51	-30	3	3	-1	.965	16	2-102/S-44,31	-0.9
■ ED MORGAN Morgan, Edward Carre b: 5/22/04, Cairo, Ill. d: 4/9/80, New Orleans, La. BR/TR, 6'0.5", 180 lbs. Deb: 4/11/28																							
1928	Cle-A	76	265	42	83	24	6	4	54	21	17	.313	.366	.494	123	8	5	5	-2	.968	1	1-36,O-21,3	0.4
1929	Cle-A	93	318	60	101	19	10	3	37	37	24	.318	.392	.469	116	8	4	3	-1	.908	-11	O-80	-0.8
1930	Cle-A	150	584	122	204	47	11	26	136	62	66	.349	.413	.601	148	41	8	4	0	.987	-3	*1-129,O-19	2.2
1931	Cle-A	131	462	87	162	33	4	11	86	83	46	.351	.451	.511	144	33	4	5	-2	.984	2	*1-117/3-3	2.1
1932	Cle-A	144	532	96	156	32	7	4	68	94	44	.293	.402	.402	102	5	7	6	-2	.985	-8	*1-142/3-1	-1.5
1933	Cle-A	39	121	10	32	3	3	1	13	7	9	.264	.305	.364	73	-5	1	1	-0	.997	2	1-32/O-1	-0.6
Total	7	771	2810	512	879	186	45	52	473	385	252	.313	.398	.467	117	76	36	25	-4	.986	-23	1-593,O-121/3	-1.2
Team	6	633	2282	417	738	158	41	49	394	304	206	.323	.405	.493	126	90	29	24	-6	.985	-16	1-456,O-121/3	1.8
■ JOE MORGAN Morgan, Joseph Michael b: 11/19/30, Walpole, Mass. BL/TR, 5'10", 170 lbs. Deb: 4/14/59 MC																							
1960	Cle-A	22	47	6	14	2	0	2	4	6	4	.298	.377	.468	131	2	0	0	0	.889	-2	3-12/O-2	0.0
1961	Cle-A	4	10	0	2	0	0	0	0	1	3	.200	.273	.200	29	-1	0	0	0	1.000	0	/O-2	-0.1
Total	4	88	187	15	36	5	3	2	10	18	31	.193	.263	.283	49	-13	0	0	0	.944	-3	/3-38,2-7,O	-1.8
Team	2	26	57	6	16	2	0	2	4	7	7	.281	.359	.421	113	1	0	0	0	.889	-2	/3-12,O-4	-0.1
■ JEFF MORONKO Moronko, Jeffrey Robert b: 8/17/59, Houston, Tex. BR/TR, 6'2", 190 lbs. Deb: 9/1/84																							
1984	Cle-A	7	19	1	3	1	0	0	3	3	5	.158	.273	.211	35	-2	0	0	0	.895	-0	/3-6,D-1	-0.2
Total	2	14	30	1	4	1	0	0	3	3	7	.133	.235	.167	12	-4	0	0	0	.926	-0	/3-9,O-2,SD	-0.4
■ JERRY MOSES Moses, Gerald Braheen b: 8/9/46, Yazoo City, Miss. BR/TR, 6'3", 210 lbs. Deb: 5/9/65																							
1972	Cle-A	52	141	9	31	3	0	4	14	11	29	.220	.290	.326	81	-3	0	0	0	.982	1	C-39/1-3	-0.2
Total	9	386	1072	89	269	48	8	25	109	63	184	.251	.297	.381	89	-19	1	4	-2	.984	3	C-328/1-4,DO	-0.5
■ HOWIE MOSS Moss, Howard Glenn b: 10/17/19, Gastonia, N.C. d: 5/7/89, Baltimore, Md. BR/TR, 5'11.5", 185 lbs. Deb: 4/14/42																							
1946	Cle-A	8	32	2	2	0	0	0	0	3	9	.063	.143	.063	-44	-6	0	1	-1	.857	0	/3-8	-0.7
Total	2	22	72	3	7	0	0	0	1	3	17	.097	.145	.097	-32	-12	0	1	-1	1.000	0	/O-9,3-8	-1.4
■ FRAN MULLINS Mullins, Francis Joseph b: 5/14/57, Oakland, Cal. BR/TR, 6', 180 lbs. Deb: 9/1/80																							
1986	Cle-A	28	40	3	7	4	0	0	5	2	11	.175	.214	.275	33	-4	0	0	0	.953	8	2-13,S-11/1D	0.4
Total	3	106	212	20	43	16	0	2	18	20	48	.203	.272	.307	61	-11	3	2	-0	.968	15	/3-49,S-39,2D1	0.5
■ EDDIE MURRAY Murray, Eddie Clarence b: 2/24/56, Los Angeles, Cal. BB/TR, 6'2", 200 lbs. Deb: 4/7/77 F																							
1994	Cle-A	108	433	57	110	21	1	17	76	31	53	.254	.304	.425	85	-11	8	4	0	.988	-2	D-82,1-26	-1.8
1995	*Cle-A	113	436	68	141	21	0	21	82	39	65	.323	.379	.516	130	19	5	1	1	.984	3	D-95,1-18	1.4
Total	19	2819	10603	1545	3071	532	34	479	1820	1257	1403	.290	.366	.482	133	484	105	43	6	.993	63	*1-2412,D-379/3O	37.1
Team	2	221	869	125	251	42	1	38	158	70	118	.289	.342	.471	108	8	13	5	1	.987	2	D-177/1-44	-0.4
■ RAY MURRAY Murray, Raymond Lee "Deacon" b: 10/12/17, Spring Hope, N.C. BR/TR, 6'3", 204 lbs. Deb: 4/25/48																							
1948	Cle-A	4	4	0	0	0	0	0	0	0	3	.000	.000	.000	-99	-1	0	0	0	.000	0	H	-0.1
1950	Cle-A	55	139	16	38	8	2	1	13	12	13	.273	.331	.381	85	-4	1	0	0	.972	-5	C-45	-0.6
1951	Cle-A	1	1	0	1	0	0	0	1	0	0	1.000	1.000	1.000	468	1	0	0	0	1.000	1	/C-1	0.1
Total	6	250	731	69	184	37	6	8	80	55	67	.252	.305	.352	75	-27	1	0	0	.987	6	C-226	-1.1
Team	3	60	144	16	39	8	2	1	14	12	16	.271	.327	.375	82	-4	1	0	0	.972	-4	/C-46	-0.6
■ GLENN MYATT Myatt, Glenn Calvin b: 7/9/1897, Argenta, Ark. d: 8/9/69, Houston, Tex. BL/TR, 5'11", 165 lbs. Deb: 4/15/20																							
1923	Cle-A	92	220	36	63	7	6	3	40	16	18	.286	.338	.414	97	-2	0	2	-1	.934	-8	C-69	-0.8
1924	Cle-A	105	342	55	117	22	7	8	73	33	12	.342	.402	.518	134	16	6	1	1	.978	-15	C-95	0.8
1925	Cle-A	106	358	51	97	15	9	11	54	29	24	.271	.329	.455	97	-4	3	1	0	.973	-18	C-98/O-1	-1.5
1926	Cle-A	56	117	14	29	5	2	0	13	13	13	.248	.323	.325	69	-5	1	0	0	1.000	-1	C-35	-0.4
1927	Cle-A	55	94	15	23	6	0	2	8	12	7	.245	.336	.372	83	-2	1	1	-0	.978	2	C-26	0.0
1928	Cle-A	58	125	9	36	7	2	1	15	13	13	.288	.355	.400	97	-0	0	2	-1	.967	-9	C-30	-0.8
1929	Cle-A	59	129	14	30	4	1	1	17	7	5	.233	.277	.302	47	-10	0	1	-1	.976	-1	C-41	-0.9
1930	Cle-A	86	265	30	78	23	2	2	37	18	17	.294	.342	.419	88	-5	2	3	-1	.977	-7	C-71	-0.6
1931	Cle-A	65	195	21	48	14	2	1	29	21	13	.246	.319	.354	73	-8	2	1	0	.991	-4	C-53	-0.8
1932	Cle-A	82	252	45	62	12	1	8	46	27	21	.246	.326	.397	81	-8	2	2	-1	.988	-8	C-65	-1.2
1933	Cle-A	40	77	10	18	4	0	0	7	15	8	.234	.372	.286	73	-2	0	1	-1	.965	-1	C-27	-0.2
1934	Cle-A	36	107	18	34	6	1	0	12	13	5	.318	.392	.393	101	1	1	0	0	.980	-1	C-34	0.2
1935	Cle-A	10	36	1	3	1	0	0	2	4	3	.083	.175	.111	-24	-7	0	0	0	1.000	-1	C-10	-0.7
Total	16	1004	2678	346	722	137	37	38	387	248	195	.270	.334	.391	85	-63	20	18	-5	.974	-78	C-734/O-38	-10.1
Team	13	850	2317	319	638	126	33	37	353	221	159	.275	.342	.406	90	-36	18	15	-4	.975	-72	C-654/O-1	-6.9
■ LOU NAGELSEN Nagelsen, Louis Marcellus (b: Louis Marcellus Nageleisen) b: 6/29/1887, Piqua, Ohio d: 10/21/65, Fort Wayne, Ind. BR/TR, 6'2", 180 lbs. Deb: 9/10/12																							
1912	Cle-A	2	3	0	0	0	0	0	0	0		.000	.000	.000	-97	-1	0			1.000	-1	/C-2	-0.2
■ RUSS NAGELSON Nagelson, Russell Charles b: 9/19/44, Cincinnati, Ohio BL/TR, 6', 205 lbs. Deb: 9/11/68																							
1968	Cle-A	5	3	0	1	0	0	0	0	2	2	.333	.600	.333	192	1	0	0	0	.000	0	H	0.1
1969	Cle-A	12	17	1	6	0	0	0	0	3	3	.353	.450	.353	123	1	0	0	0	1.000	-1	/O-3,1-1	0.0
1970	Cle-A	17	24	3	3	1	0	1	2	3	9	.125	.222	.292	39	-2	0	0	0	1.000	-0	/O-4	-0.3
Total	3	62	76	9	16	1	0	1	4	13	20	.211	.326	.263	64	-3	0	0	0	1.000	-2	/O-11,1-2	-0.6
Team	3	34	44	4	10	1	0	1	2	8	14	.227	.346	.318	84	-1	0	0	0	1.000	-1	/O-7,1-1	-0.2
■ BILL NAHORODNY Nahorodny, William Gerard b: 8/31/53, Hamtramck, Mich. BR/TR, 6'2", 200 lbs. Deb: 9/27/76																							
1982	Cle-A	39	94	6	21	5	1	4	18	2	9	.223	.240	.426	79	-3	0	0	0	1.000	-3	C-35	-0.6
Total	9	308	844	74	203	41	3	25	109	56	118	.241	.292	.385	85	-18	1	4	-2	.983	-17	C-275/1-7,D	-3.3

YEAR	TM/L	G	AB	R	H	2B	3B	HR	RBI	BB	SO	AVG	OBP	SLG	PRO+	BR/A	SB	CS	SBR	FA	FR	G/POS	TPR
■ HAL NARAGON	Naragon, Harold Richard b: 10/1/28, Zanesville, Ohio BL/TR, 6', 175 lbs. Deb: 9/23/51 C																						
1951	Cle-A	3	8	0	2	0	0	0	0	1	0	.250	.400	.250	83	-0	0	0	0	.929	0	/C-2	0.0
1954	*Cle-A	46	101	10	24	2	2	0	12	9	12	.238	.300	.297	63	-5	0	0	0	1.000	-2	C-45	-0.5
1955	Cle-A	57	127	12	41	9	2	1	14	15	8	.323	.394	.449	122	4	1	0	0	.991	-4	C-52	0.2
1956	Cle-A	53	122	11	35	3	1	3	18	13	9	.287	.360	.402	99	-0	0	0	0	.988	-12	C-48	-1.0
1957	Cle-A	57	121	12	31	1	1	0	8	12	9	.256	.328	.281	69	-5	0	0	0	.990	-2	C-39	-0.6
1958	Cle-A	9	9	2	3	0	1	0	0	0	0	.333	.333	.556	144	0	0	0	0	.000	0	H	0.0
1959	Cle-A	14	36	6	10	4	1	0	5	3	2	.278	.350	.444	121	1	0	0	0	1.000	-1	C-10	0.0
Total	10	424	985	83	262	27	11	6	87	76	62	.266	.323	.334	77	-31	1	1	-0	.991	-29	C-324	-4.9
Team	7	239	524	53	146	19	8	4	57	53	40	.279	.349	.368	93	-5	1	0	0	.991	-20	C-196	-1.9
■ KEN NASH	Nash, Kenneth Leland (Played One Game In 1912 under name of Costello) b: 7/14/1888, Weymouth, Mass. d: 2/16/77, Epsom, N.H. BB/TR, 5'8", 140 lbs. Deb: 7/4/12																						
1912	Cle-A	11	23	2	4	0	0	0	0	3		.174	.269	.174	27	-2	0			.826	-3	/S-8	-0.5
Total	2	35	74	6	18	3	1	0	6	9		.243	.325	.311	87	-1	0			.760	-10	/S-11,3-10,2	-1.1
■ CAL NEEMAN	Neeman, Calvin Amandus b: 2/18/29, Valmeyer, Ill. BR/TR, 6'1", 192 lbs. Deb: 4/16/57																						
1963	Cle-A	9	9	0	0	0	0	0	0	1	5	.000	.100	.000	-70	-2	0	0	0	1.000	3	/C-9	0.1
Total	7	376	1002	93	224	35	4	30	97	79	221	.224	.286	.356	72	-41	1	0		.988	24	C-352	-0.4
■ BERNIE NEIS	Neis, Bernard Edmund b: 9/26/1895, Bloomington, Ill. d: 11/29/72, Inverness, Fla. BB/TR, 5'7", 160 lbs. Deb: 4/14/20																						
1927	Cle-A	32	96	17	29	9	0	4	18	18	9	.302	.412	.521	140	6	0	1	-1	.978	5	O-29	0.8
Total	8	677	1825	297	496	84	18	25	210	201	186	.272	.346	.379	94	-13	46	39	-10	.950	3	O-520/2-1	-5.0
■ DAVE NELSON	Nelson, David Earl b: 6/20/44, Fort Sill, Okla. BR/TR, 5'10", 160 lbs. Deb: 4/11/68 C																						
1968	Cle-A	88	189	26	44	4	5	0	19	17	35	.233	.300	.307	85	-3	23	7	3	.987	-2	2-59,S-14	0.1
1969	Cle-A	52	123	11	25	0	0	0	6	9	26	.203	.263	.203	31	-11	4	3	-1	.966	4	2-33/O-2	-0.5
Total	10	813	2578	340	630	77	19	20	211	220	392	.244	.307	.312	81	-62	187	73	12	.976	-31	2-466,3-203/DOS1	-6.4
Team	2	140	312	37	69	4	5	0	25	26	61	.221	.285	.266	62	-14	27	10	2	.978	3	/2-92,S-14,O	-0.4
■ ROCKY NELSON	Nelson, Glenn Richard b: 11/18/24, Portsmouth, Ohio BL/TL, 5'11", 178 lbs. Deb: 4/27/49																						
1954	Cle-A	4	4	0	0	0	0	0	0	0	1	.000	.000	.000	-98	-1	0	0	0	1.000	-0	/1-2	-0.1
Total	9	620	1394	186	347	61	14	31	173	130	94	.249	.318	.379	84	-31	7	3	0	.995	-3	1-386/O-23	-5.2
■ GRAIG NETTLES	Nettles, Graig b: 8/20/44, San Diego, Cal. BL/TR, 6', 186 lbs. Deb: 9/6/67 FC																						
1970	Cle-A	157	549	81	129	13	1	26	62	81	77	.235	.336	.404	99	-1	3	1	0	**.967**	28	*3-154/O-3	2.7
1971	Cle-A	158	598	78	156	18	1	28	86	82	56	.261	.353	.435	112	10	7	4	-0	.973	**42**	*3-158	5.3
1972	Cle-A	150	557	65	141	28	0	17	70	57	50	.253	.327	.395	110	7	2	3	-1	.956	5	*3-150	1.0
Total	22	2700	8986	1193	2225	328	28	390	1314	1088	1209	.248	.332	.421	110	117	32	36	-12	.961	132	*3-2412/O-73,1DS	21.3
Team	3	465	1704	224	426	59	2	71	218	220	183	.250	.339	.412	107	16	12	8	-1	.966	75	3-462/O-3	9.0
■ MILO NETZEL	Netzel, Miles A. b: 5/12/1886, Eldred, Pa. d: 3/18/38, Oxnard, Cal. BL/TL, Deb: 9/16/09																						
1909	Cle-A	10	37	2	7	1	0	0	3	3		.189	.250	.216	46	-2	1			.800	-3	/3-6,O-2	-0.6
■ DON NEWCOMBE	Newcombe, Donald "Newk" b: 6/14/26, Madison, N.J. BL/TR, 6'4", 225 lbs. Deb: 5/20/49																						
1960	Cle-A	24	20	1	6	1	0	0	1	1	7	.300	.333	.350	88	-0	0	0	0	.889	-1	P-20	0.0
Total	10	452	878	94	238	33	3	15	108	87	147	.271	.339	.367	85	-17	2	1		.963	-6	P-344	0.0
■ SIMON NICHOLLS	Nicholls, Simon Burdette b: 7/18/1882, Germantown, Md. d: 3/12/11, Baltimore, Md. BL/TR, 5'11.5", 165 lbs. Deb: 9/18/03																						
1910	Cle-A	3	0	0	0	0	0	0	0	0		—	—	—	—	0	0			.000	-1	/S-3	-0.1
Total	6	312	1133	144	284	32	6	4	58	65		.251	.292	.300	87	-18	27			.917	-45	S-233/2-51,31	-6.6
■ MILT NIELSEN	Nielsen, Milton Robert b: 2/8/25, Tyler, Minn. BL/TL, 5'11", 190 lbs. Deb: 9/27/49																						
1949	Cle-A	3	9	1	1	0	0	0	0	2	4	.111	.273	.111	4	-1	0	0	0	1.000	-0	/O-3	-0.2
1951	Cle-A	16	6	1	0	0	0	0	0	1	1	.000	.143	.000	-63	-1	0	0	0	.000	0	H	-0.1
Total	2	19	15	2	1	0	0	0	0	3	5	.067	.222	.067	-22	-3	0	0	0	.920	-0	/O-3	-0.3
■ BOB NIEMAN	Nieman, Robert Charles b: 1/26/27, Cincinnati, Ohio d: 3/10/85, Corona, Cal. BR/TR, 5'11", 195 lbs. Deb: 9/14/51																						
1961	Cle-A	39	65	2	23	6	0	2	10	7	4	.354	.417	.538	157	5	1	0	0	.960	0	O-12	0.5
1962	Cle-A	2	1	0	0	0	0	0	1	0	1	.000	.000	.000	-99	-0	0	0	0	.000	0	H	0.0
Total	12	1113	3452	455	1018	180	32	125	544	435	512	.295	.375	.474	132	154	10	30	-15	.975	-8	O-926	8.6
Team	2	41	66	2	23	6	0	2	11	7	5	.348	.411	.530	154	5	1	0	0	.960	0	/O-12	0.5
■ HARRY NILES	Niles, Herbert Clyde b: 9/10/1880, Buchanan, Mich. d: 4/18/53, Sturgis, Mich. BR/TR, 5'8", 175 lbs. Deb: 4/24/06																						
1910	Cle-A	70	240	25	51	6	4	1	18	15		.213	.267	.283	72	-8	9			.975	-4	O-50/S-7,3	-1.6
Total	5	608	2270	278	561	58	24	12	152	163		.247	.306	.310	95	-12	107			.960	-29	O-298,2-214/3S	-6.2
■ RABBIT NILL	Nill, George Charles b: 7/14/1881, Ft.Wayne, Ind. d: 5/24/62, Fort Wayne, Ind. BR/TR, 5'7", 160 lbs. Deb: 9/27/04																						
1907	Cle-A	12	43	5	12	1	0	0	2	3		.279	.326	.302	100	0	2			.815	-4	/3-7,S-4	-0.4
1908	Cle-A	11	23	3	5	0	0	0	1	0		.217	.217	.217	41	-2	0			.833	0	/S-6,O-3,2	-0.1
Total	5	296	963	116	204	23	9	3	77	103		.212	.297	.264	82	-17	36			.943	-7	2-113/3-75,SO	-2.4
Team	2	23	66	8	17	1	0	0	3	3		.258	.290	.273	80	-1	2			.839	-3	/S-10,3-7,O2	-0.5
■ OTIS NIXON	Nixon, Otis Junior b: 1/9/59, Columbus Co., N.C. BB/TR, 6'2", 180 lbs. Deb: 9/9/83 F																						
1984	Cle-A	49	91	16	14	0	0	0	1	8	11	.154	.222	.154	6	-11	12	6	0	1.000	-2	O-46	-1.5
1985	Cle-A	104	162	34	38	4	0	3	9	8	27	.235	.271	.315	60	-9	20	11	-1	.971	-7	O-80,D-11	-1.8
1986	Cle-A	105	95	33	25	4	1	0	8	13	12	.263	.352	.326	88	-1	23	6	3	.969	-23	O-95/D-5	-2.2
1987	Cle-A	19	17	2	1	0	0	0	1	3	4	.059	.200	.059	-26	-3	2	3	-1	1.000	-4	O-17/D-2	-0.8
Total	13	1245	3444	605	920	101	16	7	217	382	477	.267	.341	.312	77	-96	444	147		.988	-33	*O-1098/D-18,S	-10.7
Team	4	277	365	85	78	8	1	3	19	32	54	.214	.277	.266	50	-25	57	26		.979	-36	O-238/D-18	-6.3
■ RUSS NIXON	Nixon, Russell Eugene b: 2/19/35, Cleves, Ohio BL/TR, 6'1", 200 lbs. Deb: 4/20/57 MC																						
1957	Cle-A	62	185	15	52	7	1	2	18	12	12	.281	.325	.362	88	-3	0	1	-1	.984	-6	C-57	-0.8
1958	Cle-A	113	376	42	113	17	4	9	46	13	38	.301	.324	.439	111	4	0	3	-2	.991	-10	*C-101	-0.2
1959	Cle-A	82	258	23	62	10	3	1	29	15	28	.240	.282	.314	66	-12	0	0	0	.985	-7	C-74	-1.5
1960	Cle-A	25	82	6	20	5	0	1	6	6	6	.244	.311	.341	79	-2	0	1	-1	.993	-0	C-25	-0.2
Total	12	906	2504	215	670	115	19	27	266	154	279	.268	.313	.361	84	-53	0	7	-4	.988	-85	C-722	-11.3
Team	4	282	901	86	247	39	8	13	99	46	84	.274	.311	.378	90	-14	0	5	-3	.988	-23	C-257	-2.7
■ JUNIOR NOBOA	Noboa, Milciades Arturo (Diaz) b: 11/10/64, Azua, D.R. BR/TR, 5'10", 160 lbs. Deb: 8/22/84																						
1984	Cle-A	23	11	3	4	0	0	0	0	0	2	.364	.364	.364	100	-0	1	0	0	1.000	4	2-19/D-1	0.4
1987	Cle-A	39	80	7	18	2	1	0	7	3	6	.225	.253	.275	40	-7	1	0	0	.983	4	2-21/S-8,3D	-0.2
Total	8	317	493	47	118	13	4	1	33	17	47	.239	.268	.288	54	-31	9	4	0	.981	10	2-129/S-28,3OD1P	-2.0
Team	2	62	91	10	22	2	1	0	7	3	8	.242	.266	.286	47	-7	2	0	1	.987	8	/2-40,S-8,3D	0.2
■ JIM NORRIS	Norris, James Francis b: 12/20/48, Brooklyn, N.Y. BL/TL, 5'10", 175 lbs. Deb: 4/7/77																						
1977	Cle-A	133	440	59	119	23	6	2	37	64	57	.270	.363	.364	102	3	26	17	-2	.982	12	*O-124/1-3	0.8

YEAR	TM/L	G	AB	R	H	2B	3B	HR	RBI	BB	SO	AVG	OBP	SLG	PRO+	BR/A	SB	CS	SBR	FA	FR	G/POS	TPR
1978	Cle-A	113	315	41	89	14	5	2	27	42	20	.283	.367	.378	111	6	12	7	-1	.988	0	O-78,D-15/1	0.2
1979	Cle-A	124	353	50	87	15	6	3	30	44	35	.246	.330	.348	83	-8	15	10	-2	.982	0	O-93,D-13	-1.3
Total	4	489	1282	173	338	57	17	7	110	173	128	.264	.351	.351	95	-5	59	37	-5	.985	-5	O-377/D-29,1	-2.9
Team	3	370	1108	150	295	52	17	7	94	150	112	.266	.354	.363	98	1	53	34	-5	.983	13	O-295/D-28,1	-0.3

■ LES NUNAMAKER Nunamaker, Leslie Grant b: 1/25/1889, Malcolm, Neb. d: 11/14/38, Hastings, Neb. BR/TR, 6'2", 190 lbs. Deb: 4/28/11

YEAR	TM/L	G	AB	R	H	2B	3B	HR	RBI	BB	SO	AVG	OBP	SLG	PRO+	BR/A	SB	CS	SBR	FA	FR	G/POS	TPR
1919	Cle-A	26	56	6	14	1	1	0	7	2	6	.250	.276	.304	59	-3	0			.927	-4	C-16	-0.7
1920	*Cle-A	34	54	10	18	3	3	0	14	4	5	.333	.379	.500	128	2	1	0	0	.963	1	C-17/1-6	0.4
1921	Cle-A	46	131	16	47	7	2	0	25	11	8	.359	.408	.443	115	3	1	1	-0	.970	4	C-46	0.8
1922	Cle-A	25	43	8	13	2	0	0	7	4	3	.302	.362	.349	85	-1	0	0	0	.936	-2	C-13	-0.3
Total	12	716	1990	194	533	75	30	2	216	176	150	.268	.332	.339	95	-12	36	12		.972	-5	C-614/1-15,O	2.4
Team	4	131	284	40	92	13	6	0	53	21	22	.324	.370	.412	102	1	2	1		.958	-2	/C-92,1-6	0.2

■ JACK O'BRIEN O'Brien, John Joseph b: 2/5/1873, Watervliet, N.Y. d: 6/10/33, Watervliet, N.Y. BL/TR, 6'1", 165 lbs. Deb: 4/14/1899

YEAR	TM/L	G	AB	R	H	2B	3B	HR	RBI	BB	SO	AVG	OBP	SLG	PRO+	BR/A	SB	CS	SBR	FA	FR	G/POS	TPR
1901	Cle-A	92	375	54	106	14	5	0	39	22		.283	.329	.347	91	-4	13			.941	-3	O-92/3-1	-1.3
Total	3	326	1226	171	317	39	14	9	133	77		.259	.308	.335	82	-29	42			.937	-5	O-295/3-16,2S	-5.4

■ PETE O'BRIEN O'Brien, Peter J. b: 6/17/1877, Binghamton, N.Y. d: 1/31/17, Jersey City, N.J. BL/TR, 5'7", 170 lbs. Deb: 9/21/01

YEAR	TM/L	G	AB	R	H	2B	3B	HR	RBI	BB	SO	AVG	OBP	SLG	PRO+	BR/A	SB	CS	SBR	FA	FR	G/POS	TPR
1907	Cle-A	43	145	9	33	5	2	0	6	7		.228	.263	.290	76	-4	1			.943	-11	2-17,3-12,S	-1.7
Total	3	249	857	60	191	18	7	3	78	63		.223	.279	.271	76	-24	30			.929	-50	2-153/3-58,S	-7.8

■ PETE O'BRIEN O'Brien, Peter Michael b: 2/9/58, Santa Monica, Cal. BL/TL, 6'1", 198 lbs. Deb: 9/3/82

YEAR	TM/L	G	AB	R	H	2B	3B	HR	RBI	BB	SO	AVG	OBP	SLG	PRO+	BR/A	SB	CS	SBR	FA	FR	G/POS	TPR
1989	Cle-A	155	554	75	144	24	1	12	55	83	48	.260	.358	.372	104	6	3	1	0	.994	3	*1-154/D-1	-0.4
Total	12	1567	5437	654	1421	254	21	169	736	641	563	.261	.340	.409	104	34	24	34		.994	49	*1-1377,D-120/O	-3.3

■ PAUL O'DEA O'Dea, Paul "Lefty" b: 7/3/20, Cleveland, Ohio d: 12/11/78, Cleveland, Ohio BL/TL, 6', 200 lbs. Deb: 4/19/44

YEAR	TM/L	G	AB	R	H	2B	3B	HR	RBI	BB	SO	AVG	OBP	SLG	PRO+	BR/A	SB	CS	SBR	FA	FR	G/POS	TPR
1944	Cle-A	76	173	25	55	9	0	0	13	23	21	.318	.401	.370	126	7	2	2	-1	.949	-5	O-41/P-3,1	0.0
1945	Cle-A	87	221	21	52	2	2	1	21	20	26	.235	.299	.276	70	-8	3	0	1	.992	2	O-53/P-1	-0.9
Total	2	163	394	46	107	11	2	1	34	43	47	.272	.345	.317	95	-1	5	2	0	.975	-2	/O-94,P-4,1	-0.9

■ BLUE MOON ODOM Odom, Johnny Lee b: 5/29/45, Macon, Ga. BR/TR, 6', 185 lbs. Deb: 9/5/64

YEAR	TM/L	G	AB	R	H	2B	3B	HR	RBI	BB	SO	AVG	OBP	SLG	PRO+	BR/A	SB	CS	SBR	FA	FR	G/POS	TPR
1975	Cle-A	3	0	0	0	0	0	0	0	0	0	—	—	—	—	0	0	0	0	1.000	-0	/P-3	0.0
Total	13	402	405	76	79	9	2	12	31	19	163	.195	.235	.316	60	-22	6	5	-1	.904	5	P-295	0.0

■ HAL O'HAGEN O'Hagen, Harry P. b: 9/30/1873, Washington, D.C. d: 1/14/13, Newark, N.J. 6', 173 lbs. Deb: 9/24/1892

YEAR	TM/L	G	AB	R	H	2B	3B	HR	RBI	BB	SO	AVG	OBP	SLG	PRO+	BR/A	SB	CS	SBR	FA	FR	G/POS	TPR
	Yr	35	119	10	22	1	3	0	10	11		.185	.254	.244	55	-6	8			1.000	2	1-31/O-4	-0.5
1902	Cle-A	3	13	2	5	2	0	0	1	0		.385	.385	.538	160	1	2			1.000	1	/1-3	0.1
Total	2	61	209	18	39	5	4	0	19	13		.187	.241	.249	51	-12	13			.981	3	/1-52,O-8,C	-1.2

■ DAVE OLIVER Oliver, David Jacob b: 4/7/51, Stockton, Cal. BL/TR, 5'11", 175 lbs. Deb: 9/25/77 C

YEAR	TM/L	G	AB	R	H	2B	3B	HR	RBI	BB	SO	AVG	OBP	SLG	PRO+	BR/A	SB	CS	SBR	FA	FR	G/POS	TPR
1977	Cle-A	7	22	2	7	0	1	0	3	4	0	.318	.444	.409	139	2	0	0	0	.949	1	/2-7	0.2

■ IVY OLSON Olson, Ivan Massie b: 10/14/1885, Kansas City, Mo. d: 9/1/65, Inglewood, Cal. BR/TR, 5'10.5", 175 lbs. Deb: 4/12/11 C

YEAR	TM/L	G	AB	R	H	2B	3B	HR	RBI	BB	SO	AVG	OBP	SLG	PRO+	BR/A	SB	CS	SBR	FA	FR	G/POS	TPR
1911	Cle-A	140	545	89	142	20	8	1	50	34		.261	.311	.332	79	-17	20			.909	-16	*S-139/3-1	-2.3
1912	Cle-A	125	467	68	118	13	1	0	33	21		.253	.291	.285	63	-23	16			.917	6	S-56,3-36,2/O	-1.3
1913	Cle-A	104	370	47	92	13	3	0	32	22	28	.249	.296	.300	72	-13	7			.953	4	3-73,1-21/2	-1.0
1914	Cle-A	89	310	22	75	6	2	1	20	13	24	.242	.275	.284	65	-14	15	9	-1	.942	12	S-31,2-23,3/O1	0.0
Total	14	1574	6111	730	1575	191	69	13	446	285	222	.258	.295	.318	74	-212	156	36		.932	-34	*S-1054,2-288,3/1O	-18.5
Team	4	458	1692	226	427	52	14	2	135	90	52	.252	.296	.303	70	-67	58	9		.915	5	S-226,3-129/21O	-4.6

■ STEVE O'NEILL O'Neill, Stephen Francis b: 7/6/1891, Minooka, Pa. d: 1/26/62, Cleveland, Ohio BR/TR, 5'10", 165 lbs. Deb: 9/18/11 FMC

YEAR	TM/L	G	AB	R	H	2B	3B	HR	RBI	BB	SO	AVG	OBP	SLG	PRO+	BR/A	SB	CS	SBR	FA	FR	G/POS	TPR
1911	Cle-A	9	27	1	4	1	0	0	1	4		.148	.281	.185	31	-2	2			.986	4	/C-9	0.2
1912	Cle-A	69	215	17	49	4	0	0	14	12		.228	.272	.247	47	-15	2			.961	9	C-68	0.0
1913	Cle-A	80	234	19	69	13	3	0	29	10	24	.295	.329	.376	103	0	5			.973	3	C-80	1.1
1914	Cle-A	87	269	28	68	12	2	0	20	15	35	.253	.292	.312	79	-8	1	3	-2	.956	0	C-82/1-1	-0.2
1915	Cle-A	121	386	32	91	14	2	2	34	26	41	.236	.293	.298	75	-13	2	3	-1	.968	5	*C-115	0.1
1916	Cle-A	130	378	30	89	23	0	0	29	24	33	.235	.288	.296	71	-14	2			.971	5	*C-128	0.0
1917	Cle-A	129	370	21	68	10	2	0	29	41	55	.184	.272	.222	47	-23	2			.980	1	*C-127	-1.3
1918	Cle-A	114	359	34	87	8	7	1	35	48	22	.242	.343	.312	89	-4	5			**.983**	1	*C-113	0.8
1919	Cle-A	125	398	46	115	35	7	2	47	48	21	.289	.373	.427	117	9	4			.977	-7	*C-123	1.3
1920	*Cle-A	149	489	63	157	39	5	3	55	69	39	.321	.408	.440	121	17	3	5	-2	.976	-5	*C-148	2.0
1921	Cle-A	106	335	39	108	22	1	1	50	57	22	.322	.424	.403	110	8	0	1	-1	.982	3	*C-105	1.6
1922	Cle-A	133	392	33	122	27	4	2	65	73	25	.311	.423	.416	118	15	2	2	-1	.974	-14	*C-130	0.6
1923	Cle-A	113	330	31	82	12	0	0	50	64	34	.248	.374	.285	75	-9	0	4	-2	.968	-12	*C-111	-1.7
Total	17	1590	4795	448	1259	248	34	13	537	592	383	.263	.349	.337	88	-61	30	23		.972	-6	*C-1532/1-1	3.1
Team	13	1365	4182	394	1109	220	33	11	458	491	351	.265	.348	.341	91	-37	30	18		.973	-5	*C-1339/1-1	4.5

■ EDDIE ONSLOW Onslow, Edward Joseph b: 2/17/1893, Meadville, Pa. d: 5/8/81, Dennison, Ohio BL/TL, 6', 170 lbs. Deb: 8/7/12 F

YEAR	TM/L	G	AB	R	H	2B	3B	HR	RBI	BB	SO	AVG	OBP	SLG	PRO+	BR/A	SB	CS	SBR	FA	FR	G/POS	TPR
1918	Cle-A	2	6	0	1	0	0	0	0	0	1	.167	.167	.167	1	-1	0			.000	-1	/O-1	-0.2
Total	4	64	207	19	48	3	2	1	22	9	10	.232	.271	.280	59	-12	4			.979	-5	/1-57,O-1	-1.9

■ JORGE ORTA Orta, Jorge (Nunez) b: 11/26/50, Mazatlan, Mexico BL/TR, 5'10", 175 lbs. Deb: 4/15/72

YEAR	TM/L	G	AB	R	H	2B	3B	HR	RBI	BB	SO	AVG	OBP	SLG	PRO+	BR/A	SB	CS	SBR	FA	FR	G/POS	TPR
1980	Cle-A☆	129	481	78	140	18	3	10	64	71	44	.291	.384	.403	116	13	6	5	-1	.982	13	*O-120/D-7	2.0
1981	Cle-A	88	338	50	92	14	3	5	34	21	43	.272	.317	.376	100	-0	4	3	-1	.994	4	O-86	0.0
Total	16	1755	5829	733	1619	267	63	130	745	500	715	.278	.338	.412	108	56	79	60		.974	-117	2-689,D-451,O/3S	-5.3
Team	2	217	819	128	232	32	6	15	98	92	87	.283	.358	.392	110	12	10	8		.987	17	O-206/D-7	2.0

■ JUNIOR ORTIZ Ortiz, Adalberto Colon b: 10/24/59, Humacao, P.R. BR/TR, 5'11", 176 lbs. Deb: 9/20/82

YEAR	TM/L	G	AB	R	H	2B	3B	HR	RBI	BB	SO	AVG	OBP	SLG	PRO+	BR/A	SB	CS	SBR	FA	FR	G/POS	TPR
1992	Cle-A	86	244	20	61	7	0	0	24	12	23	.250	.296	.279	63	-12	1	3	-2	.989	-1	C-86	-1.1
1993	Cle-A	95	249	19	55	13	0	0	20	11	26	.221	.268	.273	46	-19	1	0	0	.990	11	C-95	-0.3
Total	13	749	1894	142	484	71	4	5	186	121	222	.256	.306	.305	69	-78	8	18	-8	.986	-4	C-702/D-3	-6.2
Team	2	181	493	39	116	20	0	0	44	23	49	.235	.282	.276	54	-31	2	3	-1	.989	10	C-181	-1.4

■ HARRY OSTDIEK Ostdiek, Henry Girard b: 4/12/1881, Ottumwa, Iowa d: 5/6/56, Minneapolis, Minn. BR/TR, 5'11", 185 lbs. Deb: 9/10/04

YEAR	TM/L	G	AB	R	H	2B	3B	HR	RBI	BB	SO	AVG	OBP	SLG	PRO+	BR/A	SB	CS	SBR	FA	FR	G/POS	TPR
1904	Cle-A	7	18	1	3	0	1	0	3	3		.167	.318	.278	90	-0	1			.946	-0	/C-7	0.0
Total	2	8	21	1	3	0	1	0	3	3		.143	.280	.238	65	-1	1			.935	0	/C-8	0.0

■ JOHNNY OULLIBER Oulliber, John Andrew b: 2/24/11, New Orleans, La. d: 12/26/80, New Orleans, La. BR/TR, 5'11", 165 lbs. Deb: 7/25/33

YEAR	TM/L	G	AB	R	H	2B	3B	HR	RBI	BB	SO	AVG	OBP	SLG	PRO+	BR/A	SB	CS	SBR	FA	FR	G/POS	TPR
1933	Cle-A	22	75	9	20	1	0	0	3	4	5	.267	.313	.280	55	-5	0	0	0	1.000	-3	O-18	-0.9

■ ERNIE PADGETT Padgett, Ernest Kitchen "Red" b: 3/1/1899, Philadelphia, Pa. d: 4/15/57, E.Orange, N.J. BR/TR, 5'8", 155 lbs. Deb: 10/3/23

YEAR	TM/L	G	AB	R	H	2B	3B	HR	RBI	BB	SO	AVG	OBP	SLG	PRO+	BR/A	SB	CS	SBR	FA	FR	G/POS	TPR
1926	Cle-A	36	62	7	13	0	1	0	6	8	3	.210	.300	.242	42	-5	1	0	0	.930	2	3-29/S-2	-0.2
1927	Cle-A	7	7	1	2	0	0	0	0	0	2	.286	.286	.286	48	-1	0	0	0	1.000	-0	/2-4	-0.1
Total	5	271	838	84	223	34	17	1	81	61	75	.266	.318	.351	80	-24	8	14	-6	.957	-26	3-149/2-81,S	-4.4
Team	2	43	69	8	15	0	1	0	6	8	5	.217	.299	.246	43	-6	1	0	0	.930	2	/3-29,2-4,S	-0.3

YEAR	TM/L	G	AB	R	H	2B	3B	HR	RBI	BB	SO	AVG	OBP	SLG	PRO+	BR/A	SB	CS	SBR	FA	FR	G/POS	TPR

■ KARL PAGEL   Pagel, Karl Douglas   b: 3/29/55, Madison, Wis.   BL/TL, 6'2", 190 lbs.   Deb: 9/21/78

1981	Cle-A	14	15	3	4	0	2	1	4	4	1	.267	.421	.733	230	3	0	0	0	1.000	2	/1-6,D-1	0.4
1982	Cle-A	23	18	3	3	0	0	0	2	7	11	.167	.400	.167	63	-0	0	0	0	.970	0	1-10/D-1	-0.1
1983	Cle-A	8	20	1	6	0	0	0	1	0	5	.300	.300	.300	63	-1	0	0	0	.000	-1	/O-1,D-5	-0.2
Total	5	48	56	7	13	0	2	1	7	11	20	.232	.358	.357	99	0	0	0	0	.985	1	/1-16,D-7,O	0.0
Team	3	45	53	7	13	0	2	1	7	11	17	.245	.375	.377	110	1	0	0	0	.985	1	/1-16,D-7,O	0.1

■ LANCE PARRISH   Parrish, Lance Michael   b: 6/15/56, Clairton, Pa.   BR/TR, 6'3", 220 lbs.   Deb: 9/5/77

| 1993 | Cle-A | 10 | 20 | 2 | 4 | 1 | 0 | 1 | 2 | 4 | 5 | .200 | .333 | .400 | 97 | -0 | 1 | 0 | 0 | .950 | 4 | C-10 | 0.4 |
| Total | 19 | 1988 | 7067 | 856 | 1782 | 305 | 27 | 324 | 1070 | 612 | 1527 | .252 | .315 | .440 | 105 | 34 | 28 | 37 | -14 | .991 | 14 | *C-1818,D-123/10 | 12.0 |

■ CASEY PARSONS   Parsons, Casey Robert   b: 4/14/54, Wenatchee, Wash.   BL/TR, 6'1", 180 lbs.   Deb: 5/31/81

| 1987 | Cle-A | 18 | 25 | 2 | 4 | 0 | 0 | 1 | 5 | 0 | 5 | .160 | .160 | .280 | 13 | -3 | 0 | 0 | 0 | 1.000 | -1 | /O-2,1-1,D | -0.4 |
| Total | 4 | 63 | 53 | 9 | 10 | 1 | 0 | 2 | 10 | 3 | 11 | .189 | .259 | .321 | 57 | -3 | 0 | 0 | 0 | 1.000 | -6 | /O-29,D-7,1 | -1.0 |

■ BEN PASCHAL   Paschal, Benjamin Edwin   b: 10/13/1895, Enterprise, Ala.   d: 11/10/74, Charlotte, N.C.   BR/TR, 5'11", 185 lbs.   Deb: 8/16/15

| 1915 | Cle-A | 9 | 9 | 0 | 1 | 0 | 0 | 0 | 0 | 0 | 3 | .111 | .111 | .111 | -33 | -1 | 0 | | | .000 | 0 | H | -0.2 |
| Total | 8 | 364 | 787 | 143 | 243 | 47 | 11 | 24 | 138 | 72 | 93 | .309 | .369 | .488 | 123 | 24 | 24 | | | .953 | -19 | O-223 | -1.0 |

■ STAN PAWLOSKI   Pawloski, Stanley Walter   b: 9/6/31, Wanamie, Pa.   BR/TR, 6'1", 175 lbs.   Deb: 9/24/55

| 1955 | Cle-A | 2 | 8 | 0 | 1 | 0 | 0 | 0 | 0 | 0 | 2 | .125 | .125 | .125 | -31 | -1 | 0 | 0 | 0 | 1.000 | 1 | /2-2 | 0.0 |

■ HAL PECK   Peck, Harold Arthur   b: 4/20/17, Big Bend, Wis.   d: 4/13/95, Milwaukee, Wis.   BL/TL, 5'11", 175 lbs.   Deb: 5/13/43

1947	Cle-A	114	392	58	115	18	2	8	44	27	31	.293	.342	.411	112	5	3	3	-1	.983	-7	O-97	-0.8
1948	*Cle-A	45	63	12	18	3	0	0	8	4	8	.286	.328	.333	78	-2	1	0	0	1.000	-2	/O-9	-0.4
1949	Cle-A	33	29	1	9	1	0	0	9	3	3	.310	.375	.345	93	-0	0	0	0	1.000	-1	/O-2	-0.1
Total	7	355	1092	136	305	52	13	15	112	87	86	.279	.334	.397	106	5	10	10	-3	.965	-21	O-255	-3.4
Team	3	192	484	71	142	22	2	8	61	34	42	.293	.342	.397	106	3	4	3	-1	.984	-9	O-108	-1.3

■ ROGER PECKINPAUGH   Peckinpaugh, Roger Thorpe   b: 2/5/1891, Wooster, Ohio   d: 11/17/77, Cleveland, Ohio   BR/TR, 5'10.5", 165 lbs.   Deb: 9/15/10   M

1910	Cle-A	15	45	1	9	0	0	0	6	1		.200	.234	.200	36	-3	3			.906	-6	S-14	-1.0
1912	Cle-A	70	236	18	50	4	1	1	22	16		.212	.262	.250	45	-17	11			.924	-2	S-68	-1.4
1913	Cle-A	1	0	1	0	0	0	0	0	0		—	—	—		0	0			.000	0	H	0.0
Total	17	2012	7233	1006	1876	256	75	48	739	814	609	.259	.336	.335	87	-122	205			.949	97	*S-1982/1-2	13.2
Team	3	86	281	20	59	4	1	1	28	17	0	.210	.258	.242	44	-20	14			.921	-8	/S-82	-2.4

■ TONY PENA   Pena, Antonio Francisco (Padilla)   b: 6/4/57, Monte Cristi, D.R.   BR/TR, 6', 181 lbs.   Deb: 9/1/80   F

1994	Cle-A	40	112	18	33	8	1	2	10	9	11	.295	.347	.438	100	-0	0	1	-1	.996	5	C-40	0.6
1995	*Cle-A	91	263	25	69	15	0	5	28	14	44	.262	.302	.376	75	-10	1	0		.987	10	C-91	0.5
Total	16	1881	6229	647	1638	290	27	106	671	430	805	.263	.313	.395	86	-120	80	62		.990	108	*C-1845/1-13,OD	7.7
Team	2	131	375	43	102	23	1	7	38	23	55	.272	.316	.395	83	-10	1	1	1	.990	15	C-131	1.1

■ JACK PERCONTE   Perconte, John Patrick   b: 8/31/54, Joliet, Ill.   BL/TR, 5'10", 160 lbs.   Deb: 9/13/80

1982	Cle-A	93	219	27	52	4	4	0	15	22	25	.237	.307	.292	66	-10	9	3	1	.976	8	2-82/D-2	0.2
1983	Cle-A	14	26	1	7	1	0	0	0	5	2	.269	.387	.308	91	-0	3	1	0	.950	8	2-13	0.8
Total	7	433	1441	191	389	47	16	2	76	149	123	.270	.342	.329	86	-23	78	13	16	.982	18	2-405/D-2	2.4
Team	2	107	245	28	59	5	4	0	15	27	27	.241	.316	.294	69	-10	12	4	1	.972	16	/2-95,D-2	1.0

■ TONY PEREZCHICA   Perezchica, Antonio Llamas (Gonzales)   b: 4/20/66, Mexicali, Mex.   BR/TR, 5'11", 165 lbs.   Deb: 9/7/88

1991	Cle-A	17	22	4	8	2	0	0	3	0	5	.364	.440	.455	147	2	0	0	0	1.000	-1	/S-6,3-3,2D	0.1
1992	Cle-A	18	20	2	2	1	0	0	1	2	6	.100	.182	.150	-6	-3	0	0	0	.875	-1	/3-9,2-4,SD	-0.4
Total	4	69	101	10	23	7	1	0	5	10	26	.228	.297	.317	74	-4	0	1	-1	.944	-8	/S-25,2-20,3D	-1.1
Team	2	35	42	6	10	3	0	0	1	5	11	.238	.319	.310	76	-1	0	0	0	.889	-2	/3-12,S-10,2D	-0.3

■ BRODERICK PERKINS   Perkins, Broderick Phillip   b: 11/23/54, Pittsburg, Cal.   BL/TL, 5'10", 180 lbs.   Deb: 7/7/78

1983	Cle-A	79	184	23	50	10	0	0	24	9	19	.272	.306	.326	71	-7	1	5	-3	.991	0	1-19,O-17,D	-1.1
1984	Cle-A	58	66	5	13	1	0	0	4	7	10	.197	.284	.212	39	-5	0	0	0	1.000	-0	D-10/1-2	-0.6
Total	7	516	1255	127	340	62	8	8	157	80	116	.271	.317	.352	90	-18	9	11	-4	.993	-4	1-306/O-41,D	-4.3
Team	2	137	250	28	63	11	0	0	28	16	29	.252	.300	.296	63	-12	1	5	-3	.992	-1	/D-26,1-21,O	-1.7

■ GEORGE PERRING   Perring, George Wilson   b: 8/13/1884, Sharon, Wis.   d: 8/20/60, Beloit, Wis.   BR/TR, 6', 190 lbs.   Deb: 4/25/08

1908	Cle-A	89	310	23	67	8	5	0	19	16		.216	.255	.274	72	-10	8			.928	-6	S-48,3-41	-1.6
1909	Cle-A	88	283	26	63	10	9	0	20	19		.223	.283	.322	87	-5	6			.932	6	3-67,S-11/2	0.5
1910	Cle-A	39	122	14	27	6	3	0	8	3		.221	.240	.320	74	-4	3			.931	2	3-33/1-4	-0.2
Total	5	513	1764	198	438	75	34	9	183	154		.248	.311	.345	87	-32	34			.939	26	3-344/1-76,S2P	0.4
Team	3	216	715	63	157	24	17	0	47	38		.220	.264	.301	79	-19	17			.930	2	3-141/S-59,12	-1.3

■ HERB PERRY   Perry, Herbert Edward   b: 9/15/69, Live Oak, Fla.   BR/TR, 6'2", 210 lbs.   Deb: 5/3/94

1994	Cle-A	4	9	1	1	0	0	0	1	3	1	.111	.385	.111	36	-1	0	0	0	1.000	1	/1-2,3-2	0.0
1995	*Cle-A	52	162	23	51	13	1	3	23	13	28	.315	.380	.463	118	4	1	3	-2	1.000	0	1-45/3-1,D	-0.1
Total	2	56	171	24	52	13	1	3	24	16	29	.304	.380	.444	113	4	1	3	-2	1.000	1	/1-47,D-6,3	-0.1

■ JOHN PETERS   Peters, John William "Big Pete" or "Shotgun"   b: 7/14/1893, Kansas City, Kan.   d: 2/21/32, Kansas City, Mo.   BR/TR, 6', 192 lbs.   Deb: 5/1/15

| 1918 | Cle-A | 1 | 1 | 0 | 0 | 0 | 0 | 0 | 0 | 1 | 1 | .000 | .500 | .000 | 46 | 0 | 0 | | | .500 | -1 | /C-1 | -0.1 |
| Total | 4 | 112 | 302 | 22 | 80 | 13 | 1 | 7 | 47 | 16 | 33 | .265 | .317 | .384 | 76 | -11 | 1 | | | .934 | -18 | /C-85 | -2.4 |

■ RUSTY PETERS   Peters, Russell Dixon   b: 12/14/14, Roanoke, Va.   BR/TR, 5'11", 170 lbs.   Deb: 4/14/36

1940	Cle-A	30	71	5	17	3	2	0	7	4	14	.239	.280	.338	61	-4	1	0	0	.922	-0	/2-9,S-6,31	-0.3
1941	Cle-A	29	63	5	13	2	0	0	2	7	10	.206	.286	.238	42	-5	0	1	-1	.891	2	S-11/3-9,2	-0.3
1942	Cle-A	34	58	6	13	5	1	0	2	1	14	.224	.250	.345	70	-3	0	0	0	.944	2	S-24/2-1,3	0.0
1943	Cle-A	79	215	22	47	6	2	1	19	18	29	.219	.282	.279	69	-9	1	1	-0	.913	-6	3-46,S-14/2O	-1.5
1944	Cle-A	88	282	23	63	13	3	1	24	15	35	.223	.268	.301	65	-14	2	1	0	.976	-3	2-63,S-13/3	-1.4
1946	Cle-A	9	21	0	6	0	0	0	2	1	1	.286	.318	.286	74	-1	0	1	-1	1.000	0	/S-7	-0.1
Total	10	471	1222	123	289	53	16	8	117	98	199	.236	.295	.326	69	-57	9	9		.966	-13	2-166,S-117,3/O1	-5.6
Team	6	269	710	62	159	29	8	2	56	47	103	.224	.275	.296	64	-36	4	4		.968	-5	/2-82,S-75,3O1	-3.6

■ CAP PETERSON   Peterson, Charles Andrew   b: 8/15/42, Tacoma, Wash.   d: 5/16/80, Tacoma, Wash.   BR/TR, 6'2", 195 lbs.   Deb: 9/12/62

| 1969 | Cle-A | 76 | 110 | 8 | 25 | 3 | 0 | 4 | 24 | 18 | 25 | .227 | .370 | .282 | 82 | -1 | 0 | 0 | 0 | .977 | -2 | O-30/3-4 | -0.5 |
| Total | 8 | 536 | 1170 | 106 | 269 | 44 | 5 | 19 | 122 | 101 | 195 | .230 | .294 | .325 | 80 | -30 | 4 | 4 | -1 | .983 | -18 | O-275/3-10,21S | -6.6 |

■ LARRY PEZOLD   Pezold, Lorenz Johannes   b: 6/22/1893, New Orleans, La.   d: 10/22/57, Baton Rouge, La.   BR/TR, 5'9.5", 175 lbs.   Deb: 7/27/14

| 1914 | Cle-A | 23 | 71 | 4 | 16 | 0 | 1 | 0 | 5 | 9 | 6 | .225 | .313 | .254 | 68 | -3 | 2 | 1 | 0 | .827 | -1 | 3-20/O-1 | -0.5 |

■ KEN PHELPS   Phelps, Kenneth Allen   b: 8/6/54, Seattle, Wash.   BL/TL, 6'1", 209 lbs.   Deb: 9/20/80

| 1990 | Cle-A | 24 | 61 | 4 | 7 | 0 | 0 | 0 | 0 | 10 | 11 | .115 | .239 | .115 | 2 | -8 | 1 | 0 | 0 | 1.000 | 0 | 1-14/D-6 | -0.9 |
| Total | 11 | 761 | 1854 | 308 | 443 | 64 | 7 | 123 | 313 | 390 | 449 | .239 | .377 | .480 | 132 | 89 | 10 | 7 | -1 | .987 | -4 | D-467,1-131 | 6.4 |

YEAR	TM/L	G	AB	R	H	2B	3B	HR	RBI	BB	SO	AVG	OBP	SLG	PRO+	BR/A	SB	CS	SBR	FA	FR	G/POS	TPR
■ **DAVE PHILLEY**	Philley, David Earl b: 5/16/20, Paris, Tex. BB/TR, 6', 188 lbs. Deb: 9/6/41																						
1954	*Cle-A	133	452	48	102	13	3	12	60	57	48	.226	.312	.347	79	-13	2	4	-2	.984	-4	*O-129	-2.5
1955	Cle-A	43	104	15	31	4	2	2	9	12	10	.298	.371	.433	111	2	0	2	-1	1.000	-3	O-34	-0.3
Total	18	1904	6296	789	1700	276	72	84	729	594	551	.270	.335	.377	91	-86	101	63	-8	.981	-0	*O-1454,1-125/3	-16.7
Team	2	176	556	63	133	17	5	14	69	69	58	.239	.323	.363	85	-12	2	6	-3	.986	-7	O-163	-2.8
■ **ADOLFO PHILLIPS**	Phillips, Adolfo Emilio (Lopez) b: 12/16/41, Bethania, Panama BR/TR, 6', 177 lbs. Deb: 9/2/64																						
1972	Cle-A	12	7	2	0	0	0	0	0	2	2	.000	.222	.000	-29	-1	0	0	0	1.000	-3	O-10	-0.4
Total	8	649	1875	270	463	86	21	59	173	251	485	.247	.344	.410	110	27	82	44	-2	.980	17	O-593	1.7
■ **EDDIE PHILLIPS**	Phillips, Edward David b: 2/17/01, Worcester, Mass. d: 1/26/68, Buffalo, N.Y. BR/TR, 6', 178 lbs. Deb: 5/4/24																						
1935	Cle-A	70	220	18	60	16	1	1	41	15	21	.273	.319	.368	76	-8	0	0	0	.980	-8	C-69	-1.3
Total	6	312	997	82	236	54	6	14	126	104	115	.237	.312	.345	72	-41	3	1	0	.980	-27	C-298	-4.7
■ **BUBBA PHILLIPS**	Phillips, John Melvin b: 2/24/28, West Point, Miss. d: 6/22/93, Hattiesburg, Miss. BR/TR, 5'9", 180 lbs. Deb: 4/30/55																						
1960	Cle-A	113	304	34	63	14	1	4	33	14	37	.207	.252	.299	50	-22	1	0	0	.953	-8	3-85,O-25/S	-3.2
1961	Cle-A	143	546	64	144	23	1	18	72	29	61	.264	.307	.408	92	-8	1	0	0	.958	-18	*3-143	-2.5
1962	Cle-A	148	562	53	145	26	0	10	54	20	55	.258	.292	.358	76	-20	4	0	1	.977	-15	*3-145/O-3,2	-3.3
Total	10	1062	3278	348	835	135	8	62	356	182	314	.255	.300	.358	79	-100	25	11	1	.960	-16	3-762,O-214/2S	-12.1
Team	3	404	1412	151	352	63	2	32	159	63	153	.249	.289	.365	77	-50	6	0	2	.964	-41	3-373/O-28,2S	-9.0
■ **OLLIE PICKERING**	Pickering, Oliver Daniel b: 4/9/1870, Olney, Ill. d: 1/20/52, Vincennes, Ind. BL/TR, 5'11", 170 lbs. Deb: 8/9/1896																						
1901	Cle-A	137	547	102	169	25	6	0	40	58		.309	.383	.377	116	15	36			.949	15	*O-137	1.7
1902	Cle-A	69	293	46	75	5	2	3	26	19		.256	.306	.317	76	-9	22			.979	-2	O-64/1-2	-1.6
Total	8	885	3349	500	910	96	39	9	286	286		.272	.334	.332	97	-8	194			.949	5	O-859/1-2,2	-6.0
Team	2	206	840	148	244	30	8	3	66	77		.290	.357	.356	102	5	58			.958	12	O-201/1-2	0.1
■ **JIM PIERSALL**	Piersall, James Anthony b: 11/14/29, Waterbury, Conn. BR/TR, 6', 175 lbs. Deb: 9/7/50 C																						
1959	Cle-A	100	317	42	78	13	2	4	30	25	31	.246	.305	.338	79	-9	6	3	0	.982	0	O-91/3-1	-1.3
1960	Cle-A	138	486	70	137	12	4	18	66	24	38	.282	.316	.434	104	0	18	5	2	.992	10	*O-134	0.7
1961	Cle-A	121	484	81	156	26	7	6	40	43	46	.322	.380	.442	122	15	8	2	1	**.991**	16	*O-120	2.5
Total	17	1734	5890	811	1604	256	52	104	591	524	583	.272	.334	.386	92	-66	115	57		.990	73	*O-1614/S-30,3	-7.4
Team	3	359	1287	193	371	51	13	28	136	92	115	.288	.338	.413	105	7	32	10		.989	26	O-345/3-1	1.9
■ **LOU PINIELLA**	Piniella, Louis Victor b: 8/28/43, Tampa, Fla. BR/TR, 6'2", 198 lbs. Deb: 9/4/64 MC																						
1968	Cle-A	6	5	1	0	0	0	0	1	0	0	.000	.000	.000	-99	-1	0	0	0	1.000	-0	/O-2	-0.2
Total	18	1747	5867	651	1705	305	41	102	766	368	541	.291	.336	.409	109	61	32	41	-15	.981	21	*O-1401,D-231/1	0.3
■ **VADA PINSON**	Pinson, Vada Edward b: 8/11/38, Memphis, Tenn. d: 10/21/95, Oakland, Cal. BL/TL, 5'11", 181 lbs. Deb: 4/15/58 C																						
1970	Cle-A	148	574	74	164	28	6	24	82	28	69	.286	.322	.481	113	8	7	6	-2	.982	5	*O-141/1-7	0.4
1971	Cle-A	146	566	60	149	23	4	11	35	21	58	.263	.297	.376	82	-14	25	6	4	.978	4	*O-141/1-3	-1.5
Total	18	2469	9645	1366	2757	485	127	256	1170	574	1196	.286	.330	.442	110	106	305	122	18	.981	87	*O-2403/1-16,D	8.8
Team	2	294	1140	134	313	51	10	35	117	49	127	.275	.310	.429	98	-7	32	12	2	.980	9	O-282/1-10	-1.1
■ **DAVE POPE**	Pope, David b: 6/17/25, Talladega, Ala. BL/TR, 5'10.5", 170 lbs. Deb: 7/1/52																						
1952	Cle-A	12	34	9	10	1	1	1	4	1	7	.294	.314	.471	124	1	0	0	0	1.000	-1	O-10	-0.1
1954	*Cle-A	60	102	21	30	2	1	4	13	10	22	.294	.357	.451	118	2	2	1	0	1.000	-4	O-29	-0.2
1955	Cle-A	35	104	17	31	5	0	6	22	12	31	.298	.376	.519	134	5	0	0	0	.954	-3	O-31	0.1
1956	Cle-A	25	70	6	17	3	1	0	3	1	12	.243	.254	.314	48	-5	0	0	0	1.000	-1	O-18	-0.7
Total	4	230	551	75	146	19	7	12	73	40	113	.265	.319	.390	92	-9	7	3	0	.990	-18	O-165	-3.2
Team	4	132	310	53	88	11	3	11	42	24	72	.284	.337	.445	108	2	2	1	0	.981	-8	/O-88	-0.9
■ **JAY PORTER**	Porter, J W "J W" b: 1/17/33, Shawnee, Okla. BR/TR, 6'2", 180 lbs. Deb: 7/30/52																						
1958	Cle-A	40	85	13	17	1	0	4	19	9	23	.200	.284	.353	76	-3	0	0	0	1.000	-3	C-20/1-4,3	-0.5
Total	6	229	544	58	124	22	1	8	62	53	96	.228	.301	.316	68	-24	4	0	1	.990	-12	/C-91,O-62,13	-3.5
■ **DICK PORTER**	Porter, Richard Twilley "Wiggles" or "Twitches" b: 12/30/01, Princess Anne, Md. d: 9/24/74, Philadelphia, Pa. BL/TR, 5'10", 170 lbs. Deb: 4/16/29																						
1929	Cle-A	71	192	26	63	16	5	1	24	17	14	.328	.386	.479	117	5	3	5	-2	.941	-5	O-28,2-20	-0.3
1930	Cle-A	119	480	100	168	43	8	4	57	55	31	.350	.420	.498	127	21	3	3	-1	.962	-4	*O-118	0.7
1931	Cle-A	114	414	82	129	24	3	1	38	56	36	.312	.395	.391	102	3	6	9	-4	.970	-6	*O-109/2-1	-1.3
1932	Cle-A	146	621	106	191	42	8	4	60	64	43	.308	.373	.420	99	-1	2	4	-2	.982	-11	*O-145	-2.1
1933	Cle-A	132	499	73	133	19	6	0	41	51	42	.267	.335	.329	73	-19	4	4	-1	**.996**	-1	*O-124	-2.6
1934	Cle-A	13	44	9	10	2	1	1	6	4	5	.227	.292	.386	73	-2	0	0	0	1.000	-1	O-10	-0.4
Total	6	675	2515	426	774	159	37	11	282	268	186	.308	.376	.414	99	2	23	27	-9	.973	-35	O-599/2-21	-7.2
Team	6	595	2250	396	694	146	31	11	226	247	171	.308	.378	.416	101	7	18	25	-10	.977	-29	O-534/2-21	-6.0
■ **WALLY POST**	Post, Walter Charles b: 7/9/29, St.Wendelin, Ohio d: 1/6/82, St.Henry, Ohio BR/TR, 6'1", 203 lbs. Deb: 9/18/49																						
1964	Cle-A	5	8	1	0	0	0	0	0	3	4	.000	.273	.000	-16	-1	0	0	0	.667	-1	/O-2	-0.2
Total	15	1204	4007	594	1064	194	28	210	699	331	813	.266	.325	.485	109	39	19	13	-2	.970	46	*O-1055	3.2
■ **BOOG POWELL**	Powell, John Wesley b: 8/17/41, Lakeland, Fla. BL/TR, 6'4", 240 lbs. Deb: 9/26/61																						
1975	Cle-A	134	435	64	129	18	0	27	86	59	72	.297	.382	.524	154	31	1	3	-2	**.997**	-2	*1-121/D-5	2.0
1976	Cle-A	95	293	29	63	9	0	9	33	41	43	.215	.311	.338	91	-3	1	1	-0	.987	1	1-89	-0.9
Total	17	2042	6681	889	1776	270	11	339	1187	1001	1226	.266	.364	.462	134	310	20	21	-7	.991	-33	*1-1479,O-431/D	14.9
Team	2	229	728	93	192	27	0	36	119	100	115	.264	.353	.449	129	28	2	4	-2	.993	-1	1-210/D-5	1.1
■ **VIC POWER**	Power, Victor Pellot (b: Victor Felipe Pellot (Pove)) b: 11/1/27, Arecibo, P.R. BR/TR, 5'11", 195 lbs. Deb: 4/13/54																						
1958	Cle-A	93	385	63	122	24	6	12	53	13	11	.317	.341	.504	133	15	2	1	0	.977	6	3-42,1-41,2/SO	2.1
1959	Cle-A★	147	595	102	172	31	6	10	60	40	22	.289	.336	.412	108	5	9	13	-5	**.995**	10	*1-121,2-21/3	0.4
1960	Cle-A★	147	580	69	167	26	3	10	84	24	20	.288	.316	.395	94	-7	9	5	-0	**.996**	21	*1-147/S-5,3	0.3
1961	Cle-A	147	563	64	151	34	4	5	63	38	16	.268	.316	.369	85	-13	4	3	-1	.994	18	*1-141/2-7	-0.7
Total	12	1627	6046	765	1716	290	49	126	658	279	247	.284	.317	.411	97	-43	45	35	-7	.994	123	*1-1304,2-139,O/3S	-0.1
Team	4	534	2123	298	612	115	19	37	260	115	69	.288	.326	.413	102	1	24	22	-6	.995	55	1-450/2-55,3SO	2.1
■ **MIKE POWERS**	Powers, Ellis Foree b: 3/2/06, Toddspoint, Ky. d: 12/2/83, Louisville, Ky. BL/TL, 6'1", 185 lbs. Deb: 8/19/32																						
1932	Cle-A	14	33	4	6	4	0	0	5	2	2	.182	.229	.303	34	-3	0	0	0	.917	-2	/O-8	-0.5
1933	Cle-A	24	47	6	13	2	1	0	2	6	6	.277	.358	.362	87	-1	2	1	0	.952	-2	O-11	-0.3
Total	2	38	80	10	19	6	1	0	7	8	8	.237	.307	.338	65	-4	2	1	0	.939	-3	/O-19	-0.8
■ **JOHN POWERS**	Powers, John Calvin b: 7/8/29, Birmingham, Ala. BL/TR, 6', 190 lbs. Deb: 9/24/55																						
1960	Cle-A	8	12	2	2	1	1	0	0	2	2	.167	.286	.417	90	-0	0	0	0	1.000	-1	/O-5	-0.1
Total	6	151	215	26	42	7	2	6	14	22	48	.195	.282	.330	64	-11	0	0	0	.986	-2	/O-44	-1.6
■ **JACKIE PRICE**	Price, John Thomas Reid "Johnny" b: 11/13/12, Windborn, Miss. d: 10/2/67, San Francisco, Cal. BL/TR, 5'10.5", 150 lbs. Deb: 8/18/46																						
1946	Cle-A	7	13	1	3	0	0	0	0	0	0	.231	.231	.231	31	-1	0	0	0	.947	2	/S-4	0.0

YEAR TM/L	G	AB	R	H	2B	3B	HR	RBI	BB	SO	AVG	OBP	SLG	PRO+	BR/A	SB	CS	SBR	FA	FR	G/POS	TPR
■ RON PRUITT Pruitt, Ronald Ralph b: 10/21/51, Flint, Mich. BR/TR, 6', 185 lbs. Deb: 6/25/75																						
1976 Cle-A	47	86	7	23	1	1	0	5	16	8	.267	.382	.302	103	1	2	3	-1	1.000	2	O-26/C-6,31D	0.2
1977 Cle-A	78	219	29	63	10	2	2	32	28	22	.288	.373	.379	109	4	2	3	-1	.972	-8	O-69/C-4,3D	-0.7
1978 Cle-A	71	187	17	44	6	1	6	17	16	20	.235	.296	.374	88	-3	2	1	0	.984	-6	C-48,O-16/3D	-1.0
1979 Cle-A	64	166	23	47	7	0	2	21	19	21	.283	.357	.361	94	-1	2	0	1	.957	-5	O-29,D-14,C/3	-0.6
1980 Cle-A	23	36	1	11	1	0	0	4	4	6	.306	.375	.333	95	-0	0	0	0	1.000	0	/O-6,3-2,D	0.0
1981 Cle-A	5	9	0	0	0	0	0	0	1	2	.000	.100	.000	-70	-2	0	0	0	1.000	-1	/O-3,C-1,D	-0.3
Total 9	341	795	88	214	28	4	12	92	94	90	.269	.348	.360	97	-1	8	7	-2	.977	-19	O-162/C-89,D31	-2.6
Team 6	288	703	77	188	25	4	10	79	84	79	.267	.347	.357	97	-1	8	7	-2	.975	-17	O-149/C-70,D31	-2.4
■ FRANKIE PYTLAK Pytlak, Frank Anthony b: 7/30/08, Buffalo, N.Y. d: 5/8/77, Buffalo, N.Y. BR/TR, 5'7.5", 160 lbs. Deb: 4/22/32																						
1932 Cle-A	12	29	5	7	1	1	0	4	3	2	.241	.333	.345	71	-1	0	0	0	1.000	3	C-12	0.2
1933 Cle-A	80	248	36	77	10	6	2	33	17	10	.310	.355	.423	101	-0	3	4	-2	1.000	11	C-69	1.2
1934 Cle-A	91	289	46	75	12	4	0	35	36	11	.260	.352	.329	75	-10	11	2	2	.989	-10	C-88	-1.3
1935 Cle-A	55	149	14	44	6	1	1	12	11	4	.295	.348	.369	84	-3	3	2	-0	.984	-1	C-48	-0.2
1936 Cle-A	75	224	35	72	15	4	0	31	24	11	.321	.394	.424	101	1	5	2	0	.996	-6	C-58	-0.1
1937 Cle-A	125	397	60	125	15	6	1	44	52	15	.315	.404	.390	100	3	16	5	2	.986	10	*C-115	1.9
1938 Cle-A	113	364	46	112	14	7	1	43	36	15	.308	.376	.393	95	-2	9	5	-0	.987	-8	C-99	-0.4
1939 Cle-A	63	183	20	49	2	5	0	14	20	5	.268	.343	.333	76	-6	4	1	1	1.000	3	C-51	0.0
1940 Cle-A	62	149	16	21	2	1	0	16	17	5	.141	.234	.168	6	-21	0	1	-1	.996	7	C-58/O-1	-1.0
Total 12	795	2399	316	677	100	36	7	272	247	97	.282	.355	.363	84	-53	56	29	-1	.991	12	C-699/O-1	-0.2
Team 9	676	2032	278	582	77	35	5	232	216	78	.286	.362	.366	86	-39	51	22	2	.991	8	C-598/O-1	0.3
■ JAMIE QUIRK Quirk, James Patrick b: 10/22/54, Whittier, Cal. BL/TR, 6'4", 200 lbs. Deb: 9/4/75 C																						
1984 Cle-A	1	1	1	1	0	0	1	1	0	0	1.000	1.000	4.000	1189	1	0	0	0	.000	0	/C-1	0.1
Total 18	984	2266	193	544	100	7	43	247	177	435	.240	.300	.347	78	-68	5	16	-8	.982	28	C-525,3-118/D1OS2	-2.8
■ JOE RABBITT Rabbitt, Joseph Patrick b: 1/16/1900, Frontenac, Kan. d: 12/5/69, Norwalk, Conn. BL/TR, 5'10", 165 lbs. Deb: 9/15/22																						
1922 Cle-A	2	3	1	1	0	0	0	0	0	0	.333	.333	.333	74	-0	0	0	0	.000	-1	/O-1	-0.1
■ TOM RAFTERY Raftery, Thomas Francis b: 10/5/1881, Boston, Mass. d: 12/31/54, Boston, Mass. BR/TR, 5'10.5", 175 lbs. Deb: 4/18/09																						
1909 Cle-A	8	32	6	7	2	1	0	0	4		.219	.306	.344	101	0	1			1.000	-1	/O-8	-0.1
■ TOM RAGLAND Ragland, Thomas b: 6/16/46, Talladega, Ala. BR/TR, 5'10", 155 lbs. Deb: 4/5/71																						
1973 Cle-A	67	183	16	47	7	1	0	12	8	31	.257	.292	.306	67	-8	2	3	-1	.984	13	2-65/S-2	0.7
Total 3	102	264	20	61	9	1	0	14	13	47	.231	.272	.273	56	-15	2	4		.985	10	/2-88,S-5,3	-0.5
■ LARRY RAINES Raines, Lawrence Glenn Hope b: 3/9/30, St.Albans, W.Va. d: 1/28/78, Lansing, Mich. BR/TR, 5'10", 165 lbs. Deb: 4/16/57																						
1957 Cle-A	96	244	39	64	14	0	2	16	19	40	.262	.318	.344	82	-6	5	2	0	.922	-5	3-27,S-25,2/O	-0.9
1958 Cle-A	7	9	1	0	0	0	0	0	0	5	.000	.000	.000	-99	-2	0	1	-1	.933	4	/2-2	0.0
Total 2	103	253	40	64	14	0	2	16	19	45	.253	.308	.332	76	-9	5	3	-0	.963	-2	/3-27,S-25,2O	-0.9
■ MANNY RAMIREZ Ramirez, Manuel Aristides (Onelcida) b: 5/30/72, Brooklyn, N.Y. BR/TR, 6', 190 lbs. Deb: 9/2/93																						
1993 Cle-A	22	53	5	9	1	0	2	5	2	8	.170	.200	.302	33	-5	0	0	0	1.000	0	D-20/O-1	-0.6
1994 Cle-A	91	290	51	78	22	0	17	60	42	72	.269	.361	.521	124	10	4	2	0	.994	-1	O-84/D-5	0.7
1995 *Cle-A★	137	484	85	149	26	1	31	107	75	112	.308	.406	.558	147	35	6	6	-2	.978	-4	*O-131/D-5	2.4
Total 3	250	827	141	236	49	1	50	172	119	192	.285	.379	.528	132	39	10	8	-2	.985	-4	O-216/D-30	2.5
■ DOMINGO RAMOS Ramos, Domingo Antonio (De Ramos) b: 3/29/58, Santiago, D.R. BR/TR, 5'10", 155 lbs. Deb: 9/8/78																						
1988 Cle-A	22	46	7	12	1	0	0	5	3	7	.261	.320	.283	68	-2	0	0	0	1.000	2	2-11/1-5,S3	0.0
Total 11	507	1086	109	261	34	2	8	85	92	138	.240	.304	.297	64	-53	6	9	-4	.955	7	S-201,3-174/21DO	-3.7
■ PEDRO RAMOS Ramos, Pedro (Guerra) "Pete" b: 4/28/35, Pinar Del Rio, Cuba BB/TR, 6', 185 lbs. Deb: 4/11/55																						
1962 Cle-A	39	68	6	10	3	0	3	8	1	29	.147	.171	.324	31	-7	0	0	0	.962	0	P-37	0.0
1963 Cle-A	54	55	13	6	0	0	3	7	3	32	.109	.155	.273	17	-6	0	0	0	.963	-2	P-36	0.0
1964 Cle-A	44	39	6	7	0	0	2	2	2	22	.179	.220	.333	52	-3	0	0	0	.960	-1	P-36	0.0
Total 15	696	703	76	109	9	3	15	56	22	316	.155	.183	.240	14	-85	2	2	-1	.977	-9	P-582	0.0
Team 3	137	162	25	23	3	0	8	17	6	83	.142	.178	.309	31	-16	0	0	0	.962	-2	P-109	0.0
■ MORRIE RATH Rath, Morris Charles b: 12/25/1886, Mobeetie, Tex. d: 11/18/45, Upper Darby, Pa. BL/TR, 5'8.5", 160 lbs. Deb: 9/28/09																						
1910 Cle-A	24	67	5	13	3	0	0	0	10		.194	.299	.239	68	-2	2			.950	2	3-22/S-1	0.1
Total 6	565	2048	291	521	36	7	4	92	258		.254	.342	.285	86	-25	82			.970	25	2-510/3-36,SO	0.2
■ RUDY REGALADO Regalado, Rudolph Valentino b: 5/21/30, Los Angeles, Cal. BR/TR, 6'1", 185 lbs. Deb: 4/13/54																						
1954 *Cle-A	65	180	21	45	5	0	2	24	19	16	.250	.335	.311	76	-5	0	2	-1	.967	-5	3-50/2-2	-1.3
1955 Cle-A	10	26	2	7	2	0	0	5	2	4	.269	.321	.346	77	-1	0	0	0	.955	2	/3-8,2-1	0.1
1956 Cle-A	16	47	4	11	1	0	0	2	4	1	.234	.308	.255	49	-3	0	0	0	.783	-7	3-14/1-1	-1.0
Total 3	91	253	27	63	8	0	2	31	25	21	.249	.329	.304	71	-10	0	2	-1	.944	-10	/3-72,2-3,1	-2.2
■ HERMAN REICH Reich, Herman Charles b: 11/23/17, Bell, Cal. BR/TL, 6'2", 200 lbs. Deb: 5/3/49																						
1949 Cle-A	1	2	0	1	0	0	0	0	1	0	.500	.667	.500	215	1	0	0	0	.000	-0	/O-1	0.0
Total 1	111	390	43	109	18	2	3	34	14	33	.279	.306	.359	80	-12	4	0	1	.969	14	/1-85,O-17	0.0
■ DUKE REILLEY Reilley, Alexander Aloysius "Midget" b: 8/25/1884, Chicago, Ill. d: 3/4/68, Indianapolis, Ind. BB/TR, 5'4.5", 148 lbs. Deb: 8/28/09																						
1909 Cle-A	20	62	10	13	0	0	0	0	4		.210	.258	.210	46	-4	5			.979	2	O-18	-0.3
■ TOM REILLY Reilly, Thomas Henry b: 8/3/1884, St.Louis, Mo. d: 10/18/18, New Orleans, La. BR/TR, 5'10", Deb: 7/27/08																						
1914 Cle-A	1	1	0	0	0	0	0	0	0	0	.000	.000	.000	-96	-0	0			.000	0	H	0.0
Total 3	35	89	5	16	1	1	1	5	2	0	.180	.198	.247	44	-6	4			.875	-6	/S-34	-1.3
■ ART REINHOLZ Reinholz, Arthur August b: 1/27/03, Detroit, Mich. d: 12/29/80, New Port Richey, Fla. BR/TR, 5'10.5", 175 lbs. Deb: 9/27/28																						
1928 Cle-A	2	3	0	1	0	0	0	0	1	0	.333	.500	.333	122	0	0	0	0	.833	1	/3-2	0.1
■ PETE REISER Reiser, Harold Patrick b: 3/17/19, St.Louis, Mo. d: 10/25/81, Palm Springs, Cal. BL/TR, 5'11", 185 lbs. Deb: 7/23/40 C																						
1952 Cle-A	34	44	7	6	1	0	3	7	4	16	.136	.208	.364	61	-3	1	1	-0	1.000	-1	O-10	-0.5
Total 10	861	2662	473	786	155	41	58	368	343	369	.295	.380	.450	127	100	87	3	24	.979	-1	O-634/3-59,S	7.0
■ KEVIN RHOMBERG Rhomberg, Kevin Jay b: 11/22/55, Dubuque, Iowa BR/TR, 6', 175 lbs. Deb: 9/1/82																						
1982 Cle-A	16	18	3	6	0	0	1	1	2	4	.333	.400	.500	146	1	0	2	-1	.900	-0	/O-7,3-1,D	0.0
1983 Cle-A	12	21	2	10	0	0	0	2	2	4	.476	.522	.476	170	2	1	1	-0	1.000	-2	/O-9,D-1	0.0
1984 Cle-A	13	8	0	2	0	0	0	0	0	3	.250	.250	.250	38	-1	0	0	0	1.000	-2	/O-7,1-1,2D	-0.2
Total 3	41	47	5	18	0	0	1	3	4	11	.383	.431	.447	140	3	1	3	-2	.963	-4	/O-23,D-6,213	-0.2
■ SAM RICE Rice, Edgar Charles b: 2/20/1890, Morocco, Ind. d: 10/13/74, Rossmoor, Md. BL/TR, 5'9", 150 lbs. Deb: 8/7/15 H																						
1934 Cle-A	97	335	48	98	19	1	1	33	28	9	.293	.351	.364	83	-8	5	1	1	.963	-7	O-78	-1.6
Total 20	2404	9269	1514	2987	498	184	34	1078	708	275	.322	.374	.427	113	166	351	143	20	.965	75	*O-2270/P-9	9.1

YEAR	TM/L	G	AB	R	H	2B	3B	HR	RBI	BB	SO	AVG	OBP	SLG	PRO+	BR/A	SB	CS	SBR	FA	FR	G/POS	TPR

■ BILLY RIPKEN Ripken, William Oliver b: 12/16/64, Havre De Grace, Md. BR/TR, 6'1", 183 lbs. Deb: 7/11/87 F

| | 1995 | Cle-A | 8 | 17 | 4 | 7 | 0 | 0 | 2 | 3 | 0 | 3 | .412 | .412 | .765 | 197 | 2 | 0 | 0 | 0 | 1.000 | -3 | /2-7,3-1 | 0.0 |
| | Total | 9 | 757 | 2317 | 242 | 567 | 101 | 5 | 15 | 188 | 151 | 272 | .245 | .295 | .312 | 70 | -95 | 22 | 13 | -1 | .987 | 10 | 2-712/3-22,SD1 | -6.6 |

■ FRANK ROBINSON Robinson, Frank b: 8/31/35, Beaumont, Tex. BR/TR, 6'1", 195 lbs. Deb: 4/17/56 MCH

1974	Cle-A	15	50	6	10	1	1	2	5	10	10	.200	.333	.380	106	1	0	1	-1	.958	-1	D-11/1-4	-0.1
1975	Cle-A	49	118	19	28	5	0	9	24	29	15	.237	.388	.508	152	9	0	0	0	.000	0	D-42,M	0.8
1976	Cle-A	36	67	5	15	0	0	3	10	11	12	.224	.333	.358	104	1	0	0	0	1.000	-1	D-18/1-2,OM	-0.1
Total	21	2808	10006	1829	2943	528	72	586	1812	1420	1532	.294	.392	.537	154	744	204	77	15	.984	52	*O-2132,D-321,1/3	69.0
Team	3	100	235	30	53	6	1	14	39	50	37	.226	.361	.438	129	10	0	1	-1	.971	-1	/D-71,1-6,O	0.6

■ EDDIE ROBINSON Robinson, William Edward b: 12/15/20, Paris, Tex. BL/TR, 6'2.5", 210 lbs. Deb: 9/9/42 C

1942	Cle-A	8	8	1	1	0	0	0	2	1	0	.125	.222	.125	-1	-0	0	0	0	1.000	-0	/1-1	-0.1
1946	Cle-A	8	30	6	12	1	0	3	4	2	4	.400	.438	.733	238	5	0	0	0	.988	-2	/1-8	0.3
1947	Cle-A	95	318	52	78	10	1	14	52	30	18	.245	.314	.415	105	0	1	0	0	.994	-2	1-87	-0.4
1948	*Cle-A	134	493	53	125	18	5	16	83	36	42	.254	.307	.408	91	-9	1	0	0	**.995**	-1	*1-131	-1.0
1957	Cle-A	19	27	1	6	1	0	1	3	0	3	.222	.250	.370	68	-1	0	0	0	1.000	0	/1-7	-0.1
Total	13	1315	4282	546	1146	172	24	172	723	521	359	.268	.328	.440	113	73	10	12	-4	.990	-45	*1-1126	-1.1
Team	5	264	876	113	222	30	6	34	144	69	67	.253	.312	.418	99	-2	6	0	1	.994	-4	1-234	-1.3

■ MICKEY ROCCO Rocco, Michael Dominick b: 3/2/16, St.Paul, Minn. BL/TL, 5'11", 188 lbs. Deb: 6/5/43

1943	Cle-A	108	405	43	97	14	4	5	46	51	40	.240	.328	.331	99	-0	1	2	-1	**.995**	-5	*1-108	-1.4
1944	Cle-A	155	653	87	174	29	7	13	70	56	51	.266	.325	.392	108	5	4	8	-4	.993	17	*1-155	1.1
1945	Cle-A	143	565	81	149	28	6	10	56	52	40	.264	.326	.388	111	6	0	4	-2	**.992**	4	*1-141	-0.2
1946	Cle-A	34	98	8	24	2	0	2	14	15	15	.245	.345	.327	94	-0	1	1	-0	.996	5	1-27	0.3
Total	4	440	1721	219	444	73	17	30	186	174	146	.258	.327	.372	106	11	6	15	-7	.994	21	1-431	-0.2

■ BILL RODGERS Rodgers, Wilbur Kincaid "Rawmeat Bill" b: 4/18/1887, Pleasant Ridge, O. d: 12/24/78, Goliad, Tex. BL/TR, 5'9.5", 170 lbs. Deb: 4/15/15

| 1915 | Cle-A | 16 | 45 | 8 | 14 | 5 | 0 | 0 | 7 | 8 | 7 | .311 | .415 | .356 | 128 | 2 | 3 | 3 | -1 | .945 | -4 | 2-13 | -0.3 |
| Total | 2 | 102 | 268 | 30 | 65 | 15 | 4 | 0 | 19 | 22 | 40 | .243 | .316 | .328 | 93 | -2 | 11 | 8 | -2 | .945 | 2 | /2-75,S-7,O3 | -0.1 |

■ DAVE ROHDE Rohde, David Grant b: 5/8/64, Los Altos, Cal. BB/TR, 6'2", 180 lbs. Deb: 4/9/90

| 1992 | Cle-A | 5 | 7 | 0 | 0 | 0 | 0 | 0 | 0 | 2 | 3 | .000 | .222 | .000 | -34 | -1 | 0 | 0 | 0 | .900 | 1 | /3-5 | -0.1 |
| Total | 3 | 93 | 146 | 11 | 23 | 4 | 0 | 0 | 5 | 16 | 31 | .158 | .263 | .185 | 27 | -14 | 0 | 0 | 0 | 1.000 | 1 | /2-36,3-12,S1 | -1.3 |

■ DAN ROHN Rohn, Daniel Jay b: 1/10/56, Alpena, Mich. BL/TR, 5'7", 165 lbs. Deb: 9/2/83

| 1986 | Cle-A | 6 | 10 | 1 | 2 | 0 | 0 | 0 | 2 | 1 | 1 | .200 | .273 | .200 | 32 | -1 | 0 | 0 | 0 | .900 | 1 | /2-2,3-2,S | 0.0 |
| Total | 3 | 54 | 72 | 5 | 18 | 3 | 2 | 1 | 11 | 4 | 9 | .250 | .289 | .389 | 82 | -2 | 1 | 0 | 0 | .930 | 1 | ·/2-13,3-9,S | -0.1 |

■ RICH ROLLINS Rollins, Richard John "Red" b: 4/16/38, Mount Pleasant, Pa. BR/TR, 5'10", 185 lbs. Deb: 6/16/61

| 1970 | Cle-A | 42 | 43 | 6 | 10 | 2 | 0 | 4 | 3 | 5 | .233 | .283 | .372 | 75 | -2 | 0 | 0 | 0 | .600 | -1 | /3-5 | -0.3 |
| Total | 10 | 1002 | 3303 | 419 | 887 | 125 | 20 | 77 | 399 | 266 | 410 | .269 | .330 | .388 | 98 | -7 | 17 | 10 | -1 | .947 | -30 | 3-830/2-24,SO | -4.4 |

■ JOHNNY ROMANO Romano, John Anthony "Honey" b: 8/23/34, Hoboken, N.J. BR/TR, 5'11", 205 lbs. Deb: 9/12/58

1960	Cle-A	108	316	40	86	12	2	16	52	37	50	.272	.354	.475	126	11	0	0	0	.988	-11	C-99	0.6
1961	Cle-A★	142	509	76	152	29	1	21	80	61	60	.299	.393	.483	132	24	0	0	0	.989	-9	*C-141	2.2
1962	Cle-A★	135	459	71	120	19	3	25	81	73	64	.261	.369	.479	130	20	0	1	-1	.990	-9	*C-130	1.6
1963	Cle-A	89	255	28	55	5	2	10	34	38	49	.216	.322	.369	94	-2	4	3	-1	.993	-11	C-71/O-4	-1.1
1964	Cle-A	106	352	46	85	18	1	19	47	51	83	.241	.349	.460	124	12	2	2	-1	.991	-5	C-96/1-1	1.2
Total	10	905	2767	355	706	112	10	129	417	414	485	.255	.358	.443	123	93	7	9	-3	.990	-36	C-810/O-8,1	9.7
Team	5	580	1891	261	498	83	9	91	294	260	306	.263	.359	.461	124	65	6	6	-2	.990	-44	C-537/O-4,1	4.5

■ PHIL ROOF Roof, Phillip Anthony b: 3/5/41, Paducah, Ky. BR/TR, 6'3", 210 lbs. Deb: 4/29/61 FC

| 1965 | Cle-A | 43 | 52 | 3 | 9 | 1 | 0 | 0 | 3 | 5 | 13 | .173 | .259 | .192 | 30 | -5 | 0 | 0 | 0 | .994 | 13 | C-41 | 1.0 |
| Total | 15 | 857 | 2151 | 190 | 463 | 69 | 13 | 43 | 210 | 184 | 504 | .215 | .284 | .319 | 73 | -77 | 11 | 10 | -3 | .986 | 58 | C-835/1-3,D | 1.1 |

■ BUDDY ROSAR Rosar, Warren Vincent b: 7/3/14, Buffalo, N.Y. d: 3/13/94, Rochester, N.Y. BR/TR, 5'9", 190 lbs. Deb: 4/29/39

1943	Cle-A☆	115	382	53	108	17	1	1	41	33	12	.283	.340	.340	106	2	0	4	-2	.983	7	*C-114	1.5
1944	Cle-A	99	331	29	87	9	3	0	30	34	17	.263	.330	.308	89	-4	1	2	-1	**.989**	4	C-98	0.5
Total	13	988	3198	335	836	147	15	18	367	315	161	.261	.330	.334	84	-67	17	18	-6	.992	33	C-934	1.8
Team	2	214	713	82	195	26	4	1	71	67	29	.273	.339	.325	98	-2	1	6	-3	.986	11	C-212	2.0

■ DAVE ROSELLO Rosello, David (Rodriguez) b: 6/26/50, Mayaguez, P.R. BR/TR, 5'11", 160 lbs. Deb: 9/10/72

1979	Cle-A	59	107	20	26	6	1	3	14	15	27	.243	.336	.402	98	-0	1	0	0	.976	-5	2-33,3-14,S	-0.3
1980	Cle-A	71	117	16	29	3	0	2	12	9	19	.248	.302	.325	71	-5	0	0	0	.980	3	2-43,3-22/SD	0.0
1981	Cle-A	43	84	11	20	4	0	1	7	7	12	.238	.297	.321	79	-2	0	1	-1	.979	3	2-26/3-8,SD	0.1
Total	9	422	873	114	206	31	3	10	76	108	145	.236	.321	.313	73	-29	5	7	-3	.975	-4	2-168,S-151/3D	-1.5
Team	3	173	308	47	75	13	1	6	33	31	58	.244	.313	.351	83	-7	1	1	-0	.978	2	2-102/3-44,SD	-0.2

■ AL ROSEN Rosen, Albert Leonard "Flip" b: 2/29/24, Spartanburg, S.C. BR/TR, 5'10.5", 180 lbs. Deb: 9/10/47

1947	Cle-A	7	9	1	1	0	0	0	0	0	3	.111	.111	.111	-39	-2	0	0	0	.000	1	/3-2,O-1	-0.1
1948	*Cle-A	5	5	0	1	0	0	0	0	0	2	.200	.200	.200	7	-1	0	0	0	1.000	0	/3-2	-0.1
1949	Cle-A	23	44	3	7	2	0	0	5	7	4	.159	.275	.205	28	-5	0	1	-1	1.000	-1	3-10	-0.6
1950	Cle-A	155	554	100	159	23	4	**37**	116	100	72	.287	.405	.543	146	38	5	7	-3	.969	-20	*3-154	3.1
1951	Cle-A	154	573	82	152	30	1	24	102	85	71	.265	.362	.447	125	19	7	5	-1	.958	-15	*3-154	0.1
1952	Cle-A★	148	567	101	171	32	5	28	**105**	75	54	.302	.387	.524	162	46	8	6	-1	.958	-20	*3-147/1-4,S	2.3
1953	Cle-A★	155	599	**115**	201	27	5	**43**	**145**	85	48	.336	.422	**.613**	**181**	67	8	7	-2	.964	1	*3-154/1-1,S	**6.2**
1954	*Cle-A★	137	466	76	140	20	2	24	102	85	43	.300	.412	.506	148	33	6	2	1	.959	-14	3-87,1-46/2S	1.6
1955	Cle-A★	139	492	61	120	13	1	21	81	92	44	.244	.360	.402	103	4	4	2	0	.963	3	*3-106,1-41	0.4
1956	Cle-A	121	416	64	111	18	2	15	61	58	44	.267	.357	.428	104	2	1	3	-2	.945	-8	*3-116	-0.5
Total	10	1044	3725	603	1063	165	20	192	717	587	385	.285	.386	.495	138	202	39	33	-8	.961	-52	3-932/1-92,S2O	12.4

■ LARRY ROSENTHAL Rosenthal, Lawrence John b: 5/21/10, St.Paul, Minn. d: 3/4/92, Woodbury, Minn. BL/TL, 6'0.5", 190 lbs. Deb: 6/20/36

| 1941 | Cle-A | 45 | 75 | 10 | 14 | 3 | 1 | 1 | 8 | 9 | 10 | .187 | .274 | .293 | 53 | -5 | 1 | 0 | 0 | 1.000 | 0 | O-14/1-1 | -0.5 |
| Total | 8 | 579 | 1483 | 240 | 390 | 75 | 25 | 22 | 189 | 251 | 195 | .263 | .370 | .392 | 96 | -5 | 13 | 9 | -2 | .979 | -11 | O-410/1-1 | -3.2 |

■ DON ROSS Ross, Donald Raymond b: 7/16/14, Pasadena, Cal. BR/TR, 6'1", 185 lbs. Deb: 4/19/38

1945	Cle-A	106	363	26	95	15	1	2	43	42	15	.262	.340	.325	97	-1	0	4	-2	.958	-13	*3-106	-1.5
1946	Cle-A	55	153	12	41	7	0	3	14	17	12	.268	.341	.373	106	1	0	0	0	.944	-12	3-41/O-2	-1.1
Total	7	498	1488	129	390	63	4	12	162	166	70	.262	.338	.334	86	-26	10	6	-1	.946	-33	3-261,O-115/S21	-6.3
Team	2	161	516	38	136	22	1	5	57	59	27	.264	.340	.339	100	1	0	4	-2	.955	-25	3-147/O-2	-2.6

■ CLAUDE ROSSMAN Rossman, Claude R. b: 6/17/1881, Philmont, N.Y. d: 1/16/28, Poughkeepsie, N.Y. BL/TL, 6', 188 lbs. Deb: 9/16/04

| 1904 | Cle-A | 18 | 62 | 5 | 13 | 5 | 0 | 0 | 6 | 0 | | .210 | .210 | .290 | 58 | -3 | 0 | | | .933 | -4 | O-17 | | -0.9 |

YEAR	TM/L	G	AB	R	H	2B	3B	HR	RBI	BB	SO	AVG	OBP	SLG	PRO+	BR/A	SB	CS	SBR	FA	FR	G/POS	TPR
1906	Cle-A	118	396	49	122	13	2	1	53	17		.308	.338	.359	120	8	11			.984	-8	*1-105/O-1	-0.3
Total	5	511	1848	175	523	80	26	3	238	90		.283	.318	.359	113	21	49			.982	-26	1-471/O-20	-1.8
Team	2	136	458	54	135	18	2	1	59	17		.295	.321	.349	112	5	11			.984	-12	1-105/O-18	-1.2

■ BRAGGO ROTH

Roth, Robert Frank b: 8/28/1892, Burlington, Wis. d: 9/11/36, Chicago, Ill. BR/TR, 5'7.5", 170 lbs. Deb: 9/1/14 F

YEAR	TM/L	G	AB	R	H	2B	3B	HR	RBI	BB	SO	AVG	OBP	SLG	PRO+	BR/A	SB	CS	SBR	FA	FR	G/POS	TPR
1915	Cle-A	39	144	23	43	4	7	4	20	22	22	.299	.399	.507	168	12	14	4	2	.878	-6	O-39	0.6
1916	Cle-A	125	409	50	117	19	7	4	72	38	48	.286	.350	.396	117	8	29	14	0	.954	3	*O-112	0.6
1917	Cle-A	145	495	69	141	30	9	1	72	52	73	.285	.355	.388	118	10	51			.957	-0	*O-135	0.3
1918	Cle-A	106	375	53	106	21	12	1	59	53	41	.283	.383	.411	127	13	35			.936	-3	*O-106	0.4
Total	8	811	2831	427	804	138	73	30	422	335	389	.284	.367	.416	122	81	189	41		.944	-42	O-727/3-35	-0.1
Team	4	415	1423	195	407	74	35	10	223	165	184	.286	.366	.408	125	43	129	18		.942	-6	O-392	1.9

■ BOB ROTHEL

Rothel, Robert Burton b: 9/17/23, Columbia Station, Ohio d: 3/21/84, Huron, Ohio BR/TR, 5'10.5", 170 lbs. Deb: 4/22/45

YEAR	TM/L	G	AB	R	H	2B	3B	HR	RBI	BB	SO	AVG	OBP	SLG	PRO+	BR/A	SB	CS	SBR	FA	FR	G/POS	TPR
1945	Cle-A	4	10	0	2	0	0	0	0	3	1	.200	.385	.200	75	-0	0	0	0	.875	-1	/3-4	-0.1

■ LLOYD RUSSELL

Russell, Lloyd Opal b: 4/10/13, Atoka, Okla. d: 5/24/68, Waco, Tex. BR/TR, 5'11", 166 lbs. Deb: 4/26/38

YEAR	TM/L	G	AB	R	H	2B	3B	HR	RBI	BB	SO	AVG	OBP	SLG	PRO+	BR/A	SB	CS	SBR	FA	FR	G/POS	TPR
1938	Cle-A	2	0	0	0	0	0	0	0	0	0	—	—	—	—	0	0	0	0	.000	0	R	0.0

■ HANK RUSZKOWSKI

Ruszkowski, Henry Alexander b: 11/10/25, Cleveland, Ohio BR/TR, 6', 190 lbs. Deb: 9/26/44

YEAR	TM/L	G	AB	R	H	2B	3B	HR	RBI	BB	SO	AVG	OBP	SLG	PRO+	BR/A	SB	CS	SBR	FA	FR	G/POS	TPR
1944	Cle-A	3	8	1	3	0	0	0	1	0	1	.375	.375	.375	119	0	0	0	0	1.000	-0	/C-2	0.0
1945	Cle-A	14	49	2	10	0	0	0	5	4	9	.204	.264	.204	38	-4	0	0	0	.975	3	C-14	0.0
1947	Cle-A	23	27	5	7	2	0	3	4	2	6	.259	.310	.667	172	2	0	0	0	1.000	-2	C-16	0.1
Total	3	40	84	8	20	2	0	3	10	6	16	.238	.289	.369	91	-2	0	0	0	.981	1	/C-32	0.1

■ JIM RUTHERFORD

Rutherford, James Hollis b: 9/26/1886, Stillwater, Minn. d: 9/18/56, Cleveland, Ohio BL/TR, 6'1", 180 lbs. Deb: 7/12/10

YEAR	TM/L	G	AB	R	H	2B	3B	HR	RBI	BB	SO	AVG	OBP	SLG	PRO+	BR/A	SB	CS	SBR	FA	FR	G/POS	TPR
1910	Cle-A	1	2	0	1	0	0	0	0	0		.500	.500	.500	210	0	0			1.000	-0	/O-1	0.0

■ BUDDY RYAN

Ryan, John Budd b: 10/6/1885, Denver, Colo. d: 7/9/56, Sacramento, Cal. BL/TR, 5'9.5", 172 lbs. Deb: 4/11/12

YEAR	TM/L	G	AB	R	H	2B	3B	HR	RBI	BB	SO	AVG	OBP	SLG	PRO+	BR/A	SB	CS	SBR	FA	FR	G/POS	TPR
1912	Cle-A	93	328	53	89	12	9	1	31	30		.271	.343	.372	101	0	12			.963	5	O-90	0.0
1913	Cle-A	73	243	26	72	6	1	0	32	11	13	.296	.332	.329	91	-3	9			.986	-2	O-68/1-1	-0.8
Total	2	166	571	79	161	18	10	1	63	41	13	.282	.339	.354	97	-3	21			.973	3	O-158/1-1	-0.8

■ MARK SALAS

Salas, Mark Bruce b: 3/8/61, Montebello, Cal. BL/TR, 6', 205 lbs. Deb: 6/19/84

YEAR	TM/L	G	AB	R	H	2B	3B	HR	RBI	BB	SO	AVG	OBP	SLG	PRO+	BR/A	SB	CS	SBR	FA	FR	G/POS	TPR
1989	Cle-A	30	77	4	17	4	1	2	7	5	13	.221	.277	.377	81	-2	0	0	0	1.000	-0	D-20/C-5	-0.3
Total	8	509	1292	142	319	49	10	38	143	89	163	.247	.302	.389	86	-27	3	3		.987	-11	C-385/D-47,1O3	-2.3

■ CHICO SALMON

Salmon, Ruthford Eduardo b: 12/3/40, Colon, Panama BR/TR, 5'10", 170 lbs. Deb: 6/28/64

YEAR	TM/L	G	AB	R	H	2B	3B	HR	RBI	BB	SO	AVG	OBP	SLG	PRO+	BR/A	SB	CS	SBR	FA	FR	G/POS	TPR
1964	Cle-A	86	283	43	87	17	2	4	25	13	37	.307	.342	.424	113	4	10	6	-1	1.000	-8	O-53,2-32,1	-0.4
1965	Cle-A	79	120	20	29	8	0	3	12	5	19	.242	.283	.383	87	-2	7	4	-0	.985	-6	1-28,O-17/23	-1.0
1966	Cle-A	126	422	46	108	13	2	7	40	21	41	.256	.291	.346	82	-10	10	1	2	.958	-18	S-61,2-28,1O/3	-2.2
1967	Cle-A	90	203	19	46	13	1	2	19	17	29	.227	.290	.330	82	-5	10	4	1	1.000	1	O-28,1-24,2S/3	-0.2
1968	Cle-A	103	276	24	59	8	1	3	12	12	30	.214	.254	.283	63	-13	7	7	-2	.971	-15	2-45,3-18,SO1	-3.1
Total	9	658	1667	202	415	70	6	31	149	89	233	.249	.291	.354	84	-36	46	24	-1	.959	-75	2-164,S-137,1O/3	-10.6
Team	5	484	1304	152	329	59	6	19	108	68	156	.252	.293	.350	86	-25	44	22	0	.968	-47	2-134,O-121,1/S3	-6.9

■ RAFAEL SANTANA

Santana, Rafael Francisco (De La Cruz) b: 1/31/58, LaRomana, D.R. BR/TR, 6'1", 165 lbs. Deb: 4/5/83

YEAR	TM/L	G	AB	R	H	2B	3B	HR	RBI	BB	SO	AVG	OBP	SLG	PRO+	BR/A	SB	CS	SBR	FA	FR	G/POS	TPR
1990	Cle-A	7	13	3	3	0	0	1	3	0	0	.231	.231	.462	89	-0	0	0	0	1.000	-2	/S-7	-0.2
Total	7	668	2021	188	497	74	5	13	156	138	234	.246	.296	.307	68	-88	3	7	-3	.969	9	S-639/2-10,3	-3.1

■ GERMANY SCHAEFER

Schaefer, Herman A. b: 2/4/1877, Chicago, Ill. d: 5/16/19, Saranac Lake, N.Y. BR/TR, 5'9", 175 lbs. Deb: 10/5/01

YEAR	TM/L	G	AB	R	H	2B	3B	HR	RBI	BB	SO	AVG	OBP	SLG	PRO+	BR/A	SB	CS	SBR	FA	FR	G/POS	TPR
1918	Cle-A	1	5	2	0	0	0	0	0	0	0	.000	.000	.000	-91	-1	1			1.000	-0	/2-1	-0.2
Total	15	1150	3784	497	972	117	48	9	308	333	28	.257	.319	.320	96	-15	201			.954	4	2-588,1-145,3/SOP	-1.4

■ FRANK SCHEIBECK

Scheibeck, Frank S. b: 6/28/1865, Detroit, Mich. d: 10/22/56, Detroit, Mich. BR/TR, 5'7", 145 lbs. Deb: 5/9/1887

YEAR	TM/L	G	AB	R	H	2B	3B	HR	RBI	BB	SO	AVG	OBP	SLG	PRO+	BR/A	SB	CS	SBR	FA	FR	G/POS	TPR
1901	Cle-A	93	329	33	70	11	3	0	38	18		.213	.258	.264	47	-24	3			.897	-14	S-92	-2.7
Total	8	389	1396	213	329	37	18	2	99	182		.236	.329	.292	70	-55	88			.884	-33	S-362/O-9,23P	-5.7

■ RICHIE SCHEINBLUM

Scheinblum, Richard Alan b: 11/5/42, New York, N.Y. BB/TR, 6'1", 180 lbs. Deb: 9/1/65

YEAR	TM/L	G	AB	R	H	2B	3B	HR	RBI	BB	SO	AVG	OBP	SLG	PRO+	BR/A	SB	CS	SBR	FA	FR	G/POS	TPR
1965	Cle-A	4	1	1	0	0	0	0	0	0	0	.000	.000	.000	-99	-0	0	0	0	.000	0	H	0.0
1967	Cle-A	18	66	8	21	4	2	0	6	5	10	.318	.366	.439	136	3	0	2	-1	.943	-0	O-18	0.1
1968	Cle-A	19	55	3	12	5	0	0	5	5	8	.218	.295	.309	84	-1	0	0	0	1.000	1	O-16	-0.1
1969	Cle-A	102	199	13	37	5	1	1	13	19	30	.186	.257	.236	37	-17	0	2	-1	.974	-1	O-50	-2.3
Total	8	462	1218	131	320	52	9	13	127	149	135	.263	.346	.352	104	10	0	6	-4	.965	-4	O-299/D-25	-1.3
Team	4	143	321	25	70	14	3	1	24	29	48	.218	.285	.290	64	-15	0	4	-2	.973	-0	/O-84	-2.3

■ NORM SCHLUETER

Schlueter, Norman John "Duke" b: 9/25/16, Belleville, Ill. BR/TR, 5'10", 175 lbs. Deb: 5/28/38

YEAR	TM/L	G	AB	R	H	2B	3B	HR	RBI	BB	SO	AVG	OBP	SLG	PRO+	BR/A	SB	CS	SBR	FA	FR	G/POS	TPR
1944	Cle-A	49	122	2	15	4	0	0	11	12	22	.123	.201	.156	3	-15	0	2	-1	.985	-8	C-43	-2.4
Total	3	118	296	18	55	11	2	0	26	17	48	.186	.230	.236	24	-33	3	2	-0	.974	-10	C-109	-3.9

■ OSSEE SCHRECKENGOST

Schreckengost, Ossee Freeman (a.k.a. Ossee Schreck)
b: 4/11/1875, New Bethlehem, Pa. d: 7/9/14, Philadelphia, Pa. BR/TR, 5'10", 180 lbs. Deb: 9/8/1897

YEAR	TM/L	G	AB	R	H	2B	3B	HR	RBI	BB	SO	AVG	OBP	SLG	PRO+	BR/A	SB	CS	SBR	FA	FR	G/POS	TPR
1902	Cle-A	18	74	5	25	0	0	0	9	0		.338	.338	.338	91	-1	2			.967	-1	1-17	-0.3
Total	11	895	3057	304	829	136	31	9	338	102		.271	.297	.345	90	-42	52			.970	86	C-751/1-99,O2S	11.8

■ BILL SCHWARTZ

Schwartz, William Charles "Blab" b: 4/22/1884, Cleveland, Ohio d: 8/29/61, Nashville, Tenn. BR/TR, 6'2", 185 lbs. Deb: 5/2/04

YEAR	TM/L	G	AB	R	H	2B	3B	HR	RBI	BB	SO	AVG	OBP	SLG	PRO+	BR/A	SB	CS	SBR	FA	FR	G/POS	TPR
1904	Cle-A	24	86	5	13	2	0	0	0	0		.151	.151	.174	3	-9	4			.980	-4	1-22/3-1	-1.6

■ BOB SEEDS

Seeds, Ira Robert "Suitcase Bob" b: 2/24/07, Ringgold, Tex. d: 10/28/93, Erick, Okla. BR/TR, 6', 180 lbs. Deb: 4/19/30

YEAR	TM/L	G	AB	R	H	2B	3B	HR	RBI	BB	SO	AVG	OBP	SLG	PRO+	BR/A	SB	CS	SBR	FA	FR	G/POS	TPR
1930	Cle-A	85	277	37	79	11	3	3	32	12	22	.285	.315	.379	72	-12	1	3	-2	.953	2	O-70	-1.5
1931	Cle-A	48	134	26	41	4	1	1	10	11	11	.306	.359	.373	88	-2	1	0	0	.966	-2	O-33/1-2	-0.6
1932	Cle-A	2	4	0	0	0	0	0	0	0	0	.000	.000	.000	-94	-1	0	0	0	.000	-0	/O-1	-0.2
1934	Cle-A	61	186	28	46	8	1	0	18	21	13	.247	.327	.301	62	-10	2	1	0	.977	-4	O-48	-1.5
Total	9	615	1937	268	537	77	21	28	233	160	190	.277	.336	.382	89	-32	14	15	-5	.970	-35	O-472/1-43,3	-9.3
Team	4	196	601	91	166	23	5	4	60	44	46	.276	.327	.351	72	-26	4	4	-1	.962	-5	O-152/1-2	-3.8

■ PAT SEEREY

Seerey, James Patrick b: 3/17/23, Wilburton, Okla. d: 4/28/86, Jennings, Mo. BR/TR, 5'10", 200 lbs. Deb: 6/9/43

YEAR	TM/L	G	AB	R	H	2B	3B	HR	RBI	BB	SO	AVG	OBP	SLG	PRO+	BR/A	SB	CS	SBR	FA	FR	G/POS	TPR
1943	Cle-A	26	72	8	16	3	0	1	5	4	19	.222	.263	.306	70	-3	0	0	0	.974	1	O-16	-0.3
1944	Cle-A	101	342	39	80	16	0	15	39	19	99	.234	.276	.412	99	-3	0	2	-1	.986	1	O-86	-0.8
1945	Cle-A	126	414	56	98	22	2	14	56	66	97	.237	.342	.401	120	11	1	2	-1	.975	-15	*O-117	-1.2
1946	Cle-A	117	404	57	91	17	2	26	62	65	101	.225	.334	.470	131	15	2	3	-1	.981	-5	*O-115	0.4
1947	Cle-A	82	216	24	37	4	1	11	29	34	66	.171	.284	.352	78	-7	0	1	-1	.957	-8	O-68	-1.9
1948	Cle-A	10	23	7	6	0	0	1	6	7	8	.261	.433	.391	123	1	0	0	0	1.000	-2	/O-7	-0.1
Total	7	561	1815	236	406	73	5	86	261	259	485	.224	.321	.412	109	16	3	8	-4	.978	-27	O-504	-4.2
Team	6	462	1471	191	328	62	5	68	197	195	390	.223	.315	.411	110	14	3	8	-4	.977	-27	O-409	-3.9

■ TED SEPKOWSKI

Sepkowski, Theodore Walter (b: Theodore Walter Sczepkowski) b: 11/9/23, Baltimore, Md. BL/TR, 5'11", 190 lbs. Deb: 9/9/42

YEAR	TM/L	G	AB	R	H	2B	3B	HR	RBI	BB	SO	AVG	OBP	SLG	PRO+	BR/A	SB	CS	SBR	FA	FR	G/POS	TPR
1942	Cle-A	5	10	0	1	0	0	0	0	0	3	.100	.100	.100	-46	-2	0	0	0	.824	0	/2-2	-0.1

YEAR	TM/L	G	AB	R	H	2B	3B	HR	RBI	BB	SO	AVG	OBP	SLG	PRO+	BR/A	SB	CS	SBR	FA	FR	G/POS	TPR
1946	Cle-A	2	8	2	4	1	0	0	1	0	0	.500	.500	.625	228	1	0	0	0	.833	-1	/3-2	0.1
1947	Cle-A	10	8	0	1	1	0	0	0	1	1	.125	.222	.250	32	-1	0	0	0	.000	-0	/O-1	-0.1
Total	3	19	26	3	6	2	0	0	1	1	4	.231	.259	.308	61	-1	0	1	-1	.833	-1	/3-2,2-2,O	-0.2
Team	3	17	26	2	6	2	0	0	1	1	4	.231	.259	.308	61	-1	0	0	0	.833	-1	/3-2,2-2,O	-0.1

■ LUKE SEWELL

Sewell, James Luther b: 1/5/01, Titus, Ala. d: 5/14/87, Akron, Ohio BR/TR, 5'9", 160 lbs. Deb: 6/30/21 FMC

YEAR	TM/L	G	AB	R	H	2B	3B	HR	RBI	BB	SO	AVG	OBP	SLG	PRO+	BR/A	SB	CS	SBR	FA	FR	G/POS	TPR
1921	Cle-A	3	6	0	0	0	0	0	1	0	3	.000	.000	.000	-99	-2	0	0	0	1.000	1	/C-3	-0.1
1922	Cle-A	41	87	14	23	5	0	0	10	5	8	.264	.312	.322	65	-4	1	1	-0	.963	0	C-39	-0.3
1923	Cle-A	10	10	2	2	0	1	0	1	1	0	.200	.273	.400	76	-0	0	0	0	.833	0	/C-7	0.0
1924	Cle-A	63	165	27	48	9	1	0	17	22	13	.291	.387	.358	92	-1	1	0	0	.959	5	C-57	0.7
1925	Cle-A	74	220	30	51	10	2	0	18	33	18	.232	.337	.295	61	-12	6	2	1	.971	7	C-66/O-2	-0.2
1926	Cle-A	126	433	41	103	16	4	0	46	36	27	.238	.302	.293	55	-28	9	3	1	.983	2	*C-125	-1.7
1927	Cle-A	128	470	52	138	27	6	0	53	20	23	.294	.328	.377	82	-13	4	8	-4	.963	-2	*C-126	-0.9
1928	Cle-A	122	411	52	111	16	9	3	52	26	27	.270	.318	.375	81	-12	3	4	-2	.972	13	*C-118	0.9
1929	Cle-A	124	406	41	96	16	3	1	39	29	26	.236	.287	.298	49	-31	6	6	-2	.966	4	*C-124	-1.6
1930	Cle-A	76	292	40	75	21	2	1	43	14	9	.257	.293	.353	61	-18	5	2	0	.974	-2	C-76	-1.1
1931	Cle-A	108	375	45	103	30	4	1	53	36	17	.275	.341	.384	86	-8	1	1	-0	.980	-8	*C-104	-0.8
1932	Cle-A	87	300	36	76	20	2	2	52	38	24	.253	.337	.353	74	-11	4	5	-2	.978	4	C-84	-0.4
1939	Cle-A	16	20	1	3	1	0	0	1	3	1	.150	.261	.200	20	-2	0	0	0	.966	-1	C-15/1-1	-0.2
Total	20	1630	5383	653	1393	272	56	20	696	486	307	.259	.323	.341	70	-242	65	44	-7	.978	48	*C-1562/O-9,132	-9.4
Team	13	978	3195	381	829	171	34	8	386	263	196	.259	.320	.342	70	-145	40	32	-7	.972	24	C-944/O-2,1	-5.7

■ JOE SEWELL

Sewell, Joseph Wheeler b: 10/9/1898, Titus, Ala. d: 3/6/90, Mobile, Ala. BL/TR, 5'6.5", 155 lbs. Deb: 9/10/20 FCH

YEAR	TM/L	G	AB	R	H	2B	3B	HR	RBI	BB	SO	AVG	OBP	SLG	PRO+	BR/A	SB	CS	SBR	FA	FR	G/POS	TPR
1920	*Cle-A	22	70	14	23	4	1	0	12	9	4	.329	.412	.414	116	2	1	0	0	.884	3	S-22	0.6
1921	Cle-A	154	572	101	182	36	12	4	93	80	17	.318	.412	.444	117	17	7	6	-2	.944	-3	*S-154	2.5
1922	Cle-A	153	558	80	167	28	7	2	83	73	20	.299	.386	.385	101	3	10	12	-4	.939	12	*S-139,2-12	2.5
1923	Cle-A	153	553	98	195	41	10	3	109	98	12	.353	.456	.479	147	43	9	6	-1	.930	6	*S-151	6.0
1924	Cle-A	153	594	99	188	**45**	5	4	106	67	13	.316	.388	.429	109	9	3	3	-1	.960	**21**	*S-153	4.3
1925	Cle-A	155	608	78	204	37	7	1	98	64	4	.336	.402	.424	109	10	7	6	-2	**.967**	16	*S-153/2-3	3.8
1926	Cle-A	154	578	91	187	41	5	4	85	65	6	.324	.399	.433	116	15	17	7	1	.955	3	*S-154	3.3
1927	Cle-A	153	569	83	180	48	5	1	92	51	7	.316	.382	.424	108	7	3	16	-9	**.962**	6	*S-153	1.9
1928	Cle-A	155	588	79	190	40	2	4	70	58	9	.323	.391	.418	111	11	7	1	2	**.963**	27	*S-137,3-19	5.4
1929	Cle-A	152	578	90	182	38	3	7	73	48	4	.315	.372	.427	102	2	6	6	-2	.975	15	*3-152	2.0
1930	Cle-A	109	353	44	102	17	6	0	48	41	3	.289	.374	.371	86	-6	1	4	-2	.950	0	3-97	-0.2
Total	14	1903	7132	1141	2226	436	68	49	1055	842	114	.312	.391	.413	109	116	74	72	-21	.951	107	*S-1216,3-643/2	34.5
Team	11	1513	5621	857	1800	375	63	30	869	654	99	.320	.398	.425	111	114	71	67	-19	.951	105	*S-1216,3-268/2	32.1

■ WALLY SHANER

Shaner, Walter Dedaker "Skinny" b: 5/24/1900, Lynchburg, Va. d: 11/13/92, Las Vegas, Nev. BR/TR, 6'2", 195 lbs. Deb: 5/4/23

YEAR	TM/L	G	AB	R	H	2B	3B	HR	RBI	BB	SO	AVG	OBP	SLG	PRO+	BR/A	SB	CS	SBR	FA	FR	G/POS	TPR
1923	Cle-A	3	4	1	1	0	0	0	0	1	1	.250	.400	.250	74	-0	0	0	0	1.000	-1	/O-2,3-1	-0.1
Total	4	207	629	80	175	45	8	4	74	43	54	.278	.327	.394	89	-12	13	4	2	.959	-9	O-160/1-9,3	-3.0

■ DANNY SHAY

Shay, Daniel C. b: 11/8/1876, Springfield, Ohio d: 12/1/27, Kansas City, Mo. TR, 5'10", Deb: 4/30/01

YEAR	TM/L	G	AB	R	H	2B	3B	HR	RBI	BB	SO	AVG	OBP	SLG	PRO+	BR/A	SB	CS	SBR	FA	FR	G/POS	TPR
1901	Cle-A	19	75	4	17	2	2	0	10	2		.227	.266	.307	61	-4	0			.901	-4	S-19	-0.6
Total	4	231	775	89	186	26	5	2	62	88		.240	.325	.294	90	-6	52			.902	-31	S-164/2-54,O	-3.5

■ DANNY SHEAFFER

Sheaffer, Danny Todd b: 8/2/61, Jacksonville, Fla. BR/TR, 6' ", 185 lbs. Deb: 4/9/87

YEAR	TM/L	G	AB	R	H	2B	3B	HR	RBI	BB	SO	AVG	OBP	SLG	PRO+	BR/A	SB	CS	SBR	FA	FR	G/POS	TPR
1989	Cle-A	7	16	1	1	0	0	0	0	2	2	.063	.167	.063	-32	-3	0	0	0	.000	0	/3-2,O-1,D	-0.3
Total	5	234	616	67	141	24	2	11	79	43	80	.229	.280	.328	56	-40	2	5		.992	11	C-187/1-12,O3D	-2.2

■ PETE SHIELDS

Shields, Francis Leroy b: 9/21/1891, Swiftwater, Miss. d: 2/11/61, Jackson, Miss. BR/TR, 6', 175 lbs. Deb: 4/14/15

YEAR	TM/L	G	AB	R	H	2B	3B	HR	RBI	BB	SO	AVG	OBP	SLG	PRO+	BR/A	SB	CS	SBR	FA	FR	G/POS	TPR
1915	Cle-A	23	72	4	15	6	0	0	6	4	14	.208	.250	.292	61	-4	3	3	-1	.974	0	1-23	-0.6

■ JIM SHILLING

Shilling, James Robert b: 5/14/14, Tulsa, Okla. d: 9/12/86, Tulsa, Okla. BR/TR, 5'11", 175 lbs. Deb: 4/21/39

YEAR	TM/L	G	AB	R	H	2B	3B	HR	RBI	BB	SO	AVG	OBP	SLG	PRO+	BR/A	SB	CS	SBR	FA	FR	G/POS	TPR
1939	Cle-A	31	98	8	27	7	2	0	12	7	9	.276	.324	.388	84	-3	1	0	0	.935	4	2-27/S-3	0.2
Total	1	42	131	11	37	8	5	0	16	8	13	.282	.324	.420	94	-2	1	0	0	.936	2	/2-32,S-6,3O	0.2

■ GINGER SHINAULT

Shinault, Enoch Erskine b: 9/7/1892, Benton, Ark. d: 12/29/30, Denver, Colo. BR/TR, 5'11", 170 lbs. Deb: 7/4/21

YEAR	TM/L	G	AB	R	H	2B	3B	HR	RBI	BB	SO	AVG	OBP	SLG	PRO+	BR/A	SB	CS	SBR	FA	FR	G/POS	TPR
1921	Cle-A	22	29	5	11	1	0	0	4	6	5	.379	.486	.414	129	2	1	0	0	.917	2	C-20	0.4
1922	Cle-A	13	15	1	2	1	0	0	0	0	2	.133	.133	.200	-14	-3	0	0	0	.400	-4	C-11	-0.6
Total	2	35	44	6	13	2	0	0	4	6	7	.295	.380	.341	85	-1	1	0	0	.868	-2	/C-31	-0.2

■ BILL SHIPKE

Shipke, William Martin "Skipper Bill" or "Muskrat Bill" (b: William Martin Shipkrethaver)
b: 11/18/1882, St.Louis, Mo. d: 9/10/40, Omaha, Neb. BR/TR, 5'7", 145 lbs. Deb: 4/23/06

YEAR	TM/L	G	AB	R	H	2B	3B	HR	RBI	BB	SO	AVG	OBP	SLG	PRO+	BR/A	SB	CS	SBR	FA	FR	G/POS	TPR
1906	Cle-A	2	6	0	0	0	0	0	0	0		.000	.000	.000	-99	-1	0			.933	2	/2-2	0.0
Total	4	186	552	59	110	11	10	1	29	55		.199	.280	.261	81	-10	21			.935	5	3-179/2-3,S	0.0

■ HARRY SIMPSON

Simpson, Harry Leon "Suitcase" or "Goody" b: 12/3/25, Atlanta, Ga. d: 4/3/79, Akron, Ohio BL/TR, 6'1", 180 lbs. Deb: 4/21/51

YEAR	TM/L	G	AB	R	H	2B	3B	HR	RBI	BB	SO	AVG	OBP	SLG	PRO+	BR/A	SB	CS	SBR	FA	FR	G/POS	TPR
1951	Cle-A	122	332	51	76	7	0	7	24	45	48	.229	.325	.313	77	-10	6	4	-1	.971	-4	O-68,1-50	-1.8
1952	Cle-A	146	545	66	145	21	10	10	65	56	82	.266	.337	.396	111	6	5	3	-0	.988	-4	*O-127,1-28	-0.4
1953	Cle-A	82	242	25	55	3	1	7	22	18	27	.227	.284	.335	68	-11	0	0	0	.968	-6	O-69/1-2	-2.0
1955	Cle-A	3	1	1	0	0	0	0	0	2	0	.000	.667	.000	88	0	0	0	0	.000	0	H	0.0
Total	8	888	2829	343	752	101	41	73	381	271	429	.266	.332	.408	102	-1	17	18	-6	.974	-37	O-579,1-211	-7.8
Team	4	353	1120	143	276	31	11	24	111	121	157	.246	.323	.358	91	-15	11	7	-1	.978	-14	O-264/1-80	-4.2

■ DUKE SIMS

Sims, Duane B b: 6/5/41, Salt Lake City, Ut. BL/TR, 6'2", 205 lbs. Deb: 9/22/64

YEAR	TM/L	G	AB	R	H	2B	3B	HR	RBI	BB	SO	AVG	OBP	SLG	PRO+	BR/A	SB	CS	SBR	FA	FR	G/POS	TPR
1964	Cle-A	2	6	0	0	0	0	0	0	0	2	.000	.000	.000	-99	-2	0	0	0	1.000	1	/C-1	-0.1
1965	Cle-A	48	118	9	21	0	0	6	15	15	33	.178	.271	.331	69	-5	0	0	0	.980	-2	C-40	-0.5
1966	Cle-A	52	133	12	35	2	2	6	19	11	31	.263	.338	.444	122	4	0	1	-1	.975	-5	C-48	0.1
1967	Cle-A	88	272	25	55	8	2	12	37	30	64	.202	.295	.379	97	-1	3	3	-1	.989	-3	C-85	0.0
1968	Cle-A	122	361	48	90	21	0	11	44	62	68	.249	.367	.399	134	17	1	3	-2	.983	-1	C-84,1-31/O	2.0
1969	Cle-A	114	326	40	77	8	0	18	45	66	80	.236	.374	.426	120	10	1	2	-1	.991	-4	*C-102/O-3,1	1.2
1970	Cle-A	110	345	46	91	12	0	23	56	46	59	.264	.360	.499	128	13	0	4	-2	.993	-2	C-39,O-36,1	0.8
Total	11	843	2422	263	580	80	6	100	310	338	483	.239	.341	.401	111	38	6	16	-8	.986	-20	C-646/1-61,OD	3.9
Team	7	536	1561	180	369	51	4	76	216	230	337	.236	.344	.420	117	37	5	13	-6	.986	-15	C-399/1-61,O	3.5

■ JOEL SKINNER

Skinner, Joel Patrick b: 2/21/61, LaJolla, Cal. BR/TR, 6'4", 204 lbs. Deb: 6/12/83 F

YEAR	TM/L	G	AB	R	H	2B	3B	HR	RBI	BB	SO	AVG	OBP	SLG	PRO+	BR/A	SB	CS	SBR	FA	FR	G/POS	TPR
1989	Cle-A	79	178	10	41	10	0	1	13	9	42	.230	.271	.303	61	-9	1	1	-0	.990	-4	C-79	-1.1
1990	Cle-A	49	139	16	35	4	1	2	16	7	44	.252	.288	.338	75	-5	0	0	0	.996	0	C-49	-0.2
1991	Cle-A	99	284	23	69	14	0	1	24	14	67	.243	.281	.303	61	-15	0	2	-1	.991	1	C-99	-1.0
Total	9	564	1441	119	329	62	3	17	136	80	387	.228	.271	.311	60	-81	3	7	-3	.988	3	C-560/O-2,1	-5.3
Team	3	227	601	49	145	28	1	4	53	30	153	.241	.280	.311	64	-29	1	3	-2	.992	-3	C-227	-2.3

■ JACK SLATTERY

Slattery, John Terrence b: 1/6/1878, S.Boston, Mass. d: 7/17/49, Boston, Mass. BR/TR, 6'2", 191 lbs. Deb: 9/28/01 MC

YEAR	TM/L	G	AB	R	H	2B	3B	HR	RBI	BB	SO	AVG	OBP	SLG	PRO+	BR/A	SB	CS	SBR	FA	FR	G/POS	TPR
1903	Cle-A	4	11	1	0	0	0	0	0	0		.000	.000	.000	-99	-3	0			.885	-1	/1-2	-0.4
Total	4	103	288	14	61	5	2	0	27	6		.212	.236	.243	47	-18	3			.974	-10	/C-65,1-18	-2.4

YEAR	TM/L	G	AB	R	H	2B	3B	HR	RBI	BB	SO	AVG	OBP	SLG	PRO+	BR/A	SB	CS	SBR	FA	FR	G/POS	TPR
■ AL SMITH	Smith, Alphonse Eugene "Fuzzy" b: 2/7/28, Kirkwood, Mo. BR/TR, 6'1", 191 lbs. Deb: 7/10/53																					
1953	Cle-A	47	150	28	36	9	0	3	14	20	25	.240	.341	.360	92	-1	2	0	1	.920	-3	O-39/3-2	-0.6
1954	*Cle-A	131	481	101	135	29	6	11	50	88	65	.281	.399	.435	126	20	2	9	-5	.984	-3	*O-109,3-21/S	0.8
1955	Cle-A★	154	607	123	186	27	4	22	77	93	77	.306	.411	.473	132	30	11	6	-0	.977	-17	*O-120,3-45/S2	0.7
1956	Cle-A	141	526	87	144	26	5	16	71	84	72	.274	.382	.433	112	11	6	3	0	.981	-7	*O-122,3-28/2	-0.2
1957	Cle-A	135	507	78	125	23	5	11	49	79	70	.247	.353	.397	100	2	12	6	0	.913	-16	3-84,O-58	-1.6
1964	Cle-A	61	136	15	22	1	1	4	9	8	32	.162	.214	.272	34	-12	0	1	-1	1.000	-3	O-48/3-1	-1.9
Total	12	1517	5357	843	1458	258	46	164	676	674	768	.272	.360	.429	113	105	67	43	-6	.974	-84	*O-1118,3-378/S2	-3.7
Team	6	669	2407	432	648	115	21	67	270	372	341	.269	.376	.418	113	50	33	25	-5	.977	-49	O-496,3-181/S2	-2.8
■ ELMER SMITH	Smith, Elmer John b: 9/21/1892, Sandusky, Ohio d: 8/3/84, Columbia, Ky. BL/TR, 5'10", 165 lbs. Deb: 9/20/14																					
1914	Cle-A	13	53	5	17	3	0	0	8	2	11	.321	.345	.377	113	1	1	1	-0	1.000	1	O-13	0.1
1915	Cle-A	144	476	37	118	23	12	3	67	36	75	.248	.301	.366	97	-4	10	11	-4	.923	0	*O-123	-1.4
1916	Cle-A	79	213	25	59	15	3	3	40	18	35	.277	.336	.418	119	4	3			.966	-2	O-57	0.0
1917	Cle-A	64	161	21	42	5	1	3	22	13	18	.261	.316	.360	99	-1	6			.986	-1	O-40	-0.4
1919	Cle-A	114	395	60	110	24	6	9	54	41	30	.278	.354	.438	115	7	15			.957	-6	*O-111	-0.7
1920	*Cle-A	129	456	82	144	37	10	12	103	53	35	.316	.391	.520	135	22	5	4	-1	.970	-8	*O-129	0.5
1921	Cle-A	129	431	98	125	28	9	16	85	56	46	.290	.374	.508	121	13	0	2	-1	.971	-8	*O-127	-0.4
Total	10	1012	3195	469	881	181	62	70	541	319	359	.276	.344	.437	112	44	54	27		.957	-29	O-870	-4.5
Team	7	672	2185	328	615	135	41	46	379	219	250	.281	.350	.444	117	42	40	<u>18</u>		.957	-23	O-600	-2.3
■ SYD SMITH	Smith, Sydney E. b: 8/31/1883, Smithville, S.C. d: 6/5/61, Orangeburg, S.C. BR/TR, 5'10", 190 lbs. Deb: 4/14/08																					
1910	Cle-A	9	27	1	9	1	0	0	3	3		.333	.400	.370	140	1	0			.958	0	/C-9	0.2
1911	Cle-A	58	154	8	46	8	1	1	21	11		.299	.353	.383	104	1	0			.979	9	C-48/1-1,3	1.3
Total	5	146	397	24	98	21	1	2	40	22		.247	.291	.320	83	-8	2			.977	16	C-115/1-7,3O	1.9
Team	2	67	181	9	55	9	1	1	24	14		.304	.360	.381	109	2	0			.977	9	/C-57,3-1,1	1.5
■ TOMMY SMITH	Smith, Tommy Alexander b: 8/1/48, Albemarle, N.C. BL/TR, 6'3", 215 lbs. Deb: 9/6/73																					
1973	Cle-A	14	41	6	10	2	0	2	3	1	2	.244	.262	.439	93	-1	1	0	0	1.000	-1	O-13	-0.2
1974	Cle-A	23	31	4	3	1	0	0	0	2	7	.097	.176	.129	-11	-4	0	0	0	.938	-2	O-17/D-1	-0.7
1975	Cle-A	8	8	0	1	0	0	0	2	0	1	.125	.125	.125	-29	-1	0	0	0	1.000	-1	/O-3,D-3	-0.2
1976	Cle-A	55	164	17	42	3	1	2	12	8	8	.256	.291	.323	80	-4	8	0	2	.979	-0	O-50/D-2	-0.8
Total	5	121	271	28	63	7	2	4	21	11	24	.232	.265	.317	68	-12	9	1	2	.977	-5	/O-97,D-6	-1.9
Team	4	100	244	27	56	6	1	4	17	11	18	.230	.266	.311	67	-11	9	0	2	.975	-3	/O-83,D-6	-1.5
■ WILLIE SMITH	Smith, Willie b: 2/11/39, Anniston, Ala. BL/TL, 6', 190 lbs. Deb: 6/18/63																					
1967	Cle-A	21	32	0	7	2	0	0	2	1	10	.219	.242	.281	54	-2	0	2	-1	.800	-1	/O-4,1-3	-0.5
1968	Cle-A	33	42	1	6	2	0	0	3	3	14	.143	.217	.190	25	-4	0	0		1.000	-0	/1-7,P-2,O	-0.5
Total	9	691	1654	171	410	63	21	46	211	107	284	.248	.297	.395	94	-18	20	16	-4	.975	-24	O-339/1-93,P	-7.1
Team	2	54	74	1	13	4	0	0	5	4	24	.176	.228	.230	38	-6	0	2	-1	1.000	-1	/1-10,O-5,P	-1.0
■ CORY SNYDER	Snyder, James Cory b: 11/11/62, Inglewood, Cal. BR/TR, 6'3", 185 lbs. Deb: 6/13/86																					
1986	Cle-A	103	416	58	113	21	1	24	69	16	123	.272	.299	.500	115	6	2	3	-1	.987	-7	O-74,S-34,3/D	-0.2
1987	Cle-A	157	577	74	136	24	2	33	82	31	166	.236	.276	.456	89	-12	5	1	1	.971	2	*O-139,S-18	-1.2
1988	Cle-A	142	511	71	139	24	3	26	75	42	101	.272	.329	.483	121	13	5	1	1	.985	14	*O-141/D-7	2.3
1989	Cle-A	132	489	49	105	17	0	18	59	23	134	.215	.253	.360	70	-21	6	5	-1	**.997**	19	*O-125/S-7,D	-0.7
1990	Cle-A	123	438	46	102	27	3	14	55	21	118	.233	.271	.404	87	-10	1	4	-2	.975	2	*O-120/S-5	-1.3
Total	9	1068	3656	439	902	178	13	149	488	226	992	.247	.293	.425	95	-36	28	19	-3	.983	3	O-877/S-73,132D	-5.5
Team	5	657	2431	298	595	113	9	115	340	133	642	.245	.286	.441	96	-24	19	14	-3	.983	28	O-599/S-64,3D	-1.1
■ RUSS SNYDER	Snyder, Russell Henry b: 6/22/34, Oak, Neb. BL/TR, 6'1", 190 lbs. Deb: 4/18/59																					
1968	Cle-A	68	217	30	61	8	2	3	23	25	21	.281	.355	.364	120	6	1	1	-0	.991	4	O-54/1-1	0.7
1969	Cle-A	122	266	26	66	10	2	2	24	25	33	.248	.313	.308	72	-10	3	2	-0	.961	-4	O-84	-1.8
Total	12	1365	3631	488	984	150	29	42	319	294	438	.271	.327	.363	94	-28	58	32	-2	.981	-96	*O-1099/1-1	-18.3
Team	2	190	483	56	127	18	4	5	47	50	54	.263	.332	.333	92	-4	4	3	-0	.973	-0	O-138/1-1	-1.1
■ BILL SODD	Sodd, William b: 9/18/14, Ft.Worth, Tex. BR/TR, 6'2", 210 lbs. Deb: 9/27/37																					
1937	Cle-A	1	1	0	0	0	0	0	0	0	1	.000	.000	.000	-99	-0	0	0	0	.000	0	H	0.0
■ MOOSE SOLTERS	Solters, Julius Joseph (b: Julius Joseph Soltesz) b: 3/22/06, Pittsburgh, Pa. d: 9/28/75, Pittsburgh, Pa. BR/TR, 6', 190 lbs. Deb: 4/17/34																					
1937	Cle-A	152	589	90	190	42	11	20	109	42	56	.323	.372	.533	125	19	6	9	-4	.953	2	*O-149	1.2
1938	Cle-A	67	199	30	40	6	3	2	22	13	28	.201	.250	.291	36	-21	4	1	1	.969	1	O-46	-1.8
1939	Cle-A	41	102	19	28	7	2	2	19	9	15	.275	.333	.441	100	-0	2	1	0	.915	-3	O-25	-0.4
Total	9	938	3421	503	990	213	42	83	599	221	377	.289	.340	.449	96	-32	42	23	-1	.960	36	O-825	-3.1
Team	3	260	890	139	258	55	16	24	150	64	99	.290	.340	.469	102	-2	12	11	-3	.952	1	O-220	-1.0
■ CHICK SORRELLS	Sorrells, Raymond Edwin b: 7/31/1896, Stringtown, Okla. d: 7/20/83, Terrell, Tex. BR/TR, 5'9", 155 lbs. Deb: 9/18/22																					
1922	Cle-A	2	1	0	0	0	0	0	0	0	0	.000	.000	.000	-99	-0	0	0	0	1.000	1	/S-1	0.1
■ PAUL SORRENTO	Sorrento, Paul Anthony b: 11/17/65, Somerville, Mass. BL/TR, 6'2", 195 lbs. Deb: 9/8/89																					
1992	Cle-A	140	458	52	123	24	1	18	60	51	89	.269	.343	.443	121	12	0	3	-2	.993	-1	*1-121,D-11	0.1
1993	Cle-A	148	463	75	119	26	1	18	65	58	121	.257	.342	.434	108	5	3	1	0	.995	0	*1-144/O-3,D	-0.5
1994	Cle-A	95	322	43	90	14	0	14	62	34	68	.280	.348	.453	104	2	0	1	-1	.995	1	1-86/D-8	-0.5
1995	*Cle-A	104	323	50	76	14	0	25	79	51	71	.235	.340	.511	117	7	1	1	-0	.992	-1	1-91,D-11	-0.4
Total	7	568	1755	239	450	84	3	84	293	215	395	.256	.339	.451	110	23	5	7	-3	.994	-2	1-475/D-61,O	-1.9
Team	4	487	1566	220	408	78	2	75	266	194	349	.261	.343	.457	113	26	4	6	-2	.994	-2	1-442/D-31,O	-1.3
■ BILLY SOUTHWORTH	Southworth, William Harrison b: 3/9/1893, Harvard, Neb. d: 11/15/69, Columbus, Ohio BL/TR, 5'9", 170 lbs. Deb: 8/4/13 MC																					
1913	Cle-A	1	0	0	0	0	0	0	0	0	0	—	—	—	—	0	0			.000	0	/O-1	0.0
1915	Cle-A	60	177	25	39	2	5	0	8	36	12	.220	.352	.288	90	-1	2	4		.942	1	O-44	-0.4
Total	13	1192	4359	661	1296	173	91	52	561	402	148	.297	.359	.415	111	69	138	<u>85</u>		.965	23	*O-1115/2-2	-0.8
Team	2	61	177	25	39	2	5	0	8	36	12	.220	.352	.288	90	-1	2	<u>4</u>		.942	1	/O-45	-0.4
■ TRIS SPEAKER	Speaker, Tristram E "The Grey Eagle" b: 4/4/1888, Hubbard, Tex. d: 12/8/58, Lake Whitney, Tex. BL/TL, 5'11.5", 193 lbs. Deb: 9/14/07 MH																					
1916	Cle-A	151	546	102	**211**	**41**	8	2	79	82	20	**.386**	**.470**	.502	181	57	35	27	-6	.975	9	*O-151	**5.7**
1917	Cle-A	142	523	90	184	42	11	2	60	67	14	.352	.432	.486	168	43	30			.980	8	*O-142	4.7
1918	Cle-A	127	471	73	150	**33**	11	0	61	64	9	.318	.403	.435	140	23	27			.973	11	*O-127	3.0
1919	Cle-A	134	494	83	146	38	12	2	63	73	12	.296	.395	.433	125	18	15			.983	19	*O-134,M	2.9
1920	*Cle-A	150	552	137	214	**50**	11	8	107	97	13	**.388**	**.483**	.562	171	61	10	13	-5	.977	10	*O-148,M	5.2
1921	Cle-A	132	506	107	183	**52**	14	3	75	68	12	.362	.439	.538	146	37	2	4	-2	**.984**	10	*O-128,M	3.3
1922	Cle-A	131	426	85	161	**48**	8	11	71	77	11	.378	**.474**	.606	178	52	8	3	1	**.983**	8	*O-109,M	5.0
1923	Cle-A	150	574	133	218	**59**	11	17	130	93	15	.380	.469	.610	183	71	8	9	-3	.968	10	*O-150,M	6.4
1924	Cle-A	135	486	94	167	36	9	9	65	72	13	.344	.432	.510	141	31	5	7	-3	.963	5	*O-128,M	2.3
1925	Cle-A	117	429	79	167	35	5	12	87	70	12	.389	**.479**	.578	166	46	5	3		.967	10	O-109,M	**4.5**

YEAR	TM/L	G	AB	R	H	2B	3B	HR	RBI	BB	SO	AVG	OBP	SLG	PRO+	BR/A	SB	CS	SBR	FA	FR	G/POS	TPR
1926	Cle-A	150	539	96	164	52	8	7	86	94	15	.304	.408	.469	127	23	6	1	1	.981	10	*O-149,M	2.4
Total	22	2789	10195	1882	3514	792	222	117	1529	1381	220	.345	.428	.500	156	793	432	129		.970	248	*O-2698/1-18,P	86.5
Team	11	1519	5546	1079	1965	486	108	73	884	857	146	.354	.444	.520	157	463	151	66		.976	110	*O-1475	45.4

■ HORACE SPEED Speed, Horace Arthur b: 10/4/51, Los Angeles, Cal. BR/TR, 6'1", 180 lbs. Deb: 4/10/75

YEAR	TM/L	G	AB	R	H	2B	3B	HR	RBI	BB	SO	AVG	OBP	SLG	PRO+	BR/A	SB	CS	SBR	FA	FR	G/POS	TPR
1978	Cle-A	70	106	13	24	4	1	0	4	14	31	.226	.322	.283	72	-3	2	4	-2	.977	-12	O-61/D-3	-1.9
1979	Cle-A	26	14	6	2	0	0	0	1	5	7	.143	.368	.143	44	-1	2	1	0	.875	-5	O-16/D-4	-0.5
Total	3	113	135	21	28	5	1	0	6	20	46	.207	.318	.259	63	-6	4	5	-2	.956	-19	/O-86,D-7	-2.8
Team	2	96	120	19	26	4	1	0	5	19	38	.217	.329	.267	69	-4	4	5	-2	.962	-17	/O-77,D-7	-2.4

■ ROY SPENCER Spencer, Roy Hampton b: 2/22/1900, Scranton, N.C. d: 2/8/73, Port Charlotte, Fla BR/TR, 5'10", 168 lbs. Deb: 4/19/25

YEAR	TM/L	G	AB	R	H	2B	3B	HR	RBI	BB	SO	AVG	OBP	SLG	PRO+	BR/A	SB	CS	SBR	FA	FR	G/POS	TPR
1933	Cle-A	75	227	26	46	5	2	0	23	23	17	.203	.282	.242	38	-20	0	0	0	.990	5	C-72	-1.0
1934	Cle-A	5	7	0	1	1	0	0	2	0	1	.143	.143	.286	8	-1	0	0	0	1.000	1	/C-4	0.0
Total	12	636	1814	177	448	57	13	3	203	128	130	.247	.301	.298	56	-115	4	1	1	.984	16	C-585	-5.9
Team	2	80	234	26	47	6	2	0	25	23	18	.201	.278	.244	37	-21	0	0	0	.990	6	/C-76	-1.0

■ CHARLIE SPIKES Spikes, Leslie Charles b: 1/23/51, Bogalusa, La. BR/TR, 6'3", 220 lbs. Deb: 9/1/72

YEAR	TM/L	G	AB	R	H	2B	3B	HR	RBI	BB	SO	AVG	OBP	SLG	PRO+	BR/A	SB	CS	SBR	FA	FR	G/POS	TPR
1973	Cle-A	140	506	68	120	12	3	23	73	45	103	.237	.306	.409	98	-3	5	3	-0	.964	5	*O-111,D-26	-0.4
1974	Cle-A	155	568	63	154	23	1	22	80	34	100	.271	.320	.431	116	9	10	7	-1	.968	0	*O-154	0.2
1975	Cle-A	111	345	41	79	13	3	11	33	30	51	.229	.291	.380	88	-6	7	6	-2	.974	1	*O-103/D-2	-1.1
1976	Cle-A	101	334	34	79	11	5	3	31	23	50	.237	.296	.326	83	-7	5	6	-2	.985	1	O-98/D-2	-1.3
1977	Cle-A	32	95	13	22	2	0	3	11	11	17	.232	.324	.347	86	-2	0	2	-1	.972	-3	O-27/D-2	-0.7
Total	9	670	2039	240	502	72	12	65	256	154	388	.246	.306	.389	96	-14	27	25	-7	.969	-2	O-533/D-32	-4.9
Team	5	539	1848	219	454	61	12	62	228	143	321	.246	.306	.392	98	-9	27	24	-6	.972	5	O-493/D-32	-3.3

■ STEVE SPRINGER Springer, Steven Michael b: 2/11/61, Long Beach, Cal. BR/TR, 6', 190 lbs. Deb: 5/22/90

YEAR	TM/L	G	AB	R	H	2B	3B	HR	RBI	BB	SO	AVG	OBP	SLG	PRO+	BR/A	SB	CS	SBR	FA	FR	G/POS	TPR
1990	Cle-A	4	12	1	2	0	0	0	1	0	6	.167	.167	.167	-7	-2	0	0	0	1.000	-1	/3-3,D-1	-0.2
Total	2	8	17	1	4	1	0	0	1	0	7	.235	.235	.294	48	-1	0	0	0	1.000	-1	/3-4,2-1,D	-0.2

■ JOE SPRINZ Sprinz, Joseph Conrad "Mule" b: 8/3/02, St.Louis, Mo. d: 1/11/94, Fremont, Cal. BR/TR, 5'11", 185 lbs. Deb: 7/16/30

YEAR	TM/L	G	AB	R	H	2B	3B	HR	RBI	BB	SO	AVG	OBP	SLG	PRO+	BR/A	SB	CS	SBR	FA	FR	G/POS	TPR
1930	Cle-A	17	45	5	8	1	0	0	2	4	4	.178	.245	.200	14	-6	0	0	0	1.000	6	C-17	0.1
1931	Cle-A	1	3	0	0	0	0	0	0	0	0	.000	.000	.000	-95	-1	0	0	0	1.000	0	/C-1	-0.1
Total	3	21	53	6	9	1	0	0	2	5	5	.170	.241	.189	12	-7	0	0	0	1.000	8	/C-21	0.2
Team	2	18	48	5	8	1	0	0	2	4	4	.167	.231	.188	7	-7	0	0	0	1.000	6	/C-18	0.0

■ FREDDY SPURGEON Spurgeon, Fred b: 10/9/1900, Wabash, Ind. d: 11/5/70, Kalamazoo, Mich. BR/TR, 5'11.5", 160 lbs. Deb: 9/19/24

YEAR	TM/L	G	AB	R	H	2B	3B	HR	RBI	BB	SO	AVG	OBP	SLG	PRO+	BR/A	SB	CS	SBR	FA	FR	G/POS	TPR
1924	Cle-A	3	7	0	1	1	0	0	0	0	0	.143	.250	.286	37	-1	0	0	0	.882	1	/2-3	0.0
1925	Cle-A	107	376	50	108	9	3	0	32	15	21	.287	.315	.327	62	-22	8	5	-1	.927	-4	3-56,2-46/S	-2.0
1926	Cle-A	149	614	101	181	31	3	0	49	27	36	.295	.327	.355	77	-21	7	2	1	.962	-8	*2-149	-2.3
1927	Cle-A	57	179	30	45	6	1	1	19	18	14	.251	.323	.313	65	-9	8	1	2	.938	-8	2-52	-1.3
Total	4	316	1176	181	335	47	7	1	100	60	71	.285	.322	.339	70	-53	23	8	2	.958	-19	2-250/3-56,S	-5.6

■ FRED STANLEY Stanley, Frederick Blair b: 8/13/47, Farnhamville, Iowa BR/TR, 5'10", 167 lbs. Deb: 9/11/69 C

YEAR	TM/L	G	AB	R	H	2B	3B	HR	RBI	BB	SO	AVG	OBP	SLG	PRO+	BR/A	SB	CS	SBR	FA	FR	G/POS	TPR
1971	Cle-A	60	129	14	29	4	0	2	12	27	25	.225	.363	.302	83	-2	1	0	0	.971	7	S-55/2-3	1.1
1972	Cle-A	6	12	1	2	1	0	0	0	2	3	.167	.286	.250	58	-1	0	0	0	.917	-3	/S-5,2-1	-0.4
Total	14	816	1650	197	356	38	5	10	120	196	243	.216	.302	.263	62	-80	11	6	-0	.971	-19	S-648,2-128/301	-4.7
Team	2	66	141	15	31	5	0	2	12	29	28	.220	.357	.298	81	-2	1	0	0	.968	3	/S-60,2-4	0.7

■ DOLLY STARK Stark, Monroe Randolph b: 1/19/1885, Ripley, Miss. d: 12/1/24, Memphis, Tenn. BR/TR, 5'9", 160 lbs. Deb: 9/12/09

YEAR	TM/L	G	AB	R	H	2B	3B	HR	RBI	BB	SO	AVG	OBP	SLG	PRO+	BR/A	SB	CS	SBR	FA	FR	G/POS	TPR
1909	Cle-A	19	60	4	12	0	0	0	1	6		.200	.273	.200	48	-3	4			.875	-10	S-19	-1.5
Total	4	127	378	38	90	7	1	0	30	34		.238	.308	.262	66	-15	14			.896	-14	/S-90,2-18,3	-2.9

■ GEORGE STARNAGLE Starnagle, George Henry (b: George Henry Steuernagel)
b: 10/6/1873, Belleville, Ill. d: 2/15/46, Belleville, Ill. BR/TR, 5'11", 175 lbs. Deb: 9/14/02

YEAR	TM/L	G	AB	R	H	2B	3B	HR	RBI	BB	SO	AVG	OBP	SLG	PRO+	BR/A	SB	CS	SBR	FA	FR	G/POS	TPR
1902	Cle-A	1	3	0	0	0	0	0	0	0		.000	.000	.000	-99	-1	0			.667	-1	/C-1	-0.1

■ RED STEINER Steiner, James Harry b: 1/7/15, Los Angeles, Cal. BL/TR, 6', 185 lbs. Deb: 5/11/45

YEAR	TM/L	G	AB	R	H	2B	3B	HR	RBI	BB	SO	AVG	OBP	SLG	PRO+	BR/A	SB	CS	SBR	FA	FR	G/POS	TPR
1945	Cle-A	12	20	0	3	0	0	0	2	1	4	.150	.190	.150	-1	-3	0	0	0	1.000	1	/C-4	-0.2

■ RIGGS STEPHENSON Stephenson, Jackson Riggs "Old Hoss" b: 1/5/1898, Akron, Ala. d: 11/15/85, Tuscaloosa, Ala. BR/TR, 5'10", 185 lbs. Deb: 4/13/21

YEAR	TM/L	G	AB	R	H	2B	3B	HR	RBI	BB	SO	AVG	OBP	SLG	PRO+	BR/A	SB	CS	SBR	FA	FR	G/POS	TPR
1921	Cle-A	65	206	45	68	17	2	2	34	23	15	.330	.408	.461	119	7	4	1	1	.942	-1	2-54/3-2	0.7
1922	Cle-A	86	233	47	79	24	5	2	32	27	18	.339	.421	.511	141	15	3	0	1	.952	-6	3-34,2-25/O	1.2
1923	Cle-A	91	301	48	96	20	6	5	65	15	25	.319	.357	.475	118	6	5	5	-2	.970	11	2-66/O-3,3	1.6
1924	Cle-A	71	240	33	89	20	0	4	44	27	10	.371	.439	.504	141	15	1	2	-1	.961	-13	2-58/O-7	0.1
1925	Cle-A	19	54	8	16	3	1	1	9	7	3	.296	.387	.444	110	1	1	1	-0	.946	1	O-16	0.1
Total	14	1310	4508	714	1515	321	54	63	773	494	247	.336	.407	.473	130	206	53	9	11	.978	-21	O-913,2-203/3	12.8
Team	5	332	1034	181	348	84	14	14	184	99	71	.337	.403	.485	128	44	14	9	-1	.958	-8	2-203/3-38,O	3.7

■ SNUFFY STIRNWEISS Stirnweiss, George Henry b: 10/26/18, New York, N.Y. d: 9/15/58, Newark Bay, N.J. BR/TR, 5'8.5", 175 lbs. Deb: 4/22/43

YEAR	TM/L	G	AB	R	H	2B	3B	HR	RBI	BB	SO	AVG	OBP	SLG	PRO+	BR/A	SB	CS	SBR	FA	FR	G/POS	TPR
1951	Cle-A	50	88	10	19	1	0	1	4	22	25	.216	.373	.261	78	-2	1	0	0	.992	7	2-25/3-2	0.7
1952	Cle-A	1	0	0	0	0	0	0	0	0	0	—	—	—	—	0	0	0	0	.000	0	/3-1	0.0
Total	10	1028	3695	604	989	157	68	29	281	541	447	.268	.362	.371	102	19	134	55	7	.980	-1	2-787,3-117/S	8.2
Team	2	51	88	10	19	1	0	1	4	22	25	.216	.373	.261	78	-2	1	0	0	.992	7	/2-25,3-3	0.7

■ GEORGE STOVALL Stovall, George Thomas "Firebrand" b: 11/23/1878, Independence, Mo. d: 11/5/51, Burlington, Iowa BR/TR, 6'2", 180 lbs. Deb: 7/4/04 FM

YEAR	TM/L	G	AB	R	H	2B	3B	HR	RBI	BB	SO	AVG	OBP	SLG	PRO+	BR/A	SB	CS	SBR	FA	FR	G/POS	TPR
1904	Cle-A	52	181	18	54	10	1	1	31	2		.298	.317	.381	121	4	3			.978	-2	1-38/2-9,O3	0.1
1905	Cle-A	112	423	41	115	31	1	1	47	13		.272	.295	.357	105	1	13			.975	-5	1-60,2-46/O	-0.6
1906	Cle-A	116	443	54	121	19	5	0	37	8		.273	.288	.339	97	-3	15			.985	-5	1-55,3-30,2	-0.9
1907	Cle-A	124	466	38	110	17	6	1	36	18		.236	.267	.305	82	-11	13			.983	-4	*1-122/3-2	-2.0
1908	Cle-A	138	534	71	156	29	6	2	45	17		.292	.316	.380	126	13	14			**.990**	3	*1-132/O-5,S	1.5
1909	Cle-A	145	565	60	139	17	10	2	49	6		.246	.259	.322	80	-15	25			**.988**	10	*1-145	-0.8
1910	Cle-A	142	521	49	136	19	4	0	52	14		.261	.284	.313	86	-10	16			**.988**	7	*1-132/2-2	-0.4
1911	Cle-A	126	458	48	124	17	7	0	79	21		.271	.306	.338	79	-14	11			**.986**	7	*1-118/2-2M	-0.8
Total	12	1414	5222	547	1382	231	56	15	564	172		.265	.292	.339	89	-93	142			.986	33	*1-1217/2-78,3OS	-8.6
Team	8	955	3591	379	955	159	40	7	376	99		.266	.289	.338	94	-37	110			.986	12	1-802/2-78,3OS	-3.9

■ GEORGE STRICKLAND Strickland, George Bevan "Bo" b: 1/10/26, New Orleans, La. BR/TR, 6'1", 180 lbs. Deb: 5/7/50 MC

YEAR	TM/L	G	AB	R	H	2B	3B	HR	RBI	BB	SO	AVG	OBP	SLG	PRO+	BR/A	SB	CS	SBR	FA	FR	G/POS	TPR
1952	Cle-A	31	88	8	19	4	0	1	8	14	15	.216	.324	.295	78	-2	0	0	0	.964	10	S-30/2-1	0.9
1953	Cle-A	123	419	43	119	17	4	5	47	51	52	.284	.362	.379	103	3	0	0	0	.974	16	*S-122/1-1	2.7
1954	*Cle-A	112	361	42	77	12	3	6	37	55	62	.213	.319	.313	72	-13	2	1	0	.961	-12	*S-112	-1.6
1955	Cle-A	130	388	34	81	9	5	2	34	49	60	.209	.302	.273	54	-25	1	0	0	**.976**	8	*S-128	-0.6
1956	Cle-A	85	171	22	36	1	2	3	17	22	27	.211	.301	.292	56	-11	0	1	-1	.986	16	2-28,S-28,3	0.8
1957	Cle-A	89	201	21	47	8	2	1	19	26	29	.234	.325	.308	75	-7	0	3	-2	.980	15	2-48,S-23,3	1.1
1959	Cle-A	132	441	55	105	15	2	3	48	51	64	.238	.317	.302	74	-15	1	1	-0	.971	-9	3-80,S-50/2	-2.0

YEAR	TM/L	G	AB	R	H	2B	3B	HR	RBI	BB	SO	AVG	OBP	SLG	PRO+	BR/A	SB	CS	SBR	FA	FR	G/POS	TPR
1960	Cle-A	32	42	4	7	0	0	1	3	4	8	.167	.255	.238	35	-4	0	0	0	.962	1	S-14,3-12/2	-0.3
Total	10	971	2824	305	633	84	27	36	284	361	453	.224	.314	.311	70	-112	12	10		.963	74	S-679,2-141,3/1	1.6
Team	8	734	2111	229	491	66	18	22	213	272	317	.233	.322	.312	73	-74	4	6		.969	44	S-507,3-137/21	1.0
■ KEN SUAREZ	Suarez, Kenneth Raymond b: 4/12/43, Tampa, Fla. BR/TR, 5'9", 175 lbs. Deb: 4/14/66																						
1968	Cle-A	17	10	1	1	0	0	0	0	1	3	.100	.182	.100	-13	-1	0	0	0	1.000	1	C-12/2-1,3O	0.0
1969	Cle-A	36	85	7	25	5	0	1	9	15	12	.294	.400	.388	117	3	1	0	0	.991	6	C-36	1.0
1971	Cle-A	50	123	10	25	7	0	1	9	18	15	.203	.315	.285	65	-5	0	1	-1	.993	9	C-48	0.4
Total	7	295	661	57	150	29	1	5	60	99	97	.227	.334	.297	81	-13	5	3	-0	.984	31	C-273/O-1,32	2.8
Team	3	103	218	18	51	12	0	2	18	34	30	.234	.343	.317	82	-4	1	1	-0	.992	16	/C-96,O-1,32	1.4
■ BILL SUDAKIS	Sudakis, William Paul "Suds" b: 3/27/46, Joliet, Ill. BB/TR, 6'1", 190 lbs. Deb: 9/3/68																						
1975	Cle-A	20	46	4	9	0	0	1	3	4	7	.196	.260	.261	48	-3	0	1	-1	1.000	-1	1-12/C-6	-0.5
Total	8	530	1548	177	362	56	7	59	214	172	313	.234	.313	.393	102	2	9	6	-1	.942	6	3-217/C-83,1DO	0.5
■ DENNY SULLIVAN	Sullivan, Dennis William b: 9/28/1882, Hillsboro, Wis. d: 6/2/56, W.Los Angeles, Cal BL/TR, 5'10", Deb: 4/22/05																						
1908	Cle-A	4	6	0	0	0	0	0	0	0		.000	.000	.000	-99	-1	0			1.000	-0	/O-2	-0.2
1909	Cle-A	3	2	0	1	0	0	0	0	0		.500	.500	.500	207	0	0			.000	-1	/O-2	-0.1
Total	4	255	925	106	221	25	8	1	51	59		.239	.296	.286	87	-13	30			.978	6	O-247	-1.8
Team	2	7	8	0	1	0	0	0	0	0		.125	.125	.125	-19	-1	0			1.000	-1	/O-4	-0.3
■ BILLY SULLIVAN	Sullivan, William Joseph Jr. b: 10/23/10, Chicago, Ill. d: 1/4/94, Sarasota, Fla. BL/TR, 6', 170 lbs. Deb: 6/9/31 F																						
1936	Cle-A	93	319	39	112	32	6	2	48	16	9	.351	.382	.508	117	7	5	2	0	.968	-2	C-72/3-5,1O	0.8
1937	Cle-A	72	168	26	48	12	3	3	22	17	7	.286	.355	.446	100	-0	1	4	-2	.949	-6	C-38/1-5,3	-0.6
Total	12	962	2840	347	820	152	32	29	388	240	119	.289	.346	.395	91	-40	30	24		.972	-11	C-414,1-133,3/O2	-3.7
Team	2	165	487	65	160	44	9	5	70	33	16	.329	.372	.487	111	7	6	6		.962	-8	C-110/1-8,3O	0.2
■ HOMER SUMMA	Summa, Homer Wayne b: 11/3/1898, Gentry, Mo. d: 1/29/66, Los Angeles, Cal. BL/TR, 5'10.5", 170 lbs. Deb: 9/13/20																						
1922	Cle-A	12	46	9	16	3	3	1	6	1	1	.348	.400	.609	159	4	1	2	-1	1.000	0	O-12	0.2
1923	Cle-A	137	525	92	172	27	6	3	69	33	20	.328	.374	.419	109	6	9	13	-5	.951	-13	*O-136	-1.9
1924	Cle-A	111	390	55	113	21	6	2	38	11	16	.290	.311	.390	79	-14	4	2	0	.941	-6	O-95	-2.4
1925	Cle-A	75	224	28	74	10	1	0	25	13	6	.330	.375	.384	92	-2	3	2	-0	.966	-9	O-54/3-2	-1.3
1926	Cle-A	154	581	74	179	31	6	4	76	47	9	.308	.368	.403	100	0	15	8	-0	.975	7	*O-154	-0.3
1927	Cle-A	145	574	73	164	41	7	4	74	32	18	.286	.331	.402	89	-11	6	5	-1	.955	-8	*O-145	-2.8
1928	Cle-A	134	504	60	143	26	3	3	57	20	15	.284	.319	.365	78	-16	4	2	0	.971	-4	*O-132	-2.9
Total	10	840	3001	414	905	166	34	18	361	166	88	.302	.346	.398	92	-38	44	35	-8	.961	-36	O-773/3-2	-12.5
Team	7	768	2844	391	861	159	32	17	345	157	85	.303	.347	.399	93	-33	42	34	-8	.961	-32	O-728/3-2	-11.4
■ GEORGE SUSCE	Susce, George Cyril Methodius "Good Kid" b: 8/13/08, Pittsburgh, Pa. d: 2/25/86, Sarasota, Fla. BR/TR, 5'11.5", 200 lbs. Deb: 4/23/29 FC																						
1941	Cle-A	1	0	0	0	0	0	0	0	0	0	—	—	—	—	0	0	0	0	1.000	-0	/C-1	0.0
1942	Cle-A	2	1	1	1	0	0	0	0	1	0	1.000	1.000	1.000	492	1	0	0	0	1.000	-0	/C-2	0.1
1943	Cle-A	3	1	0	0	0	0	0	0	0	0	.000	.000	.000	-99	-0	0	0	0	1.000	1	/C-3	0.0
1944	Cle-A	29	61	3	14	1	0	0	4	2	5	.230	.254	.246	45	-4	0	0	0	.948	1	C-29	-0.2
Total	8	146	268	23	61	11	1	2	22	25	21	.228	.301	.299	60	-15	1	0	0	.974	8	C-140	-0.1
Team	4	35	63	4	15	1	0	0	4	3	5	.238	.273	.254	53	-4	0	0	0	.950	1	/C-35	-0.1
■ JOSH SWINDELL	Swindell, Joshua Ernest b: 7/5/1883, Rose Hill, Kan. d: 3/19/69, Fruita, Colo. BR/TR, 6', 180 lbs. Deb: 9/16/11																						
1911	Cle-A	4	4	0	1	0	0	0	0	0		.250	.250	.250	39	-0	0			.800	-0	/P-4	0.0
1913	Cle-A	1	0	0	0	0	0	0	0	0	0	—	—	—	—	0	0			.000	0	H	0.0
Total	2	5	4	0	1	0	0	0	0	0	0	.250	.250	.250	39	-0	0			.800	-0	/P-4	0.0
■ PAT TABLER	Tabler, Patrick Sean b: 2/2/58, Hamilton, Ohio BR/TR, 6'2", 200 lbs. Deb: 8/21/81																						
1983	Cle-A	124	430	56	125	23	5	6	65	56	63	.291	.374	.409	111	8	2	4	-2	.948	-3	O-88,3-25/2D	0.0
1984	Cle-A	144	473	66	137	21	3	10	68	47	62	.290	.358	.410	110	7	3	1	0	.998	-13	1-67,O-43,3/2D	-1.1
1985	Cle-A	117	404	47	111	18	3	5	59	27	55	.275	.323	.371	90	-5	0	6	-4	.983	1	1-92,D-18/32	-1.4
1986	Cle-A	130	473	61	154	29	2	6	48	29	75	.326	.368	.433	119	13	3	1	0	.990	1	*1-107,D-18	0.6
1987	Cle-A★	151	553	66	170	34	3	11	86	51	84	.307	.372	.439	113	12	5	2	0	.984	5	1-82,D-66	0.9
1988	Cle-A	41	143	16	32	5	1	1	17	23	27	.224	.335	.294	76	-4	1	0	0	1.000	-1	D-29,1-10	-0.6
Total	12	1202	3911	454	1101	190	25	47	512	375	559	.282	.348	.379	99	3	16	20		.988	-14	1-444,D-291,O/32	-6.4
Team	6	707	2476	312	729	130	17	39	343	233	366	.294	.359	.408	108	30	14	14		.988	-10	1-358,D-138,O/32	-1.6
■ CHUCK TANNER	Tanner, Charles William b: 7/4/29, New Castle, Pa. BL/TL, 6', 185 lbs. Deb: 4/12/55 FM																						
1959	Cle-A	14	48	6	12	2	0	1	5	2	9	.250	.280	.354	76	-2	0	0	0	1.000	-1	O-10	-0.3
1960	Cle-A	21	25	2	7	1	0	0	4	4	6	.280	.379	.320	94	-0	1	0	0	1.000	-1	/O-4	0.0
Total	8	396	885	98	231	39	5	21	105	82	93	.261	.325	.388	93	-10	2	2	-1	.983	-13	O-202	-3.2
Team	2	35	73	8	19	3	0	1	9	6	15	.260	.316	.342	83	-2	1	0	0	1.000	-2	/O-14	-0.3
■ WILLIE TASBY	Tasby, Willie b: 1/8/33, Shreveport, La. BR/TR, 5'11", 175 lbs. Deb: 9/9/58																						
1962	Cle-A	75	199	25	48	7	0	4	17	25	41	.241	.326	.337	81	-5	0	2	-1	1.000	-12	O-66/3-1	-2.2
1963	Cle-A	52	116	11	26	3	1	4	5	15	25	.224	.318	.371	93	-1	0	1	-1	.981	-5	O-37/2-1	-0.8
Total	6	583	1868	246	467	61	10	46	174	201	327	.250	.328	.367	89	-28	12	20	-8	.980	-22	O-543/2-1,3	-8.7
Team	2	127	315	36	74	10	1	8	22	40	66	.235	.323	.349	86	-6	0	3	-2	.994	-17	O-103/2-1,3	-3.0
■ EDDIE TAUBENSEE	Taubensee, Edward Kenneth b: 10/31/68, Beeville, Tex. BL/TR, 6'3", 205 lbs. Deb: 5/18/91																						
1991	Cle-A	26	66	5	16	2	1	0	8	5	16	.242	.296	.303	66	-3	0	0	0	.979	-7	C-25	-0.9
Total	5	370	1056	115	269	50	6	31	143	94	221	.255	.318	.402	95	-9	7	3	0	.989	-9	C-349/1-3	0.1
■ JACKIE TAVENER	Tavener, John Adam "Rabbit" b: 12/27/1897, Celina, Ohio d: 9/14/69, Fort Worth, Tex. BL/TR, 5'5", 138 lbs. Deb: 9/24/21																						
1929	Cle-A	92	250	25	53	9	4	2	27	26	28	.212	.289	.304	51	-19	1	4	-2	.945	23	S-89	1.1
Total	6	632	2131	254	543	88	53	13	243	186	231	.255	.318	.364	75	-82	46	31	-5	.951	58	S-626	3.7
■ SAMMY TAYLOR	Taylor, Samuel Douglas b: 2/27/33, Woodruff, S.C. BL/TR, 6'2", 185 lbs. Deb: 4/27/58																						
1963	Cle-A	4	10	1	3	0	0	0	1	0	2	.300	.300	.300	69	-0	0	0	0	1.000	-1	/C-2	-0.1
Total	6	473	1263	127	309	47	9	33	147	122	181	.245	.315	.375	84	-29	3	2	-0	.986	-55	C-387	-6.8
■ BIRDIE TEBBETTS	Tebbetts, George Robert b: 11/10/12, Burlington, Vt. BR/TR, 5'11.5", 170 lbs. Deb: 9/16/36 M																						
1951	Cle-A	55	137	8	36	6	0	2	18	8	7	.263	.308	.350	82	-4	0	0	0	.977	-1	C-44	-0.3
1952	Cle-A	42	101	4	25	4	0	1	8	12	9	.248	.339	.317	89	-1	0	1	-1	.986	-4	C-37	-0.4
Total	14	1162	3704	357	1000	169	22	38	469	389	261	.270	.341	.358	81	-103	29	23	-5	.978	19	*C-1108	-2.1
Team	2	97	238	12	61	10	0	3	26	20	16	.256	.322	.336	85	-5	0	1	-1	.981	-5	/C-81	-0.7
■ JOHNNY TEMPLE	Temple, John Ellis b: 8/8/27, Lexington, N.C. d: 1/9/94, Anderson, S.C. BR/TR, 5'11", 175 lbs. Deb: 4/15/52 C																						
1960	Cle-A	98	381	50	102	13	1	2	19	32	20	.268	.326	.323	79	-11	11	5	0	.974	-30	2-77,3-17	-3.4
1961	Cle-A★	129	518	73	143	22	3	3	30	61	36	.276	.352	.347	90	-6	9	5	-0	.969	-30	*2-129	-2.2
Total	13	1420	5218	720	1484	208	36	22	395	648	338	.284	.365	.351	91	-46	140	48	13	.974	-183	*2-1312/3-47,1OS	-11.2
Team	2	227	899	123	245	35	4	5	49	93	56	.273	.341	.337	85	-17	20	10	0	.971	-59	2-206/3-17	-5.6

YEAR	TM/L	G	AB	R	H	2B	3B	HR	RBI	BB	SO	AVG	OBP	SLG	PRO+	BR/A	SB	CS	SBR	FA	FR	G/POS	TPR
■ **PINCH THOMAS**	Thomas, Chester David b: 1/24/1888, Camp Point, Ill. d: 12/24/53, Modesto, Cal. BL/TR, 5′9.5″, 173 lbs. Deb: 4/24/12																						
1918	Cle-A	32	73	2	18	0	1	0	5	6	6	.247	.304	.274	68	-3	0			.948	1	C-24	-0.1
1919	Cle-A	34	46	2	5	0	0	0	2	4	3	.109	.180	.109	-17	-7	0			.980	-2	C-21	-0.8
1920	*Cle-A	9	9	2	3	1	0	0	0	3	1	.333	.500	.444	147	1	0	0	0	1.000	1	/C-7	0.2
1921	Cle-A	21	35	1	9	3	0	0	4	10	2	.257	.422	.343	96	0	0	0	0	.882	-6	C-19	-0.5
Total	10	481	1035	88	245	27	8	2	102	118	82	.237	.318	.284	78	-25	12	2		.973	-5	C-423/1-1	-0.3
Team	4	96	163	7	35	4	1	0	11	23	12	.215	.312	.252	56	-9	0	0		.949	-6	/C-71	-1.2
■ **GORMAN THOMAS**	Thomas, James Gorman b: 12/12/50, Charleston, S.C. BR/TR, 6′2″, 210 lbs. Deb: 4/6/73																						
1983	Cle-A	106	371	51	82	17	0	17	51	57	98	.221	.326	.404	96	-2	8	3	1	.982	12	*O-106	0.7
Total	13	1435	4677	681	1051	212	13	268	782	697	1339	.225	.328	.448	114	86	50	49	-14	.984	1	*O-1159,D-246/13	2.7
■ **VALMY THOMAS**	Thomas, Valmy b: 10/21/28, Santurce, P.R. BR/TR, 5′9″, 165 lbs. Deb: 4/16/57																						
1961	Cle-A	27	86	7	18	3	0	2	6	6	7	.209	.261	.314	54	-6	0	0	0	.988	9	C-27	0.4
Total	5	252	626	56	144	20	3	12	60	45	79	.230	.285	.329	64	-33	2	1	0	.988	29	C-249/3-1	0.5
■ **ART THOMASON**	Thomason, Arthur Wilson b: 2/12/1889, Liberty, Mo. d: 5/2/44, Kansas City, Mo. BL/TL, 5′8″, 150 lbs. Deb: 8/10/10																						
1910	Cle-A	20	70	4	12	0	1	0	2	5		.171	.227	.200	33	-5	3			.944	2	O-20	-0.5
■ **JIM THOME**	Thome, James Howard b: 8/27/70, Peoria, Ill. BL/TR, 6′3″, 190 lbs. Deb: 9/4/91																						
1991	Cle-A	27	98	7	25	4	2	1	9	5	16	.255	.298	.367	82	-2	1	1	-0	.900	1	3-27	-0.2
1992	Cle-A	40	117	8	24	3	1	2	12	10	34	.205	.279	.299	63	-6	2	0	1	.882	-6	3-40	-1.2
1993	Cle-A	47	154	28	41	11	0	7	22	29	36	.266	.396	.474	133	8	2	1	0	.950	-2	3-47	0.6
1994	Cle-A	98	321	58	86	20	1	20	52	46	84	.268	.360	.523	124	11	3	3	-1	.940	-1	3-94	0.9
1995	*Cle-A	137	452	92	142	29	3	25	73	97	113	.314	.440	.558	157	42	4	3	-1	.948	-14	*3-134/D-1	2.6
Total	5	349	1142	193	318	67	7	55	168	187	283	.278	.386	.494	130	53	12	8	-1	.934	-21	3-342/D-1	2.7
■ **JACK THONEY**	Thoney, John "Bullet Jack" (b: John Thoeny) b: 12/8/1879, Ft.Thomas, Ky. d: 10/24/48, Covington, Ky. BR/TR, 5′10″, 175 lbs. Deb: 4/26/02																						
1902	Cle-A	28	105	14	30	7	1	0	11	9		.286	.342	.371	102	0	4			.891	-15	2-14,S-11/O	-1.3
1903	Cle-A	32	122	10	25	3	0	1	9	2		.205	.218	.254	42	-9	7			.889	1	O-24/2-5,3	-0.9
Total	6	264	912	112	216	23	12	3	73	36		.237	.269	.298	75	-27	42			.929	-4	O-164/3-31,2S	-3.8
Team	2	60	227	24	55	10	1	1	20	11		.242	.277	.308	71	-8	11			.899	-14	/O-26,2-19,S3	-2.2
■ **ANDY THORNTON**	Thornton, Andre b: 8/13/49, Tuskegee, Ala. BR/TR, 6′2″, 205 lbs. Deb: 7/28/73																						
1977	Cle-A	131	433	77	114	20	5	28	70	70	82	.263	.379	.527	149	30	3	4	-2	.995	-3	*1-117/D-9	1.9
1978	Cle-A	145	508	97	133	22	4	33	105	93	72	.262	.382	.516	152	37	4	7	-3	.995	5	*1-145	3.0
1979	Cle-A	143	515	89	120	31	1	26	93	90	93	.233	.351	.449	114	11	5	4	-1	.994	-3	*1-130,D-13	-0.1
1981	Cle-A	69	226	22	54	12	0	6	30	23	37	.239	.309	.372	97	-1	3	1	0	.986	-1	D-53,1-11	-0.4
1982	Cle-A★	161	589	90	161	26	1	32	116	109	81	.273	.389	.484	139	34	6	7	-2	1.000	0	*D-152/1-8	2.5
1983	Cle-A	141	508	78	143	27	1	17	77	87	72	.281	.389	.439	123	18	4	2	0	.991	2	*D-114,1-27	1.4
1984	Cle-A★	155	587	91	159	26	0	33	99	91	79	.271	.371	.484	132	27	6	5	-1	.979	0	*D-144,1-11	2.1
1985	Cle-A	124	461	49	109	13	0	22	88	47	75	.236	.307	.408	94	-4	3	2	-0	.000	0	*D-122	-0.7
1986	Cle-A	120	401	49	92	14	0	17	66	65	67	.229	.338	.392	100	1	4	1	1	.000	0	*D-110	-0.1
1987	Cle-A	36	85	8	10	2	0	0	5	10	25	.118	.211	.141	-4	-13	1	0	0	.000	0	D-21	-1.3
Total	14	1565	5291	792	1342	244	22	253	895	876	851	.254	.364	.452	123	177	48	37		.992	14	D-738,1-729/O3	11.7
Team	10	1225	4313	650	1095	193	12	214	749	685	683	.254	.360	.453	122	140	39	33		.994	1	D-738,1-449	8.3
■ **RON TINGLEY**	Tingley, Ronald Irvin b: 5/27/59, Presque Isle, Maine BR/TR, 6′2″, 180 lbs. Deb: 9/25/82																						
1988	Cle-A	9	24	1	4	0	0	1	2	2	8	.167	.231	.292	44	-2	0	0	0	1.000	3	/C-9	0.2
Total	9	278	563	52	110	27	3	10	55	54	165	.195	.271	.307	56	-36	2	5	-2	.989	37	C-274/1-1	1.0
■ **JOE TIPTON**	Tipton, Joe Hicks b: 2/18/22, McCaysville, Ga. d: 3/1/94, Birmingham, Ala. BR/TR, 5′11″, 185 lbs. Deb: 5/2/48																						
1948	*Cle-A	47	90	11	26	3	0	1	13	4	10	.289	.333	.356	85	-2	0	0	0	.971	0	C-40	0.0
1952	Cle-A	43	105	15	26	2	0	6	22	21	21	.248	.383	.438	137	6	1	0	0	.971	-8	C-35	-0.1
1953	Cle-A	47	109	17	25	2	0	6	13	19	13	.229	.359	.413	111	2	0	0	0	1.000	-7	C-46	-0.4
Total	7	417	1117	116	264	36	5	29	125	186	142	.236	.351	.355	91	-11	3	3	-1	.984	-14	C-380	-0.9
Team	3	137	304	43	77	7	0	13	48	44	44	.253	.361	.405	112	6	1	0	0	.981	-15	C-121	-0.5
■ **CHICK TOLSON**	Tolson, Charles Julius "Toby" b: 11/6/1898, Washington, D.C. d: 4/16/65, Washington, D.C. BR/TR, 6′, 185 lbs. Deb: 7/3/25																						
1925	Cle-A	3	12	0	3	0	0	0	0	2	1	.250	.357	.250	56	-1	0	0	0	1.000	0	/1-3	-0.1
Total	5	144	275	23	78	16	1	4	45	26	39	.284	.350	.393	90	-4	1	0	0	.985	-1	/1-60	-0.9
■ **RUSTY TORRES**	Torres, Rosendo (Hernandez) b: 9/30/48, Aquadilla, P.R. BB/TR, 5′10″, 180 lbs. Deb: 9/20/71																						
1973	Cle-A	122	312	31	64	8	1	7	28	50	62	.205	.321	.304	76	-9	6	5	-1	.976	-5	*O-114	-2.0
1974	Cle-A	108	150	19	28	2	0	3	12	13	24	.187	.252	.260	48	-10	2	1	0	.959	-19	O-94/D-1	-3.3
Total	9	654	1314	159	279	45	5	35	126	164	246	.212	.303	.334	82	-30	13	20	-8	.977	-73	O-573/D-8,3	-13.3
Team	2	230	462	50	92	10	1	10	40	63	86	.199	.299	.290	67	-19	8	6	-1	.970	-24	O-208/D-1	-5.3
■ **JEFF TREADWAY**	Treadway, Hugh Jeffery b: 1/22/63, Columbus, Ga. BL/TR, 5′10″, 170 lbs. Deb: 9/4/87																						
1993	Cle-A	97	221	25	67	14	1	2	27	14	21	.303	.350	.403	102	1	1	1	-0	.933	1	3-42,2-19/D	0.2
Total	9	762	2119	244	596	103	14	28	208	140	184	.281	.329	.383	94	-17	14	13	-4	.975	-1	2-556/3-57,D	-0.5
■ **MIKE TRESH**	Tresh, Michael b: 2/23/14, Hazleton, Pa. d: 10/4/66, Detroit, Mich. BR/TR, 5′11″, 170 lbs. Deb: 9/4/38 F																						
1949	Cle-A	38	37	4	8	0	0	0	1	5	7	.216	.310	.216	41	-3	0	0	0	1.000	6	C-38	0.3
Total	12	1027	3169	326	788	75	14	2	297	402	263	.249	.335	.283	71	-113	19	21	-7	.983	22	*C-1019	-3.5
■ **MANNY TRILLO**	Trillo, Jesus Manuel Marcano (b: Jesus Manuel Marcano (Trillo)) b: 12/25/50, Caripito, Ven. BR/TR, 6′1″, 164 lbs. Deb: 6/28/73																						
1983	Cle-A★	88	320	33	87	13	1	1	29	21	46	.272	.317	.328	75	-11	1	3	-2	.989	3	2-87	-0.5
Total	17	1780	5950	598	1562	239	33	61	571	452	742	.263	.318	.345	80	-155	56	57	-17	.981	129	*2-1518,3-110/1S	3.5
■ **HAL TROSKY**	Trosky, Harold Arthur Sr. (b: Harold Arthur Troyavesky Sr.) b: 11/11/12, Norway, Iowa d: 6/18/79, Cedar Rapids, Ia. BL/TR, 6′2″, 207 lbs. Deb: 9/11/33 F																						
1933	Cle-A	11	44	6	13	1	2	1	8	2	12	.295	.340	.477	110	0	0	0	0	.990	-1	1-11	-0.1
1934	Cle-A	154	625	117	206	45	9	35	142	58	49	.330	.388	.598	149	42	2	2	-1	.986	0	*1-154	2.5
1935	Cle-A	154	632	84	171	33	7	26	113	46	60	.271	.321	.468	100	-4	1	2	-1	.993	1	*1-153	-1.9
1936	Cle-A	151	629	124	216	45	9	42	**162**	36	58	.343	.382	.644	148	41	6	5	-1	.985	1	*1-151/2-1	2.3
1937	Cle-A	153	601	104	179	36	9	32	128	65	60	.298	.367	.547	127	21	3	1	0	.993	-2	*1-152	0.2
1938	Cle-A	150	554	106	185	40	9	19	110	67	40	.334	.407	.542	138	32	5	1	1	.993	4	*1-148	1.8
1939	Cle-A	122	448	89	150	31	4	25	104	52	28	.335	.405	.589	157	37	2	3	-1	.992	11	*1-118	3.1
1940	Cle-A	140	522	85	154	39	4	25	93	79	45	.295	.392	.529	140	31	1	2	-1	.991	-7	*1-139	1.0
1941	Cle-A	89	310	43	91	17	0	11	51	44	21	.294	.383	.455	127	12	1	2	-1	.989	-3	1-85	0.3
Total	11	1347	5161	835	1561	331	58	228	1012	545	440	.302	.371	.522	130	210	28	23	-5	.991	-12	*1-1321/2-1	5.7
Team	9	1124	4365	758	1365	287	53	216	911	449	373	.313	.379	.551	135	213	21	18	-5	.990	6	*1-1111/2-1	9.2
■ **QUINCY TROUPPE**	Trouppe, Quincy Thomas b: 12/25/12, Dublin, Ga. d: 8/12/93, Creve Coeur, Mo. BB/TR, 6′2.5″, 225 lbs. Deb: 4/30/52																						
1952	Cle-A	6	10	1	1	0	0	0	0	1	3	.100	.182	.100	-22	-2	0	0	0	1.000	2	/C-6	0.1

YEAR	TM/L	G	AB	R	H	2B	3B	HR	RBI	BB	SO	AVG	OBP	SLG	PRO+	BR/A	SB	CS	SBR	FA	FR	G/POS	TPR

■ EDDIE TUCKER   Tucker, Eddie Jack "Scooter"   b: 11/18/66, Greenville, Miss.   BR/TR, 6'2", 205 lbs.   Deb: 6/14/92

| 1995 | Cle-A | 17 | 20 | 2 | 0 | 0 | 0 | 0 | 0 | 5 | 4 | .000 | .231 | .000 | -33 | -4 | 0 | 0 | 0 | .982 | 1 | C-17 | -0.2 |
| Total | 3 | 51 | 103 | 9 | 13 | 2 | 0 | 1 | 7 | 10 | 20 | .126 | .224 | .175 | 11 | -13 | 1 | 1 | -0 | .986 | -3 | /C-47 | -1.5 |

■ OLLIE TUCKER   Tucker, Oliver Dinwiddie   b: 1/27/02, Radiant, Va.   d: 7/13/40, Radiant, Va.   BL/TR, 5'11", 180 lbs.   Deb: 4/17/27

| 1928 | Cle-A | 14 | 47 | 5 | 6 | 0 | 0 | 1 | 2 | 7 | 3 | .128 | .255 | .191 | 19 | -6 | 0 | 2 | -1 | 1.000 | -0 | O-14 | -0.8 |
| Total | 2 | 34 | 71 | 6 | 11 | 2 | 0 | 1 | 10 | 11 | 5 | .155 | .277 | .225 | 33 | -7 | 0 | 2 | -1 | 1.000 | -1 | /O-19 | -1.0 |

■ THURMAN TUCKER   Tucker, Thurman Lowell "Joe E."   b: 9/26/17, Gordon, Tex.   d: 5/7/93, Oklahoma City, Okla.   BL/TR, 5'11", 170 lbs.   Deb: 4/14/42

1948	*Cle-A	83	242	52	63	13	2	1	19	31	17	.260	.347	.343	86	-5	11	2	2	1.000	-1	O-66	-0.6
1949	Cle-A	80	197	28	48	5	2	0	14	18	19	.244	.307	.289	59	-12	4	2	0	.984	3	O-42	-1.1
1950	Cle-A	57	101	13	18	2	0	1	7	14	14	.178	.284	.228	34	-10	1	0	0	.968	-5	O-34	-1.5
1951	Cle-A	1	1	0	0	0	0	0	0	0	1	.000	.000	.000	-99	-0	0	0	0	.000	0	H	0.0
Total	9	701	2231	325	570	79	24	9	179	291	237	.255	.342	.325	89	-28	77	47	-5	.988	29	O-574	-3.2
Team	4	221	541	93	129	20	4	2	40	63	51	.238	.320	.301	66	-27	16	4	2	.989	-3	O-142	-3.2

■ EDDIE TURCHIN   Turchin, Edward Lawrence "Smiley"   b: 2/10/17, New York, N.Y.   d: 2/8/82, Brookhaven, N.Y.   BR/TR, 5'10", 165 lbs.   Deb: 5/9/43

| 1943 | Cle-A | 11 | 13 | 4 | 3 | 0 | 0 | 0 | 1 | 3 | | .231 | .375 | .231 | 84 | -0 | 0 | 0 | 0 | 1.000 | 1 | /3-4,S-2 | 0.2 |

■ TERRY TURNER   Turner, Terrence Lamont "Cotton Top"   b: 2/28/1881, Sandy Lake, Pa.   d: 7/18/60, Cleveland, Ohio   BR/TR, 5'8", 149 lbs.   Deb: 8/25/01   C

1904	Cle-A	111	404	41	95	9	6	1	45	11		.235	.255	.295	74	-13	5			.940	3	*S-111	-0.7
1905	Cle-A	155	586	49	155	16	14	4	72	14		.265	.289	.360	104	0	17			.945	-25	*S-155	-2.4
1906	Cle-A	147	584	85	170	27	7	2	62	35		.291	.338	.372	124	15	27			.960	24	*S-147	4.7
1907	Cle-A	140	524	57	127	20	7	0	46	19		.242	.272	.307	84	-11	27			.950	-3	*S-139	-1.1
1908	Cle-A	60	201	21	48	11	1	0	19	15		.239	.298	.303	95	-1	18			.952	-4	O-36,S-17	-0.7
1909	Cle-A	53	208	25	52	7	4	0	16	14		.250	.304	.322	94	-2	14			.969	10	2-26,S-26	0.9
1910	Cle-A	150	574	71	132	14	6	0	33	53		.230	.301	.275	79	-13	31			.973	2	S-94,3-46/2	-0.7
1911	Cle-A	117	417	59	105	16	9	0	28	34		.252	.310	.333	78	-13	29			.970	2	3-94,2-14,S	-0.9
1912	Cle-A	103	370	54	114	14	4	0	33	31		.308	.363	.368	106	3	19			.951	-2	*3-103	0.1
1913	Cle-A	120	388	60	96	13	4	0	44	55	35	.247	.348	.302	88	-4	13			.954	16	3-71,2-25,S	1.5
1914	Cle-A	121	428	43	105	14	9	1	33	44	36	.245	.319	.327	91	-5	17	13	-3	.963	21	*3-104,2-17	1.8
1915	Cle-A	75	262	35	66	14	1	0	14	29	13	.252	.329	.313	90	-3	12	11	-3	.965	-9	2-51,3-20	-1.4
1916	Cle-A	124	428	52	112	15	3	0	38	40	29	.262	.325	.311	86	-7	15			.963	5	3-77,2-42	0.2
1917	Cle-A	69	180	16	37	7	0	0	15	14	19	.206	.262	.244	51	-11	4			.980	-2	3-40,2-23/S	-0.8
1918	Cle-A	74	233	24	58	7	2	0	23	22	15	.249	.316	.296	77	-6	6			.969	-4	3-46,2-26/S	-0.8
Total	17	1659	5921	699	1499	207	77	8	528	435	156	.253	.308	.318	89	-83	256	24		.952	37	S-741,3-604,2/0	-1.7
Team	15	1619	5787	692	1472	204	77	8	521	430	147	.254	.310	.320	90	-70	254	24		.952	34	S-722,3-601,2/0	-0.8

■ TED UHLAENDER   Uhlaender, Theodore Otto   b: 10/21/40, Chicago Heights, Ill.   BL/TR, 6'2", 190 lbs.   Deb: 9/4/65

1970	Cle-A	141	473	56	127	21	2	11	46	39	44	.268	.326	.391	92	-5	3	6	-3	.991	-14	*O-134	-3.0
1971	Cle-A	141	500	52	144	20	3	2	47	38	44	.288	.338	.352	88	-7	3	6	-3	.992	1	*O-131	-1.7
Total	8	898	2932	343	772	114	21	36	285	202	277	.263	.313	.353	86	-54	52	35	-5	.991	-3	O-793	-10.7
Team	2	282	973	108	271	41	5	13	93	77	88	.279	.332	.371	90	-13	6	12	-5	.992	-14	O-265	-4.7

■ GEORGE UHLE   Uhle, George Ernest "The Bull"   b: 9/18/1898, Cleveland, Ohio   d: 2/26/85, Lakewood, Ohio   BR/TR, 6', 190 lbs.   Deb: 4/30/19   C

1919	Cle-A	26	43	7	13	2	1	0	6	1	5	.302	.318	.395	94	-1	0			.915	0	P-26	0.0
1920	*Cle-A	27	32	4	11	0	0	0	2	2	2	.344	.382	.344	91	-0	1	0	0	1.000	0	P-27	0.0
1921	Cle-A	48	94	21	23	2	3	1	18	6	9	.245	.290	.362	64	-5	0	0	0	.938	-3	P-41	0.0
1922	Cle-A	56	109	21	29	8	2	0	14	13	6	.266	.350	.376	88	-2	1	2	-1	.932	-3	P-50	0.0
1923	Cle-A	58	144	23	52	10	3	0	22	7	10	.361	.391	.472	127	5	2	1	0	.982	0	P-54	0.0
1924	Cle-A	59	107	10	33	6	1	1	19	4	8	.308	.339	.411	92	-2	0	1	-1	1.000	1	P-28	0.0
1925	Cle-A	55	101	10	29	3	3	0	13	7	7	.287	.339	.376	81	-3	0	0	0	.943	-3	P-29	0.0
1926	Cle-A	50	132	16	30	3	0	1	11	10	12	.227	.287	.273	46	-10	2	2	-1	.933	-0	P-39	0.0
1927	Cle-A	43	79	4	21	7	1	0	14	5	12	.266	.310	.380	78	-3	0	1	-1	.974	-1	P-25	0.0
1928	Cle-A	55	98	9	28	3	2	1	17	8	4	.286	.340	.388	90	-2	0	0	0	.972	3	P-31	0.0
1936	Cle-A	24	21	1	8	1	0	0	4	2	0	.381	.435	.571	145	1	0	0	0	.000	-1	/P-7	0.0
Total	17	722	1360	172	393	60	21	9	187	98	112	.289	.336	.384	86	-29	6	8		.960	-15	P-513	0.0
Team	11	501	960	126	277	45	16	5	140	65	75	.289	.336	.384	86	-21	6	7		.957	-6	P-357	0.0

■ DEL UNSER   Unser, Delbert Bernard   b: 12/9/44, Decatur, Ill.   BL/TL, 6'1", 180 lbs.   Deb: 4/10/68   FC

| 1972 | Cle-A | 132 | 383 | 29 | 91 | 12 | 0 | 1 | 17 | 28 | 46 | .238 | .291 | .277 | 67 | -15 | 5 | 9 | -4 | .989 | 2 | *O-119 | -2.5 |
| Total | 15 | 1799 | 5215 | 617 | 1344 | 179 | 42 | 87 | 481 | 481 | 675 | .258 | .321 | .358 | 93 | -47 | 64 | 60 | -17 | .984 | 48 | *O-1407,1-168 | -8.7 |

■ WILLIE UPSHAW   Upshaw, Willie Clay   b: 4/27/57, Blanco, Tex.   BL/TL, 6', 185 lbs.   Deb: 4/9/78   C

| 1988 | Cle-A | 149 | 493 | 58 | 121 | 22 | 3 | 11 | 50 | 62 | 66 | .245 | .332 | .369 | 94 | -3 | 12 | 9 | -2 | .991 | 1 | *1-144 | -1.6 |
| Total | 10 | 1264 | 4203 | 596 | 1103 | 199 | 45 | 123 | 528 | 452 | 642 | .262 | .337 | .419 | 102 | 12 | 88 | 59 | -9 | .990 | 11 | *1-1094/O-67,D | -6.1 |

■ BOB USHER   Usher, Robert Royce   b: 3/1/25, San Diego, Cal.   BR/TR, 6'1.5", 180 lbs.   Deb: 4/16/46

| 1957 | Cle-A | 10 | 8 | 1 | 1 | 0 | 0 | 0 | 0 | 1 | 3 | .125 | .222 | .125 | -3 | -1 | 0 | 0 | -0 | 1.000 | -2 | /O-4,3-1 | -0.3 |
| Total | 6 | 428 | 1101 | 133 | 259 | 41 | 4 | 18 | 102 | 90 | 136 | .235 | .295 | .329 | 69 | -49 | 9 | 5 | -0 | .980 | -19 | O-378/3-2 | -8.6 |

■ DUTCH USSAT   Ussat, William August   b: 4/11/04, Dayton, Ohio   d: 5/29/59, Dayton, Ohio   BR/TR, 6'1", 170 lbs.   Deb: 9/13/25

1925	Cle-A	1	0	1	0	0	0	0	0	0	0	.000	.000	.000	-99	-0	0	0	0	1.000	0	/2-1	0.0
1927	Cle-A	4	16	4	3	0	1	0	2	0	1	.188	.278	.313	53	-1	0	0	0	1.000	-1	/3-4	-0.2
Total	2	5	17	4	3	0	1	0	2	0	1	.176	.263	.294	44	-1	0	0	0	.980	-1	/3-4,2-1	-0.2

■ MIKE VAIL   Vail, Michael Lewis   b: 11/10/51, San Francisco, Cal.   BR/TR, 6', 185 lbs.   Deb: 8/18/75

| 1978 | Cle-A | 14 | 34 | 2 | 8 | 2 | 1 | 0 | 2 | 1 | 9 | .235 | .257 | .353 | 71 | -1 | 1 | 1 | -0 | 1.000 | -0 | /O-9,D-1 | -0.2 |
| Total | 10 | 665 | 1604 | 146 | 447 | 71 | 11 | 34 | 219 | 81 | 317 | .279 | .315 | .400 | 95 | -17 | 3 | 17 | -9 | .968 | -5 | O-399/1-5,3D | -4.6 |

■ ELMER VALO   Valo, Elmer William   b: 3/5/21, Ribnik, Czech.   BL/TR, 5'11", 190 lbs.   Deb: 9/22/40   C

| 1959 | Cle-A | 34 | 24 | 7 | 7 | 0 | 0 | 0 | 5 | 7 | 0 | .292 | .452 | .292 | 113 | 1 | 0 | 0 | 0 | 1.000 | -1 | /O-2 | 0.1 |
| Total | 20 | 1806 | 5029 | 768 | 1420 | 228 | 73 | 58 | 601 | 942 | 284 | .282 | .399 | .391 | 114 | 142 | 110 | 79 | -14 | .977 | 1 | *O-1329 | 6.5 |

■ AL Van CAMP   Van Camp, Albert Joseph   b: 9/7/03, Moline, Ill.   d: 2/2/81, Davenport, Iowa   BR/TR, 5'11.5", 175 lbs.   Deb: 9/11/28

| 1928 | Cle-A | 5 | 17 | 0 | 4 | 1 | 0 | 0 | 2 | 1 | | .235 | .235 | .294 | 38 | -2 | 1 | 0 | 0 | .980 | -1 | /1-5 | -0.2 |
| Total | 3 | 140 | 444 | 44 | 116 | 20 | 6 | 0 | 41 | 24 | 42 | .261 | .301 | .333 | 69 | -21 | 4 | 2 | 0 | .991 | -5 | /O-59,1-55 | -3.2 |

■ OTTO VELEZ   Velez, Otoniel (Franceschi)   b: 11/29/50, Ponce, P.R.   BR/TR, 6', 195 lbs.   Deb: 9/4/73

| 1983 | Cle-A | 10 | 25 | 1 | 2 | 0 | 0 | 0 | 1 | 3 | 6 | .080 | .179 | .080 | -25 | -4 | 0 | 0 | 0 | .000 | 0 | /D-8 | -0.5 |
| Total | 11 | 637 | 1802 | 244 | 452 | 87 | 11 | 78 | 272 | 336 | 414 | .251 | .372 | .441 | 122 | 61 | 6 | 10 | -4 | .973 | -4 | O-276,D-255/13 | 3.1 |

■ MICKEY VERNON   Vernon, James Barton   b: 4/22/18, Marcus Hook, Pa.   BL/TL, 6'2", 180 lbs.   Deb: 7/8/39   MC

| 1949 | Cle-A | 153 | 584 | 72 | 170 | 27 | 4 | 18 | 83 | 58 | 51 | .291 | .357 | .443 | 113 | 9 | 9 | 7 | -2 | .991 | 19 | *1-153 | 2.4 |
| 1950 | Cle-A | 28 | 90 | 8 | 17 | 0 | 0 | 2 | 10 | 12 | 10 | .189 | .284 | .189 | 24 | -10 | 2 | 0 | 1 | .996 | 1 | 1-25 | -0.8 |

YEAR	TM/L	G	AB	R	H	2B	3B	HR	RBI	BB	SO	AVG	OBP	SLG	PRO+	BR/A	SB	CS	SBR	FA	FR	G/POS	TPR
1958	Cle-A★	119	355	49	104	22	3	8	55	44	56	.293	.374	.439	126	13	0	4	-2	.987	-2	1-96	0.4
Total	20	2409	8731	1196	2495	490	120	172	1311	955	869	.286	.359	.428	116	186	137	90	-13	.990	-32	*1-2237/O-4	3.7
Team	3	300	1029	129	291	49	7	26	148	114	117	.283	.357	.420	109	12	11	11	-3	.990	18	1-274	2.0

■ ZOILO VERSALLES

Versalles, Zoilo Casanova (Rodriguez) "Zorro"
b: 12/18/39, Veldado, Cuba d: 6/9/95, Bloomington, Minn. BR/TR, 5'10", 150 lbs. Deb: 8/1/59

YEAR	TM/L	G	AB	R	H	2B	3B	HR	RBI	BB	SO	AVG	OBP	SLG	PRO+	BR/A	SB	CS	SBR	FA	FR	G/POS	TPR
1969	Cle-A	72	217	21	49	11	1	1	13	21	47	.226	.300	.300	66	-10	3	1	0	.975	-11	2-46,3-30/S	-1.8
Total	12	1400	5141	650	1246	230	63	95	471	318	810	.242	.292	.367	82	-133	97	48	0	.956	-20	*S-1265/3-65,2	-4.8

■ TOM VERYZER

Veryzer, Thomas Martin b: 2/11/53, Port Jefferson, N.Y BR/TR, 6'1", 185 lbs. Deb: 8/14/73

YEAR	TM/L	G	AB	R	H	2B	3B	HR	RBI	BB	SO	AVG	OBP	SLG	PRO+	BR/A	SB	CS	SBR	FA	FR	G/POS	TPR
1978	Cle-A	130	421	48	114	18	4	1	32	13	36	.271	.301	.340	81	-11	1	2	-1	.963	-4	*S-129	-0.1
1979	Cle-A	149	449	41	99	9	3	0	34	34	54	.220	.281	.254	45	-34	2	5	-2	.974	4	*S-148	-1.6
1980	Cle-A	109	358	28	97	12	0	2	28	10	25	.271	.306	.321	72	-14	0	5	-3	.971	-1	*S-108	-0.5
1981	Cle-A	75	221	13	54	4	0	0	14	10	10	.244	.280	.262	58	-12	1	0	0	.970	-7	S-75	-1.1
Total	12	996	2848	250	687	84	12	14	231	143	329	.241	.285	.294	61	-148	9	23	-11	.966	-14	S-927/2-30,3	-7.8
Team	4	463	1449	130	364	43	7	3	108	67	125	.251	.293	.297	64	-71	4	12	-6	.970	-8	S-460	-3.3

■ JOSE VIDAL

Vidal, Jose (Nicolas) "Papito" b: 4/3/40, Batey Lechugas, D.R. BR/TR, 6', 190 lbs. Deb: 9/5/66

YEAR	TM/L	G	AB	R	H	2B	3B	HR	RBI	BB	SO	AVG	OBP	SLG	PRO+	BR/A	SB	CS	SBR	FA	FR	G/POS	TPR
1966	Cle-A	17	32	4	6	1	1	0	3	5	11	.188	.297	.281	67	-1	0	1	-1	1.000	-1	O-11	-0.3
1967	Cle-A	16	34	4	4	0	0	0	0	7	12	.118	.268	.118	17	-3	0	1	-1	1.000	-1	O-10	-0.6
1968	Cle-A	37	54	5	9	0	0	2	5	2	15	.167	.196	.278	43	-4	3	0	1	1.000	-5	O-26/1-1	-1.0
Total	4	88	146	20	24	1	2	3	10	18	46	.164	.261	.260	53	-8	4	3	-1	.985	-7	/O-53,1-1	-2.0
Team	3	70	120	13	19	1	1	2	8	14	38	.158	.246	.233	43	-8	3	2	-0	1.000	-6	/O-47,1-1	-1.9

■ RUBE VINSON

Vinson, Ernest Augustus b: 3/20/1879, Dover, Del. d: 10/12/51, Chester, Pa. 5'9", 168 lbs. Deb: 9/27/04

YEAR	TM/L	G	AB	R	H	2B	3B	HR	RBI	BB	SO	AVG	OBP	SLG	PRO+	BR/A	SB	CS	SBR	FA	FR	G/POS	TPR
1904	Cle-A	15	49	12	15	1	0	0	2	10		.306	.433	.327	143	3	2			1.000	3	O-15	0.6
1905	Cle-A	39	134	12	26	3	1	0	9	7		.194	.245	.231	51	-7	4			.930	-3	O-36	-1.4
Total	3	64	207	26	47	4	1	0	14	19		.227	.301	.256	77	-5	7			.919	-3	/O-58	-1.2
Team	2	54	183	24	41	4	1	0	11	17		.224	.300	.257	77	-4	6			.950	0	/O-51	-0.8

■ OMAR VIZQUEL

Vizquel, Omar Enrique (Gonzalez) b: 4/24/67, Caracas, Venez. BB/TR, 5'9", 155 lbs. Deb: 4/3/89

YEAR	TM/L	G	AB	R	H	2B	3B	HR	RBI	BB	SO	AVG	OBP	SLG	PRO+	BR/A	SB	CS	SBR	FA	FR	G/POS	TPR
1994	Cle-A	69	286	39	78	10	1	1	33	23	23	.273	.327	.325	69	-13	13	4	2	.981	-1	S-69	-0.5
1995	*Cle-A	136	542	87	144	28	0	6	56	59	59	.266	.339	.351	80	-15	29	11	2	.986	-3	*S-136	-0.3
Total	7	865	2939	349	753	98	16	13	220	255	290	.256	.317	.314	71	-113	81	49		.981	51	S-858/D-2,2	0.1
Team	2	205	828	126	222	38	1	7	89	82	82	.268	.335	.342	76	-28	42	15		.984	-4	S-205	-0.8

■ JOE VOSMIK

Vosmik, Joseph Franklin b: 4/4/10, Cleveland, Ohio d: 1/27/62, Cleveland, Ohio BR/TR, 6', 185 lbs. Deb: 9/13/30

YEAR	TM/L	G	AB	R	H	2B	3B	HR	RBI	BB	SO	AVG	OBP	SLG	PRO+	BR/A	SB	CS	SBR	FA	FR	G/POS	TPR
1930	Cle-A	9	26	1	6	2	0	0	4	1	1	.231	.259	.308	42	-2	0	0	0	.933	1	/O-5	-0.2
1931	Cle-A	149	591	80	189	36	14	7	117	38	30	.320	.363	.464	110	7	7	7	-2	.970	6	*O-147	0.1
1932	Cle-A	153	621	106	194	39	12	10	97	58	42	.312	.376	.462	109	8	2	3	-1	**.989**	24	*O-153	1.9
1933	Cle-A	119	438	53	115	20	10	4	56	42	13	.263	.331	.381	84	-10	0	2	-1	.985	6	*O-113	-1.1
1934	Cle-A	104	405	71	138	33	2	6	78	35	10	.341	.393	.477	122	13	1	1	-0	.976	-2	*O-104	0.6
1935	Cle-A★	152	620	93	**216**	**47**	**20**	10	110	59	30	.348	.408	.537	140	36	2	1	0	.986	1	*O-150	2.9
1936	Cle-A	138	506	76	145	29	7	7	94	79	21	.287	.383	.413	96	-2	5	1	1	.978	-1	*O-136	-0.6
Total	13	1414	5472	818	1682	335	92	65	874	514	272	.307	.369	.438	104	29	23	24	-8	.979	34	*O-1370	-0.9
Team	7	824	3207	480	1003	206	65	44	556	312	147	.313	.376	.459	111	48	17	15	-4	.981	34	O-808	3.6

■ GEORGE VUKOVICH

Vukovich, George Stephen b: 6/24/56, Chicago, Ill. BL/TR, 6', 198 lbs. Deb: 4/13/80

YEAR	TM/L	G	AB	R	H	2B	3B	HR	RBI	BB	SO	AVG	OBP	SLG	PRO+	BR/A	SB	CS	SBR	FA	FR	G/POS	TPR
1983	Cle-A	124	312	31	77	13	2	3	44	24	37	.247	.305	.330	72	-12	3	4	-2	.986	-13	*O-122	-2.9
1984	Cle-A	134	437	38	133	22	5	9	60	34	61	.304	.356	.439	117	10	1	4	-2	.994	14	*O-130	1.8
1985	Cle-A	149	434	43	106	22	0	8	45	30	75	.244	.295	.350	76	-14	2	2	-1	.988	-7	*O-137	-2.6
Total	6	628	1602	164	430	76	10	27	203	127	229	.268	.324	.379	92	-18	9	19	-9	.987	-22	O-528	-6.3
Team	3	407	1183	112	316	57	7	20	149	88	173	.267	.320	.378	90	-16	6	10	-4	.990	-6	O-389	-3.7

■ LEON WAGNER

Wagner, Leon Lamar b: 5/13/34, Chattanooga, Tenn. BL/TR, 6'1", 195 lbs. Deb: 6/22/58

YEAR	TM/L	G	AB	R	H	2B	3B	HR	RBI	BB	SO	AVG	OBP	SLG	PRO+	BR/A	SB	CS	SBR	FA	FR	G/POS	TPR
1964	Cle-A	163	641	94	162	19	2	31	100	56	121	.253	.319	.434	108	6	14	2	3	.959	-1	*O-163	0.0
1965	Cle-A	144	517	91	152	18	1	28	79	60	52	.294	.371	.495	143	29	12	2	2	.957	-9	*O-134	1.7
1966	Cle-A	150	549	70	153	20	0	23	66	46	69	.279	.336	.441	121	14	5	2	0	.990	-8	*O-139	0.0
1967	Cle-A	135	433	56	105	15	1	15	54	37	76	.242	.320	.386	107	4	3	3	-1	.980	-7	*O-117	-1.1
1968	Cle-A	38	49	5	9	4	0	0	6	6	6	.184	.273	.265	65	-2	0	0	0	.500	-3	O-10	-0.7
Total	12	1352	4426	636	1202	150	15	211	669	435	656	.272	.343	.455	121	117	54	24	2	.964	-44	*O-1140	1.6
Team	5	630	2189	316	581	76	4	97	305	205	324	.265	.334	.437	118	50	34	9	5	.966	-29	O-563	-0.1

■ HOWARD WAKEFIELD

Wakefield, Howard John b: 4/2/1884, Bucyrus, Ohio d: 4/16/41, Chicago, Ill. BR/TR, 6'1", 205 lbs. Deb: 9/18/05 F

YEAR	TM/L	G	AB	R	H	2B	3B	HR	RBI	BB	SO	AVG	OBP	SLG	PRO+	BR/A	SB	CS	SBR	FA	FR	G/POS	TPR
1905	Cle-A	10	26	3	4	0	0	0	1	0		.154	.185	.154	8	-3	0			.926	-3	/C-8	-0.5
1907	Cle-A	26	37	4	5	2	0	0	3	3		.135	.200	.189	24	-3	0			.930	-0	C-11	-0.3
Total	3	113	274	24	68	11	2	1	25	10		.248	.277	.314	89	-4	6			.943	-18	/C-79	-1.6
Team	2	36	63	7	9	2	0	0	4	3		.143	.194	.175	17	-6	0			.929	-3	/C-19	-0.8

■ GEE WALKER

Walker, Gerald Holmes b: 3/19/08, Gulfport, Miss. d: 3/20/81, Whitfield, Miss. BR/TR, 5'11", 188 lbs. Deb: 4/14/31 FC

YEAR	TM/L	G	AB	R	H	2B	3B	HR	RBI	BB	SO	AVG	OBP	SLG	PRO+	BR/A	SB	CS	SBR	FA	FR	G/POS	TPR
1941	Cle-A	121	445	56	126	26	11	6	48	18	46	.283	.313	.431	100	-3	12	6	0	.982	8	*O-105	-0.2
Total	15	1784	6771	954	1991	399	76	124	997	330	600	.294	.331	.430	99	-32	223	70		.961	-7	*O-1613/3-3	-10.5

■ ROXY WALTERS

Walters, Alfred John b: 11/5/1892, San Francisco, Cal. d: 6/3/56, Alameda, Cal. BR/TR, 5'8.5", 160 lbs. Deb: 9/16/15

YEAR	TM/L	G	AB	R	H	2B	3B	HR	RBI	BB	SO	AVG	OBP	SLG	PRO+	BR/A	SB	CS	SBR	FA	FR	G/POS	TPR
1924	Cle-A	32	74	10	19	2	0	0	5	10	6	.257	.345	.284	63	-4	0	1	-1	.979	6	C-25/2-7	0.2
1925	Cle-A	5	20	0	4	0	0	0	0	0	2	.200	.200	.200	2	-3	0	0	0	1.000	-0	/C-5	-0.3
Total	11	498	1426	119	317	41	6	0	116	97	151	.222	.281	.259	51	-96	13	5	1	.975	70	C-462/O-9,21	0.1
Team	2	37	94	10	23	2	0	0	5	10	8	.245	.317	.266	50	-7	0	1	-1	.982	6	/C-30,2-7	-0.1

■ BILL WAMBSGANSS

Wambsganss, William Adolph b: 3/19/1894, Cleveland, Ohio d: 12/8/85, Lakewood, Ohio BR/TR, 5'11", 175 lbs. Deb: 8/4/14

YEAR	TM/L	G	AB	R	H	2B	3B	HR	RBI	BB	SO	AVG	OBP	SLG	PRO+	BR/A	SB	CS	SBR	FA	FR	G/POS	TPR
1914	Cle-A	43	143	12	31	6	2	0	12	8	24	.217	.277	.287	67	-6	2	7	-4	.921	-1	S-36/2-4	-0.9
1915	Cle-A	121	375	30	73	4	4	0	21	36	50	.195	.272	.227	48	-23	8	9	-3	.938	7	2-78,3-35	-1.9
1916	Cle-A	136	475	57	117	14	4	0	45	41	40	.246	.313	.293	77	-13	13			.925	-8	*S-106,2-24/3	-1.6
1917	Cle-A	141	499	52	127	17	6	0	43	37	42	.255	.315	.313	85	-9	16			.951	15	*2-137/1-3	1.4
1918	Cle-A	87	315	34	93	15	2	0	40	21	21	.295	.345	.356	102	0	16			.952	-2	2-87	0.4
1919	Cle-A	139	526	60	146	17	6	2	60	32	24	.278	.323	.344	82	-13	18			.963	11	*2-139	0.5
1920	*Cle-A	153	565	83	138	16	11	1	55	54	26	.244	.316	.317	66	-28	9	18	-8	.960	8	*2-153	-2.1
1921	Cle-A	107	410	80	117	28	5	2	47	44	27	.285	.359	.393	90	-6	13	7	-0	.963	-18	*2-103/3-2	-2.0
1922	Cle-A	142	538	89	141	22	6	0	47	60	26	.262	.341	.325	74	-19	17	10	-1	.961	-9	*2-125,S-16	-2.4
1923	Cle-A	101	345	59	100	20	4	1	59	43	15	.290	.373	.380	99	0	10	9	-2	.963	5	2-88/3-4	0.4
Total	13	1491	5237	710	1359	215	59	7	520	490	357	.259	.328	.327	78	-157	140	74		.958	26	*2-1205,S-175/31	-10.2
Team	10	1170	4191	556	1083	159	50	6	429	376	295	.258	.326	.325	79	-117	122	60		.957	7	2-938,S-158/31	-8.2

■ AARON WARD

Ward, Aaron Lee b: 8/28/1896, Booneville, Ark. d: 1/30/61, New Orleans, La. BR/TR, 5'10.5", 160 lbs. Deb: 8/14/17

YEAR	TM/L	G	AB	R	H	2B	3B	HR	RBI	BB	SO	AVG	OBP	SLG	PRO+	BR/A	SB	CS	SBR	FA	FR	G/POS	TPR
1928	Cle-A	6	9	0	1	0	0	0	0	1	2	.111	.200	.111	-16	-2	0	0	0	.818	2	/3-3,S-2,2	0.1
Total	12	1059	3611	457	966	158	54	50	446	339	457	.268	.335	.383	85	-81	36	38	-12	.970	35	2-809,3-172/S10	-3.1

YEAR TM/L	G	AB	R	H	2B	3B	HR	RBI	BB	SO	AVG	OBP	SLG	PRO+	BR/A	SB	CS	SBR	FA	FR	G/POS	TPR
■ **PRESTON WARD** Ward, Preston Meyer b: 7/24/27, Columbia, Mo. BL/TR, 6'3", 198 lbs. Deb: 4/20/48																						
1956 Cle-A	87	150	18	38	10	0	6	21	16	20	.253	.325	.440	98	-1	0	0	0	.988	2	1-60,O-17	-0.1
1957 Cle-A	10	11	2	2	1	0	0	0	0	2	.182	.182	.273	23	-1	0	0	0	1.000	-0	/1-1	-0.1
1958 Cle-A	48	148	22	50	3	1	4	21	10	27	.338	.384	.453	133	6	0	1	-1	.957	-3	3-24,1-21	0.2
Total 9	744	2067	219	522	83	15	50	262	231	315	.253	.328	.380	88	-36	7	6	-2	.992	-3	1-438/O-95,3	-6.0
Team 3	145	309	42	90	14	1	10	42	26	49	.291	.348	.440	111	4	0	1	-1	.993	-1	/1-82,3-24,O	0.0
■ **TURNER WARD** Ward, Turner Max b: 4/11/65, Orlando, Fla. BB/TR, 6'2", 200 lbs. Deb: 9/10/90																						
1990 Cle-A	14	46	10	16	2	1	1	10	3	8	.348	.388	.500	147	3	3	0	1	.957	0	O-13/D-1	0.4
1991 Cle-A	40	100	11	23	7	0	0	5	10	16	.230	.300	.300	66	-4	0	0	0	1.000	-2	O-38	-0.7
Total 6	298	851	123	204	34	6	19	109	107	145	.240	.328	.361	79	-25	18	7	1	.988	-10	O-273/D-2,31	-3.8
Team 2	54	146	21	39	9	1	1	15	13	24	.267	.327	.363	91	-2	3	0	1	.989	-2	/O-51,D-1	-0.3
■ **JIMMY WASDELL** Wasdell, James Charles b: 5/15/14, Cleveland, Ohio d: 8/6/83, New Port Richey, Fla. BL/TL, 5'11", 185 lbs. Deb: 9/3/37																						
1946 Cle-A	32	41	1	11	0	0	0	4	4	4	.268	.333	.268	74	-1	1	0	0	.939	-2	/1-4,O-3	-0.3
1947 Cle-A	1	1	0	0	0	0	0	0	0	0	.000	.000	.000	-99	-0	0	0	0	.000	0	H	0.0
Total 11	888	2866	339	782	109	34	29	341	243	165	.273	.332	.365	96	-20	29	4	6	.966	-45	O-462,1-277	-11.0
Team 2	33	42	1	11	0	0	0	4	4	4	.262	.326	.262	70	-2	1	0	0	.939	-2	/1-4,O-3	-0.3
■ **RON WASHINGTON** Washington, Ronald b: 4/29/52, New Orleans, La. BR/TR, 5'11", 163 lbs. Deb: 9/10/77																						
1988 Cle-A	69	223	30	57	14	2	2	21	9	35	.256	.300	.363	82	-5	3	3	-1	.933	-14	S-54/3-8,2D	-1.6
Total 10	564	1586	190	414	65	22	20	146	65	266	.261	.294	.368	79	-49	28	18	-2	.958	-88	S-372,2-111/3D01	-11.0
■ **ROY WEATHERLY** Weatherly, Cyril Roy "Stormy" b: 2/25/15, Warren, Tex. d: 1/19/91, Woodville, Tex. BL/TR, 5'6.5", 170 lbs. Deb: 6/27/36																						
1936 Cle-A	84	349	64	117	28	6	8	53	16	29	.335	.364	.519	115	6	3	8	-4	.973	4	O-84	0.3
1937 Cle-A	53	134	19	27	4	0	5	13	6	14	.201	.246	.343	47	-12	1	1	-0	.964	-3	O-38/3-1	-1.5
1938 Cle-A	83	210	32	55	14	3	2	18	14	14	.262	.308	.386	74	-9	8	5	-1	.975	-1	O-55	-1.1
1939 Cle-A	95	323	43	100	16	6	1	32	19	23	.310	.348	.406	95	-3	7	2	1	.961	-8	O-76	-1.1
1940 Cle-A	135	578	90	175	35	11	12	59	27	26	.303	.335	.464	108	4	9	8	-2	.969	6	*O-135	0.1
1941 Cle-A	102	363	59	105	21	5	3	37	32	20	.289	.350	.399	103	1	2	5	-2	.968	-8	O-88	-1.4
1942 Cle-A	128	473	61	122	23	7	5	39	35	25	.258	.310	.368	96	-5	8	13	-5	.991	2	*O-117	-1.4
Total 10	811	2781	415	794	152	44	43	290	180	170	.286	.331	.418	99	-16	42	49	-17	.975	-10	O-676/3-1	-7.1
Team 7	680	2430	368	701	141	38	36	251	149	151	.288	.331	.422	98	-17	38	42	-14	.974	-7	O-593/3-1	-6.1
■ **SKEETER WEBB** Webb, James Laverne b: 11/4/09, Meridian, Miss. d: 7/8/86, Meridian, Miss. BR/TR, 5'9.5", 150 lbs. Deb: 7/20/32																						
1938 Cle-A	20	58	11	16	2	0	0	2	8	7	.276	.364	.310	72	-2	1	0	0	.964	-2	S-13/3-3,2	-0.3
1939 Cle-A	81	269	28	71	14	1	2	26	15	24	.264	.305	.346	68	-13	1	1	-0	.932	-9	S-81	-1.4
Total 12	699	2274	216	498	73	15	3	166	132	215	.219	.263	.268	46	-168	33	26	-6	.946	32	S-368,2-282/3	-9.9
Team 2	101	327	39	87	16	1	2	28	23	31	.266	.316	.339	69	-15	2	1	0	.936	-11	/S-94,3-3,2	-1.7
■ **MITCH WEBSTER** Webster, Mitchell Dean b: 5/16/59, Larned, Kan. BB/TL, 6', 185 lbs. Deb: 9/2/83																						
1990 Cle-A	128	437	58	110	20	6	12	55	20	61	.252	.289	.407	93	-6	22	6	3	.991	9	*O-118/1-3,D	0.4
1991 Cle-A	13	32	2	4	0	0	0	0	3	9	.125	.200	.125	-8	-5	2	2	-1	1.000	-1	O-10	-0.6
Total 13	1265	3419	504	900	150	55	70	342	325	578	.263	.332	.401	101	5	160	73	4	.980	-50	*O-1004/D-16,1	-6.8
Team 2	141	469	60	114	20	6	12	55	23	70	.243	.283	.388	86	-10	24	8	2	.992	9	O-128/1-3,D	-0.2
■ **RAY WEBSTER** Webster, Raymond George b: 11/15/37, Grass Valley, Cal. BR/TR, 6', 175 lbs. Deb: 4/17/59																						
1959 Cle-A	40	74	10	15	2	1	2	10	5	7	.203	.253	.338	63	-4	1	0	0	.929	0	2-24/3-4	-0.3
Total 2	47	77	11	15	2	1	2	11	6	7	.195	.253	.325	59	-5	1	0	0	.931	1	/2-25,3-4	-0.3
■ **RALPH WEIGEL** Weigel, Ralph Richard "Wig" b: 10/2/21, Coldwater, Ohio d: 4/15/92, Memphis, Tenn. BR/TR, 6'1", 180 lbs. Deb: 9/18/46																						
1946 Cle-A	6	12	0	2	0	0	0	0	0	2	.167	.167	.167	-7	-2	1	0	0	1.000	-1	/C-6	-0.3
Total 3	106	235	12	54	9	3	0	30	21	26	.230	.296	.294	59	-14	2	3	-1	.976	-8	/C-66,O-2	-2.0
■ **DICK WEIK** Weik, Richard Henry "Legs" b: 11/17/27, Waterloo, Iowa d: 4/21/91, Harvey, Ill. BR/TR, 6'3.5", 184 lbs. Deb: 9/8/48																						
1950 Cle-A	11	5	0	1	1	0	0	0	0	4	.200	.200	.400	52	-0	0	0	0	1.000	0	P-11	0.0
1953 Cle-A	1	0	1	0	0	0	0	0	0	0	—	—	—	—	0	0	0	0	.000	0	R	0.0
Total 5	78	53	6	12	2	1	0	3	1	16	.226	.241	.302	43	-5	0	0	0	.958	0	/P-76	0.0
Team 2	12	5	1	1	1	0	0	0	0	4	.200	.200	.400	52	-0	0	0	0	1.000	0	/P-11	0.0
■ **ELMER WEINGARTNER** Weingartner, Elmer William "Dutch" b: 8/13/18, Cleveland, Ohio BR/TR, 5'11", 178 lbs. Deb: 4/19/45																						
1945 Cle-A	20	39	5	9	1	0	0	1	4	11	.231	.302	.256	66	-2	0	0	0	.871	-3	S-20	-0.4
■ **OLLIE WELF** Welf, Oliver Henry b: 1/17/1889, Cleveland, Ohio d: 6/15/67, Cleveland, Ohio BR/TL, 5'9", 160 lbs. Deb: 8/30/16																						
1916 Cle-A	1	0	0	0	0	0	0	0	0	0	—	—	—	—	0	0			.000	0	R	0.0
■ **VIC WERTZ** Wertz, Victor Woodrow b: 2/9/25, York, Pa. d: 7/7/83, Detroit, Mich. BL/TR, 6', 186 lbs. Deb: 4/15/47																						
1954 *Cle-A	94	295	33	81	14	2	14	48	34	40	.275	.350	.478	123	8	0	2	-1	.989	2	1-83/O-5	0.5
1955 Cle-A	74	257	30	65	11	2	14	55	32	33	.253	.338	.475	112	3	1	1	-0	.984	-3	1-63/O-9	-0.4
1956 Cle-A	136	481	65	127	22	0	32	106	75	87	.264	.369	.509	127	18	0	0	0	.991	1	*1-133	1.0
1957 Cle-A★	144	515	84	145	21	0	28	105	78	88	.282	.378	.485	136	26	2	3	-1	.988	-2	*1-139	1.5
1958 Cle-A	25	43	5	12	1	0	3	12	5	7	.279	.354	.512	139	2	0	0	0	.980	0	/1-8	0.2
Total 17	1862	6099	867	1692	289	42	266	1178	828	842	.277	.366	.469	121	177	9	19		.973	12	O-889,1-715	9.4
Team 5	473	1591	217	430	69	4	91	326	224	255	.270	.363	.490	127	58	3	6		.988	-2	1-426/O-14	2.8
■ **WALLY WESTLAKE** Westlake, Waldon Thomas b: 11/8/20, Gridley, Cal. BR/TR, 6', 186 lbs. Deb: 4/15/47 F																						
1952 Cle-A	29	69	11	16	4	1	1	9	8	16	.232	.312	.362	93	-1	1	0	0	1.000	-3	O-28	-0.5
1953 Cle-A	82	218	42	72	7	1	9	46	35	29	.330	.427	.495	153	17	2	0	1	.963	-11	O-72	0.5
1954 *Cle-A	85	240	36	63	9	2	11	42	26	37	.262	.340	.454	114	4	0	1	-1	.964	-7	O-70	-0.6
1955 Cle-A	16	20	2	5	1	0	0	1	3	5	.250	.348	.300	73	-1	0	0	0	1.000	-0	/O-7	-0.1
Total 10	958	3117	474	848	107	33	127	539	317	453	.272	.346	.450	111	41	19	7	2	.983	1	O-834/3-34	0.3
Team 4	212	547	91	156	21	4	21	98	72	87	.285	.372	.453	126	20	3	1	0	.970	-21	O-177	-0.7
■ **ED WHEELER** Wheeler, Edward Raymond b: 5/24/15, Los Angeles, Cal. d: 8/4/83, Centralia, Wash. BR/TR, 5'9", 160 lbs. Deb: 4/19/45																						
1945 Cle-A	46	72	12	14	2	0	0	1	8	13	.194	.275	.222	47	-5	1	1	-0	.912	-6	3-14,S-11/2	-1.1
■ **PETE WHISENANT** Whisenant, Thomas Peter b: 12/14/29, Asheville, N.C. BR/TR, 6'2", 200 lbs. Deb: 4/16/52 C																						
1960 Cle-A	7	6	0	1	0	0	0	0	0	2	.167	.167	.167	-10	-1	0	0	0	1.000	-1	/O-2	-0.2
Total 8	475	988	140	221	46	8	37	134	86	196	.224	.287	.399	80	-30	17	5	2	.988	-20	O-343/3-1,C2	-6.3
■ **MARK WHITEN** Whiten, Mark Anthony b: 11/25/66, Pensacola, Fla. BB/TR, 6'3", 210 lbs. Deb: 7/12/90																						
1991 Cle-A	70	258	34	66	14	4	7	26	19	50	.256	.312	.422	100	-0	4	2	0	.962	11	O-67/D-3	0.9
1992 Cle-A	148	508	73	129	19	4	9	43	72	102	.254	.349	.360	101	2	16	12	-2	.980	13	*O-144/D-2	1.0
Total 6	633	2219	320	569	82	19	71	294	243	472	.256	.332	.406	99	-3	55	28	-0	.974	48	O-607/D-8	3.2
Team 2	218	766	107	195	33	8	16	69	91	152	.255	.337	.381	101	2	20	14	-2	.973	24	O-211/D-5	1.9

YEAR	TM/L	G	AB	R	H	2B	3B	HR	RBI	BB	SO	AVG	OBP	SLG	PRO+	BR/A	SB	CS	SBR	FA	FR	G/POS	TPR

■ FRED WHITFIELD Whitfield, Fred Dwight b: 1/7/38, Vandiver, Ala. BL/TL, 6'1", 190 lbs. Deb: 5/27/62

1963	Cle-A	109	346	44	87	17	3	21	54	24	61	.251	.307	.500	123	9	0	1	-1	.987	-3	1-92	0.1
1964	Cle-A	101	293	29	79	13	1	10	29	12	58	.270	.303	.423	100	-1	0	5	-3	.992	-2	1-79	-0.9
1965	Cle-A	132	468	49	137	23	1	26	90	16	42	.293	.319	.513	131	16	2	2	-1	.993	4	*1-122	1.4
1966	Cle-A	137	502	59	121	15	2	27	78	27	76	.241	.285	.440	105	1	1	2	-1	.991	-4	*1-132	-1.3
1967	Cle-A	100	257	24	56	10	0	9	31	25	45	.218	.290	.362	91	-3	3	3	-1	.993	4	1-66	-0.5
Total	9	817	2284	242	578	93	8	108	356	139	371	.253	.301	.443	107	14	7	16	-8	.990	3	1-588	-2.6
Team	5	579	1866	205	480	78	7	93	282	104	282	.257	.301	.456	112	23	6	13	-6	.991	-1	1-491	-1.2

■ DENNEY WILIE Wilie, Dennis Ernest b: 9/22/1890, Mt.Calm, Tex. d: 6/20/66, Hayward, Cal. BL/TL, 5'8", 155 lbs. Deb: 7/27/11

| 1915 | Cle-A | 45 | 131 | 14 | 33 | 4 | 1 | 2 | 10 | 26 | 18 | .252 | .384 | .344 | 115 | 4 | 2 | 6 | -3 | .910 | -2 | O-35 | -0.4 |
| Total | 3 | 103 | 230 | 26 | 56 | 7 | 3 | 2 | 19 | 41 | 38 | .243 | .372 | .326 | 102 | 6 | 2 | 5 | -2 | .925 | -8 | /O-66 | -1.2 |

■ JERRY WILLARD Willard, Gerald Duane b: 3/14/60, Oxnard, Cal. BL/TR, 6'2", 195 lbs. Deb: 4/11/84

1984	Cle-A	87	246	21	55	8	1	10	37	26	55	.224	.298	.386	86	-5	1	0	0	.981	-1	C-76/D-1	-0.2
1985	Cle-A	104	300	39	81	13	0	7	36	28	59	.270	.334	.383	97	-1	0	0	0	.990	0	C-96/D-1	0.4
Total	8	346	783	82	195	29	1	25	114	83	161	.249	.323	.384	95	-5	1	1	-0	.988	-11	C-247/D-7,13	-0.6
Team	2	191	546	60	136	21	1	17	73	54	114	.249	.318	.385	92	-6	1	0	0	.986	-0	C-172/D-2	0.2

■ RIP WILLIAMS Williams, Alva Mitchel "Buff" b: 1/31/1882, Carthage, Ill. d: 7/23/33, Keokuk, Iowa BR/TR, 5'11.5", 187 lbs. Deb: 4/12/11

| 1918 | Cle-A | 28 | 71 | 5 | 17 | 2 | 2 | 0 | 7 | 9 | 6 | .239 | .325 | .324 | 87 | -1 | 2 | | | .980 | -2 | 1-21/C-1 | -0.4 |
| Total | 7 | 498 | 1186 | 111 | 314 | 51 | 23 | 2 | 145 | 95 | 80 | .265 | .328 | .352 | 97 | -6 | 27 | | | .977 | -6 | C-212,1-144/O3 | -0.0 |

■ EDDIE WILLIAMS Williams, Edward Laquan b: 11/1/64, Shreveport, La. BR/TR, 6', 175 lbs. Deb: 4/18/86

1986	Cle-A	5	7	2	1	0	0	0	1	0	3	.143	.143	.143	-22	-1	0	0	0	.000	-2	/O-4	-0.3
1987	Cle-A	22	64	9	11	4	0	1	4	9	19	.172	.284	.281	50	-5	0	0	0	.982	2	3-22	-0.3
1988	Cle-A	10	21	3	4	0	0	0	1	0	3	.190	.190	.190	18	-2	0	0	0	1.000	3	3-10	0.0
Total	7	263	806	111	218	37	2	30	109	70	135	.270	.339	.433	108	9	1	4	-2	.989	-1	1-127,3-111/O	-0.6
Team	3	37	92	14	16	4	0	1	6	9	25	.174	.262	.250	38	-8	0	0	0	.987	2	/3-32,O-4	

■ PAPA WILLIAMS Williams, Fred b: 7/17/13, Meridian, Miss. d: 11/2/93, Meridian, Miss. BR/TR, 6'1", 200 lbs. Deb: 4/19/45

| 1945 | Cle-A | 16 | 19 | 0 | 4 | 0 | 0 | 0 | 1 | 2 | | .211 | .250 | .211 | 36 | -2 | 0 | 0 | 0 | 1.000 | 0 | /1-3 | -0.1 |

■ REGGIE WILLIAMS Williams, Reginald Dewayne b: 8/29/60, Memphis, Tenn. BR/TR, 5'11", 185 lbs. Deb: 9/2/85

| 1988 | Cle-A | 11 | 31 | 7 | 7 | 2 | 0 | 1 | 3 | 0 | 6 | .226 | .226 | .387 | 66 | -1 | 0 | 0 | 0 | 1.000 | -2 | O-11 | -0.4 |
| Total | 4 | 200 | 379 | 52 | 98 | 16 | 2 | 5 | 39 | 28 | 76 | .259 | .313 | .351 | 87 | -7 | 11 | 4 | 1 | 1.000 | -29 | O-180 | -3.9 |

■ DICK WILLIAMS Williams, Richard Hirschfeld b: 5/7/29, St.Louis, Mo. BR/TR, 6', 190 lbs. Deb: 6/10/51 MC

| 1957 | Cle-A | 67 | 205 | 33 | 58 | 7 | 0 | 6 | 17 | 12 | 19 | .283 | .326 | .405 | 99 | -1 | 3 | 4 | -2 | .973 | -3 | O-37,3-19 | -0.7 |
| Total | 13 | 1023 | 2959 | 358 | 768 | 157 | 12 | 70 | 331 | 227 | 392 | .260 | .315 | .392 | 92 | -38 | 12 | 21 | -9 | .989 | -46 | O-456,3-257,1/2 | -12.2 |

■ WALT WILLIAMS Williams, Walter Allen "No-Neck" b: 12/19/43, Brownwood, Tex. BR/TR, 5'6", 185 lbs. Deb: 4/21/64 C

| 1973 | Cle-A | 104 | 350 | 43 | 101 | 15 | 1 | 8 | 38 | 14 | 29 | .289 | .318 | .406 | 101 | -1 | 9 | 4 | 0 | .970 | 5 | O-61,D-26 | 0.1 |
| Total | 10 | 842 | 2373 | 284 | 640 | 106 | 11 | 33 | 173 | 126 | 211 | .270 | .311 | .365 | 91 | -33 | 34 | 19 | -1 | .981 | -6 | O-565/D-46,23 | -7.3 |

■ ART WILSON Wilson, Arthur Earl "Dutch" b: 12/11/1885, Macon, Ill. d: 6/12/60, Chicago, Ill. BR/TR, 5'8", 170 lbs. Deb: 9/29/08

| 1921 | Cle-A | 2 | 1 | 0 | 0 | 0 | 0 | 0 | 0 | 0 | 0 | .000 | .000 | .000 | -99 | -0 | 0 | 0 | 0 | 1.000 | 0 | /C-2 | 0.0 |
| Total | 14 | 812 | 2056 | 237 | 536 | 96 | 22 | 24 | 226 | 292 | 289 | .261 | .357 | .364 | 106 | 28 | 50 | 0 | 15 | .972 | -18 | C-738/3-6,1 | 6.4 |

■ FRANK WILSON Wilson, Francis Edward "Squash" b: 4/20/01, Malden, Mass. d: 11/25/74, Leicester, Mass. BL/TR, 6', 185 lbs. Deb: 6/20/24

| 1928 | Cle-A | 2 | 1 | 0 | 0 | 0 | 0 | 0 | 0 | 1 | 0 | .000 | .500 | .000 | 41 | 0 | 0 | 0 | 0 | .000 | 0 | H | 0.0 |
| Total | 4 | 168 | 488 | 46 | 120 | 19 | 4 | 1 | 38 | 48 | 44 | .246 | .315 | .307 | 72 | -19 | 8 | 5 | -1 | .958 | 4 | O-122 | -2.5 |

■ JIM WILSON Wilson, James George b: 12/29/60, Corvallis, Ore. BR/TR, 6'3", 230 lbs. Deb: 9/13/85

| 1985 | Cle-A | 4 | 14 | 2 | 5 | 0 | 0 | 0 | 4 | 1 | 3 | .357 | .400 | .357 | 110 | 0 | 0 | 0 | 0 | 1.000 | -1 | /1-2,D-2 | -0.1 |
| Total | 2 | 9 | 22 | 2 | 5 | 0 | 0 | 0 | 4 | 1 | 6 | .227 | .261 | .227 | 36 | -2 | 0 | 0 | 0 | .988 | -1 | /D-7,1-2 | -0.3 |

■ RED WILSON Wilson, Robert James b: 3/7/29, Milwaukee, Wis. BR/TR, 6', 200 lbs. Deb: 9/22/51

| 1960 | Cle-A | 32 | 88 | 5 | 19 | 3 | 0 | 1 | 10 | 6 | 7 | .216 | .274 | .284 | 53 | -6 | 0 | 0 | 0 | .989 | 7 | C-30 | 0.3 |
| Total | 10 | 602 | 1765 | 206 | 455 | 84 | 8 | 24 | 189 | 215 | 163 | .258 | .341 | .355 | 87 | -28 | 25 | 12 | 0 | .990 | 31 | C-580 | 2.8 |

■ RALPH WINEGARNER Winegarner, Ralph Lee b: 10/29/09, Benton, Kan. d: 4/14/88, Wichita, Kan. BR/TR, 6', 182 lbs. Deb: 9/20/30 C

1930	Cle-A	5	22	5	10	1	0	0	2	1	7	.455	.478	.500	143	2	0	0	0	.857	1	/3-5	0.2
1932	Cle-A	7	7	1	1	0	0	0	0	0	5	.143	.143	.143	-24	-1	0	0	0	.750	-0	/P-5	0.0
1934	Cle-A	32	51	9	10	2	0	1	5	3	11	.196	.241	.294	37	-5	0	0	0	1.000	-1	P-22/O-1	0.0
1935	Cle-A	65	84	11	26	4	1	3	17	9	12	.310	.376	.488	120	2	1	1	-0	.944	2	P-25/O-4,31	0.2
1936	Cle-A	18	16	0	2	0	0	0	2	1	6	.125	.176	.125	-24	-3	0	0	0	1.000	-0	/P-9	0.0
Total	6	136	185	28	51	7	1	5	28	15	43	.276	.330	.405	86	-4	1	1	-0	.952	2	/P-70,3-8,O1	0.4
Team	5	127	180	26	49	7	1	4	26	14	41	.272	.325	.389	81	-6	1	1	-0	.950	2	/P-61,3-8,O1	0.4

■ DAVE WINFIELD Winfield, David Mark b: 10/3/51, St.Paul, Minn. BR/TR, 6'6", 220 lbs. Deb: 6/19/73

| 1995 | Cle-A | 46 | 115 | 11 | 22 | 5 | 0 | 2 | 4 | 14 | 26 | .191 | .285 | .287 | 49 | -9 | 1 | 0 | 0 | .000 | 0 | D-39 | -1.0 |
| Total | 22 | 2973 | 11003 | 1669 | 3110 | 540 | 88 | 465 | 1833 | 1216 | 1686 | .283 | .355 | .475 | 130 | 440 | 223 | 96 | 9 | .982 | 34 | *O-2469,D-419/13 | 38.6 |

■ JOE WOOD Wood, Joe "Smokey Joe" (b: Howard Ellsworth Wood) b: 10/25/1889, Kansas City, Mo. d: 7/27/85, West Haven, Conn BR/TR, 5'11", 180 lbs. Deb: 8/24/08 F

1917	Cle-A	10	6	1	0	0	0	0	0	0	3	.000	.000	.000	-93	-1	0			1.000	0	/P-5	0.0
1918	Cle-A	119	422	41	125	22	4	5	66	36	38	.296	.356	.403	118	8	8			.962	0	O-95,2-19/1	0.5
1919	Cle-A	72	192	30	49	10	6	0	27	32	21	.255	.367	.370	101	1	3			.932	-8	O-64/P-1	-1.1
1920	*Cle-A	61	137	25	37	11	2	1	30	25	16	.270	.390	.401	107	2	1	1	-0	.987	-6	O-55/P-1	-0.7
1921	Cle-A	66	194	32	71	16	5	4	60	25	17	.366	.438	.562	151	15	2	0	1	.973	-13	O-64	-0.1
1922	Cle-A	142	505	74	150	33	8	8	92	50	63	.297	.367	.442	109	7	5	1	1	.960	-2	*O-141	-0.1
Total	14	696	1952	266	553	118	31	23	325	208	189	.283	.357	.411	110	25	23	3		.962	-11	O-419,P-225/21	-1.4
Team	6	470	1456	203	432	92	25	18	275	168	158	.297	.374	.431	115	32	19	2		.962	-25	O-419/2-19,P1	-1.4

■ BOB WOOD Wood, Robert Lynn b: 7/28/1865, Thorn Hill, Ohio d: 5/22/43, Churchill, Ohio BR/TR, 5'8.5", 153 lbs. Deb: 5/2/1898

1901	Cle-A	98	346	45	101	23	3	1	49	12		.292	.327	.384	101	-0	6			.952	-1	C-84/3-4,012S	0.7
1902	Cle-A	81	258	23	76	18	2	0	40	27		.295	.375	.380	114	6	1			.940	-8	C-52,1-16/O23	0.4
Total	7	382	1245	149	350	73	15	2	168	89		.281	.339	.369	102	3	15			.951	-14	C-290/3-22,102S	1.8
Team	2	179	604	68	177	41	5	1	89	39		.293	.348	.382	107	6	7			.948	-8	C-136/1-17,302S	1.1

■ ROY WOOD Wood, Roy Winton "Woody" b: 8/29/1892, Monticello, Ark. d: 4/6/74, Fayetteville, Ark. BR/TR, 6', 175 lbs. Deb: 6/16/13

1914	Cle-A	72	220	24	52	6	3	1	15	13	26	.236	.300	.305	79	-6	6	9	-4	.946	-1	O-40,1-20	-1.4
1915	Cle-A	33	78	5	15	2	1	0	3	2	13	.192	.244	.244	41	-6	1	2	-1	.990	-2	1-21/O-2	-0.9
Total	3	119	333	33	77	12	4	1	20	16	47	.231	.285	.300	73	-12	7	11		.936	-1	/O-50,1-42	-2.2
Team	2	105	298	29	67	8	4	1	18	15	39	.225	.283	.289	69	-12	7	11		.947	-2	/O-42,1-41	-2.3

YEAR	TM/L	G	AB	R	H	2B	3B	HR	RBI	BB	SO	AVG	OBP	SLG	PRO+	BR/A	SB	CS	SBR	FA	FR	G/POS	TPR

■ GENE WOODLING   Woodling, Eugene Richard   b: 8/16/22, Akron, Ohio   BL/TR, 5'9.5", 195 lbs.   Deb: 9/23/43   C

1943	Cle-A	8	25	5	8	2	1	1	5	1	5	.320	.346	.600	186	2	0	0	0	1.000	-1	/O-6	0.2
1946	Cle-A	61	133	8	25	1	4	0	9	16	13	.188	.280	.256	54	-8	1	2	-1	1.000	-3	O-37	-1.4
1955	Cle-A	79	259	33	72	15	1	5	35	36	15	.278	.372	.391	107	2	2	4	-3	.993	-3	O-70	-0.5
1956	Cle-A	100	317	56	83	17	0	8	38	69	29	.262	.398	.391	107	6	2	6	-3	.981	-0	O-85	-0.2
1957	Cle-A	133	430	74	138	25	2	19	78	64	35	.321	.412	.521	155	34	0	5	-3	.992	11	*O-113	3.5
Total	17	1796	5587	830	1585	257	63	147	830	921	479	.284	.388	.431	123	206	29	45	-18	.989	-29	*O-1566	8.8
Team	5	381	1164	176	326	60	8	33	165	186	97	.280	.384	.430	120	36	5	17	-9	.990	4	O-311	1.6

■ CHUCK WORKMAN   Workman, Charles Thomas   b: 1/6/15, Leeton, Mo.   d: 1/3/53, Kansas City, Mo.   BL/TR, 6', 175 lbs.   Deb: 9/18/38

1938	Cle-A	2	5	1	2	0	0	0	0	0	0	.400	.400	.400	103	0	0	0	0	.500	-0	/O-1	0.0
1941	Cle-A	9	4	2	0	0	0	0	0	1	1	.000	.200	.000	-45	-1	0	0	0	.000	0	H	-0.1
Total	6	526	1749	213	423	57	7	50	230	161	202	.242	.311	.368	91	-24	24	0	7	.985	-8	O-329,3-128/1	-4.8
Team	2	11	9	3	2	0	0	0	0	1	1	.222	.300	.222	37	-1	0	0	0	.500	-0	/O-1	-0.1

■ CRAIG WORTHINGTON   Worthington, Craig Richard   b: 4/17/65, Los Angeles, Cal.   BR/TR, 6', 200 lbs.   Deb: 4/26/88

1992	Cle-A	9	24	0	4	0	0	0	2	2	4	.167	.231	.167	13	-3	0	1	-1	.857	2	/3-9	-0.2
Total	6	380	1215	124	281	50	0	32	140	156	261	.231	.323	.351	91	-14	3	6	-3	.951	-22	3-369/1-4,D	-3.8

■ AB WRIGHT   Wright, Albert Owen   b: 11/16/05, Terlton, Okla.   BR/TR, 6'1.5", 190 lbs.   Deb: 4/20/35

1935	Cle-A	67	160	17	38	11	1	2	18	10	17	.237	.291	.356	65	-9	2	1	0	.984	-8	O-47	-1.7
Total	2	138	355	37	88	20	1	9	53	28	48	.248	.310	.386	85	-9	2	1	0	.974	-11	/O-94	-2.3

■ JOE WYATT   Wyatt, Loral John   b: 4/6/1900, Petersburg, Ind.   d: 12/5/70, Oblong, Ill.   BR/TR, 6'1", 175 lbs.   Deb: 9/11/24

1924	Cle-A	4	12	1	2	0	0	0	1	2	1	.167	.286	.167	18	-1	0	0	0	.833	-1	/O-4	-0.3

■ EARLY WYNN   Wynn, Early "Gus"   b: 1/6/20, Hartford, Ala.   BB/TR, 6', 200 lbs.   Deb: 9/13/39   CH

1949	Cle-A	35	70	3	10	1	0	1	7	4	10	.143	.189	.200	3	-10	0	0	0	**1.000**	1	P-26	0.0
1950	Cle-A	39	77	12	18	5	1	2	10	10	12	.234	.322	.403	87	-2	0	0	0	.932	-1	P-32	0.0
1951	Cle-A	41	108	8	20	8	1	1	13	7	9	.185	.235	.306	48	-9	0	0	0	.982	-1	P-37	0.0
1952	Cle-A	44	99	5	22	2	0	0	10	9	15	.222	.287	.242	52	-6	0	0	0	.943	-1	P-42	0.0
1953	Cle-A	37	91	11	25	2	0	3	10	7	17	.275	.327	.396	97	-1	0	0	0	**1.000**	-1	P-36	0.0
1954	*Cle-A	40	93	10	17	3	0	1	4	7	13	.183	.240	.215	25	-10	0	0	0	.957	-3	P-40	0.0
1955	Cle-A★	34	84	8	15	3	0	1	7	6	17	.179	.233	.250	29	-9	0	0	0	.944	-3	P-32	0.0
1956	Cle-A★	38	101	5	23	5	0	1	15	7	22	.228	.278	.307	53	-7	1	0	0	.955	1	P-38	0.0
1957	Cle-A★	40	86	4	10	0	0	0	4	11	23	.116	.216	.116	-7	-13	0	0	0	**1.000**	-0	P-40	0.0
1963	Cle-A	20	11	1	3	0	0	0	0	2	5	.273	.385	.273	89	-0	0	0	0	1.000	-0	P-20	0.0
Total	23	796	1704	136	365	59	5	17	173	141	330	.214	.275	.285	54	-111	1	0	0	.967	-25	P-691	0.0
Team	10	368	820	67	163	29	2	9	80	70	143	.199	.262	.272	45	-65	1	0	0	.968	-7	P-343	0.0

■ GEORGE YEAGER   Yeager, George J. "Doc"   b: 6/5/1874, Cincinnati, Ohio   d: 7/5/40, Cincinnati, Ohio   BR/TR, 5'10", 190 lbs.   Deb: 9/25/1896

1901	Cle-A	39	139	13	31	5	0	0	14	4		.223	.250	.259	43	-11	2			.964	3	C-25/1-5,O2	-0.5
Total	6	217	705	90	168	25	6	5	73	45		.238	.290	.312	69	-30	7			.953	-1	C-134/1-28,O23S	-1.8

■ ELMER YOTER   Yoter, Elmer Elsworth   b: 6/26/1900, Plainfield, Pa.   d: 7/26/66, Camp Hill, Pa.   BR/TR, 5'7", 155 lbs.   Deb: 9/9/21

1924	Cle-A	19	66	3	18	1	1	0	7	5	8	.273	.324	.318	65	-3	0	0	0	.905	-2	3-19	-0.4
Total	4	36	96	5	24	2	2	0	12	9	12	.250	.314	.313	63	-5	0	0	.915	-2	/3-31	-0.6

■ GEORGE YOUNG   Young, George Joseph   b: 4/1/1890, Brooklyn, N.Y.   d: 3/13/50, Brightwaters, N.Y.   BL/TR, 6', 185 lbs.   Deb: 8/10/13

1913	Cle-A	2	2	0	0	0	0	0	0	0	0	.000	.000	.000	-97	-0	0			.000	0	H	-0.1

■ MIKE YOUNG   Young, Michael Darren   b: 3/20/60, Oakland, Cal.   BB/TR, 6'2", 195 lbs.   Deb: 9/14/82

1989	Cle-A	32	59	2	11	0	0	1	5	6	13	.186	.273	.237	44	-4	1	2	-1	1.000	-0	D-15/O-1	-0.6
Total	8	635	1840	244	454	80	6	72	235	237	465	.247	.339	.414	107	20	22	17		.969	-18	O-402,D-148	-1.7

■ BOBBY YOUNG   Young, Robert George   b: 1/22/25, Granite, Md.   d: 1/28/85, Baltimore, Md.   BL/TR, 6'1", 175 lbs.   Deb: 7/28/48

1955	Cle-A	18	45	7	14	1	1	0	6	1	2	.311	.326	.378	86	-1	0	0	0	.983	7	2-11/3-1	0.6
1956	Cle-A	1	0	0	0	0	0	0	0	0	0	—	—	—			0	0	0	.000	0	R	0.0
Total	8	687	2447	244	609	68	28	15	137	208	212	.249	.308	.318	71	-100	18	19	-6	.980	-32	2-661/3-2	-10.5
Team	2	19	45	7	14	1	1	0	6	1	2	.311	.326	.378	86	-1	0	0	0	.983	7	/2-11,3-1	0.6

■ PAUL ZUVELLA   Zuvella, Paul   b: 10/31/58, San Mateo, Cal.   BR/TR, 6', 178 lbs.   Deb: 9/4/82

1988	Cle-A	51	130	9	30	5	1	0	7	8	13	.231	.275	.285	56	-8	0	0	0	.959	-3	S-49	-0.8
1989	Cle-A	24	58	10	16	2	0	2	6	1	11	.276	.275	.414	98	-0	0	0	0	.963	-3	S-15/3-5,D	-0.3
Total	9	209	491	41	109	17	2	2	20	34	50	.222	.275	.277	52	-32	2	0	1	.959	5	S-133/2-55,3D	-1.7
Team	2	75	188	19	46	7	1	2	13	9	24	.245	.283	.324	68	-8	0	0	0	.960	-7	/S-64,3-5,D	-1.1

CHAPTER 8

The Pitcher Register

The Indians Pitcher Register consists of the central pitching statistics of every man who has pitched for the team since 1901, without exception. Pitcher batting is expressed in Batting Runs in the Pitcher Batting column, and in the columns for base hits and batting average. Pitcher defense is expressed in Fielding Runs in the Pitcher Defense column.

The pitchers are listed alphabetically by surname and, when more than one pitcher bears the name, alphabetically by *given* name—not by "use name," by which we mean the name he may have had applied to him during his playing career. This is the standard method of alphabetizing used in other biographical reference works, and in the case of baseball it makes it easier to find a lesser-known player with a common surname like Smith or Johnson. On the whole, we have been conservative in ascribing nicknames, doing so only when the player was in fact known by that name during his playing days.

Each page of the Pitcher Register is topped at the corner by a finding aid: in capital letters, the surname of, first, the pitcher whose entry heads up the page and, second, the player whose entry concludes it. Pitcher batting and pitcher defense, because the win-denominated numbers they produce are so small, are not sorted for single-season leaders (although the all-time leaders in these categories, single season and lifetime, will be found in the separate section called "All-Time Leaders"). Symbols denoting All Star Game selection and/or play appear to the right of the team/league column. An additional finding aid is an asterisk alongside the team for which a player appeared in postseason competition, thus making for easy cross-reference to the earlier section on postseason play.

The record of a man who pitched in more than one season is given in one line for each season, plus a career total line and an Indians total line. Refer to the preceding Player Index, and ultimately to *Total Baseball*, for complete seasonal data for Indians when they wore the uniforms of other clubs. If he pitched for another team in addition to the Indians, only his total for the Indians is shown in a given year. A man who pitched in only one year has no additional career total line since it would be identical to his seasonal listing.

In *Total Baseball 1*, fractional innings were calculated for teams in the Annual Record but were rounded off to the nearest whole inning for individuals, in accordance with baseball scoring practice. In 1981, this rounding-off procedure cost Sammy Stewart of Baltimore an ERA title, as Oakland's Steve McCatty won the crown despite having a higher ERA when fractional innings were counted; this singular occurrence led to a change in baseball scoring practice. In the first edition our data base conformed to the 1976-1982 practice for all of pitching history, excepting those men who pitched only one-third of an inning in an entire season. In the second edition of *Total Baseball* we recalculated all fractional innings pitched: look for a superscript figure, either a one or a two, in the IP column to indicate thirds of innings.

Gaps remain in the official record of baseball and in the ongoing process of sabermetric reconstruction. The reader will note occasional blank elements in biographical lines; these are not typographical lapses but signs that the information does not exist or has not yet been found. However, unlike the case of batting records, there are no incomplete statistical columns for Indians pitchers. Where official statistics did not exist or the raw data have not survived, as with batters facing pitchers before 1908 in the American League and before 1903 in the National, we have constructed figures from the available raw data. For example, to obtain a pitcher's BFP—Batters Facing Pitchers—for calculating Opponents' On Base Percentage or Batting Average, we have subtracted league base hits from league at-bats, divided by league innings pitched, multiplied by the pitcher's innings and added his hits and walks allowed and hit-by-pitch, if available. Research in this area continues, and we hope one day to eliminate the need for inferential data.

For a key to the team and league abbreviations used in the Pitcher Register go to the last page of the book. For a guide to the other procedures and abbreviations employed in the Pitcher Register, review the comments on the prodigiously extended pitching record on the next page.

Looking at the biographical line for any pitcher, we see first his use name in full capitals, then his given name and nickname (and any other name he may have used or been born with, such as the matronymic of a Latin American player). His date and place of birth follow "b" and his date and place of death follow "d"; years through 1900 are expressed fully, in four digits, and years after 1900 are expressed in only their last two digits. Then come his manner of batting and throwing, abbreviated for a left-handed batter who throws right as BL/TR (a switch-hitter would be shown as BB for "bats both" and a switch thrower as TB for "throws both"). Next, and for most pitchers last, is the pitcher's debut date in the major leagues.

Some pitchers continue in major league baseball after their pitching days are through, as managers, coaches, or even umpires. A pitcher whose biographical line concludes with an M served as a major league manager, not necessarily with the Indians; one whose line bears a C served as a major league coach; and one with a U served as an umpire. (In the last case we have placed a U on the biographical line only for those pitchers who umpired in at least six games in a year.) The select few who have been enshrined in the Baseball Hall of Fame are noted with an H. An F in this line denotes family connection—father-son-grandfather-grandson or brother.

A black diamond appears at the end of the biographical line for pitchers who also appear in the Player Register by virtue of their having played in 100 or more games at

YEAR TM/L	W	L	PCT	G	GS	CG	SH	SV	IP	H	HR	BB	SO	RAT	ERA	ERA+	OAV	OOB	BH	AVG	PB	PR	/A	PD	TPI
● **RIP VAN WINKLE** Van Winkle, Rip "Half Moon" (Also Played in 1874 as Geoffrey Crayon) b: 4/30/1820, Plattekill, N.Y. d: 12/12/80, Hudson, N.Y. BL/TL, 5'5", 145 lbs. Deb: 5/7/01 MUCHF ♦																								
1901 Cle-A	27	30	.474	57	57	56	1	0	498	502	5	18		9.4	3.90	104	.258	.270	40	.167	-3	5	3		-0.1
1902 Cle-A	29	22	.569	52	51	50	2	1	450	491	4	25		10.3	4.02	106	.260	.272	50	.200	1	7	7		0.5
1904 Cle-A	5	18	.217	27	23	19	0	1	196	207	7	76	77	13.0	3.44	101	.274	.340	18	.180	-0	-3	1	0	-0.1
1905 Cle-A	5	3	.625	7	7	6	0	0	60	76	0	11	17	13.0	4.35	104	.311	.341	9	.225	2	3	1	0	0.1
1906 Cle-A	0	0	—	1	1	1	0	0	0	5	2	2	0	∞	∞	-97	1.000	1.000	1	.250	0	-2	-2	0	-0.2
1907 Cle-A	16	13	.552	35	34	18	0	2	251	224	19	78	170	10.8	2.76	126	.236	.293	30	.250	1	17	20	2	2.2
1908 Cle-A	16	12	.571	36	35	14	1	5	278	224	15	48	205	8.8	2.20	130	.215	.250	25	.200	1	24	20	-3	2.2
1909 Cle-A	25	7	.781	36	35	18	0	5	273	202	24	82	208		2.21	164	.201	.261	20	.147	-1	42	43	1	4.2
1910 Cle-A	18	12	.600	37	36	19	0	2	291	230	21	83	283	9.4	2.81	135	.211	.267	38	.277	4	40	32	1	3.6
1911 Cle-A	20	10	.667	36	35	21	0	4	286	210	18	61	289	8.6	1.76	188	.202	.246	40	.296	4	54	49	-1	5.5
1912 Cle-A	21	12	.636	35	35	13	0	3	262	215	23	77	249	10.0	2.92	116	.219	.275	34	.281	3	18	14	1	1.7
1914 Cle-A	11	11	.500	32	32	12	0	5	236	199	19	75	201	10.4	3.20	126	.226	.287	22	.227	-1	11	22	1	2.2
1915 Cle-A	22	9	.710	36	36	15	0	5	280	217	11	88	243	9.8	2.38	155	.211	.274	33	.311	3	39	41	1	4.2
1956 *Cle-A☆	7	3	.700	13	13	5	0	3	96	79	7	28	72	10.0	3.00	140	.218	.274	11	.196	1	10	13	3	1.5
1967 *Cle-A★	0	1	.000	1	1	0	0	0	⅓	5	2	1	1	180.0	108.00	1200	.833	.857	0	.000	0	-2	-2	0	-0.2
Total 16	190	128	.597	384	375	180	1	38	2903	2486	199	803	2338	10.2	2.76	134	.226	.285	294	.224	23	304	313	6	33.6
Team 15	166	111	.599	332	323	128	1	35	2509	2162	168	710	2015	10.2	2.72	138	.224	.286	243	.223	20	249	258	3	32.9

another position, including pinch hitter, or having played more than half of their total major league games at another position, or having played more games at a position other than pitcher in at least one year.

The explanations for the statistical column heads follow; for more technical information about formulas and calculations, see the next-to-last page. The vertical rules in the column-header line separate the stats into six logical groupings: year, team, league; wins and losses; game-related counting stats; inning-related counting stats; basic calculated averages; pitcher batting; sabermetric figures of more complex calculation; and run-denominated Linear Weights stats for pitching, fielding, and Total Pitcher Index.

Note that the TPI (Total Pitcher Index) has been revised to employ the Relief Ranking formula for all pitchers, not just relievers. The principal effect will be to calculate Pitcher Wins for relievers instead of Adjusted Pitcher Runs. The TPI will still be the sum of pitching, batting, fielding, and baserunning runs, but the Pitcher Runs will be expressed as Ranking Runs rather than Adjusted Pitching Runs. The net effect will be to raise the TPIs of relief closers and, to a lesser extent, starters who average a high number of innings per start, and to lower somewhat the TPIs of mopup relievers (few saves, few decisions) and starters with many no-decision games.

We have made an upward adjustment to overall league performance in the Federal League of 1914-15 (thus lowering individual ratings), because while that league is regarded as a major league, there can be no doubt that its caliber of play was not equivalent to that in the rival leagues of those years. Suffice it to say here that league earned run averages were reduced by 10 percent for the FL. Few Indians extended their careers into the FL.

YEAR   Year in which a man pitched

*   Denotes postseason play, World Series or League Championship Series.

★   Named to All Star Game, played

☆   Named to All Star Game, did not play

†   Named to All Star Game, replaced because of injury

TM/L   Team and League

W   Wins

L   Losses

PCT   Win Percentage (Wins divided by decisions)

G   Games pitched

GS   Games Started

CG   Complete Games

SH   Shutouts (Complete-game shutouts only)

SV   Saves (Employing definition in force at the time, and 1969 definition for years prior to 1969)

IP   Innings Pitched (Fractional innings included, as discussed above)

H   Hits allowed

HR   Home Runs allowed

BB   Bases on Balls allowed

SO   Strikeouts

RAT   Ratio (Hits allowed plus walks allowed per nine innings)

ERA   Earned Run Average (In a handful of cases, a pitcher will have faced one or more batters for his full season's work yet failed to retire any of them [thus having an innings-pitched figure of zero]; if any of the men he put on base came around to score earned runs, these runs produced an infinite ERA, expressed in the pitcher's record as ∞. (see Van Winkle's 1906 season)

ERA+   Adjusted Earned Run Average normalized to league average and adjusted for home-park factor. (See comments for /A.)

OAV   Opponents' Batting Average

OOB   Opponents' On Base Percentage

BH   Base Hits (as a batter)

AVG   Batting Average

PB   Pitcher Batting (Expressed in Batting Runs. Pitcher Batting is park-adjusted and weighted, for those who played primarily at other positions, by the ratio of games pitched to games played. For more technical data about Runs Per Win and Batting Run formulas, see the next-to-last page.)

PR   Pitching Runs (Linear Weights measure of runs saved *beyond* what a league-average pitcher might have saved, defined as zero. New to this edition, the formula used to calculate Relief Ranking is now employed for all pitchers; this creates small differences for starters but large differences for relievers, especially closers. Occasionally the curious figure of − 0 will appear in this column, or in the columns of other Linear Weights measures of batting, fielding, and the TPI. This "negative zero" figure signifies a run contribution that falls below the league average, but to so small a degree that it cannot be said to have cost the team a run.

/A   Adjusted (This signifies that the stat to the imme-diate left, in this instance Pitching Runs, is here normalized to league average and adjusted for home-park factor. A mark of 100 is a league-average performance, and superior marks exceed 100. An innovation for this edition is to use three-year averages for pitching park factors. If a team moved, or the park changed dramatically, then two-year averages are employed; if the park was used for only one year, then of course only that run-scoring data is used.)

PD   Pitcher Defense (Expressed in Fielding Runs. See comment above on PB.)

TPI   Total Pitcher Index (The sum, expressed in wins beyond league average, of a pitcher's Pitching Runs, Batting Runs—in the AL since 1973—and Fielding Runs, all divided by the Runs Per Win factor for that year, which is generally around 10, historically in the 9–11 range.)

Total   The lifetime record is shown alongside the notation "Total x," where *x* stands for the number of years totaled.

Team   The totals for a player while he was an Indian, from 1901 onward.

YEAR TM/L	W	L	PCT	G	GS	CG	SH	SV	IP	H	HR	BB	SO	RAT	ERA	ERA+	OAV	OOB	BH	AVG	PB	PR	/A	PD	TPI
● **PAUL ABBOTT** Abbott, Paul David b: 9/15/67, Van Nuys, Cal. BR/TR, 6'3", 185 lbs. Deb: 8/21/90																									
1993 Cle-A	0	1	.000	5	5	0	0	0	18^{1}	19	5	11	7	14.7	6.38	68	.260	.357	0	—	0	-4	-4	0	-0.2
Total 4	3	7	.300	33	15	0	0	0	111^{1}	106	11	80	88	15.2	5.25	80	.258	.381	0	—	0	-15	-13	-0	-1.9
● **AL ABER** Aber, Albert Julius "Lefty" b: 7/31/27, Cleveland, Ohio d: 5/20/93, Garfield Heights, Ohio BL/TL, 6'2", 195 lbs. Deb: 9/15/50																									
1950 Cle-A	1	0	1.000	1	1	1	0	0	9	5	0	4	4	9.0	2.00	217	.167	.265	0	.000	0	3	2	-0	0.2
1953 Cle-A	1	1	.500	6	0	0	0	0	6	6	0	9	4	22.5	7.50	50	.240	.441	0	—	1	-2	-2	0	-0.6
Total 6	24	25	.490	168	30	7	0	14	389^{1}	398	29	160	169	13.0	4.18	93	.269	.342	14	.140	-3	-11	-13	3	-2.0
Team 2	2	1	.667	7	1	1	0	0	15	11	0	13	8	14.4	4.20	98	.200	.353	0	.000	1	0	-0	0	-0.4
● **BILL ABERNATHIE** Abernathie, William Edward b: 1/30/29, Torrance, Cal. BR/TR, 5'10", 190 lbs. Deb: 9/27/52																									
1952 Cle-A	0	0	—	1	0	0	0	1	2	4	1	1	0	22.5	13.50	25	.444	.500	0	.000	-0	-2	-2	-0	-0.2
● **TED ABERNATHY** Abernathy, Theodore Wade b: 3/6/33, Stanley, N.C. BR/TR, 6'4", 215 lbs. Deb: 4/13/55																									
1963 Cle-A	7	2	.778	43	0	0	0	12	59^{1}	54	3	29	47	12.6	2.88	126	.251	.340	2	.400	1	5	5	2	1.3
1964 Cle-A	2	6	.250	53	0	0	0	11	72^{2}	66	5	46	57	14.1	4.33	83	.247	.362	0	.000	-1	-6	-6	3	-0.6
Total 14	63	69	.477	681	34	7	2	148	1147^{2}	1010	70	592	765	12.9	3.46	106	.241	.341	25	.138	-4	12	26	27	8.7
Team 2	9	8	.529	96	0	0	0	23	132	120	8	75	104	13.4	3.68	98	.249	.352	2	.182	0	-1	-1	5	0.7
● **HARRY ABLES** Ables, Harry Terrell "Hans" b: 10/4/1884, Terrell, Tex. d: 2/8/51, San Antonio, Tex. BR/TL, 6'2.5", 200 lbs. Deb: 9/4/05																									
1909 Cle-A	1	1	.500	5	3	3	0	0	29^{2}	26	1	10	24	11.2	2.12	120	.226	.294	0	.000	-1	1	1	-1	-0.2
Total 3	1	5	.167	14	8	4	0	0	71^{1}	79	1	30	41	13.9	4.04	67	.275	.346	0	.000	-4	-11	-11	-2	-1.4
● **HANK AGUIRRE** Aguirre, Henry John b: 1/31/31, Azusa, Cal. d: 9/5/94, Bloomfield Hills, Mich. BR/TL, 6'4", 205 lbs. Deb: 9/10/55 C																									
1955 Cle-A	2	0	1.000	4	1	1	1	0	12^{2}	6	0	12	6	12.8	1.42	281	.143	.333	0	.000	-1	4	4	-0	0.4
1956 Cle-A	3	5	.375	16	9	2	1	1	65^{1}	63	7	27	31	12.5	3.72	113	.253	.329	2	.111	-2	3	4	-1	0.2
1957 Cle-A	1	1	.500	10	1	0	0	0	20^{1}	26	0	13	9	17.3	5.75	65	.317	.411	0	.000	-1	-4	-5	-0	-0.5
Total 16	75	72	.510	447	149	44	9	33	1375^{2}	1216	123	479	856	11.4	3.24	116	.236	.307	33	.085	-21	67	79	-16	4.2
Team 3	6	6	.500	30	11	3	2	1	98^{1}	95	7	52	46	13.5	3.84	106	.255	.347	2	.077	-3	2	3	-1	0.1
● **DARREL AKERFELDS** Akerfelds, Darrel Wayne b: 6/12/62, Denver, Colo. BR/TR, 6'2", 210 lbs. Deb: 8/1/86																									
1987 Cle-A	2	6	.250	16	13	1	0	0	74^{2}	84	18	38	42	15.5	6.75	67	.284	.378	0	—	0	-19	-18	-0	-1.7
Total 5	9	10	.474	125	13	1	0	3	233^{2}	216	36	127	129	13.7	5.08	79	.246	.350	1	.111	-0	-28	-28	0	-2.1
● **BOB ALEXANDER** Alexander, Robert Somerville b: 8/7/22, Vancouver, B.C., Can d: 4/7/93, Oceanside, Cal. BR/TR, 6'2.5", 205 lbs. Deb: 4/11/55																									
1957 Cle-A	0	1	.000	5	0	0	0	0	7	10	0	5	1	20.6	9.00	41	.357	.471	0	.000	-0	-4	-4	-0	-0.6
Total 2	1	1	.500	9	0	0	0	0	11	18	0	7	2	22.1	10.64	35	.391	.491	0	.000	-0	-8	-8	-1	-1.5
● **JOHNNY ALLEN** Allen, John Thomas b: 9/30/05, Lenoir, N.C. d: 3/29/59, St.Petersburg, Fla BR/TR, 6', 180 lbs. Deb: 4/19/32																									
1936 Cle-A	20	10	.667	36	31	19	4	1	243	234	5	97	165	12.3	3.44	146	.256	.328	14	.161	-3	43	43	2	4.5
1937 Cle-A	15	1	**.938**	24	20	14	0	0	173	157	4	60	87	11.5	2.55	181	.244	.313	6	.090	-7	40	40	1	2.7
1938 Cle-A★	14	8	.636	30	27	13	0	0	200	189	15	81	112	12.3	4.18	111	.246	.321	20	.253	4	13	10	2	1.5
1939 Cle-A	9	7	.563	28	26	9	2	0	175	199	9	56	79	13.3	4.58	96	.291	.347	16	.225	1	1	-3	3	0.1
1940 Cle-A	9	8	.529	32	17	5	3	5	138^{2}	126	3	48	62	11.5	3.44	123	.243	.311	10	.208	0	15	12	-0	1.4
Total 13	142	75	.654	352	241	109	17	18	1950^{1}	1849	104	738	1070	12.1	3.75	113	.249	.321	124	.173	-8	138	102	6	8.9
Team 5	67	34	.663	150	121	60	9	6	929^{2}	905	36	342	505	12.2	3.65	127	.256	.325	66	.188	-4	112	101	8	10.2
● **NEIL ALLEN** Allen, Neil Patrick b: 1/24/58, Kansas City, Kan. BR/TR, 6'2", 190 lbs. Deb: 4/15/79																									
1989 Cle-A	0	1	.000	3	0	0	0	0	3	8	1	0	0	24.0	15.00	26	.500	.500	0	—	0	-4	-4	0	-1.0
Total 11	58	70	.453	434	59	7	6	75	988^{1}	985	73	417	611	12.8	3.88	97	.264	.339	15	.130	-1	-9	-11	-3	-2.9
● **BOB ALLEN** Allen, Robert Gray b: 10/23/37, Tatum, Tex. BL/TL, 6'2", 185 lbs. Deb: 4/14/61																									
1961 Cle-A	3	2	.600	48	0	0	0	3	81^{2}	96	7	40	42	15.1	3.75	105	.294	.373	2	.167	0	3	2	-0	0.1
1962 Cle-A	1	1	.500	30	0	0	0	4	30^{2}	29	5	25	23	15.8	5.87	66	.250	.383	0	.000	-1	-6	-7	0	-0.6
1963 Cle-A	1	2	.333	43	0	0	0	2	56	58	5	29	51	14.1	4.66	78	.266	.355	1	.200	-0	-6	-6	0	-0.4
1966 Cle-A	2	2	.500	36	0	0	0	5	51^{1}	56	2	13	33	12.4	4.21	82	.273	.323	1	.111	-0	-4	-4	1	-0.4
1967 Cle-A	0	5	.000	47	0	0	0	5	54^{1}	49	4	25	50	12.4	2.98	110	.243	.329	0	—	0	2	2	1	0.3
Total 5	7	12	.368	204	0	0	0	19	274	288	23	132	199	14.0	4.11	89	.270	.353	4	.129	-1	-13	-14	2	-1.0
● **LARRY ANDERSEN** Andersen, Larry Eugene b: 5/6/53, Portland, Ore. BR/TR, 6'3", 205 lbs. Deb: 9/5/75																									
1975 Cle-A	0	0	—	3	0	0	0	0	5^{2}	4	0	2	4	9.5	4.76	79	.200	.273	0	—	0	-1	-1	0	0.0
1977 Cle-A	0	1	.000	11	0	0	0	0	14^{1}	10	1	9	8	11.9	3.14	126	.200	.322	0	—	0	1	1	1	0.2
1979 Cle-A	0	0	—	8	0	0	0	0	16^{2}	25	3	4	7	15.7	7.56	56	.357	.392	0	—	0	-6	-6	0	0.0
Total 17	40	39	.506	699	1	0	0	49	995^{1}	932	58	311	758	11.4	3.15	119	.249	.309	5	.132	-0	68	68	5	8.8
Team 3	0	1	.000	22	0	0	0	0	36^{2}	39	4	15	19	13.3	5.40	75	.279	.348	0	—	0	-5	-5	1	0.2
● **BUD ANDERSON** Anderson, Karl Adam b: 5/27/56, Westbury, N.Y. BR/TR, 6'3", 210 lbs. Deb: 6/11/82																									
1982 Cle-A	3	4	.429	25	5	1	0	0	80^{2}	84	4	30	44	12.8	3.35	122	.268	.334	0	—	0	7	7	-0	0.5
1983 Cle-A	1	6	.143	39	1	0	0	7	68^{1}	64	8	32	32	12.6	4.08	104	.255	.339	0	—	0	-0	1	-1	0.0
Total 2	4	10	.286	64	6	1	0	7	149	148	12	62	76	12.7	3.68	113	.262	.337	0	—	0	6	8	-1	0.5
● **IVY ANDREWS** Andrews, Ivy Paul "Poison" b: 5/6/07, Dora, Ala. d: 11/24/70, Birmingham, Ala. BR/TR, 6'1", 200 lbs. Deb: 8/15/31																									
1937 Cle-A	3	4	.429	20	4	1	1	0	59^{2}	76	3	9	16	12.8	4.37	105	.311	.336	3	.250	1	2	2	-1	0.1
Total 8	50	59	.459	249	108	43	2	8	1041	1151	59	342	257	12.9	4.14	115	.279	.335	59	.185	-6	51	70	-9	4.4
● **NATE ANDREWS** Andrews, Nathan Hardy b: 9/30/13, Pembroke, N.C. d: 4/26/91, Winston-Salem, N.C. BR/TR, 6', 195 lbs. Deb: 5/1/37																									
1940 Cle-A	0	1	.000	6	0	0	0	0	12	16	1	6	3	16.5	6.00	70	.327	.400	0	—	0	-2	-2	1	-0.1
1941 Cle-A	0	0	—	2	0	0	0	0	2^{1}	3	0	2	1	19.3	11.57	34	.300	.417	0	.000	-0	-2	-2	-0	0.0
Total 8	41	54	.432	127	97	50	5	2	773^{1}	798	40	236	216	12.1	3.46	106	.265	.321	35	.146	-4	10	17	4	2.3
Team 2	0	1	.000	8	0	0	0	0	14^{1}	19	1	8	4	17.0	6.91	60	.322	.403	0	.000	0	-4	-4	1	-0.1
● **JOHNNY ANTONELLI** Antonelli, John August b: 4/12/30, Rochester, N.Y. BL/TL, 6', 190 lbs. Deb: 7/4/48																									
1961 Cle-A	0	4	.000	11	7	0	0	0	48	68	8	18	23	16.3	6.56	60	.338	.395	4	.267	1	-14	-14	1	-0.8
Total 12	126	110	.534	377	268	102	25	21	1992^{1}	1870	185	687	1162	11.7	3.34	116	.247	.313	121	.178	15	141	118	-1	15.7
● **LUIS APONTE** Aponte, Luis Eduardo (Yuripe) b: 6/14/53, ElTigre, Venez. BR/TR, 6', 185 lbs. Deb: 9/4/80																									
1984 Cle-A	1	0	1.000	25	0	0	0	0	50^{1}	53	5	15	25	12.3	4.11	99	.269	.324	0	—	0	-1	-0	-1	-0.1
Total 5	9	6	.600	110	0	0	0	7	220	222	17	68	113	12.0	3.27	129	.265	.323	0	—	0	18	23	3	1.3
● **PETE APPLETON** Appleton, Peter William "Jake" (a.k.a. Jablonowski In 1927-33) b: 5/20/04, Terryville, Conn. d: 1/18/74, Trenton, N.J. BR/TR, 5'11", 180 lbs. Deb: 9/14/27																									
1930 Cle-A	8	7	.533	39	7	2	0	1	118^{2}	122	8	53	45	13.7	4.02	120	.274	.357	8	.200	-1	8	11	2	1.2
1931 Cle-A	4	4	.500	29	4	3	0	0	79^{2}	100	2	29	25	14.7	4.63	100	.293	.350	5	.208	0	-2	-0	-0	0.0
1932 Cle-A	0	0	—	4	0	0	0	0	5	11	1	3	1	25.2	16.20	29	.407	.467	0	—	0	-7	-6	0	0.0
Total 14	57	66	.463	341	71	34	6	26	1141	1187	76	486	420	13.4	4.30	104	.268	.343	87	.233	7	33	19	12	4.6
Team 3	12	11	.522	72	11	5	0	1	203^{1}	233	11	85	71	14.3	4.56	104	.286	.358	13	.203	-1	-0	4	2	1.2

YEAR TM/L	W	L	PCT	G	GS	CG	SH	SV	IP	H	HR	BB	SO	RAT	ERA	ERA+	OAV	OOB	BH	AVG	PB	PR	/A	PD	TPI
● **STEVE ARLIN** Arlin, Stephen Ralph b: 9/25/45, Seattle, Wash. BR/TR, 6'3.5", 195 lbs. Deb: 6/17/69																									
1974 Cle-A	2	5	.286	11	10	1	0	0	43^2	59	1	22	20	16.7	6.60	55	.333	.407	0	—	0	-14	-14	-1	-2.0
Total 6	34	67	.337	141	123	32	11	1	788^2	792	61	373	463	13.5	4.33	78	.263	.348	32	.139	1	-69	-82	-3	-10.0
● **JACK ARMSTRONG** Armstrong, Jack William b: 3/7/65, Englewood, N.J. BR/TR, 6'5", 220 lbs. Deb: 6/21/88																									
1992 Cle-A	6	15	.286	35	23	1	0	0	166^2	176	23	67	114	13.3	4.64	84	.269	.340	0	—	0	-13	-14	1	-1.3
Total 7	40	65	.381	152	130	4	1	0	786^2	807	102	319	510	13.1	4.58	87	.265	.338	21	.114	-6	-65	-53	2	-7.2
● **MIKE ARMSTRONG** Armstrong, Michael Dennis b: 3/7/54, Glen Cove, N.Y. BR/TR, 6'3", 206 lbs. Deb: 8/12/80																									
1987 Cle-A	1	0	1.000	14	0	0	0	1	18^2	27	4	10	9	17.8	8.68	52	.333	.407	0	—	0	-9	-9	-0	-0.5
Total 8	19	17	.528	197	1	0	0	11	338	300	42	155	221	12.3	4.10	97	.240	.326	0	.000	-0	-2	-4	-3	0.3
● **BRAD ARNSBERG** Arnsberg, Bradley James b: 8/20/63, Seattle, Wash. BR/TR, 6'4", 205 lbs. Deb: 9/6/86																									
1992 Cle-A	0	0	—	8	0	0	0	0	10^2	13	6	11	5	21.9	11.81	33	.317	.481	0	—	0	-9	-9	-0	0.1
Total 6	9	6	.600	94	4	0	0	6	158^1	159	27	85	100	14.3	4.26	94	.259	.356	0	—	0	-5	-5	2	0.9
● **PAUL ASSENMACHER** Assenmacher, Paul Andre b: 12/10/60, Detroit, Mich. BL/TL, 6'3", 195 lbs. Deb: 4/12/86																									
1995 *Cle-A	6	2	.750	47	0	0	0	0	38^1	32	3	12	40	11.0	2.82	164	.225	.299	0	—	0	8	8	0	1.4
Total 10	48	36	.571	622	1	0	0	48	680	624	56	250	638	11.8	3.40	117	.245	.316	3	.083	-0	31	44	0	6.8
● **KEITH ATHERTON** Atherton, Keith Rowe b: 2/19/59, Mathews, Va. BR/TR, 6'4", 200 lbs. Deb: 7/14/83																									
1989 Cle-A	0	3	.000	32	0	0	0	2	39	48	7	13	13	14.1	4.15	95	.293	.345	0	—	0	-1	-1	-1	-0.2
Total 7	33	41	.446	342	0	0	0	26	566^1	546	75	215	349	12.3	3.99	101	.253	.324	0	.000	0	8	3	-6	0.6
● **RICK AUSTIN** Austin, Rick Gerald b: 10/27/46, Seattle, Wash. BR/TL, 6'4", 190 lbs. Deb: 6/21/70																									
1970 Cle-A	2	5	.286	31	8	1	1	3	67^2	74	10	26	53	13.7	4.79	83	.281	.353	2	.111	0	-8	-6	1	-0.5
1971 Cle-A	0	0	—	23	0	0	0	1	23	25	3	20	20	18.8	5.09	75	.291	.440	0	.000	-0	-4	-3	0	0.0
Total 4	4	8	.333	89	8	1	1	6	136	141	17	78	106	15.0	4.63	84	.273	.377	2	.105	0	-14	-11	1	-0.7
Team 2	2	5	.286	54	8	1	1	4	90^2	99	13	46	73	15.0	4.86	81	.284	.377	2	.105	0	-12	-9	1	-0.5
● **JIM BAGBY** Bagby, James Charles Jacob Jr. b: 9/8/16, Cleveland, Ohio d: 9/2/88, Marietta, Ga. BR/TR, 6'2", 170 lbs. Deb: 4/18/38 F																									
1941 Cle-A	9	15	.375	33	27	12	0	2	200^2	214	10	76	53	13.3	4.04	98	.273	.341	18	.243	2	2	-2	2	0.1
1942 Cle-A☆	17	9	.654	38	35	16	4	1	270^2	267	19	64	54	11.0	2.96	117	.258	.302	18	.189	1	21	15	0	1.5
1943 Cle-A☆	17	14	.548	36	33	16	3	1	**273**	248	15	80	70	10.9	3.10	100	.240	.296	30	.268	4	6	0	2	0.9
1944 Cle-A	4	5	.444	13	10	2	0	0	79	101	2	34	12	15.8	4.33	76	.312	.384	7	.226	1	-8	-9	0	-0.8
1945 Cle-A	8	11	.421	25	19	11	3	1	159^1	171	3	59	38	13.1	3.73	87	.279	.344	17	.293	3	-6	-8	3	-0.3
Total 10	97	96	.503	303	198	84	13	9	1666^1	1815	98	608	431	13.2	3.96	97	.278	.342	140	.226	12	-11	-23	10	0.3
Team 5	55	54	.505	145	124	57	10	5	982^2	1001	49	313	227	12.2	3.45	99	.264	.323	90	.243	11	15	-5	8	1.4
● **JIM BAGBY** Bagby, James Charles Jacob Sr. "Sarge" b: 10/5/1889, Barnett, Ga. d: 7/28/54, Marietta, Ga. BB/TR, 6', 170 lbs. Deb: 4/22/12 F																									
1916 Cle-A	16	16	.500	48	27	14	3	5	272^2	253	2	67	88	10.8	2.61	115	.251	.303	15	.167	-1	7	12	-3	1.1
1917 Cle-A	23	13	.639	49	37	26	8	7	320^2	277	6	73	83	10.0	1.96	144	.235	.283	25	.231	2	25	31	-3	3.8
1918 Cle-A	17	16	.515	**45**	31	23	2	6	271^1	274	0	78	57	11.7	2.69	112	.276	.330	21	.212	-0	3	10	-2	1.0
1919 Cle-A	17	11	.607	35	32	21	0	3	241^1	258	3	44	61	11.4	2.80	120	.275	.310	23	.258	5	12	15	-0	2.1
1920 *Cle-A	**31**	12	**.721**	**48**	38	**30**	3	0	**339^2**	338	9	79	73	11.2	2.89	132	.266	.311	33	.252	6	34	34	-7	3.8
1921 Cle-A	14	12	.538	40	26	13	0	4	191^2	238	14	44	37	13.4	4.70	91	.308	.348	15	.197	-1	-9	-9	-2	-1.4
1922 Cle-A	4	5	.444	25	10	4	0	1	98^1	134	5	39	25	16.1	6.32	63	.340	.404	11	.262	3	-25	-25	1	-1.7
Total 9	127	88	.591	316	208	133	16	29	1821^2	1884	47	458	450	11.7	3.11	110	.273	.321	144	.218	11	38	62	-15	7.8
Team 7	122	85	.589	290	201	131	16	26	1735^2	1772	39	424	424	11.6	3.02	112	.270	.318	143	.225	13	47	71	-14	8.7
● **SCOTT BAILES** Bailes, Scott Alan b: 12/18/61, Chillicothe, Ohio BL/TL, 6'2", 175 lbs. Deb: 4/9/86																									
1986 Cle-A	10	10	.500	62	10	0	0	7	112^2	123	12	43	60	13.3	4.95	84	.276	.342	0	—	0	-10	-10	-1	-1.7
1987 Cle-A	7	8	.467	39	17	0	0	6	120^1	145	21	47	65	14.7	4.64	98	.296	.362	0	—	0	-2	-2	0	-0.2
1988 Cle-A	9	14	.391	37	21	5	2	0	145	149	22	46	53	12.2	4.90	84	.266	.324	0	—	0	-15	-13	-0	-1.9
1989 Cle-A	5	9	.357	34	11	0	0	0	113^2	116	7	29	47	11.7	4.28	93	.269	.320	0	—	0	-5	-4	0	-0.5
Total 7	37	44	.457	273	59	5	2	13	617^1	679	82	235	307	13.6	4.93	84	.280	.347	0	—	0	-57	-54	-0	-6.0
Team 4	31	41	.431	172	59	5	2	13	491^2	533	62	165	225	13.0	4.70	89	.277	.337	0	—	0	-32	-28	-1	-4.3
● **STEVE BAILEY** Bailey, Steven John b: 2/12/42, Bronx, N.Y. BR/TR, 6'1", 194 lbs. Deb: 4/14/67																									
1967 Cle-A	2	5	.286	32	1	0	0	2	64^2	62	5	42	46	14.9	3.90	84	.259	.377	0	.000	-1	-5	-5	0	-0.6
1968 Cle-A	0	1	.000	2	1	0	0	0	5	4	1	2	1	10.8	3.60	82	.235	.316	0	—	0	-0	-0	-0	-0.1
Total 2	2	6	.250	34	2	0	0	2	69^2	66	6	44	47	14.6	3.88	84	.258	.373	0	.000	-1	-5	-5	-0	-0.7
● **BOCK BAKER** Baker, Charles "Smiling Bock" b: 7/17/1878, Troy, N.Y. d: 8/17/40, New York, N.Y. TL, 5'9", 181 lbs. Deb: 4/28/01																									
1901 Cle-A	0	1	.000	1	1	1	0	0	8	23	0	6	0	33.8	5.63	63	.500	.566	0	.000	-1	-2	-2	0	-0.2
● **MARK BALLINGER** Ballinger, Mark Alan b: 1/31/49, Glendale, Cal. BR/TR, 6'6", 205 lbs. Deb: 8/6/71																									
1971 Cle-A	1	2	.333	18	0	0	0	0	34^2	30	3	13	25	11.4	4.67	82	.233	.308	1	.200	-0	-5	-3	-0	-0.3
● **LEN BARKER** Barker, Leonard Harold b: 7/7/55, Fort Knox, Ky. BR/TR, 6'5", 225 lbs. Deb: 9/14/76																									
1979 Cle-A	6	6	.500	29	19	2	0	0	137^1	146	6	70	93	14.3	4.92	87	.277	.364	0	—	0	-11	-10	0	-0.8
1980 Cle-A	19	12	.613	36	36	8	1	0	246^1	237	17	92	**187**	12.1	4.17	98	.252	.320	0	—	0	-4	-3	-2	-0.5
1981 Cle-A★	8	7	.533	22	22	9	3	0	154^1	150	7	46	**127**	11.5	3.91	93	.249	.303	0	—	0	-4	-5	-0	-0.4
1982 Cle-A	15	11	.577	33	33	10	1	0	244^2	211	17	88	187	11.1	3.90	105	.232	.301	0	—	0	5	5	-0	0.5
1983 Cle-A	8	13	.381	24	24	4	1	0	149^2	150	16	52	105	12.3	5.11	83	.266	.330	0	—	0	-17	-15	-1	-2.0
Total 11	74	76	.493	248	194	35	7	5	1323^2	1289	96	513	975	12.4	4.34	93	.256	.327	3	.048	-3	-59	-48	1	-6.1
Team 5	56	49	.533	144	134	33	6	0	932^1	894	63	348	699	12.1	4.31	94	.252	.321	0	—	0	-31	-27	-3	-3.2
● **JEFF BARKLEY** Barkley, Jeffrey Carver b: 11/21/59, Hickory, N.C. BB/TR, 6'3", 185 lbs. Deb: 9/16/84																									
1984 Cle-A	0	0	—	3	0	0	0	0	4	6	0	1	4	15.8	6.75	61	.353	.389	0	—	0	-1	-1	0	-0.1
1985 Cle-A	0	3	.000	21	0	0	0	1	41	37	5	15	30	11.4	5.27	78	.243	.311	0	—	0	-5	-5	0	-0.3
Total 2	0	3	.000	24	0	0	0	1	45	43	5	16	34	11.8	5.40	76	.254	.319	0	—	0	-6	-6	0	-0.4
● **BRIAN BARNES** Barnes, Brian Keith b: 3/25/67, Roanoke Rapids, N.C. BL/TL, 5'9", 170 lbs. Deb: 9/14/90																									
1994 Cle-A	0	1	.000	6	0	0	0	0	13^1	12	2	15	5	18.2	5.40	87	.235	.409	0	—	0	-1	-1	0	-0.1
Total 5	14	22	.389	116	56	2	0	3	406^1	364	39	204	275	12.8	3.94	95	.242	.335	15	.140	1	-7	-8	1	0.0
● **RICH BARNES** Barnes, Richard Monroe b: 7/21/59, Palm Beach, Fla. BR/TL, 6'4", 186 lbs. Deb: 7/18/82																									
1983 Cle-A	1	1	.500	4	2	0	0	0	11^2	18	0	10	2	21.6	6.94	61	.375	.483	0	—	0	-4	-4	-0	-0.7
Total 2	1	3	.250	10	4	0	0	1	28^2	39	1	14	8	17.3	5.65	73	.325	.404	0	—	0	-5	-5	0	-0.8
● **LES BARNHART** Barnhart, Leslie Earl "Barney" b: 2/23/05, Hoxie, Kan. d: 10/7/71, Scottsdale, Ariz. BR/TR, 6', 180 lbs. Deb: 9/22/28																									
1928 Cle-A	0	1	.000	2	1	0	0	0	9	13	1	4	1	17.0	7.00	59	.325	.386	1	.500	0	-3	-3	-1	-0.3
1930 Cle-A	1	0	1.000	1	1	0	0	0	8^1	12	0	4	1	17.3	6.48	74	.364	.432	0	.000	-1	-2	-2	0	-0.2
Total 2	1	1	.500	3	2	0	0	0	17^1	25	1	8	2	17.1	6.75	66	.342	.407	1	.200	-0	-5	-4	-0	-0.5

● JIM BASKETTE
Baskette, James Blaine "Big Jim" b: 12/10/1887, Athens, Tenn. d: 7/30/42, Athens, Tenn. BR/TR, 6'2", 185 lbs. Deb: 9/22/11

YEAR TM/L	W	L	PCT	G	GS	CG	SH	SV	IP	H	HR	BB	SO	RAT	ERA	ERA+	OAV	OOB	BH	AVG	PB	PR	/A	PD	TPI
1911 Cle-A	1	2	.333	4	2	2	0	0	21^1	21	0	9	8	13.1	3.38	101	.273	.356	2	.333	1	-0	0	-0	0.0
1912 Cle-A	8	4	.667	29	11	7	1	1	116	109	2	46	51	12.6	3.18	107	.252	.334	5	.125	-1	2	3	-3	-0.1
1913 Cle-A	0	0	—	2	1	0	0	0	4^2	8	1	2	0	19.3	5.79	52	.400	.455	1	1.000	1	-1	-1	0	0.1
Total 3	9	6	.600	35	14	9	1	1	142	138	3	57	59	12.9	3.30	103	.261	.342	8	.170	1	0	2	-3	0.0

● BILL BAYNE
Bayne, William Lear "Beverly" b: 4/18/1899, Pittsburgh, Pa. d: 5/22/81, St.Louis, Mo. BL/TL, 5'9", 160 lbs. Deb: 9/20/19

YEAR TM/L	W	L	PCT	G	GS	CG	SH	SV	IP	H	HR	BB	SO	RAT	ERA	ERA+	OAV	OOB	BH	AVG	PB	PR	/A	PD	TPI
1928 Cle-A	2	5	.286	37	6	3	0	3	108^2	128	3	43	39	15.0	5.13	81	.309	.388	11	.367	3	-13	-12	2	-0.4
Total 9	31	32	.492	199	55	21	2	8	662	711	37	297	259	14.4	4.84	87	.283	.370	62	.290	10	-55	-45	-3	-3.4

● BELVE BEAN
Bean, Beveric Benton "Bill" b: 4/23/05, Mullin, Tex. d: 6/1/88, Comanche, Tex. BR/TR, 6'1.5", 197 lbs. Deb: 5/30/30

YEAR TM/L	W	L	PCT	G	GS	CG	SH	SV	IP	H	HR	BB	SO	RAT	ERA	ERA+	OAV	OOB	BH	AVG	PB	PR	/A	PD	TPI
1930 Cle-A	3	3	.500	23	3	1	0	2	74^1	99	7	32	19	15.9	5.45	89	.331	.396	9	.346	2	-7	-5	0	-0.2
1931 Cle-A	0	1	.000	4	0	0	0	0	7	11	0	4	3	20.6	6.43	72	.379	.471	0	.000	-0	-2	-1	0	-0.2
1933 Cle-A	1	2	.333	27	2	0	0	0	70^1	80	6	20	41	12.9	5.25	85	.300	.351	4	.182	-1	-8	-6	1	-0.2
1934 Cle-A	5	1	.833	21	1	0	0	0	51^1	53	2	21	20	13.5	3.86	118	.265	.344	3	.200	0	4	4	1	0.5
1935 Cle-A	0	0	—	1	0	0	0	0	1	2	1	0	0	18.0	9.00	50	.400	.400	0	—	0	-1	-0	-0	0.0
Total 5	11	7	.611	86	8	1	0	2	235	288	21	96	89	14.9	5.32	86	.311	.378	19	.264	4	-22	-19	1	-0.5
Team 5	9	7	.563	76	6	1	0	2	204	245	16	77	83	14.4	5.03	92	.306	.371	16	.250	1	-13	-9	2	-0.1

● GENE BEARDEN
Bearden, Henry Eugene b: 9/5/20, Lexa, Ark. BL/TL, 6'3", 204 lbs. Deb: 5/10/47

YEAR TM/L	W	L	PCT	G	GS	CG	SH	SV	IP	H	HR	BB	SO	RAT	ERA	ERA+	OAV	OOB	BH	AVG	PB	PR	/A	PD	TPI
1947 Cle-A	0	0	—	1	0	0	0	0	0^1	2	0	1	0	81.0	81.00	4	.667	.750	0	—	0	-3	-3	0	0.0
1948 *Cle-A	20	7	.741	37	29	15	6	1	229^2	187	9	106	80	11.6	**2.43**	**167**	.229	.320	23	.256	5	47	**42**	3	5.5
1949 Cle-A	8	8	.500	32	19	5	0	0	127	140	6	92	41	16.6	5.10	78	.286	.401	5	.111	-3	-13	-16	4	-1.6
1950 Cle-A	1	3	.250	14	3	0	0	0	45^1	57	5	32	10	17.7	6.15	70	.328	.432	2	.154	1	-8	-9	-1	-0.7
Total 7	45	38	.542	193	84	29	7	1	788^1	791	48	435	259	14.1	3.96	103	.266	.361	68	.236	10	17	12	7	4.2
Team 4	29	18	.617	84	51	20	6	1	402^1	386	20	231	131	13.9	3.76	108	.260	.362	30	.203	3	24	14	7	3.2

● KEVIN BEARSE
Bearse, Kevin Gerard b: 11/7/65, Jersey City, N.J. BL/TL, 6'2", 195 lbs. Deb: 4/15/90

YEAR TM/L	W	L	PCT	G	GS	CG	SH	SV	IP	H	HR	BB	SO	RAT	ERA	ERA+	OAV	OOB	BH	AVG	PB	PR	/A	PD	TPI
1990 Cle-A	0	2	.000	3	3	0	0	0	7^2	16	2	5	2	27.0	12.91	30	.421	.511	0	—	0	-8	-8	-0	-1.4

● GEORGE BECK
Beck, Ernest George B. b: 2/21/1890, South Bend, Ind. d: 10/29/73, South Bend, Ind. BR/TR, 5'11", 165 lbs. Deb: 5/15/14

YEAR TM/L	W	L	PCT	G	GS	CG	SH	SV	IP	H	HR	BB	SO	RAT	ERA	ERA+	OAV	OOB	BH	AVG	PB	PR	/A	PD	TPI
1914 Cle-A	0	0	—	1	0	0	0	0	1	1	0	0	0	18.0	0.00	—	.250	.400	0	—	0	0	0	-0	0.0

● PHIL BEDGOOD
Bedgood, Phillip Burlette b: 3/8/1898, Harrison, Ga. d: 11/8/27, Fort Pierce, Fla. BR/TR, 6'3", 218 lbs. Deb: 9/20/22

YEAR TM/L	W	L	PCT	G	GS	CG	SH	SV	IP	H	HR	BB	SO	RAT	ERA	ERA+	OAV	OOB	BH	AVG	PB	PR	/A	PD	TPI
1922 Cle-A	1	0	1.000	1	1	1	0	0	9	7	0	4	5	14.0	4.00	100	.233	.378	0	.000	-0	0	0	-0	0.0
1923 Cle-A	0	2	.000	9	2	0	0	0	18^2	16	0	14	7	15.4	5.30	75	.246	.395	1	.250	0	-3	-3	-0	-0.2
Total 2	1	2	.333	10	3	1	0	0	27^2	23	0	18	12	15.0	4.88	82	.242	.390	1	.167	0	-3	-3	-0	-0.2

● FRED BEEBE
Beebe, Frederick Leonard b: 12/31/1880, Lincoln, Neb. d: 10/30/57, Elgin, Ill. BR/TR, 6'1", 190 lbs. Deb: 4/17/06

YEAR TM/L	W	L	PCT	G	GS	CG	SH	SV	IP	H	HR	BB	SO	RAT	ERA	ERA+	OAV	OOB	BH	AVG	PB	PR	/A	PD	TPI
1916 Cle-A	5	3	.625	20	12	5	1	2	100^2	92	1	37	32	11.6	2.41	125	.251	.321	6	.214	1	5	7	-0	0.6
Total 7	62	83	.428	202	153	93	9	4	1294^1	1090	17	534	634	11.6	2.86	93	.227	.311	72	.158	-8	-28	-30	6	-3.8

● FRED BEENE
Beene, Freddy Ray b: 11/24/42, Angleton, Tex. BB/TR, 5'9", 160 lbs. Deb: 9/18/68

YEAR TM/L	W	L	PCT	G	GS	CG	SH	SV	IP	H	HR	BB	SO	RAT	ERA	ERA+	OAV	OOB	BH	AVG	PB	PR	/A	PD	TPI
1974 Cle-A	4	4	.500	32	0	0	0	2	73	68	7	26	35	11.7	4.93	73	.246	.314	0	—	0	-11	-11	1	-1.0
1975 Cle-A	1	0	1.000	19	1	0	0	1	46^2	63	4	25	20	17.6	6.94	54	.323	.408	0	—	0	-16	-16	0	-0.4
Total 7	12	7	.632	112	6	0	0	8	288	274	21	111	156	12.3	3.63	97	.253	.326	0	.000	-1	-1	-3	2	0.6
Team 2	5	4	.556	51	1	0	0	3	119^2	131	11	51	55	14.0	5.72	64	.278	.354	0	—	0	-27	-27	1	-1.4

● RICK BEHENNA
Behenna, Richard Kipp b: 3/6/60, Miami, Fla. BR/TR, 6'2", 170 lbs. Deb: 4/12/83

YEAR TM/L	W	L	PCT	G	GS	CG	SH	SV	IP	H	HR	BB	SO	RAT	ERA	ERA+	OAV	OOB	BH	AVG	PB	PR	/A	PD	TPI
1983 Cle-A	0	2	.000	5	4	0	0	0	26	22	0	14	9	12.8	4.15	102	.232	.336	0	—	0	-0	0	0	-0.2
1984 Cle-A	0	3	.000	3	3	0	0	0	9^2	17	5	8	6	24.2	13.97	29	.386	.491	0	—	0	-11	-11	0	-2.1
1985 Cle-A	0	2	.000	4	4	0	0	0	19^2	29	3	8	4	16.9	7.78	53	.354	.411	0	—	0	-8	-8	-1	-0.7
Total 3	3	10	.231	26	17	0	0	0	92^2	105	15	42	36	14.6	6.12	66	.287	.365	4	.333	2	-23	-21	-1	-3.3
Team 3	0	7	.000	12	11	0	0	0	55^1	68	8	30	19	16.3	7.16	58	.308	.395	0	—	0	-19	-18	-0	-3.0

● ERIC BELL
Bell, Eric Alvin b: 10/27/63, Modesto, Cal. BL/TL, 6'3", 195 lbs. Deb: 9/24/85

YEAR TM/L	W	L	PCT	G	GS	CG	SH	SV	IP	H	HR	BB	SO	RAT	ERA	ERA+	OAV	OOB	BH	AVG	PB	PR	/A	PD	TPI
1991 Cle-A	4	0	1.000	10	0	0	0	0	18	5	0	5	7	5.5	0.50	830	.091	.180	0	—	0	7	7	-0	1.6
1992 Cle-A	0	2	.000	7	1	0	0	0	15^1	22	1	9	10	18.8	7.63	51	.349	.438	0	—	0	-6	-6	1	-0.6
Total 6	15	18	.455	68	34	2	0	0	234^2	238	38	112	152	13.6	5.18	83	.264	.348	0	—	0	-22	-23	-2	-1.8
Team 2	4	2	.667	17	1	0	0	0	33^1	27	1	14	17	11.6	3.78	107	.229	.321	0	—	0	1	1	0	1.0

● GARY BELL
Bell, Gary b: 11/17/36, San Antonio, Tex. BR/TR, 6'1", 198 lbs. Deb: 6/1/58

YEAR TM/L	W	L	PCT	G	GS	CG	SH	SV	IP	H	HR	BB	SO	RAT	ERA	ERA+	OAV	OOB	BH	AVG	PB	PR	/A	PD	TPI
1958 Cle-A	12	10	.545	33	23	10	0	1	182	141	17	73	110	10.8	3.31	110	.213	.296	11	.196	2	9	7	-2	0.7
1959 Cle-A	16	11	.593	44	28	12	1	5	234	208	28	105	136	12.2	4.04	91	.238	.323	18	.240	3	-5	-9	-2	-0.9
1960 Cle-A★	9	10	.474	28	23	6	2	1	154^2	139	15	82	109	13.3	4.13	90	.242	.344	7	.149	-0	-4	-7	1	-0.7
1961 Cle-A	12	16	.429	34	34	11	2	0	228^1	214	32	100	163	12.6	4.10	96	.245	.326	16	.198	1	-2	-4	-1	-0.4
1962 Cle-A	10	9	.526	57	6	1	0	12	107^2	104	14	52	80	13.3	4.26	91	.264	.354	5	.208	1	-4	-5	-1	-0.8
1963 Cle-A	8	5	.615	58	7	0	0	5	119	91	13	52	98	11.1	2.95	123	.208	.298	3	.115	-1	9	9	1	1.0
1964 Cle-A	8	6	.571	56	2	0	0	4	106	106	15	53	89	13.8	4.33	83	.260	.351	6	.375	2	-8	-9	-1	-1.0
1965 Cle-A	6	5	.545	60	0	0	0	17	103^2	86	7	50	86	12.0	3.04	115	.226	.319	1	.063	-0	5	5	-1	0.6
1966 Cle-A☆	14	15	.483	40	37	12	0	0	254^1	211	19	79	194	10.4	3.22	107	.228	.291	10	.132	-1	6	6	2	0.8
1967 Cle-A	1	5	.167	9	9	1	0	0	60^2	50	7	24	39	11.1	3.71	88	.234	.314	0	.000	-2	-6	-3	1	-0.4
Total 12	121	117	.508	519	233	71	9	51	2015	1794	206	842	1378	12.0	3.68	98	.239	.320	105	.185	9	-17	-18	-3	-0.7
Team 10	96	92	.511	419	169	53	5	45	1550^1	1350	167	670	1104	12.0	3.71	99	.235	.319	77	.178	5	3	-9	-3	-1.1

● RAY BENGE
Benge, Raymond Adelphia b: 4/22/02, Jacksonville, Tex. BR/TR, 5'9.5", 160 lbs. Deb: 9/26/25

YEAR TM/L	W	L	PCT	G	GS	CG	SH	SV	IP	H	HR	BB	SO	RAT	ERA	ERA+	OAV	OOB	BH	AVG	PB	PR	/A	PD	TPI
1925 Cle-A	1	0	1.000	2	2	1	1	0	11^2	9	0	3	3	9.3	1.54	286	.205	.255	2	.400	0	4	4	-1	0.3
1926 Cle-A	1	0	1.000	8	0	0	0	0	11^2	15	0	4	3	14.7	3.86	105	.313	.365	1	.333	0	0	0	0	0.1
Total 12	101	130	.437	346	249	102	12	19	1875^1	2177	132	598	655	13.5	4.52	95	.292	.347	124	.188	-17	-89	-46	-18	-7.5
Team 2	2	0	1.000	10	2	1	1	0	23^1	24	0	7	6	12.0	2.70	157	.261	.313	3	.375	1	4	4	-1	0.4

● HENRY BENN
Benn, Henry Omer b: 1/25/1890, Viola, Wis. d: 6/4/67, Madison, Wis. BR/TR, 6', 190 lbs. Deb: 9/24/14

YEAR TM/L	W	L	PCT	G	GS	CG	SH	SV	IP	H	HR	BB	SO	RAT	ERA	ERA+	OAV	OOB	BH	AVG	PB	PR	/A	PD	TPI
1914 Cle-A	0	0	—	1	0	0	0	0	1	0	0	0	1	0.0	0.00	—	.000	.000	0	—	0	0	0	-0	0.0

● AL BENTON
Benton, John Alton b: 3/18/11, Noble, Okla. d: 4/14/68, Lynwood, Cal. BR/TR, 6'4", 215 lbs. Deb: 4/18/34

YEAR TM/L	W	L	PCT	G	GS	CG	SH	SV	IP	H	HR	BB	SO	RAT	ERA	ERA+	OAV	OOB	BH	AVG	PB	PR	/A	PD	TPI
1949 Cle-A	9	6	.600	40	11	4	2	10	135^2	116	7	51	41	11.1	2.12	188	.238	.312	5	.132	-2	31	28	-2	2.9
1950 Cle-A	4	2	.667	36	0	0	0	4	63	57	7	30	26	12.6	3.57	121	.243	.331	1	.083	-1	7	5	-1	0.4
Total 14	98	88	.527	455	167	58	10	66	1688^1	1672	106	733	697	12.9	3.66	115	.259	.336	50	.098	-39	74	102	-1	8.9
Team 2	13	8	.619	76	11	4	2	14	198^2	173	14	81	67	11.6	2.58	159	.240	.318	6	.120	-3	38	33	-3	3.3

● HEINIE BERGER
Berger, Charles b: 1/7/1882, LaSalle, Ill. d: 2/10/54, Lakewood, Ohio TR, 5'9", Deb: 5/6/07

YEAR TM/L	W	L	PCT	G	GS	CG	SH	SV	IP	H	HR	BB	SO	RAT	ERA	ERA+	OAV	OOB	BH	AVG	PB	PR	/A	PD	TPI
1907 Cle-A	3	3	.500	14	7	5	1	0	87^1	74	0	20	50	9.8	2.99	84	.231	.279	5	.179	0	-4	-5	-1	-0.5
1908 Cle-A	13	8	.619	29	24	16	0	0	199^1	152	1	66	101	10.0	2.12	113	.219	.290	8	.108	-4	6	6	-0	0.1
1909 Cle-A	13	14	.481	34	29	19	4	1	247	221	2	58	162	10.6	2.73	94	.256	.312	11	.133	-1	-7	-5	0	-0.7
1910 Cle-A	3	4	.429	13	8	2	0	0	65^1	57	0	32	24	12.7	3.03	85	.243	.341	3	.143	-1	-4	-3	-1	-0.5
Total 4	32	29	.525	90	68	42	5	1	599	504	3	176	337	10.5	2.60	96	.238	.303	27	.131	-6	-9	-7	-2	-1.6

YEAR TM/L	W	L	PCT	G	GS	CG	SH	SV	IP	H	HR	BB	SO	RAT	ERA	ERA+	OAV	OOB	BH	AVG	PB	PR	/A	PD	TPI

● **BILL BERNHARD** Bernhard, William Henry "Strawberry Bill" b: 3/16/1871, Clarence, N.Y. d: 3/30/49, San Diego, Cal. BB/TR, 6'1", 205 lbs. Deb: 4/24/1899

1902 Cle-A	17	5	.773	27	24	22	3	1	217	169	4	34	57	8.6	2.20	157	.216	.253	18	.200	-1	33	30	1	2.8
1903 Cle-A	14	6	.700	20	19	18	3	0	165²	151	1	21	60	9.3	2.12	135	.242	.267	12	.185	-1	16	14	1	1.6
1904 Cle-A	23	13	.639	38	37	35	4	0	320²	323	4	55	137	10.7	2.13	119	.263	.296	22	.177	-1	17	14	-1	1.4
1905 Cle-A	7	13	.350	22	19	17	0	0	174¹	185	5	34	56	11.4	3.36	79	.273	.309	6	.087	-6	-13	-14	0	-2.1
1906 Cle-A	16	15	.516	31	30	23	2	0	255¹	235	1	47	85	10.1	2.54	103	.248	.287	21	.212	2	4	2	2	0.7
1907 Cle-A	0	4	.000	8	4	3	0	0	42	58	0	11	19	14.8	3.21	78	.330	.369	3	.200	0	-3	-3	0	-0.3
Total 9	116	82	.586	231	200	175	14	3	1792	1860	26	365	545	11.3	3.04	102	.254	.268	129	.180	-13	23	11	7	0.9
Team 6	77	56	.579	146	133	118	12	1	1175	1121	14	202	414	10.2	2.45	114	.253	.287	82	.177	-6	53	43	3	4.1

● **JOE BERRY** Berry, Jonas Arthur "Jittery Joe" b: 12/16/04, Huntsville, Ark. d: 9/27/58, Anaheim, Cal. BL/TR, 5'10.5", 145 lbs. Deb: 9/6/42

| 1946 Cle-A | 3 | 6 | .333 | 21 | 0 | 0 | 0 | 0 | 37¹ | 32 | 4 | 21 | 16 | 12.8 | 3.38 | 98 | .235 | .338 | 2 | .286 | 0 | 1 | -0 | -1 | -0.1 |
| Total 4 | 21 | 22 | .488 | 133 | 0 | 0 | 0 | 18 | 294 | 246 | 14 | 87 | 117 | 10.3 | 2.45 | 140 | .224 | .282 | 11 | .157 | -2 | 31 | 32 | 3 | 5.6 |

● **JIM BIBBY** Bibby, James Blair b: 10/29/44, Franklinton, N.C. BR/TR, 6'5", 235 lbs. Deb: 9/4/72

1975 Cle-A	5	9	.357	24	12	2	0	1	112²	99	7	50	62	11.9	3.20	118	.235	.316	0	—	0	7	7	1	0.9
1976 Cle-A	13	7	.650	34	21	4	3	1	163¹	162	6	56	84	12.1	3.20	109	.266	.329	0	—	0	6	5	-1	0.5
1977 Cle-A	12	13	.480	37	30	9	2	2	206²	197	17	73	141	11.9	3.57	110	.250	.317	0	—	0	11	9	-2	0.8
Total 12	111	101	.524	340	239	56	19	8	1722²	1565	131	723	1079	12.2	3.76	98	.243	.323	31	.148	5	-11	-11	-8	-4.4
Team 3	30	29	.508	95	63	15	5	4	482²	458	30	179	287	12.0	3.36	112	.252	.321	0	—	0	24	21	-3	2.2

● **MIKE BIELECKI** Bielecki, Michael Joseph b: 7/31/59, Baltimore, Md. BR/TR, 6'3", 200 lbs. Deb: 9/14/84

| 1993 Cle-A | 4 | 5 | .444 | 13 | 13 | 0 | 0 | 0 | 68² | 90 | 8 | 23 | 38 | 15.1 | 5.90 | 73 | .310 | .365 | 0 | — | 0 | -12 | -12 | 0 | -1.2 |
| Total 12 | 63 | 63 | .500 | 257 | 173 | 7 | 4 | 1 | 1098¹ | 1117 | 99 | 442 | 652 | 12.9 | 4.29 | 92 | .265 | .338 | 21 | .078 | -14 | -63 | -42 | 3 | -6.4 |

● **LLOYD BISHOP** Bishop, Lloyd Clifton b: 4/25/1890, Conway Springs, Kan. d: 6/18/68, Wichita, Kan. BR/TR, 6', 180 lbs. Deb: 9/5/14

| 1914 Cle-A | 0 | 1 | .000 | 3 | 1 | 0 | 0 | 0 | 8 | 14 | 0 | 3 | 1 | 15.6 | 5.63 | 51 | .389 | .436 | 0 | .000 | 0 | -3 | -2 | -0 | -0.3 |

● **DON BLACK** Black, Donald Paul b: 7/20/16, Salix, Iowa d: 4/21/59, Cuyahoga Falls, O. BR/TR, 6', 185 lbs. Deb: 4/24/43

1946 Cle-A	1	2	.333	18	4	0	0	0	43²	45	5	21	15	13.8	4.53	73	.273	.358	2	.200	0	-5	-6	1	-0.3
1947 Cle-A	10	12	.455	30	28	8	3	0	190²	177	17	85	72	12.4	3.92	89	.249	.330	12	.182	-1	-5	-9	1	-1.0
1948 Cle-A	2	2	.500	18	10	1	0	0	52	57	5	40	16	17.0	5.37	76	.282	.403	3	.200	0	-6	-8	0	-0.5
Total 6	34	55	.382	154	113	37	4	1	797	803	46	400	263	13.7	4.35	80	.264	.352	47	.184	-4	-74	-76	0	-8.2
Team 3	13	16	.448	66	42	9	3	0	286¹	279	27	146	103	13.5	4.27	83	.259	.349	17	.187	-1	-16	-23	2	-1.8

● **BUD BLACK** Black, Harry Ralston b: 6/30/57, San Mateo, Cal. BL/TL, 6'2", 180 lbs. Deb: 9/5/81

1988 Cle-A	2	3	.400	16	7	0	0	0	59	59	6	23	44	13.1	5.03	82	.262	.341	0	—	0	-7	-6	1	-0.4
1989 Cle-A	12	11	.522	33	32	6	3	0	222¹	213	14	52	88	10.8	3.36	118	.252	.296	0	—	0	13	15	-1	1.4
1990 Cle-A	11	10	.524	29	29	5	2	0	191	171	17	58	103	11.0	3.53	111	.236	.296	0	—	0	8	8	-0	0.8
1995 Cle-A	4	2	.667	11	10	0	0	0	47¹	63	8	16	34	15.0	6.85	68	.317	.367	0	—	0	-11	-12	0	-1.2
Total 15	121	116	.511	398	296	32	12	11	2053¹	1978	217	623	1039	11.6	3.84	103	.253	.312	26	.145	-1	33	30	9	3.8
Team 4	29	26	.527	89	78	11	5	1	519²	506	45	149	269	11.5	3.93	102	.254	.309	0	—	0	3	5	0	0.6

● **GEORGE BLAEHOLDER** Blaeholder, George Franklin b: 1/26/04, Orange, Cal. d: 12/29/47, Garden Grove, Cal. BR/TR, 5'11", 175 lbs. Deb: 4/20/25

| 1936 Cle-A | 8 | 4 | .667 | 35 | 16 | 6 | 1 | 0 | 134¹ | 158 | 21 | 47 | 30 | 13.9 | 5.09 | 99 | .295 | .356 | 6 | .130 | -3 | -1 | -1 | 2 | -0.2 |
| Total 11 | 104 | 125 | .454 | 338 | 251 | 106 | 14 | 12 | 1914¹ | 2220 | 173 | 535 | 572 | 13.0 | 4.54 | 103 | .290 | .337 | 89 | .142 | -25 | -26 | 30 | 20 | 3.6 |

● **WILLIE BLAIR** Blair, William Allen b: 12/18/65, Paintsville, Ky. BR/TR, 6'1", 185 lbs. Deb: 4/11/90

| 1991 Cle-A | 2 | 3 | .400 | 11 | 5 | 0 | 0 | 0 | 36 | 58 | 7 | 10 | 13 | 17.3 | 6.75 | 62 | .377 | .418 | 0 | — | 0 | -11 | -10 | 0 | -1.3 |
| Total 6 | 23 | 35 | .397 | 200 | 50 | 1 | 0 | 3 | 521 | 592 | 56 | 189 | 339 | 13.7 | 4.75 | 90 | .287 | .351 | 5 | .060 | -6 | -43 | -28 | -5 | -4.1 |

● **FRED BLANDING** Blanding, Frederick James "Fritz" b: 2/8/1888, Redlands, Cal. d: 7/16/50, Salem, Va. BR/TR, 6', 185 lbs. Deb: 9/15/10

1910 Cle-A	2	2	.500	6	5	4	0	0	45¹	43	0	12	25	11.7	2.78	93	.254	.319	2	.111	-1	-1	-1	-1	-0.3
1911 Cle-A	7	11	.389	29	16	11	0	2	176	190	5	60	80	13.1	3.68	93	.283	.347	17	.262	2	-7	-5	0	-0.3
1912 Cle-A	18	14	.563	39	31	23	1	1	262	259	4	79	75	11.7	2.92	117	.267	.324	21	.226	1	12	14	0	1.8
1913 Cle-A	15	10	.600	41	22	14	3	0	215	234	6	72	63	12.9	2.55	119	.282	.341	21	.244	-1	4	9	-2	1.5
1914 Cle-A	3	9	.250	29	12	5	1	0	116	133	0	54	35	14.6	3.96	73	.301	.378	4	.103	-2	-16	-14	1	-1.5
Total 5	45	46	.495	144	86	57	5	4	814¹	859	15	277	278	12.7	3.13	102	.279	.341	65	.216	4	-3	6	-2	1.2

● **BERT BLYLEVEN** Blyleven, Rik Aalbert b: 4/6/51, Zeist, Holland BR/TR, 6'3", 207 lbs. Deb: 6/5/70

1981 Cle-A	11	7	.611	20	20	9	1	0	159¹	145	9	40	107	10.7	2.88	126	.245	.298	0	—	0	14	13	-2	1.4
1982 Cle-A	2	2	.500	4	4	0	0	0	20¹	16	2	11	19	12.0	4.87	84	.211	.310	0	—	0	-2	-2	0	-0.3
1983 Cle-A	7	10	.412	24	24	5	0	0	156¹	160	8	44	123	12.3	3.91	108	.267	.328	0	—	0	3	6	1	0.6
1984 Cle-A	19	7	.731	33	32	12	4	0	245	204	19	74	170	10.4	2.87	143	.224	.287	0	—	0	31	33	0	3.4
1985 Cle-A★	9	11	.450	23	23	15	4	0	179²	163	14	49	129	11.1	3.26	127	.240	.298	0	—	0	18	18	-1	1.7
Total 22	287	250	.534	692	685	242	60	0	4970	4632	430	1322	3701	11.1	3.31	117	.247	.303	59	.131	-13	271	317	1	30.8
Team 5	48	37	.565	104	103	41	9	0	760²	688	52	218	548	11.1	3.23	125	.241	.301	0	—	0	63	68	-1	6.8

● **JOE BOEHLING** Boehling, John Joseph b: 3/20/1891, Richmond, Va. d: 9/8/41, Richmond, Va. BL/TL, 5'11", 168 lbs. Deb: 6/20/12

1916 Cle-A	2	4	.333	12	9	3	0	0	60²	63	0	23	18	13.1	2.67	113	.281	.353	5	.263	1	1	2	1	0.4
1917 Cle-A	1	6	.143	12	7	1	0	0	46¹	50	1	16	11	13.4	4.66	61	.291	.361	3	.188	-0	-10	-9	-0	-1.4
1920 Cle-A	0	1	.000	3	2	0	0	0	13	16	0	10	4	18.0	4.85	78	.333	.448	2	.500	1	-2	-2	0	-0.3
Total 7	55	50	.524	162	118	57	9	5	925¹	861	13	386	396	12.5	2.97	98	.254	.337	66	.212	7	-10	-5	11	1.1
Team 3	3	11	.214	27	18	4	0	0	120	129	1	49	33	13.7	3.68	83	.291	.367	10	.256	2	-11	-9	1	-1.0

● **JOHN BOHNET** Bohnet, John Kelly b: 1/18/61, Pasadena, Cal. BB/TL, 6', 175 lbs. Deb: 5/10/82

| 1982 Cle-A | 0 | 0 | — | 3 | 3 | 0 | 0 | 0 | 11² | 11 | 4 | 7 | 4 | 14.7 | 6.94 | 59 | .250 | .365 | 0 | — | 0 | -4 | -4 | 0 | 0.0 |

● **BILL BONNESS** Bonness, William John "Lefty" b: 12/15/23, Cleveland, Ohio d: 12/3/77, Detroit, Mich. BR/TL, 6'4", 200 lbs. Deb: 9/26/44

| 1944 Cle-A | 0 | 1 | .000 | 2 | 1 | 0 | 0 | 0 | 7 | 11 | 0 | 5 | 1 | 23.1 | 7.71 | 43 | .367 | .486 | 0 | .000 | -0 | -3 | -3 | 0 | -0.4 |

● **RED BOOLES** Booles, Seabron Jesse b: 7/14/1880, Bernice, La. d: 3/16/55, Monroe, La. BL/TL, 5'10", 150 lbs. Deb: 7/30/09

| 1909 Cle-A | 0 | 1 | .000 | 4 | 1 | 0 | 0 | 0 | 22² | 20 | 0 | 8 | 6 | 11.5 | 1.99 | 129 | .235 | .309 | 1 | .167 | 0 | 1 | 1 | -0 | 0.1 |

● **DAN BOONE** Boone, James Albert b: 1/19/1895, Samantha, Ala. d: 5/11/68, Tuscaloosa, Ala. BR/TR, 6'2", 190 lbs. Deb: 9/10/19

1922 Cle-A	4	6	.400	11	10	4	2	0	75¹	87	3	19	9	12.8	4.06	99	.298	.343	5	.192	-1	-0	-0	1	-0.1
1923 Cle-A	4	6	.400	27	4	2	0	0	70¹	93	3	31	15	16.3	6.01	66	.322	.393	4	.211	0	-16	-16	3	-1.6
Total 4	8	13	.381	42	16	6	2	0	162¹	205	6	62	25	15.0	5.10	77	.315	.378	9	.180	-1	-21	-21	4	-2.0
Team 2	8	12	.400	38	14	6	2	0	145²	180	6	50	24	14.5	5.00	80	.310	.369	9	.200	-0	-16	-16	4	-1.7

● **DICK BOSMAN** Bosman, Richard Allen b: 2/17/44, Kenosha, Wis. BR/TR, 6'3", 208 lbs. Deb: 6/1/66 C

| 1973 Cle-A | 1 | 8 | .111 | 22 | 17 | 2 | 0 | 0 | 97 | 130 | 19 | 29 | 41 | 15.3 | 6.22 | 63 | .320 | .374 | 0 | — | 0 | -26 | -25 | -1 | -2.1 |
| 1974 Cle-A | 7 | 5 | .583 | 25 | 18 | 2 | 1 | 0 | 127¹ | 126 | 13 | 29 | 44 | 11.0 | 4.10 | 88 | .255 | .298 | 0 | — | 0 | -7 | -7 | -2 | -0.8 |

YEAR TM/L	W	L	PCT	G	GS	CG	SH	SV	IP	H	HR	BB	SO	RAT	ERA	ERA+	OAV	OOB	BH	AVG	PB	PR	/A	PD	TPI
1975 Cle-A	0	2	.000	6	3	0	0	0	28^2	33	3	8	11	13.8	4.08	93	.292	.355	0	—	0	-1	-1	-0	-0.1
Total 11	82	85	.491	306	229	29	10	2	1591	1594	149	412	757	11.5	3.67	93	.261	.312	41	.125	-5	-29	-46	-5	-5.7
Team 3	8	15	.348	53	38	4	1	0	253	289	35	66	108	13.0	4.91	76	.285	.335	0	—	0	-34	-33	-3	-3.0

● DENIS BOUCHER Boucher, Denis b: 3/7/68, Montreal, Que., Can. BR/TL, 6'1", 195 lbs. Deb: 4/12/91

YEAR TM/L	W	L	PCT	G	GS	CG	SH	SV	IP	H	HR	BB	SO	RAT	ERA	ERA+	OAV	OOB	BH	AVG	PB	PR	/A	PD	TPI
1991 Cle-A	1	4	.200	5	5	0	0	0	22^2	35	6	8	13	17.1	8.34	50	.350	.398	0	—	0	-11	-11	0	-1.7
1992 Cle-A	2	2	.500	8	7	0	0	0	41	48	9	20	17	15.1	6.37	61	.302	.383	0	—	0	-11	-11	-1	-0.9
Total 4	6	11	.353	35	26	0	0	0	146	170	28	54	77	14.0	5.42	76	.294	.357	2	.222	1	-22	-21	0	-2.0
Team 2	3	6	.333	13	12	0	0	0	63^2	83	15	28	30	15.8	7.07	56	.320	.389	0	—	0	-22	-22	-0	-2.6

● ABE BOWMAN Bowman, Alvah Edson b: 1/25/1893, Greenup, Ill. d: 10/11/79, Longview, Tex. BR/TR, 6'1", 190 lbs. Deb: 5/19/14

YEAR TM/L	W	L	PCT	G	GS	CG	SH	SV	IP	H	HR	BB	SO	RAT	ERA	ERA+	OAV	OOB	BH	AVG	PB	PR	/A	PD	TPI
1914 Cle-A	2	7	.222	22	10	2	1	0	72^2	74	0	45	27	15.2	4.46	65	.277	.389	1	.048	-2	-14	-13	-0	-1.7
1915 Cle-A	0	1	.000	2	1	0	0	0	1^1	1	0	3	0	27.0	20.25	15	.250	.571	0	—	0	-3	-3	1	-1.2
Total 2	2	8	.200	24	11	2	1	0	74	75	0	48	27	15.4	4.74	61	.277	.393	1	.048	-2	-16	-15	0	-2.9

● TED BOWSFIELD Bowsfield, Edward Oliver b: 1/10/35, Vernon, B.C., Canada BR/TL, 6'1", 190 lbs. Deb: 7/20/58

YEAR TM/L	W	L	PCT	G	GS	CG	SH	SV	IP	H	HR	BB	SO	RAT	ERA	ERA+	OAV	OOB	BH	AVG	PB	PR	/A	PD	TPI
1960 Cle-A	3	4	.429	11	6	1	1	0	40^2	47	1	20	14	14.8	5.09	73	.296	.374	1	.100	-0	-5	-6	1	-0.9
Total 7	37	39	.487	215	86	12	4	6	662^1	699	63	259	326	13.2	4.35	93	.270	.339	22	.127	-3	-38	-24	1	-2.9

● GARY BOYD Boyd, Gary Lee b: 8/22/46, Pasadena, Cal. BR/TR, 6'4", 200 lbs. Deb: 8/1/69

YEAR TM/L	W	L	PCT	G	GS	CG	SH	SV	IP	H	HR	BB	SO	RAT	ERA	ERA+	OAV	OOB	BH	AVG	PB	PR	/A	PD	TPI
1969 Cle-A	0	2	.000	8	3	0	0	0	11	8	1	14	9	18.0	9.00	42	.205	.415	0	.000	-0	-7	-6	-0	-1.0

● JACK BRACKEN Bracken, John James b: 4/14/1881, Cleveland, Ohio d: 7/16/54, Highland Park, Mich. BR/TR, 5'11", 175 lbs. Deb: 8/7/01

YEAR TM/L	W	L	PCT	G	GS	CG	SH	SV	IP	H	HR	BB	SO	RAT	ERA	ERA+	OAV	OOB	BH	AVG	PB	PR	/A	PD	TPI
1901 Cle-A	4	8	.333	12	12	12	0	0	100	137	4	31	18	16.0	6.21	57	.322	.381	10	.227	0	-28	-30	-1	-2.6

● BILL BRADLEY Bradley, William Joseph b: 2/13/1878, Cleveland, Ohio d: 3/11/54, Cleveland, Ohio BR/TR, 6', 185 lbs. Deb: 8/26/1899 M♦

YEAR TM/L	W	L	PCT	G	GS	CG	SH	SV	IP	H	HR	BB	SO	RAT	ERA	ERA+	OAV	OOB	BH	AVG	PB	PR	/A	PD	TPI
1901 Cle-A	0	0	—	1	0	0	0	0	1	4	0	0	0	36.0	0.00	—	.571	.571	151	.293	0	0	0	-0	0.0

● DICK BRAGGINS Braggins, Richard Realf b: 12/25/1879, Mercer, Pa. d: 8/16/63, Lake Wales, Fla. BR/TR, 5'11", 170 lbs. Deb: 5/16/01

YEAR TM/L	W	L	PCT	G	GS	CG	SH	SV	IP	H	HR	BB	SO	RAT	ERA	ERA+	OAV	OOB	BH	AVG	PB	PR	/A	PD	TPI
1901 Cle-A	1	2	.333	4	3	2	0	0	32	44	1	15	1	16.9	4.78	74	.324	.395	2	.154	-1	-4	-4	0	-0.4

● AD BRENNAN Brennan, Addison Foster b: 7/18/1881, LaHarpe, Kan. d: 1/7/62, Kansas City, Mo. BL/TL, 5'11", 170 lbs. Deb: 5/19/10

YEAR TM/L	W	L	PCT	G	GS	CG	SH	SV	IP	H	HR	BB	SO	RAT	ERA	ERA+	OAV	OOB	BH	AVG	PB	PR	/A	PD	TPI
1918 Cle-A	0	0	—	1	0	0	0	0	3	3	0	3	0	18.0	3.00	100	.333	.500	0	—	0	-0	0	-0	0.0
Total 7	37	36	.507	129	77	40	5	3	677	694	21	194	283	12.1	3.11	102	.270	.327	48	.218	4	1	4	-2	0.7

● TOM BRENNAN Brennan, Thomas Martin b: 10/30/52, Chicago, Ill. BR/TR, 6'1", 180 lbs. Deb: 9/5/81

YEAR TM/L	W	L	PCT	G	GS	CG	SH	SV	IP	H	HR	BB	SO	RAT	ERA	ERA+	OAV	OOB	BH	AVG	PB	PR	/A	PD	TPI
1981 Cle-A	2	2	.500	7	6	1	0	0	48^1	49	5	14	15	11.7	3.17	114	.259	.310	0	—	0	3	2	1	0.3
1982 Cle-A	4	2	.667	30	4	0	0	2	92^2	112	9	10	46	12.0	4.27	95	.300	.322	0	—	0	-2	-2	0	-0.1
1983 Cle-A	2	2	.500	11	5	1	1	0	39^2	45	3	8	21	12.3	3.86	110	.288	.327	0	—	0	1	2	-0	0.1
Total 5	9	10	.474	64	20	2	1	2	219	255	20	46	102	12.5	4.40	89	.294	.332	1	.125	-0	-12	-12	3	-1.1
Team 3	8	6	.571	48	15	2	1	2	180^2	206	17	32	82	12.0	3.89	103	.287	.320	0	—	0	1	2	1	0.3

● BERT BRENNER Brenner, Delbert Henry "Dutch" b: 7/18/1887, Minneapolis, Minn d: 4/11/71, St.Louis Park, Minn. BR/TR, 6', 175 lbs. Deb: 9/21/12

YEAR TM/L	W	L	PCT	G	GS	CG	SH	SV	IP	H	HR	BB	SO	RAT	ERA	ERA+	OAV	OOB	BH	AVG	PB	PR	/A	PD	TPI
1912 Cle-A	1	0	1.000	2	1	1	0	0	13	14	0	4	3	12.5	2.77	123	.286	.340	0	.000	-1	1	1	0	0.0

● LYNN BRENTON Brenton, Lynn Davis "Buck" or "Herb" b: 10/7/1890, Peoria, Ill. d: 10/14/68, Los Angeles, Cal. BR/TR, 5'10", 165 lbs. Deb: 8/10/13

YEAR TM/L	W	L	PCT	G	GS	CG	SH	SV	IP	H	HR	BB	SO	RAT	ERA	ERA+	OAV	OOB	BH	AVG	PB	PR	/A	PD	TPI
1913 Cle-A	0	0	—	1	0	0	0	0	2	4	0	0	2	18.0	9.00	34	.400	.400	0	—	0	-1	-1	-0	0.0
1915 Cle-A	2	3	.400	11	5	1	1	0	51	60	1	20	18	14.5	3.35	91	.308	.378	2	.118	-1	-2	-2	-1	-0.4
Total 4	5	12	.294	34	15	4	1	2	131^1	161	1	41	52	14.0	3.97	83	.315	.369	6	.150	-1	-9	-10	3	-1.1
Team 2	2	3	.400	12	5	1	1	0	53	64	1	20	20	14.6	3.57	85	.312	.379	2	.118	-1	-4	-3	-1	-0.4

● JOHN BRIGGS Briggs, Jonathan Tift b: 1/24/34, Natoma, Cal. BR/TR, 5'10", 175 lbs. Deb: 4/17/56

YEAR TM/L	W	L	PCT	G	GS	CG	SH	SV	IP	H	HR	BB	SO	RAT	ERA	ERA+	OAV	OOB	BH	AVG	PB	PR	/A	PD	TPI
1959 Cle-A	0	1	.000	4	1	0	0	0	12^2	12	1	3	5	10.7	2.13	173	.245	.288	0	.000	-0	2	2	-0	0.1
1960 Cle-A	4	2	.667	21	2	0	0	1	36^1	32	4	15	19	11.9	4.46	84	.250	.333	1	.125	-0	-2	-3	-1	-0.6
Total 5	9	11	.450	59	21	3	1	1	165^2	174	23	82	80	14.2	5.00	77	.275	.363	10	.208	1	-20	-21	-2	-3.4
Team 2	4	3	.571	25	3	0	0	1	49	44	5	18	24	11.6	3.86	97	.249	.321	1	.100	-1	0	-1	-1	-0.5

● LOU BRISSIE Brissie, Leland Victor b: 6/5/24, Anderson, S.C. BL/TL, 6'4", 215 lbs. Deb: 9/28/47

YEAR TM/L	W	L	PCT	G	GS	CG	SH	SV	IP	H	HR	BB	SO	RAT	ERA	ERA+	OAV	OOB	BH	AVG	PB	PR	/A	PD	TPI
1951 Cle-A	4	3	.571	54	4	1	0	9	112^1	90	5	61	50	12.3	3.20	118	.223	.329	6	.261	0	11	7	-2	0.4
1952 Cle-A	3	2	.600	42	1	0	0	2	82^2	68	5	34	28	11.1	3.48	96	.221	.299	3	.250	1	2	-1	1	0.1
1953 Cle-A	0	0	—	16	0	0	0	2	13	21	2	13	5	23.5	7.62	49	.389	.507	0	—	0	-5	-6	-0	-0.2
Total 7	44	48	.478	234	93	45	2	29	897^2	867	61	451	436	13.4	4.07	102	.254	.343	67	.227	1	19	8	-7	0.3
Team 3	7	5	.583	112	5	1	0	13	208	179	12	108	83	12.5	3.59	100	.234	.331	9	.257	1	8	0	-1	0.3

● JOHNNY BROACA Broaca, John Joseph b: 10/3/09, Lawrence, Mass. d: 5/16/85, Lawrence, Mass. BR/TR, 5'11", 190 lbs. Deb: 6/2/34

YEAR TM/L	W	L	PCT	G	GS	CG	SH	SV	IP	H	HR	BB	SO	RAT	ERA	ERA+	OAV	OOB	BH	AVG	PB	PR	/A	PD	TPI
1939 Cle-A	4	2	.667	22	2	0	0	0	46	53	5	28	13	15.8	4.70	94	.288	.382	0	.000	-2	-0	-1	-0	-0.3
Total 5	44	29	.603	121	86	42	4	3	674^1	748	51	255	258	13.4	4.08	105	.278	.341	23	.091	-21	44	15	-8	-1.5

● DICK BRODOWSKI Brodowski, Richard Stanley b: 7/26/32, Bayonne, N.J. BR/TR, 6'2", 190 lbs. Deb: 6/15/52

YEAR TM/L	W	L	PCT	G	GS	CG	SH	SV	IP	H	HR	BB	SO	RAT	ERA	ERA+	OAV	OOB	BH	AVG	PB	PR	/A	PD	TPI
1958 Cle-A	1	0	1.000	5	0	0	0	0	10	3	0	6	12	8.1	0.00	—	.100	.250	0	.000	-0	4	4	-0	0.4
1959 Cle-A	2	2	.500	18	0	0	0	5	30	19	3	21	9	12.9	1.80	205	.181	.333	2	.333	0	7	6	-1	1.0
Total 6	9	11	.450	72	15	5	0	5	215^2	212	27	124	85	14.4	4.76	84	.258	.361	15	.242	3	-23	-19	0	-0.8
Team 2	3	2	.600	23	0	0	0	5	40	22	3	27	21	11.7	1.35	272	.163	.315	2	.286	0	11	10	-1	1.4

● FRANK BROWER Brower, Frank Willard "Turkeyfoot" b: 3/26/1893, Gainesville, Va. d: 11/20/60, Baltimore, Md. BL/TR, 6'2", 180 lbs. Deb: 8/14/20 ♦

YEAR TM/L	W	L	PCT	G	GS	CG	SH	SV	IP	H	HR	BB	SO	RAT	ERA	ERA+	OAV	OOB	BH	AVG	PB	PR	/A	PD	TPI
1924 Cle-A	0	0	—	4	0	0	0	0	9^2	7	0	4	0	11.2	0.93	459	.212	.316	30	.280	1	4	4	-0	0.0

● CLINT BROWN Brown, Clinton Harold b: 7/8/03, Blackash, Pa. d: 12/31/55, Rocky River, Ohio BL/TR, 6'1", 190 lbs. Deb: 9/27/28

YEAR TM/L	W	L	PCT	G	GS	CG	SH	SV	IP	H	HR	BB	SO	RAT	ERA	ERA+	OAV	OOB	BH	AVG	PB	PR	/A	PD	TPI
1928 Cle-A	0	1	.000	2	1	1	0	0	11	14	0	2	2	13.1	4.91	84	.304	.333	1	.200	-0	-1	-1	0	-0.1
1929 Cle-A	0	2	.000	3	1	1	0	0	16^1	18	0	6	1	13.2	3.31	134	.286	.348	0	.000	-1	2	2	1	0.2
1930 Cle-A	11	13	.458	35	31	16	**3**	1	213^2	271	14	51	54	13.7	4.97	97	.314	.356	18	.247	2	-8	-3	2	0.0
1931 Cle-A	11	15	.423	39	33	12	2	0	233^1	284	10	55	50	13.1	4.71	98	.295	.333	15	.172	-2	-8	-2	4	0.0
1932 Cle-A	15	12	.556	37	32	21	1	1	262^2	298	14	50	59	12.1	4.08	116	.279	.314	25	.250	6	12	19	2	2.4
1933 Cle-A	11	12	.478	33	23	10	2	1	185	202	10	34	47	11.6	3.41	130	.276	.310	9	.145	-3	18	21	3	2.4
1934 Cle-A	4	3	.571	17	2	0	0	1	50^1	83	3	14	15	17.3	5.90	77	.359	.396	5	.294	1	-8	-8	-0	-0.8
1935 Cle-A	4	3	.571	23	5	1	0	2	49	61	3	14	20	14.0	5.14	88	.300	.349	2	.200	0	-4	-3	1	-0.4
1941 Cle-A	3	3	.500	41	0	0	0	5	74^1	77	3	28	22	12.8	3.27	120	.279	.348	2	.118	0	7	6	3	0.8
1942 Cle-A	1	1	.500	7	0	0	0	0	9	16	2	2	4	19.0	6.00	57	.356	.396	0	.000	-0	-2	-3	-0	-0.6
Total 15	89	93	.489	434	130	62	8	64	1485^2	1740	84	368	410	12.9	4.26	109	.291	.335	91	.199	5	37	60	19	9.8
Team 10	60	65	.480	237	128	62	8	11	1104^2	1324	59	256	274	13.0	4.36	105	.295	.335	77	.203	4	8	28	15	3.9

● JACKIE BROWN Brown, Jackie Gene b: 5/31/43, Holdenville, Okla. BR/TR, 6'1", 195 lbs. Deb: 7/2/70 FC

YEAR TM/L	W	L	PCT	G	GS	CG	SH	SV	IP	H	HR	BB	SO	RAT	ERA	ERA+	OAV	OOB	BH	AVG	PB	PR	/A	PD	TPI
1975 Cle-A	1	2	.333	25	3	1	0	1	69^1	72	9	29	41	13.1	4.28	88	.276	.348	0	—	0	-4	-4	-0	-0.2
1976 Cle-A	9	11	.450	32	27	5	2	0	180	193	14	55	104	12.8	4.25	82	.276	.335	0	—	0	-15	-15	-1	-1.6
Total 7	47	53	.470	214	105	26	8	3	892^2	934	82	353	516	13.2	4.18	87	.272	.343	11	.131	-3	-48	-55	-7	-6.8
Team 2	10	13	.435	57	30	6	2	1	249^1	265	23	84	145	12.9	4.26	84	.276	.338	0	—	0	-19	-19	-1	-1.8

● LLOYD BROWN Brown, Lloyd Andrew "Gimpy" b: 12/25/04, Beeville, Tex. d: 1/14/74, Opa-Locka, Fla. BL/TL, 5'9", 170 lbs. Deb: 7/17/25

YEAR	TM/L	W	L	PCT	G	GS	CG	SH	SV	IP	H	HR	BB	SO	RAT	ERA	ERA+	OAV	OOB	BH	AVG	PB	PR	/A	PD	TPI
1934	Cle-A	5	10	.333	38	15	5	0	6	117	116	7	51	39	13.0	3.85	118	.263	.342	7	.233	1	8	9	0	1.2
1935	Cle-A	8	7	.533	42	8	4	2	4	122	123	6	37	45	12.0	3.61	125	.265	.323	4	.108	-2	**11**	**12**	1	1.2
1936	Cle-A	8	10	.444	24	16	12	1	1	140^1	166	13	45	34	13.7	4.17	121	.294	.349	10	.222	2	14	14	1	1.7
1937	Cle-A	2	6	.250	31	5	2	0	0	77	107	4	27	32	16.0	6.55	70	.329	.386	4	.167	-1	-16	-17	1	-1.4
Total	12	91	105	.464	404	181	77	10	21	1693	1899	83	590	510	13.3	4.20	105	.288	.348	106	.192	6	45	42	19	6.5
Team	4	23	33	.411	135	44	23	3	11	456^1	512	30	160	150	13.5	4.34	108	.285	.347	25	.184	-0	17	18	3	2.7

● JUMBO BROWN Brown, Walter George b: 4/30/07, Greene, R.I. d: 10/2/66, Freeport, N.Y. BR/TR, 6'4", 295 lbs. Deb: 8/26/25

YEAR	TM/L	W	L	PCT	G	GS	CG	SH	SV	IP	H	HR	BB	SO	RAT	ERA	ERA+	OAV	OOB	BH	AVG	PB	PR	/A	PD	TPI
1927	Cle-A	0	2	.000	8	0	0	0	0	18^2	19	3	26	8	22.2	6.27	67	.284	.489	2	.667	1	-4	-4	0	-0.2
1928	Cle-A	0	1	.000	5	0	0	0	0	14^2	19	0	15	12	20.9	6.75	61	.365	.507	2	.667	1	-4	-4	-0	-0.1
Total	12	33	31	.516	249	23	7	2	29	597^1	619	26	300	301	13.9	4.07	99	.271	.357	32	.204	2	7	-4	-0	0.1
Team	2	0	3	.000	13	0	0	0	0	33^1	38	3	41	20	21.6	6.48	64	.319	.497	4	.667	3	-9	-9	-0	-0.3

● GARLAND BUCKEYE Buckeye, Garland Maiers "Gob" b: 10/16/1897, Heron Lake, Minn. d: 11/14/75, Stone Lake, Wis. BB/TL, 6', 260 lbs. Deb: 6/19/18

YEAR	TM/L	W	L	PCT	G	GS	CG	SH	SV	IP	H	HR	BB	SO	RAT	ERA	ERA+	OAV	OOB	BH	AVG	PB	PR	/A	PD	TPI
1925	Cle-A	13	8	.619	30	18	11	1	0	153	161	3	58	49	13.2	3.65	121	.267	.338	14	.226	2	13	13	-1	1.7
1926	Cle-A	6	9	.400	32	18	5	1	0	165^2	160	3	69	36	12.8	3.10	131	.264	.345	12	.200	2	17	18	-2	1.4
1927	Cle-A	10	17	.370	35	25	13	2	1	204^2	231	6	74	38	13.6	3.96	106	.296	.360	19	.268	3	4	6	-1	0.8
1928	Cle-A	1	5	.167	9	6	0	0	0	35	58	2	5	6	16.7	6.69	62	.389	.417	1	.111	-1	-10	-10	-0	-1.4
Total	5	30	39	.435	108	67	29	4	1	564	622	15	214	134	13.6	3.91	108	.287	.356	47	.230	7	16	19	-3	2.6
Team	4	30	39	.435	106	67	29	4	1	558^1	610	14	206	129	13.5	3.79	111	.285	.353	46	.228	7	24	26	-3	2.5

● LARRY BURCHART Burchart, Larry Wayne b: 2/8/46, Tulsa, Okla. BR/TR, 6'3", 205 lbs. Deb: 4/10/69

YEAR	TM/L	W	L	PCT	G	GS	CG	SH	SV	IP	H	HR	BB	SO	RAT	ERA	ERA+	OAV	OOB	BH	AVG	PB	PR	/A	PD	TPI
1969	Cle-A	0	2	.000	29	0	0	0	0	42^1	42	2	24	26	14.2	4.25	89	.266	.366	0	—	0	-3	-2	-1	-0.2

● TOM BUSKEY Buskey, Thomas William b: 2/20/47, Harrisburg, Pa. BR/TR, 6'3", 220 lbs. Deb: 8/5/73

YEAR	TM/L	W	L	PCT	G	GS	CG	SH	SV	IP	H	HR	BB	SO	RAT	ERA	ERA+	OAV	OOB	BH	AVG	PB	PR	/A	PD	TPI
1974	Cle-A	2	6	.250	51	0	0	0	17	93	93	10	33	40	12.3	3.19	113	.263	.327	0	—	0	4	4	1	0.7
1975	Cle-A	5	3	.625	50	0	0	0	7	77	69	7	29	29	11.6	2.57	147	.252	.326	0	—	0	10	10	2	1.4
1976	Cle-A	5	4	.556	39	0	0	0	1	94^1	88	9	34	32	11.9	3.63	96	.256	.328	0	—	0	-1	-1	1	0.0
1977	Cle-A	0	0	—	21	0	0	0	0	34	45	6	8	15	14.3	5.29	74	.313	.353	0	—	0	-5	-5	-0	0.2
Total	8	21	27	.438	258	0	0	0	34	479^1	479	57	167	212	12.3	3.66	105	.267	.332	0	—	0	9	11	4	3.1
Team	4	12	13	.480	161	0	0	0	25	298^1	295	32	104	116	12.2	3.41	107	.264	.330	0	—	0	9	8	3	2.3

● JOHN BUTCHER Butcher, John Daniel b: 3/8/57, Glendale, Cal. BR/TR, 6'4", 190 lbs. Deb: 9/8/80

YEAR	TM/L	W	L	PCT	G	GS	CG	SH	SV	IP	H	HR	BB	SO	RAT	ERA	ERA+	OAV	OOB	BH	AVG	PB	PR	/A	PD	TPI
1986	Cle-A	1	5	.167	13	8	1	1	0	50^2	86	6	13	16	18.1	6.93	60	.381	.421	0	—	0	-15	-16	-1	-1.5
Total	7	36	49	.424	164	113	23	6	6	833^2	931	79	229	363	12.7	4.42	94	.284	.334	0	—	0	-32	-24	1	-0.6

● BILL BUTLER Butler, William Franklin b: 3/12/47, Hyattsville, Md. BL/TL, 6'2", 210 lbs. Deb: 4/9/69

YEAR	TM/L	W	L	PCT	G	GS	CG	SH	SV	IP	H	HR	BB	SO	RAT	ERA	ERA+	OAV	OOB	BH	AVG	PB	PR	/A	PD	TPI
1972	Cle-A	0	0	—	6	2	0	0	0	11^2	9	1	10	6	14.7	1.54	208	.220	.373	0	.000	-0	2	2	-0	0.0
Total	7	23	35	.397	134	86	10	5	1	591^2	555	65	312	408	13.3	4.21	88	.250	.345	6	.051	-7	-37	-33	-9	-4.8

● RAY CALDWELL Caldwell, Raymond Benjamin "Rube" or "Sum" b: 4/26/1888, Corydon, Pa. d: 8/17/67, Salamanca, N.Y. BL/TR, 6'2", 190 lbs. Deb: 9/9/10 ♦

YEAR	TM/L	W	L	PCT	G	GS	CG	SH	SV	IP	H	HR	BB	SO	RAT	ERA	ERA+	OAV	OOB	BH	AVG	PB	PR	/A	PD	TPI
1919	Cle-A	5	1	.833	6	6	4	1	0	52^2	33	1	19	24	9.2	1.71	196	.181	.266	8	.348	2	9	10	-1	1.3
1920	*Cle-A	20	10	.667	34	33	20	1	0	237^2	286	9	63	80	13.4	3.86	98	.303	.350	19	.213	1	-2	-2	-3	-0.5
1921	Cle-A	6	6	.500	37	12	4	1	4	147	159	7	49	76	12.9	4.90	87	.275	.333	11	.208	0	-10	-10	-0	-0.8
Total	12	133	120	.526	343	259	184	21	9	2242	2089	59	738	1006	11.6	3.22	99	.253	.319	289	.248	31	-20	-4	-19	2.5
Team	3	31	17	.646	77	51	28	3	4	437^1	478	17	131	180	12.7	3.95	99	.281	.335	38	.230	4	-3	-2	-5	-0.0

● PAUL CALVERT Calvert, Paul Leo Emile b: 10/6/17, Montreal, Que., Can. BR/TR, 6', 185 lbs. Deb: 9/24/42

YEAR	TM/L	W	L	PCT	G	GS	CG	SH	SV	IP	H	HR	BB	SO	RAT	ERA	ERA+	OAV	OOB	BH	AVG	PB	PR	/A	PD	TPI
1942	Cle-A	0	0	—	1	0	0	0	0	2	0	0	2	2	9.0	0.00	—	.000	.286	0	—	0	1	1	-0	0.0
1943	Cle-A	0	0	—	5	0	0	0	0	8^1	6	0	6	2	14.0	4.32	72	.200	.351	0	.000	-0	-1	-1	0	0.0
1944	Cle-A	1	3	.250	35	4	0	0	0	77	89	4	38	31	14.8	4.56	72	.289	.367	4	.267	1	-10	-11	2	-0.2
1945	Cle-A	0	0	—	1	0	0	0	0	1^1	3	0	1	1	27.0	13.50	24	.429	.500	0	—	0	-2	-2	0	0.0
Total	7	9	22	.290	109	27	5	0	5	301^2	345	22	158	102	15.2	5.31	76	.287	.373	11	.149	-2	-43	-43	5	-3.4
Team	4	1	3	.250	42	4	0	0	0	88^2	98	4	47	36	14.8	4.57	72	.280	.367	4	.250	1	-11	-13	2	-0.2

● ERNIE CAMACHO Camacho, Ernest Carlos b: 2/1/55, Salinas, Cal. BR/TR, 6'1", 180 lbs. Deb: 5/22/80

YEAR	TM/L	W	L	PCT	G	GS	CG	SH	SV	IP	H	HR	BB	SO	RAT	ERA	ERA+	OAV	OOB	BH	AVG	PB	PR	/A	PD	TPI
1983	Cle-A	0	1	.000	4	0	0	0	0	5^1	5	1	2	2	13.5	5.06	84	.250	.348	0	—	0	-1	-0	-0	-0.3
1984	Cle-A	5	9	.357	69	0	0	0	23	100	83	6	37	48	10.9	2.43	168	.229	.303	0	—	0	17	18	-0	3.3
1985	Cle-A	0	1	.000	2	0	0	0	0	3^1	4	0	1	2	13.5	8.10	51	.333	.385	0	—	0	-1	-1	0	-0.3
1986	Cle-A	2	4	.333	51	0	0	0	20	57^1	60	1	31	36	14.6	4.08	101	.269	.363	0	—	0	1	0	1	0.1
1987	Cle-A	0	1	.000	15	0	0	0	1	13^2	21	1	5	9	19.1	9.22	49	.350	.426	0	—	0	-7	-7	1	-0.5
Total	10	10	20	.333	193	3	0	0	45	262^2	268	16	128	159	13.8	4.21	94	.268	.356	0	.000	-1	-8	-8	1	1.0
Team	5	7	16	.304	141	0	0	0	44	179^2	173	9	76	97	12.8	3.66	113	.256	.337	0	—	0	9	10	1	2.3

● CARDELL CAMPER Camper, Cardell b: 7/6/52, Boley, Okla. BR/TR, 6'3", 208 lbs. Deb: 9/11/77

YEAR	TM/L	W	L	PCT	G	GS	CG	SH	SV	IP	H	HR	BB	SO	RAT	ERA	ERA+	OAV	OOB	BH	AVG	PB	PR	/A	PD	TPI
1977	Cle-A	1	0	1.000	3	1	0	0	0	9^1	7	0	4	9	10.6	3.86	102	.200	.282	0	—	0	0	0	-0	0.2

● TOM CANDIOTTI Candiotti, Thomas Caesar b: 8/31/57, Walnut Creek, Cal. BR/TR, 6'3", 205 lbs. Deb: 8/8/83

YEAR	TM/L	W	L	PCT	G	GS	CG	SH	SV	IP	H	HR	BB	SO	RAT	ERA	ERA+	OAV	OOB	BH	AVG	PB	PR	/A	PD	TPI
1986	Cle-A	16	12	.571	36	34	**17**	3	0	252^1	234	18	106	167	12.4	3.57	116	.246	.326	0	—	0	17	16	3	1.9
1987	Cle-A	7	18	.280	32	32	7	2	0	201^2	193	28	93	111	12.9	4.78	95	.250	.333	0	—	0	-7	-6	0	-0.6
1988	Cle-A	14	8	.636	31	31	11	1	0	216^2	225	15	53	137	11.8	3.28	125	.272	.321	0	—	0	16	20	2	2.1
1989	Cle-A	13	10	.565	31	31	4	0	0	206	188	10	55	124	10.8	3.10	128	.242	.295	0	—	0	18	20	4	2.5
1990	Cle-A	15	11	.577	31	29	3	1	0	202	207	23	55	128	11.9	3.65	107	.263	.316	0	—	0	6	6	3	1.0
1991	Cle-A	7	6	.538	15	15	3	0	0	108^1	88	6	28	86	9.8	2.24	185	.218	.272	0	—	0	22	23	-0	2.7
Total	12	117	124	.485	331	319	64	11	0	2165^1	2054	167	707	1428	11.7	3.47	115	.250	.314	27	.122	-4	138	124	12	13.7
Team	6	72	65	.526	176	172	45	7	0	1187	1135	100	390	753	11.8	3.53	117	.251	.315	0	—	0	72	79	12	9.6

● STEVE CARLTON Carlton, Steven Norman "Lefty" b: 12/22/44, Miami, Fla. BL/TL, 6'4", 210 lbs. Deb: 4/12/65 H

YEAR	TM/L	W	L	PCT	G	GS	CG	SH	SV	IP	H	HR	BB	SO	RAT	ERA	ERA+	OAV	OOB	BH	AVG	PB	PR	/A	PD	TPI
1987	Cle-A	5	9	.357	23	14	3	0	1	109	111	17	63	71	14.5	5.37	84	.266	.364	0	—	0	-11	-10	-0	-1.2
Total	24	329	244	.574	741	709	254	55	2	5217^1	4672	414	1833	4136	11.3	3.22	115	.240	.308	346	.201	49	236	277	-18	33.2

● EDDIE CARNETT Carnett, Edwin Elliott "Lefty" b: 10/21/16, Springfield, Mo. BL/TL, 6', 185 lbs. Deb: 4/19/41 ♦

YEAR	TM/L	W	L	PCT	G	GS	CG	SH	SV	IP	H	HR	BB	SO	RAT	ERA	ERA+	OAV	OOB	BH	AVG	PB	PR	/A	PD	TPI
1945	Cle-A	0	0	—	2	0	0	0	0	2	0	0	0	1	0.0	0.00	—	.000	.000	16	.219	0	1	1	-0	0.0
Total	3	0	0	—	6	0	0	0	0	5^1	7	1	3	4	16.9	8.44	40	.304	.385	142	.268	1	-3	-3	0	0.0

● PAUL CARTER Carter, Paul Warren "Nick" b: 5/1/1894, Lake Park, Ga. d: 9/11/84, Lake Park, Ga. BL/TR, 6'3", 175 lbs. Deb: 9/15/14

YEAR	TM/L	W	L	PCT	G	GS	CG	SH	SV	IP	H	HR	BB	SO	RAT	ERA	ERA+	OAV	OOB	BH	AVG	PB	PR	/A	PD	TPI
1914	Cle-A	1	3	.250	5	4	1	0	0	24^2	35	0	5	9	14.6	2.92	99	.340	.370	0	.000	-1	-0	-0	-0	-0.1
1915	Cle-A	1	1	.500	11	2	2	0	0	42	44	1	18	14	13.3	3.21	95	.272	.344	3	.214	1	-1	-1	1	0.1
Total	7	20	26	.435	127	43	16	0	7	480	510	10	142	115	12.4	3.32	89	.283	.339	30	.195	-1	-24	-19	1	-1.7
Team	2	2	4	.333	16	6	3	0	0	66^2	79	1	23	23	13.8	3.11	96	.298	.354	3	.143	-0	-2	-1	0	0.0

● LARRY CASIAN Casian, Lawrence Paul b: 10/28/65, Lynwood, Cal. BR/TL, 6', 170 lbs. Deb: 9/9/90

YEAR	TM/L	W	L	PCT	G	GS	CG	SH	SV	IP	H	HR	BB	SO	RAT	ERA	ERA+	OAV	OOB	BH	AVG	PB	PR	/A	PD	TPI
1994	Cle-A	0	2	.000	7	0	0	0	0	8^1	16	1	4	2	21.6	8.64	55	.421	.476	0	—	0	-4	-4	0	-0.7
Total	6	10	9	.526	162	3	0	0	2	176^1	216	20	57	81	14.1	4.54	97	.307	.362	0	.000	-0	-4	-3	-0	-0.5

● PETE CENTER Center, Marvin Earl b: 4/22/12, Hazel Green, Ky. BR/TR, 6'4", 190 lbs. Deb: 9/11/42

YEAR TM/L	W	L	PCT	G	GS	CG	SH	SV	IP	H	HR	BB	SO	RAT	ERA	ERA+	OAV	OOB	BH	AVG	PB	PR	/A	PD	TPI
1942 Cle-A	0	0	—	1	0	0	0	0	3^{1}	7	0	4	0	32.4	16.20	21	.438	.571	0	.000	-0	-5	-5	-0	0.0
1943 Cle-A	1	2	.333	24	1	0	0	1	42^{1}	29	3	18	10	10.0	2.76	112	.201	.290	0	.000	-1	3	2	-1	0.0
1945 Cle-A	6	3	.667	31	8	2	0	1	85^{2}	89	2	28	34	12.4	3.99	81	.270	.329	2	.091	-2	-6	-7	-2	-1.1
1946 Cle-A	0	2	.000	21	0	0	0	1	29	29	2	20	6	15.5	4.97	67	.269	.388	0	.000	-0	-5	-5	-0	-0.4
Total 4	7	7	.500	77	9	2	0	3	160^{1}	154	7	70	50	12.7	4.10	79	.258	.338	2	.065	-3	-13	-16	-3	-1.5

● BOB CHAKALES Chakales, Robert Edward "Chick" b: 8/10/27, Asheville, N.C. BR/TR, 6'1", 185 lbs. Deb: 4/21/51

YEAR TM/L	W	L	PCT	G	GS	CG	SH	SV	IP	H	HR	BB	SO	RAT	ERA	ERA+	OAV	OOB	BH	AVG	PB	PR	/A	PD	TPI
1951 Cle-A	3	4	.429	17	10	2	1	0	68^{1}	80	3	43	32	16.2	4.74	80	.292	.388	7	.350	2	-5	-7	-0	-0.5
1952 Cle-A	1	2	.333	5	1	0	0	0	12	19	2	8	7	20.3	9.75	34	.388	.474	2	.500	1	-8	-9	-1	-1.6
1953 Cle-A	0	2	.000	7	3	1	0	0	27	28	2	10	6	13.0	2.67	141	.283	.355	2	.286	0	4	3	0	0.3
1954 Cle-A	2	0	1.000	3	0	0	0	0	10^{1}	4	0	12	3	13.9	0.87	422	.114	.340	1	.333	1	3	3	-0	0.7
Total 7	15	25	.375	171	23	3	1	10	420^{1}	445	31	225	187	14.5	4.54	85	.277	.369	26	.271	5	-28	-31	1	-2.7
Team 4	6	8	.429	32	14	3	1	0	117^{2}	131	7	73	48	15.7	4.44	84	.287	.386	12	.353	4	-6	-9	-1	-1.1

● DEAN CHANCE Chance, Wilmer Dean b: 6/1/41, Wayne, O. BR/TR, 6'3", 200 lbs. Deb: 9/11/61

YEAR TM/L	W	L	PCT	G	GS	CG	SH	SV	IP	H	HR	BB	SO	RAT	ERA	ERA+	OAV	OOB	BH	AVG	PB	PR	/A	PD	TPI
1970 Cle-A	9	8	.529	45	19	1	1	4	155	172	18	59	109	13.8	4.24	93	.287	.357	3	.071	-3	-9	-5	-1	-0.9
Total 11	128	115	.527	406	294	83	33	23	2147^{1}	1864	122	739	1534	11.2	2.92	119	.234	.305	44	.066	-37	134	131	8	10.8

● CHARLIE CHECH Chech, Charles William b: 4/27/1878, Madison, Wis. d: 1/31/38, Los Angeles, Cal. BR/TR, 5'11.5", 190 lbs. Deb: 4/14/05

YEAR TM/L	W	L	PCT	G	GS	CG	SH	SV	IP	H	HR	BB	SO	RAT	ERA	ERA+	OAV	OOB	BH	AVG	PB	PR	/A	PD	TPI
1908 Cle-A	11	7	.611	27	20	14	4	0	165^{2}	136	2	34	51	9.6	1.74	138	.229	.279	5	.104	-1	12	12	1	1.4
Total 4	33	30	.524	94	63	45	6	3	606	602	10	162	187	11.8	2.52	113	.263	.320	30	.152	-1	12	21	1	2.1

● VIRGIL CHEEVES Cheeves, Virgil Earl "Chief" b: 2/12/01, Oklahoma City, Okla. d: 5/5/79, Dallas, Tex. BR/TR, 6', 195 lbs. Deb: 9/7/20

YEAR TM/L	W	L	PCT	G	GS	CG	SH	SV	IP	H	HR	BB	SO	RAT	ERA	ERA+	OAV	OOB	BH	AVG	PB	PR	/A	PD	TPI
1924 Cle-A	0	0	—	8	1	0	0	0	17^{1}	26	2	17	2	22.8	7.79	55	.388	.518	1	.250	0	-7	-7	0	0.0
Total 6	26	27	.491	111	56	18	2	2	458^{2}	526	28	188	98	14.5	4.73	84	.300	.375	26	.184	-1	-40	-38	-5	-3.7

● MIKE CHRISTOPHER Christopher, Michael Wayne b: 11/3/63, Petersburg, Va. BR/TR, 6'5", 205 lbs. Deb: 9/10/91

YEAR TM/L	W	L	PCT	G	GS	CG	SH	SV	IP	H	HR	BB	SO	RAT	ERA	ERA+	OAV	OOB	BH	AVG	PB	PR	/A	PD	TPI
1992 Cle-A	0	0	—	10	0	0	0	0	18	17	2	10	13	13.5	3.00	130	.254	.351	0	—	0	2	2	0	0.1
1993 Cle-A	0	0	—	9	0	0	0	0	11^{2}	14	3	2	8	12.3	3.86	112	.286	.314	0	—	0	1	1	-0	0.0
Total 4	4	0	1.000	58	0	0	0	1	95	104	13	29	57	12.8	3.51	129	.280	.336	0	—	0	10	11	-0	0.5
Team 2	0	0	—	19	0	0	0	0	29^{2}	31	5	12	21	13.0	3.34	122	.267	.336	0	—	0	2	2	-0	0.1

● RUSS CHRISTOPHER Christopher, Russell Ormand b: 9/12/17, Richmond, Cal. d: 12/5/54, Richmond, Cal. BR/TR, 6'3", 180 lbs. Deb: 4/14/42 F

YEAR TM/L	W	L	PCT	G	GS	CG	SH	SV	IP	H	HR	BB	SO	RAT	ERA	ERA+	OAV	OOB	BH	AVG	PB	PR	/A	PD	TPI
1948 *Cle-A	3	2	.600	45	0	0	0	**17**	59	55	3	27	14	12.5	2.90	140	.247	.328	0	.000	-0	9	8	0	1.0
Total 7	54	64	.458	241	97	46	3	35	999^{2}	931	38	399	424	12.2	3.37	106	.248	.325	50	.158	-3	17	24	31	7.4

● CHUCK CHURN Churn, Clarence Nottingham b: 2/1/30, Bridgetown, Va. BR/TR, 6'3", 205 lbs. Deb: 4/18/57

YEAR TM/L	W	L	PCT	G	GS	CG	SH	SV	IP	H	HR	BB	SO	RAT	ERA	ERA+	OAV	OOB	BH	AVG	PB	PR	/A	PD	TPI
1958 Cle-A	0	0	—	6	0	0	0	0	8^{2}	12	1	5	4	17.7	6.23	59	.343	.425	0	—	0	-2	-2	-0	0.0
Total 3	3	2	.600	25	0	0	0	1	47^{2}	49	4	19	32	13.0	5.10	79	.285	.359	1	.143	0	-6	-6	1	-0.2

● AL CICOTTE Cicotte, Alva Warren "Bozo" b: 12/23/29, Melvindale, Mich. d: 11/29/82, Westland, Mich. BR/TR, 6'3", 185 lbs. Deb: 4/22/57

YEAR TM/L	W	L	PCT	G	GS	CG	SH	SV	IP	H	HR	BB	SO	RAT	ERA	ERA+	OAV	OOB	BH	AVG	PB	PR	/A	PD	TPI
1959 Cle-A	3	1	.750	26	1	0	0	1	44	46	4	25	23	14.9	5.32	69	.299	.403	1	.333	1	-7	-8	0	-0.6
Total 5	10	13	.435	102	16	0	0	4	260	280	30	119	149	14.0	4.36	90	.284	.364	15	.211	0	-14	-12	1	-1.1

● BRYAN CLARK Clark, Bryan Donald b: 7/12/56, Madera, Cal. BL/TL, 6'2", 185 lbs. Deb: 4/11/81

YEAR TM/L	W	L	PCT	G	GS	CG	SH	SV	IP	H	HR	BB	SO	RAT	ERA	ERA+	OAV	OOB	BH	AVG	PB	PR	/A	PD	TPI
1985 Cle-A	3	4	.429	31	3	0	0	2	62^{2}	78	8	34	24	16.1	6.32	65	.311	.393	0	—	0	-15	-15	1	-1.5
Total 8	20	23	.465	186	37	4	1	4	516^{1}	536	38	261	259	14.0	4.15	100	.272	.359	0	—	0	-8	1	7	-0.2

● GINGER CLARK Clark, Harvey Daniel b: 3/7/1879, Wooster, Ohio d: 5/10/43, Lake Charles, La. BR/TR, 5'11", 165 lbs. Deb: 8/11/02

YEAR TM/L	W	L	PCT	G	GS	CG	SH	SV	IP	H	HR	BB	SO	RAT	ERA	ERA+	OAV	OOB	BH	AVG	PB	PR	/A	PD	TPI
1902 Cle-A	1	0	1.000	1	0	0	0	0	6	10	0	3	1	21.0	6.00	57	.370	.452	2	.500	1	-2	-2	0	-0.1

● MARK CLARK Clark, Mark Willard b: 5/12/68, Bath, Ill. BR/TR, 6'5", 225 lbs. Deb: 9/6/91

YEAR TM/L	W	L	PCT	G	GS	CG	SH	SV	IP	H	HR	BB	SO	RAT	ERA	ERA+	OAV	OOB	BH	AVG	PB	PR	/A	PD	TPI
1993 Cle-A	7	5	.583	26	15	1	0	0	109^{1}	119	18	25	57	11.9	4.28	101	.279	.321	0	—	0	0	1	-2	-0.1
1994 Cle-A	11	3	.786	20	20	4	1	0	127^{1}	133	14	40	60	12.5	3.82	124	.273	.333	0	—	0	14	13	0	1.2
1995 Cle-A	9	7	.563	22	21	2	0	0	124^{2}	143	13	42	68	13.6	5.27	88	.288	.348	0	—	0	-8	-9	0	-0.9
Total 5	31	26	.544	95	78	8	2	0	497	529	60	154	242	12.5	4.44	96	.274	.331	5	.116	-1	-6	-10	-4	-1.7
Team 3	27	15	.643	68	56	7	1	0	361^{1}	395	45	107	185	12.7	4.46	103	.280	.335	0	—	0	7	5	-2	0.2

● BOB CLARK Clark, Robert William b: 8/22/1897, Newport, Pa. d: 5/18/44, Carlsbad, N.Mex. BR/TR, 6'3", 188 lbs. Deb: 5/26/20

YEAR TM/L	W	L	PCT	G	GS	CG	SH	SV	IP	H	HR	BB	SO	RAT	ERA	ERA+	OAV	OOB	BH	AVG	PB	PR	/A	PD	TPI
1920 Cle-A	1	2	.333	11	2	2	1	0	42	59	0	13	8	15.6	3.43	111	.383	.435	2	.200	-0	2	2	-0	0.0
1921 Cle-A	0	0	—	5	0	0	0	0	9^{1}	23	2	6	2	28.9	14.46	29	.511	.577	0	.000	-1	-11	-11	-0	-0.1
Total 2	1	2	.333	16	2	2	1	0	51^{1}	82	2	19	10	18.1	5.44	71	.412	.468	2	.154	-1	-9	-9	-1	-0.1

● WATTY CLARK Clark, William Watson "Lefty" b: 5/16/02, St.Joseph, La. d: 3/4/72, Clearwater, Fla. BL/TL, 6'0.5", 175 lbs. Deb: 5/28/24

YEAR TM/L	W	L	PCT	G	GS	CG	SH	SV	IP	H	HR	BB	SO	RAT	ERA	ERA+	OAV	OOB	BH	AVG	PB	PR	/A	PD	TPI
1924 Cle-A	1	3	.250	12	1	0	0	0	25^{2}	38	0	14	6	18.9	7.01	61	.345	.429	2	.222	1	-8	-8	-0	-1.0
Total 12	111	97	.534	355	206	91	14	16	1747^{1}	1897	86	383	643	11.8	3.66	112	.275	.315	117	.196	1	96	87	1	8.6

● WALTER CLARKSON Clarkson, Walter Hamilton b: 11/3/1878, Cambridge, Mass. d: 10/10/46, Cambridge, Mass. BR/TR, 5'10", 150 lbs. Deb: 7/2/04 F

YEAR TM/L	W	L	PCT	G	GS	CG	SH	SV	IP	H	HR	BB	SO	RAT	ERA	ERA+	OAV	OOB	BH	AVG	PB	PR	/A	PD	TPI
1907 Cle-A	4	6	.400	17	10	9	1	0	90^{2}	77	1	29	32	10.8	1.99	127	.232	.299	1	.036	-3	6	5	-0	0.1
1908 Cle-A	0	0	—	2	1	0	0	0	3^{1}	6	0	2	1	27.0	10.80	22	.400	.526	1	1.000	0	-3	-3	-0	0.0
Total 5	18	16	.529	78	37	23	4	1	374^{2}	340	12	132	178	11.9	3.17	88	.244	.320	20	.152	-4	-23	-16	-4	-1.6
Team 2	4	6	.400	19	11	9	1	0	94	83	1	31	33	11.4	2.30	109	.239	.311	2	.069	-3	3	2	-1	0.1

● DAVID CLYDE Clyde, David Eugene b: 4/22/55, Kansas City, Kan. BL/TL, 6'1", 185 lbs. Deb: 6/27/73

YEAR TM/L	W	L	PCT	G	GS	CG	SH	SV	IP	H	HR	BB	SO	RAT	ERA	ERA+	OAV	OOB	BH	AVG	PB	PR	/A	PD	TPI
1978 Cle-A	8	11	.421	28	25	5	0	0	153^{1}	166	4	60	83	13.4	4.28	87	.280	.350	0	—	0	-9	-9	-1	-1.1
1979 Cle-A	3	4	.429	9	8	1	0	0	45^{2}	50	7	13	17	12.6	5.91	72	.279	.332	0	—	0	-9	-8	0	-1.1
Total 5	18	33	.353	84	73	10	0	0	416^{1}	457	33	180	228	14.0	4.63	81	.285	.361	0	—	0	-39	-41	-3	-4.6
Team 2	11	15	.423	37	33	6	0	0	199	216	11	73	100	13.3	4.66	83	.280	.346	0	—	0	-18	-18	-1	-2.2

● CHRIS CODIROLI Codiroli, Christopher Allen b: 3/26/58, Oxnard, Cal. BR/TR, 6'1", 160 lbs. Deb: 9/11/82

YEAR TM/L	W	L	PCT	G	GS	CG	SH	SV	IP	H	HR	BB	SO	RAT	ERA	ERA+	OAV	OOB	BH	AVG	PB	PR	/A	PD	TPI
1988 Cle-A	0	4	.000	14	2	0	0	1	19^{1}	32	2	10	12	20.9	9.31	44	.372	.455	0	—	0	-11	-11	0	-2.2
Total 8	38	47	.447	144	108	13	2	3	670^{1}	711	76	261	312	13.4	4.87	79	.270	.341	0	—	0	-58	-76	-2	-8.8

● ROCKY COLAVITO Colavito, Rocco Domenico b: 8/10/33, New York, N.Y. BR/TR, 6'3", 190 lbs. Deb: 9/10/55 C♦

YEAR TM/L	W	L	PCT	G	GS	CG	SH	SV	IP	H	HR	BB	SO	RAT	ERA	ERA+	OAV	OOB	BH	AVG	PB	PR	/A	PD	TPI
1958 Cle-A	0	0	—	1	0	0	0	0	3	0	0	3	1	9.0	0.00	—	.000	.273	148	.303	1	1	1	0	0.0
Total 2	1	0	1.000	2	0	0	0	0	5^{2}	1	0	5	2	9.5	0.00	—	.059	.273	1730	.266	1	2	2	0	0.4

● VINCE COLBERT Colbert, Vincent Norman b: 12/20/45, Washington, D.C. BR/TR, 6'4", 200 lbs. Deb: 5/19/70

YEAR TM/L	W	L	PCT	G	GS	CG	SH	SV	IP	H	HR	BB	SO	RAT	ERA	ERA+	OAV	OOB	BH	AVG	PB	PR	/A	PD	TPI
1970 Cle-A	1	1	.500	23	0	0	0	2	31	37	4	16	17	15.7	7.26	55	.298	.383	0	.000	-0	-12	-11	0	-0.8
1971 Cle-A	7	6	.538	50	10	2	0	2	142^{2}	140	11	71	74	13.7	3.97	96	.265	.358	4	.138	-0	-8	-2	0	-0.2
1972 Cle-A	1	7	.125	22	11	1	1	0	74^{2}	74	8	38	36	14.3	4.58	70	.267	.370	4	.200	1	-13	-11	0	-1.1
Total 3	9	14	.391	95	21	3	1	4	248^{1}	251	23	125	127	14.1	4.57	80	.270	.365	8	.157	0	-33	-25	1	-2.1

● BERT COLE Cole, Albert George b: 7/1/1896, San Francisco, Cal. d: 5/30/75, San Mateo, Cal. BL/TL, 6'1", 180 lbs. Deb: 4/19/21

YEAR TM/L	W	L	PCT	G	GS	CG	SH	SV	IP	H	HR	BB	SO	RAT	ERA	ERA+	OAV	OOB	BH	AVG	PB	PR	/A	PD	TPI
1925 Cle-A	1	1	.500	13	2	0	0	1	44	55	1	25	9	16.6	6.14	72	.322	.411	2	.154	-0	-9	-8	-0	-0.4
Total 6	28	32	.467	177	47	18	4	10	605^{2}	735	26	230	119	14.6	4.67	87	.305	.370	49	.239	5	-34	-40	2	-2.8

YEAR TM/L	W	L	PCT	G	GS	CG	SH	SV	IP	H	HR	BB	SO	RAT	ERA	ERA+	OAV	OOB	BH	AVG	PB	PR	/A	PD	TPI

● **ALLAN COLLAMORE**   Collamore, Allan Edward b: 6/5/1887, Worcester, Mass.   d: 8/8/80, Battle Creek, Mich.   BR/TR, 6', 170 lbs.   Deb: 4/15/11

1914 Cle-A	3	7	.300	27	8	3	0	0	105¹	100	3	49	32	13.2	3.25	89	.264	.357	3	.094	-2	-6	-4	-1	-0.7
1915 Cle-A	2	5	.286	11	6	5	2	0	64¹	52	1	22	15	10.4	2.38	128	.235	.305	4	.174	0	4	5	1	0.6
Total 3	5	13	.278	40	14	8	2	0	171²	158	4	74	48	12.6	3.30	89	.259	.347	7	.127	-2	-9	-7	-0	-2.0
Team 2	5	12	.294	38	14	8	2	0	169²	152	4	71	47	12.1	2.92	101	.253	.338	7	.127	-2	-2	1	0	-0.1

● **HAP COLLARD**   Collard, Earl Clinton b: 8/29/1898, Williams, Ariz.   d: 7/9/68, Jamestown, Cal.   BR/TR, 6', 170 lbs.   Deb: 4/23/27

1927 Cle-A	0	0	—	4	0	0	0	0	5¹	8	0	3	2	18.6	5.06	83	.333	.407	0	—	0	-1	-1	0	0.0
1928 Cle-A	0	0	—	1	0	0	0	0	4	4	0	4	1	18.0	2.25	184	.250	.400	1	1.000	0	1	1	-0	0.0
Total 3	6	12	.333	35	15	4	0	0	136¹	200	15	46	28	16.4	6.60	81	.347	.398	10	.222	-1	-26	-19	1	-2.1
Team 2	0	0	—	5	0	0	0	0	9¹	12	0	7	3	18.3	3.86	108	.300	.404	1	1.000	0	0	0	0	0.0

● **DON COLLINS**   Collins, Donald Edward b: 9/15/52, Lyons, Ga.   BR/TL, 6'2", 195 lbs.   Deb: 5/4/77

| 1980 Cle-A | 0 | 0 | — | 4 | 0 | 0 | 0 | 0 | 6 | 9 | 0 | 7 | 0 | 24.0 | 7.50 | 54 | .346 | .485 | 0 | — | 0 | -2 | -2 | -0 | 0.0 |
| Total 2 | 3 | 9 | .250 | 44 | 6 | 0 | 0 | 2 | 76² | 91 | 8 | 48 | 27 | 16.4 | 5.28 | 84 | .303 | .401 | 0 | .000 | -1 | -12 | -7 | -1 | -1.1 |

● **JACKIE COLLUM**   Collum, Jack Dean b: 6/21/27, Victor, la.   BL/TL, 5'7", 163 lbs.   Deb: 9/21/51

| 1962 Cle-A | 0 | 0 | — | 1 | 0 | 0 | 0 | 0 | 1¹ | 4 | 0 | 0 | 1 | 27.0 | 13.50 | 29 | .571 | .571 | 0 | — | 0 | -1 | -1 | 0 | 0.0 |
| Total 9 | 32 | 28 | .533 | 171 | 37 | 11 | 2 | 12 | 464 | 480 | 44 | 173 | 171 | 13.0 | 4.15 | 101 | .273 | .344 | 29 | .246 | 8 | -4 | -1 | 6 | 2.5 |

● **STEVE COMER**   Comer, Steven Michael b: 1/13/54, Minneapolis, Minn.   BB/TR, 6'3", 205 lbs.   Deb: 4/15/78   C

| 1984 Cle-A | 4 | 8 | .333 | 22 | 20 | 1 | 0 | 0 | 117¹ | 146 | 11 | 39 | 39 | 14.5 | 5.68 | 72 | .309 | .366 | 0 | — | 0 | -22 | -21 | 0 | -1.9 |
| Total 7 | 44 | 37 | .543 | 176 | 83 | 11 | 3 | 13 | 701² | 762 | 57 | 252 | 245 | 13.2 | 4.13 | 95 | .281 | .347 | 0 | .000 | -0 | -10 | -15 | 1 | -0.4 |

● **SARGE CONNALLY**   Connally, George Walter b: 8/31/1898, McGregor, Tex.   d: 1/27/78, Temple, Tex.   BR/TR, 5'11", 170 lbs.   Deb: 9/10/21

1931 Cle-A	5	5	.500	17	9	5	0	1	85²	87	7	50	37	15.0	4.20	110	.256	.361	5	.185	0	2	4	-0	0.4
1932 Cle-A	8	6	.571	35	7	4	1	3	112¹	119	6	42	32	13.1	4.33	110	.266	.333	7	.175	-0	2	5	0	0.6
1933 Cle-A	5	3	.625	41	3	1	0	1	103	112	4	49	30	14.3	4.89	91	.271	.353	6	.231	1	-7	-5	-2	-0.5
1934 Cle-A	0	0	—	5	0	0	0	1	5¹	4	0	5	1	15.2	5.06	90	.222	.391	0	.000	-0	-0	-0	0	0.0
Total 12	49	60	.450	303	67	33	2	31	994¹	1104	32	449	345	14.4	4.30	98	.288	.368	70	.233	5	-7	-8	5	1.1
Team 4	18	14	.563	98	19	10	1	6	306¹	322	17	146	100	14.1	4.50	102	.264	.349	18	.191	1	-4	4	-2	0.5

● **ED CONNOLLY**   Connolly, Edward Joseph Jr. b: 12/3/39, Brooklyn, N.Y.   BL/TL, 6'1", 190 lbs.   Deb: 4/19/64   F

| 1967 Cle-A | 2 | 1 | .667 | 15 | 4 | 0 | 0 | 0 | 49¹ | 63 | 6 | 34 | 45 | 17.9 | 7.48 | 44 | .315 | .417 | 2 | .182 | 0 | -23 | -23 | -0 | -1.3 |
| Total 2 | 6 | 12 | .333 | 42 | 19 | 1 | 0 | 0 | 130 | 143 | 9 | 98 | 118 | 17.2 | 5.88 | 62 | .287 | .405 | 5 | .172 | 1 | -35 | -33 | -2 | -3.0 |

● **JIM CONSTABLE**   Constable, Jimmy Lee "Sheriff" b: 6/14/33, Jonesborough, Tenn.   BB/TL, 6'1", 185 lbs.   Deb: 6/24/56

| 1958 Cle-A | 0 | 1 | .000 | 6 | 2 | 0 | 0 | 0 | 9¹ | 17 | 1 | 4 | 3 | 21.2 | 11.57 | 32 | .415 | .478 | 2 | 1.000 | 1 | -8 | -8 | -0 | -0.7 |
| Total 5 | 3 | 4 | .429 | 56 | 6 | 1 | 1 | 2 | 98 | 109 | 8 | 41 | 59 | 14.4 | 4.87 | 78 | .291 | .371 | 4 | .235 | 2 | -11 | -11 | -1 | -0.4 |

● **DENNIS COOK**   Cook, Dennis Bryan b: 10/4/62, LaMarque, Tex.   BL/TL, 6'3", 185 lbs.   Deb: 9/12/88

1992 Cle-A	5	7	.417	32	25	0	0	0	158	156	29	50	96	11.8	3.82	102	.255	.314	0	—	0	2	2	-2	-0.1
1993 Cle-A	5	5	.500	25	6	0	0	0	54	62	9	16	34	13.3	5.67	76	.295	.351	0	—	0	-8	-8	-1	-1.3
1995 Cle-A	0	0	—	11	0	0	0	0	12²	16	3	10	13	19.2	6.39	72	.320	.443	0	—	0	-2	-2	-0	0.0
Total 8	32	28	.533	235	71	6	3	3	619¹	596	90	218	361	12.0	3.91	100	.255	.321	24	.250	7	2	1	-4	-0.6
Team 3	10	12	.455	68	31	1	0	0	224²	234	41	76	143	12.6	4.41	92	.269	.331	0	—	0	-8	-9	-2	-1.4

● **FRITZ COUMBE**   Coumbe, Frederick Nicholas b: 12/13/1889, Antrim, Pa.   d: 3/21/78, Paradise, Cal.   BL/TL, 6', 152 lbs.   Deb: 4/22/14

1914 Cle-A	1	5	.167	14	5	2	0	0	55¹	59	0	16	22	12.8	3.25	89	.288	.351	6	.261	1	-3	-2	1	-0.1
1915 Cle-A	4	7	.364	30	12	4	1	2	114	123	1	37	37	12.9	3.47	88	.294	.355	10	.270	1	-7	-5	3	-0.2
1916 Cle-A	7	5	.583	29	13	7	2	0	120¹	121	1	27	39	11.1	2.02	149	.279	.323	2	.057	-3	11	13	5	1.5
1917 Cle-A	8	6	.571	34	10	4	1	5	134¹	119	0	35	30	10.5	2.14	132	.251	.307	6	.154	-1	8	10	3	1.3
1918 Cle-A	13	7	.650	30	17	9	0	3	150	164	4	52	41	13.0	3.06	98	.286	.347	12	.214	-1	-5	-1	5	0.3
1919 Cle-A	1	1	.500	8	2	0	0	1	23²	32	2	9	7	15.6	5.32	63	.348	.406	3	.500	1	-6	-5	-0	-0.3
Total 8	38	38	.500	193	70	30	4	13	761¹	773	10	217	212	11.9	2.80	108	.277	.332	52	.206	-1	10	20	20	3.5
Team 6	34	31	.523	145	59	26	4	11	597²	618	8	176	176	12.1	2.83	105	.281	.338	39	.199	-3	-2	10	17	2.5

● **STAN COVELESKI**   Coveleski, Stanley Anthony (b: Stanislaus Kowalewski)
b: 7/13/1889, Shamokin, Pa.   d: 3/20/84, South Bend, Ind.   BR/TR, 5'11", 166 lbs.   Deb: 9/10/12   FH

1916 Cle-A	15	13	.536	45	27	11	1	3	232	247	6	58	76	11.9	3.41	88	.278	.323	13	.173	-0	-15	-10	2	-1.1
1917 Cle-A	19	14	.576	45	36	24	**9**	4	298¹	202	3	94	133	9.0	1.81	157	**.194**	.261	13	.134	-4	28	34	-4	3.1
1918 Cle-A	22	13	.629	38	33	25	2	1	311	261	2	76	87	9.9	1.82	165	.229	.279	21	.191	-3	33	41	-0	4.6
1919 Cle-A	24	12	.667	43	34	24	4	4	286	286	2	60	118	11.0	2.61	128	.267	.308	20	.213	4	20	23	3	3.6
1920 *Cle-A	24	14	.632	41	38	26	3	2	315	284	6	65	**133**	10.1	2.49	153	**.243**	**.285**	25	.225	3	**46**	**46**	3	**5.9**
1921 Cle-A	23	13	.639	43	40	28	2	2	315	341	6	84	99	11.6	3.37	126	.280	.329	18	.155	-6	32	31	7	3.2
1922 Cle-A	17	14	.548	35	33	21	3	2	276²	292	14	64	98	11.6	3.32	121	.274	.316	10	.101	-7	22	21	1	1.5
1923 Cle-A	13	14	.481	33	31	17	**5**	2	228	251	8	42	54	11.6	**2.76**	**143**	.282	.316	7	.089	-8	**31**	30	3	2.9
1924 Cle-A	15	16	.484	37	33	18	0	1	240¹	286	6	73	58	13.6	4.04	106	.294	.346	11	.134	-5	5	6	-0	0.2
Total 14	215	142	.602	450	385	224	38	21	3082	3055	66	802	981	11.4	2.89	128	.262	.311	168	.159	-34	259	276	16	27.5
Team 9	172	123	.583	360	305	194	31	20	2502¹	2450	53	616	856	11.1	2.80	129	.259	.306	138	.160	-25	202	228	15	23.9

● **HOWARD CRAGHEAD**   Craghead, Howard Oliver "Judge" b: 5/25/08, Selma, Cal.   d: 7/15/62, San Diego, Cal.   BR/TR, 6'2", 200 lbs.   Deb: 4/30/31

1931 Cle-A	0	0	—	4	0	0	0	0	5²	8	0	2	2	15.9	6.35	73	.320	.370	0	—	0	-1	-1	0	0.0
1933 Cle-A	0	0	—	11	0	0	0	0	17¹	19	1	10	2	15.6	6.23	71	.292	.395	0	.000	-0	-4	-3	0	0.0
Total 2	0	0	—	15	0	0	0	0	23	27	1	12	4	15.7	6.26	72	.300	.388	0	.000	-0	-5	-5	0	0.0

● **KEITH CREEL**   Creel, Steven Keith b: 2/4/59, Dallas, Tex.   BR/TR, 6'2", 180 lbs.   Deb: 5/25/82

| 1985 Cle-A | 2 | 5 | .286 | 15 | 8 | 0 | 0 | 0 | 62 | 73 | 7 | 23 | 31 | 14.2 | 4.79 | 86 | .296 | .360 | 0 | — | 0 | -4 | -5 | -1 | -0.5 |
| Total 4 | 5 | 14 | .263 | 55 | 24 | 1 | 0 | 0 | 202² | 244 | 34 | 88 | 80 | 14.9 | 5.60 | 74 | .300 | .372 | 0 | — | 0 | -33 | -33 | -2 | -2.7 |

● **BILL CRISTALL**   Cristall, William Arthur "Lefty" b: 9/12/1878, Odessa, Russia   d: 1/28/39, Buffalo, N.Y.   BL/TL, 5'7", 145 lbs.   Deb: 9/3/01

| 1901 Cle-A | 1 | 5 | .167 | 6 | 6 | 5 | 1 | 0 | 48¹ | 54 | 1 | 30 | 12 | 16.4 | 4.84 | 73 | .280 | .388 | 7 | .350 | 2 | -6 | -7 | 2 | -0.3 |

● **VICTOR CRUZ**   Cruz, Victor Manuel (b: b: 12/24/57, Rancho Viejo La Vega, D.R.   BR/TR, 5'9", 200 lbs.   Deb: 6/24/78

1979 Cle-A	3	9	.250	61	0	0	0	10	78²	70	10	44	63	13.2	4.23	100	.244	.346	0	—	0	-0	-0	0	0.0
1980 Cle-A	6	7	.462	55	0	0	0	12	86	71	10	27	88	10.6	3.45	118	.229	.297	0	—	0	6	6	-1	0.8
Total 5	18	23	.439	187	0	0	0	37	271	218	28	131	248	11.8	3.09	131	.226	.323	0	.000	-0	27	28	-2	5.2
Team 2	9	16	.360	116	0	0	0	22	164²	141	20	71	151	11.8	3.83	109	.236	.321	0	—	0	5	6	-1	0.8

● **NICK CULLOP**   Cullop, Henry Nicholas "Tomato Face" (b: Heinrich Nicholas Kolop)
b: 10/16/1900, St.Louis, Mo.   d: 12/8/78, Westerville, Ohio   BR/TR, 6', 200 lbs.   Deb: 4/14/26   ♦

| 1927 Cle-A | 0 | 0 | — | | | | | | 1 | 3 | 0 | 2 | 0 | 27.0 | 9.00 | 47 | .600 | .600 | 16 | .235 | 0 | -1 | -1 | -0 | 0.0 |

● **NICK CULLOP**   Cullop, Norman Andrew b: 9/17/1887, Chilhowie, Va.   d: 4/15/61, Tazewell, Va.   BL/TL, 5'11.5", 172 lbs.   Deb: 5/20/13

| 1913 Cle-A | 3 | 7 | .300 | 23 | 6 | 4 | 0 | 0 | 97² | 105 | 3 | 35 | 30 | 13.2 | 4.42 | 69 | .291 | .358 | 4 | .129 | -1 | -16 | -15 | 1 | -1.5 |

YEAR	TM/L	W	L	PCT	G	GS	CG	SH	SV	IP	H	HR	BB	SO	RAT	ERA	ERA+	OAV	OOB	BH	AVG	PB	PR	/A	PD	TPI
1914	Cle-A	0	1	.000	1	0	0	0	0	3^1	4	0	1	3	13.5	2.70	107	.364	.417	0	.000	-0	0	0	-0	0.0
Total	6	57	55	.509	174	121	62	9	5	1024	973	24	259	400	11.1	2.73	102	.258	.310	49	.149	-12	10	6	3	0.0
Team	2	3	8	.273	24	8	4	0	0	101	109	3	36	33	13.2	4.37	69	.293	.360	4	.125	-1	-16	-15	1	-1.5

● GEORGE CULVER
Culver, George Raymond b: 7/8/43, Salinas, Cal. BR/TR, 6'2", 185 lbs. Deb: 9/7/66

YEAR	TM/L	W	L	PCT	G	GS	CG	SH	SV	IP	H	HR	BB	SO	RAT	ERA	ERA+	OAV	OOB	BH	AVG	PB	PR	/A	PD	TPI
1966	Cle-A	0	2	.000	5	1	0	0	0	9^2	15	1	7	6	21.4	8.38	41	.357	.460	0	.000	-0	-5	-5	0	-0.9
1967	Cle-A	7	3	.700	53	1	0	0	3	75	71	2	31	41	13.0	3.96	82	.258	.346	1	.250	0	-6	-6	1	-0.7
Total	9	48	49	.495	335	57	7	2	23	789	793	42	352	451	13.6	3.62	96	.266	.352	20	.124	-4	-18	-13	8	-0.9
Team	2	7	5	.583	58	2	0	0	3	84^2	86	3	38	47	13.9	4.46	74	.271	.362	1	.167	-0	-11	-11	1	-1.6

● JACK CURTIS
Curtis, Jack Patrick b: 1/11/37, Rhodhiss, N.C. BL/TL, 5'10", 175 lbs. Deb: 4/22/61

YEAR	TM/L	W	L	PCT	G	GS	CG	SH	SV	IP	H	HR	BB	SO	RAT	ERA	ERA+	OAV	OOB	BH	AVG	PB	PR	/A	PD	TPI
1963	Cle-A	0	0	—	4	0	0	0	0	5	8	0	5	3	25.2	18.00	20	.348	.483	0	—	0	-8	-8	0	0.0
Total	3	14	19	.424	69	35	6	0	1	279	328	33	89	108	13.6	4.84	84	.297	.352	15	.183	5	-26	-24	-1	-1.3

● BILL DAILEY
Dailey, William Garland b: 5/13/35, Arlington, Va. BR/TR, 6'3", 185 lbs. Deb: 8/17/61

YEAR	TM/L	W	L	PCT	G	GS	CG	SH	SV	IP	H	HR	BB	SO	RAT	ERA	ERA+	OAV	OOB	BH	AVG	PB	PR	/A	PD	TPI
1961	Cle-A	1	0	1.000	12	0	0	0	0	19	16	0	6	7	10.4	0.95	415	.232	.293	0	.000	-0	6	6	0	0.3
1962	Cle-A	2	2	.500	27	0	0	0	1	42^2	43	0	17	24	13.1	3.59	108	.270	.348	0	.000	-0	2	1	-0	0.1
Total	4	10	7	.588	119	0	0	0	22	185^2	162	12	59	109	11.0	2.76	135	.241	.308	5	.192	1	20	20	3	2.0
Team	2	3	2	.600	39	0	0	0	1	61^2	59	0	23	31	12.3	2.77	140	.259	.332	0	.000	-1	8	8	0	0.4

● BUD DALEY
Daley, Leavitt Leo b: 10/7/32, Orange, Cal. BL/TL, 6'1", 185 lbs. Deb: 9/10/55

YEAR	TM/L	W	L	PCT	G	GS	CG	SH	SV	IP	H	HR	BB	SO	RAT	ERA	ERA+	OAV	OOB	BH	AVG	PB	PR	/A	PD	TPI
1955	Cle-A	0	1	.000	2	1	0	0	0	7	10	1	1	2	14.1	6.43	62	.333	.355	0	.000	-0	-2	-2	0	-0.2
1956	Cle-A	1	0	1.000	14	0	0	0	0	20^1	21	2	14	13	17.7	6.20	68	.273	.417	0	.000	-0	-5	-5	1	-0.1
1957	Cle-A	2	8	.200	34	10	1	0	2	87^1	99	7	40	54	15.4	4.43	84	.279	.368	4	.200	0	-6	-7	1	-0.6
Total	10	60	64	.484	248	116	36	3	10	967^1	998	100	351	549	13.1	4.03	97	.266	.339	56	.192	3	-15	-14	4	-0.7
Team	3	3	9	.250	50	11	1	0	2	114^2	130	10	55	69	15.7	4.87	78	.281	.376	4	.167	-0	-13	-13	3	-0.9

● LEE DASHNER
Dashner, Lee Claire "Lefty" b: 4/25/1887, Renault, Ill. d: 12/16/59, ElDorado, Kan. BB/TL, 5'11.5", 192 lbs. Deb: 8/4/13

YEAR	TM/L	W	L	PCT	G	GS	CG	SH	SV	IP	H	HR	BB	SO	RAT	ERA	ERA+	OAV	OOB	BH	AVG	PB	PR	/A	PD	TPI
1913	Cle-A	0	0	—	1	0	0	0	0	1^2	0	0	0	2	0.0	5.40	56	.000	.000	0	—	0	-0	-0	-0	0.0

● STEVE DAVIS
Davis, Steven Kennon b: 8/4/60, San Antonio, Tex. BL/TL, 6'1", 195 lbs. Deb: 8/25/85

YEAR	TM/L	W	L	PCT	G	GS	CG	SH	SV	IP	H	HR	BB	SO	RAT	ERA	ERA+	OAV	OOB	BH	AVG	PB	PR	/A	PD	TPI
1989	Cle-A	1	1	.500	12	2	0	0	0	25^2	34	2	14	12	16.8	8.06	49	.318	.397	0	—	0	-12	-12	-0	-0.9
Total	3	3	2	.600	25	7	0	0	0	57^1	65	9	32	39	15.2	6.44	64	.286	.375	0	—	0	-15	-15	-1	-1.1

● JOE DAWSON
Dawson, Ralph Fenton b: 3/9/1897, Bow, Wash. d: 1/4/78, Longview, Tex. BR/TR, 5'11", 182 lbs. Deb: 7/4/24

YEAR	TM/L	W	L	PCT	G	GS	CG	SH	SV	IP	H	HR	BB	SO	RAT	ERA	ERA+	OAV	OOB	BH	AVG	PB	PR	/A	PD	TPI
1924	Cle-A	1	2	.333	4	4	0	0	0	20^1	24	0	21	7	20.4	6.64	64	.300	.451	2	.286	0	-5	-5	1	-0.6
Total	4	11	17	.393	59	18	5	0	3	238^1	233	10	112	62	13.1	4.15	99	.260	.343	20	.260	3	-4	-1	-3	-0.2

● CHUBBY DEAN
Dean, Alfred Lovill b: 8/24/16, Mt.Airy, N.C. d: 12/21/70, Riverside, Cal. BL/TL, 5'11", 181 lbs. Deb: 4/14/36 ♦

YEAR	TM/L	W	L	PCT	G	GS	CG	SH	SV	IP	H	HR	BB	SO	RAT	ERA	ERA+	OAV	OOB	BH	AVG	PB	PR	/A	PD	TPI
1941	Cle-A	1	4	.200	8	8	2	0	0	53^1	57	3	24	14	13.7	4.39	90	.282	.358	4	.160	0	-1	-3	1	-0.1
1942	Cle-A	8	11	.421	27	22	8	0	1	172^2	170	7	66	46	12.3	3.81	91	.261	.329	27	.267	8	-3	-7	-3	-0.2
1943	Cle-A	5	5	.500	17	9	3	0	0	76	83	1	34	29	14.0	4.50	69	.281	.358	9	.196	1	-10	-12	-1	-1.4
Total	7	30	46	.395	162	68	23	1	9	685^2	781	52	323	195	14.5	5.08	79	.288	.364	287	.274	25	-75	-80	-1	-4.6
Team	3	14	20	.412	52	39	13	0	1	302	310	11	124	89	13.0	4.08	84	.270	.341	40	.233	10	-14	-21	-4	-1.7

● JEFF DEDMON
Dedmon, Jeffrey Linden b: 3/4/60, Torrance, Cal. BL/TR, 6'2", 200 lbs. Deb: 9/2/83

YEAR	TM/L	W	L	PCT	G	GS	CG	SH	SV	IP	H	HR	BB	SO	RAT	ERA	ERA+	OAV	OOB	BH	AVG	PB	PR	/A	PD	TPI
1988	Cle-A	1	0	1.000	21	0	0	0	1	33^2	35	3	21	17	15.8	4.54	90	.276	.391	0	—	0	-2	-2	1	0.1
Total	6	20	16	.556	250	3	0	0	12	394	387	30	186	210	13.3	3.84	105	.261	.348	7	.149	-0	-3	8	9	2.4

● BEN DeMOTT
DeMott, Benyew Harrison b: 4/2/1889, Green Village, N.J. d: 7/5/63, Somerville, N.J. BR/TR, 6', 192 lbs. Deb: 8/12/10

YEAR	TM/L	W	L	PCT	G	GS	CG	SH	SV	IP	H	HR	BB	SO	RAT	ERA	ERA+	OAV	OOB	BH	AVG	PB	PR	/A	PD	TPI
1910	Cle-A	0	3	.000	6	4	1	0	0	28^1	45	0	8	13	17.2	5.40	48	.388	.432	3	.167	-0	-9	-9	0	-0.9
1911	Cle-A	0	1	.000	1	1	0	0	0	3^2	10	0	2	2	29.5	12.27	28	.588	.632	0	.000	-0	-4	-4	0	-0.6
Total	2	0	4	.000	7	5	1	0	0	32	55	0	10	15	18.6	6.19	43	.414	.458	3	.136	-0	-13	-12	1	-1.5

● JOHN DENNY
Denny, John Allen b: 11/8/52, Prescott, Ariz. BR/TR, 6'3", 190 lbs. Deb: 9/12/74

YEAR	TM/L	W	L	PCT	G	GS	CG	SH	SV	IP	H	HR	BB	SO	RAT	ERA	ERA+	OAV	OOB	BH	AVG	PB	PR	/A	PD	TPI
1980	Cle-A	8	6	.571	16	16	4	1	0	108^2	116	4	47	59	13.9	4.39	93	.284	.365	0	—	0	-4	-4	1	-0.4
1981	Cle-A	10	6	.625	19	19	6	3	0	145^2	139	9	66	94	12.9	3.15	115	.254	.338	0	—	0	8	8	5	1.4
1982	Cle-A	6	11	.353	21	21	5	0	0	138^1	126	11	73	94	13.3	5.01	81	.240	.340	0	—	0	-14	-14	1	-1.4
Total	13	123	108	.532	325	322	62	18	0	2148^2	2093	137	778	1146	12.3	3.59	104	.258	.327	97	.170	2	25	30	31	7.0
Team	3	24	23	.511	56	56	15	4	0	392^2	381	24	186	247	13.3	4.15	94	.258	.346	0	—	0	-10	-11	6	-0.4

● SHORTY DesJARDIEN
DesJardien, Paul Raymond b: 8/24/1893, Coffeyville, Kan. d: 3/7/56, Monrovia, Cal. BR/TR, 6'4.5", 205 lbs. Deb: 5/20/16

YEAR	TM/L	W	L	PCT	G	GS	CG	SH	SV	IP	H	HR	BB	SO	RAT	ERA	ERA+	OAV	OOB	BH	AVG	PB	PR	/A	PD	TPI
1916	Cle-A	0	0	—	1	0	0	0	0	1	1	0	1	0	18.0	18.00	17	.200	.333	0	—	0	-2	-2	-0	0.0

● GEORGE DICKERSON
Dickerson, George Clark b: 12/1/1892, Renner, Tex. d: 7/9/38, Los Angeles, Cal. BR/TR, 6'1", 170 lbs. Deb: 8/2/17

YEAR	TM/L	W	L	PCT	G	GS	CG	SH	SV	IP	H	HR	BB	SO	RAT	ERA	ERA+	OAV	OOB	BH	AVG	PB	PR	/A	PD	TPI
1917	Cle-A	0	0	—	1	0	0	0	0	1	0	0	0	0	0.0	0.00	—	.000	.000	0	—	0	0	0	-0	0.0

● HARLEY DILLINGER
Dillinger, Harley Hugh "Hoke" or "Lefty"
b: 10/30/1894, Pomeroy, Ohio d: 1/8/59, Cleveland, Ohio BR/TL, 5'11", 175 lbs. Deb: 8/16/14

YEAR	TM/L	W	L	PCT	G	GS	CG	SH	SV	IP	H	HR	BB	SO	RAT	ERA	ERA+	OAV	OOB	BH	AVG	PB	PR	/A	PD	TPI
1914	Cle-A	0	1	.000	11	2	1	0	0	33^2	41	0	25	11	17.9	4.54	64	.325	.441	0	.000	-1	-7	-6	-1	-0.4

● JERRY DiPOTO
DiPoto, Gerard Peter b: 5/24/68, Jersey City, N.J. BR/TR, 6'2", 200 lbs. Deb: 5/11/93

YEAR	TM/L	W	L	PCT	G	GS	CG	SH	SV	IP	H	HR	BB	SO	RAT	ERA	ERA+	OAV	OOB	BH	AVG	PB	PR	/A	PD	TPI
1993	Cle-A	4	4	.500	46	0	0	0	11	56^1	57	0	30	41	14.1	2.40	180	.270	.364	0	—	0	12	12	1	2.1
1994	Cle-A	0	0	—	7	0	0	0	0	15^2	26	1	10	9	21.3	8.04	59	.406	.493	0	—	0	-6	-6	0	0.0
Total	3	8	10	.444	111	0	0	0	13	150^2	160	3	69	99	14.0	3.70	116	.284	.368	0	.000	-1	10	10	1	2.5
Team	2	4	4	.500	53	0	0	0	11	72	83	1	40	50	15.6	3.63	122	.302	.394	0	—	0	6	6	1	2.1

● WALT DOANE
Doane, Walter Rudolph b: 3/12/1887, Bellevue, Idaho d: 10/19/35, W.Brandywine, Pa. BL/TR, 6', 165 lbs. Deb: 9/20/09 ♦

YEAR	TM/L	W	L	PCT	G	GS	CG	SH	SV	IP	H	HR	BB	SO	RAT	ERA	ERA+	OAV	OOB	BH	AVG	PB	PR	/A	PD	TPI
1909	Cle-A	0	1	.000	1	1	0	0	0	5	10	0	1	2	19.8	5.40	47	.400	.423	1	.111	-0	-2	-2	-0	-0.3
1910	Cle-A	0	0	—	6	0	0	0	0	17^2	31	1	8	7	20.4	5.60	46	.413	.476	2	.286	1	-6	-6	-1	0.0
Total	2	0	1	.000	7	1	0	0	0	22^2	41	1	9	9	20.3	5.56	46	.410	.464	3	.188	1	-8	-8	-1	-0.3

● JOE DOBSON
Dobson, Joseph Gordon "Burrhead" b: 1/20/17, Durant, Okla. d: 6/23/94, Jacksonville, Fla. BR/TR, 6'2", 197 lbs. Deb: 4/26/39

YEAR	TM/L	W	L	PCT	G	GS	CG	SH	SV	IP	H	HR	BB	SO	RAT	ERA	ERA+	OAV	OOB	BH	AVG	PB	PR	/A	PD	TPI
1939	Cle-A	2	3	.400	35	3	0	0	1	78	87	3	51	27	16.0	5.88	75	.290	.395	1	.056	-2	-11	-13	1	-0.8
1940	Cle-A	3	7	.300	40	7	2	1	3	100	101	8	48	57	13.4	4.95	85	.268	.351	3	.125	-1	-6	-8	-0	-0.8
Total	14	137	103	.571	414	273	112	22	18	2170	2048	137	851	992	12.1	3.62	112	.250	.322	106	.152	-15	86	105	-5	10.0
Team	2	5	10	.333	75	10	2	1	4	178	188	11	99	84	14.6	5.36	80	.278	.371	4	.095	-3	-17	-21	0	-1.6

● PAT DOBSON
Dobson, Patrick Edward b: 2/12/42, Depew, N.Y. BR/TR, 6'3", 190 lbs. Deb: 5/31/67 C

YEAR	TM/L	W	L	PCT	G	GS	CG	SH	SV	IP	H	HR	BB	SO	RAT	ERA	ERA+	OAV	OOB	BH	AVG	PB	PR	/A	PD	TPI
1976	Cle-A	16	12	.571	35	35	6	0	0	217^1	226	13	65	117	12.1	3.48	100	.272	.327	0	—	0	1	0	-1	0.0
1977	Cle-A	3	12	.200	33	17	0	0	1	133^1	155	23	65	81	14.9	6.14	64	.299	.378	0	—	0	-31	-33	0	-3.1
Total	11	122	129	.486	414	279	74	14	19	2120^1	2043	197	665	1301	11.6	3.54	100	.255	.314	39	.123	-8	10	-1	-3	-1.1
Team	2	19	24	.442	68	52	6	0	1	350^2	381	36	130	198	13.2	4.49	82	.282	.347	0	—	0	-30	-32	-0	-3.1

● RED DONAHUE
Donahue, Francis Rostell b: 1/23/1873, Waterbury, Conn. d: 8/25/13, Philadelphia, Pa. BR/TR, 6', 187 lbs. Deb: 5/6/1893

YEAR	TM/L	W	L	PCT	G	GS	CG	SH	SV	IP	H	HR	BB	SO	RAT	ERA	ERA+	OAV	OOB	BH	AVG	PB	PR	/A	PD	TPI
1903	Cle-A	7	9	.438	16	15	14	4	0	136^2	142	3	12	45	10.5	2.44	117	.267	.291	8	.151	-1	8	6	1	0.7
1904	Cle-A	19	14	.576	35	32	30	6	0	277	281	2	49	127	10.9	2.40	105	.264	.299	17	.168	-1	6	4	2	0.5

YEAR	TM/L	W	L	PCT	G	GS	CG	SH	SV	IP	H	HR	BB	SO	RAT	ERA	ERA+	OAV	OOB	BH	AVG	PB	PR	/A	PD	TPI
1905	Cle-A	6	12	.333	20	18	14	1	0	137^2	132	2	25	45	10.6	3.40	77	.253	.294	4	.075	-5	-11	-12	1	-1.8
Total	13	165	175	.485	368	341	313	25	3	2975^1	3384	61	690	788	12.7	3.61	96	.285	.331	175	.152	-57	-40	-52	19	-8.0
Team	3	32	35	.478	71	65	58	11	0	551^1	555	7	86	217	10.7	2.66	99	.262	.296	29	.140	-7	3	-1	4	-0.6

● PETE DONOHUE Donohue, Peter Joseph b: 11/5/1900, Athens, Tex. d: 2/23/88, Ft.Worth, Tex. BR/TR, 6'2", 185 lbs. Deb: 7/1/21

YEAR	TM/L	W	L	PCT	G	GS	CG	SH	SV	IP	H	HR	BB	SO	RAT	ERA	ERA+	OAV	OOB	BH	AVG	PB	PR	/A	PD	TPI
1931	Cle-A	0	0	—	2	0	0	0	0	5^1	9	1	5	4	23.6	8.44	55	.429	.538	0	.000	-0	-2	-2	-0	0.0
Total	12	134	118	.532	344	270	137	16	12	2112^1	2439	68	422	571	12.4	3.87	103	.293	.330	180	.246	21	56	25	-1	4.8

● DICK DONOVAN Donovan, Richard Edward b: 12/7/27, Boston, Mass. BL/TR, 6'3", 205 lbs. Deb: 4/24/50

YEAR	TM/L	W	L	PCT	G	GS	CG	SH	SV	IP	H	HR	BB	SO	RAT	ERA	ERA+	OAV	OOB	BH	AVG	PB	PR	/A	PD	TPI
1962	Cle-A★	20	10	.667	34	34	16	**5**	0	250^2	255	23	47	94	10.9	3.59	108	.263	.299	16	.180	6	11	8	-1	1.4
1963	Cle-A	11	13	.458	30	30	7	3	0	206	211	27	28	84	10.7	4.24	85	.265	.295	9	.130	-1	-14	-14	-1	-1.7
1964	Cle-A	7	9	.438	30	23	5	0	1	158^1	181	19	29	83	12.1	4.55	79	.290	.324	7	.146	3	-16	-17	1	-1.2
1965	Cle-A	1	3	.250	12	3	0	0	0	22^2	32	6	6	12	15.1	5.96	58	.333	.373	0	.000	-1	-6	-6	-0	-1.1
Total	15	122	99	.552	345	273	101	25	5	2017^1	1988	198	495	880	11.3	3.67	104	.258	.306	113	.163	24	45	31	-0	7.3
Team	4	39	35	.527	106	90	28	8	1	637^2	679	75	110	273	11.3	4.12	90	.273	.307	32	.151	7	-26	-29	-1	-2.6

● TOM DONOVAN Donovan, Thomas Joseph b: 1/1/1873, West Troy, N.Y. d: 3/25/33, Watervliet, N.Y. BR/TR, 6'2", 168 lbs. Deb: 9/10/01 F♦

YEAR	TM/L	W	L	PCT	G	GS	CG	SH	SV	IP	H	HR	BB	SO	RAT	ERA	ERA+	OAV	OOB	BH	AVG	PB	PR	/A	PD	TPI
1901	Cle-A	0	0	—	1	0	0	0	0	7	16	0	3	0	27.0	5.14	69	.444	.512	18	.254	0	-1	-1	0	0.0

● GUS DORNER Dorner, Augustus b: 8/18/1876, Chambersburg, Pa. d: 5/4/56, Chambersburg, Pa. BR/TR, 5'10", 176 lbs. Deb: 9/17/02

YEAR	TM/L	W	L	PCT	G	GS	CG	SH	SV	IP	H	HR	BB	SO	RAT	ERA	ERA+	OAV	OOB	BH	AVG	PB	PR	/A	PD	TPI
1902	Cle-A	3	1	.750	4	4	4	1	0	36	33	1	13	5	11.8	1.25	275	.244	.315	5	.385	2	9	9	-0	1.2
1903	Cle-A	4	5	.444	12	8	4	2	0	73^2	83	4	24	28	13.2	4.52	63	.283	.340	2	.080	-2	-13	-14	0	-1.6
Total	6	36	69	.343	131	106	76	8	1	910^1	842	18	330	275	12.1	3.37	78	.250	.326	46	.149	-9	-80	-74	1	-9.5
Team	2	7	6	.538	16	12	8	3	0	109^2	116	5	37	33	12.7	3.45	88	.271	.332	7	.184	0	-3	-5	0	-0.4

● CAL DORSETT Dorsett, Calvin Leavelle "Preacher" b: 6/10/13, Lone Oak, Tex. d: 10/22/70, Elk City, Okla. BR/TR, 6', 180 lbs. Deb: 8/19/40

YEAR	TM/L	W	L	PCT	G	GS	CG	SH	SV	IP	H	HR	BB	SO	RAT	ERA	ERA+	OAV	OOB	BH	AVG	PB	PR	/A	PD	TPI
1940	Cle-A	0	0	—	1	0	0	0	0	1	1	1	0	0	9.0	9.00	47	.250	.250	0	—	0	-1	-1	-0	0.0
1941	Cle-A	0	1	.000	5	2	0	0	0	11^1	21	0	10	5	24.6	10.32	38	.382	.477	0	.000	-0	-8	-8	-0	-0.6
1947	Cle-A	0	0	—	2	0	0	0	0	1^1	3	1	3	1	40.5	27.00	13	.500	.667	0	—	0	-3	-3	0	0.0
Total	3	0	1	.000	8	2	0	0	0	13^2	25	2	13	6	25.0	11.85	33	.385	.487	0	.000	-0	-12	-12	-0	-0.6

● PETE DOWLING Dowling, Henry Peter b: St.Louis, Mo. d: 6/30/05, Hot Lake, Ore. TL , 5'11", Deb: 7/17/1897

YEAR	TM/L	W	L	PCT	G	GS	CG	SH	SV	IP	H	HR	BB	SO	RAT	ERA	ERA+	OAV	OOB	BH	AVG	PB	PR	/A	PD	TPI
1901	Cle-A	11	22	.333	33	30	28	2	0	256^1	269	1	104	99	13.6	3.86	92	.267	.344	16	.162	-4	-6	-9	0	-1.2
Total	4	39	65	.375	117	102	92	2	1	907^1	984	13	339	299	13.8	3.87	95	.274	.348	70	.199	-3	-14	-19	-1	-2.1

● LOGAN DRAKE Drake, Logan Gaffney "L.G." b: 12/26/1900, Spartanburg, S.C. d: 6/1/40, Columbia, S.C. BR/TR, 5'10.5", 165 lbs. Deb: 9/21/22

YEAR	TM/L	W	L	PCT	G	GS	CG	SH	SV	IP	H	HR	BB	SO	RAT	ERA	ERA+	OAV	OOB	BH	AVG	PB	PR	/A	PD	TPI
1922	Cle-A	0	0	—	1	0	0	0	0	3	4	0	2	1	18.0	3.00	134	.364	.462	0	.000	-0	0	0	-0	0.0
1923	Cle-A	0	0	—	4	0	0	0	0	4^1	2	0	4	2	14.5	4.15	95	.133	.350	0	—	0	-0	-0	-0	0.0
1924	Cle-A	0	1	.000	5	1	0	0	0	11^1	18	0	10	8	23.0	10.32	41	.400	.518	0	.000	-0	-8	-8	-0	-0.6
Total	3	0	1	.000	10	1	0	0	0	18^2	24	0	16	11	20.3	7.71	54	.338	.472	0	.000	-0	-7	-7	-1	-0.6

● TOM DRAKE Drake, Thomas Kendall b: 8/7/12, Birmingham, Ala. d: 7/2/88, Birmingham, Ala. BR/TR, 6'1", 185 lbs. Deb: 4/24/39

YEAR	TM/L	W	L	PCT	G	GS	CG	SH	SV	IP	H	HR	BB	SO	RAT	ERA	ERA+	OAV	OOB	BH	AVG	PB	PR	/A	PD	TPI
1939	Cle-A	0	1	.000	8	1	0	0	0	15	23	2	19	1	26.4	9.00	49	.377	.537	0	.000	-0	-7	-8	0	-0.4
Total	2	1	2	.333	18	3	0	0	0	39^2	49	4	28	13	17.9	6.13	65	.318	.429	2	.286	0	-9	-10	0	-0.5

● STEVE DUNNING Dunning, Steven John b: 5/15/49, Denver, Colo. BR/TR, 6'2", 205 lbs. Deb: 6/14/70

YEAR	TM/L	W	L	PCT	G	GS	CG	SH	SV	IP	H	HR	BB	SO	RAT	ERA	ERA+	OAV	OOB	BH	AVG	PB	PR	/A	PD	TPI
1970	Cle-A	4	9	.308	19	17	0	0	0	94^1	93	16	54	77	14.4	4.96	80	.261	.364	5	.161	-1	-13	-11	1	-1.2
1971	Cle-A	8	14	.364	31	29	3	1	1	184	173	25	109	132	14.0	4.50	85	.254	.361	10	.182	1	-21	-14	2	-1.2
1972	Cle-A	6	4	.600	16	16	1	0	0	105	98	16	43	52	12.1	3.26	99	.248	.322	9	.273	5	-2	-0	-1	0.5
1973	Cle-A	0	2	.000	4	3	0	0	0	18	17	2	13	10	15.0	6.50	60	.250	.370	0	—	0	-5	-5	-0	-0.5
Total	7	23	41	.359	136	84	7	1	1	613^2	604	82	323	390	13.8	4.56	82	.261	.355	26	.194	6	-71	-58	3	-3.6
Team	4	18	29	.383	70	65	4	1	1	401^1	381	59	219	271	13.7	4.37	85	.254	.352	24	.202	6	-42	-30	2	-2.4

● JAMIE EASTERLY Easterly, James Morris b: 2/17/53, Houston, Tex. BL/TL, 5'9", 180 lbs. Deb: 4/6/74

YEAR	TM/L	W	L	PCT	G	GS	CG	SH	SV	IP	H	HR	BB	SO	RAT	ERA	ERA+	OAV	OOB	BH	AVG	PB	PR	/A	PD	TPI
1983	Cle-A	4	2	.667	41	0	0	0	3	57	69	4	22	39	14.7	3.63	117	.309	.377	0	—	0	3	4	0	0.5
1984	Cle-A	3	1	.750	26	1	0	0	2	69^1	74	3	23	42	12.7	3.38	121	.273	.332	0	—	0	5	5	0	0.2
1985	Cle-A	4	1	.800	50	7	0	0	0	98^2	96	9	53	58	14.0	3.92	105	.264	.363	0	—	0	2	2	-0	0.2
1986	Cle-A	0	2	.000	13	0	0	0	0	17^2	27	3	12	9	19.9	7.64	54	.365	.453	0	—	0	-7	-7	-0	-0.6
1987	Cle-A	1	1	.500	16	0	0	0	0	31^2	26	4	13	22	11.4	4.55	99	.218	.301	0	—	0	-0	-0	0	0.0
Total	13	23	33	.411	321	36	0	0	14	611^1	663	48	319	350	14.7	4.62	87	.283	.373	10	.161	-1	-49	-40	-0	-3.9
Team	5	12	7	.632	146	8	0	0	5	274^1	292	23	123	170	13.9	4.04	104	.278	.358	0	—	0	3	5	0	0.3

● DENNIS ECKERSLEY Eckersley, Dennis Lee b: 10/3/54, Oakland, Cal. BR/TR, 6'2", 190 lbs. Deb: 4/12/75

YEAR	TM/L	W	L	PCT	G	GS	CG	SH	SV	IP	H	HR	BB	SO	RAT	ERA	ERA+	OAV	OOB	BH	AVG	PB	PR	/A	PD	TPI
1975	Cle-A	13	7	.650	34	24	6	2	2	186^2	147	16	90	152	11.8	2.60	145	.215	.312	0	—	0	24	24	-3	2.3
1976	Cle-A	13	12	.520	36	30	9	3	1	199^1	155	13	78	200	10.7	3.43	102	.214	.295	0	—	0	2	1	-1	0.1
1977	Cle-A★	14	13	.519	33	33	12	3	0	247^1	214	31	54	191	10.0	3.53	112	.231	**.278**	0	—	0	15	11	-3	0.9
Total	21	192	159	.547	901	361	100	20	323	3133	2916	324	716	2285.	10.6	3.48	116	.245	.291	24	.133	-1	157	194	-14	28.3
Team	3	40	32	.556	103	87	27	8	3	633^1	516	60	222	543	10.8	3.23	116	.221	.294	0	—	0	41	37	-7	3.3

● GEORGE EDMONDSON Edmondson, George Henderson "Big Ed" b: 5/18/1896, Waxahachie, Tex. d: 7/11/73, Waco, Tex. BR/TR, 6'1", 179 lbs. Deb: 8/15/22

YEAR	TM/L	W	L	PCT	G	GS	CG	SH	SV	IP	H	HR	BB	SO	RAT	ERA	ERA+	OAV	OOB	BH	AVG	PB	PR	/A	PD	TPI
1922	Cle-A	0	0	—	2	0	0	0	0	2	4	0	0	0	18.0	9.00	45	.444	.444	0	—	0	-1	-1	0	0.0
1923	Cle-A	0	0	—	1	0	0	0	0	4	8	0	3	0	27.0	11.25	35	.444	.545	0	.000	-0	-3	-3	0	0.0
1924	Cle-A	0	0	—	5	1	0	0	0	8	10	1	5	3	16.9	9.00	47	.294	.385	1	.333	0	-4	-4	-0	0.0
Total	3	0	0	—	8	1	0	0	0	14	22	1	8	3	19.9	9.64	43	.361	.443	1	.250	-0	-9	-9	0	0.0

● JIM JOE EDWARDS Edwards, James Corbette "Little Joe" b: 12/14/1894, Banner, Miss. d: 1/19/65, Sarepta, Miss. BR/TL, 6'2", 185 lbs. Deb: 5/14/22

YEAR	TM/L	W	L	PCT	G	GS	CG	SH	SV	IP	H	HR	BB	SO	RAT	ERA	ERA+	OAV	OOB	BH	AVG	PB	PR	/A	PD	TPI
1922	Cle-A	3	8	.273	25	7	0	0	0	92^2	113	1	40	44	15.3	4.47	90	.313	.389	2	.087	-2	-4	-5	-1	-0.8
1923	Cle-A	10	10	.500	38	21	8	1	1	179^1	200	5	75	68	14.1	3.71	107	.286	.359	7	.119	-5	5	5	-1	-0.1
1924	Cle-A	4	3	.571	10	7	5	1	0	57	64	3	34	15	15.5	2.84	150	.305	.402	3	.150	-1	9	9	0	0.9
1925	Cle-A	0	3	.000	13	3	1	0	0	36	60	0	23	12	21.0	8.25	54	.382	.464	1	.111	-1	-15	-15	1	-1.0
Total	6	26	37	.413	145	59	23	6	4	584^1	666	18	278	211	14.7	4.37	92	.295	.376	24	.130	-13	-19	-23	-1	-3.5
Team	4	17	24	.415	86	38	14	2	1	365	437	9	172	139	15.3	4.22	96	.306	.385	13	.117	-9	-6	-6	-1	-1.0

● HARRY EELLS Eells, Harry Archibald "Slippery" b: 2/14/1881, Ida Grove, Iowa d: 10/15/40, Los Angeles, Cal. BR/TR, 6'1", 195 lbs. Deb: 4/22/06

YEAR	TM/L	W	L	PCT	G	GS	CG	SH	SV	IP	H	HR	BB	SO	RAT	ERA	ERA+	OAV	OOB	BH	AVG	PB	PR	/A	PD	TPI
1906	Cle-A	4	5	.444	14	8	6	1	0	86^1	77	1	48	35	13.3	2.61	100	.242	.347	6	.188	1	1	0	1	0.1

● BRUCE EGLOFF Egloff, Bruce Edward b: 4/10/65, Denver, Colo. BR/TR, 6'2", 215 lbs. Deb: 4/13/91

YEAR	TM/L	W	L	PCT	G	GS	CG	SH	SV	IP	H	HR	BB	SO	RAT	ERA	ERA+	OAV	OOB	BH	AVG	PB	PR	/A	PD	TPI
1991	Cle-A	0	0	—	6	0	0	0	0	5^2	8	0	4	8	19.1	4.76	87	.333	.429	0	—	0	-0	-0	0	0.0

● JUAN EICHELBERGER Eichelberger, Juan Tyrone b: 10/21/53, St.Louis, Mo. BR/TR, 6'3", 205 lbs. Deb: 9/7/78

YEAR	TM/L	W	L	PCT	G	GS	CG	SH	SV	IP	H	HR	BB	SO	RAT	ERA	ERA+	OAV	OOB	BH	AVG	PB	PR	/A	PD	TPI
1983	Cle-A	4	11	.267	28	15	2	0	0	134	132	10	59	56	13.0	4.90	86	.259	.338	0	—	0	-13	-10	-1	-1.1
Total	7	26	36	.419	125	79	14	1	0	603^1	575	50	283	281	12.9	4.10	87	.254	.339	14	.103	-4	-29	-35	-2	-3.8

● HARRY EISENSTAT Eisenstat, Harry b: 10/10/15, Brooklyn, N.Y. BL/TL, 5'11", 185 lbs. Deb: 5/19/35

YEAR	TM/L	W	L	PCT	G	GS	CG	SH	SV	IP	H	HR	BB	SO	RAT	ERA	ERA+	OAV	OOB	BH	AVG	PB	PR	/A	PD	TPI
1939	Cle-A	6	7	.462	26	11	4	1	2	103^2	109	8	23	38	11.5	3.30	133	.265	.304	8	.250	1	15	13	-1	1.4
1940	Cle-A	1	4	.200	27	3	0	0	4	71^2	78	6	12	27	11.3	3.14	134	.282	.311	6	.273	1	**10**	9	-0	0.7
1941	Cle-A	1	1	.500	21	0	0	0	2	34	43	2	16	11	16.1	4.24	93	.312	.391	2	.333	1	-0	-1	-1	-0.1

YEAR TM/L	W	L	PCT	G	GS	CG	SH	SV	IP	H	HR	BB	SO	RAT	ERA	ERA+	OAV	OOB	BH	AVG	PB	PR	/A	PD	TPI
1942 Cle-A	2	1	.667	29	1	0	0	2	47^{2}	58	1	6	19	12.1	2.45	140	.304	.325	1	.250	0	6	5	-0	0.3
Total 8	25	27	.481	165	32	11	1	14	478^{2}	550	30	114	157	12.6	3.84	114	.287	.328	26	.211	1	30	29	0	2.4
Team 4	10	13	.435	103	15	4	1	10	257	288	17	57	95	12.2	3.22	128	.283	.322	17	.266	2	31	25	-3	2.3
● **BRUCE ELLINGSEN** Ellingsen, Harold Bruce b: 4/26/49, Pocatello, Idaho BL/TL, 6', 180 lbs. Deb: 7/4/74																									
1974 Cle-A	1	1	.500	16	2	0	0	0	42	45	5	17	16	13.3	3.21	112	.278	.346	0	—	0	2	2	-0	0.1
● **GEORGE ELLISON** Ellison, George Russell b: 1/24/1895, California d: 1/20/78, San Francisco, Cal. BR/TR, 6'3", 185 lbs. Deb: 8/21/20																									
1920 Cle-A	0	0	—	1	0	0	0	0	1	0	0	2	1	18.0	0.00	—	.000	.400	0	—	0	0	0	0	0.0
● **DICK ELLSWORTH** Ellsworth, Richard Clark b: 3/22/40, Lusk, Wyo. BL/TL, 6'4", 195 lbs. Deb: 6/22/58 F																									
1969 Cle-A	6	9	.400	34	22	3	1	0	135	162	10	40	48	13.8	4.13	91	.301	.354	6	.133	-1	-8	-6	0	-0.7
1970 Cle-A	3	3	.500	29	1	0	0	2	43^{2}	49	4	14	13	13.2	4.53	87	.299	.358	0	.000	-0	-4	-3	1	-0.3
Total 13	115	137	.456	407	310	87	9	5	2155^{2}	2274	194	595	1140	12.2	3.72	100	.272	.324	59	.088	-25	-37	-2	12	-2.2
Team 2	9	12	.429	63	23	3	1	2	178^{2}	211	14	54	61	13.7	4.23	90	.300	.355	6	.122	-2	-12	-8	1	-1.0
● **ALAN EMBREE** Embree, Alan Duane b: 1/23/70, Vancouver, Wash. BL/TL, 6'2", 185 lbs. Deb: 9/15/92																									
1992 Cle-A	0	2	.000	4	4	0	0	0	18	19	3	8	12	14.0	7.00	56	.271	.354	0	—	0	-6	-6	-1	-0.6
1995 *Cle-A	3	2	.600	23	0	0	0	1	24^{2}	23	2	16	23	14.2	5.11	91	.253	.364	0	—	0	-1	-1	0	-0.2
Total 2	3	4	.429	27	4	0	0	1	42^{2}	42	5	24	35	14.1	5.91	73	.261	.360	0	—	0	-7	-7	-1	-0.8
● **RED EMBREE** Embree, Charles Willard b: 8/30/17, ElMonte, Cal. BR/TR, 6', 165 lbs. Deb: 9/10/41																									
1941 Cle-A	0	1	.000	1	1	0	0	0	4	7	0	3	4	24.8	6.75	58	.438	.550	0	.000	-0	-1	-1	-0	-0.3
1942 Cle-A	3	4	.429	19	6	2	0	0	63	58	0	31	44	13.0	3.86	89	.242	.333	2	.133	-0	-1	-3	-0	-0.3
1944 Cle-A	0	1	.000	3	1	0	0	0	3^{1}	2	0	5	4	18.9	13.50	24	.167	.412	0	—	0	-4	-4	0	-0.9
1945 Cle-A	4	4	.500	8	8	5	1	0	70	56	3	26	42	10.5	1.93	168	.215	.287	3	.143	-1	11	10	1	1.2
1946 Cle-A	8	12	.400	28	26	8	0	0	200	170	15	79	87	11.3	3.47	95	.227	.302	13	.186	1	1	-3	-1	-0.3
1947 Cle-A	8	10	.444	27	21	6	0	0	162^{2}	137	13	67	56	11.3	3.15	110	.233	.313	9	.173	-1	10	6	1	0.5
Total 8	31	48	.392	141	90	29	1	1	707	653	50	330	286	12.6	3.72	98	.246	.331	37	.166	-4	4	-5	-2	-1.5
Team 6	23	32	.418	86	63	21	1	0	503	430	31	211	237	11.6	3.29	103	.231	.311	27	.170	-2	16	5	0	-0.1
● **JOE ENGEL** Engel, Joseph William b: 3/12/1893, Washington, D.C. d: 6/12/69, Chattanooga, Tenn BR/TL, 6'1.5", 183 lbs. Deb: 5/30/12																									
1919 Cle-A	0	0	—	1	0	0	0	0	0	0	0	3	0	—	∞	—	—	1.000	0	—	0	-2	-2	0	-0.2
Total 7	17	23	.425	102	53	10	2	4	407^{1}	344	6	242	151	13.5	3.38	88	.237	.355	7	.067	-6	-20	-18	-0	-2.1
● **JOHNNY ENZMANN** Enzmann, John "Gentleman John" b: 3/4/1890, Brooklyn, N.Y. d: 3/14/84, Riverhead, N.Y. BR/TR, 5'10", 165 lbs. Deb: 7/10/14																									
1918 Cle-A	5	7	.417	30	14	8	0	2	136^{2}	130	2	29	38	10.8	2.37	127	.263	.310	7	.149	-2	6	10	0	0.6
1919 Cle-A	3	2	.600	14	4	2	0	0	55^{1}	67	0	8	13	12.5	2.28	147	.312	.342	2	.133	-0	6	7	-1	0.4
Total 4	11	12	.478	67	21	11	0	2	269^{2}	297	4	61	91	12.4	2.84	111	.289	.338	13	.141	-3	3	10	-0	0.6
Team 2	8	9	.471	44	18	10	0	2	192	197	2	37	51	11.3	2.34	133	.277	.320	9	.145	-3	12	16	-1	1.0
● **TONY FAETH** Faeth, Anthony Joseph b: 7/9/1893, Aberdeen, S.D. d: 12/22/82, St.Paul, Minn. BR/TR, 6', 180 lbs. Deb: 8/10/19																									
1919 Cle-A	0	0	—	6	0	0	0	0	18^{1}	13	0	10	7	11.3	0.49	682	.224	.338	0	.000	-1	6	6	-0	-0.1
1920 Cle-A	0	0	—	13	0	0	0	0	25	31	0	20	14	18.7	4.32	88	.333	.456	0	.000	-1	-1	-1	-0	-0.1
Total 2	0	0	—	19	0	0	0	0	43^{1}	44	0	30	21	15.6	2.70	134	.291	.412	0	.000	-1	4	4	-0	-0.2
● **JERRY FAHR** Fahr, Gerald Warren b: 12/9/24, Marmaduke, Ark. BR/TR, 6'5", 185 lbs. Deb: 4/29/51																									
1951 Cle-A	0	0	—	5	0	0	0	0	5^{2}	11	0	2	0	20.6	4.76	80	.500	.542	0	—	0	-0	-1	-0	0.0
● **CY FALKENBERG** Falkenberg, Frederick Peter b: 12/17/1880, Chicago, Ill. d: 4/14/61, San Francisco, Cal BR/TR, 6'5", 180 lbs. Deb: 4/21/03																									
1908 Cle-A	2	4	.333	8	7	2	0	0	46^{1}	52	1	10	17	12.4	3.88	62	.284	.328	2	.118	-1	-8	-8	-1	-1.1
1909 Cle-A	10	9	.526	24	18	13	2	0	165	135	0	50	82	10.4	2.40	107	.231	.297	9	.173	-1	1	3	3	0.5
1910 Cle-A	14	13	.519	37	29	18	3	1	256^{2}	246	3	75	107	11.5	2.95	88	.261	.320	15	.183	-0	-12	-10	3	-0.8
1911 Cle-A	8	5	.615	15	13	7	0	1	106^{2}	117	0	24	46	12.2	3.29	104	.282	.326	7	.175	-1	1	1	1	0.1
1913 Cle-A	23	10	.697	39	36	23	6	0	276	238	2	88	166	10.8	2.22	137	.235	.299	10	.119	-2	22	25	-2	2.5
Total 12	130	123	.514	330	266	180	27	8	2275	2090	23	690	1164	11.3	2.68	103	.248	.310	117	.152	-23	13	20	13	1.6
Team 5	57	41	.582	123	103	63	11	2	850^{2}	788	6	247	418	11.2	2.70	104	.251	.310	43	.156	-6	4	11	3	1.2
● **HARRY FANWELL** Fanwell, Harry Clayton b: 10/16/1886, Patapsco, Md. d: 7/15/65, Baltimore, Md. BB/TR, 6', 175 lbs. Deb: 7/23/10																									
1910 Cle-A	2	9	.182	17	11	5	1	0	92	87	0	38	30	12.8	3.62	71	.260	.347	1	.033	-3	-11	-11	1	-1.4
● **ED FARMER** Farmer, Edward Joseph b: 10/18/49, Evergreen Park, Ill BR/TR, 6'5", 210 lbs. Deb: 6/9/71																									
1971 Cle-A	5	4	.556	43	4	0	0	4	78^{2}	77	9	41	48	13.8	4.35	88	.263	.359	1	.071	-1	-8	-5	-0	-0.7
1972 Cle-A	2	5	.286	46	1	0	0	7	61^{1}	51	10	27	33	11.6	4.40	73	.231	.317	1	.143	-0	-9	-8	0	-1.1
1973 Cle-A	0	2	.000	16	0	0	0	1	17^{1}	25	4	5	10	15.6	4.67	84	.325	.366	0	—	0	-2	-1	-0	-0.2
Total 11	30	43	.411	370	21	0	0	75	624	611	52	345	395	14.0	4.30	89	.257	.355	4	.085	-3	-38	-31	0	-2.6
Team 3	7	11	.389	105	5	0	0	12	157^{1}	153	23	73	91	13.2	4.40	82	.259	.344	2	.095	-1	-19	-14	-0	-2.0
● **STEVE FARR** Farr, Steven Michael b: 12/12/56, LaPlata, Md. BR/TR, 5'11", 198 lbs. Deb: 5/16/84																									
1984 Cle-A	3	11	.214	31	16	0	0	1	116	106	14	46	83	12.2	4.58	89	.245	.325	0	—	0	-8	-6	1	-0.6
1994 Cle-A	1	1	.500	19	0	0	0	4	15^{1}	17	3	15	12	20.0	5.28	89	.279	.436	0	—	0	-1	-1	0	-0.2
Total 11	48	45	.516	509	28	1	1	132	824^{1}	751	70	334	668	12.2	3.25	127	.244	.325	0	—	0	78	79	1	13.0
Team 2	4	12	.250	50	16	0	0	5	131^{1}	123	17	61	95	13.1	4.66	89	.249	.340	0	—	0	-8	-7	1	-0.8
● **JOHN FARRELL** Farrell, John Edward b: 8/4/62, Monmouth Beach, N.J. BR/TR, 6'4", 210 lbs. Deb: 8/18/87																									
1987 Cle-A	5	1	.833	10	9	1	0	0	69	68	7	22	28	12.4	3.39	133	.256	.324	0	—	0	8	9	-0	0.6
1988 Cle-A	14	10	.583	31	30	4	0	0	210^{1}	216	15	67	92	12.5	4.24	97	.269	.332	0	—	0	-6	-3	-0	-0.5
1989 Cle-A	9	14	.391	31	31	7	2	0	208	196	14	71	132	11.9	3.63	109	.244	.311	0	—	0	6	8	-2	0.5
1990 Cle-A	4	5	.444	17	17	1	0	0	96^{2}	108	10	33	44	13.2	4.28	91	.286	.345	0	—	0	-4	-4	-0	-0.3
1995 Cle-A	0	0	—	1	0	0	0	0	4^{2}	7	0	0	4	13.5	3.86	120	.368	.368	0	—	0	0	0	0	0.0
Total 7	36	44	.450	114	107	13	2	0	692^{1}	721	70	245	355	12.9	4.47	93	.268	.336	0	—	0	-33	-25	-3	-4.6
Team 5	32	30	.516	90	87	13	2	0	588^{2}	595	46	193	300	12.4	3.93	104	.262	.326	0	—	0	4	10	-3	0.3
● **BOB FELLER** Feller, Robert William Andrew (b: Robert William Feller) "Rapid Robert" b: 11/3/18, Van Meter, Iowa BR/TR, 6', 185 lbs. Deb: 7/19/36 H																									
1936 Cle-A	5	3	.625	14	8	5	0	1	62	52	1	47	76	15.0	3.34	151	.229	.371	3	.136	-2	12	12	-1	1.1
1937 Cle-A	9	7	.563	26	19	9	0	1	148^{2}	116	4	106	150	13.6	3.39	136	.218	.351	9	.170	-1	20	20	1	1.9
1938 Cle-A☆	17	11	.607	39	36	20	2	1	277^{2}	225	13	208	**240**	14.3	4.08	114	**.220**	.356	17	.181	2	22	17	-2	1.4
1939 Cle-A★	**24**	9	.727	39	35	**24**	4	1	**296^{2}**	227	13	142	**246**	11.3	2.85	154	**.210**	.303	21	.212	5	**58**	**51**	0	**5.6**
1940 Cle-A★	**27**	11	.711	**43**	37	**31**	**4**	4	**320^{1}**	245	13	118	**261**	**10.3**	**2.61**	161	**.210**	**.285**	18	.157	1	**63**	**57**	-4	**6.1**
1941 Cle-A★	**25**	13	.658	**44**	40	28	**6**	2	**343**	284	15	194	**260**	12.7	3.15	125	.226	.332	18	.150	2	38	30	-1	3.2
1945 Cle-A	5	3	.625	9	9	7	1	0	72	50	1	35	59	10.9	2.50	130	.192	.293	4	.160	-0	7	6	-1	0.5
1946 Cle-A★	**26**	15	.634	**48**	42	**36**	**10**	4	**371^{1}**	277	11	153	**348**	10.5	2.18	152	.208	.291	16	.129	-2	**55**	46	-1	4.9
1947 Cle-A†	**20**	11	.645	42	37	20	**5**	3	**299**	230	17	127	**196**	**10.9**	2.68	130	.215	.300	18	.184	3	**34**	27	2	3.1
1948 *Cle-A†	19	15	.559	44	38	18	2	3	280^{1}	255	20	116	**164**	12.0	3.56	114	.241	.317	9	.095	-8	23	15	-1	0.7
1949 Cle-A	15	14	.517	36	28	15	0	0	211	198	18	84	108	12.1	3.75	106	.248	.320	17	.236	4	10	6	-4	0.7
1950 Cle-A★	16	11	.593	35	34	16	3	0	247	230	20	103	119	12.3	3.43	126	.247	.325	10	.120	-2	32	25	-4	1.7

YEAR	TM/L	W	L	PCT	G	GS	CG	SH	SV	IP	H	HR	BB	SO	RAT	ERA	ERA+	OAV	OOB	BH	AVG	PB	PR	/A	PD	TPI
1951	Cle-A	**22**	8	**.733**	33	32	16	4	0	249^{2}	239	22	95	111	12.3	3.50	108	.253	.325	10	.123	-4	17	8	-3	0.1
1952	Cle-A	9	13	.409	30	30	11	0	0	191^{2}	219	13	83	81	14.3	4.74	71	.288	.360	7	.117	1	-23	-30	-0	-3.0
1953	Cle-A	10	7	.588	25	25	10	1	0	175^{2}	163	16	60	60	11.6	3.59	105	.251	.317	6	.107	-2	8	3	1	0.1
1954	Cle-A	13	3	.813	19	19	9	1	0	140	127	13	39	59	10.9	3.09	119	.239	.294	9	.188	1	10	9	-2	0.9
1955	Cle-A	4	4	.500	25	11	2	1	0	83	71	7	31	25	11.2	3.47	115	.235	.308	1	.048	-2	5	5	-1	0.1
1956	Cle-A	0	4	.000	19	4	2	0	1	58	63	7	23	18	13.3	4.97	85	.280	.347	0	.000	-2	-5	-5	-1	-0.6
Total	18	266	162	.621	570	484	279	44	21	3827	3271	224	1764	2581	12.0	3.25	122	.231	.319	193	.151	-7	385	301	-22	28.5

● **DON FERRARESE** Ferrarese, Donald Hugh b: 6/19/29, Oakland, Cal. BR/TL, 5'9", 170 lbs. Deb: 4/11/55

YEAR	TM/L	W	L	PCT	G	GS	CG	SH	SV	IP	H	HR	BB	SO	RAT	ERA	ERA+	OAV	OOB	BH	AVG	PB	PR	/A	PD	TPI
1958	Cle-A	3	4	.429	28	10	2	0	1	94^{2}	91	5	46	62	13.1	3.71	98	.254	.341	3	.115	-1	1	-1	-1	-0.3
1959	Cle-A	5	3	.625	15	10	4	0	0	76	58	6	51	45	13.0	3.20	115	.219	.347	7	.259	2	6	4	0	0.6
Total	8	19	36	.345	183	50	12	2	5	506^{2}	449	39	295	350	13.3	4.00	98	.241	.347	20	.156	-2	-2	-5	-1	-2.1
Team	2	8	7	.533	43	20	6	0	1	170^{2}	149	11	97	107	13.1	3.48	105	.239	.343	10	.189	1	6	3	-1	0.3

● **WES FERRELL** Ferrell, Wesley Cheek b: 2/2/08, Greensboro, N.C. d: 12/9/76, Sarasota, Fla. BR/TR, 6'2", 195 lbs. Deb: 9/9/27 F◆

YEAR	TM/L	W	L	PCT	G	GS	CG	SH	SV	IP	H	HR	BB	SO	RAT	ERA	ERA+	OAV	OOB	BH	AVG	PB	PR	/A	PD	TPI
1927	Cle-A	0	0	—	1	0	0	0	0	1	3	0	2	0	45.0	27.00	16	.600	.714	0	—	0	-3	-3	-0	0.0
1928	Cle-A	0	2	.000	2	2	1	0	0	16	15	0	5	4	11.3	2.25	184	.242	.299	1	.250	1	3	3	0	0.5
1929	Cle-A	21	10	.677	43	25	18	1	5	242^{2}	256	7	109	100	13.6	3.60	124	.279	.358	22	.237	4	17	23	3	3.4
1930	Cle-A	25	13	.658	43	35	25	1	3	296^{2}	299	14	106	143	12.3	3.31	146	.262	.325	35	.297	8	44	50	-3	6.2
1931	Cle-A	22	12	.647	40	35	**27**	2	3	276^{1}	276	9	130	123	13.3	3.75	123	.255	.336	37	.319	17	19	27	5	5.2
1932	Cle-A	23	13	.639	38	34	26	3	1	287^{2}	299	17	104	105	12.6	3.66	130	.264	.326	31	.242	5	26	35	1	4.3
1933	Cle-A☆	11	12	.478	28	26	16	1	0	201	225	8	70	41	13.3	4.21	106	.282	.341	38	.271	7	2	5	1	1.6
Total	15	193	128	.601	374	323	227	17	13	2623	2845	132	1040	985	13.4	4.04	117	.275	.343	329	.280	100	147	195	6	32.3
Team	7	102	62	.622	195	157	113	8	12	1321^{1}	1373	55	526	516	13.0	3.67	126	.267	.336	164	.274	41	110	141	7	21.2

● **TOM FERRICK** Ferrick, Thomas Jerome b: 1/6/15, New York, N.Y. BR/TR, 6'2.5", 220 lbs. Deb: 4/19/41 C

YEAR	TM/L	W	L	PCT	G	GS	CG	SH	SV	IP	H	HR	BB	SO	RAT	ERA	ERA+	OAV	OOB	BH	AVG	PB	PR	/A	PD	TPI
1942	Cle-A	3	2	.600	31	2	2	0	3	81^{1}	56	3	32	28	9.7	1.99	173	.200	.282	4	.211	0	**15**	**13**	2	1.1
1946	Cle-A	0	0	—	9	0	0	0	1	18	25	3	4	9	14.5	5.00	66	.321	.354	2	.667	1	-3	-3	0	0.1
Total	9	40	40	.500	323	7	4	1	56	674	654	44	227	245	11.8	3.47	117	.256	.317	27	.184	1	42	44	11	6.5
Team	2	3	2	.600	40	2	2	0	4	99^{1}	81	6	36	37	10.6	2.54	135	.226	.297	6	.273	2	12	10	2	1.2

● **CY FERRY** Ferry, Alfred Joseph b: 9/27/1878, Hudson, N.Y. d: 9/27/38, Pittsfield, Mass. BR/TR, 6'1", 170 lbs. Deb: 5/12/04 F

YEAR	TM/L	W	L	PCT	G	GS	CG	SH	SV	IP	H	HR	BB	SO	RAT	ERA	ERA+	OAV	OOB	BH	AVG	PB	PR	/A	PD	TPI
1905	Cle-A	0	0	—	1	1	0	0	0	2	3	1	0	2	22.5	13.50	20	.333	.455	0	.000	-0	-2	-2	0	0.0
Total	2	0	1	.000	4	2	1	0	0	15	15	1	11	6	17.4	7.20	36	.259	.403	2	.286	1	-8	-8	0	-0.3

● **CARL FISCHER** Fischer, Charles William b: 11/5/05, Medina, N.Y. d: 12/10/63, Medina, N.Y. BR/TL, 6', 180 lbs. Deb: 7/19/30

YEAR	TM/L	W	L	PCT	G	GS	CG	SH	SV	IP	H	HR	BB	SO	RAT	ERA	ERA+	OAV	OOB	BH	AVG	PB	PR	/A	PD	TPI
1937	Cle-A	0	1	.000	2	0	0	0	0	0^{2}	2	0	1	1	40.5	27.00	17	.667	.750	0	—	0	-2	-2	0	-1.4
Total	7	46	50	.479	191	105	31	3	11	823	900	53	372	376	14.0	4.63	96	.277	.354	38	.145	-12	-18	-18	-14	-4.5

● **EDDIE FISHER** Fisher, Eddie Gene b: 7/16/36, Shreveport, La. BR/TR, 6'2.5", 200 lbs. Deb: 6/22/59

YEAR	TM/L	W	L	PCT	G	GS	CG	SH	SV	IP	H	HR	BB	SO	RAT	ERA	ERA+	OAV	OOB	BH	AVG	PB	PR	/A	PD	TPI
1968	Cle-A	4	2	.667	54	0	0	0	4	94^{2}	87	8	17	42	10.1	2.85	104	.248	.286	0	.000	-1	1	1	1	0.1
Total	15	85	70	.548	690	63	7	2	81	1538^{2}	1398	149	438	812	10.9	3.41	101	.243	.299	30	.122	-5	26	5	3	0.9

● **PAUL FITZKE** Fitzke, Paul Frederick Herman "Bob" b: 7/30/1900, LaCrosse, Wis. d: 6/30/50, Sacramento, Cal. BR/TR, 5'11.5", 185 lbs. Deb: 9/1/24

YEAR	TM/L	W	L	PCT	G	GS	CG	SH	SV	IP	H	HR	BB	SO	RAT	ERA	ERA+	OAV	OOB	BH	AVG	PB	PR	/A	PD	TPI
1924	Cle-A	0	0	—	1	0	0	0	0	4	5	0	3	1	18.0	4.50	95	.313	.421	0	.000	-0	-0	-0	-0	0.0

● **AL FITZMORRIS** Fitzmorris, Alan James b: 3/21/46, Buffalo, N.Y. BB/TR, 6'2", 190 lbs. Deb: 9/8/69

YEAR	TM/L	W	L	PCT	G	GS	CG	SH	SV	IP	H	HR	BB	SO	RAT	ERA	ERA+	OAV	OOB	BH	AVG	PB	PR	/A	PD	TPI
1977	Cle-A	6	10	.375	29	21	1	0	0	133	164	12	53	54	14.8	5.41	73	.306	.369	0	—	0	-20	-22	-0	-2.0
1978	Cle-A	0	1	.000	7	0	0	0	0	14^{1}	19	3	7	5	17.0	6.28	59	.333	.415	0	—	0	-4	-4	-0	-0.2
Total	10	77	59	.566	288	159	36	11	7	1277	1284	83	433	458	12.2	3.65	101	.265	.327	24	.242	7	-1	5	12	2.5
Team	2	6	11	.353	36	21	1	0	0	147^{1}	183	15	60	59	15.0	5.50	71	.309	.374	0	—	0	-24	-26	-0	-2.2

● **RAY FLANIGAN** Flanigan, Raymond Arthur b: 1/8/23, Morgantown, W.Va. d: 3/28/93, Baltimore, Md. BR/TR, 6', 190 lbs. Deb: 9/20/46

YEAR	TM/L	W	L	PCT	G	GS	CG	SH	SV	IP	H	HR	BB	SO	RAT	ERA	ERA+	OAV	OOB	BH	AVG	PB	PR	/A	PD	TPI
1946	Cle-A	0	1	.000	3	1	0	0	0	9	11	1	8	2	19.0	11.00	30	.289	.413	1	.500	1	-7	-8	0	-0.6

● **JESSE FLORES** Flores, Jesse (Sandoval) b: 11/2/14, Guadalajara, Mexico d: 12/17/91, Orange, Cal. BR/TR, 5'10", 175 lbs. Deb: 4/16/42

YEAR	TM/L	W	L	PCT	G	GS	CG	SH	SV	IP	H	HR	BB	SO	RAT	ERA	ERA+	OAV	OOB	BH	AVG	PB	PR	/A	PD	TPI
1950	Cle-A	3	3	.500	28	2	1	1	4	53	53	3	25	27	13.4	3.74	116	.261	.345	0	.000	-2	5	4	-2	0.1
Total	7	44	59	.427	176	113	46	11	6	973	904	49	306	352	11.3	3.18	112	.246	.307	55	.181	-0	35	41	-7	3.7

● **ALAN FOSTER** Foster, Alan Benton b: 12/8/46, Pasadena, Cal. BR/TR, 6', 180 lbs. Deb: 4/25/67

YEAR	TM/L	W	L	PCT	G	GS	CG	SH	SV	IP	H	HR	BB	SO	RAT	ERA	ERA+	OAV	OOB	BH	AVG	PB	PR	/A	PD	TPI
1971	Cle-A	8	12	.400	36	26	3	0	0	181^{2}	158	19	82	97	12.1	4.16	92	.232	.318	2	.039	-4	-14	-7	-4	-1.6
Total	10	48	63	.432	217	148	26	6	0	1025^{1}	988	99	383	501	12.2	3.74	96	.254	.324	35	.119	-8	-10	-15	-9	-3.3

● **ED FOSTER** Foster, Eddy Lee "Slim" b: Georgia d: 3/1/29, Montgomery, Ala. BR/TR, 6'1", Deb: 7/31/08

YEAR	TM/L	W	L	PCT	G	GS	CG	SH	SV	IP	H	HR	BB	SO	RAT	ERA	ERA+	OAV	OOB	BH	AVG	PB	PR	/A	PD	TPI
1908	Cle-A	1	0	1.000	6	1	1	0	2	21	16	1	12	11	12.9	2.14	112	.229	.357	0	.000	-1	1	1	-1	-0.1

● **GEORGE FRAZIER** Frazier, George Allen b: 10/13/54, Oklahoma City, Okla BR/TR, 6'5", 205 lbs. Deb: 5/25/78

YEAR	TM/L	W	L	PCT	G	GS	CG	SH	SV	IP	H	HR	BB	SO	RAT	ERA	ERA+	OAV	OOB	BH	AVG	PB	PR	/A	PD	TPI
1984	Cle-A	3	2	.600	22	0	0	0	1	44^{1}	45	3	14	24	12.0	3.65	112	.259	.314	0	—	0	2	2	-1	0.0
Total	10	35	43	.449	415	0	0	0	29	675^{2}	653	54	313	449	13.1	4.20	96	.257	.342	3	.143	-1	-20	-14	-4	-4.5

● **DAVE FREISLEBEN** Freisleben, David James b: 10/31/51, Coraopolis, Pa. BR/TR, 5'11", 200 lbs. Deb: 4/26/74

YEAR	TM/L	W	L	PCT	G	GS	CG	SH	SV	IP	H	HR	BB	SO	RAT	ERA	ERA+	OAV	OOB	BH	AVG	PB	PR	/A	PD	TPI
1978	Cle-A	1	4	.200	12	10	0	0	0	44^{1}	52	4	31	19	17.3	7.11	53	.299	.411	0	—	0	-16	-17	-0	-1.6
Total	6	34	60	.362	202	121	17	6	4	865^{1}	897	67	430	430	14.1	4.30	83	.269	.357	27	.141	2	-56	-71	-1	-6.6

● **JOHNSON FRY** Fry, Johnson "Jay" b: 11/21/01, Huntington, W.Va. d: 4/7/59, Carmi, Ill. BR/TR, 6'1", 150 lbs. Deb: 8/24/23

YEAR	TM/L	W	L	PCT	G	GS	CG	SH	SV	IP	H	HR	BB	SO	RAT	ERA	ERA+	OAV	OOB	BH	AVG	PB	PR	/A	PD	TPI
1923	Cle-A	0	0	—	1	0	0	0	0	3^{2}	6	0	4	0	24.5	12.27	32	.353	.476	1	1.000	1	-3	-3	-0	0.1

● **FRANK FUNK** Funk, Franklin Ray b: 8/30/35, Washington, D.C. BR/TR, 6', 175 lbs. Deb: 9/3/60 C

YEAR	TM/L	W	L	PCT	G	GS	CG	SH	SV	IP	H	HR	BB	SO	RAT	ERA	ERA+	OAV	OOB	BH	AVG	PB	PR	/A	PD	TPI
1960	Cle-A	4	2	.667	9	0	0	0	1	31^{2}	27	3	9	18	10.2	1.99	188	.248	.305	1	.111	-0	7	6	0	1.2
1961	Cle-A	11	11	.500	56	0	0	0	11	92^{1}	79	9	31	64	11.1	3.31	119	.234	.306	1	.059	-1	7	6	0	1.4
1962	Cle-A	2	1	.667	47	0	0	0	6	80^{2}	62	11	32	49	10.9	3.24	120	.212	.298	1	.067	-1	7	6	-0	0.1
Total	4	20	17	.541	137	0	0	0	18	248^{1}	210	26	85	150	11.0	3.01	125	.233	.305	3	.067	-3	23	21	-1	2.9
Team	3	17	14	.548	112	0	0	0	18	204^{2}	168	23	72	131	10.9	3.08	126	.227	.302	3	.073	-3	20	18	-0	2.7

● **MILT GALATZER** Galatzer, Milton b: 5/4/07, Chicago, Ill. d: 1/29/76, San Francisco, Cal BL/TL, 5'10", 168 lbs. Deb: 6/25/33 ◆

YEAR	TM/L	W	L	PCT	G	GS	CG	SH	SV	IP	H	HR	BB	SO	RAT	ERA	ERA+	OAV	OOB	BH	AVG	PB	PR	/A	PD	TPI
1936	Cle-A	0	0	—	1	0	0	0	0	6	7	0	5	3	18.0	4.50	112	.292	.414	23	.237	0	0	0	0	0.0

● **DENNY GALEHOUSE** Galehouse, Dennis Ward b: 12/7/11, Marshallville, Ohio BR/TR, 6'1", 195 lbs. Deb: 4/30/34

YEAR	TM/L	W	L	PCT	G	GS	CG	SH	SV	IP	H	HR	BB	SO	RAT	ERA	ERA+	OAV	OOB	BH	AVG	PB	PR	/A	PD	TPI
1934	Cle-A	0	0	—	1	0	0	0	0	1	2	0	1	0	27.0	18.00	25	.500	.600	0	—	0	-2	-1	-0	0.0
1935	Cle-A	1	0	1.000	5	1	1	0	0	13	16	1	9	8	18.0	9.00	50	.314	.426	1	.250	-0	-7	-6	0	-0.4
1936	Cle-A	8	7	.533	36	15	5	0	1	148^{1}	161	5	68	71	14.0	4.85	104	.280	.358	8	.170	-0	3	3	-2	0.0
1937	Cle-A	9	14	.391	36	29	7	0	3	200^{2}	238	11	83	78	14.4	4.57	101	.302	.369	15	.208	-1	1	1	0	0.0
1938	Cle-A	7	8	.467	36	12	5	1	3	114	119	12	65	66	14.6	4.34	107	.275	.371	6	.154	-1	6	4	0	0.3
Total	15	109	118	.480	375	258	100	17	13	2004	2148	104	735	851	13.0	3.97	105	.275	.338	92	.138	-25	20	40	-8	1.4
Team	5	25	29	.463	114	57	18	1	7	477	536	29	226	223	14.5	4.75	100	.289	.368	30	.185	-3	2	-1	-1	-0.1

YEAR TM/L	W	L	PCT	G	GS	CG	SH	SV	IP	H	HR	BB	SO	RAT	ERA	ERA+	OAV	OOB	BH	AVG	PB	PR	/A	PD	TPI
● **MIKE GARCIA**   Garcia, Edward Miguel "The Big Bear"   b: 11/17/23, San Gabriel, Cal.   d: 1/13/86, Fairview Park, O.   BR/TR, 6'1", 200 lbs.   Deb: 10/3/48
1948 Cle-A	0	0	—	1	0	0	0	0	2	3	0	0	1	13.5	0.00	—	.333	.333	0	—	0	1	1	0	0.0
1949 Cle-A	14	5	.737	41	20	8	5	2	175²	154	6	60	94	11.1	**2.36**	169	.241	.308	12	.235	3	36	32	1	3.6
1950 Cle-A	11	11	.500	33	29	11	0	0	184	191	15	74	76	13.0	3.86	112	.266	.334	13	.200	-1	15	10	2	1.1
1951 Cle-A	20	13	.606	47	30	15	1	6	254	239	10	82	118	11.5	3.15	120	.246	.307	18	.212	2	27	18	1	2.4
1952 Cle-A☆	22	11	.667	46	36	19	**6**	4	292¹	284	9	87	143	11.6	2.37	141	.253	.310	13	.137	-2	42	32	2	3.6
1953 Cle-A★	18	9	.667	38	35	21	3	0	271²	260	18	81	134	11.4	3.25	116	.250	.307	24	.250	4	23	15	-0	1.7
1954 *Cle-A†	19	8	.704	45	34	13	**5**	5	258²	220	6	71	129	**10.2**	**2.64**	139	.229	**.284**	11	.136	-2	**31**	**30**	0	2.9
1955 Cle-A	11	13	.458	38	31	6	2	3	210²	230	17	56	120	12.3	4.02	99	.278	.327	15	.217	2	-1	-1	-1	0.0
1956 Cle-A	11	12	.478	35	30	8	4	0	197²	213	18	74	119	13.3	3.78	111	.272	.339	7	.115	-3	8	9	-0	0.6
1957 Cle-A	12	8	.600	38	27	9	1	0	211¹	221	14	73	110	12.8	3.75	99	.269	.333	12	.160	-1	1	-1	-2	-0.4
1958 Cle-A	1	0	1.000	6	1	0	0	0	8	15	2	7	2	25.9	9.00	41	.395	.500	0	.000	-0	-5	-5	0	-0.5
1959 Cle-A	3	6	.333	29	8	1	0	1	72	72	4	31	49	12.9	4.00	92	.265	.340	1	.071	-1	-1	-3	0	-0.4
Total 14	142	97	.594	428	281	111	27	23	2174²	2148	122	719	1117	12.0	3.27	117	.257	.319	127	.182	1	174	134	2	14.5
Team 12	142	96	.597	397	281	111	27	21	2138	2102	119	696	1095	11.9	3.24	118	.256	.317	126	.182	0	177	137	3	14.6
● **ROB GARDNER**   Gardner, Richard Frank   b: 12/19/44, Binghamton, N.Y.   BR/TL, 6'1", 176 lbs.   Deb: 9/1/65
1968 Cle-A	0	0	—	5	0	0	0	0	2²	5	0	2	6	23.6	6.75	44	.417	.500	0	—	0	-1	-1	-0	0.0
Total 8	14	18	.438	109	42	4	0	2	331	345	35	133	193	13.1	4.35	78	.269	.339	12	.138	-2	-34	-35	-0	-3.2
● **WAYNE GARLAND**   Garland, Marcus Wayne   b: 10/26/50, Nashville, Tenn.   BR/TR, 6', 195 lbs.   Deb: 9/13/73
1977 Cle-A	13	19	.406	38	38	21	1	0	282²	281	23	88	118	11.8	3.60	110	.261	.318	0	—	0	14	11	-0	1.1
1978 Cle-A	2	3	.400	6	6	0	0	0	29²	43	6	16	13	18.2	7.89	47	.347	.426	0	—	0	-14	-14	0	-1.8
1979 Cle-A	4	10	.286	18	14	2	0	0	94²	120	11	34	40	14.9	5.23	81	.318	.379	0	—	0	-11	-10	-1	-1.3
1980 Cle-A	6	9	.400	25	20	4	1	0	150¹	163	18	48	55	13.0	4.61	88	.276	.337	0	—	0	-10	-9	-1	-0.9
1981 Cle-A	3	7	.300	12	10	2	1	0	56	89	8	14	15	16.6	5.79	68	.374	.409	0	—	0	-13	-13	0	-2.0
Total 9	55	66	.455	190	121	43	7	6	1040	1082	89	328	450	12.4	3.89	96	.272	.330	0	—	0	-4	-18	-1	-2.2
Team 5	28	48	.368	99	88	29	3	0	613¹	696	66	200	241	13.3	4.50	88	.289	.347	0	—	0	-33	-36	-1	-4.9
● **CLARENCE GARRETT**   Garrett, Clarence Raymond "Laz"   b: 3/6/1891, Reader, W.Va.   d: 2/11/77, Moundsville, W.Va.   BR/TR, 6'5.5", 185 lbs.   Deb: 9/13/15
1915 Cle-A	2	2	.500	4	4	2	0	0	23¹	19	1	6	5	10.0	2.31	132	.224	.283	0	.000	-0	2	2	1	0.4
● **CHARLIE GASSAWAY**   Gassaway, Charles Cason "Sheriff"   b: 8/12/18, Gassaway, Ga.   d: 1/15/92, Miami, Fla.   BL/TL, 6'2.5", 210 lbs.   Deb: 9/25/44
1946 Cle-A	1	1	.500	13	6	0	0	0	50²	54	2	26	23	14.9	3.91	85	.273	.368	1	.067	-1	-2	-3	0	-0.2
Total 3	5	9	.357	39	19	4	0	0	180¹	188	9	91	80	14.2	4.04	84	.268	.357	8	.138	-3	-12	-13	-2	-1.3
● **GARY GEIGER**   Geiger, Gary Merle   b: 4/4/37, Sand Ridge, Ill.   BL/TR, 6', 168 lbs.   Deb: 4/15/58   ◆
1958 Cle-A	0	0	—	1	0	0	0	0	2	2	0	1	2	13.5	9.00	41	.286	.375	45	.231	0	-1	-1	0	0.0
● **LEFTY GEORGE**   George, Thomas Edward   b: 8/13/1886, Pittsburgh, Pa.   d: 5/13/55, York, Pa.   BL/TL, 6', 155 lbs.   Deb: 4/14/11
1912 Cle-A	0	5	.000	11	5	2	0	0	44¹	69	1	18	18	18.1	4.87	70	.373	.434	3	.214	1	-8	-7	0	-0.6
Total 4	7	21	.250	52	26	14	2	0	243	285	5	98	74	14.9	3.85	82	.281	.355	14	.152	-2	-19	-19	1	-1.9
● **AL GETTEL**   Gettel, Allen Jones   b: 9/17/17, Norfolk, Va.   BR/TR, 6'3.5", 200 lbs.   Deb: 4/20/45
1947 Cle-A	11	10	.524	31	21	9	2	0	149	122	12	62	64	11.3	3.20	109	.229	.313	15	.294	4	8	5	1	1.1
1948 Cle-A	0	1	.000	5	2	0	0	0	7²	15	2	10	4	30.5	17.61	23	.385	.520	0	.000	-0	-11	-12	-0	-1.2
Total 7	38	45	.458	184	79	31	5	6	734¹	711	72	310	310	12.7	4.28	88	.255	.334	55	.228	3	-37	-40	-1	-2.6
Team 2	11	11	.500	36	23	9	2	0	156²	137	14	72	68	12.2	3.91	90	.240	.329	15	.278	4	-3	-7	1	-0.1
● **LUKE GLAVENICH**   Glavenich, Luke Frank   b: 1/17/1893, Jackson, Cal.   d: 5/22/35, Stockton, Cal.   BR/TR, 5'9.5", 189 lbs.   Deb: 4/12/13
1913 Cle-A	0	0	—	1	0	0	0	0	1	3	0	3	1	54.0	9.00	34	.500	.667	0	—	0	-1	-1	-0	0.0
● **MARTIN GLENDON**   Glendon, Martin J.   b: 2/8/1877, Milwaukee, Wis.   d: 11/6/50, Norwood Park, Ill.   5'8", 165 lbs.   Deb: 4/18/02
1903 Cle-A	1	2	.333	3	3	3	0	0	27²	20	0	7	9	8.8	0.98	292	.202	.255	0	.000	-1	6	6	1	0.6
Total 2	1	3	.250	4	4	3	0	0	30²	25	0	11	9	10.6	2.05	140	.221	.290	0	.000	-1	3	3	1	-0.1
● **SAL GLIATTO**   Gliatto, Salvador Michael   b: 5/7/02, Chicago, Ill.   d: 11/2/95, Tyler, Tex.   BB/TL, 5'8.5", 150 lbs.   Deb: 4/19/30
1930 Cle-A	0	0	—	8	0	0	0	2	15	21	1	9	7	19.2	6.60	73	.328	.427	0	.000	-0	-3	-3	-0	-0.2
● **ED GLYNN**   Glynn, Edward Paul   b: 6/3/53, Flushing, N.Y.   BR/TL, 6'2", 180 lbs.   Deb: 9/19/75
1981 Cle-A	0	0	—	4	0	0	0	0	7²	5	0	4	4	10.6	1.17	309	.192	.300	0	—	0	2	2	-0	0.0
1982 Cle-A	5	2	.714	47	0	0	0	4	49²	43	6	30	54	13.2	4.17	98	.232	.340	0	—	0	-1	-0	-0	-0.1
1983 Cle-A	0	2	.000	11	0	0	0	0	12¹	22	2	6	13	20.4	5.84	73	.373	.431	0	—	0	-2	-2	-0	-0.5
Total 10	12	17	.414	175	8	1	0	12	264²	261	26	151	184	14.1	4.25	90	.261	.359	0	.000	-1	-13	-12	-2	-2.4
Team 3	5	4	.556	62	0	0	0	4	69²	70	8	40	71	14.2	4.13	98	.259	.355	0	—	0	-1	-1	-1	-0.6
● **BILL GOGOLEWSKI**   Gogolewski, William Joseph   b: 10/26/47, Oshkosh, Wis.   BL/TR, 6'4", 190 lbs.   Deb: 9/3/70
1974 Cle-A	0	0	—	5	0	0	0	0	13²	15	1	2	3	11.9	4.61	78	.283	.321	0	—	0	-2	-2	1	0.1
Total 6	15	24	.385	144	44	6	2	10	501	496	32	200	301	12.7	4.02	85	.260	.334	10	.127	-1	-30	-34	5	-2.2
● **RUBEN GOMEZ**   Gomez, Ruben (Colon)   b: 7/13/27, Arroyo, P.R.   BR/TR, 6', 175 lbs.   Deb: 4/17/53
1962 Cle-A	1	2	.333	15	4	0	1	0	45¹	50	5	25	21	15.3	4.37	89	.292	.389	3	.231	0	-2	-2	1	-0.1
Total 10	76	86	.469	289	205	63	15	5	1454	1436	154	574	677	12.7	4.09	97	.259	.334	95	.199	6	-17	-18	14	0.6
● **DON GORDON**   Gordon, Donald Thomas   b: 10/10/59, New York, N.Y.   BR/TR, 6'1", 175 lbs.   Deb: 4/10/86
1987 Cle-A	0	3	.000	21	0	0	0	1	39²	49	3	12	20	14.7	4.08	111	.295	.357	0	—	0	2	2	1	0.2
1988 Cle-A	3	4	.429	38	0	0	0	1	59¹	65	5	19	20	13.2	4.40	93	.284	.347	0	—	0	-3	-2	1	-0.2
Total 3	3	8	.273	78	0	0	0	3	131²	150	11	42	56	13.7	4.72	94	.286	.348	0	—	0	-8	-6	1	-0.4
Team 2	3	7	.300	59	0	0	0	2	99	114	8	31	40	13.8	4.27	100	.289	.351	0	—	0	-1	-0	1	0.1
● **AL GOULD**   Gould, Albert Frank "Pudgy"   b: 1/20/1893, Muscatine, Iowa   d: 8/8/82, San Jose, Cal.   BR/TR, 5'6.5", 160 lbs.   Deb: 7/11/16
1916 Cle-A	5	7	.417	30	9	6	1	1	106²	101	0	40	41	12.2	2.53	119	.256	.329	3	.103	-2	4	6	-1	0.4
1917 Cle-A	4	4	.500	27	7	1	0	0	94	95	1	52	24	14.4	3.64	78	.281	.382	5	.208	1	-10	-8	2	-0.5
Total 2	9	11	.450	57	16	7	1	1	200²	196	1	92	65	13.2	3.05	96	.267	.354	8	.151	-1	-7	-3	1	-0.1
● **MAURO GOZZO**   Gozzo, Mauro Paul   b: 3/7/66, New Britain, Conn.   BR/TR, 6'2", 210 lbs.   Deb: 8/8/89
1990 Cle-A	0	0	—	2	0	0	0	0	3	2	0	2	2	12.0	0.00	—	.182	.308	0	—	0	1	1	-0	0.0
1991 Cle-A	0	0	—	2	2	0	0	0	4²	9	0	7	3	30.9	19.29	22	.450	.593	0	—	0	-8	-8	-0	0.0
Total 6	7	7	.500	48	13	0	0	1	124	150	9	51	55	14.7	5.30	76	.301	.368	4	.250	1	-17	-17	-2	-1.0
Team 2	0	0	—	4	2	0	0	0	7²	11	0	9	5	23.5	11.74	35	.355	.500	0	—	0	-7	-7	-0	0.0
● **TOMMY GRAMLY**   Gramly, Bert Thomas   b: 4/19/45, Dallas, Tex.   BR/TR, 6'3", 175 lbs.   Deb: 4/18/68
1968 Cle-A	0	1	.000	3	0	0	0	0	3¹	3	0	2	1	13.5	2.70	110	.250	.357	0	—	0	0	0	-0	0.0
● **JACK GRANEY**   Graney, John Gladstone   b: 6/10/1886, St.Thomas, Ont., Can.   d: 4/20/78, Louisiana, Mo.   BL/TL, 5'9", 180 lbs.   Deb: 4/30/08   ◆
1908 Cle-A	0	0	—	2	0	0	0	0	3¹	6	0	1	0	18.9	5.40	44	.400	.438	0	—	0	-1	-1	-0	0.0

YEAR TM/L	W	L	PCT	G	GS	CG	SH	SV	IP	H	HR	BB	SO	RAT	ERA	ERA+	OAV	OOB	BH	AVG	PB	PR	/A	PD	TPI

● GEORGE GRANT Grant, George Addison b: 1/6/03, E.Tallassee, Ala. d: 3/25/86, Montgomery, Ala. BR/TR, 5'11.5", 175 lbs. Deb: 9/17/23

1927 Cle-A	4	6	.400	25	3	2	0	1	74²	85	1	40	19	15.1	4.46	94	.300	.387	2	.095	-2	-3	-2	0	-0.4
1928 Cle-A	10	8	.556	28	18	6	1	0	155¹	196	7	76	39	15.9	5.04	82	.319	.395	11	.183	-2	-17	-15	2	-1.5
1929 Cle-A	0	2	.000	12	0	0	0	0	24	41	2	23	5	24.0	10.50	42	.414	.525	0	.000	-0	-17	-16	0	-1.1
Total 7	15	20	.429	114	23	8	1	1	347¹	460	16	182	89	16.7	5.65	75	.331	.410	14	.135	-8	-59	-54	3	-4.0
Team 3	14	16	.467	65	21	8	1	1	254	322	10	139	63	16.4	5.39	78	.323	.407	13	.157	-5	-37	-34	3	-3.0

● MUDCAT GRANT Grant, James Timothy "Jim" b: 8/13/35, Lacoochee, Fla. BR/TR, 6'1", 186 lbs. Deb: 4/17/58

1958 Cle-A	10	11	.476	44	28	11	1	4	204	173	20	104	111	12.3	3.84	95	.228	.321	5	.076	-4	-2	-4	-2	-1.0
1959 Cle-A	10	7	.588	38	19	6	1	3	165¹	140	23	81	85	12.1	4.14	89	.232	.325	11	.200	1	-5	-8	-0	-0.7
1960 Cle-A	9	8	.529	33	19	5	0	0	159²	147	26	78	75	12.8	4.40	85	.243	.332	16	.281	4	-9	-12	-1	-0.9
1961 Cle-A	15	9	.625	35	35	11	3	0	244²	207	32	109	146	11.7	3.86	102	.227	.312	15	.170	1	4	2	1	0.3
1962 Cle-A	7	10	.412	26	23	6	1	0	149²	128	24	81	90	12.6	4.27	91	.233	.331	8	.151	-0	-5	-7	-0	-0.7
1963 Cle-A☆	13	14	.481	38	32	10	2	1	229¹	213	30	87	157	11.9	3.69	98	.243	.314	13	.188	3	-2	-2	-3	-0.2
1964 Cle-A	3	4	.429	13	9	1	0	0	62	82	11	25	43	15.7	5.95	60	.324	.387	6	.273	4	-16	-16	0	-1.2
Total 14	145	119	.549	571	293	89	18	53	2441²	2292	292	849	1267	11.7	3.63	100	.248	.313	135	.178	16	5	-3	-3	1.0
Team 7	67	63	.515	227	165	50	8	8	1214²	1090	166	565	707	12.4	4.09	92	.239	.325	74	.180	8	-34	-47	-6	-4.4

● JOHNNY GRAY Gray, John Leonard b: 12/11/27, W.Palm Beach, Fla. BR/TR, 6'4", 226 lbs. Deb: 7/18/54

| 1957 Cle-A | 1 | 3 | .250 | 7 | 3 | 1 | 1 | 0 | 20 | 21 | 1 | 13 | 3 | 15.3 | 5.85 | 64 | .288 | .395 | 0 | .000 | -1 | -5 | -5 | -0 | -0.9 |
| Total 4 | 4 | 18 | .182 | 48 | 24 | 6 | 1 | 0 | 169 | 172 | 16 | 142 | 75 | 16.8 | 6.18 | 64 | .271 | .405 | 2 | .043 | -5 | -45 | -42 | -1 | -5.5 |

● TED GRAY Gray, Ted Glenn b: 12/31/24, Detroit, Mich. BB/TL, 5'11", 175 lbs. Deb: 5/15/46

| 1955 Cle-A | 0 | 0 | — | 2 | 0 | 0 | 0 | 0 | 5 | 5 | 1 | 2 | 1 | 31.5 | 18.00 | 22 | .455 | .538 | 0 | — | 0 | -3 | -3 | 0 | 0.0 |
| Total 9 | 59 | 74 | .444 | 222 | 162 | 50 | 7 | 4 | 1134 | 1072 | 114 | 595 | 687 | 13.5 | 4.37 | 94 | .251 | .346 | 59 | .159 | -10 | -38 | -30 | -4 | -5.1 |

● DAVE GREGG Gregg, David Charles "Highpockets" b: 3/14/1891, Chehalis, Wash. d: 11/12/65, Clarkston, Wash. BR/TR, 6'1", 185 lbs. Deb: 6/15/13 F

| 1913 Cle-A | 0 | 0 | — | 1 | 0 | 0 | 0 | 0 | 1 | 2 | 0 | 0 | 0 | 27.0 | 18.00 | 17 | .400 | .500 | 0 | — | 0 | -2 | -2 | 0 | 0.0 |

● VEAN GREGG Gregg, Sylveanus Augustus b: 4/13/1885, Chehalis, Wash. d: 7/29/64, Aberdeen, Wash. BR/TL, 6'1", 185 lbs. Deb: 4/12/11 F

1911 Cle-A	23	7	.767	34	26	22	5	0	244²	172	2	86	125	**9.9**	**1.80**	189	.205	.286	14	.165	-4	42	44	0	4.7
1912 Cle-A	20	13	.606	37	34	26	1	2	271¹	242	4	90	184	11.3	2.59	132	.246	.316	17	.175	-3	22	25	-2	2.4
1913 Cle-A	20	13	.606	44	34	23	3	3	285²	258	2	124	166	12.4	2.24	136	.246	.334	13	.131	-4	22	25	-3	2.1
1914 Cle-A	9	3	.750	17	12	6	1	0	96²	88	4	48	56	12.9	3.07	94	.251	.347	6	.176	1	-4	-2	-0	-0.3
Total 8	92	63	.594	239	161	105	14	12	1393	1240	17	552	720	11.9	2.70	117	.248	.328	78	.171	-12	63	73	-8	6.5
Team 4	72	36	.667	132	106	77	10	5	898¹	760	8	348	531	11.5	2.31	140	.236	.317	50	.159	-10	83	92	-5	8.9

● BOB GRIM Grim, Robert Anton b: 3/8/30, New York, N.Y. BR/TR, 6'1", 185 lbs. Deb: 4/18/54

| 1960 Cle-A | 0 | 1 | .000 | 3 | 0 | 0 | 0 | 0 | 2¹ | 6 | 0 | 1 | 2 | 27.0 | 11.57 | 32 | .500 | .538 | 0 | — | 0 | -2 | -2 | 0 | -0.7 |
| Total 8 | 61 | 41 | .598 | 268 | 60 | 18 | 4 | 37 | 759² | 708 | 50 | 330 | 443 | 12.5 | 3.61 | 104 | .252 | .334 | 24 | .127 | -4 | 19 | 11 | -4 | 1.4 |

● JASON GRIMSLEY Grimsley, Jason Alan b: 8/7/67, Cleveland, Tex. BR/TR, 6'3", 180 lbs. Deb: 9/8/89

1993 Cle-A	3	4	.429	10	6	0	0	0	42¹	52	3	20	27	15.5	5.31	81	.302	.378	0	—	0	-5	-5	-0	-0.7
1994 Cle-A	5	2	.714	14	13	1	0	0	82²	91	7	34	59	14.3	4.57	103	.283	.362	0	—	0	2	1	0	0.1
1995 Cle-A	0	0	—	15	2	0	0	1	34	37	4	32	25	18.8	6.09	76	.289	.438	0	—	0	-5	-5	0	0.0
Total 6	13	18	.419	66	48	1	0	1	295²	300	21	189	201	15.3	4.75	88	.267	.379	4	.105	-1	-18	-18	2	-2.0
Team 3	8	6	.571	39	21	1	0	1	159	180	14	86	111	15.6	5.09	90	.289	.384	0	—	0	-8	-9	-0	-0.6

● ROSS GRIMSLEY Grimsley, Ross Albert Ii b: 1/7/50, Topeka, Kan. BL/TL, 6'3", 200 lbs. Deb: 5/16/71 F

| 1980 Cle-A | 4 | 5 | .444 | 14 | 11 | 2 | 0 | 0 | 74² | 103 | 11 | 24 | 18 | 15.4 | 6.75 | 60 | .331 | .381 | 0 | — | 0 | -23 | -22 | -1 | -2.3 |
| Total 11 | 124 | 99 | .556 | 345 | 295 | 79 | 15 | 3 | 2039¹ | 2105 | 202 | 559 | 750 | 11.8 | 3.81 | 92 | .270 | .320 | 45 | .127 | -10 | -29 | -67 | -1 | -7.6 |

● STEVE GROMEK Gromek, Stephen Joseph b: 1/15/20, Hamtramck, Mich. BB/TR, 6'2", 180 lbs. Deb: 8/18/41

1941 Cle-A	1	1	.500	9	2	1	0	2	23¹	25	0	11	19	13.9	4.24	93	.266	.343	1	.167	-0	-0	-1	-1	-0.2
1942 Cle-A	2	0	1.000	14	0	0	0	0	44¹	46	2	23	14	14.0	3.65	94	.267	.354	5	.333	3	0	-1	-1	0.2
1943 Cle-A	0	0	—	3	0	0	0	0	4	6	0	4	4	13.5	9.00	35	.353	.353	2	1.000	1	-3	-3	-0	0.1
1944 Cle-A	10	9	.526	35	21	12	2	1	203²	160	5	70	115	10.3	2.56	129	**.219**	.290	19	.260	5	20	17	-3	1.8
1945 Cle-A†	19	9	.679	33	30	21	3	1	251	229	6	66	101	10.7	2.55	128	.243	.295	21	.231	8	23	20	-3	2.2
1946 Cle-A	5	15	.250	29	21	5	2	4	153²	159	20	47	75	12.2	4.33	76	.264	.321	11	.196	0	-14	-18	-1	-2.2
1947 Cle-A	3	5	.375	29	7	0	0	0	84¹	77	8	36	39	12.2	3.74	93	.240	.318	7	.318	2	-0	-2	-0	-0.1
1948 *Cle-A	9	3	.750	38	9	4	1	2	130	109	10	51	50	11.5	2.84	143	.226	.307	6	.146	-1	21	18	-1	1.3
1949 Cle-A	4	6	.400	27	12	3	0	0	92	86	8	40	22	12.5	3.33	120	.250	.332	4	.167	-0	9	7	0	0.7
1950 Cle-A	10	7	.588	31	13	4	1	0	113¹	94	10	36	43	10.6	3.65	119	.226	.292	6	.158	-2	12	9	-0	0.9
1951 Cle-A	7	4	.636	27	8	4	0	1	107¹	98	6	29	40	11.0	2.77	137	.238	.295	8	.296	3	16	12	1	1.5
1952 Cle-A	7	7	.500	29	13	3	1	1	122²	109	14	28	65	10.2	3.67	91	.232	.278	3	.100	-3	0	-4	-3	-0.8
1953 Cle-A	1	1	.500	5	1	0	0	0	11	11	0	3	8	12.3	3.27	115	.268	.333	0	.000	-0	1	1	-0	0.0
Total 17	123	108	.532	447	225	92	17	23	2064²	1940	86	630	904	11.5	3.41	108	.247	.309	124	.197	15	96	63	-21	6.9
Team 13	78	67	.538	309	137	57	10	16	1340²	1209	89	440	595	11.3	3.22	111	.240	.304	93	.218	13	84	54	-12	5.4

● BOB GROOM Groom, Robert b: 9/12/1884, Belleville, Ill. d: 2/19/48, Belleville, Ill. BR/TR, 6'2", 175 lbs. Deb: 4/13/09

| 1918 Cle-A | 2 | 2 | .500 | 14 | 5 | 0 | 0 | 0 | 43¹ | 70 | 0 | 18 | 8 | 18.5 | 7.06 | 43 | .380 | .438 | 1 | .083 | -1 | -21 | -20 | 0 | -1.8 |
| Total 10 | 119 | 150 | .442 | 367 | 288 | 157 | 22 | 13 | 2336¹ | 2205 | 49 | 783 | 1159 | 11.7 | 3.10 | 93 | .254 | .319 | 98 | .128 | -35 | -61 | -58 | 2 | -9.4 |

● ERNEST GROTH Groth, Ernest William b: 5/3/22, Beaver Falls, Pa. BR/TR, 5'9", 185 lbs. Deb: 9/11/47

1947 Cle-A	0	0	—	2	0	0	0	0	1¹	0	0	1	1	6.8	0.00	—	.000	.250	0	—	0	1	1	0	0.0
1948 Cle-A	0	0	—	1	0	0	0	0	1	1	0	2	0	27.0	9.00	45	.250	.500	0	—	0	-1	-1	-0	0.0
Total 3	0	1	.000	6	0	0	0	0	7¹	4	0	2	6	12.3	4.91	82	.130	.333	0	—	0	-1	-1	-0	-0.1
Team 2	0	0	—	3	0	0	0	0	2¹	1	0	3	1	15.4	3.86	97	.143	.400	0	—	0	-0	-0	-0	0.0

● CECILIO GUANTE Guante, Cecilio (Magallane) b: 2/1/60, Villa Mella, D.R. BR/TR, 6'3", 205 lbs. Deb: 5/1/82

| 1990 Cle-A | 2 | 3 | .400 | 26 | 1 | 0 | 0 | 0 | 46² | 38 | 10 | 18 | 30 | 11.4 | 5.01 | 78 | .220 | .304 | 0 | — | 0 | -6 | -6 | 0 | -0.5 |
| Total 9 | 29 | 34 | .460 | 363 | 1 | 0 | 0 | 35 | 595 | 512 | 61 | 236 | 503 | 11.7 | 3.48 | 110 | .232 | .313 | 3 | .061 | -3 | 20 | 23 | -8 | 1.6 |

● RED GUNKEL Gunkel, Woodward William b: 4/15/1894, Sheffield, Ill. d: 4/19/54, Chicago, Ill. BB/TR, 5'8", 158 lbs. Deb: 6/18/16

| 1916 Cle-A | 0 | 0 | — | 1 | 0 | 0 | 0 | 0 | 1 | 0 | 0 | 1 | 1 | 18.0 | 0.00 | — | .000 | .500 | 0 | — | 0 | 0 | 0 | -0 | 0.0 |

● RIP HAGERMAN Hagerman, Zeriah Zequiel b: 6/20/1888, Linden, Kan. d: 1/30/30, Albuquerque, N.Mex BR/TR, 6'2", 200 lbs. Deb: 4/16/09

1914 Cle-A	9	15	.375	37	26	12	3	0	198	189	3	118	112	14.2	3.09	93	.265	.374	1	.016	-5	-8	-4	-3	-1.4
1915 Cle-A	6	14	.300	29	22	7	0	0	151	156	4	77	69	14.2	3.52	87	.277	.370	4	.105	-2	-10	-8	-3	-1.5
1916 Cle-A	0	0	—	2	0	0	0	0	3²	5	1	2	1	22.1	12.27	25	.333	.474	0	.000	-0	-4	-4	0	0.0
Total 4	19	33	.365	81	55	23	4	0	431²	414	8	225	214	13.6	3.09	93	.263	.360	8	.065	-9	-14	-10	-6	-2.4
Team 3	15	29	.341	68	48	19	3	0	352²	350	8	197	182	14.3	3.37	88	.271	.373	5	.050	-8	-21	-16	-6	-2.9

● JOHN HALLA Halla, John Arthur b: 5/13/1884, St.Louis, Mo. d: 9/30/47, ElSegundo, Cal. BL/TL, 5'11", 175 lbs. Deb: 8/18/05

| 1905 Cle-A | 0 | 0 | — | 3 | 0 | 0 | 0 | 0 | 12² | 12 | 0 | 0 | 4 | 9.2 | 2.84 | 93 | .250 | .265 | 1 | .200 | -0 | -0 | -/A | -0 | 0.0 |

YEAR TM/L	W	L	PCT	G	GS	CG	SH	SV	IP	H	HR	BB	SO	RAT	ERA	ERA+	OAV	OOB	BH	AVG	PB	PR	/A	PD	TPI

● DOC HAMANN   Hamann, Elmer Joseph b: 12/21/1900, New Ulm, Minn. d: 1/11/73, Milwaukee, Wis. BR/TR, 6'1", 180 lbs. Deb: 9/21/22

| 1922 Cle-A | 0 | 0 | — | 1 | 0 | 0 | 0 | 0 | 0 | 3 | 0 | 3 | 0 | — | ∞ | — | 1.000 | 1.000 | 0 | — | 0 | -6 | -6 | 0 | -0.5 |

● JACK HAMILTON   Hamilton, Jack Edwin b: 12/25/38, Burlington, Iowa BR/TR, 6', 200 lbs. Deb: 4/13/62

| 1969 Cle-A | 0 | 2 | .000 | 20 | 0 | 0 | 0 | 1 | 30² | 37 | 2 | 23 | 13 | 17.6 | 4.40 | 86 | .316 | .429 | 0 | .000 | -0 | -3 | -2 | -0 | -0.2 |
| Total 8 | 32 | 40 | .444 | 218 | 65 | 8 | 2 | 20 | 611² | 597 | 48 | 348 | 357 | 14.1 | 4.53 | 78 | .259 | .359 | 16 | .107 | -6 | -66 | -67 | 4 | -9.1 |

● STEVE HAMILTON   Hamilton, Steve Absher b: 11/30/35, Columbia, Ky. BL/TL, 6'7", 195 lbs. Deb: 4/23/61 C

| 1961 Cle-A | 0 | 0 | — | 2 | 0 | 0 | 0 | 0 | 3 | 2 | 0 | 3 | 4 | 15.0 | 3.00 | 131 | .200 | .385 | 1 | 1.000 | 0 | 0 | 0 | 0 | 0.1 |
| Total 12 | 40 | 31 | .563 | 421 | 17 | 3 | 1 | 42 | 663 | 556 | 51 | 214 | 531 | 10.6 | 3.05 | 114 | .229 | .295 | 14 | .125 | -2 | 36 | 32 | -1 | 2.8 |

● RICH HAND   Hand, Richard Allen b: 7/10/48, Bellevue, Wash. BR/TR, 6'1", 195 lbs. Deb: 4/9/70

1970 Cle-A	6	13	.316	35	25	3	1	3	159²	132	27	69	110	11.6	3.83	103	.228	.314	6	.146	-1	-2	2	0	0.1
1971 Cle-A	2	6	.250	15	12	0	0	0	60²	74	6	38	26	17.2	5.79	66	.311	.414	2	.125	-0	-16	-13	-1	-1.7
Total 4	24	39	.381	104	78	6	2	3	487¹	452	52	250	278	13.2	4.01	88	.249	.345	16	.147	-0	-29	-25	-1	-2.9
Team 2	8	19	.296	50	37	3	1	3	220¹	206	33	107	136	13.1	4.37	90	.252	.344	8	.140	-2	-18	-11	-1	-1.6

● MEL HARDER   Harder, Melvin Leroy "Chief" b: 10/15/09, Beemer, Neb. BR/TR, 6'1", 195 lbs. Deb: 4/24/28 MC

1928 Cle-A	0	2	.000	23	1	0	0	0	49	64	4	32	15	17.6	6.61	63	.335	.430	0	.000	-1	-14	-13	-1	-0.7
1929 Cle-A	1	0	1.000	11	0	0	0	0	17²	24	2	5	4	16.3	5.60	79	.333	.400	0	.000	-0	-3	-2	-0	-0.2
1930 Cle-A	11	10	.524	36	19	7	0	2	175¹	205	8	68	45	14.2	4.21	115	.295	.361	9	.143	-4	9	12	-1	0.8
1931 Cle-A	13	14	.481	40	24	9	0	1	194	229	8	72	63	14.2	4.36	106	.289	.352	19	.253	1	0	6	0	0.8
1932 Cle-A	15	13	.536	39	32	17	1	0	254²	277	9	68	90	12.3	3.75	127	.272	.319	17	.181	-0	21	28	3	2.9
1933 Cle-A	15	17	.469	43	31	14	2	4	253	254	10	67	81	11.5	2.95	151	.259	.309	16	.190	-1	37	42	8	5.7
1934 Cle-A★	20	12	.625	44	29	17	6	4	255¹	246	6	81	91	11.8	2.61	174	.254	.316	14	.161	-1	54	55	2	6.4
1935 Cle-A★	22	11	.667	42	35	17	4	2	287¹	313	6	53	95	11.5	3.29	137	.275	.307	21	.206	-1	37	39	5	4.4
1936 Cle-A★	15	15	.500	36	30	13	0	1	224²	294	13	71	84	14.9	5.17	97	.313	.365	11	.138	-1	-3	-3	-0	-0.7
1937 Cle-A★	15	12	.556	38	30	13	0	2	233²	269	6	86	95	13.8	4.28	108	.288	.350	15	.174	-1	9	9	2	0.9
1938 Cle-A	17	10	.630	38	29	15	2	4	240	257	16	62	102	12.2	3.83	121	.271	.319	10	.114	-5	26	22	2	1.8
1939 Cle-A	15	9	.625	29	26	12	1	1	208	213	15	64	67	12.1	3.50	126	.269	.326	10	.139	-2	26	21	-2	1.8
1940 Cle-A	12	11	.522	31	25	5	0	0	186¹	200	16	59	76	12.8	4.06	104	.278	.337	11	.177	-1	7	3	1	0.4
1941 Cle-A	5	4	.556	15	10	1	0	1	68²	76	8	37	21	15.1	5.24	75	.279	.370	2	.080	-2	-8	-10	1	-1.2
1942 Cle-A	13	14	.481	29	29	13	4	0	198²	179	8	72	74	12.0	3.44	100	.240	.317	8	.119	-3	5	0	1	-0.2
1943 Cle-A	8	7	.533	19	18	6	1	0	135¹	126	7	61	40	12.5	3.06	102	.254	.337	10	.213	2	4	1	-0	0.2
1944 Cle-A	12	10	.545	30	27	12	2	0	196¹	211	5	69	64	13.0	3.71	89	.278	.341	16	.216	1	-6	-9	-1	-0.9
1945 Cle-A	3	7	.300	11	11	2	0	0	76	93	3	23	16	13.7	3.67	88	.303	.352	2	.080	-2	-3	-4	1	-0.6
1946 Cle-A	5	4	.556	13	12	4	1	0	92¹	85	4	31	21	11.3	3.41	97	.249	.311	3	.086	-2	1	-1	-2	-0.5
1947 Cle-A	6	4	.600	15	15	4	1	0	96	91	3	27	17	11.4	4.50	77	.289	.347	5	.179	-0	-9	-9	-1	-1.1
Total 20	223	186	.545	582	433	181	25	23	3426¹	3706	161	1118	1161	12.8	3.80	113	.276	.334	199	.165	-27	190	182	18	20.0

● STEVE HARGAN   Hargan, Steven Lowell b: 9/8/42, Ft.Wayne, Ind. BR/TR, 6'3", 180 lbs. Deb: 8/3/65

1965 Cle-A	4	3	.571	17	8	1	0	2	60¹	55	2	28	37	12.5	3.43	101	.246	.332	1	.053	-1	0	0	0	-0.1
1966 Cle-A	13	10	.565	38	21	7	3	0	192	173	9	45	132	10.3	2.48	138	.241	.286	7	.121	-2	20	20	0	2.3
1967 Cle-A☆	14	13	.519	30	29	15	6	0	223	180	9	72	141	10.3	2.62	125	.224	.290	11	.164	1	15	16	1	2.3
1968 Cle-A	8	15	.348	32	27	4	2	0	158¹	139	11	81	78	12.8	4.15	71	.241	.340	9	.176	1	-21	-21	-2	-3.1
1969 Cle-A	5	14	.263	32	23	1	1	0	143²	145	14	81	76	14.3	5.70	66	.265	.363	7	.159	-1	-33	-31	2	-3.6
1970 Cle-A	11	3	.786	23	19	8	1	0	142²	101	14	53	72	9.9	2.90	136	.201	.281	5	.111	-2	13	17	1	1.5
1971 Cle-A	1	13	.071	37	16	1	0	1	113¹	138	18	56	52	15.9	6.19	62	.304	.388	2	.063	-3	-34	-30	-2	-3.8
1972 Cle-A	0	3	.000	12	1	0	0	0	20	23	1	15	10	17.1	5.85	55	.291	.404	0	.000	-0	-6	-6	1	-0.8
Total 12	87	107	.448	354	215	56	17	4	1632	1593	125	614	891	12.4	3.92	91	.257	.328	42	.129	-7	-77	-64	6	-7.6
Team 8	56	74	.431	221	144	37	13	3	1053¹	954	78	431	598	12.0	3.78	92	.244	.323	42	.132	-7	-46	-35	2	-5.3

● SPEC HARKNESS   Harkness, Frederick Harvey b: 12/13/1887, Los Angeles, Cal. d: 5/16/52, Compton, Cal. BR/TR, 5'11", 180 lbs. Deb: 6/13/10

1910 Cle-A	10	7	.588	26	16	6	1	1	136¹	132	2	55	60	12.5	3.04	85	.268	.345	7	.140	-1	-8	-7	-1	-1.1
1911 Cle-A	2	2	.500	12	6	3	0	0	53¹	62	1	21	25	14.0	4.22	81	.310	.376	6	.316	1	-5	-5	-2	-0.4
Total 2	12	9	.571	38	22	9	1	1	189²	194	3	76	85	13.0	3.37	84	.280	.354	13	.188	-0	-13	-12	-3	-1.5

● BUBBA HARRIS   Harris, Charles b: 2/15/26, Sulligent, Ala. BR/TR, 6'4", 204 lbs. Deb: 4/29/48

| 1951 Cle-A | 0 | 0 | — | 2 | 0 | 0 | 0 | 0 | 4 | 5 | 0 | 4 | 1 | 20.3 | 4.50 | 84 | .333 | .474 | 0 | — | 0 | -0 | -0 | 0 | 0.0 |
| Total 3 | 6 | 3 | .667 | 87 | 0 | 0 | 0 | 8 | 186 | 190 | 14 | 86 | 53 | 13.5 | 4.84 | 87 | .267 | .349 | 6 | .125 | -3 | -12 | -13 | 2 | -0.3 |

● MICKEY HARRIS   Harris, Maurice Charles b: 1/30/17, New York, N.Y. d: 4/15/71, Farmington, Mich. BL/TL, 6', 195 lbs. Deb: 4/23/40

| 1952 Cle-A | 3 | 0 | 1.000 | 29 | 0 | 0 | 0 | 2 | 46² | 42 | 6 | 21 | 23 | 12.3 | 4.63 | 72 | .249 | .335 | 1 | .200 | -0 | -5 | -7 | -0 | -0.4 |
| Total 9 | 59 | 71 | .454 | 271 | 109 | 42 | 2 | 21 | 1050 | 1097 | 79 | 455 | 534 | 13.4 | 4.18 | 98 | .267 | .342 | 54 | .188 | 11 | -16 | -9 | -7 | 0.3 |

● RORIC HARRISON   Harrison, Roric Edward b: 9/20/46, Los Angeles, Cal. BR/TR, 6'3", 195 lbs. Deb: 4/18/72

| 1975 Cle-A | 7 | 7 | .500 | 19 | 19 | 4 | 0 | 0 | 126 | 137 | 9 | 46 | 52 | 13.4 | 4.79 | 79 | .275 | .341 | 0 | — | 0 | -14 | -14 | -1 | -1.5 |
| Total 5 | 30 | 35 | .462 | 140 | 70 | 12 | 0 | 10 | 590 | 590 | 45 | 257 | 319 | 13.1 | 4.24 | 87 | .261 | .340 | 15 | .121 | 2 | -43 | -35 | -5 | -4.4 |

● JACK HARSHMAN   Harshman, John Elvin b: 7/12/27, San Diego, Cal. BL/TL, 6'2", 185 lbs. Deb: 9/16/48 ♦

1959 Cle-A	5	1	.833	13	6	5	1	0	66	46	6	13	35	8.0	2.59	142	.179	.219	7	.206	2	9	8	-0	0.9
1960 Cle-A	2	4	.333	15	8	0	0	0	54¹	50	7	30	25	13.3	3.98	94	.243	.339	3	.176	-0	-1	-1	-1	-0.2
Total 8	69	65	.515	217	155	61	12	7	1169¹	1025	96	539	741	12.3	3.50	109	.235	.323	76	.179	29	50	41	-5	6.1
Team 2	7	5	.583	28	14	5	1	0	120¹	96	13	43	60	10.4	3.22	115	.207	.275	10	.196	2	9	7	-1	0.7

● OSCAR HARSTAD   Harstad, Oscar Theander b: 5/24/1892, Parkland, Wash. d: 11/14/85, Corvallis, Ore. BR/TR, 6', 174 lbs. Deb: 4/23/15

| 1915 Cle-A | 3 | 5 | .375 | 32 | 7 | 4 | 0 | 1 | 82 | 81 | 1 | 35 | 35 | 12.8 | 3.40 | 90 | .270 | .348 | 2 | .125 | -1 | -4 | -3 | 2 | -0.2 |

● BILL HART   Hart, William Franklin b: 7/19/1865, Louisville, Ky. d: 9/19/36, Cincinnati, Ohio TR, 5'10", 163 lbs. Deb: 7/26/1886 U

| 1901 Cle-A | 7 | 11 | .389 | 20 | 19 | 16 | 0 | 0 | 157² | 180 | 3 | 57 | 48 | 14.1 | 3.77 | 94 | .283 | .352 | 14 | .219 | -2 | -2 | -4 | 2 | -0.3 |
| Total 8 | 66 | 120 | .355 | 206 | 190 | 162 | 5 | 3 | 1582 | 1819 | 43 | 704 | 431 | 14.8 | 4.65 | 86 | .281 | .359 | 155 | .207 | -14 | -105 | -114 | 22 | -9.5 |

● BOB HARTMAN   Hartman, Robert Louis b: 8/28/37, Kenosha, Wis. BR/TL, 5'11", 185 lbs. Deb: 4/26/59

| 1962 Cle-A | 0 | 1 | .000 | 8 | 2 | 0 | 0 | 0 | 17¹ | 14 | 1 | 8 | 11 | 11.4 | 3.12 | 124 | .209 | .293 | 0 | .000 | -1 | 2 | 1 | -0 | 0.0 |
| Total 2 | 0 | 1 | .000 | 11 | 2 | 0 | 0 | 0 | 19 | 20 | 1 | 10 | 12 | 14.2 | 5.21 | 74 | .256 | .341 | 0 | .000 | -1 | -3 | -3 | -0 | 0.0 |

● BRAD HAVENS   Havens, Bradley David b: 11/17/59, Highland Park, Mich. BL/TL, 6'1", 196 lbs. Deb: 6/5/81

1988 Cle-A	2	3	.400	28	0	0	0	1	57¹	62	7	17	30	12.4	3.14	131	.273	.324	0	—	0	5	6	-0	0.4
1989 Cle-A	0	0	—	7	0	0	0	0	13¹	18	3	7	6	16.9	4.05	98	.353	.431	0	—	0	-0	-1	1	0.0
Total 8	24	37	.393	205	61	6	2	3	590²	624	76	246	370	13.3	4.81	86	.272	.344	0	.000	-0	-54	-46	-4	-5.6
Team 2	2	3	.400	35	0	0	0	1	70²	80	10	24	36	13.2	3.31	123	.288	.344	0	—	0	5	6	0	0.4

● WYNN HAWKINS   Hawkins, Wynn Firth "Hawk" b: 2/20/36, E.Palestine, Ohio BR/TR, 6'3", 195 lbs. Deb: 4/22/60

| 1960 Cle-A | 4 | 4 | .500 | 15 | 9 | 1 | 0 | 0 | 66 | 68 | 10 | 39 | 39 | 14.7 | 4.23 | 88 | .269 | .369 | 2 | .100 | -0 | -3 | -4 | 1 | -0.4 |
| 1961 Cle-A | 7 | 9 | .438 | 30 | 21 | 3 | 1 | 1 | 133 | 139 | 16 | 59 | 51 | 13.5 | 4.06 | 97 | .270 | .347 | 4 | .108 | -2 | -1 | -2 | -1 | -0.5 |

YEAR TM/L	W	L	PCT	G	GS	CG	SH	SV	IP	H	HR	BB	SO	RAT	ERA	ERA+	OAV	OOB	BH	AVG	PB	PR	/A	PD	TPI
1962 Cle-A	1	0	1.000	3	0	0	0	0	3^{2}	9	1	1	0	24.5	7.36	53	.429	.455	0	—	0	-1	-1	-0	-0.3
Total 3	12	13	.480	48	30	4	1	1	202^{2}	216	27	99	90	14.1	4.17	93	.274	.357	6	.105	-2	-5	-7	-1	-1.2
● NEAL HEATON Heaton, Neal b: 3/3/60, Holtsville, N.Y. BL/TL, 6′1″, 205 lbs. Deb: 9/3/82																									
1982 Cle-A	0	2	.000	8	4	0	0	0	31	32	1	16	14	13.9	5.23	78	.260	.345	0	—	0	-4	-4	-0	-0.2
1983 Cle-A	11	7	.611	39	16	4	3	7	149^{1}	157	11	44	75	12.2	4.16	102	.269	.321	0	—	0	-2	1	-2	-0.2
1984 Cle-A	12	15	.444	38	34	4	1	0	198^{2}	231	21	75	75	13.9	5.21	78	.293	.354	0	—	0	-27	-25	-3	-3.3
1985 Cle-A	9	17	.346	36	33	5	1	0	207^{2}	244	19	80	82	14.3	4.90	84	.298	.365	0	—	0	-17	-18	-3	-2.1
1986 Cle-A	3	6	.333	12	12	2	0	0	74^{1}	73	8	34	24	13.1	4.24	98	.254	.335	0	—	0	-1	-1	-0	-0.1
Total 12	80	96	.455	382	202	22	6	10	1507	1589	163	524	699	12.8	4.37	91	.273	.337	32	.171	2	-72	-68	-11	-8.1
Team 5	35	47	.427	133	99	15	5	7	661	737	60	249	270	13.5	4.77	87	.283	.348	0	—	0	-50	-46	-7	-5.9
● MIKE HEDLUND Hedlund, Michael David "Red" b: 8/11/46, Dallas, Tex. BR/TR, 6′1″, 190 lbs. Deb: 5/8/65																									
1965 Cle-A	0	0	—	6	0	0	0	0	5^{1}	6	0	5	4	18.6	5.06	69	.286	.423	0	.000	-0	-1	-1	-0	0.0
1968 Cle-A	0	0	—	3	0	0	0	0	1^{2}	6	0	2	0	48.6	10.80	27	.545	.643	0	—	0	-1	-1	0	0.0
Total 6	25	24	.510	113	62	9	1	2	465^{2}	440	39	167	211	11.9	3.56	96	.253	.321	17	.123	-5	-7	-8	5	-1.5
Team 2	0	0	—	9	0	0	0	0	7	12	0	7	4	25.7	6.43	52	.375	.500	0	.000	-0	-2	-2	-0	0.0
● BOB HEFFNER Heffner, Robert Frederic b: 9/13/38, Allentown, Pa. BR/TR, 6′4″, 205 lbs. Deb: 6/19/63																									
1966 Cle-A	0	1	.000	5	1	0	0	0	13	12	1	3	7	10.4	3.46	99	.240	.283	0	.000	0	-0	-0	-1	0.0
Total 5	11	21	.344	114	31	4	2	6	353^{1}	360	45	107	241	12.0	4.51	84	.264	.320	12	.128	-1	-36	-29	-2	-2.2
● RUSS HEMAN Heman, Russell Fredrick b: 2/10/33, Olive, Cal. BR/TR, 6′4″, 200 lbs. Deb: 4/20/61																									
1961 Cle-A	0	0	—	6	0	0	0	1	10	8	0	8	4	15.3	3.60	109	.216	.370	0	.000	-0	0	0	0	0.0
● BERNIE HENDERSON Henderson, Bernard "Barnyard" b: 4/12/1899, Douglassville, Tex d: 6/6/66, Linden, Tex. BR/TR, 5′9″, 175 lbs. Deb: 9/5/21																									
1921 Cle-A	0	1	.000	2	1	0	0	0	3	5	0	0	1	15.0	9.00	47	.333	.333	0	.000	0	-2	-2	-0	-0.4
● PHIL HENNIGAN Hennigan, Phillip Winston b: 4/10/46, Jasper, Tex. BR/TR, 5′11.5″, 185 lbs. Deb: 9/2/69																									
1969 Cle-A	2	1	.667	9	0	0	0	0	16^{1}	14	0	4	10	10.5	3.31	114	.241	.302	0	.000	-0	1	1	-1	0.1
1970 Cle-A	6	3	.667	42	1	0	0	3	71^{2}	69	7	44	43	14.7	4.02	99	.263	.377	1	.143	1	-2	-0	1	0.1
1971 Cle-A	4	3	.571	57	0	0	0	14	82	80	13	51	69	14.7	4.94	77	.261	.371	0	.000	-0	-13	-10	-1	-1.3
1972 Cle-A	5	3	.625	38	1	0	0	5	67^{1}	54	8	18	44	9.9	2.67	120	.226	.286	1	.083	-0	3	4	-1	0.4
Total 5	17	14	.548	176	2	0	0	25	280^{2}	267	34	133	188	13.2	4.26	86	.257	.347	3	.100	1	-25	-18	-2	-2.0
Team 4	17	10	.630	146	2	0	0	22	237^{1}	217	28	117	166	13.0	3.91	94	.251	.346	2	.074	0	-12	-6	-2	-0.7
● EARL HENRY Henry, Earl Clifford "Hook" b: 6/10/17, Roseville, Ohio BL/TL, 5′11″, 172 lbs. Deb: 9/23/44																									
1944 Cle-A	1	1	.500	2	2	1	0	0	17^{2}	18	0	3	5	10.7	4.58	72	.269	.300	0	.000	-0	-2	-3	0	-0.3
1945 Cle-A	0	3	.000	15	1	0	0	0	21^{2}	20	0	20	10	17.0	5.40	60	.253	.410	2	.500	1	-5	-5	1	-0.5
Total 2	1	4	.200	17	3	1	0	0	39^{1}	38	0	23	15	14.2	5.03	65	.260	.365	2	.222	0	-7	-8	1	-0.8
● JEREMY HERNANDEZ Hernandez, Jeremy Stuart b: 7/6/66, Burbank, Cal. BR/TR, 6′5″, 195 lbs. Deb: 9/2/91																									
1993 Cle-A	6	5	.545	49	0	0	0	8	77^{1}	75	12	27	44	11.9	3.14	138	.261	.325	0	—	0	10	10	-0	1.5
Total 5	10	14	.417	133	0	0	0	20	193	191	20	67	122	12.2	3.64	113	.267	.333	0	.000	-1	9	10	-0	2.6
● OREL HERSHISER Hershiser, Orel Leonard Quinton b: 9/16/58, Buffalo, N.Y. BR/TR, 6′3″, 192 lbs. Deb: 9/1/83																									
1995 *Cle-A	16	6	.727	26	26	1	1	0	167^{1}	151	21	51	111	11.1	3.87	120	.244	.306	0	—	0	16	14	0	1.6
Total 13	150	108	.581	369	329	66	25	5	2323^{1}	2085	147	704	1554	11.0	3.06	119	.239	.301	144	.214	34	187	153	24	23.1
● OTTO HESS Hess, Otto C. b: 10/10/1878, Bern, Switzerland d: 2/25/26, Tucson, Ariz. BL/TL, 6′1″, 170 lbs. Deb: 8/3/02 ♦																									
1902 Cle-A	2	4	.333	7	4	4	0	0	43^{2}	67	0	23	13	18.8	5.98	58	.351	.423	1	.071	-1	-12	-12	1	-1.3
1904 Cle-A	8	7	.533	21	16	15	4	0	151^{1}	134	2	31	64	10.1	1.67	152	.238	.284	12	.120	-3	16	15	-0	1.1
1905 Cle-A	10	15	.400	26	25	22	4	0	213^{2}	179	1	72	109	11.0	3.16	83	.229	.301	44	.254	5	-12	-12	1	-0.9
1906 Cle-A	20	17	.541	43	36	33	7	**3**	333^{2}	274	4	85	167	10.3	1.83	143	.227	.291	31	.201	1	32	**29**	-2	3.3
1907 Cle-A	6	6	.500	17	14	7	0	1	93^{1}	84	1	37	36	12.8	2.89	87	.242	.336	4	.133	0	-4	-4	-1	-0.6
1908 Cle-A	0	0	—	4	0	0	0	0	7	11	0	1	2	15.4	5.14	47	.407	.429	0	.000	-1	-2	-2	0	0.0
Total 10	70	90	.438	198	165	129	18	5	1418	1355	25	448	580	12.0	2.98	98	.257	.324	154	.216	14	-11	-11	-2	0.4
Team 6	46	49	.484	118	95	81	15	4	842^{2}	749	8	249	391	11.2	2.50	106	.240	.307	92	.190	1	18	13	-1	1.6
● JOE HEVING Heving, Joseph William b: 9/2/1900, Covington, Ky. d: 4/11/70, Covington, Ky. BR/TR, 6′1″, 185 lbs. Deb: 4/29/30 F																									
1937 Cle-A	8	4	.667	40	0	0	0	5	72^{2}	92	6	30	35	15.4	4.83	95	.311	.378	5	.263	0	-2	-2	1	-0.1
1938 Cle-A	1	1	.500	3	0	0	0	0	6	10	0	5	0	22.5	9.00	52	.370	.469	0	.000	-0	-3	-3	-0	-0.7
1941 Cle-A	5	2	.714	27	3	2	1	5	70^{2}	63	2	31	18	12.1	2.29	172	.240	.323	0	.000	-1	15	13	2	1.5
1942 Cle-A	5	3	.625	27	2	0	0	3	46^{1}	52	4	25	13	15.3	4.86	71	.278	.369	0	.000	-1	-6	-7	0	-1.3
1943 Cle-A	1	1	.500	30	1	0	0	9	72	58	1	34	34	11.8	2.75	113	.230	.326	1	.071	-0	4	3	2	0.3
1944 Cle-A	8	3	.727	**63**	1	0	0	10	119^{2}	106	2	41	46	11.2	1.96	169	.239	.307	4	.182	-1	**20**	18	1	2.0
Total 13	76	48	.613	430	40	17	3	63	1038^{2}	1136	64	380	429	13.3	3.90	108	.279	.344	47	.170	-4	40	36	14	4.2
Team 6	28	14	.667	190	7	2	1	32	387^{1}	381	15	166	146	12.9	3.16	116	.260	.339	10	.128	-2	28	21	5	1.7
● JOHN HICKEY Hickey, John William b: 11/3/1881, Minneapolis, Minn. d: 12/28/41, Seattle, Wash. BR/TL, 5′10″, 170 lbs. Deb: 4/16/04																									
1904 Cle-A	0	1	.000	2	2	1	0	0	12^{1}	14	0	11	5	18.2	7.30	35	.286	.417	0	.000	-1	-6	-7	0	-0.5
● CHARLIE HICKMAN Hickman, Charles Taylor "Cheerful Charlie" or "Piano Legs" b: 3/4/1876, Taylortown, Dunkard Township, Pa. d: 4/19/34, Morgantown, W.Va. BR/TR, 5′11.5″, 215 lbs. Deb: 9/8/1897 ♦																									
1902 Cle-A	0	1	.000	1	1	1	0	0	8	11	0	5	1	19.1	7.88	44	.324	.425	161	.378	1	-4	-4	-0	-0.3
Total 6	10	8	.556	30	22	15	3	4	185	175	4	94	37	13.7	4.28	86	.249	.347	1176	.295	11	-14	-12	-1	-0.2
● DENNIS HIGGINS Higgins, Dennis Dean b: 8/4/39, Jefferson City, Mo. BR/TR, 6′4″, 190 lbs. Deb: 4/12/66																									
1970 Cle-A	4	6	.400	58	0	0	0	11	90^{1}	82	8	54	82	13.7	3.99	99	.248	.358	3	.250	1	-3	-0	1	0.1
Total 7	22	23	.489	241	2	0	0	46	410^{1}	346	32	223	339	12.8	3.42	98	.233	.340	9	.155	0	-0	-3	-1	-1.6
● ORAL HILDEBRAND Hildebrand, Oral Clyde b: 4/7/07, Indianapolis, Ind. d: 9/8/77, Southport, Ind. BR/TR, 6′3″, 175 lbs. Deb: 9/8/31																									
1931 Cle-A	2	1	.667	5	2	2	0	0	26^{2}	25	0	13	6	13.8	4.39	105	.243	.345	2	.182	-1	-0	1	-0	0.0
1932 Cle-A	8	6	.571	27	15	7	0	0	129^{1}	124	7	62	49	12.9	3.69	129	.249	.333	7	.146	-3	11	15	-2	0.9
1933 Cle-A☆	16	11	.593	36	31	15	**6**	0	220^{1}	205	8	88	90	12.0	3.76	118	.245	.318	16	.190	-1	13	17	-0	1.6
1934 Cle-A	11	9	.550	33	28	10	1	1	198	225	14	99	72	14.9	4.50	101	.282	.364	13	.171	-1	-0	1	1	0.0
1935 Cle-A	9	8	.529	34	20	8	0	5	171^{1}	171	12	63	49	12.4	3.94	114	.263	.331	9	.164	-2	10	11	-0	0.8
1936 Cle-A	10	11	.476	36	21	9	0	4	174^{2}	197	10	83	65	14.6	4.90	103	.283	.362	12	.190	0	3	3	-1	0.2
Total 10	83	78	.516	258	182	80	9	13	1430^{2}	1490	99	623	527	13.4	4.35	107	.267	.343	96	.187	-9	36	50	-8	3.4
Team 6	56	46	.549	171	117	51	7	10	920^{1}	947	51	408	331	13.4	4.18	111	.265	.342	59	.175	-8	37	47	-3	3.5
● TOM HILGENDORF Hilgendorf, Thomas Eugene b: 3/10/42, Clinton, Iowa BB/TL, 6′1″, 190 lbs. Deb: 8/15/69																									
1972 Cle-A	3	1	.750	19	5	1	0	0	47	51	4	21	25	14.2	2.68	120	.283	.365	1	.077	-1	2	3	0	0.2
1973 Cle-A	5	3	.625	48	1	1	0	6	94^{2}	87	9	36	58	12.0	3.14	125	.242	.316	0	—	0	7	8	1	0.8
1974 Cle-A	4	3	.571	35	0	0	0	3	48^{1}	58	6	17	23	14.2	4.84	75	.302	.362	0	—	0	-7	-7	0	-0.9
Total 6	19	14	.576	184	6	2	0	14	313^{2}	302	25	127	173	12.5	3.04	122	.255	.331	5	.185	1	20	24	2	2.3
Team 3	12	7	.632	102	6	2	0	9	190	196	19	74	106	13.1	3.46	106	.268	.340	1	.077	-1	3	4	2	0.1

YEAR TM/L	W	L	PCT	G	GS	CG	SH	SV	IP	H	HR	BB	SO	RAT	ERA	ERA+	OAV	OOB	BH	AVG	PB	PR	/A	PD	TPI
● **HERBERT HILL** Hill, Herbert Lee b: 8/19/1891, Hutchins, Tex. d: 9/2/70, Farmers Branch, Tex. BR/TR, 5'11.5", 175 lbs. Deb: 7/17/15																									
1915 Cle-A	0	0	—	1	0	0	0	0	2	1	0	2	0	13.5	0.00	—	.250	.500	0	—	0	1	1	-0	0.0
● **KEN HILL** Hill, Kenneth Wade b: 12/14/65, Lynn, Mass. BR/TR, 6'2", 175 lbs. Deb: 9/3/88																									
1995 *Cle-A	4	1	.800	12	11	1	0	0	74^2	77	5	32	48	13.3	3.98	116	.268	.344	0	—	0	6	5	0	0.3
Total 8	74	61	.548	198	191	11	5	0	1212	1125	84	475	720	12.1	3.67	106	.247	.322	48	.148	4	25	31	9	4.2
● **SHAWN HILLEGAS** Hillegas, Shawn Patrick b: 8/21/64, Dos Palos, Cal. BR/TR, 6'2", 208 lbs. Deb: 8/9/87																									
1991 Cle-A	3	4	.429	51	3	0	0	7	83	67	7	46	66	12.5	4.34	96	.223	.330	0	—	0	-2	-2	-0	-0.2
Total 7	24	38	.387	181	62	1	1	10	515^1	521	54	238	332	13.5	4.61	84	.264	.347	2	.069	-1	-37	-41	-6	-5.7
● **MYRIL HOAG** Hoag, Myril Oliver b: 3/9/08, Davis, Cal. d: 7/28/71, High Springs, Fla BR/TR, 5'11", 180 lbs. Deb: 4/15/31 ♦																									
1945 Cle-A	0	0	—	2	0	0	0	0	3	3	0	1	0	12.0	0.00	—	.300	.364	27	.211	0	1	1	0	0.0
Total 2	0	0	—	3	0	0	0	0	4	3	0	1	0	9.0	0.00	—	.214	.267	854	.271	1	2	2	0	0.0
● **BILL HOFFER** Hoffer, William Leopold "Chick" or "Wizard" b: 11/8/1870, Cedar Rapids, Iowa d: 7/21/59, Cedar Rapids, Ia. BR/TR, 5'9", 155 lbs. Deb: 4/26/1895																									
1901 Cle-A	3	8	.273	16	10	10	0	**3**	99	113	2	35	19	13.5	4.55	78	.283	.343	6	.136	-1	-10	-11	0	-1.1
Total 6	92	46	.667	161	142	125	10	3	1254^1	1333	22	453	314	13.2	3.75	112	.270	.339	128	.229	6	76	65	-1	6.0
● **KEN HOLLOWAY** Holloway, Kenneth Eugene (b: Kenneth Eugene Hollaway) b: 8/8/1897, Thomas County, Ga. d: 9/25/68, Thomasville, Ga. BR/TR, 6', 185 lbs. Deb: 8/27/22																									
1929 Cle-A	6	5	.545	25	11	6	2	0	119	118	2	37	32	11.9	3.03	147	.264	.323	7	.171	-2	16	19	-2	1.2
1930 Cle-A	1	1	.500	12	2	0	0	2	30	49	5	14	8	18.9	8.40	57	.374	.434	0	.000	-2	-13	-12	1	-0.9
Total 9	64	52	.552	285	110	43	4	18	1160	1370	50	397	293	14.0	4.40	95	.303	.364	63	.167	-18	-29	-30	4	-3.2
Team 2	7	6	.538	37	13	6	2	2	149	167	7	51	40	13.3	4.11	110	.289	.349	7	.132	-4	4	7	-1	0.3
● **DON HOOD** Hood, Donald Harris b: 10/16/49, Florence, S.C. BL/TL, 6'2", 180 lbs. Deb: 7/16/73																									
1975 Cle-A	6	10	.375	29	19	2	0	0	135^1	136	16	57	51	12.8	4.39	86	.268	.342	0	—	0	-9	-9	-2	-1.1
1976 Cle-A	3	5	.375	33	6	0	0	1	77^2	89	5	41	32	15.5	4.87	72	.296	.387	0	—	0	-12	-12	0	-1.1
1977 Cle-A	2	1	.667	41	5	1	0	0	105	87	3	49	62	12.0	3.00	131	.224	.317	0	—	0	12	11	-2	0.4
1978 Cle-A	5	6	.455	36	19	1	0	0	154^2	166	13	77	73	14.2	4.48	83	.278	.361	0	—	0	-12	-13	0	-0.7
1979 Cle-A	1	0	1.000	13	0	0	0	1	22	13	1	14	7	11.5	3.68	116	.169	.304	0	—	0	1	1	0	0.1
Total 10	34	35	.493	297	72	6	1	6	848^1	840	57	364	374	13.0	3.79	101	.263	.342	4	.200	-0	5	2	-1	-0.3
Team 5	17	22	.436	152	49	4	0	2	494^2	491	38	238	225	13.4	4.17	91	.262	.349	0	—	0	-20	-21	-3	-2.4
● **BOB HOOPER** Hooper, Robert Nelson b: 5/30/22, Leamington, Ont., Canada d: 3/17/80, New Brunswick, N.J BR/TR, 5'11", 195 lbs. Deb: 4/19/50																									
1953 Cle-A	5	4	.556	43	0	0	0	7	69^1	50	4	38	16	11.7	4.02	93	.206	.318	1	.083	-1	-0	-2	1	-0.3
1954 Cle-A	0	0	—	17	0	0	0	2	34^2	39	3	16	12	14.5	4.93	74	.289	.368	0	.000	-1	-5	-5	-0	-0.1
Total 6	40	41	.494	194	57	16	0	25	620^2	640	50	280	196	13.5	4.80	87	.268	.348	31	.166	-4	-48	-42	8	-4.8
Team 2	5	4	.556	60	0	0	0	9	104	89	7	54	28	12.6	4.33	86	.235	.336	1	.059	-1	-5	-7	1	-0.4
● **DAVE HOSKINS** Hoskins, David Taylor b: 8/3/25, Greenwood, Miss. d: 4/2/70, Flint, Mich. BL/TR, 6'1", 180 lbs. Deb: 4/18/53																									
1953 Cle-A	9	3	.750	26	7	3	0	1	112^2	102	9	38	55	11.5	3.99	94	.243	.312	15	.259	4	0	-3	0	0.1
1954 Cle-A	0	1	.000	14	1	0	0	0	26^2	29	3	10	9	13.2	3.04	121	.284	.348	0	.000	-1	2	2	-0	0.0
Total 2	9	4	.692	40	8	3	0	1	139^1	131	12	48	64	11.8	3.81	98	.251	.319	15	.227	3	2	-1	0	0.1
● **ART HOUTTEMAN** Houtteman, Arthur Joseph b: 8/7/27, Detroit, Mich. BR/TR, 6'2", 188 lbs. Deb: 4/29/45																									
1953 Cle-A	7	7	.500	22	13	6	1	3	109	113	4	25	40	11.8	3.80	99	.269	.318	5	.147	-1	2	-1	0	-0.2
1954 *Cle-A	15	7	.682	32	25	11	1	0	188	198	14	59	68	12.4	3.35	110	.273	.330	18	.277	5	8	7	2	1.4
1955 Cle-A	10	6	.625	35	12	3	1	0	124^1	126	15	44	53	12.5	3.98	100	.265	.330	6	.158	-1	-0	0	2	0.2
1956 Cle-A	2	2	.500	22	4	0	0	1	46^2	60	5	31	19	18.3	6.56	64	.317	.424	2	.167	-1	-12	-12	0	-1.0
1957 Cle-A	0	0	—	3	0	0	0	0	4	6	1	3	3	20.3	6.75	55	.353	.450	0	—	0	-1	-1	-0	0.0
Total 12	87	91	.489	325	181	78	14	20	1555	1646	136	516	639	12.7	4.14	99	.272	.333	99	.193	-4	-16	-11	17	1.7
Team 5	34	22	.607	114	54	20	3	4	472	503	39	162	183	12.9	3.97	97	.275	.339	31	.208	2	-4	-7	4	0.4
● **DIXIE HOWELL** Howell, Millard b: 1/7/20, Bowman, Ky. d: 3/18/60, Hollywood, Fla. BL/TR, 6'2", 210 lbs. Deb: 9/14/40																									
1940 Cle-A	0	0	—	3	0	0	0	0	5	2	0	4	2	10.8	1.80	234	.143	.333	0	—	0	1	1	0	0.0
Total 6	19	15	.559	115	2	0	0	19	226^1	236	13	103	99	13.6	3.78	104	.273	.352	18	.243	8	5	4	2	1.9
● **WILLIS HUDLIN** Hudlin, George Willis "Ace" b: 5/23/06, Wagoner, Okla. BR/TR, 6', 190 lbs. Deb: 8/15/26 C																									
1926 Cle-A	1	3	.250	8	2	1	0	0	32^1	25	1	13	6	11.1	2.78	146	.227	.320	1	.125	0	4	5	2	0.7
1927 Cle-A	18	12	.600	43	30	18	1	0	264^2	291	3	83	65	13.1	4.01	105	.283	.343	24	.250	2	4	6	3	1.1
1928 Cle-A	14	14	.500	42	26	10	0	7	220^1	231	7	90	62	13.4	4.04	103	.279	.355	14	.194	-0	0	2	2	0.5
1929 Cle-A	17	15	.531	40	33	22	2	1	280^1	299	7	73	60	12.0	3.34	133	.272	.318	19	.196	-3	28	34	7	**3.9**
1930 Cle-A	13	16	.448	37	33	13	1	1	216^2	255	12	76	60	13.8	4.57	106	.293	.351	16	.219	-1	2	6	5	1.0
1931 Cle-A	15	14	.517	44	34	15	1	4	254^1	313	14	88	83	14.2	4.60	100	.301	.356	20	.200	1	-6	1	4	0.5
1932 Cle-A	12	8	.600	33	21	12	0	2	181^2	204	10	59	65	13.1	4.71	101	.278	.332	13	.203	1	-5	1	1	0.2
1933 Cle-A	5	13	.278	34	17	6	0	1	147^1	161	7	61	44	13.7	3.97	112	.275	.346	6	.146	-1	5	8	4	1.1
1934 Cle-A	15	10	.600	36	26	15	1	4	195	210	8	65	58	12.9	4.75	96	.277	.338	14	.206	3	-6	-4	5	0.2
1935 Cle-A	15	11	.577	36	29	14	3	5	231^2	252	8	61	45	12.3	3.69	122	.277	.324	24	.279	6	20	21	0	2.7
1936 Cle-A	1	5	.167	27	7	1	0	0	64	112	1	31	20	20.4	9.00	56	.397	.460	2	.111	-1	-28	-28	1	-2.0
1937 Cle-A	12	11	.522	35	23	10	2	2	175^2	213	8	43	31	13.2	4.10	112	.295	.337	10	.169	-1	10	10	3	1.3
1938 Cle-A	8	8	.500	29	15	8	0	1	127	158	13	45	27	14.5	4.89	95	.303	.361	5	.116	-2	-1	-4	1	-0.5
1939 Cle-A	9	10	.474	27	20	7	0	3	143	175	6	42	28	13.7	4.91	90	.303	.352	9	.188	1	-5	-8	5	-0.4
1940 Cle-A	2	1	.667	4	4	2	0	0	23^2	31	3	2	8	12.5	4.94	85	.316	.330	1	.125	-0	-1	-2	-0	-0.2
Total 16	158	156	.503	491	328	155	11	31	2613^1	3011	118	846	677	13.4	4.41	102	.289	.345	180	.201	4	-0	26	42	8.2
Team 15	157	151	.510	475	320	154	11	31	2557^2	2930	108	832	662	13.4	4.34	104	.288	.345	178	.202	4	21	48	41	10.1
● **MARK HUISMANN** Huismann, Mark Lawrence b: 5/11/58, Littleton, Colo. BR/TR, 6'3", 195 lbs. Deb: 8/16/83																									
1987 Cle-A	2	3	.400	20	0	0	0	2	35^1	38	6	8	23	11.7	5.09	89	.271	.311	0	—	0	-3	-2	-0	-0.3
Total 9	13	11	.542	152	1	0	0	11	296^1	305	37	83	219	11.9	4.40	95	.266	.318	0	—	0	-9	-7	1	-0.7
● **JOHNNY HUMPHRIES** Humphries, John William b: 6/23/15, Clifton Forge, Va d: 6/24/65, New Orleans, La. BR/TR, 6'1", 185 lbs. Deb: 5/8/38																									
1938 Cle-A	9	8	.529	**45**	6	1	0	6	103^1	105	6	63	56	14.7	5.23	89	.264	.367	3	.103	-1	-5	-7	-1	-1.1
1939 Cle-A	2	4	.333	15	1	0	0	2	28^1	30	0	32	12	20.0	8.26	53	.294	.467	0	.000	-1	-11	-12	-0	-2.2
1940 Cle-A	0	2	.000	19	1	1	0	1	33^2	35	5	29	17	17.6	8.29	51	.269	.410	0	.000	-1	-15	-15	-1	-1.0
Total 9	52	63	.452	211	111	49	9	12	1002	1024	50	373	317	12.8	3.78	97	.265	.334	63	.191	4	-9	-13	-14	-3.2
Team 3	11	14	.440	79	8	2	0	9	165^1	170	11	124	85	16.2	6.37	71	.270	.394	3	.071	-3	-31	-34	-2	-4.3
● **MIKE JACKSON** Jackson, Michael Warren b: 3/27/46, Paterson, N.J. BL/TL, 6'3", 190 lbs. Deb: 5/10/70																									
1973 Cle-A	0	0	—	1	0	0	0	0	0^2	1	0	0	1	13.5	0.00	—	.333	.333	0	—	0	0	0	0	0.0
Total 4	2	3	.400	23	3	0	0	0	49^2	57	3	39	33	17.6	5.80	63	.308	.431	1	.143	-0	-12	-12	1	-0.4
● **LEFTY JAMES** James, William A. b: 7/1/1889, Glen Roy, Ohio d: 5/3/33, Glen Roy, Ohio BL/TL, 5'11.5", 175 lbs. Deb: 4/13/12																									
1912 Cle-A	0	1	.000	3	1	0	0	1	6	8	0	4	2	21.0	7.50	45	.348	.483	0	.000	-0	-3	-3	-0	-0.5

YEAR	TM/L	W	L	PCT	G	GS	CG	SH	SV	IP	H	HR	BB	SO	RAT	ERA	ERA+	OAV	OOB	BH	AVG	PB	PR	/A	PD	TPI
1913	Cle-A	2	2	.500	11	4	3	0	0	39	42	0	9	18	12.5	3.00	101	.273	.325	3	.231	-0	-0	0	-1	-0.1
1914	Cle-A	0	3	.000	17	6	1	0	0	50^2	44	0	32	16	13.9	3.20	90	.251	.373	0	.000	-1	-3	-2	1	-0.1
Total	3	2	6	.250	31	11	4	0	1	95^2	94	0	45	36	13.7	3.39	88	.267	.361	3	.107	-1	-6	-4	0	-0.7

● **BILL JAMES** James, William Henry "Big Bill" b: 1/20/1887, Detroit, Mich. d: 5/24/42, Venice, Cal. BB/TR, 6'4", 195 lbs. Deb: 6/12/11

YEAR	TM/L	W	L	PCT	G	GS	CG	SH	SV	IP	H	HR	BB	SO	RAT	ERA	ERA+	OAV	OOB	BH	AVG	PB	PR	/A	PD	TPI
1911	Cle-A	2	4	.333	8	6	4	0	0	51^2	58	1	32	21	16.0	4.88	70	.284	.387	1	.059	-1	-9	-8	-1	-1.0
1912	Cle-A	0	0	—	3	0	0	0	0	13^2	15	0	9	5	15.8	4.61	74	.288	.393	0	.000	-0	-2	-2	-1	-0.1
Total	8	65	71	.478	203	147	68	9	4	1179^2	1110	16	578	408	13.2	3.20	88	.258	.352	51	.142	-8	-44	-49	8	-5.1
Team	2	2	4	.333	11	6	4	0	0	65^1	73	1	41	26	16.0	4.82	71	.285	.388	1	.050	-2	-11	-10	-1	-1.1

● **CHARLIE JAMIESON** Jamieson, Charles Devine "Cuckoo" b: 2/7/1893, Paterson, N.J. d: 10/27/69, Paterson, N.J. BL/TL, 5'8.5", 165 lbs. Deb: 9/20/15 ♦

YEAR	TM/L	W	L	PCT	G	GS	CG	SH	SV	IP	H	HR	BB	SO	RAT	ERA	ERA+	OAV	OOB	BH	AVG	PB	PR	/A	PD	TPI
1919	Cle-A	0	0	—	4	1	0	0	0	13	12	0	8	0	13.8	5.54	60	.250	.357	6	.353	0	-3	-3	-0	0.1
1922	Cle-A	0	0	—	2	0	0	0	0	5^2	7	0	4	2	17.5	3.18	126	.318	.423	183	.323	1	1	1	-0	0.0
Total	5	2	1	.667	13	3	1	0	0	48	55	0	30	7	16.3	6.19	51	.286	.388	1990	.303	2	-17	-16	-1	-0.4
Team	2	0	0	—	6	1	0	0	0	18^2	19	0	12	2	14.9	4.82	74	.271	.378	189	.324	1	-3	-3	-1	0.1

● **HI JASPER** Jasper, Henry W. b: 11/15/1880, St.Louis, Mo. d: 5/22/37, St.Louis, Mo. BR/TR, 5'11", 180 lbs. Deb: 4/19/14

YEAR	TM/L	W	L	PCT	G	GS	CG	SH	SV	IP	H	HR	BB	SO	RAT	ERA	ERA+	OAV	OOB	BH	AVG	PB	PR	/A	PD	TPI
1919	Cle-A	4	5	.444	12	10	5	0	0	82^2	83	1	28	25	12.1	3.59	93	.269	.330	3	.103	-2	-3	-2	1	-0.4
Total	4	10	12	.455	52	21	8	0	1	237^2	210	3	99	96	12.0	3.48	84	.248	.333	12	.162	-2	-16	-15	5	-0.9

● **TEX JEANES** Jeanes, Ernest Lee b: 12/19/1900, Maypearl, Tex. d: 4/5/73, Longview, Tex. BR/TR, 6', 176 lbs. Deb: 4/20/21 ♦

YEAR	TM/L	W	L	PCT	G	GS	CG	SH	SV	IP	H	HR	BB	SO	RAT	ERA	ERA+	OAV	OOB	BH	AVG	PB	PR	/A	PD	TPI
1922	Cle-A	0	0	—	1	0	0	0	0	0	0	0	1	0	—	—	—	—	1.000	0	.000	0	0	0	0	0.0
Total	2	0	0	—	2	0	0	0	0	1	2	0	3	0	45.0	9.00	43	.400	.625	20	.274	0	-1	-1	-0	0.0

● **MIKE JEFFCOAT** Jeffcoat, James Michael b: 8/3/59, Pine Bluff, Ark. BL/TL, 6'2", 187 lbs. Deb: 8/21/83

YEAR	TM/L	W	L	PCT	G	GS	CG	SH	SV	IP	H	HR	BB	SO	RAT	ERA	ERA+	OAV	OOB	BH	AVG	PB	PR	/A	PD	TPI
1983	Cle-A	1	3	.250	11	2	0	0	0	32^2	32	1	13	9	12.7	3.31	128	.256	.331	0	—	0	3	3	-0	0.3
1984	Cle-A	5	2	.714	63	1	0	0	1	75^1	82	7	24	41	12.8	2.99	137	.281	.338	0	—	0	8	9	1	0.9
1985	Cle-A	0	0	—	9	0	0	0	0	9^2	8	1	6	4	13.0	2.79	148	.235	.350	0	—	0	1	1	1	0.1
Total	10	25	26	.490	255	45	3	2	7	500	576	49	149	242	13.3	4.37	91	.292	.346	1	.500	1	-23	-22	0	-2.1
Team	3	6	5	.545	83	3	0	0	1	117^2	122	9	43	54	12.8	3.06	135	.271	.337	0	—	0	13	14	1	1.3

● **TOMMY JOHN** John, Thomas Edward b: 5/22/43, Terre Haute, Ind. BR/TL, 6'3", 185 lbs. Deb: 9/6/63

YEAR	TM/L	W	L	PCT	G	GS	CG	SH	SV	IP	H	HR	BB	SO	RAT	ERA	ERA+	OAV	OOB	BH	AVG	PB	PR	/A	PD	TPI
1963	Cle-A	0	2	.000	6	3	0	0	0	20^1	23	1	6	9	12.8	2.21	164	.284	.333	0	.000	-1	3	3	-0	0.2
1964	Cle-A	2	9	.182	25	14	2	1	0	94^1	97	10	35	65	12.6	3.91	92	.262	.326	5	.208	0	-3	-3	1	-0.3
Total	26	288	231	.555	760	700	162	46	4	4710^1	4783	302	1259	2245	11.7	3.34	110	.265	.316	141	.157	1	214	179	53	24.8
Team	2	2	11	.154	31	17	2	1	0	114^2	120	11	41	74	12.6	3.61	100	.266	.327	5	.167	-1	0	-0	0	-0.1

● **JERRY JOHNSON** Johnson, Jerry Michael b: 12/3/43, Miami, Fla. BR/TR, 6'3", 200 lbs. Deb: 7/17/68

YEAR	TM/L	W	L	PCT	G	GS	CG	SH	SV	IP	H	HR	BB	SO	RAT	ERA	ERA+	OAV	OOB	BH	AVG	PB	PR	/A	PD	TPI
1973	Cle-A	5	6	.455	39	1	0	0	5	59^2	70	7	39	45	16.4	6.18	63	.299	.399	0	—	0	-16	-15	0	-2.8
Total	10	48	51	.485	365	39	6	2	41	770^2	779	63	389	489	13.7	4.31	83	.265	.352	15	.123	-2	-60	-62	-1	-7.5

● **BOB JOHNSON** Johnson, Robert Dale b: 4/25/43, Aurora, Ill. BL/TR, 6'4", 220 lbs. Deb: 9/19/69

YEAR	TM/L	W	L	PCT	G	GS	CG	SH	SV	IP	H	HR	BB	SO	RAT	ERA	ERA+	OAV	OOB	BH	AVG	PB	PR	/A	PD	TPI
1974	Cle-A	3	4	.429	14	10	0	0	0	72	75	12	37	36	14.4	4.38	83	.273	.365	0	—	0	-6	-6	-0	-0.6
Total	7	28	34	.452	183	76	18	2	12	692^1	644	82	269	507	12.3	3.48	102	.249	.327	15	.096	-4	9	6	-7	-0.2

● **VIC JOHNSON** Johnson, Victor Oscar b: 8/3/20, Eau Claire, Wis. BR/TL, 6', 160 lbs. Deb: 5/3/44

YEAR	TM/L	W	L	PCT	G	GS	CG	SH	SV	IP	H	HR	BB	SO	RAT	ERA	ERA+	OAV	OOB	BH	AVG	PB	PR	/A	PD	TPI
1946	Cle-A	0	1	.000	9	1	0	0	0	13^2	20	1	8	3	18.4	9.22	36	.357	.438	0	.000	-0	-9	-9	1	-0.6
Total	3	6	8	.429	42	15	4	1	2	126^1	152	5	69	31	15.9	5.06	67	.305	.392	5	.119	-3	-23	-23	2	-2.2

● **DOUG JONES** Jones, Douglas Reid b: 6/24/57, Lebanon, Ind. BR/TR, 6'3", 195 lbs. Deb: 4/9/82

YEAR	TM/L	W	L	PCT	G	GS	CG	SH	SV	IP	H	HR	BB	SO	RAT	ERA	ERA+	OAV	OOB	BH	AVG	PB	PR	/A	PD	TPI
1986	Cle-A	1	0	1.000	11	0	0	0	1	18	18	0	6	12	12.5	2.50	166	.257	.325	0	—	0	3	3	0	0.3
1987	Cle-A	6	5	.545	49	0	0	0	8	91^1	101	4	24	87	12.9	3.15	143	.281	.336	0	—	0	13	14	1	1.8
1988	Cle-A★	3	4	.429	51	0	0	0	37	83^1	69	1	16	72	9.4	2.27	181	.218	.260	0	—	0	16	17	0	3.1
1989	Cle-A★	7	10	.412	59	0	0	0	32	80^2	76	4	13	65	10.0	2.34	169	.251	.284	0	—	0	14	14	1	4.3
1990	Cle-A☆	5	5	.500	66	0	0	0	43	84^1	66	5	22	55	9.6	2.56	153	.218	.275	0	—	0	13	13	-1	2.9
1991	Cle-A	4	8	.333	36	4	0	0	7	63^1	87	7	17	48	14.8	5.54	75	.320	.360	0	—	0	-10	-10	1	-1.8
Total	11	43	58	.426	526	4	0	0	239	721^1	730	42	159	579	11.4	3.12	130	.261	.306	1	.200	0	73	74	0	16.0
Team	6	26	32	.448	272	4	0	0	128	421	417	21	98	339	11.3	3.04	136	.257	.304	0	—	0	48	52	2	10.6

● **SAM JONES** Jones, Samuel "Toothpick Sam" b: 12/14/25, Stewartsville, Ohio d: 11/5/71, Morgantown, W.Va. BR/TR, 6'4", 200 lbs. Deb: 9/22/51

YEAR	TM/L	W	L	PCT	G	GS	CG	SH	SV	IP	H	HR	BB	SO	RAT	ERA	ERA+	OAV	OOB	BH	AVG	PB	PR	/A	PD	TPI
1951	Cle-A	0	1	.000	2	1	0	0	0	8^2	4	0	5	4	9.3	2.08	182	.143	.273	0	.000	-0	2	2	-0	0.1
1952	Cle-A	2	3	.400	14	4	0	0	1	36	38	6	37	28	19.8	7.25	46	.270	.434	1	.100	-1	-14	-16	-1	-2.1
Total	12	102	101	.502	322	222	76	17	9	1643^1	1403	151	822	1376	12.5	3.59	108	.230	.328	78	.149	-11	58	50	-8	2.8
Team	2	2	4	.333	16	5	0	0	1	44^2	42	6	42	32	17.7	6.25	55	.249	.409	1	.083	-1	-12	-14	-1	-2.0

● **SAM JONES** Jones, Samuel Pond "Sad Sam" b: 7/26/1892, Woodsfield, Ohio d: 7/6/66, Barnesville, Ohio BR/TR, 6', 170 lbs. Deb: 6/13/14

YEAR	TM/L	W	L	PCT	G	GS	CG	SH	SV	IP	H	HR	BB	SO	RAT	ERA	ERA+	OAV	OOB	BH	AVG	PB	PR	/A	PD	TPI
1914	Cle-A	0	0	—	1	0	0	0	0	3^1	2	0	2	0	10.8	2.70	107	.200	.333	1	.500	0	0	0	0	0.0
1915	Cle-A	4	9	.308	48	9	2	0	4	145^2	131	0	63	42	12.0	3.65	84	.252	.334	5	.156	-0	-11	-10	0	-0.9
Total	22	229	217	.513	647	487	250	36	31	3883	4084	152	1396	1223	12.9	3.84	104	.274	.339	245	.197	25	81	61	-8	8.1
Team	2	4	9	.308	49	9	2	0	4	149	133	0	65	42	12.0	3.62	84	.251	.334	6	.176	0	-11	-10	0	-0.9

● **ADDIE JOSS** Joss, Adrian b: 4/12/1880, Woodland, Wis. d: 4/14/11, Toledo, Ohio BR/TR, 6'3", 185 lbs. Deb: 4/26/02 H

YEAR	TM/L	W	L	PCT	G	GS	CG	SH	SV	IP	H	HR	BB	SO	RAT	ERA	ERA+	OAV	OOB	BH	AVG	PB	PR	/A	PD	TPI
1902	Cle-A	17	13	.567	32	29	28	**5**	0	269^1	225	2	75	106	10.5	2.77	124	.228	.291	12	.117	-5	24	20	6	2.0
1903	Cle-A	18	13	.581	32	31	31	3	0	283^2	232	3	37	120	**8.8**	2.19	130	.223	**.256**	22	.193	0	24	21	4	2.7
1904	Cle-A	14	10	.583	25	24	20	5	0	192^1	160	0	30	83	9.2	**1.59**	159	.227	.266	10	.132	-4	22	20	0	2.2
1905	Cle-A	20	12	.625	33	32	31	3	0	286	246	4	46	132	9.5	2.01	131	.233	.273	13	.134	-0	21	20	5	2.7
1906	Cle-A	21	9	.700	34	31	28	9	1	282	220	3	43	106	8.5	1.72	152	.218	.252	21	.210	2	30	28	2	3.7
1907	Cle-A	**27**	11	.711	42	38	34	6	2	338^2	279	3	54	127	9.0	1.83	137	.226	.263	13	.114	-5	27	26	9	3.4
1908	Cle-A	24	11	.686	42	35	29	9	2	325	232	2	30	130	**7.3**	**1.16**	**206**	**.197**	**.218**	15	.155	2	45	44	2	5.9
1909	Cle-A	14	13	.519	33	28	24	4	0	242^2	198	0	31	67	8.6	1.71	150	.226	.255	8	.100	-3	21	23	0	2.4
1910	Cle-A	5	5	.500	13	12	9	1	0	107^1	96	2	18	49	9.7	2.26	114	.245	.282	4	.111	-1	3	4	2	0.4
Total	9	160	97	.623	286	260	234	45	5	2327	1888	19	364	920	8.9	1.89	142	.223	.260	118	.144	-14	216	207	30	25.4

● **KEN JUNGELS** Jungels, Kenneth Peter "Curly" b: 6/23/16, Aurora, Ill. d: 9/9/75, West Bend, Wis. BR/TR, 6'1", 180 lbs. Deb: 9/15/37

YEAR	TM/L	W	L	PCT	G	GS	CG	SH	SV	IP	H	HR	BB	SO	RAT	ERA	ERA+	OAV	OOB	BH	AVG	PB	PR	/A	PD	TPI
1937	Cle-A	0	0	—	2	0	0	0	0	3	3	0	1	0	12.0	0.00	—	.273	.333	0	—	0	2	2	0	0.0
1938	Cle-A	1	0	1.000	9	0	0	0	0	15^1	21	1	18	7	24.1	8.80	53	.339	.500	0	.000	-1	-7	-7	-0	-0.4
1940	Cle-A	0	0	—	2	0	0	0	0	3^1	3	0	1	1	10.8	2.70	156	.273	.333	0	.000	-0	1	1	0	0.0
1941	Cle-A	0	0	—	6	0	0	0	0	13^2	17	4	8	6	17.1	7.24	54	.293	.388	0	.000	-0	-5	-5	-0	-0.1
Total	5	1	0	1.000	25	0	0	0	0	49	56	5	32	21	16.7	6.80	60	.290	.399	1	.100	-1	-14	-15	-0	-0.5
Team	4	1	0	1.000	19	0	0	0	0	35^1	44	5	28	14	19.1	6.88	63	.310	.434	0	.000	-1	-9	-10	-0	-0.5

● **GEORGE KAHLER** Kahler, George Runnells "Krum" b: 9/6/1889, Athens, Ohio d: 2/7/24, Battle Creek, Va. BR/TR, 6', 183 lbs. Deb: 8/13/10

YEAR	TM/L	W	L	PCT	G	GS	CG	SH	SV	IP	H	HR	BB	SO	RAT	ERA	ERA+	OAV	OOB	BH	AVG	PB	PR	/A	PD	TPI
1910	Cle-A	6	4	.600	12	12	8	2	0	95^1	80	0	46	38	12.3	1.60	161	.237	.335	5	.143	-2	10	10	-1	0.8
1911	Cle-A	9	8	.529	30	17	10	0	1	154^1	153	1	66	97	13.5	3.27	104	.270	.360	9	.167	-2	1	3	-1	-0.1
1912	Cle-A	12	19	.387	41	32	17	3	1	246^1	263	1	121	104	14.4	3.69	92	.291	.382	9	.112	-5	-10	-8	-4	-1.7
1913	Cle-A	5	11	.313	24	15	5	0	0	117^2	118	1	32	43	11.8	3.14	97	.266	.322	2	.061	-3	-3	-1	-4	-0.9

YEAR TM/L	W	L	PCT	G	GS	CG	SH	SV	IP	H	HR	BB	SO	RAT	ERA	ERA+	OAV	OOB	BH	AVG	PB	PR	/A	PD	TPI
1914 Cle-A	0	1	.000	2	1	1	0	0	14	17	0	7	3	15.4	3.86	75	.309	.387	0	.000	-0	-2	-2	-0	-0.2
Total 5	32	43	.427	109	77	41	5	2	627^2	631	3	272	285	13.4	3.17	101	.274	.358	25	.121	-13	-4	2	-9	-2.1
● JEFF KAISER	Kaiser, Jeffrey Patrick b: 7/24/60, Wyandotte, Mich. BR/TL, 6'3", 195 lbs. Deb: 4/11/85																								
1987 Cle-A	0	0	—	2	0	0	0	0	3^1	4	1	3	2	21.6	16.20	28	.286	.444	0	—	0	-4	-4	0	0.0
1988 Cle-A	0	0	—	3	0	0	0	0	2^2	2	0	1	0	10.1	0.00	—	.286	.375	0	—	0	1	1	0	0.0
1989 Cle-A	0	1	.000	6	0	0	0	0	3^2	5	1	5	4	24.5	7.36	54	.313	.476	0	—	0	-1	-1	-0	-0.5
1990 Cle-A	0	0	—	5	0	0	0	0	12^2	16	2	7	9	16.3	3.55	110	.308	.390	0	—	0	0	1	0	0.0
Total 7	0	2	.000	50	0	0	0	2	52	68	12	46	38	20.1	9.17	43	.318	.443	0	—	0	-30	-30	1	-1.2
Team 4	0	1	.000	16	0	0	0	0	22^1	27	4	16	15	17.7	5.64	72	.303	.415	0	—	0	-4	-4	0	-0.5
● BOB KAISER	Kaiser, Robert Thomas b: 4/29/50, Cincinnati, Ohio BB/TL, 5'10", 175 lbs. Deb: 9/3/71																								
1971 Cle-A	0	0	—	5	0	0	0	0	6	8	2	3	4	19.5	4.50	85	.333	.448	0	—	0	-1	-0	0	0.0
● PAUL KARDOW	Kardow, Paul Otto "Tex" b: 9/19/15, Humble, Tex. d: 4/27/68, San Antonio, Tex. BR/TR, 6'6 ", 210 lbs. Deb: 7/1/36																								
1936 Cle-A	0	0	—	2	0	0	0	0	2	1	0	2	0	13.5	4.50	112	.167	.375	0	—	0	0	0	-0	0.0
● BENN KARR	Karr, Benjamin Joyce "Baldy" b: 11/28/1893, Mt.Pleasant, Miss. d: 12/8/68, Memphis, Tenn. BL/TR, 6', 175 lbs. Deb: 4/20/20																								
1925 Cle-A	11	12	.478	32	24	12	1	0	197^2	248	8	80	41	15.2	4.78	92	.317	.385	24	.261	4	-8	-8	2	-0.2
1926 Cle-A	5	6	.455	30	7	4	0	1	113^1	137	9	41	23	14.6	5.00	81	.291	.355	10	.222	2	-12	-12	1	-0.8
1927 Cle-A	3	3	.500	22	5	1	0	2	76^2	92	5	32	17	14.7	5.05	83	.315	.385	4	.200	1	-8	-7	2	-0.3
Total 6	35	48	.422	177	58	29	1	5	780^1	921	43	260	180	13.9	4.60	90	.303	.362	96	.245	12	-40	-39	2	-1.9
Team 3	19	21	.475	84	36	17	1	3	387^2	477	22	153	81	14.9	4.90	87	.309	.376	38	.242	6	-29	-27	5	-1.3
● DAVE KEEFE	Keefe, David Edwin b: 1/9/1897, Williston, Vt. d: 2/4/78, Kansas City, Mo. BL/TR, 5'9", 165 lbs. Deb: 4/21/17 C																								
1922 Cle-A	0	0	—	18	1	0	0	0	36^1	47	2	12	11	14.6	6.19	65	.333	.386	2	.333	1	-9	-9	-0	0.0
Total 5	9	17	.346	97	27	12	1	1	353^2	403	23	113	126	13.4	4.15	101	.294	.352	22	.206	-3	-5	2	-1	0.8
● MIKE KEKICH	Kekich, Michael Dennis b: 4/2/45, San Diego, Cal. BR/TL, 6'1", 200 lbs. Deb: 6/9/65																								
1973 Cle-A	1	4	.200	16	6	0	0	0	50	73	6	35	26	19.4	7.02	56	.349	.443	0	—	0	-18	-17	-1	-1.6
Total 9	39	51	.433	235	112	8	1	6	860^2	875	80	442	497	13.9	4.59	72	.268	.358	25	.120	-5	-108	-121	-4	-12.7
● TOM KELLEY	Kelley, Thomas Henry b: 1/5/44, Manchester, Conn. BR/TR, 6', 191 lbs. Deb: 5/5/64																								
1964 Cle-A	0	0	—	6	0	0	0	0	9^2	9	1	9	7	17.7	5.59	64	.237	.396	0	—	0	-2	-2	0	0.0
1965 Cle-A	2	1	.667	4	4	1	0	0	30	19	3	13	31	9.6	2.40	145	.186	.278	2	.222	0	4	4	-0	0.4
1966 Cle-A	4	8	.333	31	7	1	0	0	95^1	97	14	42	64	13.1	4.34	79	.264	.340	4	.143	-1	-10	-10	-1	-1.4
1967 Cle-A	0	0	—	1	0	0	0	0	1	0	0	2	0	18.0	0.00	—	.000	.500	0	—	0	0	0	0	0.0
Total 7	20	22	.476	104	45	9	1	0	408	400	38	207	234	13.4	3.75	97	.260	.349	11	.095	-6	-13	-4	-5	-1.6
Team 4	6	9	.400	42	11	2	0	0	136	125	18	66	102	12.7	3.97	87	.246	.333	6	.162	-0	-8	-8	-1	-1.0
● BOB KELLY	Kelly, Robert Edward b: 10/4/27, Cleveland, Ohio BR/TR, 6', 180 lbs. Deb: 5/4/51																								
1958 Cle-A	0	2	.000	13	3	0	0	0	27^2	29	4	13	12	14.0	5.20	70	.282	.368	1	.250	0	-4	-5	0	-0.3
Total 4	12	18	.400	123	35	7	2	2	362	374	28	152	146	13.2	4.50	90	.268	.343	16	.178	-1	-22	-18	1	-1.1
● VERN KENNEDY	Kennedy, Lloyd Vernon b: 3/20/07, Kansas City, Mo. d: 1/28/93, Mendon, Mo. BL/TR, 6', 175 lbs. Deb: 9/18/34																								
1942 Cle-A	4	8	.333	28	12	4	0	1	108	99	1	50	37	12.5	4.08	84	.244	.328	6	.200	1	-5	-8	0	-0.6
1943 Cle-A	10	7	.588	28	17	8	1	0	146^2	130	4	59	63	11.7	2.45	127	.242	.319	12	.231	1	14	11	1	1.5
1944 Cle-A	2	5	.286	12	10	2	0	0	59	66	0	37	17	15.7	5.03	66	.289	.389	2	.087	-2	-11	-11	1	-1.3
Total 12	104	132	.441	344	263	126	7	5	2025^2	2173	130	1049	691	14.4	4.67	94	.277	.363	181	.244	19	-77	-63	13	-3.3
Team 3	16	20	.444	68	39	14	1	1	313^2	295	5	146	117	12.7	3.50	93	.252	.336	20	.190	0	-2	-8	2	-0.4
● BILL KENNEDY	Kennedy, William Aulton "Lefty" b: 3/14/21, Carnesville, Ga. d: 4/9/83, Seattle, Wash. BL/TL, 6'2", 195 lbs. Deb: 4/26/48																								
1948 Cle-A	1	0	1.000	6	3	0	0	0	11^1	16	0	13	12	23.0	11.12	37	.333	.475	2	.667	1	-9	-9	0	-0.5
Total 8	15	28	.349	172	45	6	0	11	464^2	497	34	289	256	15.5	4.73	92	.275	.379	25	.208	-1	-31	-20	-2	-2.2
● JIM KERN	Kern, James Lester b: 3/15/49, Gladwin, Mich. BR/TR, 6'5", 205 lbs. Deb: 9/6/74																								
1974 Cle-A	0	1	.000	4	3	1	0	0	15^1	16	1	14	11	17.6	4.70	77	.262	.400	0	—	0	-2	-2	-0	-0.1
1975 Cle-A	1	2	.333	13	7	0	0	0	71^2	60	5	45	55	13.8	3.77	100	.233	.357	0	—	0	0	0	0	0.0
1976 Cle-A	10	7	.588	50	2	0	0	15	117^2	91	2	50	111	11.2	2.37	147	.222	.314	0	—	0	15	15	-0	2.6
1977 Cle-A★	8	10	.444	60	0	0	0	18	92	85	3	47	91	13.5	3.42	115	.260	.363	0	—	0	6	5	0	1.3
1978 Cle-A★	10	10	.500	58	0	0	0	13	99^1	77	4	58	95	12.5	3.08	121	.224	.342	0	.000	0	8	7	1	1.7
1986 Cle-A	1	1	.500	16	0	0	0	0	27^1	34	1	23	11	19.8	7.90	52	.298	.429	0	—	0	-11	-11	0	-0.6
Total 13	53	57	.482	416	14	1	0	88	793^1	670	35	444	651	13.0	3.32	115	.235	.344	0	.000	-0	48	45	2	11.1
Team 6	30	31	.492	201	12	1	0	46	423^1	363	16	237	374	13.2	3.44	109	.240	.351	0	.000	0	16	14	1	4.9
● MIKE KILKENNY	Kilkenny, Michael David b: 4/11/45, Bradford, Ont., Can. BR/TL, 6'3.5", 175 lbs. Deb: 4/11/69																								
Yr	0	0	—	2	0	0	0	0	2	1	1	0	0	4.5	4.50	67	.143	.143	0	—	0	-0	-0	-0	0.0
1972 Cle-A	4	1	.800	22	7	1	0	1	58	51	5	39	44	14.0	3.41	94	.237	.354	1	.071	-1	-2	-1	1	-0.2
1973 Cle-A	0	0	—	5	0	0	0	0	2	5	1	5	3	49.5	22.50	17	.455	.647	0	—	0	-4	-4	0	0.0
Total 5	23	18	.561	139	54	12	4	4	410	387	39	224	301	13.6	4.43	82	.248	.345	8	.070	-8	-41	-37	1	-3.6
Team 2	4	1	.800	27	7	1	0	1	60	56	6	44	47	15.2	4.05	80	.248	.373	1	.071	-1	-6	-5	1	-0.2
● ED KILLIAN	Killian, Edwin Henry "Twilight Ed" b: 11/12/1876, Racine, Wis. d: 7/18/28, Detroit, Mich. BL/TL, 5'11", 170 lbs. Deb: 8/25/03																								
1903 Cle-A	3	4	.429	9	8	7	3	0	61^2	61	1	13	18	11.4	2.48	115	.257	.307	5	.179	-1	3	3	-0	0.2
Total 8	102	78	.567	213	180	149	22	6	1598^1	1463	9	482	516	11.3	2.38	110	.245	.309	127	.209	6	36	42	-12	4.8
● ERIC KING	King, Eric Steven b: 4/10/64, Oxnard, Cal. BR/TR, 6'2", 215 lbs. Deb: 5/15/86																								
1991 Cle-A	6	11	.353	25	24	2	1	0	150^2	166	7	44	59	12.7	4.60	90	.279	.332	0	—	0	-8	-7	-2	-1.0
Total 7	52	45	.536	203	113	8	5	16	863^1	814	73	333	459	12.3	3.97	100	.249	.324	0	—	0	8	2	-3	-0.3
● DENNIS KINNEY	Kinney, Dennis Paul b: 2/26/52, Toledo, Ohio BL/TL, 6'1", 190 lbs. Deb: 4/9/78																								
1978 Cle-A	0	2	.000	18	0	0	0	5	38^2	37	3	14	19	12.1	4.42	84	.259	.329	0	—	0	-3	-3	-0	-0.2
Total 5	4	9	.308	97	0	0	0	6	154^1	153	12	71	75	13.2	4.55	78	.261	.344	1	.071	-1	-15	-17	-1	-1.4
● HARRY KIRSCH	Kirsch, Harry Louis "Casey" b: 10/17/1887, Pittsburgh, Pa. d: 12/25/25, Overbrook, Pa. BR/TR, 5'11", 170 lbs. Deb: 4/16/10																								
1910 Cle-A	0	0	—	2	0	0	0	0	3	5	0	1	5	18.0	6.00	43	.385	.429	0	—	0	-1	-1	-0	0.0
● GARLAND KISER	Kiser, Garland Routhard b: 7/8/68, Charlotte, N.C. BL/TL, 6'3", 190 lbs. Deb: 9/9/91																								
1991 Cle-A	0	0	—	7	0	0	0	0	4^2	7	0	4	3	23.1	9.64	43	.368	.500	0	—	0	-3	-3	-0	0.0
● HAL KLEINE	Kleine, Harold John b: 6/8/23, St.Louis, Mo. d: 12/10/57, St.Louis, Mo. BL/TL, 6'2", 193 lbs. Deb: 4/26/44																								
1944 Cle-A	1	2	.333	11	6	1	0	0	40^2	38	0	36	13	16.4	5.75	57	.248	.392	2	.143	-1	-11	-11	-1	-0.9
1945 Cle-A	0	0	—	3	0	0	0	0	7	8	0	7	5	19.3	3.86	84	.286	.429	1	.333	1	-0	-0	-0	0.0
Total 2	1	2	.333	14	6	1	0	0	47^2	46	0	43	18	16.8	5.48	60	.254	.397	3	.176	-0	-11	-12	-1	-0.9
● ED KLEPFER	Klepfer, Edward Lloyd "Big Ed" b: 3/17/1888, Summerville, Pa. d: 8/9/50, Tulsa, Okla. BR/TR, 6', 185 lbs. Deb: 7/4/11																								
1915 Cle-A	1	6	.143	8	7	2	0	0	43	47	0	11	13	12.1	2.09	146	.283	.328	2	.167	-0	4	5	1	0.8

YEAR	TM/L	W	L	PCT	G	GS	CG	SH	SV	IP	H	HR	BB	SO	RAT	ERA	ERA+	OAV	OOB	BH	AVG	PB	PR	/A	PD	TPI
1916	Cle-A	6	6	.500	31	13	4	1	2	143	136	0	46	62	11.7	2.52	119	.262	.327	1	.025	-4	5	8	-0	0.2
1917	Cle-A	14	4	.778	41	27	9	0	1	213	208	0	55	66	11.1	2.37	120	.264	.312	2	.032	-6	7	11	-2	0.1
1919	Cle-A	0	0	—	5	0	0	0	0	7^{1}	12	1	6	7	22.1	7.36	45	.375	.474	0	.000	-0	-3	-3	0	0.0
Total	6	22	17	.564	98	50	16	1	3	447^{2}	457	3	137	165	12.1	2.81	104	.273	.330	6	.048	-11	-2	6	-1	0.7
Team	4	21	16	.568	85	47	15	1	3	406^{1}	403	1	118	148	11.6	2.48	118	.268	.323	5	.043	-11	13	20	-1	1.1
● ED KLIEMAN	Klieman, Edward Frederick "Specs" or "Babe" b: 3/21/18, Norwood, Ohio d: 11/15/79, Homosassa, Fla. BR/TR, 6'1", 190 lbs. Deb: 9/24/43																									
1943	Cle-A	0	1	.000	1	1	1	0	0	9	8	0	5	2	13.0	1.00	311	.286	.394	0	.000	-0	2	2	-0	0.2
1944	Cle-A	11	13	.458	47	19	5	1	5	178^{1}	185	4	70	44	13.2	3.38	98	.274	.348	6	.105	-3	1	-2	1	-0.5
1945	Cle-A	5	8	.385	38	12	4	1	4	126^{1}	123	3	49	33	12.5	3.85	84	.261	.336	8	.200	1	-7	-8	3	-0.5
1946	Cle-A	0	0	—	9	0	0	0	0	15	18	0	10	2	16.8	6.60	50	.290	.389	0	.000	-0	-5	-5	-1	-0.1
1947	Cle-A	5	4	.556	**58**	0	0	0	**17**	92	78	5	39	21	11.6	3.03	115	.231	.315	2	.105	-1	7	5	2	0.7
1948	*Cle-A	3	2	.600	44	0	0	0	4	79^{2}	62	3	46	18	12.4	2.60	156	.229	.345	2	.143	-0	**15**	**13**	1	0.9
Total	8	26	28	.481	222	32	10	2	33	542	525	17	239	130	13.0	3.49	100	.261	.345	21	.146	-3	10	1	6	1.1
Team	6	24	28	.462	197	32	10	2	30	500^{1}	474	15	219	120	12.7	3.36	102	.257	.341	18	.134	-4	13	4	6	0.7
● STEVE KLINE	Kline, Steven Jack b: 10/6/47, Wenatchee, Wash. BR/TR, 6'3", 205 lbs. Deb: 7/10/70																									
1974	Cle-A	3	8	.273	16	11	1	0	0	71	70	9	31	17	13.3	5.07	71	.266	.352	0	—	0	-11	-11	1	-1.5
Total	6	43	45	.489	129	105	34	6	1	750^{1}	708	61	184	240	10.9	3.26	101	.249	.298	21	.124	-1	14	3	5	1.3
● JOHNNY KLIPPSTEIN	Klippstein, John Calvin b: 10/17/27, Washington, D.C. BR/TR, 6'1", 185 lbs. Deb: 5/3/50																									
1960	Cle-A	5	5	.500	49	0	0	0	**14**	74^{1}	53	8	35	46	10.8	2.91	129	.205	.303	2	.143	-0	8	7	0	1.2
Total	18	101	118	.461	711	161	37	6	66	1967^{2}	1915	203	978	1158	13.6	4.24	94	.258	.350	63	.125	-14	-80	-54	-0	-4.2
● ELMER KOESTNER	Koestner, Elmer Joseph "Bob" b: 11/30/1885, Piper City, Ill. d: 10/27/59, Fairbury, Ill. BR/TR, 6'1.5", 175 lbs. Deb: 4/23/10																									
1910	Cle-A	5	10	.333	27	13	8	1	2	145	145	0	63	44	13.3	3.04	85	.282	.367	15	.313	2	-8	-7	-2	-0.7
Total	2	5	10	.333	36	14	8	1	2	169^{2}	169	0	76	56	13.3	3.18	83	.279	.365	17	.315	3	-12	-10	-2	-0.6
● JOE KRAKAUSKAS	Krakauskas, Joseph Victor Lawrence b: 3/28/15, Montreal, Que., Can d: 7/8/60, Hamilton, Ont., Can BL/TL, 6'1", 203 lbs. Deb: 9/9/37																									
1941	Cle-A	1	2	.333	12	5	0	0	0	41^{2}	39	3	29	25	14.7	4.10	96	.245	.362	1	.077	-1	0	-1	1	-0.1
1942	Cle-A	0	0	—	3	0	0	0	0	7	7	1	4	2	14.1	3.86	89	.259	.355	0	.000	-0	-0	-0	1	0.0
1946	Cle-A	2	5	.286	29	5	0	0	1	47^{1}	60	2	25	20	16.2	5.51	60	.314	.394	0	.000	-1	-11	-12	1	-1.7
Total	7	26	36	.419	149	63	22	1	4	583^{2}	605	30	355	347	14.9	4.53	93	.269	.369	33	.180	2	-4	-20	-1	-1.5
Team	3	3	7	.300	44	10	0	0	1	96	106	6	58	47	15.4	4.78	75	.281	.377	1	.040	-3	-11	-13	2	-1.8
● JACK KRALICK	Kralick, John Francis b: 6/1/35, Youngstown, Ohio BL/TL, 6'2", 180 lbs. Deb: 4/15/59																									
1963	Cle-A	13	9	.591	28	27	10	3	0	197^{1}	187	19	41	116	10.4	2.92	124	.249	.288	11	.183	1	16	15	-1	1.7
1964	Cle-A☆	12	7	.632	30	29	8	3	0	190^{2}	196	17	51	119	12.1	3.21	112	.267	.322	10	.156	-1	9	8	0	0.7
1965	Cle-A	5	11	.313	30	16	1	0	0	86	106	9	21	34	13.5	4.92	71	.298	.340	3	.143	-1	-14	-14	-1	-2.5
1966	Cle-A	3	4	.429	27	4	0	0	0	68^{1}	69	9	20	31	11.9	3.82	90	.268	.324	1	.077	-1	-3	-3	1	-0.3
1967	Cle-A	0	2	.000	2	0	0	0	0	2	4	0	1	1	22.5	9.00	36	.444	.500	0	—	0	-1	-1	1	-0.9
Total	9	67	65	.508	235	169	45	12	1	1218	1238	124	318	668	11.7	3.56	108	.264	.314	62	.162	0	30	38	3	2.3
Team	5	33	33	.500	117	76	19	6	0	544^{1}	562	54	134	301	11.7	3.47	103	.267	.314	25	.158	-1	6	6	-0	-1.3
● TOM KRAMER	Kramer, Thomas Joseph b: 1/9/68, Cincinnati, Ohio BB/TR, 6', 185 lbs. Deb: 9/12/91																									
1991	Cle-A	0	0	—	4	0	0	0	0	4^{2}	10	1	6	4	30.9	17.36	24	.476	.593	0	—	0	-7	-7	-0	0.0
1993	Cle-A	7	3	.700	39	16	1	0	0	121	126	19	59	71	13.9	4.02	108	.269	.353	0	—	0	4	4	-1	0.2
Total	2	7	3	.700	43	16	1	0	0	125^{2}	136	20	65	75	14.5	4.51	96	.278	.364	0	—	0	-3	-3	-1	0.2
● GENE KRAPP	Krapp, Eugene Hamlet "Rubber Arm" b: 5/12/1887, Rochester, N.Y. d: 4/13/23, Detroit, Mich. BR/TR, 5'5", 165 lbs. Deb: 4/14/11																									
1911	Cle-A	13	9	.591	35	26	14	1	1	222	188	1	138	132	13.7	3.41	100	.232	.353	17	.230	4	-1	0	4	0.8
1912	Cle-A	2	5	.286	9	7	4	0	0	58^{2}	57	0	42	22	15.8	4.60	74	.273	.404	7	.318	1	-8	-8	2	-0.5
Total	4	40	47	.460	118	92	50	3	1	764^{1}	631	11	418	353	12.7	3.23	95	.227	.335	44	.181	-1	-19	-13	19	0.4
Team	2	15	14	.517	44	33	18	1	1	280^{2}	245	1	180	154	14.2	3.66	93	.240	.363	24	.250	5	-10	-8	7	0.3
● HARRY KRAUSE	Krause, Harry William "Hal" b: 7/12/1887, San Francisco, Cal. d: 10/23/40, San Francisco, Cal BB/TL, 5'10", 165 lbs. Deb: 4/20/08																									
1912	Cle-A	0	1	.000	2	2	0	0	0	4^{2}	11	0	2	1	25.1	11.57	29	.500	.542	0	—	0	-4	-4	-0	-0.7
Total	5	36	26	.581	85	57	39	10	2	525^{1}	446	8	146	298	10.7	2.50	107	.238	.305	36	.195	1	16	10	-9	-0.6
● RICK KREUGER	Kreuger, Richard Allen b: 11/3/48, Grand Rapids, Mich. BR/TL, 6'2", 185 lbs. Deb: 9/6/75																									
1978	Cle-A	0	0	—	6	0	0	0	0	9^{1}	6	1	3	7	8.7	3.86	97	.194	.265	0	—	0	-0	-0	0	0.0
Total	4	2	2	.500	17	4	1	0	0	44^{1}	42	4	20	20	12.6	4.47	87	.259	.341	0	—	0	-4	-3	1	-0.3
● GARY KROLL	Kroll, Gary Melvin b: 7/8/41, Culver City, Cal. BR/TR, 6'6", 220 lbs. Deb: 7/26/64																									
1969	Cle-A	0	0	—	19	0	0	0	0	24	16	3	22	28	14.3	4.13	91	.188	.355	0	—	0	-1	-1	-0	0.0
Total	4	6	7	.462	71	13	1	0	1	159^{1}	147	18	91	138	13.8	4.24	84	.244	.350	4	.125	-1	-12	-12	1	-1.1
● BUB KUHN	Kuhn, Bernard Daniel b: 10/12/1899, Vicksburg, Mich. d: 11/20/56, Detroit, Mich. BL/TR, 6'1.5", 182 lbs. Deb: 9/1/24																									
1924	Cle-A	0	1	.000	1	0	0	0	0	1	4	1	0	0	36.0	27.00	16	.667	.667	0	—	0	-3	-3	0	-1.2
● HAL KURTZ	Kurtz, Harold James "Bud" b: 8/20/43, Washington, D.C. BR/TR, 6'3", 205 lbs. Deb: 4/18/68																									
1968	Cle-A	1	0	1.000	28	0	0	0	1	38	37	2	15	16	13.5	5.21	57	.255	.345	0	.000	-0	-9	-10	-1	-0.4
● BOB KUZAVA	Kuzava, Robert Leroy "Sarge" b: 5/28/23, Wyandotte, Mich. BB/TL, 6'2", 204 lbs. Deb: 9/21/46																									
1946	Cle-A	1	0	1.000	2	2	0	0	0	12	9	0	11	4	15.8	3.00	110	.191	.356	1	.200	-0	1	0	0	0.1
1947	Cle-A	1	1	.500	4	4	1	1	0	21^{2}	22	1	9	9	13.3	4.15	84	.265	.344	1	.111	-1	-1	-2	1	-0.1
Total	10	49	44	.527	213	99	34	7	13	862	849	54	415	446	13.3	4.05	97	.260	.345	22	.086	-14	5	-12	-8	-1.6
Team	2	2	1	.667	6	6	1	1	0	33^{2}	31	1	20	13	14.2	3.74	91	.238	.349	2	.143	-1	-0	-1	1	0.0
● BOB LACEY	Lacey, Robert Joseph b: 8/25/53, Fredericksburg, Va. BR/TL, 6'5", 210 lbs. Deb: 5/13/77																									
1981	Cle-A	0	0	—	14	0	0	0	0	21^{1}	36	5	3	11	16.5	7.59	48	.371	.390	0	—	0	-9	-9	-0	0.0
Total	7	20	29	.408	284	2	1	1	22	450^{2}	464	49	139	251	12.1	3.67	103	.269	.325	2	.333	1	12	6	5	2.4
● RAY LAMB	Lamb, Raymond Richard b: 12/28/44, Glendale, Cal. BR/TR, 6'1", 175 lbs. Deb: 8/1/69																									
1971	Cle-A	6	12	.333	43	21	3	1	1	158^{1}	147	11	69	91	12.3	3.35	114	.247	.326	4	.093	-2	2	8	-2	0.5
1972	Cle-A	5	6	.455	34	9	0	0	0	107^{2}	101	5	29	64	11.0	3.09	104	.248	.299	0	.000	-1	-0	1	-1	-0.1
1973	Cle-A	3	3	.500	32	1	0	0	2	86	98	7	42	60	14.9	4.60	85	.291	.373	0	—	0	-8	-7	-0	-0.5
Total	5	20	23	.465	154	31	3	1	4	424	417	29	174	258	12.7	3.54	104	.260	.335	4	.058	-4	-1	7	-4	0.0
Team	3	14	21	.400	109	31	3	1	3	352	346	23	140	215	12.5	3.58	102	.258	.330	4	.063	-3	-6	3	-4	-0.1
● OTIS LAMBETH	Lambeth, Otis Samuel b: 5/13/1890, Berlin, Kan. d: 6/5/76, Moran, Kan. BR/TR, 6', 175 lbs. Deb: 7/16/16																									
1916	Cle-A	4	3	.571	15	9	3	0	1	74	69	1	38	28	13.4	2.92	103	.256	.354	3	.111	-1	-1	1	-2	-0.3
1917	Cle-A	7	6	.538	26	10	2	0	2	97^{1}	97	2	30	27	12.8	3.14	90	.274	.349	6	.188	-0	-5	-3	-1	-0.6
1918	Cle-A	0	0	—	2	0	0	0	0	7	10	0	6	3	20.6	6.43	47	.370	.485	1	1.000	0	-3	-3	0	0.0
Total	3	11	9	.550	43	19	5	0	3	178^{1}	176	3	74	58	13.3	3.18	92	.270	.357	10	.167	-1	-9	-5	-3	-0.9

● DAVE LaROCHE LaRoche, David Eugene b: 5/14/48, Colorado Springs, Colo. BL/TL, 6'2", 200 lbs. Deb: 5/11/70 C

YEAR TM/L	W	L	PCT	G	GS	CG	SH	SV	IP	H	HR	BB	SO	RAT	ERA	ERA+	OAV	OOB	BH	AVG	PB	PR	/A	PD	TPI
1975 Cle-A	5	3	.625	61	0	0	0	17	82^{1}	61	5	57	94	13.1	2.19	173	.210	.344	0	—	0	15	15	1	2.1
1976 Cle-A☆	1	4	.200	61	0	0	0	21	96^{1}	57	2	49	104	10.0	2.24	156	.175	.285	0	—	0	14	13	-1	1.3
1977 Cle-A	2	2	.500	13	0	0	0	4	18^{2}	15	3	7	18	10.6	5.30	74	.234	.310	0	—	0	-3	-3	-0	-0.6
Total 14	65	58	.528	647	15	1	0	126	1049^{1}	919	94	459	819	12.1	3.53	105	.239	.325	15	.246	4	26	22	-2	4.1
Team 3	8	9	.471	135	0	0	0	42	197^{1}	133	10	113	216	11.4	2.51	146	.196	.313	0	—	0	26	25	0	2.8

● FRED LASHER Lasher, Frederick Walter b: 8/19/41, Poughkeepsie, N.Y. BR/TR, 6'4", 210 lbs. Deb: 4/12/63

YEAR TM/L	W	L	PCT	G	GS	CG	SH	SV	IP	H	HR	BB	SO	RAT	ERA	ERA+	OAV	OOB	BH	AVG	PB	PR	/A	PD	TPI
1970 Cle-A	1	7	.125	43	1	0	0	5	57^{2}	57	6	30	44	14.0	4.06	98	.264	.361	0	.000	-1	-2	-1	-1	-0.3
Total 6	11	13	.458	151	1	0	0	22	202	179	18	110	148	13.2	3.88	91	.243	.347	2	.063	-2	-10	-8	0	-1.3

● BILL LASKEY Laskey, William Alan b: 12/20/57, Toledo, Ohio BR/TR, 6'5", 190 lbs. Deb: 4/23/82

YEAR TM/L	W	L	PCT	G	GS	CG	SH	SV	IP	H	HR	BB	SO	RAT	ERA	ERA+	OAV	OOB	BH	AVG	PB	PR	/A	PD	TPI
1988 Cle-A	1	0	1.000	17	0	0	0	1	24^{1}	32	0	6	17	14.1	5.18	79	.320	.358	0	—	0	-3	-3	0	-0.3
Total 6	42	53	.442	159	116	10	1	2	745^{1}	784	76	210	325	12.2	4.14	85	.272	.325	22	.105	-4	-44	-50	-2	-6.4

● BARRY LATMAN Latman, Arnold Barry b: 5/21/36, Los Angeles, Cal. BR/TR, 6'3", 210 lbs. Deb: 9/10/57

YEAR TM/L	W	L	PCT	G	GS	CG	SH	SV	IP	H	HR	BB	SO	RAT	ERA	ERA+	OAV	OOB	BH	AVG	PB	PR	/A	PD	TPI
1960 Cle-A	7	7	.500	31	20	4	0	0	147^{1}	146	19	72	94	13.7	4.03	93	.258	.348	9	.220	1	-3	-5	-1	-0.4
1961 Cle-A☆	13	5	.722	45	18	4	2	5	176^{2}	163	23	54	108	11.3	4.02	98	.244	.306	4	.073	-3	-0	-2	-3	-0.8
1962 Cle-A	8	13	.381	45	21	7	1	5	179^{1}	179	23	72	117	12.8	4.17	93	.261	.336	10	.189	2	-4	-6	-1	-0.5
1963 Cle-A	7	12	.368	38	21	4	2	2	149^{1}	146	23	52	133	12.3	4.94	73	.257	.325	8	.182	2	-22	-22	3	-2.1
Total 11	59	68	.465	344	134	28	10	16	1219	1130	142	489	829	12.3	3.91	94	.246	.325	48	.145	-1	-17	-34	-8	-6.4
Team 4	35	37	.486	159	80	19	5	12	652^{2}	634	88	250	452	12.5	4.27	89	.255	.328	31	.161	2	-28	-34	-2	-3.8

● BILL LATTIMORE Lattimore, William Hershel "Slothful Bill" b: 5/25/1884, Roxton, Tex. d: 10/30/19, Colorado Springs, Colo. BL/TL, 5'9", 165 lbs. Deb: 4/17/08

YEAR TM/L	W	L	PCT	G	GS	CG	SH	SV	IP	H	HR	BB	SO	RAT	ERA	ERA+	OAV	OOB	BH	AVG	PB	PR	/A	PD	TPI
1908 Cle-A	1	2	.333	4	4	1	1	0	24	24	0	7	5	11.6	4.50	53	.247	.298	4	.444	1	-6	-6	-1	-0.6

● RON LAW Law, Ronald David b: 3/14/46, Hamilton, Ont., Can. BR/TR, 6'2", 165 lbs. Deb: 6/29/69

YEAR TM/L	W	L	PCT	G	GS	CG	SH	SV	IP	H	HR	BB	SO	RAT	ERA	ERA+	OAV	OOB	BH	AVG	PB	PR	/A	PD	TPI
1969 Cle-A	3	4	.429	35	1	0	0	1	52^{1}	68	2	34	29	17.9	4.99	76	.325	.424	1	.143	-0	-8	-7	0	-0.9

● ROXIE LAWSON Lawson, Alfred Voyle b: 4/13/06, Donnellson, Iowa d: 4/9/77, Stockport, Iowa BR/TR, 6', 170 lbs. Deb: 8/3/30

YEAR TM/L	W	L	PCT	G	GS	CG	SH	SV	IP	H	HR	BB	SO	RAT	ERA	ERA+	OAV	OOB	BH	AVG	PB	PR	/A	PD	TPI
1930 Cle-A	1	2	.333	7	4	2	0	0	33^{2}	46	1	23	10	18.4	6.15	79	.324	.418	1	.091	-1	-6	-5	-0	-0.4
1931 Cle-A	0	2	.000	17	3	0	0	0	55^{2}	72	5	36	20	17.5	7.60	61	.304	.396	2	.143	-0	-20	-18	-1	-0.6
Total 9	47	39	.547	208	83	34	2	11	851^{2}	963	70	512	258	15.7	5.37	89	.285	.380	49	.173	-6	-67	-57	-2	-4.2
Team 2	1	4	.200	24	7	2	0	0	89^{1}	118	6	59	30	17.8	7.05	67	.311	.404	3	.120	-1	-26	-23	-1	-1.0

● BILL LAXTON Laxton, William Harry b: 1/5/48, Camden, N.J. BL/TL, 6'1", 190 lbs. Deb: 9/15/70

YEAR TM/L	W	L	PCT	G	GS	CG	SH	SV	IP	H	HR	BB	SO	RAT	ERA	ERA+	OAV	OOB	BH	AVG	PB	PR	/A	PD	TPI
1977 Cle-A	0	0	—	2	0	0	0	0	1^{2}	2	0	2	1	21.6	5.40	73	.286	.444	0	—	0	-0	-0	0	0.0
Total 5	3	10	.231	121	4	0	0	5	243^{1}	212	34	158	189	14.2	4.73	79	.236	.359	1	.200	0	-28	-26	-3	-1.8

● MIKE LEE Lee, Michael Randall b: 5/19/41, Bell, Cal. BL/TL, 6'5", 220 lbs. Deb: 5/6/60

YEAR TM/L	W	L	PCT	G	GS	CG	SH	SV	IP	H	HR	BB	SO	RAT	ERA	ERA+	OAV	OOB	BH	AVG	PB	PR	/A	PD	TPI
1960 Cle-A	0	0	—	7	0	0	0	0	9	6	1	11	6	18.0	2.00	187	.207	.439	0	—	0	2	2	-0	0.0
Total 2	1	1	.500	13	4	0	0	0	35	36	4	25	17	16.2	3.34	105	.279	.404	0	.000	-1	1	1	1	-0.1

● THORNTON LEE Lee, Thornton Starr "Lefty" b: 9/13/06, Sonoma, Cal. BL/TL, 6'3", 205 lbs. Deb: 9/19/33 F

YEAR TM/L	W	L	PCT	G	GS	CG	SH	SV	IP	H	HR	BB	SO	RAT	ERA	ERA+	OAV	OOB	BH	AVG	PB	PR	/A	PD	TPI
1933 Cle-A	1	1	.500	3	2	2	0	0	17^{1}	13	1	11	7	12.5	4.15	107	.203	.320	3	.375	1	0	1	-0	0.2
1934 Cle-A	1	1	.500	24	6	0	0	0	85^{2}	105	8	44	41	16.0	5.04	90	.308	.392	2	.095	-1	-5	-5	0	-0.2
1935 Cle-A	7	10	.412	32	20	8	1	1	180^{2}	179	6	71	81	12.7	4.04	112	.259	.331	12	.197	-1	8	9	2	0.8
1936 Cle-A	3	5	.375	43	8	2	0	3	127	138	2	67	49	14.7	4.89	103	.271	.358	5	.122	-2	**2**	2	2	0.1
Total 16	117	124	.485	374	272	155	14	10	2331^{1}	2327	121	838	937	12.4	3.56	119	.260	.326	167	.200	1	169	172	-7	16.9
Team 4	12	17	.414	102	36	12	1	4	410^{2}	435	17	193	178	14.0	4.51	104	.271	.352	22	.168	-3	6	7	4	0.9

● NORM LEHR Lehr, Norman Carl Michael "King" b: 5/28/01, Rochester, N.Y. d: 7/17/68, Livonia, N.Y. BR/TR, 6', 168 lbs. Deb: 5/20/26

YEAR TM/L	W	L	PCT	G	GS	CG	SH	SV	IP	H	HR	BB	SO	RAT	ERA	ERA+	OAV	OOB	BH	AVG	PB	PR	/A	PD	TPI
1926 Cle-A	0	0	—	4	0	0	0	0	14^{2}	11	0	4	4	9.2	3.07	132	.216	.273	0	.000	-1	2	2	1	0.0

● DUMMY LEITNER Leitner, George Michael b: 6/19/1871, Parkton, Md. d: 2/20/60, Baltimore, Md. BL/TR, 5'7", 120 lbs. Deb: 6/29/01

YEAR TM/L	W	L	PCT	G	GS	CG	SH	SV	IP	H	HR	BB	SO	RAT	ERA	ERA+	OAV	OOB	BH	AVG	PB	PR	/A	PD	TPI
1902 Cle-A	0	0	—	1	1	0	0	0	8	11	0	1	0	13.5	4.50	77	.324	.343	1	.250	0	-1	-1	0	0.0
Total 2	0	2	.000	5	3	2	0	0	32	48	0	8	4	16.6	5.34	63	.343	.391	2	.133	-1	-7	-7	0	-0.3

● BOB LEMON Lemon, Robert Granville b: 9/22/20, San Bernardino, Cal. BL/TR, 6', 185 lbs. Deb: 9/9/41 MCH♦

YEAR TM/L	W	L	PCT	G	GS	CG	SH	SV	IP	H	HR	BB	SO	RAT	ERA	ERA+	OAV	OOB	BH	AVG	PB	PR	/A	PD	TPI
1946 Cle-A	4	5	.444	32	5	1	0	1	94	77	1	68	39	13.9	2.49	133	.229	.359	16	.180	2	11	9	4	1.3
1947 Cle-A	11	5	.688	37	15	6	1	3	167^{1}	150	7	97	65	13.5	3.44	101	.242	.348	18	.321	9	5	1	4	1.6
1948 *Cle-A☆	20	14	.588	43	37	**20**	**10**	2	**293^{2}**	231	12	129	147	11.1	2.82	144	.216	.302	34	.286	14	**48**	40	8	**6.8**
1949 Cle-A☆	22	10	.688	37	33	22	2	1	279^{2}	211	19	137	138	11.4	2.99	133	.211	.309	29	.269	16	37	31	6	**5.7**
1950 Cle-A★	**23**	11	.676	44	37	**22**	3	3	**288**	281	28	146	**170**	13.4	3.84	113	.257	.345	37	.272	17	23	16	5	3.7
1951 Cle-A★	17	14	.548	42	34	17	1	2	263^{1}	244	19	124	132	12.6	3.52	108	.244	.328	21	.206	5	18	8	4	1.7
1952 Cle-A★	22	11	.667	42	36	**28**	5	4	**309^{2}**	236	15	105	131	10.1	2.50	134	**.208**	.279	28	.226	7	40	29	7	4.6
1953 Cle-A☆	21	15	.583	41	36	23	5	1	**286^{2}**	283	16	110	98	12.7	3.36	112	.262	.336	26	.232	8	20	13	8	3.2
1954 *Cle-A★	**23**	7	.767	36	33	**21**	2	0	258^{1}	228	12	92	110	11.3	2.72	135	.237	.307	21	.214	6	29	27	4	**4.1**
1955 Cle-A	**18**	10	.643	35	31	5	0	2	211^{1}	218	17	74	100	12.6	3.88	103	.266	.330	19	.244	6	2	3	2	1.1
1956 Cle-A	20	14	.588	39	35	**21**	2	3	255^{1}	230	23	89	94	11.5	3.03	139	.239	.307	18	.194	5	32	33	4	**5.2**
1957 Cle-A	6	11	.353	21	17	2	0	0	117^{1}	129	9	64	45	15.3	4.60	81	.287	.385	3	.065	-3	-11	-12	3	-1.5
1958 Cle-A	0	1	.000	11	1	0	0	0	25^{1}	41	3	16	8	20.6	5.33	68	.376	.460	3	.231	0	-4	-5	1	-0.1
Total 13	207	128	.618	460	350	188	31	22	2850	2559	181	1251	1277	12.2	3.23	119	.241	.324	274	.232	90	251	193	60	37.4

● DUTCH LEVSEN Levsen, Emil Henry b: 4/29/1898, Wyoming, Iowa d: 3/12/72, St.Louis Park, Minn. BR/TR, 6', 180 lbs. Deb: 9/28/23

YEAR TM/L	W	L	PCT	G	GS	CG	SH	SV	IP	H	HR	BB	SO	RAT	ERA	ERA+	OAV	OOB	BH	AVG	PB	PR	/A	PD	TPI
1923 Cle-A	0	0	—	3	0	0	0	0	4^{1}	4	0	0	1	8.3	0.00	—	.267	.267	0	.000	-0	2	2	1	0.1
1924 Cle-A	1	1	.500	4	1	1	0	0	16^{1}	22	0	4	3	14.3	4.41	97	.333	.371	0	.000	-1	-0	-0	0	-0.1
1925 Cle-A	1	2	.333	4	3	2	0	0	24^{1}	30	1	16	9	17.4	5.55	80	.313	.416	2	.250	0	-3	-3	-1	-0.3
1926 Cle-A	16	13	.552	33	31	18	2	0	237^{1}	235	11	85	53	12.4	3.41	119	.261	.330	17	.205	-0	16	17	-1	1.8
1927 Cle-A	3	7	.300	25	13	2	1	0	80^{1}	96	1	37	15	15.1	5.49	77	.303	.379	5	.200	-1	-12	-11	1	-1.2
1928 Cle-A	0	3	.000	11	3	0	0	0	41^{1}	39	4	31	7	15.7	5.44	76	.258	.391	0	.000	-2	-6	-6	-0	-0.6
Total 6	21	26	.447	80	51	23	3	0	404	426	17	173	88	13.6	4.17	99	.276	.354	24	.178	-4	-4	-2	1	-0.3

● DENNIS LEWALLYN Lewallyn, Dennis Dale b: 8/11/53, Pensacola, Fla. BR/TR, 6'4", 200 lbs. Deb: 9/21/75

YEAR TM/L	W	L	PCT	G	GS	CG	SH	SV	IP	H	HR	BB	SO	RAT	ERA	ERA+	OAV	OOB	BH	AVG	PB	PR	/A	PD	TPI
1981 Cle-A	0	0	—	7	0	0	0	0	13^{1}	16	1	2	11	12.2	5.40	67	.296	.321	0	—	0	-3	-3	-0	0.0
1982 Cle-A	0	1	.000	4	0	0	0	0	10^{1}	13	3	1	3	12.2	6.97	59	.310	.326	0	—	0	-3	-3	-0	-0.3
Total 8	4	4	.500	34	3	0	0	1	80^{1}	92	6	22	28	12.9	4.48	82	.287	.335	1	.077	-1	-6	-7	0	-0.4
Team 2	0	1	.000	11	0	0	0	0	23^{2}	29	4	3	14	12.2	6.08	63	.302	.323	0	—	0	-6	-6	-0	-0.3

● GLENN LIEBHARDT Liebhardt, Glenn John b: 3/10/1883, Milton, Ind. d: 7/13/56, Cleveland, Ohio BR/TR, 5'10", 175 lbs. Deb: 10/2/06 F

YEAR TM/L	W	L	PCT	G	GS	CG	SH	SV	IP	H	HR	BB	SO	RAT	ERA	ERA+	OAV	OOB	BH	AVG	PB	PR	/A	PD	TPI
1906 Cle-A	2	0	1.000	2	2	2	0	0	18	13	0	1	9	7.0	1.50	175	.206	.219	0	.000	-1	2	2	0	0.2
1907 Cle-A	18	14	.563	38	34	27	4	1	280^{1}	254	1	85	110	11.2	2.05	122	.244	.307	14	.161	-1	15	14	1	1.6
1908 Cle-A	15	16	.484	38	26	19	3	0	262	222	2	81	146	10.5	2.20	109	.235	.297	14	.175	0	6	6	1	0.7
1909 Cle-A	1	5	.167	12	4	1	0	1	52^{1}	54	0	16	15	12.2	2.92	87	.314	.376	0	.000	-2	-3	-2	-2	-0.6
Total 4	36	35	.507	90	66	49	7	2	612^{2}	543	3	183	280	10.9	2.17	114	.244	.306	28	.147	-4	21	20	0	1.9

YEAR TM/L	W	L	PCT	G	GS	CG	SH	SV	IP	H	HR	BB	SO	RAT	ERA	ERA+	OAV	OOB	BH	AVG	PB	PR	/A	PD	TPI
● DEREK LILLIQUIST Lilliquist, Derek Jansen b: 2/20/66, Winter Park, Fla. BL/TL, 6', 200 lbs. Deb: 4/13/89																									
1992 Cle-A	5	3	.625	71	0	0	0	6	61^2	39	5	18	47	8.6	1.75	223	.186	.257	0	—	0	15	15	0	2.2
1993 Cle-A	4	4	.500	56	2	0	0	10	64	64	5	19	40	11.8	2.25	192	.263	.319	0	—	0	15	15	-0	2.1
1994 Cle-A	1	3	.250	36	0	0	0	1	29^1	34	6	8	15	13.2	4.91	96	.304	.355	0	—	0	-0	-1	0	-0.1
Total 7	25	34	.424	257	52	1	1	17	480	527	58	134	260	12.6	4.11	97	.282	.333	23	.213	4	-12	-7	-4	-0.3
Team 3	10	10	.500	163	2	0	0	17	155	137	16	45	102	10.8	2.55	166	.242	.303	0	—	0	29	29	0	4.2
● LYMAN LINDE Linde, Lyman Gilbert b: 9/20/20, Beaver Dam, Wis. BR/TR, 5'11", 185 lbs. Deb: 9/11/47																									
1947 Cle-A	0	0	—	1	0	0	0	0	0^2	3	0	1	0	54.0	27.00	13	.600	.667	0	—	0	-2	-2	0	0.0
1948 Cle-A	0	0	—	3	0	0	0	0	10	9	1	4	0	11.7	5.40	75	.243	.317	0	.000	-0	-1	-1	-0	-0.1
Total 2	0	0	—	4	0	0	0	0	10^2	12	1	5	0	14.3	6.75	60	.286	.362	0	.000	-0	-3	-3	-0	-0.1
● JIM LINDSEY Lindsey, James Kendrick b: 1/24/1898, Greensburg, La. d: 10/25/63, Jackson, La. BR/TR, 6'1", 175 lbs. Deb: 5/1/22																									
1922 Cle-A	4	5	.444	29	5	0	0	1	83^2	105	4	24	29	14.2	6.02	67	.324	.376	4	.167	-1	-18	-19	-1	-1.9
1924 Cle-A	0	0	—	3	0	0	0	0	3	8	0	3	0	33.0	21.00	20	.500	.579	0	.000	-1	-6	-6	0	0.0
Total 9	21	20	.512	177	20	5	1	19	431	507	25	176	175	14.5	4.70	91	.300	.370	18	.186	-3	-23	-21	-6	-1.5
Team 2	4	5	.444	32	5	0	0	1	86^2	113	4	27	29	14.8	6.54	61	.332	.386	4	.148	-1	-24	-24	-1	-1.9
● FRED LINK Link, Edward Theodore "Laddie" b: 3/11/1886, Columbus, Ohio d: 5/22/39, Houston, Tex. BL/TL, 6', 170 lbs. Deb: 4/15/10																									
1910 Cle-A	5	6	.455	22	13	6	1	1	127^2	121	0	50	55	12.5	3.17	82	.259	.340	7	.167	-1	-9	-8	-1	-1.0
● BOBBY LOCKE Locke, Lawrence Donald b: 3/3/34, Rowes Run, Pa. BR/TR, 5'11", 185 lbs. Deb: 6/18/59																									
1959 Cle-A	3	2	.600	24	7	0	0	2	77^2	66	6	41	40	12.7	3.13	118	.233	.336	8	.333	3	6	5	0	0.7
1960 Cle-A	3	5	.375	32	11	2	2	2	123	121	10	37	53	11.7	3.37	111	.255	.311	9	.237	3	7	5	2	0.8
1961 Cle-A	4	4	.500	37	4	0	0	2	95^1	112	12	40	37	14.5	4.53	87	.300	.371	4	.211	0	-5	-6	1	-0.4
Total 9	16	15	.516	165	23	2	2	10	416^2	432	40	165	194	13.1	4.02	91	.269	.340	25	.255	8	-12	-17	4	-0.8
Team 3	10	11	.476	93	22	2	2	6	296	299	28	118	130	12.9	3.68	103	.264	.338	21	.259	7	8	4	3	1.1
● ALBIE LOPEZ Lopez, Albert Anthony b: 8/18/71, Mesa, Ariz. BR/TR, 6'1", 205 lbs. Deb: 7/6/93																									
1993 Cle-A	3	1	.750	9	9	0	0	0	49^2	49	7	32	25	14.9	5.98	72	.262	.373	0	—	0	-9	-9	-0	-0.6
1994 Cle-A	1	2	.333	4	4	1	1	0	17	20	3	6	18	14.3	4.24	111	.290	.355	0	—	0	1	1	0	0.1
1995 Cle-A	0	0	—	6	2	0	0	0	23	17	4	7	22	9.8	3.13	148	.205	.275	0	—	0	4	4	0	0.0
Total 3	4	3	.571	19	15	1	1	0	89^2	86	14	45	65	13.4	4.92	91	.254	.346	0	—	0	-4	-4	-0	-0.5
● MARCELINO LOPEZ Lopez, Marcelino Pons b: 9/23/43, Havana, Cuba BR/TL, 6'3", 210 lbs. Deb: 4/14/63																									
1972 Cle-A	0	0	—	4	2	0	0	0	8^1	8	0	10	1	19.4	5.40	60	.276	.462	0	.000	-0	-2	-2	-0	0.0
Total 8	31	40	.437	171	93	14	3	2	653	591	44	317	426	12.7	3.62	94	.243	.334	31	.171	4	-11	-15	4	-1.8
● GROVER LOWDERMILK Lowdermilk, Grover Cleveland "Slim" b: 1/15/1885, Sandborn, Ind. d: 3/31/68, Odin, Ill. BR/TR, 6'4", 190 lbs. Deb: 7/3/09 F																									
1916 Cle-A	1	5	.167	10	9	2	0	0	51^1	52	0	45	28	17.5	3.16	95	.277	.424	3	.167	-0	-2	-1	0	-0.1
Total 9	23	39	.371	122	73	30	3	0	590^1	534	4	376	296	14.4	3.58	82	.253	.375	25	.131	-8	-40	-41	5	-2.9
● JACK LUNDBOM Lundbom, John Frederick b: 3/10/1877, Manistee, Mich. d: 10/31/49, Manistee, Mich. BR/TR, 6'2", 187 lbs. Deb: 5/9/02																									
1902 Cle-A	1	1	.500	8	3	1	0	0	34	48	1	16	7	17.2	6.62	52	.333	.404	4	.267	1	-11	-12	-0	-0.6
● CHUCK MACHEMEHL Machemehl, Charles Walter b: 4/20/47, Brenham, Tex. BR/TR, 6'4", 200 lbs. Deb: 4/6/71																									
1971 Cle-A	0	2	.000	14	0	0	0	3	18^1	16	2	15	9	15.2	6.38	60	.246	.387	1	.500	0	-6	-5	0	-0.7
● SAL MAGLIE Maglie, Salvatore Anthony "The Barber" b: 4/26/17, Niagara Falls, N.Y d: 12/28/92, Niagara Falls, N.Y BR/TR, 6'2", 180 lbs. Deb: 8/9/45 C																									
1955 Cle-A	0	2	.000	10	2	0	0	2	25^2	26	0	7	11	11.9	3.86	103	.252	.306	0	.000	-0	0	0	-1	-0.1
1956 Cle-A	0	0	—	2	0	0	0	0	5	6	1	2	2	14.4	3.60	117	.300	.364	0	—	0	0	0	-0	0.0
Total 10	119	62	.657	303	232	93	25	14	1723	1591	169	562	862	11.5	3.15	127	.245	.309	76	.135	-16	156	160	-2	13.7
Team 2	0	2	.000	12	2	0	0	2	30^2	32	1	9	13	12.3	3.82	105	.260	.316	0	.000	-0	1	1	-1	-0.1
● DUSTER MAILS Mails, John Walter "Walter" or "The Great" b: 10/1/1894, San Quentin, Cal. d: 7/5/74, San Francisco, Cal BL/TL, 6', 195 lbs. Deb: 9/28/15																									
1920 *Cle-A	7	0	1.000	9	8	6	2	0	63^1	54	1	18	25	10.2	1.85	206	.230	.285	4	.200	0	14	14	-1	1.3
1921 Cle-A	14	8	.636	34	24	10	2	2	194^1	210	4	89	87	13.9	3.94	108	.283	.361	6	.094	-4	8	7	-3	0.0
1922 Cle-A	4	7	.364	26	13	4	1	0	104	122	8	40	54	14.4	5.28	76	.291	.359	5	.161	-0	-14	-15	0	-1.3
Total 7	32	25	.561	104	59	29	5	2	516	554	27	220	232	13.7	4.10	100	.277	.352	22	.133	-7	0	0	-5	-0.4
Team 3	25	15	.625	69	45	20	5	2	361^2	386	13	147	166	13.4	3.96	104	.276	.348	15	.130	-5	7	6	-4	0.0
● MORRIE MARTIN Martin, Morris Webster "Lefty" b: 9/3/22, Dixon, Mo. BL/TL, 6', 180 lbs. Deb: 4/25/49																									
1958 Cle-A	2	0	1.000	14	0	0	0	1	18^2	20	0	8	5	13.5	2.41	151	.294	.368	0	—	0	3	3	-0	0.3
Total 10	38	34	.528	250	42	8	1	15	604^2	607	56	249	245	13.1	4.29	95	.262	.341	28	.170	-6	-23	-13	1	-1.9
● DENNIS MARTINEZ Martinez, Jose Dennis (Emilia) b: 5/14/55, Granada, Nicaragua BR/TR, 6'1", 185 lbs. Deb: 9/14/76																									
1994 Cle-A	11	6	.647	24	24	7	3	0	176^2	166	14	44	92	11.1	3.52	134	.247	.301	0	—	0	25	24	0	2.0
1995 *Cle-A★	12	5	.706	28	28	3	2	0	187	174	17	46	99	11.2	3.08	150	.247	.304	0	—	0	34	32	0	2.6
Total 20	231	176	.568	610	528	120	28	6	3747^2	3601	344	1080	2022	11.5	3.60	108	.253	.311	73	.143	-3	141	113	31	14.5
Team 2	23	11	.676	52	52	10	5	0	363^2	340	31	90	191	11.1	3.29	142	.247	.302	0	—	0	59	56	0	4.6
● CARL MATHIAS Mathias, Carl Lynwood "Stubby" b: 6/13/36, Bechtelsville, Pa BB/TL, 5'11", 195 lbs. Deb: 7/31/60																									
1960 Cle-A	0	1	.000	7	0	0	0	0	15^1	14	2	8	13	12.9	3.52	106	.233	.324	0	.000	-0	1	0	0	0.0
Total 2	0	2	.000	11	3	0	0	0	29	36	5	12	20	15.2	7.14	54	.298	.366	1	.167	-0	-10	-11	0	-0.7
● JIMMY McALEER McAleer, James Robert "Loafer" b: 7/10/1864, Youngstown, Ohio d: 4/29/31, Youngstown, Ohio BR/TR, 6', 175 lbs. Deb: 4/24/1889 M♦																									
1901 Cle-A	0	0	—	1	0	0	0	0	0^1	2	0	3	0	135.0	0.00	—	.667	.833	1	.143	-0	0	0	0	0.0
● RALPH McCABE McCabe, Ralph Herbert "Mack" b: 10/21/18, Napanee, Ont., Can. d: 5/3/74, Windsor, Ont., Can. BR/TR, 6'4", 195 lbs. Deb: 9/18/46																									
1946 Cle-A	0	1	.000	1	1	0	0	0	4	5	3	2	3	18.0	11.25	29	.313	.421	0	.000	-0	-3	-4	0	-0.6
● SAM McDOWELL McDowell, Samuel Edward Thomas "Sudden Sam" b: 9/21/42, Pittsburgh, Pa. BL/TL, 6'5", 218 lbs. Deb: 9/15/61																									
1961 Cle-A	0	0	—	1	1	0	0	0	6^1	3	0	5	5	11.4	0.00	—	.136	.296	0	.000	-0	3	3	0	0.0
1962 Cle-A	3	7	.300	25	13	0	0	1	87^2	81	9	70	70	15.9	6.06	64	.243	.381	4	.154	-1	-20	-21	-0	-2.2
1963 Cle-A	3	5	.375	14	12	3	1	0	65	63	6	44	63	14.8	4.85	75	.256	.369	4	.211	0	-9	-9	-0	-1.0
1964 Cle-A	11	6	.647	31	24	6	2	1	173^1	148	8	100	177	13.0	2.70	133	.229	.336	8	.143	0	18	17	-1	1.6
1965 Cle-A★	17	11	.607	42	35	14	3	4	273	178	9	132	**325**	10.4	**2.18**	**160**	**.185**	.287	12	.126	-3	**39**	**40**	1	4.1
1966 Cle-A†	9	8	.529	35	28	8	**5**	3	194^1	130	12	102	**225**	11.0	2.87	120	**.188**	.298	12	.200	1	12	12	1	1.4
1967 Cle-A	13	15	.464	37	37	10	1	0	236^1	201	21	123	236	12.6	3.85	85	.233	.333	15	.183	1	-16	-15	-1	-1.7
1968 Cle-A★	15	14	.517	38	37	11	3	0	269	181	13	110	**283**	10.1	1.81	164	.189	.279	13	.153	0	35	34	-1	4.0
1969 Cle-A★	18	14	.563	39	38	18	4	1	285	222	13	132	**279**	10.5	2.94	128	.213	.288	16	.174	-1	22	26	-0	2.8
1970 Cle-A★	20	12	.625	39	39	19	1	0	**305**	236	25	131	**304**	11.0	2.92	136	.213	.300	13	.124	-3	27	**35**	-2	3.0
1971 Cle-A†	13	17	.433	35	31	8	2	1	214^2	160	22	153	192	13.2	3.40	113	.207	.340	13	.178	-1	2	10	-2	1.1
Total 15	141	134	.513	425	346	103	23	14	2492^1	1948	164	1312	2453	12.0	3.17	112	.215	.318	119	.154	-8	88	107	-5	10.0
Team 11	122	109	.528	336	295	97	22	11	2109^2	1603	138	1072	2159	11.6	2.99	119	.210	.311	110	.158	-6	112	132	-4	13.1

YEAR TM/L	W	L	PCT	G	GS	CG	SH	SV	IP	H	HR	BB	SO	RAT	ERA	ERA+	OAV	OOB	BH	AVG	PB	PR	/A	PD	TPI

● MARTY McHALE — McHale, Martin Joseph b: 10/30/1888, Stoneham, Mass. d: 5/7/79, Hempstead, N.Y. BR/TR, 5'11.5", 174 lbs. Deb: 9/28/10

| 1916 Cle-A | 0 | 0 | — | 5 | 0 | 0 | 0 | 0 | 11¹ | 10 | 1 | 6 | 2 | 12.7 | 5.56 | 54 | .270 | .372 | 0 | .000 | -0 | -3 | -3 | -0 | -0.1 |
| Total 6 | 12 | 30 | .286 | 64 | 44 | 23 | 1 | 1 | 358¹ | 381 | 7 | 81 | 131 | 11.8 | 3.57 | 80 | .275 | .319 | 15 | .140 | -0 | -30 | -29 | -4 | -2.7 |

● HAL McKAIN — McKain, Harold Le Roy b: 7/10/06, Logan, Iowa d: 1/24/70, Sacramento, Cal. BL/TR, 5'11", 185 lbs. Deb: 9/22/27

| 1927 Cle-A | 0 | 1 | .000 | 2 | 1 | 0 | 0 | 0 | 11 | 18 | 0 | 4 | 5 | 18.0 | 4.09 | 103 | .391 | .440 | 0 | .000 | -1 | 0 | 0 | 0 | 0.0 |
| Total 5 | 18 | 23 | .439 | 103 | 24 | 7 | 1 | 6 | 381¹ | 435 | 21 | 193 | 136 | 15.2 | 4.93 | 88 | .293 | .380 | 28 | .230 | 8 | -23 | -24 | 7 | -0.6 |

● CAL McLISH — McLish, Calvin Coolidge Julius Caesar Tuskahoma "Buster" b: 12/1/25, Anadarko, Okla. BB/TR, 6'1", 200 lbs. Deb: 5/13/44 C

1956 Cle-A	2	4	.333	37	2	0	0	1	61²	67	5	32	27	14.4	4.96	85	.282	.367	1	.111	1	-6	-5	1	-0.2
1957 Cle-A	9	7	.563	42	7	2	0	1	144¹	118	11	67	88	11.7	2.74	135	.220	.309	8	.186	3	17	16	1	2.1
1958 Cle-A	16	8	.667	39	30	13	0	1	225²	214	25	70	97	11.4	2.99	122	.251	.309	6	.094	-1	19	16	0	1.6
1959 Cle-A★	19	8	.704	35	32	13	0	1	235¹	253	26	72	113	12.6	3.63	101	.270	.326	14	.189	1	6	1	3	0.6
Total 15	92	92	.500	352	209	57	5	6	1609	1685	164	552	713	12.7	4.01	93	.270	.332	73	.149	4	-39	-50	9	-4.2
Team 4	46	27	.630	153	71	28	0	4	667	652	67	241	325	12.2	3.35	113	.255	.321	29	.153	5	37	28	5	4.1

● DON McMAHON — McMahon, Donald John b: 1/4/30, Brooklyn, N.Y. d: 7/22/87, Los Angeles, Cal. BR/TR, 6'2", 222 lbs. Deb: 6/30/57 C

1964 Cle-A	6	4	.600	70	0	0	0	16	101	67	7	52	92	10.8	2.41	150	.189	.297	2	.143	-0	14	13	-1	1.6
1965 Cle-A	3	3	.500	58	0	0	0	11	85	79	8	37	60	12.4	3.28	106	.248	.329	2	.222	0	2	2	1	0.3
1966 Cle-A	1	1	.500	12	0	0	0	1	12¹	8	1	6	5	10.2	2.92	118	.190	.292	0	.000	-0	1	1	-0	0.1
Total 18	90	68	.570	874	2	0	0	153	1310²	1054	105	579	1003	11.4	2.96	119	.221	.310	23	.137	-1	96	83	-1	10.2
Team 3	10	8	.556	140	0	0	0	28	198¹	154	16	95	157	11.4	2.81	126	.216	.310	4	.160	-1	16	16	0	2.0

● HARRY McNEAL — McNeal, John Harley b: 8/11/1877, Iberia, Ohio d: 1/11/45, Cleveland, Ohio BR/TR, 6'3", 175 lbs. Deb: 8/5/01

| 1901 Cle-A | 5 | 5 | .500 | 12 | 10 | 9 | 0 | 0 | 85¹ | 120 | 4 | 30 | 15 | 16.7 | 4.43 | 80 | .328 | .391 | 6 | .162 | -2 | -7 | -8 | -2 | -1.1 |

● GEORGE McQUILLAN — McQuillan, George Watt b: 5/1/1885, Brooklyn, N.Y. d: 3/30/40, Columbus, Ohio BR/TR, 5'11.5", 175 lbs. Deb: 5/8/07

| 1918 Cle-A | 0 | 1 | .000 | 5 | 1 | 0 | 0 | 1 | 23 | 25 | 0 | 4 | 9 | 11.3 | 2.35 | 128 | .284 | .315 | 0 | .000 | -0 | 1 | 2 | 0 | 0.1 |
| Total 10 | 85 | 89 | .489 | 273 | 173 | 105 | 17 | 14 | 1576¹ | 1382 | 23 | 401 | 590 | 10.4 | 2.38 | 114 | .241 | .294 | 55 | .117 | -14 | 62 | 59 | -9 | 4.2 |

● JOSE MESA — Mesa, Jose Ramon Nova (b: Jose Ramon Nova (Mesa)) b: 5/22/66, Pueblo Viejo, D.R. BR/TR, 6'3", 220 lbs. Deb: 9/10/87

1992 Cle-A	4	4	.500	15	15	1	1	0	93	92	5	43	40	13.3	4.16	94	.262	.346	0	—	0	-2	-3	-1	-0.2
1993 Cle-A	10	12	.455	34	33	3	0	0	208²	232	21	62	118	13.0	4.92	88	.286	.342	0	—	0	-14	-14	-0	-1.3
1994 Cle-A	7	5	.583	51	0	0	0	2	73	71	3	26	63	12.3	3.82	123	.254	.325	0	—	0	8	7	0	1.0
1995 *Cle-A★	3	0	1.000	62	0	0	0	**46**	64	49	3	17	58	9.3	1.13	412	.216	.270	0	—	0	**26**	**25**	0	**5.0**
Total 7	37	45	.451	211	95	6	2	48	708	747	61	279	406	13.3	4.55	93	.274	.345	0	—	0	-23	-27	-1	-0.4
Team 4	24	21	.533	162	48	4	1	48	438²	444	32	148	279	12.4	4.02	108	.266	.331	0	—	0	17	16	-1	4.5

● BUD MESSENGER — Messenger, Andrew Warren b: 2/1/1898, Grand Blanc, Mich. d: 11/4/71, Lansing, Mich. BR/TR, 6', 175 lbs. Deb: 7/31/24

| 1924 Cle-A | 2 | 0 | 1.000 | 5 | 2 | 1 | 0 | 0 | 25 | 28 | 4 | 14 | 4 | 15.1 | 4.32 | 99 | .283 | .372 | 1 | .125 | -0 | -0 | -0 | -0 | -0.1 |

● DEWEY METIVIER — Metivier, George Dewey b: 5/6/1898, Cambridge, Mass. d: 3/2/47, Cambridge, Mass. BL/TR, 5'11", 175 lbs. Deb: 9/15/22

1922 Cle-A	2	0	1.000	2	2	2	0	0	18	18	1	3	1	11.0	4.50	89	.265	.306	1	.167	-1	-1	-1	-1	-0.1
1923 Cle-A	4	2	.667	26	5	1	0	1	73¹	111	3	38	9	16.0	6.50	61	.368	.448	3	.150	-0	-21	-21	0	-1.5
1924 Cle-A	1	5	.167	26	6	1	0	3	76¹	110	3	34	14	17.0	5.31	81	.358	.422	3	.125	-2	-9	-9	-1	-0.9
Total 3	7	7	.500	54	13	4	0	4	167²	239	5	75	24	17.2	5.74	72	.353	.423	7	.140	-2	-31	-30	-1	-2.5

● JOHN MIDDLETON — Middleton, John Wayne "Lefty" b: 4/11/1900, Mt.Calm, Tex. d: 11/3/86, Amarillo, Tex. BL/TL, 6'1", 185 lbs. Deb: 9/6/22

| 1922 Cle-A | 0 | 1 | .000 | 2 | 1 | 0 | 0 | 0 | 7¹ | 8 | 1 | 6 | 2 | 17.2 | 7.36 | 54 | .286 | .412 | 1 | .333 | 0 | -3 | -3 | 0 | -0.3 |

● BOB MILACKI — Milacki, Robert b: 7/28/64, Trenton, N.J. BR/TR, 6'4", 220 lbs. Deb: 9/18/88

| 1993 Cle-A | 1 | 1 | .500 | 5 | 2 | 0 | 0 | 0 | 16 | 19 | 3 | 11 | 7 | 16.9 | 3.38 | 128 | .302 | .405 | 0 | — | 0 | 2 | 2 | 0 | 0.2 |
| Total 7 | 38 | 43 | .469 | 136 | 121 | 8 | 5 | 1 | 774² | 787 | 82 | 286 | 374 | 12.5 | 4.31 | 92 | .264 | .330 | 0 | — | 0 | -25 | -30 | 1 | -2.6 |

● JOHNNY MILJUS — Miljus, John Kenneth "Jovo" or "Big Serb" b: 6/30/1895, Pittsburgh, Pa. d: 2/11/76, Fort Harrison, Mont. BR/TR, 6'1", 178 lbs. Deb: 10/2/15

1928 Cle-A	1	4	.200	11	4	1	0	0	50²	46	1	20	19	11.7	2.66	156	.243	.316	3	.200	-0	8	8	-0	0.7
1929 Cle-A	8	8	.500	34	15	4	0	2	128¹	174	10	64	42	16.9	5.19	86	.331	.406	11	.256	1	-13	-11	0	-1.0
Total 7	29	26	.527	127	45	15	2	5	457¹	526	16	173	166	14.0	3.92	104	.293	.359	34	.222	0	0	7	4	1.0
Team 2	9	12	.429	45	19	5	0	3	179	220	11	84	61	15.4	4.47	97	.308	.383	14	.241	1	-6	-2	0	-0.3

● BOB MILLER — Miller, Robert Lane (b: Robert Lane Gemeinweiser) b: 2/18/39, St.Louis, Mo. d: 8/6/93, Rancho Bernardo, Cal. BR/TR, 6'1", 182 lbs. Deb: 6/26/57 C

| 1970 Cle-A | 2 | 2 | .500 | 15 | 2 | 0 | 0 | 1 | 28 | 35 | 1 | 15 | 15 | 16.1 | 4.18 | 95 | .310 | .391 | 1 | .200 | 0 | -1 | -1 | -1 | -0.2 |
| Total 17 | 69 | 81 | .460 | 694 | 99 | 7 | 0 | 51 | 1551¹ | 1487 | 101 | 608 | 895 | 12.3 | 3.37 | 105 | .255 | .328 | 33 | .110 | -8 | 38 | 31 | 18 | 5.3 |

● JAKE MILLER — Miller, Walter b: 2/28/1898, Wagram, Ohio d: 8/20/75, Venice, Fla. BL/TL, 6'2", 170 lbs. Deb: 9/11/24 F

1924 Cle-A	0	1	.000	2	1	0	0	0	12	13	0	5	4	13.5	3.00	142	.265	.333	0	.000	-1	2	2	0	0.0
1925 Cle-A	10	13	.435	32	22	13	0	2	190¹	207	4	62	51	13.1	3.31	133	.279	.340	13	.183	-3	23	23	0	2.2
1926 Cle-A	7	4	.636	18	11	5	3	1	82²	99	1	28	24	13.0	3.27	124	.307	.348	2	.083	-2	7	7	-1	0.6
1927 Cle-A	10	8	.556	34	23	11	0	0	185¹	189	4	48	53	11.8	3.21	131	.271	.324	8	.138	-4	19	21	1	1.4
1928 Cle-A	8	9	.471	25	24	8	0	1	158	203	4	43	37	14.3	4.44	93	.332	.381	7	.135	-4	-7	-5	1	-0.8
1929 Cle-A★	14	12	.538	29	29	14	2	1	206	227	7	60	58	12.8	3.58	124	.279	.334	15	.200	-3	15	20	1	2.0
1930 Cle-A	4	4	.500	24	9	1	0	0	88¹	147	6	38	31	19.3	7.13	68	.373	.433	10	.303	-1	-24	-23	2	-1.4
1931 Cle-A	2	1	.667	10	5	1	1	0	41¹	45	2	19	17	13.9	4.35	106	.273	.348	1	.077	-1	0	1	1	0.0
Total 9	60	58	.508	200	139	58	8	3	1069²	1260	33	340	305	13.8	4.09	106	.298	.355	63	.171	-19	19	30	6	2.6
Team 8	55	52	.514	174	125	54	6	3	964	1130	30	293	275	13.6	3.92	111	.298	.353	56	.169	-18	35	46	4	4.0

● AL MILNAR — Milnar, Albert Joseph "Happy" (b: Albert Joseph Mlinar) b: 12/26/13, Cleveland, Ohio BL/TL, 6'2", 195 lbs. Deb: 4/30/36

1936 Cle-A	1	2	.333	4	3	1	0	0	22	26	0	18	9	18.0	7.36	68	.286	.404	3	.300	0	-6	-6	0	-0.5
1938 Cle-A	3	1	.750	23	5	2	0	1	68¹	90	5	26	29	15.3	5.00	93	.320	.378	4	.154	-0	-2	-3	0	-0.1
1939 Cle-A	14	12	.538	37	26	12	2	3	209	212	11	99	76	13.4	3.79	116	.264	.345	20	.253	4	19	14	0	1.9
1940 Cle-A☆	18	10	.643	37	33	15	**4**	3	242¹	242	14	99	99	12.7	3.27	129	.257	.328	17	.181	-1	30	26	-3	2.1
1941 Cle-A	12	19	.387	35	30	9	1	0	229¹	236	9	116	82	13.9	4.36	90	.266	.352	14	.171	2	-5	-11	-3	-1.3
1942 Cle-A	6	8	.429	28	19	8	2	0	157	146	3	85	35	13.5	4.13	84	.251	.350	14	.171	1	-8	-12	1	-0.7
1943 Cle-A	1	3	.250	16	6	0	0	0	39	51	1	35	10	20.1	8.08	38	.329	.455	4	.211	0	-21	-22	1	-2.0
Total 8	57	58	.496	188	127	49	10	7	996¹	1043	43	495	350	14.0	4.22	98	.270	.354	79	.203	9	2	-18	-6	-1.0
Team 7	55	55	.500	180	122	47	9	7	967	1043	42	478	342	13.8	4.19	97	.268	.352	74	.195	7	8	-13	-7	-0.6

● STEVE MINGORI — Mingori, Stephen Bernard b: 2/29/44, Kansas City, Mo. BL/TL, 5'10", 170 lbs. Deb: 8/5/70

1970 Cle-A	1	0	1.000	21	0	0	0	1	20¹	17	2	12	16	13.3	2.66	149	.227	.341	0	.000	-0	2	3	0	0.2
1971 Cle-A	1	2	.333	54	0	0	0	4	56²	31	2	24	45	8.9	1.43	268	.166	.264	1	.500	0	13	15	1	1.2
1972 Cle-A	0	6	.000	41	0	0	0	10	57	67	4	36	46	16.6	3.95	91	.293	.389	1	.125	-0	-5	-5	1	-0.7
1973 Cle-A	0	0	—	5	0	0	0	0	11¹	10	3	10	5	14.3	6.17	64	.233	.377	0	—	-0	-3	-3	0	-0.3
Total 10	18	33	.353	385	0	0	0	42	584²	544	45	225	329	12.1	3.03	126	.248	.323	2	.167	-0	43	51	8	4.4
Team 4	2	8	.200	121	0	0	0	15	145²	125	11	82	112	13.0	2.97	122	.234	.340	2	.182	-0	7	10	2	0.7

YEAR TM/L	W	L	PCT	G	GS	CG	SH	SV	IP	H	HR	BB	SO	RAT	ERA	ERA+	OAV	OOB	BH	AVG	PB	PR	/A	PD	TPI
● WILLIE MITCHELL Mitchell, William b: 12/1/1889, Pleasant Grove, Miss. d: 11/23/73, Sardis, Miss. BR/TL, 6', 176 lbs. Deb: 9/22/09																									
1909 Cle-A	1	2	.333	3	3	3	0	0	23	18	0	10	8	12.5	1.57	163	.225	.340	2	.286	1	2	3	0	0.5
1910 Cle-A	12	8	.600	35	18	11	1	0	183^{2}	155	2	55	102	11.0	2.60	100	.236	.310	10	.159	-3	-2	-0	-2	-0.6
1911 Cle-A	7	14	.333	30	22	9	0	0	177^{1}	190	1	60	78	13.3	3.76	91	.284	.354	7	.109	-5	-8	-7	-1	-1.3
1912 Cle-A	5	8	.385	29	15	8	0	1	163^{2}	149	0	56	94	11.7	2.80	121	.240	.309	6	.113	-4	9	11	-3	0.1
1913 Cle-A	14	8	.636	35	22	14	4	0	217	153	1	88	141	10.3	1.91	159	.199	.288	10	.143	-2	25	27	-3	2.2
1914 Cle-A	12	17	.414	39	32	16	3	1	257	228	3	124	179	12.6	3.19	91	.238	.330	7	.086	-3	-13	-9	-5	-1.9
1915 Cle-A	11	14	.440	36	30	12	1	1	236	210	1	84	149	11.3	2.82	108	.241	.309	10	.127	-5	3	6	-4	-0.3
1916 Cle-A	2	5	.286	12	6	1	0	1	43^{2}	55	1	19	24	15.3	5.15	58	.309	.376	0	.000	-1	-11	-10	-1	-1.8
Total 11	84	92	.477	276	190	93	16	4	1632	1464	14	605	921	11.8	2.88	103	.243	.320	69	.130	-24	3	18	-23	-4.5
Team 8	64	76	.457	219	148	74	9	4	1301^{1}	1158	9	496	775	11.8	2.89	105	.241	.319	52	.121	-22	6	21	-18	-3.1
● DAVE MLICKI Mlicki, David John b: 6/8/68, Cleveland, Ohio BR/TR, 6'4", 185 lbs. Deb: 9/12/92																									
1992 Cle-A	0	2	.000	4	4	0	0	0	21^{2}	23	3	16	16	16.6	4.98	78	.280	.404	0	—	0	-3	-3	1	-0.1
1993 Cle-A	0	0	—	3	3	0	0	0	13^{1}	11	2	6	7	12.8	3.38	128	.220	.328	0	—	0	1	1	-0	0.0
Total 3	9	9	.500	36	32	0	0	0	195^{2}	194	28	76	146	12.7	4.28	97	.256	.330	2	.051	-1	-3	-3	-1	-0.4
Team 2	0	2	.000	7	7	0	0	0	35	34	5	22	23	15.2	4.37	93	.258	.376	0	—	0	-1	-1	0	-0.1
● SID MONGE Monge, Isidro Pedroza b: 4/11/51, Agua Preita, Mexico BB/TL, 6'2", 195 lbs. Deb: 9/12/75																									
1977 Cle-A	1	2	.333	33	0	0	0	3	39	47	6	27	25	17.1	6.23	63	.309	.413	0	—	0	-9	-10	-1	-0.7
1978 Cle-A	4	3	.571	48	2	0	0	6	84^{2}	71	4	51	54	13.0	2.76	135	.225	.332	0	—	0	9	9	-0	0.9
1979 Cle-A☆	12	10	.545	76	0	0	0	19	131	96	9	64	108	11.1	2.40	177	.209	.307	0	—	0	26	27	0	5.0
1980 Cle-A	3	5	.375	67	0	0	0	14	94^{1}	80	12	40	61	11.7	3.53	115	.227	.311	0	—	0	5	6	-2	0.5
1981 Cle-A	3	5	.375	31	0	0	0	4	58	58	9	21	41	12.3	4.34	83	.266	.331	0	—	0	-4	-5	-1	-0.7
Total 10	49	40	.551	435	17	4	0	56	764	708	79	356	471	12.7	3.53	107	.248	.334	2	.095	-1	25	20	-6	4.7
Team 5	23	25	.479	255	2	0	0	46	407	352	40	203	289	12.4	3.38	118	.235	.328	0	—	0	27	27	-3	5.0
● LEO MOON Moon, Leo "Lefty" b: 6/22/1899, Belmont, N.C. d: 8/25/70, New Orleans, La. BR/TL, 5'11", 165 lbs. Deb: 7/9/32																									
1932 Cle-A	0	0	—	1	0	0	0	0	5^{2}	11	0	7	1	28.6	11.12	43	.379	.500	1	.500	0	-4	-4	0	0.0
● EARL MOORE Moore, Earl Alonzo "Big Ebbie" or "Crossfire" b: 7/29/1879, Pickerington, O. d: 11/28/61, Columbus, Ohio BR/TR, 6', 195 lbs. Deb: 4/25/01																									
1901 Cle-A	16	14	.533	31	30	28	4	0	251^{1}	234	4	107	99	12.5	2.90	122	.244	.325	16	.162	-5	21	18	-4	0.9
1902 Cle-A	17	17	.500	36	34	29	4	1	293	304	8	101	84	12.7	2.95	117	.268	.331	24	.212	-0	20	16	-1	1.5
1903 Cle-A	19	9	.679	29	27	27	3	1	247^{2}	196	0	62	148	9.6	**1.74**	**164**	**.217**	.271	8	.092	-5	**34**	31	-3	2.6
1904 Cle-A	12	11	.522	26	24	22	1	0	227^{2}	186	2	61	139	10.2	2.25	113	.224	.285	12	.140	-2	9	7	-7	-0.3
1905 Cle-A	15	15	.500	31	30	28	3	0	269	232	6	92	131	11.4	2.64	100	.234	.310	10	.104	-4	1	-0	-2	-0.8
1906 Cle-A	1	1	.500	5	4	2	0	0	29^{2}	27	1	18	8	14.3	3.94	66	.245	.362	0	.000	-1	-4	-4	-1	-0.5
1907 Cle-A	1	1	.500	3	2	1	0	0	19^{1}	18	0	8	7	12.6	4.66	54	.250	.333	0	.000	-1	-5	-5	0	-0.5
Total 14	162	154	.513	388	326	230	34	7	2776	2474	57	1108	1403	12.0	2.78	110	.241	.321	134	.141	-34	88	88	-33	2.7
Team 7	81	68	.544	161	151	137	15	2	1337^{2}	1197	21	449	616	11.4	2.58	116	.239	.309	70	.141	-19	76	63	-17	2.9
● JIM MOORE Moore, James Stanford b: 12/14/03, Prescott, Ark. d: 5/19/73, Seattle, Wash. BR/TR, 6', 165 lbs. Deb: 9/21/28																									
1928 Cle-A	0	1	.000	1	1	1	0	0	9	5	0	5	1	10.0	2.00	207	.161	.278	0	.000	-0	2	2	-0	0.1
1929 Cle-A	0	0	—	2	0	0	0	0	5^{2}	6	1	4	0	15.9	9.53	47	.273	.385	0	.000	-0	-3	-3	0	0.0
Total 5	2	4	.333	46	10	3	0	1	139^{1}	147	4	49	29	12.7	4.52	97	.270	.332	4	.114	-2	-1	-2	1	0.2
Team 2	0	1	.000	3	1	1	0	0	14^{2}	11	1	9	1	12.3	4.91	87	.208	.323	0	.000	-1	-1	-1	0	0.1
● BARRY MOORE Moore, Robert Barry b: 4/3/43, Statesville, N.C. BL/TL, 6'1", 190 lbs. Deb: 5/29/65																									
1970 Cle-A	3	5	.375	13	12	0	0	0	70^{1}	70	8	46	35	15.0	4.22	94	.262	.373	2	.095	-1	-4	-2	1	-0.3
Total 6	26	37	.413	140	99	8	1	3	599^{2}	577	58	300	278	13.4	4.16	82	.256	.348	27	.151	-1	-50	-51	2	-4.6
● JACK MORRIS Morris, John Scott b: 5/16/55, St.Paul, Minn. BR/TR, 6'3", 200 lbs. Deb: 7/26/77																									
1994 Cle-A	10	6	.625	23	23	1	0	0	141^{1}	163	14	67	100	14.9	5.60	84	.292	.371	0	—	0	-13	-14	0	-1.3
Total 18	254	186	.577	549	527	175	28	0	3824	3567	389	1390	2478	11.8	3.90	104	.247	.316	0	.000	0	78	74	-4	7.1
● GUY MORTON Morton, Guy Sr. "The Alabama Blossom" b: 6/1/1893, Vernon, Ala. d: 10/18/34, Sheffield, Ala. BR/TR, 6'1", 175 lbs. Deb: 6/20/14 F																									
1914 Cle-A	1	13	.071	25	13	5	0	1	128	116	1	55	80	12.2	3.02	95	.257	.341	1	.029	-4	-4	-2	-1	-0.8
1915 Cle-A	16	15	.516	34	27	15	6	1	240	189	5	60	134	9.4	2.14	143	.216	.268	12	.146	-4	21	24	-0	2.6
1916 Cle-A	12	8	.600	27	18	9	0	0	149^{2}	139	1	42	88	11.1	2.89	104	.246	.302	12	.211	-1	-1	2	-1	0.1
1917 Cle-A	10	10	.500	35	18	6	1	2	161	158	3	59	62	12.2	2.74	103	.266	.335	4	.085	-4	-1	2	-2	-0.5
1918 Cle-A	14	8	.636	30	28	13	1	0	214^{2}	189	1	77	123	11.3	2.64	114	.240	.310	12	.156	-1	3	9	-1	0.6
1919 Cle-A	9	9	.500	26	20	9	3	0	147^{1}	128	3	47	64	10.7	2.81	119	.233	.293	9	.161	-2	7	9	-1	0.7
1920 Cle-A	8	6	.571	29	17	6	1	1	137	140	2	57	72	13.0	4.47	85	.270	.344	10	.217	-1	-10	-10	-2	-1.3
1921 Cle-A	8	3	.727	30	7	3	2	0	107^{2}	98	1	32	45	11.0	2.76	155	.244	.303	6	.171	-2	18	18	-2	1.2
1922 Cle-A	14	9	.609	38	23	13	3	0	202^{2}	218	7	85	102	13.6	4.00	100	.277	.351	13	.191	-2	1	0	3	0.2
1923 Cle-A	6	6	.500	33	14	3	2	1	129^{1}	133	3	56	54	13.3	4.24	93	.276	.354	7	.159	-2	-4	-4	-1	-0.6
1924 Cle-A	0	1	.000	10	0	0	0	0	12^{1}	12	0	13	6	18.2	6.57	65	.250	.410	0	.000	-0	-3	-3	-0	-0.3
Total 11	98	88	.527	317	185	82	19	6	1629^{2}	1520	27	583	830	11.7	3.13	108	.251	.319	86	.157	-24	27	48	-7	1.9
● DON MOSSI Mossi, Donald Louis "The Sphinx" b: 1/11/29, St.Helena, Cal. BL/TL, 6'1", 195 lbs. Deb: 4/17/54																									
1954 *Cle-A	6	1	.857	40	5	2	0	7	93	56	5	39	55	9.3	1.94	190	.176	.268	3	.158	0	**18**	**18**	-1	1.5
1955 Cle-A	4	3	.571	57	1	0	0	9	81^{2}	81	4	18	69	11.0	2.42	164	.253	.295	1	.111	0	14	14	2	1.7
1956 Cle-A	6	5	.545	48	3	0	0	11	87^{2}	79	6	33	59	11.6	3.59	117	.240	.311	3	.150	0	6	6	0	0.8
1957 Cle-A★	11	10	.524	36	22	6	1	2	159	165	16	57	97	12.7	4.13	90	.265	.329	12	.218	2	-6	-7	-1	-0.8
1958 Cle-A	7	8	.467	43	5	0	0	3	101^{2}	106	6	30	55	12.4	3.90	94	.269	.327	3	.115	-2	-1	-3	0	-0.5
Total 12	101	80	.558	460	165	55	8	50	1548	1493	156	385	932	11.0	3.43	114	.252	.299	71	.163	4	74	83	-2	7.9
Team 5	34	27	.557	224	36	8	1	32	523	487	37	177	335	11.6	3.34	114	.246	.310	22	.171	1	30	28	1	2.7
● BOB MUNCRIEF Muncrief, Robert Cleveland b: 1/28/16, Madill, Okla. BR/TR, 6'2", 190 lbs. Deb: 9/30/37																									
1948 *Cle-A	5	4	.556	21	9	1	1	0	72^{1}	76	8	31	24	13.3	3.98	102	.279	.353	2	.111	-1	2	1	-0	-0.1
Total 12	80	82	.494	288	165	67	11	9	1401^{1}	1503	108	392	525	12.3	3.80	100	.275	.325	68	.155	-10	-20	-3	-7	-2.6
● TIM MURCHISON Murchison, Thomas Malcolm b: 10/8/1896, Liberty, N.C. d: 10/20/62, Liberty, N.C. BR/TL, 6', 185 lbs. Deb: 6/21/17																									
1920 Cle-A	0	0	—	2	0	0	0	0	5	3	0	4	0	12.6	0.00	—	.200	.368	0	.000	-0	2	2	1	0.0
Total 2	0	0	—	3	0	0	0	0	6	3	0	6	2	13.5	0.00	—	.167	.375	0	.000	-0	2	2	1	0.0
● JEFF MUTIS Mutis, Jeffrey Thomas b: 12/20/66, Allentown, Pa. BL/TL, 6'2", 185 lbs. Deb: 6/15/91																									
1991 Cle-A	0	3	.000	3	3	0	0	0	12^{1}	23	1	7	6	21.9	11.68	36	.397	.462	0	—	0	-10	-10	-0	-1.7
1992 Cle-A	0	2	.000	3	2	0	0	0	11^{1}	24	4	6	8	23.8	9.53	41	.429	.484	0	—	0	-7	-7	0	-0.9
1993 Cle-A	3	6	.333	17	13	1	1	0	81	93	14	33	29	14.8	5.78	75	.289	.367	0	—	0	-13	-13	1	-1.1
Total 4	4	11	.267	58	18	1	1	0	143	191	25	61	73	16.4	6.48	66	.324	.395	0	.000	-0	-36	-35	1	-3.8
Team 3	3	11	.214	23	18	1	1	0	104^{2}	140	19	46	43	16.6	6.88	62	.321	.395	0	—	0	-31	-30	1	-3.7
● ELMER MYERS Myers, Elmer Glenn b: 3/2/1894, York Springs, Pa. d: 7/29/76, Collingswood, N.J. BR/TR, 6'2", 185 lbs. Deb: 10/6/15																									
1919 Cle-A	8	7	.533	23	15	6	1	1	134^{2}	134	3	43	38	12.5	3.74	89	.264	.334	11	.239	2	-8	-6	1	-0.3

YEAR	TM/L	W	L	PCT	G	GS	CG	SH	SV	IP	H	HR	BB	SO	RAT	ERA	ERA+	OAV	OOB	BH	AVG	PB	PR	/A	PD	TPI
1920	Cle-A	2	4	.333	16	7	2	0	1	71^2	93	1	23	16	15.1	4.77	80	.316	.374	6	.240	0	-8	-8	0	-0.6
Total	8	55	72	.433	185	127	78	8	7	1102	1148	30	440	428	13.4	4.06	80	.275	.352	93	.226	4	-102	-97	8	-9.9
Team	2	10	11	.476	39	22	8	1	2	206^1	227	4	66	54	13.4	4.10	86	.283	.348	17	.239	2	-15	-14	1	-0.9
● **CHRIS NABHOLZ** Nabholz, Christopher William b: 1/5/67, Harrisburg, Pa. BL/TL, 6'5", 210 lbs. Deb: 6/11/90																										
1994	Cle-A	0	1	.000	6	4	0	0	0	11	23	1	9	5	27.0	11.45	41	.418	.508	0	—	0	-8	-8	0	-0.6
Total	6	37	35	.514	141	100	4	2	0	611^2	542	41	278	405	12.4	3.94	96	.240	.329	19	.107	-5	-8	-9	4	-0.7
● **CHARLES NAGY** Nagy, Charles Harrison b: 5/5/67, Bridgeport, Conn. BL/TR, 6'3", 200 lbs. Deb: 6/29/90																										
1990	Cle-A	2	4	.333	9	8	0	0	0	45^2	58	7	21	26	15.8	5.91	66	.315	.388	0	—	0	-10	-10	1	-1.1
1991	Cle-A	10	15	.400	33	33	6	1	0	211^1	228	15	66	109	12.8	4.13	101	.275	.333	0	—	0	-1	1	-1	-0.1
1992	Cle-A★	17	10	.630	33	33	10	3	0	252	245	11	57	169	10.9	2.96	132	.260	.303	0	—	0	27	26	3	3.1
1993	Cle-A	2	6	.250	9	9	1	0	0	48^2	66	6	13	30	15.0	6.29	69	.322	.368	0	—	0	-11	-11	2	-1.2
1994	Cle-A	10	8	.556	23	23	3	0	0	169^1	175	15	48	108	12.1	3.45	137	.265	.320	0	—	0	25	24	0	2.2
1995	*Cle-A	16	6	.727	29	29	2	1	0	178	194	20	61	139	13.2	4.55	102	.278	.342	0	—	0	3	2	0	0.2
Total	6	57	49	.538	136	135	22	5	0	905	966	74	266	581	12.5	3.97	108	.275	.329	0	—	0	34	32	4	3.1
● **RAY NARLESKI** Narleski, Raymond Edmond b: 11/25/28, Camden, N.J. BR/TR, 6'1", 175 lbs. Deb: 4/17/54 F																										
1954	*Cle-A	3	3	.500	42	2	1	0	13	89	59	8	44	52	10.6	2.22	165	.189	.293	0	.000	-2	15	14	-1	1.1
1955	Cle-A	9	1	.900	**60**	1	1	0	**19**	111^2	91	11	52	94	11.5	3.71	108	.220	.308	7	.292	1	3	3	-2	0.3
1956	Cle-A†	3	2	.600	32	0	0	0	4	59^1	36	5	19	42	8.5	1.52	277	.170	.241	2	.250	0	**17**	**18**	-1	1.6
1957	Cle-A	11	5	.688	46	15	7	1	16	154^1	136	14	70	93	12.2	3.09	120	.235	.322	4	.093	-2	12	11	-4	0.7
1958	Cle-A★	13	10	.565	44	24	7	0	1	183^1	179	21	91	102	13.4	4.07	90	.255	.343	11	.204	1	-6	-9	-3	-1.2
Total	6	43	33	.566	266	52	17	1	58	702	606	80	335	454	12.2	3.60	106	.230	.320	26	.157	-2	19	18	-12	-0.7
Team	5	39	21	.650	224	42	16	1	53	597^2	501	59	276	383	11.9	3.22	118	.226	.314	24	.166	-1	41	37	-10	2.5
● **MIKE NAYMICK** Naymick, Michael John b: 9/6/17, Berlin, Pa. BR/TR, 6'8", 225 lbs. Deb: 9/24/39																										
1939	Cle-A	0	1	.000	2	1	1	0	0	4^2	3	0	5	3	15.4	1.93	228	.188	.381	0	.000	-0	1	1	-0	0.2
1940	Cle-A	1	2	.333	13	4	0	0	0	30	36	1	17	15	16.8	5.10	83	.290	.389	1	.167	0	-2	-3	1	-0.2
1943	Cle-A	4	4	.500	29	4	0	0	2	62^2	32	3	47	41	11.8	2.30	135	.160	.328	3	.188	-0	7	6	1	0.8
1944	Cle-A	0	0	—	7	0	0	0	0	13	16	1	10	4	18.0	9.69	34	.314	.426	0	.000	-0	-9	-9	0	0.0
Total	4	5	7	.417	52	9	1	0	2	112^1	89	5	80	64	14.0	3.93	89	.224	.362	4	.154	-1	-3	-6	1	0.8
Team	4	5	7	.417	51	9	1	0	2	110^1	87	5	79	63	14.0	3.92	89	.223	.361	4	.154	-1	-3	-5	1	0.8
● **JIM NEHER** Neher, James Gilmore b: 2/5/1889, Rochester, N.Y. d: 11/11/51, Buffalo, N.Y. BR/TR, 5'11", 185 lbs. Deb: 9/10/12																										
1912	Cle-A	0	0	—	1	0	0	0	0	1	0	0	0	0	0.0	0.00	—	.000	.000	0	—	0	0	0	-0	0.0
● **DON NEWCOMBE** Newcombe, Donald "Newk" b: 6/14/26, Madison, N.J. BL/TR, 6'4", 225 lbs. Deb: 5/20/49 ♦																										
1960	Cle-A	2	3	.400	20	2	0	0	1	54	61	6	8	27	11.5	4.33	86	.289	.315	6	.300	2	-3	-4	-1	-0.2
Total	10	149	90	.623	344	294	136	24	7	2154^2	2102	252	490	1129	11.0	3.56	114	.254	.299	238	.271	79	97	116	-6	18.9
● **HAL NEWHOUSER** Newhouser, Harold b: 5/20/21, Detroit, Mich. BL/TL, 6'2", 192 lbs. Deb: 9/29/39 H																										
1954	*Cle-A	7	2	.778	26	1	0	0	7	46^2	34	3	18	25	10.0	2.51	147	.209	.287	2	.154	-0	6	6	-0	1.3
1955	Cle-A	0	0	—	2	0	0	0	0	2^1	1	0	4	1	19.3	0.00	—	.125	.417	0	—	0	1	1	-0	0.0
Total	17	207	150	.580	488	374	212	33	26	2993	2674	137	1249	1796	11.9	3.06	130	.239	.316	201	.201	12	257	305	22	40.8
Team	2	7	2	.778	28	1	0	0	7	49	35	3	22	26	10.5	2.39	155	.205	.295	2	.154	-0	7	7	-0	1.3
● **ROD NICHOLS** Nichols, Rodney Lea b: 12/29/64, Burlington, Iowa BR/TR, 6'2", 190 lbs. Deb: 7/30/88																										
1988	Cle-A	1	7	.125	11	10	3	0	0	69^1	73	5	23	31	12.7	5.06	81	.272	.334	0	—	0	-8	-7	-0	-0.8
1989	Cle-A	4	6	.400	15	11	0	0	0	71^2	81	9	24	42	13.4	4.40	90	.285	.345	0	—	0	-4	-3	-0	-0.6
1990	Cle-A	0	3	.000	4	2	0	0	0	16	24	5	6	3	18.0	7.88	50	.343	.410	0	—	0	-7	-7	0	-1.0
1991	Cle-A	2	11	.154	31	16	3	1	1	137^1	145	6	30	76	11.9	3.54	117	.273	.319	0	—	0	8	9	-1	0.7
1992	Cle-A	4	3	.571	30	9	0	0	0	105^1	114	13	31	56	12.6	4.53	86	.273	.327	0	—	0	-7	-7	-0	-0.4
Total	7	11	31	.262	100	48	6	1	1	412^2	460	42	121	214	13.0	4.43	91	.282	.337	0	—	0	-20	-18	-1	-2.2
Team	5	11	30	.268	91	48	6	1	1	399^2	437	38	114	208	12.7	4.39	92	.278	.333	0	—	0	-18	-16	-1	-2.1
● **DICK NIEHAUS** Niehaus, Richard J. b: 10/24/1892, Covington, Ky. d: 3/12/57, Atlanta, Ga. BL/TL, 5'11", 165 lbs. Deb: 9/9/13																										
1920	Cle-A	1	2	.333	19	3	0	0	2	40	42	0	16	12	13.3	3.60	106	.269	.341	4	.444	2	1	1	-1	0.1
Total	4	4	5	.444	45	9	3	0	2	126^2	128	4	59	43	13.4	3.77	85	.268	.351	8	.235	2	-8	-8	-1	-0.4
● **PHIL NIEKRO** Niekro, Philip Henry b: 4/1/39, Blaine, Ohio BR/TR, 6'1", 180 lbs. Deb: 4/15/64 F																										
1986	Cle-A	11	11	.500	34	32	5	0	0	210^1	241	24	95	81	14.6	4.32	96	.287	.363	0	—	0	-3	-4	-1	-0.4
1987	Cle-A	7	11	.389	22	22	2	0	0	123^2	142	18	53	57	14.5	5.89	77	.286	.359	0	—	0	-20	-19	0	-2.2
Total	24	318	274	.537	864	716	245	45	29	5404^1	5044	482	1809	3342	11.6	3.35	115	.247	.312	260	.169	-6	192	299	28	35.4
Team	2	18	22	.450	56	54	7	0	0	334	383	42	148	138	14.6	4.90	87	.286	.362	0	—	0	-23	-23	-0	-2.6
● **AL NIPPER** Nipper, Albert Samuel b: 4/2/59, San Diego, Cal. BR/TR, 6', 194 lbs. Deb: 9/6/83 C																										
1990	Cle-A	2	3	.400	9	5	0	0	0	24	35	2	19	12	21.0	6.75	58	.354	.467	0	—	0	-8	-8	-0	-1.3
Total	7	46	50	.479	144	124	21	0	1	797^2	846	97	303	381	13.3	4.52	93	.271	.342	2	.087	-1	-37	-28	7	-3.6
● **RON NISCHWITZ** Nischwitz, Ronald Lee b: 7/1/37, Dayton, Ohio BB/TL, 6'3", 205 lbs. Deb: 9/4/61																										
1963	Cle-A	0	2	.000	14	0	0	0	1	16^2	17	3	8	10	13.5	6.48	56	.262	.342	0	.000	-0	-5	-5	0	-0.7
Total	4	5	8	.385	88	1	0	0	6	115^1	124	12	48	58	13.5	4.21	92	.278	.349	5	.278	1	-5	-4	0	-0.5
● **DICKIE NOLES** Noles, Dickie Ray b: 11/19/56, Charlotte, N.C. BR/TR, 6'2", 190 lbs. Deb: 7/5/79																										
1986	Cle-A	3	2	.600	32	0	0	0	0	54^2	56	9	30	32	15.0	5.10	81	.269	.374	0	—	0	-6	-6	0	-0.4
Total	11	36	53	.404	277	96	3	3	11	860	909	66	338	455	13.4	4.56	86	.272	.345	24	.136	-3	-75	-61	-2	-8.9
● **PAUL O'DEA** O'Dea, Paul "Lefty" b: 7/3/20, Cleveland, Ohio d: 12/11/78, Cleveland, Ohio BL/TL, 6', 200 lbs. Deb: 4/19/44 ♦																										
1944	Cle-A	0	0	—	3	0	0	0	0	4^1	5	0	6	0	22.8	2.08	159	.333	.524	55	.318	1	1	1	-0	0.0
1945	Cle-A	0	0	—	1	0	0	0	0	2	4	0	2	0	27.0	13.50	24	.400	.500	52	.235	0	-2	-2	0	0.0
Total	2	0	0	—	4	0	0	0	0	6^1	9	0	8	0	24.2	5.68	58	.360	.515	107	.272	1	-2	-2	-0	0.0
● **TED ODENWALD** Odenwald, Theodore Joseph "Lefty" b: 1/4/02, Hudson, Wis. d: 10/23/65, Shakopee, Minn. BR/TL, 5'10", 147 lbs. Deb: 4/13/21																										
1921	Cle-A	1	0	1.000	10	0	0	0	0	17^1	16	0	6	4	11.9	1.56	274	.262	.338	0	.000	-1	5	5	0	0.2
1922	Cle-A	0	0	—	1	0	0	0	0	1^1	6	0	2	2	54.0	40.50	10	.600	.667	0	—	0	-5	-5	0	0.0
Total	2	1	0	1.000	11	0	0	0	0	18^2	22	0	8	6	14.9	4.34	98	.310	.387	0	.000	-1	-0	-0	0	0.2
● **BLUE MOON ODOM** Odom, Johnny Lee b: 5/29/45, Macon, Ga. BR/TR, 6', 185 lbs. Deb: 9/5/64 ♦																										
1975	Cle-A	1	0	1.000	3	1	1	1	0	10^1	4	1	8	10	10.5	2.61	145	.118	.286	0	—	0	1	1	-0	0.1
Total	13	84	85	.497	295	229	40	15	1	1509	1362	103	788	857	13.0	3.70	89	.244	.341	79	.195	26	-45	-71	5	-5.8
● **JOHN O'DONOGHUE** O'Donoghue, John Eugene b: 10/7/39, Kansas City, Mo. BR/TL, 6'3", 210 lbs. Deb: 9/29/63 F																										
1966	Cle-A	6	8	.429	32	13	2	0	0	108	109	13	23	49	11.2	3.83	90	.264	.306	5	.152	-0	-5	-5	1	-0.5
1967	Cle-A	8	9	.471	33	17	5	2	2	130^2	120	10	33	81	10.7	3.24	101	.247	.298	4	.100	-0	-0	0	3	0.4
Total	9	39	55	.415	257	96	13	4	10	751	780	78	260	377	12.6	4.07	87	.269	.332	35	.170	2	-49	-44	4	-4.2
Team	2	14	17	.452	65	30	7	2	2	238^2	229	23	56	130	10.9	3.51	95	.255	.301	9	.123	-1	-5	-4	4	-0.1

YEAR	TM/L	W	L	PCT	G	GS	CG	SH	SV	IP	H	HR	BB	SO	RAT	ERA	ERA+	OAV	OOB	BH	AVG	PB	PR	/A	PD	TPI
● **BRYAN OELKERS**	Oelkers, Bryan Alois b: 3/11/61, Zaragoza, Spain BL/TL, 6'3", 192 lbs. Deb: 4/9/83																									
1986	Cle-A	3	3	.500	35	4	0	0	1	69	70	13	40	33	15.1	4.70	88	.262	.371	0	—	0	-4	-4	-1	-0.3
Total	2	3	8	.273	45	12	0	0	1	103^1	126	20	57	46	16.5	6.01	70	.303	.395	0	—	0	-21	-21	-2	-2.5
● **CHAD OGEA**	Ogea, Chad Wayne b: 11/9/70, Lake Charles, La. BR/TR, 6'2", 200 lbs. Deb: 5/3/94																									
1994	Cle-A	0	1	.000	4	1	0	0	0	16^1	21	2	10	11	17.6	6.06	78	.304	.400	0	—	0	-2	-2	0	-0.1
1995	*Cle-A	8	3	.727	20	14	1	0	0	106^1	95	11	29	57	10.6	3.05	152	.233	.286	0	—	0	20	19	0	1.7
Total	2	8	4	.667	24	15	1	0	0	122^2	116	13	39	68	11.5	3.45	135	.244	.304	0	—	0	17	16	0	1.6
● **BOB OJEDA**	Ojeda, Robert Michael b: 12/17/57, Los Angeles, Cal. BL/TL, 6'1", 190 lbs. Deb: 7/13/80																									
1993	Cle-A	2	1	.667	9	7	0	0	0	43	48	5	21	27	14.4	4.40	98	.289	.369	0	—	0	-0	-0	1	0.1
Total	15	115	98	.540	351	291	41	16	1	1884^1	1833	145	676	1128	12.1	3.65	103	.257	.323	44	.127	-4	30	24	10	2.5
● **STEVE OLIN**	Olin, Steven Robert b: 10/4/65, Portland, Ore. d: 3/22/93, Little Lake Nellie, Fla. BR/TR, 6'3", 185 lbs. Deb: 7/29/89																									
1989	Cle-A	1	4	.200	25	0	0	0	1	36	35	1	14	24	12.3	3.75	106	.255	.325	0	—	0	1	1	0	0.1
1990	Cle-A	4	4	.500	50	1	0	0	1	92^1	96	3	26	64	12.5	3.41	115	.270	.331	0	—	0	5	5	2	0.7
1991	Cle-A	3	6	.333	48	0	0	0	17	56^1	61	2	23	38	13.6	3.36	124	.274	.344	0	—	0	5	5	0	1.1
1992	Cle-A	8	5	.615	72	0	0	0	29	88^1	80	8	27	47	11.3	2.34	167	.248	.314	0	—	0	16	15	1	3.5
Total	4	16	19	.457	195	1	0	0	48	273	272	14	90	173	12.3	3.10	128	.262	.328	0	—	0	26	26	3	5.4
● **GREGG OLSON**	Olson, Greggory William b: 10/11/66, Scribner, Neb. BR/TR, 6'4", 210 lbs. Deb: 9/2/88																									
1995	Cle-A	0	0	—	3	0	0	0	0	2^2	5	1	2	0	23.6	13.50	34	.417	.500	0	—	0	-3	-3	0	0.0
Total	8	20	26	.435	359	0	0	0	164	398	328	15	190	378	11.8	2.67	151	.225	.317	0	.000	0	62	61	1	13.7
● **JESSE OROSCO**	Orosco, Jesse Russell b: 4/21/57, Santa Barbara, Cal. BR/TL, 6'2", 185 lbs. Deb: 4/5/79																									
1989	Cle-A	3	4	.429	69	0	0	0	3	78	54	7	26	79	9.5	2.08	191	.198	.272	0	—	0	16	16	1	1.6
1990	Cle-A	5	4	.556	55	0	0	0	2	64^2	58	9	38	55	13.4	3.90	101	.239	.342	0	—	0	0	0	1	0.1
1991	Cle-A	2	0	1.000	47	0	0	0	0	45^2	52	4	15	36	13.4	3.74	111	.286	.343	0	—	0	2	2	-1	0.0
Total	16	71	68	.511	819	4	0	0	133	1021^1	825	79	432	920	11.3	2.96	129	.222	.307	10	.169	2	102	97	4	16.7
Team	3	10	8	.556	171	0	0	0	5	188^1	164	20	79	170	11.8	3.11	129	.235	.315	0	—	0	17	19	2	1.7
● **HARRY OTIS**	Otis, Harry George "Cannonball" b: 10/5/1886, W.New York, N.J. d: 1/29/76, Teaneck, N.J. BR/TL, 6' ", 180 lbs. Deb: 9/5/09																									
1909	Cle-A	2	2	.500	5	3	0	0	0	26^1	26	0	18	6	16.1	1.37	187	.283	.416	1	.111	-0	3	3	-0	0.5
● **DAVE OTTO**	Otto, David Alan b: 11/12/64, Chicago, Ill. BL/TL, 6'7", 210 lbs. Deb: 9/8/87																									
1991	Cle-A	2	8	.200	18	14	1	0	0	100	108	7	27	47	12.5	4.23	98	.283	.337	0	—	0	-2	-1	-0	-0.1
1992	Cle-A	5	9	.357	18	16	0	0	0	80^1	110	12	33	32	16.1	7.06	55	.333	.396	0	—	0	-28	-28	0	-3.9
Total	8	10	22	.313	109	41	1	0	0	318^1	377	33	122	144	14.4	5.06	80	.303	.369	4	.200	1	-35	-36	0	-4.3
Team	2	7	17	.292	36	30	1	0	0	180^1	218	19	60	79	14.1	5.49	74	.306	.364	0	—	0	-29	-29	0	-4.0
● **BOB OWCHINKO**	Owchinko, Robert Dennis b: 1/1/55, Detroit, Mich. BL/TL, 6'2", 195 lbs. Deb: 9/25/76																									
1980	Cle-A	2	9	.182	29	14	1	1	0	114^1	138	13	47	66	14.7	5.27	77	.301	.368	0	—	0	-16	-15	-0	-1.3
Total	10	37	60	.381	275	104	10	4	7	890^2	937	88	363	490	13.2	4.28	85	.274	.345	22	.135	-0	-49	-66	-5	-7.0
● **PAT PAIGE**	Paige, George Lynn "Piggy" (b: George Lynn Page) b: 5/5/1882, Paw Paw, Mich. d: 6/8/39, Berlin, Wis. BL/TR, 5'10", 175 lbs. Deb: 5/20/11																									
1911	Cle-A	1	0	1.000	2	1	1	0	0	16	21	0	7	6	15.8	4.50	76	.339	.406	1	.143	-0	-2	-2	1	-0.1
● **SATCHEL PAIGE**	Paige, Leroy Robert b: 7/7/06, Mobile, Ala. d: 6/8/82, Kansas City, Mo. BR/TR, 6'3.5", 180 lbs. Deb: 7/9/48 CH																									
1948	*Cle-A	6	1	.857	21	7	3	2	1	72^2	61	2	25	45	10.8	2.48	164	.228	.297	2	.087	-2	15	13	-0	0.9
1949	Cle-A	4	7	.364	31	5	1	0	5	83	70	4	33	54	11.3	3.04	131	.230	.308	1	.063	-1	11	9	-1	1.0
Total	6	28	31	.475	179	26	7	4	32	476	429	29	183	290	11.7	3.29	124	.241	.314	12	.097	-10	37	42	-3	3.8
Team	2	10	8	.556	52	12	4	2	6	155^2	131	6	58	99	11.0	2.78	145	.229	.303	3	.077	-4	25	22	-1	1.9
● **LOWELL PALMER**	Palmer, Lowell Raymond b: 8/18/47, Sacramento, Cal. BR/TR, 6'1", 190 lbs. Deb: 6/21/69																									
1972	Cle-A	0	0	—	1	0	0	0	0	2	2	0	2	3	18.0	4.50	71	.222	.364	0	—	0	-0	-0	-0	0.0
Total	5	5	18	.217	106	25	2	1	0	316^2	302	41	202	239	15.0	5.29	69	.255	.374	10	.122	-0	-55	-57	-1	-3.8
● **FRANK PAPISH**	Papish, Frank Richard "Pap" b: 10/21/17, Pueblo, Colo. d: 8/30/65, Pueblo, Colo. BR/TL, 6'2", 192 lbs. Deb: 5/8/45																									
1949	Cle-A	1	0	1.000	25	3	1	0	1	62	54	2	39	23	13.5	3.19	125	.240	.352	1	.125	0	7	5	0	0.1
Total	6	26	29	.473	149	64	18	3	9	581	541	26	319	255	13.4	3.58	103	.249	.346	25	.154	-5	12	7	0	0.4
● **HARRY PARKER**	Parker, Harry William b: 9/14/47, Highland, Ill. BR/TR, 6'3", 190 lbs. Deb: 8/8/70																									
1976	Cle-A	0	0	—	3	0	0	0	0	7	3	0	0	5	3.9	0.00	—	.136	.136	0	—	0	3	3	0	0.0
Total	6	15	21	.417	124	30	1	0	12	315^1	315	24	128	172	12.8	3.85	94	.258	.332	6	.086	-3	-7	-8	-1	-1.4
● **CAMILO PASCUAL**	Pascual, Camilo Alberto (Lus) "Little Potato" b: 1/20/34, Havana, Cuba BR/TR, 5'11", 185 lbs. Deb: 4/15/54 FC																									
1971	Cle-A	2	2	.500	9	1	0	0	0	23^1	17	0	11	20	11.2	3.09	124	.205	.305	3	.600	1	1	2	1	0.5
Total	18	174	170	.506	529	404	132	36	10	2930^2	2703	256	1069	2167	11.8	3.63	103	.244	.314	198	.205	29	26	38	18	10.9
● **MIKE PAUL**	Paul, Michael George b: 4/18/45, Detroit, Mich. BL/TL, 6', 183 lbs. Deb: 5/27/68 C																									
1968	Cle-A	5	8	.385	36	7	0	0	3	91^2	72	11	35	87	11.0	3.93	75	.213	.296	4	.167	0	-10	-10	-1	-1.6
1969	Cle-A	5	10	.333	47	12	0	0	2	117^1	104	12	54	98	12.3	3.61	104	.241	.328	0	.000	-3	0	2	-1	-0.1
1970	Cle-A	2	8	.200	30	15	1	0	0	88	91	13	45	70	13.9	4.81	82	.271	.357	4	.154	-1	-11	-8	-2	-1.1
1971	Cle-A	2	7	.222	17	12	1	0	0	62	78	8	14	33	14.1	5.95	64	.318	.367	1	.053	-1	-17	-15	-1	-2.1
Total	7	27	48	.360	228	77	5	1	8	627^2	619	60	246	452	12.7	3.91	89	.260	.334	17	.115	-4	-35	-30	-4	-5.9
Team	4	14	33	.298	130	46	2	0	5	359	345	44	148	288	12.7	4.39	82	.255	.334	9	.094	-4	-37	-31	-4	-4.9
● **MIKE PAXTON**	Paxton, Michael De Wayne b: 9/3/53, Memphis, Tenn. BR/TR, 5'11", 190 lbs. Deb: 5/25/77																									
1978	Cle-A	12	11	.522	33	27	5	2	1	191	179	13	63	96	11.8	3.86	97	.247	.314	0	—	0	-2	-3	-1	-0.3
1979	Cle-A	8	8	.500	33	24	3	0	0	159^2	210	14	52	70	14.9	5.92	72	.315	.366	0	—	0	-30	-30	0	-2.5
1980	Cle-A	0	0	—	4	0	0	0	0	7^2	13	4	6	6	22.3	12.91	32	.394	.487	0	—	0	-8	-8	-0	0.0
Total	4	30	24	.556	99	63	10	3	1	466^1	536	38	146	230	13.4	4.71	87	.289	.345	0	—	0	-37	-32	-2	-2.6
Team	3	20	19	.513	70	51	8	2	1	358^1	402	31	121	172	13.4	4.97	80	.282	.342	0	—	0	-40	-40	-1	-2.8
● **ALEX PEARSON**	Pearson, Alexander Franklin b: 3/9/1877, Greensboro, Pa. d: 10/30/66, Rochester, Pa. BR/TR, 5'10.5", 160 lbs. Deb: 8/1/02																									
1903	Cle-A	1	2	.333	4	3	2	0	0	30^1	34	1	3	12	11.3	3.56	80	.281	.304	1	.083	-1	-2	-2	0	-0.3
Total	2	3	8	.273	15	13	10	0	0	112^1	124	1	25	36	12.3	3.85	72	.279	.323	10	.217	-0	-13	-13	-0	-1.2
● **MONTE PEARSON**	Pearson, Montgomery Marcellus "Hoot" b: 9/2/09, Oakland, Cal. d: 1/27/78, Fresno, Cal. BR/TR, 6', 175 lbs. Deb: 4/22/32																									
1932	Cle-A	0	0	—	8	0	0	0	0	8	10	1	11	5	23.6	10.13	47	.323	.500	0	—	0	-5	-5	1	0.1
1933	Cle-A	10	5	.667	19	16	10	0	0	135^1	111	5	55	54	11.0	2.33	191	.221	.297	13	.260	1	29	32	-1	3.3
1934	Cle-A	18	13	.581	39	33	19	0	2	254^2	257	16	130	140	13.7	4.52	101	.260	.346	25	.272	6	-1	1	1	0.7
1935	Cle-A	8	13	.381	30	24	10	1	0	181^2	199	9	103	90	15.0	4.90	92	.279	.371	11	.177	-0	-9	-8	2	-0.6
Total	10	100	61	.621	224	191	94	5	4	1429^2	1392	82	740	703	13.5	4.00	112	.256	.346	117	.228	19	95	75	8	9.5
Team	4	36	31	.537	96	73	39	1	2	579^2	577	31	299	289	13.6	4.21	107	.258	.346	49	.240	7	15	20	3	3.5

YEAR TM/L	W	L	PCT	G	GS	CG	SH	SV	IP	H	HR	BB	SO	RAT	ERA	ERA+	OAV	OOB	BH	AVG	PB	PR	/A	PD	TPI
● ORLANDO PENA Pena, Orlando Gregorio (Quevara) b: 11/17/33, Victoria De Las Tunas, Cuba BR/TR, 5'11", 154 lbs. Deb: 8/24/58																									
1967 Cle-A	0	3	.000	48	1	0	0	8	88^1	67	8	22	72	9.2	3.36	97	.208	.261	0	.000	-1	-1	-1	-0	-0.2
Total 14	56	77	.421	427	93	21	4	40	1202	1175	151	352	818	11.6	3.71	102	.255	.312	36	.136	-3	-7	8	-6	1.2
● KEN PENNER Penner, Kenneth William b: 4/24/1896, Boonville, Ind. d: 5/28/59, Sacramento, Cal. BL/TR, 5'11.5", 170 lbs. Deb: 9/11/16																									
1916 Cle-A	1	0	1.000	4	2	0	0	0	12^2	14	0	4	5	12.8	4.26	71	.304	.360	0	.000	-0	-2	-2	1	-0.1
Total 2	1	1	.500	9	2	0	0	0	25^1	28	1	10	8	13.5	3.55	108	.292	.358	1	.167	-0	1	1	1	0.1
● JON PERLMAN Perlman, Jonathan Samuel b: 12/13/56, Dallas, Tex. BL/TR, 6'3", 185 lbs. Deb: 9/6/85																									
1988 Cle-A	0	2	.000	10	0	0	0	0	19^2	25	0	11	10	16.5	5.49	75	.309	.391	0	—	0	-3	-3	1	-0.3
Total 3	1	2	.333	26	0	0	0	0	39^2	46	4	23	17	15.9	6.35	63	.295	.389	0	.000	-0	-11	-10	1	-1.0
● BILL PERRIN Perrin, William Joseph "Lefty" b: 6/23/10, New Orleans, La. d: 6/30/74, New Orleans, La. BR/TL, 5'11", 172 lbs. Deb: 9/30/34																									
1934 Cle-A	0	1	.000	1	1	0	0	0	5	13	0	2	3	28.8	14.40	32	.520	.571	0	.000	-0	-6	-5	0	-0.7
● GAYLORD PERRY Perry, Gaylord Jackson b: 9/15/38, Williamston, N.C. BR/TR, 6'4", 215 lbs. Deb: 4/14/62 FH																									
1972 Cle-A★	**24**	16	.600	41	40	**29**	5	1	342^2	253	17	82	234	9.1	1.92	168	.205	.261	17	.155	0	**44**	**49**	2	**7.0**
1973 Cle-A	19	19	.500	41	41	**29**	7	0	344	315	34	115	238	11.4	3.38	116	.246	.311	0	—	0	17	21	1	2.3
1974 Cle-A★	21	13	.618	37	37	28	4	0	322^1	230	25	99	216	9.4	2.51	**144**	.204	.272	0	—	0	40	**39**	1	4.4
1975 Cle-A	6	9	.400	15	15	10	1	0	121^2	120	16	34	85	11.5	3.55	106	.256	.308	0	—	0	3	3	1	0.5
Total 22	314	265	.542	777	690	303	53	11	5350^1	4938	399	1379	3534	10.8	3.11	117	.245	.297	141	.131	-16	311	305	21	34.4
Team 4	70	57	.551	134	133	96	17	1	1130^2	918	92	330	773	10.1	2.71	133	.223	.285	17	.155	0	103	113	6	14.2
● JIM PERRY Perry, James Evan b: 10/30/35, Williamston, N.C. BB/TR, 6'4", 200 lbs. Deb: 4/23/59 F																									
1959 Cle-A	12	10	.545	44	13	8	2	4	153	122	10	55	79	10.5	2.65	139	.225	.298	15	.300	3	21	18	-0	2.8
1960 Cle-A	**18**	10	**.643**	41	36	10	**4**	1	261^1	257	35	91	120	12.1	3.62	103	.260	.324	22	.242	3	7	4	0	0.6
1961 Cle-A☆	10	17	.370	35	35	6	1	0	223^2	238	28	87	90	13.3	4.71	84	.273	.343	12	.164	-1	-17	-19	-0	-2.1
1962 Cle-A	12	12	.500	35	27	7	3	0	193^2	213	21	59	74	12.7	4.14	94	.285	.339	11	.183	0	-4	-6	1	-0.5
1963 Cle-A	0	0	—	5	0	0	0	0	10^1	12	0	2	7	12.2	5.23	69	.293	.326	0	.000	-0	-2	-2	0	0.0
1974 Cle-A	17	12	.586	36	36	8	3	0	252	242	11	64	71	11.1	2.96	122	.254	.304	0	—	0	18	18	-1	2.0
1975 Cle-A	1	6	.143	8	6	0	0	0	37^2	46	8	18	11	15.3	6.69	57	.309	.383	0	—	0	-12	-12	0	-1.8
Total 17	215	174	.553	630	447	109	32	10	3285^2	3127	308	998	1576	11.5	3.45	106	.252	.312	177	.199	23	61	75	-7	9.7
Team 7	70	67	.511	204	153	39	13	5	1131^2	1130	113	376	452	12.1	3.76	100	.263	.325	60	.217	5	12	1	1	1.0
● FRITZ PETERSON Peterson, Fritz Fred (b: Fred Ingels Peterson) b: 2/8/42, Chicago, Ill. BB/TL, 6', 200 lbs. Deb: 4/15/66																									
1974 Cle-A	9	14	.391	29	29	3	0	0	152^2	187	16	37	52	13.4	4.36	83	.305	.349	0	—	0	-13	-13	1	-1.6
1975 Cle-A	14	8	.636	25	25	6	2	0	146^1	154	15	40	47	12.3	3.94	96	.275	.331	0	—	0	-3	-3	1	-0.3
1976 Cle-A	0	3	.000	9	9	0	0	0	47	59	3	10	19	13.2	5.55	63	.309	.343	0	—	0	-11	-11	-0	-0.6
Total 11	133	131	.504	355	330	90	20	1	2218^1	2217	173	426	1015	10.9	3.30	101	.261	.300	82	.159	8	40	10	15	4.1
Team 3	23	25	.479	63	63	9	2	0	346	400	34	87	118	12.9	4.34	84	.293	.340	0	—	0	-26	-26	1	-2.5
● JESSE PETTY Petty, Jesse Lee "The Silver Fox" b: 11/23/1894, Orr, Okla. d: 10/23/71, St.Paul, Minn. BR/TL, 6', 195 lbs. Deb: 4/14/21																									
1921 Cle-A	0	0	—	4	0	0	0	0	9	10	0	0	0	10.0	2.00	213	.345	.345	0	.000	-0	2	2	1	0.0
Total 7	67	78	.462	207	154	76	6	4	1208^1	1286	77	296	407	11.9	3.68	113	.275	.320	53	.128	-25	63	63	-14	2.3
● TOM PHILLIPS Phillips, Thomas Gerald b: 4/5/1889, Philipsburg, Pa. d: 4/12/29, Philipsburg, Pa. BR/TR, 6'2", 190 lbs. Deb: 9/13/15																									
1919 Cle-A	3	2	.600	22	3	2	0	0	55	55	2	34	18	15.1	2.95	114	.272	.385	4	.364	1	**2**	**2**	-1	0.2
Total 4	8	12	.400	45	15	6	1	0	161^1	164	4	71	44	13.6	3.74	95	.275	.361	8	.186	-1	-3	-3	-3	-1.0
● MARINO PIERETTI Pieretti, Marino Paul "Chick" b: 9/23/20, Lucca, Italy d: 1/30/81, San Francisco, Cal. BR/TR, 5'7", 158 lbs. Deb: 4/19/45																									
1950 Cle-A	0	1	.000	29	1	0	0	1	47^1	45	2	30	11	14.3	4.18	104	.253	.361	2	.286	0	2	1	1	0.1
Total 6	30	38	.441	194	68	21	4	8	673^2	713	34	321	188	13.9	4.53	81	.272	.353	45	.217	2	-52	-63	5	-5.1
● HORACIO PINA Pina, Horacio (Garcia) b: 3/12/45, Coahuila, Mexico BR/TR, 6'2", 177 lbs. Deb: 8/14/68																									
1968 Cle-A	1	1	.500	12	3	0	0	2	31^1	24	0	15	24	11.5	1.72	172	.218	.317	0	.000	-1	4	4	-0	0.3
1969 Cle-A	4	2	.667	31	4	0	0	1	46^2	44	6	27	32	14.7	5.21	72	.256	.373	3	.500	1	-8	-7	0	-0.8
Total 8	23	23	.500	314	7	0	0	38	432	358	28	216	278	12.6	3.25	106	.231	.336	5	.185	0	12	9	9	2.5
Team 2	5	3	.625	43	7	0	0	3	78	68	6	42	56	13.4	3.81	90	.241	.352	3	.250	0	-4	-3	0	-0.5
● STAN PITULA Pitula, Stanley b: 3/23/31, Hackensack, N.J. d: 8/15/65, Hackensack, N.J. BR/TR, 5'10", 170 lbs. Deb: 4/24/57																									
1957 Cle-A	2	2	.500	23	5	1	0	0	59^2	67	8	32	17	15.2	4.98	75	.296	.388	3	.200	0	-8	-8	-1	-0.6
● JUAN PIZARRO Pizarro, Juan Ramon (Cordova) b: 2/7/37, Santurce, P.R. BL/TL, 5'11", 190 lbs. Deb: 5/4/57																									
1969 Cle-A	3	3	.500	48	4	1	0	4	82^2	67	6	49	44	12.8	3.16	119	.229	.343	3	.200	0	4	6	0	0.5
Total 18	131	105	.555	488	245	79	17	28	2034^1	1807	201	888	1522	12.1	3.43	104	.237	.320	133	.202	29	55	33	-5	4.6
● ERIC PLUNK Plunk, Eric Vaughn b: 9/3/63, Wilmington, Cal. BR/TR, 6'5", 210 lbs. Deb: 5/12/86																									
1992 Cle-A	9	6	.600	58	0	0	0	4	71^2	61	5	38	50	12.4	3.64	107	.229	.326	0	—	0	2	2	-0	0.5
1993 Cle-A	4	5	.444	70	0	0	0	15	71	61	5	30	77	11.5	2.79	155	.226	.303	0	—	0	12	12	-1	1.8
1994 Cle-A	7	2	.778	41	0	0	0	3	71	61	3	37	73	12.7	2.54	186	.231	.330	0	—	0	18	17	0	2.0
1995 *Cle-A	6	2	.750	56	0	0	0	2	64	48	5	27	71	11.1	2.67	173	.211	.305	0	—	0	15	14	0	1.6
Total 10	57	44	.564	472	41	0	0	32	859^2	743	80	504	793	13.2	3.73	110	.234	.342	0	—	0	45	35	-7	5.6
Team 4	26	15	.634	225	0	0	0	24	277^2	231	18	132	271	12.0	2.92	150	.225	.316	0	—	0	47	45	-1	5.9
● RAY POAT Poat, Raymond Willis b: 12/19/17, Chicago, Ill. d: 4/29/90, Oak Lawn, Ill. BR/TR, 6'2", 200 lbs. Deb: 4/15/42																									
1942 Cle-A	1	3	.250	4	4	1	1	0	18^1	24	1	9	8	16.7	5.40	64	.296	.374	0	.000	-0	-4	-4	0	-0.7
1943 Cle-A	2	5	.286	17	4	1	0	0	45	44	3	20	31	12.8	4.40	71	.259	.337	2	.154	-1	-6	-6	-0	-1.0
1944 Cle-A	4	8	.333	36	6	1	0	1	80^2	82	9	37	40	13.3	5.13	64	.265	.343	0	.000	-2	-15	-16	-0	-2.5
Total 6	22	30	.423	116	47	15	4	1	400	425	48	162	178	13.3	4.55	82	.271	.340	14	.115	-3	-34	-36	-3	-4.4
Team 3	7	16	.304	57	14	3	1	1	144	150	13	66	79	13.6	4.94	66	.267	.346	2	.057	-3	-24	-27	-0	-4.2
● BUD PODBIELAN Podbielan, Clarence Anthony b: 3/6/24, Curlew, Wash. d: 10/26/82, Syracuse, N.Y. BR/TR, 6'1.5", 170 lbs. Deb: 4/25/49																									
1959 Cle-A	0	1	.000	6	0	0	0	0	12^1	17	1	2	5	13.9	5.84	63	.354	.380	0	.000	-0	-3	-3	0	-0.2
Total 9	25	42	.373	172	76	20	2	3	641	693	79	245	242	13.4	4.49	92	.279	.348	29	.154	-4	-30	-26	-2	-3.1
● JOHNNY PODGAJNY Podgajny, John Sigmund "Specs" b: 6/10/20, Chester, Pa. d: 3/2/71, Chester, Pa. BR/TR, 6'2", 173 lbs. Deb: 9/15/40																									
1946 Cle-A	0	0	—	6	0	0	0	0	9	13	0	2	4	15.0	5.00	66	.302	.333	0	—	0	-1	-2	0	0.0
Total 5	20	37	.351	115	61	20	0	0	510^1	542	22	165	129	12.8	4.20	84	.273	.334	27	.168	-3	-41	-39	3	-3.9
● LOU POLCHOW Polchow, Louis William b: 3/14/1881, Mankato, Minn. d: 8/15/12, Good Thunder, Minn 5'9", Deb: 9/14/02																									
1902 Cle-A	0	1	.000	1	1	1	0	0	8	9	0	4	2	14.6	5.63	61	.281	.361	0	.000	-1	-2	-2	-0	-0.2
● JIM POOLE Poole, James Richard b: 4/28/66, Rochester, N.Y. BL/TL, 6'2", 190 lbs. Deb: 6/15/90																									
1995 *Cle-A	3	3	.500	42	0	0	0	0	50^1	40	7	17	41	10.5	3.75	123	.217	.291	0	—	0	5	5	0	0.5
Total 6	9	6	.600	186	0	0	0	3	177	141	17	70	135	10.8	3.25	135	.220	.299	0	—	0	22	22	0	2.0

YEAR	TM/L	W	L	PCT	G	GS	CG	SH	SV	IP	H	HR	BB	SO	RAT	ERA	ERA+	OAV	OOB	BH	AVG	PB	PR	/A	PD	TPI
● **NELLIE POTT**	Pott, Nelson Adolph "Lefty" b: 7/16/1899, Cincinnati, Ohio d: 12/3/63, Cincinnati, Ohio BL/TL, 6', 185 lbs. Deb: 4/19/22																									
1922	Cle-A	0	0	—	2	0	0	0	0	2	7	1	2	0	40.5	31.50	13	.583	.643	0	—	0	-6	-6	-0	0.0
● **BILL POUNDS**	Pounds, Jeared Wells b: 3/11/1878, Paterson, N.J. d: 7/7/36, Paterson, N.J. BR/TR, 5'10.5", 178 lbs. Deb: 5/2/03																									
1903	Cle-A	0	0	—	1	0	0	0	0	5	8	0	0	2	14.4	10.80	26	.364	.364	1	.500	1	-4	-4	-0	0.1
Total	1	0	0	—	2	0	0	0	0	11	16	1	2	4	14.7	8.18	37	.356	.383	3	.600	1	-6	-6	0	0.2
● **TED POWER**	Power, Ted Henry b: 1/31/55, Guthrie, Okla. BR/TR, 6'4", 225 lbs. Deb: 9/9/81																									
1992	Cle-A	3	3	.500	64	0	0	0	6	99^1	88	7	35	51	11.5	2.54	154	.248	.322	0	—	0	15	15	0	1.2
1993	Cle-A	0	2	.000	20	0	0	0	0	20	30	2	8	11	17.1	7.20	60	.333	.388	0	—	0	-6	-6	-1	-0.6
Total	13	68	69	.496	564	85	5	3	70	1160	1159	97	452	701	12.6	4.00	97	.264	.335	14	.089	-4	-26	-14	-11	-0.5
Team	2	3	5	.375	84	0	0	0	6	119^1	118	9	43	62	12.4	3.32	120	.265	.335	0	—	0	9	9	-1	0.6
● **DICK RADATZ**	Radatz, Richard Raymond "The Monster" b: 4/2/37, Detroit, Mich. BR/TR, 6'5", 235 lbs. Deb: 4/10/62																									
1966	Cle-A	0	3	.000	39	0	0	0	10	56^2	49	6	34	49	13.7	4.61	75	.233	.348	1	.111	-0	-7	-7	-1	-0.8
1967	Cle-A	0	0	—	3	0	0	0	0	3	5	1	2	1	21.0	6.00	54	.357	.438	0	—	0	-1	-1	0	0.0
Total	7	52	43	.547	381	0	0	0	122	693^2	532	65	296	745	11.1	3.13	122	.212	.303	19	.131	-3	38	53	-9	10.8
Team	2	0	3	.000	42	0	0	0	10	59^2	54	7	36	50	14.0	4.68	73	.241	.354	1	.111	-0	-8	-8	-1	-0.8
● **ERIC RAICH**	Raich, Eric James b: 11/1/51, Detroit, Mich. BR/TR, 6'4", 225 lbs. Deb: 5/24/75																									
1975	Cle-A	7	8	.467	18	17	2	0	0	92^2	118	12	31	34	14.6	5.54	68	.320	.374	0	—	0	-18	-18	-1	-2.6
1976	Cle-A	0	0	—	1	0	0	0	0	2^2	7	1	0	1	23.6	16.88	21	.467	.467	0	—	0	-4	-4	-0	0.0
Total	2	7	8	.467	19	17	2	0	0	95^1	125	13	31	35	14.8	5.85	64	.326	.377	0	—	0	-22	-22	-1	-2.6
● **PEDRO RAMOS**	Ramos, Pedro (Guerra) "Pete" b: 4/28/35, Pinar Del Rio, Cuba BB/TR, 6', 185 lbs. Deb: 4/11/55 ♦																									
1962	Cle-A	10	12	.455	37	27	7	2	1	201^1	189	28	85	96	12.5	3.71	104	.246	.326	10	.147	2	6	4	0	0.6
1963	Cle-A	9	8	.529	36	22	5	0	0	184^2	156	29	41	169	9.8	3.12	116	.226	.273	6	.109	1	10	10	-2	0.8
1964	Cle-A	7	10	.412	36	19	3	1	0	133	144	18	26	98	11.8	5.14	70	.273	.312	7	.179	2	-22	-23	-1	-2.5
Total	15	117	160	.422	582	268	73	13	55	2355^2	2364	315	724	1305	12.1	4.08	95	.261	.320	109	.155	-0	-68	-58	-9	-6.9
Team	3	26	30	.464	109	68	15	3	1	519	489	75	152	363	11.3	3.87	96	.246	.304	23	.142	5	-6	-9	-2	-1.1
● **JERRY REED**	Reed, Jerry Maxwell b: 10/8/55, Bryson City, N.C. BR/TR, 6'1", 190 lbs. Deb: 9/11/81																									
1982	Cle-A	1	1	.500	6	1	0	0	0	15^2	15	1	3	10	10.3	3.45	118	.250	.286	0	—	0	1	1	0	0.1
1983	Cle-A	0	0	—	7	0	0	0	0	21^1	26	4	9	11	14.8	7.17	59	.310	.376	0	—	0	-7	-7	1	0.1
1985	Cle-A	3	5	.375	33	5	0	0	8	72^1	67	12	19	37	11.1	4.11	101	.245	.302	0	—	0	0	0	1	0.1
Total	9	20	19	.513	238	12	0	0	18	479^1	477	47	172	248	12.4	3.94	107	.261	.328	0	—	0	6	14	2	0.7
Team	3	4	6	.400	46	6	0	0	8	109^1	108	17	31	58	11.7	4.61	90	.259	.315	0	—	0	-6	-6	2	0.3
● **BUGS REISIGL**	Reisigl, Jacob b: 12/12/1887, Brooklyn, N.Y. d: 2/24/57, Amsterdam, N.Y. BR/TR, 5'10.5", 175 lbs. Deb: 9/20/11																									
1911	Cle-A	0	1	.000	2	1	1	0	0	13	13	1	3	6	11.1	6.23	55	.271	.314	0	.000	-1	-4	-4	-0	-0.3
● **PAUL REUSCHEL**	Reuschel, Paul Richard b: 1/12/47, Quincy, Ill. BR/TR, 6'4", 225 lbs. Deb: 7/25/75 F																									
1978	Cle-A	2	4	.333	18	6	1	0	0	89^2	95	5	22	24	11.9	3.11	120	.271	.318	0	—	0	6	6	1	0.5
1979	Cle-A	2	1	.667	17	1	0	0	1	45^1	73	7	11	22	16.7	7.94	54	.365	.398	0	—	0	-19	-19	0	-1.1
Total	5	16	16	.500	198	9	1	0	13	393	440	38	132	188	13.2	4.51	89	.286	.344	2	.063	-2	-32	-21	4	-1.0
Team	2	4	5	.444	35	7	1	0	1	135	168	12	33	46	13.5	4.73	83	.305	.347	0	—	0	-12	-12	1	-0.6
● **ALLIE REYNOLDS**	Reynolds, Allie Pierce "Superchief" b: 2/10/15, Bethany, Okla. d: 12/26/94, Oklahoma City, Okla. BR/TR, 6', 195 lbs. Deb: 9/17/42																									
1942	Cle-A	0	0	—	2	0	0	0	0	5	5	0	4	2	16.2	0.00	—	.250	.375	0	.000	-0	2	2	-0	0.0
1943	Cle-A	11	12	.478	34	21	11	3	3	198^2	140	3	109	**151**	11.6	2.99	104	**.202**	.316	10	.149	-1	7	3	-0	0.1
1944	Cle-A	11	8	.579	28	21	5	1	1	158	141	2	91	84	13.4	3.30	100	.240	.346	7	.123	-3	2	-0	-1	-0.4
1945	Cle-A†	18	12	.600	44	30	16	2	4	247^1	227	7	130	112	13.2	3.20	101	.247	.343	8	.094	-7	5	1	-1	-0.7
1946	Cle-A	11	15	.423	31	28	9	3	0	183^1	180	10	108	107	14.2	3.88	85	.259	.359	14	.222	1	-8	-12	-1	-1.5
Total	13	182	107	.630	434	309	137	36	49	2492^1	2193	133	1261	1423	12.7	3.30	110	.238	.333	140	.163	-5	149	87	-16	6.9
Team	5	51	47	.520	139	100	41	9	8	792^1	693	22	442	456	13.1	3.31	98	.238	.341	39	.142	-10	8	-6	-4	-2.5
● **BOB REYNOLDS**	Reynolds, Robert Allen b: 1/21/47, Seattle, Wash. BR/TR, 6', 205 lbs. Deb: 9/19/69																									
1975	Cle-A	0	2	.000	5	0	0	0	2	9^2	11	0	3	5	13.0	4.66	81	.289	.341	0	—	0	-1	-1	-0	-0.2
Total	6	14	16	.467	140	2	0	0	21	254^2	255	18	82	167	12.0	3.15	116	.264	.324	0	.000	-0	16	14	-3	2.7
● **BOB RHOADS**	Rhoads, Robert Barton "Dusty" b: 10/4/1879, Wooster, Ohio d: 2/12/67, San Bernardino, Cal. BR/TR, 6'1", 215 lbs. Deb: 4/19/02																									
1903	Cle-A	2	3	.400	5	5	5	0	0	41	55	2	3	21	13.2	5.27	54	.320	.339	2	.118	-1	-10	-11	-0	-1.2
1904	Cle-A	10	9	.526	22	19	18	0	0	175^1	175	1	48	72	11.7	2.87	88	.261	.315	18	.196	0	-5	-7	-1	-0.8
1905	Cle-A	16	9	.640	28	26	24	4	0	235	219	4	55	61	10.9	2.83	93	.248	.300	21	.221	4	-5	-5	0	-0.1
1906	Cle-A	22	10	.688	38	34	31	7	0	315	259	5	92	89	10.2	1.80	145	.227	.288	19	.161	-3	31	29	-2	2.4
1907	Cle-A	15	14	.517	35	31	23	5	1	275	258	0	84	76	11.7	2.29	110	.250	.315	17	.185	-1	8	7	-1	0.4
1908	Cle-A	18	12	.600	37	30	20	1	0	270	229	2	73	62	10.3	1.77	135	.239	.298	20	.222	4	19	19	2	2.9
1909	Cle-A	5	9	.357	20	15	9	2	0	133^1	124	1	50	46	12.2	2.90	88	.281	.361	7	.163	-0	-6	-5	1	-0.5
Total	8	97	82	.542	218	185	154	21	2	1691^2	1604	19	494	522	11.5	2.61	100	.256	.316	121	.188	-0	7	1	-3	0.5
Team	7	88	66	.571	185	160	130	19	1	1444^2	1319	15	405	427	11.0	2.39	107	.249	.308	104	.190	2	31	26	-1	3.1
● **DENNY RIDDLEBERGER**	Riddleberger, Dennis Michael b: 11/22/45, Clifton Forge, Va. BR/TL, 6'3", 195 lbs. Deb: 9/15/70																									
1972	Cle-A	1	3	.250	38	0	0	0	0	54	45	5	22	34	11.5	2.50	129	.237	.322	0	.000	-0	3	4	-0	0.3
Total	3	4	4	.500	103	0	0	0	1	133	119	15	56	95	12.0	2.77	119	.248	.330	0	.000	-0	8	8	-1	0.3
● **STEVE RIDZIK**	Ridzik, Stephen George b: 4/29/29, Yonkers, N.Y. BR/TR, 5'11", 170 lbs. Deb: 9/4/50																									
1958	Cle-A	0	2	.000	6	0	0	0	0	8^2	9	1	5	6	14.5	2.08	176	.257	.350	0	.000	-0	2	2	0	0.4
Total	12	39	38	.506	314	48	4	1	11	782^2	709	93	351	406	12.6	3.79	101	.243	.332	38	.192	4	2	3	-4	0.2
● **REGGIE RITTER**	Ritter, Reggie Blake b: 1/23/60, Malvern, Ark. BL/TR, 6'2", 195 lbs. Deb: 5/17/86																									
1986	Cle-A	0	0	—	5	0	0	0	0	10	14	1	4	6	17.1	6.30	66	.341	.413	0	—	0	-2	-2	0	0.2
1987	Cle-A	1	1	.500	14	0	0	0	0	26^2	33	5	16	11	16.5	6.08	74	.300	.389	0	—	0	-5	-5	0	-0.3
Total	2	1	1	.500	19	0	0	0	0	36^2	47	6	20	17	16.7	6.14	72	.311	.395	0	—	0	-7	-7	1	-0.1
● **JIM RITTWAGE**	Rittwage, James Michael b: 10/23/44, Cleveland, Ohio BR/TR, 6'3", 190 lbs. Deb: 9/7/70																									
1970	Cle-A	1	1	.500	8	3	1	0	0	26	18	0	21	16	13.5	4.15	95	.194	.342	3	.375	1	-1	-1	0	0.1
● **JOE ROA**	Roa, Joseph Rodger b: 10/11/71, Southfield, Mich. BR/TR, 6'1", 194 lbs. Deb: 9/20/95																									
1995	Cle-A	0	1	.000	1	1	0	0	0	6	9	1	2	0	16.5	6.00	77	.360	.407	0	—	0	-1	-1	0	-0.1
● **HUMBERTO ROBINSON**	Robinson, Humberto Valentino b: 6/25/30, Colon, Panama BR/TR, 6'1", 155 lbs. Deb: 4/20/55																									
1959	Cle-A	1	0	1.000	5	0	0	0	0	8^2	9	0	4	6	13.5	4.15	89	.281	.361	0	—	0	-0	-0	0	0.0
Total	5	8	13	.381	102	7	2	0	4	213	189	17	90	114	12.0	3.25	119	.241	.323	6	.158	0	16	14	2	1.6
● **RICK RODRIGUEZ**	Rodriguez, Ricardo b: 9/21/60, Oakland, Cal. BR/TR, 6'3", 190 lbs. Deb: 9/17/86																									
1988	Cle-A	1	2	.333	10	5	0	0	0	33	43	4	17	9	16.6	7.09	58	.323	.404	0	—	0	-11	-11	1	-0.8
Total	4	3	4	.429	31	8	0	0	0	77	97	9	41	22	16.4	5.73	71	.316	.400	0	—	0	-13	-14	2	-1.1

YEAR TM/L	W	L	PCT	G	GS	CG	SH	SV	IP	H	HR	BB	SO	RAT	ERA	ERA+	OAV	OOB	BH	AVG	PB	PR	/A	PD	TPI
● **BILLY ROHR** Rohr, William Joseph b: 7/1/45, San Diego, Cal. BL/TL, 6'3", 170 lbs. Deb: 4/14/67																								
1968 Cle-A	1	0	1.000	17	0	0	0	1	18¹	18	5	10	5	13.7	6.87	43	.265	.359	0	.000	-0	-8	-8	0	-0.6
Total 2	3	3	.500	27	8	2	1	1	60²	61	9	32	21	14.1	5.64	59	.258	.352	0	.000	-1	-17	-16	-0	-1.5
● **JOSE ROMAN** Roman, Jose Rafael (Sarita) b: 5/21/63, Santo Domingo, D.R. BR/TR, 6', 175 lbs. Deb: 9/5/84																								
1984 Cle-A	0	2	.000	3	2	0	0	0	6	9	1	11	3	30.0	18.00	23	.391	.588	0	—	0	-9	-9	-0	-2.0
1985 Cle-A	0	4	.000	5	3	0	0	0	16¹	13	3	14	12	14.9	6.61	63	.200	.342	0	—	0	-4	-4	-0	-0.9
1986 Cle-A	1	2	.333	6	5	0	0	0	22	23	3	17	9	16.6	6.55	63	.280	.410	0	—	0	-6	-6	-1	-0.7
Total 3	1	8	.111	14	10	0	0	0	44¹	45	7	42	24	17.9	8.12	51	.265	.413	0	—	0	-20	-20	-1	-3.6
● **RAMON ROMERO** Romero, Ramon (De Los Santos) b: 1/8/59, San Pedro De Macoris, D.R. BL/TL, 6'4", 170 lbs. Deb: 9/18/84																								
1984 Cle-A	0	0	—	1	0	0	0	0	3	0	0	3	3	3.0	0.00	—	.000	.111	0	—	0	1	1	-0	-0.1
1985 Cle-A	2	3	.400	19	10	0	0	0	64¹	69	13	38	38	15.7	6.58	63	.276	.382	0	—	0	-17	-17	-1	-1.2
Total 2	2	3	.400	20	10	0	0	0	67¹	69	13	38	41	15.1	6.28	66	.267	.374	0	—	0	-16	-16	-1	-1.3
● **VICENTE ROMO** Romo, Vicente (Navarro) "Huevo" b: 4/12/43, Santa Rosalia, Mex. BR/TR, 6'1", 195 lbs. Deb: 4/11/68 F																								
1968 Cle-A	5	3	.625	40	1	0	0	12	83¹	43	5	32	54	8.3	1.62	183	.154	.245	2	.143	-0	13	12	-0	1.7
1969 Cle-A	1	1	.500	3	0	0	0	0	8	7	0	3	7	11.3	2.25	167	.233	.303	1	.500	0	1	1	-0	0.4
Total 8	32	33	.492	335	32	4	1	52	645²	569	61	280	416	11.9	3.36	106	.239	.322	18	.149	-1	10	13	5	2.5
Team 2	6	4	.600	43	1	0	0	12	91¹	50	5	35	61	8.6	1.68	181	.161	.251	3	.188	-0	14	14	-0	2.1
● **LUTHER ROY** Roy, Luther Franklin b: 7/29/02, Ooltewah, Tenn. d: 7/24/63, Grand Rapids, Mich. BR/TR, 5'10.5", 161 lbs. Deb: 6/12/24 F																								
1924 Cle-A	0	5	.000	16	5	2	0	0	48²	62	3	31	14	17.2	7.77	55	.318	.412	4	.267	-0	-19	-19	1	-1.5
1925 Cle-A	0	0	—	6	1	0	0	0	10	14	1	11	1	22.5	3.60	123	.368	.510	0	.000	-0	1	1	-0	-0.1
Total 4	6	12	.333	56	18	3	0	0	170²	231	15	92	36	17.2	7.17	66	.328	.408	14	.264	2	-51	-47	1	-3.1
Team 2	0	5	.000	22	6	2	0	0	58²	76	4	42	15	18.1	7.06	61	.326	.429	4	.235	-0	-18	-18	-0	-1.6
● **DICK ROZEK** Rozek, Richard Louis b: 3/27/27, Cedar Rapids, Iowa BL/TL, 6'0.5", 190 lbs. Deb: 4/29/50																								
1950 Cle-A	0	0	—	12	2	0	0	0	25¹	28	3	19	14	16.7	4.97	87	.283	.398	0	.000	-1	-1	-2	-1	-0.1
1951 Cle-A	0	0	—	7	1	0	0	0	15¹	18	1	11	5	17.6	2.93	129	.286	.400	1	.333	-0	2	1	-1	0.0
1952 Cle-A	1	0	1.000	10	1	0	0	0	12²	11	0	13	5	17.1	4.97	67	.224	.387	0	.000	-0	-2	-2	-0	-0.2
Total 5	1	0	1.000	33	4	0	0	0	65¹	65	7	55	26	16.8	4.55	88	.260	.397	1	.083	-1	-3	-4	-2	-0.3
Team 3	1	0	1.000	29	4	0	0	0	53¹	57	4	43	24	17.0	4.39	90	.270	.396	1	.100	-1	-3	-3	-1	-0.3
● **DON RUDOLPH** Rudolph, Frederick Donald b: 8/16/31, Baltimore, Md. d: 9/12/68, Granada Hills, Cal BL/TL, 5'11", 195 lbs. Deb: 9/21/57																								
1962 Cle-A	0	0	—	1	0	0	0	0	0¹	1	0	0	0	27.0	0.00	—	1.000	1.000	0	—	0	0	0	0	0.0
Total 6	18	32	.360	124	57	10	2	3	450¹	485	54	102	182	11.9	4.00	96	.276	.319	20	.167	3	-11	-8	-1	-1.1
● **VERN RUHLE** Ruhle, Vernon Gerald b: 1/25/51, Coleman, Mich. BR/TR, 6'1", 187 lbs. Deb: 9/9/74																								
1985 Cle-A	2	10	.167	42	16	1	0	3	125	139	16	30	54	12.3	4.32	96	.283	.326	0	—	0	-2	-3	-0	-0.3
Total 13	67	88	.432	327	188	29	12	11	1411¹	1483	119	348	582	11.9	3.73	97	.270	.318	27	.148	6	-5	-16	-8	-3.3
● **JACK RUSSELL** Russell, Jack Erwin b: 10/24/05, Paris, Tex. d: 11/3/90, Clearwater, Fla. BR/TR, 6'1.5", 178 lbs. Deb: 5/5/26																								
1932 Cle-A	5	7	.417	18	11	6	0	1	113	146	5	27	27	13.9	4.70	101	.310	.349	12	.300	2	-3	1	1	0.4
Total 15	85	141	.376	557	182	71	3	38	2050²	2454	83	571	418	13.4	4.46	97	.299	.346	103	.167	-11	-33	-33	36	-1.2
● **JEFF RUSSELL** Russell, Jeffrey Lee b: 9/2/61, Cincinnati, Ohio BR/TR, 6'3", 210 lbs. Deb: 8/13/83																								
1994 Cle-A	1	1	.500	13	0	0	0	5	12²	13	2	3	10	11.4	4.97	95	.265	.308	0	—	0	-0	-0	0	-0.1
Total 13	53	70	.431	534	79	11	2	183	1043²	1007	95	393	670	12.1	3.77	109	.254	.325	11	.139	1	30	41	11	11.1
● **JACK RYAN** Ryan, Jack "Gulfport" b: 9/19/1884, Lawrenceville, Ill. d: 10/16/49, Hondsboro, Miss. BR/TR, 5'10", 165 lbs. Deb: 7/2/08																								
1908 Cle-A	1	1	.500	8	1	1	0	1	35²	27	3	2	7	7.6	2.27	105	.220	.238	1	.091	0	0	0	-0	0.1
Total 3	5	5	.500	24	10	3	0	1	103	101	4	26	32	11.6	2.88	87	.267	.324	5	.161	1	-4	-4	-0	-0.5
● **JACK SALVESON** Salveson, John Theodore b: 1/5/14, Fullerton, Cal. d: 12/28/74, Norwalk, Cal. BR/TR, 6'0.5", 180 lbs. Deb: 6/3/33																								
1943 Cle-A	5	3	.625	23	11	4	3	3	86	87	5	26	24	11.9	3.35	93	.266	.322	6	.231	2	-0	-2	0	0.0
1945 Cle-A	0	0	—	19	0	0	0	0	44	52	3	6	11	12.1	3.68	88	.294	.321	4	.400	3	-2	-2	1	0.4
Total 5	9	9	.500	87	19	8	3	4	272²	302	21	87	85	12.9	3.99	91	.280	.336	20	.260	2	-8	-11	2	0.1
Team 2	5	3	.625	42	11	4	3	3	130	139	8	32	35	12.0	3.46	91	.276	.322	10	.278	5	-2	-4	1	0.4
● **KEN SANDERS** Sanders, Kenneth George "Daffy" b: 7/8/41, St.Louis, Mo. BR/TR, 5'11", 185 lbs. Deb: 8/6/64																								
1973 Cle-A	5	1	.833	15	0	0	0	5	27¹	18	2	9	14	8.9	1.65	238	.188	.257	0	—	0	7	7	0	1.8
1974 Cle-A	0	1	.000	9	0	0	0	1	11	21	5	5	4	21.3	9.82	37	.404	.456	0	—	0	-8	-8	-0	-0.7
Total 10	29	45	.392	408	1	0	0	86	656²	564	49	258	360	11.5	2.97	118	.235	.314	6	.115	-0	38	39	7	7.5
Team 2	5	2	.714	24	0	0	0	6	38¹	39	7	14	18	12.4	3.99	96	.264	.327	0	—	0	-1	-1	0	1.1
● **JOSE SANTIAGO** Santiago, Jose Guillermo (Guzman) "Pants" b: 9/4/28, Coamo, P.R. BR/TR, 5'10", 175 lbs. Deb: 4/17/54																								
1954 Cle-A	0	0	—	1	0	0	0	0	1²	0	0	2	1	10.8	0.00	—	.000	.286	0	—	0	1	1	-0	0.0
1955 Cle-A	2	0	1.000	17	0	0	0	0	32²	31	1	14	19	13.8	2.48	161	.256	.357	2	.500	1	5	5	0	0.4
Total 3	3	2	.600	27	5	0	0	0	56	67	9	29	29	17.7	4.66	88	.306	.420	4	.444	2	-4	-3	0	-0.6
Team 2	2	0	1.000	18	0	0	0	0	34¹	31	1	16	20	13.6	2.36	168	.246	.354	2	.500	1	6	6	-0	0.4
● **JOE SCHAFFERNOTH** Schaffernoth, Joseph Arthur b: 8/6/37, Trenton, N.J. BR/TR, 6'4.5", 195 lbs. Deb: 4/15/59																								
1961 Cle-A	0	1	.000	15	0	0	0	0	16	14	9	16.4	4.76	83	.242	.383	0	.000	-0	-1	-2	1	0.0			
Total 3	3	8	.273	74	1	0	0	3	118	116	12	53	68	13.1	4.58	86	.264	.347	2	.125	-1	-9	-8	1	-0.7
● **DAN SCHATZEDER** Schatzeder, Daniel Ernest b: 12/1/54, Elmhurst, Ill. BL/TL, 6', 195 lbs. Deb: 9/4/77																								
1988 Cle-A	0	2	.000	15	0	0	0	3	16	26	6	2	10	16.3	9.56	43	.351	.377	0	—	0	-10	-10	-0	-1.6
Total 15	69	68	.504	504	121	18	4	10	1317	1257	128	475	748	12.0	3.74	99	.253	.321	58	.240	22	1	-4	-13	-1.8
● **KEN SCHROM** Schrom, Kenneth Marvin b: 11/23/54, Grangeville, Idaho BR/TR, 6'2", 195 lbs. Deb: 8/8/80																								
1986 Cle-A☆	14	7	.667	34	33	3	1	0	206	217	34	49	87	12.1	4.54	89	.271	.322	0	—	0	-8	-9	-3	-1.1
1987 Cle-A	6	13	.316	32	29	4	1	0	153²	185	29	57	61	14.3	6.50	70	.298	.360	0	—	0	-35	-34	-2	-3.6
Total 7	51	51	.500	176	137	22	3	1	900	963	125	320	372	13.1	4.81	89	.276	.342	0	—	0	-65	-51	-10	-6.5
Team 2	20	20	.500	66	62	7	2	0	359²	402	63	106	148	13.1	5.38	80	.283	.339	0	—	0	-43	-43	-5	-4.7
● **DON SCHULZE** Schulze, Donald Arthur b: 9/27/62, Roselle, Ill. BR/TR, 6'3", 225 lbs. Deb: 9/13/83																								
1984 Cle-A	3	6	.333	19	14	2	0	0	85²	105	9	27	39	13.9	4.83	85	.302	.352	0	—	0	-8	-7	-0	-0.7
1985 Cle-A	4	10	.286	19	18	1	0	0	94¹	128	10	19	37	14.4	6.01	69	.322	.360	0	—	0	-20	-20	1	-2.4
1986 Cle-A	4	4	.500	19	12	1	0	0	84²	88	9	34	33	13.5	5.00	83	.266	.343	0	—	0	-8	-8	-1	-0.7
Total 6	15	25	.375	76	59	4	0	0	338²	422	40	105	144	14.3	5.47	74	.306	.361	0	.000	-0	-54	-54	-0	-5.4
Team 3	11	20	.355	57	45	4	0	0	264²	321	28	80	109	13.9	5.30	78	.298	.352	0	—	0	-35	-35	-1	-3.8
● **HERB SCORE** Score, Herbert Jude b: 6/7/33, Rosedale, N.Y. BL/TL, 6'2", 185 lbs. Deb: 4/15/55																								
1955 Cle-A☆	16	10	.615	33	32	11	2	0	227¹	158	18	154	**245**	12.4	2.85	140	.194	.323	10	.119	-4	28	29	-4	2.2
1956 Cle-A★	20	9	.690	35	33	16	**5**	0	249¹	162	18	129	**263**	10.6	2.53	**166**	**.186**	.292	16	.184	-1	**45**	**46**	-4	4.8
1957 Cle-A	2	1	.667	5	5	3	1	0	36	18	3	16	39	11.3	2.00	186	.149	.304	1	.091	-0	7	7	0	0.5

YEAR TM/L	W	L	PCT	G	GS	CG	SH	SV	IP	H	HR	BB	SO	RAT	ERA	ERA+	OAV	OOB	BH	AVG	PB	PR	/A	PD	TPI
1958 Cle-A	2	3	.400	12	5	2	1	3	41	29	1	34	48	13.8	3.95	92	.197	.348	1	.091	-0	-1	-1	-1	-0.3
1959 Cle-A	9	11	.450	30	25	9	1	0	160^{2}	123	28	115	147	13.4	4.71	78	**.210**	.341	5	.096	-3	-15	-18	-3	-2.6
Total 8	55	46	.545	150	127	47	11	3	858^{1}	609	79	573	837	12.5	3.36	117	.200	.328	36	.128	-8	59	55	-12	3.8
Team 5	49	34	.590	115	100	41	10	3	714^{1}	490	65	458	742	12.0	3.17	125	.193	.318	33	.135	-6	64	62	-11	4.6
● ED SCOTT Scott, Edward b: 8/12/1870, Walbridge, Ohio d: 11/1/33, Toledo, Ohio BR/TR, 6'3", Deb: 4/19/00																									
1901 Cle-A	6	6	.500	17	16	11	0	1	124^{2}	149	2	38	23	14.0	4.40	81	.293	.350	10	.208	1	-10	-12	2	-0.7
Total 2	23	26	.469	59	51	42	0	2	439^{2}	519	12	103	110	13.2	4.01	91	.292	.338	29	.170	-4	-16	-18	11	-0.9
● SCOTT SCUDDER Scudder, William Scott b: 2/14/68, Paris, Tex. BR/TR, 6'2", 180 lbs. Deb: 6/6/89																									
1992 Cle-A	6	10	.375	23	22	0	0	0	109	134	10	55	66	15.8	5.28	74	.303	.383	0	—	0	-16	-17	0	-2.1
1993 Cle-A	0	1	.000	2	1	0	0	0	4	5	0	4	1	22.5	9.00	48	.333	.500	0	—	0	-2	-2	-0	-0.4
Total 5	21	34	.382	96	64	0	0	1	386^{1}	395	42	206	226	14.3	4.80	79	.266	.360	8	.113	-0	-46	-42	-3	-5.8
Team 2	6	11	.353	25	23	0	0	0	113	139	10	59	67	16.0	5.42	72	.304	.387	0	—	0	-18	-19	-0	-2.5
● RUDY SEANEZ Seanez, Rudy Caballero b: 10/20/68, Brawley, Cal. BR/TR, 5'10", 185 lbs. Deb: 9/7/89																									
1989 Cle-A	0	0	—	5	0	0	0	0	5	1	0	4	7	9.0	3.60	110	.071	.278	0	—	0	0	0	-0	0.0
1990 Cle-A	2	1	.667	24	0	0	0	0	27^{1}	22	2	25	24	15.8	5.60	70	.220	.381	0	—	0	-5	-5	-1	-0.5
1991 Cle-A	0	0	—	5	0	0	0	0	5	10	2	7	7	30.6	16.20	26	.385	.515	0	—	0	-7	-7	-0	0.0
Total 6	4	5	.444	91	0	0	0	3	99	104	12	65	86	15.6	6.00	65	.272	.382	0	.000	-0	-21	-23	-1	-1.7
Team 3	2	1	.667	34	0	0	0	0	37^{1}	33	4	36	38	16.9	6.75	59	.236	.395	0	—	0	-12	-12	-1	-0.5
● GORDON SEYFRIED Seyfried, Gordon Clay b: 7/4/37, Long Beach, Cal. BR/TR, 6', 185 lbs. Deb: 9/13/63																									
1963 Cle-A	0	1	.000	3	1	0	0	0	7^{1}	9	0	3	1	14.7	1.23	295	.300	.364	0	.000	-0	2	2	0	0.3
1964 Cle-A	0	0	—	2	0	0	0	0	2^{1}	4	0	0	0	15.4	0.00	—	.444	.444	0	—	0	1	1	-0	0.0
Total 2	0	1	.000	5	1	0	0	0	9^{2}	13	0	3	1	14.9	0.93	388	.333	.381	0	.000	-0	3	3	0	0.3
● JOE SHAUTE Shaute, Joseph Benjamin "Lefty" b: 8/1/1899, Peckville, Pa. d: 2/21/70, Scranton, Pa. BL/TL, 6', 190 lbs. Deb: 7/6/22																									
1922 Cle-A	0	0	—	2	0	0	0	0	3^{2}	7	2	3	3	24.5	19.64	20	.389	.476	0	.000	-0	-6	-6	-0	-0.1
1923 Cle-A	10	8	.556	33	16	7	0	0	172	176	4	53	61	12.0	3.51	113	.275	.332	11	.162	-4	9	9	-2	0.3
1924 Cle-A	20	17	.541	46	34	21	2	2	283	317	8	83	68	12.9	3.75	114	.287	.340	34	.318	9	15	16	-2	2.6
1925 Cle-A	4	12	.250	26	17	10	1	4	131	160	6	44	34	14.1	5.43	81	.304	.358	16	.302	3	-15	-15	-2	-1.4
1926 Cle-A	14	10	.583	34	25	15	1	1	206^{2}	215	9	65	47	12.3	3.53	115	.278	.337	20	.274	4	11	12	-5	1.2
1927 Cle-A	9	16	.360	45	28	14	0	2	230^{1}	255	9	75	63	13.0	4.22	100	.286	.343	27	.325	6	-2	-0	-2	0.3
1928 Cle-A	13	17	.433	36	31	21	1	2	253^{2}	295	9	68	81	13.1	4.04	102	.299	.348	21	.228	3	-0	3	1	0.7
1929 Cle-A	8	8	.500	26	24	8	0	0	162	211	6	52	43	14.7	4.28	104	.320	.370	17	.293	3	-1	3	-3	0.3
1930 Cle-A	0	0	—	4	0	0	0	0	4^{2}	8	0	4	2	23.1	15.43	31	.333	.429	0	—	0	-6	-5	0	0.0
Total 13	99	109	.476	360	208	103	5	18	1818^{1}	2097	75	534	512	13.1	4.15	99	.293	.345	170	.258	25	-18	-12	-14	0.8
Team 9	78	88	.470	252	175	96	5	11	1447	1644	53	447	402	13.1	4.11	102	.292	.347	146	.271	23	6	16	-13	3.9
● JEFF SHAW Shaw, Jeffrey Lee b: 7/7/66, Washington Court House, Ohio BR/TR, 6'2", 185 lbs. Deb: 4/30/90																									
1990 Cle-A	3	4	.429	12	9	0	0	0	48^{2}	73	11	20	25	17.2	6.66	59	.356	.413	0	—	0	-15	-15	0	-1.7
1991 Cle-A	0	5	.000	29	1	0	0	1	72^{1}	72	6	27	31	12.8	3.36	124	.262	.337	0	—	0	6	6	0	0.4
1992 Cle-A	0	1	.000	2	1	0	0	0	7^{2}	7	2	4	3	12.9	8.22	48	.259	.355	0	—	0	-4	-4	0	-0.3
Total 6	11	25	.306	203	19	0	0	5	363^{2}	380	45	125	207	12.9	4.50	92	.272	.339	3	.107	-0	-16	-14	3	-1.2
Team 3	3	10	.231	43	11	0	0	1	128^{2}	152	19	51	59	14.5	4.90	83	.300	.368	0	—	0	-13	-12	0	-1.6
● MILT SHOFFNER Shoffner, Milburn James b: 11/13/05, Sherman, Tex. d: 1/19/78, Madison, Ohio BL/TL, 6'1.5", 184 lbs. Deb: 7/20/29																									
1929 Cle-A	2	3	.400	11	3	1	0	0	44^{2}	46	4	22	15	14.3	5.04	88	.284	.380	0	.000	-2	-4	-3	0	-0.5
1930 Cle-A	3	4	.429	24	10	1	0	0	84^{2}	129	8	50	17	19.1	7.97	61	.362	.442	7	.212	1	-31	-30	-0	-1.8
1931 Cle-A	2	3	.400	12	4	1	0	0	41	55	4	26	12	18.2	7.24	64	.320	.415	1	.077	-1	-13	-12	-0	-1.3
Total 7	25	26	.490	134	51	22	2	3	577	647	34	214	180	13.6	4.59	85	.287	.352	32	.156	-0	-35	-43	-2	-2.7
Team 3	7	10	.412	47	17	3	0	0	170^{1}	230	16	98	44	17.6	7.03	67	.333	.421	8	.131	-2	-48	-44	-0	-3.6
● PAUL SHUEY Shuey, Paul Kenneth b: 9/16/70, Lima, Ohio BR/TR, 6'3", 215 lbs. Deb: 5/8/94																									
1994 Cle-A	0	1	.000	14	0	0	0	5	11^{2}	14	1	12	16	20.1	8.49	56	.280	.419	0	—	0	-5	-5	0	-0.8
1995 Cle-A	0	2	.000	7	0	0	0	0	6^{1}	5	0	5	5	14.2	4.26	109	.238	.385	0	—	0	0	0	0	0.1
Total 2	0	3	.000	21	0	0	0	5	18	19	1	17	21	18.0	7.00	67	.268	.409	0	—	0	-4	-5	0	-0.7
● SONNY SIEBERT Siebert, Wilfred Charles b: 1/14/37, St.Marys, Mo. BR/TR, 6'3", 198 lbs. Deb: 4/26/64 C																									
1964 Cle-A	7	9	.438	41	14	3	1	3	156	142	15	57	144	11.6	3.23	111	.243	.313	13	.265	5	7	6	-2	1.1
1965 Cle-A	16	8	.667	39	27	4	1	1	188^{2}	139	14	46	191	9.1	2.43	143	.206	**.262**	7	.106	-2	22	22	1	2.8
1966 Cle-A★	16	8	**.667**	34	32	11	1	1	241	193	25	62	163	9.7	2.80	123	.221	.278	11	.129	-2	17	17	2	1.7
1967 Cle-A	10	12	.455	34	26	7	1	4	185^{1}	136	17	54	136	9.5	2.38	137	.202	.268	7	.135	1	18	18	-2	2.3
1968 Cle-A	12	10	.545	31	30	8	4	0	206	145	12	88	146	10.5	2.97	100	.198	.290	11	.157	1	0	-0	1	0.2
1969 Cle-A	0	1	.000	2	2	0	0	0	14	10	1	8	6	11.6	3.21	117	.196	.305	1	.250	0	1	1	-0	0.1
Total 12	140	114	.551	399	307	67	21	16	2152	1919	197	692	1512	11.1	3.21	110	.238	.303	114	.173	18	57	73	5	10.5
Team 6	61	48	.560	181	131	33	8	9	991	765	84	315	786	10.1	2.76	121	.213	.282	50	.153	4	64	64	1	8.2
● CARL SITTON Sitton, Carl Vetter b: 9/22/1882, Pendleton, S.C. d: 9/11/31, Valdosta, Ga. BR/TR, 5'10.5", 170 lbs. Deb: 4/24/09																									
1909 Cle-A	3	2	.600	14	5	3	0	0	50	50	1	16	16	12.2	2.88	89	.263	.327	2	.154	0	-2	-2	-1	-0.2
● JOE SKALSKI Skalski, Joseph Douglas b: 9/26/64, Burnham, Ill. BR/TR, 6'3", 190 lbs. Deb: 4/10/89																									
1989 Cle-A	0	2	.000	2	1	0	0	0	6^{2}	7	0	4	3	17.6	6.75	59	.259	.394	0	—	0	-2	-2	-0	-0.5
● HEATHCLIFF SLOCUMB Slocumb, Heath b: 6/7/66, Jamaica, N.Y. BR/TR, 6'3", 210 lbs. Deb: 4/11/91																									
1993 Cle-A	3	1	.750	20	0	0	0	0	27^{1}	28	3	16	18	14.5	4.28	101	.272	.370	0	—	0	0	0	-0	0.0
Total 5	16	12	.571	225	0	0	0	34	274^{1}	279	11	134	204	13.8	3.64	113	.265	.352	1	.091	-1	11	14	2	2.9
● AL SMITH Smith, Alfred John b: 10/12/07, Belleville, Ill. d: 4/28/77, Brownsville, Tex. BL/TL, 5'11", 180 lbs. Deb: 5/5/34 C																									
1940 Cle-A	15	7	.682	31	24	11	1	2	183	187	12	55	46	12.2	3.44	122	.270	.329	19	.306	7	19	16	2	2.6
1941 Cle-A	12	13	.480	29	27	13	2	0	206^{2}	204	12	75	76	12.2	3.83	103	.256	.321	11	.155	2	7	2	2	0.6
1942 Cle-A	10	15	.400	30	24	7	1	0	168^{1}	163	9	71	66	12.8	3.96	87	.251	.329	15	.250	3	-6	-9	-1	-1.0
1943 Cle-A☆	17	7	.708	29	27	14	3	1	208^{1}	186	7	72	72	11.1	2.55	122	.239	.303	14	.206	3	17	13	-0	1.9
1944 Cle-A	7	13	.350	28	26	7	1	0	181^{2}	197	6	69	44	13.3	3.42	96	.280	.347	10	.156	-1	0	-2	1	-0.2
1945 Cle-A	5	12	.294	21	19	8	3	1	133^{2}	141	8	48	34	12.9	3.84	85	.275	.340	12	.293	4	-7	-9	2	-0.4
Total 12	99	101	.495	356	202	75	16	17	1662^{1}	1707	94	587	587	12.6	3.72	99	.267	.332	102	.191	14	17	-10	4	2.0
Team 6	66	67	.496	168	147	60	11	4	1081^{2}	1078	54	390	338	12.4	3.47	102	.261	.327	81	.221	18	31	10	6	3.5
● CHARLIE SMITH Smith, Charles Edwin b: 4/20/1880, Cleveland, Ohio d: 1/3/29, Wickliffe, Ohio BR/TR, 6'1", 185 lbs. Deb: 8/6/02 F																									
1902 Cle-A	2	1	.667	3	3	2	1	0	20	23	0	5	5	12.6	4.05	85	.287	.329	1	.125	-0	-1	-1	0	-0.2
Total 10	66	87	.431	212	148	87	10	3	1350^{1}	1309	22	353	570	11.3	2.81	94	.259	.311	67	.150	-13	-14	-24	-2	-3.8
● POP-BOY SMITH Smith, Clarence Ossie b: 5/23/1892, Newport, Tenn. d: 2/16/24, Sweetwater, Tex. BR/TR, 6'1", 176 lbs. Deb: 4/19/13																									
1916 Cle-A	1	2	.333	5	3	0	0	1	25^{2}	25	1	11	4	13.0	3.86	78	.253	.333	2	.286	0	-3	-2	-0	-0.3

YEAR	TM/L	W	L	PCT	G	GS	CG	SH	SV	IP	H	HR	BB	SO	RAT	ERA	ERA+	OAV	OOB	BH	AVG	PB	PR	/A	PD	TPI
1917	Cle-A	0	1	.000	6	0	0	0	0	8^2	14	0	4	3	19.7	8.31	34	.368	.442	0	.000	-0	-5	-5	1	-0.5
Total	3	1	4	.200	26	5	0	0	1	66^1	70	1	26	20	13.7	4.21	70	.273	.352	2	.154	-1	-10	-9	2	-0.8
Team	2	1	3	.250	11	3	0	0	1	34^1	39	1	15	7	14.7	4.98	60	.285	.364	2	.250	0	-8	-8	1	-0.8
● **CLAY SMITH** Smith, Clay Jamieson b: 9/11/14, Cambridge, Kan. BR/TR, 6'2", 190 lbs. Deb: 9/13/38																										
1938	Cle-A	0	0	—	4	0	0	0	0	11	18	1	2	3	16.4	6.55	71	.367	.392	0	.000	-0	-2	-2	0	0.0
Total	2	1	1	.500	18	1	0	0	0	39^1	50	4	15	17	15.1	5.49	86	.309	.371	0	.000	-1	-4	-3	1	-0.1
● **ROY SMITH** Smith, Le Roy Purdy b: 9/6/61, Mt.Vernon, N.Y. BR/TR, 6'3", 200 lbs. Deb: 6/23/84																										
1984	Cle-A	5	5	.500	22	14	0	0	0	86^1	91	14	40	55	13.8	4.59	89	.270	.349	0	—	0	-6	-5	-2	-0.7
1985	Cle-A	1	4	.200	12	11	1	0	0	62^1	84	8	17	28	14.7	5.34	77	.321	.364	0	—	0	-8	-8	-1	-0.6
Total	8	30	31	.492	136	93	4	1	1	618^1	707	80	202	320	13.4	4.60	90	.289	.346	0	—	0	-42	-33	-9	-4.4
Team	2	6	9	.400	34	25	1	0	0	148^2	175	22	57	83	14.2	4.90	84	.292	.356	0	—	0	-14	-13	-3	-1.3
● **BOB SMITH** Smith, Robert Walkay "Riverboat" b: 5/13/28, Clarence, Mo. BL/TL, 6', 185 lbs. Deb: 4/22/58																										
1959	Cle-A	0	1	.000	12	3	0	0	0	29^1	31	2	12	17	13.2	5.22	71	.282	.352	0	.000	-1	-4	-5	0	-0.2
Total	2	4	4	.500	30	10	1	0	0	96^2	97	6	59	60	14.5	4.75	82	.268	.371	2	.080	-2	-10	-9	1	-0.1
● **SHERRY SMITH** Smith, Sherrod Malone b: 2/18/1891, Monticello, Ga. d: 9/12/49, Reidsville, Ga. BR/TL, 6'1", 170 lbs. Deb: 5/11/11																										
1922	Cle-A	1	0	1.000	2	2	1	0	0	15^2	18	0	3	4	12.1	3.45	116	.295	.328	2	.333	1	1	1	0	0.1
1923	Cle-A	9	6	.600	30	16	10	1	1	124	129	4	37	23	12.2	3.27	121	.269	.324	11	.244	1	10	10	2	1.3
1924	Cle-A	12	14	.462	39	27	20	2	1	247^2	267	5	42	34	11.5	3.02	142	.277	.312	18	.202	-1	33	35	3	3.4
1925	Cle-A	11	14	.440	31	30	**22**	1	1	237	296	11	48	30	13.3	4.86	91	.306	.342	28	.304	7	-12	-12	-0	-0.4
1926	Cle-A	11	10	.524	27	24	16	1	0	188^1	214	8	31	25	11.9	3.73	109	.292	.324	14	.215	2	6	7	3	1.2
1927	Cle-A	1	4	.200	11	2	1	0	1	38	53	2	14	8	15.9	5.45	77	.342	.396	2	.167	-0	-6	-5	0	-0.6
Total	14	114	118	.491	373	227	142	16	21	2052^2	2234	57	440	428	11.9	3.32	108	.282	.324	165	.233	22	48	59	26	12.3
Team	6	45	48	.484	140	101	70	5	4	850^2	977	30	175	124	12.4	3.84	110	.291	.329	75	.243	9	33	35	9	5.0
● **WILLIE SMITH** Smith, Willie b: 2/11/39, Anniston, Ala. BL/TL, 6', 190 lbs. Deb: 6/18/63 ♦																										
1968	Cle-A	0	0	—	2	0	0	0	0	5	2	0	1	1	5.4	0.00	—	.125	.176	6	.143	0	2	2	0	0.0
Total	3	2	4	.333	29	3	0	0	2	61	60	7	24	39	12.5	3.10	110	.273	.347	410	.248	6	3	2	1	0.4
● **LARY SORENSEN** Sorensen, Lary Alan b: 10/4/55, Detroit, Mich. BR/TR, 6'2", 210 lbs. Deb: 6/7/77																										
1982	Cle-A	10	15	.400	32	30	6	1	0	189^1	251	19	55	62	14.7	5.61	73	.322	.369	0	—	0	-32	-32	-1	-3.7
1983	Cle-A	12	11	.522	36	34	8	1	0	222^2	238	21	65	76	12.3	4.24	100	.276	.328	0	—	0	-5	-0	2	0.1
Total	11	93	103	.474	346	235	69	10	6	1736^1	1960	147	402	569	12.4	4.15	95	.287	.329	3	.049	-4	-38	-38	1	-4.1
Team	2	22	26	.458	68	64	14	2	0	412	489	40	120	138	13.4	4.87	85	.298	.348	0	—	0	-37	-32	1	-3.6
● **ALLEN SOTHORON** Sothoron, Allen Sutton b: 4/27/1893, Bradford, Ohio d: 6/17/39, St.Louis, Mo. BB/TR, 5'11", 182 lbs. Deb: 9/17/14 MC																										
1921	Cle-A	12	4	.750	22	16	10	2	0	144^2	146	0	58	61	13.1	3.24	132	.279	.358	16	.276	2	17	17	-2	1.5
1922	Cle-A	1	3	.250	6	4	2	0	0	25^1	26	1	14	8	14.9	6.39	63	.274	.378	4	.444	1	-7	-7	-0	-0.8
Total	11	91	100	.476	264	194	102	17	9	1582^1	1583	34	596	576	12.7	3.31	105	.264	.336	113	.207	-2	29	30	-24	0.5
Team	2	13	7	.650	28	20	12	2	0	170	172	1	72	69	13.4	3.71	114	.278	.361	20	.299	3	10	10	-3	0.7
● **BY SPEECE** Speece, Byron Franklin b: 1/6/1897, West Baden, Ind. d: 9/29/74, Elgin, Ore. BR/TR, 5'11", 170 lbs. Deb: 4/21/24																										
1925	Cle-A	3	5	.375	28	3	3	0	1	90^1	106	0	28	26	13.6	4.28	103	.297	.353	5	.161	-2	1	1	0	0.0
1926	Cle-A	0	0	—	2	0	0	0	0	3	1	0	2	1	9.0	0.00	—	.125	.300	0	—	0	1	1	0	0.0
Total	4	5	6	.455	62	4	3	0	1	167^1	208	1	61	51	14.7	4.73	93	.316	.378	9	.167	-2	-6	-6	2	0.4
Team	2	3	5	.375	30	3	3	0	1	93^1	107	0	30	27	13.5	4.15	106	.293	.352	5	.161	-2	2	3	1	0.0
● **DAN SPILLNER** Spillner, Daniel Ray b: 11/27/51, Casper, Wyo. BR/TR, 6'1", 190 lbs. Deb: 5/21/74																										
1978	Cle-A	3	1	.750	36	0	0	0	3	56^1	54	2	21	48	12.1	3.67	102	.254	.323	0	—	0	1	0	-1	-0.1
1979	Cle-A	9	5	.643	49	13	3	0	1	157^2	153	16	64	97	12.6	4.62	92	.256	.331	0	—	0	-7	-6	0	-0.5
1980	Cle-A	16	11	.593	34	30	7	1	0	194^1	225	23	74	100	14.0	5.28	77	.288	.352	0	—	0	-27	-26	-2	-3.3
1981	Cle-A	4	4	.500	32	5	1	0	7	97^1	86	3	39	59	11.6	3.14	115	.240	.314	0	—	0	6	5	0	0.6
1982	Cle-A	12	10	.545	65	0	0	0	21	133^2	117	9	45	90	10.9	2.49	164	.235	.299	0	—	0	**24**	**24**	-3	4.2
1983	Cle-A	2	9	.182	60	0	0	0	8	92^1	117	7	38	48	15.3	5.07	84	.315	.382	0	—	0	-10	-9	-1	-1.3
1984	Cle-A	0	5	.000	14	8	0	0	1	51	70	3	22	23	16.2	5.65	72	.332	.395	0	—	0	-9	-9	1	-0.7
Total	12	75	89	.457	556	123	19	3	50	1492^2	1585	134	605	878	13.3	4.21	91	.275	.345	10	.077	-3	-55	-62	-11	-6.5
Team	7	46	45	.505	290	56	11	1	41	782^2	822	63	303	465	13.0	4.29	94	.271	.340	0	—	0	-24	-21	-6	-1.1
● **JACK SPRING** Spring, Jack Russell b: 3/11/33, Spokane, Wash. BR/TL, 6'1", 180 lbs. Deb: 4/16/55																										
1965	Cle-A	1	2	.333	14	0	0	0	0	21^2	21	2	10	9	12.9	3.74	93	.259	.341	1	.333	0	-1	-1	-1	-0.1
Total	8	12	5	.706	155	5	0	0	8	186	195	21	78	86	13.5	4.26	90	.273	.349	3	.107	-1	-9	-9	1	-0.3
● **LEE STANGE** Stange, Albert Lee b: 10/27/36, Chicago, Ill. BR/TR, 5'10", 170 lbs. Deb: 4/15/61 C																										
1964	Cle-A	4	8	.333	23	14	0	0	0	91^2	98	14	31	78	12.8	4.12	87	.270	.329	2	.080	-1	-5	-5	-0	-0.8
1965	Cle-A	8	4	.667	41	12	4	2	0	132	122	13	26	80	10.2	3.34	104	.247	.286	3	.107	1	2	2	-2	0.1
1966	Cle-A	1	0	1.000	8	2	1	0	0	16	17	1	3	8	11.8	2.81	122	.279	.323	1	.250	0	1	1	-0	0.1
Total	10	62	61	.504	359	125	32	8	21	1216	1172	142	344	718	11.3	3.56	102	.252	.306	24	.079	-11	-8	12	-9	-1.5
Team	3	13	12	.520	72	28	5	2	0	239^2	237	28	60	166	11.3	3.61	98	.258	.306	6	.105	1	-2	-2	-3	-0.6
● **MIKE STANTON** Stanton, Michael Thomas b: 9/25/52, Phenix City, Ala. BB/TR, 6'2", 205 lbs. Deb: 7/9/75																										
1980	Cle-A	1	3	.250	51	0	0	0	5	85^2	98	5	44	74	15.2	5.46	75	.297	.385	0	—	0	-14	-13	1	-0.6
1981	Cle-A	3	3	.500	24	0	0	0	2	43^1	43	4	18	34	12.7	4.36	83	.262	.335	0	—	0	-3	-4	-1	-0.5
Total	7	13	22	.371	277	3	0	0	31	384^1	398	27	182	304	13.8	4.61	88	.272	.356	1	.250	0	-27	-24	1	-1.7
Team	2	4	6	.400	75	0	0	0	7	129	141	9	62	108	14.4	5.09	77	.285	.369	0	—	0	-17	-17	0	-1.1
● **BILL STEEN** Steen, William John b: 11/11/1887, Pittsburgh, Pa. d: 3/13/79, Signal Hill, Cal. BR/TR, 6'0.5", 180 lbs. Deb: 4/15/12																										
1912	Cle-A	9	8	.529	26	16	6	1	0	143^1	163	3	45	61	13.1	3.77	90	.298	.352	13	.271	2	-7	-6	-1	-0.5
1913	Cle-A	4	5	.444	22	13	7	2	2	128^1	113	3	49	57	11.6	2.45	124	.237	.313	7	.171	-0	7	8	-0	0.5
1914	Cle-A	9	14	.391	30	22	13	1	0	200^2	201	0	68	97	12.2	2.60	111	.272	.337	14	.200	1	3	6	0	0.8
1915	Cle-A	1	4	.200	10	7	2	0	0	45^1	51	1	15	22	13.5	4.96	61	.290	.352	3	.188	-0	-10	-10	2	-0.8
Total	4	28	32	.467	108	65	31	4	6	597	611	7	199	265	12.4	3.05	101	.272	.334	42	.207	1	-6	2	2	0.3
Team	4	23	31	.426	88	58	28	4	2	517^2	528	7	177	237	12.4	3.09	100	.272	.337	37	.211	2	-7	-1	1	0.0
● **BRYAN STEPHENS** Stephens, Bryan Maris b: 7/14/20, Fayetteville, Ark d: 11/21/91, Santa Ana, Cal. BR/TR, 6'4", 175 lbs. Deb: 5/15/47																										
1947	Cle-A	5	10	.333	31	5	1	0	1	92	79	6	39	34	11.7	4.01	87	.230	.312	3	.111	-2	-3	-5	-1	-1.1
Total	2	8	16	.333	74	17	3	0	4	214^2	220	20	106	69	13.9	5.16	79	.264	.352	7	.119	-3	-27	-26	-2	-2.6
● **SAMMY STEWART** Stewart, Samuel Lee b: 10/28/54, Asheville, N.C. BR/TR, 6'3", 208 lbs. Deb: 9/1/78																										
1987	Cle-A	4	2	.667	25	0	0	0	3	27	25	4	21	25	15.7	5.67	80	.234	.364	0	—	0	-4	-3	0	-0.7
Total	10	59	48	.551	359	25	4	1	45	956^2	863	77	502	586	13.0	3.59	110	.245	.341	0	—	0	49	39	-1	4.4

YEAR	TM/L	W	L	PCT	G	GS	CG	SH	SV	IP	H	HR	BB	SO	RAT	ERA	ERA+	OAV	OOB	BH	AVG	PB	PR	/A	PD	TPI

● LEFTY STEWART
Stewart, Walter Cleveland b: 9/23/1900, Sparta, Tenn. d: 9/26/74, Knoxville, Tenn. BR/TL, 5'10", 160 lbs. Deb: 4/20/21

| 1935 | Cle-A | 6 | 6 | .500 | 24 | 10 | 2 | 0 | 2 | 91 | 122 | 6 | 17 | 24 | 13.8 | 5.44 | 83 | .312 | .342 | 6 | .200 | -1 | -10 | -9 | -1 | -1.3 |
| Total | 10 | 101 | 98 | .508 | 279 | 216 | 107 | 8 | 8 | 1722 | 1895 | 117 | 498 | 503 | 12.6 | 4.19 | 108 | .281 | .332 | 115 | .204 | 6 | 35 | 64 | 0 | 7.0 |

● DICK STIGMAN
Stigman, Richard Lewis b: 1/24/36, Nimrod, Minn. BR/TL, 6'3", 200 lbs. Deb: 4/22/60

1960	Cle-A☆	5	11	.313	41	18	3	0	9	133²	118	13	87	104	13.8	4.51	83	.238	.352	8	.222	2	-9	-11	-2	-1.4
1961	Cle-A	2	5	.286	22	6	0	0	0	64¹	65	9	25	48	12.6	4.62	85	.264	.332	2	.125	-1	-4	-5	0	-0.5
Total	7	46	54	.460	235	119	30	5	16	922²	819	133	406	755	12.0	4.03	93	.237	.318	32	.113	-8	-32	-29	-13	-4.0
Team	2	7	16	.304	63	24	3	0	9	198	183	22	112	152	13.4	4.55	84	.247	.346	10	.192	1	-14	-16	-1	-1.9

● TIM STODDARD
Stoddard, Timothy Paul b: 1/24/53, E.Chicago, Ind. BR/TR, 6'7", 250 lbs. Deb: 9/7/75

| 1989 | Cle-A | 0 | 0 | — | 14 | 0 | 0 | 0 | 0 | 21¹ | 25 | 1 | 7 | 12 | 13.5 | 2.95 | 134 | .313 | .368 | 0 | — | 0 | 2 | 2 | 0 | -0.1 |
| Total | 13 | 41 | 35 | .539 | 485 | 0 | 0 | 0 | 76 | 729² | 680 | 72 | 356 | 582 | 12.9 | 3.95 | 100 | .250 | .339 | 2 | .100 | -0 | 2 | -0 | -3 | -0.1 |

● JESSE STOVALL
Stovall, Jesse Cramer "Scout" b: 7/24/1875, Independence, Mo. d: 7/12/55, San Diego, Cal. BL/TR, 6', 175 lbs. Deb: 8/31/03 F

| 1903 | Cle-A | 5 | 1 | .833 | 6 | 6 | 6 | 3 | 0 | 57 | 44 | 0 | 21 | 12 | 10.7 | 2.05 | 139 | .213 | .294 | 1 | .045 | -2 | 6 | 5 | -1 | 0.2 |
| Total | 2 | 8 | 14 | .364 | 28 | 23 | 19 | 3 | 0 | 203² | 214 | 3 | 66 | 53 | 13.2 | 3.76 | 70 | .270 | .341 | 12 | .154 | -2 | -24 | -25 | -0 | -2.8 |

● OSCAR STREIT
Streit, Oscar William b: 7/7/1873, Florence, Ala. d: 10/10/35, Birmingham, Ala. BL/TL, 6'5", 190 lbs. Deb: 4/21/1899

| 1902 | Cle-A | 0 | 7 | .000 | 8 | 7 | 4 | 0 | 0 | 51² | 72 | 3 | 25 | 10 | 17.4 | 5.23 | 66 | .330 | .407 | 4 | .211 | 1 | -9 | -10 | -1 | -1.1 |
| Total | 2 | 1 | 7 | .125 | 10 | 8 | 5 | 0 | 0 | 66¹ | 87 | 4 | 40 | 10 | 17.9 | 5.56 | 65 | .316 | .412 | 4 | .154 | -0 | -14 | -14 | -1 | -1.4 |

● JIM STRICKLAND
Strickland, James Michael b: 6/12/46, Los Angeles, Cal. BL/TL, 6', 175 lbs. Deb: 5/19/71

| 1975 | Cle-A | 0 | 0 | — | 4 | 0 | 0 | 0 | 1 | 4² | 4 | 0 | 2 | 3 | 13.5 | 1.93 | 196 | .222 | .333 | 0 | — | 0 | 1 | 1 | -0 | 0.0 |
| Total | 4 | 4 | 2 | .667 | 60 | 0 | 0 | 0 | 5 | 77¹ | 63 | 9 | 44 | 60 | 12.8 | 2.68 | 128 | .223 | .333 | 1 | .250 | 1 | 6 | 7 | 0 | 0.1 |

● JAKE STRIKER
Striker, Wilbur Scott b: 10/23/33, New Washington, O. BL/TL, 6'2", 200 lbs. Deb: 9/25/59

| 1959 | Cle-A | 1 | 0 | 1.000 | 1 | 1 | 1 | 0 | 0 | 6² | 8 | 0 | 4 | 5 | 16.2 | 2.70 | 136 | .296 | .387 | 0 | .000 | 1 | 1 | 1 | -0 | 0.2 |
| Total | 2 | 1 | 0 | 1.000 | 3 | 1 | 1 | 0 | 0 | 10¹ | 13 | 1 | 5 | 6 | 16.5 | 3.48 | 107 | .317 | .404 | 0 | .000 | 1 | 0 | 0 | -0 | 0.2 |

● BRENT STROM
Strom, Brent Terry b: 10/14/48, San Diego, Cal. BR/TL, 6'3", 190 lbs. Deb: 7/31/72

| 1973 | Cle-A | 2 | 10 | .167 | 27 | 18 | 2 | 0 | 0 | 123 | 134 | 18 | 47 | 91 | 13.5 | 4.61 | 85 | .278 | .346 | 0 | — | 0 | -11 | -9 | 1 | -0.8 |
| Total | 5 | 22 | 39 | .361 | 100 | 75 | 16 | 5 | 0 | 501 | 482 | 51 | 180 | 278 | 12.0 | 3.95 | 88 | .254 | .321 | 8 | .078 | -3 | -19 | -26 | 0 | -2.3 |

● FLOYD STROMME
Stromme, Floyd Marvin "Rock" b: 8/1/16, Cooperstown, N.Dak. d: 2/7/93, Wenatchee, Wash. BR/TR, 5'11", 170 lbs. Deb: 7/5/39

| 1939 | Cle-A | 0 | 1 | .000 | 5 | 0 | 0 | 0 | 0 | 13 | 13 | 1 | 13 | 4 | 18.0 | 4.85 | 91 | .265 | .419 | 1 | .333 | 0 | -0 | -1 | -0 | 0.0 |

● CHARLEY SUCHE
Suche, Charles Morris b: 8/5/15, Cranes Mill, Tex. d: 2/11/84, San Antonio, Tex. BR/TL, 6'2", 190 lbs. Deb: 9/18/38

| 1938 | Cle-A | 0 | 0 | — | 1 | 0 | 0 | 0 | 0 | 1¹ | 4 | 0 | 3 | 1 | 47.3 | 27.00 | 17 | .571 | .700 | 1 | 1.000 | 0 | -3 | -3 | 0 | 0.1 |

● JIM SULLIVAN
Sullivan, James Richard b: 4/5/1894, Mine Run, Va. d: 2/12/72, Burtonsville, Md. BR/TR, 5'11", 165 lbs. Deb: 9/27/21

| 1923 | Cle-A | 0 | 1 | .000 | 3 | 0 | 0 | 0 | 0 | 5 | 10 | 0 | 5 | 4 | 28.8 | 14.40 | 28 | .476 | .593 | 1 | .000 | -0 | -6 | -6 | 0 | -0.9 |
| Total | 3 | 0 | 5 | .000 | 25 | 4 | 3 | 0 | 0 | 73¹ | 106 | 3 | 37 | 27 | 13.8 | 5.52 | 78 | .362 | .437 | 1 | .056 | -2 | -12 | -10 | -1 | -1.1 |

● LEFTY SULLIVAN
Sullivan, Paul Thomas b: 9/7/16, Nashville, Tenn. d: 11/1/88, Scottsdale, Ariz. BL/TL, 6'3", 204 lbs. Deb: 5/6/39

| 1939 | Cle-A | 0 | 1 | .000 | 7 | 1 | 0 | 0 | 0 | 12² | 9 | 0 | 9 | 4 | 13.5 | 4.26 | 103 | .214 | .365 | 0 | .000 | -0 | 1 | 0 | -1 | -0.1 |

● RICK SUTCLIFFE
Sutcliffe, Richard Lee b: 6/21/56, Independence, Mo. BL/TR, 6'7", 215 lbs. Deb: 9/29/76

1982	Cle-A	14	8	.636	34	27	6	1	1	216	174	16	98	142	11.5	**2.96**	138	**.226**	.317	0	—	0	**27**	27	1	2.7
1983	Cle-A☆	17	11	.607	36	35	10	2	0	243²	251	23	102	160	13.3	4.29	99	.268	.344	0	—	0	-6	-1	2	-0.2
1984	Cle-A	4	5	.444	15	15	2	0	0	94¹	111	7	46	58	15.2	5.15	79	.298	.378	0	—	0	-12	-11	-0	-1.0
Total	18	171	139	.552	457	392	72	18	6	2697²	2662	236	1081	1679	12.6	4.08	97	.260	.334	102	.181	17	-77	-34	10	-1.4
Team	3	35	24	.593	85	77	18	3	1	553²	536	46	246	360	12.9	3.92	106	.258	.340	0	—	0	8	14	2	1.5

● DARRELL SUTHERLAND
Sutherland, Darrell Wayne b: 11/14/41, Glendale, Cal. BR/TR, 6'4", 169 lbs. Deb: 6/28/64 F

| 1968 | Cle-A | 0 | 0 | — | 3 | 0 | 0 | 0 | 0 | 3¹ | 6 | 0 | 4 | 2 | 27.0 | 8.10 | 37 | .375 | .500 | 0 | — | 0 | -2 | -2 | -0 | 0.0 |
| Total | 4 | 5 | 4 | .556 | 62 | 6 | 0 | 0 | 1 | 122¹ | 131 | 11 | 58 | 60 | 14.5 | 4.78 | 75 | .282 | .371 | 5 | .238 | 1 | -17 | -17 | 3 | -0.7 |

● RUSS SWAN
Swan, Russell Howard b: 1/3/64, Fremont, Cal. BL/TL, 6'4", 210 lbs. Deb: 8/3/89

| 1994 | Cle-A | 0 | 1 | .000 | 12 | 0 | 0 | 0 | 0 | 8 | 13 | 1 | 7 | 2 | 22.5 | 11.25 | 42 | .382 | .488 | 0 | — | 0 | -6 | -6 | 0 | -0.6 |
| Total | 6 | 14 | 22 | .389 | 168 | 20 | 1 | 0 | 11 | 266² | 282 | 26 | 124 | 108 | 13.9 | 4.83 | 84 | .275 | .356 | 0 | .000 | 0 | -24 | -23 | 3 | -4.7 |

● GREG SWINDELL
Swindell, Forest Gregory b: 1/2/65, Fort Worth, Tex. BR/TL, 6'2", 225 lbs. Deb: 8/21/86

1986	Cle-A	5	2	.714	9	9	1	0	0	61²	57	9	15	46	10.7	4.23	98	.243	.291	0	—	0	-0	-1	0	0.1
1987	Cle-A	3	8	.273	16	15	4	1	0	102¹	112	18	37	97	13.2	5.10	89	.283	.346	0	—	0	-7	-7	-0	-0.7
1988	Cle-A	18	14	.563	33	33	12	4	0	242	234	18	45	180	10.4	3.20	129	.252	.287	0	—	0	21	25	-1	2.9
1989	Cle-A★	13	6	.684	28	28	5	2	0	184¹	170	16	51	129	10.8	3.37	118	.246	.298	0	—	0	11	12	-0	1.0
1990	Cle-A	12	9	.571	34	34	3	0	0	214²	245	27	47	135	12.3	4.40	89	.288	.326	0	—	0	-12	-12	-2	-1.2
1991	Cle-A	9	16	.360	33	33	7	0	0	238	241	21	31	169	10.4	3.48	119	.263	.289	0	—	0	16	18	-1	1.6
Total	10	102	94	.520	272	262	40	12	0	1748¹	1839	188	372	1188	11.4	3.80	105	.272	.311	44	.188	6	37	35	-5	3.6
Team	6	60	55	.522	153	152	32	7	0	1043	1059	109	226	756	11.1	3.79	108	.264	.304	0	—	0	28	36	-4	3.7

● JOSH SWINDELL
Swindell, Joshua Ernest b: 7/5/1883, Rose Hill, Kan. d: 3/19/69, Fruita, Colo. BR/TR, 6', 180 lbs. Deb: 9/16/11 ♦

| 1911 | Cle-A | 0 | 1 | .000 | 4 | 1 | 0 | 0 | 0 | 17¹ | 19 | 0 | 4 | 6 | 12.5 | 2.08 | 164 | .257 | .304 | 1 | .250 | -0 | 2 | 3 | -0 | 0.1 |

● JULIAN TAVAREZ
Tavarez, Julian (Carmen) b: 5/22/73, Santiago, D.R. BR/TR, 6'2", 165 lbs. Deb: 8/7/93

1993	Cle-A	2	2	.500	8	7	0	0	0	37	53	7	13	19	16.5	6.57	66	.340	.398	0	—	0	-9	-9	-0	-0.8
1994	Cle-A	0	1	.000	1	1	0	0	0	1²	6	1	1	0	37.8	21.60	22	.500	.538	0	—	0	-3	-3	0	-1.0
1995	*Cle-A	10	2	.833	57	0	0	0	0	85	76	7	21	68	10.6	2.44	190	.235	.287	0	—	0	22	21	0	2.5
Total	3	12	5	.706	66	8	0	0	0	123²	135	15	35	87	12.7	3.93	116	.274	.329	0	—	0	9	8	-0	0.7

● DUMMY TAYLOR
Taylor, Luther Haden b: 2/21/1875, Oskaloosa, Kan. d: 8/22/58, Jacksonville, Ill. BR/TR, 6'1", 160 lbs. Deb: 8/27/00

| 1902 | Cle-A | 1 | 3 | .250 | 4 | 4 | 4 | 1 | 0 | 34 | 37 | 0 | 8 | 8 | 12.4 | 1.59 | 217 | .278 | .329 | 1 | .100 | -0 | 8 | 7 | 1 | 0.9 |
| Total | 9 | 116 | 106 | .523 | 274 | 237 | 160 | 21 | 3 | 1916¹ | 1877 | 39 | 551 | 767 | 11.7 | 2.75 | 107 | .256 | .314 | 93 | .144 | -17 | 40 | 39 | 0 | 2.9 |

● RON TAYLOR
Taylor, Ronald Wesley b: 12/13/37, Toronto, Ont., Can. BR/TR, 6'1", 195 lbs. Deb: 4/11/62

| 1962 | Cle-A | 2 | 2 | .500 | 8 | 4 | 1 | 0 | 0 | 33¹ | 36 | 6 | 13 | 15 | 13.5 | 5.94 | 65 | .281 | .352 | 3 | .273 | 0 | -7 | -8 | -0 | -0.8 |
| Total | 11 | 45 | 43 | .511 | 491 | 17 | 3 | 0 | 72 | 800 | 794 | 76 | 209 | 464 | 11.5 | 3.93 | 91 | .264 | .316 | 12 | .103 | -5 | -39 | -32 | -2 | -1.5 |

● AL TEDROW
Tedrow, Allen Seymour b: 12/14/1891, Westerville, Ohio d: 1/23/58, Westerville, Ohio BR/TL, 6', 180 lbs. Deb: 9/15/14

| 1914 | Cle-A | 1 | 2 | .333 | 4 | 3 | 1 | 0 | 0 | 22¹ | 19 | 0 | 14 | 4 | 14.5 | 1.21 | 239 | .235 | .367 | 1 | .167 | 0 | 4 | 4 | -0 | 0.6 |

● RALPH TERRY
Terry, Ralph Willard b: 1/9/36, Big Cabin, Okla. BR/TR, 6'3", 195 lbs. Deb: 8/6/56

| 1965 | Cle-A | 11 | 6 | .647 | 36 | 26 | 4 | 3 | 0 | 165² | 154 | 20 | 23 | 84 | 9.7 | 3.69 | 94 | .242 | .269 | 7 | .143 | 2 | -4 | -4 | -4 | -0.6 |
| Total | 12 | 107 | 99 | .519 | 338 | 257 | 75 | 20 | 11 | 1849¹ | 1748 | 216 | 446 | 1000 | 10.8 | 3.62 | 102 | .249 | .296 | 95 | .160 | -6 | 32 | 13 | -11 | -1.6 |

● JAKE THIELMAN
Thielman, John Peter b: 5/20/1879, St.Cloud, Minn. d: 1/28/28, Minneapolis, Minn. BR/TR, 5'11", 175 lbs. Deb: 4/23/05 F

| 1907 | Cle-A | 11 | 8 | .579 | 20 | 18 | 18 | 3 | 0 | 166 | 151 | 2 | 34 | 56 | 10.4 | 2.33 | 108 | .244 | .291 | 12 | .203 | 1 | 4 | 3 | -3 | 0.2 |

YEAR TM/L	W	L	PCT	G	GS	CG	SH	SV	IP	H	HR	BB	SO	RAT	ERA	ERA+	OAV	OOB	BH	AVG	PB	PR	/A	PD	TPI
1908 Cle-A	4	3	.571	11	8	5	0	0	61^2	59	2	9	15	10.5	3.65	66	.260	.300	8	.348	4	-9	-9	2	-0.4
Total 4	30	28	.517	65	56	49	3	0	475^1	483	9	107	158	11.6	3.16	86	.266	.315	42	.240	13	-21	-23	2	-0.8
Team 2	15	11	.577	31	26	23	3	0	227^2	210	4	43	71	10.4	2.69	92	.249	.294	20	.244	5	-5	-5	-1	-0.2

● CARL THOMAS Thomas, Carl Leslie b: 5/28/32, Minneapolis, Minn. BR/TR, 6'5", 245 lbs. Deb: 4/19/60

YEAR TM/L	W	L	PCT	G	GS	CG	SH	SV	IP	H	HR	BB	SO	RAT	ERA	ERA+	OAV	OOB	BH	AVG	PB	PR	/A	PD	TPI
1960 Cle-A	1	0	1.000	4	0	0	0	0	9^2	8	1	10	5	17.7	7.45	50	.229	.413	1	.333	1	-4	-4	0	-0.3

● FAY THOMAS Thomas, Fay Wesley "Scow" b: 10/10/04, Holyrood, Kan. d: 8/16/90, Chatsworth, Cal. BR/TR, 6'2", 195 lbs. Deb: 6/27/27

YEAR TM/L	W	L	PCT	G	GS	CG	SH	SV	IP	H	HR	BB	SO	RAT	ERA	ERA+	OAV	OOB	BH	AVG	PB	PR	/A	PD	TPI
1931 Cle-A	2	4	.333	16	2	1	0	0	48^2	63	2	32	25	17.8	5.18	89	.323	.421	2	.154	-1	-4	-3	-1	-0.4
Total 4	9	20	.310	81	23	5	0	1	229	269	16	133	112	16.0	4.95	93	.299	.392	6	.107	-4	-15	-9	1	-0.9

● STAN THOMAS Thomas, Stanley Brown b: 7/11/49, Rumford, Me. BR/TR, 6'2", 185 lbs. Deb: 7/5/74

YEAR TM/L	W	L	PCT	G	GS	CG	SH	SV	IP	H	HR	BB	SO	RAT	ERA	ERA+	OAV	OOB	BH	AVG	PB	PR	/A	PD	TPI
1976 Cle-A	4	4	.500	37	7	2	0	6	105^2	88	5	41	54	11.3	2.30	152	.229	.310	0	—	0	14	14	3	1.6
Total 4	11	14	.440	111	17	3	0	9	265^1	263	16	110	123	13.0	3.70	101	.261	.340	0	—	0	1	1	3	0.6

● RICH THOMPSON Thompson, Richard Neil b: 11/1/58, New York, N.Y. BR/TR, 6'3", 225 lbs. Deb: 4/28/85

YEAR TM/L	W	L	PCT	G	GS	CG	SH	SV	IP	H	HR	BB	SO	RAT	ERA	ERA+	OAV	OOB	BH	AVG	PB	PR	/A	PD	TPI
1985 Cle-A	3	8	.273	57	0	0	0	5	80	95	8	48	30	16.8	6.30	66	.303	.405	0	—	0	-19	-19	-2	-2.6
Total 3	3	10	.231	77	1	0	0	5	114	123	10	59	45	15.0	5.05	78	.286	.382	0	.000	0	-14	-14	-2	-2.3

● LUIS TIANT Tiant, Luis Clemente (Vega) b: 11/23/40, Marianao, Cuba BR/TR, 5'11", 190 lbs. Deb: 7/19/64

YEAR TM/L	W	L	PCT	G	GS	CG	SH	SV	IP	H	HR	BB	SO	RAT	ERA	ERA+	OAV	OOB	BH	AVG	PB	PR	/A	PD	TPI
1964 Cle-A	10	4	.714	19	16	9	3	1	127	94	13	47	105	10.1	2.83	127	.207	.284	5	.111	-1	11	11	0	1.1
1965 Cle-A	11	11	.500	41	30	10	2	1	196^1	166	20	66	152	10.8	3.53	99	.228	.295	6	.088	-2	-2	-1	-0	-0.3
1966 Cle-A	12	11	.522	46	16	7	**5**	8	155	121	16	50	145	10.0	2.79	123	.213	.279	4	.111	-1	11	11	-1	1.6
1967 Cle-A	12	9	.571	33	29	9	1	2	213^2	177	24	67	219	10.3	2.74	119	.221	.282	18	.254	5	12	13	-2	1.6
1968 Cle-A★	21	9	.700	34	32	19	**9**	0	258^1	152	16	73	264	8.0	**1.60**	**185**	**.168**	**.233**	7	.080	-5	**40**	39	-3	4.2
1969 Cle-A	9	20	.310	38	37	9	1	0	249^2	229	37	129	156	13.2	3.71	101	.246	.343	19	.235	6	-3	1	-1	0.7
Total 19	229	172	.571	573	484	187	49	15	3486^1	3075	346	1104	2416	10.9	3.30	113	.236	.298	84	.164	6	116	173	-21	17.3
Team 6	75	64	.540	211	160	63	21	12	1200	939	126	432	1041	10.4	2.84	119	.214	.287	59	.152	1	69	74	-6	8.9

● DICK TIDROW Tidrow, Richard William b: 5/14/47, San Francisco, Cal. BR/TR, 6'4", 213 lbs. Deb: 4/18/72

YEAR TM/L	W	L	PCT	G	GS	CG	SH	SV	IP	H	HR	BB	SO	RAT	ERA	ERA+	OAV	OOB	BH	AVG	PB	PR	/A	PD	TPI
1972 Cle-A	14	15	.483	39	34	10	3	0	237^1	200	21	70	123	10.5	2.77	116	.230	.291	7	.100	-3	8	12	-4	0.7
1973 Cle-A	14	16	.467	42	40	13	2	0	274^2	289	31	95	138	12.8	4.42	89	.270	.334	0	—	0	-19	-15	-2	-1.7
1974 Cle-A	1	3	.250	4	4	0	0	0	19	21	4	13	8	17.1	7.11	51	.276	.396	0	—	0	-7	-7	0	-1.2
Total 13	100	94	.515	620	138	32	5	55	1746^2	1705	163	579	975	12.0	3.68	101	.257	.321	9	.095	-5	-5	7	-12	-0.1
Team 3	29	34	.460	85	78	23	5	0	531	510	56	178	269	11.9	3.78	95	.253	.318	7	.100	-3	-18	-11	-5	-2.2

● BOBBY TIEFENAUER Tiefenauer, Bobby Gene b: 10/10/29, Desloge, Mo. BR/TR, 6'2", 185 lbs. Deb: 7/14/52 C

YEAR TM/L	W	L	PCT	G	GS	CG	SH	SV	IP	H	HR	BB	SO	RAT	ERA	ERA+	OAV	OOB	BH	AVG	PB	PR	/A	PD	TPI
1960 Cle-A	0	1	.000	6	0	0	0	0	9	8	0	3	2	11.0	2.00	187	.242	.306	0	.000	0	2	2	-0	0.2
1965 Cle-A	0	5	.000	15	0	0	0	4	22^1	24	3	10	13	14.1	4.84	72	.273	.354	0	.000	-0	-3	-3	-0	-0.9
1967 Cle-A	0	1	.000	5	0	0	0	0	11^1	9	0	3	6	9.5	0.79	411	.225	.279	0	—	0	3	3	-1	0.2
Total 10	9	25	.265	179	0	0	0	23	316	312	29	87	204	11.7	3.84	94	.260	.317	1	.026	-1	-7	-9	-2	-1.2
Team 3	0	7	.000	26	0	0	0	4	42^2	41	3	16	21	12.2	3.16	110	.255	.326	0	.000	0	2	2	-1	-0.5

● TOM TIMMERMANN Timmermann, Thomas Henry b: 5/12/40, Breese, Ill. BR/TR, 6'4", 215 lbs. Deb: 6/18/69

YEAR TM/L	W	L	PCT	G	GS	CG	SH	SV	IP	H	HR	BB	SO	RAT	ERA	ERA+	OAV	OOB	BH	AVG	PB	PR	/A	PD	TPI
1973 Cle-A	8	7	.533	29	15	4	0	2	124^1	117	15	54	62	12.6	4.92	80	.251	.332	0	—	0	-15	-14	-0	-1.6
1974 Cle-A	1	1	.500	4	0	0	0	0	10	9	1	5	2	12.6	5.40	67	.250	.341	0	—	0	-2	-2	1	-0.3
Total 6	35	35	.500	228	44	8	2	35	548	508	42	208	315	12.0	3.78	96	.246	.319	8	.091	-4	-16	-10	-3	-2.7
Team 2	9	8	.529	33	15	4	0	2	134^1	126	16	59	64	12.6	4.96	79	.250	.333	0	—	0	-17	-16	0	-1.9

● DICK TOMANEK Tomanek, Richard Carl "Bones" b: 1/6/31, Avon Lake, Ohio BL/TL, 6'1", 175 lbs. Deb: 9/25/53

YEAR TM/L	W	L	PCT	G	GS	CG	SH	SV	IP	H	HR	BB	SO	RAT	ERA	ERA+	OAV	OOB	BH	AVG	PB	PR	/A	PD	TPI
1953 Cle-A	1	0	1.000	1	1	1	0	0	9	6	1	6	6	13.0	2.00	188	.176	.317	0	.000	-1	2	2	-0	0.1
1954 Cle-A	0	0	—	1	0	0	0	0	1^2	1	1	1	0	10.8	5.40	68	.167	.286	0	—	0	-0	-0	0	0.0
1957 Cle-A	2	1	.667	34	2	0	0	0	69^2	67	13	37	55	13.6	5.68	65	.248	.341	3	.231	0	-15	-15	0	-0.5
1958 Cle-A	2	3	.400	18	6	2	0	0	57^2	61	8	28	42	14.2	5.62	65	.276	.363	2	.118	0	-12	-13	0	-0.9
Total 5	10	10	.500	106	11	4	0	7	231	231	34	112	166	13.6	4.95	77	.259	.346	9	.180	1	-30	-30	1	-1.2
Team 4	5	4	.556	54	9	3	0	0	138	135	23	72	103	13.8	5.41	68	.254	.348	5	.143	-0	-25	-26	0	-1.3

● RED TORKELSON Torkelson, Chester Leroy b: 3/19/1894, Chicago, Ill. d: 9/22/64, Chicago, Ill. BR/TR, 6', 175 lbs. Deb: 8/29/17

YEAR TM/L	W	L	PCT	G	GS	CG	SH	SV	IP	H	HR	BB	SO	RAT	ERA	ERA+	OAV	OOB	BH	AVG	PB	PR	/A	PD	TPI
1917 Cle-A	2	1	.667	4	3	0	0	0	22^1	33	1	13	10	19.3	7.66	37	.333	.421	2	.222	-0	-12	-12	0	-1.3

● HAPPY TOWNSEND Townsend, John b: 4/9/1879, Townsend, Del. d: 12/21/63, Wilmington, Del. BR/TR, 6', 190 lbs. Deb: 4/19/01

YEAR TM/L	W	L	PCT	G	GS	CG	SH	SV	IP	H	HR	BB	SO	RAT	ERA	ERA+	OAV	OOB	BH	AVG	PB	PR	/A	PD	TPI
1906 Cle-A	3	7	.300	17	12	8	1	0	92^2	92	1	31	31	12.5	2.91	90	.262	.332	4	.133	-1	-2	-3	-0	-0.5
Total 6	35	82	.299	153	125	107	5	0	1137^2	1154	24	416	473	12.9	3.59	84	.264	.335	71	.166	-8	-82	-75	-7	-8.5

● MATT TURNER Turner, William Matthew b: 2/18/67, Lexington, Ky. BR/TR, 6'5", 215 lbs. Deb: 4/23/93

YEAR TM/L	W	L	PCT	G	GS	CG	SH	SV	IP	H	HR	BB	SO	RAT	ERA	ERA+	OAV	OOB	BH	AVG	PB	PR	/A	PD	TPI
1994 Cle-A	1	0	1.000	9	0	0	0	1	12^2	13	0	7	5	16.3	2.13	221	.241	.359	0	—	0	4	4	0	0.3
Total 2	5	5	.500	64	0	0	0	1	80^2	68	7	33	64	11.7	2.79	157	.230	.315	0	.000	-0	12	14	0	1.6

● DAVE TYRIVER Tyriver, David Burton b: 10/31/37, Oshkosh, Wis. d: 10/28/88, Oshkosh, Wis. BR/TR, 6' ", 175 lbs. Deb: 8/21/62

YEAR TM/L	W	L	PCT	G	GS	CG	SH	SV	IP	H	HR	BB	SO	RAT	ERA	ERA+	OAV	OOB	BH	AVG	PB	PR	/A	PD	TPI
1962 Cle-A	0	0	—	4	0	0	0	0	10^2	10	2	7	7	15.2	4.22	92	.250	.375	0	.000	-0	-0	-0	0	0.0

● GEORGE UHLE Uhle, George Ernest "The Bull" b: 9/18/1898, Cleveland, Ohio d: 2/26/85, Lakewood, Ohio BR/TR, 6', 190 lbs. Deb: 4/30/19 C♦

YEAR TM/L	W	L	PCT	G	GS	CG	SH	SV	IP	H	HR	BB	SO	RAT	ERA	ERA+	OAV	OOB	BH	AVG	PB	PR	/A	PD	TPI
1919 Cle-A	10	5	.667	26	12	7	1	0	127	129	1	43	50	12.7	2.91	115	.261	.329	13	.302	3	5	6	0	1.0
1920 *Cle-A	4	5	.444	27	6	2	0	1	84^2	98	3	29	27	14.4	5.21	73	.296	.367	11	.344	2	-13	-13	0	-1.0
1921 Cle-A	16	13	.552	41	28	13	2	2	238	288	9	63	63	13.4	4.01	106	.306	.352	23	.245	3	7	7	-3	0.7
1922 Cle-A	22	16	.579	50	40	23	**5**	3	287^1	328	6	89	82	13.5	4.07	98	.290	.348	29	.266	9	-1	-2	-3	0.1
1923 Cle-A	**26**	16	.619	54	44	**29**	1	5	**357^2**	378	8	102	109	12.4	3.77	105	.271	.326	52	.361	16	8	8	0	2.4
1924 Cle-A	9	15	.375	28	25	15	0	1	196^1	238	6	75	57	14.9	4.77	90	.306	.376	33	.308	7	-12	-11	1	-0.4
1925 Cle-A	13	11	.542	29	26	17	1	0	210^2	218	5	78	68	13.0	4.10	108	.268	.339	29	.287	6	7	7	-3	1.0
1926 Cle-A	**27**	11	**.711**	39	36	**32**	3	1	**318^1**	300	7	118	159	12.2	2.83	143	.253	.328	30	.227	4	42	43	-0	**5.2**
1927 Cle-A	8	9	.471	25	22	10	1	1	153^1	187	3	59	69	15.0	4.34	97	.310	.379	21	.266	4	-3	-2	-1	0.0
1928 Cle-A	12	17	.414	31	28	18	2	1	214^1	252	8	48	74	12.9	4.07	102	.300	.344	28	.286	7	-1	2	3	1.1
1936 Cle-A	0	1	.000	7	0	0	0	0	12^2	26	2	5	5	22.0	8.53	59	.419	.463	8	.381	4	-5	-5	-1	0.0
Total 17	200	166	.546	513	368	232	21	25	3119^2	3417	119	966	1135	13.0	3.99	105	.281	.340	393	.289	92	60	74	-15	13.5
Team 11	147	119	.553	357	267	166	16	15	2200^1	2442	58	709	763	13.3	3.92	104	.285	.346	277	.289	65	34	40	-6	10.1

● JERRY UJDUR Ujdur, Gerald Raymond b: 3/5/57, Duluth, Minn. BR/TR, 6'1", 195 lbs. Deb: 8/17/80

YEAR TM/L	W	L	PCT	G	GS	CG	SH	SV	IP	H	HR	BB	SO	RAT	ERA	ERA+	OAV	OOB	BH	AVG	PB	PR	/A	PD	TPI
1984 Cle-A	1	2	.333	4	3	0	0	0	14^1	22	1	6	6	18.8	6.91	59	.355	.429	0	—	0	-5	-4	-1	-0.9
Total 5	12	16	.429	53	40	7	0	0	261^2	268	43	110	118	13.2	4.78	84	.266	.342	0	—	0	-21	-22	-3	-2.1

● WILLIE UNDERHILL Underhill, Willie Vern b: 9/6/04, Yowell, Tex. d: 10/26/70, Bay City, Tex. BR/TR, 6'2", 185 lbs. Deb: 9/8/27

YEAR TM/L	W	L	PCT	G	GS	CG	SH	SV	IP	H	HR	BB	SO	RAT	ERA	ERA+	OAV	OOB	BH	AVG	PB	PR	/A	PD	TPI
1927 Cle-A	0	2	.000	4	1	0	0	0	8^1	12	0	11	4	24.8	9.72	43	.375	.535	0	.000	-0	-5	-5	0	-0.9
1928 Cle-A	1	2	.333	11	3	1	0	0	28	33	0	20	16	17.4	4.50	92	.306	.419	4	.364	2	-1	-1	0	0.1
Total 2	1	4	.200	15	4	1	0	0	36^1	45	0	31	20	19.1	5.70	73	.321	.448	4	.333	1	-7	-6	0	-0.8

● JERRY UPP Upp, George Henry b: 12/10/1883, Sandusky, Ohio d: 6/30/37, Sandusky, Ohio TL, Deb: 9/2/09

YEAR TM/L	W	L	PCT	G	GS	CG	SH	SV	IP	H	HR	BB	SO	RAT	ERA	ERA+	OAV	OOB	BH	AVG	PB	PR	/A	PD	TPI
1909 Cle-A	2	1	.667	7	4	2	0	0	26^2	26	0	12	13	12.8	1.69	152	.260	.339	2	.222	0	2	3	1	0.4

YEAR	TM/L	W	L	PCT	G	GS	CG	SH	SV	IP	H	HR	BB	SO	RAT	ERA	ERA+	OAV	OOB	BH	AVG	PB	PR	/A	PD	TPI

● CECIL UPSHAW Upshaw, Cecil Lee b: 10/22/42, Spearsville, La. d: 2/7/95, Lawrenceville, Ga. BR/TR, 6'6", 205 lbs. Deb: 10/1/66

| 1974 | Cle-A | 0 | 1 | .000 | 7 | 0 | 0 | 0 | 0 | 8 | 10 | 1 | 4 | 7 | 15.8 | 3.38 | 107 | .345 | .424 | 0 | — | 0 | 0 | 0 | -0 | 0.0 |
| Total | 9 | 34 | 36 | .486 | 348 | 0 | 0 | 0 | 86 | 563 | 545 | 37 | 177 | 323 | 11.9 | 3.13 | 112 | .258 | .322 | 12 | .160 | 1 | 19 | 23 | 2 | 3.2 |

● EFRAIN VALDEZ Valdez, Efrain Antonio b: 7/11/66, Nizao Bani, D.R. BL/TL, 5'11", 180 lbs. Deb: 8/13/90

1990	Cle-A	1	1	.500	13	0	0	0	0	23²	20	2	14	13	12.9	3.04	129	.233	.340	0	—	0	2	2	-0	0.2
1991	Cle-A	0	0	—	7	0	0	0	0	6	5	0	3	1	13.5	1.50	277	.238	.360	0	—	0	2	2	0	0.0
Total	2	1	1	.500	20	0	0	0	0	29²	25	2	17	14	13.0	2.73	145	.234	.344	0	—	0	4	4	-0	0.2

● SERGIO VALDEZ Valdez, Sergio Sanchez (b: Sergio Sanchez (Valdez)) b: 9/7/64, Elias Pina, D.R. BR/TR, 6', 165 lbs. Deb: 9/10/86

1990	Cle-A	6	6	.500	24	13	0	0	0	102¹	109	17	35	63	12.8	4.75	82	.276	.336	0	—	0	-10	-9	-0	-1.0
1991	Cle-A	1	0	1.000	6	0	0	0	0	16¹	15	3	5	11	11.0	5.51	75	.238	.294	0	—	0	-3	-2	-0	-0.2
Total	8	12	20	.375	116	31	1	0	0	302²	332	46	109	190	13.3	5.06	77	.279	.343	4	.121	-1	-39	-38	-1	-4.1
Team	2	7	6	.538	30	13	0	0	0	118²	124	20	40	74	12.5	4.85	81	.271	.331	0	—	0	-12	-12	-1	-1.2

● VITO VALENTINETTI Valentinetti, Vito John b: 9/16/28, W.New York, N.J. BR/TR, 6', 195 lbs. Deb: 6/20/54

| 1957 | Cle-A | 2 | 2 | .500 | 11 | 2 | 1 | 0 | 0 | 23² | 26 | 3 | 13 | 12 | 15.2 | 4.94 | 75 | .289 | .385 | 1 | .200 | -0 | -3 | -3 | 0 | -0.5 |
| Total | 5 | 13 | 14 | .481 | 108 | 15 | 3 | 0 | 3 | 257 | 266 | 35 | 122 | 94 | 13.8 | 4.73 | 81 | .273 | .358 | 12 | .218 | 1 | -27 | -26 | 0 | -2.7 |

● ED VANDE BERG Vande Berg, Edward John b: 10/26/58, Redlands, Cal. BR/TL, 6'2", 180 lbs. Deb: 4/7/82

| 1987 | Cle-A | 1 | 0 | 1.000 | 55 | 0 | 0 | 0 | 0 | 72¹ | 96 | 9 | 21 | 40 | 14.6 | 5.10 | 89 | .325 | .370 | 0 | — | 0 | -5 | -5 | 0 | 0.0 |
| Total | 7 | 25 | 28 | .472 | 413 | 17 | 2 | 0 | 22 | 519 | 572 | 52 | 200 | 314 | 13.5 | 3.92 | 104 | .284 | .351 | 0 | .000 | -0 | 8 | 10 | 3 | 1.8 |

● JOHNNY VANDER MEER Vander Meer, John Samuel "Double No-Hit" or "The Dutch Master" b: 11/2/14, Prospect Park, N.J. BB/TL, 6'1", 190 lbs. Deb: 4/22/37

| 1951 | Cle-A | 0 | 1 | .000 | 1 | 1 | 0 | 0 | 0 | 3 | 8 | 0 | 1 | 2 | 27.0 | 18.00 | 21 | .500 | .529 | 0 | .000 | -0 | -5 | -5 | 1 | -0.9 |
| Total | 13 | 119 | 121 | .496 | 346 | 285 | 131 | 29 | 2 | 2104² | 1799 | 100 | 1132 | 1294 | 12.6 | 3.44 | 107 | .232 | .332 | 104 | .152 | -9 | 63 | 53 | 3 | 6.1 |

● DIKE VARNEY Varney, Lawrence Delano (b: Lawrence Delano De Varney) b: 8/9/1880, Dover, N.H. d: 4/23/50, Long Island City, N.Y. BL/TL, 6', 165 lbs. Deb: 7/3/02

| 1902 | Cle-A | 1 | 1 | .500 | 3 | 3 | 0 | 0 | 0 | 14² | 14 | 0 | 12 | 7 | 19.0 | 6.14 | 56 | .250 | .425 | 1 | .167 | -0 | -4 | -4 | 0 | -0.5 |

● CAL VASBINDER Vasbinder, Moses Calhoun b: 7/19/1880, Scio, Ohio d: 12/22/50, Cadiz, Ohio BR/TR, 6'2", Deb: 4/27/02

| 1902 | Cle-A | 0 | 0 | — | 2 | 0 | 0 | 0 | 0 | 5 | 5 | 1 | 8 | 2 | 23.4 | 9.00 | 38 | .263 | .481 | 1 | .500 | 0 | -3 | -3 | 0 | 0.0 |

● DAVE Von OHLEN Von Ohlen, David b: 10/25/58, Flushing, N.Y. BL/TL, 6'2", 200 lbs. Deb: 5/13/83

| 1985 | Cle-A | 3 | 2 | .600 | 26 | 0 | 0 | 0 | 0 | 43¹ | 47 | 3 | 20 | 12 | 13.9 | 2.91 | 142 | .288 | .366 | 0 | — | 0 | 6 | 6 | 1 | 0.7 |
| Total | 5 | 7 | 7 | .500 | 127 | 0 | 0 | 0 | 4 | 167² | 185 | 7 | 61 | 59 | 13.4 | 3.33 | 113 | .293 | .358 | 2 | .250 | 1 | 9 | 8 | 1 | 1.3 |

● TOM WADDELL Waddell, Thomas David b: 9/17/58, Dundee, Scotland BR/TR, 6'1", 185 lbs. Deb: 4/15/84

1984	Cle-A	7	4	.636	58	0	0	0	6	97	68	12	37	59	9.8	3.06	133	.202	.283	0	—	0	10	11	-1	1.2
1985	Cle-A	8	6	.571	49	9	1	0	9	112²	104	20	39	53	11.5	4.87	85	.246	.312	0	—	0	-9	-9	0	-1.1
1987	Cle-A	0	1	.000	6	0	0	0	0	5²	7	1	7	6	23.8	14.29	32	.292	.469	0	—	0	-6	-6	-0	-0.9
Total	3	15	11	.577	113	9	1	0	15	215¹	179	33	83	118	11.1	4.30	96	.229	.305	0	—	0	-5	-4	-1	-0.8

● RICK WAITS Waits, Michael Richard b: 5/15/52, Atlanta, Ga. BL/TL, 6'3", 195 lbs. Deb: 9/17/73

1975	Cle-A	6	2	.750	16	7	3	0	1	70¹	57	3	25	34	10.6	2.94	128	.221	.292	0	—	0	7	7	0	0.8
1976	Cle-A	7	9	.438	26	22	4	2	0	123²	143	7	54	65	14.3	4.00	87	.297	.368	0	—	0	-7	-7	1	-0.9
1977	Cle-A	9	7	.563	37	16	1	0	2	135¹	132	8	64	62	13.1	3.99	99	.262	.342	0	—	0	1	-1	-0	-0.1
1978	Cle-A	13	15	.464	34	33	15	2	0	230¹	206	16	86	97	11.5	3.20	117	.240	.310	0	—	0	14	14	3	2.0
1979	Cle-A	16	13	.552	34	34	8	3	0	231	230	26	91	91	12.7	4.44	96	.264	.336	0	—	0	-6	-5	0	-0.5
1980	Cle-A	13	14	.481	33	33	9	2	0	224¹	231	18	82	109	12.6	4.45	91	.270	.335	0	—	0	-10	-10	-1	-1.1
1981	Cle-A	8	10	.444	22	21	5	1	0	126¹	173	7	44	51	15.5	4.92	74	.330	.383	0	—	0	-18	-18	2	-2.1
1982	Cle-A	2	13	.133	25	21	2	0	0	115	128	13	57	44	14.6	5.40	76	.290	.372	0	—	0	-17	-17	1	-1.8
1983	Cle-A	0	1	.000	8	0	0	0	0	19²	23	1	9	13	14.6	4.58	93	.307	.381	0	—	0	-1	-1	0	0.0
Total	12	79	92	.462	317	190	47	10	8	1427	1514	110	568	659	13.2	4.25	92	.277	.346	0	.000	0	-50	-53	6	-5.0
Team	9	74	84	.468	235	187	47	10	3	1276	1323	99	512	566	13.0	4.18	94	.272	.342	0	—	0	-37	-38	6	-3.7

● ED WALKER Walker, Edward Harrison b: 8/11/1874, Cambois, England d: 9/29/47, Akron, Ohio BL/TL, 6'5", 242 lbs. Deb: 9/26/02

1902	Cle-A	0	1	.000	1	1	1	0	0	8	11	0	3	1	15.8	3.38	102	.324	.378	1	.333	0	0	0	0	0.0
1903	Cle-A	0	0	—	3	3	0	0	0	12	13	0	10	4	17.3	5.25	54	.277	.404	0	.000	-0	-3	-3	-1	-0.1
Total	2	0	1	.000	4	4	1	0	0	20	24	0	13	5	16.6	4.50	69	.296	.394	1	.167	-0	-3	-3	-1	-0.1

● MYSTERIOUS WALKER Walker, Frederick Mitchell b: 3/21/1884, Utica, Neb. d: 2/1/58, Oak Park, Ill. BR/TR, 5'10.5", 185 lbs. Deb: 6/28/10

| 1912 | Cle-A | 0 | 0 | — | 1 | 0 | 0 | 0 | 0 | 1 | 0 | 0 | 1 | 0 | 9.0 | 0.00 | — | .000 | .200 | 0 | — | 0 | 0 | 0 | -0 | 0.0 |
| Total | 5 | 7 | 23 | .233 | 61 | 36 | 17 | 0 | 1 | 297¹ | 306 | 9 | 136 | 143 | 13.6 | 4.00 | 73 | .272 | .354 | 15 | .152 | -3 | -36 | -36 | 6 | -3.3 |

● ROY WALKER Walker, James Roy "Dixie" b: 4/13/1893, Lawrenceburg, Tenn d: 2/10/62, New Orleans, La. BR/TR, 6'1.5", 180 lbs. Deb: 9/16/12

1912	Cle-A	0	0	—	1	1	0	0	0	2	0	0	2	0	9.0	0.00	—	.000	.250	0	—	0	1	1	-0	0.0
1915	Cle-A	4	9	.308	25	15	4	0	1	131	122	1	65	57	13.3	3.98	77	.261	.360	5	.132	-2	-15	-14	-2	-1.8
Total	6	17	27	.386	91	49	17	0	5	386	408	13	155	148	13.3	3.99	85	.282	.355	17	.153	-4	-26	-26	-5	-3.8
Team	2	4	9	.308	26	15	4	0	1	133	122	1	67	58	13.3	3.92	78	.258	.358	5	.132	-2	-15	-13	-3	-1.8

● JERRY WALKER Walker, Jerry Allen b: 2/12/39, Ada, Okla. BB/TR, 6'1", 195 lbs. Deb: 7/6/57 C

1963	Cle-A	6	6	.500	39	2	0	0	1	88	92	15	36	41	13.3	4.91	74	.265	.338	2	.105	-0	-13	-13	-0	-1.7
1964	Cle-A	0	1	.000	6	0	0	0	0	9²	9	1	4	5	12.1	4.66	77	.257	.333	0	.000	-0	-1	-1	-0	-0.2
Total	8	37	44	.457	190	90	16	4	13	747	734	97	341	326	13.3	4.36	90	.259	.343	58	.230	10	-39	-36	1	-2.7
Team	2	6	7	.462	45	2	0	0	1	97²	101	16	40	46	13.2	4.88	74	.264	.337	2	.095	-1	-14	-14	-1	-1.9

● MIKE WALKER Walker, Michael Charles b: 10/4/66, Chicago, Ill. BR/TR, 6'2", 195 lbs. Deb: 9/9/88

1988	Cle-A	0	1	.000	3	1	0	0	0	8²	8	0	10	7	18.7	7.27	57	.258	.439	0	—	0	-3	-3	0	-0.4
1990	Cle-A	2	6	.250	18	11	0	0	0	75²	82	6	42	34	15.5	4.88	80	.277	.378	0	—	0	-8	-8	-0	-0.8
1991	Cle-A	0	1	.000	5	0	0	0	0	4¹	6	0	2	2	18.7	2.08	200	.316	.409	0	—	0	1	1	0	0.2
Total	4	3	11	.214	68	12	0	0	0	133¹	141	8	78	63	15.3	4.39	91	.271	.374	0	.000	-0	-6	-6	-0	-0.7
Team	3	2	8	.200	26	12	0	0	0	88²	96	6	54	43	15.9	4.97	79	.277	.386	0	—	0	-10	-10	0	-1.0

● COLBY WARD Ward, Robert Colby b: 1/2/64, Lansing, Mich. BR/TR, 6'2", 185 lbs. Deb: 7/27/90

| 1990 | Cle-A | 1 | 3 | .250 | 22 | 0 | 0 | 0 | 1 | 36 | 31 | 3 | 21 | 23 | 13.3 | 4.25 | 92 | .238 | .349 | 0 | — | 0 | -1 | -1 | -0 | -0.1 |

● CURT WARDLE Wardle, Curtis Ray b: 11/16/60, Downey, Cal. BL/TL, 6'5", 220 lbs. Deb: 8/30/84

| 1985 | Cle-A | 7 | 6 | .538 | 15 | 12 | 0 | 0 | 1 | 66 | 78 | 11 | 34 | 37 | 15.4 | 6.68 | 62 | .297 | .379 | 0 | — | 0 | -19 | -19 | -1 | -3.0 |
| Total | 2 | 8 | 9 | .471 | 52 | 12 | 0 | 0 | 1 | 119 | 130 | 22 | 62 | 89 | 14.7 | 6.13 | 69 | .281 | .369 | 0 | — | 0 | -26 | -25 | 0 | -4.1 |

● FRANK WAYENBERG Wayenberg, Frank b: 8/27/1898, Franklin, Kan. d: 4/16/75, Zanesville, Ohio BR/TR, 6'0.5", 172 lbs. Deb: 8/25/24

| 1924 | Cle-A | 0 | 0 | — | 2 | 1 | 0 | 0 | 0 | 6² | 7 | 0 | 5 | 3 | 17.6 | 5.40 | 79 | .259 | .394 | 1 | .500 | 0 | -1 | -1 | -0 | 0.0 |

YEAR TM/L	W	L	PCT	G	GS	CG	SH	SV	IP	H	HR	BB	SO	RAT	ERA	ERA+	OAV	OOB	BH	AVG	PB	PR	/A	PD	TPI
● FLOYD WEAVER Weaver, David Floyd b: 5/12/41, Ben Franklin, Tex. BR/TR, 6'4", 195 lbs. Deb: 9/30/62																									
1962 Cle-A	1	0	1.000	1	1	0	0	0	5	3	1	0	8	5.4	1.80	215	.167	.167	1	.500	0	1	1	-0	0.3
1965 Cle-A	2	2	.500	32	1	0	0	1	61^1	61	10	24	37	13.2	5.43	64	.265	.347	1	.091	0	-13	-13	-0	-0.9
Total 4	4	5	.444	85	5	0	0	1	155^1	149	21	73	108	13.3	5.21	70	.260	.351	2	.100	-0	-28	-27	-1	-1.3
Team 2	3	2	.600	33	2	0	0	1	66^1	64	11	24	45	12.6	5.16	68	.258	.336	2	.154	0	-12	-12	-0	-0.6
● LES WEBBER Webber, Lester Elmer b: 5/6/15, Kelseyville, Cal. d: 11/13/86, Santa Maria, Cal. BR/TR, 6'0.5", 185 lbs. Deb: 5/17/42																									
1946 Cle-A	1	1	.500	4	2	0	0	0	5^1	13	0	5	5	30.4	23.63	14	.464	.545	0	.000	0	-12	-12	0	-2.8
1948 Cle-A	0	0	—	1	0	0	0	0	0^2	3	0	1	1	54.0	40.50	10	.750	.800	0	—	0	-3	-3	0	0.0
Total 6	23	19	.548	154	25	7	0	14	432	434	25	201	141	13.4	4.19	83	.262	.345	15	.135	-2	-32	-34	5	-4.0
Team 2	1	1	.500	5	2	0	0	0	6	16	0	6	6	33.0	25.50	13	.500	.579	0	.000	0	-15	-15	0	-2.8
● DICK WEIK Weik, Richard Henry "Legs" b: 11/17/27, Waterloo, Iowa d: 4/21/91, Harvey, Ill. BR/TR, 6'3.5", 184 lbs. Deb: 9/8/48 ♦																									
1950 Cle-A	1	3	.250	11	2	0	0	0	26	18	1	26	16	15.6	3.81	114	.205	.391	1	.200	0	2	2	0	0.2
Total 5	6	22	.214	76	26	3	2	1	213^2	203	15	237	123	18.6	5.90	72	.260	.433	12	.226	1	-39	-39	0	-3.0
● BOB WEILAND Weiland, Robert George "Lefty" b: 12/14/05, Chicago, Ill. d: 11/9/88, Chicago, Ill. BL/TL, 6'4", 215 lbs. Deb: 9/30/28 F																									
1934 Cle-A	1	5	.167	16	7	2	0	0	70	71	5	30	42	13.0	4.11	111	.262	.336	3	.125	-0	3	3	-1	0.2
Total 12	62	94	.397	277	179	66	7	7	1388^1	1463	85	611	614	13.7	4.24	100	.272	.350	57	.129	-16	-13	2	-4	0.0
● BUTCH WENSLOFF Wensloff, Charles William b: 12/3/15, Sausalito, Cal. BR/TR, 5'11", 185 lbs. Deb: 5/2/43																									
1948 Cle-A	0	1	.000	1	0	0	0	0	1^2	2	1	3	2	27.0	10.80	38	.286	.500	0	—	0	-1	-1	-0	-0.5
Total 3	16	13	.552	41	32	19	1	1	276^2	222	11	95	125	10.3	2.60	126	.219	.287	19	.194	0	24	21	-2	1.6
● BILL WERTZ Wertz, William Charles b: 1/15/67, Cleveland, Ohio BR/TR, 6'6", 220 lbs. Deb: 5/22/93																									
1993 Cle-A	2	3	.400	34	0	0	0	0	59^2	54	5	32	53	13.1	3.62	119	.238	.335	0	—	0	5	5	-2	0.2
1994 Cle-A	0	0	—	1	0	0	0	0	4^1	9	0	1	1	20.8	10.38	45	.409	.435	0	—	0	-3	-3	0	0.0
Total 2	2	3	.400	35	0	0	0	0	64	63	5	33	54	13.6	4.08	107	.253	.343	0	—	0	2	2	-2	0.2
● HI WEST West, James Hiram b: 8/8/1884, Roseville, Ill. d: 5/25/63, Los Angeles, Cal. BR/TR, 6', 185 lbs. Deb: 9/8/05																									
1905 Cle-A	2	2	.500	6	4	4	1	0	33	43	0	10	15	15.3	4.09	64	.316	.376	1	.077	-1	-5	-5	-2	-0.9
1911 Cle-A	3	4	.429	13	8	3	0	1	64^2	84	1	18	17	14.6	3.76	91	.343	.395	3	.130	-2	-3	-2	-1	-0.5
Total 2	5	6	.455	19	12	7	1	1	97^2	127	1	28	32	14.8	3.87	81	.333	.388	4	.111	-3	-8	-8	-3	-1.4
● GUS WEYHING Weyhing, August "Cannonball" b: 9/29/1866, Louisville, Ky. d: 9/4/55, Louisville, Ky. BR/TR, 5'10", 145 lbs. Deb: 5/2/1887 F																									
1901 Cle-A	0	0	—	2	1	0	0	0	11^1	20	0	5	0	23.0	7.94	45	.377	.468	0	.000	-1	-5	-6	-0	-0.1
Total 14	264	232	.532	538	503	448	28	4	4324^1	4562	120	1566	1665	13.3	3.89	102	.264	.335	307	.166	-83	41	38	-39	-6.7
● EARL WHITEHILL Whitehill, Earl Oliver b: 2/7/1900, Cedar Rapids, Iowa d: 10/22/54, Omaha, Neb. BL/TL, 5'9.5", 174 lbs. Deb: 9/15/23 C																									
1937 Cle-A	8	8	.500	33	22	6	1	2	147	189	9	80	53	16.8	6.49	71	.322	.409	11	.224	1	-31	-31	1	-2.5
1938 Cle-A	9	8	.529	26	23	4	0	0	160^1	187	18	83	60	15.7	5.56	83	.289	.378	7	.125	-2	-14	-16	-2	-1.6
Total 17	218	185	.541	541	473	226	16	11	3564^2	3917	192	1431	1350	13.8	4.36	100	.282	.353	264	.204	4	10	6	-9	0.8
Team 2	17	16	.515	59	45	10	1	2	307^1	376	27	163	113	16.2	6.00	77	.305	.392	18	.171	-1	-44	-47	-0	-4.1
● ED WHITSON Whitson, Eddie Lee b: 5/19/55, Johnson City, Tenn. BR/TR, 6'3", 195 lbs. Deb: 9/4/77																									
1982 Cle-A	4	2	.667	40	9	1	1	2	107^2	91	6	58	61	12.5	3.26	125	.231	.330	0	—	0	10	10	-2	0.4
Total 15	126	123	.506	452	333	35	12	8	2240^1	2240	211	698	1266	11.9	3.79	97	.261	.319	72	.125	-11	-17	-28	-14	-5.4
● KEVIN WICKANDER Wickander, Kevin Dean b: 1/4/65, Fort Dodge, Iowa BL/TL, 6'2", 202 lbs. Deb: 8/10/89																									
1989 Cle-A	0	0	—	2	0	0	0	0	2^2	6	0	2	0	27.0	3.38	117	.462	.533	0	—	0	0	0	-0	-0.1
1990 Cle-A	0	1	.000	10	0	0	0	0	12^1	14	0	4	10	13.9	3.65	107	.304	.373	0	—	0	0	0	-0	0.0
1992 Cle-A	2	0	1.000	44	0	0	0	1	41	39	1	28	38	15.6	3.07	127	.258	.388	0	—	0	4	4	0	0.3
1993 Cle-A	0	0	—	11	0	0	0	0	8^2	15	3	3	3	18.7	4.15	104	.366	.409	0	—	0	0	0	-0	0.0
Total 5	3	1	.750	129	0	0	0	2	113^1	125	10	68	82	16.0	3.81	109	.285	.391	0	.000	-0	4	4	-1	-0.2
Team 4	2	1	.667	67	0	0	0	1	64^2	74	4	37	51	16.1	3.34	119	.295	.396	0	—	0	5	4	-1	0.2
● BILL WIGHT Wight, William Robert "Lefty" b: 4/12/22, Rio Vista, Cal. BL/TL, 6'1", 180 lbs. Deb: 4/17/46																									
1953 Cle-A	2	1	.667	20	0	0	0	1	26^2	29	1	16	14	15.2	3.71	101	.282	.378	0	.000	-1	1	0	0	0.0
1955 Cle-A	0	0	—	17	0	0	0	1	24	24	0	9	9	12.4	2.63	152	.261	.327	0	—	0	4	4	2	0.2
Total 12	77	99	.438	347	198	66	15	8	1563	1656	74	714	574	13.7	3.95	103	.277	.355	55	.115	-28	27	22	9	1.0
Team 2	2	1	.667	37	0	0	0	2	50^2	53	1	25	23	13.9	3.20	121	.272	.355	0	.000	-1	4	4	2	0.2
● SANDY WIHTOL Wihtol, Alexander Ames b: 6/1/55, Palo Alto, Cal. BR/TR, 6'1", 195 lbs. Deb: 9/7/79																									
1979 Cle-A	0	0	—	5	0	0	0	0	10^2	10	0	3	6	11.0	3.38	126	.238	.289	0	—	0	1	1	0	0.0
1980 Cle-A	1	0	1.000	17	0	0	0	1	35^1	35	2	14	20	13.0	3.57	114	.257	.336	0	—	0	2	2	-1	0.0
1982 Cle-A	0	0	—	6	0	0	0	0	11^2	9	1	7	8	13.1	4.63	88	.220	.347	0	—	0	-1	-1	-0	0.0
Total 3	1	0	1.000	28	0	0	0	1	57^2	54	3	24	34	12.6	3.75	110	.247	.329	0	—	0	2	2	-1	0.0
● MILT WILCOX Wilcox, Milton Edward b: 4/20/50, Honolulu, Hawaii BR/TR, 6'2", 185 lbs. Deb: 9/5/70																									
1972 Cle-A	7	14	.333	32	27	4	2	0	156	145	18	72	90	12.8	3.40	94	.251	.339	9	.200	1	-6	-3	-3	-0.6
1973 Cle-A	8	10	.444	26	19	4	0	0	134^1	143	14	68	82	14.7	5.83	67	.275	.367	0	—	0	-30	-29	1	-3.2
1974 Cle-A	2	2	.500	41	2	1	0	4	71^1	74	10	24	33	13.0	4.67	77	.271	.341	0	—	0	-8	-8	1	-0.5
Total 16	119	113	.513	394	283	73	10	6	2016^2	1991	204	770	1137	12.7	4.07	96	.260	.334	11	.177	0	-44	-33	11	-1.5
Team 3	17	26	.395	99	48	9	2	4	361^2	362	42	164	205	13.5	4.55	78	.264	.350	9	.200	1	-44	-40	-1	-4.3
● HOYT WILHELM Wilhelm, James Hoyt b: 7/26/23, Huntersville, N.C. BR/TR, 6', 195 lbs. Deb: 4/19/52 H																									
1957 Cle-A	1	0	1.000	2	0	0	0	1	3^2	2	1	1	0	9.8	2.45	151	.154	.267	0	—	0	1	1	-0	0.1
1958 Cle-A	2	7	.222	30	6	1	0	5	90^1	70	4	35	57	10.6	2.49	146	.215	.294	2	.095	-1	13	12	1	1.2
Total 21	143	122	.540	1070	52	20	5	227	2254^1	1757	150	778	1610	10.4	2.52	146	.216	.290	38	.088	-21	310	288	5	40.0
Team 2	3	7	.300	32	6	1	0	6	94	72	5	36	57	10.5	2.49	147	.213	.293	2	.095	-1	13	12	1	1.3
● ERIC WILKINS Wilkins, Eric Lamoine b: 12/9/56, St.Louis, Mo. BR/TR, 6'1", 190 lbs. Deb: 4/11/79																									
1979 Cle-A	2	4	.333	16	14	0	0	0	69^2	77	4	38	52	15.4	4.39	97	.289	.386	0	—	0	-1	-1	0	-0.1
● ROY WILKINSON Wilkinson, Roy Hamilton b: 5/8/1893, Canandaigua, N.Y. d: 7/2/56, Louisville, Ky. BR/TR, 6'1", 170 lbs. Deb: 4/29/18																									
1918 Cle-A	0	0	—	1	0	0	0	0	1	0	0	0	0	0.0	0.00	—	.000	.000	0	—	0	0	0	-0	0.0
Total 5	12	31	.279	79	37	20	1	6	380^2	466	11	142	88	14.5	4.66	86	.318	.381	18	.145	-5	-27	-28	4	-2.8
● TED WILKS Wilks, Theodore "Cork" b: 11/13/15, Fulton, N.Y. d: 8/21/89, Houston, Tex. BR/TR, 5'9.5", 178 lbs. Deb: 4/25/44 C																									
1952 Cle-A	0	0	—	7	0	0	0	1	11^2	8	0	7	6	11.6	3.86	87	.186	.300	0	—	0	-0	-1	0	0.0
1953 Cle-A	0	0	—	4	0	0	0	0	3^2	5	0	3	2	19.6	7.36	51	.278	.381	0	—	0	-1	-1	-0	0.0
Total 10	59	30	.663	385	44	22	5	46	913	832	76	283	403	11.1	3.26	118	.244	.304	27	.131	-5	55	61	-11	5.4
Team 2	0	0	—	11	0	0	0	1	15^1	13	0	10	8	13.5	4.70	73	.213	.324	0	—	0	-2	-2	-0	0.0
● STAN WILLIAMS Williams, Stanley Wilson b: 9/14/36, Enfield, N.H. BR/TR, 6'5", 230 lbs. Deb: 5/17/58 C																									
1965 Cle-A	0	0	—	3	0	0	0	0	4^1	6	1	3	1	18.7	6.23	56	.353	.450	0	—	0	-1	-1	0	0.0
1967 Cle-A	6	4	.600	16	8	2	1	1	79	64	6	24	75	10.1	2.62	125	.218	.279	2	.091	-1	5	6	-2	0.4

YEAR TM/L	W	L	PCT	G	GS	CG	SH	SV	IP	H	HR	BB	SO	RAT	ERA	ERA+	OAV	OOB	BH	AVG	PB	PR	/A	PD	TPI
1968 Cle-A	13	11	.542	44	24	6	2	9	194^1	163	14	51	147	10.4	2.50	118	.225	.285	9	.161	1	10	10	-1	1.5
1969 Cle-A	6	14	.300	61	15	3	0	12	178^1	155	25	67	139	11.8	3.94	96	.235	.317	4	.100	-1	-6	-3	-1	-0.5
Total 14	109	94	.537	482	208	42	11	43	1764^1	1527	160	748	1305	12.0	3.48	108	.232	.317	59	.118	-10	39	53	-4	5.6
Team 4	25	29	.463	124	47	11	3	22	456	388	46	145	362	11.0	3.12	107	.229	.298	15	.127	-1	8	11	-3	1.4

● LES WILLIS

Willis, Lester Evans "Wimpy" or "Lefty" b: 1/17/08, Nacogdoches, Tex. d: 1/22/82, Jasper, Tex. BL/TL, 5'9.5", 195 lbs. Deb: 4/28/47

YEAR TM/L	W	L	PCT	G	GS	CG	SH	SV	IP	H	HR	BB	SO	RAT	ERA	ERA+	OAV	OOB	BH	AVG	PB	PR	/A	PD	TPI
1947 Cle-A	0	2	.000	22	2	0	0	1	44	58	3	24	10	16.8	3.48	100	.324	.404	1	.091	-1	1	0	-1	-0.2

● FRANK WILLS

Wills, Frank Lee b: 10/26/58, New Orleans, La. BR/TR, 6'2", 202 lbs. Deb: 7/31/83

YEAR TM/L	W	L	PCT	G	GS	CG	SH	SV	IP	H	HR	BB	SO	RAT	ERA	ERA+	OAV	OOB	BH	AVG	PB	PR	/A	PD	TPI
1986 Cle-A	4	4	.500	26	0	0	0	4	40^1	43	6	16	32	13.2	4.91	84	.272	.339	0	—	0	-3	-3	0	-0.6
1987 Cle-A	0	1	.000	6	0	0	0	1	5^1	3	0	7	4	16.9	5.06	89	.176	.417	0	—	0	-0	-0	0	-0.1
Total 9	22	26	.458	154	35	1	0	6	435^2	438	50	198	281	13.3	5.06	80	.264	.344	0	—	0	-50	-50	0	-5.9
Team 2	4	5	.444	32	0	0	0	5	45^2	46	6	23	36	13.6	4.93	85	.263	.348	0	—	0	-4	-4	0	-0.7

● FRED WINCHELL

Winchell, Frederick Russell (b: Frederick Cook)
b: 1/23/1882, Arlington, Mass. d: 8/8/58, Toronto, Ont., Can. TR, 5'8", Deb: 9/16/09

YEAR TM/L	W	L	PCT	G	GS	CG	SH	SV	IP	H	HR	BB	SO	RAT	ERA	ERA+	OAV	OOB	BH	AVG	PB	PR	/A	PD	TPI
1909 Cle-A	0	3	.000	4	3	0	0	1	14^1	16	0	2	7	11.3	6.28	41	.296	.321	1	.200	0	-6	-6	-0	-1.2

● RALPH WINEGARNER

Winegarner, Ralph Lee b: 10/29/09, Benton, Kan. d: 4/14/88, Wichita, Kan. BR/TR, 6', 182 lbs. Deb: 9/20/30 C♦

YEAR TM/L	W	L	PCT	G	GS	CG	SH	SV	IP	H	HR	BB	SO	RAT	ERA	ERA+	OAV	OOB	BH	AVG	PB	PR	/A	PD	TPI
1932 Cle-A	1	0	1.000	5	1	1	0	0	17^1	7	0	13	5	10.4	1.04	457	.123	.286	1	.143	-0	7	7	-0	0.3
1934 Cle-A	5	4	.556	22	6	4	0	0	78^1	91	1	39	32	15.2	5.51	82	.289	.371	10	.196	1	-9	-8	0	-0.7
1935 Cle-A	2	2	.500	25	4	2	0	0	67^1	89	10	29	41	15.9	5.75	78	.313	.379	26	.310	4	-10	-9	0	0.0
1936 Cle-A	0	0	—	9	0	0	0	0	14^2	18	0	6	3	14.7	4.91	103	.295	.358	2	.125	-1	0	0	-0	-0.1
Total 5	8	6	.571	70	11	7	0	0	194^1	229	13	89	89	14.9	5.33	86	.290	.364	51	.276	5	-18	-16	-1	-0.4
Team 4	8	6	.571	61	11	7	0	0	177^2	205	11	87	81	14.9	5.12	90	.286	.366	39	.247	3	-12	-10	-0	-0.5

● GEORGE WINN

Winn, George Benjamin "Breezy" or "Lefty" b: 10/26/1897, Perry, Ga. d: 11/1/69, Roberta, Ga. BL/TL, 5'11", 170 lbs. Deb: 4/29/19

YEAR TM/L	W	L	PCT	G	GS	CG	SH	SV	IP	H	HR	BB	SO	RAT	ERA	ERA+	OAV	OOB	BH	AVG	PB	PR	/A	PD	TPI
1922 Cle-A	1	2	.333	8	3	1	0	0	33^2	44	2	5	7	13.1	4.54	88	.317	.340	3	.333	1	-2	-2	0	-0.1
1923 Cle-A	0	0	—	1	0	0	0	0	2	0	0	1	0	4.5	0.00	—	.000	.143	0	—	0	1	1	-0	0.0
Total 3	1	2	.333	12	3	1	0	0	40^1	50	2	7	7	12.7	4.69	83	.309	.337	3	.300	1	-3	-4	-0	-0.1
Team 2	1	2	.333	9	3	1	0	0	35^2	44	2	6	7	12.6	4.29	93	.303	.331	3	.333	1	-1	-1	-0	-0.1

● RICK WISE

Wise, Richard Charles b: 9/13/45, Jackson, Mich. BR/TR, 6'2", 195 lbs. Deb: 4/18/64

YEAR TM/L	W	L	PCT	G	GS	CG	SH	SV	IP	H	HR	BB	SO	RAT	ERA	ERA+	OAV	OOB	BH	AVG	PB	PR	/A	PD	TPI
1978 Cle-A	9	19	.321	33	31	9	1	0	211^2	226	22	59	106	12.2	4.34	86	.275	.325	0	—	0	-14	-14	-0	-1.7
1979 Cle-A	15	10	.600	34	34	9	2	0	231^2	229	24	68	108	11.6	3.73	114	.256	.309	0	—	0	12	13	0	1.3
Total 18	188	181	.509	506	455	138	30	0	3127	3227	261	804	1647	11.7	3.69	100	.267	.315	130	.195	34	-15	2	4	3.8
Team 2	24	29	.453	67	65	18	3	0	443^1	455	46	127	214	11.9	4.02	100	.265	.317	0	—	0	-1	-1	-0	-0.4

● ED WOJNA

Wojna, Edward David b: 8/20/60, Bridgeport, Conn. BR/TR, 6'1", 185 lbs. Deb: 6/16/85

YEAR TM/L	W	L	PCT	G	GS	CG	SH	SV	IP	H	HR	BB	SO	RAT	ERA	ERA+	OAV	OOB	BH	AVG	PB	PR	/A	PD	TPI
1989 Cle-A	0	1	.000	9	3	0	0	0	33	31	0	14	10	12.3	4.09	97	.254	.331	0	—	0	-1	-0	1	0.0
Total 4	4	10	.286	36	20	1	0	0	132^1	151	10	55	60	14.4	4.62	81	.288	.361	4	.129	-1	-13	-13	1	-1.7

● ERNIE WOLF

Wolf, Ernest Adolph b: 2/2/1889, Newark, N.J. d: 5/23/64, Atlantic Highlands, N.J. BR/TR, 5'11", 174 lbs. Deb: 9/10/12

YEAR TM/L	W	L	PCT	G	GS	CG	SH	SV	IP	H	HR	BB	SO	RAT	ERA	ERA+	OAV	OOB	BH	AVG	PB	PR	/A	PD	TPI
1912 Cle-A	0	0	—	1	0	0	0	0	5^2	8	0	4	1	19.1	6.35	54	.348	.444	0	.000	-0	-2	-2	-0	-0.1

● ROGER WOLFF

Wolff, Roger Francis b: 4/10/11, Evansville, Ill. d: 3/23/94, Chester, Ill. BR/TR, 6'0.5", 208 lbs. Deb: 9/20/41

YEAR TM/L	W	L	PCT	G	GS	CG	SH	SV	IP	H	HR	BB	SO	RAT	ERA	ERA+	OAV	OOB	BH	AVG	PB	PR	/A	PD	TPI
1947 Cle-A	0	0	—	7	2	0	0	0	16	15	1	10	5	15.2	3.94	88	.259	.386	0	.000	-0	-0	-1	1	0.0
Total 7	52	69	.430	182	128	63	8	13	1025^1	1018	56	316	430	11.9	3.41	100	.258	.316	41	.122	-13	8	1	-3	-1.5

● JOE WOOD

Wood, Joe "Smokey Joe" (b: Howard Ellsworth Wood)
b: 10/25/1889, Kansas City, Mo. d: 7/27/85, West Haven, Conn BR/TR, 5'11", 180 lbs. Deb: 8/24/08 F♦

YEAR TM/L	W	L	PCT	G	GS	CG	SH	SV	IP	H	HR	BB	SO	RAT	ERA	ERA+	OAV	OOB	BH	AVG	PB	PR	/A	PD	TPI
1917 Cle-A	0	1	.000	5	1	0	0	1	15^2	17	0	7	2	13.8	3.45	82	.309	.387	0	.000	-1	-1	-1	0	-0.2
1919 Cle-A	0	0	—	1	0	0	0	1	0^2	0	0	0	0	0.0	0.00	—	.000	.000	49	.255	0	0	0	0	0.1
1920 *Cle-A	0	0	—	1	0	0	0	0	2	4	0	2	1	27.0	22.50	17	.444	.545	37	.270	0	-4	-4	0	0.0
Total 11	116	57	.671	225	158	121	28	11	1436^1	1138	10	421	989	10.1	2.03	146	.220	.285	553	.283	31	150	150	14	24.3
Team 3	0	1	.000	7	1	0	0	2	18^1	21	0	9	3	14.7	5.40	55	.313	.395	86	.257	-0	-5	-5	0	-0.1

● HAL WOODESHICK

Woodeshick, Harold Joseph b: 8/24/32, Wilkes-Barre, Pa. BR/TL, 6'3", 200 lbs. Deb: 9/14/56

YEAR TM/L	W	L	PCT	G	GS	CG	SH	SV	IP	H	HR	BB	SO	RAT	ERA	ERA+	OAV	OOB	BH	AVG	PB	PR	/A	PD	TPI
1958 Cle-A	6	6	.500	14	9	3	0	0	71^2	71	4	25	27	12.8	3.64	100	.265	.341	4	.167	-1	1	0	3	0.2
Total 11	44	62	.415	427	62	7	1	61	847^1	816	40	389	484	13.2	3.56	102	.254	.342	16	.092	-7	13	7	18	3.3

● GENE WRIGHT

Wright, Clarence Eugene "Big Gene" b: 12/11/1878, Cleveland, Ohio d: 10/29/30, Barberton, Ohio BR/TR, 6'2", 185 lbs. Deb: 10/5/01

YEAR TM/L	W	L	PCT	G	GS	CG	SH	SV	IP	H	HR	BB	SO	RAT	ERA	ERA+	OAV	OOB	BH	AVG	PB	PR	/A	PD	TPI
1902 Cle-A	7	11	.389	21	18	15	1	1	148	150	6	75	52	14.2	3.95	87	.263	.357	10	.143	-2	-6	-8	-2	-1.2
1903 Cle-A	3	9	.250	15	12	8	0	0	101^2	122	1	58	42	16.3	5.75	50	.296	.388	9	.209	2	-32	-33	2	-2.9
Total 4	14	26	.350	46	40	31	2	1	323^2	361	9	152	140	14.7	4.50	70	.282	.365	23	.167	-1	-45	-49	1	-5.2
Team 2	10	20	.333	36	30	23	1	1	249^2	272	7	133	94	15.0	4.69	68	.277	.370	19	.168	0	-38	-41	-0	-4.1

● LUCKY WRIGHT

Wright, William Simmons "William The Red" or "Deacon"
b: 2/21/1880, Tontogany, Ohio d: 7/6/41, Tontogany, Ohio BR/TR, 6', 178 lbs. Deb: 4/18/09

YEAR TM/L	W	L	PCT	G	GS	CG	SH	SV	IP	H	HR	BB	SO	RAT	ERA	ERA+	OAV	OOB	BH	AVG	PB	PR	/A	PD	TPI
1909 Cle-A	0	4	.000	5	4	3	0	0	28	21	0	7	5	9.0	3.21	80	.223	.277	0	.000	-1	-2	-2	-0	-0.4

● WHIT WYATT

Wyatt, John Whitlow b: 9/27/07, Kensington, Ga. BR/TR, 6'1", 185 lbs. Deb: 9/16/29 C

YEAR TM/L	W	L	PCT	G	GS	CG	SH	SV	IP	H	HR	BB	SO	RAT	ERA	ERA+	OAV	OOB	BH	AVG	PB	PR	/A	PD	TPI
1937 Cle-A	2	3	.400	29	4	2	0	0	73	67	3	40	52	13.2	4.44	104	.244	.340	7	.389	3	1	1	0	0.3
Total 16	106	95	.527	360	210	97	17	13	1761	1684	98	642	872	12.1	3.79	105	.251	.319	133	.219	18	27	39	-6	3.8

● EARLY WYNN

Wynn, Early "Gus" b: 1/6/20, Hartford, Ala. BB/TR, 6', 200 lbs. Deb: 9/13/39 CH♦

YEAR TM/L	W	L	PCT	G	GS	CG	SH	SV	IP	H	HR	BB	SO	RAT	ERA	ERA+	OAV	OOB	BH	AVG	PB	PR	/A	PD	TPI
1949 Cle-A	11	7	.611	26	23	6	0	0	164^2	186	8	57	62	13.3	4.15	96	.282	.340	10	.143	-2	1	-3	1	-0.3
1950 Cle-A	18	8	.692	32	28	14	2	0	213^2	166	20	101	143	**11.4**	**3.20**	135	**.212**	**.305**	18	.234	7	33	27	0	3.6
1951 Cle-A	20	13	.606	37	34	21	3	1	**274^1**	227	18	107	133	11.1	3.02	126	.225	.301	20	.185	2	**34**	23	-1	2.6
1952 Cle-A	23	12	.657	42	33	19	4	3	285^2	239	23	132	153	11.7	2.90	115	.231	.318	22	.222	5	25	14	-1	2.1
1953 Cle-A	17	12	.586	36	34	16	1	0	251^2	234	19	107	138	12.3	3.93	95	.245	.324	25	.275	9	2	-5	-1	0.2
1954 *Cle-A	**23**	11	.676	40	36	20	3	2	**270^2**	225	21	83	155	10.2	2.73	135	.225	.284	17	.183	1	30	29	-3	3.3
1955 Cle-A★	17	11	.607	32	31	16	6	0	230	207	19	80	122	11.3	2.82	142	.240	.307	15	.179	1	29	30	-3	3.3
1956 Cle-A★	20	9	.690	38	35	18	4	2	277^2	233	19	91	158	10.7	2.72	154	.228	.294	23	.228	3	44	46	1	5.1
1957 Cle-A★	14	17	.452	40	37	13	1	1	263	270	32	104	**184**	13.0	4.31	86	.265	.336	10	.116	-2	-15	-17	-1	-2.1
1963 Cle-A	1	2	.333	20	5	1	0	1	55^1	50	2	15	29	10.6	2.28	159	.250	.302	3	.273	1	8	8	-0	0.5
Total 23	300	244	.551	691	612	290	49	15	4564	4291	338	1775	2334	12.1	3.54	106	.248	.321	365	.214	72	170	112	-25	16.6
Team 10	164	102	.617	343	296	144	24	10	2286^2	2037	181	877	1277	11.6	3.24	118	.238	.311	163	.199	26	190	151	-7	18.3

● RICH YETT

Yett, Richard Martin b: 10/6/62, Pomona, Cal. BR/TR, 6'2", 187 lbs. Deb: 4/13/85

YEAR TM/L	W	L	PCT	G	GS	CG	SH	SV	IP	H	HR	BB	SO	RAT	ERA	ERA+	OAV	OOB	BH	AVG	PB	PR	/A	PD	TPI
1986 Cle-A	5	3	.625	39	3	1	1	1	78^2	84	10	37	50	14.0	5.15	80	.275	.355	0	—	0	-8	-9	-1	-0.9
1987 Cle-A	3	9	.250	37	11	2	0	1	97^2	96	21	49	59	13.6	5.25	86	.257	.347	0	—	0	-9	-8	-1	-0.9
1988 Cle-A	9	6	.600	23	22	0	0	0	134^1	146	11	55	71	13.5	4.62	89	.275	.344	0	—	0	-10	-8	-2	-1.0
1989 Cle-A	5	6	.455	32	12	1	0	0	99	111	10	47	47	14.5	5.00	79	.283	.363	0	—	0	-12	-11	-1	-1.4
Total 6	22	24	.478	136	49	4	1	2	414^1	444	53	191	229	13.9	4.95	84	.274	.353	0	—	0	-39	-36	-5	-4.7
Team 4	22	24	.478	131	48	4	1	2	409^2	437	52	188	227	13.9	4.97	84	.273	.352	0	—	0	-39	-36	-5	-4.2

YEAR TM/L	W	L	PCT	G	GS	CG	SH	SV	IP	H	HR	BB	SO	RAT	ERA	ERA+	OAV	OOB	BH	AVG	PB	PR	/A	PD	TPI
● **EARL YINGLING** Yingling, Earl Hershey "Chink" b: 10/29/1888, Chillicothe, Ohio d: 10/2/62, Columbus, Ohio BL/TL, 5'11.5", 180 lbs. Deb: 4/12/11																									
1911 Cle-A	1	0	1.000	4	3	1	0	0	22¹	30	1	9	6	16.1	4.43	77	.326	.392	3	.273	0	-3	-3	0	-0.1
Total 5	25	34	.424	94	61	31	5	0	568	611	19	141	192	12.1	3.22	98	.281	.328	72	.267	16	-8	-4	-3	1.2
● **MIKE YORK** York, Michael David b: 9/6/64, Oak Park, Ill. BR/TR, 6'1", 187 lbs. Deb: 8/17/90																									
1991 Cle-A	1	4	.200	14	4	0	0	0	34²	45	2	19	19	17.1	6.75	62	.333	.423	0	—	0	-10	-10	-0	-1.3
Total 2	2	5	.286	18	5	0	0	0	47¹	58	2	24	23	16.2	5.70	70	.319	.407	1	.333	0	-9	-9	-0	-1.1
● **CLIFF YOUNG** Young, Clifford Raphael b: 8/2/64, Willis, Tex. d: 11/4/93, Montgomery Co., Tex. BL/TL, 6'4", 200 lbs. Deb: 7/14/90																									
1993 Cle-A	3	3	.500	21	7	0	0	1	60¹	74	9	18	31	14.2	4.62	94	.298	.353	0	—	0	-2	-2	-1	-0.2
Total 3	5	4	.556	49	7	0	0	1	103²	126	14	28	56	13.7	4.25	97	.302	.352	0	—	0	-1	-1	-1	0.0
● **CY YOUNG** Young, Denton True b: 3/29/1867, Gilmore, Ohio d: 11/4/55, Newcomerstown, Ohio BR/TR, 6'2", 210 lbs. Deb: 8/6/1890 MH																									
1909 Cle-A	19	15	.559	35	34	30	3	0	295	267	4	59	109	10.2	2.26	113	.250	.294	21	.196	-0	7	10	-1	1.0
1910 Cle-A	7	10	.412	21	20	14	1	0	163¹	149	0	27	58	9.9	2.53	102	.252	.289	8	.145	-0	-0	1	1	0.2
1911 Cle-A	3	4	.429	7	7	4	0	0	46¹	54	2	13	20	13.2	3.88	88	.298	.349	1	.063	-2	-3	-2	-0	-0.5
Total 22	511	316	.618	906	815	749	76	17	7356²	7092	138	1217	2803	10.4	2.63	138	.252	.286	623	.210	-22	754	820	19	79.9
Team 3	29	29	.500	63	61	48	4	0	504²	470	6	99	187	10.4	2.50	106	.255	.298	30	.169	-3	4	8	-1	0.7
● **MATT YOUNG** Young, Matthew John b: 8/9/58, Pasadena, Cal. BL/TL, 6'3", 205 lbs. Deb: 4/6/83																									
1993 Cle-A	1	6	.143	22	8	0	0	0	74¹	75	8	57	65	16.3	5.21	83	.266	.395	0	—	0	-7	-7	0	-0.6
Total 10	55	95	.367	333	163	20	5	25	1189²	1207	99	565	857	13.7	4.40	94	.265	.350	0	.000	-0	-46	-35	-3	-4.1
● **CARL YOWELL** Yowell, Carl Columbus "Sundown" b: 12/20/02, Madison, Va. d: 7/27/85, Jacksonville, Tex. BL/TL, 6'4", 180 lbs. Deb: 9/5/24																									
1924 Cle-A	1	1	.500	4	2	2	0	0	27	37	1	13	8	16.7	6.67	64	.343	.413	2	.182	-1	-7	-7	-0	-0.5
1925 Cle-A	2	3	.400	12	4	1	0	0	36¹	40	1	17	12	14.4	4.46	99	.310	.395	1	.125	-1	-0	-0	0	-0.1
Total 2	3	4	.429	16	6	3	0	0	63¹	77	2	30	20	15.3	5.40	81	.325	.403	3	.158	-1	-8	-7	0	-0.6
● **JIMMY ZINN** Zinn, James Edward b: 1/21/1895, Benton, Ark. d: 2/26/91, Memphis, Tenn. BL/TR, 6'0.5", 195 lbs. Deb: 9/4/19																									
1929 Cle-A	4	6	.400	18	11	6	1	2	105¹	150	8	33	29	15.9	5.04	88	.340	.390	16	.381	7	-9	-7	-0	0.0
Total 5	13	16	.448	66	26	15	2	7	299	390	15	80	108	14.4	4.30	92	.324	.369	34	.283	9	-15	-12	-3	-0.9
● **SAM ZOLDAK** Zoldak, Samuel Walter "Sad Sam" b: 12/8/18, Brooklyn, N.Y. d: 8/25/66, New Hyde Park, N.Y. BL/TL, 5'11.5", 185 lbs. Deb: 5/13/44																									
1948 Cle-A	9	6	.600	23	12	4	1	0	105²	104	6	24	17	10.9	2.81	144	.261	.303	5	.139	-2	17	15	2	1.9
1949 Cle-A	1	2	.333	27	0	0	0	0	53	60	4	18	11	13.2	4.25	94	.291	.348	3	.375	1	-0	-1	3	0.3
1950 Cle-A	4	2	.667	33	3	0	0	4	63²	64	6	21	15	12.2	3.96	109	.259	.320	3	.188	0	4	3	-0	0.2
Total 9	43	53	.448	250	93	30	5	8	929¹	956	64	301	207	12.2	3.54	112	.267	.325	50	.175	-7	34	45	7	5.2
Team 3	14	10	.583	83	15	4	1	4	222¹	228	16	63	43	11.8	3.48	118	.268	.319	11	.183	-1	21	16	4	2.4
● **BILL ZUBER** Zuber, William Henry "Goober" b: 3/26/13, Middle Amana, Iowa d: 11/2/82, Cedar Rapids, Iowa BR/TR, 6'2", 195 lbs. Deb: 9/16/36																									
1936 Cle-A	1	1	.500	2	2	1	0	0	13²	14	0	15	5	19.1	6.59	76	.269	.433	1	.200	-0	-2	-2	-0	-0.3
1938 Cle-A	0	3	.000	15	0	0	0	1	28²	33	0	20	14	16.6	5.02	92	.295	.402	0	.000	-1	-1	-1	-0	-0.2
1939 Cle-A	2	0	1.000	16	1	0	0	0	31²	41	2	19	16	17.3	5.97	74	.323	.415	1	.200	0	-5	-6	1	-0.2
1940 Cle-A	1	1	.500	17	0	0	0	0	24	25	3	14	12	14.6	5.63	75	.260	.355	1	.333	0	-3	-4	0	-0.3
Total 11	43	42	.506	224	65	23	3	6	786	767	35	468	383	14.2	4.28	87	.260	.362	31	.135	-6	-51	-50	-8	-5.5
Team 4	4	5	.444	50	3	1	0	1	98	113	5	68	47	16.7	5.69	79	.292	.399	3	.150	-0	-11	-13	-0	-1.0
● **GEORGE ZUVERINK** Zuverink, George b: 8/20/24, Holland, Mich. BR/TR, 6'4", 200 lbs. Deb: 4/21/51																									
1951 Cle-A	0	0	—	16	0	0	0	0	25¹	24	2	13	14	13.5	5.33	71	.253	.349	0	—	0	-3	-4	0	0.0
1952 Cle-A	0	0	—	1	0	0	0	0	1¹	1	0	0	1	6.8	0.00	—	.200	.200	0	—	0	1	0	0	0.0
Total 8	32	36	.471	265	31	9	2	40	642¹	660	56	203	223	12.5	3.54	105	.271	.334	21	.148	-2	23	13	7	2.4
Team 2	0	0	—	17	0	0	0	0	26²	25	2	13	15	13.2	5.06	74	.250	.342	0	—	0	-3	-4	1	0.0

The Annual Roster

This valuable presentation of a team's personnel history and development makes its first appearance in *Total Indians*. The reader may see at a glance who played for the franchise in each year of its existence, how many games he played at various positions, how effectively he played or managed, how he came to join the club, and where his travels may have taken him next.

Each page of the Annual Roster is topped at the corner by a finding aid: first, the year of the Indians team that heads up the page; second, the year which concludes that page. Remember that major league teams which may have played in Cleveland in leagues other than the American League are excluded; these teams are not of the same franchise as the Indians, which has a direct line of descent from the first year of the American League, declared as a major league in 1901.

In compact style, the year-by-year flow of stars and spares may be traced, and reference to other sections of this book for additional data becomes simple enough. The expanded record of every player in these lists may be found in the Player Register, Pitcher Register, and Player Index. Superior players may be found as well in the All-Time Leaders section to follow, or in the capsule biographies of Indians Greats.

Below is a sample entry from the Annual Roster.

Note that to the right of the team year and city is a parenthetical grouping of three figures, representing games played, won-lost mark, and place in the standings. The manager is listed immediately below, and his won-lost record is identical to the team's record if he was the only manager that season, as Tris Speaker was for the champion Indians. (In seasons characterized by managerial changes, the won-lost mark of each manager is presented.) Coaches, if any, are listed at the end of each seasonal entry.

The column headings otherwise describe players by use name (proper names are available in the Registers), followed by games played ("G"). Next comes a measure of appearance frequency, AB/IP: at bats for position players, innings pitched for pitchers.

The "P/E" column contains a dual measure of efficiency: Production (on base average plus slugging percentage) for position players, Earned Run Average for pitchers. Other measures might have appeared here, but these are the single best shorthand means of identifying batting or pitching excellence. Note that Production is expressed, for all but superlative seasons, as numbers less than 1.000 (three figures to the right of a decimal point), while ERA is expressed as a whole number followed by a decimal and two decimal places.

"G/POS" stands for games by position, expressed in descending order of frequency. If a man pitched and played a regular position, the statistic provided in the "P/E" column will be determined by which position he played more often. In G/POS for outfielders, the position is shown as left, center, or right field based on which outfield position he played more often. (If game data is missing for more than two games, "OF" is the abbreviation shown.) Beyond the expected abbreviations, note that "H" stands for a pinch hitter who did not take the field and "R" for a pinch runner who did not have a plate appearance.

In the column marked "From," the letter "A" signifies a player's major league debut, as with Joe Sewell of the 1920 Indians. "B" means he played for the Indians as his last or only club the previous year, as with Jack Graney. If he came from another major league club, that club is shown in abbreviated form; if the abbreviation is preceded by an "x," then he has come to the Indians during the season, as with George Burns. A key to these abbreviations may be found on the final page of this book.

In the column marked "To," the letter "C" signifies that this season marked the close of his major league career (see Joe Boehling). If the player moved on to another club during the season, the abbreviation for that club is preceded by an "x" (see Elmer Myers). If the column is blank, the reader knows the player returned to the Indians the following season.

Name	G	AB/IP	P/E	G/POS	From	To
◆ 1920 CLEVELAND (154 98-56 1) ATT: 912,832						
Tris Speaker				M		
Jim Bagby	49	340	2.89	P-48(31-12)	B	
Joe Boehling	3	13	4.85	P-3(0-1)	B	C
George Burns	44	64	.714	1-12,RF-1	xPhi-A	
Ray Caldwell	41	238	3.86	P-34(20-10)	B	
Ray Chapman	111	530	.803	S-111	B	C
Bob Clark	11	42	3.43	P-11(1-2)	A	
Stan Coveleski	41	315	2.49	P-41(24-14)	B	
George Ellison	1	1	0.00	P-1	A	C
Joe Evans	56	189	.910	LF-43,S-6	B	
Tony Faeth	13	25	4.32	P-13	B	C
Larry Gardner	154	683	.781	3-154	B	
Jack Graney	62	191	.794	LF-47	B	
Charlie Jamieson	108	425	.799	LF-98,1-4	B	
Doc Johnston	147	593	.718	1-147	B	
Harry Lunte	23	76	.447	S-21,2-2	B	C
Duster Mails	9	63	1.85	P-9(7-0)	Bro-N	
Guy Morton	29	137	4.47	P-29(8-6)	B	
Tim Murchison	2	5	0.00	P-2	StL-N	C
Elmer Myers	16	72	4.77	P-16(2-4)	B	xBos-A
Dick Niehaus	19	40	3.60	P-19(1-2)	StL-N	C
Les Nunamaker	34	59	.879	C-17,1-6	B	
Steve O'Neill	149	576	.848	C-148	B	
Joe Sewell	22	83	.827	S-22	A	
Elmer Smith	129	525	.910	RF-129	B	
Tris Speaker	150	674	1.045	CF-148	B	
Pinch Thomas	9	12	.944	C-7	B	
George Uhle	27	85	5.21	P-27(4-5)	B	
Bill Wambsganss	153	664	.633	2-153	B	
Joe Wood	61	176	.792	RF-55,P-1	B	

Coach: Jack McCallister

1901 CLEVELAND (138 55-82 7) ATT: 131,380

Name	G	AB/IP	P/E	G/POS	From	To
Jimmy McAleer				M		
Bock Baker	1	8	5.63	P-1(0-1)	A	xPhi-A
Erve Beck	135	567	.720	2-132	Bro-N	Cin-N
Jack Bracken	12	100	6.21	P-12(4-8)	A	C
Bill Bradley	133	551	.739	3-133,P-1	Chi-N	
Dick Braggins	4	32	4.78	P-4(1-2)	A	C
Ed Cermak	1	4	.000	RF-1	A	C
Joe Connor	37	133	.382	C-32,RF-4,S-1	xMil-A	NY-A
Bill Cristall	6	48	4.84	P-6(1-5)	A	C
Frank Cross	1	5	1.200	RF-1	A	C
Tom Donovan	18	72	.577	RF-18,P-1	A	C
Pete Dowling	33	256	3.86	P-33(11-22)	xMil-A	C
Truck Eagan	5	19	.488	2-5,3-1	xPit-N	C
Shorty Gallagher	2	4	.000	RF-2	A	C
Frank Genins	26	113	.562	CF-26	Pit-N	C
Russ Hall	1	4	1.000	S-1	StL-N	C
Bill Hallman	5	21	.496	S-5	Bro-N	xPhi-N
Bill Hart	20	158	3.77	P-20(7-11)	Pit-N	C
Erwin Harvey	45	182	.851	RF-45	xChi-A	
Bill Hoffer	17	99	4.55	P-16(3-8),S-1	Pit-N	C
Harry Hogan	1	4	.000	RF-1	A	C
Candy LaChance	133	564	.696	1-133	Bal-N	Bos-A
Paddy Livingston	1	3	.333	C-1	A	Cin-N
Jimmy McAleer	3	7	.286	CF-2,P-1,3-1	Cle-N	StL-A
Jack McCarthy	86	396	.784	LF-86	Chi-N	
Jim McGuire	18	69	.493	S-18	A	C
Harry McNeal	12	85	4.43	P-12(5-5)	A	C
Earl Moore	31	251	2.90	P-31(16-14)	A	
Jack O'Brien	92	405	.676	RF-92,3-1	xWas-A	Bos-A
Ollie Pickering	137	618	.760	CF-137	Cle-N	
Frank Scheibeck	93	359	.522	S-92	Was-N	Det-A
Ed Scott	17	125	4.40	P-17(6-6)	Cin-N	C
Danny Shay	19	80	.572	S-19	A	StL-N
Gus Weyhing	2	11	7.94	P-2	Bro-N	xCin-N
Bob Wood	98	368	.711	C-84,3-4,RF-3,1-1,2-1,S-1	Cin-N	
George Yeager	39	146	.509	C-25,1-5,RF-3,2-2	Bos-N	xPit-N

1902 CLEVELAND (137 69-67 5) ATT: 275,395

Name	G	AB/IP	P/E	G/POS	From	To
Bill Armour				M		
Harry Bay	108	510	.678	CF-107	xCin-N	
Harry Bemis	93	353	.770	C-87,RF-2,2-1	A	
Bill Bernhard	27	217	2.20	P-27(17-5)	xPhi-A	
Frank Bonner	34	140	.637	2-34	Was-N	xPhi-A
Bill Bradley	137	597	.890	3-137	B	
Ginger Clark	1	6	6.00	P-1(1-0)	A	C
Gus Dorner	4	36	1.25	P-4(3-1)	A	
Elmer Flick	110	482	.779	RF-110	xPhi-A	
John Gochnauer	127	506	.485	S-127	Bro-N	
Peaches Graham	2	7	.762	2-1	A	Chi-N
Erwin Harvey	12	50	.779	RF-12	B	C
Charlie Hemphill	25	102	.590	LF-19	Bos-A	xStL-A
Otto Hess	7	44	5.98	P-7(2-4)	A	
Charlie Hickman	102	449	.958	1-98,2-3,P-1(0-1)	xBos-A	
Addie Joss	33	269	2.77	P-32(17-13),1-1	A	
Nap Lajoie	86	381	.990	2-86	xPhi-A	
Dummy Leitner	1	8	4.50	P-1	NY-N	xChi-A
Jack Lundbom	8	34	6.62	P-8(1-1)	A	C
Jack McCarthy	95	401	.727	LF-95	B	
Earl Moore	36	293	2.95	P-36(17-17)	B	
Hal O'Hagen	3	13	.923	1-3	xNY-N	xNY-N
Ollie Pickering	69	316	.623	CF-64,1-2	B	Phi-A
Lou Polchow	1	8	5.63	P-1(0-1)	A	C
Ossee Schreckengost	18	74	.676	1-17	Bos-A	xPhi-A
Charlie Smith	3	20	4.05	P-3(2-1)	A	Was-A
George Starnagle	1	3	.000	C-1	A	C
Oscar Streit	8	52	5.23	P-8(0-7)	Bos-N	C
Dummy Taylor	4	34	1.59	P-4(1-3)	NY-N	xNY-N
Jack Thoney	28	115	.714	2-14,S-11,RF-2	A	xBal-A
Dike Varney	3	15	6.14	P-3(1-1)	A	C
Cal Vasbinder	2	5	9.00	P-2	A	C
Ed Walker	1	8	3.38	P-1(0-1)	A	C
Bob Wood	81	295	.754	C-52,1-16,RF-2,2-1,3-1	B	Det-A
Gene Wright	23	148	3.95	P-21(7-11),1-1	Bro-N	

1903 CLEVELAND (140 77-63 3) ATT: 311,280

Name	G	AB/IP	P/E	G/POS	From	To
Bill Armour				M		
Fred Abbott	77	276	.583	C-71,1-3	A	
Harry Bay	140	636	.693	CF-140	B	
Harry Bemis	92	332	.648	C-74,1-10,2-1	B	
Bill Bernhard	20	166	2.12	P-20(14-6)	B	
Bill Bradley	136	587	.844	3-136	B	
Billy Clingman	21	78	.715	2-11,S-7,3-3	Was-A	C
Red Donahue	16	137	2.44	P-16(7-9)	xStL-A	
Gus Dorner	12	74	4.52	P-12(4-5)	B	Cin-N
Elmer Flick	140	593	.781	RF-140	B	
Martin Glendon	3	28	0.98	P-3(1-2)	Cin-N	C
John Gochnauer	134	512	.505	S-134	B	C
Jack Hardy	5	20	.411	RF-5	A	Chi-N
Charlie Hickman	131	552	.790	1-125,2-7	B	
Hugh Hill	1	1	.000	H	A	StL-N
Happy Iott	3	12	.533	CF-3	A	C
Addie Joss	34	284	2.19	P-32(18-13),1-1	B	
Ed Killian	10	62	2.48	P-9(3-4)	A	Det-A
Nap Lajoie	125	525	.896	2-122,1-1,3-1	B	
Jack McCarthy	108	461	.651	LF-108	B	xChi-N
Earl Moore	29	248	1.74	P-29(19-9)	B	
Alex Pearson	4	30	3.56	P-4(1-2)	StL-N	C
Bill Pounds	1	5	10.80	P-1	A	xBro-N
Bob Rhoads	5	41	5.27	P-5(2-3)	xStL-N	
Jack Slattery	4	11	.000	1-2	Bos-A	xChi-A
Jesse Stovall	6	57	2.05	P-6(5-1)	A	Det-A
Jack Thoney	32	124	.472	CF-24,2-5,3-2	Bal-A	Was-A
Ed Walker	3	12	5.25	P-3	B	C
Gene Wright	15	102	5.75	P-15(3-9)	B	xStL-A

1904 CLEVELAND (154 86-65 4) ATT: 264,749

Name	G	AB/IP	P/E	G/POS	From	To
Bill Armour				M		
Fred Abbott	41	141	.437	C-33,1-7	B	Phi-N
Harry Bay	132	563	.625	CF-132	B	
Harry Bemis	97	362	.554	C-79,1-13,2-1	B	
Bill Bernhard	38	321	2.13	P-38(23-13)	B	
Bill Bradley	154	667	.738	3-154	B	
Fritz Buelow	42	137	.479	C-42	xDet-A	
Charlie Carr	32	127	.533	1-32	xDet-A	
Red Donahue	35	277	2.40	P-35(19-14)	B	
Mike Donovan	2	2	.000	S-1	A	NY-A
Elmer Flick	150	659	.820	RF-145,2-6	B	
Otto Hess	34	151	1.67	P-21(8-7),LF-12	B	
John Hickey	2	12	7.30	P-2(0-1)	A	C
Charlie Hickman	86	361	.766	2-45,1-40,LF-1	B	xDet-A
Addie Joss	28	192	1.59	P-25(14-10),1-3	B	
Nap Lajoie	140	594	.965	2-95,S-44,1-2	B	
Billy Lush	138	577	.684	LF-138	Det-A	C
Earl Moore	26	228	2.25	P-26(12-11)	B	
Harry Ostdiek	7	22	.596	C-7	A	Bos-A
Bob Rhoads	29	175	2.87	P-22(10-9),CF-5	B	
Claude Rossman	18	65	.500	RF-17	A	
Bill Schwartz	24	88	.326	1-22,3-1	A	C
George Stovall	52	191	.698	1-38,2-9,LF-3,3-1	A	
Terry Turner	111	434	.550	S-111	Pit-N	
Rube Vinson	15	60	.760	LF-15	A	

1905 CLEVELAND (155 76-78 5) ATT: 316,306

Name	G	AB/IP	P/E	G/POS	From	To
Nap Lajoie				M(58 37-21 1)		
Bill Bradley				M(41 20-21 2)		
Nap Lajoie				M(56 19-36 5)		
Jap Barbeau	11	40	.641	2-11	A	
Harry Bay	144	623	.719	CF-144	B	
Harry Bemis	70	249	.720	C-58,2-4,3-2,1-1	B	
Bill Bernhard	22	174	3.36	P-22(7-13)	B	
Bill Bradley	146	604	.674	3-146	B	
Fritz Buelow	75	254	.408	C-60,RF-8,1-3,3-2	B	
Charlie Carr	89	334	.577	1-87	B	Cin-N
Nig Clarke	5	10	.422	C-5	A	xDet-A
Nig Clarke	37	126	.529	C-37	xDet-A	
Bunk Congalton	12	49	.749	RF-12	Chi-N	
Red Donahue	20	138	3.40	P-20(6-12)	B	Det-A
Cy Ferry	1	2	13.50	P-1	Det-A	C
Elmer Flick	132	573	.845	RF-131,2-1	B	
Eddie Grant	2	8	.750	2-2	A	Phi-N
John Halla	3	13	2.84	P-3	A	C
Otto Hess	54	185	.638	LF-28,P-26(10-15)	B	
Jim Jackson	109	470	.634	LF-106,3-3	NY-N	
Addie Joss	35	286	2.01	P-33(20-12),1-1,3-1	B	
Nick Kahl	40	142	.507	2-32,S-1,CF-1	A	C
Nap Lajoie	65	271	.795	2-59,1-5	B	
Emil Leber	2	7	.143	3-2	A	C
Earl Moore	31	269	2.64	P-31(15-15)	B	
Bob Rhoads	33	235	2.83	P-28(16-9),OF-1	B	
George Stovall	112	445	.652	1-60,2-46,CF-4	B	
Terry Turner	155	621	.649	S-155	B	
Rube Vinson	39	148	.476	LF-36	B	Chi-A
Howard Wakefield	10	27	.593	C-8	A	Was-A
Hi West	6	33	4.09	P-6(2-2)	A	

1906 CLEVELAND (157 89-64 3) ATT: 325,733

Name	G	AB/IP	P/E	G/POS	From	To
Nap Lajoie				M		
Jap Barbeau	42	143	.536	3-32,S-6	B	Pit-N
Harry Bay	68	321	.662	CF-68	B	
Harry Bemis	93	318	.685	C-81	B	
Bill Bernhard	31	255	2.54	P-31(16-15)	B	
Joe Birmingham	10	42	.748	LF-9,3-1	A	
Bill Bradley	82	340	.685	3-82	B	
Fritz Buelow	34	101	.436	C-33,1-1	B	StL-A
Ben Caffyn	30	118	.524	LF-29	A	C
Nig Clarke	57	195	.890	C-54	B	
Bunk Congalton	117	470	.757	RF-114	B	
Harry Eells	14	86	2.61	P-14(4-5)	A	C
Elmer Flick	157	700	.813	CF-150,2-8	B	
Otto Hess	53	334	1.83	P-43(20-17),CF-5	B	
Jim Jackson	105	428	.549	LF-104	B	C
Addie Joss	36	282	1.72	P-34(21-9),CF-2	B	
Malachi Kittridge	5	10	.200	C-5	xWas-A	C
Nap Lajoie	152	655	.857	2-130,3-15,S-7	B	
Glenn Liebhardt	2	18	1.50	P-2(2-0)	A	
Earl Moore	5	30	3.94	P-5(1-1)	B	
Bob Rhoads	38	315	1.80	P-38(22-10)	B	
Claude Rossman	118	431	.697	1-105,CF-1	B	Det-A
Bill Shipke	2	7	.000	2-2	A	Was-A
George Stovall	116	469	.626	1-55,3-30,2-19	B	
Happy Townsend	17	93	2.91	P-17(3-7)	Was-A	C
Terry Turner	147	643	.709	S-147	B	

1907 CLEVELAND (158 85-67 4) ATT: 382,046

Name	G	AB/IP	P/E	G/POS	From	To
Nap Lajoie				M		
Harry Bay	34	112	.482	CF-31	B	
Harry Bemis	65	189	.574	C-51,1-2	B	
Heinie Berger	14	87	2.99	P-14(3-3)	A	
Bill Bernhard	8	42	3.21	P-8(0-4)	B	C
Joe Birmingham	136	503	.565	CF-130,S-5	B	
Bill Bradley	139	588	.553	3-139	B	
Nig Clarke	120	430	.704	C-115	B	
Walter Clarkson	17	91	1.99	P-17(4-6)	xNY-A	
Bunk Congalton	9	26	.490	RF-6	B	xBos-A
Frank Delahanty	15	56	.444	LF-15	NY-A	NY-A
Elmer Flick	147	637	.798	RF-147	B	
Otto Hess	19	93	2.89	P-17(6-6),LF-2	B	
Harry Hinchman	15	58	.599	2-15	A	C

Name	G	AB/IP	P/E	G/POS	From	To
Bill Hinchman	152	592	.616	LF-148,1-4,2-1	Cin-N	
Addie Joss	42	339	1.83	P-42(27-11)	B	
Nap Lajoie	137	558	.738	2-128,1-9	B	
Glenn Liebhardt	38	280	2.05	P-38(18-14)	B	
Pete Lister	22	71	.627	1-22	A	C
Earl Moore	3	19	4.66	P-3(1-1)	B	xNY-A
Rabbit Nill	12	47	.628	3-7,S-4	xWas-A	
Pete O'Brien	43	158	.553	2-17,3-12,S-11	StL-A	xWas-A
Bob Rhoads	35	275	2.29	P-35(15-14)	B	
George Stovall	124	500	.572	1-122,3-2	B	
Jake Thielman	21	166	2.33	P-20(11-8),LF-1	StL-N	
Terry Turner	140	561	.579	S-139	B	
Howard Wakefield	26	40	.389	C-11	Was-A	C

♦ **1908 CLEVELAND** (157 90-64 2) ATT: 422,262

Name	G	AB/IP	P/E	G/POS	From	To
Nap Lajoie				M		
Dave Altizer	29	109	.548	CF-24,S-3	xWas-A	Chi-A
Harry Bay	2	0	†	R	B	C
Harry Bemis	91	298	.517	C-76,1-2	B	
Heinie Berger	29	199	2.12	P-29(13-8)	B	
Joe Birmingham	122	446	.510	CF-121,S-1	B	
Bill Bradley	148	650	.614	3-118,S-30	B	
Charlie Chech	27	166	1.74	P-27(11-7)	Cin-N	Bos-A
Nig Clarke	97	328	.635	C-90	B	
Josh Clarke	131	581	.628	LF-131	StL-N	
Walter Clarkson	2	3	10.80	P-2	B	C
Homer Davidson	9	4	.000	C-5,RF-1	A	C
Cy Falkenberg	8	46	3.88	P-8(2-4)	xWas-A	
Elmer Flick	9	39	.604	RF-9	B	
Ed Foster	6	21	2.14	P-6(1-0)	A	C
Wilbur Good	46	175	.695	RF-42	NY-A	
Jack Graney	2	3	5.40	P-2	A	
Otto Hess	9	7	5.14	P-4,RF-4	B	Bos-N
Charlie Hickman	65	209	.575	RF-28,1-20,2-1	Chi-A	C
Bill Hinchman	137	530	.655	RF-75,S-51,1-4	B	
Addie Joss	42	325	1.16	P-42(24-11)	B	
Nap Lajoie	157	667	.727	2-156,1-1	B	
Grover Land	8	17	.375	C-8	A	
Bill Lattimore	4	24	4.50	P-4(1-2)	A	C
Glenn Liebhardt	38	262	2.20	P-38(15-16)	B	
Deacon McGuire	1	4	.750	1-1	xBos-A	
Rabbit Nill	11	25	.435	S-6,LF-3,2-1	B	C
George Perring	89	331	.529	S-48,3-41	A	
Bob Rhoads	37	270	1.77	P-37(18-12)	B	
Jack Ryan	8	36	2.27	P-8(1-1)	A	Bos-A
George Stovall	138	584	.697	1-132,CF-5,S-1	B	
Denny Sullivan	4	6	.000	LF-2	xBos-A	
Jake Thielman	13	62	3.65	P-11(4-3),RF-2	B	xBos-A
Terry Turner	60	226	.602	RF-36,S-17	B	

♦ **1909 CLEVELAND** (155 71-82 6) ATT: 354,627

Name	G	AB/IP	P/E	G/POS	From	To
Nap Lajoie				M(114 57-57 4)		
Deacon McGuire				M(41 14-25 6)		
Harry Ables	5	30	2.12	P-5(1-1)	StL-A	NY-A
Neal Ball	96	357	.613	S-95	xNY-A	
Harry Bemis	42	126	.446	C-36	B	
Heinie Berger	34	247	2.73	P-34(13-14)	B	
Joe Birmingham	100	370	.689	CF-98	B	
Red Booles	4	23	1.99	P-4(0-1)	A	C
Bill Bradley	95	376	.458	3-87,1-3,2-3	B	
Nig Clarke	55	179	.639	C-44	B	
Josh Clarke	4	14	.143	LF-4	B	Bos-N
Walt Doane	4	10	.311	LF-2,P-1(0-1)	A	
Ted Easterly	98	308	.684	C-76	A	
Cy Falkenberg	24	165	2.40	P-24(10-9)	B	
Elmer Flick	66	259	.637	RF-61	B	
Wilbur Good	94	360	.560	RF-80	B	Bos-N
Bob Higgins	8	23	.174	C-8	A	Bro-N
Bill Hinchman	139	524	.703	LF-131,S-6	B	Pit-N
Addie Joss	33	243	1.71	P-33(14-13)	B	
Nap Lajoie	128	521	.809	2-120,1-8	B	
Grover Land	1	4	1.000	C-1	B	
Glenn Liebhardt	12	52	2.92	P-12(1-5)	B	C
Bris Lord	69	270	.628	LF-67	Phi-A	
Willie Mitchell	3	23	1.57	P-3(1-2)	A	
Milo Netzel	10	40	.466	3-6,LF-2	A	C
Harry Otis	5	26	1.37	P-5(2-2)	A	C
George Perring	88	316	.605	3-67,S-11,2-4	B	
Tom Raftery	8	36	.649	RF-8	A	C
Duke Reilley	20	71	.467	LF-18	A	C
Bob Rhoads	20	133	2.90	P-20(5-9)	B	C
Carl Sitton	14	50	2.88	P-14(3-2)	A	C
Dolly Stark	19	68	.473	S-19	A	Bro-N
George Stovall	145	595	.581	1-145	B	
Denny Sullivan	3	2	1.000	RF-2	B	C
Terry Turner	53	226	.626	2-26,S-26	B	
Jerry Upp	7	27	1.69	P-7(2-1)	A	C
Fred Winchell	4	14	6.28	P-4(0-3)	A	C
Lucky Wright	5	28	3.21	P-5(0-4)	A	C
Cy Young	35	295	2.26	P-35(19-15)	Bos-A	

♦ **1910 CLEVELAND** (161 71-81 5) ATT: 293,456

Name	G	AB/IP	P/E	G/POS	From	To
Deacon McGuire				M		
Bert Adams	5	13	.462	C-5	A	
Neal Ball	53	134	.518	S-27,2-6,CF-6,3-3	B	
Harry Bemis	61	178	.514	C-46	B	C
Heinie Berger	13	65	3.03	P-13(3-4)	B	C
Joe Birmingham	104	406	.553	CF-103,3-1	B	
Fred Blanding	6	45	2.78	P-6(2-2)	A	
Bill Bradley	61	233	.446	3-61	B	Bro-F
Herman Bronkie	5	10	.522	3-3,S-1	A	
Dave Callahan	13	51	.470	LF-12	A	
Nig Clarke	21	69	.447	C-17	B	StL-A
Ben DeMott	9	28	5.40	P-6(0-3),CF-2	A	
Walt Doane	6	18	5.60	P-6	B	C

Name	G	AB/IP	P/E	G/POS	From	To
Pat Donahue	2	6	.333	C-2,1-1	xPhi-A	xPhi-A
Ted Easterly	110	398	.727	C-65,RF-32	B	
Cy Falkenberg	37	257	2.95	P-37(14-13)	B	
Harry Fanwell	17	92	3.62	P-17(2-9)	A	C
Elmer Flick	24	78	.727	RF-18	B	C
Jack Graney	116	499	.604	LF-114	B	
Spec Harkness	26	136	3.04	P-26(10-7)	A	
Eddie Hohnhorst	18	68	.755	1-18	A	
Joe Jackson	20	86	1.032	CF-20	Phi-A	
Addie Joss	13	107	2.26	P-13(5-5)	B	C
George Kahler	12	95	1.60	P-12(6-4)	A	
Harry Kirsch	2	3	6.00	P-2	A	C
Cotton Knaupp	18	71	.660	S-18	A	
Elmer Koestner	27	145	3.04	P-27(5-10)	A	Chi-N
Art Kruger	47	198	.439	LF-47	Cin-N	xBos-N
Art Kruger	15	61	.586	LF-15	xBos-N	KC-F
Nap Lajoie	159	677	.960	2-149,1-10	B	
Grover Land	34	119	.435	C-33	B	
Fred Link	22	128	3.17	P-22(5-6)	A	xStL-A
Bris Lord	58	230	.592	RF-56	B	xPhi-A
Deacon McGuire	1	4	.833	C-1	B	Det-A
Willie Mitchell	35	184	2.60	P-35(12-8)	B	
Simon Nicholls	3	0	†	S-3	Phi-A	C
Harry Niles	70	261	.551	RF-50,S-7,3-5	xBos-A	C
Roger Peckinpaugh	15	50	.434	S-14	A	
George Perring	39	126	.560	3-33,1-4	B	KC-F
Morrie Rath	24	78	.538	3-22,S-1	xPhi-A	Chi-A
Jim Rutherford	1	2	1.000	CF-1	A	C
Syd Smith	9	30	.770	C-9	StL-A	
George Stovall	142	566	.597	1-132,2-2	B	
Art Thomason	20	76	.427	RF-20	A	C
Terry Turner	150	651	.576	S-94,3-46,2-9	B	
Cy Young	21	163	2.53	P-21(7-10)	B	

♦ **1911 CLEVELAND** (156 80-73 3) ATT: 406,296

Name	G	AB/IP	P/E	G/POS	From	To
Deacon McGuire				M(17 6-11 7)		
George Stovall				M(139 74-62 3)		
Bert Adams	2	7	.533	C-2	B	
Neal Ball	116	452	.735	2-94,3-17,S-1	B	
Jim Baskette	4	21	3.38	P-4(1-2)	A	
Joe Birmingham	125	481	.714	CF-102,3-16	B	
Fred Blanding	30	176	3.68	P-29(7-11)	B	
Herman Bronkie	2	6	.333	3-2	B	
Hank Butcher	38	147	.664	LF-34	B	
Dave Callahan	6	17	.669	CF-4	B	C
Ben DeMott	2	4	12.27	P-1(0-1),CF-1	B	C
Ted Easterly	99	306	.780	RF-54,C-22	B	
Cy Falkenberg	16	107	3.29	P-15(8-5)	B	
Gus Fisher	70	220	.623	C-58,1-1	A	NY-A
Jack Graney	146	620	.704	LF-142	B	
Vean Gregg	34	245	1.80	P-34(23-7)	A	
Art Griggs	27	74	.698	2-11,RF-4,3-3,1-1	StL-A	
Spec Harkness	12	53	4.22	P-12(2-2)	B	C
Tim Hendryx	4	8	.571	3-3	A	
Joe Jackson	147	641	1.058	RF-147	B	
Bill James	8	52	4.88	P-8(2-4)	A	
George Kahler	30	154	3.27	P-30(9-8)	B	
Cotton Knaupp	13	40	.231	S-13	B	C
Gene Krapp	36	222	3.41	P-35(13-9)	A	
Nap Lajoie	90	353	.874	1-41,2-37	B	
Grover Land	35	112	.351	C-34,1-1	B	
Bill Lindsay	19	68	.537	3-15,2-1	A	C
Jack Mills	13	19	.663	3-7	A	C
Willie Mitchell	32	177	3.76	P-30(7-14)	B	
Ivy Olson	140	610	.643	S-139,3-1	A	
Steve O'Neill	9	33	.466	C-9	A	
Pat Paige	2	16	4.50	P-2(1-0)	A	C
Bugs Reisigl	2	13	6.23	P-2(0-1)	A	C
Syd Smith	58	172	.736	C-48,1-1,3-1	B	Pit-N
George Stovall	126	492	.644	1-118,2-2	B	StL-A
Josh Swindell	4	17	2.08	P-4(0-1)	A	
Terry Turner	117	470	.643	3-94,2-14,S-10	B	
Hi West	13	65	3.76	P-13(3-4)	A	C
Earl Yingling	6	22	4.43	P-4(1-0),CF-1	A	Bro-N
Cy Young	7	46	3.88	P-7(3-4)	B	xBos-N

♦ **1912 CLEVELAND** (155 75-78 5) ATT: 336,844

Name	G	AB/IP	P/E	G/POS	From	To
Harry Davis				M(127 54-71 6)		
Joe Birmingham				M(28 21-7 5)		
Bert Adams	20	62	.536	C-20	B	Phi-N
Howard Baker	11	35	.452	3-10	A	Chi-A
Neal Ball	40	145	.549	2-37	B	xBos-A
Jim Baskette	29	116	3.18	P-29(8-4)	B	
Joe Birmingham	107	415	.641	CF-96,1-9	B	
Fred Blanding	39	262	2.92	P-39(18-14)	B	
Bert Brenner	2	13	2.77	P-2(1-0)	A	C
Herman Bronkie	6	19	.059	3-6	B	Chi-N
Hank Butcher	26	91	.555	LF-21	B	C
Fred Carisch	24	72	.634	C-23	Pit-N	
Ray Chapman	31	132	.797	S-31	A	
Harry Davis	2	5	.000	1-2	Phi-A	Phi-A
Ted Easterly	65	199	.678	C-51	B	xChi-A
Hack Eibel	1	3	.000	RF-1	A	Bos-A
Lefty George	11	44	4.87	P-11(0-5)	StL-A	Cin-N
Jack Graney	78	321	.674	LF-75	B	
Vean Gregg	37	271	2.59	P-37(20-13)	B	
Art Griggs	89	314	.795	1-71	B	Bro-F
Harvey Grubb	1	1	1.000	3-1	A	C
Arthur Hauger	15	19	.161	CF-5	A	C
Tim Hendryx	23	86	.758	CF-22	B	NY-A
Eddie Hohnhorst	15	57	.454	1-15	B	C
Bill Hunter	21	69	.503	CF-16	A	C
Joe Jackson	154	653	1.036	RF-150	B	
Lefty James	3	6	7.50	P-3(0-1)	A	
Bill James	3	14	4.61	P-3	B	StL-A

Name	G	AB/IP	P/E	G/POS	From	To
Doc Johnston	43	182	.716	1-41	Cin-N	
George Kahler	41	246	3.69	P-41(12-19)	B	
Jack Kibble	5	9	.111	3-4,2-1	A	C
Gene Krapp	13	59	4.60	P-9(2-5)	B	Buf-F
Harry Krause	2	5	11.57	P-2(0-1)	xPhi-A	C
Nap Lajoie	117	500	.876	2-97,1-20	B	
Paddy Livingston	20	54	.599	C-14	Phi-A	StL-N
Moxie Meixell	3	2	1.000	OF-1	A	C
Willie Mitchell	29	164	2.80	P-29(5-8)	B	
Lou Nagelsen	2	3	.000	C-2	A	C
Ken Nash	11	26	.443	S-8	A	StL-N
Jim Neher	1	1	0.00	P-1	A	C
Ivy Olson	125	522	.575	S-56,3-36,2-21,LF-3	B	
Steve O'Neill	69	233	.518	C-68	B	
Roger Peckinpaugh	70	258	.512	S-68	B	
Buddy Ryan	93	376	.715	LF-90	A	
Bill Steen	26	143	3.77	P-26(9-8)	A	
Terry Turner	103	419	.731	3-103	B	
Mysterious Walker	1	1	0.00	P-1	Cin-N	Bro-N
Roy Walker	1	2	0.00	P-1	A	
Ernie Wolf	1	6	6.35	P-1	A	C

◆ 1913 CLEVELAND (155 86-66 3) ATT: 541,000

Name	G	AB/IP	P/E	G/POS	From	To
Joe Birmingham				M		
Jim Baskette	2	5	5.79	P-2	B	C
Johnny Bassler	1	2	.000	C-1	A	
Ray Bates	27	35	.565	3-12,CF-2	A	Phi-A
Johnny Beall	6	6	.333	H	A	xChi-A
Josh Billings	1	3	.000	C-1	A	
Joe Birmingham	47	148	.690	CF-36	B	
Fred Blanding	41	215	2.55	P-41(15-10)	B	
Lynn Brenton	1	2	9.00	P-1	A	
Fred Carisch	82	246	.539	C-79	B	
Ray Chapman	141	601	.662	S-138,OF-1	B	
Nick Cullop	23	98	4.42	P-23(3-7)	A	
Lee Dashner	1	2	5.40	P-1	A	C
George Dunlop	7	17	.529	S-4,3-3	A	
Eddie Edmonson	2	5	.000	1-1,OF-1	A	C
Cy Falkenberg	39	276	2.22	P-39(23-10)	B	Ind-F
Luke Glavenich	1	1	9.00	P-1	A	C
Jack Graney	148	583	.701	LF-148	B	
Dave Gregg	1	1	18.00	P-1	A	C
Vean Gregg	44	286	2.24	P-44(20-13)	B	
Joe Jackson	148	623	1.011	RF-148	B	
Lefty James	11	39	3.00	P-11(2-2)	B	
Doc Johnston	133	583	.657	1-133	B	
George Kahler	24	118	3.14	P-24(5-11)	B	
Larry Kopf	6	10	.700	2-4,3-1	A	Phi-A
Ernie Krueger	5	6	.000	C-4	A	NY-A
Nap Lajoie	137	525	.802	2-126	B	
Grover Land	17	56	.576	C-17	B	Bro-F
Nemo Leibold	93	312	.649	CF-74	A	
Jack Lelivelt	23	23	.870	CF-1	xNY-A	
Willie Mitchell	35	217	1.91	P-35(14-8)	B	
Ivy Olson	104	411	.596	3-73,1-21,2-1	B	
Steve O'Neill	80	253	.705	C-80	B	
Roger Peckinpaugh	1	0	†	R	B	xNY-A
Buddy Ryan	73	268	.661	CF-68,1-1	B	C
Billy Southworth	1	0	†	OF-1	A	
Bill Steen	22	128	2.45	P-22(4-5)	B	
Josh Swindell	1	0	†	R	B	C
Terry Turner	120	481	.650	3-71,2-25,S-21	B	
George Young	2	2	.000	H	A	C

◆ 1914 CLEVELAND (157 51-102 8) ATT: 185,997

Name	G	AB/IP	P/E	G/POS	From	To
Joe Birmingham				M		
Walter Barbare	15	58	.769	3-14,S-1	A	
Johnny Bassler	43	93	.543	C-25,3-1,RF-1	B	Det-A
George Beck	1	1	0.00	P-1	A	C
Henry Benn	1	1	0.00	P-1	A	C
Josh Billings	11	9	.708	C-3	B	
Joe Birmingham	19	50	.291	RF-14	B	C
Lloyd Bishop	3	8	5.63	P-3(0-1)	A	C
Rivington Bisland	18	64	.313	S-15,3-1	StL-A	C
Fred Blanding	30	116	3.96	P-29(3-9)	B	C
Abe Bowman	22	73	4.46	P-22(2-7)	A	
Fred Carisch	40	117	.583	C-38	B	Det-A
Paul Carter	5	25	2.92	P-5(1-3)	A	
Ray Chapman	106	442	.745	S-72,2-33	B	
Allan Collamore	27	105	3.25	P-27(3-7)	Phi-A	
Fritz Coumbe	14	55	3.25	P-14(1-5)	xBos-A	
Nick Cullop	1	3	2.70	P-1(0-1)	B	xKC-F
Al Cypert	1	1	.000	3-1	A	C
Harley Dillinger	11	34	4.54	P-11(0-1)	A	C
George Dunlop	1	4	.250	S-1	B	C
Ben Egan	29	95	.549	C-27	Phi-A	
Tinsley Ginn	2	1	.000	OF-2	A	C
Jack Graney	130	536	.714	LF-127	B	
Vean Gregg	17	97	3.07	P-17(9-3)	B	xBos-A
Rip Hagerman	37	198	3.09	P-37(9-15)	Chi-N	
Bruce Hartford	8	26	.535	S-8	A	C
Joe Jackson	122	512	.862	RF-119	B	
Lefty James	17	51	3.20	P-17(0-3)	B	C
Doc Johnston	103	384	.605	1-90,CF-2	B	Pit-N
Sam Jones	1	3	2.70	P-1	A	
George Kahler	2	14	3.86	P-2(0-1)	B	C
Jay Kirke	67	254	.639	LF-42,1-18	Bos-N	
Nap Lajoie	121	468	.619	2-80,1-31	B	Phi-A
Nemo Leibold	115	464	.665	CF-107	B	
Jack Lelivelt	34	87	.786	CF-13,1-1	B	C
Frank Mills	4	9	.347	C-2	A	C
Willie Mitchell	39	257	3.19	P-39(12-17)	B	
Guy Morton	25	128	3.02	P-25(1-13)	A	
Ivy Olson	89	331	.559	S-31,2-23,3-19,LF-6,1-3	B	Cin-N
Steve O'Neill	87	286	.605	C-82,1-1	B	

Name	G	AB/IP	P/E	G/POS	From	To
Larry Pezold	23	82	.566	3-20,RF-1	A	C
Tom Reilly	1	1	.000	H	StL-N	C
Elmer Smith	13	56	.723	CF-13	A	
Bill Steen	30	201	2.60	P-30(9-14)	B	
Al Tedrow	4	22	1.21	P-4(1-2)	A	C
Terry Turner	121	512	.646	3-104,2-17	B	
Bill Wambsganss	43	159	.564	S-36,2-4	A	
Roy Wood	72	241	.605	RF-40,1-20	Pit-N	

◆ 1915 CLEVELAND (155 57-95 7) ATT: 159,285

Name	G	AB/IP	P/E	G/POS	From	To
Joe Birmingham				M(28 12-16 6)		
Lee Fohl				M(127 45-79 7)		
Walter Barbare	77	274	.446	3-68,1-1	B	
Josh Billings	8	24	.429	C-7,CF-1	B	
Abe Bowman	2	1	20.25	P-2(0-1)	B	C
Lynn Brenton	11	51	3.35	P-11(2-3)	B	Cin-N
Paul Carter	12	42	3.21	P-11(1-1)	B	Chi-N
Ray Chapman	154	669	.723	S-154	B	
Allan Collamore	13	64	2.38	P-11(2-5)	B	C
Fritz Coumbe	35	114	3.47	P-30(4-7)	B	
Ben Egan	42	132	.297	C-40	B	C
Jim Eschen	15	50	.581	CF-10	A	C
Joe Evans	42	138	.712	3-30,2-2	A	
Clarence Garrett	4	23	2.31	P-4(2-2)	A	C
Lee Gooch	2	2	1.000	H	A	Phi-A
Jack Graney	116	476	.708	LF-115	B	
Rip Hagerman	29	151	3.52	P-29(6-14)	B	
Jack Hammond	35	92	.485	2-19	A	
Oscar Harstad	32	82	3.40	P-32(3-5)	A	C
Howie Haworth	7	9	.476	C-5	A	C
Herbert Hill	1	2	0.00	P-1	A	C
Tex Hoffman	9	15	.368	3-3	A	C
Joe Jackson	83	337	.858	RF-49,1-30	B	xChi-A
Sam Jones	48	146	3.65	P-48(4-9)	B	Bos-A
Jay Kirke	87	369	.742	1-87	B	NY-N
Ed Klepfer	8	43	2.09	P-8(1-6)	xChi-A	
Nemo Leibold	57	237	.658	CF-52	B	xChi-A
Willie Mitchell	36	236	2.82	P-36(11-14)	B	
Guy Morton	34	240	2.14	P-34(16-15)	B	
Steve O'Neill	121	426	.590	C-115	B	
Ben Paschal	9	9	.222	H	A	Bos-A
Bill Rodgers	16	55	.771	2-13	A	xBos-A
Braggo Roth	39	173	.906	CF-39	xChi-A	
Pete Shields	23	78	.542	1-23	A	C
Elmer Smith	144	528	.666	RF-123	B	
Billy Southworth	60	214	.640	CF-44	B	Pit-N
Bill Steen	10	45	4.96	P-10(1-4)	B	xDet-A
Terry Turner	75	305	.642	2-51,3-20	B	
Roy Walker	25	131	3.98	P-25(4-9)	B	Chi-A
Bill Wambsganss	121	423	.499	2-78,3-35	B	
Denney Wilie	45	161	.727	CF-35	StL-N	C
Roy Wood	33	83	.475	1-21,LF-2	B	C

◆ 1916 CLEVELAND (157 77-77 6) ATT: 492,106

Name	G	AB/IP	P/E	G/POS	From	To
Lee Fohl				M		
Milo Allison	14	25	.736	RF-5	Chi-N	
Jim Bagby	51	273	2.61	P-48(16-16)	Cin-N	
Walter Barbare	13	54	.538	3-12	B	Bos-A
Fred Beebe	20	101	2.41	P-20(5-3)	Phi-N	C
Al Bergman	8	16	.670	2-3	A	C
Josh Billings	22	35	.373	C-12	B	
Joe Boehling	13	61	2.67	P-12(2-4)	xWas-A	
Jack Bradley	2	3	.000	C-1	A	C
Ray Chapman	109	437	.619	S-52,3-36,2-16	B	
Larry Chappell	3	3	.333	H	Chi-A	xBos-N
Bob Coleman	19	36	.657	C-12	Pit-N	
Fritz Coumbe	31	120	2.02	P-29(7-5),RF-1	B	
Stan Coveleski	45	232	3.41	P-45(15-13)	Phi-A	
Tom Daly	31	75	.490	C-25,RF-1	Chi-A	Chi-N
Hank DeBerry	15	39	.779	C-14	A	
Shorty DesJardien	1	1	18.00	P-1	A	C
Clyde Engle	11	28	.308	3-7,1-2,RF-1	Buf-F	C
Joe Evans	33	94	.372	3-28	B	
Chick Gandil	146	601	.653	1-145	Was-A	Chi-A
Al Gould	30	107	2.53	P-30(5-7)	A	
Jack Graney	155	702	.739	LF-154	B	
Lou Guisto	6	23	.462	1-6	A	
Red Gunkel	1	1	0.00	P-1	A	C
Rip Hagerman	2	4	12.27	P-2	B	C
Ivon Howard	81	294	.571	2-65,1-7	StL-A	
Marty Kavanagh	19	46	.692	2-9,1-3,3-1	xDet-A	
Ed Klepfer	31	143	2.52	P-31(6-6)	B	
Otis Lambeth	16	74	2.92	P-15(4-3)	A	
Joe Leonard	3	2	.000	2-1	Pit-N	xWas-A
Howard Lohr	3	7	.286	RF-3	Cin-N	C
Grover Lowdermilk	10	51	3.16	P-10(1-5)	xDet-A	StL-A
Marty McHale	5	11	5.56	P-5	xBos-A	C
Willie Mitchell	12	44	5.15	P-12(2-5)	B	xDet-A
Danny Moeller	25	36	.267	LF-8,2-1	xWas-A	C
Guy Morton	27	150	2.89	P-27(12-8)	B	
Steve O'Neill	130	417	.584	C-128	B	
Ken Penner	4	13	4.26	P-4(1-0)	A	Chi-N
Braggo Roth	125	465	.746	RF-112	B	
Pop-Boy Smith	5	26	3.86	P-5(1-2)	Chi-A	
Elmer Smith	79	238	.754	RF-57	B	xWas-A
Tris Speaker	151	647	.972	CF-151	Bos-A	
Terry Turner	124	495	.636	3-77,2-42	B	
Bill Wambsganss	136	551	.605	S-106,2-24,3-5	B	
Ollie Welf	1	0	†	R	A	C

◆ 1917 CLEVELAND (156 88-66 3) ATT: 477,298

Name	G	AB/IP	P/E	G/POS	From	To
Lee Fohl				M		
Milo Allison	32	46	.461	CF-11	B	C
Jim Bagby	49	321	1.96	P-49(23-13)	B	
Josh Billings	66	147	.475	C-48	B	

Name	G	AB/IP	P/E	G/POS	From	To
Joe Boehling	14	46	4.66	P-12(1-6)	B	
Ray Chapman	156	691	.779	S-156	B	
Fritz Coumbe	35	134	2.14	P-34(8-6)	B	
Stan Coveleski	46	298	1.81	P-45(19-14),RF-1	B	
Hank DeBerry	25	36	.667	C-9	B	Bro-N
George Dickerson	1	1	0.00	P-1	A	C
Fred Eunick	1	2	.000	3-1	A	C
Joe Evans	132	460	.513	3-127	B	
Al Gould	27	94	3.64	P-27(4-4)	B	C
Jack Graney	146	648	.673	LF-145	B	
Lou Guisto	73	233	.507	1-59	B	
Joe Harris	112	435	.783	1-95,RF-5,3-2	NY-A	
Ivon Howard	27	44	.269	3-6,2-4,CF-4	B	C
Marty Kavanagh	14	17	.176	CF-2	B	
Ed Klepfer	41	213	2.37	P-41(14-4)	B	
Otis Lambeth	26	97	3.14	P-26(7-6)	B	
Ray Miller	19	29	.652	1-4	A	xPit-N
Guy Morton	35	161	2.74	P-35(10-10)	B	
Steve O'Neill	129	429	.494	C-127	B	
Braggo Roth	145	569	.743	RF-135	B	
Pop-Boy Smith	6	9	8.31	P-6(0-1)	B	C
Elmer Smith	64	181	.676	RF-40	xWas-A	
Tris Speaker	142	612	.918	CF-142	A	
Red Torkelson	4	22	7.66	P-4(2-1)	A	C
Terry Turner	69	202	.507	3-40,2-23,S-1	B	
Bill Wambsganss	141	570	.628	2-137,1-3	B	
Joe Wood	10	16	3.45	P-5(0-1)	Bos-A	

◆ 1918 CLEVELAND (129 73-54 2) ATT: 295,515

Name	G	AB/IP	P/E	G/POS	From	To
Lee Fohl				M		
Jim Bagby	47	271	2.69	P-45(17-16)	B	
Bob Bescher	25	78	.887	RF-17	StL-N	C
Josh Billings	2	3	.667	C-1	B	StL-A
Ad Brennan	1	3	3.00	P-1	xWas-A	C
Ray Chapman	128	571	.742	S-128,CF-1	B	
Fritz Coumbe	32	150	3.06	P-30(13-7),LF-1	B	
Stan Coveleski	38	311	1.82	P-38(22-13)	B	
Johnny Enzmann	30	137	2.37	P-30(5-7)	Bro-N	
Joe Evans	79	281	.702	3-74	B	
Jack Farmer	7	10	.522	LF-3	Pit-N	C
Gus Getz	6	20	.550	3-5	Cin-N	xPit-N
Jack Graney	70	211	.673	LF-45	B	
Bob Groom	14	43	7.06	P-14(2-2)	StL-A	C
Al Halt	26	78	.472	3-14,2-4,S-4,1-2	Bro-F	C
Doc Johnston	74	315	.587	1-73	Pit-N	
Marty Kavanagh	13	48	.611	1-12	B	xStL-N
Otis Lambeth	2	7	6.43	P-2	B	C
George McQuillan	5	23	2.35	P-5(0-1)	Phi-N	C
Ed Miller	32	111	.654	1-22,RF-4	StL-A	C
Guy Morton	30	215	2.64	P-30(14-8)	B	
Steve O'Neill	114	420	.655	C-113	B	
Eddie Onslow	2	6	.333	LF-1	Det-A	Was-A
John Peters	1	2	.500	C-1	Det-A	Phi-N
Braggo Roth	106	448	.794	RF-106	B	Phi-A
Germany Schaefer	1	5	.000	2-1	NY-A	C
Tris Speaker	127	549	.839	CF-127	B	
Pinch Thomas	32	82	.578	C-24	Bos-A	
Terry Turner	74	269	.613	3-46,2-26,S-1	B	Phi-A
Bill Wambsganss	87	356	.701	2-87	B	
Roy Wilkinson	1	1	0.00	P-1	A	Chi-A
Rip Williams	28	86	.649	1-21,C-1	Was-A	C
Joe Wood	119	481	.759	LF-95,2-19,1-4	B	

◆ 1919 CLEVELAND (139 84-55 2) ATT: 538,135

Name	G	AB/IP	P/E	G/POS	From	To
Lee Fohl				M(78 44-34 3)		
Tris Speaker				M(61 40-21 2)		
Jim Bagby	37	241	2.80	P-35(17-11)	B	
Ray Caldwell	6	53	1.71	P-6(5-1)	xBos-A	
Ray Chapman	115	517	.772	S-115	B	
Fritz Coumbe	8	24	5.32	P-8(1-1)	B	Cin-N
Stan Coveleski	43	286	2.61	P-43(24-12)	B	
Joe Engel	1	0	/	P-1	Cin-N	Was-A
Johnny Enzmann	14	55	2.28	P-14(3-2)	B	Phi-N
Joe Evans	21	16	.259	S-6	B	
Tony Faeth	6	18	0.49	P-6	A	
Larry Gardner	139	597	.745	3-139	Phi-A	
Jack Graney	128	585	.703	LF-125	B	
Joe Harris	62	227	.962	1-46,S-4	B	Bos-A
Charlie Jamieson	26	13	5.54	P-4,CF-3	Phi-A	
Hi Jasper	12	83	3.59	P-12(4-5)	StL-N	C
Doc Johnston	102	381	.743	1-98	B	
Ed Klepfer	5	7	7.36	P-5	B	C
Harry Lunte	26	83	.436	S-24	A	
Guy Morton	26	147	2.81	P-26(9-9)	B	
Elmer Myers	23	135	3.74	P-23(8-7)	Phi-A	
Les Nunamaker	26	59	.579	C-16	StL-A	
Steve O'Neill	125	461	.800	C-123	B	
Tom Phillips	22	55	2.95	P-22(3-2)	StL-A	Was-A
Elmer Smith	114	451	.792	RF-111	B	
Tris Speaker	134	595	.828	CF-134	B	
Pinch Thomas	34	52	.289	C-21	B	
George Uhle	26	127	2.91	P-26(10-5)	A	
Bill Wambsganss	139	587	.667	2-139	B	
Joe Wood	72	235	.737	RF-64,P-1	B	

◆ 1920 CLEVELAND (154 98-56 1) ATT: 912,832

Name	G	AB/IP	P/E	G/POS	From	To
Tris Speaker				M		
Jim Bagby	49	340	2.89	P-48(31-12)	B	
Joe Boehling	3	13	4.85	P-3(0-1)	B	C
George Burns	44	64	.714	1-12,RF-1	xPhi-A	
Ray Caldwell	41	238	3.86	P-34(20-10)	B	
Ray Chapman	111	530	.803	S-111	B	C
Bob Clark	11	42	3.43	P-11(1-2)	A	
Stan Coveleski	41	315	2.49	P-41(24-14)	B	
George Ellison	1	1	0.00	P-1	A	C
Joe Evans	56	189	.910	LF-43,S-6	B	
Tony Faeth	13	25	4.32	P-13	B	C
Larry Gardner	154	683	.781	3-154	B	
Jack Graney	62	191	.794	LF-47	B	
Charlie Jamieson	108	425	.799	LF-98,1-4	B	
Doc Johnston	147	593	.718	1-147	B	
Harry Lunte	23	76	.447	S-21,2-2	B	C
Duster Mails	9	63	1.85	P-9(7-0)	Bro-N	
Guy Morton	29	137	4.47	P-29(8-6)	B	
Tim Murchison	2	5	0.00	P-2	StL-N	C
Elmer Myers	16	72	4.77	P-16(2-4)	B	xBos-A
Dick Niehaus	19	40	3.60	P-19(1-2)	StL-N	C
Les Nunamaker	34	59	.879	C-17,1-6	B	
Steve O'Neill	149	576	.848	C-148	B	
Joe Sewell	22	83	.827	S-22	A	
Elmer Smith	129	525	.910	RF-129	B	
Tris Speaker	150	674	1.045	CF-148	B	
Pinch Thomas	9	12	.944	C-7	B	
George Uhle	27	85	5.21	P-27(4-5)	B	
Bill Wambsganss	153	664	.633	2-153	B	
Joe Wood	61	176	.792	RF-55,P-1	B	

Coach: Jack McCallister

◆ 1921 CLEVELAND (154 94-60 2) ATT: 748,705

Name	G	AB/IP	P/E	G/POS	From	To
Tris Speaker				M		
Jim Bagby	41	192	4.70	P-40(14-12)	B	
George Burns	84	265	.877	1-73	B	Bos-A
Ray Caldwell	38	147	4.90	P-37(6-6)	B	C
Bob Clark	5	9	14.46	P-5	B	C
Stan Coveleski	43	315	3.37	P-43(23-13)	B	
Joe Evans	57	174	.816	LF-47	B	
Larry Gardner	153	686	.828	3-152	B	
Jack Graney	68	133	.797	LF-32	B	
Lou Guisto	2	2	1.000	1-1	B	
Bernie Henderson	3	3	9.00	P-2(0-1)	A	C
Charlie Jamieson	140	608	.802	LF-137	B	
Tex Jeanes	5	5	1.750	CF-5	A	
Doc Johnston	118	444	.754	1-116	B	Phi-A
Duster Mails	34	194	3.94	P-34(14-8)	B	
Guy Morton	30	108	2.76	P-30(8-3)	B	
Les Nunamaker	46	148	.851	C-46	B	
Ted Odenwald	10	17	1.56	P-10(1-0)	A	
Steve O'Neill	106	405	.827	C-105	B	
Jesse Petty	4	9	2.00	P-4	A	Bro-N
Luke Sewell	3	7	.000	C-3	A	
Joe Sewell	154	683	.856	S-154	B	
Ginger Shinault	22	36	.900	C-20	A	
Elmer Smith	129	505	.882	RF-127	B	Bos-A
Allen Sothoron	22	145	3.24	P-22(12-4)	xBos-A	
Tris Speaker	132	588	.977	CF-128	B	
Riggs Stephenson	65	240	.869	2-54,3-2	A	
Pinch Thomas	21	46	.765	C-19	B	C
George Uhle	48	238	4.01	P-41(16-13)	B	
Bill Wambsganss	107	500	.752	2-103,3-2	B	
Art Wilson	2	1	.000	C-2	Bos-N	C
Joe Wood	66	229	1.000	RF-64	B	

Coach: Jack McCallister

◆ 1922 CLEVELAND (155 78-76 4) ATT: 528,145

Name	G	AB/IP	P/E	G/POS	From	To
Tris Speaker				M		
Jim Bagby	25	98	6.32	P-25(4-5)	B	Pit-N
Phil Bedgood	1	9	4.00	P-1(1-0)	A	
Dan Boone	11	75	4.06	P-11(4-6)	Det-A	
Uke Clanton	1	1	.000	1-1	A	C
Joe Connolly	12	51	.653	CF-12	NY-N	
Stan Coveleski	35	277	3.32	P-35(17-14)	B	
Bill Doran	3	3	1.167	3-2	A	C
Logan Drake	1	3	3.00	P-1	A	
George Edmondson	2	2	9.00	P-2	A	
Jim Joe Edwards	25	93	4.47	P-25(3-8)	A	
Joe Evans	75	164	.645	LF-49	B	Was-A
Larry Gardner	137	538	.732	3-128	B	
Jack Graney	37	71	.435	RF-13	B	C
Lou Guisto	35	90	.669	1-24	B	
Doc Hamann	1	0	/	P-1	A	C
Jack Hammond	1	4	.500	2-1	B	xPit-N
Charlie Jamieson	145	641	.816	LF-144,P-2	B	
Tex Jeanes	1	0	†	P-1,LF-1	B	Was-A
Ike Kahdot	4	2	.000	3-2	A	C
Dave Keefe	18	36	6.19	P-18	Phi-A	C
Jim Lindsey	29	84	6.02	P-29(4-5)	A	
Duster Mails	26	104	5.28	P-26(4-7)	B	StL-N
Stuffy McInnis	142	580	.715	1-140	Bos-A	Bos-N
Pat McNulty	22	71	.707	CF-22	A	
Dewey Metivier	2	18	4.50	P-2(2-0)	A	
John Middleton	2	7	7.36	P-2(0-1)	A	C
Guy Morton	38	203	4.00	P-38(14-9)	B	
Les Nunamaker	25	49	.711	C-13	B	C
Ted Odenwald	1	1	40.50	P-1	A	C
Steve O'Neill	133	477	.839	C-130	B	
Nellie Pott	2	2	31.50	P-2	A	C
Joe Rabbitt	2	3	.667	LF-1	A	C
Luke Sewell	41	95	.634	C-39	B	
Joe Sewell	153	656	.771	S-139,2-12	B	
Joe Shaute	5	4	19.64	P-2,RF-2	A	
Ginger Shinault	13	15	.333	C-11	B	
Sherry Smith	2	16	3.45	P-2(1-0)	xBro-N	
Chick Sorrells	2	1	.000	S-1	A	C
Allen Sothoron	6	25	6.39	P-6(1-3)	B	StL-N
Tris Speaker	131	516	1.080	CF-109	B	
Riggs Stephenson	86	267	.932	3-34,2-25,LF-3	B	
Homer Summa	12	50	1.009	RF-12	Pit-N	
George Uhle	56	287	4.07	P-50(22-16)	B	
Bill Wambsganss	142	644	.666	2-125,S-16	B	

Name	G	AB/IP	P/E	G/POS	From	To
George Winn	8	34	4.54	P-8(1-2)	Bos-A	
Joe Wood	142	583	.809	RF-141	B	C
Coaches: Jack McCallister						

♦ 1923 CLEVELAND (153 82-71 3) ATT: 558,856

Name	G	AB/IP	P/E	G/POS	From	To
Tris Speaker				M		
Phil Bedgood	9	19	5.30	P-9(0-2)	B	C
Dan Boone	27	70	6.01	P-27(4-6)	B	C
Frank Brower	126	476	.901	1-112,RF-4	Was-A	
Sumpter Clarke	1	3	.000	OF-1	Chi-N	
Joe Connolly	52	129	.872	RF-39	B	Bos-A
Stan Coveleski	33	228	2.76	P-33(13-14)	B	
Logan Drake	4	4	4.15	P-4	B	
George Edmondson	1	4	11.25	P-1	B	
Jim Joe Edwards	38	179	3.71	P-38(10-10)	B	
Johnson Fry	1	4	12.27	P-1	A	C
Jackie Gallagher	1	1	2.000	LF-1	A	C
Larry Gardner	52	93	.693	3-19	B	
Lou Guisto	40	164	.478	1-40	B	C
Tom Gulley	2	3	1.000	CF-1	A	
Kenny Hogan	1	0	†	R	Cin-N	
Charlie Jamieson	152	742	.869	LF-152	B	
Ray Knode	22	45	.772	1-21	A	
Dutch Levsen	3	4	0.00	P-3	A	
Rube Lutzke	143	596	.675	3-141,S-2	A	
Dewey Metivier	26	73	6.50	P-26(4-2)	B	
Guy Morton	33	129	4.24	P-33(6-6)	B	
Glenn Myatt	92	240	.751	C-69	Phi-A	
Steve O'Neill	113	404	.659	C-111	B	Bos-A
Luke Sewell	10	11	.673	C-7	B	
Joe Sewell	153	682	.935	S-151	B	
Wally Shaner	3	5	.650	LF-2,3-1	A	Bos-A
Joe Shaute	33	172	3.51	P-33(10-8)	B	
Sherry Smith	30	124	3.27	P-30(9-6)	B	
Tris Speaker	150	693	1.079	CF-150	B	
Riggs Stephenson	91	327	.832	2-66,RF-3,3-2	B	
Jim Sullivan	3	5	14.40	P-3(0-1)	Phi-A	C
Homer Summa	137	589	.793	RF-130	B	
George Uhle	58	358	3.77	P-54(26-16)	B	
Bill Wambsganss	101	418	.753	2-88,3-4	B	Bos-A
George Winn	1	2	0.00	P-1	B	C
Coaches: Jack McCallister, Frank Roth						

♦ 1924 CLEVELAND (153 67-86 6) ATT: 481,905

Name	G	AB/IP	P/E	G/POS	From	To
Tris Speaker				M		
Frank Brower	66	136	.910	1-26,P-4,LF-3	B	C
George Burns	129	529	.807	1-127	Bos-A	
Virgil Cheeves	8	17	7.79	P-8	Chi-N	NY-A
Watty Clark	12	26	7.01	P-12(1-3)	A	Bro-N
Sumpter Clarke	35	113	.580	RF-33	B	C
Stan Coveleski	37	240	4.04	P-37(15-16)	B	Was-A
Joe Dawson	4	20	6.64	P-4(1-2)	A	Pit-N
Logan Drake	5	11	10.32	P-5(0-1)	B	C
George Edmondson	5	8	9.00	P-5	B	C
Jim Joe Edwards	10	57	2.84	P-10(4-3)	B	
Frank Ellerbe	46	127	.612	3-39,2-2	xStL-A	C
Chick Fewster	101	357	.641	2-94,3-5	Bos-A	
Paul Fitzke	1	4	4.50	P-1	A	C
Larry Gardner	38	55	.473	3-8,2-6	B	C
Tom Gulley	8	23	.511	RF-5	B	Chi-A
Kenny Hogan	2	1	.000	H	B	C
Charlie Jamieson	143	660	.865	LF-139	B	
Ray Knode	11	40	.570	1-10	B	
Bub Kuhn	1	1	27.00	P-1(0-1)	A	C
Dutch Levsen	4	16	4.41	P-4(1-1)	B	
Jim Lindsey	3	3	21.00	P-3	A	StL-N
Rube Lutzke	106	396	.642	3-103,2-3	B	
Pat McNulty	101	337	.694	RF-75	B	
Bud Messenger	5	25	4.32	P-5(2-0)	A	C
Dewey Metivier	26	76	5.31	P-26(1-5)	B	C
Jake Miller	2	12	3.00	P-2(0-1)	A	
Guy Morton	10	12	6.57	P-10(0-1)	B	C
Glenn Myatt	105	384	.919	C-95	B	
Luther Roy	16	49	7.77	P-16(0-5)	A	
Luke Sewell	63	194	.745	C-57	B	
Joe Sewell	153	685	.817	S-153	B	
Joe Shaute	46	283	3.75	P-46(20-17)	B	
Sherry Smith	40	248	3.02	P-39(12-14)	B	
Tris Speaker	135	575	.943	CF-128	B	
Freddy Spurgeon	3	8	.536	2-3	A	
Riggs Stephenson	71	272	.943	2-58,RF-7	B	
Homer Summa	111	409	.701	RF-95	B	
George Uhle	59	196	4.77	P-28(9-15)	B	
Roxy Walters	32	87	.629	C-25,2-7	Bos-A	
Frank Wayenberg	2	7	5.40	P-2	A	C
Joe Wyatt	4	16	.452	RF-4	A	C
Elmer Yoter	19	74	.642	3-19	Phi-A	Chi-N
Carl Yowell	4	27	6.67	P-4(1-1)	A	
Coaches: Jack McCallister, Frank Roth						

♦ 1925 CLEVELAND (155 70-84 6) ATT: 419,005

Name	G	AB/IP	P/E	G/POS	From	To
Tris Speaker				M		
Gene Bedford	2	3	.000	2-2	A	C
Ray Benge	2	12	1.54	P-2(1-0)	A	
Garland Buckeye	30	153	3.65	P-30(13-8)	Was-A	
George Burns	127	523	.844	1-126	B	
Bert Cole	13	44	6.14	P-13(1-1)	xDet-A	Chi-A
Jim Joe Edwards	13	36	8.25	P-13(0-3)	B	xChi-A
Ike Eichrodt	15	55	.586	CF-13	A	
Chick Fewster	93	343	.650	2-83,3-10,RF-1	B	Bro-N
Harvey Hendrick	25	38	.819	1-3	NY-A	Bro-N
Johnny Hodapp	37	146	.590	3-37	A	
Charlie Jamieson	138	643	.759	LF-135	B	

Name	G	AB/IP	P/E	G/POS	From	To
Benn Karr	46	198	4.78	P-32(11-12)	Bos-A	
Joe Klugmann	38	96	.869	2-29,1-4,3-2	Bro-N	C
Ray Knode	45	121	.610	1-34	B	
Cliff Lee	77	258	.870	RF-70	Cin-N	
Dutch Levsen	4	24	5.55	P-4(1-2)	B	
Rube Lutzke	81	283	.564	3-69,2-10	B	
Frank McCrea	1	5	.400	C-1	A	C
Pat McNulty	118	432	.813	RF-111	B	
Jake Miller	32	190	3.31	P-32(10-13)	B	
Glenn Myatt	106	396	.784	C-98,LF-1	B	
Luther Roy	6	10	3.60	P-6	B	Chi-N
Luke Sewell	74	262	.633	C-66,LF-2	B	
Joe Sewell	155	699	.827	S-153,2-3	B	
Joe Shaute	29	131	5.43	P-26(4-12)	B	
Sherry Smith	31	237	4.86	P-31(11-14)	B	
Tris Speaker	117	518	1.057	CF-109	B	
By Speece	28	90	4.28	P-28(3-5)	Was-A	
Freddy Spurgeon	107	406	.642	3-56,2-46,S-3	B	
Riggs Stephenson	19	64	.832	RF-16	B	Chi-N
Homer Summa	75	246	.759	RF-54,3-2	B	
Chick Tolson	3	14	.607	1-3	A	Chi-N
George Uhle	55	211	4.10	P-29(13-11)	B	
Dutch Ussat	1	1	.000	2-1	A	
Roxy Walters	5	20	.400	C-5	B	C
Carl Yowell	12	36	4.46	P-12(2-3)	B	C
Coaches: Jack McCallister, Frank Roth						

♦ 1926 CLEVELAND (154 88-66 2) ATT: 627,426

Name	G	AB/IP	P/E	G/POS	From	To
Tris Speaker				M		
Chick Autry	3	8	.393	C-3	NY-A	
Ray Benge	8	12	3.86	P-8(1-0)	B	Phi-N
Garland Buckeye	32	166	3.10	P-32(6-9)	B	
George Burns	151	657	.889	1-151	B	
Ike Eichrodt	37	85	.754	LF-27	B	
Johnny Hodapp	3	5	.400	3-3	B	
Willis Hudlin	8	32	2.78	P-8(1-3)	A	
Charlie Jamieson	143	628	.756	LF-143	B	
Benn Karr	31	113	5.00	P-30(5-6)	B	
Ray Knode	31	27	.866	1-11	B	C
Guy Lacy	13	31	.551	2-11,3-2	A	C
Cliff Lee	21	46	.558	LF-9,C-3	B	C
Norm Lehr	4	15	3.07	P-4	A	C
Dutch Levsen	33	237	3.41	P-33(16-13)	B	
Rube Lutzke	142	536	.658	3-142	B	
Pat McNulty	48	63	.633	CF-9	B	
Jake Miller	18	83	3.27	P-18(7-4)	B	
Glenn Myatt	56	132	.648	C-35	B	
Ernie Padgett	36	70	.542	3-29,S-2	Bos-N	
Luke Sewell	126	499	.596	C-125	B	
Joe Sewell	154	672	.832	S-154	B	
Joe Shaute	34	207	3.53	P-34(14-10)	B	
Sherry Smith	27	188	3.73	P-27(11-10)	B	
Tris Speaker	150	661	.877	CF-149	B	Was-A
By Speece	2	3	0.00	P-2	B	Phi-N
Freddy Spurgeon	149	678	.682	2-149	B	
Homer Summa	154	652	.771	RF-154	B	
George Uhle	50	318	2.83	P-39(27-11)	B	
Coaches: Harry Mathews, Jack McCallister						

♦ 1927 CLEVELAND (153 66-87 6) ATT: 373,138

Name	G	AB/IP	P/E	G/POS	From	To
Jack McCallister				M		
Chick Autry	16	46	.651	C-14	B	
Jumbo Brown	8	19	6.27	P-8(0-2)	Chi-N	
Garland Buckeye	35	205	3.96	P-35(10-17)	B	
Johnny Burnett	17	8	.000	2-2	A	
George Burns	140	607	.810	1-139	B	
Hap Collard	4	5	5.06	P-4	A	
Nick Cullop	32	80	.730	CF-20,P-1	xWas-A	Bro-N
Ike Eichrodt	85	293	.572	CF-81	B	Chi-A
Wes Ferrell	1	1	27.00	P-1	A	
Lew Fonseca	112	459	.737	2-96,1-13	Phi-N	
George Gerken	6	15	.481	CF-5	A	
Johnny Gill	21	69	.636	LF-17	A	
George Grant	25	75	4.46	P-25(4-6)	StL-A	
Johnny Hodapp	79	261	.797	3-67,1-4	B	
Willis Hudlin	43	265	4.01	P-43(18-12)	B	
Baby Doll Jacobson	32	116	.601	CF-31	xBos-A	xPhi-A
Charlie Jamieson	127	572	.775	LF-127	B	
Benn Karr	22	77	5.05	P-22(3-3)	B	C
Sam Langford	20	77	.735	CF-20	Bos-A	
Dutch Levsen	25	80	5.49	P-25(3-7)	B	
Carl Lind	12	44	.391	2-11,S-1	A	
Rube Lutzke	100	359	.615	3-98	B	C
Hal McKain	2	11	4.09	P-2(0-1)	A	Chi-A
Pat McNulty	19	46	.719	CF-12	B	C
Jake Miller	34	185	3.21	P-34(10-8)	B	
Glenn Myatt	55	109	.709	C-26	B	
Bernie Neis	32	122	.933	CF-29	Bos-N	xChi-A
Ernie Padgett	7	7	.571	2-4	B	
Luke Sewell	128	512	.705	C-126	B	
Joe Sewell	153	652	.805	S-153	B	
Joe Shaute	45	230	4.22	P-45(9-16)	B	
Sherry Smith	11	36	5.45	P-11(1-4)	B	C
Freddy Spurgeon	57	221	.636	2-52	B	C
Homer Summa	145	640	.734	RF-145	B	
George Uhle	43	153	4.34	P-25(8-9)	B	
Willie Underhill	4	8	9.72	P-4(0-2)	A	
Dutch Ussat	4	18	.590	3-4	B	C
Coach: Harry Mathews						

♦ 1928 CLEVELAND (155 62-92 7) ATT: 375,907

Name	G	AB/IP	P/E	G/POS	From	To
Roger Peckinpaugh				M		
Chick Autry	22	63	.795	C-18	B	Chi-A
Les Barnhart	2	9	7.00	P-2(0-1)	A	

Name	G	AB/IP	P/E	G/POS	From	To
Bill Bayne	37	109	5.13	P-37(2-5)	StL-A	Bos-A
Cecil Bolton	4	15	.728	1-4	A	C
Clint Brown	2	11	4.91	P-2(0-1)	A	
Jumbo Brown	5	15	6.75	P-5(0-1)	B	NY-A
Garland Buckeye	9	35	6.69	P-9(1-5)	B	xNY-N
Johnny Burnett	3	10	1.000	S-2	B	
George Burns	82	238	.711	1-53	B	xNY-A
Bruce Caldwell	18	31	.633	RF-10,1-1	A	Bro-N
Hap Collard	1	4	2.25	P-1	B	Phi-N
Red Dorman	25	87	.872	CF-24	A	C
Wes Ferrell	2	16	2.25	P-2(0-2)	B	
Lew Fonseca	75	288	.825	1-56,3-15,S-4,2-1	B	
George Gerken	38	132	.626	CF-34	B	C
Johnny Gill	2	2	.000	H	B	Was-A
Jonah Goldman	7	25	.619	S-7	A	
George Grant	29	155	5.04	P-28(10-8)	B	
Mel Harder	23	49	6.61	P-23(0-2)	A	
Luther Harvel	40	148	.543	CF-39	A	C
Johnny Hodapp	116	481	.784	3-101,1-13	B	
Willis Hudlin	42	220	4.04	P-42(14-14)	B	
Charlie Jamieson	112	501	.762	LF-111	B	
Sam Langford	110	461	.694	CF-107	B	C
Dutch Levsen	11	41	5.44	P-11(0-3)	B	C
Carl Lind	154	713	.706	2-154	B	
Johnny Miljus	11	51	2.66	P-11(1-4)	xPit-N	
Jake Miller	25	158	4.44	P-25(8-9)	A	
Ed Montague	32	60	.613	S-15,3-9	A	
Jim Moore	1	9	2.00	P-1(0-1)	A	
Ed Morgan	76	296	.860	1-36,CF-21,3-14	A	
Glenn Myatt	58	138	.755	C-30	B	
Art Reinholz	2	4	.833	3-2	A	C
Luke Sewell	122	457	.693	C-118	B	
Joe Sewell	155	678	.809	S-137,3-19	B	
Joe Shaute	36	254	4.04	P-36(13-17)	B	
Homer Summa	134	553	.684	RF-132	B	Phi-A
Ollie Tucker	14	56	.446	RF-14	Was-A	C
George Uhle	55	214	4.07	P-31(12-17)	B	Det-A
Willie Underhill	11	28	4.50	P-11(1-2)	B	C
Al VanCamp	5	18	.529	1-5	A	Bos-A
Aaron Ward	6	11	.311	3-3,S-2,2-1	Chi-A	C
Frank Wilson	2	2	.500	H	Bos-N	xStL-A

Coaches: Grover Hartley, Howie Shanks

♦ **1929 CLEVELAND** (152 81-71 3) ATT: 536,210
Roger Peckinpaugh — M

Name	G	AB/IP	P/E	G/POS	From	To
Earl Averill	151	680	.936	CF-151	A	
Clint Brown	3	16	3.31	P-3(0-2)	B	
Johnny Burnett	19	35	.382	S-10,2-8	B	
Bibb Falk	125	488	.881	LF-120	Chi-A	
Wes Ferrell	47	243	3.60	P-43(21-10)	B	
Lew Fonseca	148	643	.959	1-147	B	
Ray Gardner	82	296	.638	S-82	A	
George Grant	12	24	10.50	P-12(0-2)	B	Pit-N
Mel Harder	11	18	5.60	P-11(1-0)	B	
Grover Hartley	24	35	.648	C-13	Bos-A	
Joe Hauser	37	53	.821	1-8	Phi-A	C
Johnny Hodapp	90	316	.817	2-72	B	
Ken Holloway	25	119	3.03	P-25(6-5)	Det-A	
Willis Hudlin	40	280	3.34	P-40(17-15)	B	
Charlie Jamieson	102	422	.735	LF-93	B	
Dan Jessee	1	0	†	R	A	C
Carl Lind	66	249	.566	2-64,3-1	B	
Johnny Miljus	34	128	5.19	P-34(8-8)	B	C
Jake Miller	29	206	3.58	P-29(14-12)	B	
Jim Moore	2	6	9.53	P-2	B	Chi-A
Ed Morgan	93	360	.861	RF-80	B	
Glenn Myatt	59	141	.580	C-41	B	
Dick Porter	71	214	.865	RF-28,2-20	A	
Luke Sewell	124	457	.585	C-124	B	
Joe Sewell	152	672	.800	3-152	B	
Joe Shaute	26	162	4.28	P-26(8-8)	B	
Milt Shoffner	11	45	5.04	P-11(2-3)	A	
Jackie Tavener	92	292	.593	S-89	Det-A	C
Jimmy Zinn	20	105	5.04	P-18(4-6)	Pit-N	C

Coaches: Grover Hartley, Howie Shanks

♦ **1930 CLEVELAND** (154 81-73 4) ATT: 528,657
Roger Peckinpaugh — M

Name	G	AB/IP	P/E	G/POS	From	To
Pete Appleton	39	119	4.02	P-39(8-7)	Cin-N	
Earl Averill	139	605	.941	CF-134	B	
Les Barnhart	1	8	6.48	P-1(1-0)	B	C
Belve Bean	23	74	5.45	P-23(3-3)	A	
Clint Brown	35	214	4.97	P-35(11-13)	B	
Johnny Burnett	54	194	.766	3-27,S-19	B	
George DeTore	3	13	.417	3-3	A	
Bibb Falk	82	218	.858	LF-42	B	
Wes Ferrell	53	297	3.31	P-43(25-13)	B	
Lew Fonseca	40	140	.696	1-28,3-6	B	
Ray Gardner	33	14	.154	S-22,2-5,3-1	B	C
Sal Gliatto	10	15	6.60	P-8	A	C
Jonah Goldman	111	351	.622	S-93,3-20	B	
Mel Harder	36	175	4.21	P-36(11-10)	B	
Grover Hartley	1	4	1.500	C-1	B	StL-A
Johnny Hodapp	154	687	.889	2-154	B	
Ken Holloway	12	30	8.40	P-12(1-1)	B	xNY-A
Willis Hudlin	37	217	4.57	P-37(13-16)	B	
Charlie Jamieson	103	417	.742	LF-95	B	
Roxie Lawson	7	34	6.15	P-7(1-2)	A	
Carl Lind	24	75	.568	S-22,2-2	B	C
Jake Miller	24	88	7.13	P-24(4-4)	B	
Ed Montague	58	223	.721	S-46,3-13	B	
Ed Morgan	150	666	1.014	1-129,RF-19	B	
Glenn Myatt	86	288	.760	C-71	B	
Dick Porter	119	552	.918	RF-118	B	
Bob Seeds	85	296	.694	LF-70	A	

Name	G	AB/IP	P/E	G/POS	From	To
Luke Sewell	76	315	.646	C-76	B	
Joe Sewell	109	414	.745	3-97	B	NY-A
Joe Shaute	4	5	15.43	P-4	B	Bro-N
Milt Shoffner	24	85	7.97	P-24(3-4)	B	
Joe Sprinz	17	51	.445	C-17	A	
Joe Vosmik	9	27	.567	CF-5	A	
Ralph Winegarner	5	24	.978	3-5	A	

Coaches: Grover Hartley, Mickey O'Neil, Howie Shanks

♦ **1931 CLEVELAND** (155 78-76 4) ATT: 483,027
Roger Peckinpaugh — M

Name	G	AB/IP	P/E	G/POS	From	To
Pete Appleton	30	80	4.63	P-29(4-4)	B	
Earl Averill	155	701	.979	CF-155	B	
Belve Bean	4	7	6.43	P-4(0-1)	B	
Moe Berg	10	14	.297	C-8	Chi-A	Was-A
Clint Brown	39	233	4.71	P-39(11-15)	B	
Johnny Burnett	111	470	.749	S-63,2-35,3-21,RF-1	B	
Sarge Connally	17	86	4.20	P-17(5-5)	Chi-A	
Bruce Connatser	12	52	.674	1-12	A	
Howard Craghead	4	6	6.35	P-4	A	
George DeTore	30	64	.734	3-13,S-10,2-3	B	C
Pete Donohue	2	5	8.44	P-2	xNY-N	Bos-A
Bibb Falk	79	179	.806	RF-33	B	C
Wes Ferrell	48	276	3.75	P-40(22-12)	B	
Lew Fonseca	26	120	.919	1-26	B	xChi-A
Jonah Goldman	30	70	.327	S-30	B	C
Odell Hale	25	102	.764	3-15,2-10,S-1	A	
Mel Harder	40	194	4.36	P-40(13-14)	B	
Oral Hildebrand	5	27	4.39	P-5(2-1)	A	
Johnny Hodapp	122	502	.701	2-121	B	
Willis Hudlin	44	254	4.60	P-44(15-14)	B	
Bill Hunnefield	21	82	.649	S-21,2-1	Chi-A	xBos-N
Charlie Jamieson	28	48	.770	LF-7	B	
Willie Kamm	114	486	.782	3-114	xChi-A	
Roxie Lawson	17	56	7.60	P-17(0-2)	B	Det-A
Jake Miller	10	41	4.35	P-10(2-1)	B	Chi-A
Ed Montague	64	225	.731	S-64	B	
Ed Morgan	131	552	.961	1-117,3-3	B	
Glenn Myatt	65	217	.673	C-53	B	
Dick Porter	114	478	.786	RF-109,2-1	B	
Bob Seeds	48	146	.732	RF-33,1-2	B	
Luke Sewell	108	422	.725	C-104	B	
Milt Shoffner	12	41	7.24	P-12(2-3)	B	Bos-N
Joe Sprinz	1	3	.000	C-1	B	StL-N
Fay Thomas	16	49	5.18	P-16(2-4)	NY-N	Bro-N
Joe Vosmik	149	640	.827	LF-147	B	

Coaches: Howie Shanks, C. Wolgamot

♦ **1932 CLEVELAND** (153 87-65 4) ATT: 468,953
Roger Peckinpaugh — M

Name	G	AB/IP	P/E	G/POS	From	To
Pete Appleton	4	5	16.20	P-4	B	xBos-A
Earl Averill	153	712	.961	CF-153	B	
Boze Berger	1	1	.000	S-1	A	
Joe Boley	1	4	.500	S-1	xPhi-A	C
Clint Brown	39	263	4.08	P-37(15-12)	B	
Johnny Burnett	129	573	.744	S-103,2-26	B	
Bill Cissell	131	576	.794	2-129,S-6	xChi-A	
Sarge Connally	35	112	4.33	P-35(8-6)	B	
Bruce Connatser	23	64	.598	1-14	B	C
Wes Ferrell	55	288	3.66	P-38(23-13)	B	
Mel Harder	39	255	3.75	P-39(15-13)	B	
Oral Hildebrand	27	129	3.69	P-27(8-6)	B	
Johnny Hodapp	7	18	.313	2-7	B	xChi-A
Willis Hudlin	33	182	4.71	P-33(12-8)	B	
Charlie Jamieson	16	19	.336	RF-2	B	C
Willie Kamm	148	615	.781	3-148	B	
Ed Montague	66	225	.607	S-57,3-11	B	C
Leo Moon	1	6	11.12	P-1	A	C
Ed Morgan	144	637	.804	1-142,3-1	B	
Glenn Myatt	82	292	.723	C-65	B	
Monte Pearson	8	8	10.13	P-8	A	
Dick Porter	146	700	.793	RF-145	B	
Mike Powers	14	35	.532	RF-8	A	
Frankie Pytlak	12	36	.678	C-12	A	
Jack Russell	18	113	4.70	P-18(5-7)	xBos-A	Was-A
Bob Seeds	2	4	.000	RF-1	B	xChi-A
Luke Sewell	87	343	.691	C-84	B	Was-A
Joe Vosmik	153	690	.838	LF-153	B	
Ralph Winegarner	7	17	1.04	P-5(1-0)	B	

Coaches: Howie Shanks, C. Wolgamot

♦ **1933 CLEVELAND** (151 75-76 4) ATT: 387,936
Roger Peckinpaugh — M(51 26-25 5)
Bibb Falk — M(1 1-0 5)
Walter Johnson — M(99 48-51 4)

Name	G	AB/IP	P/E	G/POS	From	To
Earl Averill	151	658	.837	CF-149	B	
Belve Bean	27	70	5.25	P-27(1-2)	B	
Harley Boss	112	470	.657	1-110	Was-A	C
Clint Brown	34	185	3.41	P-33(11-12)	B	
Johnny Burnett	83	292	.674	S-41,2-17,3-12	B	
Bill Cissell	112	449	.624	2-62,S-46,3-1	B	Bos-A
Sarge Connally	41	103	4.89	P-41(5-3)	B	
Howard Craghead	11	17	6.23	P-11	B	C
Wes Ferrell	61	201	4.21	P-28(11-12),LF-13	B	Bos-A
Milt Galatzer	57	186	.615	RF-40,1-5	A	
Odell Hale	98	386	.795	2-73,3-21	B	
Mel Harder	44	253	2.95	P-43(15-17)	B	
Oral Hildebrand	36	220	3.76	P-36(16-11)	B	
Willis Hudlin	34	141	3.97	P-34(5-13)	B	
Willie Kamm	133	517	.695	3-131	B	
Bill Knickerbocker	80	303	.581	S-80	A	
Thornton Lee	3	17	4.15	P-3(1-1)	A	
Odell Hale						
Ed Morgan	39	129	.668	1-32,LF-1	B	Bos-A
Glenn Myatt	40	94	.658	C-27	B	
Johnny Oulliber	22	82	.592	LF-18	A	C

Name	G	AB/IP	P/E	G/POS	From	To
Monte Pearson	19	135	2.33	P-19(10-5)	B	
Dick Porter	132	563	.663	RF-124	B	
Mike Powers	24	53	.720	RF-11	B	C
Frankie Pytlak	80	267	.778	C-69	B	
Roy Spencer	75	258	.524	C-72	Was-A	
Hal Trosky	11	47	.818	1-11	A	
Joe Vosmik	119	485	.713	LF-113	B	

Coaches: Bibb Falk, Patsy Gharrity, C. Wolgamot

♦ 1934 CLEVELAND (154 85-69 3) ATT: 391,338

Name	G	AB/IP	P/E	G/POS	From	To
Walter Johnson				M		
Earl Averill	154	702	.982	CF-154	B	
Belve Bean	21	51	3.86	P-21(5-1)	B	
Moe Berg	29	100	.575	C-28	xWas-A	Bos-A
Bill Brenzel	15	55	.520	C-15	Pit-N	
Clint Brown	17	50	5.90	P-17(4-3)	B	
Lloyd Brown	38	117	3.85	P-38(5-10)	Bos-A	
Johnny Burnett	72	229	.761	3-42,S-9,2-3,LF-2	B	StL-A
Kit Carson	5	20	.850	RF-4	A	
Sarge Connally	5	5	5.06	P-5	B	C
Milt Galatzer	49	222	.686	RF-49	B	
Denny Galehouse	1	1	18.00	P-1	A	
Bob Garbark	5	12	.083	C-5	A	
Odell Hale	143	616	.827	2-137,3-5	B	
Mel Harder	44	255	2.61	P-44(20-12)	B	
Oral Hildebrand	33	198	4.50	P-33(11-9)	B	
Dutch Holland	50	142	.725	RF-31	Bos-N	C
Willis Hudlin	36	195	4.75	P-36(15-10)	B	
Willie Kamm	121	457	.716	3-118	B	
Bill Knickerbocker	146	632	.755	S-146	B	
Thornton Lee	24	86	5.04	P-24(1-1)	B	
Eddie Moore	27	75	.451	2-18,3-3,S-2	NY-N	C
Glenn Myatt	36	121	.784	C-34	B	
Monte Pearson	39	255	4.52	P-39(18-13)	B	
Bill Perrin	1	5	14.40	P-1(0-1)	A	C
Dick Porter	13	49	.678	RF-10	B	xBos-A
Frankie Pytlak	91	335	.680	C-88	B	
Sam Rice	97	367	.715	RF-78	Was-A	C
Bob Seeds	61	213	.628	LF-48	xBos-A	NY-A
Roy Spencer	5	7	.429	C-4	B	NY-N
Hal Trosky	154	685	.987	1-154	B	
Joe Vosmik	104	449	.870	LF-104	B	
Bob Weiland	16	70	4.11	P-16(1-5)	xBos-A	StL-A
Ralph Winegarner	32	78	5.51	P-22(5-4),RF-1	B	

Coach: Patsy Gharrity

♦ 1935 CLEVELAND (156 82-71 3) ATT: 397,615

Name	G	AB/IP	P/E	G/POS	From	To
Walter Johnson				M(96 46-48 5)		
Steve O'Neill				M(60 36-23 3)		
Earl Averill	140	638	.863	CF-139	B	
Belve Bean	1	1	9.00	P-1	B	xWas-A
Boze Berger	124	504	.681	2-120,S-3,1-2,3-1	B	
Bill Brenzel	52	154	.518	C-51	B	C
Clint Brown	23	49	5.14	P-23(4-3)	B	Chi-A
Lloyd Brown	42	122	3.61	P-42(8-7)	B	
Bruce Campbell	80	343	.887	RF-75	StL-A	
Kit Carson	16	24	.610	RF-4	B	C
Milt Galatzer	93	302	.748	RF-81	B	
Denny Galehouse	5	13	9.00	P-5(1-0)	B	
Bob Garbark	6	23	.867	C-6	B	Chi-N
Greek George	2	0	†	C-1	A	
Odell Hale	150	646	.847	3-149,2-1	B	
Mel Harder	42	287	3.29	P-42(22-11)	B	
Oral Hildebrand	34	171	3.94	P-34(9-8)	B	
Willis Hudlin	37	232	3.69	P-36(15-11)	B	
Roy Hughes	82	293	.713	2-40,S-29,3-1	A	
Willie Kamm	6	18	.667	3-4	B	C
Bill Knickerbocker	132	577	.701	S-128	B	
Thornton Lee	32	181	4.04	P-32(7-10)	B	
Glenn Myatt	10	40	.286	C-10	B	xNY-N
Monte Pearson	30	182	4.90	P-30(8-13)	B	NY-A
Eddie Phillips	70	235	.687	C-69	Was-A	C
Frankie Pytlak	55	164	.717	C-48	B	
Lefty Stewart	24	91	5.44	P-24(6-6)	xWas-A	C
Hal Trosky	154	680	.789	1-153	B	
Joe Vosmik	152	688	.946	LF-150	B	
Ralph Winegarner	65	67	5.75	P-25(2-2),LF-4,3-1,1-1	B	
Ab Wright	67	177	.647	RF-47	A	Bos-N

Coaches: Patsy Gharrity, Steve O'Neill

♦ 1936 CLEVELAND (157 80-74 5) ATT: 500,391

Name	G	AB/IP	P/E	G/POS	From	To
Steve O'Neill				M		
Johnny Allen	37	243	3.44	P-36(20-10)	NY-A	
Earl Averill	152	682	1.065	CF-150	B	
Joe Becker	22	55	.595	C-15	A	
Boze Berger	28	53	.400	1-8,2-8,3-7,S-2	B	Chi-A
George Blaeholder	35	134	5.09	P-35(8-4)	Phi-A	C
Lloyd Brown	24	140	4.17	P-24(8-10)	B	
Bruce Campbell	76	194	1.028	RF-47	B	
Bob Feller	14	62	3.34	P-14(5-3)	A	
Milt Galatzer	49	112	.632	RF-42,P-1,1-1	B	Cin-N
Denny Galehouse	36	148	4.85	P-36(8-7)	B	
Greek George	23	86	.513	C-22	B	Bro-N
Jim Gleeson	41	158	.783	RF-33	A	Chi-N
Odell Hale	153	693	.887	3-148,2-3	B	
Mel Harder	36	225	5.17	P-36(15-15)	B	
Jeff Heath	12	44	1.021	LF-12	A	
Oral Hildebrand	36	175	4.90	P-36(10-11)	B	StL-A
Willis Hudlin	27	64	9.00	P-27(1-5)	B	
Roy Hughes	152	708	.734	2-152	B	
Paul Kardow	2	2	4.50	P-2	A	C
Bill Knickerbocker	155	686	.754	S-155	B	StL-A
Thornton Lee	43	127	4.89	P-43(3-5)	B	Chi-A
Al Milnar	4	22	7.36	P-4(1-2)	A	
Frankie Pytlak	75	255	.819	C-58	B	

Name	G	AB/IP	P/E	G/POS	From	To
Billy Sullivan	93	339	.890	C-72,3-5,1-3,LF-1	Cin-N	
Hal Trosky	151	671	1.026	1-151,2-1	B	
George Uhle	24	13	8.53	P-7(0-1)	NY-A	C
Joe Vosmik	138	591	.796	LF-136	B	StL-A
Roy Weatherly	84	366	.883	RF-84	A	
Ralph Winegarner	18	15	4.91	P-9	B	StL-A
Bill Zuber	2	14	6.59	P-2(1-1)	A	

Coaches: Wally Schang, George Uhle

♦ 1937 CLEVELAND (156 83-71 4) ATT: 564,849

Name	G	AB/IP	P/E	G/POS	From	To
Steve O'Neill				M		
Hugh Alexander	7	11	.182	RF-3	A	C
Johnny Allen	24	173	2.55	P-24(15-1)	B	
Ivy Andrews	20	60	4.37	P-20(3-4)	StL-A	xNY-A
Earl Averill	156	702	.880	CF-156	B	
Joe Becker	18	37	.860	C-12	B	C
Lloyd Brown	31	77	6.55	P-31(2-6)	B	Phi-N
Bruce Campbell	134	519	.863	RF-123	B	
Bob Feller	26	149	3.39	P-26(9-7)	B	
Carl Fischer	2	2	27.00	P-2(0-1)	Chi-A	xWas-A
Denny Galehouse	36	201	4.57	P-36(9-14)	B	
Odell Hale	154	626	.706	3-90,2-64	B	
Mel Harder	38	234	4.28	P-38(15-12)	B	
Jeff Heath	20	61	.607	RF-14	B	
Joe Heving	40	73	4.83	P-40(8-4)	Chi-A	
Willis Hudlin	35	176	4.10	P-35(12-11)	B	
Roy Hughes	104	395	.708	3-58,2-32	B	StL-A
Ken Jungels	2	3	0.00	P-2	A	
Ken Keltner	1	1	.000	3-1	B	
John Kroner	86	315	.606	2-64,3-11	Bos-A	
Lyn Lary	156	741	.799	S-156	StL-A	
Blas Monaco	5	8	.946	2-3	A	
Frankie Pytlak	125	463	.794	C-115	B	
Bill Sodd	1	1	.000	H	A	C
Moose Solters	152	644	.905	LF-149	StL-A	
Billy Sullivan	72	190	.801	C-38,1-5,3-1	B	StL-A
Hal Trosky	153	670	.915	1-152	B	
Roy Weatherly	53	145	.590	RF-38,3-1	B	
Earl Whitehill	33	147	6.49	P-33(8-8)	Was-A	
Whit Wyatt	29	73	4.44	P-29(2-3)	Chi-A	Bro-N

Coaches: Wally Schang, George Uhle

♦ 1938 CLEVELAND (153 86-66 3) ATT: 652,006

Name	G	AB/IP	P/E	G/POS	From	To
Ossie Vitt				M		
Johnny Allen	30	200	4.18	P-30(14-8)	B	
Earl Averill	134	567	.965	CF-131	B	
Lou Boudreau	1	2	.500	3-1	A	
Bruce Campbell	133	575	.820	RF-122	B	
Bob Feller	39	278	4.08	P-39(17-11)	B	
Denny Galehouse	36	114	4.34	P-36(7-8)	B	Bos-A
Oscar Grimes	4	12	.733	2-2,1-1	A	
Odell Hale	130	559	.737	2-127	B	
Mel Harder	39	240	3.83	P-38(17-10)	B	
Jeff Heath	126	538	.985	LF-122	B	
Hank Helf	6	14	.220	C-5	A	
Rollie Hemsley	66	230	.776	C-58	StL-A	
Joe Heving	3	6	9.00	P-3(1-1)	B	xBos-A
Willis Hudlin	29	127	4.89	P-29(8-8)	B	
Johnny Humphries	45	103	5.23	P-45(9-8)	A	
Tommy Irwin	3	12	.444	S-3	A	C
Ken Jungels	9	15	8.80	P-9(1-0)	B	
Ken Keltner	149	619	.815	3-149	B	
John Kroner	51	137	.763	2-31,1-7,3-3,S-1	B	C
Lyn Lary	141	661	.727	S-141	B	
Ray Mack	2	6	1.000	2-2	A	
Al Milnar	24	68	5.00	P-23(3-1)	B	
Frankie Pytlak	113	406	.769	C-99	B	
Lloyd Russell	2	0	†	R	A	C
Clay Smith	4	11	6.55	P-4	A	Det-A
Moose Solters	67	214	.541	LF-46	B	
Charley Suche	1	1	27.00	P-1	A	C
Hal Trosky	150	626	.948	1-148	B	
Roy Weatherly	83	228	.694	CF-55	B	
Skeeter Webb	20	66	.674	S-13,3-3,2-2	StL-N	
Earl Whitehill	26	160	5.56	P-26(9-8)	B	Chi-N
Chuck Workman	2	5	.800	RF-1	A	
Bill Zuber	15	29	5.02	P-15(0-3)	B	

Coaches: Johnny Bassler, Wally Schang

♦ 1939 CLEVELAND (154 87-67 3) ATT: 563,926

Name	G	AB/IP	P/E	G/POS	From	To
Ossie Vitt				M		
Johnny Allen	34	175	4.58	P-28(9-7)	B	
Earl Averill	24	61	.817	RF-11	B	xDet-A
Lou Boudreau	53	256	.700	S-53	B	
Johnny Broaca	22	46	4.70	P-22(4-2)	NY-A	C
Bruce Campbell	130	527	.832	RF-115	B	Det-A
Ben Chapman	149	654	.802	CF-146	Bos-A	
Joe Dobson	35	78	5.88	P-35(2-3)	A	
Tom Drake	8	15	9.00	P-8(0-1)	A	Bro-N
Harry Eisenstat	26	104	3.30	P-26(6-7)	xDet-A	
Bob Feller	39	297	2.85	P-39(24-9)	B	
Oscar Grimes	119	432	.753	2-48,1-43,S-37,3-3	B	
Odell Hale	108	286	.813	2-73,3-2	B	
Mel Harder	29	208	3.50	P-29(15-9)	B	
Jeff Heath	121	472	.848	LF-108	B	
Rollie Hemsley	107	432	.651	C-106	B	
Willis Hudlin	27	143	4.91	P-27(9-10)	B	
Johnny Humphries	15	28	8.26	P-15(2-4)	B	
Ken Keltner	154	648	.868	3-154	B	
Lyn Lary	3	2	.000	S-2	B	xBro-N
Ray Mack	36	126	.472	2-34,3-1	B	
Al Milnar	41	209	3.79	P-37(14-12),LF-1	B	
Mike Naymick	2	5	1.93	P-2(0-1)	A	
Frankie Pytlak	63	210	.676	C-51	B	
Luke Sewell	16	25	.461	C-15,1-1	Chi-A	StL-A

Name	G	AB/IP	P/E	G/POS	From	To
Jim Shilling	31	106	.712	2-27,S-3	A	xPhi-N
Moose Solters	41	111	.775	LF-25	B	xStL-A
Floyd Stromme	5	13	4.85	P-5(0-1)	A	C
Lefty Sullivan	7	13	4.26	P-7(0-1)	A	C
Hal Trosky	122	511	.994	1-118	B	
Roy Weatherly	95	344	.754	LF-76	B	
Skeeter Webb	81	292	.651	S-81	B	Chi-A
Bill Zuber	16	32	5.97	P-16(2-0)	B	

Coaches: Johnny Bassler, Ski Melillo, Luke Sewell

◆ **1940 CLEVELAND** (155 89-65 2) ATT: 902,576

Name	G	AB/IP	P/E	G/POS	From	To
Ossie Vitt				M		
Johnny Allen	32	139	3.44	P-32(9-8)	B	StL-A
Nate Andrews	6	12	6.00	P-6(0-1)	StL-N	
Beau Bell	120	482	.697	RF-97,1-14	Det-A	
Lou Boudreau	155	706	.814	S-155	B	
Soup Campbell	35	69	.546	LF-16	A	
Ben Chapman	143	631	.781	LF-140	B	Was-A
Joe Dobson	40	100	4.95	P-40(3-7)	B	Bos-A
Cal Dorsett	1	1	9.00	P-1	A	
Harry Eisenstat	27	72	3.14	P-27(1-4)	B	
Bob Feller	43	320	2.61	P-43(27-11)	B	
Oscar Grimes	11	13	.000	1-4,3-1	B	
Odell Hale	48	55	.611	3-3	B	Bos-A
Mel Harder	31	186	4.06	P-31(12-11)	B	
Jeff Heath	100	396	.697	LF-90	B	
Hank Helf	1	1	.000	C-1	B	StL-A
Rollie Hemsley	119	443	.671	C-117	B	
Dixie Howell	3	5	1.80	P-3	A	Cin-N
Willis Hudlin	4	24	4.94	P-4(2-1)	B	xWas-A
Johnny Humphries	19	34	8.29	P-19(0-2)	B	Chi-A
Ken Jungels	2	3	2.70	P-2	B	
Ken Keltner	149	608	.740	3-148	B	
Ray Mack	146	583	.755	2-146	B	
Al Milnar	37	242	3.27	P-37(18-10)	B	
Mike Naymick	13	30	5.10	P-13(1-2)	B	
Rusty Peters	30	75	.618	2-9,S-6,3-6,1-1	Phi-A	
Frankie Pytlak	62	172	.401	C-58,RF-1	B	Bos-A
Al Smith	31	183	3.44	P-31(15-7)	Phi-N	
Hal Trosky	140	608	.920	1-139	B	
Roy Weatherly	135	615	.799	CF-135	B	
Bill Zuber	17	24	5.63	P-17(1-1)	B	Was-A

Coaches: Johnny Bassler, Ski Melillo, Luke Sewell

◆ **1941 CLEVELAND** (155 75-79 4) ATT: 745,948

Name	G	AB/IP	P/E	G/POS	From	To
Roger Peckinpaugh				M		
Nate Andrews	2	2	11.57	P-2	B	Bos-N
Jim Bagby	35	201	4.04	P-33(9-15)	Bos-A	
Beau Bell	48	118	.558	RF-14,1-10	B	C
Lou Boudreau	148	681	.770	S-147	B	
Clint Brown	41	74	3.27	P-41(3-3)	Chi-A	
Soup Campbell	104	363	.649	CF-78	B	C
Jack Conway	2	2	1.000	S-2	A	
Chubby Dean	17	53	4.39	P-8(1-4)	xPhi-A	
Gene Desautels	66	211	.514	C-66	Bos-A	
Cal Dorsett	5	11	10.32	P-5(0-1)	B	
Hank Edwards	16	72	.552	RF-16	A	
Harry Eisenstat	21	34	4.24	P-21(1-1)	B	
Red Embree	1	4	6.75	P-1(0-1)	A	
Bob Feller	44	343	3.15	P-44(25-13)	B	
Les Fleming	2	8	.625	1-2	Det-A	
Vern Freiburger	2	8	.250	1-2	A	C
Buck Frierson	5	12	.697	LF-3	A	C
Fabian Gaffke	4	6	.750	CF-2	Bos-A	
Oscar Grimes	77	291	.693	1-62,2-13,3-1	B	
Steve Gromek	9	23	4.24	P-9(1-1)	A	
Mel Harder	15	69	5.24	P-15(5-4)	B	
Jeff Heath	151	643	.982	RF-151	B	
Jim Hegan	16	53	.798	C-16	A	
Rollie Hemsley	98	309	.614	C-96	B	Cin-N
Joe Heving	27	71	2.29	P-27(5-2)	Bos-A	
Oris Hockett	2	8	.833	CF-2	Bro-N	
Red Howell	11	11	.831	H	A	C
Ken Jungels	6	14	7.24	P-6	B	Pit-N
Ken Keltner	149	644	.815	3-149	B	
Joe Krakauskas	12	42	4.10	P-12(1-2)	Was-A	
Bob Lemon	5	4	.500	3-1	A	
Ray Mack	145	565	.645	2-145	B	
Al Milnar	35	229	4.36	P-35(12-19)	B	
Rusty Peters	29	70	.524	S-11,3-9,2-3	B	
Larry Rosenthal	45	86	.567	CF-14,1-1	xChi-A	NY-A
Al Smith	30	207	3.83	P-29(12-13)	B	
George Susce	1	0	†	C-1	StL-A	
Hal Trosky	89	355	.838	1-85	B	Chi-A
Gee Walker	121	472	.744	LF-105	Was-A	Cin-N
Roy Weatherly	102	404	.750	CF-88	B	
Chuck Workman	9	5	.200	H	B	Bos-N

Coaches: Luke Sewell, George Susce, Earl Whitehill, Dutch Zwilling

◆ **1942 CLEVELAND** (156 75-79 4) ATT: 459,447

Name	G	AB/IP	P/E	G/POS	From	To
Lou Boudreau				M		
Jim Bagby	39	271	2.96	P-38(17-9)	B	
Lou Boudreau	147	604	.749	S-146	B	
Clint Brown	7	9	6.00	P-7(1-1)	B	C
Paul Calvert	1	2	0.00	P-1	A	
Pete Center	1	3	16.20	P-1	A	
Chubby Dean	70	173	3.81	P-27(8-11)	B	
Otto Denning	92	234	.564	C-78,LF-2	A	
Gene Desautels	62	181	.581	C-61	B	
Hank Edwards	13	53	.654	CF-12	B	
Harry Eisenstat	29	48	2.45	P-29(2-1)	B	C
Red Embree	19	63	3.86	P-19(3-4)	A	
Tom Ferrick	31	81	1.99	P-31(3-2)	Phi-A	
Les Fleming	156	662	.845	1-156	B	
Fabian Gaffke	40	74	.437	RF-16	B	C

Name	G	AB/IP	P/E	G/POS	From	To
Oscar Grimes	51	100	.491	2-24,3-8,1-1,S-1	B	NY-A
Steve Gromek	14	44	3.65	P-14(2-0)	B	
Mel Harder	29	199	3.44	P-29(13-14)	B	
Jeff Heath	147	634	.792	LF-146	B	
Jim Hegan	68	184	.467	C-66	B	
Joe Heving	27	46	4.86	P-27(5-3)	B	
Oris Hockett	148	654	.650	RF-145	B	
Ken Keltner	152	663	.695	3-151	B	
Vern Kennedy	33	108	4.08	P-28(4-8)	Was-A	
Joe Krakauskas	3	7	3.86	P-3	B	
Bob Lemon	5	5	.000	3-1	B	
Ray Mack	143	531	.579	2-143	B	
Buster Mills	80	220	.687	CF-53	NY-A	
Al Milnar	40	157	4.13	P-28(6-8)	B	
Rusty Peters	34	60	.595	S-24,2-1,3-1	B	
Ray Poat	4	18	5.40	P-4(1-3)	A	
Allie Reynolds	2	5	0.00	P-2	A	
Eddie Robinson	8	9	.347	1-1	A	
Ted Sepkowski	5	10	.200	2-2	A	
Al Smith	30	168	3.96	P-30(10-15)	B	
George Susce	2	2	2.000	C-2	B	
Roy Weatherly	128	514	.678	CF-117	B	NY-A

Coaches: Ski Melillo, Burt Shotton, George Susce

◆ **1943 CLEVELAND** (153 82-71 3) ATT: 438,894

Name	G	AB/IP	P/E	G/POS	From	To
Lou Boudreau				M		
Jim Bagby	41	273	3.10	P-36(17-14),S-1	B	
Lou Boudreau	152	649	.776	S-152,C-1	B	
Paul Calvert	5	8	4.32	P-5	B	
Pete Center	24	42	2.76	P-24(1-2)	B	
Roy Cullenbine	138	598	.811	RF-121,1-13	NY-A	
Chubby Dean	41	76	4.50	P-17(5-5)	B	C
Otto Denning	37	137	.555	1-34	B	C
Gene Desautels	68	199	.499	C-66	B	
Frank Doljack	3	8	.125	LF-2	Det-A	C
Hank Edwards	92	329	.750	CF-74	B	
Jimmy Grant	15	26	.497	3-5	xChi-A	
Steve Gromek	3	4	9.00	P-3	B	
Mel Harder	19	135	3.06	P-19(8-7)	B	
Jeff Heath	118	488	.850	LF-111	B	
Joe Heving	30	72	2.75	P-30(1-1)	B	
Oris Hockett	141	657	.685	CF-139	B	
Ken Keltner	110	469	.692	3-107	B	
Vern Kennedy	38	147	2.45	P-28(10-7)	B	
Ed Klieman	1	9	1.00	P-1(0-1)	A	
Ray Mack	153	608	.596	2-153	B	
Jim McDonnell	2	3	.667	C-1	A	
Al Milnar	19	39	8.08	P-16(1-3)	B	xStL-A
Mike Naymick	29	63	2.30	P-29(4-4)	B	
Rusty Peters	79	241	.561	3-46,S-14,2-6,LF-2	B	
Ray Poat	17	45	4.40	P-17(2-5)	B	
Allie Reynolds	39	199	2.99	P-34(11-12)	B	
Mickey Rocco	108	469	.658	1-108	A	
Buddy Rosar	115	419	.680	C-114	NY-A	
Jack Salveson	23	86	3.35	P-23(5-3)	Chi-A	
Pat Seerey	26	76	.569	LF-16	A	
Al Smith	30	208	2.55	P-29(17-7)	B	
George Susce	3	1	.000	C-3	B	
Eddie Turchin	11	16	.606	3-4,S-2	A	C
Gene Woodling	8	27	.946	RF-6	A	

Coaches: Del Baker, Burt Shotton, George Susce

◆ **1944 CLEVELAND** (155 72-82 5) ATT: 475,272

Name	G	AB/IP	P/E	G/POS	From	To
Lou Boudreau				M		
Jim Bagby	14	79	4.33	P-13(4-5)	B	
Steve Biras	2	2	2.000	2-1	A	C
Bill Bonness	2	7	7.71	P-2(0-1)	A	C
Lou Boudreau	150	681	.843	S-149,C-1	B	
Paul Calvert	35	77	4.56	P-35(1-3)	B	
Roy Cullenbine	154	666	.825	RF-151	B	
Jim Devlin	1	1	.000	C-1	A	C
Red Embree	3	3	13.50	P-3(0-1)	B	
Jimmy Grant	61	113	.761	2-20,3-4	B	C
Steve Gromek	44	204	2.56	P-35(10-9)	B	
Mel Harder	30	196	3.71	P-30(12-10)	B	
Jeff Heath	60	170	.892	LF-37	B	
Earl Henry	4	18	4.58	P-2(1-1)	A	
Joe Heving	63	120	1.96	P-63(8-3)	B	Bos-N
Myril Hoag	67	308	.697	CF-66	xChi-A	
Oris Hockett	124	497	.720	CF-110	B	Chi-A
Ken Keltner	149	632	.821	3-149	B	
Vern Kennedy	15	59	5.03	P-12(2-5)	B	xPhi-N
Hal Kleine	14	41	5.75	P-11(1-2)	A	
Ed Klieman	47	178	3.38	P-47(11-13)	B	
Russ Lyon	7	12	.432	C-3	A	C
Ray Mack	83	319	.608	2-83	B	
Jim McDonnell	20	47	.530	C-13	B	
Mike Naymick	7	13	9.69	P-7	B	xStL-N
Paul O'Dea	76	198	.771	LF-41,P-3,1-3	A	
Rusty Peters	88	310	.569	2-63,S-13,3-8	B	
Ray Poat	36	81	5.13	P-36(4-8)	B	NY-N
Allie Reynolds	41	158	3.30	P-28(11-8)	B	
Mickey Rocco	155	721	.717	1-155	B	
Buddy Rosar	99	375	.647	C-98	B	Phi-A
Hank Ruszkowski	3	8	.750	C-2	A	
Norm Schlueter	49	135	.357	C-43	Chi-A	C
Pat Seerey	101	365	.689	LF-86	B	
Al Smith	28	182	3.42	P-28(7-13)	B	
George Susce	29	68	.500	C-29	B	C

Coaches: Del Baker, Burt Shotton, George Susce

◆ **1945 CLEVELAND** (147 73-72 5) ATT: 558,182

Name	G	AB/IP	P/E	G/POS	From	To
Lou Boudreau				M		
Jim Bagby	25	159	3.73	P-25(8-11)	B	Bos-A
Stan Benjamin	14	21	.762	LF-4	Phi-N	C

Name	G	AB/IP	P/E	G/POS	From	To
Lou Boudreau	97	402	.783	S-97	B	
Paul Calvert	1	1	13.50	P-1	B	Was-A
Eddie Carnett	30	76	.565	LF-16,P-2	Chi-A	C
Pete Center	31	86	3.99	P-31(6-3)	B	
Al Cihocki	92	307	.507	S-41,3-29,2-23	A	C
Roy Cullenbine	8	24	.654	RF-4,3-3	B	xDet-A
Gene Desautels	10	10	.311	C-10	B	Phi-A
Red Embree	8	70	1.93	P-8(4-4)	B	
Bob Feller	9	72	2.50	P-9(5-3)	B	
Les Fleming	42	153	.874	RF-33,1-5	B	
Steve Gromek	37	251	2.55	P-33(19-9)	B	
Mel Harder	11	76	3.67	P-11(3-7)	B	
Frankie Hayes	119	450	.688	C-119	xPhi-A	
Jeff Heath	102	429	.906	LF-101	B	Was-A
Earl Henry	16	22	5.40	P-15(0-3)	B	C
Myril Hoag	40	143	.575	CF-33,P-2	B	C
Hal Kleine	3	7	3.86	P-3	B	C
Ed Klieman	38	126	3.85	P-38(5-8)	B	
Felix Mackiewicz	120	411	.723	CF-112	Phi-A	
Jim McDonnell	28	55	.462	C-23	B	C
Dutch Meyer	130	567	.760	2-130	Det-A	
Paul O'Dea	87	250	.575	RF-53,P-1	B	C
Allie Reynolds	44	247	3.20	P-44(18-12)	B	
Mickey Rocco	143	628	.713	1-141	B	
Don Ross	106	417	.665	3-106	xDet-A	
Bob Rothel	4	13	.585	3-4	A	C
Hank Ruszkowski	14	53	.468	C-14	B	
Jack Salveson	19	44	3.68	P-19	B	C
Pat Seerey	126	485	.743	RF-117	B	
Al Smith	22	134	3.84	P-21(5-12)	B	C
Red Steiner	12	21	.340	C-4	A	xBos-A
Elmer Weingartner	20	44	.559	S-20	A	C
Ed Wheeler	46	81	.497	3-14,S-11,2-3	A	C
Papa Williams	16	20	.461	1-3	A	C

Coaches: Ski Melillo, Burt Shotton, George Susce

◆ **1946 CLEVELAND** (156 68-86 6) ATT: 1,057,289

Name	G	AB/IP	P/E	G/POS	From	To
Lou Boudreau				M		
Heinz Becker	50	172	.782	1-44	xChi-N	
Joe Berry	21	37	3.38	P-21(3-6)	xPhi-A	C
Don Black	18	44	4.53	P-18(1-2)	Phi-A	
Lou Boudreau	140	571	.755	S-139	B	
Charlie Brewster	3	3	.333	S-1	Chi-N	C
George Case	118	528	.576	LF-118	Was-A	Was-A
Pete Center	21	29	4.97	P-21(0-2)	B	C
Jack Conway	68	282	.544	2-50,S-14,3-3	B	
Hank Edwards	124	502	.870	RF-123	B	
Red Embree	28	200	3.46	P-28(8-12)	B	
Bob Feller	48	371	2.18	P-48(26-15)	B	
Tom Ferrick	9	18	5.00	P-9	B	xStL-A
Ray Flanigan	3	9	11.00	P-3(0-1)	A	C
Les Fleming	99	358	.827	1-80,RF-1	B	
Charlie Gassaway	13	51	3.91	P-13(1-1)	Phi-A	C
Steve Gromek	37	154	4.33	P-29(9-15)	B	
Mel Harder	13	92	3.41	P-13(5-4)	B	
Frankie Hayes	51	181	.736	C-50	B	xChi-A
Jim Hegan	88	292	.597	C-87	B	
Vic Johnson	9	14	9.22	P-9(0-1)	Bos-A	C
Tom Jordan	14	39	.577	C-13	xChi-A	StL-A
Ken Keltner	116	435	.681	3-112	B	
Ed Klieman	9	15	6.60	P-9	B	
Joe Krakauskas	29	47	5.51	P-29(2-5)	B	C
Bob Kuzava	2	12	3.00	P-2(1-0)	A	
Bob Lemon	55	94	2.49	P-32(4-5),CF-12	B	
Sherm Lollar	28	70	.686	C-24	A	NY-A
Ray Mack	61	194	.580	2-61	B	NY-A
Felix Mackiewicz	78	280	.654	CF-72	B	
Ralph McCabe	1	4	11.25	P-1(0-1)	A	C
Dutch Meyer	72	235	.606	2-64	B	C
Buster Mills	9	25	.633	LF-6	B	C
Dale Mitchell	11	45	.944	CF-11	A	
Blas Monaco	12	7	.143	H	B	C
Howie Moss	8	35	.205	3-8	xCin-N	C
Rusty Peters	9	22	.604	S-7	B	StL-A
Johnny Podgajny	6	9	5.00	P-6	Pit-N	C
Jackie Price	7	14	.462	S-4	A	C
Allie Reynolds	35	183	3.88	P-31(11-15)	B	NY-A
Eddie Robinson	8	34	1.171	1-8	B	
Mickey Rocco	34	116	.672	1-27	B	C
Don Ross	55	172	.714	3-41,RF-2	B	C
Pat Seerey	117	476	.804	RF-115	B	
Ted Sepkowski	2	8	1.125	3-2	B	
Jimmy Wasdell	32	45	.602	1-4,RF-3	xPhi-N	
Les Webber	4	5	23.63	P-4(1-1)	xBro-N	
Ralph Weigel	6	12	.333	C-6	A	Chi-A
Gene Woodling	61	155	.536	CF-37	B	Pit-N

Coaches: Ski Melillo, C. Mills, Max Patkin, George Susce

◆ **1947 CLEVELAND** (157 80-74 4) ATT: 1,521,978

Name	G	AB/IP	P/E	G/POS	From	To
Lou Boudreau				M		
Gene Bearden	1	0	81.00	P-1	A	
Heinz Becker	2	2	.000	H	B	C
Don Black	30	191	3.92	P-30(10-12)	B	
Eddie Bockman	46	71	.704	3-12,2-4,S-1,LF-1	NY-A	Pit-N
Lou Boudreau	150	623	.811	S-148	B	
Jack Conway	34	56	.446	S-24,2-5,3-1	B	NY-N
Larry Doby	29	33	.369	2-4,1-1,S-1	A	
Cal Dorsett	2	1	27.00	P-2	B	C
Hank Edwards	108	427	.735	RF-100	B	
Red Embree	28	163	3.15	P-27(8-10)	B	NY-A
Bob Feller	42	299	2.68	P-42(20-11)	B	
Les Fleming	103	337	.711	1-77	B	Pit-N
Joe Frazier	9	15	.276	RF-5	A	StL-N
Al Gettel	34	149	3.20	P-31(11-10)	NY-A	
Joe Gordon	155	626	.842	2-155	NY-A	

Name	G	AB/IP	P/E	G/POS	From	To
Steve Gromek	30	84	3.74	P-29(3-5)	B	
Ernest Groth	2	1	0.00	P-2	A	
Mel Harder	15	80	4.50	P-15(6-4)	B	C
Jim Hegan	135	426	.668	C-133	B	
Ken Keltner	151	613	.714	3-150	B	
Ed Klieman	58	92	3.03	P-58(5-4)	B	
Bob Kuzava	4	22	4.15	P-4(1-1)	B	Chi-A
Bob Lemon	47	167	3.44	P-37(11-5),CF-2	B	
Lyman Linde	1	1	27.00	P-1	A	
Al Lopez	61	136	.581	C-57	Pit-N	C
Felix Mackiewicz	2	6	.000	CF-2	B	xWas-A
Catfish Metkovich	126	515	.664	CF-119,1-1	Bos-A	Chi-A
Dale Mitchell	123	518	.742	LF-115	B	
Hal Peck	114	422	.753	RF-97	Phi-A	
Eddie Robinson	95	355	.729	1-87	B	
Al Rosen	7	9	.222	3-2,LF-1	A	
Hank Ruszkowski	23	29	.977	C-16	B	C
Pat Seerey	82	251	.636	LF-68	B	
Ted Sepkowski	10	9	.472	H	B	xNY-A
Bryan Stephens	31	92	4.01	P-31(5-10)	A	StL-A
Jimmy Wasdell	1	1	.000	H	B	C
Les Willis	22	44	3.48	P-22(0-2)	A	
Roger Wolff	7	16	3.94	P-7	Was-A	xPit-N

Coaches: Mel Harder, Bill McKechnie, Ski Melillo, Max Patkin, George Susce

◆ **1948 CLEVELAND** (156 97-58 1) ATT: 2,620,627

Name	G	AB/IP	P/E	G/POS	From	To
Lou Boudreau				M		
Gene Bearden	37	230	2.43	P-37(20-7)	B	
Johnny Berardino	66	179	.607	2-20,1-18,S-12,3-3	StL-A	
Don Black	18	52	5.37	P-18(2-2)	B	C
Ray Boone	6	5	1.000	S-4	B	
Lou Boudreau	152	676	.987	S-151,C-1	B	
Russ Christopher	45	59	2.90	P-45(3-2)	Phi-A	C
Allie Clark	81	298	.807	RF-65,3-5,1-1	NY-A	
Larry Doby	121	500	.873	CF-114	B	
Hank Edwards	55	179	.753	RF-41	B	
Bob Feller	44	280	3.56	P-44(19-15)	B	
Mike Garcia	1	2	0.00	P-1	A	
Al Gettel	5	8	17.61	P-5(0-1)	B	xChi-A
Joe Gordon	144	633	.879	2-144,S-2	B	
Steve Gromek	38	130	2.84	P-38(9-3)	B	
Ernest Groth	2	1	9.00	P-1	B	Chi-A
Jim Hegan	144	524	.724	C-142	B	
Wally Judnich	79	281	.782	CF-49,1-20	StL-A	Pit-N
Ken Keltner	153	656	.917	3-153	B	
Bob Kennedy	66	80	.735	RF-50,2-2,1-1	xChi-A	
Bill Kennedy	6	11	11.12	P-6(1-0)	A	xStL-A
Ed Klieman	44	80	2.60	P-44(3-2)	B	Was-A
Bob Lemon	52	294	2.82	P-43(20-14)	B	
Lyman Linde	3	10	5.40	P-3	B	C
Dale Mitchell	141	656	.814	LF-140	B	
Bob Muncrief	21	72	3.98	P-21(5-4)	StL-A	Pit-N
Ray Murray	4	4	.000	H	A	
Satchel Paige	21	73	2.48	P-21(6-1)	A	
Hal Peck	45	68	.662	RF-9	B	Was-A
Eddie Robinson	134	540	.715	1-131	B	Was-A
Al Rosen	5	5	.400	3-2	B	
Pat Seerey	10	31	.825	RF-7	B	xChi-A
Joe Tipton	47	97	.689	C-40	A	Chi-A
Thurman Tucker	83	274	.690	CF-66	Chi-A	
Les Webber	1	1	40.50	P-1	B	C
Butch Wensloff	1	2	10.80	P-1(0-1)	NY-A	C
Sam Zoldak	23	106	2.81	P-23(9-6)	xStL-A	

Coaches: Mel Harder, Bill McKechnie, Ski Melillo, Muddy Ruel, George Susce

◆ **1949 CLEVELAND** (154 89-65 3) ATT: 2,233,771

Name	G	AB/IP	P/E	G/POS	From	To
Lou Boudreau				M		
Bobby Avila	31	15	.481	2-5	A	
Gene Bearden	32	127	5.10	P-32(8-8)	B	
Al Benton	40	136	2.12	P-40(9-6)	Det-A	
Johnny Berardino	50	134	.563	3-25,2-8,S-3	B	
Ray Boone	86	307	.697	S-76	B	
Lou Boudreau	134	561	.745	S-88,3-38,1-6,2-1	B	
Allie Clark	35	78	.488	RF-17,1-1	B	
Larry Doby	147	650	.857	CF-147	B	
Luke Easter	21	54	.629	RF-12	A	
Hank Edwards	5	16	.779	RF-5	B	xChi-N
Bob Feller	36	211	3.75	P-36(15-14)	B	
Mike Garcia	41	176	2.36	P-41(14-5)	B	
Joe Gordon	148	632	.762	2-145	B	
Steve Gromek	27	92	3.33	P-27(4-6)	B	
Jim Hegan	152	529	.635	C-152	B	
Ken Keltner	80	292	.717	3-69	B	Bos-A
Bob Kennedy	121	469	.752	RF-98,3-21	B	
Bob Lemon	46	280	2.99	P-37(22-10)	B	
Fred Marsh	1	0	†	R	A	StL-A
Minnie Minoso	9	20	.725	RF-7	A	
Dale Mitchell	149	685	.788	LF-149	B	
Milt Nielsen	3	11	.384	CF-3	A	
Satchel Paige	31	83	3.04	P-31(4-7)	B	StL-A
Frank Papish	25	62	3.19	P-25(1-0)	Chi-A	Pit-N
Hal Peck	33	32	.720	RF-2	B	C
Herman Reich	1	3	1.167	RF-1	xWas-A	xChi-N
Al Rosen	23	51	.479	3-10	B	
Mike Tresh	38	43	.526	C-38	Chi-A	C
Thurman Tucker	80	217	.596	CF-42	B	
Mickey Vernon	153	659	.801	1-153	Was-A	
Early Wynn	35	165	4.15	P-26(11-7)	Was-A	
Sam Zoldak	27	53	4.25	P-27(1-2)	B	

Coaches: Mel Harder, Bill McKechnie, Steve O'Neill, Muddy Ruel, George Susce

◆ **1950 CLEVELAND** (155 92-62 4) ATT: 1,727,464

Name	G	AB/IP	P/E	G/POS	From	To
Lou Boudreau				M		
Al Aber	1	9	2.00	P-1(1-0)	A	

Name	G	AB/IP	P/E	G/POS	From	To
Bobby Avila	80	239	.773	2-62,S-2	B	
Gene Bearden	14	45	6.15	P-14(1-3)	B	xWas-A
Al Benton	36	63	3.57	P-36(4-2)	B	Bos-A
Johnny Berardino	4	6	.900	2-1,3-1	B	xPit-N
Ray Boone	109	425	.827	S-102	B	
Lou Boudreau	81	295	.695	S-61,1-8,2-2,3-2	B	Bos-A
Allie Clark	59	175	.639	LF-41	B	
Herb Conyers	7	10	1.067	1-1	A	C
Larry Doby	142	609	.986	CF-140	B	
Luke Easter	141	623	.860	1-128,RF-13	B	
Bob Feller	35	247	3.43	P-35(16-11)	B	
Jesse Flores	28	53	3.74	P-28(3-3)	Phi-A	C
Mike Garcia	33	184	3.86	P-33(11-11)	B	
Joe Gordon	119	429	.770	2-105	B	C
Steve Gromek	31	113	3.65	P-31(10-7)	B	
Jim Hegan	131	469	.674	C-129	B	
Bob Kennedy	146	609	.764	RF-144	B	
Jim Lemon	12	37	.537	LF-10	A	
Bob Lemon	72	288	3.84	P-44(23-11)	B	
Dale Mitchell	130	577	.789	LF-127	B	
Ray Murray	55	153	.712	C-45	B	
Marino Pieretti	30	47	4.18	P-29(0-1)	Chi-A	C
Al Rosen	155	668	.948	3-154	B	
Dick Rozek	12	25	4.97	P-12	A	
Thurman Tucker	57	116	.512	CF-34	B	
Mickey Vernon	28	105	.473	1-25	B	xWas-A
Dick Weik	11	26	3.81	P-11(1-3)	xWas-A	
Early Wynn	39	214	3.20	P-32(18-8)	B	
Sam Zoldak	33	64	3.96	P-33(4-2)	B	Phi-A

Coaches: Mel Harder, Ski Melillo, Muddy Ruel, Al Simmons

◆ 1951 CLEVELAND (155 93-61 2) ATT: 1,704,984

Name	G	AB/IP	P/E	G/POS	From	To
Al Lopez			M			
Bobby Avila	141	615	.783	2-136	B	
Ray Boone	151	603	.631	S-151	B	
Lou Brissie	54	112	3.20	P-54(4-3)	xPhi-A	
Bob Chakales	17	68	4.74	P-17(3-4)	A	
Sam Chapman	94	274	.650	CF-84,1-1	xPhi-A	C
Allie Clark	3	11	1.164	RF-3	B	xPhi-A
Merl Combs	19	31	.483	S-16	Was-A	
Larry Doby	134	551	.941	CF-132	B	
Luke Easter	128	532	.814	1-125	B	
Jerry Fahr	5	6	4.76	P-5	A	C
Bob Feller	33	250	3.50	P-33(22-8)	B	
Mike Garcia	47	254	3.15	P-47(20-13)	B	
Steve Gromek	27	107	2.77	P-27(7-4)	B	
Doug Hansen	3	0	†	R	A	C
Bubba Harris	2	4	4.50	P-2	xPhi-A	C
Jim Hegan	133	457	.648	C-129	B	
Sam Jones	2	9	2.08	P-2(0-1)	A	
Bob Kennedy	108	359	.703	RF-106	B	
Lou Klein	2	2	.000	H	StL-N	xPhi-A
Paul Lehner	12	14	.516	LF-1	xStL-A	Bos-A
Bob Lemon	56	263	3.52	P-42(17-14)	B	
Clarence Maddern	11	12	.333	LF-1	Chi-N	C
Barney McCosky	31	69	.567	RF-16	xCin-N	
Minnie Minoso	8	17	1.101	1-7	B	xChi-A
Dale Mitchell	134	570	.782	LF-124	B	
Ray Murray	1	1	2.000	C-1	B	xPhi-A
Hal Naragon	3	10	.650	C-2	A	
Milt Nielsen	16	7	.143	H	B	C
Al Rosen	154	661	.809	3-154	B	
Dick Rozek	7	15	2.93	P-7	B	
Harry Simpson	122	381	.638	RF-68,1-50	A	
Snuffy Stirnweiss	50	111	.634	2-25,3-2	StL-A	
Birdie Tebbetts	55	146	.659	C-44	Bos-A	
Thurman Tucker	1	1	.000	H	B	C
Johnny Vander Meer	1	3	18.00	P-1(0-1)	Chi-N	C
Early Wynn	41	274	3.02	P-37(20-13)	B	
George Zuverink	16	25	5.33	P-16	A	

Coaches: Jake Flowers, Mel Harder, Bill Lobe, Al Simmons

◆ 1952 CLEVELAND (155 93-61 2) ATT: 1,444,607

Name	G	AB/IP	P/E	G/POS	From	To
Al Lopez			M			
Bill Abernathie	1	2	13.50	P-1	A	C
Bobby Avila	150	684	.787	2-149	B	
Johnny Berardino	35	42	.403	2-8,S-8,3-4,1-2	StL-A	xPit-N
Ray Boone	103	375	.739	S-96,3-2,2-1	B	
Lou Brissie	42	83	3.48	P-42(3-2)	B	
Bob Chakales	5	12	9.75	P-5(1-2)	B	
Merl Combs	52	155	.450	S-49,2-3	B	C
Larry Doby	140	611	.924	CF-136	B	
Luke Easter	127	486	.850	1-118	B	
Bob Feller	30	192	4.74	P-30(9-13)	B	
Jim Fridley	62	193	.642	LF-54	A	Bal-A
Mike Garcia	46	292	2.37	P-46(22-11)	B	
Bill Glynn	44	98	.701	1-32	Phi-N	
Steve Gromek	30	123	3.67	P-29(7-7)	B	
Mickey Harris	29	47	4.63	P-29(3-0)	xWas-A	C
Jim Hegan	112	364	.612	C-107	B	
Sam Jones	14	36	7.25	P-14(2-3)	B	Chi-N
Bob Kennedy	22	49	.854	RF-13,3-3	B	
Bob Lemon	54	310	2.50	P-42(22-11)	B	
Hank Majeski	36	62	.710	3-11,2-3	xPhi-A	
Barney McCosky	54	88	.609	LF-19	B	
Dale Mitchell	134	571	.801	LF-128	B	
Dave Pope	12	35	.785	RF-10	A	
Pete Reiser	34	48	.572	CF-10	Pit-N	C
Al Rosen	148	649	.911	3-147,1-4,S-3	B	
Dick Rozek	10	13	4.97	P-10(1-0)	B	Phi-A
Harry Simpson	146	607	.733	RF-127,1-28	B	
Snuffy Stirnweiss	1	0	†	3-1	B	C
George Strickland	31	103	.619	S-30,2-1	xPit-N	
Birdie Tebbetts	42	117	.656	C-37	B	C

Name	G	AB/IP	P/E	G/POS	From	To
Joe Tipton	43	129	.821	C-35	xPhi-A	
Quincy Trouppe	6	11	.282	C-6	A	C
Wally Westlake	29	80	.674	RF-28	xCin-N	
Ted Wilks	7	12	3.86	P-7	xPit-N	
Early Wynn	44	286	2.90	P-42(23-12)	B	
George Zuverink	2	1	0.00	P-1	B	Cin-N

Coaches: Tony Cuccinello, Jake Flowers, Mel Harder, Bill Lobe

◆ 1953 CLEVELAND (155 92-62 2) ATT: 1,069,176

Name	G	AB/IP	P/E	G/POS	From	To
Al Lopez			M			
Al Aber	6	6	7.50	P-6(1-1)	B	xDet-A
Bobby Avila	141	633	.735	2-140	B	
Dick Aylward	4	3	.000	C-4	A	C
Ray Boone	34	139	.768	S-31	B	xDet-A
Lou Brissie	16	13	7.62	P-16	B	C
Bob Chakales	7	27	2.67	P-7(0-2)	B	
Larry Doby	149	617	.873	CF-146	B	
Luke Easter	68	230	.806	1-56	B	
Bob Feller	25	176	3.59	P-25(10-7)	B	
Hank Foiles	7	8	.393	C-7	xCin-N	
Owen Friend	34	73	.641	2-19,S-8,3-1	xDet-A	Bos-A
Mike Garcia	38	272	3.25	P-38(18-9)	B	
Joe Ginsberg	46	127	.692	C-39	xDet-A	
Bill Glynn	147	474	.633	1-135,LF-2	B	
Steve Gromek	5	11	3.27	P-5(1-1)	B	xDet-A
Jim Hegan	112	329	.628	C-106	B	
Bob Hooper	43	69	4.02	P-43(5-4)	Phi-A	
Dave Hoskins	38	113	3.99	P-26(9-3)	A	
Art Houtteman	23	109	3.80	P-22(7-7)	xDet-A	
Bob Kennedy	100	181	.643	RF-89	B	
Jim Lemon	16	49	.485	LF-11,1-2	B	Was-A
Bob Lemon	51	287	3.36	P-41(21-15)	B	
Hank Majeski	50	55	.792	2-10,3-7,LF-1	B	
Barney McCosky	22	22	.561	H	B	C
Dale Mitchell	134	542	.800	LF-125	B	
Al Rosen	155	688	1.034	3-154,1-1,S-1	B	
Harry Simpson	82	264	.618	RF-69,1-2	B	
Al Smith	47	173	.701	RF-39,3-2	A	
George Strickland	123	482	.741	S-122,1-1	B	
Joe Tipton	47	131	.772	C-46	B	Was-A
Dick Tomanek	1	9	2.00	P-1(1-0)	A	
Dick Weik	1	0	†	R	B	xDet-A
Wally Westlake	82	259	.923	LF-72	B	
Bill Wight	20	27	3.71	P-20(2-1)	xDet-A	
Ted Wilks	4	4	7.36	P-4	B	C
Early Wynn	37	252	3.93	P-36(17-12)	B	

Coaches: Tony Cuccinello, Mel Harder, Red Kress, Bill Lobe

◆ 1954 CLEVELAND (156 111-43 1) ATT: 1,335,472

Name	G	AB/IP	P/E	G/POS	From	To
Al Lopez			M			
Bobby Avila	143	638	.882	2-141,S-7	B	
Bob Chakales	3	10	0.87	P-3(2-0)	B	xBal-A
Sam Dente	68	194	.660	S-60,2-7	Chi-A	
Larry Doby	153	675	.852	CF-153	B	
Jim Dyck	2	2	2.000	H	StL-A	Bal-A
Luke Easter	6	6	.333	1-4	B	C
Bob Feller	19	140	3.09	P-19(13-3)	B	
Mike Garcia	45	259	2.64	P-45(19-8)	B	
Joe Ginsberg	3	3	2.167	C-1	B	KC-A
Bill Glynn	111	185	.681	1-96,RF-1	B	C
Mickey Grasso	4	8	1.333	C-4	Was-A	NY-N
Jim Hegan	139	468	.665	C-137	B	
Bob Hooper	17	35	4.93	P-17	B	Cin-N
Dave Hoskins	15	27	3.04	P-14(0-1)	B	C
Art Houtteman	32	188	3.35	P-32(15-7)	B	
Bob Kennedy	1	0	†	LF-1	B	xBal-A
Bob Lemon	40	258	2.72	P-36(23-7)	B	
Hank Majeski	57	129	.709	2-25,3-10	B	
Dale Mitchell	53	69	.727	LF-6,1-1	B	
Don Mossi	40	93	1.94	P-40(6-1)	A	
Hal Naragon	46	113	.597	C-45	B	
Ray Narleski	42	89	2.22	P-42(3-3)	A	
Rocky Nelson	4	4	.000	1-2	Bro-N	Bro-N
Hal Newhouser	26	47	2.51	P-26(7-2)	Det-A	
Dave Philley	133	522	.660	RF-129	Phi-A	
Dave Pope	60	114	.808	LF-29	B	
Rudy Regalado	65	208	.646	3-50,2-2	B	
Al Rosen	137	566	.918	3-87,1-46,2-1,S-1	B	
Jose Santiago	1	0	0.00	P-1	A	
Al Smith	131	583	.834	LF-109,3-21,S-4	B	
George Strickland	112	433	.632	S-112	B	
Dick Tomanek	1	2	5.40	P-1	B	
Vic Wertz	94	335	.828	1-83,RF-5	xBal-A	
Wally Westlake	85	274	.794	LF-70	B	
Early Wynn	40	271	2.73	P-40(23-11)	B	

Coaches: Tony Cuccinello, Mel Harder, Red Kress, Bill Lobe

◆ 1955 CLEVELAND (154 93-61 2) ATT: 1,221,780

Name	G	AB/IP	P/E	G/POS	From	To
Al Lopez			M			
Hank Aguirre	4	13	1.42	P-4(2-0)	A	
Joe Altobelli	42	84	.579	1-40	A	
Bobby Avila	141	643	.771	2-141	B	
Rocky Colavito	5	9	1.111	RF-2	A	
Bud Daley	2	7	6.43	P-2(0-1)	A	
Sam Dente	73	121	.629	S-53,3-13,2-4	B	C
Larry Doby	131	560	.877	CF-129	B	Chi-A
Hoot Evers	39	70	.834	LF-25	xBal-A	
Ferris Fain	56	162	.733	1-51	xDet-A	C
Bob Feller	25	83	3.47	P-25(4-4)	B	
Hank Foiles	62	132	.729	C-41	B	
Mike Garcia	38	211	4.02	P-38(11-13)	B	
Ted Gray	3	2	18.00	P-2	xChi-A	xNY-A
Billy Harrell	13	22	.921	S-11	A	
Jim Hegan	116	352	.638	C-111	B	
Art Houtteman	35	124	3.98	P-35(10-6)	B	

Name	G	AB/IP	P/E	G/POS	From	To
Ralph Kiner	113	390	.822	LF-87	Chi-N	C
Kenny Kuhn	4	7	.762	S-4	A	
Bob Lemon	49	211	3.88	P-35(18-10)	B	
Stu Locklin	16	21	.508	CF-7	A	
Sal Maglie	10	26	3.86	P-10(0-2)	xNY-N	
Hank Majeski	36	59	.682	3-9,2-4	B	xBal-A
Dale Mitchell	61	63	.634	1-8,LF-3	B	
Don Mossi	57	82	2.42	P-57(4-3)	B	
Hal Naragon	57	143	.843	C-52	B	
Ray Narleski	60	112	3.71	P-60(9-1)	B	
Hal Newhouser	2	2	0.00	P-2	B	C
Stan Pawloski	2	8	.250	2-2	A	C
Dave Philley	43	117	.803	RF-34	B	xBal-A
Dave Pope	35	118	.895	CF-31	B	xBal-A
Rudy Regalado	10	28	.668	3-8,2-1	B	
Al Rosen	139	596	.770	3-106,1-41	B	
Jose Santiago	17	33	2.48	P-17(2-0)	B	KC-A
Herb Score	33	227	2.85	P-33(16-10)	A	
Harry Simpson	3	3	.667	H	B	xKC-A
Al Smith	154	725	.884	RF-120,3-45,S-5,2-1	B	
George Strickland	130	455	.575	S-128	B	
Vic Wertz	74	295	.813	1-63,RF-9	B	
Wally Westlake	16	23	.648	LF-7	B	xBal-A
Bill Wight	17	24	2.63	P-17	B	xBal-A
Gene Woodling	79	303	.774	LF-70	xBal-A	
Early Wynn	34	230	2.82	P-32(17-11)	B	
Bobby Young	18	47	.704	2-11,3-1	xBal-A	

Coaches: Tony Cuccinello, Mel Harder, Red Kress, Bill Lobe

◆ 1956 CLEVELAND (155 88-66 2) ATT: 865,467

Name	G	AB/IP	P/E	G/POS	From	To
Al Lopez				M		
Hank Aguirre	16	65	3.72	P-16(3-5)	B	
Earl Averill	42	110	.740	C-34	A	
Bobby Avila	138	597	.641	2-135	B	
Jim Busby	135	546	.656	CF-133	Chi-A	
Joe Caffie	12	44	.774	LF-10	A	
Chico Carrasquel	141	544	.648	S-141,3-1	Chi-A	
Rocky Colavito	101	380	.906	RF-98	B	
Bud Daley	14	20	6.20	P-14(1-0)	B	
Hoot Evers	3	1	1.000	H	B	xBal-A
Bob Feller	19	58	4.97	P-19(0-4)	B	C
Hank Foiles	1	0	†	C-1	B	xPit-N
Mike Garcia	35	198	3.78	P-35(11-12)	B	
Jim Hegan	122	368	.667	C-118	B	
Art Houtteman	23	47	6.56	P-22(2-2)	B	
Kenny Kuhn	27	22	.591	S-17,2-5	B	
Bob Lemon	43	255	3.03	P-39(20-14)	B	
Stu Locklin	9	6	.333	RF-1	B	C
Sal Maglie	2	5	3.60	P-2	B	xBro-N
Cal McLish	39	62	4.96	P-37(2-4)	Chi-N	
Sam Mele	57	128	.746	LF-20,1-8	Cin-N	C
Dale Mitchell	38	37	.431	LF-1	B	xBro-N
Don Mossi	48	88	3.59	P-48(6-5)	B	
Hal Naragon	53	140	.762	C-48	B	
Ray Narleski	32	59	1.52	P-32(3-2)	B	
Dave Pope	25	72	.568	CF-18	xBal-A	C
Rudy Regalado	16	52	.563	3-14,1-1	B	C
Al Rosen	121	481	.784	3-116	B	C
Herb Score	35	249	2.53	P-35(20-9)	B	
Al Smith	141	616	.815	RF-122,3-28,2-1	B	
George Strickland	85	199	.593	2-28,S-28,3-26	B	
Preston Ward	87	170	.765	1-60,LF-17	xPit-N	
Vic Wertz	136	568	.878	1-133	B	
Gene Woodling	100	399	.790	LF-85	B	
Early Wynn	38	278	2.72	P-38(20-9)	B	
Bobby Young	1	0	†	R	B	Phi-N

Coaches: Tony Cuccinello, Mel Harder, Red Kress, Bill Lobe

◆ 1957 CLEVELAND (153 76-77 6) ATT: 722,256

Name	G	AB/IP	P/E	G/POS	From	To
Kerby Farrell				M		
Hank Aguirre	10	20	5.75	P-10(1-1)	B	Det-A
Bob Alexander	5	7	9.00	P-5(0-1)	Bal-A	C
Joe Altobelli	83	97	.545	1-56,CF-7	B	Min-A
Bobby Avila	129	528	.690	2-107,3-16	B	
Dick Brown	34	121	.692	C-33	A	
Jim Busby	30	78	.524	CF-26	B	xBal-A
Joe Caffie	32	95	.717	RF-19	B	C
Chico Carrasquel	125	454	.734	S-122	B	
Rocky Colavito	134	544	.823	RF-130	B	
Bud Daley	34	87	4.43	P-34(2-8)	B	KC-A
Mike Garcia	38	211	3.75	P-38(12-8)	B	
Johnny Gray	7	20	5.85	P-7(1-3)	KC-A	Phi-N
Billy Harrell	22	62	.680	S-14,3-6,2-1	B	
Jim Hegan	58	167	.637	C-58	B	Det-A
Art Houtteman	3	4	6.75	P-3	B	xBal-A
Kenny Kuhn	40	59	.398	2-14,3-2,S-1	B	C
Bob Lemon	25	117	4.60	P-21(6-11)	B	
Roger Maris	116	424	.751	CF-112	A	
Cal McLish	44	144	2.74	P-42(9-7)	B	
Don Mossi	36	159	4.13	P-36(11-10)	B	
Hal Naragon	57	136	.609	C-39	B	
Ray Narleski	46	154	3.09	P-46(11-5)	B	
Russ Nixon	62	199	.687	C-57	A	
Stan Pitula	24	60	4.98	P-23(2-2)	A	C
Larry Raines	96	266	.662	3-27,S-25,2-10,LF-8	A	
Eddie Robinson	19	29	.620	1-7	xDet-A	xBal-A
Herb Score	5	36	2.00	P-5(2-1)	B	
Al Smith	135	605	.729	3-84,CF-58	B	Chi-A
George Strickland	89	230	.633	2-48,S-23,3-19	B	
Dick Tomanek	34	70	5.68	P-34(2-1)	B	
Bob Usher	10	10	.347	CF-4,3-1	Chi-N	xWas-A
Vito Valentinetti	11	24	4.94	P-11(2-2)	xChi-N	Det-A
Preston Ward	10	11	.455	1-1	B	
Vic Wertz	144	606	.864	1-139	B	xStL-N
Hoyt Wilhelm	2	4	2.45	P-2(1-0)	xStL-N	

Name	G	AB/IP	P/E	G/POS	From	To
Dick Williams	67	220	.731	CF-37,3-19	xBal-A	Bal-A
Gene Woodling	133	506	.933	LF-113	B	Bal-A
Early Wynn	40	263	4.31	P-40(14-17)	B	Chi-A

Coaches: Mel Harder, Red Kress, Eddie Stanky

◆ 1958 CLEVELAND (153 77-76 4) ATT: 663,805

Name	G	AB/IP	P/E	G/POS	From	To
Bobby Bragan				M(67 31-36 6)		
Joe Gordon				M(86 46-40 4)		
Earl Averill	17	60	.559	3-17	B	Chi-N
Bobby Avila	113	445	.716	2-82,3-33	B	Bal-A
Gary Bell	33	182	3.31	P-33(12-10)	A	
Dick Brodowski	5	10	0.00	P-5(1-0)	Was-A	
Dick Brown	68	193	.693	C-62	B	
Chico Carrasquel	49	173	.651	S-32,3-14	B	xKC-A
Chuck Churn	6	9	6.23	P-6	Pit-N	LA-N
Rocky Colavito	143	578	1.027	RF-129,1-11,P-1	B	
Jim Constable	6	9	11.57	P-6(0-1)	xSF-N	xWas-A
Larry Doby	89	276	.842	CF-68	Chi-A	Det-A
Don Ferrarese	28	95	3.71	P-28(3-4)	Bal-A	
Mike Garcia	6	8	9.00	P-6(1-0)	B	
Gary Geiger	91	229	.605	CF-53,3-2,P-1	A	Bos-A
Rod Graber	4	9	.347	CF-2	A	C
Mudcat Grant	54	204	3.84	P-44(10-11)	A	
Carroll Hardy	27	58	.630	CF-17	B	
Billy Harrell	101	248	.600	3-46,S-45,2-7,RF-1	B	Bos-A
Fred Hatfield	3	9	.347	3-2	Chi-A	xCin-N
Woodie Held	67	166	.587	CF-43,S-14,3-4	xKC-A	
Billy Hunter	76	214	.533	S-75,3-2	xKC-A	C
Randy Jackson	29	94	.695	3-24	xLA-N	
Bob Kelly	13	28	5.20	P-13(0-2)	xCin-N	C
Bob Lemon	15	25	5.33	P-11(0-1)	B	C
Roger Maris	51	202	.704	CF-47	B	xKC-A
Morrie Martin	14	19	2.41	P-14(2-0)	xStL-N	Chi-N
Cal McLish	39	226	2.99	P-39(16-8)	B	
Minnie Minoso	149	638	.868	LF-147,3-1	Chi-A	
Billy Moran	115	279	.543	2-74,S-38	A	
Don Mossi	43	102	3.90	P-43(7-8)	B	Det-A
Hal Naragon	9	9	.889	C	B	
Ray Narleski	44	183	4.07	P-44(13-10)	B	Det-A
Russ Nixon	113	395	.763	C-101	B	
Jay Porter	40	96	.637	C-20,1-4,3-1	Det-A	Was-A
Vic Power	93	405	.845	3-42,1-41,2-27,S-2,LF-1	xKC-A	
Larry Raines	7	9	.000	2-2	B	C
Steve Ridzik	6	9	2.08	P-6(0-2)	NY-N	Was-A
Herb Score	12	41	3.95	P-12(2-3)	B	
Dick Tomanek	20	58	5.62	P-18(2-3)	B	xKC-A
Mickey Vernon	119	404	.814	1-96	Bos-A	Mil-N
Preston Ward	48	162	.836	3-24,1-21	B	xKC-A
Vic Wertz	25	48	.866	1-8	B	Bos-A
Hoyt Wilhelm	30	90	2.49	P-30(2-7)	B	xBal-A
Hal Woodeshick	14	72	3.64	P-14(6-6)	Det-A	Was-A

Coaches: Mel Harder, Red Kress, Eddie Stanky, Jo-Jo White

◆ 1959 CLEVELAND (154 89-65 2) ATT: 1,497,976

Name	G	AB/IP	P/E	G/POS	From	To
Joe Gordon				M		
Jim Baxes	77	270	.764	2-48,3-22	xLA-N	C
Gary Bell	44	234	4.04	P-44(16-11)	B	
Jim Bolger	8	8	.125	H	Chi-N	xPhi-N
John Briggs	4	13	2.13	P-4(0-1)	Chi-N	
Dick Brodowski	18	30	1.80	P-18(2-2)	B	C
Dick Brown	48	157	.666	C-48	B	Chi-A
Al Cicotte	26	44	5.32	P-26(3-1)	Det-A	StL-N
Rocky Colavito	154	664	.851	RF-154	B	Det-A
Gordy Coleman	6	16	1.229	1-3	A	Cin-N
Don Dillard	10	10	.800	H	A	
Don Ferrarese	15	76	3.20	P-15(5-3)	B	Chi-A
Ed Fitz Gerald	49	143	.699	C-45	xWas-A	C
Tito Francona	122	443	.985	CF-64,1-35	Det-A	
Mike Garcia	29	72	4.00	P-29(3-6)	B	Chi-A
Mudcat Grant	42	165	4.14	P-38(10-7)	B	
Granny Hamner	27	69	.430	S-10,2-7,3-5	xPhi-N	KC-A
Carroll Hardy	32	57	.476	CF-15	B	
Jack Harshman	21	66	2.59	P-13(5-1)	xBos-A	
Woodie Held	143	577	.779	S-103,3-40,CF-6,2-3	B	
Randy Jackson	3	7	.286	3-2	B	xChi-N
Willie Jones	11	19	.541	3-4	xPhi-N	xCin-N
Gene Leek	13	38	.652	3-13,S-1	A	LA-A
Bobby Locke	24	78	3.13	P-24(3-2)	A	
Billy Martin	73	259	.693	2-67,3-4	Det-A	Cin-N
Cal McLish	35	235	3.63	P-35(19-8)	B	Cin-N
Minnie Minoso	148	650	.848	LF-148	B	Chi-A
Billy Moran	11	17	.588	2-6,S-5	B	LA-A
Hal Naragon	14	41	.794	C-10	B	xWas-A
Russ Nixon	82	280	.596	C-74	B	
Jim Perry	44	153	2.65	P-44(12-10)	A	
Jim Piersall	100	354	.643	CF-91,3-1	Bos-A	
Bud Podbielan	6	12	5.84	P-6(0-1)	Cin-N	C
Vic Power	147	645	.748	1-121,2-21,3-7	B	xPhi-N
Humberto Robinson	5	9	4.15	P-5(1-0)	Mil-N	xPhi-N
Herb Score	30	161	4.71	P-30(9-11)	B	Chi-A
Bob Smith	12	29	5.22	P-12(0-1)	xChi-N	C
George Strickland	132	501	.619	3-80,S-50,2-4	B	
Jake Striker	1	7	2.70	P-1(1-0)	A	
Chuck Tanner	14	50	.634	CF-10	Chi-N	
Elmer Valo	34	33	.743	RF-2	LA-N	NY-A
Ray Webster	40	80	.591	2-24,3-4	A	Bos-A

Coaches: Mel Harder, Red Kress, Jo-Jo White

◆ 1960 CLEVELAND (154 76-78 4) ATT: 950,985

Name	G	AB/IP	P/E	G/POS	From	To
Joe Gordon				M(95 49-46 4)		
Jo-Jo White				M(1 1-0 4)		
Jimmy Dykes				M(58 26-32 4)		
Ken Aspromonte	117	521	.769	2-80,3-36	xWas-A	LA-A
Gary Bell	30	155	4.13	P-28(9-10)	B	

Name	G	AB/IP	P/E	G/POS	From	To
Walt Bond	40	149	.673	RF-36	A	
Ted Bowsfield	11	41	5.09	P-11(3-4)	xBos-A	LA-A
Rocky Bridges	10	29	.690	S-7,3-3	xDet-A	xStL-N
John Briggs	21	36	4.46	P-21(4-2)	B	xKC-A
Ty Cline	7	27	.731	CF-6	A	
Mike DeLa Hoz	49	178	.731	S-38,3-8	A	
Steve Demeter	4	5	.000	3-3	Det-A	C
Don Dillard	6	8	.393	RF-1	B	
Hank Foiles	24	76	.685	C-22	xKC-A	xDet-A
Tito Francona	147	624	.835	LF-138,1-13	B	
Frank Funk	9	32	1.99	P-9(4-2)	A	
Mudcat Grant	47	160	4.40	P-33(9-8)	B	
Bob Grim	3	2	11.57	P-3(0-1)	KC-A	xCin-N
Bob Hale	70	77	.729	1-5	Bal-A	
Carroll Hardy	29	20	.367	CF-17	B	xBos-A
Jack Harshman	15	54	3.98	P-15(2-4)	B	C
Wynn Hawkins	15	66	4.23	P-15(4-4)	A	
Woodie Held	109	430	.814	S-109	B	
Marty Keough	65	164	.638	CF-42	xBos-A	Was-A
Johnny Klippstein	49	74	2.91	P-49(5-5)	LA-N	Was-A
Harvey Kuenn	126	537	.797	RF-119,3-5	Det-A	SF-N
Barry Latman	31	147	4.03	P-31(7-7)	Chi-A	
Mike Lee	7	9	2.00	P-7	A	LA-A
Bobby Locke	35	123	3.37	P-32(3-5)	B	
Carl Mathias	7	15	3.52	P-7(0-1)	A	Was-A
Joe Morgan	22	54	.845	3-12,RF-2	xPhi-N	
Don Newcombe	24	54	4.33	P-20(2-3)	xCin-N	C
Russ Nixon	25	92	.653	C-25	B	xBos-A
Jim Perry	42	261	3.62	P-41(18-10)	B	
Bubba Phillips	113	330	.551	3-85,LF-25,S-1	Chi-A	
Jim Piersall	138	522	.750	CF-134	B	
Vic Power	147	625	.711	1-147,S-5,3-4	B	
John Powers	8	14	.702	LF-5	xBal-A	C
Johnny Romano	108	361	.829	C-99	Chi-A	
Dick Stigman	41	134	4.51	P-41(5-11)	A	
George Strickland	32	47	.493	S-14,3-12,2-2	B	C
Chuck Tanner	21	30	.699	LF-4	B	LA-A
Johnny Temple	98	425	.649	2-77,3-17	Cin-N	
Carl Thomas	5	10	7.45	P-4(1-0)	A	C
Bobby Tiefenauer	6	9	2.00	P-6(0-1)	StL-N	StL-N
Pete Whisenant	7	6	.333	LF-2	xCin-N	xWas-A
Red Wilson	32	98	.558	C-30	xDet-A	C

Coaches: Luke Appling, Ed Fitzgerald, Mel Harder, Red Kress, Bob Lemon, Jo-Jo White, Ted Wilks

♦ 1961 CLEVELAND (161 78-83 5) ATT: 725,547

Name	G	AB/IP	P/E	G/POS	From	To
Jimmy Dykes				M(160 77-83 5)		
Mel Harder				M(1 1-0 5)		
Bob Allen	48	82	3.75	P-48(3-2)	A	
Johnny Antonelli	12	48	6.56	P-11(0-4)	SF-N	xMil-N
Ken Aspromonte	22	78	.632	2-21	xLA-A	
Gary Bell	34	228	4.10	P-34(12-16)	B	
Walt Bond	38	60	.617	RF-12	B	
Ty Cline	12	51	.636	CF-12	B	
Bill Dailey	12	19	0.95	P-12(1-0)	A	
Mike DeLa Hoz	61	183	.667	2-17,S-17,3-16	B	
Don Dillard	74	162	.788	CF-39	B	
Chuck Essegian	60	181	.894	CF-49	xKC-A	
Tito Francona	155	667	.824	LF-138,1-14	B	
Frank Funk	56	92	3.31	P-56(11-11)	B	
Mudcat Grant	48	245	3.86	P-35(15-9)	B	
Bob Hale	42	40	.377	H	B	xNY-A
Steve Hamilton	2	3	3.00	P-2	A	Was-A
Wynn Hawkins	30	133	4.06	P-30(7-9)	B	
Woodie Held	146	590	.826	S-144	B	
Russ Heman	6	10	3.60	P-6	A	xLA-A
Hal Jones	12	37	.559	1-10	A	
Willie Kirkland	146	585	.797	RF-138	SF-N	
Jack Kubiszyn	25	44	.464	3-8,S-7,2-2	A	
Barry Latman	45	177	4.02	P-45(13-5)	B	
Bobby Locke	37	95	4.53	P-37(4-4)	B	StL-N
Al Luplow	5	20	.206	RF-5	A	
Sam McDowell	1	6	0.00	P-1	A	
Joe Morgan	4	11	.473	CF-2	B	StL-N
Bob Nieman	39	72	.955	LF-12	xStL-N	
Jim Perry	35	224	4.71	P-35(10-17)	B	
Bubba Phillips	143	590	.715	3-143	B	
Jim Piersall	121	536	.822	CF-120	B	Was-A
Vic Power	147	622	.685	1-141,2-7	B	Min-A
Johnny Romano	142	580	.862	C-141	B	
Joe Schaffernoth	15	17	4.76	P-15(0-1)	xChi-N	C
Dick Stigman	22	64	4.62	P-22(2-5)	B	Min-A
Johnny Temple	129	588	.700	2-129	B	Bal-A
Valmy Thomas	27	92	.575	C-27	Bal-A	C

Coaches: Luke Appling, Mel Harder, Mel McGaha

♦ 1962 CLEVELAND (162 80-82 6) ATT: 716,076

Name	G	AB/IP	P/E	G/POS	From	To
Mel McGaha				M(160 78-82 6)		
Mel Harder				M(2 2-0 6)		
Tommie Agee	5	14	.429	LF-3	A	
Bob Allen	30	31	5.87	P-30(1-1)	B	
Max Alvis	12	53	.500	3-12	B	
Ken Aspromonte	20	35	.508	2-6,3-3	B	xMil-A
Gary Bell	57	108	4.26	P-57(10-9)	B	
Walt Bond	12	54	1.226	RF-12	B	Hou-N
Ty Cline	118	411	.639	CF-107	B	Mil-N
Jackie Collum	1	1	13.50	P-1	xMin-A	C
Marlan Coughtry	3	3	1.167	H	xKC-A	C
Bill Dailey	27	43	3.59	P-27(2-2)	B	Min-A
Mike DeLa Hoz	12	12	.167	2-2	B	
Don Dillard	95	185	.632	LF-50	B	Mil-N
Dick Donovan	34	251	3.59	P-34(20-10)	Was-A	
Doc Edwards	53	154	.702	C-39	A	
Chuck Essegian	106	391	.863	LF-90	B	KC-A
Tito Francona	158	690	.731	1-158	B	

Name	G	AB/IP	P/E	G/POS	From	To
Frank Funk	47	81	3.24	P-47(2-1)	B	Mil-N
Ruben Gomez	16	45	4.37	P-15(1-2)	Phi-N	xMin-A
Mudcat Grant	30	150	4.27	P-26(7-10)	B	
Gene Green	66	152	.870	RF-33,1-2	Was-A	
Bob Hartman	8	17	3.12	P-8(0-1)	Mil-N	C
Wynn Hawkins	3	4	7.36	P-3(1-0)	B	C
Woodie Held	139	555	.769	S-133,3-5,CF-1	B	
Hal Jones	5	17	.728	1-4	B	C
Jerry Kindall	154	588	.641	2-154	Chi-N	
Willie Kirkland	137	470	.652	RF-125	B	
Jack Kubiszyn	25	65	.489	S-18,3-1	B	C
Barry Latman	45	179	4.17	P-45(8-13)	B	
Al Luplow	97	362	.836	LF-86	B	
Jim Mahoney	41	80	.692	S-23,2-8,3-1	Was-A	Hou-N
Sam McDowell	25	88	6.06	P-25(3-7)	B	
Bob Nieman	2	2	.000	H	B	xSF-N
Jim Perry	35	194	4.14	P-35(12-12)	B	
Bubba Phillips	148	599	.650	3-145,CF-3,2-1	B	Det-A
Pedro Ramos	39	201	3.71	P-37(10-12)	Min-A	
Johnny Romano	135	548	.848	C-130	B	
Don Rudolph	1	0	0.00	P-1	Cin-N	xWas-A
Willie Tasby	75	225	.663	CF-66,3-1	xWas-A	
Ron Taylor	8	33	5.94	P-8(2-2)	A	StL-N
Dave Tyriver	4	11	4.22	P-4	A	C
Floyd Weaver	1	5	1.80	P-1(1-0)	A	

Coaches: Mel Harder, Ray Katt, Salty Parker

♦ 1963 CLEVELAND (162 79-83 5) ATT: 562,507

Name	G	AB/IP	P/E	G/POS	From	To
Birdie Tebbetts				M		
Ted Abernathy	43	59	2.88	P-43(7-2)	Was-A	
Joe Adcock	97	317	.743	1-78	Mil-N	LA-A
Tommie Agee	13	29	.503	RF-13	B	
Bob Allen	43	56	4.66	P-43(1-2)	B	
Max Alvis	158	660	.786	3-158	B	
Joe Azcue	94	339	.782	C-91	xKC-A	
Gary Bell	58	119	2.95	P-58(8-5)	B	
Larry Brown	74	281	.659	S-46,2-27	A	
Ellis Burton	26	35	.673	LF-16	StL-N	xChi-N
Bob Chance	16	54	.783	RF-14	A	
Jack Curtis	4	5	18.00	P-4	Mil-N	C
Vic Davalillo	90	394	.747	CF-89	A	
Mike DeLa Hoz	67	161	.746	2-34,3-6,S-2,LF-2	B	Mil-N
Dick Donovan	31	206	4.24	P-30(11-13)	B	
Doc Edwards	10	33	.626	C-10	B	xKC-A
Tito Francona	142	553	.643	LF-122,1-11	B	
Mudcat Grant	53	229	3.69	P-38(13-14)	B	
Gene Green	43	85	.582	RF-18	B	xCin-N
Woodie Held	133	493	.790	2-96,LF-35,S-5,3-3	B	
Dick Howser	49	190	.633	S-44	xKC-A	
Tommy John	6	20	2.21	P-6(0-2)	A	
Jerry Kindall	86	263	.563	S-46,2-37,1-4	B	
Willie Kirkland	127	478	.679	CF-112	B	Bal-A
Jack Kralick	28	197	2.92	P-28(13-9)	xMin-A	
Barry Latman	38	149	4.94	P-38(7-12)	B	LA-A
Jim Lawrence	2	0	†	C-2	A	C
Bob Lipski	2	1	.000	C-2	A	C
Al Luplow	100	333	.656	RF-85	B	
Tony Martinez	43	151	.369	S-41	A	
Sam McDowell	15	65	4.85	P-14(3-5)	B	
Cal Neeman	9	11	.100	C-9	Pit-N	xWas-A
Ron Nischwitz	14	17	6.48	P-14(0-2)	Det-A	Det-A
Jim Perry	5	10	5.23	P-5	B	xMin-A
Pedro Ramos	54	185	3.12	P-36(9-8)	B	
Johnny Romano	89	300	.691	C-71,LF-4	B	
Gordon Seyfried	3	7	1.23	P-3(0-1)	A	
Willie Tasby	52	134	.689	LF-37,2-1	B	C
Sammy Taylor	4	10	.600	C-2	xCin-N	C
Jerry Walker	39	88	4.91	P-39(6-6)	KC-A	
Fred Whitfield	109	383	.807	1-92	StL-N	
Early Wynn	20	55	2.28	P-20(1-2)	Chi-A	C

Coaches: Mel Harder, George Strickland, Elmer Valo

♦ 1964 CLEVELAND (164 79-83 6) ATT: 653,293

Name	G	AB/IP	P/E	G/POS	From	To
George Strickland				M(73 33-39 8)		
Birdie Tebbetts				M(91 46-44 6)		
Ted Abernathy	53	73	4.33	P-53(2-6)	B	Chi-N
Tommie Agee	13	12	.333	RF-12	B	Chi-A
Max Alvis	107	419	.761	3-105	B	
Joe Azcue	83	294	.676	C-76	B	
George Banks	9	23	1.184	LF-3,2-1,3-1	xMin-A	
Gary Bell	56	106	4.33	P-56(8-6)	B	
Larry Brown	115	367	.664	2-103,S-4	B	
Bob Chance	120	439	.784	1-81,RF-31	B	Was-A
Vic Davalillo	150	622	.666	CF-143	B	
Paul Dicken	11	11	.000	H	A	
Dick Donovan	31	158	4.55	P-30(7-9)	B	
Tito Francona	111	320	.762	RF-69,1-17	B	StL-N
Vern Fuller	2	1	.000	H	A	
Mudcat Grant	20	62	5.95	P-13(3-4)	B	xMin-A
Woodie Held	118	415	.749	2-52,CF-41,3-30	B	Was-A
Dick Howser	162	735	.656	S-162	B	
Tommy John	25	94	3.91	P-25(2-9)	B	Chi-A
Tom Kelley	6	10	5.59	P-6	A	
Jerry Kindall	23	27	1.047	1-23	B	xMin-A
Jack Kralick	30	191	3.21	P-30(12-7)	B	
Al Luplow	19	19	.269	RF-5	B	
Tony Martinez	14	14	.500	2-4,S-1	B	
Sam McDowell	31	173	2.70	P-31(11-6)	B	
Don McMahon	70	101	2.41	P-70(6-4)	Hou-N	
Billy Moran	69	195	.559	3-42,2-15,1-2	xLA-A	
Wally Post	5	11	.273	RF-2	Min-A	C
Pedro Ramos	44	133	5.14	P-36(7-10)	B	xNY-A
Johnny Romano	106	415	.809	C-96,1-1	B	Chi-A
Chico Salmon	86	302	.766	RF-53,2-32,1-13	A	
Gordon Seyfried	2	2	0.00	P-2	B	C

Name	G	AB/IP	P/E	G/POS	From	To
Sonny Siebert	42	156	3.23	P-41(7-9)	A	
Duke Sims	2	6	.000	C-1	A	
Al Smith	61	147	.486	RF-48,3-1	Bal-A	xBos-A
Lee Stange	24	92	4.12	P-23(4-8)	xMin-A	
Luis Tiant	19	127	2.83	P-19(10-4)	A	
Leon Wagner	163	710	.752	LF-163	LA-A	
Jerry Walker	6	10	4.66	P-6(0-1)	B	C
Fred Whitfield	101	311	.726	1-79	B	

Coaches: Solly Hemus, George Strickland, Elmer Valo, Early Wynn

♦ **1965 CLEVELAND** (162 87-75 5) ATT: 934,786

Name	G	AB/IP	P/E	G/POS	From	To
Birdie Tebbetts				M		
Max Alvis	159	670	.708	3-156	B	
Joe Azcue	111	371	.562	C-108	B	
George Banks	4	6	.733	3-1	B	
Ray Barker	11	8	.250	1-3	Bal-A	xNY-A
Gary Bell	60	104	3.04	P-60(6-5)	B	
Larry Brown	124	490	.683	S-95,2-26	B	
Cam Carreon	19	62	.710	C-19	Chi-A	Bal-A
Lou Clinton	12	37	.537	LF-9	xKC-A	NY-A
Rocky Colavito	162	695	.855	RF-162	KC-A	
Vic Davalillo	142	550	.719	CF-134	B	
Bill Davis	10	10	.700	H	A	
Dick Donovan	12	23	5.96	P-12(1-3)	B	C
Ralph Gagliano	1	0	†	R		
Pedro Gonzalez	116	432	.630	2-112,RF-3,3-2	xNY-A	
Steve Hargan	17	60	3.43	P-17(4-3)	A	
Mike Hedlund	6	5	5.06	P-6	A	
Chuck Hinton	133	493	.786	CF-72,1-40,2-23,3-1	Was-A	
Dick Howser	107	377	.640	S-73,2-17	B	
Tom Kelley	4	30	2.40	P-4(2-1)	B	
Jack Kralick	30	86	4.92	P-30(5-11)	B	
Al Luplow	53	48	.432	RF-6	B	NY-N
Tony Martinez	4	3	.000	H	B	
Sam McDowell	43	273	2.18	P-42(17-11)	B	
Don McMahon	58	85	3.28	P-58(3-3)	B	
Billy Moran	22	27	.347	2-7,S-1	B	C
Phil Roof	43	61	.451	C-41	xCal-A	KC-A
Chico Salmon	79	133	.667	1-28,LF-17,2-5,3-5	B	
Richie Scheinblum	4	1	.000	H	A	
Sonny Siebert	40	188	2.43	P-39(16-8)	B	
Duke Sims	48	133	.601	C-40	B	
Jack Spring	14	22	3.74	P-14(1-2)	StL-N	C
Lee Stange	41	132	3.34	P-41(8-4)	B	
Ralph Terry	30	166	3.69	P-30(11-6)	NY-A	KC-A
Luis Tiant	41	196	3.53	P-41(11-11)	B	
Bobby Tiefenauer	15	22	4.84	P-15(0-5)	xNY-A	
Leon Wagner	144	583	.866	LF-134	B	
Floyd Weaver	32	61	5.43	P-32(2-2)	B	Chi-A
Fred Whitfield	132	492	.832	1-122	B	
Stan Williams	3	4	6.23	P-3	NY-A	

Coaches: Solly Hemus, George Strickland, Early Wynn

♦ **1966 CLEVELAND** (162 81-81 5) ATT: 903,359

Name	G	AB/IP	P/E	G/POS	From	To
Birdie Tebbetts				M(123 66-57 3)		
George Strickland				M(39 15-24 5)		
Bob Allen	36	51	4.21	P-36(2-2)	B	
Max Alvis	157	655	.683	3-157	B	
Joe Azcue	98	330	.728	C-97	B	
George Banks	4	4	.500	H	B	C
Gary Bell	40	254	3.22	P-40(14-15)	B	
Buddy Booker	18	30	.731	C-12	A	Chi-A
Larry Brown	105	384	.600	S-90,2-10	B	
Rocky Colavito	151	614	.768	RF-146	B	
Del Crandall	50	122	.681	C-49	Pit-N	C
George Culver	5	10	8.38	P-5(0-2)	A	
Tony Curry	19	19	.388	H	Phi-N	C
Vic Davalillo	121	354	.616	CF-108	B	
Bill Davis	23	45	.536	1-9	B	SD-N
Paul Dicken	2	2	.000	H	B	C
Vern Fuller	16	56	.804	2-16	B	
Jim Gentile	33	52	.488	1-9	xHou-N	C
Pedro Gonzalez	110	374	.555	2-104,3-1,RF-1	B	
Steve Hargan	38	192	2.48	P-38(13-10)	B	
Bob Heffner	5	13	3.46	P-5(0-1)	Bos-A	Cal-A
Chuck Hinton	123	389	.728	CF-104,1-6,2-2	B	
Dick Howser	67	161	.653	2-26,S-26	B	NY-A
Tom Kelley	31	95	4.34	P-31(4-8)	B	
Jack Kralick	27	68	3.82	P-27(3-4)	B	
Jim Landis	85	180	.639	CF-61	KC-A	Det-A
Tony Martinez	17	18	.627	S-5,2-4	B	C
Sam McDowell	36	194	2.87	P-35(9-8)	B	
Don McMahon	12	12	2.92	P-12(1-1)	B	xBos-A
John O'Donoghue	32	108	3.83	P-32(6-8)	KC-A	
Dick Radatz	39	57	4.61	P-39(0-3)	xBos-A	
Chico Salmon	126	463	.637	S-61,2-28,1-24,LF-10,3-6	B	
Sonny Siebert	34	241	2.80	P-34(16-8)	B	
Duke Sims	52	148	.781	C-48	B	
Lee Stange	8	16	2.81	P-8(1-0)	B	xBos-A
Luis Tiant	46	155	2.79	P-46(12-11)	B	
Jose Vidal	17	37	.579	RF-11	A	
Leon Wagner	150	599	.776	LF-139	B	
Fred Whitfield	137	538	.725	1-132	B	

Coaches: George Strickland, Early Wynn

♦ **1967 CLEVELAND** (162 75-87 8) ATT: 662,980

Name	G	AB/IP	P/E	G/POS	From	To
Joe Adcock				M		
Bob Allen	47	54	2.98	P-47(0-5)	B	C
Max Alvis	161	697	.705	3-161	B	
Joe Azcue	86	324	.747	C-86	B	
Steve Bailey	32	65	3.90	P-32(2-5)	A	
Gary Bell	9	61	3.71	P-9(1-5)	B	xBos-A
Larry Brown	152	562	.622	S-150	B	
Rocky Colavito	63	216	.695	RF-50	B	xChi-A
Ed Connolly	15	49	7.48	P-15(2-1)	Bos-A	C

Name	G	AB/IP	P/E	G/POS	From	To
George Culver	53	75	3.96	P-53(7-3)	B	Cin-N
Vic Davalillo	139	375	.687	CF-125	B	
Don Demeter	51	130	.619	CF-35,3-1	xBos-A	C
Ray Fosse	7	16	.125	C-7	A	
Vern Fuller	73	232	.675	2-64,S-2	B	
Gus Gil	51	107	.354	2-49,1-1	A	Sea-A
Pedro Gonzalez	80	208	.552	2-64,1-4,3-4,S-3	B	C
Steve Hargan	30	223	2.62	P-30(14-13)	B	
Chuck Hinton	147	552	.662	RF-136,2-5	B	
Tony Horton	106	387	.744	1-94	xBos-A	
Tom Kelley	1	1	0.00	P-1	B	Atl-N
Jim King	19	22	.325	RF-1	xChi-A	C
Jack Kralick	2	2	9.00	P-2(0-2)	B	C
Gordy Lund	3	8	.625	S-2	A	Sea-A
Lee Maye	115	326	.765	RF-77,2-1	Hou-N	
Sam McDowell	37	236	3.85	P-37(13-15)	B	
John O'Donoghue	33	131	3.23	P-33(8-9)	B	Bal-A
Orlando Pena	48	88	3.36	P-48(0-3)	xDet-A	Pit-N
Dick Radatz	3	3	6.00	P-3	B	xChi-N
Chico Salmon	90	224	.620	LF-28,1-24,2-24,S-14,3-4	B	
Richie Scheinblum	18	73	.806	RF-18	B	
Sonny Siebert	34	185	2.38	P-34(10-12)	B	
Duke Sims	88	310	.674	C-85	B	
Willie Smith	21	33	.524	LF-4,1-3	Cal-A	
Luis Tiant	33	214	2.74	P-33(12-9)	B	
Bobby Tiefenauer	5	11	0.79	P-5(0-1)	B	Chi-N
Jose Vidal	16	41	.386	LF-10	B	
Leon Wagner	135	488	.705	LF-117	B	
Fred Whitfield	100	284	.652	1-66	B	Cin-N
Stan Williams	16	79	2.62	P-16(6-4)	B	

Coaches: Clay Bryant, Pat Mullin, Del Rice, George Strickland

♦ **1968 CLEVELAND** (162 86-75 3) ATT: 857,994

Name	G	AB/IP	P/E	G/POS	From	To
Alvin Dark				M		
Max Alvis	131	503	.621	3-128	B	
Joe Azcue	115	389	.674	C-97	B	
Steve Bailey	2	5	3.60	P-2(0-1)	B	C
Larry Brown	154	553	.621	S-154	B	
Jose Cardenal	157	629	.659	CF-153	Cal-A	
Vic Davalillo	51	186	.572	RF-49	B	xCal-A
Eddie Fisher	54	95	2.85	P-54(4-2)	Bal-A	Cal-A
Ray Fosse	1	0	†	C-1	B	
Vern Fuller	97	278	.611	2-73,3-23,S-4	B	
Rob Gardner	5	3	6.75	P-5	Chi-N	NY-A
Tommy Gramly	4	3	2.70	P-3(0-1)	A	C
Jimmie Hall	53	121	.526	LF-29	xCal-A	
Steve Hargan	32	158	4.15	P-32(8-15)	B	
Tommy Harper	130	266	.672	LF-115,2-2	Cin-N	Sea-A
Billy Harris	38	103	.562	2-27,3-10,S-1	A	KC-A
Mike Hedlund	3	2	10.80	P-3	B	KC-A
Tony Horton	133	517	.714	1-128	B	
Lou Johnson	65	218	.698	LF-57	xChi-N	Cal-A
Lou Klimchock	11	17	.321	3-4,1-1,2-1	NY-N	
Hal Kurtz	30	38	5.21	P-28(1-0)	A	C
Eddie Leon	6	1	.000	S-6	A	
Lee Maye	109	316	.695	LF-80,1-1	B	
Sam McDowell	38	269	1.81	P-38(15-14)	B	
Russ Nagelson	5	5	.933	H	A	
Dave Nelson	88	216	.606	2-59,S-14	A	
Mike Paul	36	92	3.93	P-36(5-8),1-1	A	
Horacio Pina	12	31	1.72	P-12(1-1)	A	
Lou Piniella	6	6	.000	LF-2	Bal-A	KC-A
Billy Rohr	17	18	6.87	P-17(1-0)	Bos-A	C
Vicente Romo	40	83	1.62	P-40(5-3)	xLA-N	
Chico Salmon	103	297	.560	2-45,3-18,S-15,LF-13,1-11	B	Bal-A
Richie Scheinblum	19	64	.604	RF-16	B	
Sonny Siebert	33	206	2.97	P-31(12-10)	B	
Duke Sims	122	429	.766	C-84,1-31,LF-4	B	
Willie Smith	33	47	.408	1-7,P-2,LF-1	B	xChi-N
Russ Snyder	68	246	.719	RF-54,1-1	xChi-A	
Ken Suarez	17	11	.282	C-12,2-1,3-1,LF-1	KC-A	
Darrell Sutherland	3	3	8.10	P-3	NY-N	C
Luis Tiant	34	258	1.60	P-34(21-9)	B	
Jose Vidal	37	56	.474	RF-26,1-1	B	Sea-A
Leon Wagner	38	55	.538	LF-10	B	xChi-A
Stan Williams	44	194	2.50	P-44(13-11)	B	

Coaches: Johnny Lipon, Jack Sanford, George Strickland

♦ **1969 CLEVELAND** (161 62-99 6E) ATT: 619,970

Name	G	AB/IP	P/E	G/POS	From	To
Alvin Dark				M		
Max Alvis	66	207	.550	3-58,S-1	B	Mil-A
Joe Azcue	7	28	.810	C-6	B	xBos-A
Frank Baker	52	189	.688	LF-46	A	
Gary Boyd	8	11	9.00	P-8(0-2)	A	C
Larry Brown	132	521	.600	S-101,3-29,2-5	B	
Larry Burchart	29	42	4.25	P-29(0-2)	A	C
Lou Camilli	13	15	.000	3-13	A	
Jose Cardenal	146	616	.690	CF-142,3-5	B	StL-N
Dick Ellsworth	34	135	4.13	P-34(6-9)	xBos-A	
Ray Fosse	37	126	.482	C-37	B	
Vern Fuller	108	280	.632	2-102,3-7	B	
Jimmie Hall	4	12	.167	LF-3	B	xNY-A
Jack Hamilton	20	31	4.40	P-20(0-2)	Cal-A	xChi-A
Steve Hargan	34	144	5.70	P-32(5-14)	B	
Ken Harrelson	149	621	.762	RF-144,1-16	xBos-A	
Jack Heidemann	3	4	.250	S-3	A	
Phil Hennigan	9	16	3.31	P-9(2-1)	A	
Chuck Hinton	94	132	.696	LF-40,3-14	Cal-A	
Tony Horton	159	669	.782	1-157	B	
Lou Klimchock	90	279	.756	3-56,2-21,C-1	B	
Gary Kroll	19	24	4.13	P-19	Hou-N	C
Ron Law	35	52	4.99	P-35(3-4)	A	C
Eddie Leon	64	236	.612	S-64	B	
Lee Maye	43	118	.632	LF-28	B	xWas-A
Sam McDowell	39	285	2.94	P-39(18-14)	B	

Name	G	AB/IP	P/E	G/POS	From	To
Russ Nagelson	12	20	.803	RF-3,1-1	B	
Dave Nelson	52	137	.466	2-33,LF-2	B	Was-A
Mike Paul	47	117	3.61	P-47(5-10)	B	
Cap Peterson	76	137	.652	LF-30,3-4	Was-A	C
Horacio Pina	31	47	5.21	P-31(4-2)	B	Was-A
Juan Pizarro	48	83	3.16	P-48(3-3)	xBos-A	xOak-A
Vicente Romo	3	8	2.25	P-3(1-1)	B	xBos-A
Richie Scheinblum	102	222	.493	LF-50	B	Was-A
Sonny Siebert	2	14	3.21	P-2(0-1)	B	xBos-A
Duke Sims	114	399	.801	C-102,LF-3,1-1	B	
Russ Snyder	122	293	.621	LF-84	B	Mil-A
Ken Suarez	36	102	.788	C-36	B	
Luis Tiant	38	250	3.71	P-38(9-20)	B	Min-A
Zoilo Versalles	72	242	.600	2-46,3-30,S-3	LA-N	xWas-A
Stan Williams	61	178	3.94	P-61(6-14)	B	Min-A

Coaches: L. Easter, Johnny Lipon, Jack Sanford, George Strickland

♦ **1970 CLEVELAND** (162 76-86 5E) ATT: 729,752

Name	G	AB/IP	P/E	G/POS	From	To
Alvin Dark				M		
Rick Austin	31	68	4.79	P-31(2-5)	A	
Buddy Bradford	75	186	.666	CF-64,3-1	xChi-A	
Larry Brown	72	180	.659	S-27,3-17,2-16	B	
Lou Camilli	16	17	.118	S-3,2-2,3-1	B	
Dean Chance	45	155	4.24	P-45(9-8)	Min-A	xNY-N
Vince Colbert	23	31	7.26	P-23(1-1)	A	
Steve Dunning	19	94	4.96	P-19(4-9)	A	
Dick Ellsworth	29	44	4.53	P-29(3-3)	B	xMil-A
Ted Ford	26	50	.485	RF-12	A	
Ray Fosse	120	497	.832	C-120	B	
Roy Foster	139	545	.825	LF-131	A	
Vern Fuller	29	36	.583	2-16,3-4,1-1	B	C
Rich Hand	35	160	3.83	P-35(6-13)	A	
Steve Hargan	28	143	2.90	P-23(11-3)	B	
Ken Harrelson	17	45	.762	1-13	B	
Jack Heidemann	133	495	.562	S-132	B	
Phil Hennigan	42	72	4.02	P-42(6-3)	B	
Dennis Higgins	58	90	3.99	P-58(4-6)	Was-A	StL-N
Chuck Hinton	107	224	.872	1-40,RF-35,C-4,2-3,3-2	B	
Tony Horton	115	452	.777	1-112	B	C
Lou Klimchock	41	61	.431	1-5,2-5	B	C
Fred Lasher	43	58	4.06	P-43(1-7)	xDet-A	Cal-A
Eddie Leon	152	624	.663	2-141,S-23,3-1	B	
John Lowenstein	17	44	.715	2-10,3-2,LF-2,S-1	A	
Sam McDowell	40	305	2.92	P-39(20-12),1-1,2-1	B	
Bob Miller	15	28	4.18	P-15(2-2)	Min-A	xChi-A
Steve Mingori	21	20	2.66	P-21(1-0)	A	
Barry Moore	13	70	4.22	P-13(3-5)	Was-A	xChi-A
Russ Nagelson	17	27	.514	RF-4	B	xDet-A
Graig Nettles	157	633	.741	3-154,LF-3	Min-A	
Mike Paul	30	88	4.81	P-30(2-8)	B	
Vada Pinson	148	611	.803	RF-141,1-7	StL-N	
Jim Rittwage	8	26	4.15	P-8(1-1),3-1	A	C
Rich Rollins	42	46	.655	3-5	xMil-A	C
Duke Sims	110	398	.859	C-39,LF-36,1-29	B	LA-N
Ted Uhlaender	141	524	.717	CF-134	Min-A	

Coaches: Cot Deal, Hoot Evers, M. Farrell, Johnny Lipon

♦ **1971 CLEVELAND** (162 60-102 6E) ATT: 591,361

Name	G	AB/IP	P/E	G/POS	From	To
Alvin Dark				M(103 42-61 6)		
Johnny Lipon				M(59 18-41 6)		
Rick Austin	23	23	5.09	P-23	B	Mil-A
Frank Baker	73	195	.567	RF-51	B	C
Mark Ballinger	18	35	4.67	P-18(1-2)	A	C
Kurt Bevacqua	55	145	.534	2-36,RF-5,3-3,S-2	A	
Buddy Bradford	20	44	.536	CF-18	B	xCin-N
Larry Brown	13	54	.518	S-13	B	xOak-A
Lou Camilli	39	89	.492	S-23,2-16	B	
Chris Chambliss	111	459	.749	1-108	A	
Jim Clark	13	20	.528	LF-3,1-1	A	C
Vince Colbert	52	143	3.97	P-50(7-6)	B	
Steve Dunning	32	184	4.50	P-31(8-14)	B	
Ed Farmer	43	79	4.35	P-43(5-4)	A	
Ted Ford	74	206	.484	RF-55	B	Tex-A
Ray Fosse	133	529	.728	C-126,1-4	B	
Alan Foster	37	182	4.16	P-36(8-12)	LA-N	Cal-A
Roy Foster	125	439	.755	RF-107	B	
Rich Hand	16	61	5.79	P-15(2-6)	B	Tex-A
Steve Hargan	37	113	6.19	P-37(1-13)	B	
Ken Harrelson	52	187	.607	1-40,LF-7	B	C
Jack Heidemann	81	260	.489	S-81	B	
Phil Hennigan	57	62	4.94	P-57(4-3)	B	
Chuck Hinton	88	167	.692	1-20,LF-20,C-5	B	C
Gomer Hodge	80	90	.536	1-3,3-3,2-2	A	C
Bob Kaiser	5	6	4.50	P-5	A	C
Ray Lamb	43	158	3.35	P-43(6-12)	LA-N	
Eddie Leon	131	476	.643	2-107,S-24	B	
John Lowenstein	58	159	.576	2-29,RF-18,S-3	B	
Chuck Machemehl	14	18	6.38	P-14(0-2)	A	C
Sam McDowell	35	215	3.40	P-35(13-17)	B	SF-N
Steve Mingori	54	57	1.43	P-54(1-2)	B	
Graig Nettles	158	690	.788	3-158	B	
Camilo Pascual	9	23	3.09	P-9(2-2)	LA-N	C
Mike Paul	17	62	5.95	P-17(2-7)	B	Tex-A
Vada Pinson	146	599	.673	CF-141,1-3	B	Cal-A
Fred Stanley	60	160	.665	S-55,2-3	Mil-A	
Ken Suarez	50	146	.599	C-48	B	Tex-A
Ted Uhlaender	141	541	.690	LF-131	B	Cin-N

Coaches: Cot Deal, M. Farrell, Bobby Hofman, Johnny Lipon, Joe Lutz

♦ **1972 CLEVELAND** (156 72-84 5E) ATT: 626,354

Name	G	AB/IP	P/E	G/POS	From	To
Ken Aspromonte				M		
Buddy Bell	132	505	.673	RF-123,3-6	A	
Kurt Bevacqua	19	38	.384	LF-11,3-1	B	KC-A
Jack Brohamer	136	567	.566	2-132,3-1	A	
Bill Butler	6	12	1.54	P-6	KC-A	Min-A

Name	G	AB/IP	P/E	G/POS	From	To
Lou Camilli	39	45	.400	S-8,2-2	B	C
Chris Chambliss	121	499	.726	1-119	B	
Vince Colbert	23	75	4.58	P-22(1-7)	B	C
Frank Duffy	130	428	.622	S-126	SF-N	
Steve Dunning	20	105	3.26	P-16(6-4)	B	
Ed Farmer	46	61	4.40	P-46(2-5)	B	
Ray Fosse	134	508	.667	C-124,1-3	B	Oak-A
Roy Foster	73	169	.667	RF-45	B	C
Steve Hargan	12	20	5.85	P-12(0-3)	B	Tex-A
Jack Heidemann	10	23	.411	S-10	B	
Phil Hennigan	38	67	2.67	P-38(5-3)	B	NY-N
Tom Hilgendorf	19	47	2.68	P-19(3-1)	StL-N	
Alex Johnson	108	384	.625	LF-95	Cal-A	Tex-A
Larry Johnson	1	2	1.000	C-1	A	
Mike Kilkenny	22	58	3.41	P-22(4-1)	xSD-N	
Ray Lamb	34	108	3.09	P-34(5-6)	B	
Eddie Leon	89	251	.539	2-36,S-35	B	Chi-A
Ron Lolich	24	85	.501	RF-22	Chi-A	
Marcelino Lopez	4	8	5.40	P-4	Mil-A	C
John Lowenstein	68	172	.701	RF-58,1-2	B	
Tommy McCraw	129	442	.706	LF-84,1-38	Was-A	Cal-A
Steve Mingori	42	57	3.95	P-41(0-6),LF-1	B	
Jerry Moses	52	157	.617	C-39,1-3	Cal-A	NY-N
Graig Nettles	150	623	.722	3-150	B	NY-A
Lowell Palmer	2	2	4.50	P-1	xStL-N	SD-N
Gaylord Perry	41	343	1.92	P-41(24-16)	SF-N	
Adolfo Phillips	12	9	.222	LF-10	Mon-N	C
Denny Riddleberger	38	54	2.50	P-38(1-3)	Was-A	C
Fred Stanley	6	15	.536	S-5,2-1	B	xSD-N
Dick Tidrow	39	237	2.77	P-39(14-15)	A	
Del Unser	132	422	.568	CF-119	Was-A	Phi-N
Milt Wilcox	32	156	3.40	P-32(7-14)	Cin-N	

Coaches: Bobby Hofman, Joe Lutz, Warren Spahn

♦ **1973 CLEVELAND** (162 71-91 6E) ATT: 615,107

Name	G	AB/IP	P/E	G/POS	From	To
Ken Aspromonte				M		
Alan Ashby	11	31	.536	C-11	A	
Buddy Bell	156	689	.720	3-154,CF-2	B	
Dick Bosman	22	97	6.22	P-22(1-8)	xTex-A	
Jack Brohamer	102	340	.602	2-97	B	
Leo Cardenas	72	212	.500	S-67,3-5	Cal-A	Tex-A
Chris Chambliss	155	636	.733	1-154	B	
Frank Duffy	116	395	.571	S-115	B	
Dave Duncan	95	383	.728	C-86,D-9	Oak-A	
Steve Dunning	4	18	6.50	P-4(0-2)	B	xTex-A
John Ellis	127	494	.746	C-72,D-38,1-12	NY-A	
Ed Farmer	16	17	4.67	P-16(0-2)	B	xDet-A
Ted Ford	11	44	.537	CF-10	Tex-A	C
Oscar Gamble	113	432	.794	D-70,RF-37	Phi-N	
George Hendrick	113	473	.763	CF-110	Oak-A	
Tom Hilgendorf	48	95	3.14	P-48(5-3)	B	
Mike Jackson	1	1	0.00	P-1	xKC-A	C
Jerry Johnson	39	60	6.18	P-39(5-6)	SF-N	Hou-N
Mike Kekich	19	50	7.02	P-16(1-4)	xNY-A	Tex-A
Jerry Kenney	5	19	.708	2-5	NY-A	C
Mike Kilkenny	5	2	22.50	P-5	B	C
Ray Lamb	32	86	4.60	P-32(3-3)	B	C
Ron Lolich	61	148	.587	RF-32,D-15	B	C
John Lowenstein	98	334	.751	RF-51,2-25,3-8,1-1,D-4	B	
Steve Mingori	5	12	6.17	P-5	B	xKC-A
Gaylord Perry	41	344	3.38	P-41(19-19)	B	
Tom Ragland	67	198	.598	2-65,S-2	Tex-A	C
Ken Sanders	15	27	1.65	P-15(5-1)	xMin-A	
Tommy Smith	14	42	.701	CF-13	A	
Charlie Spikes	140	561	.715	LF-111,D-26	NY-A	
Brent Strom	27	123	4.61	P-27(2-10)	NY-N	SD-N
Dick Tidrow	42	275	4.42	P-42(14-16)	B	
Tom Timmermann	29	124	4.92	P-29(8-7)	xDet-A	
Rusty Torres	122	376	.625	RF-114	NY-A	
Milt Wilcox	27	134	5.83	P-26(8-10)	B	
Walt Williams	104	371	.724	LF-61,D-26	Chi-A	NY-A

Coaches: Rocky Colavito, Joe Lutz, Warren Spahn

♦ **1974 CLEVELAND** (162 77-85 4E) ATT: 1,114,262

Name	G	AB/IP	P/E	G/POS	From	To
Ken Aspromonte				M		
Luis Alvarado	61	125	.495	2-46,S-7,D-3	xStL-N	StL-N
Dwain Anderson	2	3	.667	2-1	SD-N	C
Steve Arlin	11	44	6.60	P-11(2-5)	xSD-N	C
Alan Ashby	10	8	.393	C-9	B	
Fred Beene	33	73	4.93	P-32(4-4)	xNY-A	
Buddy Bell	116	471	.675	3-115,D-1	B	
Ossie Blanco	18	43	.520	1-16,D-1	Chi-A	C
Dick Bosman	25	127	4.10	P-25(7-5)	B	
Jack Brohamer	101	350	.662	2-99	B	
Tom Buskey	51	93	3.19	P-51(2-6)	xNY-A	
Rico Carty	33	96	.846	D-14,1-8	Oak-A	
Chris Chambliss	17	72	.763	1-17	B	xNY-A
Ed Crosby	37	95	.505	3-18,S-13,2-3	Cin-N	
Frank Duffy	158	596	.583	S-158	B	
Dave Duncan	136	474	.616	C-134,1-3,D-1	B	Bal-A
Bruce Ellingsen	16	42	3.21	P-16(1-1)	A	C
John Ellis	128	513	.753	1-69,C-42,D-21	B	
Oscar Gamble	135	509	.834	D-115,LF-13	B	
Bill Gogolewski	5	14	4.61	P-5	Tex-A	Chi-A
Jack Heidemann	12	11	.182	3-6,S-4,1-1,2-1	B	xStL-N
George Hendrick	139	534	.770	CF-133,D-1	B	
Remy Hermoso	48	135	.526	2-45	Mon-N	C
Tom Hilgendorf	35	48	4.84	P-35(4-3)	B	Phi-N
Johnny Jeter	6	18	.801	LF-6	Chi-A	C
Larry Johnson	1	0	†	R	B	Mon-N
Bob Johnson	14	72	4.38	P-14(3-4)	Pit-N	Atl-N
Jim Kern	4	15	4.70	P-4(0-1)	A	
Steve Kline	16	71	5.07	P-16(3-8)	xNY-A	Atl-N
Duane Kuiper	10	24	1.133	2-8	A	

Name	G	AB/IP	P/E	G/POS	From	To
Leron Lee	79	248	.633	LF-62,D-2	SD-N	
Joe Lis	57	123	.687	1-31,3-9,LF-1,D-9	xMin-A	
John Lowenstein	140	574	.641	LF-100,3-28,1-12,2-4	B	
Tommy McCraw	45	120	.794	1-38,CF-1	xCal-A	
Gaylord Perry	37	322	2.51	P-37(21-13)	B	
Jim Perry	36	252	2.96	P-36(17-12)	Det-A	
Fritz Peterson	29	153	4.36	P-29(9-14)	xNY-A	
Frank Robinson	15	61	.713	D-11,1-4	xCal-A	
Ken Sanders	9	11	9.82	P-9(0-1)	B	xCal-A
Tommy Smith	23	35	.306	LF-17,D-1	B	
Charlie Spikes	155	612	.752	RF-154	B	
Dick Tidrow	4	19	7.11	P-4(1-3)	B	xNY-A
Tom Timmermann	4	10	5.40	P-4(1-1)	C	
Rusty Torres	108	169	.512	CF-94,D-1	B	Cal-A
Cecil Upshaw	7	8	3.38	P-7(0-1)	Hou-N	xNY-A
Milt Wilcox	41	71	4.67	P-41(2-2)	B	Chi-N

Coaches: Clay Bryant, Larry Doby, Tony Pacheco

♦ **1975 CLEVELAND** (159 79-80 4E) ATT: 977,039

Name	G	AB/IP	P/E	G/POS	From	To
Frank Robinson				M		
Larry Andersen	3	6	4.76	P-3	A	
Alan Ashby	90	301	.639	C-87,1-2,3-1,D-1	B	
Fred Beene	20	47	6.94	P-19(1-0)	B	C
Buddy Bell	153	619	.710	3-153	B	
Ken Berry	25	42	.463	LF-18,D-5	Mil-A	C
Jim Bibby	24	113	3.20	P-24(5-9)	xTex-A	
Dick Bosman	6	29	4.08	P-6(0-2)	B	xOak-A
Jack Brohamer	69	234	.640	2-66	B	Chi-A
Jackie Brown	25	69	4.28	P-25(1-2)	xTex-A	
Tom Buskey	50	77	2.57	P-50(5-3)	B	
Rico Carty	118	436	.888	D-72,1-26,LF-12	B	
Rick Cerone	7	14	.641	C-7	A	
Ed Crosby	61	145	.563	S-30,2-19,3-13	B	
Frank Duffy	146	521	.589	S-145	B	
Dennis Eckersley	34	187	2.60	P-34(13-7)	A	
John Ellis	92	316	.614	C-84,1-2,D-3	B	Tex-A
Oscar Gamble	121	405	.816	LF-82,D-29	B	NY-A
Roric Harrison	19	126	4.79	P-19(7-7)	xAtl-N	Min-A
George Hendrick	145	613	.739	CF-143	B	
Don Hood	35	135	4.39	P-29(6-10)	Bal-A	
Jim Kern	13	72	3.77	P-13(1-2)	B	
Duane Kuiper	90	388	.691	2-87,D-1	B	
Dave LaRoche	61	82	2.19	P-61(5-3)	Chi-N	
Leron Lee	13	26	.405	LF-5,D-3	B	xLA-N
Joe Lis	9	18	1.394	1-8,D-1	B	
John Lowenstein	91	297	.718	LF-36,D-31,3-8,2-2	B	
Rick Manning	120	535	.706	CF-118,D-1	A	
Tommy McCraw	23	59	.813	1-16,LF-3	B	C
Blue Moon Odom	3	10	2.61	P-3(1-0)	xOak-A	xAtl-N
Gaylord Perry	15	122	3.55	P-15(6-9)	B	xTex-A
Jim Perry	8	38	6.69	P-8(1-6)	B	xOak-A
Fritz Peterson	25	146	3.94	P-25(14-8)	B	
Boog Powell	134	502	.906	1-121,D-5	Bal-A	
Eric Raich	18	93	5.54	P-18(7-8)	A	
Bob Reynolds	5	10	4.66	P-5(0-2)	xDet-A	C
Frank Robinson	49	149	.896	D-42	B	
Tommy Smith	8	9	.250	RF-3,D-3	B	
Charlie Spikes	111	378	.670	RF-103,D-2	B	
Jim Strickland	4	5	1.93	P-4	Min-A	C
Bill Sudakis	20	50	.521	1-12,C-6	xCal-A	C
Rick Waits	16	70	2.94	P-16(6-2)	Tex-A	

Coaches: Dave Garcia, Harvey Haddix, Tommy McCraw, Jeff Torborg

♦ **1976 CLEVELAND** (159 81-78 4E) ATT: 948,776

Name	G	AB/IP	P/E	G/POS	From	To
Frank Robinson				M		
Alan Ashby	89	283	.630	C-86,1-2,3-1	B	Tor-A
Buddy Bell	159	661	.698	3-158,1-2	B	
Jim Bibby	34	163	3.20	P-34(13-7)	B	
Larvell Blanks	104	371	.734	S-56,2-46,3-2,D-3	Atl-N	
Jackie Brown	32	180	4.25	P-32(9-11)	B	Mon-N
Tom Buskey	39	94	3.63	P-39(5-4)	B	
Rico Carty	152	628	.827	D-137,1-12,LF-1	B	Tor-A
Rick Cerone	7	16	.250	C-6,D-1	B	C
Ed Crosby	2	2	1.000	3-1,D-1	B	
Pat Dobson	35	217	3.48	P-35(16-12)	NY-A	
Frank Duffy	133	437	.535	S-132	B	
Dennis Eckersley	36	199	3.43	P-36(13-12)	B	Oak-A
Ray Fosse	90	300	.710	C-85,1-3,D-1	Oak-A	
Orlando Gonzalez	28	75	.581	1-15,RF-7,D-2	A	Phi-N
Alfredo Griffin	12	4	.500	S-6,D-4	A	
George Hendrick	149	611	.776	LF-146,D-3	B	SD-N
Don Hood	34	78	4.87	P-33(3-5)	B	
Doug Howard	39	99	.500	1-32,RF-2,D-4	StL-N	C
Jim Kern	50	118	2.37	P-50(10-7)	B	
Duane Kuiper	135	555	.618	2-128,1-5,D-2	B	
Dave LaRoche	61	96	2.24	P-61(1-4)	B	
Joe Lis	20	60	.858	1-17,D-1	B	Sea-A
John Lowenstein	93	257	.567	RF-61,D-11,1-9	B	
Rick Manning	138	606	.734	CF-136	B	
Harry Parker	3	7	0.00	P-3	StL-N	C
Fritz Peterson	9	47	5.55	P-9(0-3)	B	xTex-A
Boog Powell	95	343	.649	1-89	B	LA-N
Ron Pruitt	47	104	.685	RF-26,C-6,3-6,1-1,D-4	Tex-A	
Eric Raich	1	3	16.88	P-1	B	C
Frank Robinson	36	79	.692	D-18,1-2,LF-1	B	C
Tommy Smith	55	173	.614	RF-50,D-2	B	Sea-A
Charlie Spikes	101	365	.622	RF-98,D-2	B	
Stan Thomas	37	106	2.30	P-37(4-4)	Tex-A	Sea-A
Rick Waits	36	124	4.00	P-26(7-9),D-7	B	

Coaches: Rocky Colavito, Dave Garcia, Harvey Haddix, Jeff Torborg

♦ **1977 CLEVELAND** (161 71-90 5E) ATT: 900,365

Name	G	AB/IP	P/E	G/POS	From	To
Frank Robinson				M(57 26-31 5)		
Jeff Torborg				M(104 45-59 5)		
Larry Andersen	11	14	3.14	P-11(0-1)	B	

Name	G	AB/IP	P/E	G/POS	From	To
Buddy Bell	129	538	.780	3-118,LF-11	B	
Jim Bibby	37	207	3.57	P-37(12-13)	B	Pit-N
Larvell Blanks	105	351	.725	S-66,3-18,2-12,D-6	B	
Bruce Bochte	112	444	.763	LF-76,1-36,D-1	xCal-A	Sea-A
Tom Buskey	21	34	5.29	P-21	B	Tor-A
Cardell Camper	3	9	3.86	P-3(1-0)	A	C
Rico Carty	127	521	.790	D-123,1-2	B	Tor-A
Paul Dade	134	508	.695	RF-99,3-26,2-1,D-7	Cal-A	
Pat Dobson	33	133	6.14	P-33(3-12)	B	C
Frank Duffy	122	369	.535	S-121	B	Bos-A
Dennis Eckersley	34	247	3.53	P-33(14-13)	B	Bos-A
Al Fitzmorris	29	133	5.41	P-29(6-10)	KC-A	
Ray Fosse	78	257	.673	C-77,1-1,D-1	B	xSea-A
Wayne Garland	38	283	3.60	P-38(13-19)	Bal-A	
Alfredo Griffin	14	44	.375	S-13,D-1	B	
Johnny Grubb	34	113	.887	LF-28,D-4	SD-N	
Don Hood	42	105	3.00	P-41(2-1),D-1	B	
Fred Kendall	103	346	.612	C-102,D-1	SD-N	Bos-A
Jim Kern	60	92	3.42	P-60(8-10)	B	
Duane Kuiper	148	679	.658	2-148	B	
Dave LaRoche	13	19	5.30	P-13(2-2)	B	xCal-A
Bill Laxton	2	2	5.40	P-2	xSea-A	Tex-A
John Lowenstein	81	172	.711	LF-39,D-19,1-1	B	
Rick Manning	68	283	.623	CF-68	B	
Bill Melton	50	154	.659	1-15,D-14,3-13	Cal-A	C
Sid Monge	33	39	6.23	P-33(1-2)	xCal-A	
Jim Norris	133	517	.727	CF-124,1-3	A	
Dave Oliver	7	29	.854	2-7	A	C
Ron Pruitt	78	253	.752	RF-69,C-4,3-1,D-4	B	
Charlie Spikes	32	109	.671	RF-27,D-2	B	Det-A
Andy Thornton	131	517	.906	1-117,D-9	Mon-N	
Rick Waits	38	135	3.99	P-37(9-7),D-1	B	

Coaches: Rocky Colavito, Harvey Haddix, Joe Nossek, Jeff Torborg

♦ **1978 CLEVELAND** (159 69-90 6E) ATT: 800,584

Name	G	AB/IP	P/E	G/POS	From	To
Jeff Torborg				M		
Gary Alexander	90	364	.765	C-66,D-25	xOak-A	
Buddy Bell	142	606	.721	3-139,D-1	B	Tex-A
Larvell Blanks	70	212	.627	S-43,2-17,3-3,D-1	B	Tex-A
Dan Briggs	15	53	.492	RF-15	Cal-A	SD-N
Wayne Cage	36	108	.757	D-20,1-11	A	
Bernie Carbo	60	197	.766	D-49,RF-4	xBos-A	StL-N
David Clyde	29	153	4.28	P-28(8-11)	Tex-A	
Ted Cox	82	253	.564	LF-38,3-20,D-12,1-7,S-1	Bos-A	
Paul Dade	93	349	.661	RF-81,D-9	B	
Bo Diaz	44	133	.575	C-44	Bos-A	
Al Fitzmorris	7	14	6.28	P-7(0-1)	B	xCal-A
Dave Freisleben	12	44	7.11	P-12(1-4)	xSD-N	Tor-A
Wayne Garland	6	30	7.89	P-6(2-3)	B	
Alfredo Griffin	5	6	1.417	S-2	B	Tor-A
Johnny Grubb	113	449	.816	LF-110	B	xTex-A
Ron Hassey	25	83	.546	C-24	A	
Don Hood	36	155	4.48	P-36(5-6)	B	xOak-A
Willie Horton	50	186	.692	D-48	Tex-A	Oak-A
Jim Kern	58	99	3.08	P-58(10-10)	B	Tex-A
Dennis Kinney	18	39	4.42	P-18(0-2)	A	xSD-N
Rick Kreuger	6	9	3.86	P-6	Bos-A	C
Duane Kuiper	149	589	.650	2-149	B	
Larry Lintz	3	0	†	D-1	Oak-A	C
Rick Manning	148	616	.648	CF-144	B	
Sid Monge	48	85	2.76	P-48(4-3)	B	
Jim Norris	113	365	.745	RF-78,D-15,1-6	B	
Mike Paxton	33	191	3.86	P-33(12-11)	Bos-A	
Ron Pruitt	71	205	.670	C-48,LF-16,3-2,D-5	B	
Paul Reuschel	18	90	3.11	P-18(2-4)	xChi-N	
Horace Speed	70	124	.605	RF-61,D-3	SF-N	
Dan Spillner	36	56	3.67	P-36(3-1)	xSD-N	
Andy Thornton	145	617	.898	1-145	B	
Mike Vail	14	37	.610	RF-9,D-1	NY-N	xChi-N
Tom Veryzer	130	458	.640	S-129	Det-A	
Rick Waits	35	230	3.20	P-34(13-15),D-1	B	
Rick Wise	33	212	4.34	P-33(9-19)	Bos-A	

Coaches: Rocky Colavito, Dave Duncan, Harvey Haddix, Joe Nossek

♦ **1979 CLEVELAND** (161 81-80 6E) ATT: 1,011,644

Name	G	AB/IP	P/E	G/POS	From	To
Jeff Torborg				M(95 43-52 6)		
Dave Garcia				M(66 38-28 6)		
Gary Alexander	110	415	.710	C-91,D-13,LF-2	B	
Dell Alston	54	74	.792	LF-30,D-7	Oak-A	
Larry Andersen	8	17	7.56	P-8	B	Sea-A
Len Barker	29	137	4.92	P-29(6-6)	Tex-A	
Bobby Bonds	146	631	.834	RF-116,D-29	Tex-A	StL-N
Wayne Cage	29	61	.617	1-7,D-9	B	C
David Clyde	9	46	5.91	P-9(3-4)	B	
Ted Cox	78	208	.580	3-52,LF-16,2-4,D-1	B	Sea-A
Victor Cruz	61	79	4.23	P-61(3-9)	Tor-A	
Paul Dade	44	185	.700	LF-37,3-2,D-4	B	xSD-N
Bo Diaz	15	35	.425	C-15	B	
Wayne Garland	18	95	5.23	P-18(4-10)	B	
Mike Hargrove	100	413	.938	LF-65,1-28,D-7	xSD-N	
Toby Harrah	149	635	.835	3-127,S-33,D-9	Tex-A	
Ron Hassey	75	249	.747	C-68,1-2,D-1	B	
Don Hood	13	22	3.68	P-13(1-0)	B	xNY-A
Cliff Johnson	72	274	.887	D-62,C-1	xNY-A	
Duane Kuiper	140	528	.608	2-140	B	
Rick Manning	144	632	.630	CF-141,D-1	B	
Sid Monge	76	131	2.40	P-76(12-10)	B	
Jim Norris	124	406	.678	LF-93,D-13	B	Tex-A
Mike Paxton	33	160	5.92	P-33(8-8)	B	
Ron Pruitt	64	188	.718	LF-29,D-14,C-11,3-3	B	
Paul Reuschel	17	45	7.94	P-17(2-1)	B	C
Dave Rosello	59	134	.738	2-33,3-14,S-11	Chi-N	
Horace Speed	26	19	.511	LF-16,D-4	B	C
Dan Spillner	49	158	4.62	P-49(9-5)	B	
Andy Thornton	143	617	.800	1-130,D-13	B	

Name	G	AB/IP	P/E	G/POS	From	To
Tom Veryzer	149	501	.535	S-148	B	
Rick Waits	34	231	4.44	P-34(16-13)	B	
Sandy Wihtol	5	11	3.38	P-5	A	
Eric Wilkins	16	70	4.39	P-16(2-4)	A	C
Rick Wise	34	232	3.73	P-34(15-10)	B	SD-N

Coaches: Dave Duncan, Dave Garcia, Chuck Hartenstein, Tommy McCraw, Joe Nossek

♦ 1980 CLEVELAND (160 79-81 6E) ATT: 1,033,827
Dave Garcia — M

Name	G	AB/IP	P/E	G/POS	From	To
Gary Alexander	76	198	.652	D-40,C-13,LF-2	B	Pit-N
Dell Alston	52	64	.626	LF-26,D-6	B	C
Alan Bannister	81	297	.828	2-41,RF-40,3-3,S-2	xChi-A	
Len Barker	36	246	4.17	P-36(19-12)	B	
Jack Brohamer	53	161	.591	2-47,D-1	xBos-A	C
Joe Charboneau	131	512	.850	LF-67,D-57	A	
Don Collins	4	6	7.50	P-4	Atl-N	C
Victor Cruz	55	86	3.45	P-55(6-7)	B	Pit-N
John Denny	16	109	4.39	P-16(8-6)	StL-N	
Bo Diaz	76	221	.595	C-75	B	
Miguel Dilone	132	566	.808	LF-118,D-11	Chi-N	
Jerry Dybzinski	114	278	.568	S-73,2-29,3-4,D-2	A	
Wayne Garland	25	150	4.61	P-25(6-9)	B	
Gary Gray	28	57	.471	1-6,LF-6,D-9	Tex-A	Sea-A
Ross Grimsley	14	75	6.75	P-14(4-5)	xMon-N	Bal-A
Mike Hargrove	160	720	.825	1-160	B	
Toby Harrah	160	675	.763	3-156,S-2,D-3	B	
Ron Hassey	130	447	.842	C-113,1-3,D-7	B	
Cliff Johnson	54	203	.689	D-45	B	xChi-N
Duane Kuiper	42	166	.655	2-42	B	
Rick Manning	140	555	.632	CF-139	B	
Sid Monge	67	94	3.53	P-67(3-5)	B	
Andres Mora	9	18	.222	LF-3	Bal-A	C
Jorge Orta	129	564	.788	RF-120,D-7	Chi-A	
Bob Owchinko	29	114	5.27	P-29(2-9)	SD-N	Oak-A
Mike Paxton	4	8	12.91	P-4	B	C
Ron Pruitt	23	42	.708	RF-6,3-2,D-2	B	xChi-A
Dave Rosello	71	131	.626	2-43,3-22,S-3,D-1	B	
Dan Spillner	34	194	5.28	P-34(16-11)	B	
Mike Stanton	51	86	5.46	P-51(1-3)	Hou-N	
Tom Veryzer	109	383	.627	S-108	B	
Rick Waits	33	224	4.45	P-33(13-14)	B	
Sandy Wihtol	17	35	3.57	P-17(1-0)	B	

Coaches: Dave Duncan, Tommy McCraw, Joe Nossek, Denny Sommers

♦ 1981 CLEVELAND (103 52-51 5E) ATT: 661,395
Dave Garcia — M(50 26-24 6) 1st half
Dave Garcia — M(53 26-27 5) 2nd half

Name	G	AB/IP	P/E	G/POS	From	To
Chris Bando	21	51	.521	C-15,D-2	A	
Alan Bannister	68	250	.642	LF-35,2-30,1-2,S-1	B	
Len Barker	22	154	3.91	P-22(8-7)	B	
Bert Blyleven	20	159	2.88	P-20(11-7)	Pit-N	
Tom Brennan	7	48	3.17	P-7(2-2)	A	
Joe Charboneau	48	147	.611	LF-27,D-14	B	
John Denny	19	146	3.15	P-19(10-6)	B	
Bo Diaz	63	199	.895	C-51,D-3	B	Phi-N
Miguel Dilone	72	289	.680	LF-56,D-11	B	
Jerry Dybzinski	48	67	.653	S-34,2-3,3-3,D-1	B	
Mike Fischlin	22	48	.538	S-19,2-1	Hou-N	
Wayne Garland	12	56	5.79	P-12(3-7)	B	C
Ed Glynn	4	8	1.17	P-4	NY-N	
Mike Hargrove	94	398	.832	1-88,D-4	B	
Toby Harrah	103	427	.777	3-101,S-3,D-1	B	
Ron Hassey	61	215	.570	C-56,1-5,D-1	B	
Von Hayes	43	131	.746	D-21,LF-13,3-5	A	
Pat Kelly	48	90	.644	D-18,RF-8	Bal-A	C
Duane Kuiper	72	219	.571	2-72	B	SF-N
Bob Lacey	14	21	7.59	P-14	Oak-A	xTex-A
Dennis Lewallyn	7	13	5.40	P-7	Tex-A	
Larry Littleton	26	27	.115	LF-24	A	C
Rick Manning	103	404	.656	CF-103	B	
Sid Monge	31	58	4.34	P-31(3-5)	B	Phi-N
Jorge Orta	88	370	.692	RF-86	B	LA-N
Karl Pagel	14	19	1.154	1-6,D-1	Chi-N	
Ron Pruitt	5	10	.100	LF-3,C-1,D-1	Chi-A	SF-N
Dave Rosello	43	96	.618	2-26,3-8,S-4,D-4	B	C
Dan Spillner	32	97	3.14	P-32(4-4)	B	
Mike Stanton	24	43	4.36	P-24(3-3)	B	Sea-A
Andy Thornton	69	256	.681	D-53,1-11	B	
Tom Veryzer	75	239	.543	S-75	B	NY-N
Rick Waits	22	126	4.92	P-22(8-10)	B	

Coaches: Dave Duncan, Tommy McCraw, Joe Nossek, Denny Sommers

♦ 1982 CLEVELAND (162 78-84 6E) ATT: 1,044,021
Dave Garcia — M

Name	G	AB/IP	P/E	G/POS	From	To
Bud Anderson	25	81	3.35	P-25(3-4)	A	
Chris Bando	66	212	.607	C-63,3-2	B	
Alan Bannister	101	398	.701	LF-55,2-48,S-2,3-1,D-1	B	
Len Barker	33	245	3.90	P-33(15-11)	B	
Bert Blyleven	4	20	4.87	P-4(2-2)	B	
John Bohnet	3	12	6.94	P-3	A	C
Tom Brennan	30	93	4.27	P-30(4-2)	B	
Carmen Castillo	47	129	.549	RF-43,D-2	A	
Joe Charboneau	22	63	.683	LF-18,D-1	B	C
Rod Craig	49	71	.537	LF-22,D-4	Sea-A	Chi-A
John Denny	21	138	5.01	P-21(6-11)	B	xPhi-N
Miguel Dilone	104	412	.592	LF-97,D-1	B	
Jerry Dybzinski	80	246	.588	S-77,3-3	B	Chi-A
Mike Fischlin	112	322	.671	S-101,3-8,2-6,C-1	B	
Ed Glynn	47	50	4.17	P-47(5-2)	B	
Mike Hargrove	160	705	.718	1-153,D-5	B	
Toby Harrah	162	708	.890	3-159,2-3,S-2	B	
Ron Hassey	113	382	.711	C-105,1-2,D-2	B	
Von Hayes	150	583	.700	RF-139,3-5,1-4	B	Phi-N
Neal Heaton	8	31	5.23	P-8(0-2)	A	

Name	G	AB/IP	P/E	G/POS	From	To
Dennis Lewallyn	4	10	6.97	P-4(0-1)	B	C
Rick Manning	152	619	.687	CF-152	B	
Bake McBride	27	88	.850	RF-22	Phi-N	
Larry Milbourne	82	319	.669	2-63,S-21,3-9,D-1	xMin-A	Phi-N
Bill Nahorodny	39	98	.665	C-35	Atl-N	Det-A
Karl Pagel	23	25	.567	1-10,D-1	B	
Jack Perconte	93	251	.599	2-82,D-2	LA-N	
Jerry Reed	6	16	3.45	P-6(1-1)	xPhi-N	
Kevin Rhomberg	16	20	.900	LF-7,3-1,D-4	A	
Lary Sorensen	32	189	5.61	P-32(10-15)	StL-N	
Dan Spillner	65	134	2.49	P-65(12-10)	B	
Rick Sutcliffe	34	216	2.96	P-34(14-8)	LA-N	
Andy Thornton	161	708	.872	D-152,1-8	B	
Rick Waits	25	115	5.40	P-25(2-13)	B	
Ed Whitson	40	108	3.26	P-40(4-2)	SF-N	SD-N
Sandy Wihtol	6	12	4.63	P-6	B	C

Coaches: Johnny Goryl, Tommy McCraw, Mel Queen, Denny Sommers

♦ 1983 CLEVELAND (162 70-92 7E) ATT: 768,941
Mike Ferraro — M(100 40-60 7)
Pat Corrales — M(62 30-32 7)

Name	G	AB/IP	P/E	G/POS	From	To
Bud Anderson	39	68	4.08	P-39(1-6)	B	C
Chris Bando	48	138	.718	C-43	B	
Alan Bannister	117	422	.719	LF-91,2-27,1-3,D-3	B	Hou-N
Len Barker	24	150	5.11	P-24(8-13)	B	xAtl-N
Rich Barnes	4	12	6.94	P-4(1-1)	Chi-A	C
Rick Behenna	5	26	4.15	P-5(0-2)	xAtl-N	
Bert Blyleven	24	156	3.91	P-24(7-10)	B	
Tom Brennan	11	40	3.86	P-11(2-2)	B	Chi-A
Ernie Camacho	4	5	5.06	P-4(0-1)	Pit-N	
Carmen Castillo	23	41	.838	RF-19,D-1	B	
Wil Culmer	7	20	.211	RF-4,D-2	A	C
Miguel Dilone	32	78	.560	LF-19	B	xChi-A
Jamie Easterly	41	57	3.63	P-41(4-2)	xMil-A	
Juan Eichelberger	28	134	4.90	P-28(4-11)	SD-N	Atl-N
Jim Essian	48	112	.633	C-47,3-1	Sea-A	Oak-A
Mike Fischlin	95	266	.572	2-71,S-15,3-4,D-1	B	
Julio Franco	149	598	.696	S-149	Phi-N	
Ed Glynn	11	12	5.84	P-11(0-2)	B	Mon-N
Mike Hargrove	134	566	.760	1-131,D-1	B	
Toby Harrah	138	615	.730	3-137,2-1,D-1	B	NY-A
Ron Hassey	117	388	.731	C-113,D-1	B	
Neal Heaton	39	149	4.16	P-39(11-7)	B	
Mike Jeffcoat	11	33	3.31	P-11(1-3)	A	
Rick Manning	50	209	.645	CF-50	B	xMil-A
Bake McBride	70	243	.669	RF-46,D-15	B	C
Karl Pagel	8	20	.600	LF-1,D-5	B	C
Jack Perconte	14	31	.695	2-13	B	Sea-A
Broderick Perkins	79	197	.632	1-19,RF-17,D-16	SD-N	
Jerry Reed	7	21	7.17	P-7	B	
Kevin Rhomberg	12	24	.998	LF-9,D-1	B	
Lary Sorensen	36	223	4.24	P-36(12-11)	B	Oak-A
Dan Spillner	60	92	5.07	P-60(2-9)	B	
Rick Sutcliffe	36	243	4.29	P-36(17-11)	B	Chi-N
Pat Tabler	124	492	.783	LF-88,3-25,2-2,D-6	Chi-N	
Gorman Thomas	106	437	.731	CF-106	xMil-A	Sea-A
Andy Thornton	141	605	.828	D-114,1-27	B	
Manny Trillo	88	347	.645	2-87	Phi-N	xMon-N
Otto Velez	10	28	.259	D-8	Tor-A	C
George Vukovich	124	345	.635	RF-122	Phi-N	
Rick Waits	8	20	4.58	P-8(0-1)	B	xMil-A

Coaches: Chuck Estrada, Johnny Goryl, Don McMahon, Ed Napoleon, Denny Sommers

♦ 1984 CLEVELAND (163 75-87 6E) ATT: 734,079
Pat Corrales — M

Name	G	AB/IP	P/E	G/POS	From	To
Luis Aponte	25	50	4.11	P-25(1-0)	Bos-A	C
Chris Bando	75	260	.888	C-63,1-1,3-1,D-1	B	
Jeff Barkley	3	4	6.75	P-3	A	
Rick Behenna	3	10	13.97	P-3(0-3)	B	
Tony Bernazard	140	497	.580	2-136,D-1	Sea-A	
Bert Blyleven	33	245	2.87	P-33(19-7)	B	
Brett Butler	159	709	.720	CF-156	Atl-N	
Ernie Camacho	69	100	2.43	P-69(5-9)	B	
Joe Carter	66	257	.776	LF-59,1-7	Chi-N	
Carmen Castillo	87	237	.798	RF-70,D-2	B	
Steve Comer	22	117	5.68	P-22(4-8)	Phi-N	C
Jamie Easterly	26	69	3.38	P-26(3-1)	B	
Steve Farr	31	116	4.58	P-31(3-11)	A	KC-A
Mike Fischlin	85	150	.598	2-55,3-17,S-15	B	
Julio Franco	160	718	.683	S-159,D-1	B	
George Frazier	22	44	3.65	P-22(3-2)	NY-A	xChi-N
Mel Hall	83	299	.747	LF-69,D-9	xChi-N	
Mike Hargrove	133	410	.698	1-124	B	
Ron Hassey	48	165	.625	C-44,1-1,D-1	B	xChi-N
Neal Heaton	38	199	5.21	P-38(12-15)	B	
Brook Jacoby	126	483	.688	3-126,S-1	Atl-N	
Mike Jeffcoat	63	75	2.99	P-63(5-2)	B	
Jeff Moronko	7	23	.483	3-6,D-1	A	NY-A
Otis Nixon	49	103	.376	LF-46	NY-A	
Junior Noboa	23	12	.727	2-19,D-1	A	
Broderick Perkins	58	76	.496	D-10,1-2	B	C
Jamie Quirk	1	1	5.000	C-1	xChi-A	KC-A
Kevin Rhomberg	13	8	.500	LF-7,1-1,2-1,D-1	B	C
Jose Roman	3	6	18.00	P-3(0-2)	A	
Ramon Romero	1	3	0.00	P-1	A	
Don Schulze	19	86	4.83	P-19(3-6)	xChi-N	
Roy Smith	22	86	4.59	P-22(5-5)	A	
Dan Spillner	14	51	5.65	P-14(0-5)	B	xChi-A
Rick Sutcliffe	15	94	5.15	P-15(4-5)	B	xChi-A
Pat Tabler	144	528	.768	1-67,LF-43,3-36,2-1,D-1	B	
Andy Thornton	155	689	.854	D-144,1-11	B	
Jerry Ujdur	4	14	6.91	P-4(1-2)	Det-A	C
George Vukovich	134	474	.795	RF-130	B	
Tom Waddell	58	97	3.06	P-58(7-4)	A	

Name	G	AB/IP	P/E	G/POS	From	To
Jerry Willard	87	275	.684	C-76,D-1		A

Coaches: Bobby Bonds, Johnny Goryl, Don McMahon, Ed Napoleon, Denny Sommers

♦ **1985 CLEVELAND** (162 60-102 7E) ATT: 655,181

Name	G	AB/IP	P/E	G/POS	From	To
Pat Corrales				M		
Benny Ayala	46	81	.709	LF-20,D-3	Bal-A	C
Chris Bando	73	199	.409	C-67	B	
Jeff Barkley	21	41	5.27	P-21(0-3)	B	C
Rick Behenna	4	20	7.78	P-4(0-2)	B	C
Butch Benton	31	73	.453	C-26	Chi-N	C
Tony Bernazard	153	579	.767	2-147,S-1	B	
Bert Blyleven	23	180	3.26	P-23(9-11)	B	xMin-A
Brett Butler	152	666	.810	CF-150,D-1	B	
Ernie Camacho	2	3	8.10	P-2(0-1)	B	
Joe Carter	143	523	.709	LF-135,1-11,2-1,3-1,D-7	B	
Carmen Castillo	67	198	.760	RF-51,D-9	B	
Bryan Clark	31	63	6.32	P-31(3-4)	Tor-A	Chi-A
Keith Creel	15	62	4.79	P-15(2-5)	KC-A	Tex-A
Jamie Easterly	50	99	3.92	P-50(4-1)	B	
Mike Fischlin	73	69	.562	2-31,S-22,1-6,3-3,D-5	B	NY-A
Julio Franco	160	703	.728	S-151,2-8,D-1	B	
Mel Hall	23	75	.801	LF-15,D-5	B	C
Mike Hargrove	107	326	.724	1-85	B	
Neal Heaton	36	208	4.90	P-36(9-17)	B	
Brook Jacoby	161	662	.753	3-161,2-1	B	
Mike Jeffcoat	9	10	2.79	P-9	B	xSF-N
Johnnie LeMaster	11	21	.300	S-10	xSF-N	xPit-N
Otis Nixon	104	174	.585	LF-80,D-11	B	
Jerry Reed	33	72	4.11	P-33(3-5)	B	Sea-A
Jose Roman	5	16	6.61	P-5(0-4)	B	
Ramon Romero	19	64	6.58	P-19(2-3)	B	C
Vern Ruhle	42	125	4.32	P-42(2-10)	Hou-N	Cal-A
Don Schulze	19	94	6.01	P-19(4-10)	B	
Roy Smith	12	62	5.34	P-12(1-4)	B	Min-A
Pat Tabler	117	438	.695	1-92,D-18,3-4,2-1	B	
Rich Thompson	57	80	6.30	P-57(3-8)	A	Mon-N
Andy Thornton	124	514	.715	D-122	B	
Dave VonOhlen	26	43	2.91	P-26(3-2)	StL-N	Oak-A
George Vukovich	149	470	.645	RF-137	B	C
Tom Waddell	49	113	4.87	P-49(8-6)	B	
Curt Wardle	15	64	6.68	P-15(7-6)	xMin-A	C
Jerry Willard	104	334	.718	C-96,D-1	B	Oak-A
Jim Wilson	4	15	.757	1-2,D-2	A	Sea-A

Coaches: Jack Aker, Bobby Bonds, Doc Edwards, Johnny Goryl, Fred Koenig, Don McMahon, Ed Napoleon, Denny Sommers

♦ **1986 CLEVELAND** (163 84-78 5E) ATT: 1,471,805

Name	G	AB/IP	P/E	G/POS	From	To
Pat Corrales				M		
Andy Allanson	101	323	.543	C-99	A	
Scott Bailes	62	113	4.95	P-62(10-10)	A	
Chris Bando	92	290	.655	C-86	B	
Jay Bell	5	16	1.152	2-2,D-2	A	
Tony Bernazard	146	636	.823	2-146	B	
John Butcher	13	51	6.93	P-13(1-5)	xMin-A	C
Brett Butler	161	683	.733	CF-159	B	
Ernie Camacho	51	57	4.08	P-51(2-4)	B	
Tom Candiotti	36	252	3.57	P-36(16-12)	Mil-A	
Joe Carter	162	709	.853	RF-104,1-70	B	
Carmen Castillo	85	217	.751	RF-37,D-35	B	
Dave Clark	18	68	.802	RF-10,D-7	A	
Jamie Easterly	13	18	7.64	P-13(0-2)	B	
Julio Franco	149	636	.763	S-134,2-13,D-3	B	
Mel Hall	140	480	.841	LF-126,D-7	B	
Neal Heaton	12	74	4.24	P-12(3-6)	B	xMin-A
Brook Jacoby	158	641	.791	3-158	B	
Doug Jones	11	18	2.50	P-11(1-0)	Mil-A	
Jim Kern	16	27	7.90	P-16(1-1)	Mil-A	C
Fran Mullins	28	44	.489	2-13,S-11,1-1,D-1	SF-N	C
Phil Niekro	34	210	4.32	P-34(11-11)	NY-A	Tor-A
Otis Nixon	105	110	.678	LF-95,D-5	B	
Dickie Noles	32	55	5.10	P-32(3-2)	Tex-A	Chi-N
Bryan Oelkers	35	69	4.70	P-35(3-3)	Min-A	C
Reggie Ritter	5	10	6.30	P-5	A	
Dan Rohn	6	11	.473	2-2,3-2,S-1	Chi-N	C
Jose Roman	6	22	6.55	P-6(1-2)	B	C
Ken Schrom	34	206	4.54	P-34(14-7)	Min-A	B
Don Schulze	19	85	5.00	P-19(4-4)	B	NY-N
Cory Snyder	103	433	.799	RF-74,S-34,3-11,D-1	A	
Greg Swindell	9	62	4.23	P-9(5-2)	A	
Pat Tabler	130	508	.802	1-107,D-18	B	
Andy Thornton	120	475	.730	D-110	B	
Eddie Williams	5	7	.286	LF-4	A	
Frank Wills	26	40	4.91	P-26(4-4)	Sea-A	B
Rich Yett	39	79	5.15	P-39(5-3)	Min-A	B

Coaches: Jack Aker, Bobby Bonds, Doc Edwards, Johnny Goryl, Fred Koenig

♦ **1987 CLEVELAND** (162 61-101 7E) ATT: 1,077,898

Name	G	AB/IP	P/E	G/POS	From	To
Pat Corrales				M(87 31-56 7)		
Doc Edwards				M(75 30-45 7)		
Darrel Akerfelds	16	75	6.75	P-16(2-6)	Oak-A	Tex-A
Andy Allanson	50	172	.670	C-50	B	
Mike Armstrong	14	19	8.68	P-14(1-0)	NY-A	C
Scott Bailes	39	120	4.64	P-39(7-8)	B	
Chris Bando	89	229	.592	C-86	B	
Jay Bell	38	137	.621	S-38	B	
Tony Bernazard	79	324	.700	2-78	B	xOak-A
Brett Butler	137	618	.826	CF-136	B	SF-N
Ernie Camacho	15	14	9.22	P-15(0-1)	B	Hou-N
Tom Candiotti	32	202	4.78	P-32(7-18)	B	
Steve Carlton	23	109	5.37	P-23(5-9)	Chi-A	xMin-A
Joe Carter	149	629	.786	1-84,LF-62,D-5	B	
Carmen Castillo	89	241	.778	D-43,RF-23	B	
Dave Clark	29	89	.593	RF-13,D-12	B	
Rick Dempsey	60	170	.566	C-59	Bal-A	LA-N

Name	G	AB/IP	P/E	G/POS	From	To
Brian Dorsett	5	12	.879	C-4	A	Cal-A
Jamie Easterly	16	32	4.55	P-16(1-1)	B	C
John Farrell	10	69	3.39	P-10(5-1)	A	
Julio Franco	128	560	.821	S-111,2-9,D-8	B	
Doug Frobel	29	46	.450	RF-12,D-5	Mon-N	C
Dave Gallagher	15	39	.352	CF-14	A	Chi-A
Don Gordon	21	40	4.08	P-21(0-3)	xTor-A	
Mel Hall	142	508	.749	LF-122,D-14	B	
Tommy Hinzo	67	280	.655	2-67	A	
Mark Huismann	20	35	5.09	P-20(2-3)	xSea-A	Det-A
Brook Jacoby	155	620	.929	3-144,1-7,D-4	B	
Doug Jones	49	91	3.15	P-49(6-5)	B	
Jeff Kaiser	2	3	16.20	P-2	Oak-A	
Phil Niekro	22	124	5.89	P-22(7-11)	xTor-A	xAtl-N
Otis Nixon	19	20	.259	LF-17,D-2	B	Mon-N
Junior Noboa	39	88	.528	2-21,S-8,3-5,D-1	B	Cal-A
Casey Parsons	18	25	.440	CF-2,1-1,D-5	Chi-A	C
Reggie Ritter	14	27	6.07	P-14(1-1)	B	C
Ken Schrom	32	154	6.50	P-32(6-13)	B	
Cory Snyder	157	615	.732	RF-139,S-18	B	
Sammy Stewart	25	27	5.67	P-25(4-2)	Bos-A	C
Greg Swindell	16	102	5.10	P-16(3-8)	B	
Pat Tabler	151	618	.812	1-82,D-66	B	
Andy Thornton	36	97	.352	D-21	B	C
Ed Vande Berg	55	72	5.10	P-55(1-0)	LA-N	Tex-A
Tom Waddell	6	6	14.29	P-6(0-1)	B	C
Eddie Williams	22	75	.565	3-22	B	
Frank Wills	6	5	5.06	P-6(0-1)	B	Tor-A
Rich Yett	37	98	5.25	P-37(3-9)	B	

Coaches: Jack Aker, Bobby Bonds, Steve Comer, Doc Edwards, Johnny Goryl, Luis Isaac

♦ **1988 CLEVELAND** (162 78-84 6E) ATT: 1,411,610

Name	G	AB/IP	P/E	G/POS	From	To
Doc Edwards				M		
Andy Allanson	133	474	.630	C-133	B	
Rod Allen	5	11	.273	D-4	Det-A	C
Scott Bailes	37	145	4.90	P-37(9-14)	B	
Chris Bando	32	86	.403	C-32	B	xDet-A
Jay Bell	73	236	.571	S-72,D-1		Pit-N
Bud Black	16	59	5.03	P-16(2-3)	xKC-A	
Tom Candiotti	31	217	3.28	P-31(14-8)	B	
Joe Carter	157	670	.795	CF-156	B	
Carmen Castillo	66	182	.683	LF-45,D-9	B	Min-A
Dave Clark	63	174	.694	D-27,RF-23	B	
Chris Codiroli	14	19	9.31	P-14(0-4)	Oak-A	KC-A
Jeff Dedmon	21	34	4.54	P-21(1-0)	Atl-N	C
John Farrell	31	210	4.24	P-31(14-10)	B	
Dan Firova	1	0	†	C-1	Sea-A	C
Julio Franco	152	676	.773	2-151,D-1	B	Tex-A
Terry Francona	62	221	.690	D-38,1-5,LF-5	Cin-N	Mil-A
Don Gordon	38	59	4.40	P-38(3-4)	B	C
Mel Hall	150	553	.709	LF-141,D-6	B	NY-A
Brad Havens	28	57	3.14	P-28(2-3)	xLA-N	
Brook Jacoby	152	606	.638	3-151	B	
Houston Jimenez	9	22	.095	2-7,S-2	Pit-N	C
Doug Jones	51	83	2.27	P-51(3-4)	B	C
Scott Jordan	7	10	.222	CF-6	A	C
Jeff Kaiser	3	3	0.00	P-3	B	
Ron Kittle	75	254	.863	D-63	NY-A	Chi-A
Tom Lampkin	4	5	.200	C-3	A	SD-N
Bill Laskey	17	24	5.18	P-17(1-0)	SF-N	C
Luis Medina	16	56	.917	1-16	A	
Rod Nichols	11	69	5.06	P-11(1-7)	A	
Jon Perlman	10	20	5.49	P-10(0-2)	SF-N	C
Domingo Ramos	22	52	.603	2-11,1-5,S-4,3-2	Sea-A	xCal-A
Rick Rodriguez	10	33	7.09	P-10(1-2)	Oak-A	SF-N
Dan Schatzeder	15	16	9.56	P-15(0-2)	Min-A	xMin-A
Cory Snyder	142	558	.812	RF-141,D-1	B	
Greg Swindell	33	242	3.20	P-33(18-14)	B	
Pat Tabler	41	168	.629	D-29,1-10	B	xKC-A
Ron Tingley	9	26	.522	C-9	SD-N	Cal-A
Willie Upshaw	149	564	.701	1-144	Tor-A	C
Mike Walker	3	9	7.27	P-3(0-1)	A	
Ron Washington	69	241	.663	S-54,3-8,2-7,D-1	Bal-A	Hou-N
Eddie Williams	10	23	.418	3-10	B	Chi-A
Reggie Williams	11	31	.613	LF-11	LA-N	C
Rich Yett	23	134	4.62	P-23(9-6)	B	
Paul Zuvella	51	146	.560	S-49	NY-A	

Coaches: Johnny Goryl, Luis Isaac, Charlie Manuel, Tom Spencer, Mark Wiley

♦ **1989 CLEVELAND** (162 73-89 6E) ATT: 1,285,542

Name	G	AB/IP	P/E	G/POS	From	To
Doc Edwards				M(143 65-78 6)		
John Hart				M(19 8-11 6)		
Luis Aguayo	47	112	.513	3-19,S-15,2-10,D-2	NY-A	C
Andy Allanson	111	359	.586	C-111	B	Det-A
Neil Allen	3	3	15.00	P-3(0-1)	NY-A	C
Beau Allred	13	26	.683	LF-5,D-2	A	
Keith Atherton	32	39	4.15	P-32(0-3)	Min-A	C
Scott Bailes	34	114	4.28	P-34(5-9)	B	Cal-A
Albert Belle	62	234	.666	RF-44,D-17	A	
Bud Black	33	222	3.36	P-33(12-11)	B	
Jerry Browne	153	685	.761	2-151,D-2	Tex-A	
Tom Candiotti	31	206	3.10	P-31(13-10)	B	
Joe Carter	162	705	.759	CF-146,1-11,D-8	B	Chi-N
Dave Clark	102	285	.697	D-55,LF-21	B	Chi-N
Pete Dalena	5	7	.429	D-1	A	C
Steve Davis	12	26	8.06	P-12(1-1)	Tor-A	C
John Farrell	31	208	3.63	P-31(9-14)	B	
Felix Fermin	156	562	.563	S-153,2-2	Pit-N	
Denny Gonzalez	8	19	.686	3-1,D-6	Pit-N	C
Brad Havens	7	13	4.05	P-7	B	xDet-A
Dave Hengel	12	28	.345	LF-9,D-3	Sea-A	C
Mark Higgins	6	11	.282	1-5	A	C
Tommy Hinzo	18	21	.105	2-6,S-1,D-1	B	C
Brook Jacoby	147	592	.769	3-144,D-3	B	

Name	G	AB/IP	P/E	G/POS	From	To
Dion James	71	271	.768	LF-37,D-27,1-2	xAtl-N	
Doug Jones	59	81	2.34	P-59(7-10)	B	
Jeff Kaiser	6	4	7.36	P-6(0-1)	B	
Pat Keedy	9	16	.670	LF-3,3-2,1-1,S-1,D-1	Chi-A	C
Brad Komminsk	71	227	.742	CF-68	Mil-A	SF-N
Tom Magrann	9	10	.000	C-9	A	C
Oddibe McDowell	69	270	.595	LF-64,D-2	Tex-A	xAtl-N
Luis Medina	30	89	.620	D-25,RF-3,1-1	B	
Rod Nichols	15	72	4.40	P-15(4-6)	B	
Pete O'Brien	155	646	.730	1-154,D-1	Tex-A	Sea-A
Steve Olin	25	36	3.75	P-25(1-4)	A	
Jesse Orosco	69	78	2.08	P-69(3-4)	LA-N	
Mark Salas	30	83	.654	D-20,C-5	Chi-A	Det-A
Rudy Seanez	5	5	3.60	P-5	A	
Danny Sheaffer	7	19	.229	3-2,LF-1,D-3	Bos-A	Col-N
Joe Skalski	2	7	6.75	P-2(0-2)	A	C
Joel Skinner	79	189	.575	C-79	NY-A	
Cory Snyder	132	518	.613	RF-125,S-7,D-2	B	
Tim Stoddard	14	21	2.95	P-14	NY-A	C
Greg Swindell	28	184	3.37	P-28(13-6)	B	
Kevin Wickander	2	3	3.38	P-2	A	
Ed Wojna	9	33	4.09	P-9(0-1)	SD-N	C
Rich Yett	32	99	5.00	P-32(5-6)	B	Min-A
Mike Young	32	66	.510	D-15,LF-1	Mil-A	C
Paul Zuvella	24	60	.714	S-15,3-5,D-3	B	KC-A

Coaches: Jim Davenport, Luis Isaac, Charlie Manuel, Tom Spencer, Mark Wiley

♦ **1990 CLEVELAND** (162 77-85 4E) ATT: 1,225,240

Name	G	AB/IP	P/E	G/POS	From	To
John McNamara				M		
Beau Allred	4	18	.715	CF-4	B	
Sandy Alomar	132	483	.748	C-129	SD-N	
Carlos Baerga	108	338	.698	3-50,S-48,2-8	A	
Kevin Bearse	3	8	12.91	P-3(0-2)	A	C
Albert Belle	9	25	.513	LF-1,D-6	B	
Bud Black	29	191	3.53	P-29(11-10)	B	xTor-N
Tom Brookens	64	172	.685	3-35,2-21,S-3,1-2,D-1	NY-A	C
Jerry Browne	140	610	.732	2-139	B	
Tom Candiotti	31	202	3.65	P-31(15-11)	B	
Alex Cole	63	256	.736	CF-59,D-1	A	
John Farrell	17	97	4.28	P-17(4-5)	B	Cal-A
Felix Fermin	148	458	.604	S-147,2-1	B	
Mauro Gozzo	2	3	0.00	P-2	Tor-A	
Cecilio Guante	26	47	5.01	P-26(2-3)	Tex-A	C
Keith Hernandez	43	145	.521	1-42	NY-N	C
Brook Jacoby	155	624	.794	3-99,1-78	B	
Dion James	87	280	.711	1-35,LF-33,D-10	B	NY-A
Chris James	140	569	.786	D-124,LF-14	SD-N	
Stan Jefferson	49	112	.761	LF-34,D-5	xBal-A	Cin-N
Doug Jones	66	84	2.56	P-66(5-5)	B	
Jeff Kaiser	5	13	3.55	P-5	B	Det-A
Candy Maldonado	155	651	.780	LF-134,D-20	SF-N	Mil-A
Jeff Manto	30	97	.786	1-25,3-5	A	
Mark McLemore	8	12	.333	3-4,2-3,D-1	xCal-A	Hou-N
Charles Nagy	9	46	5.91	P-9(2-4)	A	
Rod Nichols	4	16	7.87	P-4(0-3)	B	
Al Nipper	9	24	6.75	P-9(2-3)	Chi-N	C
Steve Olin	50	92	3.41	P-50(4-4)	B	
Jesse Orosco	55	65	3.90	P-55(5-4)	B	
Ken Phelps	24	71	.354	1-14,D-6	xOak-A	C
Rafael Santana	7	13	.692	S-7	NY-A	C
Rudy Seanez	24	27	5.60	P-24(2-1)	B	
Jeff Shaw	12	49	6.66	P-12(3-4)	A	
Joel Skinner	49	146	.626	C-49	B	
Cory Snyder	123	468	.675	RF-120,S-5	B	Chi-A
Steve Springer	4	13	.333	3-3,D-1	A	NY-N
Greg Swindell	34	215	4.40	P-34(12-9)	B	
Efrain Valdez	13	24	3.04	P-13(1-1)	A	
Sergio Valdez	24	102	4.75	P-24(6-6)	xAtl-N	
Mike Walker	18	76	4.88	P-18(2-6)	B	
Colby Ward	22	36	4.25	P-22(1-3)	A	C
Turner Ward	14	49	.888	RF-13,D-1	A	
Mitch Webster	128	477	.696	CF-118,1-3,D-3	Chi-A	
Kevin Wickander	10	12	3.65	P-10(0-1)	B	

Coaches: Rich Dauer, Mike Hargrove, Luis Isaac, Jose Morales, Mark Wiley

♦ **1991 CLEVELAND** (162 57-105 7E) ATT: 1,051,863

Name	G	AB/IP	P/E	G/POS	From	To
John McNamara				M(77 25-52 7)		
Mike Hargrove				M(85 32-53 7)		
Mike Aldrete	85	222	.706	1-47,LF-16,D-7	xSD-N	Oak-A
Beau Allred	48	156	.692	RF-42,D-1	B	C
Sandy Alomar	51	199	.532	C-46,D-4	B	
Carlos Baerga	158	654	.746	3-89,2-75,S-2	B	
Eric Bell	10	18	0.50	P-10(4-0)	Bal-A	
Albert Belle	123	496	.866	LF-89,D-32	B	
Willie Blair	11	36	6.75	P-11(2-3)	Tor-A	Hou-N
Denis Boucher	5	23	8.34	P-5(1-4)	xTor-A	
Jerry Browne	107	334	.565	2-47,LF-17,3-15,D-7	B	Oak-A
Tom Candiotti	15	108	2.24	P-15(7-6)	B	xTor-A
Alex Cole	122	452	.742	LF-107,D-6	B	
Bruce Egloff	6	6	4.76	P-6	A	C
Jose Escobar	10	17	.450	S-5,2-4,3-1	A	C
Felix Fermin	129	469	.611	S-129	B	
Jose Gonzalez	33	81	.545	RF-32	xPit-N	Cal-A
Mauro Gozzo	2	5	19.29	P-2	B	Min-A
Glenallen Hill	37	140	.758	CF-33,D-1	xTor-A	
Shawn Hillegas	51	83	4.34	P-51(3-4)	Chi-A	NY-A
Mike Huff	51	119	.701	CF-48,2-2	LA-N	xChi-A
Brook Jacoby	66	249	.622	1-55,3-15	B	xOak-A
Chris James	115	463	.593	D-60,LF-39,1-15	B	SF-N
Reggie Jefferson	26	105	.508	1-26	xCin-N	
Doug Jones	36	63	5.54	P-36(4-8)	B	Hou-N
Eric King	25	151	4.60	P-25(6-11)	Chi-A	Det-A
Wayne Kirby	21	47	.500	RF-21	A	
Garland Kiser	7	5	9.64	P-7	A	C
Tom Kramer	4	5	17.36	P-4	A	

Name	G	AB/IP	P/E	G/POS	From	To
Mark Lewis	84	336	.616	2-50,S-36	A	
Luis Lopez	35	89	.557	C-12,1-10,3-1,LF-1,D-6	LA-N	C
Ever Magallanes	3	3	.333	S-2	A	C
Jeff Manto	47	148	.621	3-32,1-14,C-5,LF-1	B	Phi-N
Carlos Martinez	72	275	.713	D-41,1-31	Chi-A	
Luis Medina	5	18	.180	D-5	B	C
Jeff Mutis	3	12	11.68	P-3(0-3)	A	
Charles Nagy	33	211	4.13	P-33(10-15)	B	
Rod Nichols	31	137	3.54	P-31(2-11)	B	
Steve Olin	48	56	3.36	P-48(3-6)	B	
Jesse Orosco	47	46	3.74	P-47(2-0)	B	Mil-A
Dave Otto	18	100	4.23	P-18(2-8)	Oak-A	
Tony Perezchica	17	25	.895	S-6,3-3,2-2,D-1	xSF-N	
Rudy Seanez	5	5	16.20	P-5	B	SD-N
Jeff Shaw	29	72	3.36	P-29(0-5)	B	
Joel Skinner	99	305	.584	C-99	B	C
Greg Swindell	33	238	3.48	P-33(9-16)	B	Cin-N
Eddie Taubensee	26	73	.599	C-25	A	Hou-N
Jim Thome	27	104	.665	3-27	B	
Efrain Valdez	7	6	1.50	P-7	B	C
Sergio Valdez	6	16	5.51	P-6(1-0)	B	Mon-N
Mike Walker	5	4	2.08	P-5(0-1)	B	Chi-N
Turner Ward	40	114	.600	RF-38	B	xTor-A
Mitch Webster	13	36	.325	LF-10	B	xPit-N
Mark Whiten	70	281	.734	RF-67,D-3	xTor-A	
Mike York	14	35	6.75	P-14(1-4)	Pit-N	C

Coaches: Dom Chiti, Rich Dauer, Mike Hargrove, Luis Isaac, Gordy MacKenzie, Jose Morales, Mark Wiley

♦ **1992 CLEVELAND** (162 76-86 4E) ATT: 1,224,094

Name	G	AB/IP	P/E	G/POS	From	To
Mike Hargrove				M		
Sandy Alomar	89	320	.618	C-88,D-1	B	
Jack Armstrong	35	167	4.64	P-35(6-15)	Cin-N	Fla-N
Brad Arnsberg	8	11	11.81	P-8	Tex-A	C
Carlos Baerga	161	716	.814	2-160,D-1	B	
Eric Bell	7	15	7.63	P-7(0-2)	B	Hou-N
Albert Belle	153	650	.801	D-100,LF-52	B	
Denis Boucher	8	41	6.37	P-8(2-2)	B	Mon-N
Mike Christopher	10	18	3.00	P-10	LA-N	
Alex Cole	41	109	.504	LF-24,D-4	B	xPit-N
Dennis Cook	32	158	3.82	P-32(5-7)	LA-N	
Alan Embree	4	18	7.00	P-4(0-2)	A	
Felix Fermin	79	245	.650	S-55,3-17,2-7,1-2	B	
Jose Hernandez	3	4	.000	S-3	Tex-A	Chi-N
Glenallen Hill	102	394	.724	LF-59,D-34	B	
Thomas Howard	117	387	.656	LF-97,D-2	xSD-N	
Brook Jacoby	120	327	.655	3-111,1-10	Oak-A	C
Reggie Jefferson	24	91	.835	1-15,D-7	B	
Wayne Kirby	21	21	.675	LF-2,D-4	B	
Jesse Levis	28	43	.721	C-21,D-1	A	
Mark Lewis	122	446	.662	S-121,3-1	B	
Derek Lilliquist	71	62	1.75	P-71(5-3)	SD-N	
Kenny Lofton	148	651	.727	CF-143	Hou-N	
Carlos Martinez	69	241	.665	1-37,3-28,D-4	B	
Jose Mesa	15	93	4.16	P-15(4-4)	xBal-A	
Dave Mlicki	4	22	4.98	P-4(0-2)	A	
Jeff Mutis	3	11	9.53	P-3(0-2)	B	
Charles Nagy	33	252	2.96	P-33(17-10)	B	
Rod Nichols	30	105	4.53	P-30(4-3)	B	LA-N
Steve Olin	72	88	2.34	P-72(8-5)	B	C
Junior Ortiz	86	262	.575	C-86	Min-A	
Dave Otto	18	80	7.06	P-18(5-9)	B	Pit-N
Tony Perezchica	18	24	.332	3-9,2-4,S-4,D-1	B	C
Eric Plunk	58	72	3.64	P-58(9-6)	NY-A	
Ted Power	64	99	2.54	P-64(3-3)	Cin-N	
Dave Rohde	5	9	.222	3-5	Hou-N	C
Scott Scudder	23	109	5.28	P-23(6-10)	Cin-N	
Jeff Shaw	2	8	8.22	P-2(0-1)	B	Mon-N
Paul Sorrento	140	514	.786	1-121,D-11	Min-A	
Jim Thome	40	131	.578	3-40	B	
Mark Whiten	148	588	.709	RF-144,D-2	B	StL-N
Kevin Wickander	44	41	3.07	P-44(2-0)	B	
Craig Worthington	9	26	.397	3-9	Bal-A	Cin-N

Coaches: Rick Adair, Dom Chiti, Ron Clark, Jose Morales, Dave Nelson, Jeff Newman

♦ **1993 CLEVELAND** (162 76-86 6E) ATT: 2,177,908

Name	G	AB/IP	P/E	G/POS	From	To
Mike Hargrove				M		
Paul Abbott	5	18	6.38	P-5(0-1)	Min-A	C
Sandy Alomar	64	237	.719	C-64	B	
Carlos Baerga	154	680	.847	2-150,D-4	B	
Albert Belle	159	693	.930	LF-150,D-9	B	
Mike Bielecki	13	69	5.90	P-13(4-5)	Atl-N	Atl-N
Mike Christopher	9	12	3.86	P-9	B	Det-A
Mark Clark	26	109	4.28	P-26(7-5)	StL-N	
Dennis Cook	25	54	5.67	P-25(5-5)	B	Chi-A
Jerry DiPoto	46	56	2.40	P-46(4-4)	A	
Alvaro Espinoza	129	283	.682	3-99,S-35,2-2	NY-A	
Felix Fermin	140	514	.620	S-140	B	Sea-A
Jason Grimsley	10	42	5.31	P-10(3-4)	Phi-N	
Jeremy Hernandez	49	77	3.14	P-49(6-5)	xSD-N	Fla-N
Glenallen Hill	66	191	.648	RF-39,D-18	B	xChi-N
Sam Horn	12	36	1.334	D-11	Bal-A	Tex-A
Thomas Howard	74	194	.610	RF-47,D-7	B	xCin-N
Reggie Jefferson	113	403	.682	D-88,1-15	B	Sea-A
Wayne Kirby	131	511	.698	RF-123,D-5	B	
Tom Kramer	39	121	4.02	P-39(7-3)	B	C
Jesse Levis	31	67	.406	C-29	B	
Mark Lewis	14	53	.596	S-13	B	
Derek Lilliquist	56	64	2.25	P-56(4-4)	B	
Kenny Lofton	148	657	.818	CF-146	B	
Albie Lopez	9	50	5.98	P-9(3-1)	A	
Candy Maldonado	28	94	.794	RF-26,D-2	xChi-N	
Carlos Martinez	80	285	.638	3-35,1-22,D-19	B	Cal-A
Jose Mesa	34	209	4.92	P-34(10-12)	B	

Name	G	AB/IP	P/E	G/POS	From	To
Bob Milacki	5	16	3.38	P-5(1-1)	Bal-A	KC-A
Randy Milligan	19	61	1.132	1-18,D-1	xCin-N	Mon-N
Dave Mlicki	3	13	3.38	P-3	B	NY-N
Jeff Mutis	17	81	5.78	P-17(3-6)	B	Fla-N
Charles Nagy	9	49	6.29	P-9(2-6)	B	
Bob Ojeda	9	43	4.40	P-9(2-1)	LA-N	NY-A
Junior Ortiz	95	270	.541	C-95	B	Tex-A
Lance Parrish	10	24	.733	C-10	Sea-A	Pit-N
Eric Plunk	70	71	2.79	P-70(4-5)	B	
Ted Power	20	20	7.20	P-20(0-2)	B	xSea-A
Manny Ramirez	22	55	.502	D-20,RF-1	A	
Scott Scudder	2	4	9.00	P-2(0-1)	B	C
Heathcliff Slocumb	20	27	4.28	P-20(3-1)	xChi-N	Phi-N
Paul Sorrento	148	527	.776	1-144,RF-3,D-1	B	
Julian Tavarez	8	37	6.57	P-8(2-2)	A	
Jim Thome	47	192	.870	3-47	B	
Jeff Treadway	97	240	.753	3-42,2-19,D-4	Atl-N	LA-N
Bill Wertz	34	60	3.62	P-34(2-3)	A	
Kevin Wickander	11	9	4.15	P-11	B	xCin-N
Cliff Young	21	60	4.62	P-21(3-3)	Cal-A	C
Matt Young	22	74	5.21	P-22(1-6)	Bos-A	C

Coaches: Rick Adair, Dom Chiti, Ron Clark, Jose Morales, Dave Nelson, Jeff Newman, Dan Williams

◆ **1994 CLEVELAND** (113 66-47 2C) ATT: 1,995,174

Name	G	AB/IP	P/E	G/POS	From	To
Mike Hargrove				M		
Sandy Alomar	80	320	.838	C-78	B	
Ruben Amaro	26	25	.802	CF-12,D-3	Phi-N	
Carlos Baerga	103	469	.863	2-102,D-1	B	
Brian Barnes	6	13	5.40	P-6(0-1)	Mon-N	xLA-N
Albert Belle	106	480	1.156	LF-104,D-2	B	
Larry Casian	7	8	8.64	P-7(0-2)	xMin-A	Chi-N
Mark Clark	20	127	3.82	P-20(11-3)	B	
Jerry DiPoto	7	16	8.04	P-7	B	NY-N
Alvaro Espinoza	90	244	.568	3-37,S-36,2-20,1-3	B	
Steve Farr	19	15	5.28	P-19(1-1)	NY-A	xBos-A
Rene Gonzales	22	30	1.073	3-13,1-4,S-4,2-1	Cal-A	Cal-A
Jason Grimsley	14	83	4.57	P-14(5-2)	B	
Wayne Kirby	78	207	.745	RF-68,D-2	B	
Jesse Levis	1	1	2.000	H	B	
Mark Lewis	20	76	.542	S-13,3-6,2-1	B	Cin-N
Derek Lilliquist	36	29	4.91	P-36(1-3)	B	Bos-A
Kenny Lofton	112	523	.953	CF-112	B	
Albie Lopez	4	17	4.24	P-4(1-2)	B	
Candy Maldonado	42	111	.768	D-25,LF-5	B	Tor-A
Dennis Martinez	24	177	3.52	P-24(11-6)	Mon-N	
Matt Merullo	4	13	.350	C-4	Chi-A	Min-A
Jose Mesa	51	73	3.82	P-51(7-5)	B	
Jack Morris	23	141	5.60	P-23(10-6)	Tor-A	C
Eddie Murray	108	467	.729	D-82,1-26	NY-N	
Chris Nabholz	6	11	11.45	P-6(0-1)	Mon-N	xBos-A
Charles Nagy	23	169	3.45	P-23(10-8)	B	
Chad Ogea	4	16	6.06	P-4(0-1)	A	
Tony Pena	40	126	.785	C-40	Bos-A	
Herb Perry	4	14	.496	1-2,3-2	A	
Eric Plunk	41	71	2.54	P-41(7-2)	B	
Manny Ramirez	91	336	.882	RF-84,D-5	B	

Name	G	AB/IP	P/E	G/POS	From	To
Jeff Russell	13	13	4.97	P-13(1-1)	xBos-A	Tex-A
Paul Shuey	14	12	8.49	P-14(0-1)	A	
Paul Sorrento	95	360	.802	1-86,D-8	B	
Russ Swan	12	8	11.25	P-12(0-1)	Sea-A	C
Julian Tavarez	1	2	21.60	P-1(0-1)	B	
Jim Thome	98	369	.883	3-94	B	
Matt Turner	9	13	2.13	P-9(1-0)	Fla-N	C
Omar Vizquel	69	322	.652	S-69	Sea-A	
Bill Wertz	1	4	10.38	P-1	B	C

Coaches: Buddy Bell, Luis Isaac, Charlie Manuel, Dave Nelson, Jeff Newman, Phil Regan

◆ **1995 CLEVELAND** (144 100-44 1C) ATT: 2,842,725

Name	G	AB/IP	P/E	G/POS	From	To
Mike Hargrove				M		
Sandy Alomar	66	218	.811	C-61	B	
Ruben Amaro	28	68	.573	CF-22,D-3	B	
Paul Assenmacher	47	38	2.82	P-47(6-2)	Chi-A	
Carlos Baerga	135	600	.810	2-134,D-1	B	
David Bell	2	2	.000	3-2	A	xStL-N
Albert Belle	143	629	1.094	LF-142,D-1	B	
Bud Black	11	47	6.85	P-11(4-2)	SF-N	
Jeromy Burnitz	9	7	1.286	LF-6,D-2	NY-N	
Mark Clark	22	125	5.27	P-22(9-7)	B	
Dennis Cook	11	13	6.39	P-11	Chi-A	xTex-A
Alan Embree	23	25	5.11	P-23(3-2)	B	
Alvaro Espinoza	66	150	.589	2-22,3-22,S-19,1-2,D-3	B	
John Farrell	1	5	3.86	P-1	Cal-A	
Brian Giles	6	9	1.444	RF-3,D-1	A	
Jason Grimsley	15	34	6.09	P-15	B	
Orel Hershiser	26	167	3.87	P-26(16-6)	LA-N	
Ken Hill	12	75	3.98	P-12(4-1)	xStL-N	
Wayne Kirby	101	205	.560	RF-68,D-7	B	
Jesse Levis	12	22	.813	C-12	B	
Kenny Lofton	118	529	.817	CF-114,D-2	B	
Albie Lopez	6	23	3.13	P-6	B	
Dennis Martinez	28	187	3.08	P-28(12-5)	B	
Jose Mesa	62	64	1.13	P-62(3-0)	B	
Eddie Murray	113	480	.895	D-95,1-18	B	
Charles Nagy	29	178	4.55	P-29(16-6)	B	
Chad Ogea	20	106	3.05	P-20(8-3)	B	
Gregg Olson	3	3	13.50	P-3	Atl-N	xKC-A
Tony Pena	91	279	.679	C-91	B	
Herb Perry	52	184	.843	1-45,3-1,D-6	B	
Eric Plunk	56	64	2.67	P-56(6-2)	B	
Jim Poole	42	50	3.75	P-42(3-3)	Bal-A	
Manny Ramirez	137	571	.964	RF-131,D-5	B	
Billy Ripken	8	17	1.176	2-7,3-1	Tex-A	
Joe Roa	1	6	6.00	P-1(0-1)	A	
Paul Shuey	7	6	4.26	P-7(0-2)	B	
Paul Sorrento	104	378	.850	1-91,D-11	B	
Julian Tavarez	57	85	2.44	P-57(10-2)	B	
Jim Thome	137	557	.998	3-134,D-1	B	
Eddie Tucker	17	27	.231	C-17	xHou-N	
Omar Vizquel	136	622	.689	S-136	B	
Dave Winfield	46	130	.572	D-39	Min-A	

Coaches: Buddy Bell, Luis Isaac, Charlie Manuel, Dave Nelson, Jeff Newman, Mark Wiley

CHAPTER 10

The All-Time Leaders

This section is divided into two parts: lifetime leaders and single-season leaders. Both groups command our attention and convey the pleasures of the game, which lie as much in contemplation of the past as in experiencing the present: Henry Aaron, 755; Babe Ruth, 714; Willie Mays, 660—this is no mere aggregation of names and numbers, as in a telephone directory . . . it comprises the romance and lore of the home run, and of baseball itself. Bob Gibson, 1.12, 1968; Nolan Ryan, 383; Greg Maddux, 1.56, 1994 . . . you can fill in the blanks that tell the story of pitching's most glorious seasons.

What follows are the all-time great Indians achievements, in both the traditional statistics and the new. For most categories we will give the top 20 lifetime and the top 10 single season. Some categories will be dominated by players of a certain era (for example, slugging average by batters of the 1920s and 1930s, earned run average by pitchers of 1900–1919). So, for many stats we will offer a second kind of ranking, broken down into five distinct eras of baseball, with the top five leaders in each. For example, breaking down single-season home runs this way on a major-league level would produce lists topped by these men:

> 1901–1919: Babe Ruth, 29, 1919
> 1920–1941: Babe Ruth, 60, 1927
> 1942–1960: Ralph Kiner, 54, 1949
> 1961–1976: Roger Maris, 61, 1961
> 1977–1995: George Foster, 52, 1977

To be eligible for a lifetime pitching category that is stated as an average, a man must have pitched 750 or more innings, or 375 or more innings if he is a relief pitcher, for the Indians. For a counting statistic, he must simply have attained the necessary quantity to crack the list. For a single-season category expressed as an average, he must have pitched one inning per league scheduled game or have attained the necessary quantity (wins, strikeouts, saves) to head a counted list.

To be eligible for a lifetime batting category that is stated as an average, a man must have played in 500 or more games; for counting stats such as strikeouts, a Rob Deer earned his place on the major-league list before he played his 1,000th game. For Pitcher Batting Average, the criterion is 750 innings pitched or 50 hits. And to reach the single-season batting lists, a man must have 3.1 plate appearances per scheduled game.

We provide tables of the top fielding performances, too, sorted by position as you would expect (and including only games played at the position). But we go one step further and rank several *batting* categories by position, thus recognizing and illustrating the greater demands for fielding skill at such positions as shortstop, catcher, and second base, and the comparatively plentiful supply of batting talent in the outfield and at first base. As we establish a 500-game minimum for inclusion in all but a few batting and baserunning categories, we likewise establish for these positional rankings a minimum of 500 games played at the position.

For the three principal categories—Total Player Rating, Total Pitcher Index, and Total Baseball Ranking—ties are calculated to as many decimal places as needed to break them, but averages are shown to only three places. When two or more players are tied in an averaged category with a narrow base of data, such as a season's won-lost percentage, the reader can presume a numerical dead heat. But where there is a tie for batting average, earned run average, or any of the sabermetric measures, the reader may assume that the man listed above the other(s) has the minutely higher average.

Here are the stats carried in this section that are not carried in the Registers, with definitions where the terms are not self-explanatory:

Batting, Baserunning, Fielding

Runs (Scored) Per Game   Broken down by era
Home Run Percentage   Home runs per 100 at bats
Bases on Balls Percentage   Walks (most) per 100 appearances (at bats plus walks)
At-Bats Per Strikeout   Broken down by era
Relative Batting Average   Normalized to league average
Isolated Power   Slugging average minus batting average
Extra Base Hits
Pinch Hits
Pinch Hit Batting Average
Pinch Hit Home Runs
Strikeout Percentage
Total Player Rating Per 150 Games   Highlighting the achievements of modern players and those with comparatively short careers (though at least 500 games)
Total Chances Per Game   Broken down by position
Chances Accepted Per Game   Broken down by position
Putouts   Broken down by position
Putouts Per Game   Broken down by position
Assists   Broken down by position
Assists Per Game   Broken down by position
Double Plays   Broken down by position

Pitching

Wins Above Team   How many wins a pitcher garnered beyond those expected of an average pitcher for that team; the formula is weighted so that a pitcher on a good team has a chance to compete with pitchers on poor teams who otherwise would benefit from the larger potential spread between their team's won-lost percentage and their own; see next-to-last page for more information.
Wins Above League   A pitcher's won-lost record restated by adding his Pitching Wins above the league average to the record that a league-average pitcher would have had with the same number of decisions (for example, Dennis Martinez goes 20–10 with 7 Pitching Wins; applying the 7 wins to a 15–15 mark in the same 30 decisions results in a WAL of 22–8).
Percentage of Team Wins
Relief Games
Pitchers' Batting Runs
Pitchers' Fielding Runs
Relief Wins   This statistic, like the relief stats below, includes only games in relief.
Relief Losses
Relief Innings Pitched
Relief Points   Relief wins plus saves minus losses

Games

1	Terry Turner	1619
2	Nap Lajoie	1614
3	Lou Boudreau	1560
4	Jim Hegan	1526
5	Tris Speaker	1519
6	Ken Keltner	1513
	Joe Sewell	1513
8	Earl Averill	1509
9	Charlie Jamieson	1483
10	Jack Graney	1402
11	Steve O'Neill	1365
12	Brook Jacoby	1240
13	Larry Doby	1235
14	Bill Bradley	1231
15	Andy Thornton	1225
16	Bobby Avila	1207
17	Bill Wambsganss	1170
18	Hal Trosky	1124
19	Dale Mitchell	1108
20	Rick Manning	1063

At Bats

1	Nap Lajoie	6034
2	Earl Averill	5909
3	Terry Turner	5787
4	Lou Boudreau	5754
5	Ken Keltner	5655
6	Joe Sewell	5621
7	Charlie Jamieson	5551
8	Tris Speaker	5546
9	Jack Graney	4705
10	Bill Bradley	4648
11	Jim Hegan	4459
12	Hal Trosky	4365
13	Bobby Avila	4356
14	Larry Doby	4315
15	Brook Jacoby	4314
16	Andy Thornton	4313
17	Bill Wambsganss	4191
18	Steve O'Neill	4182
19	Rick Manning	3997
20	Dale Mitchell	3960

Runs

1	Earl Averill	1154
2	Tris Speaker	1079
3	Charlie Jamieson	942
4	Nap Lajoie	865
5	Joe Sewell	857
6	Lou Boudreau	823
7	Larry Doby	808
8	Hal Trosky	758
9	Ken Keltner	735
10	Jack Graney	706
11	Terry Turner	692
12	Bobby Avila	688
13	Ray Chapman	671
14	Andy Thornton	650
15	Bill Bradley	649
16	Al Rosen	603
17	Bill Wambsganss	556
18	Dale Mitchell	552
19	Jeff Heath	546
20	Elmer Flick	535

Runs per Game (by era)

1901-1919

1	Joe Jackson	.70
2	Ray Chapman	.64
3	Harry Bay	.61
4	Elmer Flick	.57
5	Nap Lajoie	.54

1920-1941

1	Earl Averill	.76
2	Tris Speaker	.71
3	Hal Trosky	.67
4	Dick Porter	.67
5	Ed Morgan	.66

1942-1960

1	Larry Doby	.65
2	Al Smith	.65
3	Al Rosen	.58
4	Bobby Avila	.57
5	Joe Gordon	.56

1961-1976

1	George Hendrick	.52
2	Leon Wagner	.50
3	Tito Francona	.49
4	Buddy Bell	.47
5	Johnny Romano	.45

1977-1995

1	Kenny Lofton	.78
2	Brett Butler	.65
3	Toby Harrah	.62
4	Albert Belle	.62
5	Carlos Baerga	.60

Hits

1	Nap Lajoie	2046
2	Tris Speaker	1965
3	Earl Averill	1903
4	Joe Sewell	1800
5	Charlie Jamieson	1753
6	Lou Boudreau	1706
7	Ken Keltner	1561
8	Terry Turner	1472
9	Hal Trosky	1365
10	Bill Bradley	1265
11	Dale Mitchell	1237
12	Bobby Avila	1236
13	Larry Doby	1234
14	Jack Graney	1178
	Brook Jacoby	1178
16	Steve O'Neill	1109
17	Andy Thornton	1095
18	Bill Wambsganss	1083
19	Al Rosen	1063
20	Elmer Flick	1058

Doubles

1	Tris Speaker	486
2	Nap Lajoie	424
3	Earl Averill	377
4	Joe Sewell	375
5	Lou Boudreau	367
6	Ken Keltner	306
7	Charlie Jamieson	296
8	Hal Trosky	287
9	Bill Bradley	238
10	Odell Hale	235
11	George Burns	230
12	Steve O'Neill	220
13	Jack Graney	219
14	Joe Vosmik	206
15	Terry Turner	204
16	Jeff Heath	194
17	Andy Thornton	193
18	Brook Jacoby	192
19	Larry Doby	190
20	Albert Belle	185

Triples

1	Earl Averill	121
2	Tris Speaker	108
3	Elmer Flick	106
4	Joe Jackson	89
5	Jeff Heath	83
6	Ray Chapman	81
7	Jack Graney	79
8	Nap Lajoie	78
9	Terry Turner	77
10	Bill Bradley	74
	Charlie Jamieson	74
12	Ken Keltner	69
13	Lou Boudreau	65
	Joe Vosmik	65
15	Joe Sewell	63
16	Dale Mitchell	61
17	Hal Trosky	53
18	Odell Hale	51
19	Bill Wambsganss	50
20	3 players tied	45

Triples (by era)

1901-1919

1	Elmer Flick	106
2	Joe Jackson	89
3	Ray Chapman	81
4	Jack Graney	79
5	Nap Lajoie	78

1920-1941

1	Earl Averill	121
2	Tris Speaker	108
3	Jeff Heath	83
4	Charlie Jamieson	74
5	Joe Vosmik	65

1942-1960

1	Ken Keltner	69
2	Lou Boudreau	65
3	Dale Mitchell	61
4	Larry Doby	45
	Jim Hegan	45

1961-1976

1	Buddy Bell	27
2	Max Alvis	22
3	Vic Davalillo	20
4	Tito Francona	19
5	Woodie Held	16

1977-1995

1	Brett Butler	45
2	Kenny Lofton	38
3	Julio Franco	31
4	Rick Manning	29
5	Duane Kuiper	26

Home Runs

1	Earl Averill	226
2	Hal Trosky	216
3	Larry Doby	215
4	Andy Thornton	214
5	Albert Belle	194
6	Al Rosen	192
7	Rocky Colavito	190
8	Ken Keltner	163
9	Joe Carter	151
10	Woodie Held	130
11	Jeff Heath	122
12	Brook Jacoby	120
13	Cory Snyder	115
14	Max Alvis	108
15	Joe Gordon	100
16	Leon Wagner	97
17	Carlos Baerga	93
	Luke Easter	93
	Fred Whitfield	93
20	2 players tied	91

Home Runs (by era)

1901-1919

1	Elmer Smith	46
2	Nap Lajoie	34
3	Bill Bradley	26
	Charlie Hickman	26
5	Joe Jackson	24

1920-1941

1	Earl Averill	226
2	Hal Trosky	216
3	Jeff Heath	122
4	Tris Speaker	73
5	Odell Hale	72

1942-1960

1	Larry Doby	215
2	Al Rosen	192
3	Rocky Colavito	190
4	Ken Keltner	163
5	Joe Gordon	100

1961-1976

1	Woodie Held	130
2	Max Alvis	108
3	Leon Wagner	97
4	Fred Whitfield	93
5	Johnny Romano	91

1977-1995

1	Andy Thornton	214
2	Albert Belle	194
3	Joe Carter	151
4	Brook Jacoby	120
5	Cory Snyder	115

Home Run Percentage

1	Albert Belle	6.83
2	Rocky Colavito	5.97
3	Al Rosen	5.15
4	Fred Whitfield	4.98
5	Larry Doby	4.98
6	Andy Thornton	4.96
7	Hal Trosky	4.95
8	Joe Gordon	4.95
9	Duke Sims	4.87
10	Johnny Romano	4.81
11	Cory Snyder	4.73
12	Woodie Held	4.64
13	Joe Carter	4.64
14	Leon Wagner	4.43
15	George Hendrick	4.35
16	Earl Averill	3.82
17	Tony Horton	3.62
18	Jeff Heath	3.50
19	Charlie Spikes	3.35
20	Chuck Hinton	3.28

Home Run Pctg. (by era)

1901-1919

1	Elmer Smith	2.11
2	Joe Jackson	0.96
3	Nap Lajoie	0.56
4	Bill Bradley	0.56
5	Elmer Flick	0.54

1920-1941

1	Hal Trosky	4.95
2	Earl Averill	3.82
3	Jeff Heath	3.50
4	Ed Morgan	2.15
5	Odell Hale	2.01

1942-1960

1	Rocky Colavito	5.97
2	Al Rosen	5.15
3	Larry Doby	4.98
4	Joe Gordon	4.95
5	Bob Lemon	3.13

1961-1976

1	Fred Whitfield	4.98
2	Duke Sims	4.87
3	Johnny Romano	4.81
4	Woodie Held	4.64
5	Leon Wagner	4.43

1977-1995

1	Albert Belle	6.83
2	Andy Thornton	4.96
3	Cory Snyder	4.73
4	Joe Carter	4.64
5	Carlos Baerga	2.92

Total Bases

1	Earl Averill	3200
2	Tris Speaker	2886
3	Nap Lajoie	2728
4	Ken Keltner	2494
5	Hal Trosky	2406
6	Lou Boudreau	2392
7	Joe Sewell	2391
8	Charlie Jamieson	2251
9	Larry Doby	2159
10	Andy Thornton	1954
11	Terry Turner	1854
12	Al Rosen	1844
13	Brook Jacoby	1778
14	Jeff Heath	1766
15	Bill Bradley	1729
16	Bobby Avila	1706
17	Dale Mitchell	1650
18	Albert Belle	1620
19	Jack Graney	1609
20	Odell Hale	1599

Runs Batted In

1	Earl Averill	1084
2	Nap Lajoie	919
3	Hal Trosky	911
4	Tris Speaker	884
5	Joe Sewell	869
6	Ken Keltner	850
7	Larry Doby	776
8	Andy Thornton	749
9	Lou Boudreau	740
10	Al Rosen	717
11	Jeff Heath	619
12	Albert Belle	603
13	Rocky Colavito	574
14	Odell Hale	563
15	Joe Vosmik	556
16	Joe Carter	530
17	Brook Jacoby	524
18	Terry Turner	521
19	Carlos Baerga	505
20	Jim Hegan	499

Runs Batted In (by era)

1901-1919

1	Nap Lajoie	919
2	Terry Turner	521
3	Bill Bradley	473
4	Steve O'Neill	458
5	Bill Wambsganss	429

1920-1941

1	Earl Averill	1084
2	Hal Trosky	911
3	Tris Speaker	884
4	Joe Sewell	869
5	Jeff Heath	619

1942-1960

1	Ken Keltner	850
2	Larry Doby	776
3	Lou Boudreau	740
4	Al Rosen	717
5	Rocky Colavito	574

1961-1976

1	Woodie Held	401
2	Buddy Bell	386
3	Tito Francona	378
4	Max Alvis	361
5	Leon Wagner	305

1977-1995

1	Andy Thornton	749
2	Albert Belle	603
3	Joe Carter	530
4	Brook Jacoby	524
5	Carlos Baerga	505

Runs Batted In per Game

1	Hal Trosky	.81
2	Albert Belle	.80
3	Earl Averill	.72
4	Al Rosen	.69
5	Joe Vosmik	.67
6	Jeff Heath	.65
7	Joe Gordon	.63
8	Joe Carter	.63
9	Rocky Colavito	.63
10	Larry Doby	.63
11	Ed Morgan	.62
12	Carlos Baerga	.62
13	Andy Thornton	.61
14	Larry Gardner	.60
15	Johnny Hodapp	.58
16	Tris Speaker	.58
17	Joe Sewell	.57
18	Nap Lajoie	.57
19	George Burns	.57
20	Elmer Smith	.56

Walks

1	Tris Speaker	857
2	Lou Boudreau	766
3	Earl Averill	725
4	Jack Graney	712
5	Larry Doby	703
6	Andy Thornton	685
7	Joe Sewell	654
8	Charlie Jamieson	627
9	Al Rosen	587
10	Bobby Avila	527
11	Ken Keltner	511
12	Mike Hargrove	505
13	Steve O'Neill	491
14	Rocky Colavito	468
15	Ray Chapman	452
16	Hal Trosky	449
17	Jim Hegan	437
18	Terry Turner	430
19	Brook Jacoby	428
20	Nap Lajoie	408

Walk Percentage

1	Mike Hargrove	14.64
2	Larry Doby	14.01
3	Andy Thornton	13.71
4	Al Rosen	13.61
5	Toby Harrah	13.52
6	Al Smith	13.39
7	Tris Speaker	13.38
8	Jack Graney	13.14
9	Duke Sims	12.84
10	Rocky Colavito	12.81
11	Willie Kamm	12.50
12	Joe Gordon	12.09
13	Johnny Romano	12.09
14	Brett Butler	11.87
15	Ed Morgan	11.76
16	Lou Boudreau	11.75
17	George Strickland	11.41
18	Bruce Campbell	11.15
19	Woodie Held	11.14
20	Earl Averill	10.93

Strikeouts

1	Larry Doby	805
2	Brook Jacoby	738
3	Andy Thornton	683
4	Jim Hegan	664
5	Max Alvis	642
	Cory Snyder	642
7	Woodie Held	629
8	Albert Belle	535
9	Joe Carter	516
10	Rick Manning	487
11	Rocky Colavito	478
12	Ken Keltner	474
13	Earl Averill	470
14	Jeff Heath	438
15	Julio Franco	386
16	Al Rosen	385
17	Hal Trosky	373
18	Larry Brown	370
19	Pat Tabler	366
20	Tito Francona	358

At Bats per Strikeout

1	Joe Sewell	56.8
2	Dale Mitchell	34.1
3	Homer Summa	33.5
4	Vic Power	30.8
5	Frankie Pytlak	26.1
6	Charlie Jamieson	22.5
7	Joe Vosmik	21.8
8	Felix Fermin	20.2
9	Lou Boudreau	19.4
10	Johnny Hodapp	18.8
11	George Burns	18.1
12	Luke Sewell	16.3
13	Roy Weatherly	16.1
14	Willie Kamm	15.5
15	Bill Knickerbocker	15.5
16	Glenn Myatt	14.6
17	Bill Wambsganss	14.2
18	Duane Kuiper	13.8
19	Dick Porter	13.2
20	George Uhle	12.8

Batting Average

1	Joe Jackson	.375
2	Tris Speaker	.354
3	Nap Lajoie	.339
4	George Burns	.327
5	Ed Morgan	.323
6	Earl Averill	.322
7	Joe Sewell	.320
8	Johnny Hodapp	.318
9	Charlie Jamieson	.316
10	Kenny Lofton	.316
11	Joe Vosmik	.313
12	Hal Trosky	.313
13	Dale Mitchell	.312
14	Dick Porter	.308
15	Bruce Campbell	.305
16	Carlos Baerga	.305
17	Homer Summa	.303
18	Larry Gardner	.301
19	Elmer Flick	.299
20	Jeff Heath	.298

Batting Average (by era)

1901-1919

1	Joe Jackson	.375
2	Nap Lajoie	.339
3	Elmer Flick	.299
4	Elmer Smith	.281
5	Ray Chapman	.278

1920-1941

1	Tris Speaker	.354
2	George Burns	.327
3	Ed Morgan	.323
4	Earl Averill	.322
5	Joe Sewell	.320

1942-1960

1	Dale Mitchell	.312
2	Lou Boudreau	.296
3	Vic Power	.288
4	Larry Doby	.286
5	Al Rosen	.285

1961-1976

1	Tito Francona	.284
2	Vic Davalillo	.278
3	Buddy Bell	.274
4	Tony Horton	.269
5	Ray Fosse	.269

1977-1995

1	Kenny Lofton	.316
2	Carlos Baerga	.305
3	Julio Franco	.295
4	Pat Tabler	.294
5	Mike Hargrove	.292

Batting Average (by position)

Second Base

1	Nap Lajoie	.339
2	Carlos Baerga	.305
3	Bobby Avila	.284
4	Duane Kuiper	.274
5	Tony Bernazard	.264

Shortstop

1	Joe Sewell	.320
2	Lou Boudreau	.296
3	Julio Franco	.295
4	Bill Knickerbocker	.293
5	Ray Chapman	.278

Third Base

1	Larry Gardner	.301
2	Al Rosen	.285
3	Willie Kamm	.284
4	Toby Harrah	.281
5	Ken Keltner	.276

Outfield

1	Joe Jackson	.375
2	Tris Speaker	.354
3	Earl Averill	.322
4	Charlie Jamieson	.316
5	Kenny Lofton	.316
6	Joe Vosmik	.313
7	Dale Mitchell	.312
8	Dick Porter	.308
9	Homer Summa	.303
10	Elmer Flick	.299

Catcher

1	Frankie Pytlak	.286
2	Glenn Myatt	.275
3	Ron Hassey	.271
4	Ray Fosse	.269
5	Joe Azcue	.266

Relative Batting Average

1	Joe Jackson	140.4
2	Nap Lajoie	131.2
3	Tris Speaker	125.5
4	Kenny Lofton	118.4
5	Dale Mitchell	116.3
6	Elmer Flick	116.2
7	Carlos Baerga	115.3
8	Julio Franco	112.4
9	Ed Morgan	111.9
10	Pat Tabler	111.9
11	Earl Averill	111.4
12	Vic Davalillo	111.3
13	George Burns	110.9
14	Mike Hargrove	110.4
15	Lou Boudreau	110.2
16	Albert Belle	109.9
17	Vic Power	109.9
18	Brett Butler	109.6
19	Tito Francona	109.1
20	Johnny Hodapp	109.0

On Base Percentage

1	Tris Speaker	.444
2	Joe Jackson	.441
3	Ed Morgan	.405
4	Mike Hargrove	.400
5	Earl Averill	.399
6	Joe Sewell	.398
7	Larry Doby	.390
8	Charlie Jamieson	.388
	Nap Lajoie	.388
	Kenny Lofton	.388
11	Toby Harrah	.386
	Al Rosen	.386
13	Bruce Campbell	.385
14	Lou Boudreau	.382
15	Hal Trosky	.379
16	Dick Porter	.378
17	Al Smith	.376
	Joe Vosmik	.376
19	3 players tied	.375

Slugging Average

1	Albert Belle	.571
2	Hal Trosky	.551
3	Joe Jackson	.542
4	Earl Averill	.542
5	Tris Speaker	.520
6	Jeff Heath	.506
7	Larry Doby	.500
8	Al Rosen	.495
9	Rocky Colavito	.495
10	Ed Morgan	.493
11	Bruce Campbell	.478
12	Joe Carter	.472
13	Joe Gordon	.463
14	Johnny Romano	.461
15	Joe Vosmik	.459
16	Fred Whitfield	.456
17	George Burns	.455
18	Carlos Baerga	.454
19	Andy Thornton	.453
20	Nap Lajoie	.452

Production

1	Joe Jackson	.983
2	Tris Speaker	.965
3	Earl Averill	.940
4	Albert Belle	.935
5	Hal Trosky	.930
6	Ed Morgan	.898
7	Larry Doby	.890
8	Al Rosen	.882
9	Jeff Heath	.872
10	Bruce Campbell	.863
11	Rocky Colavito	.858
12	Nap Lajoie	.841
13	Joe Vosmik	.835
14	George Burns	.830
15	Kenny Lofton	.823
	Joe Sewell	.823
17	Johnny Romano	.820
18	Joe Gordon	.817
19	Andy Thornton	.813
20	2 players tied	.803

Adjusted Production

1	Joe Jackson	181
2	Tris Speaker	157
3	Nap Lajoie	155
4	Albert Belle	148
5	Elmer Flick	145
6	Larry Doby	141
7	Jeff Heath	139
8	Al Rosen	138
9	Rocky Colavito	137
10	Earl Averill	135
	Hal Trosky	135
12	Ed Morgan	126
13	Johnny Romano	124
14	Lou Boudreau	123
15	Andy Thornton	122
16	Joe Gordon	120
	Toby Harrah	120
	Kenny Lofton	120
19	Bruce Campbell	118
	Leon Wagner	118

Batting Runs

1	Tris Speaker	502
2	Nap Lajoie	393
3	Earl Averill	338
4	Joe Jackson	270
5	Larry Doby	234
6	Hal Trosky	207
7	Al Rosen	188
8	Elmer Flick	187
9	Albert Belle	182
10	Rocky Colavito	157
11	Lou Boudreau	153
12	Jeff Heath	147
13	Andy Thornton	139
14	Joe Sewell	126
15	Ed Morgan	111
16	Mike Hargrove	94
17	Toby Harrah	89
18	Ray Chapman	76
19	Rico Carty	69
20	Joe Vosmik	67

Adjusted Batting Runs

1	Tris Speaker	463
2	Nap Lajoie	387
3	Earl Averill	305
4	Joe Jackson	255
5	Larry Doby	254
6	Hal Trosky	213
7	Al Rosen	202
8	Elmer Flick	191
9	Lou Boudreau	190
10	Albert Belle	183
11	Jeff Heath	173
12	Rocky Colavito	162
13	Andy Thornton	140
14	Joe Sewell	114
15	Mike Hargrove	91
16	Ed Morgan	90
17	Toby Harrah	87
18	Ken Keltner	76
19	Dale Mitchell	75
20	Rico Carty	72

Batting Wins

1	Tris Speaker	50.3
2	Nap Lajoie	42.3
3	Earl Averill	31.2
4	Joe Jackson	28.0
5	Larry Doby	23.3
6	Elmer Flick	20.1
7	Hal Trosky	19.1
8	Al Rosen	18.7
9	Albert Belle	17.8
10	Rocky Colavito	16.3
11	Lou Boudreau	15.4
12	Jeff Heath	14.5
13	Andy Thornton	13.9
14	Joe Sewell	11.9
15	Ed Morgan	10.3
16	Mike Hargrove	9.4
17	Toby Harrah	8.9
18	Ray Chapman	8.1
19	Rico Carty	7.1
20	Charlie Hickman	6.7

Adjusted Batting Wins

1	Tris Speaker	46.4
2	Nap Lajoie	41.7
3	Earl Averill	28.1
4	Joe Jackson	26.5
5	Larry Doby	25.3
6	Elmer Flick	20.5
7	Al Rosen	20.1
8	Hal Trosky	19.7
9	Lou Boudreau	19.1
10	Albert Belle	17.9
11	Jeff Heath	17.0
12	Rocky Colavito	16.9
13	Andy Thornton	14.0
14	Joe Sewell	10.8
15	Mike Hargrove	9.1
16	Toby Harrah	8.7
17	Ed Morgan	8.4
18	Ken Keltner	7.5
19	Dale Mitchell	7.4
20	Rico Carty	7.4

Runs Created

1	Tris Speaker	1336
2	Earl Averill	1291
3	Nap Lajoie	1179
4	Joe Sewell	982
5	Lou Boudreau	957
6	Hal Trosky	923
7	Larry Doby	892
8	Charlie Jamieson	890
9	Ken Keltner	839
10	Al Rosen	729
11	Andy Thornton	718
12	Terry Turner	673
13	Jeff Heath	667
14	Elmer Flick	654
15	Bill Bradley	649
16	Joe Jackson	643
17	Bobby Avila	637
18	Dale Mitchell	620
19	Jack Graney	610
20	Ray Chapman	595

Total Average

1	Joe Jackson	1.112
2	Tris Speaker	1.061
3	Earl Averill	.977
4	Hal Trosky	.947
5	Albert Belle	.925
6	Ed Morgan	.920
7	Larry Doby	.911
8	Kenny Lofton	.896
9	Al Rosen	.875
10	Bruce Campbell	.863
11	Nap Lajoie	.859
12	Jeff Heath	.852
13	Elmer Flick	.847
14	Rocky Colavito	.840
15	Toby Harrah	.812
16	Joe Vosmik	.811
17	Joe Sewell	.801
18	Johnny Romano	.797
19	Andy Thornton	.794
20	Joe Gordon	.788

Runs Produced

1	Earl Averill	2012
2	Tris Speaker	1890
3	Nap Lajoie	1750
4	Joe Sewell	1696
5	Lou Boudreau	1500
6	Hal Trosky	1453
7	Ken Keltner	1422
8	Charlie Jamieson	1416
9	Larry Doby	1369
10	Terry Turner	1205
11	Andy Thornton	1185
12	Al Rosen	1128
13	Jack Graney	1108
14	Bill Bradley	1096
15	Bobby Avila	1056
16	Jeff Heath	1043
17	Odell Hale	1024
18	Ray Chapman	1018
19	Joe Vosmik	992
20	Bill Wambsganss	979

Clutch Hitting Index

1	Larry Gardner	134
2	Ron Hassey	124
3	George Uhle	119
4	Mike Hargrove	116
	Rube Lutzke	116
	Pat Tabler	116
7	Elmer Smith	115
8	Joe Azcue	113
	Mel Hall	113
	Nap Lajoie	113
11	Harry Bemis	112
12	Julio Franco	111
	Willie Kamm	111
14	Luke Sewell	110
	Joe Sewell	110
16	Glenn Myatt	109
17	Carlos Baerga	108
	George Burns	108
	Steve O'Neill	108
	Joe Vosmik	108

Isolated Power

1	Albert Belle	.279
2	Hal Trosky	.238
3	Rocky Colavito	.227
4	Earl Averill	.219
5	Larry Doby	.214
6	Al Rosen	.210
7	Jeff Heath	.208
8	Joe Carter	.203
9	Joe Gordon	.201
10	Andy Thornton	.199
11	Fred Whitfield	.199
12	Johnny Romano	.198
13	Cory Snyder	.196
14	Woodie Held	.188
15	Duke Sims	.184
16	George Hendrick	.176
17	Bruce Campbell	.173
18	Leon Wagner	.171
19	Ed Morgan	.170
20	Tony Horton	.169

Pinch Hits

1	Dale Mitchell	41
2	Glenn Myatt	40
3	Chuck Hinton	36
4	Don Dillard	31
5	Bob Lemon	31

Pinch Hit Average
(75 at-bats minimum)

1	Bibb Falk	.346
2	Don Dillard	.326
3	Jack Graney	.315
4	Bob Lemon	.284
5	George Uhle	.283

Pinch Hit Home Runs

1	Fred Whitfield	8
2	Gene Green	4
3	Ted Uhlaender	3
	Ron Kittle	3

Total Player Rating / 150g

1	Nap Lajoie	6.12
2	Joe Jackson	5.36
3	Tris Speaker	4.48
4	Lou Boudreau	3.98
5	Kenny Lofton	3.65
6	Albert Belle	3.62
7	Joe Sewell	3.18
8	Rocky Colavito	2.43
9	Larry Doby	2.40
10	Carlos Baerga	2.29
11	Elmer Flick	2.28
12	Ray Chapman	2.20
13	Brett Butler	2.09
14	Earl Averill	1.96
15	Jeff Heath	1.80
16	Al Rosen	1.78
17	Bill Bradley	1.24
18	Mike Hargrove	1.23
19	Hal Trosky	1.23
20	Woodie Held	1.21

Stolen Bases

1	Terry Turner	254
2	Kenny Lofton	250
3	Nap Lajoie	240
4	Ray Chapman	233
5	Elmer Flick	207
6	Harry Bay	165
7	Brett Butler	164
8	Bill Bradley	157
9	Tris Speaker	151
10	Jack Graney	148
11	Rick Manning	142
12	Joe Jackson	138
13	Julio Franco	131
14	Joe Carter	126
15	Bill Wambsganss	122
16	George Stovall	110
17	Joe Birmingham	108
18	Charlie Jamieson	107
19	Doc Johnston	89
20	Toby Harrah	82

Stolen Base Average

1	Kenny Lofton	82.5
2	Joe Carter	79.2
3	Toby Harrah	76.6
4	Frankie Pytlak	69.9
5	Julio Franco	69.3
6	Rick Manning	68.3
7	Vic Davalillo	64.3
8	George Burns	62.0
9	Bobby Avila	59.1
10	John Lowenstein	56.7

Stolen Base Runs

1	Kenny Lofton	43
2	Joe Carter	18
3	Toby Harrah	10
4	Carlos Baerga	6
5	Julio Franco	5
	Leon Wagner	5
7	Rick Manning	3
8	Tito Francona	2
	Frankie Pytlak	2

Stolen Base Wins

1	Kenny Lofton	4.2
2	Joe Carter	1.8
3	Toby Harrah	1.0
4	Carlos Baerga	0.6
5	Leon Wagner	0.5
6	Julio Franco	0.5
7	Rick Manning	0.3
8	Tito Francona	0.2
9	Frankie Pytlak	0.2

Games

First Base

1	Hal Trosky	1111
2	George Stovall	802
3	Mike Hargrove	769
4	Doc Johnston	698
5	George Burns	681

Second Base

1	Nap Lajoie	1385
2	Bobby Avila	1098
3	Bill Wambsganss	938
4	Duane Kuiper	774
5	Ray Mack	767

Shortstop

1	Lou Boudreau	1486
2	Joe Sewell	1216
3	Ray Chapman	957
4	Frank Duffy	797
5	Terry Turner	722

Third Base

1	Ken Keltner	1492
2	Bill Bradley	1193
3	Brook Jacoby	1109
4	Max Alvis	935
5	Al Rosen	932

Outfield

1	Earl Averill	1483
2	Tris Speaker	1475
3	Charlie Jamieson	1386
4	Jack Graney	1282
5	Larry Doby	1165
6	Rick Manning	1051
7	Dale Mitchell	929
8	Elmer Flick	911
9	Jeff Heath	892
10	Rocky Colavito	871

Catcher

1	Jim Hegan	1491
2	Steve O'Neill	1339
3	Luke Sewell	944
4	Glenn Myatt	654
5	Frankie Pytlak	598

Pitcher

1	Mel Harder	582
2	Bob Feller	570
3	Willis Hudlin	475
4	Bob Lemon	460
5	Gary Bell	419

Fielding Average

First Base

1	Mike Hargrove	.993
2	Hal Trosky	.990
3	Doc Johnston	.989
4	George Burns	.988
5	George Stovall	.986

Second Base

1	Duane Kuiper	.984
2	Bobby Avila	.979
3	Tony Bernazard	.977
4	Joe Gordon	.975
5	Carlos Baerga	.975

Shortstop

1	Frank Duffy	.979
2	Lou Boudreau	.973
3	Felix Fermin	.971
4	George Strickland	.969
5	Larry Brown	.964

Third Base

1	Willie Kamm	.969
2	Ken Keltner	.965
3	Toby Harrah	.963
4	Al Rosen	.961
5	Terry Turner	.961

Outfield

1	Brett Butler	.993
2	George Hendrick	.987
3	Bob Kennedy	.986
4	Vic Davalillo	.986
5	Rick Manning	.986
6	Tito Francona	.985
7	Dale Mitchell	.985
8	Larry Doby	.983
9	Cory Snyder	.983
10	Joe Vosmik	.981

Extra Base Hits

1	Earl Averill	724
2	Tris Speaker	667
3	Hal Trosky	556
4	Ken Keltner	538
5	Nap Lajoie	536
6	Lou Boudreau	495
7	Joe Sewell	468
8	Larry Doby	450
9	Andy Thornton	419
10	Jeff Heath	399
11	Albert Belle	392
12	Charlie Jamieson	388
13	Al Rosen	377
14	Odell Hale	358
15	Bill Bradley	338
16	Joe Carter	337
17	Brook Jacoby	336
18	Rocky Colavito	335
19	Jack Graney	316
20	Joe Vosmik	315

Catcher

1	Ron Hassey	.994
2	Joe Azcue	.994
3	Frankie Pytlak	.991
4	Johnny Romano	.990
5	Jim Hegan	.990

Pitcher
1. Mike Garcia .... .978
2. Stan Coveleski .... .976
3. Bob Lemon .... .969
4. Early Wynn .... .968
5. Bob Rhoads .... .965

Total Chances per Game

First Base
1. George Stovall 11.46
2. George Burns 10.19
3. Doc Johnston 10.09
4. Hal Trosky 9.77
5. Mike Hargrove 8.81

Second Base
1. Nap Lajoie 5.90
2. Bill Wambsganss 5.70
3. Carlos Baerga 5.43
4. Ray Mack 5.40
5. Bobby Avila 5.26

Shortstop
1. Ray Chapman 5.74
2. Joe Sewell 5.64
3. Terry Turner 5.45
4. Bill Knickerbocker 5.35
5. Lou Boudreau 5.30

Third Base
1. Rube Lutzke 3.64
2. Bill Bradley 3.55
3. Larry Gardner 3.35
4. Terry Turner 3.35
5. Buddy Bell 3.31

Outfield
1. Brett Butler 2.95
2. Rick Manning 2.86
3. Tris Speaker 2.82
4. Kenny Lofton 2.77
5. Earl Averill 2.71
6. Larry Doby 2.65
7. Joe Carter 2.50
8. Roy Weatherly 2.46
9. George Hendrick 2.40
10. Joe Birmingham 2.37

Catcher
1. Joe Azcue 7.25
2. Ray Fosse 6.75
3. Johnny Romano 6.06
4. Harry Bemis 5.51
5. Ron Hassey 5.45

Pitcher
1. Addie Joss 3.60
2. Bill Bernhard 3.14
3. Bob Rhoads 2.94
4. Stan Coveleski 2.42
5. Bob Lemon 2.19

Chances Accepted per Game

First Base
1. George Stovall 11.29
2. George Burns 10.07
3. Doc Johnston 9.97
4. Hal Trosky 9.68
5. Mike Hargrove 8.75

Second Base
1. Nap Lajoie 5.70
2. Bill Wambsganss 5.45
3. Carlos Baerga 5.29
4. Ray Mack 5.22
5. Bobby Avila 5.15

Shortstop
1. Ray Chapman 5.39
2. Joe Sewell 5.37
3. Terry Turner 5.19
4. Lou Boudreau 5.16
5. Bill Knickerbocker 5.11

Third Base
1. Rube Lutzke 3.44
2. Bill Bradley 3.34
3. Terry Turner 3.22
4. Larry Gardner 3.20
5. Buddy Bell 3.17

Outfield
1. Brett Butler 2.93
2. Rick Manning 2.82
3. Tris Speaker 2.76
4. Kenny Lofton 2.71
5. Earl Averill 2.63
6. Larry Doby 2.60
7. Joe Carter 2.45
8. Roy Weatherly 2.40
9. George Hendrick 2.37
10. Joe Vosmik 2.32

Catcher
1. Joe Azcue 7.20
2. Ray Fosse 6.65
3. Johnny Romano 6.00
4. Ron Hassey 5.41
5. Harry Bemis 5.32

Putouts

First Base
1. Hal Trosky 10085
2. George Stovall 8498
3. Doc Johnston 6578
4. George Burns 6371
5. Mike Hargrove 6158

Second Base
1. Nap Lajoie 3641
2. Bobby Avila 2689
3. Bill Wambsganss 2265
4. Ray Mack 1839
5. Duane Kuiper 1733

Shortstop
1. Lou Boudreau 3052
2. Joe Sewell 2591
3. Ray Chapman 2204
4. Terry Turner 1352
5. Frank Duffy 1229

Third Base
1. Ken Keltner 1568
2. Bill Bradley 1488
3. Al Rosen 970
4. Max Alvis 947
5. Buddy Bell 752

Outfield
1. Tris Speaker 3837
2. Earl Averill 3784
3. Charlie Jamieson 3011
4. Larry Doby 2947
5. Rick Manning 2892
6. Jack Graney 2488
7. Dale Mitchell 1903
8. Jeff Heath 1890
9. Joe Vosmik 1806
10. Brett Butler 1712

Catcher
1. Jim Hegan 6959
2. Steve O'Neill 5313
3. Joe Azcue 3757
4. Ray Fosse 3508
5. Luke Sewell 3206

Pitcher
1. Bob Lemon 263
2. Mel Harder 209
3. Stan Coveleski 153
4. Willis Hudlin 149
5. Bob Feller 146
   Addie Joss 146

Putouts per Game

First Base
1. George Stovall 10.60
2. Doc Johnston 9.43
3. George Burns 9.36
4. Hal Trosky 9.08
5. Mike Hargrove 8.01

Second Base
1. Nap Lajoie 2.63
2. Bobby Avila 2.45
3. Bill Wambsganss 2.42
4. Ray Mack 2.40
5. Duane Kuiper 2.24

Shortstop
1. Ray Chapman 2.31
2. Joe Sewell 2.14
3. Lou Boudreau 2.06
4. Bill Knickerbocker 1.92
5. Terry Turner 1.88

Third Base
1. Bill Bradley 1.25
2. Rube Lutzke 1.23
3. Terry Turner 1.14
4. Willie Kamm 1.09
5. Ken Keltner 1.06

Outfield
1. Brett Butler 2.85
2. Rick Manning 2.76
3. Kenny Lofton 2.62
4. Tris Speaker 2.61
5. Earl Averill 2.56
6. Larry Doby 2.53
7. Joe Carter 2.38
8. Roy Weatherly 2.32
9. George Hendrick 2.30
10. Joe Vosmik 2.24

Catcher
1. Joe Azcue 6.70
2. Ray Fosse 6.08
3. Johnny Romano 5.59
4. Ron Hassey 4.97
5. Jim Hegan 4.67

Pitcher
1. Bob Lemon 0.58
2. Addie Joss 0.52
3. Stan Coveleski 0.43
4. George Uhle 0.40
5. Jim Bagby 0.39
6. Bob Rhoads 0.39

Assists

First Base
1. Hal Trosky 662
2. Mike Hargrove 564
3. George Stovall 556
4. George Burns 481
5. Doc Johnston 379

Second Base
1. Nap Lajoie 4243
2. Bobby Avila 2965
3. Bill Wambsganss 2844
4. Ray Mack 2158
5. Duane Kuiper 2136

Shortstop
1. Lou Boudreau 4606
2. Joe Sewell 3933
3. Ray Chapman 2950
4. Terry Turner 2389
5. Frank Duffy 2337

Third Base
1. Ken Keltner 3060
2. Bill Bradley 2489
3. Brook Jacoby 1980
4. Buddy Bell 1918
5. Al Rosen 1773

Outfield
1. Tris Speaker 222
2. Charlie Jamieson 160
3. Jack Graney 151
4. Joe Birmingham 130
5. Joe Jackson 111
6. Earl Averill 108
7. Elmer Flick 105
8. Larry Doby 79
9. Homer Summa 72
10. Harry Bay 68

Catcher
1. Steve O'Neill 1535
2. Luke Sewell 698
3. Jim Hegan 642
4. Harry Bemis 626
5. Glenn Myatt 374

Pitcher
1. Addie Joss 845
2. Mel Harder 734
3. Willis Hudlin 720
4. Bob Lemon 709
5. Stan Coveleski 695

Assists per Game

First Base
1. Mike Hargrove 0.74
2. George Burns 0.71
3. George Stovall 0.70
4. Hal Trosky 0.60
5. Doc Johnston 0.55

Second Base
1. Carlos Baerga 3.12
2. Nap Lajoie 3.07
3. Bill Wambsganss 3.04
4. Joe Gordon 2.95
5. Tony Bernazard 2.84

Shortstop
1. Terry Turner 3.31
2. Joe Sewell 3.24
3. Bill Knickerbocker 3.19
4. Lou Boudreau 3.10
5. Ray Chapman 3.09

Third Base
1. Buddy Bell 2.28
2. Rube Lutzke 2.21
3. Larry Gardner 2.16
4. Bill Bradley 2.09
5. Terry Turner 2.09

Outfield
1. Joe Birmingham 0.19
2. Joe Jackson 0.18
3. Tris Speaker 0.16
4. Elmer Flick 0.12
5. Jack Graney 0.12
6. Charlie Jamieson 0.12
7. Harry Bay 0.11
8. Elmer Smith 0.11
9. Cory Snyder 0.11
10. Kenny Lofton 0.10
11. Homer Summa 0.10

Catcher
1. Steve O'Neill 1.15
2. Harry Bemis 1.07
3. Luke Sewell 0.74
4. Frankie Pytlak 0.59
5. Glenn Myatt 0.58

Pitcher
1. Addie Joss 2.96
2. Bill Bernhard 2.61
3. Bob Rhoads 2.45
4. Stan Coveleski 1.94
5. Bob Lemon 1.55

Double Plays

First Base
1. Hal Trosky 961
2. Mike Hargrove 611
3. George Burns 497
4. George Stovall 457
5. Doc Johnston 383

Second Base
1. Bobby Avila 754
2. Nap Lajoie 701
3. Ray Mack 582
4. Duane Kuiper 496
5. Carlos Baerga 482

Shortstop
1. Lou Boudreau 1135
2. Joe Sewell 665
3. Frank Duffy 470
4. Julio Franco 437
5. Felix Fermin 362

Third Base
1. Ken Keltner 306
2. Buddy Bell 182
3. Bill Bradley 160
4. Al Rosen 159
5. Brook Jacoby 158

Outfield
1. Tris Speaker 69
2. Joe Birmingham 38
3. Jack Graney 34
4. Earl Averill 29
5. Charlie Jamieson 28
6. Elmer Flick 26
7. Larry Doby 22
8. Joe Jackson 20
   Homer Summa 20
10. Harry Bay 19
   Elmer Smith 19

Catcher
1. Steve O'Neill 175
2. Jim Hegan 126
3. Luke Sewell 79
4. Frankie Pytlak 57
5. Ray Fosse 47

Pitcher
1. Bob Lemon 78
2. Willis Hudlin 54
3. Mel Harder 38
4. George Uhle 34
5. Stan Coveleski 32

Fielding Runs

1	Nap Lajoie	252
2	Jim Hegan	137
3	Lou Boudreau	135
4	Tris Speaker	110
5	Joe Sewell	105
6	Buddy Bell	79
7	Rick Manning	77
8	Graig Nettles	75
9	Bob Lemon	62
10	Brett Butler	60
11	Mike Fischlin	59
12	Vic Power	55
13	Joe Birmingham	46
14	Odell Hale	44
	George Strickland	44
16	Rube Lutzke	42
17	Vic Davalillo	41
18	Carlos Baerga	39
	Kenny Lofton	39
20	Ken Keltner	37

Fielding Runs (by position)

First Base

1	Mike Hargrove	31
2	George Stovall	29
3	George Burns	16
4	Hal Trosky	4

Second Base

1	Nap Lajoie	250
2	Carlos Baerga	43
3	Bill Wambsganss	16

Shortstop

1	Lou Boudreau	137
2	Joe Sewell	83
3	Frank Duffy	35
4	George Strickland	26
5	Ray Chapman	24

Third Base

1	Buddy Bell	73
2	Rube Lutzke	43
3	Bill Bradley	37
	Ken Keltner	37
5	Terry Turner	22

Outfield

1	Tris Speaker	109
2	Rick Manning	76
3	Brett Butler	60
4	Joe Birmingham	44
	Cory Snyder	44
6	Vic Davalillo	42
7	Kenny Lofton	39
8	Rocky Colavito	37
9	Joe Vosmik	35
10	Albert Belle	30

Catcher

1	Jim Hegan	138
2	Ray Fosse	26
3	Luke Sewell	23
4	Ron Hassey	19
5	Joe Azcue	12

Pitcher

1	Bob Lemon	59
2	Willis Hudlin	42
3	Addie Joss	30
4	Mel Harder	19
5	Stan Coveleski	15

Fielding Wins

1	Nap Lajoie	27.1
2	Jim Hegan	13.7
3	Lou Boudreau	13.6
4	Tris Speaker	11.0
5	Joe Sewell	10.0
6	Buddy Bell	8.2
7	Graig Nettles	8.1
8	Rick Manning	7.8
9	Bob Lemon	6.2
10	Mike Fischlin	5.9
11	Brett Butler	5.9
12	Vic Power	5.6
13	Joe Birmingham	4.9
14	George Strickland	4.4
15	Vic Davalillo	4.4
16	Odell Hale	4.0
17	Rube Lutzke	4.0
18	Carlos Baerga	3.8
19	Kenny Lofton	3.8
20	Terry Turner	3.7

Total Player Rating

1	Nap Lajoie	65.9
2	Tris Speaker	45.4
3	Lou Boudreau	41.4
4	Joe Sewell	32.1
5	Joe Jackson	24.1
6	Larry Doby	19.8
7	Earl Averill	19.7
8	Albert Belle	18.2
9	Ray Chapman	15.4
10	Rocky Colavito	14.8
11	Elmer Flick	14.2
12	Kenny Lofton	12.8
13	Carlos Baerga	12.5
14	Al Rosen	12.4
15	Ken Keltner	11.8
16	Jeff Heath	11.5
17	Bill Bradley	10.2
18	Hal Trosky	9.2
19	Graig Nettles	9.0
20	Brett Butler	8.5
21	Andy Thornton	8.3
22	Mike Hargrove	7.3
23	Odell Hale	7.2
24	Woodie Held	6.9
25	Minnie Minoso	6.7
26	Bobby Avila	5.8
27	Rico Carty	5.6
28	Buddy Bell	5.4
29	Charlie Hickman	5.0
30	Roy Cullenbine	4.9
31	Steve O'Neill	4.5
	Johnny Romano	4.5
33	Mike Fischlin	4.4
	Johnny Hodapp	4.4
35	Les Fleming	4.1
	Joe Harris	4.1
37	Joe Azcue	3.8
38	Ray Fosse	3.7
	Riggs Stephenson	3.7
40	Joe Vosmik	3.6
41	Jerry Dybzinski	3.5
	Jim Hegan	3.5
	Duke Sims	3.5
44	Ron Hassey	3.4
45	Nig Clarke	3.3
	Joe Gordon	3.3
47	Oscar Gamble	3.2
48	Vic Wertz	2.8
49	Willie Kamm	2.7
	Jim Thome	2.7

Total Player Rating (alpha.)

Earl Averill	19.7
Bobby Avila	5.8
Joe Azcue	3.8
Carlos Baerga	12.5
Buddy Bell	5.4
Albert Belle	18.2
Lou Boudreau	41.4
Bill Bradley	10.2
Brett Butler	8.5
Rico Carty	5.6
Ray Chapman	15.4
Nig Clarke	3.3
Rocky Colavito	14.8
Roy Cullenbine	4.9
Larry Doby	19.8
Jerry Dybzinski	3.5
Mike Fischlin	4.4
Les Fleming	4.1
Elmer Flick	14.2
Ray Fosse	3.7
Oscar Gamble	3.2
Joe Gordon	3.3
Odell Hale	7.2
Mike Hargrove	7.3
Joe Harris	4.1
Ron Hassey	3.4
Jeff Heath	11.5
Jim Hegan	3.5
Woodie Held	6.9
Charlie Hickman	5.0
Johnny Hodapp	4.4
Joe Jackson	24.1
Willie Kamm	2.7
Ken Keltner	11.8
Nap Lajoie	65.9
Kenny Lofton	12.8
Minnie Minoso	6.7
Graig Nettles	9.0
Steve O'Neill	4.5
Johnny Romano	4.5
Al Rosen	12.4
Joe Sewell	32.1
Duke Sims	3.5
Tris Speaker	45.4
Riggs Stephenson	3.7
Jim Thome	2.7
Andy Thornton	8.3
Hal Trosky	9.2
Joe Vosmik	3.6
Vic Wertz	2.8

Total Player Rating (by era)

1901-1919

1	Nap Lajoie	65.9
2	Joe Jackson	24.1
3	Ray Chapman	15.4
4	Elmer Flick	14.2
5	Bill Bradley	10.2

1920-1941

1	Tris Speaker	45.4
2	Joe Sewell	32.1
3	Earl Averill	19.7
4	Jeff Heath	11.5
5	Hal Trosky	9.2

1942-1960

1	Lou Boudreau	41.4
2	Larry Doby	19.8
3	Rocky Colavito	14.8
4	Al Rosen	12.4
5	Ken Keltner	11.8

1961-1976

1	Graig Nettles	9.0
2	Woodie Held	6.9
3	Rico Carty	5.6
4	Buddy Bell	5.4
5	Johnny Romano	4.5

1977-1995

1	Albert Belle	18.2
2	Kenny Lofton	12.8
3	Carlos Baerga	12.5
4	Brett Butler	8.5
5	Andy Thornton	8.3

Wins

1	Bob Feller	266
2	Mel Harder	223
3	Bob Lemon	207
4	Stan Coveleski	172
5	Early Wynn	164
6	Addie Joss	160
7	Willis Hudlin	157
8	George Uhle	147
9	Mike Garcia	142
10	Jim Bagby	122
	Sam McDowell	122
12	Wes Ferrell	102
13	Guy Morton	98
14	Gary Bell	96
15	Bob Rhoads	88
16	Earl Moore	81
17	Steve Gromek	78
	Joe Shaute	78
19	Bill Bernhard	77
20	Luis Tiant	75

Losses

1	Mel Harder	186
2	Bob Feller	162
3	Willis Hudlin	151
4	Bob Lemon	128
5	Stan Coveleski	123
6	George Uhle	119
7	Sam McDowell	109
8	Early Wynn	102
9	Addie Joss	97
10	Mike Garcia	96
11	Gary Bell	92
12	Guy Morton	88
	Joe Shaute	88
14	Jim Bagby	85
15	Rick Waits	84
16	Willie Mitchell	76
17	Steve Hargan	74
18	Earl Moore	68
19	3 players tied	67

Winning Percentage

1	Vean Gregg	.667
2	Johnny Allen	.663
3	Addie Joss	.623
4	Wes Ferrell	.622
5	Bob Feller	.621
6	Bob Lemon	.618
7	Early Wynn	.617
8	Mike Garcia	.597
9	Jim Bagby	.589
10	Stan Coveleski	.583
11	Cy Falkenberg	.582
12	Bill Bernhard	.579
13	Bob Rhoads	.571
14	Bert Blyleven	.565
15	Sonny Siebert	.560
16	George Uhle	.553
17	Gaylord Perry	.551
18	Oral Hildebrand	.549
19	Mel Harder	.545
20	Earl Moore	.544

Games

1	Mel Harder	582
2	Bob Feller	570
3	Willis Hudlin	475
4	Bob Lemon	460
5	Gary Bell	419
6	Mike Garcia	397
7	Stan Coveleski	360
8	George Uhle	357
9	Early Wynn	343
10	Sam McDowell	336
11	Guy Morton	317
12	Steve Gromek	309
13	Jim Bagby	290
	Dan Spillner	290
15	Addie Joss	286
16	Doug Jones	272
17	Sid Monge	255
18	Joe Shaute	252
19	Clint Brown	237
20	Rick Waits	235

Games Started

1	Bob Feller	484
2	Mel Harder	433
3	Bob Lemon	350
4	Willis Hudlin	320
5	Stan Coveleski	305
6	Early Wynn	296
7	Sam McDowell	295
8	Mike Garcia	281
9	George Uhle	267
10	Addie Joss	260
11	Jim Bagby	201
12	Rick Waits	187
13	Guy Morton	185
14	Joe Shaute	175
15	Tom Candiotti	172
16	Gary Bell	169
17	Mudcat Grant	165
18	Bob Rhoads	160
	Luis Tiant	160
20	Wes Ferrell	157

Games Started (by era)

1901-1919

1	Addie Joss	260
2	Jim Bagby	201
3	Guy Morton	185
4	Bob Rhoads	160
5	Earl Moore	151

1920-1941

1	Mel Harder	433
2	Willis Hudlin	320
3	Stan Coveleski	305
4	George Uhle	267
5	Joe Shaute	175

1942-1960

1	Bob Feller	484
2	Bob Lemon	350
3	Early Wynn	296
4	Mike Garcia	281
5	Al Smith	147

1961-1976

1	Sam McDowell	295
2	Gary Bell	169
3	Mudcat Grant	165
4	Luis Tiant	160
5	Jim Perry	153

1977-1995

1	Rick Waits	187
2	Tom Candiotti	172
3	Greg Swindell	152
4	Charles Nagy	135
5	Len Barker	134

Complete Games

1	Bob Feller	279
2	Addie Joss	234
3	Stan Coveleski	194
4	Bob Lemon	188
5	Mel Harder	181
6	George Uhle	166
7	Willis Hudlin	154
8	Early Wynn	144
9	Earl Moore	137
10	Jim Bagby	131
11	Bob Rhoads	130
12	Bill Bernhard	118
13	Wes Ferrell	113
14	Mike Garcia	111
15	Sam McDowell	97
16	Gaylord Perry	96
	Joe Shaute	96
18	Guy Morton	82
19	Otto Hess	81
20	Vean Gregg	77

Complete Games (by era)

1901-1919

1	Addie Joss	234
2	Earl Moore	137
3	Jim Bagby	131
4	Bob Rhoads	130
5	Bill Bernhard	118

1920-1941

1	Stan Coveleski	194
2	Mel Harder	181
3	George Uhle	166
4	Willis Hudlin	154
5	Wes Ferrell	113

1942-1960

1	Bob Feller	279
2	Bob Lemon	188
3	Early Wynn	144
4	Mike Garcia	111
5	Al Smith	60

1961-1976

1	Sam McDowell	97
2	Gaylord Perry	96
3	Luis Tiant	63
4	Gary Bell	53
5	Mudcat Grant	50

1977-1995

1	Rick Waits	47
2	Tom Candiotti	45
3	Bert Blyleven	41
4	Len Barker	33
5	Greg Swindell	32

Shutouts

1	Addie Joss	45
2	Bob Feller	44
3	Stan Coveleski	31
	Bob Lemon	31
5	Mike Garcia	27
6	Mel Harder	25
7	Early Wynn	24
8	Sam McDowell	22
9	Luis Tiant	21
10	Guy Morton	19
	Bob Rhoads	19
12	Gaylord Perry	17
13	Jim Bagby	16
	George Uhle	16
15	Otto Hess	15
	Earl Moore	15
17	Steve Hargan	13
	Jim Perry	13
19	Bill Bernhard	12
20	3 players tied	11

Saves

1	Doug Jones	128
2	Ray Narleski	53
3	Jose Mesa	48
	Steve Olin	48
5	Jim Kern	46
	Sid Monge	46
7	Gary Bell	45
8	Ernie Camacho	44
9	Dave LaRoche	42
10	Dan Spillner	41
11	Joe Heving	32
	Don Mossi	32
13	Willis Hudlin	31
14	Ed Klieman	30
15	Don McMahon	28
16	Jim Bagby	26
17	Tom Buskey	25
18	Eric Plunk	24
19	Ted Abernathy	23
	Mel Harder	23

Innings Pitched

1	Bob Feller	3827.0
2	Mel Harder	3426.1
3	Bob Lemon	2850.0
4	Willis Hudlin	2557.2
5	Stan Coveleski	2502.1
6	Addie Joss	2327.0
7	Early Wynn	2286.2
8	George Uhle	2200.1
9	Mike Garcia	2138.0
10	Sam McDowell	2109.2
11	Jim Bagby	1735.2
12	Guy Morton	1629.2
13	Gary Bell	1550.1
14	Joe Shaute	1447.0
15	Bob Rhoads	1444.2
16	Steve Gromek	1340.2
17	Earl Moore	1337.2
18	Wes Ferrell	1321.1
19	Willie Mitchell	1301.1
20	Rick Waits	1276.0

Innings Pitched (by era)

1901-1919

1	Addie Joss	2327.0
2	Jim Bagby	1735.2
3	Guy Morton	1629.2
4	Bob Rhoads	1444.2
5	Earl Moore	1337.2

1920-1941

1	Mel Harder	3426.1
2	Willis Hudlin	2557.2
3	Stan Coveleski	2502.1
4	George Uhle	2200.1
5	Joe Shaute	1447.0

1942-1960

1	Bob Feller	3827.0
2	Bob Lemon	2850.0
3	Early Wynn	2286.2
4	Mike Garcia	2138.0
5	Steve Gromek	1340.2

1961-1976

1	Sam McDowell	2109.2
2	Gary Bell	1550.1
3	Mudcat Grant	1214.2
4	Luis Tiant	1200.0
5	Jim Perry	1131.2

1977-1995

1	Rick Waits	1276.0
2	Tom Candiotti	1187.0
3	Greg Swindell	1043.0
4	Len Barker	932.1
5	Charles Nagy	905.0

Hits per Game

1	Sam McDowell	6.84
2	Sonny Siebert	6.95
3	Luis Tiant	7.04
4	Addie Joss	7.30
5	Gaylord Perry	7.31
6	Vean Gregg	7.61
7	Bob Feller	7.69
8	Gary Bell	7.84
9	Allie Reynolds	7.87
10	Otto Hess	8.00
11	Willie Mitchell	8.01
12	Early Wynn	8.02
13	Earl Moore	8.05
14	Mudcat Grant	8.08
15	Bob Lemon	8.08
16	Steve Gromek	8.12
17	Bert Blyleven	8.14
18	Steve Hargan	8.15
19	Bob Rhoads	8.22
20	Cy Falkenberg	8.34

Home Runs Allowed

1	Bob Feller	224
2	Bob Lemon	181
	Early Wynn	181
4	Gary Bell	167
5	Mudcat Grant	166
6	Mel Harder	161
7	Sam McDowell	138
8	Luis Tiant	126
9	Mike Garcia	119
10	Jim Perry	113
11	Greg Swindell	109
12	Willis Hudlin	108
13	Tom Candiotti	100
14	Rick Waits	99
15	Gaylord Perry	92
16	Steve Gromek	89
17	Sonny Siebert	84
18	Steve Hargan	78
19	Charles Nagy	74
20	Cal McLish	67

Home Runs Allowed (by era)

1901-1919

1	Jim Bagby	39
2	Guy Morton	27
3	Earl Moore	21
4	Addie Joss	19
5	2 players tied	15

1920-1941

1	Mel Harder	161
2	Willis Hudlin	108
3	Clint Brown	59
4	George Uhle	58
5	Wes Ferrell	55

1942-1960

1	Bob Feller	224
2	Bob Lemon	181
	Early Wynn	181
4	Mike Garcia	119
5	Steve Gromek	89

1961-1976

1	Gary Bell	167
2	Mudcat Grant	166
3	Sam McDowell	138
4	Luis Tiant	126
5	Jim Perry	113

1977-1995

1	Greg Swindell	109
2	Tom Candiotti	100
3	Rick Waits	99
4	Charles Nagy	74
5	2 players tied	63

Walks

1	Bob Feller	1764
2	Bob Lemon	1251
3	Mel Harder	1118
4	Sam McDowell	1072
5	Early Wynn	877
6	Willis Hudlin	832
7	George Uhle	709
8	Mike Garcia	696
9	Gary Bell	670
10	Stan Coveleski	616
11	Guy Morton	583
12	Mudcat Grant	565
13	Wes Ferrell	526
14	Rick Waits	512
15	Willie Mitchell	496
16	Al Milnar	478
17	Herb Score	458
18	Earl Moore	449
19	Joe Shaute	447
20	Allie Reynolds	442

Fewest Walks per Game

1901-1919

1	Addie Joss	1.41
2	Bill Bernhard	1.55
3	Jim Bagby	2.20
4	Bob Rhoads	2.52
5	Cy Falkenberg	2.61

1920-1941

1	Sherry Smith	1.85
2	Clint Brown	2.09
3	Stan Coveleski	2.22
4	Jake Miller	2.74
5	Joe Shaute	2.78

1942-1960

1	Jim Bagby, Jr.	2.87
2	Mike Garcia	2.93
3	Steve Gromek	2.95
4	Al Smith	3.24
5	Early Wynn	3.45

1961-1976

1	Gaylord Perry	2.63
2	Sonny Siebert	2.86
3	Jim Perry	2.99
4	Luis Tiant	3.24
5	Steve Hargan	3.68

1977-1995

1	Greg Swindell	1.95
2	Bert Blyleven	2.58
3	Charles Nagy	2.65
4	Tom Candiotti	2.96
5	Len Barker	3.36

Ratio

1	Addie Joss	8.9
2	Gaylord Perry	10.1
	Sonny Siebert	10.1
4	Bill Bernhard	10.2
5	Luis Tiant	10.4
6	Bob Rhoads	11.0
7	Bert Blyleven	11.1
	Stan Coveleski	11.1
	Greg Swindell	11.1
10	Cy Falkenberg	11.2
	Otto Hess	11.2
12	Steve Gromek	11.3
13	Earl Moore	11.4
14	Vean Gregg	11.5
15	Jim Bagby	11.6
	Sam McDowell	11.6
	Early Wynn	11.6
18	Guy Morton	11.7
19	Tom Candiotti	11.8
	Willie Mitchell	11.8

Strikeouts

1	Bob Feller	2581
2	Sam McDowell	2159
3	Bob Lemon	1277
	Early Wynn	1277
5	Mel Harder	1161
6	Gary Bell	1104
7	Mike Garcia	1095
8	Luis Tiant	1041
9	Addie Joss	920
10	Stan Coveleski	856
11	Guy Morton	830
12	Sonny Siebert	786
13	Willie Mitchell	775
14	Gaylord Perry	773
15	George Uhle	763
16	Greg Swindell	756
17	Tom Candiotti	753
18	Herb Score	742
19	Mudcat Grant	707
20	Len Barker	699

Strikeouts per Game

1	Sam McDowell	9.21
2	Luis Tiant	7.81
3	Sonny Siebert	7.14
4	Len Barker	6.75
5	Greg Swindell	6.52
6	Bert Blyleven	6.48
7	Gary Bell	6.41
8	Gaylord Perry	6.15
9	Bob Feller	6.07
10	Charles Nagy	5.78
11	Tom Candiotti	5.71
12	Willie Mitchell	5.36
13	Dan Spillner	5.35
14	Vean Gregg	5.32
15	Mudcat Grant	5.24
16	Allie Reynolds	5.18
17	Steve Hargan	5.11
18	Early Wynn	5.03
19	Johnny Allen	4.89
20	Mike Garcia	4.61

Earned Run Average (by era)

1901-1919
1	Addie Joss	1.89
2	Vean Gregg	2.31
3	Bob Rhoads	2.39
4	Bill Bernhard	2.45
5	Otto Hess	2.50

1920-1941
1	Stan Coveleski	2.80
2	Johnny Allen	3.65
3	Wes Ferrell	3.67
4	Mel Harder	3.80
5	Sherry Smith	3.84

1942-1960
1	Steve Gromek	3.22
2	Bob Lemon	3.23
3	Mike Garcia	3.24
	Early Wynn	3.24
5	Bob Feller	3.25

1961-1976
1	Gaylord Perry	2.71
2	Sonny Siebert	2.76
3	Luis Tiant	2.84
4	Sam McDowell	2.99
5	Gary Bell	3.71

1977-1995
1	Bert Blyleven	3.23
2	Tom Candiotti	3.53
3	Greg Swindell	3.79
4	Charles Nagy	3.97
5	Rick Waits	4.18

Earned Run Average

1	Addie Joss	1.89
2	Vean Gregg	2.31
3	Bob Rhoads	2.39
4	Bill Bernhard	2.45
5	Otto Hess	2.50
6	Earl Moore	2.58
7	Cy Falkenberg	2.70
8	Gaylord Perry	2.71
9	Sonny Siebert	2.76
10	Stan Coveleski	2.80
11	Luis Tiant	2.84
12	Willie Mitchell	2.89
13	Sam McDowell	2.99
14	Jim Bagby	3.02
15	Fred Blanding	3.13
	Guy Morton	3.13
17	Steve Gromek	3.22
18	Bert Blyleven	3.23
	Bob Lemon	3.23
20	2 players tied	3.24

Adjusted Earned Run Average

1	Addie Joss	142
2	Vean Gregg	140
3	Gaylord Perry	133
4	Stan Coveleski	129
5	Johnny Allen	127
6	Wes Ferrell	126
7	Bert Blyleven	125
8	Bob Feller	122
9	Sonny Siebert	121
10	Bob Lemon	119
	Sam McDowell	119
	Luis Tiant	119
13	Mike Garcia	118
	Early Wynn	118
15	Tom Candiotti	117
16	Earl Moore	116
17	Bill Bernhard	114
18	Mel Harder	113
19	Jim Bagby	112
20	3 players tied	111

Adjusted ERA (by era)

1901-1919
1	Addie Joss	142
2	Vean Gregg	140
3	Earl Moore	116
4	Bill Bernhard	114
5	Jim Bagby	112

1920-1941
1	Stan Coveleski	129
2	Johnny Allen	127
3	Wes Ferrell	126
4	Mel Harder	113
5	2 players tied	111

1942-1960
1	Bob Feller	122
2	Bob Lemon	119
3	Mike Garcia	118
	Early Wynn	118
5	Steve Gromek	111

1961-1976
1	Gaylord Perry	133
2	Sonny Siebert	121
3	Sam McDowell	119
	Luis Tiant	119
5	Jim Perry	100

1977-1995
1	Bert Blyleven	125
2	Tom Candiotti	117
3	Charles Nagy	108
	Greg Swindell	108
5	3 players tied	94

Pitching Runs

1	Bob Feller	385
2	Bob Lemon	251
3	Addie Joss	216
4	Stan Coveleski	202
5	Mel Harder	190
	Early Wynn	190
7	Mike Garcia	177
8	Johnny Allen	112
	Sam McDowell	112
10	Wes Ferrell	110
11	Gaylord Perry	103
12	Steve Gromek	84
13	Vean Gregg	83
14	Earl Moore	76
15	Tom Candiotti	72
16	Luis Tiant	69
17	Herb Score	64
	Sonny Siebert	64
19	Bert Blyleven	63
20	Dennis Martinez	59

Adjusted Pitching Runs

1	Bob Feller	301
2	Stan Coveleski	228
3	Addie Joss	207
4	Bob Lemon	193
5	Mel Harder	182
6	Early Wynn	151
7	Wes Ferrell	141
8	Mike Garcia	137
9	Sam McDowell	132
10	Gaylord Perry	113
11	Johnny Allen	101
12	Vean Gregg	92
13	Tom Candiotti	79
14	Luis Tiant	74
15	Jim Bagby	71
16	Bert Blyleven	68
17	Sonny Siebert	64
18	Earl Moore	63
19	Herb Score	62
20	Dennis Martinez	56

Pitching Wins

1	Bob Feller	37.5
2	Bob Lemon	25.0
3	Addie Joss	23.4
4	Stan Coveleski	20.5
5	Early Wynn	19.0
6	Mel Harder	18.1
7	Mike Garcia	17.7
8	Sam McDowell	12.0
9	Gaylord Perry	10.9
10	Wes Ferrell	10.2
11	Johnny Allen	10.2
12	Steve Gromek	8.6
13	Vean Gregg	8.5
14	Earl Moore	7.7
15	Luis Tiant	7.5
16	Tom Candiotti	7.2
17	Sonny Siebert	7.0
18	Herb Score	6.4
19	Bert Blyleven	6.4
20	Bill Bernhard	5.6

Adjusted Pitching Wins

1	Bob Feller	29.3
2	Stan Coveleski	23.1
3	Addie Joss	22.4
4	Bob Lemon	19.2
5	Mel Harder	17.3
6	Early Wynn	15.1
7	Sam McDowell	14.1
8	Mike Garcia	13.7
9	Wes Ferrell	13.1
10	Gaylord Perry	12.0
11	Vean Gregg	9.4
12	Johnny Allen	9.2
13	Luis Tiant	8.0
14	Tom Candiotti	7.9
15	Jim Bagby	7.4
16	Sonny Siebert	7.0
17	Bert Blyleven	6.9
18	Earl Moore	6.4
19	Herb Score	6.2
20	Steve Gromek	5.5

Opponents' Batting Average

1	Sam McDowell	.210
2	Sonny Siebert	.213
3	Luis Tiant	.214
4	Addie Joss	.223
	Gaylord Perry	.223
6	Bob Feller	.231
7	Gary Bell	.235
8	Vean Gregg	.236
9	Allie Reynolds	.238
	Early Wynn	.238
11	Mudcat Grant	.239
	Earl Moore	.239
13	Steve Gromek	.240
	Otto Hess	.240
15	Bert Blyleven	.241
	Bob Lemon	.241
	Willie Mitchell	.241
18	Steve Hargan	.244
19	Bob Rhoads	.249
20	3 players tied	.251

Opponents' On Base Pctg.

1	Addie Joss	.260
2	Sonny Siebert	.282
3	Gaylord Perry	.285
4	Bill Bernhard	.287
	Luis Tiant	.287
6	Bert Blyleven	.301
7	Steve Gromek	.304
	Greg Swindell	.304
9	Stan Coveleski	.306
10	Otto Hess	.307
11	Bob Rhoads	.308
12	Earl Moore	.309
13	Cy Falkenberg	.310
14	Sam McDowell	.311
	Early Wynn	.311
16	Tom Candiotti	.315
17	Mike Garcia	.317
	Vean Gregg	.317
19	Jim Bagby	.318
20	4 players tied	.319

Wins Above Team

1	Bob Feller	36.8
2	Addie Joss	28.7
3	Wes Ferrell	19.8
4	Vean Gregg	18.8
5	Sam McDowell	15.1
6	George Uhle	14.7
7	Bob Lemon	13.8
8	Johnny Allen	13.5
9	Gaylord Perry	12.8
10	Stan Coveleski	11.0
11	Bert Blyleven	10.3
12	Mel Harder	10.0
13	Greg Swindell	9.6
14	Tom Candiotti	9.4
15	Cy Falkenberg	8.8
	Cal McLish	8.8
17	Luis Tiant	8.2
	Early Wynn	8.2
19	Ray Narleski	8.0
20	Earl Moore	7.4

Wins Above League

1	Bob Feller	214.0
2	Mel Harder	204.5
3	Bob Lemon	167.5
4	Willis Hudlin	154.0
5	Stan Coveleski	147.5
6	George Uhle	133.0
	Early Wynn	133.0
8	Addie Joss	128.5
9	Mike Garcia	119.0
10	Sam McDowell	115.5
11	Jim Bagby	103.5
12	Gary Bell	94.0
13	Guy Morton	93.0
14	Joe Shaute	83.0
15	Wes Ferrell	82.0
16	Rick Waits	79.0
17	Bob Rhoads	77.0
18	Earl Moore	74.5
19	Steve Gromek	72.5
20	Willie Mitchell	70.0

Relief Games

1	Doug Jones	268
2	Sid Monge	253
3	Dan Spillner	234
4	Eric Plunk	225
5	Steve Olin	194
6	Jim Kern	189
7	Don Mossi	188
8	Joe Heving	183
9	Ray Narleski	182
10	Ed Klieman	165

Relief Wins

1	Gary Bell	34
2	Jim Kern	28
3	Joe Heving	26
	Eric Plunk	26
5	Dan Spillner	25
6	Doug Jones	23
	Sid Monge	23
8	Ray Narleski	21
9	Frank Funk	17
	Phil Hennigan	17

Relief Losses

1	Doug Jones	31
2	Jim Kern	27
3	Sid Monge	24
4	Dan Spillner	23
5	Gary Bell	20
6	Steve Olin	19
7	Ernie Camacho	16
	Victor Cruz	16
9	Eric Plunk	15
10	2 players tied	14

Relief Innings Pitched

1	Dan Spillner	447.1
2	Gary Bell	442.1
3	Sid Monge	395.1
4	Doug Jones	390.0
5	Jim Kern	351.0
6	Joe Heving	347.2
7	Ray Narleski	319.1
8	Don Mossi	316.0
9	Tom Buskey	298.1
10	Ed Klieman	281.1

Relief Points

1	Doug Jones	271
2	Ray Narleski	142
3	Gary Bell	138
4	Jim Kern	121
5	Sid Monge	114
6	Jose Mesa	111
7	Dan Spillner	109
8	Steve Olin	107
9	Joe Heving	104
10	Dave LaRoche	91

Relief Ranking

1	Doug Jones	88
2	Jose Mesa	62
	Eric Plunk	62
4	Sid Monge	51
5	Steve Olin	46
6	Derek Lilliquist	44
7	Jim Kern	43
	Ray Narleski	43
9	Dan Spillner	42
10	Gary Bell	41

Relievers' Runs

1	Doug Jones	47
	Steve Mingori	47
	Eric Plunk	47
4	Ray Narleski	42
5	Don Mossi	41
6	Jose Mesa	33
7	Gary Bell	31
8	Al Benton	29
	Sid Monge	29
10	Derek Lilliquist	27

Adjusted Relievers' Runs

1	Doug Jones	50
2	Eric Plunk	45
3	Ray Narleski	42
4	Don Mossi	40
5	Jose Mesa	33
6	Gary Bell	29
	Sid Monge	29
8	Derek Lilliquist	27
	Dan Spillner	27
10	2 players tied	26

Clutch Pitching Index

1	Bob Rhoads	119
2	Fred Blanding	115
3	Otto Hess	113
4	Vean Gregg	112
5	Jake Miller	110
6	Wes Ferrell	108
	Earl Moore	108
8	Mel Harder	106
	Al Smith	106
10	Jim Perry	105
11	Jim Bagby	104
	Bill Bernhard	104
	Mike Garcia	104
	Bob Lemon	104
	Charles Nagy	104
16	Al Milnar	103
17	6 players tied	101

Pitcher Batting Runs

1	Bob Lemon	90
2	George Uhle	65
3	Wes Ferrell	41
4	Jim Wynn	26
5	Joe Shaute	23
6	Al Smith	18
7	Jim Bagby	13
	Steve Gromek	13
9	Jim Bagby, Jr.	11
10	Sherry Smith	9
11	Mudcat Grant	8
12	Garland Buckeye	7
	Al Milnar	7
	Monte Pearson	7
15	Gary Bell	5
	Cal McLish	5
	Jim Perry	5
18	4 players tied	4

Pitcher Fielding Runs

1	Bob Lemon	60
2	Willis Hudlin	41
3	Addie Joss	30
4	Mel Harder	18
5	Fritz Coumbe	17
6	Clint Brown	15
	Stan Coveleski	15
8	Tom Candiotti	12
9	Sherry Smith	9
10	Johnny Allen	8
	Jim Bagby, Jr.	8
12	Gene Bearden	7
	Wes Ferrell	7
14	Ed Klieman	6
	Gaylord Perry	6
	Al Smith	6
	Rick Waits	6
18	4 players tied	5

Pitcher Batting Average

1	George Uhle	.289
2	Wes Ferrell	.274
3	Joe Shaute	.271
4	Jim Bagby, Jr.	.243
	Sherry Smith	.243
6	Bob Lemon	.232
7	Jim Bagby	.225
8	Al Smith	.221
9	Steve Gromek	.218
10	Jim Perry	.217
11	Fred Blanding	.216
12	Clint Brown	.203
13	Willis Hudlin	.202
14	Early Wynn	.199
15	Al Milnar	.195
16	Otto Hess	.190
	Bob Rhoads	.190
18	Johnny Allen	.188
19	Mike Garcia	.182
20	Mudcat Grant	.180

Total Pitcher Index

1	Bob Lemon	37.4
2	Bob Feller	28.5
3	Addie Joss	25.4
4	Stan Coveleski	23.9
5	Wes Ferrell	21.2
6	Mel Harder	20.0
7	Early Wynn	18.3
8	Mike Garcia	14.6
9	Gaylord Perry	14.2
10	Sam McDowell	13.1
11	Doug Jones	10.6
12	Johnny Allen	10.2
13	Willis Hudlin	10.1
	George Uhle	10.1
15	Tom Candiotti	9.6
16	Vean Gregg	8.9
	Luis Tiant	8.9
18	Jim Bagby	8.7
19	Sonny Siebert	8.2
20	Bert Blyleven	6.8
21	Eric Plunk	5.9
22	Steve Gromek	5.4
	Steve Olin	5.4
24	Sid Monge	5.0
	Sherry Smith	5.0
26	Jim Kern	4.9
27	Dennis Martinez	4.6
	Herb Score	4.6
29	Jose Mesa	4.5
30	Derek Lilliquist	4.2
31	Bill Bernhard	4.1
	Cal McLish	4.1
33	Jake Miller	4.0
34	Clint Brown	3.9
	Joe Shaute	3.9
36	Greg Swindell	3.7
37	Oral Hildebrand	3.5
	Monte Pearson	3.5
	Al Smith	3.5
40	Al Benton	3.3
	Dennis Eckersley	3.3
42	Gene Bearden	3.2
43	Charles Nagy	3.1
	Bob Rhoads	3.1
45	Earl Moore	2.9
46	Dave LaRoche	2.8
47	Lloyd Brown	2.7
	Frank Funk	2.7
	Don Mossi	2.7
50	3 players tied	2.5

Total Pitcher Index (alpha.)

Johnny Allen	10.2
Jim Bagby	8.7
Gene Bearden	3.2
Al Benton	3.3
Bill Bernhard	4.1
Bert Blyleven	6.8
Clint Brown	3.9
Lloyd Brown	2.7
Tom Candiotti	9.6
Stan Coveleski	23.9
Dennis Eckersley	3.3
Bob Feller	28.5
Wes Ferrell	21.2
Frank Funk	2.7
Mike Garcia	14.6
Vean Gregg	8.9
Steve Gromek	5.4
Mel Harder	20.0
Oral Hildebrand	3.5
Willis Hudlin	10.1
Doug Jones	10.6
Addie Joss	25.4
Jim Kern	4.9
Bob Lemon	37.4
Derek Lilliquist	4.2
Dave LaRoche	2.8
Dennis Martinez	4.6
Jose Mesa	4.5
Jake Miller	4.0
Sid Monge	5.0
Earl Moore	2.9
Don Mossi	2.7
Sam McDowell	13.1
Cal McLish	4.1
Charles Nagy	3.1
Steve Olin	5.4
Monte Pearson	3.5
Gaylord Perry	14.2
Eric Plunk	5.9
Bob Rhoads	3.1
Herb Score	4.6
Joe Shaute	3.9
Sonny Siebert	8.2
Al Smith	3.5
Sherry Smith	5.0
Greg Swindell	3.7
Luis Tiant	8.9
George Uhle	10.1
Early Wynn	18.3

Total Pitcher Index (by era)

1901-1919

1	Addie Joss	25.4
2	Vean Gregg	8.9
3	Jim Bagby	8.7
4	Bill Bernhard	4.1
5	Bob Rhoads	3.1

1920-1941

1	Stan Coveleski	23.9
2	Wes Ferrell	21.2
3	Mel Harder	20.0
4	Johnny Allen	10.2
5	Willis Hudlin	10.1
	George Uhle	10.1

1942-1960

1	Bob Lemon	37.4
2	Bob Feller	28.5
3	Early Wynn	18.3
4	Mike Garcia	14.6
5	Steve Gromek	5.4

1961-1976

1	Gaylord Perry	14.2
2	Sam McDowell	13.1
3	Luis Tiant	8.9
4	Sonny Siebert	8.2
5	Dennis Eckersley	3.3

1977-1995

1	Doug Jones	10.6
2	Tom Candiotti	9.6
3	Bert Blyleven	6.8
4	Eric Plunk	5.9
5	Steve Olin	5.4

Total Baseball Ranking

1	Nap Lajoie	65.9
2	Tris Speaker	45.4
3	Lou Boudreau	41.4
4	Bob Lemon	36.9
5	Joe Sewell	32.1
6	Bob Feller	28.5
7	Addie Joss	25.4
8	Joe Jackson	24.1
9	Stan Coveleski	23.9
10	Wes Ferrell	21.2
11	Mel Harder	20.0
12	Larry Doby	19.8
13	Earl Averill	19.7
14	Early Wynn	18.3
15	Albert Belle	18.2
16	Ray Chapman	15.4
17	Rocky Colavito	14.8
18	Mike Garcia	14.6
19	Gaylord Perry	14.2
	Elmer Flick	14.2
21	Sam McDowell	13.1
22	Kenny Lofton	12.8
23	Carlos Baerga	12.5
24	Al Rosen	12.4
25	Ken Keltner	11.8
26	Jeff Heath	11.5
27	Doug Jones	10.6
28	Johnny Allen	10.2
	Bill Bradley	10.2
30	Willis Hudlin	10.1
	George Uhle	10.1
32	Tom Candiotti	9.6
33	Hal Trosky	9.2
34	Graig Nettles	9.0
35	Vean Gregg	8.9
	Luis Tiant	8.9
37	Jim Bagby	8.7
38	Brett Butler	8.5
39	Andy Thornton	8.3
40	Sonny Siebert	8.2
41	Mike Hargrove	7.3
42	Odell Hale	7.2
43	Woodie Held	6.9
44	Bert Blyleven	6.8
45	Minnie Minoso	6.7
46	Eric Plunk	5.9
47	Bobby Avila	5.8
48	Rico Carty	5.6
49	Steve Gromek	5.4
	Steve Olin	5.4
	Buddy Bell	5.4
52	Sid Monge	5.0
	Sherry Smith	5.0
	Charlie Hickman	5.0
55	Jim Kern	4.9
	Roy Cullenbine	4.9
57	Dennis Martinez	4.6
	Herb Score	4.6
59	Jose Mesa	4.5
	Steve O'Neill	4.5
	Johnny Romano	4.5
62	Mike Fischlin	4.4
	Johnny Hodapp	4.4
64	Derek Lilliquist	4.2
65	Bill Bernhard	4.1
	Cal McLish	4.1
	Les Fleming	4.1
	Joe Harris	4.1
69	Jake Miller	4.0
70	Clint Brown	3.9
	Joe Shaute	3.9
72	Joe Azcue	3.8
73	Greg Swindell	3.7
	Ray Fosse	3.7
	Riggs Stephenson	3.7
76	Joe Vosmik	3.6
77	Oral Hildebrand	3.5
	Monte Pearson	3.5
	Al Smith	3.5
	Jerry Dybzinski	3.5
	Jim Hegan	3.5
	Duke Sims	3.5
83	Ron Hassey	3.4
84	Al Benton	3.3
	Dennis Eckersley	3.3
	Nig Clarke	3.3
	Joe Gordon	3.3
88	Gene Bearden	3.2
	Oscar Gamble	3.2
90	Charles Nagy	3.1
	Bob Rhoads	3.1
92	Earl Moore	2.9
93	Dave LaRoche	2.8
	Vic Wertz	2.8
95	Lloyd Brown	2.7
	Frank Funk	2.7
	Don Mossi	2.7
	Willie Kamm	2.7
	Jim Thome	2.7
100	4 players tied	2.5

Total Baseball Rank (alpha.)

Johnny Allen	10.2
Earl Averill	19.7
Bobby Avila	5.8
Joe Azcue	3.8
Carlos Baerga	12.5
Jim Bagby	8.7
Gene Bearden	3.2
Buddy Bell	5.4
Albert Belle	18.2
Al Benton	3.3
Bill Bernhard	4.1
Bert Blyleven	6.8
Lou Boudreau	41.4
Bill Bradley	10.2
Clint Brown	3.9
Lloyd Brown	2.7
Brett Butler	8.5
Tom Candiotti	9.6
Rico Carty	5.6
Ray Chapman	15.4
Nig Clarke	3.3
Rocky Colavito	14.8
Stan Coveleski	23.9
Roy Cullenbine	4.9
Larry Doby	19.8
Jerry Dybzinski	3.5
Dennis Eckersley	3.3
Bob Feller	28.5
Wes Ferrell	21.2
Mike Fischlin	4.4
Les Fleming	4.1
Elmer Flick	14.2
Ray Fosse	3.7
Frank Funk	2.7
Oscar Gamble	3.2
Mike Garcia	14.6
Joe Gordon	3.3
Vean Gregg	8.9
Steve Gromek	5.4
Odell Hale	7.2
Mel Harder	20.0
Mike Hargrove	7.3
Joe Harris	4.1
Ron Hassey	3.4
Jeff Heath	11.5
Jim Hegan	3.5
Woodie Held	6.9
Charlie Hickman	5.0
Oral Hildebrand	3.5
Johnny Hodapp	4.4

Willis Hudlin	10.1
Joe Jackson	24.1
Doug Jones	10.6
Addie Joss	25.4
Willie Kamm	2.7
Ken Keltner	11.8
Jim Kern	4.9
Nap Lajoie	65.9
Bob Lemon	36.9
Derek Lilliquist	4.2
Kenny Lofton	12.8
Dave LaRoche	2.8
Dennis Martinez	4.6
Jose Mesa	4.5
Jake Miller	4.0
Minnie Minoso	6.7
Sid Monge	5.0
Earl Moore	2.9
Don Mossi	2.7
Sam McDowell	13.1
Cal McLish	4.1
Charles Nagy	3.1
Graig Nettles	9.0
Steve O'Neill	4.5
Steve Olin	5.4
Monte Pearson	3.5
Gaylord Perry	14.2
Eric Plunk	5.9
Bob Rhoads	3.1
Johnny Romano	4.5
Al Rosen	12.4
Herb Score	4.6
Joe Sewell	32.1
Joe Shaute	3.9
Sonny Siebert	8.2
Duke Sims	3.5
Al Smith	3.5
Sherry Smith	5.0
Tris Speaker	45.4
Riggs Stephenson	3.7
Greg Swindell	3.7
Jim Thome	2.7
Andy Thornton	8.3
Luis Tiant	8.9
Hal Trosky	9.2
George Uhle	10.1
Joe Vosmik	3.6
Vic Wertz	2.8
Early Wynn	18.3

Total Baseball Rank (by era)

1901-1919

1	Nap Lajoie	65.9
2	Addie Joss	25.4
3	Joe Jackson	24.1
4	Ray Chapman	15.4
5	Elmer Flick	14.2
6	Bill Bradley	10.2
7	Vean Gregg	8.9
8	Jim Bagby	8.7
9	Charlie Hickman	5.0
10	Steve O'Neill	4.5

1920-1941

1	Tris Speaker	45.4
2	Joe Sewell	32.1
3	Stan Coveleski	23.9
4	Wes Ferrell	21.2
5	Mel Harder	20.0
6	Earl Averill	19.7
7	Jeff Heath	11.5
8	Johnny Allen	10.2
9	Willis Hudlin	10.1
	George Uhle	10.1

1942-1960

1	Lou Boudreau	41.4
2	Bob Lemon	36.9
3	Bob Feller	28.5
4	Larry Doby	19.8
5	Early Wynn	18.3
6	Rocky Colavito	14.8
7	Mike Garcia	14.6
8	Al Rosen	12.4
9	Ken Keltner	11.8
10	Minnie Minoso	6.7

1961-1976

1	Gaylord Perry	14.2
2	Sam McDowell	13.1
3	Graig Nettles	9.0
4	Luis Tiant	8.9
5	Sonny Siebert	8.2
6	Woodie Held	6.9
7	Rico Carty	5.6
8	Buddy Bell	5.4
9	Johnny Romano	4.5
10	Joe Azcue	3.8

1977-1995

1	Albert Belle	18.2
2	Kenny Lofton	12.8
3	Carlos Baerga	12.5
4	Doug Jones	10.6
5	Tom Candiotti	9.6
6	Brett Butler	8.5
7	Andy Thornton	8.3
8	Mike Hargrove	7.3
9	Bert Blyleven	6.8
10	Eric Plunk	5.9

At Bats

1	Joe Carter, 1986	663
2	Julio Franco, 1984	658
3	Carlos Baerga, 1992	657
4	Mike Rocco, 1944	653
5	Joe Carter, 1989	651
6	Carl Lind, 1928	650
7	Charlie Jamieson, 1923	644
	Lyn Lary, 1937	644
9	Leon Wagner, 1964	641
10	Dale Mitchell, 1949	640
11	Roy Hughes, 1936	638
12	Dick Howser, 1964	637
	Max Alvis, 1967	637
14	Julio Franco, 1985	636
15	Johnny Hodapp, 1930	635
16	Hal Trosky, 1935	632
17	Earl Averill, 1932	631
	Buddy Bell, 1973	631
19	Hal Trosky, 1936	629
20	2 players tied	627

Runs

1	Earl Averill, 1931	140
2	Tris Speaker, 1920	137
3	Earl Averill, 1936	136
4	Tris Speaker, 1923	133
5	Charlie Jamieson, 1923	130
6	Earl Averill, 1934	128
7	Joe Jackson, 1911	126
	Odell Hale, 1936	126
9	Hal Trosky, 1936	124
10	Al Smith, 1955	123
11	Ed Morgan, 1930	122
12	Joe Jackson, 1912	121
	Earl Averill, 1937	121
	Albert Belle, 1995	121
15	Hal Trosky, 1934	117
16	Earl Averill, 1932	116
	Lou Boudreau, 1948	116
	Kenny Lofton, 1993	116
19	Al Rosen, 1953	115
20	2 players tied	112

Runs per Game

1901-1919

1	Joe Jackson, 1911	.86
2	Joe Jackson, 1912	.79
3	Bill Bradley, 1902	.76
4	Ollie Pickering, 1901	.74
5	Bill Bradley, 1903	.74

1920-1941

1	Tris Speaker, 1920	.91
2	Earl Averill, 1931	.90
3	Earl Averill, 1936	.89
4	Tris Speaker, 1923	.89
5	Ray Chapman, 1920	.87

1942-1960

1	Al Smith, 1955	.80
2	Bobby Avila, 1954	.78
3	Larry Doby, 1950	.77
4	Al Smith, 1954	.77
5	Lou Boudreau, 1948	.76

1961-1976

1	Jim Piersall, 1961	.67
2	Leon Wagner, 1965	.63
3	Dick Howser, 1964	.62
4	Leon Wagner, 1964	.58
5	Willie Kirkland, 1961	.58

1977-1995

1	Kenny Lofton, 1994	.94
2	Albert Belle, 1994	.85
3	Albert Belle, 1995	.85
4	Kenny Lofton, 1995	.79
5	Carlos Baerga, 1994	.79

Hits

1	Joe Jackson, 1911	233
2	Earl Averill, 1936	232
3	Nap Lajoie, 1910	227
4	Joe Jackson, 1912	226
5	Johnny Hodapp, 1930	225
6	Charlie Jamieson, 1923	222
7	Tris Speaker, 1923	218
8	George Burns, 1926	216
	Joe Vosmik, 1935	216
	Hal Trosky, 1936	216
11	Nap Lajoie, 1906	214
	Tris Speaker, 1920	214
13	Charlie Jamieson, 1924	213
14	Tris Speaker, 1916	211
15	Lew Fonseca, 1929	209
	Earl Averill, 1931	209
17	Nap Lajoie, 1904	208
18	Hal Trosky, 1934	206
19	Carlos Baerga, 1992	205
20	3 players tied	204

Doubles

1	George Burns, 1926	64
2	Tris Speaker, 1923	59
3	Tris Speaker, 1921	52
	Tris Speaker, 1926	52
	Albert Belle, 1995	52
6	Nap Lajoie, 1910	51
	George Burns, 1927	51
	Johnny Hodapp, 1930	51
9	Tris Speaker, 1920	50
	Odell Hale, 1936	50
11	Nap Lajoie, 1904	49
12	Nap Lajoie, 1906	48
	Tris Speaker, 1922	48
	Joe Sewell, 1927	48
	Earl Averill, 1934	48
16	Ed Morgan, 1930	47
	Joe Vosmik, 1935	47
18	Lyn Lary, 1937	46
	Lou Boudreau, 1940	46
20	7 players tied	45

Triples (by era)

1901-1919

1	Joe Jackson, 1912	26
2	Bill Bradley, 1903	22
	Elmer Flick, 1906	22
4	Joe Jackson, 1911	19
5	2 players tied	18

1920-1941

1	Joe Vosmik, 1935	20
	Jeff Heath, 1941	20
3	Jeff Heath, 1938	18
4	Earl Averill, 1933	16
5	3 players tied	15

1942-1960

1	Dale Mitchell, 1949	23
2	Hank Edwards, 1946	16
3	Jeff Heath, 1942	13
4	Bobby Avila, 1952	11
5	3 players tied	10

1961-1976

1	Tito Francona, 1961	8
2	6 players tied	7

1977-1995

1	Brett Butler, 1985	14
	Brett Butler, 1986	14
3	Kenny Lofton, 1995	13
4	4 players tied	9

Triples

1	Joe Jackson, 1912	26
2	Dale Mitchell, 1949	23
3	Bill Bradley, 1903	22
	Elmer Flick, 1906	22
5	Joe Vosmik, 1935	20
	Jeff Heath, 1941	20
7	Joe Jackson, 1911	19
8	Elmer Flick, 1905	18
	Elmer Flick, 1907	18
	Jeff Heath, 1938	18
11	Elmer Flick, 1904	17
	Joe Jackson, 1913	17
	Ray Chapman, 1915	17
14	Elmer Flick, 1903	16
	Earl Averill, 1933	16
	Hank Edwards, 1946	16
17	Nap Lajoie, 1904	15
	Lew Fonseca, 1929	15
	Earl Averill, 1936	15
	Earl Averill, 1938	15

Home Runs

1	Albert Belle, 1995	50
2	Al Rosen, 1953	43
3	Hal Trosky, 1936	42
	Rocky Colavito, 1959	42
5	Rocky Colavito, 1958	41
6	Albert Belle, 1993	38
7	Al Rosen, 1950	37
8	Albert Belle, 1994	36
9	Hal Trosky, 1934	35
	Joe Carter, 1989	35
11	Albert Belle, 1992	34
12	Andy Thornton, 1978	33
	Andy Thornton, 1984	33
	Cory Snyder, 1987	33
15	10 players tied	32

Home Runs (by era)

1901-1919

1	Charlie Hickman, 1903	12
2	Bill Bradley, 1902	11
3	Elmer Smith, 1919	9
4	Charlie Hickman, 1902	8
5	4 players tied	7

1920-1941

1	Hal Trosky, 1936	42
2	Hal Trosky, 1934	35
3	Earl Averill, 1931	32
	Earl Averill, 1932	32
	Hal Trosky, 1937	32

1942-1960

1	Al Rosen, 1953	43
2	Rocky Colavito, 1959	42
3	Rocky Colavito, 1958	41
4	Al Rosen, 1950	37
5	4 players tied	32

1961-1976

1	Leon Wagner, 1964	31
2	Rocky Colavito, 1966	30
3	Leon Wagner, 1965	28
	Graig Nettles, 1971	28
5	5 players tied	27

1977-1995

1	Albert Belle, 1995	50
2	Albert Belle, 1993	38
3	Albert Belle, 1994	36
4	Joe Carter, 1989	35
5	Albert Belle, 1992	34

Home Run Percentage

1	Albert Belle, 1995	9.16
2	Albert Belle, 1994	8.74
3	Rocky Colavito, 1958	8.38
4	Al Rosen, 1953	7.18
5	Rocky Colavito, 1959	7.14
6	Luke Easter, 1952	7.09
7	Al Rosen, 1950	6.68
8	Hal Trosky, 1936	6.68
9	Vic Wertz, 1956	6.65
10	Andy Thornton, 1978	6.50
11	Andy Thornton, 1977	6.47
12	Manny Ramirez, 1995	6.40
13	Albert Belle, 1993	6.40
14	Jim Thome, 1994	6.23
15	Boog Powell, 1975	6.21
16	Larry Doby, 1952	6.17
17	Brook Jacoby, 1987	5.93
18	Joe Gordon, 1948	5.82
19	Albert Belle, 1992	5.81
20	Cory Snyder, 1987	5.72

Home Run Pctg.(by era)

1901-1919

1	Charlie Hickman, 1903	2.30
2	Elmer Smith, 1919	2.28
3	Bill Bradley, 1902	2.00
4	Charlie Hickman, 1902	1.88
5	Nap Lajoie, 1903	1.44

1920-1941

1	Hal Trosky, 1936	6.68
2	Hal Trosky, 1934	5.60
3	Hal Trosky, 1939	5.58
4	Hal Trosky, 1937	5.32
5	Earl Averill, 1934	5.18

1942-1960

1	Rocky Colavito, 1958	8.38
2	Al Rosen, 1953	7.18
3	Rocky Colavito, 1959	7.14
4	Luke Easter, 1952	7.09
5	Al Rosen, 1950	6.68

1961-1976

1	Boog Powell, 1975	6.21
2	Rocky Colavito, 1966	5.63
3	Johnny Romano, 1962	5.45
4	Leon Wagner, 1965	5.42
5	Fred Whitfield, 1966	5.38

1977-1995

1	Albert Belle, 1995	9.16
2	Albert Belle, 1994	8.74
3	Andy Thornton, 1978	6.50
4	Andy Thornton, 1977	6.47
5	Manny Ramirez, 1995	6.40

Total Bases

1	Hal Trosky, 1936	405
2	Earl Averill, 1936	385
3	Albert Belle, 1995	377
4	Hal Trosky, 1934	374
5	Al Rosen, 1953	367
6	Earl Averill, 1931	361
7	Earl Averill, 1932	359
8	Ed Morgan, 1930	351
9	Tris Speaker, 1923	350
10	Jeff Heath, 1941	343
11	Joe Carter, 1986	341
12	Earl Averill, 1934	340
13	Joe Jackson, 1911	337
14	Joe Vosmik, 1935	333
15	Joe Jackson, 1912	331
16	Hal Trosky, 1937	329
17	Albert Belle, 1993	328
18	Earl Averill, 1929	321
19	Johnny Hodapp, 1930	319
20	2 players tied	314

Runs Batted In

1	Hal Trosky, 1936	162
2	Al Rosen, 1953	145
3	Earl Averill, 1931	143
4	Hal Trosky, 1934	142
5	Ed Morgan, 1930	136
6	Tris Speaker, 1923	130
7	Albert Belle, 1993	129
8	Hal Trosky, 1937	128
9	Earl Averill, 1936	126
	Larry Doby, 1954	126
	Albert Belle, 1995	126
12	Earl Averill, 1932	124
	Joe Gordon, 1948	124
14	Jeff Heath, 1941	123
15	Johnny Hodapp, 1930	121
	Joe Carter, 1986	121
17	Larry Gardner, 1921	120
18	Earl Averill, 1930	119
	Ken Keltner, 1948	119
20	Larry Gardner, 1920	118

Runs Batted In per Game

1	Hal Trosky, 1936	1.07
2	Albert Belle, 1994	.95
3	Al Rosen, 1953	.94
4	Earl Averill, 1931	.92
5	Hal Trosky, 1934	.92
6	Charlie Hickman, 1902	.92
7	Ed Morgan, 1930	.91
8	Jeff Heath, 1938	.89
9	Albert Belle, 1995	.88
10	Tris Speaker, 1923	.87
11	Joe Gordon, 1948	.86
12	Earl Averill, 1930	.86
13	Hal Trosky, 1939	.85
14	Hal Trosky, 1937	.84
15	Earl Averill, 1936	.83
16	Larry Doby, 1954	.82
17	Jeff Heath, 1941	.81
18	Albert Belle, 1993	.81
19	Earl Averill, 1932	.81
20	Luke Easter, 1951	.80

Strikeout Percentage

1901-1919

1	Elmer Smith, 1915	15.76
2	Braggo Roth, 1917	14.75
3	Ray Chapman, 1915	14.39
4	Doc Johnston, 1913	12.26
5	Jack Graney, 1916	12.22

1920-1941

1	Boze Berger, 1935	21.04
2	Ray Mack, 1940	14.53
3	Ray Mack, 1941	13.80
4	Ken Keltner, 1938	13.02
5	Joe Wood, 1922	12.48

1942-1960

1	Larry Doby, 1953	23.59
2	Pat Seerey, 1945	23.43
3	Woodie Held, 1959	22.48
4	Larry Doby, 1952	21.39
5	Larry Doby, 1955	20.37

1961-1976

1	Woodie Held, 1962	22.96
2	Woodie Held, 1961	21.81
3	Charlie Spikes, 1973	20.36
4	Jerry Kindall, 1962	20.19
5	Max Alvis, 1968	20.13

1977-1995

1	Cory Snyder, 1987	28.77
2	Cory Snyder, 1989	27.40
3	Jim Thome, 1994	26.17
4	Paul Sorrento, 1993	26.13
5	Bobby Bonds, 1979	25.09

Walks

1 Mike Hargrove, 1980 111
2 Andy Thornton, 1982 109
3 Les Fleming, 1942 106
4 Jack Graney, 1919 105
5 Jack Graney, 1916 102
6 Larry Doby, 1951 101
  Mike Hargrove, 1982 101
8 Al Rosen, 1950 100
9 Earl Averill, 1934 99
10 Joe Sewell, 1923 98
  Lou Boudreau, 1948 98
  Larry Doby, 1950 98
  Toby Harrah, 1980 98
14 Tris Speaker, 1920 97
  Jim Thome, 1995 97
16 Roy Cullenbine, 1943 . . . 96
  Larry Doby, 1953 96
18 Ken Harrelson, 1969 95
19 3 players tied 94

Strikeouts

1 Cory Snyder, 1987 166
2 Brook Jacoby, 1986 137
3 Bobby Bonds, 1979 135
4 Cory Snyder, 1989 134
  Candy Maldonado, 1990 . 134
6 Albert Belle, 1992 128
7 Cory Snyder, 1986 123
8 Larry Doby, 1953 121
  Leon Wagner, 1964 121
  Max Alvis, 1965 121
  Paul Sorrento, 1993 121
12 Brook Jacoby, 1985 120
13 Woodie Held, 1959 118
  Cory Snyder, 1990 118
15 Jim Thome, 1995 113
16 Joe Carter, 1989 112
  Manny Ramirez, 1995 112
18 Larry Doby, 1952 111
  Woodie Held, 1961 111
20 Max Alvis, 1963 109

At Bats per Strikeout

1901-1919
1 Tris Speaker, 1918 . . . . . 52.3
2 Tris Speaker, 1919 . . . . . 41.2
3 Tris Speaker, 1917 . . . . . 37.4
4 Nap Lajoie, 1913 . . . . . . 27.4
5 Tris Speaker, 1916 . . . . . 27.3

1920-1941
1 Joe Sewell, 1925 . . . . 152.0
2 Joe Sewell, 1929 . . . . 144.5
3 Stuffy McInnis, 1922 . . . . . 107.4
4 Joe Sewell, 1926 . . . . 96.3
5 Joe Sewell, 1927 . . . . 81.3

1942-1960
1 Lou Boudreau, 1948 . . . . . 62.2
2 Dale Mitchell, 1949 . . . . . 58.2
3 Dale Mitchell, 1952 . . . . . 56.8
4 Lou Boudreau, 1947 . . . . . 53.8
5 Lou Boudreau, 1949 . . . . . 47.5

1961-1976
1 Vic Power, 1961 . . . . 35.2
2 Dick Howser, 1964 . . . . . . 16.3
3 Buddy Bell, 1972 . . . . 16.1
4 Johnny Temple, 1961 . . . 14.4
5 Buddy Bell, 1973 . . . . 13.4

1977-1995
1 Felix Fermin, 1993 . . . . . . 34.3
2 Mike Hargrove, 1981 . . . . . 20.1
3 Carlos Baerga, 1995 . . . . 18.0
4 Felix Fermin, 1989 . . . . . . 17.9
5 Duane Kuiper, 1979 . . . . . 17.7

Batting Average

1 Joe Jackson, 1911 408
2 Joe Jackson, 1912 395
3 Tris Speaker, 1925 389
4 Tris Speaker, 1920 388
5 Tris Speaker, 1916 386
6 Nap Lajoie, 1910 384
7 Tris Speaker, 1923 380
8 Charlie Hickman, 1902 378
  Tris Speaker, 1922 378
10 Earl Averill, 1936 378
11 Nap Lajoie, 1904 376
12 Joe Jackson, 1913 373
13 Lew Fonseca, 1929 369
14 Nap Lajoie, 1912 368
15 Tris Speaker, 1921 362
16 Charlie Jamieson, 1924 . . .359
17 George Burns, 1926 358
18 Albert Belle, 1994 357
19 Nap Lajoie, 1906 355
20 Lou Boudreau, 1948 355

Batting Average (by era)

1901-1919
1 Joe Jackson, 1911 408
2 Joe Jackson, 1912 395
3 Tris Speaker, 1916 386
4 Nap Lajoie, 1910 384
5 Charlie Hickman, 1902 378

1920-1941
1 Tris Speaker, 1925 389
2 Tris Speaker, 1920 388
3 Tris Speaker, 1923 380
4 Tris Speaker, 1922 378
5 Earl Averill, 1936 378

1942-1960
1 Lou Boudreau, 1948 355
2 Bobby Avila, 1954 341
3 Al Rosen, 1953 336
4 Dale Mitchell, 1948 336
5 Lou Boudreau, 1944 327

1961-1976
1 Jim Piersall, 1961 322
2 Rico Carty, 1976 310
3 Vic Davalillo, 1965 301
4 Tito Francona, 1961 301
5 Johnny Romano, 1961 299

1977-1995
1 Albert Belle, 1994 357
2 Kenny Lofton, 1994 349
3 Miguel Dilone, 1980 341
4 Pat Tabler, 1986 326
5 Kenny Lofton, 1993 325

Relative Batting Average

1 Nap Lajoie, 1910 . . . . 1.537
2 Tris Speaker, 1916 . . . . . . 1.506
3 Nap Lajoie, 1904 . . . . 1.499
4 Joe Jackson, 1911 . . . . . . 1.452
5 Joe Jackson, 1912 . . . . . . 1.451
6 Joe Jackson, 1913 . . . . . . 1.411
7 Nap Lajoie, 1906 . . . . 1.390
8 Tris Speaker, 1917 . . . . . . 1.380
9 Nap Lajoie, 1912 . . . . 1.353
10 Charlie Hickman, 1902 . . . 1.334
11 Tris Speaker, 1920 . . . . . . 1.330
12 Joe Jackson, 1914 . . . . . . 1.317
13 Tris Speaker, 1923 . . . . . . 1.310
14 Nap Lajoie, 1903 . . . . 1.309
15 Albert Belle, 1994 . . . . . . 1.309
16 Lou Boudreau, 1948 . . . . . 1.302
17 Tris Speaker, 1925 . . . . . . 1.300
18 Tris Speaker, 1922 . . . . . . 1.290
19 Bobby Avila, 1954 . . . . . . 1.284
20 Nap Lajoie, 1909 . . . . 1.283

Batting Average (by position)

First Base
1 Lew Fonseca, 1929 369
2 George Burns, 1926 358
3 Ed Morgan, 1931 351
4 Ed Morgan, 1930 349
5 Hal Trosky, 1936 343

Second Base
1 Nap Lajoie, 1910 384
2 Nap Lajoie, 1906 355
3 Johnny Hodapp, 1930 354
4 Nap Lajoie, 1903 344
5 Bobby Avila, 1954 341

Shortstop
1 Lou Boudreau, 1948 355
2 Joe Sewell, 1923 353
3 Joe Sewell, 1925 336
4 Lou Boudreau, 1944 327
5 Joe Sewell, 1926 324

Third Base
1 Bill Bradley, 1902 340
2 Al Rosen, 1953 336
3 Ken Keltner, 1939 325
4 Johnny Hodapp, 1928 323
5 Larry Gardner, 1921 319

Outfield
1 Joe Jackson, 1911 408
2 Joe Jackson, 1912 395
3 Tris Speaker, 1925 389
4 Tris Speaker, 1920 388
5 Tris Speaker, 1916 386
6 Tris Speaker, 1923 380
7 Tris Speaker, 1922 378
8 Earl Averill, 1936 378
9 Joe Jackson, 1913 373
10 Tris Speaker, 1921 362

Catcher

1 Steve O'Neill, 1921 322
2 Steve O'Neill, 1920 321
3 Ron Hassey, 1980 318
4 Frankie Pytlak, 1937 315
5 Steve O'Neill, 1922 311

On Base Percentage

1 Tris Speaker, 1920 483
2 Tris Speaker, 1925 479
3 Tris Speaker, 1922 474
4 Tris Speaker, 1916 470
5 Tris Speaker, 1923 469
6 Joe Jackson, 1911 468
7 Joe Jackson, 1913 460
8 Joe Jackson, 1912 458
9 Joe Sewell, 1923 456
10 Lou Boudreau, 1948 453
11 Ed Morgan, 1931 451
12 Nap Lajoie, 1910 445
13 Albert Belle, 1994 442
14 Larry Doby, 1950 442
15 Jim Thome, 1995 440
16 Tris Speaker, 1921 439
17 Earl Averill, 1936 438
18 Tris Speaker, 1924 432
19 Tris Speaker, 1917 432
20 Mike Hargrove, 1981 432

Slugging Average

1 Albert Belle, 1994 714
2 Albert Belle, 1995 690
3 Hal Trosky, 1936 644
4 Earl Averill, 1936 627
5 Rocky Colavito, 1958 620
6 Al Rosen, 1953 613
7 Tris Speaker, 1923 610
8 Tris Speaker, 1922 606
9 Jeff Heath, 1938 602
10 Ed Morgan, 1930 601
11 Hal Trosky, 1934 598
12 Joe Jackson, 1911 590
13 Hal Trosky, 1939 589
14 Jeff Heath, 1941 586
15 Joe Jackson, 1912 579
16 Tris Speaker, 1925 578
17 Earl Averill, 1931 576
18 Earl Averill, 1932 569
19 Earl Averill, 1934 569
20 Tris Speaker, 1920 562

Production

1 Albert Belle, 1994 . . . . . . 1.156
2 Albert Belle, 1995 . . . . . . 1.094
3 Tris Speaker, 1922 . . . . . 1.080
4 Tris Speaker, 1923 . . . . . 1.079
5 Earl Averill, 1936 . . . . . . 1.065
6 Joe Jackson, 1911 . . . . . . 1.058
7 Tris Speaker, 1925 . . . . . 1.057
8 Tris Speaker, 1920 . . . . . 1.045
9 Joe Jackson, 1912 . . . . . . 1.036
10 Al Rosen, 1953 . . . . 1.034
11 Rocky Colavito, 1958 . . . . 1.027
12 Hal Trosky, 1936 . . . . 1.026
13 Ed Morgan, 1930 . . . . 1.014
14 Joe Jackson, 1913 . . . . . . 1.011
15 Jim Thome, 1995 998
16 Hal Trosky, 1939 994
17 Lou Boudreau, 1948 987
18 Hal Trosky, 1934 987
19 Larry Doby, 1950 986
20 Jeff Heath, 1938 985

Adjusted Production

1 Nap Lajoie, 1904 205
2 Nap Lajoie, 1910 198
3 Joe Jackson, 1911 192
4 Albert Belle, 1994 191
5 Joe Jackson, 1913 190
6 Joe Jackson, 1912 190
7 Tris Speaker, 1923 183
8 Rocky Colavito, 1958 183
9 Al Rosen, 1953 181
10 Tris Speaker, 1916 181
11 Tris Speaker, 1922 178
12 Albert Belle, 1995 178
13 Tris Speaker, 1920 171
14 Charlie Hickman, 1902 . . . 170
15 Nap Lajoie, 1906 170
16 Nap Lajoie, 1903 170
17 Tris Speaker, 1917 168
18 Lou Boudreau, 1948 166
19 Larry Doby, 1952 166
20 Tris Speaker, 1925 166

Batting Runs

1 Joe Jackson, 1911 72
2 Tris Speaker, 1923 71
3 Joe Jackson, 1912 70
4 Nap Lajoie, 1910 68
5 Tris Speaker, 1920 66
6 Joe Jackson, 1913 66
7 Tris Speaker, 1916 65
8 Al Rosen, 1953 63
9 Nap Lajoie, 1904 62
10 Albert Belle, 1995 61
11 Earl Averill, 1936 56
12 Albert Belle, 1994 56
13 Rocky Colavito, 1958 53
14 Tris Speaker, 1922 53
15 Lou Boudreau, 1948 53
16 Tris Speaker, 1917 51
17 Earl Averill, 1931 48
18 Tris Speaker, 1925 47
19 Ed Morgan, 1930 46
20 Earl Averill, 1934 46

Adjusted Batting Runs

1 Tris Speaker, 1923 71
2 Joe Jackson, 1911 70
3 Al Rosen, 1953 67
4 Nap Lajoie, 1910 66
5 Joe Jackson, 1912 66
6 Nap Lajoie, 1904 64
7 Joe Jackson, 1913 62
8 Tris Speaker, 1920 61
9 Albert Belle, 1995 60
10 Tris Speaker, 1916 57
11 Lou Boudreau, 1948 56
12 Albert Belle, 1994 56
13 Rocky Colavito, 1958 56
14 Earl Averill, 1936 55
15 Tris Speaker, 1922 52
16 Jeff Heath, 1941 51
17 Nap Lajoie, 1906 46
18 Tris Speaker, 1925 46
19 Al Rosen, 1952 46
20 Larry Doby, 1950 46

Batting Wins

1 Nap Lajoie, 1910 . . . . 7.6
2 Tris Speaker, 1916 . . . . . 7.1
3 Joe Jackson, 1911 . . . . . . 7.1
4 Joe Jackson, 1912 . . . . . . 7.0
5 Nap Lajoie, 1904 . . . . 7.0
6 Joe Jackson, 1913 . . . . . . 7.0
7 Tris Speaker, 1923 . . . . . 6.9
8 Tris Speaker, 1920 . . . . . 6.4
9 Al Rosen, 1953 . . . . 6.3
10 Tris Speaker, 1917 . . . . . 5.7
11 Albert Belle, 1995 . . . . . . 5.7
12 Rocky Colavito, 1958 . . . . 5.5
13 Albert Belle, 1994 . . . . . . 5.2
14 Tris Speaker, 1922 . . . . . 5.1
15 Lou Boudreau, 1948 . . . . . 5.1
16 Earl Averill, 1936 . . . . 5.0
17 Nap Lajoie, 1906 . . . . 4.9
18 Earl Averill, 1931 . . . . 4.5
19 Tris Speaker, 1925 . . . . . 4.3
20 Jeff Heath, 1941 . . . . 4.3

Adjusted Batting Wins

1 Nap Lajoie, 1910 . . . . 7.4
2 Nap Lajoie, 1904 . . . . 7.1
3 Joe Jackson, 1911 . . . . . . 6.9
4 Tris Speaker, 1923 . . . . . 6.9
5 Al Rosen, 1953 . . . . 6.7
6 Joe Jackson, 1912 . . . . . . 6.6
7 Joe Jackson, 1913 . . . . . . 6.6
8 Tris Speaker, 1916 . . . . . 6.3
9 Tris Speaker, 1920 . . . . . 5.9
10 Rocky Colavito, 1958 . . . . 5.8
11 Albert Belle, 1995 . . . . . . 5.7
12 Lou Boudreau, 1948 . . . . . 5.5
13 Albert Belle, 1994 . . . . . . 5.2
14 Nap Lajoie, 1906 . . . . 5.1
15 Tris Speaker, 1922 . . . . . 5.0
16 Jeff Heath, 1941 . . . . 4.9
17 Earl Averill, 1936 . . . . 4.9
18 Tris Speaker, 1917 . . . . . 4.8
19 Al Rosen, 1952 . . . . 4.8
20 Larry Doby, 1952 . . . . 4.7

Runs Created

1	Joe Jackson, 1911	175
2	Earl Averill, 1936	168
3	Joe Jackson, 1912	166
4	Tris Speaker, 1923	166
5	Al Rosen, 1953	155
6	Tris Speaker, 1920	152
7	Hal Trosky, 1936	150
8	Nap Lajoie, 1910	147
9	Earl Averill, 1934	145
10	Hal Trosky, 1934	145
11	Ed Morgan, 1930	144
12	Earl Averill, 1931	144
13	Albert Belle, 1995	144
14	Lou Boudreau, 1948	143
15	Nap Lajoie, 1904	142
16	Joe Jackson, 1913	140
17	Earl Averill, 1932	140
18	Jeff Heath, 1941	138
19	Joe Vosmik, 1935	137
20	Tris Speaker, 1916	132

Total Average

1	Joe Jackson, 1911	1.308
2	Albert Belle, 1994	1.304
3	Tris Speaker, 1922	1.272
4	Joe Jackson, 1912	1.249
5	Tris Speaker, 1925	1.231
6	Tris Speaker, 1923	1.222
7	Joe Jackson, 1913	1.215
8	Earl Averill, 1936	1.171
9	Tris Speaker, 1920	1.165
10	Albert Belle, 1995	1.150
11	Jim Thome, 1995	1.106
12	Kenny Lofton, 1994	1.101
13	Ed Morgan, 1930	1.089
14	Nap Lajoie, 1910	1.085
15	Rocky Colavito, 1958	1.078
16	Al Rosen, 1953	1.078
17	Earl Averill, 1934	1.075
18	Larry Doby, 1950	1.073
19	Nap Lajoie, 1904	1.070
20	Hal Trosky, 1936	1.065

Runs Produced

1	Earl Averill, 1931	251
2	Tris Speaker, 1923	246
3	Hal Trosky, 1936	244
4	Tris Speaker, 1920	236
5	Earl Averill, 1936	234
6	Ed Morgan, 1930	232
7	Hal Trosky, 1934	224
8	Johnny Hodapp, 1930	223
9	Larry Gardner, 1921	218
10	Al Rosen, 1953	217
11	Earl Averill, 1934	210
12	Joe Jackson, 1912	208
	Earl Averill, 1932	208
14	George Burns, 1926	207
15	Joe Sewell, 1923	204
	Lou Boudreau, 1948	204
17	Joe Jackson, 1911	202
	Earl Averill, 1930	202
19	Joe Sewell, 1924	201
20	2 players tied	200

Clutch Hitting Index

1	George Stovall, 1911	163
2	John Gochnauer, 1903	155
3	Nap Lajoie, 1912	145
4	Larry Gardner, 1920	144
5	Larry Gardner, 1921	141
6	Julio Franco, 1985	137
7	Julio Franco, 1984	132
8	Steve O'Neill, 1922	132
9	Lou Boudreau, 1940	130
10	Bill Bradley, 1904	129
11	Chick Gandil, 1916	129
12	Mike Hargrove, 1981	129
13	Willie Kamm, 1931	128
14	Von Hayes, 1982	128
15	Joe Wood, 1922	126
16	George Strickland, 1959	126
17	Larry Gardner, 1922	125
18	Braggo Roth, 1917	125
	Rick Manning, 1980	125
20	2 players tied	125

Isolated Power

1	Albert Belle, 1995	.374
2	Albert Belle, 1994	.357
3	Rocky Colavito, 1958	.317
4	Hal Trosky, 1936	.300
5	Al Rosen, 1953	.277
6	Hal Trosky, 1934	.269
7	Larry Doby, 1952	.266
8	Andy Thornton, 1977	.263
9	Albert Belle, 1993	.263
10	Jeff Heath, 1938	.259
11	Al Rosen, 1950	.256
12	Earl Averill, 1934	.256
13	Jim Thome, 1994	.255
14	Earl Averill, 1932	.255
15	Rocky Colavito, 1959	.255
16	Hal Trosky, 1939	.254
17	Andy Thornton, 1978	.254
18	Ed Morgan, 1930	.252
19	Manny Ramirez, 1995	.250
20	Hal Trosky, 1937	.250

Extra Base Hits

1	Albert Belle, 1995	103
2	Hal Trosky, 1936	96
3	Hal Trosky, 1934	89
4	Tris Speaker, 1923	87
5	Earl Averill, 1934	85
6	Ed Morgan, 1930	84
7	Earl Averill, 1932	83
8	Earl Averill, 1936	82
9	Earl Averill, 1931	78
10	Joe Vosmik, 1935	77
	Odell Hale, 1936	77
	Hal Trosky, 1937	77
	Albert Belle, 1993	77
14	Jeff Heath, 1941	76
15	Al Rosen, 1953	75
16	Earl Averill, 1929	74
	Joe Carter, 1986	74
18	Joe Jackson, 1912	73
	Moose Solters, 1937	73
	Albert Belle, 1994	73

Pinch Hits

1	Bob Hale, 1960	19
2	Gomer Hodge, 1971	16
3	Don Dillard, 1961	15
4	Bibb Falk, 1932	14
	Dale Mitchell, 1954	14
	Richie Scheinblum, 1969	14

Pinch Hit Average
(20 at-bats minimum)

1	Don Dillard, 1961	.429
2	George Uhle, 1924	.423
3	Willie Kirkland, 1963	.400
4	Ralph Kiner, 1955	.393
5	Bibb Falk, 1930	.382

Pinch Hit Home Runs

1	Gene Green, 1962	3
	Fred Whitfield, 1965	3
	Ted Uhlaender, 1970	3
	Ron Kittle, 1988	3

Total Player Rating / 150g

1	Nap Lajoie, 1903	10.08
2	Nap Lajoie, 1906	8.39
3	Nap Lajoie, 1910	8.02
4	Lou Boudreau, 1944	7.80
5	Nap Lajoie, 1904	7.71
6	Nap Lajoie, 1908	7.45
7	Nap Lajoie, 1907	7.23
8	Albert Belle, 1994	7.08
9	Joe Jackson, 1911	6.94
10	Lou Boudreau, 1948	6.81
11	Joe Jackson, 1912	6.72
12	Lou Boudreau, 1943	6.61
13	Tris Speaker, 1923	6.40
14	Albert Belle, 1995	6.29
15	Joe Jackson, 1913	6.08
16	Al Rosen, 1953	6.00
17	Joe Sewell, 1923	5.88
18	Tris Speaker, 1925	5.77
19	Tris Speaker, 1922	5.73
20	Tris Speaker, 1916	5.66

Stolen Bases

1	Kenny Lofton, 1993	70
2	Kenny Lofton, 1992	66
3	Miguel Dilone, 1980	61
4	Kenny Lofton, 1994	60
5	Kenny Lofton, 1995	54
6	Ray Chapman, 1917	52
	Brett Butler, 1984	52
8	Braggo Roth, 1917	51
9	Brett Butler, 1985	47
10	Harry Bay, 1903	45
11	Elmer Flick, 1907	41
	Joe Jackson, 1911	41
13	Jose Cardenal, 1968	40
14	Elmer Flick, 1906	39
15	Elmer Flick, 1904	38
	Harry Bay, 1904	38
17	Josh Clarke, 1908	37
18	5 players tied	36

Stolen Base Average

1	Frank Duffy, 1976	100.0
2	Toby Harrah, 1981	92.3
3	Chico Salmon, 1966	90.9
	Andy Allanson, 1986	90.9
5	Toby Harrah, 1980	89.5
6	Rick Manning, 1981	89.3
7	Alan Bannister, 1981	88.9
8	Leon Wagner, 1964	87.5
9	Miguel Dilone, 1982	86.8
10	3 players tied	85.7

Stolen Base Runs

1	Kenny Lofton, 1992	13
	Kenny Lofton, 1993	13
3	Kenny Lofton, 1994	11
4	Miguel Dilone, 1980	8
5	Kenny Lofton, 1995	7
6	Jose Cardenal, 1969	7
7	Miguel Dilone, 1982	7
8	Rick Manning, 1981	6
	Joe Carter, 1987	6
10	Joe Carter, 1988	5

Stolen Base Wins

1	Kenny Lofton, 1992	1.3
2	Kenny Lofton, 1993	1.2
3	Kenny Lofton, 1994	1.0
4	Jose Cardenal, 1969	0.8
5	Miguel Dilone, 1980	0.7
6	Miguel Dilone, 1982	0.7
7	Kenny Lofton, 1995	0.7
8	Rick Manning, 1981	0.6
9	Joe Carter, 1987	0.5
10	Joe Carter, 1988	0.5

Fielding Average

First Base

1	Boog Powell, 1975	.997
2	Stuffy McInnis, 1922	.997
3	Mike Hargrove, 1982	.996
4	Vic Power, 1960	.996
5	Mike Rocco, 1943	.995

Second Base

1	Duane Kuiper, 1979	.988
2	Duane Kuiper, 1976	.987
3	Bobby Avila, 1953	.986
4	Jerry Browne, 1990	.985
5	Duane Kuiper, 1977	.985

Shortstop

1	Frank Duffy, 1973	.986
2	Omar Vizquel, 1995	.986
3	Frank Duffy, 1976	.983
4	Lou Boudreau, 1947	.982
5	Frank Duffy, 1974	.980

Third Base

1	Willie Kamm, 1933	.984
2	Willie Kamm, 1934	.978
3	Bubba Phillips, 1962	.977
4	Larry Gardner, 1920	.976
5	Brook Jacoby, 1988	.975

Outfield

1	Rocky Colavito, 1965	1.000
2	Brett Butler, 1985	.998
3	Cory Snyder, 1989	.997
4	Dick Porter, 1933	.996
5	Larry Doby, 1954	.995
6	Rick Manning, 1978	.995
7	Dale Mitchell, 1949	.994
8	George Vukovich, 1984	.994
9	Jorge Orta, 1981	.994
10	Larry Doby, 1955	.994

Catcher

1	Joe Azcue, 1967	.999
2	Jim Hegan, 1955	.997
3	Sandy Alomar, 1992	.996
4	Joe Azcue, 1968	.996
5	Sandy Alomar, 1994	.996

Pitcher

1	Stan Coveleski, 1921	.992
2	Willis Hudlin, 1927	.989
3	Stan Coveleski, 1916	.989
4	Bob Rhoads, 1908	.983
5	Bob Lemon, 1952	.982

Total Chances per Game

First Base

1	George Stovall, 1908	12.20
2	George Stovall, 1907	12.08
3	Charlie Hickman, 1902	11.90
4	Chick Gandil, 1916	11.52
5	Claude Rossman, 1906	11.51

Second Base

1	Odell Hale, 1934	6.78
2	Nap Lajoie, 1903	6.59
3	Nap Lajoie, 1908	6.57
4	Bill Cissell, 1932	6.47
5	Johnny Hodapp, 1930	6.43

Shortstop

1	Terry Turner, 1906	6.07
2	Ray Chapman, 1917	6.07
3	Ray Chapman, 1918	6.00
4	Joe Sewell, 1924	5.88
5	Lou Boudreau, 1944	5.87

Third Base

1	Bill Bradley, 1902	4.05
2	Rube Lutzke, 1923	4.04
3	Rube Lutzke, 1924	4.02
4	Bill Bradley, 1901	3.96
5	Ken Keltner, 1944	3.72

Outfield

1	Tris Speaker, 1925	3.10
2	Kenny Lofton, 1992	3.09
3	Rick Manning, 1979	3.06
4	Rick Manning, 1981	3.06
5	Larry Doby, 1952	3.05
6	Brett Butler, 1985	3.05
7	Tris Speaker, 1919	3.04
8	Catfish Metkovich, 1947	2.98
9	Rick Manning, 1975	2.98
10	Brett Butler, 1984	2.98

Catcher

1	Joe Azcue, 1967	8.07
2	Johnny Romano, 1964	7.91
3	Ray Fosse, 1970	7.78
4	Joe Azcue, 1968	7.75
5	Duke Sims, 1967	7.34

Pitcher

1	Addie Joss, 1905	4.06
2	Addie Joss, 1907	3.98
3	Addie Joss, 1903	3.97
4	Addie Joss, 1902	3.78
5	Red Donahue, 1903	3.63

Chances Accepted per Game

First Base

1	George Stovall, 1908	12.08
2	George Stovall, 1907	11.88
3	Charlie Hickman, 1902	11.49
4	Chick Gandil, 1916	11.46
5	Claude Rossman, 1906	11.33

Second Base

1	Odell Hale, 1934	6.48
2	Nap Lajoie, 1908	6.33
3	Nap Lajoie, 1903	6.30
4	Johnny Hodapp, 1930	6.23
5	Bill Cissell, 1932	6.23

Shortstop

1	Terry Turner, 1906	5.83
2	Lou Boudreau, 1944	5.74
3	Ray Chapman, 1917	5.69
4	Joe Sewell, 1924	5.64
5	Ray Chapman, 1918	5.62

Third Base

1	Rube Lutzke, 1924	3.81
2	Rube Lutzke, 1923	3.79
3	Bill Bradley, 1902	3.74
4	Bill Bradley, 1901	3.68
5	Graig Nettles, 1971	3.61

Outfield

1	Brett Butler, 1985	3.04
2	Kenny Lofton, 1992	3.03
3	Rick Manning, 1979	3.02
4	Rick Manning, 1981	3.02
5	Larry Doby, 1952	3.01
6	Tris Speaker, 1925	3.00
7	Tris Speaker, 1919	2.99
8	Brett Butler, 1984	2.96
9	Catfish Metkovich, 1947	2.95
10	Brett Butler, 1987	2.92

Catcher

1	Joe Azcue, 1967	8.06
2	Johnny Romano, 1964	7.83
3	Joe Azcue, 1968	7.72
4	Ray Fosse, 1970	7.70
5	Duke Sims, 1967	7.26

Pitcher

1	Addie Joss, 1905	3.94
2	Addie Joss, 1907	3.90
3	Addie Joss, 1903	3.75
4	Addie Joss, 1902	3.59
5	Addie Joss, 1906	3.50

Putouts

First Base

1	Hal Trosky, 1935	1567
2	Chick Gandil, 1916	1557
3	George Stovall, 1908	1508
4	Les Fleming, 1942	1503
5	George Burns, 1926	1499

Second Base

1	Nap Lajoie, 1908	450
2	Roy Hughes, 1936	421
3	Bill Wambsganss, 1920	414
4	Odell Hale, 1934	408
5	Johnny Hodapp, 1930	403

Shortstop

1	Ray Chapman, 1915	378
2	Joe Sewell, 1927	361
3	Ray Chapman, 1917	360
4	Joe Sewell, 1924	349
5	Lou Boudreau, 1944	339

Third Base

1	Bill Bradley, 1901	192
2	Bill Bradley, 1902	188
	Bill Bradley, 1905	188
	Bubba Phillips, 1961	188
5	Ken Keltner, 1939	187

Outfield

1	Brett Butler, 1984	448
2	Joe Carter, 1988	444
3	Brett Butler, 1985	437
4	Brett Butler, 1986	434
5	Joe Vosmik, 1932	432
6	Kenny Lofton, 1992	420
7	Rick Manning, 1979	417
8	Earl Averill, 1932	412
9	Larry Doby, 1954	411
10	Earl Averill, 1934	410

Catcher

1	Ray Fosse, 1970	854
2	Johnny Romano, 1961	752
3	Ray Fosse, 1971	748
4	Johnny Romano, 1964	714
	Joe Azcue, 1965	714

Pitcher

1	Lary Sorensen, 1983	36
2	Bob Lemon, 1949	34
3	Bob Lemon, 1952	32
4	Bob Lemon, 1953	31
5	George Uhle, 1926	30

Putouts per Game

First Base

1	George Stovall, 1908	11.42
2	George Stovall, 1907	11.32
3	Charlie Hickman, 1902	11.01
4	Claude Rossman, 1906	10.90
5	Chick Gandil, 1916	10.74

Second Base

1	Nap Lajoie, 1903	3.00
2	Odell Hale, 1934	2.98
3	Nap Lajoie, 1908	2.88
4	Roy Hughes, 1936	2.77
5	Nap Lajoie, 1906	2.72

Shortstop

1	Ray Chapman, 1918	2.51
2	Ray Chapman, 1915	2.45
3	Joe Sewell, 1927	2.36
4	Ray Chapman, 1917	2.31
5	Joe Sewell, 1924	2.28

Third Base

1	Rube Lutzke, 1924	1.50
2	Bill Bradley, 1901	1.44
3	Bill Bradley, 1902	1.37
4	Terry Turner, 1914	1.33
5	Bubba Phillips, 1961	1.31

Outfield

1	Rick Manning, 1981	2.96
2	Rick Manning, 1979	2.96
3	Kenny Lofton, 1992	2.94
4	Catfish Metkovich, 1947	2.93
5	Larry Doby, 1952	2.93
6	Brett Butler, 1985	2.91
7	Brett Butler, 1987	2.89
8	Brett Butler, 1984	2.87
9	Tris Speaker, 1925	2.85
10	Joe Carter, 1988	2.85

Catcher

1	Johnny Romano, 1964	7.44
2	Joe Azcue, 1967	7.40
3	Joe Azcue, 1968	7.21
4	Ray Fosse, 1970	7.12
5	Joe Azcue, 1965	6.61

Pitcher

1	Lary Sorensen, 1983	1.00
2	Bob Lemon, 1949	0.92
3	Tom Candiotti, 1989	0.90
4	Otto Hess, 1905	0.85
5	Willis Hudlin, 1939	0.78

Assists

First Base

1	Mickey Vernon, 1949	155
2	Vic Power, 1960	145
3	Vic Power, 1961	142
4	Mike Rocco, 1944	138
5	Tito Francona, 1962	127

Second Base

1	Johnny Hodapp, 1930	557
2	Nap Lajoie, 1908	538
3	Carl Lind, 1928	505
4	Jerry Kindall, 1962	494
5	Bill Wambsganss, 1920	489

Shortstop

1	Terry Turner, 1906	570
2	Joe Sewell, 1925	529
3	Ray Chapman, 1917	528
4	Lou Boudreau, 1944	516
5	Joe Sewell, 1924	514

Third Base

1	Graig Nettles, 1971	412
2	Ken Keltner, 1944	369
3	Buddy Bell, 1973	363
4	Larry Gardner, 1920	362
5	Graig Nettles, 1970	358

Outfield

1	Joe Jackson, 1911	32
2	Joe Jackson, 1912	30
3	Joe Birmingham, 1907	28
	Joe Jackson, 1913	28
5	Tris Speaker, 1923	26
6	Tris Speaker, 1916	25
	Tris Speaker, 1919	25
8	Joe Birmingham, 1910	24
	Tris Speaker, 1920	24
10	Tris Speaker, 1917	23

Catcher

1	Steve O'Neill, 1915	175
2	Steve O'Neill, 1916	154
	Steve O'Neill, 1918	154
4	Steve O'Neill, 1917	145
5	Steve O'Neill, 1914	134

Pitcher

1	Addie Joss, 1907	143
2	Addie Joss, 1908	109
3	Stan Coveleski, 1921	108
4	Addie Joss, 1903	107
5	Addie Joss, 1902	106
	Addie Joss, 1905	106

Assists per Game

First Base

1	Mickey Vernon, 1949	1.01
2	Vic Power, 1961	1.01
3	Vic Power, 1960	0.99
4	Vic Power, 1959	0.91
5	Mike Rocco, 1944	0.89

Second Base

1	Bill Cissell, 1932	3.68
2	Johnny Hodapp, 1930	3.62
3	Nap Lajoie, 1907	3.60
4	Odell Hale, 1934	3.50
5	Boze Berger, 1935	3.49

Shortstop

1	Terry Turner, 1906	3.88
2	Bill Knickerbocker, 1935	3.54
3	John Gochnauer, 1902	3.52
4	Lou Boudreau, 1944	3.46
5	Joe Sewell, 1925	3.46

Third Base

1	Graig Nettles, 1971	2.61
2	Buddy Bell, 1978	2.55
3	Rube Lutzke, 1923	2.51
4	Ken Keltner, 1944	2.48
5	Buddy Bell, 1974	2.38

Outfield

1	Joe Birmingham, 1910	0.23
2	Joe Jackson, 1911	0.22
3	Joe Birmingham, 1907	0.22
4	Nemo Leibold, 1914	0.21
5	Joe Jackson, 1912	0.20
6	Charlie Jamieson, 1928	0.20
7	Joe Jackson, 1913	0.19
8	Tris Speaker, 1919	0.19
9	Braggo Roth, 1916	0.18
10	Tris Speaker, 1923	0.17

Catcher

1	Steve O'Neill, 1914	1.63
2	Steve O'Neill, 1915	1.52
3	Steve O'Neill, 1913	1.49
4	Fred Carisch, 1913	1.44
5	Harry Bemis, 1902	1.38

Pitcher

1	Addie Joss, 1907	3.40
2	Addie Joss, 1903	3.34
3	Addie Joss, 1902	3.31
4	Addie Joss, 1905	3.21
5	Red Donahue, 1903	3.13

Double Plays

First Base

1	Mickey Vernon, 1949	168
2	Mike Rocco, 1944	158
3	Tito Francona, 1962	157
4	Chris Chambliss, 1973	153
5	Les Fleming, 1942	152

Second Base

1	Carlos Baerga, 1992	138
2	Ray Mack, 1943	123
	Joe Gordon, 1949	123
4	Carl Lind, 1928	116
5	Bobby Avila, 1953	114
	Jerry Kindall, 1962	114

Shortstop

1	Lou Boudreau, 1944	134
2	Lou Boudreau, 1943	122
3	Lou Boudreau, 1947	120
4	Lou Boudreau, 1948	119
5	Lou Boudreau, 1940	116
	Julio Franco, 1984	116

Third Base

1	Graig Nettles, 1971	54
2	Buddy Bell, 1973	44
3	Ken Keltner, 1939	40
	Graig Nettles, 1970	40
5	Ken Keltner, 1942	38
	Al Rosen, 1953	38

Outfield

1	Tris Speaker, 1916	10
2	Ollie Pickering, 1901	9
	Tris Speaker, 1925	9
4	Joe Birmingham, 1907	8
	Joe Birmingham, 1910	8
	Joe Jackson, 1911	8
	Elmer Smith, 1919	8
	Tris Speaker, 1920	8
9	Elmer Flick, 1907	7
	Tris Speaker, 1923	7
	Tris Speaker, 1926	7
	Jose Cardenal, 1968	7
	Albert Belle, 1993	7

Catcher

1	Steve O'Neill, 1916	36
2	Frankie Hayes, 1945	23
3	Steve O'Neill, 1914	22
4	Steve O'Neill, 1917	19
	Steve O'Neill, 1920	19

Pitcher

1	Bob Lemon, 1953	15
2	Gene Bearden, 1948	11
3	Willis Hudlin, 1931	10
4	George Uhle, 1923	9
5	Willis Hudlin, 1929	8
	Willis Hudlin, 1934	8
	Bob Lemon, 1948	8
	Bob Lemon, 1954	8

Fielding Wins

1	Nap Lajoie, 1908	5.6
2	Nap Lajoie, 1907	5.0
3	Graig Nettles, 1971	4.6
4	Nap Lajoie, 1903	4.2
5	Nap Lajoie, 1906	3.5
6	Lou Boudreau, 1943	3.1
7	Buddy Bell, 1978	2.9
8	Graig Nettles, 1970	2.9
9	Nap Lajoie, 1902	2.8
10	Ray Chapman, 1917	2.7
11	Lou Boudreau, 1944	2.7
12	Joe Sewell, 1928	2.6
13	Terry Turner, 1906	2.6
14	Buddy Bell, 1973	2.5
15	Odell Hale, 1934	2.4
16	Odell Hale, 1937	2.4
17	Terry Turner, 1914	2.4
18	Jim Hegan, 1950	2.3
19	Alvaro Espinoza, 1994	2.3
20	Jackie Tavener, 1929	2.2

Fielding Runs

1	Nap Lajoie, 1908	49.3
2	Nap Lajoie, 1907	45.0
3	Graig Nettles, 1971	42.3
4	Nap Lajoie, 1903	40.1
5	Nap Lajoie, 1906	31.9
6	Nap Lajoie, 1902	29.6
7	Lou Boudreau, 1943	28.3
	Buddy Bell, 1978	28.3
9	Graig Nettles, 1970	27.8
10	Joe Sewell, 1928	27.0
11	Odell Hale, 1937	25.9
12	Lou Boudreau, 1944	25.8
13	Odell Hale, 1934	25.7
14	Ray Chapman, 1917	24.4
	Alvaro Espinoza, 1994	24.4
16	Buddy Bell, 1973	24.3
17	Jim Hegan, 1950	24.2
18	Joe Vosmik, 1932	23.8
19	Terry Turner, 1906	23.6
20	Jackie Tavener, 1929	23.4

Fielding Runs

First Base

1	Vic Power, 1960	21
2	Mickey Vernon, 1949	19
3	Mike Rocco, 1944	17
4	Vic Power, 1961	17
5	Vic Power, 1959	15

Second Base

1	Nap Lajoie, 1908	48
2	Nap Lajoie, 1907	43
3	Nap Lajoie, 1903	39
4	Nap Lajoie, 1906	26
5	Odell Hale, 1934	26

Shortstop

1	Lou Boudreau, 1943	28
2	Lou Boudreau, 1944	26
3	Ray Chapman, 1917	24
4	Terry Turner, 1906	24
5	Joe Sewell, 1924	21

Third Base

1	Graig Nettles, 1971	42
2	Graig Nettles, 1970	29
3	Buddy Bell, 1978	28
4	Buddy Bell, 1973	25
5	Ken Keltner, 1941	22

Outfield

1	Joe Vosmik, 1932	24
2	Brett Butler, 1985	22
3	Charlie Jamieson, 1928	20
4	Albert Belle, 1993	19
5	Tris Speaker, 1919	19
6	Cory Snyder, 1989	18
7	Kenny Lofton, 1992	17
8	Minnie Minoso, 1959	16
9	Vic Davalillo, 1964	16
10	Jim Piersall, 1961	16

Catcher

1	Jim Hegan, 1950	24
2	Jim Hegan, 1948	21
3	Jim Hegan, 1956	16
4	Fred Carisch, 1913	13
5	Jim Hegan, 1954	13

Pitcher

1	Addie Joss, 1907	9
2	Bob Lemon, 1948	8
3	Bob Lemon, 1953	8
4	Mel Harder, 1933	8
5	Stan Coveleski, 1921	7

Total Player Rating

1	Nap Lajoie, 1906	8.5
	Nap Lajoie, 1910	8.5
3	Nap Lajoie, 1903	8.4
4	Nap Lajoie, 1908	7.8
	Lou Boudreau, 1944	7.8
6	Nap Lajoie, 1904	7.2
7	Joe Jackson, 1912	6.9
	Lou Boudreau, 1948	6.9
9	Joe Jackson, 1911	6.8
10	Lou Boudreau, 1943	6.7
11	Nap Lajoie, 1907	6.6
12	Tris Speaker, 1923	6.4
13	Nap Lajoie, 1902	6.3
14	Al Rosen, 1953	6.2
15	Joe Jackson, 1913	6.0
	Joe Sewell, 1923	6.0
	Albert Belle, 1995	6.0
18	Tris Speaker, 1916	5.7
19	Ray Chapman, 1917	5.4
	Joe Sewell, 1928	5.4

Total Player Rating (alpha.)

Albert Belle, 1995	6.0
Lou Boudreau, 1943	6.7
Lou Boudreau, 1944	7.8
Lou Boudreau, 1948	6.9
Ray Chapman, 1917	5.4
Joe Jackson, 1911	6.8
Joe Jackson, 1912	6.9
Joe Jackson, 1913	6.0
Nap Lajoie, 1902	6.3
Nap Lajoie, 1903	8.4
Nap Lajoie, 1904	7.2
Nap Lajoie, 1906	8.5
Nap Lajoie, 1907	6.6
Nap Lajoie, 1908	7.8
Nap Lajoie, 1910	8.5
Al Rosen, 1953	6.2
Joe Sewell, 1923	6.0
Joe Sewell, 1928	5.4
Tris Speaker, 1916	5.7
Tris Speaker, 1923	6.4

Total Player Rating (by era)

1901-1919
1	Nap Lajoie, 1906	8.5
	Nap Lajoie, 1910	8.5
3	Nap Lajoie, 1903	8.4
4	Nap Lajoie, 1908	7.8
5	Nap Lajoie, 1904	7.2

1920-1941
1	Tris Speaker, 1923	6.4
2	Joe Sewell, 1923	6.0
3	Joe Sewell, 1928	5.4
4	Tris Speaker, 1920	5.2
5	Tris Speaker, 1922	5.0

1942-1960
1	Lou Boudreau, 1944	7.8
2	Lou Boudreau, 1948	6.9
3	Lou Boudreau, 1943	6.7
4	Al Rosen, 1953	6.2
5	Larry Doby, 1952	5.1

1961-1976
1	Graig Nettles, 1971	5.3
2	Rocky Colavito, 1965	3.1
3	Graig Nettles, 1970	2.7
4	Jim Piersall, 1961	2.5
	Rico Carty, 1976	2.5

1977-1995
1	Albert Belle, 1995	6.0
2	Albert Belle, 1993	5.2
3	Albert Belle, 1994	5.0
4	Kenny Lofton, 1994	4.2
5	Kenny Lofton, 1993	4.1

Wins

1	Jim Bagby, 1920	31
2	Addie Joss, 1907	27
	George Uhle, 1926	27
	Bob Feller, 1940	27
5	George Uhle, 1923	26
	Bob Feller, 1946	26
7	Wes Ferrell, 1930	25
	Bob Feller, 1941	25
9	Addie Joss, 1908	24
	Stan Coveleski, 1919	24
	Stan Coveleski, 1920	24
	Bob Feller, 1939	24
	Gaylord Perry, 1972	24
14	10 players tied	23

Wins (by era)

1901-1919
1	Addie Joss, 1907	27
2	Addie Joss, 1908	24
	Stan Coveleski, 1919	24
4	4 players tied	23

1920-1941
1	Jim Bagby, 1920	31
2	George Uhle, 1926	27
	Bob Feller, 1940	27
4	George Uhle, 1923	26
5	2 players tied	25

1942-1960
1	Bob Feller, 1946	26
2	Bob Lemon, 1950	23
	Early Wynn, 1952	23
	Early Wynn, 1954	23
	Bob Lemon, 1954	23

1961-1976
1	Gaylord Perry, 1972	24
2	Luis Tiant, 1968	21
	Gaylord Perry, 1974	21
4	Dick Donovan, 1962	20
	Sam McDowell, 1970	20

1977-1995
1	Len Barker, 1980	19
	Bert Blyleven, 1984	19
3	Greg Swindell, 1988	18
4	Rick Sutcliffe, 1983	17
	Charles Nagy, 1992	17

Losses

1	Pete Dowling, 1901	22
2	Luis Tiant, 1969	20
3	George Kahler, 1912	19
	Al Milnar, 1941	19
	Gaylord Perry, 1973	19
	Wayne Garland, 1977	19
	Rick Wise, 1978	19
8	Tom Candiotti, 1987	18
9	Earl Moore, 1902	17
	Otto Hess, 1906	17
	Willie Mitchell, 1914	17
	Joe Shaute, 1924	17
	Garland Buckeye, 1927	17
	Joe Shaute, 1928	17
	George Uhle, 1928	17
	Mel Harder, 1933	17
	Early Wynn, 1957	17
	Jim Perry, 1961	17
	Sam McDowell, 1971	17
	Neal Heaton, 1985	17

Winning Percentage

1	Bill Bernhard, 1902	.773
2	Vean Gregg, 1911	.767
	Bob Lemon, 1954	.767
4	Gene Bearden, 1948	.741
5	Bob Feller, 1951	.733
6	Bert Blyleven, 1984	.731
7	Bob Feller, 1939	.727
	Orel Hershiser, 1995	.727
	Charles Nagy, 1995	.727
10	Jim Bagby, 1920	.721
11	Addie Joss, 1907	.711
	George Uhle, 1926	.711
	Bob Feller, 1940	.711
14	Al Smith, 1943	.708
15	Mike Garcia, 1954	.704
	Calvin McLish, 1959	.704
17	Addie Joss, 1906	.700
	Luis Tiant, 1968	.700
19	Cy Falkenberg, 1913	.697
20	Early Wynn, 1950	.692

Winning Percentage (by era)

1901-1919
1	Bill Bernhard, 1902	.773
2	Vean Gregg, 1911	.767
3	Addie Joss, 1907	.711
4	Addie Joss, 1906	.700
5	Cy Falkenberg, 1913	.697

1920-1941
1	Bob Feller, 1939	.727
2	Jim Bagby, 1920	.721
3	George Uhle, 1926	.711
	Bob Feller, 1940	.711
5	Wes Ferrell, 1929	.677

1942-1960
1	Bob Lemon, 1954	.767
2	Gene Bearden, 1948	.741
3	Bob Feller, 1951	.733
4	Al Smith, 1943	.708
5	2 players tied	.704

1961-1976
1	Luis Tiant, 1968	.700
2	Dick Donovan, 1962	.667
	Sonny Siebert, 1965	.667
	Sonny Siebert, 1966	.667
5	Sam McDowell, 1970	.625

1977-1995
1	Bert Blyleven, 1984	.731
2	Orel Hershiser, 1995	.727
	Charles Nagy, 1995	.727
4	Charles Nagy, 1992	.630
5	Len Barker, 1980	.613

Games

1	Sid Monge, 1979	76
2	Steve Olin, 1992	72
3	Derek Lilliquist, 1992	71
4	Don McMahon, 1964	70
	Eric Plunk, 1993	70
6	Ernie Camacho, 1984	69
	Jesse Orosco, 1989	69
8	Sid Monge, 1980	67
9	Doug Jones, 1990	66
10	Dan Spillner, 1982	65
11	Ted Power, 1992	64
12	Joe Heving, 1944	63
	Mike Jeffcoat, 1984	63
14	Scott Bailes, 1986	62
	Jose Mesa, 1995	62
16	Stan Williams, 1969	61
	Dave LaRoche, 1975	61
	Dave LaRoche, 1976	61
	Victor Cruz, 1979	61
20	4 players tied	60

Games (by era)

1901-1919
1	Jim Bagby, 1917	49
2	Sam Jones, 1915	48
	Jim Bagby, 1916	48
4	3 players tied	45

1920-1941
1	George Uhle, 1923	54
2	George Uhle, 1922	50
3	Jim Bagby, 1920	48
4	Joe Shaute, 1924	46
5	2 players tied	45

1942-1960
1	Joe Heving, 1944	63
2	Ray Narleski, 1955	60
3	Ed Klieman, 1947	58
4	Don Mossi, 1955	57
5	Lou Brissie, 1951	54

1961-1976
1	Don McMahon, 1964	70
2	Stan Williams, 1969	61
	Dave LaRoche, 1975	61
	Dave LaRoche, 1976	61
5	Gary Bell, 1965	60

1977-1995
1	Sid Monge, 1979	76
2	Steve Olin, 1992	72
3	Derek Lilliquist, 1992	71
4	Eric Plunk, 1993	70
5	2 players tied	69

Games Started

1	George Uhle, 1923	44
2	Bob Feller, 1946	42
3	Gaylord Perry, 1973	41
4	Stan Coveleski, 1921	40
	George Uhle, 1922	40
	Bob Feller, 1941	40
	Gaylord Perry, 1972	40
	Dick Tidrow, 1973	40
9	Sam McDowell, 1970	39
10	Addie Joss, 1907	38
	Stan Coveleski, 1920	38
	Jim Bagby, 1920	38
	Bob Feller, 1948	38
	Sam McDowell, 1969	38
	Wayne Garland, 1977	38
16	12 players tied	37

Games Started (by era)

1901-1919
1	Addie Joss, 1907	38
2	Bill Bernhard, 1904	37
	Jim Bagby, 1917	37
4	3 players tied	36

1920-1941
1	George Uhle, 1923	44
2	Stan Coveleski, 1921	40
	George Uhle, 1922	40
	Bob Feller, 1941	40
5	2 players tied	38

1942-1960
1	Bob Feller, 1946	42
2	Bob Feller, 1948	38
3	4 players tied	37

1961-1976
1	Gaylord Perry, 1973	41
2	Gaylord Perry, 1972	40
	Dick Tidrow, 1973	40
4	Sam McDowell, 1970	39
5	Sam McDowell, 1969	38

1977-1995
1	Wayne Garland, 1977	38
2	Len Barker, 1980	36
3	Rick Sutcliffe, 1983	35
4	6 players tied	34

Complete Games

1	Bob Feller, 1946	36
2	Bill Bernhard, 1904	35
3	Addie Joss, 1907	34
4	Otto Hess, 1906	33
5	George Uhle, 1926	32
6	Addie Joss, 1903	31
	Addie Joss, 1905	31
	Bob Rhoads, 1906	31
	Bob Feller, 1940	31
10	Red Donahue, 1904	30
	Cy Young, 1909	30
	Jim Bagby, 1920	30
13	Earl Moore, 1902	29
	Addie Joss, 1908	29
	George Uhle, 1923	29
	Gaylord Perry, 1972	29
	Gaylord Perry, 1973	29
18	9 players tied	28

Complete Games (by era)

1901-1919
1	Bill Bernhard, 1904	35
2	Addie Joss, 1907	34
3	Otto Hess, 1906	33
4	3 players tied	31

1920-1941
1	George Uhle, 1926	32
2	Bob Feller, 1940	31
3	Jim Bagby, 1920	30
4	George Uhle, 1923	29
5	2 players tied	28

1942-1960
1	Bob Feller, 1946	36
2	Bob Lemon, 1952	28
3	Bob Lemon, 1953	23
4	Bob Lemon, 1949	22
	Bob Lemon, 1950	22

1961-1976
1	Gaylord Perry, 1972	29
	Gaylord Perry, 1973	29
3	Gaylord Perry, 1974	28
4	Luis Tiant, 1968	19
	Sam McDowell, 1970	19

1977-1995
1	Wayne Garland, 1977	21
2	Tom Candiotti, 1986	17
3	Rick Waits, 1978	15
	Bert Blyleven, 1985	15
5	3 players tied	12

Shutouts

1	Bob Feller, 1946	10
	Bob Lemon, 1948	10
3	Addie Joss, 1906	9
	Addie Joss, 1908	9
	Stan Coveleski, 1917	9
	Luis Tiant, 1968	9
7	Jim Bagby, 1917	8
8	Bob Rhoads, 1906	7
	Otto Hess, 1906	7
	Gaylord Perry, 1973	7
11	11 players tied	6

Saves

1	Jose Mesa, 1995	46
2	Doug Jones, 1990	43
3	Doug Jones, 1988	37
4	Doug Jones, 1989	32
5	Steve Olin, 1992	29
6	Ernie Camacho, 1984	23
7	Dave LaRoche, 1976	21
	Dan Spillner, 1982	21
9	Ernie Camacho, 1986	20
10	Ray Narleski, 1955	19
	Sid Monge, 1979	19
12	Jim Kern, 1977	18
13	Ed Klieman, 1947	17
	Russ Christopher, 1948	17
	Gary Bell, 1965	17
	Tom Buskey, 1974	17
	Dave LaRoche, 1975	17
	Steve Olin, 1991	17
19	Ray Narleski, 1957	16
	Don McMahon, 1964	16

Innings Pitched

1	Bob Feller, 1946	371.1
2	George Uhle, 1923	357.2
3	Gaylord Perry, 1973	344.0
4	Bob Feller, 1941	343.0
5	Gaylord Perry, 1972	342.2
6	Jim Bagby, 1920	339.2
7	Addie Joss, 1907	338.2
8	Otto Hess, 1906	333.2
9	Addie Joss, 1908	325.0
10	Gaylord Perry, 1974	322.1
11	Bill Bernhard, 1904	320.2
	Jim Bagby, 1917	320.2
13	Bob Feller, 1940	320.1
14	George Uhle, 1926	318.1
15	Bob Rhoads, 1906	315.0
	Stan Coveleski, 1920	315.0
	Stan Coveleski, 1921	315.0
18	Stan Coveleski, 1918	311.0
19	Bob Lemon, 1952	309.2
20	Sam McDowell, 1970	305.0

Innings Pitched (by era)

1901-1919

1	Addie Joss, 1907	338.2
2	Otto Hess, 1906	333.2
3	Addie Joss, 1908	325.0
4	Bill Bernhard, 1904	320.2
	Jim Bagby, 1917	320.2

1920-1941

1	George Uhle, 1923	357.2
2	Bob Feller, 1941	343.0
3	Jim Bagby, 1920	339.2
4	Bob Feller, 1940	320.1
5	George Uhle, 1926	318.1

1942-1960

1	Bob Feller, 1946	371.1
2	Bob Lemon, 1952	309.2
3	Bob Feller, 1947	299.0
4	Bob Lemon, 1948	293.2
5	Mike Garcia, 1952	292.1

1961-1976

1	Gaylord Perry, 1973	344.0
2	Gaylord Perry, 1972	342.2
3	Gaylord Perry, 1974	322.1
4	Sam McDowell, 1970	305.0
5	Sam McDowell, 1969	285.0

1977-1995

1	Wayne Garland, 1977	282.2
2	Tom Candiotti, 1986	252.1
3	Charles Nagy, 1992	252.0
4	Dennis Eckersley, 1977	247.1
5	Len Barker, 1980	246.1

Hits per Game

1	Luis Tiant, 1968	5.30
2	Herb Score, 1956	5.85
3	Sam McDowell, 1965	5.87
4	Sam McDowell, 1966	6.02
5	Sam McDowell, 1968	6.06
6	Stan Coveleski, 1917	6.09
7	Herb Score, 1955	6.26
8	Vean Gregg, 1911	6.33
9	Sonny Siebert, 1968	6.33
10	Allie Reynolds, 1943	6.34
11	Willie Mitchell, 1913	6.35
12	Gaylord Perry, 1974	6.42
13	Addie Joss, 1908	6.42
14	Sonny Siebert, 1967	6.60
15	Sonny Siebert, 1965	6.63
16	Gaylord Perry, 1972	6.64
17	Sam McDowell, 1971	6.71
18	Bob Feller, 1946	6.71
19	Bob Lemon, 1949	6.79
20	Bob Lemon, 1952	6.86

Hits per Game (by era)

1901-1919

1	Stan Coveleski, 1917	6.09
2	Vean Gregg, 1911	6.33
3	Willie Mitchell, 1913	6.35
4	Addie Joss, 1908	6.42
5	Heinie Berger, 1908	6.86

1920-1941

1	Bob Feller, 1940	6.88
2	Bob Feller, 1939	6.89
3	Bob Feller, 1938	7.29
4	Bob Feller, 1941	7.45
5	Stan Coveleski, 1920	8.11

1942-1960

1	Herb Score, 1956	5.85
2	Herb Score, 1955	6.26
3	Allie Reynolds, 1943	6.34
4	Bob Feller, 1946	6.71
5	Bob Lemon, 1949	6.79

1961-1976

1	Luis Tiant, 1968	5.30
2	Sam McDowell, 1965	5.87
3	Sam McDowell, 1966	6.02
4	Sam McDowell, 1968	6.06
5	Sonny Siebert, 1968	6.33

1977-1995

1	Rick Sutcliffe, 1982	7.25
2	Bert Blyleven, 1984	7.49
3	Len Barker, 1982	7.76
4	Dennis Eckersley, 1977	7.79
5	Rick Waits, 1978	8.05

Home Runs Allowed

1	Luis Tiant, 1969	37
2	Jim Perry, 1960	35
3	Gaylord Perry, 1973	34
	Ken Schrom, 1986	34
5	Early Wynn, 1957	32
	Gary Bell, 1961	32
	Mudcat Grant, 1961	32
8	Dick Tidrow, 1973	31
	Dennis Eckersley, 1977	31
10	Mudcat Grant, 1963	30
11	Pedro Ramos, 1963	29
	Ken Schrom, 1987	29
	Dennis Cook, 1992	29
14	Bob Lemon, 1950	28
	Gary Bell, 1959	28
	Herb Score, 1959	28
	Jim Perry, 1961	28
	Pedro Ramos, 1962	28
	Tom Candiotti, 1987	28
20	3 players tied	27

Home Runs Allowed (by era)

1901-1919

1	Earl Moore, 1902	8
2	5 players tied	6

1920-1941

1	George Blaeholder, 1936	21
2	Earl Whitehill, 1938	18
3	Wes Ferrell, 1932	17
4	3 players tied	16

1942-1960

1	Jim Perry, 1960	35
2	Early Wynn, 1957	32
3	Bob Lemon, 1950	28
	Gary Bell, 1959	28
	Herb Score, 1959	28

1961-1976

1	Luis Tiant, 1969	37
2	Gaylord Perry, 1973	34
3	Gary Bell, 1961	32
	Mudcat Grant, 1961	32
5	Dick Tidrow, 1973	31

1977-1995

1	Ken Schrom, 1986	34
2	Dennis Eckersley, 1977	31
3	Ken Schrom, 1987	29
	Dennis Cook, 1992	29
5	Tom Candiotti, 1987	28

Walks

1	Bob Feller, 1938	208
2	Bob Feller, 1941	194
3	Herb Score, 1955	154
4	Bob Feller, 1946	153
	Sam McDowell, 1971	153
6	Bob Lemon, 1950	146
7	Bob Feller, 1939	142
8	Gene Krapp, 1911	138
9	Bob Lemon, 1949	137
10	Early Wynn, 1952	132
	Sam McDowell, 1965	132
12	Sam McDowell, 1970	131
13	Wes Ferrell, 1931	130
	Monte Pearson, 1934	130
	Allie Reynolds, 1945	130
16	Bob Lemon, 1948	129
	Herb Score, 1956	129
	Luis Tiant, 1969	129
19	Bob Feller, 1947	127
20	3 players tied	124

Fewest Walks/Game (by era)

1901-1919

1	Addie Joss, 1908	0.83
2	Bill Bernhard, 1903	1.14
3	Addie Joss, 1909	1.15
4	Addie Joss, 1903	1.17
5	Addie Joss, 1906	1.37

1920-1941

1	Sherry Smith, 1926	1.48
2	Sherry Smith, 1924	1.53
3	Clint Brown, 1933	1.65
4	Stan Coveleski, 1923	1.66
5	Mel Harder, 1935	1.66

1942-1960

1	Jim Bagby, Jr., 1942	2.13
2	Steve Gromek, 1945	2.37
3	Mike Garcia, 1955	2.39
4	Mike Garcia, 1954	2.47
5	Jim Bagby, Jr., 1943	2.64

1961-1976

1	Dick Donovan, 1963	1.22
2	Ralph Terry, 1965	1.25
3	Dick Donovan, 1962	1.69
4	Jack Kralick, 1963	1.87
5	Pedro Ramos, 1963	2.00

1977-1995

1	Greg Swindell, 1991	1.17
2	Greg Swindell, 1988	1.67
3	Dennis Eckersley, 1977	1.96
4	Greg Swindell, 1990	1.97
5	Charles Nagy, 1992	2.04

Ratio

1	Addie Joss, 1908	7.31
2	Luis Tiant, 1968	7.98
3	Addie Joss, 1906	8.49
4	Bill Bernhard, 1902	8.63
5	Addie Joss, 1909	8.64
6	Addie Joss, 1903	8.82
7	Stan Coveleski, 1917	8.96
8	Addie Joss, 1907	9.04
9	Sonny Siebert, 1965	9.06
10	Gaylord Perry, 1972	9.11
11	Addie Joss, 1904	9.22
12	Bill Bernhard, 1903	9.34
13	Gaylord Perry, 1974	9.35
14	Guy Morton, 1915	9.41
15	Sonny Siebert, 1967	9.52
16	Addie Joss, 1905	9.53
17	Earl Moore, 1903	9.56
18	Charlie Chech, 1908	9.62
19	Ralph Terry, 1965	9.67
20	Sonny Siebert, 1966	9.75

Strikeouts

1	Bob Feller, 1946	348
2	Sam McDowell, 1965	325
3	Sam McDowell, 1970	304
4	Sam McDowell, 1968	283
5	Sam McDowell, 1969	279
6	Luis Tiant, 1968	264
7	Herb Score, 1956	263
8	Bob Feller, 1940	261
9	Bob Feller, 1941	260
10	Bob Feller, 1939	246
11	Herb Score, 1955	245
12	Bob Feller, 1938	240
13	Gaylord Perry, 1973	238
14	Sam McDowell, 1967	236
15	Gaylord Perry, 1972	234
16	Sam McDowell, 1966	225
17	Luis Tiant, 1967	219
18	Gaylord Perry, 1974	216
19	Dennis Eckersley, 1976	200
20	Bob Feller, 1947	196

Strikeouts (by era)

1901-1919

1	Vean Gregg, 1912	184
2	Willie Mitchell, 1914	179
3	Otto Hess, 1906	167
4	Cy Falkenberg, 1913	166
	Vean Gregg, 1913	166

1920-1941

1	Bob Feller, 1940	261
2	Bob Feller, 1941	260
3	Bob Feller, 1939	246
4	Bob Feller, 1938	240
5	Johnny Allen, 1936	165

1942-1960

1	Bob Feller, 1946	348
2	Herb Score, 1956	263
3	Herb Score, 1955	245
4	Bob Feller, 1947	196
5	Early Wynn, 1957	184

1961-1976

1	Sam McDowell, 1965	325
2	Sam McDowell, 1970	304
3	Sam McDowell, 1968	283
4	Sam McDowell, 1969	279
5	Luis Tiant, 1968	264

1977-1995

1	Dennis Eckersley, 1977	191
2	Len Barker, 1980	187
	Len Barker, 1982	187
4	Greg Swindell, 1988	180
5	Bert Blyleven, 1984	170

Strikeouts per Game

1	Sam McDowell, 1965	10.71
2	Sam McDowell, 1966	10.42
3	Herb Score, 1955	9.70
4	Herb Score, 1956	9.49
5	Sam McDowell, 1968	9.47
6	Luis Tiant, 1967	9.22
7	Luis Tiant, 1968	9.20
8	Sam McDowell, 1964	9.19
9	Sonny Siebert, 1965	9.11
10	Dennis Eckersley, 1976	9.03
11	Sam McDowell, 1967	8.99
12	Sam McDowell, 1970	8.97
13	Sam McDowell, 1969	8.81
14	Bob Feller, 1946	8.43
15	Pedro Ramos, 1963	8.24
16	Herb Score, 1959	8.23
17	Sam McDowell, 1971	8.05
18	Bob Feller, 1938	7.78
19	Bob Feller, 1939	7.46
20	Len Barker, 1981	7.41

Strikeouts per Game (by era)

1901-1919

1	Willie Mitchell, 1914	6.27
2	Vean Gregg, 1912	6.10
3	Heinie Berger, 1909	5.90
4	Willie Mitchell, 1913	5.85
5	Willie Mitchell, 1915	5.68

1920-1941

1	Bob Feller, 1938	7.78
2	Bob Feller, 1939	7.46
3	Bob Feller, 1940	7.33
4	Bob Feller, 1941	6.82
5	Johnny Allen, 1936	6.11

1942-1960

1	Herb Score, 1955	9.70
2	Herb Score, 1956	9.49
3	Bob Feller, 1946	8.43
4	Herb Score, 1959	8.23
5	Allie Reynolds, 1943	6.84

1961-1976

1	Sam McDowell, 1965	10.71
2	Sam McDowell, 1966	10.42
3	Sam McDowell, 1968	9.47
4	Luis Tiant, 1967	9.22
5	Luis Tiant, 1968	9.20

1977-1995

1	Len Barker, 1981	7.41
2	Charles Nagy, 1995	7.03
3	Dennis Eckersley, 1977	6.95
4	Len Barker, 1982	6.88
5	Len Barker, 1980	6.83

Earned Run Average

1	Addie Joss, 1908	1.16
2	Addie Joss, 1904	1.59
3	Luis Tiant, 1968	1.60
4	Addie Joss, 1909	1.71
5	Addie Joss, 1906	1.72
6	Charlie Chech, 1908	1.74
7	Earl Moore, 1903	1.74
8	Bob Rhoads, 1908	1.77
9	Bob Rhoads, 1906	1.80
10	Vean Gregg, 1911	1.80
11	Sam McDowell, 1968	1.81
12	Stan Coveleski, 1917	1.81
13	Stan Coveleski, 1918	1.82
14	Addie Joss, 1907	1.83
15	Otto Hess, 1906	1.83
16	Willie Mitchell, 1913	1.91
17	Gaylord Perry, 1972	1.92
18	Jim Bagby, 1917	1.96
19	Addie Joss, 1905	2.01
20	Glenn Liebhardt, 1907	2.05

Earned Run Average (by era)

1901-1919

1	Addie Joss, 1908	1.16
2	Addie Joss, 1904	1.59
3	Addie Joss, 1909	1.71
4	Addie Joss, 1906	1.72
5	Charlie Chech, 1908	1.74

1920-1941

1	Stan Coveleski, 1920	2.49
2	Johnny Allen, 1937	2.55
3	Mel Harder, 1934	2.61
4	Bob Feller, 1940	2.61
5	Stan Coveleski, 1923	2.76

1942-1960

1	Bob Feller, 1946	2.18
2	Mike Garcia, 1949	2.36
3	Mike Garcia, 1952	2.37
4	Gene Bearden, 1948	2.43
5	Bob Lemon, 1952	2.50

1961-1976

1	Luis Tiant, 1968	1.60
2	Sam McDowell, 1968	1.81
3	Gaylord Perry, 1972	1.92
4	Sam McDowell, 1965	2.18
5	Sonny Siebert, 1967	2.38

1977-1995

1	Bert Blyleven, 1984	2.87
2	Bert Blyleven, 1981	2.88
3	Rick Sutcliffe, 1982	2.96
4	Charles Nagy, 1992	2.96
5	Dennis Martinez, 1995	3.08

Adjusted Earned Run Average

1	Addie Joss, 1908	206
2	Vean Gregg, 1911	189
3	Luis Tiant, 1968	185
4	Johnny Allen, 1937	181
5	Mel Harder, 1934	174
6	Mike Garcia, 1949	169
7	Gaylord Perry, 1972	168
8	Gene Bearden, 1948	167
9	Herb Score, 1956	166
10	Stan Coveleski, 1918	165
11	Sam McDowell, 1968	164
12	Earl Moore, 1903	164
13	Bob Feller, 1940	161
14	Sam McDowell, 1965	160
15	Addie Joss, 1904	159
16	Willie Mitchell, 1913	159
17	Bill Bernhard, 1902	157
18	Stan Coveleski, 1917	157
19	Early Wynn, 1956	154
20	Bob Feller, 1939	154

Adjusted ERA (by era)

1901-1919

1	Addie Joss, 1908	206
2	Vean Gregg, 1911	189
3	Stan Coveleski, 1918	165
4	Earl Moore, 1903	164
5	Addie Joss, 1904	159

1920-1941

1	Johnny Allen, 1937	181
2	Mel Harder, 1934	174
3	Bob Feller, 1940	161
4	Bob Feller, 1939	154
5	Stan Coveleski, 1920	153

1942-1960

1	Mike Garcia, 1949	169
2	Gene Bearden, 1948	167
3	Herb Score, 1956	166
4	Early Wynn, 1956	154
5	Bob Feller, 1946	152

1961-1976

1	Luis Tiant, 1968	185
2	Gaylord Perry, 1972	168
3	Sam McDowell, 1968	164
4	Sam McDowell, 1965	160
5	Dennis Eckersley, 1975	145

1977-1995

1	Dennis Martinez, 1995	150
2	Bert Blyleven, 1984	143
3	Rick Sutcliffe, 1982	138
4	Charles Nagy, 1994	137
5	Dennis Martinez, 1994	134

Pitching Runs

1	Bob Feller, 1940	63.0
2	Bob Feller, 1939	58.3
3	Bob Feller, 1946	54.5
4	Mel Harder, 1934	53.6
5	Bob Lemon, 1948	47.9
6	Gene Bearden, 1948	47.4
7	Stan Coveleski, 1920	45.9
8	Herb Score, 1956	45.2
9	Addie Joss, 1908	44.5
10	Early Wynn, 1956	44.3
11	Wes Ferrell, 1930	44.3
12	Gaylord Perry, 1972	43.5
13	Johnny Allen, 1936	43.0
14	Mike Garcia, 1952	42.4
15	George Uhle, 1926	42.2
16	Vean Gregg, 1911	41.9
17	Bob Lemon, 1952	40.4
18	Johnny Allen, 1937	39.8
19	Gaylord Perry, 1974	39.5
20	Luis Tiant, 1968	39.5

Adjusted Pitching Runs

1	Bob Feller, 1940	57.1
2	Mel Harder, 1934	55.0
3	Bob Feller, 1939	51.1
4	Wes Ferrell, 1930	50.1
5	Gaylord Perry, 1972	49.5
6	Herb Score, 1956	46.5
7	Bob Feller, 1946	46.4
8	Stan Coveleski, 1920	46.0
9	Early Wynn, 1956	45.7
10	Addie Joss, 1908	44.3
11	Vean Gregg, 1911	43.8
12	George Uhle, 1926	43.5
13	Johnny Allen, 1936	43.0
14	Mel Harder, 1933	41.9
15	Gene Bearden, 1948	41.5
16	Stan Coveleski, 1918	40.8
17	Bob Lemon, 1948	40.4
18	Johnny Allen, 1937	39.6
19	Sam McDowell, 1965	39.5
20	Gaylord Perry, 1974	39.4

Pitching Wins

1	Bob Feller, 1940	5.9
2	Bob Feller, 1946	5.7
3	Bob Feller, 1939	5.4
4	Addie Joss, 1908	5.1
5	Mel Harder, 1934	5.0
6	Gaylord Perry, 1972	5.0
7	Bob Lemon, 1948	4.6
8	Gene Bearden, 1948	4.6
9	Luis Tiant, 1968	4.5
10	Stan Coveleski, 1920	4.4
11	Herb Score, 1956	4.4
12	Mike Garcia, 1952	4.4
13	Early Wynn, 1956	4.3
14	Bob Lemon, 1952	4.2
15	Sam McDowell, 1965	4.1
16	Gaylord Perry, 1974	4.1
17	Vean Gregg, 1911	4.1
18	George Uhle, 1926	4.1
19	Sam McDowell, 1968	4.0
20	Wes Ferrell, 1930	4.0

Adjusted Pitching Wins

1	Gaylord Perry, 1972	5.6
2	Bob Feller, 1940	5.4
3	Mel Harder, 1934	5.1
4	Addie Joss, 1908	5.0
5	Bob Feller, 1946	4.9
6	Bob Feller, 1939	4.7
7	Herb Score, 1956	4.6
8	Stan Coveleski, 1918	4.5
9	Wes Ferrell, 1930	4.5
10	Early Wynn, 1956	4.5
11	Luis Tiant, 1968	4.5
12	Stan Coveleski, 1920	4.5
13	Vean Gregg, 1911	4.3
14	Sam McDowell, 1965	4.2
15	George Uhle, 1926	4.2
16	Gaylord Perry, 1974	4.1
17	Gene Bearden, 1948	4.0
18	Mel Harder, 1933	4.0
19	Sam McDowell, 1968	3.9
20	Bob Lemon, 1948	3.9

Opponents' Batting Average

1	Luis Tiant, 1968	.168
2	Sam McDowell, 1965	.185
3	Herb Score, 1956	.186
4	Sam McDowell, 1966	.188
5	Sam McDowell, 1968	.189
6	Stan Coveleski, 1917	.194
7	Herb Score, 1955	.194
8	Addie Joss, 1908	.197
9	Sonny Siebert, 1968	.198
10	Willie Mitchell, 1913	.199
11	Allie Reynolds, 1943	.202
12	Sonny Siebert, 1967	.202
13	Gaylord Perry, 1974	.204
14	Vean Gregg, 1911	.205
15	Gaylord Perry, 1972	.205
16	Sonny Siebert, 1965	.206
17	Sam McDowell, 1971	.207
18	Bob Feller, 1946	.208
19	Bob Lemon, 1952	.208
20	Bob Feller, 1940	.210

Opponents' On Base Pctg.

1	Addie Joss, 1908	.218
2	Luis Tiant, 1968	.233
3	Addie Joss, 1906	.252
4	Bill Bernhard, 1902	.253
5	Addie Joss, 1909	.255
6	Addie Joss, 1903	.256
7	Gaylord Perry, 1972	.261
8	Stan Coveleski, 1917	.261
9	Sonny Siebert, 1965	.262
10	Addie Joss, 1907	.263
11	Addie Joss, 1904	.266
12	Bill Bernhard, 1903	.267
13	Guy Morton, 1915	.268
14	Sonny Siebert, 1967	.268
15	Ralph Terry, 1965	.269
16	Earl Moore, 1903	.271
17	Gaylord Perry, 1974	.272
18	Addie Joss, 1905	.273
19	Pedro Ramos, 1963	.273
20	Sonny Siebert, 1966	.278

Wins Above Team

1	Bob Feller, 1946	8.6
2	Vean Gregg, 1911	8.5
3	Addie Joss, 1907	7.8
4	Bob Feller, 1941	7.6
5	George Uhle, 1926	7.4
6	Bob Feller, 1940	7.2
7	Bob Feller, 1939	7.1
8	Johnny Allen, 1937	7.0
	Bert Blyleven, 1984	7.0
10	Bill Bernhard, 1902	6.4
	Jim Bagby, 1920	6.4
	Wes Ferrell, 1930	6.4
	Gaylord Perry, 1972	6.4
14	Luis Tiant, 1968	6.1
15	Cy Falkenberg, 1913	5.9
16	Wes Ferrell, 1931	5.8
	Dick Donovan, 1962	5.8
18	Wes Ferrell, 1929	5.6
	Steve Gromek, 1945	5.6
	Bob Feller, 1951	5.6

Wins Above League

1	Gaylord Perry, 1972	25.6
2	Bob Feller, 1946	25.4
3	Jim Bagby, 1920	24.8
4	Bob Feller, 1940	24.4
5	Wes Ferrell, 1930	23.5
6	Stan Coveleski, 1920	23.5
7	George Uhle, 1926	23.2
8	Addie Joss, 1908	22.5
9	Stan Coveleski, 1918	22.0
10	Bob Feller, 1941	21.9
11	Addie Joss, 1907	21.8
12	George Uhle, 1923	21.7
13	Otto Hess, 1906	21.7
14	Jim Bagby, 1917	21.4
15	Bob Feller, 1939	21.2
16	Wes Ferrell, 1932	21.2
17	Gaylord Perry, 1973	21.1
18	Gaylord Perry, 1974	21.1
19	Mel Harder, 1934	21.1
20	Bob Lemon, 1948	20.9

Relief Games

1	Sid Monge, 1979	76
2	Steve Olin, 1992	72
3	Derek Lilliquist, 1992	71
4	Don McMahon, 1964	70
	Eric Plunk, 1993	70
6	Ernie Camacho, 1984	69
	Jesse Orosco, 1989	69
8	Sid Monge, 1980	67
9	Doug Jones, 1990	66
10	Dan Spillner, 1982	65

Relief Wins

1	Sid Monge, 1979	12
	Dan Spillner, 1982	12
3	Frank Funk, 1961	11
4	Jim Kern, 1978	10
	Scott Bailes, 1986	10
	Julian Tavarez, 1995	10
7	Gary Bell, 1962	9
	Jim Kern, 1976	9
	Eric Plunk, 1992	9
10	6 players tied	8

Relief Losses

1	Frank Funk, 1961	11
2	Jim Kern, 1977	10
	Jim Kern, 1978	10
	Sid Monge, 1979	10
	Dan Spillner, 1982	10
	Doug Jones, 1989	10
7	Stan Williams, 1969	9
	Victor Cruz, 1979	9
	Dan Spillner, 1983	9
	Ernie Camacho, 1984	9

Relief Innings Pitched

1	Dan Spillner, 1982	133.2
2	Sid Monge, 1979	131.0
3	Joe Heving, 1944	113.2
4	Jim Kern, 1976	105.2
5	Gary Bell, 1965	103.2
6	Ray Narleski, 1955	102.2
7	Don McMahon, 1964	101.0
8	Ernie Camacho, 1984	100.0
9	Jim Kern, 1978	99.1
	Ted Power, 1992	99.1

Relief Points

1	Jose Mesa, 1995	98
2	Doug Jones, 1990	91
3	Doug Jones, 1988	76
4	Steve Olin, 1992	69
5	Doug Jones, 1989	68
6	Dan Spillner, 1982	56
7	Ray Narleski, 1955	53
8	Sid Monge, 1979	52
9	Ernie Camacho, 1984	47
10	2 players tied	42

Relief Ranking

1	Jose Mesa, 1995	50.9
2	Sid Monge, 1979	49.5
3	Dan Spillner, 1982	43.2
4	Doug Jones, 1989	40.4
5	Ernie Camacho, 1984	32.7
6	Steve Olin, 1992	31.6
7	Doug Jones, 1988	30.0
8	Doug Jones, 1990	28.1
9	Julian Tavarez, 1995	26.4
10	Jim Kern, 1976	23.9

Relievers' Runs

1. Sid Monge, 1979 .... 26.3
2. Jose Mesa, 1995 .... 25.5
3. Dan Spillner, 1982 .... 23.5
4. Julian Tavarez, 1995 ..... 21.5
5. Joe Heving, 1944 .... 21.3
6. Don Mossi, 1955 .... 18.5
7. Eric Plunk, 1994 .... 17.9
8. Ray Narleski, 1956 .... 17.4
9. Ernie Camacho, 1984 .... 17.3
10. Doug Jones, 1988 .... 15.7

Adjusted Relievers' Runs

1. Sid Monge, 1979 .... 26.9
2. Jose Mesa, 1995 .... 24.9
3. Dan Spillner, 1982 .... 23.6
4. Julian Tavarez, 1995 ..... 20.8
5. Joe Heving, 1944 .... 19.7
6. Don Mossi, 1955 .... 18.7
7. Ernie Camacho, 1984 .... 18.4
8. Ray Narleski, 1956 .... 17.7
9. Eric Plunk, 1994 .... 17.2
10. Doug Jones, 1988 .... 17.1

Clutch Pitching Index

1. Fred Blanding, 1913 ..... 140.8
2. Bob Rhoads, 1908 ..... 136.8
3. Gene Bearden, 1948 ..... 132.3
4. Bill Bernhard, 1904 ..... 130.4
5. Vean Gregg, 1913 ..... 130.0
6. Mike Garcia, 1952 ..... 127.3
7. Mel Harder, 1934 .... 126.5
8. Rip Hagerman, 1914 ..... 125.7
9. Bob Rhoads, 1906 ..... 125.5
10. Glenn Liebhardt, 1907 ... 124.7
11. Otto Hess, 1906 .... 124.1
12. Mike Garcia, 1949 ..... 123.4
13. Bill Steen, 1914 .... 123.0
14. Sam McDowell, 1964 ..... 122.6
15. Stan Coveleski, 1923 ..... 120.6
16. Calvin McLish, 1958 ..... 120.4
17. Johnny Allen, 1937 ..... 120.3
18. George Kahler, 1912 ..... 119.6
19. Bob Rhoads, 1907 .... 119.5
    Fritz Coumbe, 1918 ..... 119.5

Pitcher Batting Runs

1. Wes Ferrell, 1931 .... 17.8
2. George Uhle, 1923 .... 16.4
3. Bob Lemon, 1950 .... 15.6
4. Bob Lemon, 1949 .... 14.7
5. Bob Lemon, 1948 .... 12.6
6. Joe Shaute, 1924 .... 8.8
7. George Uhle, 1922 .... 8.6
8. Wes Ferrell, 1930 .... 8.5
9. Early Wynn, 1953 .... 8.0
10. Bob Lemon, 1947 .... 7.9
11. Chubby Dean, 1942 .... 7.7
12. Wes Ferrell, 1933 .... 7.6
13. Bob Lemon, 1953 .... 7.5
14. George Uhle, 1928 .... 7.3
15. George Uhle, 1924 .... 7.2
16. Sherry Smith, 1925 .... 6.8
17. Early Wynn, 1950 .... 6.5
18. Al Smith, 1940 .... 6.5
19. Clint Brown, 1932 .... 6.2
20. George Uhle, 1925 .... 6.1

Pitcher Fielding Runs

1. Addie Joss, 1907 .... 8.6
2. Bob Lemon, 1948 .... 8.4
3. Bob Lemon, 1953 .... 7.9
4. Mel Harder, 1933 .... 7.7
5. Stan Coveleski, 1921 .... 6.7
   Willis Hudlin, 1929 .... 6.7
7. Bob Lemon, 1952 .... 6.5
8. Bob Lemon, 1949 .... 6.2
9. Addie Joss, 1902 .... 6.1
10. Willis Hudlin, 1934 .... 5.4
11. Fritz Coumbe, 1918 .... 5.3
12. Wes Ferrell, 1931 .... 5.1
    Mel Harder, 1935 .... 5.1
14. Addie Joss, 1905 .... 4.9
    Fritz Coumbe, 1916 ..... 4.9
    Bob Lemon, 1950 .... 4.9
17. Willis Hudlin, 1939 ..... 4.8
18. Willis Hudlin, 1930 ..... 4.5
    John Denny, 1981 .... 4.5
20. 2 players tied 4.4

Total Pitcher Index

1. Gaylord Perry, 1972 ..... 7.0
2. Bob Lemon, 1948 .... 6.8
3. Mel Harder, 1934 .... 6.4
4. Wes Ferrell, 1930 .... 6.2
5. Bob Feller, 1940 .... 6.1
6. Addie Joss, 1908 .... 5.9
   Stan Coveleski, 1920 ..... 5.9
8. Mel Harder, 1933 .... 5.7
   Bob Lemon, 1949 .... 5.7
10. Bob Feller, 1939 .... 5.6
11. Gene Bearden, 1948 ..... 5.5
12. George Uhle, 1926 ...... 5.2
    Wes Ferrell, 1931 .... 5.2
    Bob Lemon, 1956 .... 5.2
15. Early Wynn, 1956 .... 5.1
16. Sid Monge, 1979 .... 5.0
    Jose Mesa, 1995 .... 5.0
18. Bob Feller, 1946 .... 4.9
19. Herb Score, 1956 .... 4.8
20. Vean Gregg, 1911 .... 4.7

Total Pitcher Index (alpha.)

Gene Bearden, 1948 .... 5.5
Stan Coveleski, 1920 .... 5.9
Bob Feller, 1939 .... 5.6
Bob Feller, 1940 .... 6.1
Bob Feller, 1946 .... 4.9
Wes Ferrell, 1930 .... 6.2
Wes Ferrell, 1931 .... 5.2
Vean Gregg, 1911 .... 4.7
Mel Harder, 1933 .... 5.7
Mel Harder, 1934 .... 6.4
Addie Joss, 1908 .... 5.9
Bob Lemon, 1948 .... 6.8
Bob Lemon, 1949 .... 5.7
Bob Lemon, 1956 .... 5.2
Jose Mesa, 1995 .... 5.0
Sid Monge, 1979 .... 5.0
Gaylord Perry, 1972 .... 7.0
Herb Score, 1956 .... 4.8
George Uhle, 1926 .... 5.2
Early Wynn, 1956 .... 5.1

Total Pitcher Index (by era)

1901-1919
1. Addie Joss, 1908 .... 5.9
2. Vean Gregg, 1911 .... 4.7
3. Stan Coveleski, 1918 .... 4.6
4. Jim Bagby, 1917 .... 3.8
5. Addie Joss, 1906 .... 3.7

1920-1941
1. Mel Harder, 1934 .... 6.4
2. Wes Ferrell, 1930 .... 6.2
3. Bob Feller, 1940 .... 6.1
4. Stan Coveleski, 1920 .... 5.9
5. Mel Harder, 1933 .... 5.7

1942-1960
1. Bob Lemon, 1948 .... 6.8
2. Bob Lemon, 1949 .... 5.7
3. Gene Bearden, 1948 ..... 5.5
4. Bob Lemon, 1956 .... 5.2
5. Early Wynn, 1956 .... 5.1

1961-1976
1. Gaylord Perry, 1972 ..... 7.0
2. Gaylord Perry, 1974 ..... 4.4
3. Luis Tiant, 1968 .... 4.2
4. Sam McDowell, 1965 ..... 4.1
5. Sam McDowell, 1968 .... 4.0

1977-1995
1. Sid Monge, 1979 .... 5.0
   Jose Mesa, 1995 .... 5.0
3. Doug Jones, 1989 .... 4.3
4. Dan Spillner, 1982 .... 4.2
5. Steve Olin, 1992 .... 3.5

Total Baseball Ranking

1. Nap Lajoie, 1906 .... 8.5
   Nap Lajoie, 1910 .... 8.5
3. Nap Lajoie, 1903 .... 8.4
4. Nap Lajoie, 1908 .... 7.8
   Lou Boudreau, 1944 ..... 7.8
6. Nap Lajoie, 1904 .... 7.2
7. Gaylord Perry, 1972 ..... 7.0
8. Joe Jackson, 1912 ...... 6.9
   Lou Boudreau, 1948 ..... 6.9
10. Bob Lemon, 1948 .... 6.8
    Joe Jackson, 1911 ...... 6.8
12. Lou Boudreau, 1943 ..... 6.7
13. Nap Lajoie, 1907 .... 6.6
14. Mel Harder, 1934 .... 6.4
    Tris Speaker, 1923 .... 6.4
16. Nap Lajoie, 1902 .... 6.3
17. Wes Ferrell, 1930 .... 6.2
    Al Rosen, 1953 .... 6.2
19. Bob Feller, 1940 .... 6.1
20. 3 players tied 6.0

Total Baseball Rank (alpha.)

Lou Boudreau, 1943 ..... 6.7
Lou Boudreau, 1944 ..... 7.8
Lou Boudreau, 1948 ..... 6.9
Bob Feller, 1940 .... 6.1
Wes Ferrell, 1930 .... 6.2
Mel Harder, 1934 .... 6.4
Joe Jackson, 1911 ...... 6.8
Joe Jackson, 1912 ...... 6.9
Nap Lajoie, 1902 .... 6.3
Nap Lajoie, 1903 .... 8.4
Nap Lajoie, 1904 .... 7.2
Nap Lajoie, 1906 .... 8.5
Nap Lajoie, 1907 .... 6.6
Nap Lajoie, 1908 .... 7.8
Nap Lajoie, 1910 .... 8.5
Bob Lemon, 1948 .... 6.8
Gaylord Perry, 1972 ..... 7.0
Al Rosen, 1953 .... 6.2
Tris Speaker, 1923 .... 6.4

Total Baseball Rank (by era)

1901-1919
1. Nap Lajoie, 1906 .... 8.5
   Nap Lajoie, 1910 .... 8.5
3. Nap Lajoie, 1903 .... 8.4
4. Nap Lajoie, 1908 .... 7.8
5. Nap Lajoie, 1904 .... 7.2

1920-1941
1. Mel Harder, 1934 .... 6.4
   Tris Speaker, 1923 .... 6.4
3. Wes Ferrell, 1930 .... 6.2
4. Bob Feller, 1940 .... 6.1
5. Joe Sewell, 1923 .... 6.0

1942-1960
1. Lou Boudreau, 1944 ..... 7.8
2. Lou Boudreau, 1948 ..... 6.9
3. Bob Lemon, 1948 .... 6.8
4. Lou Boudreau, 1943 ..... 6.7
5. Al Rosen, 1953 .... 6.2

1961-1976
1. Gaylord Perry, 1972 ..... 7.0
2. Graig Nettles, 1971 ...... 5.3
3. Gaylord Perry, 1974 ..... 4.4
4. Luis Tiant, 1968 .... 4.2
5. Sam McDowell, 1965 .... 4.1

1977-1995
1. Albert Belle, 1995 .... 6.0
2. Albert Belle, 1993 .... 5.2
3. Sid Monge, 1979 .... 5.0
   Jose Mesa, 1995 .... 5.0
   Albert Belle, 1994 .... 5.0

Indians All Stars

1933 AL
Earl Averill
Wes Ferrell*
Oral Hildebrand*

1934 AL
Earl Averill
Mel Harder

1935 AL
Earl Averill†
Mel Harder
Joe Vosmik

1936 AL
Earl Averill
Mel Harder

1937 AL
Earl Averill
Mel Harder

1938 AL
Johnny Allen
Earl Averill
Bob Feller*

1939 AL
Bob Feller
Rollie Hemsley*

1940 AL
Lou Boudreau
Bob Feller
Rollie Hemsley
Ken Keltner
Ray Mack
Al Milnar*

1941 AL
Lou Boudreau
Bob Feller
Jeff Heath
Ken Keltner

1942 AL
Jim Bagby*
Lou Boudreau
Ken Keltner

1943 AL
Jim Bagby*
Lou Boudreau*
Jeff Heath
Ken Keltner
Buddy Rosar*
Al Smith*

1944 AL
Lou Boudreau*
Roy Cullenbine*
Oris Hockett*
Ken Keltner

1945 AL
Lou Boudreau*
Steve Gromek*
Frankie Hayes*
Jeff Heath*
Allie Reynolds*

1946 AL
Bob Feller
Frankie Hayes
Ken Keltner

1947 AL
Lou Boudreau
Bob Feller†
Joe Gordon
Jim Hegan*

1948 AL
Lou Boudreau
Bob Feller†
Joe Gordon
Ken Keltner
Bob Lemon*

1949 AL
Larry Doby
Joe Gordon
Jim Hegan*
Bob Lemon*
Dale Mitchell

1950 AL
Larry Doby
Bob Feller
Jim Hegan
Bob Lemon

1951 AL
Larry Doby
Jim Hegan
Bob Lemon

1952 AL
Bobby Avila
Larry Doby
Mike Garcia*
Jim Hegan*
Bob Lemon
Dale Mitchell
Al Rosen

1953 AL
Larry Doby
Mike Garcia
Bob Lemon*
Al Rosen

1954 AL
Bobby Avila
Larry Doby
Mike Garcia†
Bob Lemon
Al Rosen

1955 AL
Bobby Avila
Larry Doby*
Al Rosen
Herb Score*
Al Smith
Early Wynn

1956 AL
Ray Narleski†
Herb Score
Early Wynn

1957 AL
Don Mossi
Vic Wertz
Early Wynn

1958 AL
Ray Narleski
Mickey Vernon

1959 AL (Game 1)
Rocky Colavito
Minnie Minoso
Vic Power

1959 AL (Game 2)
Rocky Colavito
Cal McLish
Minnie Minoso*
Vic Power

1960 AL (Game 1)
Gary Bell
Harvey Kuenn
Vic Power*
Dick Stigman*

1960 AL (Game 2)
Gary Bell
Harvey Kuenn
Vic Power
Dick Stigman*

1961 AL (Game 1)
Jim Perry*
Johnny Romano
Johnny Temple

1961 AL (Game 2)
Tito Francona*
Barry Latman*
Johnny Romano
Johnny Temple

1962 AL (Game 1)
Dick Donovan
Johnny Romano

1962 AL (Game 2)
Dick Donovan*
Johnny Romano*

1963 AL
Mudcat Grant*

1964 AL
Jack Kralick*

1965 AL
Max Alvis
Rocky Colavito
Vic Davalillo
Sam McDowell

1966 AL
Gary Bell*
Rocky Colavito
Sam McDowell†
Sonny Siebert

1967 AL
Max Alvis
Steve Hargan*

1968 AL
Joe Azcue
Sam McDowell
Luis Tiant

1969 AL
Sam McDowell

1970 AL
Ray Fosse
Sam McDowell

1971 AL
Ray Fosse†
Sam McDowell†

1972 AL
Gaylord Perry

1973 AL
Buddy Bell

1974 AL
George Hendrick
Gaylord Perry

1975 AL
George Hendrick

1976 AL
Dave La Roche*

1977 AL
Dennis Eckersley
Jim Kern

1978 AL
Jim Kern

1979 AL
Sid Monge*

1980 AL
Jorge Orta*

1981 AL
Len Barker
Bo Diaz

1982 AL
Toby Harrah*
Andy Thornton

1983 AL
Rick Sutcliffe*
Manny Trillo

1984 AL
Andy Thornton

1985 AL
Bert Blyleven

1986 AL
Brook Jacoby
Ken Schrom*

1987 AL
Pat Tabler

1988 AL
Doug Jones

1989 AL
Doug Jones
Greg Swindell

1990 AL
Sandy Alomar
Brook Jacoby
Doug Jones*

1991 AL
Sandy Alomar

1992 AL
Sandy Alomar
Carlos Baerga
Charles Nagy

1993 AL
Carlos Baerga
Albert Belle

1994 AL
Albert Belle
Kenny Lofton

1995 AL
Carlos Baerga
Albert Belle
Kenny Lofton
Dennis Martinez
Jose Mesa
Manny Ramirez

* Named to All Star Game, did not play.
† Named to All Star Game, replaced because of injury.

Formulas and Technical Information

Batting Runs $= (.47)1B + (.78)2B + (1.09)3B + (1.40)HR + (.33)(BB + HB) - (.25)(AB - H) - (.50)(OOB)$

Clutch Hitting Index Calculated for individuals, actual RBIs over expected RBIs, adjusted for league average and slot in batting order; 100 is a league-average performance. The spot in the batting order is figured as: $5 - (9 \times BFPGP - BFPGT)$, where BFPGP is the batters facing pitcher per game for the player, or plate appearances divided by games, and BFPGT is the batters facing pitcher per game of the entire team. Expected RBIs are calculated as (.25 singles + .50 doubles + .75 triples + 1.75 homers) $\times$ LGAV $\times$ EXPSL where LGAV (league average) = league RBIs divided by (.25 singles + .50 doubles + .75 triples + 1.75 homers), and EXPSL (expected RBIs by slot number) = .88 for the leadoff batter, and for the remaining slots, descending to ninth, .90, .98, 1.08, 1.08, 1.04, 1.04, 1.04, and 1.02.

Calculated for teams, Clutch Hitting Index is actual runs scored over Batting Runs.

Clutch Pitching Index Expected runs allowed over actual runs allowed, with 100 being a league-average performance. Expected runs are figured on the basis of the pitcher's opposing at bats, hits, walks, and hit batsmen (doubles and triples are estimated at league average).

Fielding Runs Calculated to take account of the particular demands of the different positions. (For a full explanation, see *Total Baseball*.) For second basemen, shortstops and third basemen, the formula begins by calculating the league average for each position as follows:

$$\text{League Average} = \left(\frac{.20 (PO + 2A - E + DP) \text{ league at position}}{PO \text{ league total} - K \text{ league total}} \right)$$

where PO = putouts, A = assists, E = errors, DP = double plays, and K = strikeouts. Then we estimate the number of innings for each player at each position based upon each player's entire fielding record and his number of plate appearances. So, if the team played 1,500 innings and one player was calculated to have played 1,000 of those innings at a given position, his Fielding Runs (FR) would be calculated as:

$$FR = .20 (PO + 2A - E + DP) \text{ player} - \text{avg. pos. lg.} \times \left(\frac{PO}{\text{team}} - \frac{K}{\text{team}} \right) \frac{\text{innings, player}}{\text{innings, team}}$$

Assists are doubly weighted because more fielding skill is generally required to get one than to record a putout.

For catchers, the above formula is modified by removing strikeouts from their formulas and subtracting not only errors but also passed balls divided by two. Also incorporated in the catcher's Fielding Runs is one tenth of the adjusted Pitching Runs for the team, times the percentage of games behind the plate by that catcher.

For pitchers, the above formula is modified to subtract individual pitcher strikeouts from the total number of potential outs (otherwise, exceptional strikeout pitchers like Nolan Ryan or Bob Feller would see their Fielding Runs artificially depressed). Also, pitchers' chances are weighted less than an infielder's assists because a pitcher's style may produce fewer ground balls. Thus the formula for pitchers is .10(PO + 2A − E + DP), whereas for second basemen, shortstops, and third basemen it is .20(PO + 2A − E + DP).

For first basemen, because putouts and double plays require so little skill in all but the odd case, these plays are eliminated, leaving only .20(2A − E) in the numerator.

For outfielders, the formula becomes .20(PO + 4A − E + 2DP). The weighting for assists is boosted here because a good outfielder can prevent runs through the threat of assists that are never made; for them, unlike infielders, the assist is essentially an elective play, like the stolen base.

Isolated Power Total bases minus hits, divided by at bats; or more simply, Slugging Average minus Batting Average.

On-Base Percentage The editors employ the version created by Allan Roth and Branch Rickey in the early 1950s: hits plus walks plus hit by pitch divided by at bats plus walks, without regard to sacrifice flies.

Park Factor Calculated separately for batters and pitchers and abbreviated PF. The computation of Park Factor is daunting and what follows is probably of interest to few readers but here's a taste; for the full explanation, consult the Glossary of *Total Baseball*.

Step 1: Find games, losses, and runs scored and allowed for each team at home and on the road. Take runs per game scored and allowed at home over runs per game scored and allowed on the road. This is the initial figure, but requires two corrections.

Step 2: The first correction is for innings pitched at home and on the road. First, find the team's home winning percentage (wins at home over

games at home). Do the same for road games. Then calculate the Innings Pitched Corrector (IPC):

$$\text{IPC} = \frac{(18.5 - \text{Wins at home} / \text{Games at home})}{(18.5 - \text{Losses on road} / \text{Games on road})}$$

If the number is greater than 1, this means that the innings pitched on the road are higher because the other team is batting more often in the last of the ninth. The 18.5 figure is the average number of half innings per game that the home team always bats in the bottom of the ninth.

Step 3: Correct for the fact that the other road parks' total difference from the league average is offset by the park rating of the club being rated. Multiply this rating by the Other Parks Corrector (OPC):

$$\text{OPC} = \frac{\text{No. of teams}}{\text{No. of teams} - 1 + \text{Run Factor, team}}$$

Pitching Runs = Innings Pitched $\times$ (League ERA/9) − Earned Runs Allowed. An alternative version is: Innings Pitched/9 $\times$ (League ERA − Individual ERA).

Production = On-Base Percentage plus Slugging Average. When PRO, as it is abbreviated, is adjusted, the calculation is modified slightly to create a baseline of 100 for league average performance. For PRO/A, the equation is:

$$\frac{\text{Player On Base Pct.}}{\text{League On Base Pct.}} + \frac{\text{Player Slugging Avg.}}{\text{League Slugging Avg.}} - 1$$

Relief Ranking = Relief Runs x (9 $\times$ [Wins + Losses + Saves/4] / Innings Pitched)

Runs Created Bill James's formulation runs to fourteen separate versions; see the Glossary of *Total Baseball* for a full accounting. For 1963-1989, the years covered by the Player and Pitcher Registers, the formula is:

$$\frac{(H + BB + HBP - CS - GIDP) (TB + .26[BB - IBB + HBP] + .52[SH + SF + SB])}{AB + BB + HBP + SH + SF}$$

Runs per Win Calculated on a league-wide basis as the square root of (2 $\times$ runs per inning) multiplied by 10. The runs per inning is multiplied by two to account for the scoring of each team. Historically, the average number of runs per inning is one-half, or 4.5 runs per game per team, so the Runs per Win equation is generally the square root of a number very close to one times 10 or 10 runs per win. In a year with a lot of scoring, the Runs per Win figure will move closer to 11 and in low scoring years the figure will move closer to 9, but 10 is a good estimate for any season.

For individuals, the Runs per Win calculation adjusts the runs per inning to reflect the contribution of the pitcher or batter. A pitcher who allows 45 runs less than average over the course of 25 games lowers the runs per game by 1.8, which is .2 runs per inning, so the Runs per Win figure is 10 times the square root of average runs per inning for both teams minus the pitcher's rating. (A pitcher who allowed 45 more runs than average would have his runs per inning added to the league average.) If the league average was one run per inning, then the Runs per Win for that pitcher would become the square root of .8 runs per inning times 10, which is 8.9. Dividing his 45 pitching runs by 8.9 runs per wins gives him 5.1 linear weights wins. Similarly a batter who produces 45 runs more than average in 150 games contributes .3 runs per game or .03 per inning, which is added to the league average of one run per inning. His Runs per Win equation becomes 10 times the square root of 1.03, which is 10.1. Dividing his 45 batter runs over 10.1 runs per win gives him 4.4 linear weights wins. Although the batter and pitcher contribute the same number of linear weights runs to their team, the pitcher comes out with more linear weights wins, and is statistically more valuable to his team, because he contributes his runs over fewer games and because, as the number of runs scored decreases, each run becomes more valuable.

Slugging Average = Total Bases divided by At Bats.

Total Average = (Total Bases + Walks + Stolen Bases + HBP − Caught Stealing) / (At Bats − Hits + Caught Stealing + GIDP)

Wins Above Team For a pitcher with a winning percentage better than his team (a positive WAT):

Pitcher Decisions $\times$ ([Pitcher pct. − Team pct.] / [2 − 2 $\times$ Team pct.])

For a pitcher with a winning percentage lower than his team's winning percentage (a negative WAT), the equation is:

Pitcher Decisions $\times$ ([Pitcher pct. − Team pct.] / [2 $\times$ Team pct.])

Team and League Abbreviations

These are the 146 franchises, seven principal leagues, and their abbreviations as used throughout this book.

NATIONAL ASSOCIATION, 1871–1875 (shown as n or NA)

Abbrev.	First	Last	Team
ATH n	1871	1875	Philadelphia Athletics
ATL n	1872	1875	Brooklyn Atlantics
BAL n	1872	1874	Baltimore Lord Baltimores
BOS n	1871	1875	Boston Red Stockings
CEN n	1875	1875	Philadelphia Centennials
CHI n	1871	1871	Chicago White Stockings
CHI n	1874	1875	Chicago White Stockings
CLE n	1871	1872	Cleveland Forest City
ECK n	1872	1872	Brooklyn Eckfords
HAR n	1874	1875	Hartford Dark Blues
KEK n	1871	1871	Fort Wayne Kekiongas
MAN n	1872	1872	Middletown (Conn.) Mansfields
MAR n	1873	1873	Baltimore Marylands
MUT n	1871	1875	New York Mutuals
NAT n	1872	1872	Washington, D.C., Nationals
NH n	1875	1875	New Haven Elm City
OLY n	1871	1872	Washington, D.C., Olympics
PHI n	1873	1875	Philadelphia White Stockings
RES n	1873	1873	Elizabeth (N.J.) Resolutes
ROK n	1871	1871	Rockford (Ill.) Forest City
RS n	1875	1875	St. Louis Red Stockings
STL n	1875	1875	St. Louis Brown Stockings
TRO n	1871	1872	Troy Haymakers
WAS n	1873	1873	Washington Washingtons
WAS n	1875	1875	Washington Washingtons
WES n	1875	1875	Keokuk (Iowa) Westerns

NATIONAL LEAGUE, 1876– (shown as N or NL)

Abbrev.	First	Last	Team
ATL N	1966		Atlanta
BAL N	1892	1899	Baltimore
BOS N	1876	1952	Boston (transferred to Milwaukee)
BRO N	1890	1957	Brooklyn (transferred to Los Angeles)
BUF N	1879	1885	Buffalo
CHI N	1876		Chicago
CIN N	1876	1880	Cincinnati
CIN N	1890		Cincinnati
CLE N	1879	1884	Cleveland
CLE N	1889	1899	Cleveland
COL N	1993		Colorado
DET N	1881	1888	Detroit
FLA N	1993		Florida
HAR N	1876	1877	Hartford (played in Brooklyn in 1877)
HOU N	1962		Houston
IND N	1878	1878	Indianapolis
IND N	1887	1889	Indianapolis
KC N	1886	1886	Kansas City
LA N	1958		Los Angeles
LOU N	1876	1877	Louisville
LOU N	1892	1899	Louisville
MIL N	1878	1878	Milwaukee
MIL N	1953	1965	Milwaukee (transferred to Atlanta)
MON N	1969		Montreal
NY N	1876	1876	New York (played in Brooklyn)
NY N	1883	1957	New York (transferred to San Francisco)
NY N	1962		New York
PHI N	1876	1876	Philadelphia
PHI N	1883		Philadelphia
PIT N	1887		Pittsburgh
PRO N	1878	1885	Providence
STL N	1876	1877	St. Louis
STL N	1885	1886	St. Louis
STL N	1892		St. Louis
SD N	1969		San Diego
SF N	1958		San Francisco
SYR N	1879	1879	Syracuse
TRO N	1879	1882	Troy (N.Y.)
WAS N	1886	1889	Washington, D.C.
WAS N	1892	1899	Washington, D.C.
WOR N	1880	1882	Worcester (Mass.)

AMERICAN ASSOCIATION, 1882-1891 (shown as a or AA)

Abbrev.	First	Last	Team
BAL a	1882	1889	Baltimore
BAL a	1890	1890	Baltimore (combined with Brooklyn, shown as BB)
BAL a	1891	1891	Baltimore (transferred to National League)
BOS a	1891	1891	Boston
BRO a	1884	1889	Brooklyn (transferred to National League)
BRO a	1890	1890	Brooklyn (combined with Baltimore, shown as BB)
CIN a	1882	1889	Cincinnati (transferred to National League)
CIN a	1891	1891	Cincinnati
CLE a	1887	1888	Cleveland (transferred to National League)
COL a	1883	1884	Columbus (Ohio)
COL a	1889	1891	Columbus (Ohio)
IND a	1884	1884	Indianapolis
KC a	1888	1889	Kansas City
LOU a	1882	1891	Louisville (transferred to National League)
MIL a	1891	1891	Milwaukee
NY a	1883	1887	New York
PHI a	1882	1891	Philadelphia
PIT a	1882	1886	Pittsburgh (transferred to National League)
RIC a	1884	1884	Richmond
ROC a	1890	1890	Rochester
STL a	1882	1891	St. Louis (transferred to National League)
SYR a	1890	1890	Syracuse
TOL a	1884	1884	Toledo
TOL a	1890	1890	Toledo
WAS a	1884	1884	Washington, D.C.
WAS a	1891	1891	Washington, D.C. (transferred to National League)

UNION ASSOCIATION, 1884 (shown as U or UA)

Abbrev.	First	Last	Team
ALT U	1884	1884	Altoona (Pa.)
BAL U	1884	1884	Baltimore
BOS U	1884	1884	Boston
CHI U	1884	1884	Chicago (combined with Pittsburgh, shown as CP)
CIN U	1884	1884	Cincinnati
KC U	1884	1884	Kansas City
MIL U	1884	1884	Milwaukee
PHI U	1884	1884	Philadelphia
PIT U	1884	1884	Pittsburgh (combined with Chicago, shown as CP)
STL U	1884	1884	St. Louis
STP U	1884	1884	St. Paul (Minn.)
WAS U	1884	1884	Washington, D.C.
WIL U	1884	1884	Wilmington (Del.)

PLAYERS LEAGUE, 1890 (shown as P or PL)

Abbrev.	First	Last	Team
BOS P	1890	1890	Boston
BRO P	1890	1890	Brooklyn
BUF P	1890	1890	Buffalo
CHI P	1890	1890	Chicago
CLE P	1890	1890	Cleveland
NY P	1890	1890	New York
PHI P	1890	1890	Philadelphia
PIT P	1890	1890	Pittsburgh

AMERICAN LEAGUE, 1901– (shown as A or AL)

Abbrev.	First	Last	Team
BAL A	1901	1902	Baltimore (replaced by New York)
BAL A	1954		Baltimore
BOS A	1901		Boston
CAL A	1965		California
CHI A	1901		Chicago
CLE A	1901		Cleveland
DET A	1901		Detroit
KC A	1955	1967	Kansas City (transferred to Oakland)
KC A	1969		Kansas City
LA A	1961	1964	Los Angeles (transferred to California)
MIL A	1901	1901	Milwaukee (replaced by St. Louis)
MIL A	1970		Milwaukee
MIN A	1961		Minnesota
NY A	1903		New York
OAK A	1968		Oakland
PHI A	1901	1954	Philadelphia (transferred to Kansas City)
STL A	1902	1953	St. Louis (transferred to Baltimore)
SEA A	1969	1969	Seattle (transferred to Milwaukee)
SEA A	1977		Seattle
TEX A	1972		Texas
TOR A	1977		Toronto
WAS A	1901	1960	Washington, D.C. (transferred to Minnesota)
WAS A	1961	1971	Washington, D.C. (transferred to Texas)

FEDERAL LEAGUE, 1914-1915 (shown as F or FL)

Abbrev.	First	Last	Team
BAL F	1914	1915	Baltimore
BRO F	1914	1915	Brooklyn
BUF F	1914	1915	Buffalo
CHI F	1914	1915	Chicago
IND F	1914	1914	Indianapolis (transferred to Newark)
KC F	1914	1915	Kansas City
NEW F	1915	1915	Newark
PIT F	1914	1915	Pittsburgh
STL F	1914	1915	St. Louis